LONDON RECOLLECTED

THE VILLAGE LONDON SERIES

Other titles already published in hard back are:

VILLAGE LONDON Volume I
VILLAGE LONDON Volume II
LONDON RECOLLECTED Volume I
LONDON RECOLLECTED Volume II
LONDON RECOLLECTED Volume III
LONDON RECOLLECTED Volume IV

Other titles already published in paperback

VILLAGE LONDON Pt. 1 West and North
VILLAGE LONDON Pt. 2 North and East
VILLAGE LONDON Pt. 3 South-East
VILLAGE LONDON Pt. 4 South-West

OLD FLEET STREET
CHEAPSIDE AND ST. PAUL'S
THE TOWER AND EAST END

HAMPSTEAD, FROM THE KILBURN ROAD.

LONDON RECOLLECTED

ITS HISTORY, LORE AND LEGEND

by
EDWARD WALFORD.

VOLUME V

THE ALDERMAN PRESS
London

First published in 1872-8 by Cassell, Petter, Galpin & Co.
under the title *Old and New London.*

British Library Cataloguing in Publication Data.

Walford, Edward.
[Old and new London] London Recollected: its
history, lore and legend.
Vol 5.
1. London (England)____________History
I. Title
942.1 DA677

ISBN 0-946619-06-9

Published by The Alderman Press, 1987
1/7 Church Street, London N9 9DR

Printed in Great Britain by
Robert Hartnoll (1985) Ltd,
Bodmin, Cornwall.

CONTENTS.

THE WESTERN AND NORTHERN SUBURBS.

CONTENTS.

CHAPTER XXIV.

CAMDEN TOWN AND KENTISH TOWN.

CHAPTER XXV.

ST. PANCRAS.

CHAPTER XXVI.

SOMER'S TOWN AND EUSTON SQUARE.

CHAPTER XXVII.

THE FOUNDLING HOSPITAL AND NEIGHBOURHOOD.

CHAPTER XXVIII.

AGAR TOWN AND THE MIDLAND RAILWAY.

CHAPTER XXIX.

HOLLOWAY.

CHAPTER XXX.

HIGHGATE.

CONTENTS.

CHAPTER XXXVIII.

HAMPSTEAD (*continued*).—ROSSLYN HILL, &c.

CHAPTER XXXIX.

HAMPSTEAD (*continued*).—BELSIZE AND FROGNAL.

CHAPTER XL.

THE NORTH-EASTERN SUBURBS.—HAGGERSTON, HACKNEY, &c.

CHAPTER XLI.

THE NORTH-EASTERN SUBURBS.—HACKNEY (*continued*).

CHAPTER XLII.

HOXTON, KINGSLAND, DALSTON, &c.

CHAPTER XLIII.

STOKE NEWINGTON.

CHAPTER XLIV.

STOKE NEWINGTON (*continued*), AND STAMFORD HILL.

CHAPTER XLV.

TOTTENHAM.

PAGE

CHAPTER XLVI.

NORTH TOTTENHAM, EDMONTON, &c.

CHAPTER XLVII.

THE LEA, STRATFORD-LE-BOW, &c.

LIST OF ILLUSTRATIONS.

LONDON.

THE WESTERN SUBURBS.

CHAPTER I.

BELGRAVIA.

> "'Tis hard to say—such space the city wins—
> Where country ends and where the town begins."
>
> "*Prolusiones Paulinæ*," 1876.

Prefatory Remarks—The Building of the District—De Moret, and his Flying-machine—Nature of the Soil of Belgravia—"Slender Billy"—The Spanish Monkey "Mukako" and Tom Cribb's Fighting Dogs—The Grosvenor Family—Enormous Rent-rolls—Belgravia and Bethnal Green compared—Lanesborough House—St. George's Hospital—Old "Tattersall's"—St. George's Place—Liston, the Comedian—Pope's School-days—The Alexandra Hotel—The Old Toll-gate at Hyde Park Corner—Grosvenor Place—The "Feathers" Tavern," and how George Prince of Wales was made an Odd Fellow there—Arabella Row—A Witty Lord Chancellor—The "Bag o' Nails"—The "Three Compasses"—Belgrave Square—"Gentleman Jones"—Eccleston Street—Sir Francis Chantrey—St. Paul's Church, Wilton Place—The Pantechnicon—Halkin Street—Upper and Lower Belgrave Streets—Suicide of Lord Munster—Eaton Square—Chester Square—Ebury Street—Lowndes Square—Cadogan Place—William Wilberforce—The Locality in Former Times.

HAVING, in the previous volume, completed our peregrination of what may be called the *interior gyrus*—the innermost circle—of the great metropolis, we may now venture on a somewhat wider journey afield, and roam over that portion of the next circle—but still far from the outermost of all—which, not above half a century ago, certainly was *not* London, but as certainly now forms part of it. We hope, at all events, to find much that will be interesting to our readers even in modern "Belgravia;" but Knightsbridge and Paddington, Chelsea and Kensington, are each and all old enough to have histories of their own; and the two last-named villages have played a conspicuous part in the annals of the Court under our Hanoverian sovereigns, and in those of the aristocracy for even a longer period.

We purpose, therefore, to traverse in turn the fashionable area which has its centre fixed about Eaton and Belgrave Squares; then the undefined region of Knightsbridge, and that portion of Hyde Park which lies to the south of the Serpentine, and formed the site of the first Great Exhibition of 1851. Then across Pimlico to Chelsea, rich in its memories of Sir Hans Sloane and Nell Gwynne; to look in upon the household of good Sir Thomas More; and to speak of Chelsea's famous bun-house, and its ancient china-ware. Next we shall visit Brompton, the "Montpelier" of the metropolis; and then be off to the "old Court suburb" of Kensington, familiar to all Englishmen and Englishwomen as the home of William III., and of most of our Hanoverian sovereigns, and dear to them as the birthplace of Queen Victoria. We shall linger for a time under the shade of the trees which compose its pleasant gardens, and call up the royal memories of nearly two centuries. Then, bearing westwards, we shall look in upon the long galleries of Holland House, and see the chamber in which Addison died, and the rooms in which Charles James Fox and the leading Whigs of the last three reigns talked politics and fashionable news; thence to Percy Cross, and Walham Green and Parsons' Green, and to Fulham, for a thousand years the country seat of the Bishops of London both before and since the Reformation. Then we will saunter about the quaint old suburban village of Hammersmith, with its red-brick cottages and cedar-planted lawns, and so work our way round by way of Shepherd's Bush and Notting Hill—two names of truly rural sound—to Paddington and St. John's Wood—once the property of the Knights of St. John—and so to Kilburn, Hampstead, and Highgate, and Camden and Kentish Towns, till we once more arrive at St. Pancras.

With these few words by way of preface to the present volume, we again take our staff in hand, and turning our back on the "congestion" of traffic at Hyde Park Corner, which has lately been an object of legislation in Parliament, we turn our faces westward, and prepare to go on our way.

The name of "Belgravia" was originally applied as a *sobriquet* to Belgrave and Eaton Squares and the streets radiating immediately from them, but is now received as a collective popular appellation of that "City of Palaces" which lies to the south-west of Hyde Park Corner, stretching away towards Pimlico and Chelsea. The district was first laid out and built by Messrs. Cubitt, under a special Act of Parliament, passed in 1826, empowering Lord Grosvenor to drain the site, raise the level, and erect bars, &c. "During the late reign—that of George IV.," observes a writer in 1831—"Lord Grosvenor has built a new and elegant town on the site of fields of no healthy aspect, thus connecting London and Chelsea, and improving the western entrance to the metropolis, at a great expense."

Where now rise Belgrave and Eaton Squares, the most fashionable in the metropolis, there was, down to about the year above mentioned, an open and rural space, known as the "Five Fields." It was infested, as recently as the beginning of the present century, by footpads and robbers. These fields formed the scene of one of the first, but unsuccessful, attempts at ballooning in London. De Moret, a Frenchman, and a bit of an adventurer, proposed, in 1784, to ascend from some tea-gardens in this place, having attached to his balloon a car, not unlike some of the unwieldy summer-houses which may be seen in suburban gardens, and even provided with wheels, so that, if needful, it could be used as a travelling carriage. "Whether," says Chambers, in his "Book of Days," "M. Moret ever really intended to attempt an ascent in such an unwieldy machine, has never been clearly ascertained. . . . However, having collected a considerable sum of money, he was preparing for his ascent, on the 10th of August in that year, when his machine caught fire and was burnt; the unruly mob avenging their disappointment by destroying the adjoining property. The adventurer himself made a timely escape; and a caricature of the day represents him flying off to Ostend with a bag of British guineas, leaving the Stockwell Ghost, the Bottle Conjurer, Elizabeth Canning, Mary Toft, and other cheats, enveloped in the smoke of his burning balloon."

There was a time, and not so very distant in the lapse of ages, when much of Belgravia, and other parts of the valley bordering upon London, was a "lagoon of the Thames;" * indeed, the clayey swamp in this particular region retained so much water that no one would build there. At length, Mr. Thomas Cubitt found the strata to consist of gravel and clay, of inconsiderable depth. The clay

* In this lagoon there were many islands, as Chels*ey*, Bermonds*ey*, &c.

he removed and burned into bricks, and by building upon the substratum of gravel, he converted this spot from the most unhealthy to one of the most healthy in the metropolis, in spite of the fact that its surface is but a few feet above the level of the river Thames at high water, during spring-tides.

This mine of wealth—the present suburb, or rather city, of Belgravia, for such it has become—passed into the possession of the Grosvenor family in 1656, when the daughter and sole heiress of Alexander Davies, Esq., of Ebury Farm, married Sir Thomas Grosvenor, the ancestor of the present Duke of Westminster. This Mr. Davies died in 1663, three years after the Restoration, little conscious of the future value of his five pasturing fields. "In Queen Elizabeth's time," observes a writer in the *Belgravia* magazine, "this sumptuous property was only plain Eabury, or Ebury Farm, a plot of 430 acres, meadow and pasture, let on lease to a troublesome 'untoward' person named Wharle; and he, to her farthingaled Majesty's infinite annoyance, had let out the same to various other scurvy fellows, who insisted on enclosing the arable land, driving out the ploughs, and laying down grass, to the hindrance of all pleasant hawking and coursing parties. Nor was this all the large-hearted queen alone cared about; she had a feeling for the poor, and she saw how these enclosures were just so much sheer stark robbery of the poor man's right of common after Lammas-tide. In the Regency, when Belgrave Square was a ground for hanging out clothes, all the space between Westminster and Vauxhall Bridge was known as 'Tothill Fields,' or 'The Downs.' It was a dreary tract of stunted, dusty, trodden grass, beloved by bull-baiters, badger-drawers, and dog-fighters. Beyond this Campus Martius of prize-fighting days loomed a garden region of cabbage-beds, stagnant ditches fringed with pollard withes. There was then no Penitentiary at Millbank, no Vauxhall Bridge, but a haunted house half-way to Chelsea, and a halfpenny hatch, that led through a cabbage-plot to a tavern known by the agreeable name of 'The Monster.' Beyond this came an embankment called the Willow Walk (a convenient place for quiet murder); and at one end of this lived that eminent public character, Mr. William Aberfield, generally known to the sporting peers, thieves, and dog-fanciers of the Regency as 'Slender Billy.' Mr. Grantley Berkeley once had the honour of making this gentleman's acquaintance, and visited his house to see the great Spanish monkey 'Mukako' ('Muchacho') fight Tom Cribb's dogs, and cut their throats one after the other—apparently, at least—for the 'gentleman' who really bled the dogs and the peers was Mr. Cribb himself, who had a lancet hidden in his hand, with which, under the pretence of rendering the bitten and bruised dogs help, he contrived, in a frank and friendly way, to open the jugular vein. A good many of the Prince Regent's friends were Slender Billy's also. Mr. Slender Billy died, however, much more regretted than the Regent, being a most useful and trusty member of a gang of forgers."

The Grosvenors, as already mentioned by us,* are one of the most ancient of the untitled English aristocracy, their ancestor having been the chief hunter (*Le Gros veneur*) to the Dukes of Normandy before the Conquest. It was not till a century ago that they condescended to bear a title, but since that time their growth to the very foremost rank in the peerage has been steady and well-earned, if personal worth and high honour, combined with immense wealth, are to be reckoned as any claim to a coronet.

The chief wealth of the Grosvenors, prior to the marriage of their head with Miss Davies, of Ebury Farm, was drawn out of the bowels of the earth in the north of England. Hence Pope writes—

"All Townshend's turnips, and all Grosvenor's mines."

There can be little doubt that, in right of his Manor of Ebury, the Duke of Westminster enjoys one of the largest rent-rolls, if not the very largest, in the kingdom. The current rumour of the day sets it down at £1,000 a day, or £365,000 a year. Other noblemen, especially the Dukes of Sutherland, Buccleuch, and Northumberland, are thought to approach very nearly to a like rental. As far back as the year 1819, the head of the Grosvenors was returned to the property-tax commissioners as one of the four richest noblemen in the kingdom, the three others being the Duke of Northumberland, the Marquis of Stafford (afterwards Duke of Sutherland), and the Earl of Bridgewater, the annual income in each case being in excess of £100,000. No other peers exceeded that sum at that time; but now, owing to the increased value of land in London, and the steady growth of the productiveness of the agricultural and mining industries, the owners of the above properties have much larger rent-rolls; and the probability is that there are ten or, perhaps, a dozen other peers whose incomes would reach the above-mentioned standard. A very different state of things, it must be said, from that which prevailed when Charles II. was on the throne, if Macaulay may be trusted when he writes of the year 1683:—"The greatest estates in the kingdom then very

* See Vol. IV., p. 371.

little exceeded twenty thousand a year. The Duke of Ormond had twenty-two thousand a year. The Duke of Buckingham, before his extravagance had impaired his great property, had nineteen thousand six hundred a year. George Monk, Duke of Albemarle, who had been rewarded for his eminent services with immense grants of crown land, and who had been notorious both for covetousness and for parsimony, left fifteen thousand a year of real estate, and sixty thousand pounds in money, which probably yielded seven per cent. These three dukes were supposed to be three of the very richest subjects in England." The building of this great city of Belgravia, for such we are compelled to call it, fully justified William IV. in bestowing on his lordship the territorial title of "Marquis of Westminster," which has blossomed into a dukedom under Queen Victoria.

Viewing the great metropolis as a world in itself, as Addison and Dr. Johnson, and, indeed, all observant and thoughtful persons for these two centuries past have done, Belgravia and Bethnal Green become, both morally and physically, the opposite poles of the sphere of London—the frigid zones, so to speak, of the capital: the former, icy cold, from its stiff and unbending habit of fashion, form, and ceremony; the other, wrapped in a perpetual winter of never-ending poverty and squalor.

But it is now time for us to proceed with our perambulation. Close by Hyde Park Corner, at the north end of Grosvenor Place, stands St. George's Hospital. It was built upon the site of a pleasant suburban residence of the first Lord Lanesborough, who died in 1723. Here he was out of the sound of the noisy streets, and could enjoy in private his favourite amusement of dancing. The reader will not forget the line of Pope, in which he is immortalised as—

"Sober Lanesborough, dancing with the gout."

Mr. Jesse writes: "So paramount is said to have been his lordship's passion for dancing, that when Queen Anne lost her Consort, Prince George of Denmark, he seriously advised her Majesty to dispel her grief by applying to his favourite exercise." But this may be possibly a piece of scandal and a *canard* of the day. Lord Lanesborough's house was beyond the turnpike gate, and Pennant says it was his lordship's "country house."

In 1733, Lanesborough House was converted into an infirmary by some seceding governors of Westminster Hospital. The old house for many years formed the central part of the hospital, two wings having been added to it when it was converted to its new purposes. A report of the governors for the year 1734, for which we are indebted to Maitland, tells us that "the hospital is now fitted up, and made much more complete than could have been expected out of a dwelling-house. It will at present contain sixty patients; but, as the boundaries of their grounds will admit of new buildings for several spacious and airy wards, the subscribers propose to erect such buildings as soon as their circumstances shall enable them." These extra wards have since been supplied at a considerable expense, and in process of time the entire building has been reconstructed. From its commencement the hospital has been mainly dependent upon voluntary contributions, not being richly endowed like Guy's, St. Bartholomew's, and St. Thomas's. Fifty years after its foundation, the subscriptions amounted to a little over £2,000 a year. The hospital was aided by one-third of the proceeds of musical entertainments in the Abbey. In its first half century it had numbered 150,000 patients. The present edifice was commenced towards the end of the reign of George IV., by William Wilkins, R.A., the architect of the National Gallery, University College in Gower Street, and other important buildings; but several additions have since been made to the original design, the latest being the erection of a new wing on the south-west side, in Grosvenor Crescent, which was completed about the year 1868.

The principal front of the hospital, facing the Green Park, is now nearly 200 feet in length, and forms a rather handsome elevation. The building contains a lecture theatre and an anatomical museum. The expenses of the institution are defrayed by voluntary contributions, and by the interest of funded property arising from legacies. In the year 1880, including some special gifts, its income amounted to upwards of £23,000; and the number of persons benefited during the year was above 20,000.

Mr. John Timbs, in his "Curiosities of London," mentions an "ingenious telegraph," which has been devised here for the transmission of orders through the different wards. "In the hall," he writes, "is a column three feet high, with a dial of engraved signals, and on the walls of the different wards are corresponding dials; so that when the pointer to the hall dial is moved to any signal, all the others move accordingly, and a little hammer strikes a bell, by which means about fifty signals are transmitted daily to each ward, without the possibility of error or the least noise."

The Atkinson Morley Convalescent Home at Wimbledon is connected with this hospital, and there is also a medical school in connection with the institution. Of the many celebrated men whose names are more or less intimately associated with St. George's Hospital, may be mentioned those of Dr. Baily, Dr. W. Hunter, and his brother, John Hunter (who died here suddenly, having been violently excited by a quarrel in the board-room, while suffering under disease of the heart), Sir Benjamin Brodie, Sir Everard Home, and Dr. James Hope, the author of "A Treatise on the Diseases of the Heart," and on "Morbid Anatomy," who was chiefly instrumental in overcoming the prejudice that formerly existed in England, and especially at this hospital, against the use of the stethoscope in the examination of diseases of the chest.

In June, 1876, a curious accident occurred here. Through the bursting of a large tank on the roof, several tons of water suddenly broke through and deluged the lower floors, injuring some of the patients and the medical students, and causing the death of two or three of the patients. It need scarcely be added that, in the sanitary arrangements of the hospital, and also more especially in the important matter of ventilation, recourse has been had to the latest scientific improvements and discoveries.

Like other London hospitals, St. George's draws its patients very largely from the most unfriended classes in its vicinity, very much from the poor of all parts of London, and in no small degree from the poor of all parts of England. In 1870, an inquiry showed that there were above 330 in-patients. Of these, 100 resided within a mile of the hospital; 150 beyond that radius, but within four miles of Charing Cross; while the remainder came from all parts of the country.

At the south-eastern corner of St. George's Hospital, where now is Grosvenor Crescent, was formerly the entrance to Tattersall's celebrated auction-mart, "so renowned through all the breadth and length of horse-loving, horse-breeding, horse-racing Europe," which from all parts sends hither its representatives, when the more important sales are going on, and, with a confidence justified by the known character of the house, commissions the proprietor himself to procure for the nobles and gentry of the Continent fresh supplies for their studs of the finest English horses. The building itself, at the back, occupied part of the grounds of Lanesborough House. The entry was through an arched passage and down an inclined "drive," at the bottom of which was a public-house or "tap," designated "The Turf," for the accommodation of the throngs of grooms, jockeys, and poorer horse-dealers and horse-fanciers. On the left, an open gateway led into a garden-like enclosure, with a single tree in the centre rising from the middle of a grass-plot, surrounded by a circular path of yellow sand or gravel. Immediately beyond the gateway was the subscription-room; this building, though small, was admirably adapted for the purposes for which it was designed, and it contained merely a set of desks arranged in an octagonal form in the centre, where bets were recorded, and money paid over. On the right of the passage, a covered gateway led into the court-yard, where the principal business of the place was carried on; this was surrounded on three sides by a covered way, and at the extremity of one side stood the auctioneer's rostrum, overlooking the whole area. The stables, where the horses to be sold were kept in the interim, were close at hand, and admirably arranged for light and ventilation. In the centre of the enclosure was a domed structure to an humble but important appendage—a pump, and the structure itself was crowned by a bust of George IV. About the year 1864, "Tattersall's"—as this celebrated auction-mart was familiarly called throughout Europe—was removed further westward to Knightsbridge, where we shall come to it shortly.

The public days at old "Tattersall's" were the Mondays in each week through the year, with the addition of Thursday during the height of the season. The horses of the chief sale, that of the Monday, arrived on the Friday previous. "When the settling-times arrive," observes a writer in the *Penny Magazine* for 1831, "great is the bustle and excitement that prevails throughout Tattersall's. Vehicles of all kinds dash to and fro in incessant motion, or linger altogether inactive in rows about the neighbourhood, while their masters are bidding for a good hunter or a pair of carriage-horses. A more motley assemblage than the buyers or lookers-on at such times it would be impossible to find. Noblemen and ambitious costermongers, bishops and blacklegs, horse-breeders, grooms, jockeys, mingling promiscuously with the man of retired and studious habits fond of riding and breeding the wherewithal to ride; tradesmen about to set up their little pleasure-chaise or business-cart; and commercial travellers, whose calling has inoculated them with a passion for dabbling in horseflesh, and who, in their inns on the road, talk with great gusto and decision of all that pertains to Tattersall's, on the strength of some occasional half-hour's experience in the court-yard."

Richard Tattersall, the founder of the above establishment, was training-groom to the last Duke of Kingston, brother of Lady Mary Wortley Montagu, and husband of the notorious duchess. On the death of his patron, in 1773, he appears to have opened his auction-mart; but the foundation of his fortune was laid by his purchase of the racehorse "Highflyer," for the enormous sum of £2,500, and, it is supposed, on credit—an evidence of the high character for integrity which he must have already acquired. "Of his personal qualities," it has been observed, "perhaps the establishment itself is the best testimony; what Tattersall's is now, it seems to have essentially been from the very outset—a place where men of honour might congregate without breathing, or, at all events, in but a greatly lessened degree, the pestilential vapour that usually but too often surrounds the stable; where men of taste might enjoy the glimpses afforded of the most beautiful specimens of an exquisitely beautiful race, without being perpetually disgusted with the worst of all things—that of the jockey or horse-dealer." We shall have more to say of "Tattersall's," however, when we come to Knightsbridge.

St. George's Place, or Terrace, now a series of princely mansions, was, till lately, a long row of low brick houses, of only one or two storeys, on the west side of the hospital, fronting Hyde Park, and extended as far as the Alexandra Hotel. Here Dr. Parr used to stay when he came up to London from his parsonage at Hatton. Here, too, lived for some years John Liston, the comedian, who had removed hither after his retirement from the stage. "He had long outlived the use of his faculties," writes Leigh Hunt, "and used to stand at his window at 'the Corner' sadly gazing at the tide of human existence which was going by, and which he had once helped to enliven." Mr. Planché, who was one of his most intimate friends, writes thus of this singular monomaniac: "His sole occupation was sitting all day long at the window of his residence, timing the omnibuses, and expressing the greatest distress and displeasure if any of them happened to be late. This had become a sort of monomania; his spirits had completely forsaken him. He never smiled or entered into conversation, and eventually he sunk into a lethargy, from which he woke no more in this world."

In this terrace, probably, was the school to which Pope was sent at ten or eleven years of age, and where, as he tells us, he forgot nearly all that he had learnt from his first instructor, a worthy priest;

ENTRANCE TO OLD "TATTERSALL'S." (*See page* 5.)

ST. GEORGE'S HOSPITAL, 1745. (*See page* 4.)

and it is to his stay at this school that the poet thus refers later in life :—

> "Soon as I enter at my country door,
> My mind resumes the thread it dropt before;
> Thoughts, which at Hyde Park Corner I forgot,
> Meet and rejoin me in my pensive grot."

The Alexandra Hotel, which covers the ground formerly occupied by some half-dozen of the houses in St. George's Place, is one of the most important and largest hotels in the metropolis. It was built shortly after the marriage of the Prince of Wales with the Princess Alexandra of Denmark, after whom it is named. The hotel is largely patronised by families of distinction from the country, and also by foreign notabilities, who, during their stay in London, desire to be within easy reach of the Court and the principal quarters of the West End. A few short yards westward beyond the Alexandra Hotel the roadway enters Knightsbridge, which we shall deal with in the next chapter.

The old toll-gate at Hyde Park Corner, between Piccadilly and Knightsbridge, considerably narrowed the entrance into Piccadilly at its western end; and its removal, as we have mentioned in our account of that thoroughfare,* was a great improvement not only to Piccadilly itself, but to Knightsbridge as well. Our illustration (see page 10) shows the auctioneer in the act of brandishing his hammer, and exclaiming, *de more*, "Once, twice, thrice! Going, going, gone!" to the great satisfaction, no doubt, of the speculative contractor who purchased the old materials in order to mend the roads.

Grosvenor Place forms the eastern boundary of Belgravia, extending southward from St. George's Hospital, and overlooking the gardens of Buckingham Palace, of which we have already spoken. It was till recently described as "a pleasant row of houses," mostly built during the Grenville Administration, in the early part of the present century. "When George III. was adding a portion of the Green Park to the new garden at Buckingham House," says Mr. Peter Cunningham, quoting from Walpole's "George III.," "the fields on the opposite side of the road were to be sold, at the price of £20,000. This sum Grenville refused to issue from the Treasury. The ground was consequently leased to builders, and a new row of houses, overlooking the king in his private walks, was erected, to his great annoyance."

Lord Hatherton removed, in 1830, from Portman Square to a house in Grosvenor Place, which Macaulay terms a palace. Macaulay tells about this neighbourhood a good story, which would not gratify the pride of the head of the house of Grosvenor. "When Lord Hatherton changed his residence his servants gave him warning, as they could not, they said, go into such an unheard-of part of the world as Grosvenor Place. I can only say that I have never been in a finer house." Verily there is as much truth to-day, as there was two thousand years ago, in the old Roman satirist's line—

> "Maxima quæque domus servis est plena superbis."

Lord Hatherton continued to reside here for many years. He had a choice gallery of paintings, which are mentioned, in some detail, by Dr. Waagen, in his work on "Art and Artists in England."

During the years 1873-76 the appearance of a great part of this street was totally changed. In place of some dozen or so houses of ordinary appearance, which formerly stood at the north end, five princely mansions have been erected, in the most ornate Italian style; one of these is occupied by the Duke of Grafton, and another by the Duke of Northumberland, since his expulsion from Charing Cross. Lower down is the residence of the head of the Rothschild family. In the adjoining house lived for some time the late Earl Stanhope (better known by his courtesy title of Lord Mahon), the historian and essayist, author of a "History of the War of the Succession in Spain," "A History of England, from the Peace of Utrecht," and other works. Lord Stanhope, who was many years President of the Society of Antiquaries, was grandson of the inventor of the Stanhope printing-press.

At the southern end, in Hobart Place, formerly Grosvenor Street West, was an inn called "The Feathers," about which a good story is told by Mr. J. Larwood in his "History of Sign-boards:"—"A lodge of Odd Fellows was held at this house, into the private chamber of which George Prince of Wales one night intruded very abruptly, with a roystering friend. The society at that moment was celebrating some of its awful mysteries, which no uninitiated eye might behold, and these were witnessed by the profane intruders. The only way to repair the sacrilege was to make the Prince and his companion 'Odd Fellows'—a title which they certainly deserved as richly as any members of the club. The initiatory rites were quickly gone through, and the Prince was chairman for the remainder of the evening. In 1851 the old public-house was pulled down, and a new gin-palace built on its site, in the parlour of which," adds Mr. Larwood, "the chair used by the distinguished 'Odd Fellow' is still preserved, along with a portrait of his Royal High-

* See Vol. IV., p. 290.

ness in the robes of the order." Another public-house in Grosvenor Street perpetuated, writes Mr. J. Larwood, the well-known fable of the "Wolf and the Lamb," which was pictured by a sign representing a lion and a kid. The house was known as the "Lion and Goat."

At the bottom of Grosvenor Place, and reaching to Buckingham Palace Road, is a large triangular piece of ground, intersected by a part of Ebury Street, and covered with lofty and handsomely-constructed houses, known respectively as Grosvenor Gardens and Belgrave Mansions. On the east side of this triangular plot is Arabella Row, one side of which is occupied by the royal stables of Buckingham Palace, which we have already described.* This row was once, not so very long ago, well tenanted. Among others, here lived Lord Erskine, after he had ceased to hold the seals as Lord Chancellor. His lordship, who held them only a year, was not only an orator, but a wit, as the following anecdote will show:—Captain Parry was once at dinner in his company, when Lord Erskine asked him what he and his crew lived upon in the Frozen Sea. Parry said that they lived upon seals. "And capital things, too, seals are, if you only keep them long enough," was the reply. One of the houses in Arabella Row is the official residence of the Queen's Librarian at Windsor Castle.

At the corner of Arabella Row and Buckingham Palace Road, is a public-house, rejoicing in the once common sign of the "Bag o' Nails"—a perversion of "The Bacchanals" of Ben Jonson. "About fifty years ago," writes the author of "Tavern Anecdotes," in 1825, "the original sign might have been seen at the front of the house; it was a Satyr of the Woods, with a group of 'jolly dogs,' ycleped Bacchanals. But the Satyr having been painted black, and with cloven feet, it was called by the common people 'The Devil;' while the Bacchanalian revellers were transmuted, by a comic process, into the 'Bag of Nails.'"

In Grosvenor Row, a thoroughfare which has disappeared in the march of modern improvements that have recently taken place in this neighbourhood, was another inn, "The Three Compasses," well known as a starting-point for the Pimlico omnibuses. It was generally known as the "Goat and Compasses"—possibly a corruption of the text, "God encompasseth us;" though Mr. P. Cunningham sees in it a reproduction of the arms of the Wine Coopers' Company, as they appear on a vault in the Church of S. Maria di Capitolo, at Cologne—a shield, with a pair of compasses, an axe, and a dray, or truck, with goats for supporters. "In a country like England, dealing so much at one time in Rhenish wine, a more likely origin," he observes, "could hardly be imagined." Mr. Larwood, however, points out that possibly the "Goat" was the original sign, and that the host afterwards added the Masonic "Compasses," as is often done now.

Belgrave Square, into which we now pass, was so named after the Viscountcy of Belgrave, the second title of Earl Grosvenor before he was raised to his superior titles. It was built in the year 1825, and covers an area of about ten acres. It was designed by George Basevi, the detached mansions at the angles being the work of Hardwick, Kendall, and others. It is nearly 700 feet in length by a little over 600. The houses are uniform, except the large detached mansions at the angles. Those in the sides are adorned with Corinthian columns and capitals.

Belgrave Square has always been occupied by the heads of the highest titled nobility, and by many foreigners of distinction. Lord Ellesmere lived here till he built Bridgewater House. Among other notabilities who have resided here may be named the first Lord Combermere, Sir Roderick Murchison, the geologist, Sir Charles Wood, afterwards Lord Halifax, and General Sir George Murray, who acted as Quartermaster-General to the British army during the Peninsular War. At the south-west corner lived for some years another distinguished General, Lord Hill, the hero of Almarez. In this square the Count de Chambord and his mother held their court, during a short visit which they paid to England in 1843. The Austrian Embassy has been for several years located in this square.

In Chapel Street, which runs from the south-east corner of Belgrave Square into Grosvenor Place, resided Mr. Richard Jones, a teacher of elocution, generally known as "Gentleman Jones," who is mentioned by Lord William Lennox, and by nearly all the writers of modern London anecdote. Here he used to have scores of pupils practising for the pulpit, the bar, or the senate. "Under his able tuition," says Lord W. Lennox, "many a reverend gentleman, who mumbled over the service, became a shining light; many an embryo lawyer, who spoke as if he had a ball of worsted in his mouth, became a great orator; and many a member of Parliament, who 'hummed and hawed,' and was unintelligible in the gallery, turned out a distinguished speaker."

Eccleston Street derives its name from Eccleston,

* See Vol. IV., p. 69.

in Cheshire, where the Grosvenors own a property. The large house at the corner of this street was for many years the residence of Sir Francis Chantrey, the sculptor. He was born at Norton, near Sheffield, in 1781, and, as a boy, used to ride a donkey, carrying milk into the town. "On a certain day, when returning home upon his donkey, Chantrey was observed by a gentleman to be very intently engaged in cutting a stick with his penknife. Excited by his curiosity, he asked the lad what he was doing, when, with great simplicity of manner, but with courtesy, the lad replied, 'I am cutting *old Foxe's head.*' Foxe was the schoolmaster of the village. On this, the gentleman asked to see what he had done, pronounced it to be an excellent likeness, and presented the youth with *sixpence;* and this may, perhaps, be reckoned the first money which Chantrey ever obtained for his ingenuity."

He took up his residence here shortly after his marriage in 1809. The house was then two separate residences—Nos. 29 and 30, Lower Belgrave Place—but Chantrey threw the two houses into one, and named them anew as part of Eccleston Street. In the studios at the back, all his best works—his bust of Sir Walter Scott, his "Sleeping Children," and his statue of Watt—were executed. There is, or was, in it a small gallery with a lanthorn, by Sir John Soane. Sir F. Chantrey was pronounced by the "Foreigner," who is known as the author of "An Historical and Literary Tour in England," to be the only English sculptor of his age who was distinguished by true originality, though still young in reputation.

Macaulay tells a good story of him, and one most creditable to his magnanimity, which kept him from being ashamed of his early struggles in life. When Chantrey dined with Rogers, he took particular notice of a certain vase, and of the table on which it stood, and asked Rogers who made the latter. "A common carpenter," said Rogers. "Do you remember the making of it?" asked Chantrey. "Certainly," replied Rogers, in some surprise; "I was in the room while it was finished with the chisel, and gave the workmen directions about placing it." "Yes," said Chantrey, "I was the carpenter; I remember the room well, and all the circumstances." Chantrey died at the close of the year 1841: he expired whilst sitting in an easy-chair in his drawing-room. By his will Sir Francis left a considerable sum to the Royal Academy, to be devoted to endowing the Presidentship of that institution, and in other ways to "the encouragement of British Fine Art in Painting and Sculp-

SALE OF HYDE PARK TURNPIKE. (*See page* 8.)

ture," the bequest to take effect on the death or second marriage of his wife. Lady Chantrey died in 1875, when the above legacy, which had gone on accumulating, became available for the purposes to which it was to be devoted.

On the north-west side of Belgrave Square are Wilton Crescent and Wilton Place. In the latter, which opens into Knightsbridge Road, a little westward of the Alexandra Hotel, is St. Paul's Church, which is deserving of notice, from the fact of its clergy having always been prominent leaders of the Ritualistic or extreme "high church" party. The first incumbent was the Rev. W. J. E. Bennett, who was succeeded by the Hon. and Rev. Robert Liddell, and he by Lord Russell's son-in-law, Mr. Villiers. The church, which was consecrated in 1843, is built in the Early Perpendicular style, and was erected at a cost of £11,000. It consists only of a nave and chancel, and a lofty tower crowned with eight pinnacles; the windows are filled with stained glass, and the interior is rich in ornamentation. This church has been the scene of many a strong conflict between the parishioners and the incumbent respecting the ceremonials carried on here, which culminated in one of the vestrymen, more courageous than the rest—a Mr. Westerton—bringing the matter in dispute before the courts of law.

Between Motcomb, Lowndes, and Kinnerton Streets, all of which are on the western side of the square, is a large building, called the Pantechnicon, used of late years for storing furniture, carriages, works of art, &c. It was originally built about the year 1834, as a bazaar, and was established principally for the sale of carriages and household furniture. There was also a "wine department," consisting of a range of dry vaults for the reception and display of wines; and the bazaar contained likewise a "toy department." The building, which covered about two acres, was burnt to the ground in 1874, when a large quantity of valuable property was destroyed. The work of rebuilding was soon afterwards commenced, the new structure being erected on detached blocks, and of fire-proof materials, so that the chances of the building being again destroyed in a similar way are considerably reduced.

Halkin Street, on the northern side of the square, was so called from Halkin Castle, in Flintshire, one of the seats of the ducal owner. In this street is a chapel, which has been since 1866 used by the Presbyterian body. The building is somewhat singular in shape, neither square nor oblong, the end opposite the entrance being considerably wider than the other.

Connecting the south-east corner of Belgrave Square with Ebury Street, and skirting the east ends of Eaton and Chester Squares, are Upper and Lower Belgrave Streets. In the former, in 1842, the Earl of Munster committed suicide. He was the eldest son of William IV. by Mrs. Jordan. He married Miss Wyndham, one of the natural daughters of Lord Egremont, with whom he had a fortune of £40,000 or £50,000. He had the place of Constable of Windsor Castle, which was continued to him by the Queen, and he had just been appointed to the command of the troops at Plymouth, with which he was much pleased. Mr. Raikes, in his "Journal," speaks of him as "a very amiable man in private life, not without some talent, and given to study Eastern languages." As Colonel Fitz-Clarence, he had shown great bravery and energy in arresting the leaders of the Cato Street conspiracy. He was raised to a peerage on his father's accession to the throne.

Eaton Square was designed and built by Messrs. Cubitt in 1827. It was named after Eaton Hall, in Cheshire, the principal seat of the Duke of Westminster. It occupies an oblong piece of ground, and the centre is divided by roadways into six separate enclosures. No. 71 was for some time, during the rebuilding of the Houses of Parliament, the official residence of the Speaker of the House of Commons. Most of the mansions, in fact, have at different times been occupied by members of one or other division of the Legislature. No. 75 was for many years the residence of the late Mr. Ralph Bernal, M.P. for Rochester, and Chairman of Committees in the House of Commons. He was a distinguished antiquary and connoisseur, and made here his superb collection of works of art, including china, armour, articles of *virtu*, and antiquities of every description, the sale of which, occupying thirty-two days, was one of the "events" of the season of 1855.

At No. 83 lived, during the closing years of his life, the late Lord Truro. The son of an attorney on College Hill, in London, Thomas Wilde began life in his father's office; but having afterwards studied for the higher branch of the profession, he was, at the age of thirty-five, called to the bar at the Inner Temple. In 1820 he was engaged as one of the counsel for Queen Caroline on her "trial" in the House of Lords, which, doubtless, brought him a handsome fee; and he is said to have had a retaining fee of 3,000 guineas in the case of the British Iron Company against Mr. John Attwood. Before his accession to the Upper House on being made Lord Chancellor, he sat in the House of Commons as member for Newark.

and also for the City of Worcester. He died in 1855, immensely rich, having married, as his second wife, a daughter of the late Duke of Sussex.

At the east end of the square is St. Peter's Church, an Ionic building designed by Hakewill, and consecrated in 1827. The altar-piece, "Christ crowned with thorns," was painted by W. Hilton, R.A., and presented to the church by the British Institution.

INTERIOR OF THE COURT-YARD OF OLD "TATTERSALL'S." (*See page* 5.)

Chester Square, which almost abuts upon the north side of Eaton Square, was commenced about the year 1840, and was so called after the City of Chester, near which place Eaton Hall is situated. The picturesque Gothic church of St. Michael, which stands in a commanding position at the western end of the square, was erected in 1844, the foundation-stone being laid by Earl Grosvenor, father of the present Duke of Westminster; and it was built from the designs of Mr. Thomas Cundy in the Decorated style of the fourteenth century. Its principal external feature is the tower, with a lofty spire, which, till some additions to the body of the church were made in 1874, appeared to be somewhat out of proportion to the remainder of the fabric.

Ebury Street and Ebury Square were so called from Ebury or Eabery Farm, which stood on this site. The farm embraced upwards of 400 acres, meadow and pasture, and was let on lease by Queen Elizabeth for the sum of £21 per annum, to a person named Whashe, by whom, as Strype tells us, "the same was let to divers persons, who, for their private commodity, did inclose the same and had made pastures of arable land; thereby not only annoying her Majesty in her walks and passages, but to the hindrance of her game, and great injury to the common, which at Lammas was wont to be laid open." In Ebury Street there was formerly an open-air skating-rink and club-house, called the "Belgravia." Its career, however, was but of short duration, as the skating-rink mania soon passed away. The Manor House of the Eabury Estate stood between Hobart Place and the bottom of Grosvenor Place.

The western limits of Belgravia are Lowndes Square, Cadogan Place, and the few connecting streets on the east side of Sloane Street. Lowndes Square itself dates from about the year 1838, when it was built on a vacant piece of ground, described in Rocque's "Map of London and its Environs," engraved in 1746, as then belonging to "—Lowndes, Esq.;" and it was so called, says Mr. Peter Cunningham, "after Mr. Lowndes, of The Bury, near Chesham, in Buckinghamshire, the ground landlord, a descendant of William Lowndes, Secretary to the Treasury in the reign of Queen Anne." "The site of this square," as Mr. John Timbs informs us, "was once a coppice, which supplied the Abbot and Convent of Westminster with wood for fuel."

Lowndes Square has numbered among its residents at different times men who have distinguished themselves in their several walks of life. Of them we may mention Sir John Rennie, the architect of New London Bridge; Sir William Tite, another distinguished architect, and some time M.P. for Bath; General Lord Airey; Thomas Brassey, the engineer; and the Right Hon. Robert Lowe, M.P. for London University.

At the corner of Lowndes Square and Cadogan Place, we quit the Duke of Westminster's estate. Cadogan Place, which occupies an extensive area of ground, is open on the west side to Sloane Street. It is called after the family of Lord Cadogan, into whose hands the manor of Chelsea came, by the marriage of the first Lord Cadogan with the heiress of Sir Hans Sloane.

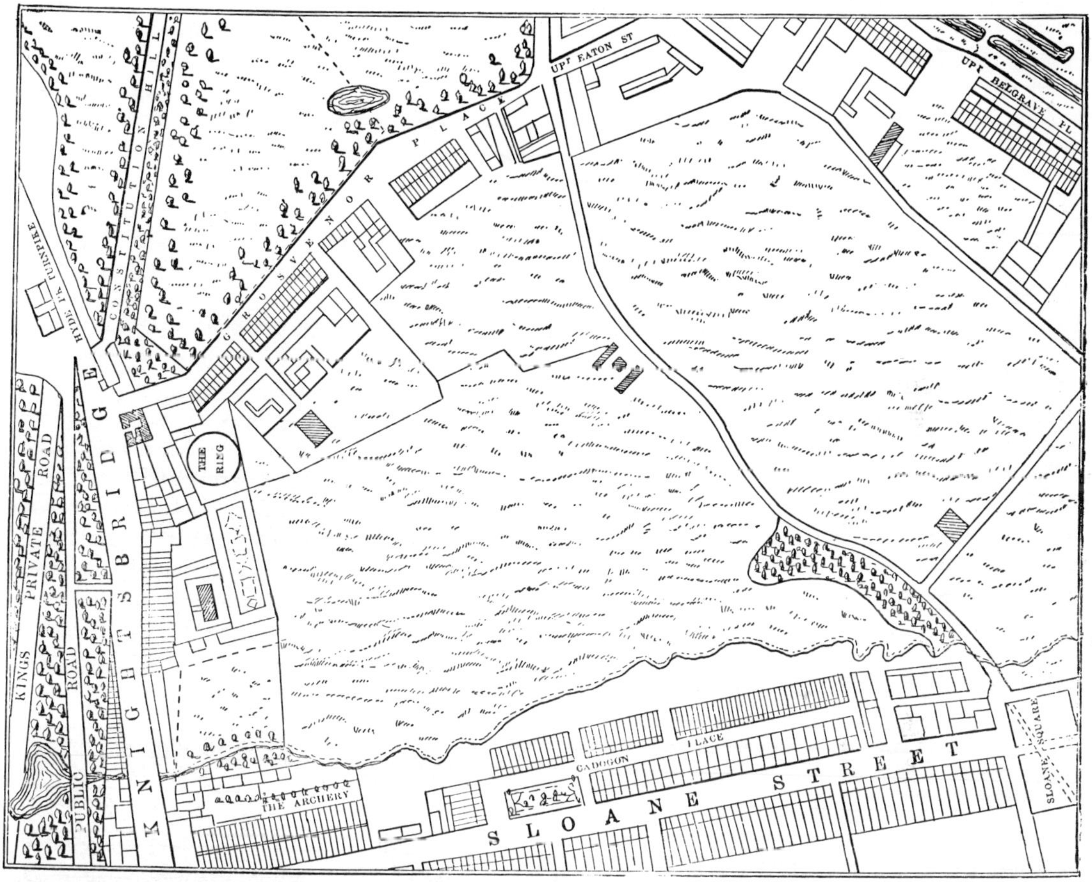

MAP OF BELGRAVIA, 1814.

Here lived Mr. and Mrs. Zachary Macaulay from about 1818 to 1823, when they removed to Great Ormond Street, as already stated. From Cadogan Place, the young Macaulays used to walk on a Sunday—or, as they were taught to call the day, the "Sabbath"—across the "Five Fields," now Belgrave Square, to the Lock Chapel, then situated in Grosvenor Place.

In a house in Cadogan Place, on the 29th of July, 1833, died William Wilberforce, the eminent philanthropist, many years M.P. for Yorkshire, who is best known for his devotion to the abolition of the slave-trade. There is something peculiarly touching in the fact that Wilberforce died—*felix opportunitate mortis*—just as the abolition of the slave-trade was in the act of being carried through Parliament, and the last fetters struck from the slaves' hands and feet. His funeral took place on the 3rd of August, in Westminster Abbey. On that day, his friend's son, Thomas Babington Macaulay, writes :—"We have laid him side by side with Canning, at the feet of Pitt, and within two steps of Fox and Grattan. He died with the promised land full in view." Before the end of the next month the British Parliament formally abolished slavery throughout the dominions of the Crown, and the last touch was put to the work that had consumed so many pure and noble lives. It was agreed that he should have been buried in the grave of his friends the Stephens, at Stoke Newington, but the voice of the country ruled otherwise. A subscription was immediately opened among Mr. Wilberforce's friends in London, and his statue has been placed in Westminster Abbey. At York, a County Asylum for the Blind has been founded in honour of him, while his townsmen of Hull have raised a column to his memory. Great part of our coloured population in the West Indies went into mourning at the news of his death; and the same was the case at New York, where also an eulogium was pronounced upon him by a person publicly selected for the task.

In Cadogan Place lived Sir Herbert Taylor, the Private Secretary and attached friend of King William IV. Here, too, was the last London residence of the celebrated actress, Mrs. Jordan. Another resident in Cadogan Place, in more recent times, was Mr. Wynn Ellis, of Tankerton Castle, Whitstable, formerly M.P. for Leicester. He had for many years a mania for collecting pictures, chiefly the works of the old masters, of which he was an excellent connoisseur. Dr. Waagen (1835), in his "Art and Artists in England," mentions a visit paid by him to Mr. Wynn Ellis's gallery:—"He possesses, besides many good old pictures, the best copy of Wilson's celebrated landscape, together with the 'Children of Niobe,' formerly in the possession of the Duke of Gloucester."

Mr. Wynn Ellis died in 1875, having by his will left to the nation, for exhibition in the National Gallery, his large collection of the works of the old masters. These alone number some four or five hundred. The mere mention of the names of certain of the artists tell their own tale; for among the collection there are more than one painting, in some cases several, from the brushes of Raphael, Rubens, Murillo, Claude, Van der Velde, Hobbima, Holbein, Guido, Leonardo da Vinci, the Poussins, and a score of others. Mr. Ellis's collection of works by modern artists was brought to the hammer at Christie's, and the sale formed one of the events of the season. Mr. Ellis began life as a warehouseman on Ludgate Hill, and accumulated a large fortune, many thousands of which he left to different charities.

Of Sloane Square, at the south end of Cadogan Place, we shall speak in a future chapter, when dealing with Sloane Street.

In a map of London and its neighbourhood, published in 1804, the whole of the site of Belgravia, between Grosvenor Place and Sloane Street, appears still covered with fields. They are crossed by "the King's private road," which is now occupied by Hobart Place, the roadway in the centre of Eaton Square, and Westbourne Place, terminating in Sloane Square. About the centre of Grosvenor Place, at that time, stood the Lock Hospital or Asylum, which was founded in 1787 by the Rev. Thomas Scott, the commentator; a little to the south, at the corner of the "King's private road," was the Duke's Hospital. What is now Ebury Street was then an open roadway, called Ranelagh Street, having a few houses on one side only. Twenty years later the whole character of this locality was considerably changed. Belgrave Square and Wilton Crescent had sprung into existence, as also had Cadogan Square and Cadogan Place, together with a few connecting streets. Sir Richard Phillips, in his "Walk from London to Kew," published in 1817, speaks of the creeks which at that time ran from the Thames "in the swamps opposite Belgrave Place," and adds that they "once joined the canal in St. James's Park, and, passing through Whitehall, formed by their circuit the ancient isle of St. Peter's. Their course," he continues, "has been filled up between the wharf of the water-works and the end of the canal in St. James's Park, and the isle of St. Peter's is no longer to be traced." The cut on the preceding page shows the locality in 1814.

CHAPTER II.

KNIGHTSBRIDGE.

"Cubat hic in colle Quirini,
Hic extremo in Aventino; visendus uterque:
Intervalla vides humanè commoda."—*Horace.*

Derivation of the Name of Knightsbridge—Early History of the Locality—The Old Bridge—Insecurity of the Roads, and Bad Reputation of the Innkeepers—Historical Events connected with Knightsbridge—The Old "Swan" Inn—Electioneering Riots—An Eccentric Old Lady—The "Spring Garden" and the "World's End"—Knightsbridge Grove—Mrs. Cornelys as a Vendor of Asses' Milk—Albert Gate—The "Fox and Bull"—The French Embassy—George Hudson, the "Railway King"—The Cannon Brewery—Dunn's Chinese Gallery—Trinity Chapel and the Lazar House—"Irregular" Marriages—Knightsbridge Barracks—Smith and Barber's Floor-cloth Manufactory—Edward Stirling, the "Thunderer" of the *Times*—Kent House—Kingston House—Rutland Gate—Ennismore Place—Brompton Oratory—Brompton Church—Count Rumford and other Distinguished Residents—New "Tattersall's"—The Green—Chalker House—The "Rose and Crown" Inn—The "Rising Sun"—Knightsbridge Cattle Market.

In the early Saxon days, when "Chelsey," and "Kensing town," and "Charing" were country villages, there lay between all three a sort of "No Man's Land," which in process of time came to be called "Knightsbridge," although it never assumed, or even claimed, parochial honours, nor indeed could be said to have had a recognised existence. It was a district of uncertain extent and limits; but it is, nevertheless, our purpose to try and "beat the bounds" on behalf of its former inhabitants.

The name of Knightsbridge, then, must be taken as indicating, not a parish, nor yet a manor, but only a certain locality adjoining a bridge which formerly stood on the road between London and far distant Kensington. There is much difficulty as to the derivation of the name, for in the time of Edward the Confessor, if old records are correctly deciphered, it was called "Kyngesburig;" while some hundred years or so later we find it spoken of as "Knightsbrigg," in a charter of Herbert, Abbot of Westminster. A local legend, recorded by Mr. Davis, in his "History of Knightsbridge," says that: "In ancient time certain knights had occasion to go from London to wage war for some holy purpose. Light in heart, if heavy in arms, they passed through this district on their way to receive the blessing awarded to the faithful by the Bishop of London at Fulham. For some cause or other, however, a quarrel ensued between two of the band, and a combat was determined upon to decide the dispute. They fought on the bridge which spanned the stream of the Westbourne, whilst from its banks the struggle was watched by their partisans. Both fell, if the legend may be trusted; and the place was ever after called Knightsbridge, in remembrance of their fatal feud."

Another possible derivation of the name is quoted from Norden, the topographer, by the Rev. M. Walcott, in his "Memorials of Westminster:"—"Kingsbridge, commonly called Stonebridge, near Hyde Park Corner, [is a place] where I wish no true man to walk too late without good guard, as did Sir H. Knyvett, Knight, who valiantly defended himself, there being assaulted, and slew the master thief with his own hands." However, in all probability the name is of older date than either of the above events; therefore we may be content to leave the question for the solution of future topographers, merely remarking that whether it was originally "Knightsbrigg," or "Kyngesbrigg," King Edward the Confessor held lands here, and possibly may have built a bridge for the use of the monks of Westminster, to whom he devised a portion of his acres. That such was the case we learn from a charter preserved in the British Museum, which conveyed to the monks of Westminster, along with the manor of Chelsea, "every third tree, and every horse-load of fruit grown in an adjacent wood at Kyngesbyrig, as heretofore by law accustomed."

"Knightsbridge," observes Mr. Davis, in his "History," "is not mentioned in Domesday Book, neither are Westbourne, or Hyde, or Paddington, these places being probably included in the surrounding manors." Moreover, we read that "Knightsbridge lies in the manor of Eia or Ea, formerly a portion of Cealcyth (Chelcheth or Chelsey), and now known as Eabury or Ebury." The manor of Ea, as confirmed to the Abbey of Westminster by the Conqueror, seems to have included all the lands lying between the Westbourne on the west, and the Tyburn on the east, from the great road which ran from Tyburn towards Uxbridge down to the Thames. Yet, curiously enough, as Mr. Davis tells us, though given thus early to the Abbey, the manor was not included in the franchise of the city of Westminster, though Knightsbridge, which lay partly, at least, beyond it, was so included. The fact is the more strange, as a large part of Knightsbridge belonged for many centuries, and indeed still in theory belongs, to the parish of St. Margaret, Westminster.

In the course of time the monks of Westminster

appear to have claimed and exercised further rights over this district, including the holding of market and a fair, the erection of a gallows-tree, and those of imprisoning evil-doers, and of seizing the goods of condemned persons and runaways. They further appropriated sundry lay fees in "Knythbrigg, Padyngton, Eya, and Westbourne, without licence of the king." In 1222 the Tyburn stream was laid down as the west boundary of that parish, excepting the hamlet of Knightsbridge, which lay beyond it.

The manor of Ea, or Eabury, was afterwards included in St. Martin's-in-the-Fields, when the latter was cut off from St. Margaret's; but when St. George's, Hanover Square, was carved out of St. Martin's, in 1724, both Knightsbridge and Eabury were assigned to the parish of St. George's. The rivulet, however, being made the western boundary between St. George's parish and Chelsea, it came about that Knightsbridge stands partly in all the three parishes above mentioned. When the bounds of St. Margaret's and other parishes were beaten, the parochial authorities passed through one part or other of the hamlet; and we may be sure that many a Knightsbridge urchin was whipped at the frontiers in order to impress the exact limits indelibly on his memory. Indeed, in the parish books of St. Margaret's there are several entries of sums spent by the beadles, &c., at Knightsbridge, on the "perambulation." Knightsbridge was, at all events, cut off, at a very early date, from St. Margaret's parish. It would appear, therefore, that only a portion of the hamlet was within the manor of Ea, including, as nearly as possible, all that now forms the parish of St. George's, Hanover Square. In Domesday Book it is given as ten hides; it was afterwards divided into three manors —viz., Neyte, Eabury, and Hyde. The first-named manor was near the Thames; and Hyde, with certain lands taken from Knightsbridge, formed Hyde Park. All these manors belonged to the Abbey till the Reformation, when they "escheated to"—*i.e.*, were seized by—the king. They were afterwards exchanged by his most gracious and rapacious majesty for the dissolved Priory of Hurley, in Berkshire.

Somehow or other, however, though the time and the way are not known, Knightsbridge reverted to its former owners, the Abbey of Westminster, in whose hands it has since remained, with the exception of the few years of the Puritan Protectorate, though the outlying lands about Kensington Gore passed into lay hands, as also did the manor of Eabury, in which it would seem that there was abundance of game, and large portions of waste land laid open to them for the pasturage of their cattle. Be this as it may, however, the manor passed into the hands first of the Whashes, or Walshes, and then into those of a family named Davis, the last male of whom, Alexander Davis, left an only daughter and heiress, Mary, who, in 1676, was married, at St. Clement Danes' Church, to Sir Thomas Grosvenor, into whose hands she carried the manor, as already stated. Her lineal descendants, it is almost needless to state, are the present Duke of Westminster and Lord Ebury.

The bridge which spanned the Westbourne, and gave its name to the hamlet of Knightsbridge, is described by Strype as of stone, and probably is the same which lasted down to our own day. It stood where now is Albert Gate, and probably portions of it are still embedded in the high road a few yards south of that entrance, and opposite to Lowndes Square. The stream is now little more than the surplus water of the Serpentine, which passes here in a covered drain under the high road; but Mr. Davis tells us that, as lately as 1809, it overflowed its banks so much that the "neighbourhood became a lake, and that foot-passengers were for several days rowed from Chelsea by Thames boatmen."

As far back as the reign of Edward III. (1361), we find Knightsbridge spoken of as "a town;" for during the plague in that reign a royal edict was issued from the Palace at Westminster, to the effect "that all bulls, oxen, hogs, and other grass creatures to be slain for the sustenance of the people, be led as far as the town of Stratford on the one side of London, *and the town of Knightsbridge* on the other, to be slain."

In Thornton's "Survey of London," published in 1780, Knightsbridge is described as "a village a little to the east of Kensington, with many public-houses and several new buildings lately erected, but none of them sufficiently remarkable to admit of particular description." Indeed, it was not till quite the end of the last century, or, perhaps, early in the present, that Knightsbridge became fairly joined on to the metropolis. A letter, in 1783, describes the place as "quite out of London." And so it must have been, for as late as that date, writes Mr. Davis, "the stream ran open, the streets were unpaved and unlighted, and a May-pole was still on the village green. It is not ten years [he wrote in 1854] since the hawthorn hedge has disappeared entirely from the Gore, and the blackbird and starling might still be heard. . . . . Few persons imagine, perhaps, that within the recollection of some who have not long passed from us, snipes and woodcocks might occasionally be found. Forty years since there was neither a draper's nor a butcher's shop between Hyde Park Corner and Sloane Street, and only one in the whole locality where a newspaper or writing-paper could be bought. There was no conveyance to London but a kind of stage-coach; the roads were dimly lighted by oil; and the modern paving to be seen only along Knightsbridge Terrace. Till about 1835 a watch-house and pound remained at the east end of Middle Row; and the stocks were to be seen, as late as 1805, at the end of Park-side, almost opposite the Conduit."

The high road which led through Knightsbridge towards Kensington, and so on to Brentford, was, two centuries ago, very badly kept and maintained, as regards both its repairs and the security of those who passed along it. There was no lack of inns about Knightsbridge; but the reputation of their keepers would not bear much inquiry, as it is almost certain that they were in league with the highwaymen who infested the road. As a proof of the former part of our assertion, it may be mentioned that when Sir Thomas Wyatt brought up his forces to attack London, this was the route by which they came. "The state of the road," we are told, "materially added to their discomfiture, and so great was the delay thereby occasioned that the Queen's party were able to make every preparation, and when Wyatt's men reached London, their jaded appearance gained them the name of 'Draggle-tails.'" In this condition, however, things remained for more than a century and a half; for, in 1736, when the Court had resided at Kensington for nearly fifty years, Lord Hervey writes to his mother thus, under date November 27th:—"The road between this place (Kensington) and London is grown so infamously bad, that we live here in the same solitude we should do if cast on a rock in the middle of the ocean; and all the Londoners tell us there is between them and us a great impassable gulf of mud. There are two roads through the park; but the new one is so convex, and the old one so concave, that by this extreme of faults they agree in the common one of being, like the high road, impassable."

As to the danger from footpads to which travellers were exposed on the high road between Kensington and London, we will quote the following proofs. In the register of burials at Kensington is the following entry, which speaks for itself:—"1687, 25th November.—Thomas Ridge, of Portsmouth, who was killed by thieves almost at Knightsbridge." John Evelyn, too, writes in his "Diary," November 25th, 1699:—"This week robberies were committed between the many lights which were fixed between London and Kensington on both sides, and while coaches and travellers were passing." Lady Cowper, too, has the following entry in her "Diary," in October, 1715:—"I was at Kensington, where I intended to stay as long as the camp was in Hyde Park, the roads being so secure by it that we might come from London at any time of the night without danger, which I did very often."

It is clear, from the *Gentleman's Magazine* for April, 1740, that about a quarter of a century later matters were as bad as ever. "The Bristol mail," writes Sylvanus Urban, "was robbed, a little beyond Knightsbridge, by a man on foot, who took the Bath and Bristol bags, and, mounting the postboy's horse, rode off towards London." Four years later three men were executed for highway robberies committed here; and in another attempted highway robbery, a little westward of the bridge at Knightsbridge, we read of a footpad being shot dead.

This being the case, we need not be surprised to find, from the *Morning Chronicle* of May 23, 1799, that it was necessary at the close of last century to order a party of light horse to patrol every night the road from Hyde Park Corner to Kensington; and Mr. Davis, in his work already quoted, states that persons then (1854) alive well remembered when "pedestrians walked to and from Kensington in bands sufficient to ensure mutual protection, starting on their journey only at known intervals, of which a bell gave due warning." It would, however, be unfair to suppose that Knightsbridge, in this respect, was worse than any other suburb of London at that time, as we have already shown in our accounts of Marylebone, Tottenham Court Road, and other parts.

In proof of the bad character of the innkeepers of Knightsbridge, we may mention that Sheffield, Duke of Buckingham, tells us that when about to be engaged in a duel with the Earl of Rochester, he and his second "lay over-night at Knightsbridge privately, to avoid being secured at London upon any suspicion;" adding, that he and his friend "had the appearance of highwaymen, for which the people of the house liked us all the better." So also in *The Rehearsal*, written to satirise Dryden, we find the following dialogue, the drift of which is obvious:—

Smith: But pray, Mr. Bayes, is not this a little difficult, that you were saying e'en now, to keep an army thus concealed in Knightsbridge?

Bayes: In Knightsbridge? No, not if the innkeeper be his friends.

The "wood at Kyngesbrigg," of which we have

spoken, and which modern topographers identify with the spot where now stands Lowndes Square, may give us some clue to the character of the neighbourhood six or seven hundred years ago. No doubt, it formed a portion of that forest with which, as we learn from Fitz-Stephen, London was surrounded on almost every side. "It owned no lord," says Mr. Davis, "and the few inhabitants enjoyed free chase and other rights in it. It was disafforested by order of Henry III.; and in the reign of his son, Edward I., if we may trust Mr. Lysons, Knightsbridge was a manor belonging to the Abbey. To their lands here, in the course of the next half century or so, the monks added others at Westbourne, and both were jointly erected into a manor—that of 'Knightsbridge and Westbourne'—a name still retained in legal documents." Mr. Davis adds that "the whole of the isolated parts of St. Margaret's parish—including a part of Kensington, its palace, and gardens—are included in this manor."

As we have already related, Knightsbridge was the last halting-place of Sir Thomas Wyatt and his Kentish followers, before his foolish assault on London in the reign of Queen Mary; and there is every reason to believe, both from local tradition, and also from the helmets, swords, &c., which from time to time have been dug up in the neighbourhood, that it was the scene of more than one encounter between the Royal and Parliamentary forces in the time of Charles I. Here, too, was the house occupied by the "infamous" Lord Howard, of Escrick, by whose perjured evidence so noble a patriot as Algernon Sidney was sent to the block. Roger North, in his "Examen," tells us that when the Rye House Plot became known, the king commanded that Howard should be arrested, and that accordingly his house was searched by the Serjeant-at-Arms, to whom he surrendered at discretion. He saved his own life by despicably turning round upon the partners of his guilt. Many allusions to his conduct on this occasion will be found in the satires and ballads of the day, of which the following may be taken as an average specimen :—

THE SPRING GARDEN, "WORLD'S END." *From a Drawing in the Crace Collection.* (*See page* 21.)

"Was it not a d—— thing
That Russell and Hampden
Should serve all the projects of hot-headed Tory?
But much more untoward
To appoint my Lord Howard
Of his own purse and credit to raise men and money?

THE NORTH SIDE OF KNIGHTSBRIDGE IN 1820, FROM THE CANNON BREWERY TO HYDE PARK CORNER.
(From a Drawing in the Crace Collection.)

Who at Knightsbridge did hide
Those brisk boys unspy'd,
That at Shaftesbury's whistle were ready to follow
But when aid he should bring,
Like a true Brentford king,
He was here with a whoop and there with a hollo!"

Through Knightsbridge passed the corpse of Henry VIII., on its way to its last resting-place at Windsor. The fact is thus recorded in the parish books of St. Margaret's:—"Paid to the poor men that did bere the copis (copes) and other necessaries to Knightsbridge, when that the King was brought to his buryal to Wynsor, and to the men that did ring the bells, 3 shillings."

The next historical event connected with this neighbourhood is the intended assassination of William III. by two Jacobite gentlemen—curiously enough, named Barclay and Perkins—in 1694. Their plan was to waylay the king on his return to Kensington from some hunting expedition, and to shoot him. The plot, however, was revealed by one of their accomplices, who met at the "Swan Inn," Knightsbridge, to arrange the time and place; and the two principals were hung at Tyburn, though they never carried their plot into execution.

The "Swan," two centuries ago, was an inn of so bad a reputation, as to be the terror of jealous husbands and anxious fathers, and is often alluded to as such in some of the comedies of the time; as, for instance, in Otway's *Soldier of Fortune*, where Sir David Dance says: "I have surely lost her (my daughter), and shall never see her more; she promised me strictly to stay at home till I came back again. . . . For aught I know, she may be taking the air as far as Knightsbridge, with some smooth-faced rogue or another. 'Tis a bad house, that Swan; the Swan at Knightsbridge is a confounded house." The house has also the honour, such as it is, of being mentioned by Tom Brown in his "School Days," and also by Peter Pindar.

More recently, Knightsbridge has gained some celebrity, as the scene of one or two passing riots, as, for instance, in the year 1768, on the election of Wilkes for Middlesex. "It was customary," writes Mr. Davis, "for a London mob to meet the Brentford mob in or about Knightsbridge; and as Wilkes' opponent was riding through with a body of his supporters, one of them hoisted a flag, on which was inscribed 'No Blasphemer,' and terrible violence instantly ensued." Again, in 1803, another election riot, in which one or two lives were lost, took place in the High Street, Sir Francis Burdett being the popular favourite. Another riot took place here in 1821, at the funeral of two men who had been shot by the soldiers at the funeral of Queen Caroline.

It should, perhaps, be mentioned here, in illustration of the strongly-marked character of the inhabitants of the locality, that in the days of Burdett, when politics ran high, the people of Knightsbridge were mostly "Radicals of the first water." At that time "Old Glory," as Sir Francis Burdett was called before his conversion to Toryism, was in every respect the man of their choice as member for Westminster. And it was in compliment to the inhabitants of Knightsbridge, and in acknowledgment of their support, that he and his colleague, Sir John Hobhouse, on one occasion, when "chaired," chose to make their start from the corner of Sloane Street.

From a chance allusion in Butler's "Hudibras" to this place, it may be inferred that in the Puritan times it formed the head-quarters of one of the hundred-and-one sects into which the "religious world" of that day was divided; for the dominant faction are there accused of having—

"Filled Bedlam with predestination
And Knightsbridge with illumination."

As stated in the previous chapter, the commencement of the Knightsbridge Road is about fifty yards west of the Alexandra Hotel. Here, at the corner of the main road and of Wilton Place, stood formerly a tobacconist's shop, which very much narrowed the thoroughfare, and was not removed till about the year 1840. It was occupied by an eccentric old woman, a Mrs. Dowell, who was so extremely partial to the Duke of Wellington, that she was constantly devising some new plan by which to show her regard for him. She sent him from time to time patties, cakes, and other delicacies of the like kind; and as it was found impossible to defeat the old woman's pertinacity, the duke's servants took in her presents. To such a pitch did she carry her mania, that she is said to have laid a knife and fork regularly for him at her own table day by day, constantly expecting that the duke would sooner or later do her the honour of dropping in and "taking pot luck" with her. In this hope, however, we believe we may safely assert that she was doomed to disappointment to the last.

At the back of the above-mentioned house was in former times one of the most noted suburban retreats in the neighbourhood of London, called the "Spring Garden," a place of amusement formed in the grounds of an old mansion which stood on the north side of what is now Lowndes Square. Dr. King, of Oxford, mentions it in his diary as "an excellent spring garden;" and among the entries of the Virtuosi, or St. Luke's Club, founded by Vandyck, is the following item:—"Paid—Spent at Spring Gardens, by Knightsbridge, forfeiture, £3 15s." Pepys also, no doubt, refers to these same gardens in his "Diary," when he writes:—"I lay in my drawers and stockings and waistcoat [at Kensington] till five of the clock, and so up; and being well pleased with our frolic, walked to Knightsbridge, and there ate a mess of cream; and so on to St. James's." Again, too, on another occasion:—"From the town, and away out of the Park, to Knightsbridge, and there ate and drank in the coach; and so home." It is probable that the sign of the house in this Spring Garden was the "World's End," for the following entry in Mr. Pepys' "Diary" can hardly refer to any other place but this:—"Forth to Hyde Park, but was too soon to go in; so went on to Knightsbridge, and there ate and drank at the 'World's End,' where we had good things; and then back to the Park, and there till night, being fine weather, and much company." And again, the very last entry in his "Diary," under date of May 31st, 1669:—"To the Park, Mary Botelier and a Dutch gentleman, a friend of hers, being with us. Thence to the 'World's End,' a drinking-house by the Park, and there merry, and so home late."

Whether the tavern attached to this Spring Garden enjoyed the doubtful reputation of the "World's End" at Chelsea is not quite certain.

The house to which this garden was attached, having been successively occupied as a museum of anatomy, an auction-room, and a carpenter's workshop, was pulled down about the year 1826, in order to lay out the ground for building. Lowndes Square, however, was not begun till about 1838, or completed till 1848 or 1849. The stream which ran along the west side of Spring Gardens had along its banks a path leading down to Bloody Bridge, and thence to Ranelagh. On grand gala nights this path was protected by a patrol, or by the more able of the Chelsea pensioners. It only remains to add that various relics of the Civil War have been discovered upon this site, such as swords, spurs, and bits, and other relics telling of more modern and more prosaic encounters, such as staves and handcuffs, tokens of successful or unsuccessful struggles between footpads and constables.

A little west of Wilton Place, a narrow roadway, called Porter's Lane, led into some fields, in which stood an old mansion, known as Knightsbridge Grove, and approached from the highway by an avenue of fine trees. This is the house which, about 1790, was taken by the celebrated Mrs. Cornelys, under the assumed name of Mrs. Smith, as a place for company to drink new asses' milk. After the failure of all her plans and schemes to secure the support of the world of fashion for her masquerades and concerts at Carlisle House, in Soho Square, as we have already seen,* and not cast down by the decree of the Court of Chancery, under which her house and furniture were sold by auction in 1785, here she fitted up a suite of rooms for the reception of visitors who wished to breakfast in public. But the manners of the age were changed, and her taste had not adapted itself to the varieties of fashion. After much expense incurred in the gaudy embellishment of her rooms after the foreign fashion, she was obliged to abandon her scheme, and to seek a refuge from her merciless creditors. A former queen—or rather empress—of fashion, she closed her eccentric and varied career a prisoner for debt in the Fleet Prison, in August, 1797. The house was afterwards kept by a sporting character, named Hicks, under whom it was frequently visited by George, Prince Regent, and his friends.

The entrance into Hyde Park, opposite Lowndes Square, is named Albert Gate, after the late Prince Consort; the houses which compose it stand as nearly as possible on the site of the old bridge over the Westbourne, which gave its name to the locality. We gave a view of this old bridge in our last volume, page 402. Mr. Davis, in his "Memorials of Knightsbridge," tells us that there was also another bridge across this brook, just inside the park to the north, erected in 1734. At the west end of the former bridge stood, at one time, a celebrated inn, known as the "Fox and Bull," traditionally said to have been founded in the reign of Elizabeth, and to have been used by her on her visits to Lord Burleigh at Brompton. The house is referred to in the *Tatler*, No. 259, and it is said to be the only inn that bore that sign. "At the 'Fox and Bull,'" writes Mr. Davis, "for a long while was maintained that Queen Anne style of society where persons of 'parts' and reputation were to be met with in rooms open to all. A Captain Corbet was for a long time its head; a Mr. Shaw, of the War Office, supplied the *London Gazette*, and W. Harris, of Covent Garden Theatre, his play-bills." Among its visitors may be named George Morland, and his patron, Sir W. W. Wynn, and occasionally Sir Joshua Reynolds, who painted its sign, which was blown down in a storm in 1807. The "Fox and Bull," it may be added, served for some years as a receiving-house

* See Vol. III., p. 188.

of the Royal Humane Society, in Hyde Park. Hither was brought the body of the first wife of the poet Shelley, after she had drowned herself in the Serpentine; and here the judicial business of the locality was conducted, a magistrate sitting once a week for that purpose. The old house was Elizabethan in structure, and contained rooms and ceilings panelled and carved in the style of her day, and with large fire-places and fire-dogs. The house stood till the year 1835. The skeletons of several men were found beneath it in the course of some excavations in the early part of the present century, these were supposed to have been those of soldiers killed here in the Civil War.

On the east side of the old bridge was a low court of very old houses, named after the "White Hart Inn," but these were swept away about 1841. The stags on the side pedestals of the gate, we learn from the "Memorials of Knightsbridge," were modelled from a pair of prints by Bartolozzi, and formerly kept watch and ward in Piccadilly, at the entrance to the Ranger's Lodge in the Green Park.*

When this entrance was first formed, the late Mr. Thomas Cubitt designed and built two very lofty mansions on either side, which were sneeringly styled the "Two Gibraltars," because it was prophesied that they never would or could be "taken." Taken, however, they were; that on the eastern side was the town residence of the "Railway King," George Hudson, before his fall; it has since been occupied as the French Embassy. Queen Victoria paid a visit to the Embassy in state in 1854, and the Emperor Louis Napoleon held a levée here, on his visit to London, in the summer of the following year.

"The career of George Hudson, ridiculously styled the 'Railway King,'" writes Mr. J. Timbs, in his "Romance of London," "was one of the *ignes fatui* of the railway mania of 1844-5. He was born in a lowly house in College Street, York, in 1800; here he served his apprenticeship to a linendraper, and subsequently carried on the business as principal, amassing considerable wealth. His fortune was next increased by a bequest from a distant relative, which sum he invested in North-Midland Railway shares. Mr. Smiles describes Hudson as a man of some local repute when the line between Leeds and York was projected. His views as to railways were then extremely moderate, and his main object in joining the undertaking was to secure for York the advantages of the best railway communication. . . . The grand test by which the shareholders judged him was the dividends which he paid, although subsequent events proved that these dividends were, in many cases, delusive, intended only to make things pleasant. The policy, however, had its effect. The shares in all the lines of which he was chairman went to a premium; and then arose the temptation to create new shares in branch and extension lines, often worthless, which were issued at a premium also. Thus he shortly found himself chairman of nearly 600 miles of railways, extending from Rugby to Newcastle, and at the head of numerous new projects, by means of which paper wealth could be created, as it were, at pleasure. He held in his own hands almost the entire administrative power of chairman, board, manager, and all. Mr. Hudson was voted praises, testimonials, and surplus shares alike liberally, and scarcely a word against him could find a hearing.

"The Hudson testimonial was a taking thing, for Mr. Hudson had it in his power to allot shares (selling at a premium) to the subscribers to the testimonial. With this fund he bought of Mr. Thomas Cubitt, for £15,000, the lofty house on the east of Albert Gate, Hyde Park. There he lived sumptuously, and went his round of visits among the peerage.

"Mr. Hudson's brief reign soon drew to a close. The speculation of 1845 was followed by a sudden reaction. Shares went down faster than they had gone up: the holders of them hastened to sell in order to avoid payment of the calls; and many found themselves ruined. Then came repentance, and a sudden return to virtue. The golden calf was found to be of brass, and hurled down, Hudson's own toadies and sycophants eagerly joining in the chorus of popular indignation; and the bubbles having burst, the railway mania came to a sudden and ignominious end."

The rest of the site now covered by Albert Gate was occupied by the Cannon Brewery—so called from a cannon which surmounted it—and was surrounded by low and filthy courts with open cellars. The celebrated Chinese collection of Mr. Dunn was located here in the interval between the removal of the brewery and the erection of the present sumptuous edifices.

It is not a little singular that among all the changes as to the limits of parishes, it should have been forgotten that, from time immemorial, there was a chapel in the main street of Knightsbridge which could very easily, at any time, have been made parochial. This edifice, known as Trinity Chapel, still stands, though much altered, between the north side of the main street and

* See Vol. IV., p. 180.

the park; it was, in ancient times, attached to a lazar-house, of the early history of which little or nothing is known. No doubt it was formed before the Reformation, though the earliest notice of it in writing is in a grant of James I., to be seen in the British Museum, ordering "the hospital for sick, lame, or impotent people at Knightsbridge" to be supplied with water by an underground pipe, laid on from the conduit in Hyde Park. Lysons, however, tells us, in his "Environs of London," that there is among the records of the Chapter of Westminster a short MS. statement of the condition of the hospital in the latter part of Elizabeth's reign, from which it appears that it generally had about thirty-five inmates, and that it was supported by the contributions of charitable persons, being quite unendowed. The patients, it appears from this document, attended prayers mornings and evenings in the chapel, the neighbours also being admitted to the services on Sunday. The inmates dined on "warm meat and porrege," and each one had assigned to him, or her, a separate "dish, platter, and tankard, to kepe the broken for the whole."

A few notes on the disbursement made on behalf of the poor inmates, taken from the parish books of St. Margaret's, will be found in Mr. Nichols' "Illustrations of the Manners and Experiences of Ancient Times." The latter history of the hospital is almost as uncertain as its earlier chapters. We know even the names of a few of the "cripples," and other inmates—mostly wayfarers—who were discharged from it, after having been relieved; but although it was certainly in existence when Newcourt was collecting materials for his "Repertorium," in the reign of George I., no further trace of its existence or of its demolition can be found. It is traditionally asserted, however, that in the time of the Great Plague of 1665, the lazar-house was used as a hospital for those stricken by that disorder, and that such as died within its walls were buried in the enclosed triangular plot of ground which was once part of Knightsbridge Green. A writer in the first volume of *Notes and Queries* states that in the case of leprosy arising in London, the infected persons were taken off speedily into one of the lazar-houses in the suburbs. "The law was strictly carried out, and where resistance was made the sufferers were tied to horses, and dragged thither by force."

The chapel, being "very old and ruinous," was rebuilt by a subscription among the inhabitants of Knightsbridge, and opened as a chapel of ease by the authority of Laud, then Bishop of London, who licensed a minister to perform service in it. During the Commonwealth it was served by a minister appointed by the Parliament, and afterwards passed into lay hands. In the end, however, it was given back to the Dean and Chapter of Westminster; this body still appoints the incumbent, who is supported by a small endowment and the pew-rents.

The present chapel, now called the Church of Holy Trinity, was entirely restored and remodelled in 1861, from the designs of Messrs. Brandon and Eyton. It is a handsome Gothic building, with accommodation for about 650 worshippers, and was erected at a cost of about £3,300. The principal peculiarity about it is the roof, which is so constructed as to have a continuous range of clerestory lights the whole length of the church. These are accessible from the outside, so as to regulate the ventilation.

The chapel possesses some good communion plate. In the list of its ministers occur no names of note, unless it be worth while to record that of the Rev. Dr. Symons, who read the funeral service over Sir John Moore at Corunna.

In the registers of the chapel is recorded only one burial, under date 1667. It is probable that those who died in this hamlet were buried at St. Margaret's, Westminster, or at Chelsea, or Kensington. Mr. Davis, however, mentions a tradition that the enclosure on Knightsbridge Green was formerly used as a burying-ground. If this be so, the records of the fact have long since been lost. The statement, however, may have reference to the victims of the plague, as stated above.

The registers of baptisms are still in existence, and so are those of the marriages solemnised here—some of them, as might be expected, rather irregular, especially before the passing of Lord Hardwicke's Marriage Act in 1753, which seems to have put an extinguisher on such scandals. With reference to these irregular or "stolen" marriages, a writer in the *Saturday Review* observes:—"This was one of the places where irregular marriages were solemnised, and it is accordingly often noticed by the old dramatists. Thus in Shadwell's *Sullen Lovers*, Lovell is made to say, 'Let's dally no longer; there is a person in Knightsbridge that pokes all stray people together. We'll to him; he'll dispatch us presently, and send us away as lovingly as any two fools that ever yet were condemned to marriage.' Some of the entries in this marriage register are suspicious enough—'secrecy for life,' or 'great secrecy,' or 'secret for fourteen years,' being appended to the names. Mr. Davis, in his 'Memorials of Knightsbridge,' was the first to exhume from this document the name of the adventuress, 'Mrs. Mary Ayliss,' whom Sir Samuel Morland married as his fourth wife, in 1687. The readers of Pepys will remember how pathetically Morland wrote, eighteen days after the wedding, that, when he had expected to marry an heiress, 'I was, about a fortnight since, led as a fool to the stocks, and married a coachman's daughter not worth a shilling.' In 1699, an entry mentions one 'Storey at ye Park Gate.' This worthy it was who gave his name to what is now known as Storey's Gate. He was keeper of the aviary to Charles II., whence was derived the name of the Birdcage Walk. In the same year, Cornelius Van der Velde, limner, was married here to Bernada Van der Hagen. This was a brother of the famous William Van der Velde, the elder, and himself a painter of nautical pictures, in the employment of Charles II."

Among those who were married here, with more or less of secrecy or privacy, not mentioned in the above extract, were Sir John Lenthall, son of the Speaker of the House of Commons under Cromwell; the widow of the second Earl of Derwentwater—this lady was the youngest natural daughter of Charles II., by the actress, Mrs. Davis, known before her marriage as Lady Mary Tudor; and lastly, the great Sir Robert Walpole, to a daughter of the Lord Mayor of London, by whom he became the father of Horace Walpole. Many of the marriages here solemnised were runaway matches, and, as such, are marked in the registers with the words "private" and "secresy."

Of the barracks at Knightsbridge, facing the Park, usually occupied by one of the regiments of the Guards, there is little to say, except that they are badly placed, and were long an eyesore to the neighbourhood. They originally consisted of a range of dull heavy brick buildings, erected in 1794–5. In the centre of the building is an oblong parade-ground, around which are apartments for the private soldiers, placed over the stables. At the west-end is a riding-school, and a wing cut up into residences for the officers. New barracks were erected here in 1879–80, and are said to be the best of the kind in Europe. They form an extensive quadrangle, and there are reading-rooms for both the non-commissioned officers and privates.

THE "WHITE HART," KNIGHTSBRIDGE, 1820. (*See page* 22.

At the corner of South Place and Hill Street, nearly opposite the barracks, stands the celebrated floor-cloth manufactory of Messrs. Smith and

Barber. It was established as far back as the year 1754, and is said to be the oldest manufactory of the kind in London. The first block used for patterns was cut by its founder, Mr. Abraham Smith, and is still preserved in the factory. An illustration of it is given in Dodd's "British Manufactures," where the process of the manufacture will be found minutely described. In the adjoining house, No. 2, lived the Rev. Mr. Gamble, one of the incumbents of Knightsbridge Chapel; and after him Mr. Edward Stirling, known as the "Thunderer" of the *Times*, from whom it passed to his son, the gifted and amiable John Stirling, whose early death was so much lamented. There he used to receive among his visitors Professor Maurice, John Stuart Mill, and Thomas Carlyle; and here Sir Colin Campbell took up his residence for a time between his Crimean and his last Indian campaign.

Kent House, so called after the late Duke of Kent, who for a short time resided in it, and added considerably to its size, stands only a few yards to the west of South Place. It was for many years the residence of a brother of the late Earl of Clarendon, and afterwards of his widow, Lady Theresa Villiers (author of "The Friends and Contemporaries of Lord Chancellor Clarendon"), who married as her second husband Sir George C. Lewis, M.P., some time Chancellor of the Exchequer. He died here in 1863. Next door to it is Stratheden House, so named after the wife of Lord Chancellor Campbell, who wrote here his "Lives of the Chancellors." He died here suddenly in June, 1861. The mansion had previously been owned by Lord De Dunstanville.

KINGSTON HOUSE, KNIGHTSBRIDGE.

It was at Kingston House—situated some little distance westward of Kent House—that, on the 26th of September, 1842, the eminent statesman, the Marquis Wellesley, died, at the age of eighty-two. He was the elder brother of the "great" Duke of Wellington. Mr. Raikes tells us, in his "Journal:" "He had in his time filled various offices in the State at home, had been Governor-General of India, and twice Lord-Lieutenant of Ireland. He was a man of considerable talent and acquirements, particularly in the Latin and Greek languages. His first wife was a French lady—a Madame Roland—formerly his mistress. His second wife was an American—Mrs. Patterson."

Rutland Gate, a row of houses standing a little westward of the barracks, on the south side of the road, was built about 1840, and was so called from a large mansion which formerly stood on the site, belonging to the Dukes of Rutland. Here was the picture-gallery of Mr. John Sheepshanks, bequeathed by him to the nation, and now housed in the Sheepshanks Gallery at the South Kensington Museum. It was rich in works by Mulready, Leslie, and Landseer.

Ennismore Place, close by Prince's Gate, is so called from the second title of the Earl of Listowel, to whom the ground on which it stands belongs or belonged.

Brompton Road is the name given to a row of houses built about the year 1840, on what was a garden a century ago. At a house here, then numbered 45, Brompton Row, but now 168, Brompton Road, lived the celebrated philanthropist and philosopher, Count Rumford, and afterwards his daughter Sarah, Countess Rumford. The count had come to England as an exiled loyalist from America, and having risen to high employ in England, had been sent, in 1798, as Ambassador to London from Bavaria. Here he entertained Sir William Pepperell, and other American loyalists. Owing to George III.'s opposition to his appointment as a diplomatic representative of Bavaria, he lived in a private capacity. He died in France in 1814. The house is minutely described, in 1801, by M. Pictet, an intimate friend of the count, in a life of Count Rumford, published in 1876. It is still full, from top to bottom, of all sorts of cleverly-contrived cupboards, writing-desks, &c., fixed in the walls, and with fireplaces on a plan unlike those in the adjoining dwellings. It remains very much in the same state as in the count's time, though a stucco front appears to have been added. "The house had been let by Count Rumford to the Rev. William Beloe, the translator of Herodotus, who quitted possession of it in 1810. The countess, his daughter, lived in it and let it alternately, among her tenants being Sir Richard Phillips and Mr. Wilberforce. She disposed of the lease in 1837 to its present owners."

On the south side of Ennismore Place is Brompton Square, which consists of houses open at the south end to the Brompton Road, and terminating at the northern end with a semi-circular sweep, with a gateway leading to Prince's Terrace and Ennismore Gardens. At No. 22 in this square died, in 1836, George Colman "the Younger," the author of *John Bull*. Here also lived Mr. Luttrell, the friend of Sam Rogers, and the most brilliant of conversationalists *temp.* George IV. In consequence of the salubrity of the air in this neighbourhood, Brompton Square has long been a favourite abode for singers and actors. Behind the west side stands Brompton Church, a poor semi-Gothic structure, dating from about 1830. It was built from the designs of Professor Donaldson, and has a lofty tower and stained-glass windows of ancient design and colour. The church is approached by a fine avenue of lime-trees, and its churchyard contains a very large number of tombs; all, however, are modern, and few are of interest to the antiquary. John Reeve, the comic actor, who died in 1838, is buried here. Adjoining the parish church stands a building in the Italian style, known as the Oratory of St. Philip Neri, consisting of a large chapel, very secular in appearance, and a fine residence in the Italian style. They cover the site of a country house standing in its own grounds, which as lately as the year 1851 was used as a school. The clergy attached to the Oratory are secular priests, living voluntarily in a community, but not tied by religious vows. The first rector, and indeed the founder of this community in London, was the Rev. Frederick William Faber, formerly of University College, Oxford, and well known as the author of "The Cherwell Water-Lily," and other poems. He died in 1863.

Knightsbridge, however, has in its time numbered many other distinguished residents. Among them, Lady Anne Hamilton, the faithful friend and attendant of the Princess Caroline of Brunswick; the artist Chalon; Paul Bedford, the actor; McCarthy, the sculptor; and Ozias Humfrey, the Royal Academician (the friend of Reynolds, Dr. Johnson, and Romney), who is thus celebrated by the poet Hayley, when abandoning miniatures for oil portraits:—

> "Thy graces, Humfrey, and thy colours clear,
> From miniature's small circle disappear;
> May thy distinguished merit still prevail,
> And shine with lustre on a larger scale."

Here died, in 1805, at the age of upwards of eighty, Arthur Murphy, the author, who was a friend of Johnson, Reynolds, Burke, and others. Boswell thus relates the manner in which an acquaintance first commenced between Dr. Johnson and Mr. Murphy:—"During the publication of the *Gray's Inn Journal*, a periodical paper which was successfully carried on by Mr. Murphy alone, when a very young man, he happened to be in the country with Mr. Foote; and having mentioned that he was obliged to go to London in order to get ready for the press one of the numbers of that journal, Foote said to him, 'You need not go on that account. Here is a French magazine, in which you will find a very pretty Oriental tale; translate that, and send it to your printer.' Mr. Murphy having read the tale, was highly pleased with it, and followed Foote's advice. When he returned to town, this tale was pointed out to him in the *Rambler*, from whence it had been translated into the French magazine. Mr. Murphy then waited upon Johnson, to explain this curious incident. His talents, literature, and gentleman-like manners were soon perceived by Johnson, and a friendship was formed which was never broken."

Here, at a farm-house which supplied the royal family with milk, the fair Quakeress, Hannah Lightfoot, is said to have resided, after she had captivated the susceptible heart of George III., in the first year of his reign; but the story is discredited.

At the junction of Brompton Road with the main road through Knightsbridge, and near to Albert Gate, stands the great sporting rendezvous and auction-mart for horses, "Tattersall's." It was removed to this spot in 1865 from Grosvenor Place, where, as we have seen in the preceding chapter, it was originally established. The building occupies a site previously of comparatively little value, and has before its entrance a small triangular space planted with evergreens. The building in itself is arranged upon much the same plan as that of its predecessor, which we have already described. Immediately on the right of the entrance is the subscription-room and counting-house, both of which are well designed to meet their requirements; whilst beyond is a spacious covered court-yard, with a small circular structure in the centre, in which is a pump, surmounted by the figure of a fox; the dome which covers it bears a bust of George IV. The fox, it is presumed, belongs to the poetry of Tattersall's, suggesting, as it does, breezy rides over hill and dale and far-stretching moorlands. The royal bust above refers to more specific facts of which the establishment can boast; it is a type of the lofty patronage that has been acceded to the house from its earliest days. The bust represents the "first gentleman of Europe," as he has been, absurdly enough, called, in his eighteenth year, when the prince was a constant attendant at Tattersall's. The yard itself is surrounded by stabling for the horses, and galleries for carriages which may be there offered for sale. The great public horse auction is on Mondays throughout the year, with the addition of Thursdays in the height of the season. The subscription to the "Rooms," which is regulated by the Jockey Club, is two guineas annually; and the betting at Tattersall's, we need scarcely add, regulates the betting throughout the country.

The Green, as the triangular plot of ground in front of Tattersall's, mentioned above, is called, was once really a village-green, and it had its village may-pole, at all events, down to the end of the last century. It was larger in its extent in former days, several encroachments having been made upon its area. At its east end there stood, till 1834, a watch-house and pound, to which Addison refers in a very amusing paper in the *Spectator* (No. 142). Pretending, by way of jest, to satisfy by home news the craving for foreign intelligence which the late war had created in 1712, he writes: "By my last advices from Knightsbridge, I hear that a horse was clapped into the pound there on the 3rd inst., and that he was not recovered when the letters came away." A large part of what once was the Green is now covered by some inferior cottages, styled Middle Row; on the north side was an old inn, which rejoiced in the sign of the "Marquis of Granby," with reference to which we may be pardoned for quoting Byron's lines:—

"Vernon, the 'Butcher' Cumberland, Wolfe, Hawke,
  Prince Ferdinand, Granby, Burgoyne, Keppel, Howe,
Evil and good, have had their tithe of talk,
  And filled the sign-posts then as Wellesley now."

The small portion on the north side, fenced in by rails, is probably the old burial-ground belonging to the Lazar House, already mentioned.

Of Knightsbridge Terrace, now a row of shops, old inhabitants tell us that, when Her Majesty came to the throne, it consisted wholly of private houses. Here was Mr. Telfair's College for the Deaf and Dumb, and here lived Maurice Morgan, one of the secretaries to Lord Shelburne when the latter was Premier, and honourably mentioned by Boswell in his "Life of Johnson." Close to the corner of Sloane Street, too, lived Rodwell, the composer.

Among the oldest dwellings in this hamlet are some of the irregular houses on the south side of the road, between the Green and Rutland Gate. Mr. Davis, writing in the year 1859, in his "History of Knightsbridge," mentions Chalker House, built in 1688, now a broker's, and for many years a boarding-house. "Three doors beyond it," he continues, "is an ancient inn, now known as the 'Rose and Crown,' but formerly as the 'Oliver Cromwell,' but which has borne a licence for above three hundred years. It is the oldest house in Knightsbridge, and was formerly its largest inn, and not improbably was the house which sheltered Wyatt, while his unfortunate Kentish followers rested on the adjacent green. A tradition, told by all old inhabitants of the locality, that Cromwell's body-guard was once quartered here, is still very prevalent: an inscription to that effect was till lately painted on the front of the house; and on an ornamental piece of plaster-work was formerly emblazoned the great Lord Protector's coat of arms." Mr. Davis does not guarantee the literal truth of this tradition, though he holds that nothing is more certain than that Knightsbridge was the scene of frequent skirmishes during the Civil War. This was natural enough, considering that the hamlet was the first place on the great western road from London. We know for certain that the army of the Parliament was encamped about the neighbourhood in 1647, and that the head-quarters of Fairfax were at Holland House; and the same was the case just before and after the fight at Brentford. It was on the strength of this, and other traditions, that Mr. E. H. Corbould made this inn the subject of a painting, "The Old Hostelrie at Knightsbridge," exhibited in 1849. "He laid the scene as early as 1497. Opposite the inn is a well, surmounted by a figure of St. George; while beyond is the spacious green, the meandering stream, and the bridge over it, surmounted by an embattled tower; further off appears the old hospital and chapel. . . . . . The house of late," continues Mr. Davis, "has been much modernised, and in 1853 had a narrow escape from destruction by fire; but enough still remains, in its peculiar chimneys, oval-shaped windows, its low rooms, its large yard and extensive stabling, with galleries above and office-like places beneath, to testify to its antiquity and former importance." It was pulled down about the year 1865. Another hostelry in the main street was the "Rising Sun;" though a wooden inn, it was an ancient house, and its staircase and the panelling of its walls were handsomely carved. On the spot now occupied by the Duke of Wellington's stables, there was also, in former times, an inn known as the "Life Guardsman," and previously as the "Nag's Head."

We may mention that a market for cattle was held at Knightsbridge every Thursday till an early year in the present century, and that the last pen posts were not removed till 1850.

The air of this neighbourhood has always been regarded as pure and healthy. Swift brought his friend Harrison to it for the benefit of pure air; and half a century later it maintained the same character, for we read that Lady Hester Stanhope sent a faithful servant thither, with the same object in view. In sooth, "Constitution" Hill at one end, and "Montpelier" Square at the other, both derive their names from this peculiarity. The fact is that the main street of Knightsbridge stands on a well-defined terrace of the London clay, between the gravel of Hyde Park and that of Pimlico, resting on thick layers of sand, which cause the soil to be porous, and rapidly to absorb the surface-water.

The water-supply of Knightsbridge has always been remarkably good, being drawn from several conduits in and about Park-side and to the south of Rotten Row. One of these, known as St. James's, for the Receiving Conduit, supplied the royal palaces and the Abbey with water.

CHAPTER III.

THE GREAT EXHIBITION OF 1851.

> "Anon, out of the earth a fabric huge
> Rose like an exhalation."—*Milton.*

Previous Exhibitions of a somewhat similar Character—The Marquis d'Aveze's projected Exhibition—Various French Expositions—Competitive Exhibitions in England—Prince Albert's Proposal for holding an Industrial Exhibition of All Nations—His Royal Highness becomes Chairman of the Royal Commission—Banquet at the Mansion House—Lecturers and Agents sent all over the Country, to Explain the Objects of the Exhibition—Reception of Plans and Designs—Mr. Paxton's Design accepted—Realisation of one of the Earliest Poetical Dreams in the English Language—General Description of the Building—Opening of the Exhibition by Her Majesty—Number of Visitors—Removal of the Building—The National Albert Memorial.

THAT portion of Hyde Park, between Prince's Gate and the Serpentine, running parallel with the main road through Knightsbridge and Kensington, is memorable as having been the site of the great Industrial Exhibition of 1851, wherein were brought together, for the first time, under one spacious roof, for the purposes of competition, the various productions of the inventive genius and industry of nearly all the nations of the earth.

Before proceeding with a description of the building and an epitome of its principal contents, it may not be out of place to take a brief glance at some previous exhibitions of a similar character, which had been held in France, at various times, within the preceding hundred years. As far back as the year 1756—about the same time that our Royal Academy opened to the public its galleries of painting, engraving, and sculpture—the productions of art and skill were collected and displayed in London, for the purpose of stimulating public industry and inventiveness; and although these exhibitions were, to a certain extent, nothing more than would now be termed "bazaars," they were found to answer so successfully the ends for which they were instituted, that the plan was adopted in France, and there continued, with the happiest results, even long after it had been abandoned in England. When the first French Revolution was at its height, the Marquis d'Aveze projected an exhibition of tapestry and porcelain, as a means of raising funds for relieving the distress then existing among the workers in those trades. Before, however, he could complete his arrangements, he was denounced, and on the very day on which his exhibition was to have been opened, he was compelled to fly from the vengeance of the Directory. So firm a hold, however, had the idea taken on the public mind, that it was not allowed to die out. A few years afterwards, on his return to Paris, the marquis resumed his labours, and in 1798 actually succeeded in opening a National Exposition in the house and gardens of the Maison d'Orsay. The people flocked in great numbers to view the show, which altogether proved a complete success. In that same year, too, the French Government organised its first official Exposition of national manufacture and the works of industry. It was held on the Champ de Mars, in a building constructed for the purpose, called the Temple of Industry. Three years later a second Exposition took place, and more than two hundred exhibitors competed for the prizes offered for excellence. In the following year a third Exposition was held on the same spot, the number of exhibitors increasing to upwards of four hundred. So great was the success of these several shows, that out of them arose an institution similar to our Society of Arts, called the *Société d'Encouragement*, a society to which the working classes of France are largely indebted for the taste which they have acquired for the beautiful in art, and for the cultivation of science as a handmaid to industry. In 1806 the fourth French Exposition was held in a building erected in front of the Hôpital des Invalides; this was even more successful than its predecessors; for while the previous Expositions had each remained open only about a week, this one was kept open for twenty-four days, and was visited by many thousands of people. The number of exhibitors rose from about five hundred to nearly fifteen hundred, and nearly every department of French industry was represented. At different periods between the years 1819 and 1849, seven other Expositions were held in France, the last of which was restricted to national products. The Industrial Show of 1855, however, was, like our own Great Exhibition of 1851, international.

During all this time there had grown up in England exhibitions, consisting chiefly of agricultural implements and cattle, together with local exhibitions of arts and manufactures. In Birmingham, Leeds, Manchester, Dublin, and other great centres of industry, bazaars, after the French pattern, had been successfully held from time to time. The one which most nearly approached the idea of the French Exposition, in the variety and extent of the national productions displayed, was the Free Trade Bazaar, held for twelve days, in 1845, in Covent Garden Theatre—an exhibition which excited considerable public interest, and doubtless did much to make the London public acquainted with many arts and manufactures of which they had hitherto had but a very confused and imperfect knowledge.

Roused from their remissness by the success that had attended the various French Expositions, the English people, during the years 1847 and 1848, re-opened their exhibitions, chiefly at the instigation and by the aid of the Society of Arts, by whom the plan had been revived. So great was now the importance of these industrial displays, that they became a subject of national consideration; but it was felt that something more was necessary than France or England had as yet attempted to give them their proper development and effect.

At this point, an idea was entertained by the late Prince Consort of gathering together into one place the best specimens of contemporary art and skill, and the natural productions of every soil and climate, instead of the mere local or national productions of France and England. "It was to be a whole world of nature and art collected at the call of the queen of cities—a competition in which every country might have a place, and every variety of intellect its claim and chance of distinction. Nothing great, or beautiful, or useful, be its native home where it might; not a discovery or invention, however humble or obscure; not a candidate, however lowly his rank, but would obtain admission, and be estimated to the full amount of genuine worth. It was to be to the nineteenth what the tournament had been to the fourteenth and fifteenth centuries—a challenge at once and welcome to all comers, and to which every land could send, not its brightest dame and bravest lance, as of yore, but its best produce and happiest device for the promotion of universal happiness and brotherhood."*

* "Comprehensive History of England," vol. iv., p. 798.

The undertaking received Her Majesty's royal sanction on the 3rd of January, 1850; on the 11th of the same month the Royal Commissioners held their first meeting; and on the 14th of February Prince Albert sat as Chairman of the Commission. On the 21st of March the Lord Mayor of London invited the mayors of nearly all the cities, boroughs, and towns of the United Kingdom to a banquet at the Mansion House to meet the Prince, and upon that occasion his Royal Highness lucidly explained the object of the proposed undertaking.

COURTYARD OF THE "ROSE AND CROWN," 1820. (*See page* 27.)

The Exhibition, it was announced, was to belong exclusively to the people themselves of every nation, instead of being supported and controlled by their respective governments; and in order that nothing might be wanting in its character as a great competitive trial, the sum of £20,000 was set apart for the expense of prizes, which were to be awarded to the successful competitors. At first, the real magnitude and the great difficulties of the project were not fully perceived; and the proposal was scarcely made public by the Society of Arts, of which Prince Albert was at the head, before impediments began to rise up in their way, and for more than a year they were beset with difficulties. At first, many manufacturers and merchants in foreign countries were exceedingly averse to the proposed Exhibition; but, as was the case with those at home, discussion and better information led to more enlightened views. Prince Albert, in his speech at a banquet held at York, said, in the name of the Royal Commission:—"Although we perceive in some countries an apprehension that the advantages to be derived from the Exhibition will be mainly reaped by England, and a consequent distrust in the effects of our scheme upon their own interests, we must, at the same time, freely and gratefully acknowledge, that our invitation has been received by all nations, with whom communication was possible, in that spirit of liberality and friendship in which it was tendered, and that they are making great exertions, and incurring great expenses, in order to meet our plans." Upon the same occasion, Lord Carlisle, one of the most enlightened men of the age, expressed a hope that "the promoters of this Exhibition were giving a new impulse to civilisation, and bestowing an additional reward upon industry, and supplying a fresh guarantee to the amity of nations. Yes, the nations were stirring

EXTERIOR OF THE GREAT EXHIBITION OF 1851.

at their call, but not as the trumpet sounds to battle; they were summoning them to the peaceful field of a nobler competition; not to build the superiority or predominance of one country on the depression and prostration of another, but where all might strive who could do most to embellish, improve, and elevate their common humanity."

At a meeting held in Birmingham, Mr. Cobden, in speaking of the advantages that might be expected to flow from this Exhibition, said, "We shall by that means break down the barriers that have separated the people of different nations, and witness one universal republic; the year 1851 will be a memorable one, indeed: it will witness a triumph of industry instead of a triumph of arms. We shall not witness the reception of the allied sovereigns after some fearful conflict, men bowing their heads in submission; but, instead, thousands and tens of thousands will cross the Channel, to whom we will give the right hand of fellowship, with the fullest conviction that war, rather than a national aggrandisement, has been the curse and the evil which has retarded the progress of liberty and of virtue; and we shall show to them that the people of England—not a section of them, but hundreds of thousands—are ready to sign a treaty of amity with all the nations on the face of the earth."

Lecturers and competent agents were now sent throughout the country to explain the objects of the Exhibition, and the advantages likely to arise from it; besides which, the subject had been proclaimed in every country far and wide—in fact, a challenge had been given, such as men had never heard, to an enterprise in which every nation might hope to be the victor. It was arranged that the great competition should be opened in London on the 1st of May, 1851; but as yet a place for the accommodation of the specimens and the spectators had to be erected. The directors of the Exhibition were for a time perplexed, for they found, on calculation, that no building on earth would be sufficiently large to contain a tithe of its contents. After many expedients had been proposed and rejected, Mr. (afterwards Sir Joseph) Paxton, the celebrated horticulturist at Chatsworth, came forward with a simple plan, which effectually solved all the difficulty.

The number of plans and designs sent in to the Committee appointed by the Royal Commission amounted to nearly two hundred and fifty, including several foreigners; but none of these appeared to be satisfactory. Accordingly, the Committee set to work and perfected a design for themselves, from the various suggestions afforded by the competing architects, adding, as a contribution "entirely their own," a dome of gigantic proportions. This dome at once became so unpopular with the public, and the contest about its site grew so fierce, that the whole scheme of the Exhibition seemed at one time likely to have collapsed. At "the eleventh hour," however, Mr. Paxton, as we have stated above, came forward with a plan, which he considered would meet all the requirements of the Committee, and avoid all the objections of the public. "It was not," said Mr. Paxton himself, at a meeting of the Derby Institute, "until one morning, when I was present with my friend, Mr. Ellis, at an early sitting in the House of Commons, that the idea of sending in a design occurred to me. A conversation took place between us, with reference to the construction of the new House of Commons, in the course of which I observed, that I was afraid they would also commit a blunder in the building for the Industrial Exhibition; I told him that I had a notion in my head, and that if he would accompany me to the Board of Trade I would ascertain whether it was too late to send in a design. I asked the Executive Committee whether they were so far committed to the plans as to be precluded from receiving another; the reply was, 'Certainly not; the specifications will be out in a fortnight, but there is no reason why a clause should not be introduced, allowing of the reception of another design.' I said, 'Well, if you will introduce such a clause, I will go home, and, in nine days hence, I will bring you my plans all complete.' No doubt the Executive thought me a conceited fellow, and that what I had said was nearer akin to romance than to common sense. Well, this was on Friday, the 11th of June. From London I went to the Menai Straits, to see the third tube of the Britannia Bridge placed, and on my return to Derby I had to attend to some business at the Board Room, during which time, however, my whole mind was devoted to this project; and whilst the business proceeded, I sketched the outline of my design on a large sheet of blotting-paper. Well, having sketched this design, I sat up all night, until I had worked it out to my own satisfaction; and, by the aid of my friend Mr. Barlow, on the 15th, I was enabled to complete the whole of the plans by the Saturday following, on which day I left Rowsley for London. On arriving at the Derby station, I met Mr. Robert Stephenson, a member of the Building Committee, who was also on his way to the metropolis. Mr. Stephenson minutely examined the plans, and became thoroughly engrossed with them, until at length he exclaimed that the design was just the thing, and he only wished it had been submitted to the Committee in time. Mr. Stephenson, however, laid the plans before the Committee, and at first the idea was rather pooh-poohed; but the plans gradually grew in favour, and by publishing the design in the *Illustrated London News*, and showing the advantage of such an erection over one composed of fifteen millions of bricks and other materials, which would have to be removed at a great loss, the Committee did, in the end, reject the abortion of a child of their own, and unanimously recommended my bantling. I am bound to say that I have been treated by the Committee with great fairness. Mr. Brunel, the author of the great dome, I believe, was at first so wedded to his own plan that he would hardly look at mine. But Mr. Brunel was a gentleman and a man of fairness, and listened with every attention to all that could be urged in favour of my plans. As an instance of that gentleman's very creditable conduct, I will mention that a difficulty presented itself to the Committee as to what was to be done with the large trees, and it was gravely suggested that they should be walled in. I remarked that I could cover the trees without any difficulty; when Mr. Brunel asked, 'Do you know their height?' I acknowledged that I did not. On the following morning Mr. Brunel called at Devonshire House, and gave me the measurement of the trees, which he had taken early in the morning, adding—'Although I mean to try to win with my own plan, I will give you all the information I can.' Having given this preliminary explanation of the origin and execution of my design, I will pass over the question of merit, leaving that to be discussed and decided by others when the whole shall have been completed."

Notwithstanding that Sir Robert Peel and Prince Albert strongly favoured Mr. Paxton's scheme, it was at first but coldly received by the Building Committee, who still clung to their own plan. Nothing daunted, Mr. Paxton appealed to the British public; and this he did by the aid of the woodcuts and pages of the *Illustrated London News*. Everybody but the Committee was at once convinced of the practicability, simplicity, and beauty of Mr. Paxton's plan, which, in fact, was but a vast expansion of a conservatory design, built by him at Chatsworth for the flowering of the Victoria Lily. The people and the Prince were heartily with him; and, thus encouraged, Mr. Paxton resolved to make another effort with the Building Committee. It happened that the Committee had invited candidates for raising their edifice to suggest any improvements in it that might occur to them. This opened a crevice for the tender of Mr. Paxton's plan as an "improvement" on that of the Committee. After some discussion, the result was that the glazed "palace" was chosen unanimously, not only by the Building Committee, but by the Royal Commissioners also. Mr. Paxton's design, as everybody knows, was that of a huge building in the style of a garden conservatory, in which iron and glass should be almost the sole materials, wood being introduced only in the fittings. This method was at once adopted, and the result was a building in Hyde Park, nearly twice the breadth and fully four times the length of St. Paul's Cathedral. The edifice—which was appropriately called the "Crystal Palace"—covered nearly twenty acres of ground, and contained eight miles of tables. It was erected and finished in the short space of seven months. "With its iron framework, that rose towards the sky in dark slender lines, and its walls of glittering crystal, that seemed to float in mid-air like a vapour, it appeared, indeed, an exhalation which a breath of wind might disperse—a *fata morgana* that would disappear with a sudden shift of sunshine. But on looking more nearly it was seen to be a solid edifice, the iron pillars of which were rooted deep in the earth; while within the combination of light and lofty arches, with ribs forming a graceful metallic net-work, gave strength and security to the edifice." It is a curious fact that the edifice realised the conceptions of one of the earliest poetical dreams in the English language; and one would almost believe that when Chaucer, four centuries and a half ago, wrote the following lines in his "House of Fame," he was endowed with a prophetic as well as a poetic faculty:—

"I dreamt I was
Within a *temple made of glass*,
In which there were more images
Of *gold* standing in sundry stages,
In more rich tabernacles,
And with *jewels*, more pinnacles,
And more curious *portraitures*,
And quaint manner of figures
Of gold-work than I saw ever.

* * * * *

"Then saw I stand on either side
Straight down to the doors wide
From the daïs many a pillar
Of metal that shone out full clear.

* * * * *

"Then gan I look about and see
That there came ent'ring in the hall,
A right great company withal,
And that of sundry regions

Of all kinds of conditions,
That dwell in earth beneath the moon,
Poor and rich.
* * * * *
"*Such a great congregation*
Of folks as I saw roam about,
Some within and some without,
Was never seen or shall be more!"

The superintendence of the construction of the building was entrusted to Mr. (afterwards Sir) Matthew Digby Wyatt, and the construction itself was undertaken by Messrs. Fox, Henderson, and Co., of Birmingham. The ground-plan of the building was a parallelogram, 1,851 feet long—a fact worthy of mention, seeing that the number corresponds with the date of the year in which the Exhibition was held—by 456 feet wide in the broadest part, with a transept upwards of 400 feet long and 72 feet wide intersecting the building at right angles in the middle. The side walls rose in three stages: the outer wall rising from the ground twenty-four feet, the second twenty feet higher, and the third twenty feet higher still, or sixty-four feet from the bottom of its supporting pillars, giving within the building a great central avenue or nave seventy-two feet wide, and on each side of it three avenues twenty-four feet wide, and two of forty-eight feet; the transept, having a semi-circular roof, being 108 feet high, to give ample room for three or four trees in the Park which remained enclosed under it. The edifice was a trifle longer than Portland Place. "I walked out one evening," says Sir Charles Fox, "and there setting out the 1,848 feet upon the pavement, found it the same length within a few yards; and then considered that the Great Exhibition building would be three times the width of that fine street, and the nave as high as the houses on either side."

As no brick and mortar were used, and all the proportions of the building depended upon its iron pillars and girders, nearly all the materials arrived on the spot ready to be placed and secured in their destined positions. Yet vast operations were necessary even then in its construction, and called forth the most admirable display of scientific ingenuity, systematic arrangements, and great energy. Hardly any scaffolding was used, the columns, as they were set up, answering their purpose. Machines for performing all the preparatory operations required to be done on the spot were introduced in the building, and some of them invented for the occasion; such, for instance, as the sash-bar machine, gutter-machine, mortising-machine, painting-machine, glazing-machine, and other ingenious contrivances for economising labour.

Throughout the progress of the building it was visited by many of the most distinguished persons in the country; and the contractors finding that the numbers who flocked to it impeded in some degree their operations, determined to make a charge of five shillings for admission, the proceeds of which were to constitute an accident-relief fund for the workmen. A very considerable sum was thus raised, though the number of accidents was very small, and the nature of the accidents not at all serious. During the months of December and January upwards of 2,000 persons were employed upon the building.

Whatever wonders the Exhibition was to contain, the building itself, when completed, was looked upon as the greatest wonder of all. Shortly before it was opened to the public, the *Times* observed that, "Not the least wonderful part of the Exhibition will be the edifice within which the specimens of the industry of all nations are to be collected. Its magnitude, the celerity with which it is to be constructed, and the materials of which it is to be composed, all combine to ensure for it a large share of that attention which the Exhibition is likely to attract, and to render its progress a matter of great public interest. A building designed to cover 753,984 superficial feet, and to have an exhibiting surface of about twenty-one acres, to be roofed in, and handed over to the Commissioners within little more than three months from its commencement; to be constructed almost entirely of glass and iron, the most fragile and the strongest of working materials; to combine the lightness of a conservatory with the stability of our most permanent structures—such a building will naturally excite much curiosity as to the mode in which the works connected with it are conducted, and the advances which are made towards its completion. Enchanted palaces that grow up in a night are confined to fairy-land, and in this material world of ours the labours of the bricklayer and the carpenter are notoriously never-ending. It took 300 years to build St. Peter's at Rome, and thirty-five to complete our own St. Paul's. The New Palace of Westminster has already been fifteen years in hand, and still is unfinished. We run up houses, it is true, quickly enough in this country; but if there be a touch of magic in the time occupied, there is none in the appearance of so much stucco and brick-work as our streets exhibit. Something very different from this was promised for the great edifice in Hyde Park. Not only was it to rise with extraordinary rapidity, but in every other respect is to be suggestive of 'Arabian Nights' remembrances."

The decoration of the building, both in design and in execution, was entrusted to Mr. Owen Jones, about 500 painters being employed upon the work. The under sides of the girders were painted red, the round portions of the columns yellow, and the hollows of the capitals blue, in due proportions. All the stalls were covered with red cloth, or pink calico; by which means not only was the unsightly woodwork concealed, but a warmth of colouring was given to the whole ground area of the building, which, combined with the mass of blue overhead, and the yellow stripes of the columns, produced a most harmonious effect, which was further softened by covering the roof and south side with unbleached calico, to prevent the glare of light which would necessarily take place in a building whose roof and sides were chiefly of glass. Mr. Jones also displayed great knowledge in his profession by the judicious distribution of various large articles and groups of articles, with a view to their effect upon the general internal aspect of the Exhibition.

The first column of the edifice was fixed on the 26th of September, 1850, and by the middle of January, 1851, notwithstanding various alterations in some of the details of the plan, little of the exterior of the vast structure remained to be finished, and by the 1st of May everything was complete; the contributions from all nations were in their places; and the Exhibition was opened by Her Majesty Queen Victoria in person, attended by her Royal Consort, the Archbishop of Canterbury, Her Majesty's ministers and great officers of state, the foreign ambassadors and ministers, the Royal Commissioners, &c. The opening ceremony took place with a punctuality which was the source of much congratulation. A chair of state had been placed upon a daïs of three steps, on the north of the centre facing the south transept, and over it was suspended, by invisible rods, a canopy of blue and silver. In front, in the centre of the transept, was a large glass fountain, and on either side, a little in the rear, were equestrian statues of Her Majesty and the Prince Consort. The doors of the "Crystal Palace" were opened on the morning of that eventful day at nine o'clock for the admission of the purchasers of season tickets, of which about 20,000 had been sold. The visitors were so judiciously sprinkled over the different parts of the building, by the tickets assigning to every person the staircase or section he was to repair to, that there was nothing like crushing in any part of the building, with one temporary exception of a rush of persons beyond the barriers before the platform, which was soon set right by a party of sappers. The following particulars of the opening ceremony we here quote from the *Gentleman's Magazine*:—"The Queen left Buckingham Palace in state at twenty minutes before twelve, accompanied by Prince Albert and their two eldest children, the Prince and Princess of Prussia, Prince Frederick William of Prussia, and their respective suites. They were conveyed in nine carriages. Some time before Her Majesty entered, the heralds in their tabards, the officers of state, Her Majesty's ministers, the foreign ambassadors, and the officers of the household troops, in their full costumes, with the Executive Committee and other functionaries of the Exhibition, the architect and contractors in court dresses, and the Lord Mayor and Aldermen in their robes, had assembled round the platform, and the 'beef-eaters' were ranged behind. At length a flourish of trumpets announced the Queen's arrival at the north door of the building, and Her Majesty and her Royal Consort, leading by the hand the Prince of Wales and the Princess Royal, appeared before the vast assemblage of her subjects, and 'the crystal bow' rang with enthusiastic shouts, overpowering the sound of the cannon discharged on the other side of the Serpentine. It was a moment of intense excitement. In the midst of the grandest temple ever raised to the peaceful arts, surrounded by thousands of her subjects and men of all nations, was the ruler of this realm and its vast dependencies, herself the centre of the great undertaking. Her emotions, as she gracefully and repeatedly acknowledged her people's gratulations, were very evident. The Prince Consort having conducted Her Majesty to the throne, the National Anthem was sung by a choir of near a thousand voices, accompanied by the organ of Messrs. Gray and Davidson." Prince Albert then quitted the Queen's side, and, advancing at the head of the Royal Commissioners, over whose deliberations he had indefatigably presided, delivered in an emphatic tone of voice the report of the completion of their labours, from which it appears that the number of exhibitors whose productions it had been found possible to accommodate was about 15,000, of whom nearly one-half were British. The remainder represented the productions of more than forty foreign countries, comprising almost the whole of the civilised nations of the globe. In arranging the space allotted to each, the report stated that the Commissioners had taken into consideration both the nature of its productions and the facilities of access to this country afforded by its geographical position. The productions of Great Britain and her dependencies were arranged in the western portion of the building, and those of foreign countries in the eastern. The Exhibition was divided into four great classes, viz.:—1. Raw Materials; 2. Machinery; 3. Manufactures; 4. Sculpture and the Fine Arts. With regard to the distribution of rewards to deserving exhibitors, the report went on to state that the Commissioner had decided that they should be given in the form of medals, not with reference to merely individual competition, but as rewards for excellence, in whatever shape it might present itself. The selection of the persons to be so rewarded was entrusted to juries, composed equally of British subjects and of foreigners, many of whose names were a guarantee of the impartiality with which the rewards would be assigned. Her Majesty's reply to the address was followed by a prayer, offered up by the Archbishop of Canterbury; and that finished, the majestic "Hallelujah Chorus" burst forth, its strains reverberating through the arched transept and "long-drawn aisles" of the building.

NAVE OF THE GREAT EXHIBITION OF 1851.

"The state procession was then formed, and passed down the northern avenue of the west nave. The spectators were arranged on either side, and as Her Majesty passed along, the cheers were taken up in succession by the whole of the long array, and seconded with waving of hats and handkerchiefs from the galleries. Her Majesty and the Prince acknowledged these gratulations by continual bowing. The various objects of interest around were for a time almost disregarded, but the effect of the whole upon the eye, as the Sovereign and her attendants threaded their way between the living throng, and the lines of statuary and other works of art, and the rich assemblage

THE ALBERT MEMORIAL. (*See page* 38.)

of the products of industry, was exceedingly impressive; and the ovation of industry far outshone all the splendours of old Rome, with no fettered captives in the rear, or wailing widows and orphans at home to dim its lustre. The Duke of Wellington and the Marquis of Anglesey (who joined the procession as Commander-in-Chief and Master-General of the Ordnance), united arm-in-arm in this triumph of peace, were the objects of much attraction. When the procession reached the west end, the magnificent organ by Mr. Willis, with its 4,700 pipes, commenced playing the National Anthem, which was heard to the remotest end of the building. The procession returned by the south side to the transept, round the southern part of which it passed, amidst the cheers of the people, the peals of two organs, and the voices of 700 choristers, to the eastern or foreign division of the nave, where the French organ took up the strain, and the delicate lady, whose tempered sway is owned by a hundred millions of men, pursued her course amongst the contributions of all the civilised world. As she passed the gigantic equestrian figure of Godfrey de Bouillon, by the Belgian sculptor, Simonis, which seems the very impersonation of physical strength, we could not but be struck by the contrast, and by the reflection how far the prowess of the crusader is transcended by the power of well-defined liberty and constitutional law. The brilliant train having at length made the complete circuit of the building, Her Majesty again ascended the throne, and pronounced the Exhibition opened. The announcement was repeated by the Marquis of Breadalbane as Lord Steward, followed immediately by a burst of acclamations, the bray of trumpets, and a royal salute across the Serpentine. The royal party then withdrew; the National Anthem was again repeated; and the visitors dispersed themselves through the building, to gratify their curiosity without restraint."

It would be impossible, and indeed superfluous, within the space at our command, to attempt to give anything even like a *résumé* of the multifarious articles here brought together; suffice it to say, that the Exhibition comprised most of the best productions in the different branches of art, manufactures, &c., from all parts of the civilised globe, and that it became properly enough called the "World's Fair," for it attracted visitors from all parts of the world. We have already mentioned the glass fountain in the transept; that object, from its central position, was invariably fixed upon as the rendezvous, or meeting-place, by family groups or parties of visitors, in case of their losing sight of one another in the labyrinth of tables and articles which thronged the building. Another object, which we cannot well pass over, was the famous Koh-i-noor, or "Mountain of Light," which had been specially lent by Her Majesty. This royal gem—the value of which has been variously stated at from £1,500,000 to £3,000,000—appeared to be one of the greatest curiosities of the Exhibition, judging from the numbers congregated around it during the day. The Exhibition was open for 144 days, being closed on the 11th of October. The entire number of visitors was above 6,170,000, averaging 43,536 per day. The largest number of visitors in one day was 109,760, on the 8th of October; and at two o'clock on the previous day 93,000 persons were present at one time. The entire money drawn for tickets of admission amounted to £506,100; and after all expenses were defrayed, a balance of £213,300 was left over, to be applied to the promotion of industrial art.

At the time when the Exhibition was over, so firm a hold had the fairy-like palace obtained upon the good opinion of the public, that a general desire for its preservation sprung up. Application was made to Government that it should be purchased and become the property of the nation; but it was ruled otherwise. The building was, however, not doomed to disappear altogether, for a few enterprising gentlemen having stepped forward, it was rescued from destruction. It was decided that the building should be removed to some convenient place within an easy distance of London, and accordingly it was transferred to Sydenham, where a fine estate of three hundred acres had been purchased, on which the edifice was raised again in increased grandeur and beauty, and where, under the name of the Crystal Palace, it soon became one of the most popular places of recreation in or near the metropolis.

The whole building was removed from Hyde Park before the close of 1852; and in the following year it was proposed to place upon the site a memorial of the Exhibition, to include a statue of Prince Albert—the originator of this display of the industry of all nations. The spot ultimately chosen for the memorial, however, is somewhat to the west of the ground covered by the Exhibition building; in fact, it is just within the south-eastern enclosure of Kensington Gardens, directly opposite the centre of the Horticultural Gardens, and looking upon the South Kensington establishments, in the promotion of which the Prince Consort always took so deep an interest. The memorial, which took upwards of twenty years before it was completed, and cost upwards of £130,000, was erected from the designs of Sir Gilbert Scott. It consists of a lofty and wide-spreading pyramid of three quadrangular ranges of steps, forming, as it were, the base of the monument, which may be described as a colossal statue of the Prince, placed beneath a vast and gorgeous Gothic canopy, about thirty feet square, supported at the angles by groups of columns of polished granite, and "surrounded by works of sculpture, illustrating those arts and sciences which he fostered, and the great undertakings which he originated." The memorial partakes somewhat, in the richness of its colours, decorations, and mosaics, of the Renaissance Gothic style; and its whole height from the roadway is 176 feet. The first flight of granite steps, forming the basement, is 212 feet wide, with massive abutments of solid granite. At the four corners of the second flight of steps are gigantic square masses of carved granite, occupied with colossal groups of marble statuary, emblematical of Europe, Asia, Africa, and America, and executed respectively by Messrs. Macdowell, Foley, Theed, and Bell. Above the topmost flight of steps rises the memorial itself, the podium or pedestal of which is carved with nearly 200 figures, life-size, and all more or less in high relief. They are all portrait-statues of celebrities in the different walks of art, literature, science, &c. At the four corners of this, again, as on the base below, are allegorical groups of statuary—one of Commerce, by Thornycroft; one of Manufactures, by Weekes; one of Agriculture, by Marshall; and one of Engineering, by Lawlor. The statue of the Prince—which was not completed till early in the year 1876—is richly gilt, and rests upon a pedestal fifteen feet high; it represents the Prince sitting on a chair of state, and attired in his regal-looking robes as a Knight of the Garter. This great work was entrusted to Mr. Foley. The roof of the canopy is decorated with mosaics, representing the royal arms and those of the Prince on a ground of blue and gold. At the angles of the four arches above the canopy are marble figures, life-size. The spandrils of the arches above the trefoil are filled in with rich and elaborate glass mosaics on a gilt ground, portraying Poetry, Painting, Sculpture, and Architecture. One of the main features of the whole design is the beautiful spire, in which every portion of the metal surface is covered with ornament; the surface in many parts is coated with colours in enamel, with coloured marbles and imitation gem-work; and up to the very cross itself, which surmounts the whole, there is the same amount of extraordinary detail and finish, as if each part were meant for the most minute and close inspection.

CHAPTER IV.

PIMLICO.

"I'll have thee, Captain Gilthead, and march up
And take in Pimlico."—*Old Play.*

Etymology of Pimlico—The Locality Half a Century Ago—Warwick Square—Vauxhall Bridge Road—The Army Clothing Depôt—St. George's Square—The Church of St. James the Less—Victoria Railway Station—New Chelsea Bridge—The Western Pumping Station, and Metropolitan Main-Drainage Works—St. Barnabas Church—St. Barnabas Mission House and Orphanage—Bramah, the Engineer and Locksmith—Thomas Cubitt, the Builder—The "Monster" Tavern—The "Gun," the "Star and Garter," and the "Orange" Tea-Gardens—"Jenny's Whim"—Tart Hall—Stafford Row—St. Peter's Chapel and Dr. Dodd—Richard Heber and his famous Library.

THE name Pimlico is clearly of foreign derivation, and it has not a little puzzled topographers. Gifford, in a note in his edition of Ben Jonson, tells us that "Pimlico is sometimes spoken of as a person, and may not improbably have been the master of a house once famous for ale of a particular description;" and we know, from Dodsley's "Old Plays," and from Ben Jonson's writings, that there was another Pimlico at Hoxton, or (as the place was then termed) Hogsdon, where, indeed, to the present day there is a "Pimlico Walk." It is evident, from a reference to *The Alchemist* of Ben Jonson, that the place so named at "Hogsdon" was a place of resort of no very good repute, and constantly frequented by all sorts of people, from knights, ladies, and gentlewomen, down to oyster-wenches:—

"Gallants, men, and women,
And of all sorts, tag-rag, been seen to flock here,
In these ten weeks, as to a second Hogsdon,
In days of Pimlico."

In another play of about the same period a worthy knight is represented as sending his daughter to Pimlico "to fetch a draught of Derby ale." It is antecedently probable, therefore, that the district lying between Chelsea and St. James's Park should have got the name from an accidental resemblance to its antipodes at Hoxton. And this supposition is confirmed by Isaac Reed, who tells us, in Dodsley's "Old Plays," how that "a place near Chelsey is still called Pimlico, and was resorted to within these few years on the same account as the former at Hogsdon." It may be added that Pimlico is still celebrated for its ales, and also that the district is not mentioned by the name of Pimlico in any existing document prior to the year 1626.

"At this time"—*i.e.* the reign of Charles I., writes Mr. Peter Cunningham—"Pimlico was quite uninhabited, nor is it introduced into the rate-books of St. Martin's (to which it belonged) until the year 1680, when the Earl of Arlington—previously rated as residing in the Mulberry Gardens—is rated, though still living in the same house, under the head of Pimlico. In 1687, seven years later, four people are described as living in what was then called Pimlico—the Duke of Grafton, Lady Stafford, Thomas Wilkins, and Dr. Crispin. The Duke of Grafton, having married the only child of the Earl of Arlington, was residing in Arlington House; and Lady Stafford in what was then and long before known as Tart Hall." Arlington House, as we have seen,* was ultimately developed into Buckingham Palace.

The district of Pimlico may be regarded as embracing the whole of Belgravia, which we have already dealt with in a previous chapter, as well as the locality extending from Buckingham Palace Road to the Thames, and stretching away westward to Chelsea. This latter portion includes the Grosvenor Road and the Eccleston sub-district of squares, terraces, and streets, nearly all of which have sprung up within the last half-century.

In the map appended to Coghlan's "Picture of London," published in the year 1834, the whole of this division of Pimlico, between Vauxhall Bridge Road and Chelsea (now Buckingham Palace) Road, appears unbuilt upon, with the exception of a few stray cottages here and there, and a few blocks of houses near the river; the rest of the space is marked out as gardens and waste land, intersected by the Grosvenor Canal, the head of which, forming an immense basin, is now entirely covered by the Victoria Railway Station. Its rustic character at the above date may be inferred from the fact, that a considerable portion of the space between the two roads above mentioned is described as "osier beds," whilst a straight thoroughfare connecting the two roads is called Willow Walk. These osier beds are now covered by Eccleston Square and a number of small streets adjacent to it; whilst "Willow Walk" has been transformed into shops and places of business, and is now known as Warwick Street. On the north side of Warwick Street, covering part of the "old Neat House" Gardens, to which we have already referred,† is Warwick Square, which is bounded on the north-east by Belgrave Road, and on the south-west by St. George's Road. In Warwick Square stands St. Gabriel's Church, a large building of Early English architecture, erected from the designs of Mr. Thomas Cundy, who was also the architect of St. Saviour's Church, in St. George's Square, close by. Vauxhall Bridge Road, which dates from the erection of the bridge, about the year 1816, is a broad and well-built thoroughfare, opening up a direct communication, by way of Grosvenor Place, between Hyde Park Corner and Vauxhall Bridge, and so on to Kennington and the southern suburbs of London. Of Vauxhall Bridge, and of Trinity Church, in Bessborough Gardens, close by, we have already spoken.‡

Not far from St. George's Square stands an extensive range of buildings, known as the Army Clothing Depôt—one of the largest institutions that has ever been established for the organisation and utilisation of women's work. "Previous to the year 1857," observes a writer in the *Queen* newspaper, "all the clothes for the British army were made by contractors, whose first thought seemed to be how to amass a fortune at the expense of the makers and the wearers of the clothes primarily, and of the British public indirectly. But in that year the Army Clothing Depôt was established, somewhat experimentally, in Blomberg Terrace, Vauxhall Road; the experiment answering so well, that an extension of the premises became imperative. In 1859 the present depôt was opened, although since then it has largely increased, and has not yet, apparently, come to the full stage of its development. The whole of the premises occupy about seven acres, the long block of buildings on the one side being used as the Government stores, while the corresponding block consists of the factory. The main feature of the latter is a large glass-roofed central hall of three storeys, with spacious galleries all round on each storey. The ventilation is ensured by louvres, so that the whole atmosphere can be renewed in the space of five minutes or so; the temperature is kept at an average of 60° to 63°, and each operative enjoys 1,200 cubic feet of air, so that we have at the outset the three requirements of light, air, and warmth, in strongly-marked contrast to the crowded rooms of the contractor, or the more wretched chamber of the home-worker. Five hundred and twenty-seven women are at present working in the central hall, and five hundred in the side rooms, which also accommodate about two hundred men. This forms the working staff of the factory, which comprises, therefore, what may be called the pick of the sewing-machine population in London. It may well be imagined that the prospect of so comfortable an abiding place would attract great numbers of workpeople; and, indeed, this has been so much the case that very rigorous rules have been obliged to be made to guard against unworthy admissions. 'The good of the public service' is the motto of the factory, and everything else must yield to that; so that, both for in-door and out-door hands, all candidates must first of

* See Vol. IV., p. 62. † See Vol. IV., p. 3.

‡ See Vol. IV., p. 9.

all appear before a committee, consisting of the matron, the foreman cutter, the foreman viewer, and the instructor, who are held responsible for the selection of proper persons. In-door candidates as needlewomen must be healthy and strong, and, if single, between the ages of seventeen and thirty; if married or widows, they must have no children at home young enough to demand their care. These points being settled, the candidates are examined as to any previous training or fitness for army work, and are required to show what they can do. If all these requirements are satisfactory, the matron inquires into their character, and finally they are examined by the doctor, who certifies to their fitness, after which they are placed in a trial division in the factory for further report and promotion."

St. George's Square, with its trees and shrubs, presents a healthful and cheering aspect, almost bordering on the Thames, just above Vauxhall Bridge. It covers a considerable space of ground, and is bounded on the north side by Lupus Street—a thoroughfare so called after a favourite Christian name in the Grosvenor family, perpetuating the memory of Hugh Lupus, Earl of Chester after the Norman Conquest. St. Saviour's Church, which was built in 1865, is in the Decorated style of Gothic architecture, and with its elegant tower and spire forms a striking object, as seen from the river.

In Upper Garden Street, which runs parallel with Vauxhall Bridge Road, is the Church of St. James the Less, built in 1861, from the designs of Mr. G. E. Street, R.A. The edifice was founded by the daughters of the late Bishop of Gloucester and Bristol (Dr. Monk) as a memorial to their father, who was also a Canon of Westminster. It is constructed of brick, with dressings of stone, marble, and alabaster; and it consists of a nave, side aisles, a semi-circular apse, and a lofty tower and spire. The roof of the chancel is groined, and is a combination of brick and stone. A very considerable amount of elaborate detail pervades the interior. The chancel is surrounded by screens of brass and iron, and over the chancel-arch is a well-executed fresco painting, by Mr. G. F. Watts, R.A., of "Our Saviour attended by Angels." Some of the windows are filled with stained glass. The building, including the decorations, cost upwards of £9,000.

The Victoria Railway Station, situated at the northern end of Vauxhall Bridge Road, covers, as we have stated above, a considerable portion of the basin of the old Grosvenor Canal; it unites the West-end of London with the lines terminating at London Bridge and Holborn Viaduct, and also serves as the joint terminus of the Brighton Railway and of the London, Chatham, and Dover Railway. Like the stations at Charing Cross and Cannon Street, which we have already described, the Victoria Railway Station has a "monster" hotel—"The Grosvenor"—built in connection with it. The lines of railway, soon after leaving the station, are carried across the Thames by an iron bridge of four arches, called the Victoria Bridge, and then diverge.

On the western side of the railway bridge is a handsome new bridge, which now connects this populous and increasing neighbourhood with Battersea and Vauxhall. The railway bridge somewhat mars the structural beauty of the one under notice; but when looked at from the embankment on either side, "above bridge," or, better still, from a boat in the middle of the river, the bridge appears like a fairy structure, with its towers gilded and painted to resemble light-coloured bronze, and crowned with large globular lamps. The bridge, which is constructed on the suspension principle, is built of iron, and rests upon piers of English elm and concrete enclosed within iron casings. The two piers are each nearly ninety feet in length by twenty in width, with curved cutwaters. The roadway on the bridge is formed by two wrought-iron longitudinal girders, upwards of 1,400 feet, which extend the whole length of the bridge, and are suspended by rods from the chains. At either end of the bridge are picturesque lodge-houses, for the use of the toll-collectors. The bridge was built from the designs of Mr. Page, and finished in 1857, at a cost of £88,000.

Nearly the whole of the river-side between Vauxhall Bridge and Chelsea Bridge forms a broad promenade and thoroughfare, very similar in its construction to the Victoria Embankment, which we have already described, and of which it is, so to speak, a continuation—the only break in the line of roadway being about a quarter of a mile between Millbank and the Houses of Parliament, where the river is not embanked on the north side. This roadway is known partly as Thames Bank, or Thames Parade, and partly as the Grosvenor Road. One of the principal buildings erected upon it is the Western Pumping Station, which was finished in 1874-5, completing the main-drainage system of the metropolis. The foundation-stone of the structure was laid in 1873, and the works cost about £183,000. This station provides pumping power to lift the sewage and a part of the rainfall contributed by the district, together estimated at 38,000 gallons per minute, a height of eighteen feet in the Low Level Sewer, which extends from Pimlico to the Abbey Mills Pumping Station, near Barking, in Essex. The requisite power is obtained from four high-pressure condensing beam-engines of an aggregate of 360-horse power. Supplementary power, to be used in case of accident to the principal engines, or on any similar emergency, is provided by an additional high-pressure, non-condensing engine of 120-horse power, supplied from two boilers similar to those for the principal engines. This engine and its boilers are erected in a separate building to the rear of the main buildings, near the canal. The works further comprise coal vaults, settling pond, and reservoirs for condensing water, repairing-shops, stores, and dwelling-houses for the workmen and superintendent in charge of the works. In all they cover nearly four acres. The principal engine-house is situate facing the main road and river, and the height of this building rises to upwards of seventy-one feet. But all this is dwarfed by the chimney-shaft, which is very nearly the height of the Monument, being only ten feet short of it. The shaft is square, and the sides are relieved by three recessed panels, arched over a short distance below the entablature which surmounts the shaft. Altogether, this chimney really makes a most conspicuous and beautiful object as one comes down the river. The foundations of this great pile of brickwork are carried down into the London clay, and even then bedded in a mass of concrete cement 35 feet square.

THE "MONSTER" TEA GARDENS, 1820. (*See page* 45.)

The system of the main-drainage of London, which has been carried out by the Metropolitan Board of Works, comprises 117 square miles of sewers, and, as each was concluded, it added to the health and comfort of the inhabitants of the metropolis. The main sewers are eighty-two miles long, and cost about £4,607,000; and the local boards and vestries assisted in completing the work, which comprised 635 miles of sewers.

At the western extremity of Buckingham Palace Road, near Ebury Square, stands a handsome Gothic church, built in the severest Early English style, which has acquired some celebrity as "St. Barnabas, Pimlico." It was built in 1848-50, as a chapel of ease to St. Paul's, Knightsbridge, under the auspices of its then incumbent, the Rev. W. J. E. Bennett. Attached to it are large schools, a presbytery or college for the officiating clergy,

"JENNY'S WHIM" BRIDGE, 1750. (*See page* 45.)

who must almost of necessity be celibates. The church gained some notoriety during the earlier part of the Ritualistic movement, and, indeed, the services were not allowed to be carried on without sundry popular outbursts of indignation. Of late, however, this church has ceased to occupy the public attention, having been fairly eclipsed by other churches, which are marked by a still more "advanced" Ritual. The church is a portion of a college founded on St. Barnabas' Day, 1846, and is built upon ground presented by the first Marquis of Westminster. The fabric has a Caen-stone tower and spire, 170 feet high, with a peal of ten bells, the gifts of as many parishioners. The windows throughout are filled with stained glass, with subjects from the life of St. Barnabas. An oak screen, richly carved, separates the nave from the chancel; the open roof is splendidly painted, and the superb altar-plate, the font, the illuminated "office" books, and other costly ornaments, were the gifts of private individuals.

In Blomfield Place, close by St. Barnabas' Church, are two or three useful institutions, of modern growth, which must not be overlooked. One of these is St. John's School for girls, which was established in 1859, under the auspices of the Sisterhood of St. John, and with the sanction of the Bishop of London. The school is "specially adapted for the children of clergymen, professional men; for those whose parents are abroad, who need home-training and care; also for young ladies desirous of improving their education, or to be fitted for governesses." Adjoining the school-house is St. Barnabas' Mission House, and also the St. Barnabas' Orphanage. The latter institution was established in 1860, and is supported by ladies living in the immediate neighbourhood. It is also placed under the care of the "sisters" of St. John.

In 1815, according to the "Beauties of England and Wales," the "chief ornament of this neighbourhood" was the "amazingly extensive and interesting manufactory of Mr. Bramah, the engineer, locksmith, and engine-maker. . . . These works have been deemed worthy the inspection of royalty, and have excited the admiration of the most powerful emperor of Christendom, Alexander of Russia." John Joseph Bramah, the founder of these engineering works, was nephew of Joseph Bramah, "a many-sided mechanist, one who did the world large service, and who, aided by a good business faculty in buying and selling, did himself and his heirs service also;" whose bust, modelled by Chantrey, was destroyed (but for what reason does not appear) by Lady Chantrey, after the sculptor's death. The younger Bramah inherited the business faculty of his uncle, and his love for mechanism, if not his inventive skill. He it was who here gathered together a huge business in railway plant, with the aid and help of the two Stephensons, George and Robert, and subsequently transferred it to Smethwick, near Birmingham, as the "London Works," joining with himself Charles Fox and John Henderson as his partners; and out of their works finally grew up the original Crystal Palace, as we have shown in the last chapter.

Another large establishment, which flourished for many years at Thames Bank, was that of Mr. Thomas Cubitt, the founder of the well-known firm in Gray's Inn Road which bears his name. The large engagements which resulted in the laying-out and erection of Belgrave Square were commenced by Mr. Cubitt, in 1825. Mr. Cubitt died towards the close of 1855. "Through life," observes a writer in the *Builder*, "he had been the real friend of the working man; and among his own people he did much to promote their social, intellectual, and moral progress. He established a workman's library; school-room for workmen's children; and by an arrangement to supply generally to his workmen soup and cocoa at the smallest rate at which these could be produced, assisted in establishing a habit of temperance, and superseding, to a great extent, the dram-drinking which previously existed among them. Although his kindness was appreciated by many, yet at times his motives have been misconstrued, and unkind remarks have been made. In alluding to these, he has often said to one who was about him and possessed his confidence, 'If you wait till people thank you for doing anything for them, you will never do anything. It is right for me to do it, whether they are thankful for it or not.' To those under him, and holding responsible situations, he was most liberal and kind. He was a liberal benefactor at all times to churches, schools, and charities, in those places with which he was connected, and always valued, in a peculiar degree, the advantages resulting to the poor from the London hospitals." Mr. Cubitt was a man of unassuming demeanour, and bore his great prosperity with becoming modesty. One instance of his equanimity occurred when his premises were unfortunately burnt down, in the year before his death. He was in the country at the time, and was immediately telegraphed for to town. The shock to most minds, on seeing the great destruction which occurred, attended with pecuniary loss to the amount of £30,000, would have been overpowering. Mr. Cubitt's first words on entering the premises, however, were, "Tell the men they shall be at work within a week, and I will subscribe £600 towards buying them new tools."

So late as 1763, Buckingham House enjoyed an uninterrupted prospect south and west to the river, there being only a few scattered cottages and the "Stag" Brewery between it and the Thames. Lying as it did at the distance of only a short walk from London, and on the way to rural Chelsea, this locality was always a great place for taverns and tea-gardens. The "Monster" Tavern, at one period an inn of popular resort, at the corner of St. George's Row and Buckingham Palace Road, and for many years the starting-point of the "Monster" line of omnibuses, is probably a corruption, perhaps an intentional one, of the "Monastery." Mr. Larwood writes thus, in his "History of Sign-boards:"—"Robert de Heyle, in 1368, leased the whole of the Manor of Chelsea to the Abbot and Monastery or Convent of Westminster for the term of his own life, for which they were to pay him the sum of £20 a year, to provide him every day with two white loaves, two flagons of convent ale, and once a year a robe of esquire's silk. At this period, or shortly after, the sign of the 'Monastery' may have been set up, to be handed down from generation to generation, until the meaning and proper pronunciation were alike forgotten, and it became the 'Monster.' . . This tavern," he adds, "I believe, is the only one with such a sign."

We have already spoken of the Mulberry Gardens, which occupied the site of Buckingham Palace.* Here also were the "Gun" Tavern and Tea-gardens, with convenient "arbours and costume figures." These gardens were removed to make way for improvements at Buckingham Gate. Then there was the "Star and Garter" Tavern, at the end of Five-Fields' Row, which was at one time famous for its fireworks, dancing, and equestrianism; and the "Orange," as nearly as possible upon the site of St. Barnabas' Church.

Another tavern or place of public entertainment in this neighbourhood, in former times, was "Jenny's Whim." This establishment, which bore the name down to the beginning of the present century, occupied the site now covered by St. George's Row, near to Ebury Bridge, which spanned the canal at the north end of the Commercial Road. This bridge was formerly known as the "Wooden Bridge," and also as "Jenny's Whim Bridge" (see page 43); and down to about the year 1825, a turnpike close by bore the same lady's name.

A hundred years ago, as is clear from allusions to it in the *Connoisseur* and other periodicals, "Jenny's Whim" was a very favourite place of amusement for the middle classes. At a somewhat earlier date, it would appear to have been frequented alike by high and low, by lords and gay ladies, and by City apprentices; and indeed was generally looked upon as a very favourite place of recreation. The derivation of the name is a little uncertain; but Mr. Davis, in his "History of Knightsbridge," thus attempts to solve it:—"I never could unearth the origin of its name, but I presume the tradition told me by an old inhabitant of the neighbourhood is correct, namely, that it was so called after its first landlady, who caused the gardens round her house to be laid out in so fantastic a manner, as to cause the expressive little noun to be affixed to the pretty and familiar Christian name that she bore."

In the "Reminiscences" of Angelo, however, it is said that the founder of "Jenny's Whim" was not a lady at all, but a celebrated pyrotechnist, who lived in the reign of George I. If so, this assertion carries back the existence of the "Whim" as a place of amusement to a very respectable antiquity. Angelo states that it was "much frequented from its novelty, being an inducement to allure the curious to it by its amusing deceptions." "Here," he adds, "was a large garden; in different parts were recesses; and by treading on a spring—taking you by surprise—up started different figures, some ugly enough to frighten you outright—a harlequin, a Mother Shipton, or some terrific animal." Something of the same kind, it may here be remarked, was to be seen in the days of Charles I., in the Spring Garden near Charing Cross.† "In a large piece of water facing the tea alcoves," adds Mr. Angelo, "large fish or mermaids were showing themselves above the surface." Horace Walpole, in his letters, occasionally alludes to "Jenny's Whim," in terms which imply that he was among "the quality" who visited it. In one of his epistles to his friend Montagu, he writes, rather spitefully and maliciously, it must be owned, to the effect that at Vauxhall he and his party picked up Lord Granby, who had arrived very drunk from "Jenny's Whim." In 1755, a satirical tract was published, entitled, "Jenny's Whim; or a Sure Guide to the Nobility, Gentry, and other Eminent Persons in this Metropolis." "Jenny's Whim" has occasionally served the novelist for an illustration of the manners of the age. Let us take the following passage from "Maids of Honour," a tale *temp.* George I.:—

* See Vol. IV., p. 62.

† See Vol. IV., p. 77.

"Attached to the place there were gardens and a bowling-green," writes the author; "and parties were frequently made, composed of ladies and gentlemen, to enjoy a day's amusement there in eating strawberries and cream, cake, syllabub, and taking other refreshments, of which a great variety could be procured, with cider, perry, ale, wine, and other liquors in abundance. The gentlemen played at bowls—some employed themselves at skittles; whilst the ladies amused themselves with a swing, or walked about the garden, admiring the sunflower and hollyhocks, and the Duke of Marlborough cut out of a filbert-tree, and the roses and daisies, currants and gooseberries, that spread their alluring charms in every part."

No doubt, therefore, we may conclude that a century, or a century and a half ago, "Jenny's Whim" was a favourite meeting-place for lovers in the happy courting seasons, and that a day's pleasure near Ebury Bridge was considered by the fair damsels of Westminster and Knightsbridge one of the most attractive amusements that could be offered to them by their beaux; and many a heart which was obdurate elsewhere, gave way to gentle pressure beneath the influence of its attractions, aided by the *genius loci*, who is always most complaisant and benignant on such occasions. "Sometimes," writes Mr. Davis, "all its chambers were filled, and its gardens were constantly thronged by gay and sentimental visitors." We may be sure, therefore, that always during the season—in other words, from Easter-tide till the end of St. Martin's summer, when the long evenings drew on—"Jenny's Whim" was largely frequented by the young people of either sex, and that its "arbours" and "alcoves" witnessed and overheard many a tale of love. It is well perhaps that garden walls have not tongues as well as ears. But, in any case, it is perhaps a little singular that a place, once so well known and so popular, should have passed away, clean forgotten from the public memory.

All that appears to be known in detail about the house is, that it contained a large room for parties to breakfast in; and that the grounds, though not large, were fairly diversified, as they contained a bowling-green, several alcoves and arbours, and straight, prim flower-beds, with a fish-pond in the centre, where the paths met at right angles. There was also a "cock-pit" in the garden, and in a pond adjoining the brutal sport of duck-hunting was carried on. This feature of the garden is specially mentioned in a short and slight sketch of the place to be found in the *Connoisseur* of March 15th, 1775:—"The lower part of the people have their Ranelaghs and Vauxhalls as well as 'the quality.' Perrott's inimitable grotto may be seen for only calling for a pint of beer; and the royal diversion of duck-hunting may be had into the bargain, together with a decanter of Dorchester [ale] for your sixpence at 'Jenny's Whim.'"

Mr. Davis states, in his work above quoted, that the house was still partly standing in 1859, when his book was published, and might be easily identified by its "red brick and lattice-work."

Notwithstanding all the attractions which the district of Pimlico thus afforded to the Londoners, to betake themselves thither in order to enjoy the good things provided for their entertainment, access to it must have been somewhat difficult and dangerous in the last century—a state of things, as we have more than once remarked, that seems to have been pretty similar in all the suburbs of the metropolis; for we read in the *London Magazine* that, as lately as 1773, two persons were sentenced to death for a highway robbery in "Chelsea Fields," as that part of Pimlico bordering the Chelsea Road was then called. It is also not a matter of tradition, but of personal remembrance, that for the first twenty years of the present century persons who resided in the "suburb" of Pimlico rarely thought of venturing into London at night, so slight was the protection afforded them by the watchmen and "Charlies," aided by the faint glimmer of oil lamps, few and far between.

Not far from the Mulberry Gardens, on the west side of what is now James Street, as we have stated in the previous volume,* stood a mansion, called Tart Hall, which was built, or, at all events, extensively altered and enlarged, in the reign of Charles I., for the wife of Thomas, "the magnificent Earl of Arundel." On her death it passed into the hands of her second son, William, Lord Stafford, one of the victims of the plot of the infamous Titus Oates, in 1680, and whose memory is still kept up in the names of Stafford Place and Stafford Row. Strange to say, that John Evelyn himself, usually so circumstantial in all matters of detail, dismisses this legal murder without a single remark, beyond the dry entry in his "Diary," under December 20th, 1680: "The Viscount Stafford was beheaded on Tower Hill." It is said that the old gateway, which stood till early in the last century, was never opened after the condemned nobleman passed through it for the last time.

The building is described in the "New View of London" (1708), as being "near the way leading out of the Park to Chelsea;" and its

* See Vol. IV., p 25.

site is marked in Faithorne's Map of London, published in 1658.

In his "Morning's Walk from London to Kew" (1817), Sir Richard Phillips writes:—"The name of Stafford Row reminded me of the ancient distinction of Tart Hall, once the rival in size and splendour of its more fortunate neighbour, Buckingham House. . . . It faced the Park, on the present site of James Street; its garden-wall standing where Stafford Row is now built, and the extensive livery-stables being once the stables of its residents."

The origin of Tart Hall is unknown; but the name is probably a corruption or abridgment of a longer word. It is noted, as to situation, in "Walpole's Anecdotes," as "without the gate of St. James's Park, near Buckingham House," and is described by him as "very large, and having a very venerable appearance."

After the removal of the Arundel marbles and other treasures from Arundel House, in the neighbourhood of the Strand,* the remainder of the collection, as Walpole tells us, was kept at Tart Hall; but they were sold in 1720, and the house was subsequently pulled down. From the same authority we learn that some carved seats, by Inigo Jones, purchased at this sale, were placed by Lord Burlington in his villa at Chiswick. In the Harleian MSS., in the British Museum, is to be seen "A Memorial of all the Roomes at Tart Hall, and an Inventory of all the household stuffs and goods there, except of six Roomes at the North end of the ould Building (which the Right Honourable the Countess hath reserved unto her peculiar use), and Mr. Thomas Howard's Closett, &c.," dated September, 1641. The memorial is curious as giving a catalogue, not only of the picture-gallery, but of the carpets and decorations of this once magnificent palace. It is, however, too long in its details to be reprinted here.

In Stafford Row, which lies immediately at the back of Buckingham Palace Hotel, lived, in the year 1767, William Wynne Ryland, the engraver, who was executed for forgery in 1783; here, too, during the early part of the present century, died Mrs. Radcliffe, the author of "The Mysteries of Udolpho." Richard Yates, the actor, who was famous in the last century for his delineation of "old men," died at his residence in this Row in 1796. The following singular story of the ill fortune which attended the actor and his family is told by Peter Cunningham, in his "Hand-book of London:"—"Yates had ordered eels for dinner, and died the same day of rage and disappointment, because his housekeeper was unable to obtain them. The actor's great-nephew was, a few months afterwards—August 22nd, 1796—killed while endeavouring to effect an entrance into the house from the back garden. The great-nephew, whose name was Yates, claimed a right to the house, as did also a Miss Jones, and both lived in the house for some months after Yates' death. Yates, while strolling in the garden, was bolted out after an early dinner, and, while forcing his way in, was wounded by a ball from a pistol, which caused his death. The parties were acquitted."

St. Peter's Chapel, on the west side of Charlotte Street, which runs southwards out of Buckingham Palace Road, just opposite to the Palace, and skirts the west end of Stafford Place, enjoys a melancholy celebrity, as having been the scene of the ministrations of Dr. Dodd, of whose execution for a forgery on Lord Chesterfield we shall have to make fuller mention when we come to speak of "Tyburn Tree." The following account of the life of Dr. Dodd is said to have been sketched by himself while lying in Newgate, awaiting his execution, and to have been finished by Dr. Johnson:—"I entered very young on public life, very innocent—very ignorant—and very ingenuous. I lived many happy years at West Ham, in an uninterrupted and successful discharge of my duty. A disappointment in the living of that parish obliged me to exert myself, and I engaged for a chapel near Buckingham Gate. Great success attended the undertaking; it pleased and elated me. At the same time Lord Chesterfield, to whom I was personally unknown, offered me the care of his heir, Mr. Stanhope. By the advice of my dear friend, now in heaven, Dr. Squire, I engaged, under promises which were not performed. Such a distinction, too, you must know, served to increase a young man's vanity. I was naturally led into more extensive and important connections, and, of course, with greater expenses and more dissipations. Indeed, before I never dissipated at all—for many, many years, never seeing a playhouse, or any public place, but living entirely in Christian duties. Thus brought to town, and introduced to gay life, I fell into its snares. Ambition and vanity led me on. My temper, naturally cheerful, was pleased with company; naturally generous, it knew not the use of money; it was a stranger to the useful science of economy and frugality; nor could it withhold from distress what it too much (often) wanted itself.

"Besides this, the habit of uniform, regular,

* See Vol. III., p. 73.

sober piety, and of watchfulness and devotion, wearing off, amidst this unavoidable scene of dissipation, I was not, as at West Ham, the innocent man that I lived there. I committed offences against my God, which yet, I bless Him, were always, on reflection. detestable to me.

"But my greatest evil was expense. To supply it, I fell into the dreadful and ruinous mode of raising money by annuities. The annuities devoured me. Still, I exerted myself by every means to do what I thought right, and built my hopes of perfect extrication from all my difficulties when my young and beloved pupil should come of age. But, alas! during this interval, which was not very long, I declare with solemn truth that I never varied from the steady belief of the Christian doctrines. I preached them with all my power, and kept back nothing from my congregations which I thought might tend to their best welfare; and I was very successful in this way during the time. Nor, though I spent in dissipation many hours which I ought not, but to which my connections inevitably led, was I idle during this period; as my 'Commentary on the Bible,' my 'Sermons to Young Men,' and several other publications prove. I can say, too, with pleasure, that I studiously employed my interest, through the connections I had, for the good of others. I never forgot or neglected the cause of the distressed; many, if need were, could bear me witness. Let it suffice to say, that during this period I instituted the Charity for the Discharge of Debtors."

Close by Charlotte Street, in a small gloomy house, inside the gates of Messrs. Elliot's Brewery, between Brewer Street, Pimlico, and York Street, Westminster, lived Richard Heber, some time M.P. for the University of Oxford, and the owner of one of the finest private libraries in the world. Here he kept a portion of his library; a second part occupying an entire house in James Street, Buckingham Gate; a third portion, from kitchen to attics, was at his country seat at Hodnet, in Shropshire; and a fourth at Paris. "Nobody," he used to say, "could do without three copies of a book—one for show at his country house, one for personal use, and the third to lend to his friends." And this library, as we learn from "A Century of Anecdote," had but a small beginning—the accidental purchase of a chance volume

THE "GUN TAVERN," 1820. (*See page* 45.)

picked up for a few pence at a bookstall, and about which Mr. Heber was for some time in doubt whether to buy it or not. The catalogue of Mr. Heber's library was bound up in five thick octavo volumes. Dr. Dibdin once addressed to him a letter entitled "Bibliomania;" but he was no bibliomaniac, but a ripe and accomplished scholar. Mr. Heber took an active part in founding the Athenæum Club, and he was also a member of several other literary societies; indeed, to use the phrase of Dr. Johnson, "He was an excellent clubber." He was the half-brother of Reginald Heber, Bishop of Calcutta, and died a bachelor in 1833, in the sixtieth year of his age. His extensive library was dispersed by auction in London. The sale commenced upon the 10th of April, 1834, and occupied *two hundred and two days*, and extended through a period of more than *two years*. The catalogue of this remarkable sale filled more than two thousand printed octavo pages, and contained no less than 52,672 lots.

Mr. Peter Cunningham, in noticing the growth of this locality in his "Hand-book of London," says: "George IV. began the great alterations in Pimlico by rebuilding Buckingham House, and drawing the courtiers from Portland Place and Portman Square to the splendid mansions built by Messrs. Basevi and Cubitt, in what was known at that time, and long before, as the 'Five Fields.' It seems but the other day," he adds, "that the writer of this brief notice of the place played at cricket in the Five Fields, 'where robbers lie in wait,' or pulled bulrushes in the 'cuts' of the Willow Walk, in Pimlico."

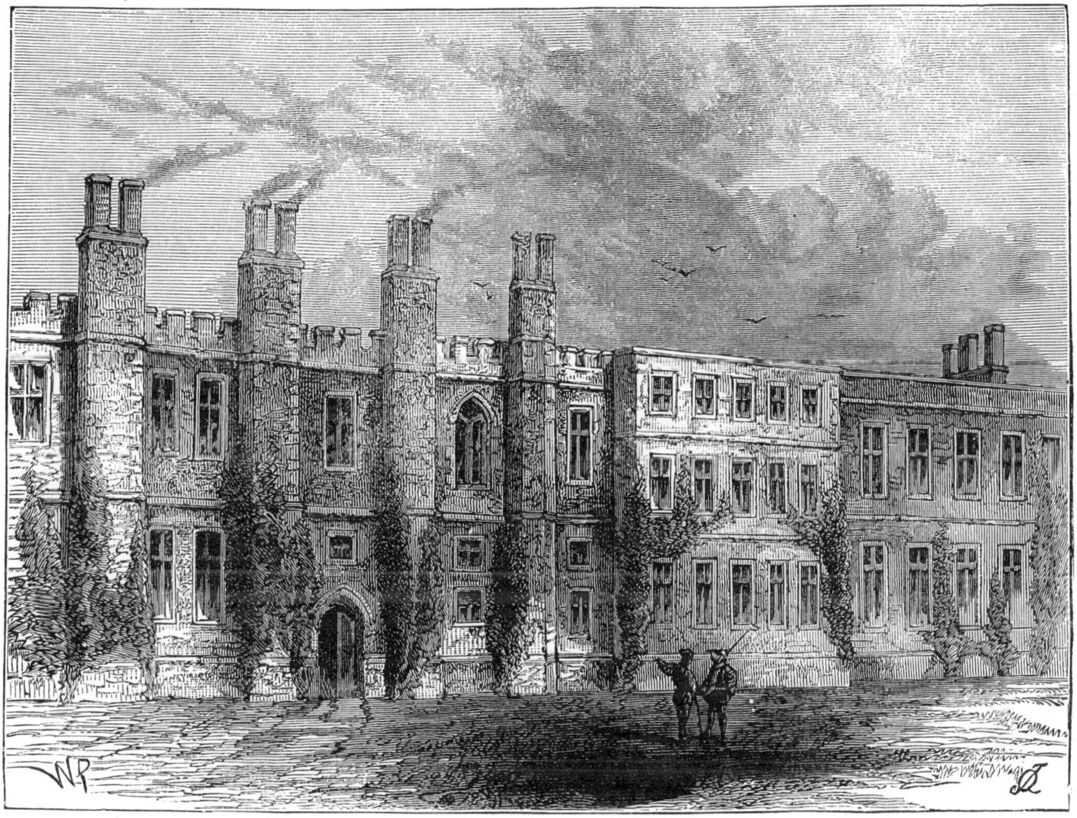

THE OLD CHELSEA MANOR HOUSE. (*See page* 52.)

As might be naturally expected, the removal of King William and his Court from St. James's to Buckingham Palace, on his accession to the throne in 1830, gave a considerable impetus to the improvement of Pimlico, although a town of palaces had already been commenced upon the "Five Fields," as that dreary region had been formerly called. The ground landlord of a considerable portion of the land thus benefited by these metropolitan improvements was Lord Grosvenor, who, in the year 1831, was created Marquis of Westminster, and who, as we have already stated in our description of Grosvenor House in a former chapter, was grandfather of the present ducal owner.*

* See Vol. IV., p. 371.

CHAPTER V.

CHELSEA.

"The sands of Chelsey Fields."—*Ben Jonson.*

Boundary of the Parish—Etymology of its Name—Charles II. and Colonel Blood—Chelsea Fields—The "Dwarf's Tavern"—Chapels of French Huguenot Refugees—Gardens and Nurseries—Appearance of Chelsea from the River—Chelsea in the Last Century—A Stag Hunt in Chelsea—History of the Manor—The Old Manor House and its Eminent Residents—Lord Cremorne's Farm at Chelsea—Lady Cremorne—Lindsey House—The Moravians—The Duchess of Mazarine—Sir Robert Walpole's House—Shrewsbury House—Winchester House—Beaufort House and the "Good" Sir Thomas More—Anecdotes of Sir Thomas More—The Old and New Parish Churches.

Few, if any, of the suburban districts of the metropolis can lay claim to greater interest, biographical as well as topographical, than the locality upon which we have now entered. In Faulkner's "History of Chelsea," we read that the parish is "bounded on the north by the Fulham Road, which separates it from Kensington; on the east by a rivulet, which divides it from St. George's, Hanover Square, and which enters the Thames near Ranelagh; on the west a brook, which rises near Wormholt Scrubs, and falls into the Thames facing Battersea Church, divides this parish from that of Fulham; and on the south it is bounded by the Thames." Lysons observes that the most ancient record in which he has seen the name of this place mentioned is a charter of Edward the Confessor, in which it is written "Cealchylle."* The name seems to have puzzled the Norman scribes, for in Domesday Book it is written both "Cercehede" and "Chelched;" and in certain documents of a later date it is called "Chelcheth," or "Chelcith." "The word 'Chelsey,'" observes Mr. Norris Brewer, in the "Beauties of England and Wales," "was first adopted in the sixteenth century, and the present mode of spelling the name appears to have grown into use about a century back." It may here be remarked that the name of Chelsea has been derived by some writers from "Shelves" of sand, and "ey," or "ea," land situated near the water. But Lysons prefers the etymology of Norden, who says that "it is so called from the nature of the place, its strand being like the chesel [*ceosel*, or *cesol*], which the sea casteth up of sand and pebble stones, thereof called Chevelsey, briefly Chelsey." In like manner it may be added that the beach of pebbles thrown up by the action of the sea outside Weymouth harbour, is styled the Chesil bank. Perhaps it is the same word at bottom as Selsey, the name of a peninsula of pebbles on the Sussex coast, near Chichester.

As a symbol of infinity, Ben Jonson, in his "Forest," speaks of

"All the grass that Romney yields,
Or the sands of Chelsey Fields."

Macaulay reminds us that, at the end of the reign of Charles II., Chelsea was a "quiet country village, with about a thousand inhabitants; the baptisms averaging little more than forty in the year." At that time the Thames was sufficiently clear and pure for bathing above Westminster. We are told that, on one occasion, Charles II. was bathing at Chelsea, when the notorious Colonel Blood lay hid among the reeds at Battersea, in order to shoot him. Notwithstanding its remoteness from the metropolis, however, Chelsea does not appear to have escaped the ravages of the "Great Plague," for it raged here as well as in other suburbs of London, as Pepys informs us, in his "Diary," under date of April 9th, 1666:—"Thinking to have been merry at Chelsey; but, being almost come to the house by coach, near the waterside, a house alone, I think the 'Swan,' a gentleman walking by called out to us that the house was shut up because of the sickness."

Chelsea Fields must have been quite a rustic spot even to a yet later date, for Gay thus addresses his friend Pulteney:—

"When the sweet-breathing spring unfolds the buds,
Love flies the dusty town for shady woods;
Then . . . .
. . . Chelsea's meads o'erhear perfidious vows,
And the press'd grass defrauds the grazing cows."

In "Chelsea Fields" was formerly a tavern, known as "The Dwarf's," kept by John Coan, a diminutive manikin from Norfolk. "It seems to have been a place of some attraction," says Mr. Larwood, "since it was honoured by the repeated visits of an Indian king." Thus the *Daily Advertiser* of July 12, 1762, says: "On Friday last the Cherokee king and his two chiefs were so greatly pleased with the curiosities of the Dwarf's Tavern, in Chelsea Fields, that they were there again on Sunday, at seven in the evening, to drink tea, and will be there again in a few days." The reputation of the tavern, under its pygmean proprietor, was but brief, as the "unparalleled" Coan, as he is styled, died within two years from the above date.

* "Environs of London," vol. ii., p. 70.

In the reign of William III., the French Huguenot refugees had two chapels in Chelsea: the one in "Cook's Grounds," now used by the Congregationalists, and another at Little Chelsea, not far from Kensington.

"Chelsea," observes a writer in the *Mirror*, in 1833, "though now proverbial for its dulness, was formerly a place of great gaiety. Thousands flocked to Salter's—or, as it was dubbed, 'Don Saltero's'—coffee-house in Cheyne Walk; the Chelsea buns were eaten by princesses; and the public were allowed to walk in thirteen acres of avenues of limes and chestnut-trees in the gardens adjoining the College. This privilege was disallowed in 1806; but within the last few weeks these grounds have been again thrown open to the public." The ground round about Chelsea and its neighbourhood, like that of Bermondsey, and other low-lying districts bordering upon the Thames, is peculiarly adapted for the growth of vegetables, fruits, and flowers; indeed, Chelsea has long been remarkable for its gardens and nurseries. Dr. Mackay, in his "Extraordinary Popular Delusions," tells us that about the time of Her Majesty's accession, there was a gardener in the King's Road, Chelsea, in whose catalogue a single tulip was marked at two hundred guineas—a remnant, perhaps, of the tulip-mania, which, two centuries before, had ruined half of the merchants of Holland, and threatened to prove as disastrous here as the "South Sea Bubble." It may be added, too, that the first red geranium seen in England is said to have been raised by a Mr. Davis here, about the year 1822.

Chelsea, which was once a rustic and retired village, has been gradually absorbed into the metropolis by the advance of the army of bricklayers and mortar-layers, and now forms fairly a portion of London, Pimlico and Belgravia having supplied the connecting link. Environed though it is by the growing suburbs, the place has still an old-fashioned look about it, which the modern, trimly-laid-out flower-gardens on the new embankment only tend to increase. Looked at from the Battersea side of the river, with the barges floating lazily along past the solid red-brick houses, screened by sheltering trees, Chelsea presents such a picture as the old Dutch "masters" would have revelled in, especially as the Thames here widens into a fine "reach," well known to oarsmen for the rough "seas" which they encounter there on those occasions when the wind meets the tide; in fact, the river is wider at this particular spot than anywhere "above bridge." In the reign of Charles II. it was such a fashionable rendezvous that it was frequently called "Hyde Park on the Thames."

Bowack thus writes, in an account of Chelsea, published in 1705:—"The situation of it upon the Thames is very pleasant, and standing in a small bay, or angle, made by the meeting of Chelsea and Battersea Reaches, it has a most delightful prospect on that river for near four miles, as far as Vauxhall eastward, and as Wandsworth to the west."

In the last century, Chelsea being, in fact, quite a suburban place, had its own society; "its many honourable and worthy inhabitants," as we are told by Bowack, "being not more remarkable for their titles, estates, and employments, than for their civility and condescension, and their kind and facetious tempers, living in a perfect amity among themselves, and having a general meeting every day at a coffee-house near the church, well known for a pretty collection of varieties in nature and art, some of which are very curious." The coffee-house here mentioned was the renowned Don Saltero's, of which we shall have more to say in the next chapter.

Mr. Peter Cunningham speaks of Chelsea as "at one time the Islington of the West-end," and thus enumerates the articles for which it has from time to time been famous:—Its manor house, its college, its botanic garden, its hospital, its amusements at Ranelagh, its waterworks, its buns, its china, and its custards.

"About the year 1796," writes Faulkner, in his "History of Chelsea," "I was present at a stag-hunt in Chelsea. The animal swam across the river from Battersea, and made for Lord Cremorne's grounds. Upon being driven from thence, he ran along the water-side as far as the church, and turning up Church Lane, at last took refuge in Mrs. Hutchins's barn, where he was taken alive."

The connection of Chelsea with Westminster, already stated in our account* of the "Monster" Tavern, Pimlico, is probably of very old standing, for even during the rule of our Norman kings it appears to have been one of the manors belonging to the abbey of St. Peter. Little, however, is known with certainty of the history of this now extensive parish till the time of Henry VII., when the manor was held by Sir Reginald Bray, from whom it descended to Margaret, only child of his next brother, John, who married William, Lord Sandys. From Lord Sandys the manor passed, in exchange for other lands, to that rapacious king, Henry VIII., by whom it was assigned to Katharine

* See above, p. 45.

Parr, as part of her marriage jointure. Faulkner, in his work above quoted, says that "Henry was probably induced to possess this manor from having observed, in his frequent visits to Sir Thomas More, the pleasantness of the situation on the bank of the Thames; and, from the salubrity of the air, deeming it a fit residence for his infant daughter, the Princess Elizabeth, then between three and four years of age. But after having obtained it, finding that the manor house was ancient, and at that time in the possession of the Lawrence family, he erected a new manor house, on the eastern side of the spot where Winchester House lately stood, and supplied it with water from a spring at Kensington." The manor was subsequently held by John Dudley, Duke of Northumberland; by Anne, Duchess of Somerset, widow of the "Protector;" by John, first Lord Stanhope, of Harrington; by Katharine, Lady Howard, wife of the Lord Admiral; by James, first Duke of Hamilton; by Charles, Viscount Cheyne; and by Sir Hans Sloane, the celebrated physician, who purchased it in 1712 from the Cheyne family, and from whom it passed by marriage to Charles, second Lord Cadogan, of Oakley, through which alliance the manor of Chelsea became vested in the Cadogans, with whom it still remains.

The old manor house stood near the church, and was sold by Henry VIII. to the Lawrence family, after whom Lawrence Street derives its name. The new manor house stood on that part of Cheyne Walk fronting the Thames, between the Pier Hotel and the house formerly known as "Don Saltero's Coffee-house." The building, of which a view of the north front is engraved in Faulkner's "History of Chelsea" (see page 49), was of a quadrangular form, enclosing a spacious court, and was partly embattled. The mansion was pulled down shortly after the death of Sir Hans Sloane, in the middle of the last century, and a row of houses erected on the site.

Like Kensington, Chelsea has been from time to time the residence of many individuals of high rank, who were attracted to it on account of its nearness to the Court, and its easiness of access at a time when the roads of the suburbs were bad, and the Thames was the "silent highway" to families who could afford to keep their barge. So far as rank and station are concerned, perhaps the first and foremost of its residents was the Princess (afterwards Queen) Elizabeth. After her father's death, Miss Lucy Aikin tells us, in her "Memoirs of the Court" of that sovereign, the princess "had been consigned to the care and protection of the Queen Dowager (Katharine Parr), with whom she usually made her abode at one or other of her jointure houses at Chelsea, or at Hanworth, near Hounslow."

In the reign of Elizabeth, the Lord High Admiral, the Earl of Effingham, was among the residents of this place; and we are told by Bishop Goodman that, in her "progresses" from Richmond to Whitehall, the "Virgin Queen" would often dine with his lordship at Chelsea, and afterwards set out thence towards London, late at night, by torchlight, in order that the Lord Mayor and aldermen, and the other loyal citizens, might not see those wrinkles and that ugly throat of hers, with which Horace Walpole has made us familiar in his representation of a coin struck shortly before her death.

Thomas Beauchamp, Earl of Warwick, who acquired high renown at the battles of Cressy and Poictiers, appears to have occasionally resided at Chelsea. It is supposed that he occupied a house and premises which afterwards belonged to Richard Beauchamp, Bishop of Salisbury, and which were granted by Richard III. to Elizabeth, widow of Thomas Mowbray, Duke of Norfolk, for life, "to be held by the service of a red rose." The site of this mansion, however, is now unknown, as also is the spot once occupied by a house in Chelsea which was possessed by William, Marquis of Berkeley, an adherent of the Earl of Richmond (afterwards Henry VII.).

In April, 1663, we find Lord Sandwich at his Chelsea lodging, eating cakes made by the mistress of the house, and, it may be added, the mother of his own mistress—cakes so good that, says Pepys, "they were fit to present to my Lady Castlemaine"—a curious parody of the lines of the old nursery rhyme:—

> "Now was not that a dainty dish
> To set before a king?"

Among the residents of Chelsea in the last century was Lord Cremorne, who occupied a house called Chelsea Farm, which was situated at a short distance from the bridge on the site long covered by Cremorne Gardens. Lady Cremorne is celebrated in the "Percy Anecdotes" as the best mistress of a household that ever lived. She had a servant, Elizabeth Palfrey, who had lived with her for forty-eight years, during the latter half of the time as housekeeper, and who so regulated affairs that in all that long time not one of the female servants was known to have left her place, except in order to be married. Such mistresses are rare now, and probably were not common even in her day. As late as 1826, the name of Viscountess Cremorne appears in the "Royal Blue Book," with

"Chelsea Farm" as her country residence. The edifice, which was built of brick, overlooked the river, from which it was separated by a lawn, pleasantly shaded by stately trees. The house had a somewhat irregular appearance externally, and little to boast of in the way of architecture; but the interior was commodious, and the best suite of rooms well adapted to the use of a distinguished family. Here was a small but judicious collection of pictures, formed by Viscount Cremorne, among which were some by noted Flemish and Italian masters.

Lindsey Row and Lindsey Place, facing the river immediately westward of Battersea Bridge, mark the site of Lindsey House, the residence of the Berties, Earls of Lindsey. About the middle of the last century the mansion was purchased by Count Zinzendorf, a leader of the peculiar sect known as Moravians, for the purpose of establishing a settlement of that society in Chelsea; but the project failed; the building was again sold, and subsequently demolished, or cut up into private tenements.

In a small house in Chelsea, rented from Lord Cheyne, died, in difficulties, the beautiful Duchess of Mazarine, one of the frail beauties of the Court of Charles II.

In Lyson's "Environs," we read that about the year 1722 Sir Robert Walpole, the well-known prime minister of George II., "became possessed of a house and garden in the stable-yard at Chelsea." The house was "next the college," adjoining Gough House. Sir Robert frequently resided there, improved and added to the house, and considerably enlarged the gardens by a purchase of some land from the Gough family; he erected an octagonal summer-house at the head of the terrace, and a large green-house, where he had a fine collection of exotics. A good story is told about Queen Caroline, when dining one day here with Lady Walpole. Sir Paul Methuen, who was one of the company, was remarkable for his love of romances. The queen asked him what he had been reading of late in his own way. "Nothing, madam," said Sir Paul; "I have now commenced, instead of romances, a very foolish study, 'The History of the Kings and Queens of England.'" Horace Walpole informs us that he remembered La Belle Jennings (afterwards Duchess of Marlborough) coming to his parents' house to solicit a pension.

Shrewsbury House, or, as it was sometimes called, Alston House, in Cheyne Walk, near the waterside, if we may trust Priscilla Wakefield's "Perambulations in London," was a paper manufactory at the time of its demolition in 1814. It was an irregular brick building, forming three sides of a quadrangle. The principal room was upwards of 100 feet long, and was originally wainscoted with carved oak. One of the rooms was painted in imitation of marble, and others were ornamented with certain "curious portraits on panel." Leading from the premises towards the King's Road was a subterranean passage, which is traditionally said to have communicated with a cave, or dungeon, situated at some distance from the house.

Winchester House, the Palace of the Bishops of Winchester from about the middle of the seventeenth down to the commencement of the present century, stood on the spot now occupied by the Pier Hotel, and its gardens adjoined Shrewsbury House. It was a heavy brick building, of low proportions, and quite devoid of any architectural ornament. The interior was fairly commodious, and "much enriched by the collection of antiques and specimens of natural history" placed there by Bishop North, the last prelate who occupied it. Bishop Hoadley, who died here in 1761, was so lax in his ideas of Church authority, that some free-thinking Christians were wittily styled by Archbishop Secker, "Christians secundum usum Winton," in allusion to the customary title of books printed "for the use of the Winchester scholars."

The chief interest of Chelsea, however, not only to the antiquary, but to the educated Englishman, must lie in the fact that it was the much-loved home of that great man whose memory English history will never allow to die, Sir Thomas More. Here he resided, surrounded by his family, in a house about midway between the Thames and the King's Road, on the site of what is now Beaufort Street. In Aubrey's "Letters from the Bodleian," we read:—"His country house was at Chelsey, in Middlesex, where Sir John Danvers built his house. The chimney-piece, of marble, in Sir John's chamber, was the chimney-piece of Sir Thomas More's chamber, as Sir John himself told me. Where the gate is now, adorned with two noble pyramids, there stood anciently a gate-house, which was flatt on the top, leaded, from whence was a most pleasant prospect of the Thames and the fields beyond; on this place the Lord Chancellor More was wont to recreate himself and contemplate."

Erasmus—himself one of the most cherished friends of Sir Thomas—describes the house as "neither mean nor subject to envy, yet magnificent and commodious enough." The building, which was erected early in the sixteenth century, was successively called Buckingham House and Beaufort House, and was pulled down about the middle of the last century. At the end of the garden Sir Thomas erected a pile of buildings, consisting of a chapel, gallery, and library, all being designed for his own retirement. His piety, staunch and firm as was his adherence to the Roman Catholic creed, is acknowledged even by Protestant writers. Wood, in his "Ecclesiastical Antiquities," says:—"More rose early, and assembled his family morning and evening in the chapel, when certain prayers and Psalms were recited. He heard mass daily himself, and expected all his household to do so on Sundays and festivals; whilst, on the eves of great feasts, all watched till matins. Every Friday, as was also his custom on some other occasions, he retired to the new buildings, where he spent the whole day in prayer and meditation."

Sir Thomas usually attended Divine service on Sundays at Chelsea Church, and very often assisted at the celebration of mass. The Duke of Norfolk coming one day to dine with him during his chancellorship, found him in church with a surplice on, and singing in the choir. "God's body, my Lord Chancellor!" said the duke, as they returned to his house. "What! a parish clerk! a parish clerk! you dishonour the king and his office." "Nay," said Sir Thomas, "you may not think your master and mine will be offended with me for serving God, his master, or thereby count his office dishonoured."

CHELSEA FARM, 1829. (*See page* 53.)

OLD MANSIONS IN CHELSEA. (*From Faulkner's "Chelsea."*)

1. Church Place, 1641. 2. Gough House, 1760. 3. Shrewsbury House, 1540. 4. Beaufort House, 1628. 5. Winchester House.

In later years the chapel in More's house appears to have been free to the public, for in various marriage licences, granted towards the commencement of the last century, persons were to be married "in the parish church, in the chapel of Chelsea College, or the chapel of Beaufort House." The only fragment of the house remaining down to the present century was a portion of the cellars, which existed beneath the house No. 17, forming one of the line of dwellings now known by the name of Beaufort Row. An avenue, with a high wall on each side, constituted the chief approach to the house, or that from the river-side; and fronting the entrance of this avenue were the stairs used by Sir Thomas More when descending to his barge. A terrace-walk, which stretched from the house towards the east, is described in the legal writings of the estate as being so much raised that it was ascended by several steps. After the demolition of the house a portion of the ground was occupied as a burial-place for the Moravian Society, and the remains of the stables were converted into public schools.

The most important circumstances in the life of Sir Thomas More are too well known to need repetition in these pages. His domestic life at Chelsea has been described by Erasmus in the following words:—"There he converses with his wife, his son, his daughter-in-law, his three daughters and their husbands, with eleven grandchildren. There is not any man living so affectionate as he, and he loveth his old wife as well as if she was a young maid. You would say there was in that place Plato's Academy; but I do his house an injury in comparing it to Plato's Academy, where there were only disputations of numbers and geometrical figures, and sometimes of moral virtues. I should rather call his house a school, or university of Christian religion, for though there is none therein but readeth or studieth the liberal sciences, their special care is piety and virtue; there is no quarrelling or intemperate words heard; none seen idle; that worthy gentleman doth not govern with proud and lofty words, but with well-timed and courteous benevolence; everybody performeth his duty, yet is there always alacrity; neither is sober mirth anything wanting."

Erasmus was the correspondent of Sir Thomas More long before he was personally acquainted with his illustrious friend; and although strongly dissimilar in religious opinions, when the great reformer and scholar visited England he was the frequent guest of Sir Thomas at Chelsea. The house of More was, indeed, the resort of all who were conspicuous for learning and taste. Collet, Linacre, and Tunstall often partook of the hospitality of his table. Here Sir Thomas often entertained "Master John Heywood," the early English playwright, and cracked with him many a joke. It is said that it was through Sir Thomas More that he was introduced to the Lady Mary, and so was brought under the notice of Henry VIII., who appointed him the Court jester. Those were, indeed, strange days, when a buffoon dared to laugh in the face of a sovereign who could send to the scaffold so venerable, so grave and learned a scholar, and so loyal a subject of the Crown. The wit of Sir Thomas More was almost boundless, and he was also no mean actor. It is related of him that when an interlude was performed he would "make one among the players, occasionally coming upon them by surprise, and without rehearsal fall into a character, and support the part by his extemporaneous invention, and acquit himself with credit." It was probably by his intercourse with Heywood that the latent dramatic powers of the great Lord Chancellor were called out.

Henry VIII., to whom More owed his rise and fall, frequently came to Chelsea, and spent whole days in the most familiar manner with his learned friend; and "it is supposed," says Faulkner, in his "History of Chelsea," "that the king's answer to Luther was prepared and arranged for the public eye, with the assistance of Sir Thomas, during these visits." Notwithstanding all this familiarity, Sir Thomas understood the temper of his royal master very well, as the following anecdote sufficiently testifies:—"One day the king came unexpectedly to Chelsea, and dined with him, and after dinner walked in his garden for the space of an hour, holding his arm about his neck. As soon as his Majesty was gone, Sir Thomas's son-in-law observed to him how happy he was, since the king had treated him with that familiarity he had never used to any person before, except Cardinal Wolsey, with whom he once saw his Majesty walk arm-in-arm." "I thank our Lord," answered Sir Thomas, "I find his grace my very good lord indeed; and I believe he doth as singularly love me as any subject within this realm; however, son Roper, I may tell thee I have no cause to be proud thereof, for if my head would win him a castle in France, it should not fail to go off."

Sir Thomas More is said to have converted one part of his house into a prison for the restraint of heretics; and according to a passage in "Foxe's Book of Martyrs," he here kept in prison, and whipped in his garden, one John Baynham, a lawyer, who was suspected of holding the doctrines of Wycliffe, and who was ultimately burnt at Smithfield. But it must be remembered that he lived in an age when religious persecution was practised by all parties, and when, as Byron writes—

"Christians did burn each other, quite persuaded
That all th' Apostles would have done as they did.

More's fondness for animals is an interesting and curious peculiarity. Erasmus tells us, that watching their growth, development, and dispositions, was one of his chief pleasures. "At Chelsea may be seen many varieties of birds, and an ape, a fox, a weasel, and a ferret. Moreover, if anything foreign, or otherwise remarkable, comes in his way, he greedily buys it up, and he has his house completely furnished with these objects; so that, as you enter, there is everywhere something to catch the eye, and he renews his own pleasure as often as he becomes a witness to the delight of others." With one of his favourite dogs, Sir Thomas would frequently sit in fine weather on the top of the gate-house, in order to enjoy the agreeable prospect. A curious story is told in the "Percy Anecdotes," which will bear repeating:—"It happened one day that a 'Tom o' Bedlam,' a maniac vagrant, got upstairs while Sir Thomas was there, and coming up to him, cried out, 'Leap, Tom, leap!' at the same time, attempting to throw his lordship over the battlements. Sir Thomas, who was a feeble old man, and incapable of much resistance, had the presence of mind to say, 'Let us first throw this little dog over.' The maniac threw the dog down immediately. 'Pretty sport,' said the Lord Chancellor; 'now go down and bring him up; then we'll try again.' While the poor madman went down for the dog, his lordship made fast the door of the stairs, and, calling for help, saved his life."

Sir Thomas More is to be remembered also with gratitude on quite another score, and on higher grounds; for he was the generous patron of Holbein, the Court painter, who occupied rooms in his house for three years, and was employed in drawing portraits of his patron and his family.

Hoddesdon, in his "History of More," says:—"He seldom used to feast noble men, but his poor neighbours often, whom he would visit in their houses, and bestow upon them his large liberality—not groats, but crowns of gold—even more than according to their wants. He hired a house also for many aged people in Chelsea, whom he daily relieved, and it was his daughter Margaret's charge to see them want nothing; and when he was a private lawyer he would take no fees of poor folks, widows, nor pupils."

By indefatigable application Sir Thomas More cleared the Court of Chancery of all its causes. One day, having ended a cause, he called for the next, and was told that "there was no other depending in the court." He was delighted to hear it, and ordered it to be inserted in the records of the court. This gave rise to the epigram—not the worst in the English language—which we have already quoted in our account of Lincoln's Inn.* After having held the Great Seal for two years and a half, Sir Thomas, on being pressed by the king to hasten on his divorce from Catherine of Arragon, resigned his office in May, 1532. He retired cheerfully to the privacy of domestic life, and to the studies which he was not long to enjoy. On the day after he resigned the chancellorship, Sir Thomas went to church, as usual, with his wife and family, none of whom he had yet informed of his resignation. During the service, as was his custom, he sat in the choir in a surplice. After the service it was usual for one of his attendants to go to her ladyship's pew and say, "My lord is gone before." But this day the ex-Chancellor came himself, and, making a low bow said, "Madam, my lord is gone." Then, on their way home, we are told, "to her great mortification, he unriddled his mournful pleasantry, by telling her his lordship was gone, in the loss of his official dignities." He was included in the bill of attainder introduced into Parliament to punish Elizabeth Barton—"the holy maid of Kent"—and her accomplices; but on his disclaiming any surviving faith in the nun, or any share in her treasonable designs, his name was ultimately struck out of the bill. On the passing of the Act of Succession, which declared the king's marriage with Catherine invalid, and fixed the succession in the children of Anne Boleyn, More declined to accept it, and refused to take the oath. A few days afterwards he was committed to the Tower, and in the space of a few short months, as is known to every reader of English history, was placed on his trial for high treason, found guilty, and executed on Tower Hill. More retained his mild and characteristic jocularity to the last. "Going up the scaffold, which was so weak that it was ready to fall," we read in Roper's "Life of More," "he said hurriedly to the lieutenant, 'I pray you, Master Lieutenant, see me safe up; and for my coming down, let me shift for myself.' When the axe of the executioner was about to fall, he asked for a moment's delay while he moved aside his beard. 'Pity that should be cut,' he murmured; '*that* surely has not committed treason.'"

"Thou art the cause of this man's death," said Henry VIII. to Anne Boleyn when the news of his execution was brought to the guilty couple; and

* See Vol. III., p. 50.

the king rose, left his paramour, and shut himself up in his chamber "in great perturbation of spirit." At that perturbation we need not wonder—the greatest man of the realm had been beheaded as a victim to the royal lust. It may be truly said that during the reign of Henry VIII. there lived and moved, in a prominent position, but one man whose memory is held in high esteem by all parties, and that man was Sir Thomas More. Protestants as well as Roman Catholics alike venerated his name, while they held his life up as a model for all time, and even the more extreme Protestants had less to say in his disfavour than about any other leading son of the Church. Risen through his own exertions from comparative obscurity, Sir Thomas More held the highest lay position in the land, bore off the palm in learning as in probity, was faithful to his God as well as to his king and to his own lofty principles, and died because he would not and could not make his conscience truckle to the lewd desires of his earthly master. A grand lawyer, a great statesman, a profound politician, an example of domesticity for all generations, a deep student of the things of the spiritual as well as of the temporal life, and a Catholic of Catholics—Sir Thomas More earned and commanded, and will continue to command, the profoundest respect of all high-minded Englishmen. Sir Thomas More, indeed, was justly called by Thomson, in his "Seasons"—

"A dauntless soul erect, who smiled on death."

Sir Thomas More's house appears to have become afterwards the residence of royalty. Anne of Cleves died here in 1557; and Katharine Parr occupied it after her re-marriage with Admiral Seymour, having charge of the Princess Elizabeth, then a child of thirteen.

The old parish church of Chelsea, dedicated to St. Luke, stands parallel with the river. It is constructed chiefly of brick, and is by no means conspicuous for beauty. It appears to have been erected piecemeal at different periods, and the builders do not seem to have aimed in the slightest degree at architectural arrangement; nevertheless, though the building is sadly incongruous and much barbarised, its interior is still picturesque. The chancel and a part of the north aisle are the only portions which can lay claim to antiquity; the former was rebuilt shortly before the Reformation. The eastern end of the north aisle is the chapel of the Lawrence family, which was probably founded in the fourteenth century. The southern aisle was erected at the cost of good Sir Thomas More, who also gave the communion plate. With a forecast of the coming troubles, he remarked, "Good men give these things, and bad men will soon take them away." At the commencement of the present century modern windows, with frames of woodwork, were introduced. These, it need hardly be said, in no way improved the already mean appearance of the fabric. More's chapel, which was an absolute freehold, and beyond the control of the bishop, was allowed to fall into a very dilapidated condition; but it has recently been purchased by a Mr. R. H. Davies, who has transferred it to the rector, churchwardens, and trustees of the new church of St. Luke, under whose charge the old parish church is placed; and it has since been partially restored. The church was considerably enlarged in the middle of the seventeenth century, at which time the heavy brick tower at the west end was erected. The interior consists of a nave, chancel, and two aisles, comprehending the two chapels above mentioned. The roof of the chancel is arched, and it is separated from the nave by a semi-circular arch, above which hang several escutcheons and banners; the latter, very faded and tattered, are said to have been the needlework of Queen Charlotte, by whom they were presented to the Royal Volunteers. They were deposited here on the disbandment of the regiment. Near the south-west corner of the church, resting upon a window-sill, is an ancient book-case and desk, on which are displayed a chained Bible, a Book of Homilies, and some other works, including "Foxe's Book of Martyrs." In the porch, placed upon brackets on the wall, is a bell, which was presented to the church by the Hon. William Ashburnham, in 1679, in commemoration of his escape from drowning. It appears, from a tablet on the wall, that Mr. Ashburnham was walking on the bank of the Thames at Chelsea one very dark night in winter, apparently in a meditative mood, and had strayed into the river, when he was suddenly brought to a sense of his situation by hearing the church clock strike nine. Mr. Ashburnham left a sum of money to the parish to pay for the ringing of the bell every evening at nine o'clock, but the custom was discontinued in 1825. The bell, after lying neglected for many years in the clock-room, was placed in its present position after a silence of thirty years.

The monuments in the church are both numerous and interesting. On the north side of the chancel is an ancient altar-tomb without any inscription, but supposed to belong to the family of Bray, of Eaton. On the south wall of the chancel is a tablet of black marble, surmounted by a flat Gothic arch, in memory of Sir Thomas More. It was originally erected by himself, in 1532, some three years before his death; but being much worn, it was restored, at the expense of Sir John Lawrence, of Chelsea, in the reign of Charles I., and again by subscription, in 1833.

The Latin inscription was written by More himself; but an allusion to "heretics," which it contained, is stated to have been purposely omitted when the monument was restored. A blank space is left for the word. Although More's first wife lies buried here, the place of interment of Sir Thomas himself is somewhat doubtful. Weever and Anthony Wood say that his daughter, Margaret Roper, removed his body to Chelsea. Earlier writers, however, differ as to the precise spot of his burial, some saying that he was interred in the belfry, and others near the vestry of the chapel of St. Peter, in the Tower. It is recorded that his daughter took thither the body of Bishop Fisher, that it might lie near her father's, and, therefore, it is probable that the Tower still contains his ashes. The head of Sir Thomas More is deposited in St. Dunstan's Church at Canterbury, where it is preserved in a niche in the wall, secured by an iron grate, near the coffin of Margaret Roper.

In the south aisle is a fine monument to Lord and Lady Dacre, dated 1594. It was this Lady Dacre who erected the almshouses in Westminster which bore her name.* She was sister to Thomas Sackville, Earl of Dorset, the poet. In the north aisle is the monument of Lady Jane Cheyne, daughter of William Cavendish, Duke of Newcastle, and wife of Charles Cheyne, after whom Cheyne Row is named. The monument is the work of Bernini, and is said to have cost £500. Here is buried Adam Littleton, Prebendary of Westminster and Rector of Chelsea, the author of a once celebrated Latin Dictionary. He was at one time "usher" of Westminster School; and after the Restoration he took pupils at Chelsea. He wrote the preface to Cicero's Works, as edited by Gale, and was a perfect master of the Latin style. Collier says of him that his erudition gained for him the title of "the Great Dictator of Learning." In the churchyard is a monument to Sir Hans Sloane, the physician. It consists of an inscribed pedestal, upon which is placed a large vase of white marble, entwined with serpents, and the whole is surmounted by a portico supported by four pillars.

In the old burial-ground lie Andrew Millar, the eminent London bookseller, and John B. Cipriani, one of the earliest members of the Royal Academy.†

The new church of St. Luke, situated between King's Road and Fulham Road, was built by James Savage, in 1820, in imitation of the style of the fourteenth and fifteenth centuries, and has a pinnacled tower, nearly 150 feet high. It is, however, a poor specimen of modern Gothic. The most remarkable feature of the building is the roof of the nave, which is vaulted with stone, with a clear height of sixty feet from the pavement to the crown of the vault. The porch extends the whole width of the west front, and is divided by piers and arches into five bays, the central one of which forms the lower storey of the tower. The large east window is filled with stained glass, and beneath it is a fine altar-screen of antique design. Immediately over the altar is a painting, "The Entombing of Christ," said to be by Northcote. The church will seat about 2,000 persons, and was erected at a cost of about £40,000—the first stone being laid by the Duke of Wellington. The first two rectors of the new church were Dr. Gerard V. Wellesley (whose name is still retained in Wellesley Street), brother of the Duke of Wellington, and the Rev. Charles Kingsley, father of Charles Kingsley, Canon of Westminster, and author of "Alton Locke," &c.

CHAPTER VI.

CHELSEA (*continued*).

"Then, farewell, my trim-built wherry;
 Oars, and coat, and badge, farewell!
Never more at Chelsea Ferry
 Shall your Thomas take a spell."—*Dibdin*.

Cheyne Walk—An Eccentric Miser—Dominicetti, an Italian Quack—Don Saltero's Coffee House and Museum—Catalogue of Rarities in the Museum—Thomas Carlyle—Chelsea Embankment—Albert Bridge—The Mulberry Garden—The "Swan" Inn—The Rowing Matches for Doggett's Coat and Badge—The Botanic Gardens—The Old Bun-house.

VISITORS to Chelsea by water, landing at the Cadogan Pier, will not fail to be struck by the antique appearance of the long terrace of houses stretching away eastward, overlooking the river, and screened by a row of trees. This is Cheyne Walk, so named after Lord Cheyne, who owned the

* See Vol. IV., p 12.

† See Faulkner's "History of Chelsea," vol. ii., p 38.

manor of Chelsea near the close of the seventeenth century. The houses are mostly of dark-red brick, with heavy window-frames, and they have about them altogether an old-fashioned look, such as we are accustomed to find in buildings of the time of Queen Anne. The place, from its air of repose and seclusion, has always reckoned among its inhabitants a large number of successful artists and literary celebrities.

Here, in a large house very scantily furnished, lived during the latter portion of his existence—we can scarcely call it life—Mr. John Camden Neild, the eccentric miser, who, at his decease in August, 1852, left his scrapings and savings, amounting to half a million sterling, to the Queen, "begging Her Majesty's most gracious acceptance of the same for her sole use and benefit, and that of her heirs." He was buried at North Marston, near Aylesbury, where he held a landed property, and where the Queen ordered a painted window to be put up to his memory. A sketch of the career of this modern rival of John Elwes will be found in Chambers' "Book of Days." Here, too, lived Dominicetti, an Italian quack, who made a great noise in his day by the introduction of medicated baths, which he established in Cheyne Walk, in 1765. It is thus immortalised in Boswell's "Life of Johnson:"—"There was a pretty large circle this evening. Dr. Johnson was in very good humour, lively, and ready to talk upon all subjects. Dominicetti being mentioned, he would not allow him any merit. 'There is nothing

CHEYNE WALK AND CADOGAN PIER, 1860.

in all this boasted system. No, sir; medicated baths can be no better than warm water; their only effect can be that of tepid moisture.' One of the company took the other side, maintaining that medicines of various sorts, and some, too, of most powerful effect, are introduced into the human fumigated; but be sure that the steam be directed to thy head, for *that* is the *peccant part.*' This produced a triumphant roar of laughter from the motley assembly of philosophers, printers, and dependents, male and female." Dominicetti is said to have had under his care upwards of 16,000 persons,

CARLYLE'S HOUSE, GREAT CHEYNE ROW. (*See page* 64.)

frame by the medium of the pores; and therefore, when warm water is impregnated with salutiferous substances, it may produce great effects as a bath. The Doctor, determined to be master of the field, had recourse to the device which Goldsmith imputed to him in the witty words of one of Cibber's comedies, 'There is no arguing with Johnson; for when his pistol misses fire, he knocks you down with the butt-end of it.' He turned to the gentleman: 'Well, sir, go to Dominicetti, and get thyself including Edward, Duke of York. He spent some £37,000 on his establishment, but became bankrupt in 1782, when he disappeared.

In the middle of Cheyne Walk is, or was till recently (for it was doomed to destruction in 1866), the house known to readers of anecdote biography as "Don Saltero's Coffee House," celebrated not only as a place of entertainment, but also as a repository of natural and other curiosities. John Salter, its founder, was an old and trusty servant of

Sir Hans Sloane, who, from time to time, gave him all sorts of curiosities. With these he adorned the house, which he opened as a suburban coffee-house, about the year 1690. The earliest notice of Salter's Museum is to be found in the thirty-fourth number of the *Tatler*, published in June, 1709, in which its owner figures as "Don Saltero," and several of its curious contents are specified by the writer, Sir Richard Steele. Beside the donations of Sir Hans Sloane, at the head of the "Complete List of Benefactors to Don Saltero's Coffee-room of Curiosities," printed in 1739, figure the names of Sir John Cope, Baronet, and his son, "the first generous benefactors." There is an account of the exhibition in the *Gentleman's Magazine* for 1799, where it is stated that Rear-Admiral Sir John Munden, and other officers who had been much upon the coasts of Spain, enriched it with many curiosities, and gave its owner the name of "Don Saltero;" but the list of donors does not include the admiral, though the name of "Mr. Munden" occurs in the list subjoined to the nineteenth edition of the catalogue. The title by which Salter was so well known in his own day may be accounted for even at this distance of time by the notice of him and his collection, as immortalised in the pages of Sir Richard Steele. "When I came into the coffee-house," he says, "I had not time to salute the company before my eye was diverted by ten thousand gimcracks, round the room and on the ceiling." The Don was famous for his punch, and his skill on the fiddle. "Indeed," says Steele, "I think he does play the 'Merry Christ-Church Bells' pretty justly; but he confessed to me he did it rather to show he was orthodox than that he valued himself upon the music itself." This description is probably faithful, as well as humorous, since he continues, "When my first astonishment was over, there comes to me a sage, of a thin and meagre countenance, which aspect made me doubtful whether reading or fretting had made it so philosophic."

In the *Weekly Journal* of Saturday, June 22nd, 1723, we read the following poetical announcement of the treasures to be seen at this coffee-house, which may be regarded as authentic and literally true, since it is sanctioned by the signature of the proprietor himself:—

"Sir,

Fifty years since to Chelsea great,
From Rodman, on the Irish main,
I strolled, with maggots in my pate,
Where, much improved, they still remain.

"Through various employs I've passed—
A scraper, virtuoso, projector,
Tooth-drawer, trimmer, and at last,
I'm now a gimcrack whim collector.

"Monsters of all sorts here are seen,
Strange things in nature as they grow so,
Some relicks of the Sheba queen,
And fragments of the famed Bob Crusoe.

"Knicknacks, too, dangle round the wall,
Some in glass cases, some on shelf;
But what's the rarest sight of all,
Your humble servant shows himself.

"On this my chiefest hope depends—
Now if you will my cause espouse,
In journals pray direct your friends
To my Museum Coffee-house;

"And, in requital for the timely favour,
I'll gratis bleed, draw teeth, and be your shaver:
Nay, that your pate may with my noddle tally,
And you shine bright as I do—marry! shall ye
Freely consult your revelation, Molly;
Nor shall one jealous thought create a huff,
For she has taught me manners long enough."

"Chelsea Knackatory." "Don Saltero.

The date of Salter's death does not appear to be known precisely, but the museum was continued by his daughter, a Mrs. Hall, until about the accession of George III. We know little of the subsequent history of the house until January, 1799, when the whole place, with the museum of curiosities, was sold by auction by Mr. Harwood. They are described in the catalogue as follows:—"A substantial and well-erected dwelling-house and premises, delightfully situate, facing the river Thames, commanding beautiful views of the Surrey hills and the adjacent country, in excellent repair, held for a term of thirty-nine years from Christmas last, at a ground-rent of £3 10s. per annum. Also the valuable collection of curiosities, comprising a curious model of our Saviour's sepulchre, a Roman bishop's crosier, antique coins and medals, minerals, fossils, antique fire-arms, curious birds, fishes, and other productions of nature, and a large collection of various antiquities and curiosities, glass-cases, &c. N.B. The curiosities will be sold the last day. May be viewed six days preceding the sale. Catalogues at sixpence each." The number of lots was a hundred and twenty-one; and the entire produce of the sale appears to have been little more than £50. The highest price given for a single lot was £1 16s.—lot 98, consisting of "a very curious model of our Blessed Saviour's sepulchre at Jerusalem, very neatly inlaid with mother of pearl."

"It is not improbable," writes Mr. Smith in his "Historical and Literary Curiosities," "that this very celebrated collection was not preserved either entire or genuine until the time of its dispersion;

since the gift of John Pennant, of Chelsea, the great-uncle of Thomas Pennant, the topographical writer, appears to have been wanting in the forty-seventh edition of the catalogue of the museum. This donation consisted of a part of a root of a tree, shaped like a swine, and sometimes called 'a lignified hog;' but the several editions of the catalogue differ considerably in the insertion or omission of various articles. The exhibition was contained chiefly in glass cases ranged on the tables, placed in the front room of the first floor of the building; but the walls also were covered with curiosities, and the entrance passage displayed an alligator suspended from the ceiling, with a variety of ancient and foreign weapons hung at the sides."

Perhaps, however, the most novel and interesting particulars which can now be given concerning this museum may be gleaned from the "Exhibition Catalogue" itself, which shows that it consisted rather of strange and wonderful, than of really valuable specimens. The title is "A Catalogue of Rarities, to be seen at Don Salter's Coffee house in Chelsea; to which is added a complete list of the donors thereof. Price 2d.

"'O Rare!'"

In the *first glass* were contained the model of the holy sepulchre, and a variety of curiosities of a similar character: such as "painted ribbands from Jerusalem, with a pillar to which our Saviour was tied when scourged, with a motto on each;" "boxes of relicks from Jerusalem;" "a piece of a saint's bone in nun's work;" several pieces of the holy cross in a frame, glazed; a rose of Jericho; dice of the Knights Templars; an Israelitish shekel; and the Lord's Prayer in an ivory frame, glazed. There were also several specimens of carving on cherry-stones, representing the heads of the four Evangelists and effigies of saints; with some cups and baskets made out of the same minute materials. The same case also contained a number of fine coins and medals, both British and foreign, and "a model of Governor Pitt's great diamond," which was taken out of the sale. There were also a few natural curiosities, as "a bone of an angel-fish; a sea-horse; a petrified crab from China; a small pair of horns, and several legs of guinea-deer; a handkerchief made of the asbestus rock, which fire cannot consume; a piece of rotten wood not to be consumed by fire; the rattle of a rattlesnake with twenty-seven joints; a large worm that eats into the keels of ships in the West Indies; serpents' tongues; the bark of a tree, which when drawn out appears like fine lace; a salamander; a fairy's or elf's arrow; a little skull, very curious." The most remarkable artificial rarities contained in the *second glass* were "a piece of Solomon's temple; Queen Katherine's wedding shoes; King Charles the Second's band which he wore in disguise; and a piece of a coat of mail one hundred and fifty times doubled." Of foreign productions this case contained "a Turkish almanack; a book in Chinese characters; letters in the Malabar language; the effigies and hand of an Egyptian mummy; forty-eight cups, one in another; and an Indian hatchet used by them before iron was invented." The natural curiosities included "a little whale; a giant's tooth; a curious ball of fish-bones found near Plymouth; Job's tears that grow on a tree, wherewith they make anodyne necklaces; a nut of the sand-box tree; several petrified plumes and olives; a young frog in a tobacco-stopper; and a piece of the caul of an elephant." The *third glass* comprised "black and white scorpions; animals in embryo; the worm that eats into the piles in Holland; the tarantula; a nest of snakes; the horns of a shamway; the back-bone of a rattlesnake."

The *fourth glass* consisted of artificial curiosities, and included "a nun's whip; a pair of garters from South Carolina; a Chinese dodgin, which they weigh their gold in; a little Sultaness; an Indian spoon of equal weight with gold; a Chinese nun, very curious; Dr. Durham's paper made of nettles." The *fifth glass* contained "a Muscovy snuff-box, made of an elk's hoof; a humming-bird's nest, with two young ones in it; a starved swallow; the head of an Egyptian; a lock of hair of a Goa goat; belts of wampum; Indian money; the fruit of the horn-tree."

The following curiosities were also disposed in various parts of the coffee-room, with many others less remarkable in their names and appearance—"King James's coronation sword; King William's coronation sword and shoes; Henry VIII.'s coat of mail, gloves, and spurs; Queen Elizabeth's Prayer-book, stirrup, and strawberry dish; the Pope's infallible candle; a set of beads, consecrated by Clement VII., made of the bones of St. Anthony of Padua; a piece of the royal oak; a petrified child, or the figure of death; a curious piece of metal, found in the ruins of Troy; a pair of Saxon stockings; William the Conqueror's family sword; Oliver's broad-sword; the King of Whiddaw's staff; Bistreanier's staff; a wooden shoe, put under the Speaker's chair in James II.'s time; the Emperor of Morocco's tobacco pipe; a curious flea-trap; an Indian prince's crown; a starved cat, found between the walls of Westminster Abbey when the east end was repaired; the jaws of a wild boar that was starved to death by his tusks growing inward;

a frog, fifteen inches long, found in the Isle of Dogs; the Staffordshire almanack, used when the Danes were in England; the lance of Captain Tow-How-Sham, king of the Darien Indians, with which he killed six Spaniards, and took a tooth out of each head, and put in his lance as a trophy of his valour; a coffin of state for a friar's bones; a cockatrice serpent; a large snake, seventeen feet long, taken in a pigeon-house in Sumatra—it had in its belly fifteen fowls and five pigeons; a dolphin with a flying-fish at his mouth; a gargulet, that Indians used to cool their water with; a whistling arrow, which the Indians use when they would treat of peace; a negro boy's cap, made of a rat-skin; Mary Queen of Scots' pin-cushion; a purse made of a spider from Antigua; manna from Canaan; a jaw of a skate, with 500 teeth; the mermaid fish; the wild man of the woods; the flying bull's head; and, last of all, a snake's skin, ten feet and a half long—a most excellent hydrometer." It may be added that, according to Pennant, the ex-Protector, Richard Cromwell, was one of the regular visitors at Don Saltero's coffee-house in its earliest days. The place was one of the exhibitions which Benjamin Franklin went to see when working as a journeyman printer in London.

In Cheyne Walk is the Cheyne Hospital for Sick and Incurable Children. Lindsey House, built about 1660, and named after the Berties, Earls of Lindsey, was afterwards used as a conference hall by the Moravian missionaries, and subsequently cut up into tenements.

At No. 5, Great Cheyne Row, an old-fashioned red-brick house, lived for many years Thomas Carlyle, who so far identified himself with this neighbourhood as to be known to the world in common parlance as "The Philosopher of Chelsea." The house and the habits of its tenant are thus described by a writer who signs himself "Quiz," in the *West Middlesex Advertiser*:—

"The house tenanted by Carlyle has on its front an appearance of antiquity, which would lead us to ascribe it to the days of Queen Anne. In one of his later pamphlets, 'Shooting Niagara,' associated with a hit at modern brick-makers and brick-layers, Carlyle has an allusion to the wall at the end ('head,' as he writes) of his garden, made of bricks burnt in the reign of Henry VIII., and still quite sound, whereas bricks of London manufacture in our day are used up in about sixty years. This wall was, of course, the boundary wall of the old park or garden belonging to Chelsea Manor-house. But this remark only comes incidentally, and we know scarcely anything about Carlyle's house and its belongings from himself. Other people have reported a variety of particulars, not to be credited without large deductions, concerning his home and personal habits. Thus, an American divine, giving an account of an interview he had with the Chelsea sage, indulges in minutiæ such as the following:—'We were shown into a plainly-furnished room, on whose walls hung a rugged portrait of Oliver Cromwell. Presently an old man, apparently over threescore years and ten, walked very slowly into the room. He was attired in a long blue woollen gown, reaching down to his feet. His grey hair was in an uncombed mop on his head. His clear blue eye was sharp and piercing. A bright tinge of red was on his thin cheek, and his hand trembled as he took our own. This most singular-looking personage reminded us of an old alchemist, &c.' Much in the Yankee mannerism, certainly, yet it comes as a slight retribution, that one who has been so hard on America should be commented on in true Yankee fashion. Others have given us accounts of rooms in the house heaped up with books, not at all marshalled in the regular order we should have expected, when they belonged to a man so fond of the drill-sergeant. One correspondent of a London paper tells us of a collection of portraits of great men, gathered by degrees from picture-galleries, shops, and book-stalls. As it is rumoured, the contrivances resorted to by some of Carlyle's admirers, at the period of life when most of us are inclined to be enthusiastic in our likings, with the intent of seeing the interior of his house, or coming into personal communication with him, have been both ingenious and ludicrous. Some have, it is said, called at his house, and inquired for an imaginary Jones or Smith, in the hope that they might catch a glimpse at the interior, or see the man himself in the background. Possibly, there have been those who have made friends with the 'dustmen,' so that they may glean up some scraps of MSS. from the miscellaneous contents of his waste-basket. I have not heard, though, whether any one ever went so far as to assume the garb of a policeman, to ensnare the affections of some damsel at 5, Great Cheyne Row, and in this way make discoveries about the philosopher's personal habits.

"Mr. J. C. Hotten, in some notes on Carlyle, states that 'he always walks at night, carrying an enormous stick, and generally with his eyes on the ground.' This is an exaggeration of the stick, and so far from being only out at night, those accustomed to be in the streets of Chelsea know that Carlyle has, for years past, taken a stroll in all weathers in the morning, and in the afternoon he is frequently to be seen wending his way towards

St. James's Park. Hence certain persons have waylaid him in these walks from curiosity, the Chelsea sage himself being supremely unconscious of being watched. He has been seen to conduct a blind man over a crossing, the person being necessarily ignorant as to who was showing him a kindness, and a little knot of human beings will touch his sympathies, and cause him to pause. I saw Carlyle once step up to a shop-window, around which several individuals stood looking at something. This something was a new portrait of himself, as he quickly perceived; but before they were awake to the fact that the original was close by, he had moved off, giving his stick a rather contemptuous twirl."

The connection of Thomas Carlyle with Chelsea is, at all events, of upwards of forty years' duration, as he was a resident there in the early part of 1834; two years previously, when in London, he visited Leigh Hunt, who at that time lived close to Cheyne Row; and, probably, it was at that time that he resolved to make it his fixed abode. The two writers were neighbours here until 1840, when Leigh Hunt removed to Kensington, which he has immortalised under the title of the "Old Court Suburb;" and their friendship continued until Hunt's death.

At Chelsea, it is almost needless to add, Carlyle wrote his history of "The French Revolution," "Past and Present," his "Life of John Stirling," "Oliver Cromwell's Letters and Speeches," and his "Life of Frederick the Great;" in fact, nearly all the works which have made his name famous through the world.

His wife died at Chelsea suddenly in April, 1866, just as she heard of the delivery of his inaugural address as Lord Rector of Edinburgh University. She left a work unfinished. Charles Dickens admired her literary talents very much. He writes to his friend Forster: "It was a terrible shock to me, and poor dear Carlyle has been in my mind ever since. How often have I thought of the unfinished novel! No one now to finish it. None of the writing women come near her at all." Mr. Forster adds: "No one could doubt this who had come within the fascinating influence of that sweet and noble nature. With some of the highest gifts of intellect, and the charm of a most varied knowledge of books and things, there was something beyond. No one who knew Mrs. Carlyle could replace her loss when she had passed away."

On the 4th of December, 1875, Thomas Carlyle completed his eightieth year (having been born in 1795, in the once obscure village of Ecclefechan, in Scotland), on which occasion he received congratulations from a number of the chief *littérateurs* of Germany, and also a present of a gold medal, struck in honour of the day, from a number of English friends and admirers. He died here on the 5th of February, 1881, and was buried at Ecclefechan.

Sir John Goss, who was many years organist at St. Paul's Cathedral, was for some time a resident in Cheyne Row.

The embankment facing Cheyne Walk, extending from Battersea Bridge, close by old Chelsea Church, to the grounds of Chelsea Hospital, a distance of nearly a mile, presents a pleasing contrast to the red-bricked houses of which we have been speaking. Although the proposition to embank the northern shore of the Thames between Chelsea Hospital and Battersea Bridge was first made by the Commissioners of Her Majesty's Woods and Forests in 1839, the practical execution of the idea was not commenced even on a small scale until some twenty years afterwards. These works originally formed a portion of a scheme for which the Commissioners of Woods and Forests obtained an Act of Parliament in 1846, and which embodied the formation of an embankment and roadway between Vauxhall and Battersea bridges, and the construction of a suspension bridge at Chelsea. The funds which it was estimated would be required were procured, but they proved insufficient for the whole of the work, the bridge costing more than was anticipated. A narrow embankment and roadway were therefore constructed as far as the western end of the Chelsea Hospital gardens, where they terminated in a *cul de sac*. In time, however, the necessity arose for making a sewer to intercept the sewage of the district west of Cremorne, and to help it on its way to Barking. But there was no good thoroughfare from Cremorne eastwards along which to construct it; so it was proposed to form a route for the sewer, and at the same time to complete an unfinished work by continuing the embankment and road on to Battersea. Application was made to Government for the return of £38,150, a sum which remained unexpended from the amount originally raised for the bridge and embankment, and which would have assisted in the prosecution of the new work. The application, however, was unsuccessful, and Sir William Tite, who from the first took a very active interest in the matter, appealed to the Metropolitan Board of Works to undertake the work independently of Government assistance. The Board, therefore, made several applications to Parliament for an Act, which they succeeded in obtaining in 1868. The designs for the embankment, roadway, and sewer were at once prepared by Mr. (afterwards Sir James) Bazalgette, the engineer to the Board, and the whole work was completed and opened to the public in 1874.

At its commencement by Battersea Bridge very little land has been reclaimed from the Thames; but a great change has been effected in the appearance of the spot by doing away with the old awkward approach to the steamboat pier under the archway of a private house, the pontoon being now moored close to the wall. A picturesque block of houses, too, which stood between this spot and Chelsea Church has been entirely removed. They formed a narrow quaint-looking old thoroughfare, called Lombard Street, one part of which was spanned by the upper rooms of an old house. The backs of one side of this thoroughfare overlooked, and here and there overhung, the river; but they have all been cleared away, and the narrow street converted into a broad one, so that one side of it faces the river. After passing the church the road widens out, and as the space between the houses and the embankment wall becomes greater, a piece of land has been laid out as a garden, so that there are two roads, one in front of the shops, the other between the garden and the granite wall. This garden extends nearly to Oakley Street, which the road rises gradually to meet, while the path falls slightly in order to pass under the shore end of the new Albert Bridge. There is another pretty little piece of garden at this part of the route. After this the reclaimed land becomes of yet greater extent as Cheyne Row is reached. From this spot the Embankment and its surroundings can be seen to the best advantage. The rough hammer-dressed granite wall runs in a straight line from here to where it meets the old roadway formed by the Office of Woods and Forests. In the ground beneath the pavement have been planted trees on both sides of the road, similar to those planted on the Victoria Embankment. But nothing adds so much to the picturesqueness of this part of the Thames-side roadway, and helps to relieve the appearance of newness which is so marked a feature in the Victoria Embankment, as the line of old trees planted on what was formerly the edge of the river, with the background formed by a fine old row of private houses. The trees are now in the garden divided by a gravel walk, which fills up the space between the two roadways. At the end of Cheyne Walk the

THE BOTANICAL GARDENS, CHELSEA, 1790. (*See page* 68.

Queen's Road branches off to the left, and runs into the bottom of Lower Sloane Street. At the junction of two roads, but where was formerly the diverging point of one from the river-side, stood the "Swan" tavern, famous as the goal of many a hotly-contested aquatic race from its namesake near London Bridge. Not far from this time-honoured inn are the Botanical Gardens of the Society of Apothecaries.

The Albert Bridge, opposite Oakley Street, constructed upon the suspension principle, was opened in 1873; it forms a useful communication between Chelsea and Battersea Park. Cadogan Pier, close to the bridge, serves as a landing-place for passengers on the river steamboats.

Near the river and Cheyne Walk was a large mulberry-garden, one of those established in the suburbs of London by order of James I., about the year 1610. Thoresby, writing in 1723, tells us in his diary that he saw "at Mr. Gate's a sample of the satin made at Chelsea of English silkworms for the Princess of Wales, very rich and beautiful." But it has long disappeared, owing to the steady progress of bricks and mortar.

As late as 1824, there was to be seen near Chelsea Bridge a sign of "The Cricketers," painted by George Morland. "At the above date," says Mr. Larwood, "this painting by Morland had been removed inside the house, and a copy of it hung up for the sign. Unfortunately, however, the landlord used to travel about with the original, and put it up before his booth at Staines and Egham races, cricket matches, and similar occasions"—all of which removals, it may be presumed, did no great good to it.

The "Old Swan" inn, which was the goal of Doggett's annual rowing match, stood on the east side of the Botanical Gardens, and was long since

THOMAS CARLYLE. (*See page* 64.)

turned into a brewery, and the race, down to about the year 1873, ended at the new "Swan," higher up the river, as mentioned above.

The "Swan," very naturally, was a favourite sign for inns by the waterside, and Mr. J. T. Smith, in his "Book for a Rainy Day," or rather a waterman who speaks in his pages, enumerates a goodly list of "Swans" between London and Battersea bridges in 1829:—"Why, let me see, master," he writes, "there's the 'Old Swan' at London Bridge—that's one; then there's the 'Swan' in Arundel Street—that's two; then our's here" (at Hungerford Stairs), "three; the 'Swan' at Lambeth—that's down though. Well, then there's the 'Old Swan' at Chelsea, but that has been long turned into a brewhouse; though that was where our people" (the watermen) "rowed to formerly, as mentioned in Doggett's will; now they row to the sign of the 'New Swan' beyond the Physic Garden—we'll say that's four. Then there's two 'Swans' at Battersea—six."

We have already spoken at some length of Tom Doggett, the famous comedian,* and of the annual rowing match by Thames watermen for the honour of carrying off the "coat and badge," which, in pursuance of his will, have been competed for on the 1st of August for the last 150 years; suffice it to say, then, that in the year 1873 the old familiar "Swan" inn was demolished to make room for the new embankment. The old "Swan" tavern enjoyed a fair share of public favour for many years. Pepys, in his "Diary," thus mentions it, under date April 9, 1666:—"By coach to Mrs. Pierce's, and with her and Knipp, and Mrs. Pierce's boy and girl abroad, thinking to have been merry at Chelsea; but being come almost to the house by coach, near the waterside, a house alone, I think the 'Swan,' a gentleman walking by called to us to tell us that the house was shut up because of the sickness. So we, with great affright, turned back, being holden to the gentleman, and went away (I, for my part, in great disorder) to Kensington." In 1780 the house was converted into the Swan Brewery; and the landing of the victor in the aquatic contest thenceforth took place, as above stated, at a house bearing the same sign nearer to Cheyne Walk. Since the demolition of this house the race has been ended close to the spot where the old tavern stood. This rowing match—although not to be compared in any way to the great annual aquatic contest between the Universities of Oxford and Cambridge—occasions a very lively scene, the river being covered with boats, and the utmost anxiety evinced by the friends of the contending parties. In former times it was customary for the winner on his arrival to be saluted with shouts of applause by the surrounding spectators, and carried in triumph on the shoulders of his friends into the tavern.

On a vacant space of ground in front of the Swan Brewery stood formerly a mansion, erected in the reign of Queen Anne, which was for many years inhabited by Mrs. Banks, the mother of Sir Joseph Banks.

"The Physic Garden," to which we now come, was originated by Sir Hans Sloane, the celebrated physician, and was handed over in 1721 by him, by deed of gift, to the Apothecaries' Company, who still own and maintain it. The garden, which bears the name of the "Royal Botanic," was presented to the above company on condition that it "should at all times be continued as a physic-garden, for the manifestation of the power, and wisdom, and goodness of God in creation; and that the apprentices might learn to distinguish good and useful plants from hurtful ones." Various additions have been made to the "Physic Garden" at different periods, in the way of greenhouses and hot-houses; and in the centre of the principal walk was erected a statue of Sir Hans Sloane, by Michael Rysbraeck.

"We visited," writes P. Wakefield in 1814, "the 'Physic or Botanic Garden,' commenced by the Company of Apothecaries in 1673, and patronised by Sir Hans Sloane, who granted the freehold of the premises to the company on condition that they should present annually to the Royal Society specimens of fifty new plants till their number should amount to two thousand. From a sense of gratitude they erected in the centre of the garden a marble statue of their benefactor. Above the spacious greenhouse is a library, furnished with a large collection of botanical works, and with numerous specimens of dried plants. We could not quit these gardens without admiring two cedars of great size and beauty."

"At the time the garden was formed," writes the author of "London Exhibited in 1851," "it must have stood entirely in the country, and had every chance of the plants in it maintaining a healthy state. Now, however, it is completely in the town, and but for its being on the side of the river, and lying open on that quarter, it would be altogether surrounded with common streets and houses. As it is, the appearance of the walls, grass, plants, and houses is very much that of most London gardens—dingy, smoky, and, as regards the plants, impoverished and starved. It is, however,

* See Vol. III., p. 308.

interesting for its age, for the few old specimens it contains, for the medical plants, and, especially, because the houses are being gradually renovated, and collections of ornamental plants, as well as those which are useful in medicine, formed and cultivated on the best principles, under the curatorship of Mr. Thomas Moore, one of the editors of the 'Gardener's Magazine of Botany.'" In spite of the disadvantages of its situation, here are still grown very many of the drugs which figure in the "London Pharmacopœia." The two cedars of Lebanon, which have now reached the age of upwards of 150 years, are said to have been presented to the garden by Sir Joseph Banks, the distinguished naturalist, who here studied the first principles of botany. Of Sir Hans Sloane, and of his numerous public benefactions, we have already spoken in our account of the British Museum.* It only remains, therefore, to add that he was a contributor of natural specimens of rocks from the Giant's Causeway to Pope's Grotto at Twickenham; that he attended Queen Anne in her last illness at Kensington; and that he was the first member of the medical profession on whom a baronetcy was conferred.

During the last century, and early in the present, a pleasant walk across green fields, intersected with hedges and ditches, led the pedestrian from Westminster and Millbank to "The Old Bun House" at Chelsea. This far-famed establishment, which possessed a sort of rival museum to Don Saltero's, stood at the end of Jew's Row (now Pimlico Road), not far from Grosvenor Row. The building was a one-storeyed structure, with a colonnade projecting over the foot pavement, and was demolished in 1839, after having enjoyed the favour of the public for more than a century and a half. Chelsea has been famed for its buns since the commencement of the last century. Swift, in his "Journal to Stella," 1712, writes, "Pray are not the fine buns sold here in our town as the rare Chelsea buns? I bought one to-day in my walk," &c. It was for many years the custom of the Royal Family, and the nobility and gentry, to visit the Bun-house in the morning. George II., Queen Caroline, and the princesses frequently honoured the proprietor, Mrs. Hand, with their company, as did also George III. and Queen Charlotte; and her Majesty presented Mrs. Hand with a silver half-gallon mug, with five guineas in it. On Good Friday mornings the Bun-house used to present a scene of great bustle—upwards of 50,000 persons have assembled here, when disturbances often arose among the London mob; and in one day more than £250 has been taken for buns.

The following curious notice was issued on Wednesday, March 27th, 1793:—"Royal Bun House, Chelsea, Good Friday.—No Cross Buns. Mrs. Hand respectfully informs her friends and the public, that in consequence of the great concourse of people which assembled before her house at a very early hour, on the morning of Good Friday last, by which her neighbours (with whom she has always lived in friendship and repute) have been much alarmed and annoyed; it having also been intimated, that to encourage or countenance a tumultuous assembly at this particular period might be attended with consequences more serious than have hitherto been apprehended; desirous, therefore, of testifying her regard and obedience to those laws by which she is happily protected, she is determined, though much to her loss, not to sell *Cross Buns* on that day to any person whatever, but Chelsea buns as usual."

The Bun-house was much frequented during the palmy days of Ranelagh, after the closing of which the bun trade declined. Notwithstanding this, on Good Friday, April 18th, 1839, upwards of 24,000 buns were sold here. Soon after, the Bun-house was sold and pulled down; and at the same time was dispersed a collection of pictures, models, grotesque figures, and modern antiques, which had for a century added the attractions of a museum to the bun celebrity. Another bun-house was built in its place, but the olden charm of the place had fled, and Chelsea buns are now only matters of history.

Sir Richard Phillips, in his "Morning's Walk from London to Kew," a few years before the demolition of the old Bun-house, after describing his ramble through Pimlico, writes: "I soon turned the corner of a street which took me out of sight of the space on which once stood the gay Ranelagh. . . . Before me appeared the shop so famed for Chelsea buns, which for above thirty years I have never passed without filling my pockets. In the original of these shops—for even of Chelsea buns there are counterfeits—are preserved mementoes of domestic events in the first half of the past century. The bottle-conjuror is exhibited in a toy of his own age; portraits are also displayed of Duke William and other noted personages; a model of a British soldier, in the stiff costume of the same age; and some grotto-works, serve to indicate the taste of a former owner, and were, perhaps, intended to rival the neighbouring exhibition at Don Saltero's. These buns have afforded a competency, and even wealth, to four generations of the same family;

* See Vol. IV., p. 494.

and it is singular that their delicate flavour, lightness, and richness, have never been successfully imitated."

In the *Mirror* for April 6, 1839, are two views of the old Bun-house, which were taken just before its demolition.

Chelsea would seem at one time to have enjoyed a reputation not only for buns, but for custards, if we may judge from the following allusion to them by Gay, in his "Trivia:"—

> "When W—— and G——, mighty names, are dead,
> Or but at Chelsea under custards read."

CHAPTER VII.

CHELSEA (*continued*).—THE HOSPITAL, &c.

> "Go with old Thames, view Chelsea's glorious pile,
> And ask the shattered hero whence his smile."
>
> *Rogers's "Pleasures of Memory."*

Foundation of the Hospital—The Story of Nell Gwynne and the Wounded Soldier—Chelsea College—Archbishop Bancroft's Legacy—Transference of the College to the Royal Society—The Property sold to Sir Stephen Fox, and afterwards given as a Site for the Hospital—Lord Ranelagh's Mansion—Dr. Monsey—The Chudleigh Family—The Royal Hospital described—Lying in State of the Duke of Wellington—Regulations for the Admission of Pensioners—A few Veritable Centenarians—The "Snow Shoes" Tavern—The Duke of York's School—Ranelagh Gardens, and its Former Glories—The Victoria Hospital for Sick Children.

On the west side of the Physic Garden, with its lawns and flower-beds stretching almost down to the river, stands a noble hospital, the counterpart of that at Greenwich, still providing an asylum for invalid soldiers—as its rival did, till recently, for sailors worn out in the service of their country.

It is well known that the foundation of this splendid institution was the work of Charles II. John Evelyn has the following entry in his "Diary," under date 27th of January, 1682:—"This evening Sir Stephen Fox acquainted me againe with his Majesty's resolution of proceeding in the erection of a royal hospital for merited soldiers, on that spot of ground which the Royal Society had sold to his Majesty for £1,300, and that he would settle £5,000 per annum on it, and build to the value of £20,000, for the reliefe and reception of four companies—viz., 400 men, to be as in a colledge or monasterie." It appears that Evelyn was largely consulted by the king and Sir Stephen Fox as to the details of the new building, the growth of whose foundations and walls he watched constantly, as he tells us in his "Diary."

It was not without a pang that the British public saw Greenwich "disestablished;" and, observes a writer in the *Times*, "the parting with the wooden-legged veterans, in their antique garb, and with their garrulous prattle—too often, it is to be feared, apocryphal—about Nelson, Duncan, Jervis, and Collingwood, was like the parting from old friends. The associations connected with Chelsea Hospital," continues the writer, "possess nearly the same historical interest with those awakened by Greenwich. Both piles—although that upon the river-bank is by far the more splendid edifice—were built by Sir Christopher Wren. Chelsea has yet a stronger claim upon our sympathies, since, according to popular tradition, the first idea of converting it into an asylum for broken-down soldiers sprang from the charitable heart of Nell Gwynne, the frail actress, with whom, for all her frailties, the English people can never be angry. As the story goes, a wounded and destitute soldier hobbled up to Nellie's coach-window to ask alms, and the kind-hearted woman was so pained to see a man who had fought for his country begging his bread in the street that she prevailed on Charles II. to establish at Chelsea a permanent home for military invalids. We should like to believe the story; and, indeed, its veracity may not be incompatible with a far less pleasant report, that the second Charles made a remarkably good thing, in a pecuniary sense, out of Chelsea Hospital."

Before entering upon an account of Chelsea Hospital, it may be desirable to notice here a collegiate building which formerly occupied the site of this great national edifice. This college was originated, soon after the commencement of the seventeenth century, by Dr. Matthew Sutcliffe, Dean of Exeter, for the study of polemical divinity. King James I. laid the first stone of the edifice, in May, 1609, and bestowed on it the name of "King James's College at Chelsey." According to the Charter of Incorporation, the number of members was limited to a provost and nineteen fellows, seventeen of whom were required to be in holy orders; the other two might be either laymen or divines, and they were to be employed in recording the chief historical events of the era. Dr. Sutcliffe was himself the first provost, and Camden and Hayward were the first historians. Archbishop Laud called the institution "Controversy College;" and, according to "Alleyn's Life," "the Papists, in derision, gave it the name of an alehouse."

It is, perhaps, worthy of a passing note that Archbishop Bancroft left the books which formed the nucleus of the library at Lambeth Palace, to his successors in the see of Canterbury, with the condition that if certain stipulations were not complied with, his legacy should go to Chelsea College, if built within six years of his own decease.

From a print of the original design, prefixed to Darley's "Glory of Chelsey College new Revived" (a copy of which is published in Faulkner's "History of Chelsea"), it would appear that the buildings were originally intended to combine two quadrangles, of different, but spacious, dimensions, with a piazza along the four sides of the smaller court. Only one side of the first quadrangle, however, was completed, and the whole collegiate establishment very soon collapsed. Evelyn tells us that the plan of Chelsea College embraced a quadrangle, with accommodation for 440 persons, "after the dimensions of the larger quadrangle at Christchurch, Oxford." Shortly after the death of the third provost, Dr. Slater, which occurred in 1645, suits were commenced in the Court of Chancery respecting the title to the ground on which the college stood, when it was decreed that Dr. Sutcliffe's estates should revert to his rightful heirs, upon their paying to the college a certain sum of money. The college buildings were afterwards devoted to various inappropriate purposes, being at one time used as a receptacle for prisoners of war, and at another as a riding-house.

Its next destination would appear to have been of a higher order; for it appears that the king gave it, or offered it, to the then newly-founded Royal Society. John Evelyn writes, in his "Diary," under date September 24th, 1667:—"Returned to London, where I had orders to deliver the possession of Chelsey Colledge (used as my prison during the warr with Holland, for such as were sent from the Fleete to London) to our Society [the Royal Society], as a gift of his Majesty, our founder." And again, under date September, 14th, 1681, Evelyn writes:—"Din'd with Sir Stephen Fox, who proposed to me the purchasing of Chelsey College, which his Majesty had some time since given to our Society, and would now purchase it again to build a hospital or infirmary for soldiers there, in which he desired my assistance, as one of the council of the Royal Society."

On the failure of the college, the ground escheated to the Crown, by whom, as stated above, it was afterwards granted to the Royal Society. This body, in turn, sold the property to Sir Stephen Fox, for Charles II., who "generously gave" it as a site for a Royal Hospital for Aged and Disabled Soldiers, but at the same time pocketing Dr. Sutcliffe's endowment, and leaving the building to be erected at the cost of the nation.

On part of the site of the college was erected, towards the close of the seventeenth century, the mansion of the Earls of Ranelagh, whose name was perpetuated in that of the gardens which were ultimately opened to the public on that spot.

We read in the *Weekly Post*, of 1714, a rumour to the effect that "the Duke and Duchess of Marlborough are to have the late Earl of Ranelagh's house at Chelsea College;" but the arrangement does not appear to have been carried out, for in 1730 an Act was passed, vesting the estates of the Earl of Ranelagh in trustees; and a few years later the house and premises were sold in lots, and shortly afterwards opened as a place of public entertainment, of which we shall have more to say presently. Lord Ranelagh's house and gardens are thus described by Bowack, in 1705:—"The house, built with brick and cornered with stone, is not large, but very convenient, and may well be called a cabinet. It stands a good distance from the Thames. In finishing the whole, his lordship has spared neither labour nor cost. The very greenhouses and stables, adorned with festoons and urns, have an air of grandeur not to be seen in many princes' palaces."

Again, in Gibson's "View of the Gardens near London," published in 1691, these grounds are thus described:—"My Lord Ranelagh's garden being but lately made, the plants are but small, but the plats, border, and walks are curiously kept and elegantly designed, having the advantage of opening into Chelsea College walks. The kitchen-garden there lies very fine, with walks and seats; one of which, being large and covered, was then under the hands of a curious painter. The house there is very fine within, all the rooms being wainscoted with Norway oak, and all the chimneys adorned with carving, as in the council-chamber in Chelsea College." The staircase was painted by Noble, who died in 1700.

A portion of the old college seems to have remained standing for many years, and ultimately to have become the residence of Dr. Messenger Monsey, one of Dr. Johnson's literary acquaintances, and many years Physician to the Royal Hospital.

From Boswell's "Life of Johnson" we learn that the character of Dr. Monsey, in point of natural humour, is thought to have borne a near resemblance to that of Dean Swift; and like him, he too will be long remembered for the vivid powers of his mind and the marked peculiarity of his manners. "His classical abilities were indeed enviable, his memory throughout life was wonderfully retentive, and upon a variety of occasions enabled him, with an inexhaustible flow of words, to pour forth the treasures of erudition acquired by reading, study, and experience; insomuch that he was truly allowed to be a storehouse of anecdote, a reservoir of curious narrative for all weathers; the living chronicle, in short, of other times. The exuberance of his wit, which, like the web of life, was of a mingled yarn, often rendered his conversation exceedingly entertaining, sometimes indeed alarmingly offensive, and at other times pointedly pathetic and instructive; for, at certain happy intervals, the doctor could lay aside Rabelais and Scarron to think deeply on the most important subjects, and to open a very serious vein." The following anecdote, told in Faulkner's "History of Chelsea," is very characteristic of the doctor's turn of temper, and is said to be well attested:—"He lived so long in his office of Physician to Chelsea Hospital, that, during many changes of administration, the reversion of his place had been successively promised to several medical friends of the Paymaster-General of the Forces. Looking out of his window one day, and observing a gentleman below examining the college and gardens, who he knew had secured the reversion of his place, the doctor came down stairs, and going out to him, accosted him thus:—'Well, sir, I see you are examining your house and gardens, that *are to be*, and I will assure you that they are both very pleasant and very convenient. But I must tell you one circumstance: you are the fifth man that has had the reversion of the place, and I have buried them all. And what is more,' continued he, looking very scientifically at him, 'there is something in your face that tells me I shall bury you too.' The event justified the prediction, for the gentleman died some years after; and what is more extraordinary, at the time of the doctor's death there was not a person who seems to have even solicited the promise of the reversion."

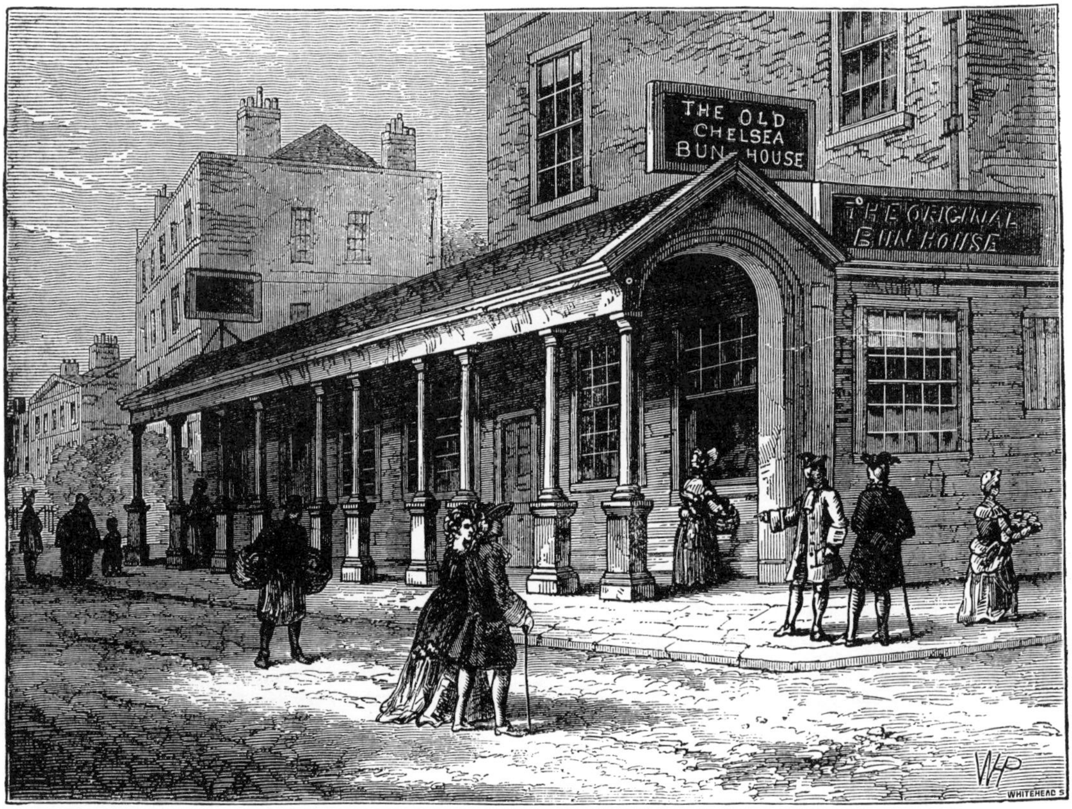

THE CHELSEA BUN-HOUSE, 1810. (*From the Crace Collection.*)

Dr. Monsey's death is recorded as having taken place in December, 1788, "at his apartments in Chelsea College," at the great age of ninety-five. Johnson, though he admired his intellect, disliked

CHELSEA HOSPITAL.

his private character; and Boswell quotes him, saying of old Dr. Monsey, of Chelsea College, that he was "a fellow who swore and talked indecently." Here, as Taylor tells us in his "Recollections," the Doctor "had a large box in his chamber, full of air-holes, for the purpose of carrying his body to his friend, Mr. Forster, in case he should be in a trance when supposed to be dead. It was provided with poles, like a sedan-chair. In his will, which is to be seen in the *Gentleman's Magazine* (vol. 50), he gave instructions that his body should not be buried with any funeral ceremony, but be dissected, and then thrown into the Thames, or wherever the surgeon who operated might please. "It is surprising," observes John Wilson Croker, "that this coarse and crazy humourist should have been an intimate friend and favourite of the elegant and pious Mrs. Montagu." In all probability, however, he knew how to conduct himself in the presence of ladies and bishops, for Dr. Percy, the Bishop of Dromore, says that he never knew him guilty of the vices ascribed to him by Johnson.

The Chudleighs, the father and mother of Elizabeth, Duchess of Kingston,* lived in the College, and the future duchess, as a girl, used to romp and play in its galleries and gardens. They were friends of Sir Robert Walpole, who resided at no great distance.

Here died, in 1833, John Heriot, Comptroller of the Hospital. He was a native of Haddington, in Scotland, and wrote some novels. He was the first editor of the *Sun*, when that paper was started as an evening paper in the interest of Pitt's Administration, and it soon rose to 4,000 a day—a very large circulation for the time, considering the scarcity of educated readers and the heavy stamp-duty then imposed on newspapers.

As we have already observed, a considerable part of the old college grounds, and probably part of the college itself, ultimately became the site of the Royal Hospital for Wounded and Superannuated Soldiers. Dr. Jortin, with his usual sprightliness, observed on this that, "with a very small and easy alteration it was made a receptacle of maimed and discarded soldiers. For if the king's project had been put into execution, the house would most probably have become a house of discord, and 'peace be within thy walls' would have been a fruitless wish, and a prayer bestowed in vain upon it."

King Charles himself laid the first stone of the new building (which had been designed by Wren), in the presence of the chief nobility and gentry of the kingdom, and the whole structure was finished in 1690, at a cost, it is said, of £150,000. The building is of red brick, with stone quoins, cornices, pediments, and columns; and consists of three courts, two of which are spacious quadrangles; the third, the central one, is open on the south side towards the river, and has its area laid out in gardens and walks. A Latin inscription on the frieze of the large quadrangle tells us that the building was founded by Charles II., augmented by James II., and completed by William and Mary, for the aid and relief of soldiers worn out by old age or by the labours of war. In the central area is a bronze statue of Charles II. in Roman imperial armour, supposed to be the work of Grinling Gibbons; and in the grounds is a granite obelisk erected to the memory of the officers and men who fell in the Indian campaigns. There is also here a statue, by Noble, to Sir J. McGrigor, the Physician-General to the army under Wellington in Spain. In the eastern and western wings of this court are the wards of the pensioners; they are sixteen in number, and are both spacious and airy.

At the extremity of the eastern wing is the governor's house. The ceiling of the principal room is divided into oblong compartments, appropriately ornamented, and the walls are hung with several portraits of royalty, from the time of King Charles II. In the western wing are the apartments of the lieutenant-governor.

The north front is of great extent, and faced by avenues of limes and chestnut-trees. In the centre of the structure is a handsome portico of the Doric order, surmounted by a lofty clock turret in the roof. Beneath are the principal entrances. On the eastern side of the vestibule, a short flight of steps leads to the chapel. This is a lofty apartment, with an arched ceiling; it is rather over 100 feet in length, by about thirty in width, and is paved with black and white marble. The pews for the various officers of the establishment are ranged along the sides, and the pensioners sit in the middle on benches. Over the communion-table is a painting of the Ascension, by Sebastian Ricci. King James II. presented a handsome service of plate, an altar-cloth, pulpit-cloth, several velvet cushions, and four handsomely-bound prayer-books. From the walls on either side of the chapel are suspended a large number of colours captured by the British army, including thirteen "eagles" captured from the French at Barossa, Talavera, and Waterloo. The dining-hall is on the western side of the vestibule, and is of the same dimensions as the chapel.

* See Vol. III., p. 552.

The furniture of this room is massive and simple. Above the doorway, at the eastern end, is a gallery; the upper end is occupied by a large painting, which was presented by the Earl of Ranelagh. It was designed by Verrio, and finished by Henry Cooke, an artist who studied Salvator Rosa. The chief figure of the composition is King Charles II., mounted on a richly-caparisoned horse; in the background is a perspective view of the Royal Hospital; and fanciful representations of Hercules, Minerva, Peace, and "Father Thames," are introduced, by way of allegory. The sides of the hall are hung with numerous engravings of military subjects, and there is also a large painting of the Battle of Waterloo, and an allegorical picture of the victories of the Duke of Wellington, by James Ward, R.A. A dinner for the pensioners is regularly placed in this hall every day (with the exception of Sunday), at twelve o'clock; but they do not dine in public, as every man is allowed to take his meal in his own apartment in the wards. The hall serves also as a reading-room for the old pensioners, and here they are allowed to sit and smoke—for they are allowed one penny a day for tobacco, which is called "Her Majesty's bounty"—and while away the time with card-playing and other amusements, and also with the perusal of books and newspapers. In this hall the remains of the "great" Duke of Wellington were deposited, in November, 1852, preparatory to the public funeral in St. Paul's Cathedral. Her Majesty, accompanied by Prince Albert, the Prince of Wales, and Princess Royal, visited Chelsea Hospital during part of the ceremony of lying in state; afterwards the veterans of Chelsea were admitted; on one day the admission was restricted to those who were provided with tickets from the Lord Chamberlain's office; and then, for four days, the public were admitted without tickets, when the crush was so great that several persons were killed in the attempt to gain admission.

The east, or "Light Horse" court, comprises the apartments of many official persons connected with the institution, such as the governor, the deputy-treasurer, secretary, chaplain, apothecary, comptroller, steward, and other officials. The west court is partly occupied by the board-room, used by the commissioners for their meetings, and by the apartments of various officers connected with the establishment. Still further to the west is the stable-yard; and, on the site of the mansion formerly occupied by Sir Robert Walpole is the infirmary, which is admirably adapted for the patients admitted within its walls.

Chelsea Hospital affords a refuge for upwards of 500 inmates. The number of out-pensioners, from whom they are selected, is about 64,000; and of these, on an average, nearly 8,000 are over seventy years of age. Here the veterans, whether wounded, disabled, or merely advanced in years, find a home, and for their accommodation, comfort, and medical treatment, a liberal provision is made. An applicant for admission must be on the permanent pension list, must be of good character, must have no wife or children dependent on him for support, and he must be incapable of supplementing his pension by labour. He must show that he has given good service "by flood and field." A monthly list of applications is kept, in the order in which they are received; and at the end of the month the commissioners, having regard to the number of vacancies and the eligibility of the candidates, according to the terms of the Royal Warrant of 1862, sanction the selection and admission of the most meritorious. All the wants of the inmates are liberally provided for. Their clothing is certainly rather of an antique style; but, nevertheless, it is picturesque. They wear long scarlet coats, lined with blue, and the original three-cornered cocked hat of the last century; but then, as the quarter-master once said to the War Office Committee, "they are old men." Their diet consists of beef on Sundays and mutton on week-days; but, in order to break the monotony, at their own request, bacon has been substituted for mutton on one week-day. A pint of porter daily is the allowance for each man; and there is a fund of about £540 a year, derived from private legacies, which is devoted to maintaining the library and providing extra personal comforts and amusements. The pensioners are divided into six companies, the captains and other officers of each company being responsible for the cleanliness of the ward and the preservation of order.

The expenditure of the hospital is chiefly met by an annual Parliamentary vote; but the institution enjoys a small independent income from property and interest on unclaimed prize-money. With all this liberal provision, however, it appears, from the War Office Committee reports which have been published, that Chelsea Hospital is not popular with soldiers. The inmates, indeed, are contented; but it is admitted that soldiers serving under the colours look forward to out-pensions at the close of their military career, and that the severance of home-ties, the monastic character of the institution, and a certain amount of disciplinary restraint, outweigh the advantages of the hospital, except in the instance of men (perhaps who have earned only small pensions) aged, infirm, and helpless, without family or friends able and willing to support them. Even the very old prefer providing for themselves out of the hospital if they can; there are only about 230 men in the hospital over seventy—generally fewer than that.

Adjoining the hospital is a burial-ground for the pensioners, wherein repose a few veritable centenarians, if the records of their deaths are to be relied upon. Thomas Asbey, died 1737, aged 112; Robert Comming, died 1767, aged 116; Peter Dowling, died 1768, aged 102; a soldier who fought at the battle of the Boyne, died 1772, aged 111; and Peter Bennet, died 1773, aged 107.

In Pimlico Road—or, as it was formerly called, Jew's Row, or Royal Hospital Row—"there is," writes Larwood, in 1866, in his "History of Signboards," "a sign which greatly mystifies the maimed old heroes of Waterloo and the Peninsula, and many others besides. I refer to the 'Snow Shoes.' But this hostelry is historic in its origin. Its sign was set up during the excitement of the American War of Independence, when 'Snow Shoes' formed a leading article in the equipment of the troops sent out to fight the battles of King George, against old Washington and his rebels." John Timbs, in his "Curiosities of London," says that the tradition of the foundation of the hospital being due to the influence of Nell Gwynne is kept in countenance by the head of that royal favourite having been for very many years the sign of a public-house in Grosvenor Row. More than one entry in Evelyn's "Diary," however, proves that Sir Stephen Fox "had not only the whole managing" of the plan, but was himself "a grand benefactor" to it. He was mainly advised by Evelyn, who arranged the offices, "would needes have a library, and mentioned several bookes."

North of the hospital is the Duke of York's School, or Royal Military Asylum. This institution was founded by the late Duke of York, for the support and education of children of soldiers of the regular army, who remain there until of a suitable age, when they are apprenticed, or sent into service. The building is constructed chiefly of brick, with stone dressings and embellishments, and it comprises three sides of a quadrangle. In the centre of the chief front is a stone portico of the Doric order; four massive pillars support the pediment, the frieze of which is inscribed as follows—"The Royal Military Asylum for the Children of Soldiers of the Regular Army;" and the whole is surmounted with the royal arms. In this part of the building are the dining-rooms and school-rooms for the children, and also bath-rooms and a committee-room. The north and south wings contain the dormitories for the boys and girls, and apartments for several officers of the establishment. In the front the ground is laid out in grass plats and gravel walks, and planted with trees; attached to each wing is a spacious play-ground for exercise, with cloistral arcades for the protection of the children in inclement seasons. The affairs of the Royal Military Asylum are regulated by commissioners appointed by the Government, who have to apply to Parliament for an annual grant for the support of the institution. The commissioners also have the selection of the children, whose admission is regulated in accordance with the following rules:—Orphans, or those whose fathers have been killed, or have died on foreign stations; those who have lost their mothers, and whose fathers are absent on duty abroad; those whose fathers are ordered on foreign service, or whose parents have other children to maintain." The children are supported, lodged, and educated, until they are of a suitable age to be disposed of as servants and apprentices. The boys undergo a regular military training; and it is a pleasing sight to witness them going through their exercises, with their military band of juvenile performers. According to the original intention of the founders of this institution, the number of children admitted into the asylum is not to exceed seven hundred boys and three hundred girls, exclusive of such as, on an exigency, may be admitted to the branch establishment in the Isle of Wight. The boys are clothed in red jackets, blue breeches, blue stockings, and black caps; and the girls in red gowns, blue petticoats, straw hats, &c. The latter are taught the ordinary branches of needlework and household work.

A considerable part of the grounds lying immediately at the south-east corner of Chelsea Hospital once formed the site of Ranelagh Gardens, as we have already observed. "Ranelagh," writes Mr. Lambert, in his "History of London and its Environs," published in 1806, "was the seat of an Irish nobleman of that title, in whose time the gardens were extensive. On his death the estate was sold, and the principal part of the gardens was converted into fields, though the house remained unaltered. Part of the gardens also was permitted to remain. Some gentlemen and builders having become the purchasers of these, a resolution was taken to convert them into a place of entertainment. Accordingly, Mr. William Jones, architect to the East India Company, drew the plan of the present Rotunda, which is an illustrious monument of his genius and fancy. The chief material employed was wood, and it was erected in 1740." He describes it as "a noble edifice, somewhat resembling the Pantheon at Rome, with a diameter externally of 185 feet, and internally of 150 feet. The entrances," he adds, "are by four Doric porticoes opposite each other, and the first storey is rustic. Round the whole on the outside is a gallery, the stairs to which are at the porticoes; and overhead is a slated covering which projects from the body of the Rotunda. Over the gallery are the windows, sixty in number, and over these the slated roof. The interior is elegantly decorated, and, when well illuminated and full of company, presents a most brilliant spectacle. Indeed, it may be said of Ranelagh that, as a public place of amusement, it is not to be equalled in Europe for beauty, elegance, and grandeur. Before the Act of Parliament passed in 1752, which prohibited all places of entertainment from being opened before a certain hour in the afternoon, the Rotunda was open every day for public breakfasts. It was not, however, a place of much note until it was honoured with the famous masquerades in the late reign, which brought it into vogue. But the immorality so frequently practised at masquerades has lessened their reputation, and they are not now attended, as formerly, by persons of rank and fashion. The entertainments consist of music and singing, and upon particular occasions fireworks also are exhibited; and during the summer season the gardens may be seen in the day-time on payment of a shilling. The price of admittance in the evening is half-a-crown, including tea and coffee, which are the only refreshments allowed; but on extraordinary occasions the price is raised."

Sir Richard Phillips, in his "Modern London," published in 1804, in noticing Ranelagh, writes:— "This place is situated about two miles west of London, in the village of Chelsea. It consists of a splendid Rotunda and gardens. The Rotunda itself, used as a promenade, is very spacious, and brilliantly illuminated, with a neat orchestra. The amusements of Ranelagh, generally speaking, are limited to miscellaneous performances, vocal and instrumental; and in the gardens there are fireworks and illuminations. Masquerades are sometimes given in a very good style; but the genius of the English people seems not well calculated for this species of amusement. Ranelagh has lately been engaged by the 'Pic-Nic Society,' and it is supposed will be appropriated to their entertainments."

Besides the Rotunda there was a small Venetian pavilion in a lake, to which the company were rowed in boats, and the grounds were planted with trees. The decorations of the various buildings were designed by Capon, an eminent scene-painter. In each of the refreshment-boxes was a painting; in the centre of the Rotunda was a heating apparatus, concealed by arches, porticoes, and niches, paintings, &c.; and supporting the ceiling, which was decorated with celestial figures, festoons of flowers, and arabesques, and lighted by circles of chandeliers.

In the *Gentleman's Magazine* for 1742 is the following description of Ranelagh Gardens from a foreigner's point of view:—"I repaired to the rendezvous, which was the park adjoining to the Palace Royal, and which answers to our Tuilleries, where we sauntered, with a handful of fine company, till it was almost twilight—a time, I thought, not a little unseasonable for a tour into the country. We had no sooner quitted the park but we found ourselves in a road full of people, illuminated with lamps on each side; the dust was the only inconvenience; but in less than half an hour we found ourselves at a gate where money was demanded, and paid for our admittance; and immediately my eyes were struck with a large building, of an orbicular figure, with a row of windows round the attic storey, through which it seemed to be liberally illuminated within, and altogether presented to the eye such an image as a man of a whimsical imagination would not scruple to call a giant's lanthorn. Into this enchanted palace we entered, with more haste than ceremony; and at the first glance I, for my part, found myself dumb with surprise and astonishment, in the middle of a vast amphitheatre; for structure, Roman; for decorations of paint and gilding, gay as the Asiatic; four grand portals, in the manner of the ancient triumphal arches, and four times twelve boxes, in a double row, with suitable pilasters between, form the whole interior of this wonderful fabric, save that in the middle a magnificent orchestra rises to the roof, from which descend several large branches, which contain a great number of candles enclosed in crystal glasses, at once to light and adorn this spacious Rotunda. Groups of well-dressed persons were dispersed in the boxes; numbers covered the area; all manner of refreshments were within call; and music of all kinds echoed, though not intelligibly, from every one of those elegant retreats, where Pleasure seemed to beckon her wanton followers. I have acknowledged myself charmed at my entrance; you will wonder, therefore, when I tell you that satiety followed. In five minutes I was familiar with the whole and every part; in the five next indifference took place; in five more my eyes grew dazzled, my head became giddy, and all night I dreamed of Vanity Fair."

The Rotunda was first opened with a public breakfast in April, 1742; and, for a short time, morning concerts were given, consisting of selections from oratorios. Walpole, in a letter to Sir Horace Mann, written during the next month, gives us the following particulars of this once famous place of amusement:—"There is a vast amphitheatre, finely gilt, painted, and illuminated, into which everybody that loves eating, drinking, staring, or crowding, is admitted for twelve pence. The building and disposition of the gardens cost sixteen thousand pounds. . . . I was there last night, but did not find the joy of it. Vauxhall is a little better, for the garden is pleasanter, and one goes by water." Ranelagh, however, appears soon to have eclipsed its rival on the other side of the water, for two years later we find the following record by the same gossiping chronicler:—"Every night constantly I go to Ranelagh, which has totally beat Vauxhall. Nobody goes anywhere else—everybody goes there. My Lord Chesterfield is so fond of it that he says he has ordered all his letters to be directed thither." And again, some four years afterwards, he tells us: "Ranelagh is so crowded, that in going there t'other night in a string of coaches, we had a stop of six-and-thirty minutes."

A CARD OF INVITATION TO RANELAGH. (*See page* 80.)

The Jubilee Masquerade, "after the Venetian manner," held here in 1749, about seven years after the gardens were first opened, is thus described by gossiping Horace Walpole:—"It was by far the best understood and prettiest spectacle I ever saw

THE ROTUNDA, RANELAGH GARDENS, IN 1750. (*See page* 77.)

—nothing in a fairy tale ever surpassed it. One of the proprietors, who is a German, and belongs to court, had got my Lady Yarmouth to persuade the king to order it. It began at three o'clock; at about five, people of fashion began to go. When you entered, you found the whole garden filled with marquees and spread with tents, which remained all night very commodely. In one quarter was a May-pole, dressed with garlands, and people dancing round it to a tabour and pipe, and rustic music, all masked, as were all the various bands of music that were disposed in different parts of the garden; some like huntsmen, with French horns; some like peasants; and a troop of harlequins and scaramouches in the little open temple on the mount. On the canal was a sort of gondola, adorned with flags and streamers, and filled with music, rowing about. All round the outside of the amphitheatre were shops, filled with Dresden china, japan, &c., and all the shopkeepers in masks; the amphitheatre was illuminated, and in the middle was a circular bower, composed of all kinds of firs, in tubs, from twenty to thirty feet high; under them orange-trees, with small lamps in each orange, and below them all sorts of auriculas in pots; and festoons of natural flowers hanging from tree to tree. Between the arches, too, were firs, and smaller ones in the balconies above. There were booths for tea and wine, gaming-tables and dancing, and about two thousand persons present. In short, it pleased me more than the finest thing I ever saw."

Not many weeks after this there was another "Subscription Masquerade" here, also described at some length by the same old Court gossip, Walpole:—"The king was well disguised in an old-fashioned English habit, and much pleased with somebody who desired him to hold their cups as they were drinking tea. The Duke [of Cumberland] had a dress of the same kind, but was so immensely corpulent that he looked like 'Cacofoco,' the drunken captain in *Rule a Wife and Have a Wife.* The Duchess of Richmond was a Lady Mayoress of the time of James I.; and Lord De la Warr, Queen Elizabeth's 'Garter,' from a picture in the Guard Chamber at Kensington; they were admirable masks. Lord Rochford, Miss Evelyn, Miss Bishopp, Lady Stafford, and Miss Pitt, were in vast beauty, particularly the last, who had a red veil, which made her look gloriously handsome. I forgot Lady Kildare. Mr. Conway was the 'Duke' in *Don Quixote*, and the finest figure that I ever saw. Miss Chudleigh was 'Iphigenia,' and so lightly clad that you would have taken her for Andromeda. . . . The maids of honour were so offended they would not speak to her. Pretty Mrs. Pitt looked as if she came from heaven, but was only thither in the habit of a Chanoineness. Lady Betty Smithson (Seymour) had such a pyramid of baubles upon her head that she was exactly the Princess of Babylon in Grammont."

In 1754 the evening amusements here were advertised under the name of Comus's Court; and in 1759 a burlesque ode on St. Cecilia's Day, written by Bonnell Thornton, was performed; and we are told that "among the instruments employed there was a band of marrow-bones and cleavers, whose endeavours were admitted by the *cognoscenti* to have been a great success."

From Boswell we learn that even the sage and grave Dr. Johnson was as fond of Ranelagh as he was of the Pantheon. When somebody said, cynically, that there "was not half a guinea's worth of pleasure in seeing Ranelagh," he replied, "No; but there is half a guinea's worth of inferiority to other people in not having seen it." Indeed, if we may believe the statement of his friend, Dr. Maxwell, some time assistant preacher at the Temple, Dr. Johnson "often went to Ranelagh, which he deemed a place of innocent recreation." But this is rather a proof of Dr. Johnson's own purity than a testimony to the morals of the place, for "to the pure all things are pure." The gardens were constantly visited also by Oliver Goldsmith; even when he was in difficulties, he would take an Irish cousin there, and treat her to the admission. Sometimes poor Oliver would stroll thither with Dr. Johnson and Sir Joshua Reynolds, to see the great world of which he at once knew so much and so little.

The King of Denmark and his suite paid a visit to Ranelagh in 1768, when, we are told, his Majesty "examined the Temple and other buildings, which gave him great satisfaction."

The scene of the finish of the first Regatta on the Thames, in June, 1775, must have been one of the crowning glories of Ranelagh. The admission ticket on the occasion, engraved by Bartolozzi, was long held in high estimation by collectors. Plans of the regatta were sold, from a shilling to a penny each, and songs on the occasion sung, in which "Regatta" was the rhyme for "Ranelagh," and "Royal Family" echoed to "liberty." "On the return of the wager boats," writes Mr. Faulkner, in his "History of Chelsea," "the whole procession moved, in picturesque irregularity, towards Ranelagh. The Thames was now a floating town. The company landed at the stairs about nine o'clock, when they joined the assembly which came by land in the Temple of Neptune a temporary octagon kind of building, erected about twenty yards below the Rotunda, lined with striped linen of the different-coloured flags of the navy, ornamented with streamers of the same kind loosely flowing, and lustres hanging between each. This room discovered great taste. At half after ten the Rotunda was opened for supper, which displayed three circular tables, of different elevations, elegantly set out. The Rotunda was finely illuminated with parti-coloured lamps; the centre was solely appropriated for one of the fullest and finest bands of music, vocal and instrumental, ever collected in these kingdoms, the number being 240, in which were included the first masters, led by Giardini, and the whole directed by Mr. Simpson. . . . . Supper being over, a part of the company retired to the Temple, where they danced without any regard to precedence; while others entertained themselves in the great room. Several temporary structures were erected in the gardens, such as bridges, palm-trees, &c., which were intended to discover something novel in the illumination style, but the badness of the evening prevented their being exhibited."

In 1802 an *afternoon breakfast* was given here, under the auspices of the Pic-Nic Society, at which about two thousand persons of distinction were present. On this occasion M. Garnerin and Captain Snowden made an ascent in a balloon, and alighted at Colchester in less than an hour. "This," as Hone in his "Year-Book" observes, "was the most memorable ascent in England from the time of Lunardi."

In the following year a magnificent ball was held in the Rotunda; it was given by the knights of the Order of the Bath, on the occasion of an "installation," and is said to have been a "gala of uncommon splendour." But even this was surpassed in brilliancy by an entertainment given shortly afterwards by the Spanish Ambassador. "The whole external front of the house," we read, "was illuminated in a novel manner, and the portico immediately leading to the Rotunda was filled on each side with rows of aromatic shrubs. The Rotunda itself, at the first opening to the sight, exhibited a most superb appearance. The lower boxes formed a Spanish camp, striped blue and red, each tent guarded by a boy dressed in the Spanish uniform. The gallery formed a Temple of Flora, lighted by a number of gold baskets containing wax tapers. The queen's box was hung with crimson satin, lined with white, which hung in festoons richly fringed with gold, and at the top was a regal crown. In the orchestra, which was converted into a magnificent pavilion, a table of eighteen covers was laid for the Royal Family. Opposite to Her Majesty's box was a light temple or stage, on which a Spanish dance was performed by children; at another part were beautiful moving transparencies; and a third was a lottery of valuable trinkets, consisting of six hundred prizes. Women, ornamented with wreaths of flowers, made tea; and one hundred valets, in scarlet and gold, and as many footmen, in sky-blue and silver, waited on the company."

From about the year 1780 down to the close of the last century Ranelagh was in the height of its glory. It was visited by royalty, and all the nobility and gentry. "As no place was ever better calculated for the display of female beauty and elegance," writes Mr. Faulkner, in his work above quoted, "it followed, of course, the greatest belles of the day frequented Ranelagh, at the head of whom was the celebrated and beautiful Duchess of Devonshire, a lady eminent for every grace that could adorn the female, and not a few candidates for admiration were in her train." The Rotunda was subsequently used for late evening concerts, and as an assembly-room, and the gardens for the display of fireworks and other out-door amusements. The place soon ceased to be the attractive promenade it had formerly been, and the brilliant display of beauty it had made for years was no more. The whole of the premises were taken down about the year 1805.

Many persons will remember the description of the ideal "Old Gentleman," in Hone's "Table-Book." "He has been induced to look in at 'Vauxhall' again, but likes it still less than he did years back, and cannot bear it in comparison with Ranelagh! He thinks everything looks poor, flaring, and jaded. 'Ah!' says he, with a sort of triumphant sigh, 'ah! Ranelagh was a noble place! Such taste! such elegance! and such beauty! There was the Duchess of A——, the finest woman in England, sir; and Mrs. B——, a mighty fine creature; and Lady Susan what's-her-name, who had that unfortunate affair with Sir Charles. Yes, indeed, sir, they came swimming by you like swans. Ranelagh for me!'"

Whether it be true or not that ladies of *bon ton* "came swimming by you like swans," there can be no doubt that Ranelagh, in its palmy days, was a favourite haunt of the "upper ten thousand," and that "duchesses" and "Lady Susans" in plenty jostled there against the troops of plebeian City and country dames.

A writer in the *Connoisseur* (No. 22) complains: "The modest excesses of these times [the reign of George II.] are in their nature the same with those which were formerly in vogue. The present races of 'bucks,' 'bloods,' and 'free-thinkers' are but the spawn of the Mohocks and Hell-fire Clubs; and if our modern fine ladies have had their masquerades, their Vauxhalls, their Sunday tea-drinking at Ranelagh, and their morning chocolate in the Haymarket, they have only improved upon the 'Ring,' the Spring Gardens, the New Exchange assignations, and the morning Puppet-show, which enjoyed the attention of their grandmothers. And so, as it is not apparent that our people of fashion are more wicked, so neither are they more wise than their predecessors." The fall of Ranelagh—like other enchanting places of amusement, the description of whose assemblages give us such graphic pictures of the frail beauties of the last century—is thus mournfully set forth in Murphy's "Prologue to Zobeide:"—

> "Adieu, Almack's! Cornelys' masquerade!
> Sweet Ranelagh!"

The picture of ruin and desolation which the site of Ranelagh presented after the demolition of the Rotunda and the dismantling of its gardens, is ably reproduced by Sir Richard Phillips, in his "Walk from London to Kew." "On entering Chelsea," he writes, "I was naturally led to inquire for the site of the once gay Ranelagh. I passed up the avenue of trees, which I remember often to have seen blocked up with carriages. At its extremity I looked for the Rotunda and its surrounding buildings; but, as I could not see them, I concluded that I had acquired but an imperfect idea of the place in my nocturnal visits! I went forward, on an open space, but still could discern no Ranelagh. At length, on a spot covered with nettles, thistles, and other rank weeds, I met a working man, who, in answer to my inquiries, told me that he could see I was a stranger, or I should have known that Ranelagh had been pulled down, and that I was then standing on the site of the Rotunda! Reader, imagine my feelings, for I cannot analyse them! This vile place, I exclaimed, the site of the once enchanting Ranelagh! It cannot be! The same eyes were never destined to see such a metamorphosis! All was desolation! A few inequalities appeared in the ground, indicative of some former building, and holes filled with muddy water showed the foundation-walls; but the rest of the space, making about two acres, was covered with clusters of tall nettles, thistles, and docks. On a more accurate survey I traced the circular foundation of the Rotunda, and at some distance discovered the broken arches of some cellars, once filled with the choicest wines, but now with dirty water. Further on were marks against a garden wall, indicating that the water-boilers for tea and coffee had once been heated there. I traced, too, the site of the orchestra, where I had often been ravished by the finest performances of vocal and instrumental music. My imagination brought the objects before me; I fancied I could still hear an air of Mara's. I turned my eye aside, and what a contrast appeared! No glittering lights! no brilliant happy company! no peals of laughter from thronged boxes! no chorus of a hundred instruments and voices! All was death-like stillness! Is such, I exclaimed, the end of human splendour? Yes, truly, all is vanity; and here is a striking example. Here are ruins and desolation, even without antiquity! I am not mourning, said I, over the remains of Babylon or Carthage—ruins sanctioned by the unsparing march of time; but here it was all glory and splendour, even yesterday! Here, but seven years have flown away, and I was myself one of three thousand of the gayest mortals ever assembled in one of the gayest scenes which the art of man could devise—ay, on this very spot; yet the whole is now changed into the dismal scene of desolation before me!"

Although not a vestige of the gardens remains, its memory is preserved by naming after it some of the streets, roads, and places which have been built near its site. Mr. Jesse, in his work on "London," published in 1871, tells us that "a single avenue of trees, formerly illuminated by a thousand lamps, and over-canopying the wit, the rank, and the beauty of the last century, now forms an almost solitary memento of the departed glories of Ranelagh. Attached to these trees, the author discovered one or two solitary iron fixtures, from which the variegated lamps were formerly suspended."

According to Mr. John Timbs' "Club Life of London," there was subsequently opened in the neighbourhood a New Ranelagh; but it would appear to have been short-lived, as its memory has quite passed away.

Such, however, was the celebrity of the old Ranelagh, that another Ranelagh, like a second Salamis, was established in the suburbs of Paris; as witness the following extract from a French writer in 1875:—"The name of Ranelagh Gardens, almost forgotten in England, will soon be equally so in Paris. Or rather, it would be, but for the inscription on the neighbouring street, preserving a title which no revolution need trouble to alter. Some alterations now undertaken by the Parisian authorities in the street recall to mind the chequered fortunes of the French Ranelagh. It was started in the summer of 1774 by a simple gardener of the Bois de Boulogne as a private speculation, the name, of course, being borrowed from Chelsea. The gardener was patronised by the Prince de Soubise, and the concerts and balls were at first a great success. But the novelty died out, and about nine years afterwards the proprietor was fain to escape ruin by becoming manager to a private club, with a more select *clientèle.* Thenceforth, till the Revolution, the place was a success. Marie Antoinette had been seen there, and the club invitations were much sought after. The Republic, pure and simple, would have been fatal to the gardens had not the Directory come to the rescue. Under its less rigid *régime* came Trénitz, with his troop of Muscadins and Merveilleuses. Morisart died just before the fall of the Empire, and in time to escape the sight of the Cossacks trampling his pet flower-beds and lawns. From 1816 to 1830 another aristocratic club held its *réunions* at Ranelagh, and under the Orleans dynasty it became again a public place of entertainment. At last came M. Thiers' scheme of fortifying Paris, and his ramparts cut the gardens in half. This was in 1840; and twenty years later a decree suppressed for ever the last lingering vestige of gaiety, and consigned the ground to building purposes."

Queen's Road West (formerly called Paradise Row) has been the residence of many of the "nobility and gentry" of Chelsea in former times. In a large mansion adjoining Robinson's Lane, lived the Earl of Radnor in the time of Charles II., and here his lordship entertained the king "most sumptuously" in September, 1660. The parish register contains several entries of baptisms and deaths in the Radnor family.

Sir Francis Windham had a house in this road at the commencement of the last century. After the battle of Worcester he entertained Charles II. at Trent, where the king remained concealed for several days. Dr. Richard Mead, the eminent physician, of whom we have already spoken in our account of Great Ormond Street,* resided in this neighbourhood for some time, as appears by the parish books. Another physician of note who lived here about the same time was Dr. Alexander Blackwell, who resided in a house near the Botanic Garden. Dr. Blackwell became involved in difficulties; and after leaving Chelsea he went to Sweden, where he was appointed physician to the king. Subsequently, however, he was found guilty of high treason, "in plotting to overturn the constitution of the kingdom, and sentenced to be broken alive on the wheel."

In the Queen's Road, adjoining the Royal Hospital, with its gardens stretching down towards the river, and close by the spot where formerly stood the residence of Sir Robert Walpole, is the Victoria Hospital for Sick Children. The building, which was converted to its present use in 1866, was formerly known as Gough House. It was built by John, Earl of Carberry—one of the "noble authors" mentioned by Horace Walpole—at the commencement of the last century. The estate afterwards came into the possession of the Gough family, and the house subsequently was made use of for many years as a school for young ladies. The house has lately been raised a storey, and additional wards have been provided. These improvements were effected at an expense of about £3,000, and the hospital was formally re-opened by the Princess Louise.

At the eastern end of Queen's Road, forming one side of a broad and open thoroughfare, connecting Sloane Street with new Chelsea Bridge, stand some fine barracks for the Foot Guards, erected about the year 1863. They are constructed in a substantial manner with light-coloured brick, relieved with rustic quoins of red brick, and they consist of several commodious blocks of buildings, the largest of which contains quarters for the officers, &c. They afford accommodation for about 1,000 men. It has been said, perhaps with some truth till lately, that this is the only handsome structure in the way of barracks to be seen in the entire metropolis. If so, the assertion is not very creditable to our character as a nation, considering the duties that we owe to those who defend our homes and our commerce in the field.

In 1809, the Serpentine — which joined the Thames by Ranelagh—rose so high as to overflow its banks, and boats were employed in carrying passengers between the old Bun-house and Chelsea Hospital.

Mr. Larwood, in his "History of Sign-boards," says that there is, or, at all events, was in 1866, in Bridge Row, a public-house bearing the sign of the "Chelsea Water-works." These water-works, after which it was named, were constructed about the year 1724. A canal was dug from the Thames, near Ranelagh to Pimlico, where an engine was placed for the purpose of raising the water into pipes, which conveyed it to Chelsea, Westminster, and other parts of western London. The reservoirs in Hyde Park and the Green Park were supplied by pipes from the Chelsea Waterworks, which, in 1767, yielded daily 1,750 tons of water.

* See Vol. IV., p. 560.

CHELSEA WATER-WORKS, IN 1750. (*See page* 83.)

CHAPTER VIII.

CHELSEA (*continued*).—CREMORNE GARDENS, &c.

"Where smiling Chelsea spreads the cultured lands,
Sacred to Flora, a pavilion stands;
And yet a second temple neighb'ring near
Nurses the fragrance of the various year."—*Anon.*

Chelsea Farm, the Residence of Lord Cremorne—Cremorne Gardens—Attempts at Aërial Navigation—Ashburnham House—The Ashburnham Tournament—The "Captive" Balloon—Turner's Last Home—Noted Residents in Lindsey Row—The King's Road—The Old Burial-ground—St. Mark's College—The "World's End" Tavern—Chelsea Common—Famous Nurseries—Chelsea Park—The "Goat in Boots"—The Queen's Elm—The Jews' Burial-ground—Shaftesbury House—The Workhouse—Sir John Cope—Robert Boyle, the Philosopher and Chemist—The Earl of Orrery—Mr. Adrian Haworth—Dr. Atterbury—Shadwell, the Poet—The "White Horse" Inn—Mr. H. S. Woodfall—The Original of "Strap the Barber" in "Roderick Random"—Danvers Street—Justice Walk—The Old Wesleyan Chapel—Chelsea China—Lawrence Street—Tobias Smollett—Old Chelsea Stage-coaches—Sir Richard Steele and other Noted Residents—The Old Clock-house—The Glaciarium—Hospital for Diseases of Women—Chelsea Vestry Hall, and Literary and Scientific Institution—Congregational Church—Royal Avenue Skating-rink—Sloane Square—Bloody Bridge—Chelsea, Brompton, and Belgrave Dispensary—Royal Court Theatre—Hans Town—Sloane Street—Trinity Church—Sloane Terrace Wesleyan Chapel—Sir C. W. Dilke, Bart.—Ladies' Work Society—Hans Town School of Industry for Girls—"Count Cagliostro"—An Anecdote of Professor Porson—Chelsea House—St. Mary's Roman Catholic Chapel—The "Marlborough Tavern"—Hans Place—Miss Letitia E. Landon—The Pavilion—St. Saviour's Church—Prince's Cricket-ground and Skating-rink—The "South Australian."

A FEW hundred yards to the west of old Battersea Bridge, on the north side of the river, were the celebrated Cremorne Gardens, so named after Thomas Dawson, Lord Cremorne, the site of whose former suburban residence and estate they covered. They proved, to a very great extent, the successors of "Kuper's," Vauxhall, and Ranelagh. In the early part of the present century, Lord Cremorne's mansion, known as Chelsea Farm, was often visited by George III., Queen Charlotte, and the Prince of Wales. In 1825 the house and grounds devolved on Mr. Granville Penn, a cousin of Lady Cremorne, who much improved the estate, but subsequently disposed of it. The natural beauty of the situation soon afterwards led to the grounds being opened to the public as the "Stadium," and a few years later the gardens were laid out with great taste; the tavern adjoining them was enlarged, and the place became the resort of a motley crowd of pleasure-seekers, and generally well attended. To a recent period it retained most of its original features. At night during the summer months the grounds were illuminated with numberless coloured lamps, and there were various ornamental buildings, grottoes, &c., together with a theatre, concert-room, and dining-hall. The amusements provided were of a similar character to those which were presented at Vauxhall Gardens in its palmy days: such as vocal and instrumental concerts, balloon ascents, dancing, fireworks, &c. Several remarkable balloon ascents were made from these grounds, notably among them being that of Mr. Hampton, who, in 1839, ascended with a balloon and parachute, by which he descended from a height of about two miles. More recently an attempt at aerial navigation was made from Cremorne by a foreigner, M. de Groof. The apparatus was suspended beneath the car of a balloon, and when the aeronaut had reached a considerable height, the machine was liberated; but owing to some defect in its construction, it immediately collapsed and fell to the ground with a fearful crash, killing its unfortunate occupant on the spot.

Ashburnham House, which stood on the west of the gardens, was built about the middle of the last century by Dr. Benjamin Hoadley, an eminent physician, after whose death it was purchased by Sir Richard Glynn, who sold it to the Earl of Ashburnham, from whom it obtained its present name. It was next in the possession of Dr. Cadogan, and again changing hands at different periods, ultimately became the residence of the Hon Leicester Stanhope, afterwards Earl of Harrington. A strip of waste ground between Ashburnham House and the river, called the "Lots," was for many years "a bone of contention" between the residents in the neighbourhood and the Chelsea Vestry, in consequence of the disgraceful scenes carried on by a large number of "roughs" who were in the habit of meeting there. Here, in 1863, in a large pavilion prettily draped with the flags of all nations and a variety of heraldic trophies and allegorical devices, a sensational entertainment on a scale of great splendour was given, in the shape of a revival of the Eglinton "tournament." A large number of persons took part in it as heralds, seneschals, yeomen, pages, men-at-arms, squires, and banner-bearers, clad in an almost endless variety of shining

THE "WORLD'S END," IN 1790. (*See page* 87.)

armour and mediæval costume. In 1869, a monster balloon, nearly 100 feet in diameter, made daily ascents for some time from these grounds. The balloon, appropriately called "The Captive," was secured by a rope about 2,000 feet long, which was let out and wound in by steam power. The Captive balloon, however, one day escaped from its moorings, and the exhibition was discontinued.

In a small house close to Cremorne Pier, Mr. J. M. W. Turner, R.A., resided for some time, under an assumed name, and here, as we have already stated,* he died in 1851. Whilst living here, Turner would not see any person, excepting a very few intimate friends, and, in fact, was too reserved to allow himself to be recognised. This inclination at the close of his life, perhaps, was only natural. Doubtless, Chelsea is proud to add his name to its list of distinguished residents.

Close by, in Lindsey Row, lived Sir Mark Isambard Brunel, the originator and designer of the Thames Tunnel; and Mr. Timothy Bramah, the distinguished locksmith. Here, too, resided Mr. John Martin, R.A. The Rev. A. C. Coxe, in his "Impressions of England," published in 1851, speaking of Chelsea, says:—"We landed not far from this church, and called upon John Martin, whose illustrations of Milton and 'Belshazzar's Feast' have rendered him celebrated as a painter of a certain class of subjects, and in a very peculiar style. He was engaged on a picture of 'The Judgment,' full of his mannerism, and sadly blemished by offences against doctrinal truth, but not devoid of merit or of interest. He asked about Allston and his 'Belshazzar,' and also made inquiries about Morse, of whose claim as the inventor of the electric telegraph he was entirely ignorant."

Mr. Henry Constantine Jennings, an antiquary and virtuoso, settled in Lindsey Row at the close of the last century. His "museum," which comprised a large collection of shells, minerals, preserved birds, quadrupeds, &c., was disposed of by auction in 1820.

Leading from the site of Cremorne Gardens eastward through Chelsea, is a broad thoroughfare, called the King's Road; and by this road we shall now proceed on our way backward towards Sloane Street, picking up such scraps of information respecting the neighbourhood on either side as the records of the district have left for our use. Respecting the King's Road itself, we may state that, prior to the reign of Charles II., it was only a narrow lane through the fields, for the convenience of the farmers and gardeners who had lands in the neighbourhood. Soon after the Restoration, however, it was found that it might be made to serve as a more direct road for the king between St. James's or Whitehall and Hampton Court Palace; and, accordingly, after some discussion between the Government and the parishioners of Chelsea, it was converted into an ordinary coach-road. It continued to be the private road of royalty down to the reign of George III. Pass tickets, admitting passengers along it by sufferance, are still in existence; they bear on the one side a crown and "G. R," and on the other, as a legend, "The King's Private Road."

Along this road is the burial-ground belonging to the parish of Chelsea, in which lies Andrew Millar, the original publisher of Hume's "History of England," Thomson's "Seasons," and some of Fielding's novels.

The Duke of York was thrown from his horse whilst riding along this road towards Fulham; he had two ribs broken. John Timbs records that, "near the spot where is now the Vestry Hall, the Earl of Peterborough was stopped by highwaymen in what was then a narrow lane; and the robbers, being watched by some soldiers, who formed a part of the guard at Chelsea College, were fired at from behind the hedge. One of these highwaymen turned out to be a student in the Temple, whose father having lost his estate, his son lived by 'play, sharping, and a little on the highway'—the desperate resources of the day."

Nearly opposite Ashburnham House, on the north side of the King's Road, is St. Mark's College, which was established in 1841 by the National Society, as a training institution for schoolmasters. The residence of the principal was formerly known as Stanley House, and was originally built in the reign of Queen Elizabeth, by Sir Arthur Gorges, whose family at that time possessed considerable property in Chelsea. About the middle of the last century it became the property of the Countess of Strathmore, who afterwards married Captain A. R. Bowes, whose barbarity to her drew on him the execration of the country. About the year 1815, Stanley House was sold to Mr. William Hamilton, from whom it subsequently passed to the National Society. The college accommodates about 110 students, and the period of training is for two years, according to the provisions of the Committee of Council on Education. The chapel, which abuts on the Fulham Road, is an unpretending building; but a certain amount of effect is produced in the interior by the stained-glass windows. The buildings of the college form a quadrangle, erected in the Italian style; and there

* See Vol. IV., p. 448.

is also in the grounds an octagonal building, used as a practising school. The first Principal of the college, and indeed its joint-founder, the Rev. Derwent Coleridge, a son of the poet, died in 1883.

In the King's Road, near Milman Street, is an inn styled "The World's End." The old tavern, like the "World's End" at Knightsbridge, already described,* was a noted house of entertainment in the reign of Charles II. The tea-gardens and grounds were extensive, and elegantly fitted up. The house was probably called "The World's End" on account of its then considerable distance from London, and the bad state of the roads and pathways leading to it. It figures in a dialogue in Congreve's "Love for Love" in a manner which implies that it bore no very high character.

At the commencement of the present century, the King's Road was a very different place from what it is now. The line of road was almost exclusively occupied by nurserymen and florists, and it became, in consequence, to a certain extent, a fashionable resort for the nobility and gentry. The road, in most parts, was very narrow, and the different grounds were mostly enclosed in wooden palings. At night there were only a few gloomy oil-lamps, and the lives and property of the inhabitants were principally entrusted to a small number of private watchmen. Northward of the King's Road, at no very distant date, a considerable extent of land, stretching away to the Fulham Road, was a vast open heath, known as Chelsea Common. Standing in the central space, which has, singularly enough, been left as a memorial of the old common, and looking at the streets now branching off in various directions, it is not easy to call up visions of the past—say two hundred years ago—when this locality was probably as agreeable a spot as Clapham or Wimbledon Commons in our own time.

Faulkner conjectures that the Fulham Road formed the north boundary of the common, and on the south it reached to some nursery grounds abutting on the King's Road, which said nursery grounds, one may conjecture, had been cut off the common by some party or parties in the days when land boundaries were not always kept with care. Westward, the common must have extended about to the line of Robert and Sydney Streets, and eastward to "Blackland's Lane," as it was first called, afterwards Marlborough Road; or perhaps originally the common was bounded by the road or lane which is now Sloane Street. It is first spoken of as "Chelsea Heath," and it appears to have been covered, at least in part, with heath and furze, therein resembling some of the Surrey commons. One of the earliest records concerning Chelsea Common tells us the fact that the City train-bands used to repair to it for exercise, and that, in the disturbed times of Charles I., reviews of troops were more than once held there.

This common was used in former times as a means of raising money for the benefit of the parish. We have particulars relating to such a usage as far back as the reign of Charles II., when the re-building of the church having been resolved upon, Lord Lindsey, Charles Cheyne, and those interested in the common, agreed to enclose it for twenty-one years, the term commencing in March, 1674. On the expiration in 1695, the ground was again thrown open. Somewhat more than a century later—namely, in 1713—articles were drawn up, Sir Hans Sloane being then lord of the manor, in which, amid sundry other recitals, it is stated that the ground at Chelsea Common having been put to various unlawful uses, the holders decide to let it for three years to one John Hugget. It was stipulated that he was to fence the common "with a good bank and a ditch all around," which it is probable that he did, to the satisfaction of all parties, as he had his term renewed from time to time.

An Act passed in the reign of George I., which empowered the surveyor of the London roads to dig up gravel on any common or waste land convenient to him, gave rise to some disputes in Chelsea. The parties interested in the common were informed that much gravel had been removed from Chelsea, and they objected to this, but the Government paid little heed to the complaint. The agents of the surveyor were warned off, though not expelled by physical force; and they went away for awhile, to come back at the next good opportunity. This matter was not finally settled till 1736; for some years previous to that, however, a regular account was kept of all the gravel removed, and payment demanded (and obtained) from those who kept the roads. It was also in the early part of the eighteenth century that an enterprising individual, probably short of money, set up an experimental turnpike on part of the waste ground on the common near Blackland's Lane. The Chelsea authorities fined him heavily, and his scheme was forthwith abandoned.

It was not until some years after an Act had been obtained for the purpose, that the first streets were formed on what had been Chelsea Common. The earliest building lease appears to bear date in 1790, being to the Hon. George Cadogan. The streets, square, grove (for there is at least one of

* See page 21, *ante.*

each of these—Marlborough Square and Whitehead's Grove), and the bye-lanes, display all the variety to be expected under the circumstances, as a number of men took sites of very different sizes, and no general plan was attempted to be carried out.

About the spot now occupied by Pond Place, there were, as may be conjectured, one or more ponds, which supplied water to the cattle grazing on the common. It is worthy of being remembered that William Curtis, the botanist, once lived in Pond Place; he was originally an apothecary's assistant, but his fondness for botany led him to give himself entirely to its study, as soon as his means allowed him. He was one of the pioneers in the formation of those Natural History Societies which have spread themselves in every part of our islands; and his "Botanical Magazine," begun in 1787, met with a sale which in that day was looked upon as something remarkable. Curtis at first opened a botanical garden in Lambeth Marsh, and subsequently removed his collection of plants to a nursery-ground at Queen's Elm, Brompton.

Two noted nurseries in the King's Road abutted on Chelsea Common, which were favourite resorts in the reign of George III. and later. Colvill's nursery, at the end of Blackland's Lane, had, at the beginning of the present century, what was considered a large and splendid conservatory, in which the visitor was told there might be counted five hundred species of geranium. Also, there was a green-house, specially arranged so as to show the mode of growth of exotic parasitical plants. The memory of this nursery was kept up by "Colvill Terrace," now extinguished by the uniform numbering of the King's Road. To the west of that ground was Davey's nursery, also fronting the King's Road.

Beyond these nursery-grounds, and also surrounding Chelsea Common on the south side, were large orchards; but these shared the fate of the waste land, and are now, for the most part, covered with houses. Jubilee Place was built about 1810, and doubtless received its name in memory of the attainment by George III. of the fiftieth year of his sovereignty. King Street, too, in the immediate locality, we may suppose received its name in honour of that particular monarch. Russell Street was originally called Wellesley Street, a name meant to do honour to a family bearing an illustrious name, which, as we have already stated, once furnished Chelsea with a rector. The names of Marlborough, Blenheim, and College Street, applied to some of the streets and places hereabouts, may perhaps lead to the belief that they were so named by persons who have had to do with the Royal Hospital.

Chelsea Park, also situated on the north side of the King's Road, was part of the property of Sir Thomas More. It originally consisted of about thirty acres, and was enclosed with a brick wall, but this has gradually given way to the erection of buildings. Towards the beginning of the last century a manufactory for raw silk was established here, and a number of mulberry-trees were planted for the purpose, but the scheme proved unsuccessful. Park Walk, which now crosses this locality from the King's Road to Fulham Road, appears in old maps as "Lover's Walk," and was planted with trees. The "Goat in Boots" is the sign of a public-house at the end of Park Walk, in the Fulham Road. It is said that the old sign was painted by George Morland, in order to liquidate a bill incurred during a residence here. In old deeds the inn is called simply "The Goat."

A short distance eastward, at the corner of Upper Church Street, is the Queen's Elm Hotel, which keeps in remembrance a story traditionally told respecting the Virgin Queen. The tavern is mentioned in the parish books of Chelsea as far back as 1667, under the name of the Queen's Tree, and the tradition is that it derived its name from the fact of Queen Elizabeth, on her way to or from a visit to Lord Burleigh at Brompton Hall, being caught in a shower of rain, and taking shelter under the branches of a wide-spreading and friendly elm which grew on the spot. The Queen's Elm, it may be added, is mentioned in the parish books of Chelsea as far back as the year 1586, where it is stated that "the tree at the end of Duke's Walk, in Chelsea parish, is called the Queen's Tree," and that "there was an arbour built round it by one Bostocke, at the charge of the parish." There was formerly a turnpike-gate at Queen's Elm; and "a court of guard" there is mentioned among the defences around London that were ordered to be prepared by the Parliament in 1642.

The Jews' burial-ground, situate at Queen's Elm, was formed, early in the present century, on a piece of land purchased for that purpose. Much of the ground hereabouts, now known as West Brompton, was in former times called the hamlet of Little Chelsea. Towards the end of the seventeenth century, Lord Shaftesbury, the author of "Characteristics," purchased an estate here. He rebuilt the house, and generally resided there during the sitting of Parliament. Locke here wrote part of his "Essay," and Addison several of the "Spectators." Of Lord Shaftesbury's letters there are several extant, dated from Chelsea, in 1708. The mansion was subsequently converted into an additional workhouse for the parish of St. George, Hanover Square.

Mrs. S. Carter Hall, in her "Pilgrimages to English Shrines," gives us the following account of Shaftesbury House:—"The lodge at the entrance, as you see, is peculiar, the gate being of old wrought iron. The porter permitted us to pass in; and while he sought the master, we had leisure to look around us. The stone steps are of old times: they are wide, and much worn; a low wall flanks either side; and on the right, downwards, are steps of narrower dimensions leading to the underground apartments. When we entered, we perceived that the hall is panelled in, so as to form a passage; but this is a modern innovation; there can be no doubt of its having been, in Lord Shaftesbury's time, a good-sized hall; the banisters and supporters of the very handsome staircase are in admirable preservation, delicately rather than richly carved in oak, and not at all injured; the stairs are also of oak. What remains of the old house is chopped up, as it were, into small apartments, but there are rich and varied indications of the 'light of other days' to illumine the whole. Over several of the doors are strips of paintings, which, as well as can be seen through thick varnish, are the productions of no feeble pencil. With a little trouble these old paintings can be made out, but they would seem bitter mockeries, occupied as the house at present is; and yet one of the inmates said, 'She liked to look up at that bit of picture when she was sick a-bed: it took away the notion of a workhouse.' Surely art might be made even a teacher here. Some of the rooms retain an antique air."

In 1733, a workhouse was erected on a piece of ground "near the conduit in the King's Road," which had been given by Sir Hans Sloane. Over the chimney-piece was a picture, by a Flemish painter, of a woman spinning thread, with the legend, "Waste not, want not."

A noted resident in Little Chelsea, at the commencement of the last century, was Sir John Cope, so famous in the rebellion of 1745. His house, having been subsequently used as a private asylum, was pulled down; on its site Odell's Place was erected. Mr. Robert Boyle, the distinguished philosopher and chemist, a son of Richard, Earl of Cork, resided here in 1660. Here he was visited by the learned and eminent of his time—amongst others, by M. de Monconys, who, in his "Travels," after informing us how that, after dinner, he went with his son and Mr. Oldenburg "two miles from London in a stage-coach, for five shillings, to a village called Little Chelsea, to visit Mr. Boyle," gives an account of several experiments which that gentleman made in his presence, and then proceeds:—"He has a very fine laboratory, where he makes all his extracts and other operations, one of which he showed me with salt, which being put in quite dry with gold leaves sixteen times thicker than that used by gilders into a crucible on a slow fire, even over a lighted candle, the salt calcined the gold so perfectly that water afterwards dissolved them both and became impregnated with them, in the same manner as with common salt." Evelyn, in his "Diary," has also recorded a visit to the same place. "I went," he writes, "with that excellent person and philosopher, Sir Robert Murray, to visit Mr. Boyle at Chelsea, and saw divers effects of the Eolipile, for weighing air."

Charles, fourth Earl of Orrery, grand-nephew of Mr. Boyle, was born at Little Chelsea in 1676. He was the improver of an instrument or machine which had been constructed for the purpose of exhibiting the motions of the planets round the sun, and which henceforth was called the Orrery, in his honour; the instrument, which was held in high repute in the last century, is, however, now regarded as little more than an ingenious toy. Edward Hyde, third Earl of Clarendon, died at his house at Little Chelsea in 1723.

Another resident of this part of Chelsea, at the beginning of the present century, was Mr. Adrian Haworth, the eminent entomologist and botanist, author of "Lepidoptera Britannica," "Miscellanea Naturalia," and other important works. He was a native of Hull, lived to a great age, and here he died.

But even greater names are connected with Chelsea. Within only a short distance from where we are now, stood the abodes of Pym, Locke, Addison, Steele, Swift, and Atterbury; and the extinct hamlet of Little Chelsea was gilded by the greater lights of the Augustan age of British literature.

That part of Church Street which lies between the King's Road and the river has in its time had some distinguished residents. The thoroughfare itself appears to have been built at a very early period. Here, for several years, lived Dr. Atterbury, afterwards Bishop of Rochester, whose committal to the Tower on suspicion of being concerned in a plot in favour of the Pretender was one of the principal events at the commencement of the last century. It was whilst living here that Dr. Atterbury became acquainted with Dean Swift, who, in 1711, took up his residence opposite the doctor's house. Previous to becoming a resident at Chelsea,

Swift was a frequenter of its rural scenes. He writes, in May, 1711:—"I leave my best gown and periwig at Mrs. Van Homrigh's (in Suffolk Street),* then walk up Pall Mall, out at Buckingham House, and so to Chelsea, a little beyond the church. I set out about sunset, and get there in something less than an hour; it is two good miles, and just 5,748 steps."

Shadwell, the poet laureate of the seventeenth century, was another inhabitant of Church Street or Church Lane. He lived in a house which had been previously occupied by Dr. Arbuthnot.

The old "White Horse" inn, in this street, which was burnt down some years since—a new one being substituted for it—was a very ancient structure, built in the Tudor style of architecture. The house was rich in ancient panelling, together with grotesque ornaments and carving, in the form of brackets. In the principal room, which was large, and consequently well adapted for such a purpose, the old Parochial Guardian Society mostly held its meetings.

Another remarkable old inn in the same street was the "Black Lion," which was situated opposite the rectory garden wall, and was pulled down a few years ago to make room for the present

CHELSEA CHURCH, 1860. (*See page* 58.)

* See Vol. IV., p. 227.

OLD CHELSEA IN 1750.

1. The Clock House. 2. The Moravian Chapel. 3. The White Horse Inn.

tavern, which still retains the name. It is supposed that the old tavern was in its full glory during the reign of Charles II.; for, in an old house situated at the corner of Danvers Street, coeval with it, was an old pump, which the present proprietor, who has resided there for sixty years, recently pulled down. It bore the date of 1697 on a leaden panel of the pump. The old tea-gardens was, no doubt, the resort of the many fashionable families which lived in the neighbourhood; and attached to it was an extensive bowling-green for those who enjoyed that fashionable game.

At the bottom of Church Lane, close by the old church in Lombard Street, lived, during the last twelve years of his life, Mr. Henry Sampson Woodfall, whose name was brought prominently before the public as the printer of the celebrated "Letters of Junius." He used jocularly to say to his Chelsea friends that he had been *fined* and *confined* by the Court of King's Bench, fined by the Houses of Lords and Commons, and indicted at the Old Bailey.

Mr. W. Lewis, bookbinder, the intimate friend of Dr. Smollett, and his fellow-companion whilst journeying from Edinburgh to London, lived for many years in this street. Lewis figures in the novel of "Roderick Random," under the character of "Strap the Barber." The description of the hero of the novel and of Strap, upon their arrival in London, and of their escapes from dangers and impositions, must be familiar to all who have read that work.

Danvers Street takes its name from Danvers Gardens, on the site of which it was built in the latter end of the seventeenth century. Danvers House adjoined, if it was not actually part of, the property of Sir Thomas More, or that of his son-in-law, Roper. Sir John Danvers, who possessed this property early in the reign of Elizabeth, is said to have first introduced into this country the Italian method of horticulture, of which his garden, as represented by Kip, was a beautiful specimen. Danvers House passed from the Danvers family to the first Marquis of Wharton, in the reign of Queen Anne. The house was pulled down early in the last century.

Justice Walk, which extends from Church Street to Lawrence Street, was so named from a magistrate who lived in it. An avenue of lime-trees formerly adorned it, and rendered it an agreeable promenade for strollers. In this thoroughfare there is a commodious Wesleyan Chapel, built in 1841. The exterior is plain and unpretending; and beneath the chapel is a spacious school-room. The old Wesleyan Chapel of Chelsea was of some antiquity, and deserves mention as one of the favourite places of the founder of that community. In its pulpit John Wesley preached for the last time on February 18th, 1791, a fortnight before his death.

Several houses at the corner of Justice Walk and Lawrence Street were formerly used as the show-rooms and manufactory of Chelsea china. The whole of the premises were pulled down towards the close of the last century, and new houses erected on the site. "The manufactory of Chelsea porcelain," says Mr. Faulkner, in his work already quoted, "was set on foot and carried on by a Mr. Spremont, a foreigner. The establishment employed a great number of hands; but the original proprietor, having acquired a large fortune, retired from the concern; and his successors, wanting his enterprise and spirit, did not so well succeed, and in a few years finally abandoned it. Previous to the dissolution of the establishment, the proprietors presented a memorial respecting it to the Government, requesting protection and assistance, in which they stated that 'the manufacture in England has been carried on by great labour and a large expense; it is in many respects to the full as good as the Dresden; and the late Duke of Orleans told Colonel York that the metal or earth had been tried in his furnace, and was found to be the best made in Europe. It is now daily improving, and already employs at least one hundred hands, of which is a nursery of thirty lads, taken from the parishes and charity schools, and bred to designing and painting—arts very much wanted here, and which are of the greatest use in our silk and printed linen manufactories.' Specimens of this porcelain have always been much esteemed, and still retain a great value. At the sale of the effects of Queen Charlotte, the articles in Chelsea china, of which her Majesty had a large collection, brought very high prices." It is recorded that Dr. Johnson had conceived a notion that he was capable of improving on the manufacture of china. He even applied to the directors of the Chelsea China Works, and was allowed to *bake* his compositions in their ovens in Lawrence Street. He was accordingly accustomed to go down with his housekeeper, about twice a week, and stay the whole day, she carrying a basket of provisions with her. The doctor, who was not allowed to enter the *mixing* room, had access to every other part of the premises, and formed his composition in a particular apartment, without being overlooked by any one. He had also free access to the oven, and superintended the whole of the process; but he completely failed, both as to composition and baking, for his materials always yielded to the intensity of the heat, while those of the Company came out of the furnace perfect and complete. Dr. Johnson retired in disgust, but not in despair, for he afterwards gave a dissertation on this very subject in his works.

Chelsea china seems to have been manufactured as far back as the reign of Queen Anne, but was not brought out to anything like perfection till the reign of George II. He and the Duke of Cumberland were the great patrons of the Chelsea China Works, and took much interest in promoting the success of this interesting manufacture. Beaumont painted some of the best landscapes on it; Nollekens' father worked there; and Sir James Thornhill was also employed in designing for it. The clay for the Chelsea china was brought from China by merchant captains, who procured it ostensibly for ballast. The productions of the Chelsea furnaces were thought worthy to vie with those of the celebrated manufactories of Germany. Walpole, in his correspondence with Sir Horace Mann, mentions a service of Chelsea porcelain sent by the King and Queen to the Duke of Mecklenburg, which cost £1,200. Possibly, it was in order to encourage the manufacture that George II. had his coffee-pot of Chelsea china on board the royal yacht. It was evidently *made* for the ship, as it has "ship" burnt in at the bottom. In Mr. Forster's notes to the catalogue of the sale at Stowe, in 1848—where the finest specimens of "rare old china," a pair of small vases, painted with Roman triumphs, sold for £23 10s.—it is stated that George II. brought over artificers from Brunswick and Saxony; whence, probably, M. Brongniart terms Chelsea a "Manufacture Royale." In 1745 the celebrity of Chelsea porcelain was regarded with jealousy by the manufacturers of France, who, therefore, petitioned Louis XV. to concede to them exclusive privileges.

Chelsea ware has always held a high rank among the varieties of English pottery. It reached its perfection about the year 1750; some fifteen years later, owing to the influx of foreign china, and the death of the director of the Chelsea works, Spremont, the workmen were transferred to Derby, where afterwards arose the celebrated Chelsea-Derby manufacture, which marked the first twenty years of the reign of George III., and of which Dr. Johnson remarked that it was "very beautiful, but nearly as dear as silver."

Lawrence Street derives its name from having been erected on the site of the residence of the Lawrence family, which flourished here in the days of bluff King Hal. It is uncertain when this family first settled in Chelsea; but as the "Lawrence Chapel," in the old parish church, is built in the style of architecture which prevailed at the beginning of the fourteenth century, it was probably about that period, or, at all events, some time before they purchased the old manor house. At the "great house" in this street—commonly called Monmouth House—lived Ann, Duchess of Monmouth and Buccleuch, widow of James, Duke of Monmouth. Gay was for some time secretary to the duchess, as stated in Johnson's Life of the poet. Dr. Tobias Smollett afterwards resided in the same house.

A view of the old mansion, which was taken down in 1833, and a fac-simile of an autograph letter, dated thence in 1756, and addressed to Richardson, the actor, are to be seen in Smith's "Historical and Literary Curiosities." The letter is of more than ordinary interest, as Smollett writes thus frankly on a literary subject:—"I was extremely concerned to find myself suspected of a silly, mean insinuation against Mr. Richardson's writings, which appeared some time ago in the *Critical Review;* and I desired my friend, Mr. Millar, to assure you, in my name, that it was inserted without my privity or concurrence." It is pleasant to know that this frank letter was received as kindly as it was intended, and that one of those many "Quarrels of Authors," which have afforded subjects without end to satirists and essayists, was thus avoided. Smollett has immortalised this spot by making it the scene of one of the chapters in his "Humphrey Clinker." Here Smollett wrote his "Adventures of Ferdinand, Count Fathom," the "Reprisals, or the Tars of Old England," and his continuation of Hume's "History of England." He was editor of the *Briton*, a paper set up to support Lord Bute's ministry, and which Wilkes answered by his celebrated *North Briton.*

Between Lawrence Street and Church Street, in former times, was the stabling for the old Chelsea stage-coaches. The fare for inside passengers was 1s. 6d.; outside, 1s.; and no intermediate fare of a lower sum was taken. Such are the changes, however, brought about by the "whirligig of time," that passengers can now go almost from one extremity of London to the other for sixpence, and Chelsea can now be reached by steamboat for the moderate sum of twopence.

Besides the residents in this part of Chelsea in former times, of whom we have already spoken, a few more remain to be mentioned. Sir Richard Steele occupied a house not far from the waterside. In a letter to Lady Steele, dated 14th of February, 1716, Sir Richard writes:—"Mr. Fuller and I came hither to dine in the air, but the mail has been so slow that we are benighted, and chuse to lie here rather than go this road in the dark. I lie at our own house, and my friend at a relation's in the town." Addison, Steele's coadjutor on the *Spectator*, lived for some time close by. Macaulay says that he (Addison) enjoyed nothing so much as the quiet and seclusion of his villa at Chelsea.

At the house of a clergyman here, Mrs. Darby, the mother of Mary Robinson, better known as "Perdita," took up her home, with her children, on being deserted by her husband at Bristol. Soon afterwards she opened a girls' school in the neighbourhood, in which she was aided by her daughter.

In 1823, Mrs. Somerville went to live in Chelsea, her husband being appointed Physician to Chelsea Hospital. She speaks of it as a "dreary and unhealthy situation," and adds that she suffered from sick headaches all the time. Here she numbered among her friends and visitors Lady Noel Byron and her daughter Ada, the Napiers, Maria Edgeworth, Lady Bunbury, and Sir James Mackintosh. Here Gilray, the caricaturist, is supposed to have been born, in 1757. We have already spoken of the unfortunate career of this celebrity in our account of St. James's Street.*

John Pym, a distinguished member of the House of Commons in the seventeenth century, resided here for several years. Count D'Estrades, who came to England to negotiate the sale of Dunkirk, as ambassador from Louis XIV., fixed his abode at Chelsea during the years 1661 and 1662. "It was usual for the foreign ambassadors at that time to make their public entry from the Tower of London, but on this occasion the king sent his own coaches to Chelsea to carry the ambassador, and the count was accompanied by the equipages of the whole of the foreign diplomatic corps at that time in London."†

The Rev. David Williams, the founder of the Royal Literary Fund,‡ lived here for some time, keeping a school. Here he had Franklin for a guest at the time when the American philosopher was subjected to the abuse of Wedderburn before the Privy Council.

Besides its literary celebrities, Chelsea has also had its heroines, of whom mention of one or two will suffice. In the year 1739 was interred, in the College burying-ground, Christian Davies, *alias* Mother Ross, who, according to her own narrative, served in several campaigns under King William and the Duke of Marlborough, and behaved with signal bravery. During the latter portion of her life she resided here, her third husband being a pensioner in the college. At this time she subsisted, as she tells us, principally on the benevolence of "the quality" at Court, whither she went twice a week in a hackney-coach, old age and infirmities having rendered her unable to walk.

The famous Hannah Snell, whose history is recorded in various publications of the year 1750, was actually at that time put upon the out-pensioners' list at Chelsea, on account of the wounds which she received at the siege of Pondicherry. Her singular story excited a considerable share of public attention, and she was engaged to sing and perform the military exercises at various places of public entertainment; some time afterwards she married one Eyles, a carpenter, at Newbury. A lady of fortune, who admired the heroism and eccentricity of her conduct, having honoured her with particular notice, became godmother to her son, and contributed liberally to his education. Mrs. Eyles, to the day of her death, continued to receive her pension, which, in the year 1786, was augmented by a special grant to a shilling a day. In the latter part of her life she discovered symptoms of insanity, and was admitted a patient into Bethlehem Hospital, where she died in 1792.

In Smith Street died, in 1855, Mr. Thomas Faulkner, bookseller, the author of "Histories of Chelsea, Hammersmith, Putney, and Fulham," &c. As a topographer he contributed in the number of his works probably more than any other person to the illustration of the history and antiquities of the western parts of Middlesex, and had his powers of combination and comparison been equal to his industry and perseverance, his labours would have been truly valuable. He began his literary career in 1797, by communications to the *Gentleman's Magazine*, in which, for more than half a century, he occasionally wrote essays and reviews. His contributions also frequently appeared in various volumes of the early series of the *New Monthly Magazine*.

Returning to the King's Road, we may here state that the house adjoining the entrance to the Moravian Chapel and burial-ground, at the north end of Milman's Row, and some few years since pulled down, was for many years in the occupation of the Howard family, of the Society of Friends. The elder Mr. Howard was gardener to Sir Hans Sloane; his brother, having a natural genius for mechanics, became a clockmaker, and made the clock in the old parish church, in 1761, for £50. In front of Howard's house was placed a large clock, and hence the building came to be known as

* See Vol. IV., p. 167. † Faulkner's "History of Chelsea."
‡ See Vol. IV., p. 543.

the "Clock-house," a name now applied to what was once the Moravian chapel.

A plot of land behind the old Clock-house formed part of what was formerly Queen Elizabeth's nursery-ground, and on it still exists a mulberry-tree said to have been planted by that queen.

At No. 178, King's Road, was established in 1871 the Chelsea Hospital for Diseases of Women. The institution is open gratuitously to those without means, small fees for medical treatment being required from such as can afford to pay. In 1883 this hospital was removed to a new building near the Queen's Elm, in Fulham Road.

On the south side of the King's Road, nearly opposite Robert Street and the Workhouse, is the Vestry Hall, a handsome and spacious building in the Italian style, constructed of red brick with stone dressings. It was built from the designs of Mr. W. Pocock. A portion of the building is occupied by the Chelsea Literary and Scientific Institution, for the use of which a rental is paid. The whole interior is well arranged and admirably adapted for the requirements of the parish. Adjoining the Vestry Hall are some commodious swimming-baths, which were constructed under the superintendence of Mr. E. Perrett, the designer of the floating-baths at Charing Cross.

In Markham Square, abutting on the King's Road, is the Chelsea Congregational Church. The edifice stands in a very prominent position, and covers a large piece of ground. The form of the building is slightly cruciform, having transepts projecting about five feet from the body of the chapel. The prominent feature of the exterior is a tower and spire, rising from the west side of the southern transept to the height of about 130 feet. The style of the building is in the second period of the Gothic, and the exterior is constructed entirely of stone. There are lofty and spacious school-rooms, with the requisite offices, beneath the chapel.

In the Royal Avenue, a turning on the south side of the road leading towards the Royal Hospital, a skating-rink was formed about 1875, having an area of about 3,000 square yards, laid with Green and King's patent ice.

At the eastern end of the King's Road is Sloane Square, which, together with Sloane Street and Hans Place, all bear testimony to the memory of the eminent physician, Sir Hans Sloane, of whom we have already had occasion to speak.* In 1712 Sir Hans Sloane bought the manor of Chelsea, to which he retired thirty years later, having resigned his public offices and employments. Thither he removed his museum, and there he received the visits of the royal family and persons of high rank, learned foreigners, and distinguished literary and scientific men; nor did he refuse admittance and advice to either rich or poor who went to consult him respecting their health. At ninety his health began to decline sensibly, and he died here, at the age of ninety-two, in January, 1753.

In the early part of the present century, the houses around Sloane Square were nearly the same in appearance as at the present time; but the square was an open space, simply enclosed with wooden posts, connected by iron chains. Here Queen Charlotte's Royal Volunteers often assembled, and marched off in military order to Hyde Park, headed by their band. On the eastern side of the square, at that time, was the bridge, of which we have already spoken,† called Bloody Bridge. It was about twelve or fourteen feet wide, and had on either side a wall of sufficient height to protect passengers from falling into the narrow rivulet which it spanned, and which belonged to the Commissioners of Sewers. In old records this structure is called "Blandel Bridge;" and it probably received its more sanguinary appellation in consequence of the numerous robberies and murders formerly committed on the spot. In more recent times it has assumed the name of "Grosvenor Bridge," from the extensive adjoining property of the Grosvenors.

In 1812 the Chelsea, Brompton, and Belgrave Dispensary was established in Sloane Square, principally through the great exertions of the Rev. George Clark, the then chaplain of the Royal Military Asylum. The objects of the institution, as officially set forth, are "the relief of sick poor (not paupers), the delivery of married women at their own homes, and attention to diseases of women and children." Mr. William Wilberforce, whose name will be for ever associated with the abolition of slavery, took a leading part in the foundation of the dispensary. The earliest annual average of patients relieved at this admirable institution did not exceed 1,200; the number benefited yearly amounts now to nearly 7,000.

The Royal Court Theatre, in this square, was opened in January, 1871, for the performance of comedies, farces, and the lighter order of dramas. The building, which was originally erected in the year 1818 as a chapel, replaced a theatre at the beginning, and, singularly enough, the chapel has been replaced by a theatre at its close. The station on the Metropolitan District Railway, close

* See Vol. IV., p. 490.

† See p. 21, *ante*.

by, doubtless confers great advantages on the surrounding neighbourhood.

At the beginning of the present century considerable addition was made to the parish of Chelsea by the erection of houses in this direction, and most of the new buildings were called Hans Town. Sloane Street is a long and wide thoroughfare, running from north to south, and connecting Knightsbridge with the west part of Pimlico and the east end of Chelsea. On the east side the houses are made to recede, so as to form three sides of a square, called Cadogan Place, of which we have already spoken.* At the south end of Sloane Street, near the square, is Trinity Church, of which the Rev. Henry Blunt was the first incumbent. The edifice, which was consecrated in 1830, is a brick building of Gothic architecture. The western front consists of a centre, flanked by two wide towers rising to a level with the roof, and terminating with lofty octagonal spires. Sittings are provided for about 1,500 worshippers. Sloane Terrace Wesleyan Chapel, which dates from 1811, is a neat and substantial building, and its erection is attributed to the liberality of several beneficent gentlemen, among whom may be named Mr. Joseph Butterworth, who at that time resided principally at Chelsea.

At No. 72, Sloane Street, lived, for many years, Sir Charles Wentworth Dilke, Bart. In early life Sir Charles was associated with the literary labours of his father, who was the chief proprietor, and at one time editor, of the *Athenæum* newspaper. He was one of the earliest promoters of the first Great Exhibition, and, indeed, took a leading share in the work of the Executive Committee. For the ability he displayed in that capacity, the honour of knighthood was offered to him, at the suggestion of the late Prince Consort. This honour, however, he declined, together with all pecuniary remuneration. Mr. Dilke was likewise associated with the second Industrial Exhibition, as one of the five Royal Commissioners appointed by Her Majesty. Almost immediately after the death of the Prince Consort, Her Majesty was pleased to confer a baronetcy on Mr. Dilke, "in recognition of the Prince's friendship and personal regard for him." Sir Charles was M.P. for the borough of Wallingford for a short time, and died in 1869 at St. Petersburg. His son and successor was

THE "BLACK LION," CHURCH STREET, CHELSEA, IN 1820. (*See page* 90.)

* See p. 13, *ante*.

elected in 1868 as one of the first members for the newly-enfranchised constituency of Chelsea. He is the author of a work on "Greater Britain," and of pamphlets on social and political topics, and a member of the Gladstone ministry.

At No. 31 is the Ladies' Work Society, an institution established for the sale of needlework, embroidery, and other articles, the production of ladies in necessitous circumstances. Its president is her Royal Highness the Princess Louise (Marchioness of Lorne), who herself has designed much of the ornamental work. The institution was established in the year 1871, in North Audley Street, and removed hither in 1875. The members of the society can do their work at home, and send it to Sloane Street for sale—the name of the exhibitors being known only to the ladies who form the committee. An annual subscription of 7s. 6d. constitutes a membership; and when an article is sold at the price set upon it by the exhibitor, a penny in the shilling is deducted towards defraying the necessary expenses of the establishment. In the earlier period of its career the society had a somewhat hard struggle for existence, but it gradually grew in proportion to the publicity given of the good work it was doing, so that now (1876), under its royal patronage and presidency, the number of members, which at first were 200, have increased to 1,000.

No. 103 is the Hans Town School of Industry for Girls. This institution was founded in the year 1804, and its special object is the training of young girls for servants. A sum of two guineas is charged on admission, and the number of children benefited by this institution amounts to about fifty annually.

THE PAVILION, HANS PLACE, IN 1800. (*See page* 99.)

In this street the arch-impostor, Count Cagliostro, was living in the year 1786, when he published his celebrated "Letter to the English People," so cruelly criticised by M. de Morande, the editor of the *Courrier de l'Europe*, and thus defended by himself in the *Public Advertiser*, under date September 3rd, 1786:—"In physics and chemistry, Mr. Joker, arguments go for little and sneers for nothing—experience is all. Permit me, then, to propose a little experiment, which will divert the public, either at your expense or at mine. I invite you to breakfast for the 9th November next, at nine o'clock in the morning: you will furnish the wine and the accessories; I will furnish one dish in my own style—a little sucking pig, fattened according to my method. Two hours before breakfast I will present him to you alive, fat, and healthy. You will engage to have him killed and cooked, and I will not go near him till the moment when he is put on the table; you shall cut him yourself into four pieces, choose that which attracts you the most, and give me any piece you please. The day after this breakfast one of four things will have happened: either we shall be both dead or both alive, or I shall be dead and you alive, or you dead and I alive. Out of these four chances I give you three, and I bet 5,000 guineas that the day after the breakfast you will be dead and I shall be in good health. You will confess that no fairer offer could be made, and that you must either accept the wager or confess your ignorance, and that you have foolishly and dully cut your jokes upon a subject beyond your knowledge." This characteristic letter failed to persuade M. de Morande to breakfast, and he was fain to back out as best he might, getting well laughed at for his pains.

Count Cagliostro—or, to give him his proper name, Joseph Balsamo—used to advertise in the London newspapers that he was prepared to sell "the Egyptian pill of life at thirty shillings a dram;" doubtless about as efficacious as the preparation called "mummy," which was actually dispensed as a curative for sores, by physicians duly provided with diplomas, so late as the reign of Queen Anne. Cagliostro's doings as a quack of quacks took place just after the "diamond necklace" affair; and through the bursting of that bubble he was temporarily "down on his luck." No legal proceedings were taken against him in England, but subsequently he went to Rome, where he was flung into prison by the Inquisition, not, oddly enough, because he was a charlatan—the Piazza Navona and the Corso swarmed every day with vendors of Elixirs of Life and Love—but because he pretended to be a spirit-rapper. A very different state of things prevails at the present day in our own country.

The following story, having reference to this particular street, we give for what it is worth:—"I had invited Porson," says an English author, "to meet a party of friends in Sloane Street, where I lived; but the eccentric professor had mistaken the day, and made his appearance in full costume the preceding one. We had already dined, and were at our cheese. When he discovered his error, he made his usual exclamation of a *whooe!* as long as my arm, and turning to me, with great gravity, said, 'I advise you in future, sir, when you ask your friends to dinner, to ask your wife to write your cards. Sir, your penmanship is abominable; it would disgrace a cobbler. I swear that your day is written Thursday, not Friday,' at the same time pulling the invitation out of his pocket. It turned out, however, that he was wrong, which he was obliged to admit."

Towards the commencement of the century, a considerable part of Sloane Street, between the square and Cadogan Place, was laid out as a botanical garden by a Mr. Salisbury. The extent of the grounds was about six acres, and at one time formed an agreeable promenade for company.

At the corner of Cadogan Place and Lowndes Street is Chelsea House, the town residence of Earl Cadogan, whose family formerly had a mansion on the site of the Royal Military Asylum. The house was rebuilt in 1874, from the designs of Mr. W. Young. The principal entrance, in Cadogan Place, is marked by a tetrastyle portico, which is carried up to the first floor as a bay window; another bay window on the same front is carried up two storeys, and finished with balustrades. The front to Lowndes Street has a semi-octagonal bay at each end, carried up the whole height of the building. The ground storey is of rustic stonework, and at the level of the first floor is a stone balcony carried all round the building. The drawing-room windows, which are well studied in proportion and design, have a most imposing effect. The chief rooms are large and lofty, and the principal staircase is of Sicilian marble.

The manor and estate of Chelsea came into the possession of Lord Cadogan's family on the death of Mr. Hans Sloane by his own hand, Charles, second Lord Cadogan, having married Elizabeth, the daughter and co-heir of Sir Hans Sloane. It may be noted here that Horace Walpole was one of the trustees under Sir Hans Sloane's will.

On the west side of the street, in Cadogan Terrace, is the Roman Catholic Chapel of St. Mary's, an unpretending structure, dating from 1811, and one of the oldest of the missionary chapels of that religion. Not far from the chapel are the convent and schools, together with a Roman Catholic burial-ground, with some large vaults and catacombs. The chapel itself was built by M. Voyaux de Franous, one of the French *émigré* clergy. Before its erection, mass was said in a room above a shop. The Duchess of Angoulême was a generous contributor to the building, and laid the first stone. Dr. Poynter, then Vicar-Apostolic of the London district, officiated at the consecration. Poor as the building was, it cost £6,000. It was specially designed for the use of the French veterans confined at Chelsea. Among the assistant clergy here were Cardinal Weld, the late Bishop of Troy, Dr. Cox, Mgr. Eyre, and Bishop Patterson. St. Mary's Church has been lately improved and enlarged.

In Cadogan Street stood formerly an ancient house, which, in its latter days, was known as the "Marlborough Tavern;" the grounds adjoining were used for the purposes of cricket, &c. It is probable that the house was first established as a tavern during the lifetime of the great Duke of Marlborough, who, it is said, at one time resided in Chelsea, though his house is not identified. Marlborough Road, Blenheim Street, &c.—all contiguous in this neighbourhood—doubtless hence received their names. The old "Admiral Keppel" tavern, with its tea-gardens, in Marlborough Road, was demolished in 1856, and on its site a large inn has been erected.

Hans Place, at the north-west corner, between Sloane Street and Brompton Road, is an irregular octagonal space, laid out after the fashion of a London square. Here (at the house No. 25, according to Mr. Peter Cunningham) was born, in August, 1802, Miss Letitia E. Landon, the "L. E. L." of "Annual" celebrity. She went to school three doors off (No. 22), under a Miss Rowden, the same who numbered amongst her pupils Miss Mary R. Mitford. Miss Landon was the daughter of an army agent, and niece of the late Dr. Whittington Landon, Dean of Exeter and Provost of Worcester College, Oxford, who took a sincere interest in the welfare and fame of his relative. Having had the misfortune to lose her father when very young, and her brilliant talents soon becoming manifest, she appeared before the world, while little more than a child, as an enthusiastic and delightful literary labourer. Her first efforts were made in the pages of the *Literary Gazette*. "To her honour, it must be added," says the editor of the *Athenæum*, "that the fruits of her incessant exertion were neither selfishly hoarded nor foolishly trifled away, but applied to the maintenance and advancement of her family." Hans Place is associated with all the earliest recollections of Miss Landon, whose home it was, in fact, until her marriage, in 1838, with Captain George Maclean, Governor of Cape Coast Castle, on the west coast of Africa. She died in October of the same year, universally beloved on account of her amiable and gifted nature, and as simple as a child. Her poems live, and *will* live.

Mr. and Mrs. Alfred Wigan, the popular actor and actress, resided for some time in Hans Place.

Adjoining Hans Place is the Pavilion, formerly the residence of Lady Charlotte Denys, and now of the Earl of Arran. This building was erected in the latter part of the last century by a Mr. Holland, who had taken from Lord Cadogan a lease of one hundred acres of land hereabouts, formerly called "Blacklands," and now Upper Chelsea, for the purpose of forming new streets, &c. Mr. Holland reserved to himself twenty-one acres of land, on which he erected an elegant house for his own residence. The front of the house was originally built as a model for the Pavilion at Brighton, and was ornamented by a colonnade of the Doric order, extending the whole length of the building. The mansion consisted of three sides of a quadrangle, open to the north, and the approach was from Hans Place. The south front of the house faced an extensive and beautifully-planted lawn, gently rising to the level of the colonnade and principal floor. On the west side of the lawn was an ice-house, round which was erected a representation of the ruins of an ancient "priory," in which the appearance of age and decay is said to have been strikingly reproduced. The Gothic stonework was brought from the ancient but now demolished residence of Cardinal Wolsey, at Esher, in Surrey. The lawn was ornamented by a fine sheet of water, besides which the grounds had about them "considerable variety of fanciful intricate paths and scenery, properly ornamented with shrubs, and had a private communication with the house by the walks of the shrubbery."

On the north side of Hans Place, near to Walton Street, is St. Saviour's Church. It was built about the year 1840, and has no particular pretensions to architectural effect. It has no spire, but two dwarf towers flank the entrance facing Walton Place. The interior is perfectly plain. Deep galleries, supported on octagonal pillars and iron girders, extend round three sides. The pillars supporting the front of the galleries are extended upwards, and from their capitals spring pointed arches along each side. In connection with this church there are some excellent schools and charitable societies.

Close by is Prince's Cricket Ground, which was lately one of the principal centres of attraction and conversation during the London "season." The place has always been a cricket-ground of more or less importance, but more than once of late it has been suggested that it would not be bad to transfer to it the "Eton and Harrow Match" from "Lord's." Besides this, there is every accommodation for lawn-tennis, Badminton, and other games. A few years ago a "skating-rink," with artificial ice, for practice at all seasons of the year, was added to the other attractions of "Prince's;" its career, however, was but of short duration. "Prince's" was always rather select and exclusive, but latterly its exclusiveness increased, the price of admission being raised, and all sorts of stringent regulations being introduced by the committee, in order to keep it "select." So "select" indeed had it become, that a cricketing husband, though an old subscriber, might not take his wife into its precincts, nor could a skating wife introduce her husband, or even her daughter. Nay, further, an edict was issued from the despots of "Prince's"—"That no lady was to be admitted at all unless she has been presented at Court." Of course, therefore, the members became "very select:" no "nobodies" were there; "Lady Clara Vere de Vere" had the skating-rink all to herself, or shared it only with other "daughters of a hundred earls." How delightful! Yes, delightful for Lady Clara and her friend, but not so for the outside public.

The "South Australian" is the sign of a small inn not far from Prince's Grounds. This building tells its own tale, having been put up about the year 1835, when the colony of South Australia was founded, by some one who had a pecuniary interest in it.

CHAPTER IX.

WEST BROMPTON, SOUTH KENSINGTON MUSEUM, &c.

"Uplift a thousand voices, full and sweet,
In this wide hall, with Earth's inventions stored,
And praise th' invisible universal Lord,
Who lets once more in peace the nations meet,
Where Science, Art, and Labour have outpour'd
Their myriad horns of plenty at our feet."—*Tennyson.*

Situation of Brompton—Its Nurseries and Flower-gardens—Cromwell or Hale House—Thistle Grove—The Boltons—Westminster and West London Cemetery—Brompton Hall—St. Michael's Grove—Brompton Grove—John Sidney Hawkins—Gloucester Lodge—The Hospital for Consumption—The Cancer Hospital—Pelham Crescent—Onslow Square—Eagle Lodge—Thurloe Place and Square—Cromwell Road—The International Exhibition of 1862—Annual International Exhibitions—A School of Cookery—Exhibition of Scientific Apparatus—The National Portrait Gallery—The Meyrick Collection of Arms and Armour—The Indian Museum—South Kensington Museum—The Raphael Cartoons—The Sheepshanks, Ellison, and Vernon Galleries—Ancient and Modern Jewellery—The Museum of Patents—The Science and Art Schools—The Royal Albert Hall—The National Training School for Music—Royal Horticultural Gardens—The Fisheries Exhibition.

BROMPTON, which is—or, rather, was till lately—a hamlet to the parish of Kensington, is situated on the north side of Little Chelsea, and on the west of Sloane Street. It has long been celebrated for its soft air, and for its nurseries and flower-gardens; indeed, "Brompton, with its two centuries of nursery-garden fame," writes Mr. John Timbs, "lasted to our times; southward, among 'the groves,' were the 'Florida,' the 'Hoop and Toy,' and other taverns, with tea-gardens attached; there still (1866) remains the 'Swan,' with its bowling-green." At the commencement of the present century the "village" of Brompton was considerably increased by building, and became nominally divided into two parts, termed Old and New Brompton. The latter division of the hamlet chiefly consisted of rows of houses crowded together more closely than was perhaps desirable. "Old Brompton," writes the author of the "Beauties of England and Wales," in 1816, "still retains a similitude of rural aspect, and is yet celebrated for well-cultivated nursery and garden grounds. In this part of the village," continues the writer, "are many handsome detached houses; and here is likewise a domestic building, of comparative antiquity, which requires notice. This is termed Hale House, but is often called Cromwell House, and is traditionally said to have been the residence of Oliver Cromwell. But for such a tradition there appears no sort of authority. Mr. Lysons* shows that this house was the property of the Methwold family during Cromwell's time; and the same writer observes that 'if there are *any* grounds for the tradition, it may be that *Henry* Cromwell occupied the house before he went out to Ireland the second time.' It appears from the register of this parish that 'Mr. Henry Cromwell and Elizabeth Russell' were married on the 10th of May, 1653; and it may be observed that General Lambert, an eminent supporter of the Cromwell family, is known to have possessed a residence near Earl's Court. Hale House is now divided into two parts, each of which is occupied by a separate family. William Methwold, Esq., who died possessed of the above house in 1652, founded, near his residence, an almshouse for six poor women."

Mr. H. G. Davis, writing on the subject of Cromwell House in *Notes and Queries*, gives the

* "Environs of London," vol. ii., p. 507.

following version of the story as that which he had always heard:—"That on some occasion Cromwell's troop was quartered at Knightsbridge, and he one day venturing to stray along the lanes of Brompton, was met by some cavaliers who knew him, and pursued him to this house, where he was sheltered till assistance came from Knightsbridge and liberated him." Faulkner, in his "History of Kensington," describing this house, says: "Over the mantelpiece there is a recess, formed by the curve of the chimney, in which it is said that the Protector used to conceal himself when he visited this house; but why his Highness chose this place for concealment the tradition has not condescended to inform us. This recess is concealed by the wainscot, and is still used as a cupboard." Mr. Faulkner then goes on to state that, though the tradition is "very strong and universal," all documents he has consulted "seem to show that there is not the least foundation for this conjecture;" and presumes "from the marriage of Henry Cromwell having taken place in this parish, that he resided here;" and hence the whole of the story. Mrs. Samuel Carter Hall, mentioning the tradition in her "Pilgrimages to English Shrines," says:—"Upon closer investigation how grieved we have been to discover the truth. . . . We found that Oliver never resided there, but that his son *Richard* had, and *was a ratepayer* to the parish of Kensington some time." Even this latter statement is doubted, for, according to Dr. Rimbault, it is not recorded in the parochial books. Dr. Rimbault, in *Notes and Queries*, states that "the house was known as Hale House in 1596, when a rent-charge of 20s. per annum was laid upon it for the poor of Kensington parish. In 1630 it was purchased by William Methwold, Esq., of the executors of Sir William Blake, who died in that year. This gentleman seems to have been its constant occupant till the period of his death, which occurred in 1652. He is described of Hale House in his will. On May 10, 1653, immediately after his return from Ireland, 'Mr. Henry Cromwell was married to Elizabeth Russell, daughter of Sir Thomas Russell,' at Kensington Church; after which, according to Noble, 'he chiefly resided at Whitehall.' In the following year (1654) he returned to Ireland, and upon his taking leave of that kingdom, he retired to Spinney Abbey, near Soham, in Cambridgeshire, where he died in 1673. The chances of *Henry* Cromwell having resided at Hale House are, therefore, but slender. In 1668 Hale House appears to have been inhabited by the Lawrences, of Shurdington, in Gloucestershire; in 1682 it was in the occupation of Francis Lord Howard of Effingham, the birth of whose son is thus recorded in the parish registers:—'July 7, 1682. The Honble Thomas Howard, son of the R^t^ Honourable Francis, Ld Howard, Baron of Effingham, and the Lady Philadelphia, was born at Hale House, in this parish.' Hale House was still the property of the Methwold family, who, in 1754, sold it to John Fleming, Esq., afterwards created a baronet; and in 1790 it was the joint property of the Earl of Harrington and Sir Richard Worsley, Bart., who married his daughters and co-heirs." Such is the brief history of the proprietors and inhabitants of Cromwell House. It was a pleasant rural seat in 1794, when Edmund Burke's only and beloved son died there of a rapid consumption a few days after his election to Parliament. The father's hopes were blasted by the blow, and his own death followed within two years. The house itself was pulled down about the year 1853, to make room for new improvements. The site of its grounds is now marked by part of Cromwell Road.

Brompton is briefly dispatched by Priscilla Wakefield with the remark that "it is a hamlet to Kensington, and has been much recommended to invalids for the softness of the air." An extensive botanical garden, containing also a botanical library, was established here by a Mr. Curtis, in the reign of George III., and was supported by subscriptions for many years.*

What with its nurseries, its groves, and its pleasant detached mansions or cottages, standing apart in their own grounds, this neighbourhood, down to very recent times, presented much of the appearance of a suburban retreat.

Thistle Grove, a turning out of the Fulham Road, nearly opposite the "Queen's Elm" Hotel, covers the site of what was known a century or more ago as "Brompton Heath." Here lived Mr. John Burke, the author of the "Peerage" and the "Commoners" of England. On the west side of Thistle Grove is "The Boltons," a sort of park, comprising two neat-built rows of houses on either side of an oval-shaped inclosure, in which stands St. Mary's Church, a handsome Gothic edifice.

Further westward is the Westminster and West of London Cemetery. It covers about forty acres of ground, and was consecrated in 1840. It has a domed chapel, with semi-circular colonnades of imposing design. In the grounds is a large monument, consisting of an altar-tomb, with athlete figures, and a pompous epitaph, to the memory of Jackson, the prize-fighter, who kept the "Cock"

* See page 88, *ante*.

Inn, at Sutton, near Epsom, from which he retired with a fortune, having obtained the patronage of George Prince of Wales and many leaders of the sporting world. Sir Roderick Murchison, the eminent geologist, lies buried here.

Brompton Hall, the residence of the great Lord Burleigh, which stood near Earl's Court, is described by Faulkner as retaining at that time (1829) some marks of its ancient splendour. "There was till lately," adds the author, "a grand porch at the entrance. The hall, or saloon, is a step lower than the rooms upon the same floor. The dining-room has a richly-carved ceiling of oak, displaying in the centre the rose and crown, and in its other compartments the fleur-de-lys and portcullis; and on taking down some ancient tapestry a few years since, the arms of Queen Elizabeth, carved in oak, and curiously inlaid with gold, were discovered above the chimney-piece. There are also in another room the relics of a very curious old wainscot, in small compartments."

In St. Michael's Grove lived Douglas Jerrold; and it was in his house that Charles Dickens first made his acquaintance, in or about 1835, when staying at home invalided.

Mr. J. R. Planché was living in Brompton Crescent about the year 1826; and near him, in Brompton Grove (now covered by the houses of Ovington Square), lived William Jerdan, the editor of the *Literary Gazette* in its palmy days. At their houses Mr. T. Crofton Croker, Tom Hood, the Rev. Dr. Croly, Miss Landon (the unfortunate "L. E. L."), used to meet constantly, to discuss the last new play or poem, and literary subjects in general. Jerdan died in June, 1869, at the age of eighty-eight, nearly twenty years after resigning his editorial chair. His Autobiography, published in four volumes, contains many pleasant notices of his contemporaries. In Brompton Grove, too, lived Major Shadwell Clarke, the hospitable friend at whose table Theodore Hook was an ever welcome guest, and where he dined the last time that he ever left his house.

ENTRANCE TO BROMPTON CEMETERY.

In Lower Grove, Brompton, lived and died the antiquary, John Sidney Hawkins, the eldest son of Sir John Hawkins, Dr. Johnson's friend and biographer. He died about the year 1842, at an advanced age. He published several works on architectural subjects.

At Gloucester Lodge, was living, in 1809, George

THE CONSUMPTION HOSPITAL, BROMPTON. (*See page* 104.)

Canning, when he fought the duel with his colleague, Lord Castlereagh, and both before and during his premiership. Mr. Rush, in his "Court of London," gives us many accounts of his official interviews with Mr. Canning here, and also of his dinner parties, at which he met all that was illustrious and brilliant in the society of the time. While residing here too, at a later date, Canning's son, the future Governor-General of India, was born; and here he received several visits from the Princess of Wales, whose cause he so nobly and honourably espoused.

In the Fulham Road, near Pelham Crescent, is the Hospital for Consumption. The original building, on the north side of the road, is a beautiful Elizabethan structure, consisting of a centre and wings, about 200 feet in width. It stands on a square piece of ground, about three acres in extent. The foundation-stone of the hospital was laid by the late Prince Consort in 1841. On the ground floor, the west wing contains physicians' rooms, laboratory, museums, rooms for the resident medical officer and clinical assistants, and servants' hall; and the east wing contains the apartments of the lady superintendent, store-rooms, secretary's office, board-room, &c. The kitchen and sculleries abut on the north side of the central basement corridor, and are built altogether outside the hospital. The first floor is devoted exclusively to female patients, and the second floor to male patients, the total number of beds being 210. The wards, galleries, and corridors are well lighted, and fitted up with every attention to the comfort and convenience of the patients. The chapel, which stands on the north side of the hospital, parallel with the central portion, was founded in 1849 by the Rev. Sir Henry Foulis, Bart., in memory of a near relative. It is approached from the hospital by a corridor, so that the patients may not be exposed to external air in bad weather. It is fitted up with wide cushioned seats for the patients, and is capable of accommodating the whole of the inmates and a few visitors.

In 1879, the first stone of a new extension building of the hospital was laid on the opposite side of the road. It was built mainly from the proceeds of a bequest of Miss Read, and was completed in 1882. This building is constructed of red brick, and is connected with the parent hospital by a subway. It is about 200 feet in length, and 100 feet high, and besides increasing the accommodation to nearly 350 beds, contains a large out-patient department, lecture theatre, &c.

The Hospital receives patients from all parts of the kingdom, and is almost entirely dependent on voluntary contributions, the expenditure being about £10,000 a year more than the fixed annual income.

On the south side of the road is another of those excellent institutions which minister to the most formidable "ills that flesh is heir to." This is the Cancer Hospital. This building, which was founded in 1851, is constructed of plain white Suffolk bricks, relieved with bands of red bricks, and keystones and cornices of terra-cotta. The principal ground floor, approached by a flight of steps, contains the hall and a handsome stone staircase, apartments for the house surgeon and medical officers, and wards for patients. Apparatus for heating and ventilating the building is provided—everything, in short, that is calculated to add to the comforts and assist the recovery of the patients. The Archbishop of Canterbury, preaching on behalf of the funds of this hospital, observed, "There is no disease more pitiable than that to which this institution is specially devoted. This, therefore, is a case in which I may justly ask your liberal contributions." Chelsea Hospital for Women, a handsome red-brick building in the Fulham Road, was built in 1880.

Large property round about this neighbourhood belongs to Lord Onslow's family; Onslow Square is so named in consequence, and Cranley Place is so called after the second title of Lord Onslow.

In Pelham Crescent died, in 1869, aged seventy-four, Mr. Robert Keeley, the comic actor. Hard by, in Onslow Square, at No. 36, Thackeray was living in 1858, when he stood his unsuccessful contest for Oxford city, and when he commenced the editorship of the *Cornhill Magazine.*

Eagle Lodge was at one time tenanted by Mr. Bunn, so well known as the lessee of Drury Lane Theatre. Here he used to entertain Malibran, Thalberg, De Beriot, Mr. J. R. Planché, and other friends of music and the drama.

Thurloe Place and Thurloe Square, near the junction of the Fulham, Cromwell, and Brompton Roads, are of too modern a growth to have any historic associations. Cromwell Road, a long and open thoroughfare, extending from Thurloe Square westward to Earl's Court, was doubtless so named after the Cromwellian associations connected with the neighbourhood, as described above. At the eastern end of the road, a considerable space of ground lying between it and the gardens of the Royal Horticultural Society, was the site of the International Exhibition of 1862. The site was purchased by the Royal Commissioners of the Exhibition of 1851, with a portion of the surplus money arising from the receipts of that exhibition. The edifice, which was altogether different from its predecessor in Hyde Park, was built from the designs of Captain Fowke, R.E. It was constructed chiefly of brick, and the ground plan in its general form was that of the letter L, the short limb being the annexe for the machinery in motion. It consisted of a nave and two transepts, each point of intersection at the extremities of the nave being marked by a polygonal hall, surmounted by an immense dome. The southern façade ran along the Cromwell Road, and the building had also a frontage on the east in the Exhibition Road, and on the west in Prince Albert's Road (now Queen's Gate). Between this and the Horticultural Society's boundary was a semi-detached portion of the building, comprising the departments for implements and machinery in motion, extending over an entrance by a covered way or bridge, so that this section was kept entirely separate from the main body of the building. Its entire length was only about 1,150 feet, or 700 feet shorter than its crystal prototype in Hyde Park. The external appearance of the structure was not very striking. It was massive; but its unbroken length left a feeling of painful monotony on the observer, which the enormous domes at either end, 260 feet in height and 160 feet in diameter, failed to vary. Almost in the centre of this mass of brickwork was the grand entrance or portico, built according to an Italian plan. The picture-galleries occupied the first compartment in the front portion of the building, facing the Cromwell Road, and were two in number; they were lighted by clerestory windows in the roof, and formed perhaps the most attractive feature of the Exhibition. The basement storey of this part of the building was devoted to the exhibition of carriages, carts, and other descriptions of road vehicles. Adjoining the picture-gallery, but on the ground floor, was a large space, upwards of 1,000 feet in length, glazed from end to end, which was devoted to manufactures and art productions from every country in the world. Advancing across this court, the nave was reached; this extended the whole length of the building, and was 80 feet in width, or eight feet wider than that of the Crystal Palace of 1851. The nave was 100 feet high, and was crossed at its extremities by two transepts, each 692 feet long by 85 feet in width, and 100 feet high, resembling the nave in the last two respects. At each of the points of their intersection with the nave, rose octagonal halls 160 feet in diameter, each surmounted by a magnificent glass dome 200 feet in height internally, and 250 feet externally, reaching to the top of the pinnacle. These were the largest domes ever built; St. Paul's being only 108 feet in diameter at the base, St. Peter's at Rome being 139 feet, and that of the British Museum reading-room 140 feet. The floors of these dome-covered halls being raised sixteen feet above the floor of the rest of the nave and transepts, afforded an admirable opportunity to the spectator for taking in grand views of the main lines of the building. The extreme ends of the building presented an extraordinary and beautiful appearance when viewed from the floors of these halls. At the angles of these halls were staircases, communicating with the galleries of the main building. On the side walls beneath the roof of the nave and transept were the clerestory windows, twenty-five feet high, of iron and glass, very light and elegant, which, together with the light from the glass domes, brought out in soft relief the architectural and artistic decorations. The nave and transepts were roofed in with wood, coated with felt, meeting in an angle at the centre; this roof was supported by semi-circular arches of timber, springing from iron columns, in pairs, by which the roof was supported at a height of sixty feet from the floor. A very pleasing effect was produced by the combination of the circular ribs and the angular girders carrying the roof; these double columns, girders and ribs, were repeated sixteen times in the nave, and their decorations produced fine polychromatic effects. The *coup d'œil* standing under either of the domes, and looking down the nave, was one of unequalled beauty; the fine proportions of the columns made the immense vista appear as if looking along a kind of iron lace-work. The columns supported on each side of the nave galleries fifty feet in width, one side commanding a view of the nave, and the other looking upon the industrial courts on the ground floor.

The principal entrance, in the Exhibition Road, was situated in the centre of the eastern transept, and led directly to the orchestra erected for the opening ceremony, under the eastern dome, which took place on the 1st of May, 1862. Space will not permit us to do more than notice a few of the most important objects here brought together. In the centre of the nave stood a trophy of small arms by the Birmingham gunmakers, flanked on either side by an Armstrong and a Whitworth gun. The Armstrong was mounted on its carriage of polished wood, and presented in every detail the delicate finish of a trinket. Indeed, the Exhibition seems to have been rich in the display of these marvellous weapons. Elaborate fountains and trophies of a more peaceful kind—such as articles of food, and animal and vegetable substances employed in manufacture, together with others of different manufactured articles—made up the miscellaneous collection. Dividing the British from the foreign portion of the nave was a huge screen in iron-work of elaborate design. At this end of the nave were some noble groups of bronze statues from various countries, and some magnificent candelabra and columns in polished jasper and porphyry from Russia. A very fine collection of Berlin porcelain manufactures was placed on raised counters under the western dome. Sèvres, Vienna, Berlin, and Dresden made great efforts to recover their lost ground in their previous competitions with the English porcelain manufacturers. The attractions of the western dome balanced very fairly the features of interest at the other end of the building. The central object was a circular stand, displaying the Prince of Prussia's collection of China, all of Berlin manufacture, which rivals the richest and most delicate Sèvres. An adjacent parterre was appropriated to the exhibition of the silver objects presented by the City of Berlin to the Princess of Prussia as a wedding gift. The great Koh-i-noor diamond was placed in the English portion of the nave near the jewellery classes, and created, doubtless, as much interest as it occasioned in 1851. Her Majesty's magnificent dessert service of Worcester porcelain was exhibited near here: it is said to eclipse the finest specimen that Sèvres, Dresden, or Vienna have yet produced.

That this second International Exhibition was a success no one will pretend to say; it is enough to admit that with the first great gathering in 1851 the charm of novelty was worn off, and that even the lapse of eleven years was not sufficient to cause a repetition of that great influx of visitors to London from every part of the civilised world, which we have already noticed.

Although the building was so substantially constructed, it was not destined to remain standing in its entirety long after the closing of the Exhibition in October. Piece by piece it gradually disappeared, till only the inner portion, which had served chiefly as refreshment departments, overlooking the gardens, was left; and this part has since been made to serve various purposes.

In 1870 it was announced that a series of annual International Exhibitions should be held here, commencing from the following year (1871), under the direction of Her Majesty's Commissioners for the Exhibition of 1851. Hitherto, as we learn from the official announcement of this series of exhibitions, the exhibition of works of Fine Art had been too much limited to the display of pictures and sculpture, dissociated from purposes of utility; and it might be doubted whether a picture on enamel or on pottery, destined to be applied to a piece of furniture, or a sculpture in wood intended for a picture-frame, however great its merits, would find any place in the Exhibitions of the Royal Academy of London, or in any of the numerous other exhibitions of the works of artists. Still less would a Cashmere shawl or a Persian carpet, the chief excellence of which depended upon its combination of colours, find in any of these exhibitions its proper place. Such a complete separation of artistic work from objects of utility might indeed be said to be only the characteristic of modern times; for in the ancient and mediæval periods the highest art is to be found in alliance with the meanest materials of manufacture. The Etruscans painted on vases of clay subjects which still charm us by their beauty of composition and skilful drawing; and the finest works of Raffaele were designed as decorations for hangings to be made of wool. It was intended that these exhibitions should furnish the opportunity of stimulating the revival of the application of the artist's talents to give beauty and refinement to every description of objects of utility, whether domestic or monumental. In these annual Exhibitions it was contended that every work in which Fine Art is a dominant feature would find proper provision made for its display. Painting, on whatever surface, or in any method; sculpture in every description of material, engravings of all kinds, architectural design as a Fine Art, every description of textile fabric of which Fine Art is a characteristic feature—in short, every work, whether of utility or pleasure, which is entitled to be considered a work of excellence from the artistic point of view, might be displayed in the exhibitions under the division of Fine Art. The industrial portion of these exhibitions was to be confined to educational works and appliances, and new inventions and scientific discoveries. Every artist-workman, moreover, it was stated, would be able to exhibit a work of merit as his own production, and every manufacturer might distinguish himself as a patron of art by his alliance with the artistic talent of the country. In the Fine Art section the artist might exhibit a vase for its beauty of painting, or form, or artistic invention; whilst a similar vase might appear in its appropriate place among manufactures on account of its cheapness, or the novelty of its material.

It was arranged that these annual Exhibitions should take place in permanent buildings erected on either side of the Horticultural Gardens, connecting that part of the building of 1862 which remained standing with a new and lofty structure, on the north side of the gardens, called the Royal

Albert Hall, of which we shall have more to say presently. On the south side of the Albert Hall, and facing the gardens, is the splendid conservatory of the Royal Horticultural Society, and at each end are long curved arcades, named respectively the East and West Quadrants. Flanking these, and enclosing the gardens, are the buildings in which the principal part of the Exhibition was held. They consist of lower and upper galleries, about 550 feet long and twenty feet wide, with corridors open to the gardens. The lower storeys have side lights; the upper are lighted from the roof. The whole of the Exhibition buildings are in the Decorated Italian style, and harmonise well with the adjacent South Kensington Museum. The mouldings, cornices, and courses are in light-coloured terra-cotta, and red brick is the material used in the construction.

The first of these annual Exhibitions was held in 1871, and in addition to the two permanent features mentioned above, included woollen and worsted manufactures, pottery, and educational apparatus. These were replaced in 1872 by cotton and cotton fabrics; jewellery, including articles worn as personal ornaments, made of precious metals, precious stones, or their imitations; musical instruments of all kinds; acoustic apparatus and experiments; paper, stationery and printing. These various classes comprised also the raw materials, machinery, and processes used in their production.

The third Exhibition of the series, held in 1873, comprehended several classes of subjects not included in the displays of the two previous years. The fine arts, scientific inventions and discoveries, and galleries of painting and sculpture by British and foreign artists, continued as special features of the Exhibition, as before; but this year visitors were enabled to add to the knowledge they had gained of the processes employed in one great department of the textile manufactures which forms so important a part of our national industry, an acquaintance with the mode of producing the beautiful fabrics silk and velvet. Cutlery and edged tools, for which this country has been famous for centuries, were exhibited, Fine-art furniture and decorative work, and stained glass—not entirely absent from the previous Exhibitions, but appearing there in a subordinate position—had now more justice afforded to their claims on our attention.

One novel feature in the Exhibition of 1873 was a School of Cookery, where lectures were delivered and admirably illustrated by the practical experiments of neat-handed cooks. Ladies, naturally, formed a large portion of the audience, and Her Majesty and other members of the Royal Family did not fail to give the sanction of their presence to these novel lectures. The building used for these lectures was subsequently placed at the service of the National Training School for Cookery, by whom the work has since been carried on.

The manufactures selected for the fourth Exhibition, which was opened in the year 1874, were lace, the show of which was magnificent; civil engineering, architecture, and building, including sanitary apparatus and constructions on the one hand, and decorative work on the other; heating by all methods and every kind of fuel, selected in consequence of the high price of coal and the necessity for teaching economy in the combustion of fuel; leather and saddlery, harness, and other articles made of leather; bookbinding; and foreign wines.

Whether these Annual International Exhibitions were successful or not in imparting that knowledge as to the *best* means employed in various arts and trades, and the *best* results achieved, we will not pretend to say. They were not, however, sufficiently attractive to the masses of the people to warrant their continuance year after year, and with the Exhibition of 1874 the series terminated, and the various buildings were set apart for other purposes. In one series of rooms is the National Portrait Gallery, which was originally established in Great George Street, Westminster, in 1859. It is a most interesting collection, from an artistic as well as an historic point of view, and embraces the "counterfeit presentment" of many of England's greatest worthies, whether as sovereigns, statesmen, warriors, poets, authors, &c. Here are the famous Chandos portrait of Shakespeare, several of Queen Elizabeth, and between four and five hundred likenesses of some of the most remarkable men and women in English history, many of them executed by the first painters of the periods. Besides the portraits, there are a few highly interesting casts of effigies from monuments in Westminster Abbey, Canterbury Cathedral, and other places; and also an interesting collection of autographs.

In 1868 was deposited in the building the Meyrick collection of arms and armour, from Goodrich Court, Herefordshire, formed by the late Sir Samuel Meyrick, the author of "A Critical Inquiry into Ancient Armour," and lent to the Museum by its then owner, Colonel Meyrick. It was arranged for exhibition here by Mr. J. R. Planché. The collection of naval models, and of the munitions of war, lent by the War Department, and on view here, contains examples of British ship-building, from the earliest period down to the construction of the turret-ship of the ill-fated Captain Coles.

That portion of the Exhibition galleries overlooking the gardens on the eastern side was made, in 1875, the receptacle of the India Museum. This collection of objects was originally formed by the East India Company, and after its removal from Leadenhall Street, was for a time stowed away in Whitehall Yard, and in various cellars and warerooms, and in the topmost storey of the new India Office. In these rooms were deposited for exhibition the numerous costly presents brought from India by the Prince of Wales after his tour in that country in 1875-6.

In 1881 a portion of the buildings on this side the Horticultural Gardens was taken as the site of the Central Institution of the City and Guilds of London, for the purposes of technical education, and to serve as a focus for uniting the different technical schools in the metropolis already in existence, and as a central establishment also to which promising students from the provinces may, by the aid of scholarships, be brought to benefit by the superior instruction which London can command.

The site of the main portion of the Exhibition Buildings is now occupied by the Museum of Natural History, which was erected to contain the Natural History collections hitherto preserved in the British Museum, where the accommodation for many years past had become too restricted, and the necessity for a larger building keenly felt. The new museum, built from the designs of Mr. A. Waterhouse, fronts the Cromwell Road, and is about 650 feet in length. It is constructed of brick, faced with terra-cotta, of a highly ornamental character, and consists of three storeys, in addition to the basement. The main part of the building has a tower at each end, and there are also two central towers rising on either side of the entrance. The Mineralogical, Botanical, and Geological collections were removed hither from the British Museum in 1881, and have since been followed by the Zoological specimens.

THE INTERNATIONAL EXHIBITION OF 1862.

On the eastern side of the Exhibition Road, and with its principal entrance in Cromwell Road, is the South Kensington Museum, together with the various Science and Art Schools which have been established, under Government, in connection therewith.

This Museum, which now contains upwards of 20,000 rare and choice examples of mediæval and

THE COURT OF THE SOUTH KENSINGTON MUSEUM.

202

Modern Art workmanship, originated in the year 1852 with a small collection, exhibited in Marlborough House in connection with the Schools of Art. In 1857 the collection was transferred hither to some temporary iron buildings which had been erected for its reception, which, from their material, and from some peculiarities of construction, became popularly known as the "Brompton Boilers." These temporary buildings have been gradually replaced by a permanent edifice. From the year 1853 the Museum has included objects contributed on loan by private owners. In 1862—the year of the second International Exhibition—a special "loan exhibition" of works, chiefly of Mediæval and Renaissance Art, was held here; and since that time the number of objects on loan has always been considerable. By this means very many of the rarest and most precious examples of art workmanship in this country have been generously permitted by their owners to be seen and leisurely studied by the public. In addition to the "loans," many objects have been acquired by purchase, gift, and bequest; besides which are reproductions, by the electrotype process and in plaster, of objects in other collections which have been judged to be of special interest and value to the art student.

The plan of the Museum is somewhat irregular, and covers a large space of ground—about twelve acres in extent—acquired by the Government, at a cost of £60,000, being a portion of the estate purchased by Her Majesty's Commissioners for the Exhibition of 1851, out of the surplus proceeds of that undertaking. The buildings, with their courts and galleries, are constructed chiefly of brick, somewhat profusely ornamented with terra-cotta, and were built from the designs of Captain Fowke, R.E. The art collections are chiefly contained in three large courts and a long range of cloisters on the ground floor; but many rare and valuable objects are shown in the picture-galleries, and also in what is called the Prince Consort Gallery. The visitor, on entering the Museum from the Cromwell Road, passes through a corridor to the New or Architectural Court. This is divided by a central passage and gallery. The majority of the objects it contains are full-size reproductions (in plaster) of architectural works of large dimensions designed for erection in the open air, or in large halls or churches, including the famous Trajan Column at Rome, and the "'Prentice Pillar" in Roslin Chapel, Scotland; there is also a full-size copy (by photography) of the Bayeux Tapestry, coloured in imitation of the original needlework.

From this Court we enter the South Court, a lofty and spacious building, surrounded with galleries, and rich in ornamentation. The upper portion of the walls is divided into thirty-six alcoves, (eighteen on either side), containing portraits, in mosaic, of eminent men of all ages connected with the arts, especially those who have been distinguished as ornamentalists, or as workers in bronze, marble, or pottery. These portraits, which include such men as Phidias, the sculptor of the Elgin marbles, William of Wykeham, Donatello, Torrigiano, Albert Dürer, Michael Angelo, Titian, Hogarth, Sir Joshua Reynolds, and Mulready, are from designs by some of the first artists of the day. This court is divided into two parts by a broad passage which crosses it, above which is the Prince Consort Gallery above mentioned. It would be impossible to give, within the limits at our disposal, a list of the various objects here exhibited, and indeed such a task would be needless, as they are all detailed in the various catalogues sold at the Museum; suffice it to say that here are deposited the numerous and costly objects comprising the "Loan Collections," together with a miscellaneous assortment of art manufactures. The "Oriental Courts," appropriately decorated by Mr. Owen Jones, contain some examples of the art workmanship of the East Indies, China, Japan, Persia, &c.

The North Court is specially appropriated to the exhibition of Italian sculpture, and architectural models and casts. Many of the most beautiful of these objects are, so to speak, incorporated into the building, the decoration of which is much simpler than that of the South Court. In the east arcade of this court are some textile or woven fabrics, of European origin, including several ecclesiastical vestments and rare fragments of mediæval embroidery. Through the windows of the north arcade is seen the "fernery," which was designed to enable the students in training as art-teachers to draw from plants at all seasons. A considerable portion of the west arcade forms the reading-room of the Art Library. The staircase leading to the galleries is lighted by a large stained-glass window, the subject of which was suggested by a passage in Ecclesiasticus, chapter xxxviii., descriptive of trades. The keramic, or pottery gallery, contains a large collection of Wedgwood's jasper and other wares, and also examples of the porcelain of Bow, Chelsea, Bristol, Plymouth, Worcester, and Derby. Here, too, are represented the great manufacturers of pottery of the present day in Italy, France, and England. The next gallery into which the visitor passes contains a collection of Venetian, German, and other ancient glass vessels. In the Prince

Consort Gallery are placed many of the most interesting and costly possessions of the Museum, in enamel, gold, and silversmith's work, jewellery, watches, clocks, &c. The South Gallery, which we now enter, is filled with cases containing examples of ancient and mediæval ivories. The gallery of the Architectural Court is devoted to examples of art iron-work. From an arched opening at the north end of the Prince Consort Gallery a view of the North Court is obtained. The balcony here is the Singing Gallery from Florence. To the right is the grand fresco of the Industrial Arts as applied to War, by Sir Frederick Leighton, P.R.A. It is a lunette, thirty-five feet long at the base and sixteen feet high. "The scene," observes a writer in the *Athenæum*, "is the entrance to a town or fortress of Italian Gothic architecture; and the figures wear those Italian costumes of the fourteenth century which are dear to artists in designs of the Early Renaissance. The effect of brilliant open daylight has been rendered with peculiar splendour; the colouration is vivid and in a bright, pure key; the treatment is at once severe and elegant, decorative, and monumental, without achaism and without those Mantegnesque affectations of which we have seen much of late. The composition of the figures, not less than that of the chiaroscuro, general colouring, and light and shade, is architectonic; the lines throughout and the arrangement of the groups are adapted to the pedimental form of the lunette; even the shadow of the overhanging arch has been considered in the disposition of the white clouds and buildings in the distance." The companion subject, The Industrial Arts as applied to Peace, is destined to fill the corresponding space on the other side of the north end of the South Court.

Three staircases in different parts of the building lead to the Picture Galleries, which are above the cloisters of the North and South Courts. Several rooms or galleries are devoted to the National Collection of Pictures by British artists. Critical notices of many of the paintings here exhibited will be found in Redgrave's "Century of British Art." In the north gallery are hung the Raphael cartoons. From the authorised "Guide to the Museum" we glean the following particulars concerning these celebrated productions. They are drawn with chalk upon strong paper, and coloured in distemper, and are the original designs, executed by Raphael and his scholars for Pope Leo X., in the year 1513, as copies for tapestry work. Each cartoon is about twelve feet high. They were originally ten, but three are lost—viz., "The Stoning of St. Stephen," the "Conversion of St. Paul," and "St. Paul in his Dungeon at Philippi." A copy in tapestry of Christ's "Charge to Peter" is hung opposite the original cartoon; and also a tapestry from the Imperial manufactory, the Gobelins, at Paris, a copy of the "Holy Family" by Raphael in the Louvre.

The tapestries, worked in wool, silk, and gold, were hung in the Sistine Chapel at Rome in the year 1519, the year before Raphael died. These are now in the Vatican.

The cartoons remained neglected in the warehouse of the manufacturer at Arras, and were seen there by Rubens, who advised Charles I. to purchase them for the use of a tapestry manufactory which was then established at Mortlake. On the death of Charles I., Cromwell bought them for £300 for the nation. They remained for a long time in a lumber-room at Whitehall, till, by command of William III., Sir Christopher Wren erected a room for them at Hampton Court, in which they hung till Her Majesty permitted them to be removed hither.

Passing through the door at the east end of the gallery, we enter the rooms containing the Sheepshanks' Collection of Paintings. A bust, by Foley, of the late John Sheepshanks, the donor of the pictures, has been placed in this gallery by Miss Sheepshanks. The south-eastern gallery contains the Jones Collection of furniture, Sèvres, and other porcelain, enamelled miniatures, paintings, sculpture, bronzes, &c. It was bequeathed to the Museum in 1882 by Mr. John Jones, of Piccadilly. In five rooms at the south end of the Western Galleries are placed the Dyce and Forster collections. The former collection, bequeathed to the Museum by the Rev. Alexander Dyce, the eminent scholar and editor of Shakespeare, consists of oil paintings, miniatures, drawings, engravings, &c., a few manuscripts, and a library containing upwards of 11,000 volumes. The Forster collection, bequeathed to the Museum in 1876, by Mr. John Forster, the friend and biographer of Charles Dickens, consists of oil and water-colour paintings, drawings, manuscripts, autographs, and a library of 18,000 volumes. Oliver Goldsmith's chair, desk, and walking-cane, bequeathed by Goldsmith to his friend Dr. Hawes, and given to the Museum by Lady Hawes, are exhibited in this gallery. A painting by Maclise, representing "Caxton's Printing-office in the Almonry at Westminster," was bequeathed by Mr. Forster to Lord Lytton, and has been lent by his lordship to the Museum.

The reading-room for the Dyce and Forster libraries is open from 10 a.m. till 5 p.m. daily.

The Historical Collection of British Water-colour Drawings, exhibited in two rooms facing the head of the staircase, is for the most part composed of the gifts of Mrs. Ellison, of Sudbrooke Holme, Lincolnshire, Mr. William Smith, Mrs. Tatlock, Miss Twining, Mr. C. T. Maud, the bequests of the Rev. C. H. Townshend and Mr. J. M. Parsons; examples of Gainsborough, Rooker, Barret, Gilpin, De Loutherbourg, Sandby, Payne, Dayes, Rowlandson, Cerres, and Cipriani; and on a screen several original sketches by the late John Leech.

The Museum of Patents, adjoining the South Court, is a collection illustrative of the progress of national invention, and contains not only models, but several original machines which have been the means of developing our prosperity, and have given new life to the world. As examples may be mentioned the first steam-engine to which James Watt applied his condenser; the first locomotive, "Puffing Billy," and its successor, George Stephenson's "Rocket;" the first engine ever used in steam navigation, the first Bramah's press, and many other pieces of mechanism of not less historical value.

On the west side of the main buildings of the Museum, facing the Exhibition Road, is a large edifice, containing class-rooms for instruction in various branches of science. This structure was built on the site of the "International Bazaar," a building which was constructed in 1862, and filled with a choice selection of works by persons whose application for space in the Exhibition could not be complied with. The Art Schools extend along the north side of the Museum, and have separate apartments for male and female students.

The Science and Art Department is a division of the Education Department, under the direction of the Lord President of the Council and the Vice-President of the Committee of Council on Education. It was established in 1852. A sum of money is voted annually by Parliament, in aid of local efforts to promote science and art applied to productive industry, such efforts originating with the localities. Payments are made upon results of instruction in science and art, as tested by examination by properly-appointed officials. The National Art Training School was established for the purpose of training art-masters and mistresses for the United Kingdom, and for the instruction of students in designing, &c., to which male and female students are admitted when properly qualified, receiving an allowance in aid of their maintenance, which is proportioned to their attainments, and to their qualification for the duties of teaching required from them. When such students have obtained certificates of qualification, they may be appointed teachers to the local Schools of Art throughout the United Kingdom. The object of the Science Schools and Classes is to promote instruction in science, especially among the industrial classes, in such subjects as Mathematics, Geometry, Naval Architecture, Mechanics, Chemistry, Botany, and the like. The assistance granted by the Science and Art Department to that end is in the form of public examinations, in which Queen's medals and Queen's prizes are awarded; payments on the results of examination and on attendance; scholarships and exhibitions; building grants; grants towards the purchase of apparatus, &c., and supplementary grants in certain subjects; and special aid to teachers and students. The sum voted by Parliament, for the year 1882-3, for the Science and Art Department, amounted to nearly £351,400. The department, it may be added, has the advantage of the services of gentlemen of the highest standing in their several professions, as examiners both for Science and Art Schools, and as official referees for the purchases made for the collections.

The Royal Albert Hall of Arts and Sciences, to which we now pass, owes its origin to the fund, which was raised in 1862, for the purpose of erecting in Hyde Park the national memorial to the late Prince Consort, which we have already described. With every desire that this recognition of the debt which English art, science, and industry owed to the Prince should be, in every sense of the word, such a memorial as the country itself preferred, the Queen requested a committee of gentlemen to suggest the form which the testimonial should assume. After deliberating upon the matter, the committee recommended the erection of a personal memorial to the Prince Consort in Hyde Park, opposite to what was best known as the Central Hall of Arts and Sciences. Naturally enough, it was expected that large subscriptions would flow in towards the object in view. These expectations were not fully realised, the amount subscribed at that period being less than £70,000. To this sum Parliament added £50,000; and with the £120,000 thus obtained it was resolved to place in Hyde Park the monument of which we have spoken. Further efforts were yet to be made, and in these the Prince of Wales took the initiative. In the year 1865 the Prince of Wales called together a number of gentlemen, who were asked and consented to become vice-patrons of the proposed memorial building. A statement of the intentions of the promoters of the undertaking was issued: the Royal Commissioners of the Exhibition of

1851 gave three acres of land as a site for the building, at the nominal rent of 1s. a year, on a long lease, and subscriptions came in towards the much-cherished object. A provisional committee, consisting of twelve members, was formed, of which the Prince of Wales was president. They held several meetings at Marlborough House; £110,000 was soon subscribed; and there was every prospect of the intentions of the committee being quickly realised, when a sudden stop was put to the efforts of the promoters by the memorable panic of 1866. For a while all further proceedings ceased. In the plans of the proposed hall provision was made for a certain number of sittings; and at the beginning of the year 1867 Messrs. Lucas, the great contractors, came forward, and consented to purchase sittings valued at £38,000, on the understanding that they should receive the contract for the building, the total cost of which was not to exceed £200,000. These terms were agreed to by the provisional committee; the public nobly came forward and subscribed £112,000, the Royal Commissioners of the 1851 Exhibition gave £50,000, Messrs. Lucas' proposition was worth £38,000; and on the 20th of May, 1867, the Queen laid the foundation-stone of the building, the original plans for which came from the late Captain Fowke, R.E.; Colonel Scott, R.E., being the architect. From that time the scheme was successful. A pardonable degree of curiosity was aroused respecting the ultimate destiny of the hall; but this was set aside when it was announced that the new building was intended, amongst other things, to accommodate science congresses, to provide a suitable arena for musical performances, and to serve other equally useful artistic and scientific purposes. For this the building is admirably adapted, from the immense disposable space it offers. Between 6,000 and 7,000 persons can be seated in the hall, and besides this, when the necessity arises, it is possible to place as many as 2,000 spectators in comfortable positions on an inclined staging in the picture-gallery, which runs nearly round the hall.

Guided by the principles upon which the Romans constructed those amphitheatric buildings, the remains of which strike modern spectators with awe and admiration, the designers of the Albert Hall have succeeded in raising a structure of eminently beautiful and attractive proportions. Seen from the Park or the Kensington Road, the hall stands boldly out in all the magnificence which invests a building in the style of Italian Renaissance. The base is of plain red brick, with single-headed windows, the keystone of which is formed of the crown and cushion and the letter "V.," above which the principal floor is divided by terra-cotta pilasters, between which are semicircular-headed windows. An idea of the vast character of the building may be obtained from the knowledge that 70,000 blocks of terra-cotta were used in its construction. The frieze, which is about 800 feet long and about 6 feet wide, was made in sections of 50 feet, of encaustic *tesseræ*, by Messrs. Minton and Co., who employed in its working the female students of the School of Art at Kensington. Above these is the entablature, having a widely-projecting balcony four feet across. Surrounding the building, and high above the balcony, is mosaic work, representing various allegories descriptive of the arts, commerce, and manufactures. These mosaics are from the designs of Messrs. Horsley, Armitage, Yeames, Marks, Poynter, Pickersgill, and Armstead. Round the frieze of the building runs the following inscription in large letters:—"This hall was erected for the advancement of the arts and sciences, and for the works of industry of all nations, in fulfilment of the intentions of Albert, Prince Consort. The site was purchased by the proceeds of the Great Exhibition of the year 1851. The first stone of the hall was laid by Her Majesty Queen Victoria, on the 20th day of May, 1867, and it was opened by Her Majesty the Queen, on the 29th day of March, in the year 1871."

Above the frieze, in terra-cotta, in letters a foot high, is the sacred text: "Thine, O Lord, is the greatness, and the power, and the glory, and the victory, and the majesty: for all that is in the heaven and in the earth is Thine. The wise and their works are in the hand of God. Glory be to God on high, and on earth peace."

In the plan of the interior, it can be seen at once that the architect has taken for his model the old Roman amphitheatre, though with such important modifications as, happily, quite another kind of entertainment, and, unhappily, less genial skies, required. Roman plebeians and aristocrats were mere spectators, looking down on the fierce and bloody spectacles provided for their amusement in the arena. Here it was necessary so to provide that people might both hear and see, but above all things hear. Such a condition gives the key to the arrangement of the interior. Imagine, then, within an outer shell of staircases, corridors, refreshment and retiring rooms, a vast hall, in shape of a graceful oval, of which the southern end is all but filled by the organ and an orchestra rising upwards in tiers of seats. Fronting this orchestra is the auditorium, of horse-shoe form, composed of arena, a level space; the amphitheatre, or, as it might be better termed, the stalls, sloping upwards towards the boxes; three tiers of boxes; above them the balcony; and lastly, above it, what is called the picture-gallery. This gallery is not within the proper limits of the ellipse forming the interior, but is built over the staircases and corridors which form an outer zone to the portions of the auditorium below. It runs, therefore, round the whole of the interior; and the thirty Italian arches, with their scagliola pillars, through which the body of the hall is seen, are really its great ornament.

The boxes and balcony project from the wall into the ellipse, each tier extending three feet beyond that above it. Such an arrangement enables the occupants of each tier to see without much difficulty, and be seen by those above them. One of the most remarkable features of the hall, in fact, is the perfect view of the interior, and of all within it, which can be had from any point. The boxes and stalls were taken by subscription. One of the latter, comprising the right to a revolving chair, like a music stool with arms, in the amphitheatre, cost £100; a *loggia* box, holding eight persons, £800; a box on the grand tier, with ten places, £1,000; and one with five places on the second tier, £500. Thus the unit of £100 is taken as the cost per seat in each case. The subscription season is rather a long one—999 years.

One of the most striking features in the interior is the organ, which stands in the centre of the orchestra, supported by a framework of the lightest and simplest kind, itself its only ornament. It is said to be the largest organ in the world, and was constructed by Mr. Henry Willis, the builder of the organ at St. George's Hall, Liverpool. Some idea of the size of the instrument may be formed when we say that it contains about 120 registers, about 8,000 pipes, distributed over four manuals and a pedal organ. The pipes vary in length from about thirty-four feet to three-quarters of an inch. The only organ in England which approaches it in size is that at the Alexandra Palace, built by the same maker; and it is about double the size of the fine organ of St. Paul's Cathedral. In this

THE HORTICULTURAL GARDENS AND EXHIBITION BUILDING.

organ the builder, for the first time, made use of pneumatic tubes for the connection of the manuals and pedals with pipes at a distance, instead of the old long tracker movement; and it is probable that this invention will, in the course of time, cause important changes in the construction of such gigantic instruments. With its vistas of polished pipes of all sizes, some of them gleaming like silver, the organ arrests the eye at once on entering the building; and when one hears that the motive power is supplied by two steam-engines, one might be led to expect such a volume of sound as would almost blow the roof off.

The lighting of the hall is a novelty in itself. Thirty gold-coloured chandeliers, one in each arch, surround the picture-gallery, each having fifteen lights. There is a third ring of sixty chandeliers, with twenty-one lights each; and altogether there are nearly 7,000 gas jets, which can all be lit by electricity in ten seconds.

The spaces over the porches on the east and west sides of the hall have been in each case arranged as a lecture theatre, having a raised floor, with a platform or stage, and holding about 200 people. At its widest part the hall measures 200 feet, the shorter length is 180 feet, and there is a distance of 140 feet between the floor of the arena and the dome.

Since the day of the opening of the hall by Her Majesty, when the orchestra was occupied by 1,200 instrumentalists and vocalists, concerts on a grand and extensive scale have been the chief use to which the building has been put; and it was also used for part of the display in the annual industrial Exhibitions of 1871-4. The grandest scenes, perhaps, which have taken place within its walls were on the occasions of the state concerts given in honour of the visits to England of the Shah of Persia, the Czar of Russia, &c.; another brilliant ceremony witnessed here was the installation of the Prince of Wales as Grand Master of the Lodge of Freemasons of England.

INTERIOR OF THE ALBERT HALL.

Close by the Royal Albert Hall, on a plot of ground granted by the Commissioners of the Exhibition of 1851, is the National Training School for Music, of which the Duke of Edinburgh was the first president. The building was constructed in 1875, at the cost of Sir Charles Freake. The Council of the Society of Arts undertook the supervision of the foundation of scholarships.

The Royal Horticultural Society, whose gardens, as we have already stated, are enclosed by the Exhibition buildings on the south side of the Royal Albert Hall, was established in 1804, and incorporated by royal charter soon afterwards. The society was instituted for the improvement of horticulture in all its branches, and it has an extensive experimental garden at Chiswick, five miles from London, laid out tastefully, and filled with many rare plants. These gardens have acquired great celebrity from their having been established at a period when gardening was in a very low condition in this country, and from having been the means of raising it to its present greatly-improved state. Previously to purchasing the land at Chiswick, the Horticultural Society had temporarily occupied a small piece of ground at Brompton, not far from the gardens which we are about to notice. In 1859 the society obtained (through the late Prince Consort) possession of about twenty acres of land on this site, and new and splendid gardens were laid out. These were opened in the summer of 1862, forming a charming retreat from the bustle of the Exhibition.

Between the Kensington Road and Cromwell Road the ground falls about forty feet, and using this fact in aid of a general effect, the ground has been divided into three principal levels. The entrances to the gardens are on the lower level in Exhibition Road and Queen's Gate, and the central pathway, upwards of seventy-five feet wide, ascending through terraces to the third great level, leads to the winter garden or conservatory. The whole garden is surrounded by Italian arcades, each of the three levels having arcades of a different character. The upper, or north arcade, where the boundary is semi-circular in form, is a modification of the arcades of the Villa Albani at Rome. The central arcade is almost wholly of Milanese brick-work, interspersed with terra-cotta, majolica, &c., while the design for the south arcade has been adapted from the beautiful cloisters of St. John Lateran at Rome. None of these arcades are less than twenty feet wide and twenty-five feet high, and they give a promenade, sheltered from all weathers, more than three-quarters of a mile in length. The arcades and earthworks were executed by the Commissioners for the Exhibition of 1851, at a cost of £50,000, while the laying-out of the gardens and construction of the conservatory were executed by the Horticultural Society, and cost about the same sum. On the upper terrace, in front of the conservatory, and at the head of a lake, stands a memorial of the late Prince Consort, the work of Mr. Joseph Durham, sculptor, originally intended only to commemorate the International Exhibition of 1851. The death of the Prince having occurred before the work was completed, the memorial was made into a lasting tribute to the "great founder of the Exhibition." The idea embodied is Britannia (typified by the Prince) supported by the four quarters of the globe—signifying that the Exhibition originated in England, and was supported by all other nations. The monument stands upwards of forty feet in height, and represents the Prince in his robes as Grand Master of the Order of the Bath. The body of the memorial is of grey granite, with columns and panels of red polished Aberdeen granite; the statue of the Prince, and also those of the figures representing each quarter of the globe, being of bronze.

In 1883 a large portion of the gardens of the Horticultural Society was utilised for the purposes of an International Fisheries Exhibition, which was opened by the Prince of Wales on the 12th of May. The exhibition was held in several temporary buildings, covering nearly twelve acres of ground. It was designed with the view of illustrating sea and fresh-water fishing in all its branches, fish-culture, fishing-boats, fish-curing, fishing-tackle and apparatus of all kinds, lifeboats and life-saving apparatus, diving apparatus, indeed, everything immediately relating to and connected with the actual working of all kinds of fishing. Among the more interesting features of the exhibition were the aquaria of sea and fresh water, well stocked with fish, anemones, aquatic plants, &c.; also the fine collection of pictures of marine subjects, and the collection of stuffed and preserved fish, and casts, and drawings; together with specimens and representations illustrative of the relations between extinct and existing fishes. The boat used by Grace Darling and her father, in 1838, in their gallant rescue of nine of the sufferers from the wreck of the *Forfarshire* among the Farne Islands, was exhibited, as also was the old Royal state barge which was built in the reign of James II. Prizes were offered for essays connected with the objects of the Exhibition: on such subjects as the natural history of commercial sea fishes of Great Britain and Ireland, with special reference to such parts of their natural history as bear upon their production and commercial use; as to the effect of the laws for the regulation and protection of fisheries; on improved facilities for the capture and economic distribution of sea fishes; and on improved fishery harbour accommodation. Conferences were also held for reading and discussing papers on subjects connected with the exhibitions; and instruction in cooking fish was given.

OLD GORE HOUSE, IN 1830.

CHAPTER X.

"THE OLD COURT SUBURB."—KENSINGTON.

"When shall we walk to Totnam, or crosse o'er
The water? or take coach to Kensington
Or Paddington? or to some one or other
O' th' City out-leaps for an afternoon?"
Brome's "New Academy" (a play), 1658.

Descent of the Manor—A Parochial Enigma—Derivation of the Name of Kensington—Thackeray's "Esmond"—Leigh Hunt's Reminiscences—Gore House—Mr. Wilberforce, the Philanthropist—Lord Rodney—The Countess of Blessington and her Admirers—An Anecdote of Louis Napoleon—Count D'Orsay's Picture—A Touching Incident—Sale of the Contents of Gore House, and Death of the Countess of Blessington—M. Soyer's "Symposium"—Sale of the Gore House Estate—Park House—Hamilton Lodge, the Residence of John Wilkes—Batty's Hippodrome—St. Stephen's Church—Orford Lodge—Christ Church.

KENSINGTON, which is technically described as a suburb of London, in the Hundred of Ossulston, has long enjoyed distinction from its Palace, in which several successive sovereigns of the Hanoverian line held their court, and which was the birth-place of Queen Victoria. In the time of the Domesday survey the manor of Kensington was owned by the Bishop of Coutances, to whom it was granted by William the Conqueror. It was at that time held by Aubrey de Vere, and subsequently, as history tells us, it became the absolute property of the De Veres, who afterwards gave twenty Earls of Oxford to the English peerage. Aubrey de Vere was Grand Justiciary of England, and was created Earl of Oxford by the Empress Maud. Upon the attainder of John, Earl of Oxford, who was beheaded during the struggle for power between the houses of York and Lancaster, the manor was bestowed by Edward IV. on his brother Richard, Duke of Gloucester. After passing through the hands of the Marquis of Berkeley and Sir Reginald Bray, the property returned (as is supposed by purchase) to John, Earl of Oxford, son of the attainted nobleman above mentioned. The manor is said to have again passed from that family, probably by sale, in the reign of Elizabeth; and early in the seventeenth century the Earl of Argyll and three other persons joined in a conveyance of the property to Sir Walter Cope, whose daughter conveyed it by marriage to Henry Rich, Earl of Holland. The manor subsequently passed into the hands of Lord Kensington, who was maternally descended from Robert Rich, last Earl of Warwick and Holland, and whose barony, singularly enough, is an Irish one, although the title is derived from this place.

Parochially considered, Kensington is somewhat of an enigma, for it is not only more than Kensington in some places, but it is not Kensington itself in others. In Kensington parish, for instance, are included Earl's Court, Little Chelsea, Old and New Brompton, Kensal Green, and even some of the houses in Sloane Street; while, on the other hand, Kensington Palace and Kensington Gardens are not in Kensington, but in the parish of St. Margaret's, Westminster.

The place, which now forms, as it were, part and parcel of London, was down to comparatively recent times a village, one mile and a half from Hyde Park Corner. The name is stated by some topographers to be derived from Kœnnigston, or from the Saxon *Kyning's*-tun, a term synonymous with King's End Town, and to be the same word as Kennington and Kingston; our monarchs from the earliest date having had residences at all three places. Possibly, however, the "Ken" may be an equivalent to "Kaen," or "Caen," which lies at the root of "Kentish" Town, "Caen-wood," &c.; but we will leave the origin of the name to be discussed by antiquaries, and pass on to a survey of the district in detail.

"Whatever was the origin of its name," writes Leigh Hunt, in the "Old Court Suburb," "there is no doubt that the first inhabited spot of Kensington was an inclosure from the great Middlesex forest which once occupied this side of London, and which extended northwards as far as Barnet." Kensington has been always a favourite, not only with royalty, but with those who more or less bask in the sunshine of princes—poets, painters, &c. The healthfulness and fashion of the place attracted numerous families of distinction; and its importance was completed when William III. bought the house and grounds of the Finch family (Earls of Nottingham), and converted the former into a palace, and the latter into royal gardens. It is emphatically "the old Court suburb," and is familiar to all readers of Thackeray, who has portrayed its features in many of his writings, especially in "Esmond." Leigh Hunt observes that "there is not a step of the way, from its commencement at Kensington Gore to its termination beyond Holland House, in which you are not greeted with the face of some pleasant memory. Here, to 'minds' eyes' conversant with local biography, stands a beauty looking out of a window; there, a wit talking with other wits at a garden-gate; there, a poet on the green sward, glad to get out of the London smoke and find himself among trees. Here come De Veres of the times of old; Hollands and Davenants, of the Stuart and Cromwell times; Evelyn, peering about him soberly, and Samuel Pepys in a bustle. Here advance Prior, Swift, Arbuthnot, Gay, Sir Isaac Newton; Steele, from visiting Addison; Walpole, from visiting the Foxes; Johnson, from a dinner with Elphinstone; 'Junius,' from a communication with Wilkes. Here, in his carriage, is King William III. going from the palace to open Parliament; Queen Anne, for the same purpose; George I. and George II. (we shall have the pleasure of looking at all these personages a little more closely); and there, from out of Kensington Gardens, comes bursting, as if the whole recorded polite world were in flower at one and the same period, all the fashion of the gayest times of those sovereigns, blooming with chintzes, full-blown with hoop-petticoats, towering with topknots and toupees. Here comes 'Lady Mary,' quizzing everybody; and Lady Suffolk, looking discreet; there, the lovely Bellendens and Lepels; there, Miss Howe, laughing with Nancy Lowther (who made her very grave afterwards); there Chesterfield, Hanbury Williams, Lord Hervey; Miss Chudleigh, not over clothed; the Miss Gunnings, drawing crowds of admirers; and here is George Selwyn, interchanging wit with my Lady Townshend, the 'Lady Bellaston' (so, at least, it has been said) of 'Tom Jones.'" Probably there is not an old house in Kensington in which some distinguished person has not lived, during the reigns in which the Court resided there; but the houses themselves are, as Leigh Hunt puts it, "but dry bones, unless invested with interests of flesh and blood."

The Royal Albert Hall and the gardens of the Horticultural Society occupy the site of Gore House and grounds. This is probably the estate called the Gara, or the Gare, which Herbert, Abbot of Westminster, gave to the nuns of Kilburn. The spot was, according to John Timbs, anciently called Kyng's Gore. Old Gore House was a low, plain, and unpretending building, painted white, and abutted on the roadway, about 150 yards to the east of the chief public entrance to the Albert Hall. Its external beauty, if it had any, belonged to its southern, or garden side. Standing close to the roadside, it looked as if meant originally for the lodge of some great mansion which had never actually been built: and the row, of which it formed a part, as Leigh Hunt observes, in his "Old Court Suburb," might easily lead one to imagine that it had been divided into apartments for the retainers of the Court, and that either a supernumerary set of maids of honour had lived there, or else that some four or five younger brothers of lords of the bed-chamber had been the occupants, and expecting places in reversion. "The two houses," adds the writer, "seem to be nothing but one large drawing-room. They possess, however, parlours and second storeys at the back, and they have good gardens, so that, what with their flowers behind them, the park in front, and their own neatness and elegance, the miniature aristocracy of their appearance is not ill borne out."

Here, for the best part of half a century, distinguished statesmen and philanthropists, and afterwards the light and frivolous butterflies of West-end society, used to mix with men of letters and the votaries of science. Here the "lions" of the day were entertained from time to time; and there were few houses to which the *entrée* was more coveted. At the end of the last century it was little more than a cottage, with a pleasant garden in the rear attached to it, and it was tenanted by a Government contractor, who does not seem to have cared to go to any expense in keeping it in order. Early in the present century it was enlarged on coming into the possession of Mr. Wilberforce, who soon grew very fond of the spot, and here used to entertain Mr. Pitt, Lord Auckland (who lived hard by), and such eminent philanthropists as Clarkson, Stephen, Zachary Macaulay, and Romilly; indeed, it has often been said that the agitation which ended in the abolition of West Indian slavery was commenced in the library of Gore House. Of this place Mr. Wilberforce often speaks in his private correspondence; and in one place he mentions his *rus in urbe* in the following terms:—"We are just one mile from the turnpike at Hyde Park Corner, having about three acres of pleasure-ground around our house, or rather behind it, and several old trees, walnut and mulberry, of thick foliage. I can sit and read under their shade with as much admiration of the beauties of Nature as if I were down in Yorkshire, or anywhere else 200 miles from the great city." Here, too, his four sons, including the future Bishop of Oxford and of Winchester, were mainly brought up in their childhood and boyhood; and in the later years of its hospitable owner's life it is on record that "its costliness made him at times uneasy, lest it should force him to curtail his charities," a thing which he was always most anxious to avoid. Mrs. Wilberforce supported in this mansion a school for poor girls, which was under her own personal superintendence. At Gore House the gallant admiral, Lord Rodney, was for some time "laid up in port."

Mr. Wilberforce having occupied the house for thirteen years, from 1808 down to 1821, it next passed into the hands of a new meditator, but not so much on the beauties of nature as on those of art and literature—one who was more *spirituelle* in *salons*, that "spiritual" in Wilberforce's sense of the term—the "gorgeous" Countess of Blessington became in turn its proprietor. She lived here during her widowhood, surrounded by a bright and fashionable crowd of aristocratic and literary admirers. Gore House became indeed a centre of attraction to the world of letters; for besides giving such dinners as Dr. Johnson would have thought "worth being asked to," Lady Blessington prided herself on her success in "bringing people together," in order to please and be pleased in turn. Here were such men of the last generation as Lord Melbourne, the poet Campbell, Samuel Rogers, and many of the *beaux* of "the Regency" and of the reign of George IV., including Count D'Orsay, who married Lady Blessington's daughter, and made the house his home.

"At Gore House," writes Mr. Blanchard Jerrold, "Prince Louis Napoleon met most of the intellectual society of the time, and became the friend of Count D'Orsay, Sir E. Lytton Bulwer, Sir Henry Holland, Albany Fonblanque, and many others who formed Lady Blessington's circle." The Prince dined at Gore House with a small party of West-end friends and acquaintances, including Lord Nugent and "Poodle" Byng, on the evening before he started off on his wild and abortive effort to make a descent on Boulogne in August, 1840. "It was the fashion in that day," says Mr. Planché, in his "Recollections," "to wear black satin handkerchiefs for evening dress; and that of the Prince was fastened by a large spread eagle in diamonds, clutching a thunderbolt of rubies. There was in England at that time but one man who, without the impeachment of coxcombry, could have sported so magnificent a jewel; and though to my knowledge I had never seen him before, I felt convinced that he could be no other than Prince Louis Napoleon. Such was the fact. . . . There was a general conversation on indifferent matters for some twenty minutes, during which the Prince spoke but little, and then took his departure with Count Montholon. Shortly afterwards, Lord Nugent, Mr. Byng, and I, said good night, and walked townward together. As we went along, one of my companions said to the other, 'What could Louis Napoleon mean by asking us to dine with him at the Tuileries on this day twelve months?' Four days afterwards the question was answered. The news arrived of the abortive landing at Boulogne and the captivity of the Prince." On the first day after his escape from Ham (1846), and his arrival in London, Prince Louis Napoleon again dined here at a party, with Lady Blessington, Count D'Orsay, Walter Savage Landor, Mr. John Forster, &c., whom he amused by recounting his recent adventure in detail.

THE OLD TURNPIKE, KENSINGTON, IN 1820.

Mr. Madden, in his "Life and Correspondence of the Countess of Blessington," says:—"For nineteen years Lady Blessington had maintained, at first in Seamore Place, and afterwards at Kensington, a position almost queen-like in the world of intellectual distinction, in fashionable literary society, reigning over the best circles of London celebrities, and reckoning among her admiring friends, and the frequenters of her *salons*, the most eminent men of England in every walk of literature, art, and science, in statesmanship, in the military profession, and in every learned pursuit. For nineteen years she had maintained in London establishments seldom equalled, and still more rarely surpassed, in all the appliances of a state of society brilliant in the highest degree; but, alas! it must be acknowledged, at the same time, a state of splendid misery for a great portion of that time to the mistress of those elegant and luxurious establishments. And now, at the end of that time, we find her forced to abandon that position, to leave all the elegancies and refinements of her home to become the property of strangers, and in fact to make a departure from the scene of all her former triumphs, with a privacy which must have been most painful and humiliating."

Count D'Orsay painted a large garden view of Gore House, with portraits of the Duke of Wellington, Lords Chesterfield, Douro, and Brougham, Sir E. Landseer, the Miss Powers, and other members of the fashionable circle that gathered there. "In the foreground, to the right," says a description of the picture, "are the great Duke and Lady Blessington; in the centre, Sir E. Landseer, seated, in the act of sketching a fine cow, with a calf by her side; Count D'Orsay himself, with two favourite dogs, is seen on the right of the group, and Lord Chesterfield on the left: nearer the house are the two Miss Powers (nieces of Lady Blessington), reading a letter, a gentleman walking behind. Further to the left are Lord Brougham, Lord Douro, &c., seated under a tree, engaged in conversation."

and Albert Smith and Thackeray, Charles Dickens and William Jerdan, Mr. Monckton Milnes, Mr. A. Baillie Cochrane, Mr. N. P. Willis, the Countess Guiccioli (Byron's *chere amie*), Lords Brougham, Lyndhurst, and Chesterfield, and all the other celebrities, who, being added up together into one sum, made up, what Joseph Hume would have styled, the "tottle of the whole" of the Gore House circle. Mr. N. P. Willis thus records an incident during an evening here:—"We all sat round the piano, and, after two or three songs of Lady Blessington's choosing, Moore rambled over the keys awhile, and then sang 'When first I met thee,' with a pathos that beggars description. When the last word had faltered out, he rose and

THE "HALFWAY HOUSE," KENSINGTON, 1850.

Mr. Madden, in his book above quoted, gives us anecdotes of, or letters from, most of the visitors at Gore House when it was in its prime. Thomas Moore, who sang so touchingly as to unlock the fount of tears in the drawing-room, was often there; so were Horace and James Smith, the authors of the "Rejected Addresses;" so was Sir Henry Lytton Bulwer and his brother, the late Lord Lytton. Walter Savage Landor would repair thither, with his stern eyebrows and kindly heart;

took Lady Blessington's hand, said good-night, and was gone before a word was uttered. . . . I have heard of women fainting at a song of Moore's; and if the burden of it answered by chance to a secret in the bosom of the listener, I should think, from its comparative effect upon so old a stager as myself, that the heart would break with it."

Lady Blessington's "curiosities" and treasures—the contents of the once favourite mansion—were disposed of by auction in the summer of 1849; and she herself went off to Paris, to die in debt, and deserted by her butterfly admirers, but a few weeks afterwards. The contents of the mansion are thus described in the catalogue of the sale:—"Costly and elegant effects: comprising all the magnificent furniture, rare porcelain, sculpture in marble, bronzes, and an assemblage of objects of art and decoration; a casket of valuable jewellery and *bijouterie*, services of rich chased silver and silver-gilt plate, a superbly-fitted silver dressing-case; collection of ancient and modern pictures, including many portraits of distinguished persons, valuable original drawings, and fine engravings, framed and in portfolios; the extensive and interesting library of books, comprising upwards of 5,000 volumes, expensive table services of china and rich cut glass, and an infinity of useful and valuable articles. All the property of the Right Hon. the Countess of Blessington, retiring to the Continent."

In 1851, during the time of the Great Exhibition, Gore House was made a "Symposium," or *restaurant*, by M. Alexis Soyer, whose *cuisine*, whilst *chef* of the Reform Club, enjoyed European fame.* Its walls were once more adorned with a splendour and costliness which it had not known for some years, though, possibly, not with equal taste as that which was so conspicuous under the *régime* of the clever and brilliant lady who had made it a home. Soyer first came to England on a visit to his brother, who was then cook to the Duke of Cambridge; and at Cambridge House he cooked his first dinner in England for the then Prince George. Soyer afterwards entered the service of various noblemen: amongst others, of Lord Ailsa, Lord Panmure, &c. He then was employed by the Reform Club, and the breakfast given by that club, on the occasion of the Queen's coronation, obtained him high commendation. Mr. Mark Boyd, in his "Social Gleanings," tells a good story about M. Soyer. "Meeting him in an omnibus, after his return from the Crimea, I congratulated him on the laurels he had gained with our army, and was anxious to learn how he had managed this under the privations to which our brave fellows were exposed from short rations, and often from no rations at all! 'Dere is my merit, Monsieur Boyd,' he replied, 'for I did make good dishes out of nothing.'" It is to be feared that his words were literally true.

The Gore House estate, comprising some twenty-one acres, was purchased in 1852 by the Commissioners of the Great Exhibition, out of the surplus fund of that Exhibition, for the sum of £60,000, as a site for a new National Gallery; and the Baron de Villars' estate, adjoining, nearly fifty acres, fronting the Brompton Road, was bought for £153,500, as a site for a Museum of Manufactures; "these localities being recommended for the dryness of the soil, and as the only ground safe for future years amidst the growth of the metropolis." On the latter site, as we have shown in the previous chapter, the South Kensington Museum and the Schools of Art and Science have been erected; but instead of the National Gallery, the ground at Kensington Gore was made to serve as the site for the Albert Hall, &c.

Park House, at the eastern end of the Gore, close by Prince's Gate, indicates the northern boundary of the once famous Kensington or Brompton Park Nursery, which figures in the pages of the *Spectator* as the establishment of Messrs. Loudon and Wise, the most celebrated gardeners of their time. Near to this was Noel House, so called from having been built by one of the Campdens. Hamilton Lodge, Kensington Gore, was the occasional residence of John Wilkes, who here entertained Counts Woronzow and Nesselrode, and Sir Philip Francis. At Palace Gate lives Mr. J. E. Millais, R.A. De Vere Gardens, close by, perpetuate the memory of the Veres, Earls of Oxford.

A little to the west of Kensington Gore, immediately opposite to the broad walk of Kensington Gardens, was, in 1850–1, Batty's Grand National Hippodrome. Its site, which lies at the back of the Prince of Wales' Terrace, covering a considerable space of ground between the two thoroughfares known as Palace Gate and Victoria Road, was for many years used as a riding school, but was ultimately given up for building purposes. Near the old turnpike, which stood a little westward of Gore House, was a small inn known as the halfway house between London and Hammersmith. It was a curious and picturesque structure, but was swept away about the year 1860.

Opposite Queen's Gate Gardens, and adjoining the Gloucester Road, on the west side of the

* See Vol. IV., p. 149.

Horticultural Gardens, is St. Stephen's Church, built in 1866, from the designs of Mr. Joseph Peacock, and is an architectural ornament to the neighbourhood. In this immediate locality was Orford Lodge, built on the site of the "Old Florida Tea Gardens," for the late Duchess of Gloucester, after whom Gloucester Road is named. The Lodge was subsequently tenanted by the Princess Sophia, and also by the Right Hon. George Canning, who was here visited by Queen Caroline. The house was taken down in the year 1852. The thoroughfare which connected Chelsea with the great western road through the village between the Gore and Kensington Square rejoiced in the not very pleasant-sounding name of "Hogmire Lane"—a name, however, suggestive of farm-yards and piggeries, which then, doubtless, were plentiful in the neighbourhood.

Christ Church, in the Victoria Road, is a fine edifice, of Gothic design, dating from the year 1851, and accommodating about 800 persons. All its seats are open. It was built from the designs of Mr. Benjamin Ferrey. The architecture is of the Decorated style, varying from geometrical to flowing. It comprises a nave and chancel, tower and spire. The windows throughout are of flowered quarries; that at the east end is a rich diaper pattern, copied from one in York Minster.

CHAPTER XI.

KENSINGTON (*continued*).

"Faith, and it's the Old Court Suburb that you spoke of, is it? Sure, an' it's a mighty fine place for the quality."—*Old Play.*

The Old Court Suburb—Pepys at "Kingly Kensington"—The High Street—Thackeray's "Esmond"—Palace Gate—Colby House—Singular Death—Kensington House: its Early History—Famous Inhabitants—Old Kensington Bedlam—The New House—Young Street—Kensington Square—Famous Inhabitants—Talleyrand—An Aged Waltzer—Macaulay's Description of Talleyrand—The New Parish Church—The Old Building—The Monuments—The Bells—The Parish Registers—The Charity School—Campden House—"The Dogs"—Sir James South's Observatory—A Singular Sale—Other Noted Residents at Kensington—Insecurity of the Kensington Road—A Remarkable Dramatic Performance—A Ghost Story—The Crippled Boys' Home—Scarsdale House—The Roman Catholic University College—Roman Catholic Chapels—The Pro-Cathedral—The "Adam and Eve."

HITHERTO, since leaving the side of the river at Chelsea, we have been mostly passing over modern ground, which a century ago was scantily dotted with private residences, and which, therefore, can scarcely be expected as yet to have much of a past history. But now, as we look round the "Old Court Suburb" of Kensington, and its venerable and somewhat narrow High Street, we find ourselves again confronted with houses and persons of an earlier era, and, consequently, we shall be able to dwell at greater length on the annals and anecdotes of which Kensington has been the scene. The Palace and the Church, of course, will form our central objects, to which, perhaps, we ought to add that old-world haunt of fashion, Kensington Square. The old town of Kensington consisted principally of one long street, extending about three-quarters of a mile in length, from the Gore to Earl's Terrace; but even that thoroughfare is of comparatively modern growth, for the only highway for travellers westward, in former times, was the old Roman (or present Uxbridge) Road, then bending southerly (as it still branches) to Turnham Green. Within the last century a number of small streets have been built on either side. Bowack, in his "History of Middlesex," thus describes the place in the middle of the last century:—"This town, standing in a wholesome air, not above three miles from London, has ever been resorted to by persons of quality and citizens, and for many years past honoured with several fine seats belonging to the Earls of Nottingham and Warwick. We cannot, indeed, find it was ever taken notice of in history, except for the great western road through it, nor hath anything occurred in it that might perpetuate its name, till his late Majesty, King William, was pleased to ennoble it with his court and royal presence. Since which time it has flourished even almost beyond belief, and is inhabited by gentry and persons of note; there is also abundance of shopkeepers, and all sorts of artificers in it, which makes it appear rather like part of London than a country village. It is, with its dependencies, about three times as big as Chelsea, in number of houses, and in summer time extremely filled with lodgers, for the pleasure of the air, walks, and gardens round it, to the great advantage of its inhabitants. The buildings are chiefly of brick, regular, and built into streets; the largest is that through which the road lies, reclining back from the Queen's House, a considerable way beyond the church. From the church runs a row of buildings towards the north, called Church Lane; but the most beautiful part of it is the Square, south of the road, which, for beauty of buildings, and worthy inhabitants, exceed several noted squares in London."

Kensington—"kingly Kensington," as Dean Swift called it—is not very frequently mentioned by Pepys, as that country village had not, in his days, become the "court suburb." He mentions, however, accompanying "my lord" (the Earl of Sandwich) to dine at Kensington with Lord Campden, at Campden House, and afterwards to call at Holland House. With two other trivial exceptions, this is all that we learn about Kensington from the old gossip's "Diary;" neither does the place figure in the "Memoirs of the Count de Gramont." It is on record that George II. admired the flat grounds of Kensington and Kew, as reminding him of "Yarmany." It is described by Bowack, in 1705, as being about three times as big as Chelsea. The manor of Abbots' Kensington, which occupies an area of about 1,140 acres in all, extends northwards so far as to include all the Gravel Pits and Notting Hill.

Although Kensington is so near London, and contains so many new buildings, the High Street has a considerable resemblance to that of a country town. The houses, for the most part, are of moderate size, and considerable variety is displayed in the style of building, so that the fronts of scarcely any two houses are alike. Faulkner, writing in 1820, remarks: "The town, being in the direct road for the western parts of England, is in a considerable bustle, and resembles the most populous streets in London, especially in an evening, when the mail-coaches are setting out for their various destinations." The chief coaching-inn and posting-house, at that time, was the "Red Lion," at the back of which is still to be seen a curious sun-dial, bearing the date 1713. Readers of Thackeray's "Esmond" will not have forgotten the picture he has given of the scene which might have been witnessed from the tavern at the corner of the old High Street, on the occasion of the accession of King George I.:—"Out of the window of the tavern, and looking over the garden wall, you can see the green before Kensington Palace, the palace gate (round which the ministers' coaches are standing), and the barrack building. As we were looking out from this window in gloomy distraction, we heard presently the trumpets blowing, and some of us ran to the window of the front room looking into the High Street, and saw a regiment of horse coming. 'It's Ormond's Guards,' says one. 'No, by G—; it's Argyle's old regiment!' says my general, clapping down his crutch. It was indeed Argyle's regiment that was brought up from Westminster, and that took the part of the regiment at Kensington." The sequel is soon told, and it shall here be told, in the words of "Esmond:"—"With some delays in procuring horses, we got to Hammersmith about four o'clock on Sunday morning, the 1st of August (1714), and half an hour after, it then being bright day, we rode by my Lady Warwick's house, and so down the street of Kensington. Early as the hour was, there was a bustle in the street, and many people moving to and fro. Round the gate leading to the palace, where the guard is, there was especially a great crowd; and the coach ahead of us stopped, and the bishop's man got down, to know what the concourse meant. Then presently came out from the gate horse-guards with their trumpets, and a company of heralds with their tabards. The trumpets blew, and the herald-at-arms came forward, and proclaimed 'George, by the grace of God, of Great Britain, France, and Ireland, King, Defender of the Faith.' And the people shouted 'God save the King!'" Thus was the first sovereign of the Hanoverian line proclaimed in the High Street of Kensington; and there, with the sound of King George's trumpets, were the last hopes of the Stuart line scattered to the winds of heaven. The spot where this proclamation took place is surely an object of historic interest to after ages.

Almost at the entrance of the High Street is the Palace Gate, with its sentinels on duty, and opposite to it stood, till recently, a good, moderate-sized house—a sort of undergrown mansion—which, as Leigh Hunt says, looked as if it "had been made for some rich old bachelor who chose to live alone, but liked to have everything about him strong and safe." Such was probably the case, for it was called Colby House, and was the abode of Sir Thomas Colby, of whom Dr. King tells us in his "Anecdotes of his Own Times," that being worth £200,000, and having no near relatives, he met with his death by getting up from his warm bed on a winter night to fetch the key of his cellar, which he had forgotten, for fear his servant might help himself to a bottle of wine. The house was inhabited, when Faulkner wrote his "History of Kensington," by one of the leading magistrates of the county. Its former eccentric owner was buried in the parish church. The house was standing till about 1872, when it was pulled down, along with the large red house, Kensington House, adjoining, to make a site for Baron Grant's mansion.

Kensington House, a dull and heavy building of red brick on the south side of the high road, nearly facing the Palace gates, was for some years inhabited by the notorious Duchess of Portsmouth, one of the many mistresses of Charles II. The house was long and low in proportion, and was screened from the road by a high wall. It is recorded that King Charles supped here the night before he was seized with the illness which proved his last. The house was afterwards turned into a school, kept by Elphinstone, who was known as the translator of Martial, and as a friend of Dr. Jortin, Benjamin Franklin, and Dr. Johnson. He was ludicrously caricatured by Smollett, in "Roderick Random," which was consequently a forbidden book in his school. At the outbreak of the first French Revolution the house was occupied by some French emigrant priests, members of the Jesuit Order, who kept here a college for the youth of the French and some of the English aristocracy, under the assumed name of "Les Pères de la Foi." The late Mr. Richard Lalor Sheil was sent here when a boy, and he tells us how the school was visited by "Monsieur"—as Charles X., afterwards King of France, was then called—in his brother's lifetime.

The building has been described as follows by Mr. Sheil*:—"I landed at Bristol, and with a French clergyman, the Abbé de Grimeau, who had been my tutor, I proceeded to London. The abbé informed me that I was to be sent to Kensington House, a college established by the Pères de la Foi—for so the French Jesuits settled in England at that time called themselves—and that he had directions to leave me there upon his way to Languedoc, from whence he had been exiled in the Revolution, and to which he had been driven by the *maladie de pays* to return. Accordingly, we set off for Kensington House, which is situated exactly opposite the avenue leading to the palace, and has the beautiful garden attached to it in front. A large iron gate, wrought into rustic flowers, and other fantastic forms, showed that the Jesuit school had once been the residence of some person of distinction. . . . It was a large old-fashioned house, with many remains of decayed splendour. In a beautiful walk of trees, which ran down from the rear of the building through the play-ground, I saw several French boys playing at swing-swang; and the moment I entered, my ears were filled with the shrill vociferations of some hundreds of little emigrants, who were engaged in their various amusements, and babbled, screamed, laughed, and shouted, in all the velocity of their rapid and joyous language. I did not hear a word of English, and at once perceived that I was as much amongst Frenchmen as if I had been suddenly transferred to a Parisian college. Having got this peep at the gaiety of the school into which I was to be introduced, I was led, with my companion, to a chamber covered with faded gilding, and which had once been richly tapestried, where I found the head of the establishment, in the person of a French nobleman, Monsieur le Prince de Broglie."

Here, in 1821, whilst the house was still in the hands of the Jesuits, died—it is said, from the effects of tight lacing—Mrs. Inchbald, the authoress of the "Simple Story." She had resided in several other houses in Kensington before coming here. She had written many volumes, which she had by her in manuscript; but on her death-bed, from some motive or other, she requested a friend to tear them to pieces before her eyes, not having the strength to perform the heroic deed of immolation with her own hands. Mr. and Mrs. Cosway, too, resided here for a short time, after leaving Stratford Place, and before settling down in the Edgware Road.

The building was subsequently turned into a private lunatic asylum, and was then popularly known as Old Kensington Bedlam. It was purchased in 1873 by "Baron" Albert Grant, who pulled it down and erected a modern Italian palace on its site. The cost of the building and grounds is stated to have exceeded one million sterling. The mansion contained a grand hall and staircase, built entirely of white marble, drawing-rooms, library, picture-gallery, three dining-rooms *en suite*, and a spacious ball-room. In the construction of the windows, numbering over a hundred, no less than three tons of stone were used. In the formation of the grounds, which are twelve acres in extent, Mr. Grant purchased an Irish colony situated in the rear of the Kensington High Street—formerly called the "Rookery" and "Jenning's Buildings"—both of which had been a nuisance to the parish for years past. These places were entirely demolished, and the ground was converted into a picturesque lake, three acres in extent, with two small islands in the centre. Baron Grant got into difficulties, and the house, after various efforts to secure a sale, in order that it might be converted into a club or hotel, was sold piecemeal as so much old materials, and finally pulled down in 1883 to make way for smaller houses.

Continuing our way westward, we come to the turning at Young Street, which leads into the square above alluded to. It is an old-fashioned, oblong enclosure, and bears the name of Ken-

* Quoted by Leigh Hunt, in "The Old Court Suburb."

sington Square. It was commenced in the reign of James II., and finished about 1698, as appeared by a date at one time affixed at the north-east corner. It is described by Bowack, in 1705, as "the most beautiful part of the parish south of the main road," and as "exceeding several noted squares in London for beauty of its buildings and (for) worthy inhabitants." While the Court was at Kensington, most of the houses were inhabited by some of Montaigne's "Essays." It is said that, finding little or no information in the chapters as to the subjects their titles promised, he closed the book more confused than satisfied. "What think you of this famous French author?" said a gentleman present. "Think?" said he, smiling: "why, that a pair of manacles, or a stone doublet, would probably have been of some service to that author's infirmity." "Would you imprison a man

INTERIOR OF KENSINGTON CHURCH, 1850.

"persons of quality," ambassadors, gentry, and clergy; and at one time, as Faulkner tells us, upwards of forty carriages were kept by residents in and about the neighbourhood. In the reigns of William and Anne and the first two Georges, this square was the most fashionable spot in the suburbs; indeed, in the time of George II., the demand for lodgings here was so great, "that an ambassador, a bishop, and a physician have been known to occupy apartments in the same house." The celebrated Duchess de Mazarin appears to have resided here in 1692; and here she probably had among her visitors her "adoring old friend, Saint Evremond, with his white locks, little skull cap, and the great wen on his forehead." Here, too, Addison lodged for some time; and here it was that he read over for singularity in writing?" "Why, let me tell you," replied Addison, "if he had been a horse he would have been pounded for straying; and why he ought to be more favoured because he is a man, I cannot understand." We shall have more, however, to say of Addison when we come to Holland House.

Somewhere about the south-west corner of the square lived, for several years, physician to King William III., and butt of all the wits of the time, Sir Richard Blackmore, the poet, of whom we have spoken in our account of Earl's Court. Hough, the good old Bishop of Winchester, lived here for many years; as also did Mawson, Bishop of Ely; and Dr. Herring, Bishop of Bangor, and afterwards Archbishop of Canterbury. Among other noted

OLD KENSINGTON CHURCH, ABOUT 1750.

OLD VIEW OF KENSINGTON, ABOUT 1750.

residents were the Rev. W. Beloe, the translator of Herodotus; and the Earl of Clanricarde.

Another resident in Kensington Square, during the early part of the present century, was Prince de Talleyrand, at one time Bishop of Autun, in France, and subsequently Ambassador-Extraordinary for that country to the Court of St. James's. Lord Palmerston used to declare that he was "exceedingly quiet and courteous, but he had a strange versatility not revealed to the world at large." When eighty years of age, and extremely lame, he still was fond of sharing the amusements of the young, and his smile was then so benign as quite to discredit the "sarcastic sneer" for which he was famous. "One night at the Duchess of Gramont's," writes Lady Clementina Davies, in her "Recollections of Society," "a game of forfeits was proposed. The duchess joined in the game, and lost her king. She asked how she could get it back. She was told she must ask some gentleman in the room to take a *tour de valse* with her, and she invited the lame and aged diplomatist to dance with her. He smiled, and instantly rose to comply. Several young men offered to take his place, but neither he nor the gay little duchess would allow of this, and Talleyrand seemed able to perform his share in the valse, and to be pleased with the exertion. He remained with his partner, and conversed with her in a style of brilliant animation. When Louis XVIII. was restored to the French throne, the sage minister said to him, 'Now, sir, as a king of the French people, you must learn to forget!' The Bourbons might have fared better could they have taken this wise counsel!"

Lady Clementina Davies, who lived on terms of intimacy with the Prince, declares that it is quite an error to suppose that he was a mere political hypocrite, or that he transferred his services from one sovereign to another with reckless indifference; but that, on the contrary, his only motive was a patriotic desire to advance the interests of his country. He was shamefully used by his parents on account of his club-foot; he was deprived of all his rights as the eldest son, and forced against his will to become a priest. In spite of his cynicism, the great diplomatist was a remarkably pleasant-tempered man, full of kindness to children, and possessing conversational powers of the highest orders.

Talleyrand, in the year 1831, is thus described by Macaulay among the guests he met at Holland House:—"He is certainly the greatest curiosity that I ever fell in with. His head is sunk down between two high shoulders. One of his feet is hideously distorted. His face is as pale as that of a corpse, and wrinkled to a frightful degree. His eyes have an odd glassy stare, quite peculiar to them. His hair, thickly powdered and pomatumed, hangs down his shoulders on each side as straight as a pound of tallow candles. His conversation, however, soon makes you forget his ugliness and infirmities. There is a poignancy without effort in all that he says, which reminds me a little of the character which the wits of Johnson's circle give of Beauclerk. . . . He told several stories about the political men of France, not of any great value in themselves; but his way of telling them was beyond all praise—concise, pointed, and delicately satirical. . . . I could not help breaking out into admiration of his talent for relating anecdotes. Lady Holland said that he had been considered for nearly forty years as the best teller of a story in Europe."

In this square, also, resided James Mill, the historian of British India, and father of Mr. John Stuart Mill, M.P., the political economist. He died in 1836, and was buried in the parish church. Here, too, lived for some years the Rev. J. R. Green, author of "The Making of England," and of other works. He died in 1883.

Part of the western side of the square is occupied by the front of the Kensington Proprietary Grammar School; and three or four of the largest mansions near the south-west angle form now the Convent of the Dames de Sacré Cœur, on whose garden a handsome Roman Catholic church, and also a convent chapel, have been built.

It is in Kensington Square that Thackeray, in his "Esmond," lays the scene which presents us with James Stuart, "the Prince" from Saint Germains, as lodging, and passing for the time as Lord Castlewood, holding himself in readiness for action when the death of Queen Anne was expected. He pictures the Prince walking restlessly upon "the Mall" at Kensington. The "little house in Kensington Square" figures from first to last in the above-mentioned work as the residence of Lady Castlewood and of Beatrix Esmond, and is the centre at once of love-making and of political plots, in the interest of the exiled Stuarts.

About the middle of the High Street stands Kensington Church, dedicated to St. Mary the Virgin. The present fabric dates only from the year 1869, having replaced an older structure. It was built from the designs of Sir Gilbert Scott, and has about it a degree of architectural dignity which befits the importance of the parish as the "Old Court Suburb," the abode of royalty, and a quarter inhabited by many wealthy and aristocratic families.

The style of design is that which was in vogue towards the close of the thirteenth century, and known as the Decorated, though it is freely adapted to present uses. It consists of a large nave and chancel, each with aisles, and additional aisles at the eastern part of the nave, which at that part, consequently, has double aisles on each side. The whole is of very lofty proportions, with clerestory both to nave and chancel. The tower and spire, which are on a considerable scale, are at the north-east angle, and connected with the chancel by an extra aisle, which contains the organ. The cost of the building was nearly £50,000, towards which Her Majesty the Queen gave £200, and the late vicar of the parish, Archdeacon Sinclair, made a donation of £1,000.

The old parish church of St. Mary's, though a plain and unpretending edifice, which Bishop Blomfield used to designate the ugliest in his diocese, was an interesting structure, not only on account of the numerous monuments which it contained, but far more on account of the historical reminiscences connected with it. What with partial rebuildings and wholesale repairs, it had been altered a dozen times in less than two centuries. It superseded a previous building of which little or nothing is recorded. It is more than probable that the ancient parish church of Kensington stood nearly on the spot in Holland Street now occupied by the church of the Carmelite Fathers, and opposite the vicarage. At all events, it stood a little to the north of the parish church of subsequent centuries, and not far from the Manor House, to which the vicarage is a successor; through there is a tradition, but unconfirmed, that the original parish church stood some distance to the north, near the Gravel Pits, and was removed hither at the time of the Conquest. The road, by its very narrowness and curvings, shows that it is an ancient way, and it is still traditionally called, or at all events was called within the memory of the present generation, the "Parson's Yard." It will not be a little singular if hereafter it should be discovered that the Carmelites have been building on the old foundations. The resolution to build this church was adopted by the vestry in 1696, and among the contributors were William III. and Queen Mary, as well as the Princess Anne. The king and queen not only subscribed to the building fund, but presented the reading-desk and pulpit, which had crowns carved upon them, with the initials "W." and "M. R." A pew, curtained round in the fashion of old times, was, in consequence, set apart for the royal family, and long continued to be occupied by residents in Kensington Palace, amongst whom were the Duke and Duchess of Kent and the late Duke of Cambridge. It was in this church that the Duchess of Kent returned thanks after the birth of Queen Victoria.

Here were monuments to Edward, eighth Earl of Warwick and Holland, who died in 1759; and to "the three Colmans:" Francis Colman, some time British Minister to the Court of Florence; his son, George, "the Elder," and his grandson, George, "the Younger." The two latter wrote several comedies, and were proprietors of the Haymarket Theatre. Here also was buried one Sir Manhood Penruddock, who was "slain at Notting Wood, in fight, in the year 1608." At that time the nation was at peace; the "fight" which is recorded in the parish register probably means a "duel." Two interesting monuments by Chantrey, which were erected in the old parish church, have been replaced in the new edifice: the one in memory of a former vicar, Dr. T. Rennell; the other to a Peninsular officer, Colonel Hutchins, a native of Earl's Court.

Near one of the entrances to the church was a tablet recording a reputed donation of lands to the parish by Oliver Cromwell, of which Lysons states: "An anonymous benefactor, in 1652, gave some land at Kensington Gravel-pits, on which was formerly a malthouse. This is called Cromwell's gift, and a tradition has prevailed that is was given by Oliver Cromwell; but the parish have no evidence to ascertain it."

The peal of bells was cast by Janeway, of Chelsea, in 1772. In the parish books are several entries of sums paid for ringing the church bells on public occasions since the Revolution. The Battle of the Boyne, for instance, is thus recorded: "May 2, 1690.—Paid William Reynolds for the ringers on that day the news came of the victory gained by his Majesty at and near the Boyne, 12s." And again, the Battle of Blenheim is thus noted: "1704.—Paid Mr. Jackman for a barrel of beer for the victory over the French and Bavarians, 15s." Another entry runs as follows: "For Limerick's being taken, and 'twas false," (*sic*): on this occasion the ringers were contented with eighteen pence. Various sums are mentioned as having been paid on the arrival of King William and his Queen, such as became the royal parish, "kingly Kensington." In Murray's "Environs of London" it is stated that this church has had its "Vicar of Bray," in one Thomas Hodges, collated to the living by Archbishop Juxon. He kept his preferment during the Civil War and interregnum, by joining alternately with either party Although a frequent preacher before the Long Parliament, and one of the Assembly of Divines, he was made Dean of Hereford after the Restoration, but continued Vicar of Kensington.

Amongst the many interesting associations of the old church are several of the present century. Mr. Wilberforce, who, as we have stated, resided at Kensington Gore, is still remembered by many of the old inhabitants as sitting in the pew appropriated to the Holland House family. George Canning, who resided at Gloucester Lodge, might often be seen sitting in the royal pew; Coke, of Norfolk, the eminent agriculturist, had a pew here, which he regularly occupied. Professor Nassau W. Senior, the political economist, although living so far distant as Hyde Park Gate, might often be seen, in company with the late Mr. Thackeray, attending the early service; but neither of these eminent writers, it is said, rented a pew in the church. Lord Macaulay, too, whilst living at Holly Lodge, Campden Hill, regularly attended here during the last two summers of his life.

To the churchyard, in 1814, was added a new cemetery, where was previously an avenue of elms, through which ran the original approach from the town to Campden House. In the churchyard is a monument to Mrs. Elizabeth Inchbald, who is truthfully and touchingly described on it as "a beauty, a virtue, a player, and authoress of 'A Simple Story.'" She commenced her career as an actress in 1777, on the York circuit, but quitted the stage in 1789, continuing, however, for many years to entertain the public in the character of a dramatic author. Mrs. Inchbald died on the 1st of March, 1821, as we have stated above, at old Kensington House. The following instances of longevity are to be found in the registers of burials:—1786, Margaret Smart, aged 103; 1804, Jane Hartwell, from Methwold's Almshouses, aged 100; 1807, William Griffiths, of the Gravel-pits, aged 103. The present vicarage, built about 1774, superseded a humble structure little more than a cottage with latticed windows.

Returning again into the High Street, we notice, a few yards beyond the church, a curious-looking brick building, of two storeys, above which is a square tower, probably intended to hold a bell; this was the old Kensington Charity School, built by Sir John Vanbrugh. It is now a savings'-bank, with a new school-room by the side of it. Adjoining this building is the Vestry Hall, which has been recently erected in the Jacobean style. A new Town Hall adjoining it was built in 1879–80.

On the opposite side of the way, in a house which stood on the site of the Metropolitan Railway Station, lived for some years the celebrated political writer, William Cobbett, whom we have mentioned above. In a garden at the back of his house, and also at a farm which he possessed at the same time at Barn-Elms, Cobbett cultivated his Indian corn, his American forest-trees, his pigs, poultry, and butchers' meat, all which he pronounced to be the best that were ever beheld; but the aristocratic suburb, we are told, did not prove a congenial soil, and he quitted it a bankrupt. He entered Parliament as member for Oldham, but did not live long afterwards, dying in 1835.

Campden House—which stands on the western side of Church Street, in its own grounds—is mentioned in the "New View of London," published in 1708, among the noble palaces belonging to Her Majesty, Queen Anne, "for the Court to reside in at pleasure." But this statement is not quite true. The house never absolutely belonged to royalty. It was the residence of Baptist Hicks, Viscount Campden, after whom it was called, and who was the founder of Hicks's Hall, in Clerkenwell;* and it caused his name to be given to the neighbourhood as Campden Hill. The mansion, which underwent considerable alterations in its exterior at the beginning of the present century, was spacious and picturesque, with its bay windows and turrets; several of the rooms had ceilings richly worked in stucco, and chimney-cases much ornamented. It was built about the year 1612, for Sir Baptist Hicks, whose arms (with that date), and those of his sons-in-law, Edward Lord Noel and Sir Charles Morison, figured in one of the windows. In the great dining-room it is said that Charles II. more than once supped with Lord Campden. It has fine wainscoat panels, and the ceiling was divided into compartments, in which figured the arms of the family, and their alliances. The house was rented from the Noel family by the Princess of Denmark (afterwards Queen Anne), who resided there about five years with her son, the Duke of Gloucester; and about that time, according to Lysons, the adjoining house, afterwards the residence of Mrs. Pitt, is said to have been built for the accommodation of Her Majesty's household. The amusements and pursuits of the Duke of Gloucester, who died in early boyhood, were principally of a military cast, for he is said to have formed a regiment of his youthful companions, chiefly from Kensington, who seem to have been upon constant duty at Campden House. At the beginning of the eighteenth century Campden House was in the occupation of the Dowager Countess of Burlington and her son, Richard Boyle, afterwards Earl, famous for his taste in the

* See Vol. II., p. 322.

fine arts. The house was afterwards held by the Noels, who parted with it to Nicholas Lechmere, the politician, who was created Lord Lechmere, and who resided here for several years. His lordship, probably, is now best remembered by the place he occupies in Gay's (or Swift's) ballad, entitled "Duke upon Duke," where, having challenged one Sir John Guise to fight a duel, he contrives to give his foe the slip :—

"Back in the dark, by Brompton Park,
He turned up through the Gore;
So slunk to Campden House so high,
All in his coach and four."

Towards the close of the last century the mansion became a boarding-school for ladies. George Selwyn speaks of going there to see a *protégé* of his, Maria Fagniani, who was held to be a very lucky person, for he and his friend Lord March (afterwards Duke of Queensberry—"Old Q.") took themselves respectively for her father, and each of them left her a fortune. She afterwards married the Marquis of Hertford.* In the *Mirror* for 1840, we read: "There are two dogs, carved out of stone, on the end walls of the gate or entrance, leading to Campden House, near Campden Hill, Kensington; they are pointer dogs, and very beautifully carved. The boys in the neighbourhood have done them much damage by pelting them with stones for fun, but they have stood all their knocks well—their legs are nearly worn away. From these two dogs the entrance is generally called by the inhabitants 'The Dogs,' by way of distinction. 'The House,' the entrance-lane to which they guard, was formerly occupied by Queen Anne; it is a plain substantial house, and now occupied as a ladies' school." Later on it was again converted into a private residence. It contained in all about thirty rooms, besides a private theatre, in which the Campden amateur artists used to perform for charitable objects. The terrace steps and parapets were extremely massive and handsome, and in the garden, which was sheltered and sunny, the wild olive is said to have flourished. A caper-tree long produced fruit here. The building was destroyed by fire in 1862, but was rebuilt immediately.

At Campden Hill was the observatory of Sir James South, one of the founders of the Royal Astronomical Society. Among his working instruments here was a 7-feet transit instrument, a 4-feet transit circle, and one of the equatorials with which, between the years 1821 and 1823, he and Sir John Herschel made a catalogue of 380 double stars. It was about the year 1825 that Sir James settled at Campden Hill; but in the equipment of his observatory he appears to have been unfortunate, for one large equatorial instrument, constructed at great expense, which became the subject of a lawsuit, gave him such dissatisfaction that he ordered it to be broken up, and the parts sold by auction. Large printed placards were posted throughout the neighbourhood of Kensington, and advertisements also appeared in the daily papers, announcing that on such a day (named) a sale of an extraordinary nature would take place at the observatory. These placards, from their singular character, attracted much attention. The following is a copy :—

"Observatory, Campden Hill, Kensington.

"To shycock toy-makers, smoke-jack makers, mock-coin makers, dealers in old metals, collectors of and dealers in artificial curiosities, and to such Fellows of the Astronomical Society as, at the meeting of that most learned and equally upright body, on the 13th of May last, were enlightened by Mr. Airy's (the Astronomer Royal) profound *exposé* of the mechanical incapacity of English astronomical instrument-makers of the present day:—To be sold by hand, on the premises, by Mr. M'Lelland, on Wednesday, December 21, 1842, between eleven and twelve o'clock in the forenoon, several hundred-weight of brass, gun-metal, &c., being the metal of the great equatorial instrument made for the Kensington Observatory by Messrs. Troughton and Simms; the wooden polar axis of which, by the same artists, and its botchings, cobbled up by their assistants (Mr. Airy and the Rev. R. Sheepshanks) were, in consequence of public advertisements, on the 8th of July, 1839, purchased by divers vendors of old clothes, and licensed dealers in dead cows and horses, &c., with the exception of a fragment of mahogany, specially reserved at the request of several distinguished philosophers, which, on account of the great anxiety expressed by foreign astronomers and foreign astronomical instrument-makers, to possess when converted into snuff-boxes as a *souvenir piquante* of the state of the art of astronomical instrument-making in England during the nineteenth century, will, at the conclusion of the sale, be disposed of at per pound."

At the hour appointed a number of marine-store dealers and other dealers in metal (some of whom had come in carts from town), with a sprinkling of astronomical instrument-makers, and scientific persons, were assembled outside Sir James South's residence, and were admitted into the grounds by a small door in the hedge close to the well-known circular building in which the equatorial instrument

* See Vol. IV., p. 287.

was at first placed. On entering the grounds, to the left appeared the wreck of the instrument which a few years ago excited the interest of men of science throughout the world, lying arranged in lots numbered from 0 to 14, lot 15 being the fragment of mahogany spoken of in the bill, and lot 16 a plaster bust of Professor Airy, which was mounted on the ledge of a window above the centre lot. On the right, on the spacious lawn, tainly be futile. Even the portions of the enormous tube were bored with holes, and battered to attain that object. Sir James South, in answer to an inquiry by a gentleman present as to the cause of so much deterioration in the value of the property having been made, said he had been told that he should get only the value of old metal for it; and knowing that those who purchased the material, had the parts been sold in a perfect state, would take

CAMPDEN HOUSE, 1720. (*See page* 130.)

was erected a large beam and scales, with weights for the purpose of ascertaining the weights of the different metals. Sir James South was present during the sale. He appeared in high spirits, and conversed with the company with his accustomed urbanity. The sale not being conducted by hammer, but by hand, was a very silent proceeding, and afforded no scope for either the eloquence or ingenuity of the auctioneer. The iron portion of the instrument, consisting of bolts, screws, &c., as well as the copper part, was unmutilated. The former fetched £3, and the latter 7d. per pound. The great equatorial instrument itself—viz., the tube, circle, &c., made of brass, had been broken into numerous pieces, which were divided into several lots, so that any attempt to reunite them would most cer-

them to the manufacturers, and from them receive a valuable consideration for them, he therefore determined to prevent its being devoted to any such ignoble purpose, and had mutilated it so that it should be of no value to any one beyond the intrinsic value of the metal. Notwithstanding these singular proceedings, one of Sir James's "equatorials" still remained mounted in his observatory, besides a few other instruments, including a transit circle, celebrated as having formerly belonged to Mr. Groombridge, and as having been the instrument with which the observations were made for the formation of the catalogue of circumpolar stars which bear his name. Sir James, whose contributions to scientific literature are well known, died here in 1867, at an advanced age. Kensington, of late years, has recovered some of its aristocratical character as a place of residence. Argyll Lodge, on Campden Hill, is the town-house of the Duke of Argyll, and Bedford Lodge, close by, was for many years the mansion of the Dowager Duchess of Bedford.

desired to have a list of the parochial charities, and a seat in the parish church. Although confined to the house by asthma during the winter, he was, as we have stated above, very regular in his attendance during the summer. A few days before his death, discussing the subject of church-

KENSINGTON HIGH STREET, IN 1860.

At Holly Lodge, Campden Hill, on the 28th of December, 1859, died Thomas Babington, Lord Macaulay, the essayist, orator, and historian, of whom we have already had occasion to speak in our accounts of the Albany and of Great Ormond Street.* When, after having been raised to the peerage, he went to reside at Holly Lodge, he

* See Vol. IV., pp. 259, 562.

rates, he said, "Church-rates cannot last; and the proper substitute for them is a large subscription—I will give £100 as my share. I am not an exclusive, but of all Christian communions I consider the Church of England to be the best."

Lord Macaulay took great delight in his house and garden here; and he was never more pleased than when in his library, surrounded by his nephews and nieces.

At a house in Orbell's Buildings, previously called Pitt's Buildings, on the south-east side of Campden Hill, died, March 20th, 1727, the great Sir Isaac Newton, at the age of eighty-five. His house seems to have had a back entrance in Church Street, where a gateway next the "George" Tavern is inscribed "Newton House." His estate at Kensington he left to a daughter of his nephew, Mr. Conduit, who married Lord Lymington, afterwards Earl of Portsmouth; and hence it is that the manuscripts of the great philosopher have been kept in the custody of the Wallop family.

A writer in the *Times* stated, in 1870, that the house actually occupied by Sir Isaac Newton was not the house named after him, but Bullingham House, where, he adds, "a slab put up in remembrance of him may still be seen in the garden wall."

The neighbourhood of Kensington Gravel Pits, by which name is understood a district of some extent bordering on the Uxbridge Road, has long been noted for salubrity of the air, and was a favourite residence of artists half a century ago. The high road through this district, known as High Street, Notting Hill, forms a kind of second Kensington High Street, being to the northern boundary of the suburb what the High Street, in the road to Hammersmith, is to Kensington proper.

Swift had lodgings in the Gravel Pits during the winter of 1712-13; and Lord Chatham's sister, Anne Pitt, is recorded to have died "at her house in Pitt Place, Kensington Gravel Pits," in 1780. To the south of the Gravel Pits was the Mall, which still exists as a street running at right angles to the Uxbridge Road.

Sheffield House, which stood between Church Street and Kensington Gravel Pits, owed its name to property possessed in this quarter by Sheffield, Duke of Buckingham, with the descendants of whose family it long remained. The house, however, has disappeared, and in its place have risen rows of houses overlooking Campden House Gardens and Palace Green.

Time was, and not so very long ago, when the artist body made their homes at Kentish and Camden Town, at Highgate, Hampstead, and St. John's Wood; but of late years they have flocked in far larger numbers to Kensington, no doubt on account of the convenience of access thence to all parts of the town, and of the good northern light which is secured to them by Kensington Gardens and the Park round Holland House. The Royal Academy Catalogue for 1876 shows that out of the total number of exhibitors, about a hundred lived in and around Kensington.

At his residence in the Mall, in 1844, died Sir Augustus Callcott, R.A., the eminent English landscape painter. Sir Augustus and his brother John W. Callcott, the musician, were the sons of a builder who resided near the "Gravel Pits," Kensington, where they were born in 1779 and 1766 respectively. At the time of the fire at Campden House, above mentioned, the adjoining mansion was in the occupation of Mr. Augustus Egg, a distinguished Royal Academician, and fears were entertained for the safety of his house and its valuable contents.

Sir David Wilkie was living in Kensington in 1834. Here he showed to his friends his picture of "John Knox preaching to his Congregation" before sending it in to the Academy. Mr. J. R. Planché, who was among the visitors, drew his attention to certain anachronisms in the armour, which the painter promised to alter; but time went on, the promise was never fulfilled, and the painting still exists to hand down a wilful blunder to posterity. Wilkie's first residence here was in Lower Phillimore Place, near the milestone; there he painted his "Chelsea Pensioners," his "Reading of the Will," his "Distraining for Rent," and his "Blind-man's Buff." He afterwards removed to Shaftesbury House, on the Terrace, and here the sunny hours of his life were spent. We get a glimpse of his daily habits in a letter which he wrote to his sister soon after settling here: "I dine, as formerly," he tells her, "at two o'clock, paint two hours in the forenoon and two hours in the afternoon, and take a short walk in the Park or through the fields twice a day." His last residence here, as Peter Cunningham tells us, was a detached mansion in Vicarage Place, at the head of Church Lane; there he took leave of his friends before his visit to the Holy Land, which shortly preceded his death.

At Kensington, John Evelyn, as he tells us in his "Diary," went to visit Dr. Tenison (afterwards Archbishop of Canterbury), "whither he had retired to refresh himself after he had been sick of the small-pox." This was just before the erection of the school in Leicester Square which bears Tenison's name. Kensington was the birthplace of Lord Chancellor Camden, who died in 1794, at the age of eighty. Sir John Fielding, the well-known magistrate, was also a resident here. Here, too, lived, and here died at an advanced age, Lady Margaret Macdonald, the mother of Chief Baron Macdonald, a lady who was visited by Dr. Johnson in his tour to the Hebrides. She was buried in the centre vault of the old church, close to the reading-desk, which was given to the parish by William III. It was her attendant and connection,

Flora Macdonald, who so heroically aided the escape of "Bonny Prince Charlie," after his defeat at Culloden.

Another Kensingtonian was Robert Nelson, the author of "Fasts and Festivals," and one of the founders of the Society for Promoting Christian Knowledge. He died in 1715, and was a man of such polished and courtly manners, that Dr. Johnson affirms him to have been the original whence Samuel Richardson drew his "Sir Charles Grandison."

It is worthy of note that the high road between London and Kensington was the first place where oil lamps with glazed lights were placed, for the convenience of the Court as they travelled backwards and forwards to St. James's and Whitehall. This was about the year 1694. The old method of lighting the thoroughfare with lanterns and wicks of cotton was then gradually laid aside. It does not appear, however, that the example of Kensington was at all speedily followed by the rest of the metropolis at the West End; for more than a quarter of a century later, in 1718, we find Lady Mary Wortley Montagu* contrasting the lighting of London at night with that of Paris in most unfavourable terms. If Chelsea, as Thackeray observes in his "Esmond," was even in Anne's time "distant from London, and the roads to it were bad, and infested by footpads," the same was true also of Kensington. Indeed, as a proof of the insecurity of the roads in the suburbs until after the introduction of gas and the establishment of a police force, we may be pardoned for informing our readers, on the authority of Walker's "Original," that, "at Kensington, within the memory of man, on Sunday evenings a bell used to be rung at intervals to muster the people returning to town. As soon as a band was assembled sufficiently numerous to ensure mutual protection, it set off, and so on till all had passed." So insecure was the state of the road—in fact, in spite of the patrol—that we read of a plot being concocted for the purpose of robbing Queen Anne as she returned from London to Kensington in her coach. Indeed, even as late as the end of the last century, a journey from London to the suburbs after night-fall was not accomplished without danger to purse and person too. Horace Walpole often travelled along this road in his carriage between Berkeley Square and Strawberry Hill. On one occasion, as he intimates in one of his letters to the Miss Berrys, he composed a long set of verses in praise of General Conway, then in chief command at the Horse Guards, whilst in his carriage, having "conceived and executed them between Hammersmith and Hyde Park Corner."

We learn from a private letter in the Record Office, descriptive of the Fire of London, that on that occasion a great quantity of the goods and property of the citizens was brought as far westward as Kensington for safety. The writer adds: "Had your lordship been at Kensington you would have thought for five days—for so long the fire lasted—that it had been Doomsday, and that the heavens themselves had been on fire; and the fearful cries and howlings of undone people did much increase the resemblance. My walks and gardens were almost covered with the ashes of papers, linen, &c., and pieces of ceiling and plaster-work, blown thither by the tempest."

"In a curious little nook of the 'Court Suburb,' wherein the drama had furtively taken root," writes Mr. J. R. Planché, in his "Recollections," "I witnessed the performance of a piece entitled the 'Queen's Lover,' by a company of actors, all previously unknown to me, even by name, but who generally exhibited talent, and one, in my humble opinion, genius." Mr. Planché went thither in the company of Madame Vestris and Mr. Alfred Bunn, who at the time had succeeded to the united stage kingdom of Covent Garden and of Drury Lane. The person of "genius" was Henry Gaskell Denvil, in whom Bunn thought that he had found a second Kean. Instead, however, of encouraging him, he crushed his spirits and drove him out of life.

It would, perhaps, be a little singular if such an interesting "old-world" sort of place as Kensington should be without its "ghost-story;" and it may be gratifying to find that it is not. Here is one, of no older date than the year 1868, which we quote from the newspaper reports at the time:—"In a small house, about twenty yards away from the main road, live an old lady, eighty-four years of age, and her daughter, with one servant. They have lived in the same house for nearly twenty years without any annoyance; but for the last few months they are being constantly startled by a sharp loud knocking upon the panel of the street-door. Upon opening the door, however quickly, no sign of any one is to be discovered. No sooner are the ladies quietly settled again than rap-rap-rap! comes upon the door. And this is repeated at irregular intervals through the evening. For some time it was attributed to some imps of school-boys, who are always ready for mischief, and but little notice was taken of it; but the continuance of what was only annoying became at last a serious nuisance. The most nimble efforts were made, without success,

* Works, edited by Lord Wharncliffe, vol. ii., p. 118.

to 'catch' the offenders, but until a few nights ago the attacks were so arranged as never to take place in the presence of male visitors; consequently the ladies received much pity, but little sympathy, from their friends. After a time they became nervous, and at last really frightened. On Thursday evening a gentleman, the son of the old lady, called, and found them quite ill from nervous excitement, and was comforting them as well as he could, when a quick rap-rap-rap! at the front door made him jump up. In two seconds he was at the door, rushed out, looking in every direction without discovering a sound or a trace of any human being in any of the adjacent roads. Then, for the first time, he was able to understand from what his mother and sister had suffered, and set to work to examine the approaches to the door inside and out, and to solve the mystery, if possible. No sooner had he gone back to the little dining-room, and placed a chair in the open doorway, with a big stick handy to 'trounce' the perpetrator the next time, and begun to discuss what it was, than rap-rap-rap! sent him flying out into the street, to the astonishment of a passing cabman, who must have thought a madman had just escaped his keeper. This happened four or five times more; in fact, it only ceased about a quarter to eleven. He went round to the police-station, and had an officer put on special duty opposite the house for the next day, and spent the following morning in calling upon the neighbours, and carefully examining the gardens and walls which abutted upon the 'haunted' house. Not a mark of any sort was to be found, and he was quite convinced that the door could not have been reached from any point but right in front from the street, as there is no cellar or drain under the house. In the evening he took a friend down with him, and two more of his friends looked in later. The ladies were found in a painful state of nervous fright, as the nuisance had already been going on, and the maid-servant was crying. Altogether, it was a scene of misery. In the course of conversation the following facts came out:—It began on a Friday, the 18th of October, and has never missed a Friday since then. It has never been heard on Sunday, seldom on Saturday; never before the gas-lamps are lit, never after eleven. Just as all were talking at once, rap-rap-rap! In an instant all four gentlemen were in the front garden; the policeman was quietly standing opposite the door; the lady of the house opposite watching the door from her portico, and another gentleman from the leads. All declared that not a living creature had been near the house for at least a quarter of an hour. The whole thing seems inexplicable, and has created quite a sensation in the neighbourhood." The mystery was afterwards solved, for it appeared that the servant-girl had caused the rapping by means of wires.

In Scarsdale Terrace, Wright's Lane, near the railway station, Kensington High Street, is the Crippled Boys' National Industrial Home. This charity was instituted in 1865, and was originally located in a house in the High Street. There are about fifty crippled boys in the Home, received from all parts of the kingdom, once destitute, neglected, or ill treated in their own dwellings, without any chance of rising, like other youths, to social independence by their own exertions, but now happily engaged for a term of three years in learning an industrial employment for this end. This charity has, notwithstanding its limited means, been of great service to many, the greater portion of whom are seen or heard of from time to time; and it is astonishing to find how many crippled children there are throughout the country, whose anxious appeals to the committee for admission are very distressing.

Scarsdale House, a small mansion close by, was for many years a boarding-school, and as such, says Leigh Hunt, it must have been an eyesore to William Cobbett, the political writer, the back of whose premises in the High Street it overlooked. Scarsdale House, now no longer a boarding-school, appears to have returned to the occupation of the family who are understood to have built it, for its present inmate is the Hon. Edward Cecil Curzon, brother of the late Lord Zouche. It is conjectured that the house was built by the Earl of Scarsdale, whose family name was Leake, the Scarsdale celebrated by Pope for his love of the bottle—

> "Each mortal has his pleasure;—none deny
> Scarsdale his bottle, Darty his ham-pie."

The short-lived Roman Catholic University College, which was formally inaugurated in 1874, stood on the site of Abingdon House, in Wright's Lane. The building, although comparatively small, was very complete in its arrangements, and comprised a theatre, lecture-rooms, a school of science, a discussion-room, and a chapel. A number of rooms were also set apart for the amusement or edification of the students in various ways. The college, which received the support and patronage of all the English Roman Catholic bishops, was founded mainly through the instrumentality of Monsignor Capel, who was appointed its first rector. It, however, failed after a brief career of usefulness, and, as its difficulties were found to be insurmountable, the institution was given up, and the buildings were pulled down about the year 1880. The site has since been built over.

Kensington always has had a large Irish element, and of late years, owing to the increasing population of the place, rapid strides have been made by the Roman Catholic body in augmenting their numbers.

The *London Review* of 1865 gives the following account of the progress of the Roman Catholic body of Kensington at that time:—"Formerly, for the accommodation of the whole of the Roman Catholics of this parish, there was but one small chapel near the High Street, which appeared amply sufficient for the members of that creed. But ten or twelve years ago a Roman Catholic builder purchased, at an enormous price, a plot of ground, about three acres in extent, beside the Church of the Holy Trinity, Brompton. For a time considerable mystery prevailed as to the uses it was to be applied to; but, shortly after the buildings were commenced, they were discovered to be the future residence and church of the Oratorian Fathers, removed to it from their former dwelling; and the chapel, a small and commodious erection, was opened for divine service. At first the congregation was of the scantiest description: even on Sundays at high mass, small as the chapel was, it was frequently only half filled; while on week days, at many of the services, it was no uncommon circumstance to find the attendance scarcely more numerous than the number of priests serving at the altar. By degrees the congregation increased, till the chapel was found too small for their accommodation, and extensive alterations were made to it; but these, again, were soon filled to overflowing, and further alterations had to be made, till at last the building was capable of holding, without difficulty, from 2,000 to 2,500 persons. It is now frequently so crowded at high mass that it is difficult for an individual entering it after the commencement of the service to find even standing room. In the meantime the monastery itself, if that is the proper term, was completed—a splendid appearance it presents—and we believe is fully occupied. The Roman Catholic population in the parish or mission, under the spiritual direction of the Fathers of the Oratory, now comprise between 7,000 and 8,000 souls. The average attendance at mass on Sunday is about 5,000, and the average number of communicants for the last two years has been about 45,000 annually. But in addition to this church, Kensington has three others—St. Mary's, Upper Holland Street; St. Simon Stock, belonging to the Carmelite Friars; and the Church of St. Francis Assisi, in Notting Hill. Of monasteries, or religious communities of men, it has the Oratorians before mentioned, and the Discalced Carmelites, in Vicarage Place. Of convents of ladies it has the Assumption, in Kensington Square; the Poor Clares Convent, in Edmond Terrace; the Franciscan Convent, in Portobello Road; and the Sisters of Jesus, in Holland Villas. Of schools, the Roman Catholics possess, in the parish of Kensington, the Orphanage, in the Fulham Road; the Industrial School of St. Vincent de Paul; as well as the large Industrial School for Girls in the southern ward. All these schools are very numerously attended; the gross number of pupils amounting to 1,200, those of the Oratory alone being 1,000. The kindness and consideration shown by the Roman Catholic teachers to the children of the poor is above all praise, not only in Kensington, but in all localities where they are under their charge; and the love they receive from their pupils in return forms one of their most powerful engines in their system of proselytising."

The chapel of St. Mary's above mentioned, in Holland Street, is close to the principal street in Kensington, and is thus described in the "Catholic Hand book," published in 1857:—"It is a plain, unpretending edifice, the cross upon its front being the only feature to distinguish it from an ordinary Dissenting meeting-house. Its interior has a remarkable air of neatness. The building itself is an oblong square, built north and south, and capable of accommodating about 300 persons. It is lit by three windows at the northern end, and one window at the eastern and western sides. It is devoid of ornament, except at the south end, where the altar is raised between two pillars. The body of the chapel is fitted with low open seats, and at the northern end is a spacious gallery." Being superseded by other and larger ecclesiastical edifices, the old chapel is now used as a school-room. It was built about 1812 by the family of Mr. Wheble, the manufacturer of the celebrated Kensington candles, who began life with a small shop in High Street, but died worth a quarter of a million.

In Newland Terrace, on the south side of the main road, is the Church of Our Lady of Victories, which serves as a pro-cathedral, superseding the Church of St. Mary's, Moorfields. It is a lofty Gothic structure of the Early English type, with some details approaching more nearly to the Decorated style. It consists of a nave and side aisles, and a shallow chancel, in which is the throne of the archiepiscopal see of Westminster. The windows of the apse are filled with stained glass.

In the Kensington Road is the "Adam and Eve" public-house, where Sheridan, on his way to or from Holland House, regularly stopped for a dram; and there he ran up a long bill, which, as we learn from Moore's diary, Lord Holland had to pay.

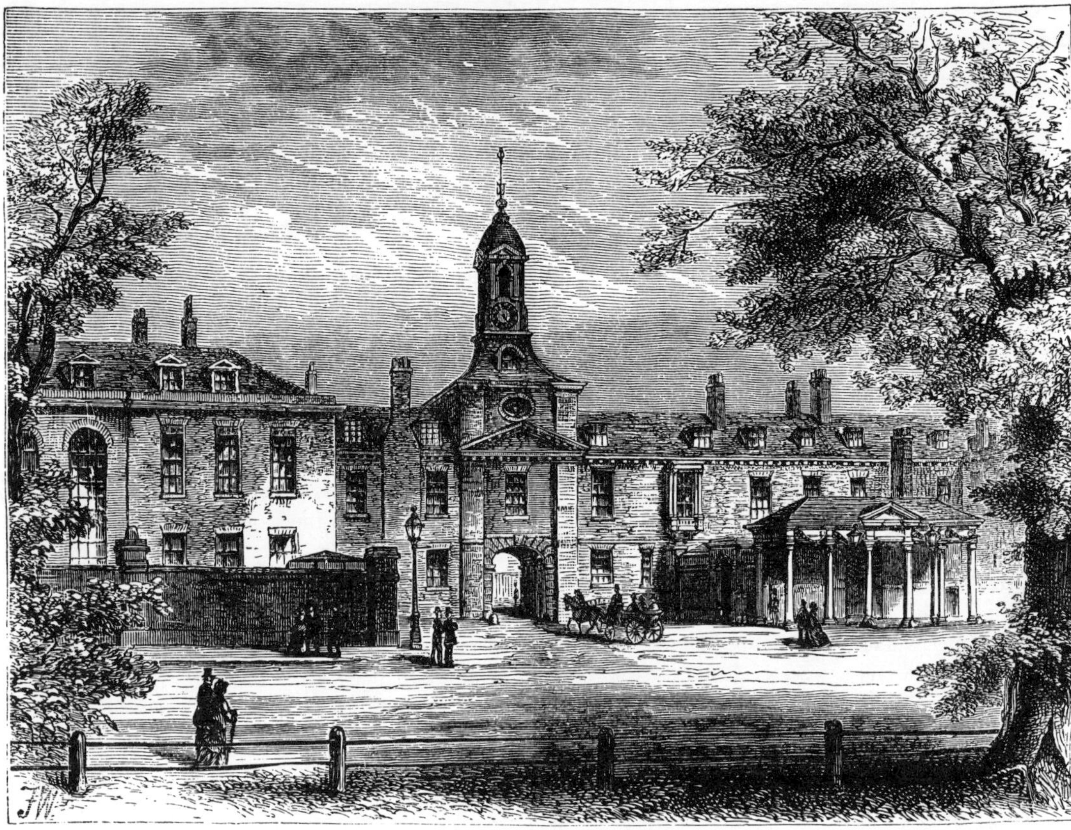

WEST FRONT OF KENSINGTON PALACE.

CHAPTER XII.

KENSINGTON PALACE.

"High o'er the neighbouring lands,
'Midst greens and sweets, a regal fabric stands."—*Tickell.*

Situation of Kensington Palace—Houses near it—Kensington Palace Gardens—The "King's Arms"—Henry VIII.'s Conduit—Palace Green—The Kensington Volunteers—The Water Tower—Thackeray's House: his Death—Description of the Palace—The Chapel—The Principal Pictures formerly shown here—Early History of the Building—William III. and Dr. Radcliffe—A "Scene" in the Royal Apartments—Death of Queen Mary and William III.—Queen Anne and the Jacobites—"Scholar Dick," and his Fondness for the Bottle—Lax Manners of the Court under the Early Georges—Death of George II.—The Princess Sophia—Caroline, Princess of Wales—Balls and Parties given by her Royal Highness—An Undignified Act—The Duke of Sussex's Hospitality—Birth of the Princess Victoria—Her Baptism—Death of William IV., and Accession of Queen Victoria—Her First Council—Death of the Duke of Sussex—The Duchess of Inverness—Other Royal Inhabitants.

As in France, so also in England, nearly all the palaces of royalty are located outside the city. Greenwich, Eltham, Hatfield, Theobalds, Nonsuch, Enfield, Havering-atte-Bower, Oatlands, Hampton Court, Kew, Richmond, all in turn, as well as Kensington, have been chosen as residences for our sovereigns. Kensington Palace, though actually situated in the parish of St. Margaret, Westminster, is named from the adjoining town, to which it would more naturally seem to belong, and it stands in grounds about 350 acres in extent.

Palace Gate House, a spacious mansion, with ornamental elevation, standing on the north side of the High Street, near the entrance to the Palace, was long the residence of the late Mr. John Forster, the historian, biographer, and critic, and the friend of Charles Dickens. A broad roadway, leading from the High Street of Kensington to the Bayswater Road, and known as Kensington Palace Gardens, contains several costly mansions, including one of German-Gothic design, built for the Earl of Harrington in 1852.

In the High Street, close by the entrance to the Palace, is the "King's Arms" Tavern, at which Addison was a frequent visitor, when he took up his abode in his adopted home at Holland House as the husband of Lady Warwick.

On the west side of Palace Green, in what was

formerly called the King's Garden, Henry VIII. is said to have built a conduit, or bath, for the use of the Princess Elizabeth, when a child. It was a low building, with walls of great thickness, and the roof covered with bricks. The interior was in good preservation when Faulkner wrote his "History of Kensington," and afforded a favourable specimen of the brickwork of the period. It is clear, from an entry in the parish books, though unnoticed by Faulkner, that Queen Elizabeth, at least on one occasion subsequent to her childhood, stayed within the parish, for the parish officers are rebuked and punished for not ringing "when Her Majesty left Kensington." Probably this entry refers to some visit which she paid to Holland House, where no doubt she was entertained as a guest by the then owner, the old Earl of Holland, or by Sir Walter Cope, who built the original mansion. On Palace Green are the barracks for foot-soldiers, who still regularly mount guard at the Palace. The Green, called in ancient documents the "Moor," was the military parade when the Court resided here, and the royal standard was hoisted on it daily.

Among the historical associations of this place must not be overlooked the Old Kensington Volunteers, which was formed towards the close of the last century. In 1801 an engraving was published, showing the presentation of colours to the regiment; the original painting, together with the colours themselves—which were worked by the Duchess of Gloucester and her daughter, the Princess Sophia Matilda—are now in the Vestry Hall. In 1876 these colours were placed in front of the Princess Louise, when she opened the New National Schools here, and the vicar of Kensington drew the attention of her Royal Highness to this work of her ancestors. Dr. Callcott, whom we have already mentioned as living near the Gravel Pits, was band-master in the above corps, which was disbanded at the Peace of Amiens, and also in the Kensington Corps of Volunteer Infantry, which was established in 1803.

KENSINGTON PALACE, FROM THE GARDENS.

On this green there stood formerly a water-tower of singular construction; it was built in the reign of Queen Anne, but had long ceased to be used when Faulkner wrote his "History of Kensington" in 1820. It was of red brick, and consisted of three storeys, surrounded by two heavy battlemented turrets; it is said to have been designed by Sir John Vanbrugh. The tower was removed in 1850.

In 1846, Thackeray removed from London to Kensington, taking up his abode at No. 13, Young Street, which connects the Square with the High Street, occupying also by day, for working purposes, chambers at 10, Crown Office Row, Temple. He afterwards removed to Onslow Square, Brompton; but about 1861, or the following year, he again removed to the more congenial neighbourhood of Kensington Palace, and took up his permanent abode in the "Old Court Suburb," about which Leigh Hunt has gossiped so pleasantly. He took on a long lease a somewhat dilapidated mansion, on the west side of Palace Gardens. His intention at first was to repair and improve it, but he finally resolved to pull it down, and build a new house in its place. This, a handsome, solid mansion of choice red brick, with stone facings, was built from his own designs, and he occupied it until his death. "It was," remarks Mr. James Hannay, "a dwelling worthy of one who really represented literature in the great world, and who, planting himself on his books, yet sustained the character of his profession with all the dignity of a gentleman." A friend who called on him there from Edinburgh, in the summer of 1862, knowing of old his love of the poet of Venusia, playfully reminded him what Horace says of those who, regardless of their death, employ themselves in building houses :—

"Sepulchri
Immemor struis domos."

"Nay," said he, "I am *memor sepulchri*, for this house will always let for so many hundreds"—mentioning the sum—"a year." Thackeray was always of opinion, that notwithstanding the somewhat costly proceeding of pulling down and re-erecting, he had achieved the result, rare for a private gentleman, of building for himself a house which, regarded as an investment of a portion of his fortune, left no cause for regret.

HENRY VIII.'S CONDUIT. (*See page* 139.)

Mr. John Forster has told us, in his "Life of Charles Dickens," how the latter met Thackeray at the Athenæum Club, just a week before his death, and shook hands with him at parting, little thinking that it was for the last time. "There had been some estrangement between them since the autumn of 1858. . . . Thackeray, justly indignant at a published description of himself by a member of a club to which both he and Dickens belonged (the Garrick), referred the matter to the committee, who decided to expel the writer. Dickens, thinking expulsion too harsh a penalty for an offence thoughtlessly given, and, as far as might be, manfully atoned for by withdrawal and regret, interposed to avert the extremity. Thackeray resented the interference, and Dickens was justly hurt at the manner in which he did so. Neither," adds Mr. Forster, "was wholly in the right, nor was either altogether in the wrong." The affair, however, is scarcely worth being added as a fresh chapter to the "Quarrels of Authors." Thackeray had often suffered from serious illness, so that his daughter was not much alarmed at finding him in considerable pain and suffering on Wednesday, the 23rd of December, 1863. He complained of pain when his servant left his room, wishing him "good-night," and in the morning, on entering, the man-servant found him dead. He had passed away in the night from an effusion of blood on the brain.

Mr. Hannay wrote :—"Thackeray is dead; and the purest English prose writer of the nineteenth century, and the novelist with a greater knowledge of the human heart as it really is than any one—with the exception, perhaps, of Shakespeare and Balzac—is suddenly struck down in the midst of us. In the midst of us! No long illness, no lingering decay, no gradual suspension of power; almost pen in hand, like Kempenfelt, he went down. Well said the *Examiner*—'Whatever little feuds may have gathered about Mr. Thackeray's public life lay lightly on the surface of the minds that chanced to be in contest with him. They could be thrown off in a moment, at the first shock of the news that he was dead.' It seemed impossible to realise the fact. No other celebrity—be he writer, statesman, artist, actor—seemed so thoroughly a portion of London. That 'good grey head which all men knew' was as easy of recognition as his to whom the term applied, the Duke of Wellington. Scarcely a day passed without his being seen in the Pall-Mall districts; and a Londoner showing to 'country cousins' the wonders of the metropolis, generally knew how to arrange for them to get a sight of the great English writer."

The palace has been described as a "plain brick building, of no particular style or period, but containing a heterogeneous mass of dull apartments, halls, and galleries, presenting externally no single feature of architectural beauty; the united effect of its ill-proportioned divisions being irregular and disagreeable in the extreme." This criticism can hardly be considered too severe. Certain portions of the exterior, it is true, are admired as fine specimens of brickwork in their way; but it cannot be concealed that the general effect of the brick is mean and poor.

The following particulars of the interior of the palace, some of which stand good even at the present day, we glean from John Timbs' "Curiosities of London," published in 1855:—"The great staircase, of black and white marble, and graceful ironwork (the walls painted by Kent with mythological subjects in chiaroscuro, and architectural and sculptural decoration), leads to the suite of twelve state apartments, some of which are hung with tapestry, and have painted ceilings. The 'Presence Chamber' has a chimney-piece richly sculptured by Gibbons, with flowers, fruits, and heads; the ceiling is diapered red, blue, and gold upon a white field, copied by Kent from Herculaneum; and the pier-glass is wreathed with flowers, by Jean Baptiste Monnoyer. The 'King's Gallery,' in the south front, has an elaborately painted allegorical ceiling, and a circular fresco of a Madonna, after Raphael. 'The Cube Room' is forty feet in height, and contains gilded statues and busts, and a marble bas-relief of a Roman marriage, by Rysbrack. The 'King's Great Drawing-room' was hung with the then new paper, in imitation of the old velvet flock. The 'Queen's Gallery,' in the rear of the eastern front, continued northwards, has above the doorway the monogram of William and Mary; and the pediment is enriched with fruits and flowers in high relief and wholly detached, probably carved by Gibbons. The 'Green Closet' was the private closet of William III., and contained his writing table and escritoire; and the 'Patchwork Closet' had its walls and chairs covered with tapestry worked by Queen Mary."

The palace contains a comfortable though far from splendid or tasteful suite of state apartments, the ceilings and staircases of which are ornamented with paintings by Kent. The grand staircase leads from the principal entrance to the palace, on the west, by a long corridor, the sides of which are painted to represent a gallery crowded with spectators on a Court day, in which the artist has introduced portraits of himself; of "Peter, the Wild Boy;" of Ulric, a Polish lad, page to George I.; and of the Turks Mahomet and Mustapha, two of his personal attendants, who were taken prisoners by the Imperialists in Hungary, and who, having become converts to Christianity, obtained posts at Court. Mahomet was extremely charitable, and Pope thus records his personal worth:—

> "From peer or bishop 'tis no easy thing
> To draw the man who loves his God and king.
> Alas! I copy (or my draught would fail)
> From honest Mahomet or from Parson Hale."

The chapel royal is as plain and ordinary an apartment as a Scottish Presbyterian would wish to see; but it is remarkable for containing some fine communion plate. Divine service is performed here regularly by a chaplain to the household, and the public are admitted.

The fine collection of historical paintings which once adorned the walls of Kensington Palace is unrecorded in Dr. Waagen's "Art and Artists in England." The fact is that they have been, for the most part, dispersed, and many of them now are to be found at the Palace of Hampton Court, and other public buildings. Mr. George Scharf, F.S.A., in his "Notes on the Royal Picture Galleries," states that Kensington Palace, during the reign of George II., appears to have contained many, if not most, of the finest pictures. He especially notes Vandyck's pictures of King Charles and his Queen, Cupid and Psyche, and the same painter's "Three Children of Charles I.;" Queen Elizabeth in a Chinese dress, drawn when she was a prisoner at Woodstock; Kneller's portraits of King William and Queen Mary, in their coronation robes (Kneller was knighted for painting these pictures); Tintoretto's grand pictures of "Esther fainting before Ahasuerus," and "Apollo and the Nine Muses." It appears that about the time of the fire at Whitehall, the series of old heads and foreign portraits were transferred to Kensington, as Vertue—on the title to his engravings of them, in "Rapin," published in 1736—mentions them as being in the latter palace; and Walpole, in the first edition of his "Anecdotes" (1762), especially alludes to the early royal portraits at Kensington. He also speaks of a chamber of very ancient portraits—among them one of the Duke of Norfolk—as then existing in the Princess Dowager's house at Kew. A catalogue of these pictures was taken by Benjamin West, at the king's desire, in 1818. Unlike the portraits in most galleries, many of those at Kensington had no names attached to them; and thus, if we may judge from a complaint made by the unfortunate Princess Caroline of Wales, their interest was in a great measure destroyed. The fine collection of Holbein's original drawings and designs for the portraits of the leading personages in the Court of Henry VIII., now in the Royal Library at Windsor, was accidentally discovered by Queen Caroline in a bureau here, shortly after the accession of George II.

The palace has a character of its own among the other residences of the royal family. Leigh Hunt hits the right nail on the head when he speaks of it as possessing "a Dutch solidity." "It can be imagined full of English comfort," he adds; "it is quiet, in a good air, and, though it is a palace, no tragical history is connected with it; all which considerations give it a sort of homely, fireside character, which seems to represent the domestic side of royalty itself, and thus renders an interesting service to what is not always so well recommended by cost and splendour. Windsor Castle is a place to receive monarchs in; Buckingham Palace, to see fashion in; Kensington Palace seems a place to drink tea in; and this is by no means a state of things in which the idea of royalty comes least home to the good wishes of its subjects."

The original mansion was the suburban residence of Lord Chancellor Finch, afterwards Earl of Nottingham, and as such it bore the name of "Nottingham House," of which the lower portion of the present north wing is part. It was purchased for the sum of £20,000 from his successor by William III.; and, as Northouck writes, "for its convenience and healthful situation for the king to reside in during the sitting of Parliament." Shortly after its purchase by the Crown, the house was nearly destroyed by fire, and the king himself had a narrow escape from being burned in his bed. The building was at first, comparatively speaking, small, and the grounds only occupied a few acres. Evelyn, in his "Memoirs," under date February 25, 1690-1, says: "I went to Kensington, which King William has bought of Lord Nottingham, and altered, but was yet a patched-up building, but with the gardens, however, it is a very neat villa." The king found its sequestered situation congenial with his moody and apathetic disposition, and therefore resolved to make it a royal residence superseding Whitehall. The palace was considerably enlarged by William III., at the suggestion of Queen Mary, from designs by Sir Christopher Wren, and surrounded by straight cut solitary lawns, and formal stately gardens, laid out with paths and flower-beds at right angles, after the stiffest Dutch fashion. Queen Anne added very largely to the size of the house, and also to the beauty of the gardens, such as that beauty may have been. The orangery, a fine detached building at a little distance on the north side, was built for her by Sir Christopher Wren. The eastern front of the palace itself was added by George I., from the designs of Kent. The north-western angle was added by George II., in order to form a nursery for his children; and to his queen, Caroline of Anspach, we owe the introduction of the ornamental water into the gardens and pleasure-grounds. The house, which had been growing all this time in size, was finally brought to its present size or appearance by the Duke of Sussex, who added or rebuilt the rooms that form the angle on the south-west. The Duchess of Kent's apartments were in the south-east part of the palace, under the King's Gallery. A melancholy interest hangs about the irregular pile, for within its walls died William III. and his wife, Queen Mary; her sister, Queen Anne, and her consort, Prince George of Denmark, who was carried hence to his tomb in Westminster Abbey; George II.; and lastly, the Queen's favourite uncle, the Duke of Sussex.

Such, then, is a rough outline of the history of the once favourite residence of the House of Hanover. "In the metropolis of commerce," observes Macaulay, "the point of convergence is the Exchange; in the metropolis of fashion it is the Palace." This was eminently true, as we have seen, of the Palace at Whitehall in the days of the second Charles, who made his Court the centre of fashionable gaiety as well as of political intrigue. Under the first of our Hanoverian kings this centre was transferred to Kensington. But the centre had lost much of its attractiveness under them. "The Revolution," Macaulay writes, "gave us several kings, unfitted by their education and habits to be gracious and affable hosts. They had been born and bred upon the Continent. They never felt themselves at home on our island. If they spoke our language, they spoke it inelegantly and with effort. Our national character they never understood; our national manners they hardly attempted to acquire. The most important part of their duty they performed better than any ruler that had preceded them: for they governed strictly according to law; but they could not be the first gentlemen of the realm—the heads of polite society. If ever they unbent, it was in a very small circle, where hardly an English face was to be seen; and they were never so happy as when they could escape for a summer to their native land. They had, indeed, their days of reception for our nobility and gentry; but the reception was a matter of form, and became at last as solemn a ceremony as a funeral." To the head-quarters of the Court at Kensington these remarks are to be applied quite literally.

William III. usually held his Courts at Kensington, and the decoration of the apartments of its palace was one of the chief amusements of his royal consort. And yet, fond as he was of Kensington, King William would often say that he preferred to be hunting on the shores of Guelderland rather than riding over the glades of this place or Hampton Court—a taste in which he was followed by George II. Indeed, with a natural love for his Dutch home, William made this palace and the gardens surrounding it look as much like his native country as he could.

Although William was not over-fond of his new subjects, and his Court, for the most part, was as gloomy as his gardens, yet there still might occasionally be seen here some of the liveliest wits and courtiers that have left a name in history. Here came the Earl of Dorset, Prior's friend, who had been one of the wits of the Court of Charles II.; Prior himself, too, was there, and succeeded in obtaining an appointment as one of the "gentlemen of the king's bedchamber;" Congreve, whose plays were admired by Queen Mary; Halifax, who is spoken of as a "minor wit, but no mean statesman;" Swift, and Sir William Temple; Burnet, the gossiping historian, who afterwards became a bishop; the Earl of Devonshire, "whose nobler zeal," as Leigh Hunt puts it, "had made him a duke, one of a family remarkable for their constant and happy combination of popular politics with all the graces of their rank." Among other visitors here at this period, too, were Lord Monmouth, afterwards Earl of Peterborough, "the friend of Swift and Pope, conqueror of Spain, and lover, at the age of seventy, of Lady Suffolk;" Sheffield, afterwards Duke of Buckinghamshire, "a minor wit and poet, in love with (the rank of) the Princess Anne;" and last not least, Peter the Great, the "semi-barbarian, the premature forcer of Russian pseudo-civilisation, who came to England in order to import the art of shipbuilding into his dominions in his own proper mechanical person." Peter is stated to have frequently dined at Kensington Palace; and it has been wondered how the two sovereigns got on so well together. Leigh Hunt tells a story how that one day the king took the Russian monarch to the House of Lords, when the latter, owing to a natural shyness, made the lords and the king himself laugh, by peeping strangely at them out of a window in the roof. He got the same kind of sight at the House of Commons; and even at a ball at Kensington, on the Princess Anne's birthday, he contrived to be invisibly present in a closet prepared for him on purpose, where he could see without being seen.

Here, when William was ill with the dropsy, he called in the Court physician, Dr. Radcliffe, to pay him a professional visit. Showing him his swollen ankles, he exclaimed, "Doctor, what do you think of these?" "Why, truly," answered Radcliffe, "I would not have your Majesty's two legs for your three kingdoms." With this ill-timed jest, though it passed unnoticed at the moment, it is needless to add that the doctor's attendance on the Court at Kensington ceased. It is true that in 1714 he was sent for by Queen Anne upon her death-bed; but he was too ill to leave his house at Carshalton. His refusal, however, nearly exposed him to "lynch law," for the mob at the West End threatened to kill him if he came to London. The mob, however, was disappointed, for a few months later he died of the gout.

The following story, relating to a scene which happened in the royal apartments here, we tell in the words of Lord Sackville, as they stand recorded in the gossiping pages of Sir N. W. Wraxall:—"My father, having lost his own mother when very young, was brought up chiefly by the Dowager Countess of Northampton, his grandmother, who being particularly acceptable to Queen Mary, she commanded the countess always to bring her little grandson, Lord Buckhurst, to Kensington Palace, though at that time hardly four years of age; and he was allowed to amuse himself with a child's cart in the gallery. King William, like almost all Dutchmen, never failed to attend the tea-table every evening. It happened that her Majesty having one afternoon, by his desire, made tea, and waiting for the king's arrival, who was engaged in business in his cabinet, at the other extremity of the gallery, the boy, hearing the queen express her impatience at the delay, ran away to the closet, dragging after him the cart. When he arrived at the door, he knocked, and the king asked, 'Who is there?' 'Lord Buck,' answered he. 'And what does Lord Buck want with me?' replied his Majesty. 'You must come to tea directly,' said he; 'the queen is waiting for you.' King William immediately laid down his pen, and opened the door; then taking the child in his arms, placed Lord Buckhurst in the cart, and seizing the pole, drew them both along the gallery, quite to the room in which were seated the queen, Lady Northampton, and the company. But no sooner had he entered the apartment than, exhausted with the effort, which had forced the blood upon his lungs, and being naturally asthmatic, threw himself into a chair, and for some minutes was incapable of uttering a word, breathing with the utmost difficulty. The Countess of Northampton, shocked at the consequences of her grandson's indiscretion, which threw the whole circle into great consternation, would have punished him; but the king interposed in his behalf; and the story is chiefly interesting because (as serving to show how kindly he could behave to a troublesome child) it places that prince in a more amiable point of view than he is commonly represented in history."

Queen Mary, consort of William III., died here of the small-pox, and the king's attachment to the palace is said to have increased, from the circumstance of its having been the scene of the last acts of the queen, who was justly entitled to his affection. It was here that the king also died, in consequence of an accident in riding at Hampton Court a few days previously. The readers of Macaulay will not have forgotten the picture which he draws in the very last page of his history, when William, knowing that death was approaching, sent for his friends Albemarle, Auverquerque, and Bentinck, while Bishops Burnet and Tillotson read the last prayers by his bedside. After his Majesty's death, bracelets composed of the queen's hair were found upon his arm.

QUEEN CAROLINE'S DRAWING-ROOM, KENSINGTON PALACE.

The Court at Kensington in Queen Anne's time was not much livelier than it had been in that of King William. Swift describes Anne, in a circle of twenty visitors, as sitting with her fan in her mouth, saying about three words once a minute to those that were near her, and then, upon hearing that dinner was ready, going out. Addison and Steele might have been occasionally seen at her

Kensington levees, among the Whigs; and Swift, Prior, and Bolingbroke among the Tories. Marlborough would be there also; his celebrated duchess, Sarah Jennings, had entered upon a court life at an early age as one of the companions of Anne during the princess's girlhood.

The last memorable interview between Queen Anne and the Duke of Marlborough took place here. When Queen Anne was lying in the agonies of death, and the Jacobite party were correspondingly in the agonies of hope and expectation, two noblemen of the highest rank—John, Duke of Argyll, and the "proud" Duke of Somerset, who had been superseded in office at the time of the union with Scotland—suddenly, and unbidden, appeared at the council, and their unexpected presence is said to have stifled Lord Bolingbroke's designs, if he ever entertained any, of recalling the exiled Stuarts. On such slight events—accidents as we often call them—do the fates of dynasties, and indeed of whole nations, depend.

We learn from Thackeray's "Esmond" that while the royal guard had a very splendid table laid out for them at St. James's, the gentlemen ushers who waited on King William, and afterwards on Queen Anne, had their dinner here; and he tells us that Richard Steele liked the latter far better than his own chair at the former, "where there was less wine and more ceremony." Steele, who came to London in the suite of the Duke of Ormond, figures in the above work as "Scholar Dick;" he was one of the gentlemen ushers or members of the king's guard at Kensington.

When Esmond comes to England, after being wounded at Blenheim, he finds Mrs. Beatrix installed as a lady-in-waiting at the palace, and thenceforth "all his hopes and desires lay within Kensington Park wall."

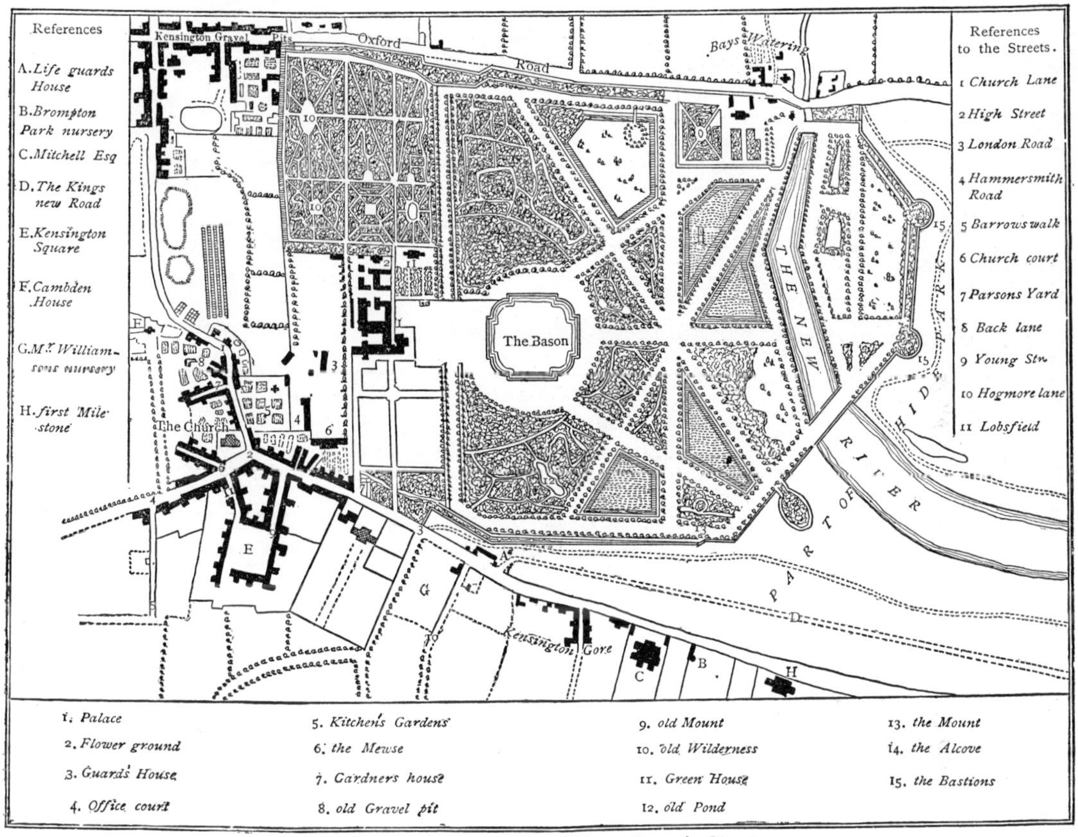

KENSINGTON IN 1764. (*From Rocque's Map.*)

George I., whose additions to the palace were the cupola-room and the great staircase, frequently resided here, as also did his successor, George II. Here, free from the restraint caused by Sir Robert Walpole's presence, the latter king, when angry with his ministers or his attendants, would fly into furious rages, expending his anger even on his innocent wig; whilst his clever spouse, Queen Caroline, stood by, maintaining her dignity and self-possession, and, consequently, her ascendancy over him, and acting as a "conducting wire" between the sovereign and the premier. A good story is told by Horace Walpole, showing the lax and romping manners of the Court under the early Georges:—"There has been a great fracas at Kensington (he writes in 1742). One of the mesdames (the princesses) pulled the chair from under Countess Deloraine at cards, who, being provoked that her monarch was diverted with her disgrace, with the malice of a hobby-horse gave him just such another fall. But, alas! the monarch, like Louis XIV., is mortal in the part that touched the ground, and was so hurt and so angry, that the countess is disgraced, and her German rival remains in the sole and quiet possession of her royal master's favour." The Countess of Deloraine was governess to the young princesses, daughters of George II., and was a favourite with the king, with whom she generally played cards in the evenings in the princesses' apartments. Sir Robert Walpole considered her as a dangerous person about the Court, for she possessed, said the shrewd minister, "a weak head, a pretty face, a lying tongue, and a false heart." Lord Hervey, in his "Court Ballad," written in 1742, sarcastically styles her "*virtuous*, and *sober*, and *wise* Deloraine;" and in his "Memoirs," under date of 1735, he describes her as "one of the vainest as well as one of the simplest women that ever lived; but to this wretched head," he adds, "there was certainly joined one of the prettiest faces that ever was formed, which, though she was now five-and-thirty, had a bloom upon it, too, that not one woman in ten thousand has at fifteen."

George II. died quite suddenly as he sat at breakfast in the palace, on Saturday, October 25, 1760. The building underwent considerable alterations during his reign, and he was the last monarch who resided here, George III. having chosen as his homes St. James's Palace, Kew Gardens, and Buckingham House.

The palace, too, was the home of the Princess Sophia, the poor blind daughter of George III. Miss Amelia Murray, in her "Recollections," speaks of having constantly spent an evening with her in her apartments here, and bears testimony to the goodness of her disposition, as "an example of patient and unmurmuring endurance such as can rarely be met with."

Here, too, the unfortunate Caroline, Princess of Wales, was living from 1810 down to 1814, when she removed to Connaught Place. Here she held, if we may so speak, her rival Court, and kept up a kind of triangular duel with her royal husband, and her wayward child, the Princess Charlotte, not at all to the edification of those around her, who were obliged to feel and to own that, injured as she undoubtedly was by one who had sworn to love and cherish her, she did but little to win the respect and regard of either the Court or the nation at large. The hangers-on of the Princess would seem to have been of the ordinary type of "summer friends." At all events, one of her ladies in waiting writes thus, with a vein of unconscious sarcasm: "These noblemen and their wives continued to visit her royal highness the Princess of Wales till the old king was declared too ill to reign, and the Prince became in fact regent; then those ladies disappeared that moment from Kensington, and were never seen there more. It was the besom of expediency which swept them all away." It appears, however, that the Princess of Wales was well aware that her hangers-on were not very disinterested. At all events, she writes: "Unless I do show dem de knife and fork, no company has come to Kensington or Blackheath, and neither my purse nor my spirits can always afford to hang out de offer of 'an ordinary.'"

The friends of the Princess formed a circle by themselves. It included Lord and Lady Henry Fitz-Gerald, Lady C. Lindsay, Lord Rivers, Mr. H. (afterwards Lord) Brougham, Lord and Lady Abercorn, Sir Humphry Davy, Lady Anne Hamilton, Mr. (afterwards Sir William) Gell, Mr. Craven, Sir J. Mackintosh, Mr. R. Payne Knight, Mr. and Lady E. Whitbread, Lord and Lady Grey, and Lord Erskine—a most strange and heterogeneous medley. Very frequently the dinners at Kensington were exceedingly agreeable, the company well chosen, and sufficient liberty given to admit of their conversing with unrestrained freedom. This expression does not imply a licentious mode of conversation, although sometimes discretion and modesty were trenched upon in favour of wit. Still, that was by no means the general turn of the discourse.

One of the ladies of the Princess Caroline writes, under date of 1810: "The Princess often does the most extraordinary things, apparently for no other purpose than to make her attendants stare. Very frequently she will take one of her ladies with her to walk in Kensington Gardens, who are accordingly dressed [it may be] in a costume very unsuited to the public highway; and, all of a sudden, she will bolt out at one of the smaller gates, and walk all over Bayswater, and along the Paddington Canal, at the risk of being insulted, or, if known, mobbed, enjoying the terror of the unfortunate attendant who may be destined to walk after her. One day, her royal highness inquired at all the doors of Bayswater and its neighbourhood if there were any houses to be let, and went into many of them, till at last she came to one where some children of a friend of hers (Lord H. F.) were placed for change of air, and she was quite enchanted to be known by them, and to boast of her extraordinary mode of walking over the country."

Her royal highness gave plenty of balls and parties whilst residing here, and amused herself pretty well as she chose. In 1811 she is thus described by Lady Brownlow, in her "Reminiscences of a Septuagenarian:"—"I had scarcely ever seen the Princess, and hardly knew her by sight. At the time of which I speak, her figure was fat and somewhat shapeless; her face had probably been pretty in youth, for her nose was well formed, her complexion was good, and she had bright blue eyes; but their expression was bold—this, however, might be partly caused by the quantity of rouge which she wore. Her fair hair hung in masses of curls on each side of her throat, like a lion's mane. Everybody, before the peace with France, dressed much according to their individual taste; and her royal highness was of a showy turn: her gowns were generally ornamented with gold or silver spangles, and her satin boots were also embroidered with them. Sometimes she wore a scarlet mantle, with a gold trimming round it, hanging from her shoulders; and as she swam, so attired, down an English dance, with no regard to the figure, the effect was rather strange. . . . The princess's parties themselves," Lady Brownlow continues, "were marvellously heterogeneous in their composition. There were good people, and very bad ones, fine ladies and fine gentlemen, humdrums and clever people; among the latter the Rev. Sydney Smith, who, I thought, looked out of place there. . . . Her royal highness made rather a fuss with us, and we both always supped at her table. On one occasion I was much amused at seeing my father opposite to me, seated between the Duchess of Montrose and Lady Oxford. Sure never were there more incongruous supporters; and my father's countenance was irresistibly comic. 'Methought,' said he, as we drove home, 'that I was Hercules between Virtue and Vice.'"

The following anecdote of her royal highness shows how little of good sense or dignity she possessed:—"One day, the Princess set out to walk, accompanied by myself and one of her ladies, round Kensington Gardens. At last, being wearied, her royal highness sat down on a bench occupied by two old persons, and she conversed with them, to my infinite amusement, they being perfectly ignorant who she was. She asked them all manner of questions about herself, to which they replied favourably; but her lady, I observed, was considerably alarmed, and was obliged to draw her veil over her face to prevent betraying herself; and every moment I was myself afraid that something not so favourable might be expressed by these good people. Fortunately, this was not the case, and her royal highness walked away undiscovered, having informed them that, if they would be at such a door at such an hour at the palace on any day, they would meet with the Princess of Wales, to see whom they expressed the strongest desire. This Haroun Al-Raschid expedition passed off happily, but I own I dreaded its repetition."

On another occasion her royal highness made a party to go to a small cottage in the neighbourhood of Bayswater, where she could feel herself unshackled by the restraints of royalty and etiquette; there she received a set of persons wholly unfit to be admitted to her society. It is true that, since the days of Mary of Scotland (when Rizzio sang in the Queen's closet), and in the old time before her, all royal persons have delighted in some small retired place or apartment, where they conceived themselves at liberty to cast off the cares of their high station, and descend from the pedestal of power and place to taste the sweets of private life. But in all similar cases, this attempt to be what they were not has only proved injurious to them: every station has its price—its penalty. By the Princess, especially, a more unwise or foolish course could not have been pursued, than this imitation of her unfortunate sister-queen of France. All the follies, though not the elegance and splendour, of Le Petit Trianon were aped in the rural retreat of Bayswater; and the Princess's foes were not backward at seizing upon this circumstance, and turning it (as well they might) to effect her downfall.

"Monk" Lewis, under date November, 1811, writes: "I have neither seen nor heard anything of the Princess since she removed to Blackheath, except a report that she is in future to reside at Hampton Court, because the Princess Charlotte wants the apartments at Kensington; but I cannot believe that the young princess, who has been always described to me as so partial to her mother, would endure to turn her out of her apartments, or suffer it to be done. I have also been positively assured, that the Prince has announced that the first exertion of his power will be to decide the fate of the Princess; and that Perceval, even though he demurred at endeavouring to bring about a divorce, gave it to be understood that he should have no objection to her being excluded from the coronation, and exiled to Holyrood House." Here the Princess was living in 1813, when she received the address of sympathy from the citizens of London—an address which was regarded by the Prince as the first step towards defying his authority.

The Duke of Sussex, whilst occupying apartments here, used to entertain his friends hospitably. Among others who dined here was Mr. Rush, ambassador from the United States in 1819-25, who gives us the following sketch :—

"The duke sat at the head of his table in true old English style, and was full of cordiality and conversation. . . . General principles of government coming to be spoken of, he expatiated on the blessings of free government, declaring that as all men, kings as well as others, were prone to abuse power when they got to possess it, the only safe course was to limit its exercise by the strictest constitutional rules. In the palace of kings, and from the son and brother of a king," adds the honest and sensible republican, "I should not have been prepared for this declaration, but that it was not the first time that I had heard him converse in the same way." The duke continued to reside in this palace till his death. He was very fond of the long room on the first floor, which he made his library, and where he received visitors. The interior of the room has been often engraved.

But that which invests Kensington Palace with the greatest interest is the fact that it was the residence of the late Duke and Duchess of Kent, in the year 1819, and consequently the birth-place of her present Majesty, who spent here nearly all her infancy, and the greater part of her youthful days. In the Gardens, as a child, the Princess Victoria used daily to take her walk, or ride in a goat or donkey carriage, attended by her nurses. Her most gracious Majesty was born at a quarter past four o'clock in the morning of the 24th of May, 1819, and on the 24th of the following month she was christened in the grand saloon of the palace by the name of Alexandrina Victoria. The reason of the choice of these two names is thus explained by the Hon. Amelia Murray, in her "Recollections :"—"It was believed that the Duke of Kent wished to name his child Elizabeth, that being a popular name with the English people. But the Prince Regent, who was not kind to his brothers, gave notice that he should stand in person as one godfather, and that the Emperor of Russia was to be another. At the baptism, when asked by the Archbishop of Canterbury to name the infant, the Prince Regent gave only the name of 'Alexandrina;' but the duke requested that one other name might be added: 'Give her her mother's also, then; but,' he added, 'it cannot precede that of the Emperor.' The Queen, on her accession, commanded that she should be proclaimed as 'Victoria' only."

We learn incidentally from Mr. Raikes' "Journal" that on the Princess Victoria coming of age, on the 24th of May, 1837, it was proposed by her uncle, the king, to form for her here an establishment of her own; but that the idea was "combated by her mother, as it would have given the nomination of the appointments to the then Court party." The death of King William, however, which happened very shortly afterwards, put an end to the idea. On the 20th of June following, only a month after attaining her majority, as a girl of eighteen, she was waited upon here early in the morning by the Archbishop of Canterbury, and the then Lord Chamberlain, the Marquis of Conyngham, to receive the news that she was Queen of England!

For the following longer and more detailed account of the affair we are indebted to the "Diary of a Lady of Quality:"—"At Kensington Palace the Princess Victoria received the intelligence of the death of William IV., June, 1837. On the 20th, at 2 a.m., the scene closed, and in a very short time the Archbishop of Canterbury and Lord Conyngham, the Chamberlain, set out to announce the event to their young sovereign. They reached Kensington Palace about five; they knocked, they rang, they thumped for a considerable time before they could rouse the porter at the gate; they were again kept waiting in the court-yard; they turned into one of the lower rooms, where they seemed forgotten by everybody. They rang the bell, desired that the attendant of the Princess Victoria might be sent to inform H.R.H. that they requested an audience on business of importance. After another delay, and another ringing to inquire the cause, the attendant was summoned, who stated that the *Princess* was in such a sweet sleep she could not venture to disturb her. Then they said, 'We are come to the *Queen* on business of state, and even her sleep must give way to that.' It did; and, to prove that *she* did not keep them waiting, in a few minutes she came into the room in a loose white nightgown and shawl, her nightcap thrown off, and her hair falling upon her shoulders, her feet in slippers, tears in her eyes, but perfectly collected and dignified."

In this trying moment, though supported by her mother's presence, she gave vent to the feelings of her heart by bursting into a flood of tears as she thought of the responsibilities which had devolved upon her, and begged the Archbishop's prayers.

The story of Her Majesty's accession, and the

account of her first council, is thus told in the "Greville Memoirs:"—"1837, June 21. The King died at twenty minutes after two yesterday morning, and the young Queen met the council at Kensington Palace at eleven. Never was anything like the first impression she produced, or the chorus of praise and admiration which is raised about her manner and behaviour, and certainly not without justice. It was very extraordinary and far beyond what was looked for. Her extreme youth and inexperience, and the ignorance of the world concerning her, naturally excited intense curiosity to see how she would act on this trying occasion, and there was a considerable assemblage at the palace, notwithstanding the short notice that was given. The first thing that was to be done was to teach her her lesson, which, for this purpose, Melbourne had himself to learn. I gave him the council papers, and explained all that was to be done, and he went and explained all this to her. He asked her if she would enter the room accompanied by the great officers of state, but she said she would come in alone. When the lords were assembled, the Lord President informed them of the King's death, and suggested, as they were so numerous, that a few of them should repair to the presence of the Queen, and inform her of the event, and that their lordships were assembled in consequence; and, accordingly, the two royal dukes, the two archbishops, the chancellor, and Melbourne, went with him. The Queen received them in the adjoining room alone. As soon as they had returned, the proclamation was read, and the usual order passed, when the doors were thrown open, and the Queen entered, accompanied by her two uncles, who advanced to meet her. She bowed to the lords, took her seat, and then read her speech in a clear, distinct, and audible voice, and without any appearance of fear or embarrassment. She was quite plainly dressed, and in mourning. After she had read her speech and taken and signed the oath for the security of the Church of Scotland, the Privy Councillors were sworn, the two royal dukes first by themselves; and as these two old men, her uncles, knelt before her, swearing allegiance and kissing her hand, I saw her blush up to the eyes, as if she felt the contrast between their several and natural relations; and this was the only sign of emotion she evinced. Her manner to them was very graceful and engaging. She kissed them both, and moved towards the Duke of Sussex, who was furthest from her seat, and too infirm to reach her. She seemed rather bewildered at the multitude of men who were sworn, and who came one after another to kiss her hand; but she did not speak to anybody, nor did she make the slightest difference in her manner, or show any in her countenance to any individual of any rank, station, or party. I particularly watched her when Melbourne and her ministers, and the Duke of Wellington and Peel approached her. She went through the whole ceremony, occasionally looking at Melbourne for instructions when she had any doubt what to do, and with perfect calmness and self-possession, but, at the same time, with a modesty and propriety particularly interesting and ingratiating. When the business was done she retired as she had entered, and I could see that no one was in the adjoining room."

The scene at Kensington Palace on the above occasion is thus described by Mr. Rush, from the lips of the late Lord Clarendon, one of the Privy Councillors present at the time:—"Lord Lansdowne, the president, announced to the council that they had met on the occasion of the demise of the crown; then with some others of the body, including the Premier, he left the council for a short time, when all returned with the Princess. She entered, leaning upon the arm of her uncle, the Duke of Sussex. The latter had not before been in the council-room, but resides in the same palace, and had been with the Princess in an adjoining apartment. He conducted her to a chair at the head of the council. A short time after she took her seat, she read the declaration which the sovereign makes on coming to the throne, and took the oath to govern the realm according to law, and cause justice to be executed in mercy. The members of the council then successively kneeled, one knee bending, and kissed the young queen's hand as she extended it to each —for now she was the veritable Queen of England. Lord Clarendon described the whole ceremony as performed in a very appropriate and graceful manner by the young lady. Some timidity was discernible at first, as she came into the room in the presence of the cabinet and privy councillors; but it soon disappeared, and a becoming self-possession took its place. He noticed her discretion in not talking, except as the business of the ceremonial made it proper, and confining herself chiefly, when she spoke, to Lord Melbourne, as official head of the Ministry, and to her uncle, the Duke of Sussex."

The author of "The Diary of a Lady of Quality" thus describes the first meeting of the Privy Council of the youthful queen, which differs only in some slight particulars from the accounts given above: "The first act of the reign was, of course, the summoning of the council, and most of the summonses were not received till after the early hour fixed for its meeting. The Queen was, upon the opening of the doors, found sitting at the head of the table. She received first the homage of the Duke of Cumberland, who, I suppose, was not king of Hanover when he knelt to her; the Duke of Sussex rose to perform the same ceremony, but the Queen, with admirable grace, stood up, and preventing him from kneeling, kissed him on the forehead. The crowd was so great, the arrangements were so ill-made, that my brothers told me the scene of swearing allegiance to their young sovereign was more like that of the bidding at an auction than anything else."

The state document signed by the youthful sovereign is to be seen in the Record Office. Sir David Wilkie has painted the scene, but with a difference. The picture, it may be added, is well known to the public, thanks to the engraver's art. It may be a matter of wonder that the Lord Mayor of London (Alderman Kelly), should have figured in this picture; but on the sovereign's death the Lord Mayor is the only officer in the kingdom whose commission still holds good; and as such he takes his place, by virtue of his office, at the Privy Council board until the new sovereign is proclaimed.

Here, on the 21st of April, 1843, died, at the age of seventy, Augustus Frederick, Duke of Sussex. Mr. T. Raikes, in his "Journal," says of him: "He was a stout, coarse-looking man, of a free habit, plethoric, and subject to asthma. He lived at Kensington Palace, and was married to Lady Cecilia Gore, who had been made Duchess of Inverness by the Whigs. He had married previously, in 1793, Lady Augusta Murray; but that marriage had been dissolved on the plea of the duke not obtaining his father's consent. He was always on bad terms with George IV., and under the weak government of William IV. he took the Radical line, courted the Whigs, and got the rangership of a royal park." He was buried at Kensal Green. His royal highness was, perhaps, the most popular of the sons of George III. He had a magnificent library at Kensington, including one of the finest collections of Bibles in the world, which was dispersed, soon after his death, under the hammer of the auctioneer. His widow, the Duchess of Inverness, was allowed to occupy his apartments until her death, in 1873. Under date of Sunday, 29th March, 1840, Mr. Raikes writes in his "Journal: "The Duke of Sussex claims

THE ROUND POND, KENSINGTON GARDENS.

from the Whig Ministry the public acknowledgment of his marriage with Lady Cecilia Underwood, and an addition of £6,000 a year to his income. This is the explanation: on the question of Prince Albert's precedence they first applied to the Duke of Sussex for his acquiescence, which he most violently refused. They then went to the Duke of Cambridge with the same request, to which he made less difficulty, saying, that he wished to promote harmony in the family, and as it could not prevent him from being the son of his father, if the Duke of Sussex consented, he should not object. Lord Melbourne then returned to the latter, saying that the Duke of Cambridge had agreed at once; upon which Sussex, finding that he should lose all the merit of the concession, went straight to the Queen, and professed to be the first to meet her wishes, but stipulating also that he expected a great favour for himself in return. This now proves to have been his object in view."

Shortly after the death of the duke, the following paragraph, headed "The late 'Duchess of Sussex,'" appeared in the *Times* newspaper: "As the fact is becoming a matter of general discussion, that in the event of the death of the King of Hanover, and of the Crown Prince, his son, the question of the title of Sir Augustus D'Este to the throne of that kingdom will create some controversy, the following letter from her royal highness (the Countess d'Ameland) to Sir S. J. Dillon, will not be uninteresting. It is dated so long since as December 16, 1811: 'My dear Sir,—I wished to have

SCOTCH FIRS, KENSINGTON GARDENS.

answered your last letter, but having mislaid your first, I did not know how to direct to you. I am sure you must believe that I am delighted with your pamphlet; but I must confess I do not think you have stated the fact quite exactly when you say (page 25) "that the question is at rest between me and the Duke of Sussex, because the connection has not only been declared illegal by sentence of the Ecclesiastical Court, but has been dissolved by consent—that I have agreed to abandon all claims to his name," &c. Now, my dear sir, had I believed the sentence of the Ecclesiastical Court to be anything but a stretch of power, my girl would not have been born. Lord Thurlow told me my marriage was good abroad—religion taught me it was good at home, and not one decree of any powerful enemy could make me believe otherwise, nor ever will. By refusing me a subsistence they forced me to take a name—not the Duke of Sussex's—but they have not made me believe that I had no right to his. My children and myself were to starve, or I was to obey; and I obeyed; but I am not convinced. Therefore, pray don't call this "an act of mutual consent," or say "the question is at rest." The moment my son wishes it, I am ready to declare that it was debt, imprisonment, arrestation, necessity (force like this, in short), which obliged me to seem to give up my claims, and not my conviction of their fallacy. When the banns were published in the most frequented church in London, and where all the town goes, is not that a permission asked? And why were they not forbid? I believe my marriage at Rome good; and I shall never feel "the question at rest" till this is acknowledged. Prince Augustus is now sent to Jersey, as Lieutenant D'Este, in the 7th Fusiliers. Before he went, he told his father he had no objection to go under any name they chose to make him take; but that he knew what he was, and the time, he trusted, would come when himself would see justice done to his mother and sister, and his own birth.'"

George III. having made St. James's and Buckingham Palace the head-quarters of royalty and the court, henceforward Kensington became the occasional or permanent residence of some of the younger branches of the royal family.

Kensington Palace, we need hardly add, is maintained at the cost of the nation; and, though no longer used actually as a royal residence, it is appropriated to the use of certain pensioned families, favoured by royalty, and a lady who is distantly connected with the highest court circles holds the envied and not very laborious post of housekeeper. It may safely be assumed, we think, that she is "at the top of her profession." The Right Hon. John Wilson Croker lived here for some time. The Duke and Duchess of Teck and the Marquis and Marchioness of Lorne have since occupied those apartments which formerly were inhabited by the distinguished personages mentioned above.

CHAPTER XIII.

KENSINGTON GARDENS.

"Where Kensington, luxuriant in her bowers,
Sees snow of blossoms, and a wild of flowers;
The dames of Britain oft in crowds repair
To gravel walks and unpolluted air:
Here, while the town in damps and darkness lies,
They breathe in sunshine and see azure skies;
Each walk, with robes of various dyes bespread,
Seems from afar a moving tulip-bed,
Where rich brocades and glossy damasks glow,
And chintz, the rival of the showery bow."—*Tickell.*

"Military" Appearance of the Gardens, as laid out by Wise and Loudon—Addison's Comments on the Horticultural Improvements of his Time—The Gardens as they appeared at the Beginning of the Last Century—Queen Anne's Banqueting House—Statue of Dr. Jenner—Bridgeman's Additions to the Gardens—The "Ha! ha!"—"Capability" Brown—The Gardens first opened to the Public—A Foreigner's Opinion of Kensington Gardens—"Tommy Hill" and John Poole—Introduction of Rare Plants and Shrubs—Scotch Pines and other Trees—A Friendly Flash of Lightning—The Reservoir and Fountains—Tickell, and his Poem on Kensington Gardens—Chateaubriand—Introduction of Hooped Petticoats—The Broad Walk becomes a Fashionable Promenade—Eccentricities in Costume—The Childhood of Queen Victoria, and her Early Intercourse with her Future Subjects—A Critical Review of the Gardens.

THE gardens attached to Kensington Palace, when purchased by William III., did not exceed twenty-six acres. They were immediately laid out according to the royal taste; and this being entirely military, the consequence was that closely-cropped yews, and prim holly hedges, were taught, under the auspices of Loudon and Wise, the royal gardeners, to imitate the lines, angles, bastions, scarps, and counter-scarps of regular fortifications. This curious upper garden, we are told, was long "the admiration of every lover of that kind of horticultural embellishment," and, indeed, influenced the general taste of the age; for Le Nautre, or Le Notre, who was gardener to the Tuileries, and had been personally favoured by Louis XIV., in conjunction with the royal gardeners, was employed by most of the nobility, during the reign of William, in laying out their gardens and grounds. Addison, in No. 477 of the *Spectator*, thus speaks of the horticultural improvements of this period:—"I think there are as many kinds of gardening as of poetry: your makers of pastures and flower-gardens are epigrammatists and sonneteers in this art; contrivers of bowers and grottoes, treillages and cascades, are romantic writers; Wise and Loudon are our heroic poets; and if, as a critic, I may single out any passage of their works to commend, I shall take notice of that part in the upper garden at Kensington which was at first nothing but a gravel-pit. It must have been a fine genius for gardening that could have thought of forming such an unsightly hollow into so beautiful an area, and to have hit the eye with so uncommon and agreeable a scene as that which it is now wrought into."

In 1691 these gardens are thus described:—"They are not great, nor abounding with fine plants. The orange, lemon, myrtle, and what other trees they had there in summer, were all removed to London, or to Mr. Wise's greenhouse at Brompton Park, a little mile from there. But the walks and grass were very fine, and they were digging up a plot of four or five acres to enlarge their gardens." Queen Anne added some thirty acres more, which were laid out by her gardener, Wise. Bowack, in 1705, describes here "a noble collection of foreign plants, and fine neat greens, which makes it pleasant all the year. . . . Her Majesty has been pleased lately to plant near thirty acres more to the north, separated from the rest only by a stately greenhouse, not yet finished." It appears from this passage that, previous to the above date, Kensington Gardens did not extend further to the north than the conservatory, which, as stated in the previous chapter, was originally built for a banqueting-house, and was frequently used as such by Queen Anne. This banqueting-house was completed in the year 1705, and is considered a fine specimen of brickwork. The south front has rusticated columns supporting a Doric pediment, and the ends have semi-circular recesses. "The interior, decorated with Corinthian columns," Mr. John Timbs tells us in his "Curiosities," "was fitted up as a drawing-room, music-room, and ball-room; and thither the queen was conveyed in her chair from the western end of the palace. Here were given full-dress *fêtes à la Watteau*, with a profusion of 'brocaded robes, hoops, fly-caps, and fans,' songs by the court lyrists, &c." When the Court left Kensington, this building was converted into an orangery and greenhouse.

Just within the boundary of the gardens at the south-eastern corner, on slightly rising ground, is the Albert Memorial, which we have already described,* and not far distant is the statue of Dr. Jenner, the originator of vaccination. This statue, which is of bronze, represents the venerable doctor in a sitting posture. It is the work of William Calder Marshall, and was originally set up in Trafalgar Square in 1858, but was removed hither about four years afterwards.

The eastern boundary of the gardens would seem to have been in Queen Anne's time nearly in the line of the broad walk which crosses them on the east side of the palace. The kitchen-gardens, which extended north of the palace, towards the gravel-pits, but are now occupied by some elegant villas and mansions, and the thirty acres lying north of the conservatory, added by Queen Anne to the pleasure-gardens, may have been the fifty-five acres "detached and severed from the park, lying in the north-west corner thereof," granted in the reign of Charles II. to Hamilton, the Ranger of Hyde Park, and Birch, the auditor of excise, "to be walled and planted with 'pippins and red-streaks,' on condition of their furnishing apples or cider for the king's use." This portion of the garden is thus mentioned in Tickell's poem:—

"That hollow space, where now, in living rows,
Line above line, the yew's sad verdure grows,
Was, ere the planter's hand its beauty gave,
A common pit, a rude unfashion'd cave.
The landscape, now so sweet, we well may praise;
But far, far sweeter, in its ancient days—
Far sweeter was it when its peopled ground
With fairy domes and dazzling towers was crown'd.
Where, in the midst, those verdant pillars spring,
Rose the proud palace of the Elfin king;
For every hedge of vegetable green,
In happier years, a crowded street was seen;
Nor all those leaves that now the prospect grace
Could match the numbers of its pigmy race."

At the end of the avenue leading from the south part of the palace to the wall on the Kensington Road is an alcove built by Queen Anne's orders; so that the palace, in her reign, seems to have stood in the midst of fruit and pleasure gardens, with pleasant alcoves on the west and south, and

* See p. 38, *ante*.

the stately banqueting-house on the east, the whole confined between the Kensington and Uxbridge Roads on the north and south, with Palace Green on the west; the line of demarcation on the east being the broad walk before the east front of the palace.

Bridgeman, who succeeded Wise as the fashionable designer of gardens, was employed by Queen Caroline, consort of George II., to plant and lay out, on a larger scale than had hitherto been attempted, the ground which had been added to the gardens by encroaching upon Hyde Park. Bridgeman's idea of the picturesque led him to abandon "verdant sculpture," and he succeeded in effecting a complete revolution in the formal and square precision of the foregoing age, although he adhered in parts to the formal Dutch style of straight walks and clipped hedges. A plan of the gardens, published in 1762, shows on the north-east side a low wall and fosse, reaching from the Uxbridge Road to the Serpentine, and effectually shutting in the gardens. Across the park, to the east of Queen Anne's Gardens, immediately in front of the palace, a reservoir was formed with the "round pond;" thence, as from a centre, long vistas or avenues were carried through the wood that encircled the water—one as far as the head of the Serpentine; another to the wall and fosse above mentioned, affording a view of the park; a third avenue led to a mount on the south-east side, which was raised with the soil dug in the formation of the adjoining canal, and planted with evergreens by Queen Anne. This mount, which has since been levelled again, or, at all events, considerably reduced, had on the top a revolving "prospect house." There was also in the gardens a "hermitage:" a print of it is to be seen in the British Museum. The low wall and fosse was introduced by Bridgeman as a substitute for a high wall, which would shut out the view of the broad expanse of park as seen from the palace and gardens; and it was deemed such a novelty that it obtained the name of a "Ha! ha!" derived from the exclamation of surprise involuntarily uttered by disappointed pedestrians. At each angle of this wall and fosse, however, semicircular projections were formed, which were termed bastions, and in this particular the arrangement accorded with the prevailing military taste. Bridgeman's plan of gardening, however, embraced the beauties of flowers and lawns, together with a wilderness and open groves; but the principal embellishments were entrusted to Mr. Kent, and subsequently carried out by a gentleman well known by the familiar appellation of "Capability" Brown. The gardens, it may be added, are still sufficiently rural to make a home for the nightingale, whose voice is often heard in the summer nights, especially in the part nearest to Kensington Gore.

> "Here England's daughter, darling of the land,
> Sometimes, surrounded with her virgin band,
> Gleams through the shades. She, towering o'er the rest,
> Stands fairest of the fairer kind confest;
> Form'd to gain hearts that Brunswick's cause denied,
> And charm a people to her father's side.
>
> "Long have these groves to royal guests been known,
> Nor Nassau, first, preferred them to a throne.
> Ere Norman banners waved in British air;
> Ere lordly Hubba with the golden hair
> Pour'd in his Danes; ere elder Julius came;
> Or Dardan Brutus gave our isle a name;
> A prince of Albion's lineage graced the wood,
> The scene of wars, and stained with lover's blood."

On King William taking up his abode in the palace, the neighbouring town of Kensington and the outskirts of Hyde Park became the abode of fashion and of the hangers-on at the Court, whilst the gardens themselves became the scene of a plot for assassinating William, and replacing James II. on the throne. The large gardens laid out by Queen Caroline were opened to the public on Saturdays, when the King and Court went to Richmond, and on these occasions all visitors were required to appear in full dress. When the Court ceased to reside here, the gardens were thrown open in the spring and summer; they, nevertheless, long continued to retain much of their stately seclusion. The gardens are mentioned in the following terms by the poet Crabbe, in his "Diary:"—"Drove to Kensington Gardens: . . . effect new and striking. Kensington Gardens have a very peculiar effect; not exhilarating, I think, yet alive [lively] and pleasant." It seems, however, that the public had not always access to this pleasant place; for, in the "Historical Recollections of Hyde Park," by Thomas Smith, we find a notice of one Sarah Gray having had granted her a pension of £18 a year, as a compensation for the loss of her husband, who was "accidentally shot by one of the keepers while hunting a fox in Kensington Gardens."

According to Sir Richard Phillips, in "Modern London," published in 1804, the gardens were open to the public at that time only from spring to autumn; and, curiously enough, servants in livery were excluded, as also were dogs. Thirty years later the gardens are described as being open "all the year round, to all respectably-dressed persons, from sunrise till sunset." About that time, when it happened that the hour for closing the gates was eight o'clock, the following lines, purporting to have been written "by a young lady aged nineteen," were discovered affixed to one of the seats:—

"Poor Adam and Eve were from Eden turned out,
As a punishment due to their sin;
But here after eight, if you loiter about,
As a punishment you 'll be locked in."

It may be added that now, on stated days during the "London season," the scene in these gardens is enlivened by the exhilarating strains of military bands. It is stated by Count de Melfort, in his "Impressions of England," published in the reign of William IV., that the Duke of St. Albans—we suppose, as Grand Falconer of England—is the only subject, except members of the royal family, who has the right of entering Kensington Palace Gardens in his carriage. The fact may be true, but it wants verifying.

The author of an agreeable "Tour of a Foreigner in England," published in 1825, remarks:—"The Palais Royale gives a better idea of the London squares than any other part of Paris. The public promenades are St. James's Park, Hyde Park, and Kensington Gardens, which communicate with each other. I am sometimes tempted to prefer these parks to the gardens of the Luxembourg and the Tuileries, which, however, cannot give you any idea of them. St. James's Park, Hyde Park, and Kensington Gardens are to me the Tuileries, the Champs Élysees, and the Jardin des Plantes united. On Sundays the crowd of carriages which repair thither, and the gentlemen of fashion who exhibit their horsemanship with admirable dexterity in the ride, remind me of Long Champs; but hackney coaches are not allowed to enter here to destroy the fine spectacle which so many elegant carriages afford. Sheep graze tranquilly in Hyde Park, where it is also pleasing to see the deer bounding about. At Kensington Gardens you are obliged to leave your horse or carriage standing at the gate. Walking through its shady alleys I observed with pleasure that the fashionable ladies pay, in regard to dress, a just tribute to our fair countrywomen. Judging from the costumes of the ladies, you might sometimes fancy yourself walking under the chestnut trees of the Tuileries. A line of Tasso may very well be applied to Kensington Gardens:—

'L'arte che tutto fa, nulla si scuopre.'"

Within the last half century these gardens have been greatly improved by drainage, relaying, and replanting. Much of the surrounding walls, too, have been removed, and in their place handsome iron railings have been substituted. The leading features of the gardens at the present time are the three avenues above mentioned, radiating from the east front of the palace, through dense masses of trees. Immediately in front of the palace is a quaintly-designed flower garden, separated from the Kensington Road by some fine old elm-trees. The broad walk, fifty feet in width, was once the fashionable promenade. "Tommy Hill," and his friend John Poole, who made him his great character in *Paul Pry*, with "I hope I don't intrude," used to walk daily together here. All the surrounding parts are filled in with stately groups of ancient trees; and the total absence of anything that indicates the proximity of the town, renders this spot particularly pleasant and agreeable for a stroll on a summer's evening. Keeping along the eastern margin of the gardens, and crossing the end of the broad avenue, the visitor soon reaches a new walk formed about the time of the first Great Exhibition. Here will be found a large number of new and rarer kind of shrubs, with their popular and technical names all legibly inscribed. Weale, in his work on London, published in 1851, says:—"It is in the introduction of these rarer plants that the idea of a 'garden' is, perhaps, better sustained than in most of the other features of the place, which are those of a park. The demand, indeed, for evergreens and undergrowth in these gardens is most urgent; and if (which we greatly doubt) there exists a well-founded objection to the use of shrubs and bushes in tufts or in single plants, there certainly can be no reason why solitary specimens, or varied groups of the many kinds of thorn, pyrus, mespilus, laburnum, pine and fir, evergreen, oaks, hollies, yews, &c., should not be most extensively planted, and a large portion of the younger and smaller trees in the densest parts cut away to make room for them." With reference to the trees in these gardens, a correspondent of the *Times* newspaper, in May, 1876, observes:—"The crowds who flock to Bushy Park or Kew do not see anything more fair than the tree-pictures now in Kensington Gardens, to which I beg to call the attention of all lovers of trees. The hawthorns and horse-chestnuts are now in marvellous beauty, though one rarely sees anybody taking the least notice of them. All the blaze of the autumnal 'bedding out' is in point of beauty as nothing to what is now afforded here by a few kinds of ordinary hardy trees that cost little at first and take care of themselves afterwards. There is a little open lawn with a small lime-tree in its centre, quite near the 'Row' corner of the gardens, around which there are several charming aspects of tree-beauty. One hawthorn is about forty feet high. Some of the central and unfrequented portions of the gardens are the most attractive. Nobody can despair of growing flowering trees to his heart's content in London after seeing the mountains of horse-chestnut bloom and other masses of tree-flowers here. Let those interested see the old trees in the central parts as well as the newer plantations, which, however, are also beautiful."

At the north side, nearly facing Porchester Terrace, there are some fine trees, including Scotch pines, which, a few years ago, were a glory to the neighbourhood, and are duly celebrated by Mr. Matthew Arnold in his verses on Kensington Gardens. Some of these, however, became so decayed that they were cut down by order of Her Majesty's Woods and Forests, in 1875.

The author of "Reminiscences of Fifty Years" tells an amusing story with reference to one of the trees in this part of the gardens. He was one day praising the charming view which some friends of his commanded from their drawing-room window overlooking the gardens. "Yes, the view would be perfect, if the branch of that large tree," to which they specially drew his attention, "did not interrupt it." "Well," remarked the other, "it is somewhat singular that I walked to your door with the nearest relative in London of the Chief Commissioner of Woods and Forests (the Right Hon. Mr. Milne), and I shall ask him to inquire whether the branch can be removed without injury to the royal tree." "I accordingly wrote to my friend in the evening (Tuesday)," continues the author, "and on Thursday morning my friends discovered, to their infinite satisfaction, that the obtrusive branch had disappeared; and, as a natural sequence, I came in for a warm benediction, and the Woods and Forests for their full share of praise as an exceptional department of the State, where red tape was not used, and circumlocution unknown. The Chief Commissioner, on reading my note to his relative, gave orders on the Wednesday to the superintendent of Kensington Gardens to look at the tree, and if the branch could be taken off without serious prejudice, it was to be done. The superintendent reported at head-quarters on the Thursday that on visiting the tree at an early hour that morning he found the branch in question lying on the ground, having been struck off by lightning during the heavy storm of the previous night. The Chief Commissioner wrote an amusing letter on the occasion, alleging that I really must be one 'who could call spirits from the vasty deep,' and had evidently transferred my powers to Kensington Gardens, acting on the suggestion given in

THE FLOWER WALKS, KENSINGTON GARDENS.

Richard III., 'With lightning strike the murderer dead.' The same day," adds the author, "I visited the tree, which appeared, saving the amputation of the large branch, to have escaped all other injury. Had other trees not suffered severely in Kensington Gardens that night, it might have led to a special inquiry or inquest to ascertain whether it was lightning or a saw that I had employed in obliging my friends. I told them they owed everything to the lightning; as I was much inclined to think that the Chief Commissioner, with every desire to meet their wishes, might possibly have deemed it his duty to postpone the consideration of the removal of so large and umbrageous a branch from the royal demesne to the Greek Calends."

Of the bridge over the Serpentine, at the north-east corner of the Gardens, we have already given an illustration.* At some distance on the west side of this bridge, as it leaves the Uxbridge Road, the Serpentine has been divided into a series of four large basins or reservoirs, of octangular form, each of which has a small fountain in the centre, encompassed with marble. In the central pathway, running between the basins, there is a larger fountain, of octagonal form. The end of the reservoir nearest the bridge forms an ornamental façade, enriched with vases of various patterns, filled with flowers. The centre of this façade has two draped female figures, seated, holding vases, from which flow streams; and between these two figures, but projecting forward, is another large fountain. The height of this balustraded façade is about eight feet above the water-level. At the other end of the reservoirs is an engine-house, containing engines for working the fountains. This building is of Italian design, and roofed with red Italian tiles. It stands just within the Gardens, at a short distance from the Bayswater Road.

OUTFALL OF WESTBOURNE. 1850.

Kensington Gardens have been celebrated by Tickell in the poem which bears their name, and from which we have quoted above; "verses," says Charles Knight, "full of fairies and their dwarfs, and Dryads and Naiads; verses made to order, and which have wholly perished as they deserve to perish." Tickell enjoyed the patronage of Addison, contributed papers to the *Spectator*, was contemporary with Pope, and published a translation of the "First Book of the Iliad," from his own pen, in

* See Vol. IV., p. 396.

apparent opposition to Pope's "Homer," of which the first part was published at the same time. As we read in Johnson's "Lives of the Poets," "Addison declared that the rival versions were both good, but Tickell's was the best. His poem on 'Kensington Gardens,' with the fairy tale introduced, is much admired; the versification is smooth and elegant. He is said to have been a man of gay conversation, but in his domestic relations without censure." Musical attractions were not wanting here in Tickell's time, if we may judge from the following couplet, which refers to Kensington Gardens:—

> "Nor the shrill corn-pipe, echoing loud to arms,
> To rank and file reduce the straggling swarms."

Readers of the "Life of Chateaubriand" will remember that he was one of those who admired and enjoyed the repose of the leafy walks of these Gardens. Professor Robertson, in his "Lectures on Modern History and Biography," tells us how the venerable sage "would stroll under these beautiful trees, where in the days of his exile he used to meet his fellow-sufferers, the French priests, reciting their breviary—those trees under which he had indulged in many a reverie, under which he had breathed many a sigh for his home in La Belle France, under which he had finished 'Atala,' and had composed 'Réné.'"

Kensington Palace and its Gardens were the first places where the hooped petticoats of our great-grandmother's days were displayed by ladies of fashion and "quality." We do not purpose giving here a history of Englishwomen's dress; but it may be as well to record the fact that the hoop appears to have been the invention of a Mrs. Selby, whose novelty is made the subject of a pamphlet, published at Bath, under the title of "The Farthingale Reviewed; or, more Work for the Cooper: a Panegyrick on the late but most admirable invention of the Hooped Petticoat." The talented lady who invented it died in 1717, and is thus mentioned by a Mrs. Stone, in the "Chronicles of Fashion:" "How we yearn to know something more of Mrs. Selby, her personal appearance, her whereabouts, her habits, and her thoughts. Can no more be said of her, whose inventive genius influenced the empire for well-nigh a century, who, by the potency of a rib of whalebone, held the universal realm of fashion against the censures of the press, the admonitions of the pulpit, and the common sense of the whole nation? Mrs. Tempest, the milliner, had her portrait taken by Kent, and painted on the staircase of Kensington Palace; and what was Mrs. Tempest that her lineaments should be preserved, whilst those of Mrs. Selby, the inventor of the hoop, are suffered to fall into oblivion?"

It was during the reign of George I. that the fashionable promenades in the Gardens became so popular, and the glittering skirts, which still lived in the recollection of our grandparents, would seem to have made their first appearance. Caroline of Anspach, the Prince of Wales's consort, probably introduced them, when she came with her bevy of maidens to Court. People would throng to see them; the ladies would take the opportunity of showing themselves, like pea-hens, in the walks; persons of fashion, privileged to enter the Gardens, would avail themselves of the privilege; and at last the public would obtain admission, and the raree-show would be complete. The full-dress promenade, it seems, was at first confined to Saturdays; it was afterwards changed to Sundays, and continued on that day till the custom went out with the closing days of George III.

In fact, during the last century the broad walk in Kensington Gardens had become almost as fashionable a promenade as the Mall in St. James's Park had been a century earlier, under Charles II. There might, probably, have been seen here, on one and the same day, during the portentous year 1791, Wilkes and Wilberforce; George Rose and Mr. Holcroft; Mr. Reeve and Mr. Godwin; Burke, Warren Hastings, and Tom Paine; Horace Walpole and Hannah More (whom he introduced to the Duke of Queensberry); Mary Wolstonecroft and Miss Burney (Madame d'Arblay), the latter avoiding the former with all her might; the Countess of Albany (the widow of the Pretender); the Margravine of Anspach; Mrs. Montagu; Mrs. Barbauld; Mrs. Trimmer; Emma Harte (Lady Hamilton), accompanied by her adoring portrait-painter, Romney; and poor Madame du Barry, mistress of Louis XV., come to look after some jewels of which she has been robbed, and little thinking she would return to be guillotined. The fashions of this half century, with the exception of an occasional broad-brimmed hat worn both by gentlemen and ladies, comprised the ugliest that ever were seen in the old Court suburb. Head-dresses became monstrous compounds of paste-board, flowers, feathers, and pomatum; the hoop degenerated into little panniers; and about the year 1770, a set of travelled fops came up, calling themselves Macaronis (from their intimacy with the Italian eatable so called), who wore ridiculously little hats, large pigtails, and tight-fitting clothes of striped colours. The lesser pigtail, long or curly, prevailed for a long time among elderly gentlemen, making a powdered semicircle between the shoulders; a plain cocked-hat adorned their heads; and, on a sudden, at the beginning of the new century, some of the ladies took to wearing turbans, surmounted with ostrich feathers, and bodies literally without a waist, the girdle coming directly under the arms. There was a song in those days, beginning—

"Shepherds, I have lost my love;
Have you seen my Anna?"

This song was parodied by one beginning—

"Shepherds, I have lost my waist;
Have you seen my body?"

Lady Brownlow, in her "Reminiscences of a Septuagenarian," tells us that after the Peace of Amiens, in 1802, she here met the celebrated Madame Recamier, who created a sensation at the West-end, partly by her beauty, but still more by her dress, which was vastly unlike the unsophisticated style and *poke* bonnets of the English ladies. "She appeared in Kensington Gardens *à l'antique*, a muslin gown clinging to her form like the folds of drapery on a statue; her hair in a plait at the back, and falling in small ringlets round her face, and greasy with *huile antique;* a large veil thrown over her head completed her attire, which not unnaturally caused her to be followed and stared at." No doubt, dressed in such a costume, and at such a period, Madame Recamier might well have been the "cynosure of neighbouring eyes."

During the early childhood of Her Majesty Queen Victoria, when living with her royal mother in Kensington Palace, the little princess was daily to be seen running about these gardens, or riding on her donkey about its walks; and her intercourse with the visitors there, we are assured by the author of an "Anecdotal Memoir of Her Majesty," was of a very interesting description. Some anecdotes upon this subject may be well introduced by the following remarks of a correspondent to the editor of a daily newspaper, when the princess was nearly three years old:—

"Passing accidentally through Kensington Gardens, a few days since, I observed at some distance a party, consisting of several ladies, a young child, and two men-servants, having in charge a donkey, gaily caparisoned with blue ribbons, and accoutred for the use of the infant. The appearance of the party, and the general attention they attracted, led me to suspect they might be the royal inhabitants of the palace; I soon learnt that my conjectures were well founded, and that her Royal Highness the Duchess of Kent was in maternal attendance, as is her daily custom, upon her august and interesting daughter, in the enjoyment of her healthful exercise. On approaching the royal party, the infant princess, observing my respectful recognition, nodded, and wished me a 'good morning' with much liveliness, as she skipped along between her mother and her sister, the Princess Feodore, holding a hand of each. Having passed on some paces, I stood a moment to observe the actions of the royal child, and was pleased to see that the gracious notice with which she honoured me was extended, in a greater or less degree, to almost every person she met: thus does this fair scion of our royal house, while yet an infant, daily make an impression on the hearts of many individuals which will not easily be forgotten. Her Royal Highness is remarkably beautiful, and her gay and animated countenance bespeaks perfect health and good temper. Her complexion is excessively fair, her eyes large and expressive, and her cheeks blooming. She bears a very striking resemblance to her late royal father, and, indeed, to every member of our reigning family; but the soft beauty, and (if I may be allowed the term) the dignity of her infantine countenance, peculiarly reminded me of our late beloved Princess Charlotte."

"This favourite donkey," we are further told by the above-mentioned authority, "a present from the Duke of York, bore his royal mistress daily round the gardens, to her great delight; so fond, indeed, was she of him, and of the exercise which he procured for her, that it was generally necessary to persuade her that the donkey was tired or hungry in order to induce her to alight. Even at this very early age, the princess took great pleasure in mixing with the people generally, and seldom passed anybody in the gardens, either when riding in her little carriage or upon her donkey, without accosting them with, 'How do you do?' or 'Good-morning, sir,' or 'lady;' and always seemed pleased to enter into conversation with strangers, returning their compliments or answering their questions in the most distinct and good-humoured manner. The young princess showed her womanly nature as a particular admirer of children, and rarely allowed an infant to pass her without requesting permission to inspect it and to take it in her arms. She expressed great delight at meeting a young ladies' school, and always had something to say to most of the children, but particularly to the younger ones. When a little older, she was remarkable for her activity, as, holding her sister Feodore in one hand, and the string of her little cart in the other, with a moss-rose fastened into her bosom, she would run with astonishing rapidity the whole length of the broad gravel walk, or up and down the green hills with which the gardens abound, her eyes sparkling with animation and glee, until the attendants, fearful of the effects of such violent exercise, were compelled to put a stop to it, much against the will of the little romp; and although a large assemblage of well-dressed ladies, gentlemen, and children would, on such occasions, form a semicircle round the scene of amusement, their presence never seemed in any way to disconcert the royal child, who would continue her play, occasionally speaking to the spectators as though they were partakers in her enjoyment, which, in very truth, they were. If, whilst amusing herself in the enclosed lawn, she observed, as sometimes happened, many persons collected round the green railings, she would walk close up to it, and curtsey and kiss her hand to the people, speaking to all who addressed her; and when her nurse led her away, she would again and again slip from her hand, and return to renew the mutual greetings between herself and her future subjects, who, as they contemplated with delight her bounding step and merry healthful countenance, the index of a heart full of innocence and joy, were ready unanimously to exclaim—

"'Long may it be ere royal state
That cherub smile shall dissipate;
Long ere that bright eye's peerless blue,
A sovereign's anxious tear bedew;
Ere that fair form of airy grace,
Assume the regal measured pace;
Or that young, open, cloudless brow,
With truth and joy that glitters now,
The imperial diadem shall wear
Beset with trouble, grief, and care.'"

In an article on Kensington Palace and Gardens, in the *Monthly Register* for September, 1802, the writer somewhat critically remarks:—"All the views from the south and east façades of the edifice suffer from the absurdity of the early inspectors of these grounds. The three vistas opening from the latter, without a single wave in the outline, without a clump or a few insulated trees to soften the glare of the champagne, or diminish the oppressive weight of the incumbent grove, are among the greatest deformities. The most exquisite view in the Gardens is near the north east angle; at the ingress of the Serpentine river, which takes an easy wind towards the park, and is ornamented on either side by sloping banks, with scenery of a different character. To the left the wood presses boldly on the water, whose polished bosom seems timidly to recede from the dark intruder; to the right, a few truant foresters interrupt the uniformity of the parent grove, which rises at some distance on the more elevated part of the shore; and through the boles of the trees are discovered minute tracts of landscape, in which the eye of taste can observe sufficient variety of light and shade of vegetable and animal life to gratify the imagination, and disappoint the torpor, which the more sombre scenery to the east is accustomed to invite.

"The pencil of Claude and Poussin was employed on general landscape; and the transport inspired by their works is from the composition and general effect, not from the exact resemblance of objects, to which Swanevelt and Watteau were so scrupulously attentive. In the landscape of nature, as well as in the feeble imitations of the artist, individuals deserve some attention. The largest and most beautiful of all the productions of the earth is a tree. As the effulgent tints of the insect must yield to the elegance and proportion of the other orders of animals, when contemplated by our imperfect optics, so the gorgeous radiance of the flower must bend its coronal honours to this gigantic offspring of nature, whose ample foliage receives all the splendid effects of light and shade, and gives arrangement and composition to landscape. The trees that conduce to the sublime in scenery are the oak, the ash, the elm, and the beech. It is a defect in the gardens at Kensington that, excepting the elm, the whole of this beautiful fraternity is excluded, so that all the variety of tint in the spring and autumn is lost, and the gardens burst into the luxuriance of summer, and hasten to the disgrace of winter, without those gradations which indulgent Nature has contrived to moderate our transport on the approach of the one, and to soften our griefs on the appearance of the other. The dusky fir is the only melancholy companion the elm is here permitted to possess, who seems to raise his tall funereal head to insult his more lively associate with approaching decay. If in spring we have not here all the colours of the rainbow, in the forms of nascent existence; if in autumn the yellow of the elm, the orange of the beech, and the glowing brown of the oak do not blend their fading honours, it must be acknowledged that the elm is one of the noblest ornaments of the forest; it is the medium between the massive unyielding arm of the oak and the versatile pliancy of the ash; it out-tops the venerable parent of the grove, and seems to extend its mighty limbs towards heaven, in bold defiance of the awful monarch of the wood.

"Besides the disadvantage from the uniformity in the umbrageous furniture of these gardens, there is another, which we hardly know whether to attribute to design or accident. A tree rising like an artificial pillar from the smooth earth, without exposing any portion of the bold angles of its root, not only loses half its strength, but almost all its dignity. Pliny, endeavouring to give a grand idea of the Hercynian forest, describes the magnitude of the trees in that ancient domain of the Sylvani to be sufficient to admit mounted cavalry to pass beneath the huge radical curves. Whatever ornament Pliny's extravagance might attribute in this respect on the broad expanse of solitary Nature, this gigantic wildness would not be at all adapted to these pigmy haunts of man; but some resemblance, some approach, should be attempted to the magnificence of her operations.

"'———A huge oak, dry and dead,
Still cull'd with relics of its trophies old,
Lifting to heaven its aged hoary head.'

"Such an object, with some of our readers, would be considered a venerable inmate of these gardens, and to us it would be infinitely preferable to the trim expedients of art. The insulated majesty of this ancient possessor of the soil would prevent the intrusion of the timid hand of man, and the character which this parent of the forest would impart to the general scenery would secure it from sacrilegious profanation."

CHAPTER XIV.

HOLLAND HOUSE, AND ITS HISTORICAL ASSOCIATIONS.

"Here Rogers sat, and here for ever dwell
With me those pleasures that he sang so well."—*Lord Holland.*

Earl's Court—John Hunter's House—Mrs. Inchbald—Edwardes Square—Warwick Road and Warwick Gardens—Addison Road—Holland House—An Antique Relic—The Pictures and Curiosities—The Library—The Rooms occupied by Addison, Charles Fox, Rogers, and Sheridan—Holland House under the Family of Rich—Theatrical Performances carried on by Stealth during the Commonwealth—Subsequent Owners of the Mansion—Oliver Goldsmith—Addison—The House purchased by Henry Fox, afterwards Lord Holland—The Story of Henry Fox's Elopement with the Daughter of the Duke of Richmond—Lady Sarah Lennox and the Private Theatricals—Charles James Fox—Henry Richard, third Lord Holland, and his Imperious Wife—Lord Macaulay, and other Distinguished Guests—"Who is Junius?"—Lord Holland and the Emperor Napoleon—Death of Lord Holland, and his Character, as written by a Friend—A Curious Custom—The Duel between Lord Camelford and Captain Best—Rogers' Grotto—The Gardens and Grounds—Canova's Bust of Napoleon—The Highland and Scottish Societies' Sports and Pastimes—A Tradition concerning Cromwell and Ireton—Little Holland House—The Residence of General Fox—The Nursery-grounds.

RETRACING our steps along the Kensington Road, we come to Earl's Court Road, a thoroughfare communicating with the western end of Cromwell Road, which comprises several highly respectable detached mansions. It probably owes its name to the Earls of Warwick and Holland, whose mansion faces it. Sir Richard Blackmore, the poet, appears to have had a residence here, for Pope writes, in his "Imitations of Horace"—

"Blackmore himself, for any grave effort,
Would drink and doze at Tooting or Earl's Court."

In later times Earl's Court afforded a retirement to the eminent surgeon, John Hunter, who here made several experiments in natural history, and formed in the grounds surrounding his villa a menagerie of rare and valuable foreign animals. In the kitchen of Hunter's house the great surgeon literally boiled down the Irish giant, O'Brien, whose skeleton we have mentioned in our account of the Museum* in Lincoln's Inn Fields. Even the copper in which the operation was performed is religiously kept, and shown to curious visitors. After the death of Mr. Hunter, the house in which he resided was for some time occupied occasionally by the Duke of Richmond, who purchased the estate. The house, it may be added, has since been a *maison de santé.*

* See Vol. III., p. 46.

In Leonard's Place, and also in Earl's Court Terrace, Mrs. Inchbald resided for some time, in boarding-houses. At the back of Earl's Terrace is Edwardes Square, so called after the family name of Lord Kensington. This square is chiefly remarkable for the largeness as well as the cultivated look of the enclosure, which affords to the residents, and also to the inhabitants of the Terrace, who have the right of entry, the advantages of a larger kind of garden. Leigh Hunt mentions a tradition as current in Kensington that Coleridge once had lodgings in Edwardes Square; but, he adds, "we do not find the circumstance in his biographies, though he once lived in the neighbouring village of Hammersmith."

Warwick Road and Warwick Gardens, which lie on the west side of Edwardes Square, are so named after the Earls of Warwick, the former owners of Holland House. In Warwick Gardens is a well-built Wesleyan chapel. Running parallel with Warwick Road, crossing by a bridge the Kensington Road, and continuing its course by Holland Road, is the West London Railway, and this we fix upon as the limits of our perambulations in the "far west." Addison Road, of course, is so named after another and a distinguished occupant of Holland House, of which we shall presently speak; and it forms a communication between the Kensington and Uxbridge Roads, skirting the west side of Holland Park. St. Barnabas Church, which stands in this road, and dates from about the year 1827, is built in the "late Perpendicular" style of Gothic architecture.

Having been built only in the early part ot the seventeenth century, shortly after the death of Queen Elizabeth, Holland House has no history that carries us back beyond the first of the Stuarts; nor, indeed, did the mansion become really celebrated till the reign of George I., when the widow of its owner, Rich, Earl of Holland and Warwick, married Addison, who died here. It afterwards came into the possession of the family of Fox, Lord Holland, firstly as tenants, and subsequently as owners of the freehold. The first Lord Holland and his lady were both persons of ability; and before the end of the reign of George II., Holland House had risen into a celebrity which it has never since lost.

The mansion takes its name from Henry Rich, Earl of Holland, by whose father-in-law, Sir Walter Cope, it was built, in the year 1607, from the designs of John Thorpe, the famous architect of several of the baronial mansions of England which were erected about that time. Although scarcely two miles distant from London, with its smoke, its din, and its crowded thoroughfares, Holland House still has its green meadows, its sloping lawns, and its refreshing trees; and the view of the quaint old pile which meets the wayfarer in passing along the Kensington Road, on his road towards or from Hammersmith, is highly suggestive of rural solitude, and the effect is enhanced by the note of the nightingale, which is frequently heard in the grounds which surround the mansion. From Sir Walter Cope the property passed to his son-in-law, above mentioned, who much improved the house, and completed its internal decorations. The building follows the form so usually adopted at the era of its construction, and may be best described by saying that it resembles one-half of the letter H. The material is brick, with dressings and embellishments of stone and stucco. The projection in the central compartment of the principal division of the house forms at once a tower and porch. There is a building at each end of

EARL'S COURT HOUSE (FORMERLY JOHN HUNTER'S). (*See page* 161.)

OLD KENSINGTON.

1. Manor House. 2. Old Tavern. 3. Little Holland House.

the same division, with shingled and steep-roofed turrets, surmounted by a vane. A projecting arcade, terminated by a parapet of carved stone-work, ranges along the principal faces of the building; and the original court is bounded by a palisade. The present terrace in front of the house was raised about 1848, when the old foot-path, which ran immediately in front of its windows, was diverted from its course. The following are the particulars of the interior of this interesting mansion, as given in "Homes and Haunts of the Poets:"—"There is a fine entrance-hall, a library behind it, and another library extending the whole length of one of the wings and the house up-stairs, one hundred and fifty feet in length. The drawing-room over the entrance-hall, called the gilt-room, extends from front to back of the house, and commands views of the gardens both ways; those to the back are very beautiful." There was evidently a chapel attached to the house in former times, for there are some remnants of arches still existing, built into the walls of rooms which now serve a very different purpose. The old bronze font, or "stoup," for holy water, too, stands by the staircase in the inner hall, supported by a comparatively modern tripod of the same material. It appears to have been made in the year 1484, by a Fleming, named Cassel, or Caselli; "around it, far interspersed with odd old Scriptural and armorial devices, is written, in Gothic letters, an abbreviated rendering of the passage in the Psalm, so familiar to Catholic ears: 'Asperges me hyssopo, et mundabor; lavabis me, et super nivem dealbabor.'" Many of the pictures which adorn the walls are by some of the best masters. One apartment, called "The Sir Joshua Room," contains several of Reynolds's works, the best of which are considered "Muscipula," a child holding up a mouse in a cage, with puss looking wistfully on from below; a portrait of Baretti, author of the Italian Dictionary, who was tried for murder,* but received favourable testimony from Dr. Johnson, Burke, and Garrick, and was acquitted; and the beautiful Lady Sarah Lennox, whom George III. noticed with admiration when a little girl in Kensington Gardens. His Majesty, it is related, requested to see her again in later years, and, in fact, wished much to marry her when she had grown into a young lady. She was one of the bridesmaids at his wedding, when, if report be true, he kept his eyes steadily fixed on her during the ceremony of his own marriage with Charlotte of Mecklenburg. This room contains also Murillo's "Vision of St. Antony of Padua." The gilt-room—which has lost some of its former glories, in the shape of frescoes on the chimney-piece, supposed to represent the Aldobrandini Marriage, and which are presumed to be buried underneath a coating of plaster—was prepared by the first Earl of Holland of the line of Rich for the purpose of giving a ball to Prince Charles on the occasion of his marriage with Henrietta Maria of France; the ball, however, for some unexplained reason, never came off. This apartment is now said to be tenanted by the solitary ghost of its first lord, who, according to tradition, "issues forth at midnight from behind a secret door, and walks slowly through the scenes of former triumphs, with his head in his hand." This, however, is not the only "ghost story" connected with Holland House, for credulous old Aubrey tells us: "The beautiful Lady Diana Rich, as she was walking in her father's garden at Kensington, to take the fresh air before dinner, about eleven o'clock, being then very well, met with her own apparition, habit, and every thing, as in a looking-glass. About a month after, she died of the small-pox. And it is said that her sister, the Lady Elizabeth Thynne, saw the like of herself before she died. This account," he adds, "I had from a person of honour."

Among the most noticeable pictures which abound in the map-room and the picture-room, are some by Watts, who is considered by many one of the greatest of contemporary English artists. In the latter room mass was said daily during the brief stay of Marie Amélie, the late Queen of the French, in the house in 1862. In the print-room are some specimens of the Italian, German, Dutch, Flemish, French, Spanish, and English schools; the Rembrandts being the most worthy of note. Hogarth is represented in the next room. Here, among the portraits, are those of Tom Moore, by Shee, and of Rogers, by Hoffner; there are also some fine Dutch sea-pieces. The library, a very handsome long room, contains, besides its literary treasures, among other relics, a table used by Addison at the Temple. There is a glowing notice of this room by Macaulay, too long for quotation. In the yellow drawing-room there is "a pair of candlesticks in Byzantine ware, which belonged to Mary Queen of Scots. They were in her possession at Fotheringay Castle, and thus were witnesses to the last hours of her life's tragedy." There is, too, "an ancient poison-ring," with a death's head in carbuncle, supposed to have been sent to the same unfortunate queen. Here are also numerous relics of the great Napoleon: among them is a locket, containing some of his hair, a ring, and a

* See Vol. IV., p. 220.

cross worn by him in his island prison at St. Helena. The miniature-room, it need scarcely be added, has its treasures; as have also "Lady Holland's private rooms" and the "blue-room." The former had a narrow escape from destruction by fire a few years ago. Among the remaining curiosities and works of art preserved here, is an interesting collection of fans, some of which are very beautifully painted. "One of these," as the Princess Marie Lichstenstein informs us in her account of Holland House, "is historically interesting, having been painted by a daughter of George III., before the union of Ireland with England. It bears the rose and the thistle, but no shamrock; and the motto, 'Health is restored to one, happiness to millions,' seems to indicate the occasion for which it was painted." Autographs, too, and manuscripts of famous characters, are not wanting: among them are those of Catherine, Empress of Russia; Napoleon I., Voltaire, Addison, Petrarch, letters of Philip II., III., and IV. of Spain; and music by Pergolese, copied by Rousseau.

"The library," says Leigh Hunt, in his "Old Court Suburb," "must originally have been a greenhouse or conservatory; for, in its first condition, it appears to have been scarcely anything but windows, and it is upwards of ninety feet long, by only seventeen feet four inches wide, and fourteen feet seven inches in height. The moment one enters it, one looks at the two ends, and thinks of the tradition about Addison's pacings in it to and fro. It represents him as meditating his 'Spectators' between two bottles of wine, and comforting his ethics by taking a glass of each as he arrived at each end of the room. The regularity of this procedure is, of course, a jest; but the main circumstance is not improbable, though Lord Holland seems to have thought otherwise. He says (for the words in Faulkner's 'Kensington' are evidently his):—'Fancy may trace the exquisite humour which enlivens his papers to the mirth inspired by wine; but there is too much sober good sense in all his lucubrations, even when he indulges more in pleasantry, to allow us to give implicit credit to a tradition invented, probably, as excuse for intemperance by such as can empty two bottles of wine, but never produce a 'Spectator' or a 'Freeholder.'" Of other apartments which have any particular interest attached to them, is the chamber in which Addison died; the bed-room occupied by Charles Fox; that of Rogers, the poet, who was a frequent visitor here; and also that of Sheridan, "in the next room to which," as Leigh Hunt informs us "a servant was regularly in attendance all night, partly to furnish, we believe, a bottle of champagne to the thirsty orator, in case he should happen to call for one betwixt his slumbers (at least, we heard so a long while ago, and it was quite in keeping with his noble host's hospitality; but we forgot to verify the anecdote on this occasion), and partly—of which there is no doubt—to secure the bed-curtains from being set on fire by his candle."

In a previous chapter we have narrated the descent of the manor of Kensington from the time of the Conquest, when it was held by the De Veres, down to the present day. Sir Walter Cope, the purchaser of the Vere property in Kensington, was a master of the Court of Wards in the time of James I., and one of the Chamberlains of the Exchequer. He built the centre of the house and the turrets, and bequeathed it, as already stated, to Sir Henry Rich, the husband of his daughter and heiress, Isabel. Not long afterwards, Sir Henry was raised to the peerage, when he assumed his title of nobility from his wife's inheritance—that of Lord Kensington. The wings and arcades were added by this nobleman, who also completed the internal decorations. His lordship was a courtier, and had the honour of being employed to negotiate a marriage between Prince Charles and the Infanta of Spain; but the negotiation proved abortive. Lord Kensington's services were, nevertheless, appreciated and rewarded by an earl's coronet and the insignia of the Garter. The new title chosen by his lordship was Holland, and thence the manor house of Kensington received its present appellation. This Earl of Holland was a younger son of Robert Rich, first Earl of Warwick, by his marriage with Penelope, daughter of Queen Elizabeth's favourite, the Earl of Essex, and the "Stella" of Sir Philip Sidney. He was a favourite with King James's "Steenie," Duke of Buckingham, whom he almost rivalled in coxcombry. During the prosperous portion of Rich's career, Holland House, no doubt, was the centre of rank and fashion. The name of Bassompierre, the French ambassador, figures among the guests here at that time. The earl was a political waverer in the "troublous times" of Charles I. He was twice made a prisoner in the house: first by Charles, in 1633, upon the occasion of his challenging Lord Weston, and a second time by command of the Parliament, after the unsuccessful issue of his attempt to restore the king, in 1648. In the following year he lost his life on the scaffold in Palace Yard, Westminster; foppish to the last, he is reported to have died in a white satin waistcoat or doublet, and a cap made of the same material, trimmed with silver lace. Within a few months of the earl's execution, Holland House became the head-quarters of the Parliamentary army, General Fairfax becoming its occupant. In the *Perfect Diurnal*, a journal of the day, is this entry:—"The Lord-General (Fairfax) is removed from Queen Street to the late Earl of Holland's house at Kensington, where he intends to reside." The mansion, however, was soon restored to the earl's widow and children; and it remained quietly in the possession of the family almost as long as they lasted.

It is well known that throughout the gloomy reign of Puritanism, under Oliver Cromwell, the dramatic profession was utterly proscribed. We are told that during this period the actors, who had been great loyalists, contrived to perform secretly and by stealth at noblemen's houses, where purses were collected for the benefit of "the poor players." In the "Historia Histrionica," published in 1699, it is stated that, "In Oliver's time they [the players] used to act privately, three or four miles or more out of town, now here, now there, sometimes in noblemen's houses, in particular, Holland House at Kensington, where the nobility and gentry who met (but in no great numbers) used to make a sum for them, each giving a broad piece, or the like."

From the Restoration to the time of the Georges, Holland House appears to have been let by the noble owners on short leases to a variety of persons, and sometimes even in apartments to lodgers. Leigh Hunt, in his work already quoted, mentions the names of several who, in this manner, resided here: among them, Arthur Annesley, the first Earl of Anglesey; Sir John Chardin, the traveller; Catherine Darnley, Duchess of Buckinghamshire; William Penn, the founder of Pennsylvania; and Shippen, the famous Jacobite, whom Pope has immortalised for his sincerity and honesty. Robert Rich, the son and successor of the first Earl of Holland, succeeded his cousin as Earl of Warwick, in consequence of failure of the elder branch, and thus united the two coronets of his family. He was the father of Edward Rich, Earl of Warwick and Holland, whose widow, Charlotte, daughter of Sir Thomas Myddleton, of Chirk Castle, Denbighshire, married, in 1716, the Right Honourable Joseph Addison, and thus, "by linking with the associations of Kensington the memory of that illustrious man, has invested with a classic halo the groves and shades of Holland House." Edward Henry, the next earl—to whom, as we have stated, there is a monument in Kensington Church—was succeeded by his kinsman, Edward Rich; and the daughter and only child of this nobleman dying unmarried, the earldom became extinct in the middle of the last century. Holland House then came into the possession of the youthful earl's first cousin, William Edwardes (a Welsh gentleman, who was created a Peer of Ireland, as Baron Kensington), and was eventually sold to the Right Honourable Henry Fox, the distinguished politician of the time of George II., who, on being created a peer, adopted the title of Holland, and with his descendants the mansion has continued ever since.

To the literary circle, of which this house was the centre, it is impossible to say how many poets, essayists, and other writers have owed their first celebrity. It is said that even Goldsmith's charming novel, "The Vicar of Wakefield," here found its earliest admirer. This beautiful little work remained unnoticed, and was attacked by the reviews, until Lord Holland, who had been ill, sent to his bookseller for some amusing book. This was supplied, and he was so pleased that he spoke of it in the highest terms to a large company who dined with him a few days after. The consequence was that the whole impression was sold off in a few days.

It has been said that Addison obtained an introduction to his future wife in the capacity of tutor to her son, the young Earl of Warwick; but this supposition appears to be negatived by two letters written by Addison to the earl, when a boy, wherein the writer evinces an entire ignorance of the advances which his correspondent might have made in classical attainment. The letters are dated 1708. Addison had been appointed Under-Secretary of State two years previously, and it seems improbable that he should have undertaken the office of tutor at a subsequent period. His courtship of the countess, however, is said to have been marked by tedious formalities; and it is further asserted that her ladyship at first encouraged his overtures with a view of extracting amusement from the diffidence and singularity of his character. From the following anecdote, which is told respecting Addison's courtship, there would seem to be a show of truth in the story. The tenor of this anecdote is that "he endeavoured to fathom her sentiments by reading to her an article in a newspaper (which he himself had caused to be inserted), stating the probability of a marriage taking place between the reader and the auditress! From a comparison of dates, and a further examination of internal evidence," adds the narrative, "there is reason to suppose that Addison meant as a playful description of his own courtship that of Sir Roger de Coverley to the widow with a white hand; and, if so, how highly is the world indebted to the warm fancy of the one party, and the want of determination in the other!" It was, in all probability, at this period of his life that Addison had a cottage at Fulham; at all events, he figures in "Esmond," as walking thither from Kensington at night-time. "When the time came to take leave, Esmond marched homewards to his lodgings, and met Mr. Addison on the road, walking to a cottage which he had at Fulham, the moon shining on his handsome serene face. 'What cheer, brother!' says Addison, laughing; 'I thought it was a footpad advancing in the dark, and, behold, it is an old friend! We may shake hands, colonel, in the dark, 'tis better than fighting by daylight. Why should we quarrel because I am a Whig and thou art a Tory? Turn thy steps and walk with me to Fulham, where there is a nightingale still singing in the garden, and a cool bottle in a cave I know of. You shall drink to the Pretender, if you like; I will drink my liquor in my own way!'"

The growing renown of Addison—perhaps his fame as a writer, or, more probably, his accession of political importance—assisted in persuading the countess to become his wife. But the marriage was productive of little comfort; and this unfortunate marriage is said to have been the cause of his indulging to excess in drink. Be that as it may, Addison himself wrote vehemently against cowardice seeking strength "in the bottle;" yet it is asserted that he often withdrew from the bickerings of his Countess to the coffee-house or the tavern. His favourite places of resort are said to have been the White Horse Inn, at the bottom of Holland House Lane, and Button's Coffee-house, in Russell Street, Covent Garden, where we have already made his acquaintance.* The fruit of this unpropitious union was one daughter, who died, at an advanced age, at Bilton, an estate in Warwickshire which Addison had purchased some years previously. Addison himself died at the end of three years after his marriage. The story of his death-bed here has been often told, but very probably it is a little apocryphal in its details. Lord Warwick was a young man of very irregular life, and of loose opinions. Addison, for whom he did not want respect, had very diligently endeavoured to reclaim him; but his arguments and expostulations had no effect. One experiment, however, remained to be tried. When he found his life near its end, he directed the young lord to be called, and told him, "I have sent for you that you may see how a Christian can die." It was to this young nobleman that Somerville addressed his "Elegiac Lines on the Death of Mr. Addison," wherein occur the lines having reference to his burial in Westminster Abbey:—

"Can I forget the dismal night that gave
My soul's best part for ever to the grave?
How silent did his old companions tread,
By midnight lamps, the mansions of the dead,
Thro' breathing statues, then unheeded things,
Thro' rows of warriors, and thro' walks of kings!
What awe did the slow, solemn knell inspire,
The pealing organ, and the pausing choir;
The duties by the lawn-rob'd prelate paid,
And the last words, that dust to dust convey'd!"

A short time before his death, Addison sent to request a visit from the poet Gay, and told him, on their meeting, that he had once done him an injury, but that if he survived his present affliction he would endeavour to repair it. Gay did not know the nature of the injury which had been inflicted, but supposed that he might have lost some appointment through the intervention of Addison.

"Addison," writes Leigh Hunt, "it must be owned, did not shine during his occupation of Holland House. He married, and was not happy; he was made Secretary of State, and was not a good one; he was in Parliament, and could not speak in it; he quarrelled with, and even treated contemptuously, his old friend and associate, Steele, who declined to return the injury. Yet there, in Holland House, he lived and wrote, nevertheless, with a literary glory about his name, which never can desert the place; and to Holland House, while he resided in it, must have come all the distinguished men of the day, for, though a Whig, he was personally 'well in,' as the phrase is, with the majority of all parties. He was in communication with Swift, who was a Tory, and with Pope, who was neither Tory nor Whig. It was now that the house and its owners began to appear in verse. Rowe addressed stanzas to Addison's bride; and Tickell, after his death, touchingly apostrophizes the place—

"'Thou hill, whose brow the antique structures grace,
Rear'd by bold chiefs of Warwick's noble race;
Why, once so loved, whene'er thy bower appears,
O'er my dim eyeballs glance the sudden tears?'

* * * * * *

"It seems to have been in Holland House (for he died shortly afterwards) that Addison was visited by Milton's daughter, when he had requested her to bring him some evidences of her birth. The moment he beheld her, he exclaimed, 'Madame, you need no other voucher; your face is a sufficient testimonial whose daughter you are.

* See Vol. III., p. 277.

It must have been very pleasing to Addison to befriend Milton's daughter; for he had been the first to popularise the great poet by his critiques on 'Paradise Lost,' in the *Spectator*."

After the death of Addison, Holland House remained in the possession of the Warwick family, and of their heir, Lord Kensington, until, as we have stated above, it was purchased by Henry Fox, who subsequently became a lord himself, and took his title from the mansion. This was towards the close of the reign of George II.

Henry Fox, the first Lord Holland of the new creation, was the youngest son of Sir Stephen Fox, a distinguished politician during the reigns of Charles II., James II., William III., and Queen Anne. After having had a numerous offspring by one wife, Sir Stephen married another at the age of seventy-six, and had three more children, two of whom founded the noble families of Holland and Ilchester. It was reported that Stephen Fox had been a singing-boy in one of our English cathedrals; Walpole says he was a footman; and the late Lord Holland, who was a man of too noble a nature to affect ignorance of such traditions, candidly owns that he was a man of "very humble origin." Henry Fox was the political opponent of the first William Pitt, afterwards Earl of Chatham. The chief transactions of his lordship's public life are all duly recorded in the pages of history. Leigh Hunt, in his own lively manner, writes thus of

ROGERS' SEAT AND INIGO JONES' GATEWAY, HOLLAND HOUSE.

HOLLAND HOUSE.

him:—"Fox had begun life as a partisan of Sir Robert Walpole; and in the course of his career held lucrative offices under Government—that of Paymaster of the Forces, for one—in which he enriched himself to a degree which incurred a great deal of suspicion." A good story is told concerning Fox whilst he held the above-mentioned office; it is one which will bear repeating here. After Admiral Byron's engagement in the West Indies, there arose a great clamour about the badness of the ammunition served out. Soon afterwards, Mr. Fox fought a duel with a Mr. Adam. The former received his adversary's ball, which, happily, made but a very slight impression. "Egad, sir!" observed Fox, "it would have been all over with me if we had not charged our pistols with Government powder."

Fox, however, was latterly denounced, in a City address, as the "defaulter of unaccounted millions." "Public accounts, in those times, were strangely neglected; and the family have said that his were in no worse condition than those of others; but they do not deny that he was a jobber. Fox, however, for a long time did not care. The joyousness of his temperament, together with some very lax notions of morality, enabled him to be at ease with himself as long as his blood spun so well. He jobbed and prospered; ran away with a duke's daughter; contrived to reconcile himself with the family (that of Richmond); got his wife made a baroness; was made a lord himself—Baron Holland, of Foxley; was a husband, notwithstanding his jobbing, loving and beloved; was an indulgent father; a gay and social friend—in short, had as happy a life of it as health and spirits could make, till, unfortunately, health and spirits failed, and then there seems to have been a remnant of his father's better portion within him, which did not allow him to be so well satisfied with himself in his decline." The story of Henry Fox's elopement with the Duke of Richmond's daughter, Lady Georgiana Caroline Lennox, is thus told in the "Old Court Suburb:"—"The duke was a grandson of Charles II., and both he and the duchess had declined to favour the suit of Mr. Fox, the son of the equivocal Sir Stephen. They reckoned on her marrying another man, and an evening was appointed on which the suitor in question was to be formally introduced to her. Lady Caroline, whose affections the dashing statesman had secretly engaged, was at her wits' end to know how to baffle this interview. She had evaded the choice of the family as long as possible, but this appointment looked like a crisis. The gentleman is to come in the evening; the lady is to prepare for his reception by a more than ordinary attention to her toilet. This gives her the cue to what is to be done. The more than ordinary attention is paid; but it is in a way that renders the interview impossible. She has cut off her eyebrows. How can she be seen by anybody in such a trim? The indignation of the duke and duchess is great; but the thing is manifestly impossible. She is accordingly left to herself for the night; she has perfected her plan, in expectation of the result; and the consequence is, that when next her parents inquire for her, she has gone. Nobody can find her. She is off for Mr. Fox." This runaway marriage took place in the Fleet Prison, in the year 1744. In January, 1761, two years before the elevation of Mr. Fox to the peerage, Horace Walpole was present at a performance of private theatricals at Holland House—a sight which greatly entertained him. The play selected to be performed by children and very young ladies was *Jane Shore*, Lady Sarah Lennox, a sister of Lady Georgiana Fox, enacting the heroine; while the boy afterwards eminent as Charles James Fox played the part of "Hastings," and his brother, Henry Edward, then six years old, enacted the "Bishop of Ely," dressed in lawn sleeves, and with a square cap (this little boy died a general in the army in 1811). Walpole praises the acting of the performers, but particularly that of Lady Sarah Lennox, who, he says, "was more beautiful than you can conceive, . . . in white, with her hair about her ears, and on the ground; no Magdalen by Correggio was half so lovely and expressive." The charms of this lovely person had already made an impression on the heart of George III., then newly come to the throne at two-and-twenty. There seems no reason to doubt that the young monarch formed the design of raising his lovely cousin (for such she was, in a certain sense) to a share of the throne. The following story concerning the pair we quote from Timbs' "Romance of London:"—"Early in the winter of 1760-1, the king took an opportunity of speaking to Lady Sarah's cousin, Lady Susan Strangways, expressing a hope at the drawing-room that her ladyship was not soon to leave town. She said that she should be leaving soon. 'But,' said the king, 'you will return in summer for the coronation.' Lady Susan answered that 'she did not know—she hoped so.' 'But,' said the king again, 'they talk of a wedding. There have been many proposals; but I think an English match would do better than a foreign one. Pray, tell Lady Sarah Lennox I say so.' Here was a sufficiently broad hint to inflame the hopes of a family, and to raise the head of a blooming girl of sixteen to the fifth heavens. It happened, however, that Lady Sarah had already allowed her heart to be pre-occupied, having formed a girlish attachment for the young Lord Newbottle, grandson of the Marquis of Lothian. She did not, therefore, enter into the views of her family with all the alacrity which they desired. According to the narrative of Mr. Grenville, she went the next drawing-room to St. James's, and stated to the king, in as few words as she could, the inconveniences and difficulties in which such a step would involve him. He said that was his business; he would stand them all; his part was taken, and he wished to hear hers was likewise. In this state it continued, whilst she, by the advice of her friends, broke off with Lord Newbottle, very reluctantly, on her part. She went into the country for a few days, and by a fall from her horse broke her leg. The absence which this occasioned gave time and opportunities for her enemies to work; they instilled jealousy into the king's mind upon the subject of Lord Newbottle, telling him that Lady Sarah Lennox still continued her intercourse with him; and immediately the marriage with the Princess of Strelitz was set on foot; and at Lady Sarah's return from the country, she found herself deprived of her crown and her lover, Lord Newbottle, who complained as much of her as she did of the king. While this was in agitation, Lady Sarah used to meet the king in his rides early in the morning, driving a little chaise with Lady Susan Strangways; and once, it is said, that, wanting to speak to him, she went dressed like a servant-maid, and stood amongst the crowd in the guard-room, to say a few words to him as he passed by." Walpole also relates that Lady Sarah would sometimes appear as a haymaker in the park at Holland House, in order to attract the attention of the king as he rode past; but the opportunity was lost. The gossiping chronicler adds also, that his Majesty blushed scarlet red at his wedding-service when allusion was made to "Abraham and *Sarah*." The lady survived her disappointment, and became the mother of the gallant Napiers.

Three children were the fruit of Lord Holland's marriage with Lady Georgiana Lennox, and he proved the fondest of parents. When his lordship was dangerously ill, he was informed that George Selwyn had called at his door to inquire after him. Selwyn, as is well known, was notorious for his passion for "being in at the death" of all his acquaintances, and for attending, more especially, every execution that took place. "Be so good," said his lordship, "in case Mr. Selwyn calls again, to show him up without fail; for if I am alive, I shall be delighted to see him, and if I am dead, I am sure he will be very pleased to see me.'

Of Stephen, second Lord Holland, we have nothing to say, beyond that he was good-natured and whimsical, and that he died before reaching his thirtieth year. His brother, the celebrated Charles James Fox, the "man of the people," is not much associated with Holland House, except as a name. Here, it is true, he passed his boyhood and part of his youth, during which period he was allowed to have pretty much his own way; in fact, he was what is generally styled a "spoilt child." His father is said never to have thwarted his will in anything. Thus, the boy expressing a desire one day to "smash a watch," the father, after ascertaining that the little gentleman did positively feel such a desire, and was not disposed to give it up, said, "Well, if you must, I suppose you must;" and the watch was at once smashed. On another occasion, his father, having resolved to take down the wall before Holland House, and to have an iron railing put up in its stead, found it necessary to use gunpowder to facilitate the work. He had promised his son, Charles James, that he should be present whenever the explosion took place. Finding that the labourers had blasted the brickwork in his absence, he ordered the wall to be rebuilt; and, when it was thoroughly cemented, had it blown up again for the gratification of his favourite boy; at the same time advising those about him never, on any account, to break a promise with children.

Henry Richard Fox, the third lord, who came to the title before he was a year old, lived to rescue the mansion from the ruin which at one time threatened it, and may be said to have resided in it during the whole of his life, in the enjoyment of his books, and dispensing his hospitalities to wits and worthies of all parties. His lordship married Elizabeth, the daughter and heiress of Mr. Richard Vassall, whose name he afterwards assumed; his children retaining the name of Fox. It is, perhaps, to this nobleman, with the exception of Addison, that Holland House owes most of its celebrity and its literary interest. Among the visitors round its hospitable board, Macaulay mentions the name of Prince Talleyrand, Lord Lansdowne, Lord John Russell, Lord Melbourne, the Marchioness of Clanricarde (Canning's daughter, who for many years did not forget to take vengeance on the colleagues and political opponents who had killed her father); Lord King, the bishop-hater; Wilberforce, the philanthropist; Lord Radnor, Charles Grant, and Mackintosh. Byron and Campbell, too, were guests here; and the name of Lord Holland is embalmed by the former in his dedication of "The Bride of Abydos," and by the latter in that of "Gertrude of Wyoming."

It is evident from Macaulay, Tom Moore, and the other members of the Holland House clique, that, though they were nominally the guests of Lord Holland, their real entertainer was her ladyship, in whom was illustrated the proverb which declares that "the grey mare is often the better horse." In fact, she was not only lady paramount in the house, but often insolently imperious towards her guests, whom, as one man wittily remarked, she treated like her *vassals*, though she was only a *Vassall* herself, alluding, of course, to her maiden name. "The centurion," it has been remarked, "did not keep his soldiers in better order than she keeps her guests. It is to one, 'Go,' and he goeth; and to another, 'Do this,' and it is done. 'Ring the bell, Mr. Macaulay.' 'Lay down the screen, Lord Russell; you will spoil it.' 'Mr. Allen, take a candle, and show Mr. Cradock the pictures of Buonaparte.'" Lord Holland was, on the other hand, all kindness, simplicity, and vivacity. One of the occasional visitors here, Mr. Granville Penn, said about her ladyship a good thing, which, while it helped to establish his credit as a wit, excluded him from its hospitable doors for ever. "Holland House," a friend remarked to him, "is really a most pleasant place; and in Lord Holland's company you might imagine yourself inside the home of Socrates." "It certainly always seemed so to me; for I often seemed to hear Xanthippe talking rather loud in the adjoining room," was Mr. Penn's reply. In fact, Lady Holland herself, who presided at the *réunions* of Holland House, was most arbitrary and domineering in her manner, and, consequently, made herself unpopular with some of her guests. When she heard that Sir Henry Holland was about to be made a baronet, she expressed herself vexed that there would be "two Lady Hollands." But that could not be helped. Ugo Foscolo, in spite of having obtained the *entrée* of Holland House, could not help regarding her with aversion, and once said, with a strong emphasis, that, "though he could go anywhere"—even to a certain place, which shall be nameless—"with his lordship, he should be sorry to go to heaven with Lady Holland."

Macaulay did not find an *entrée* here till after he had made his mark in Parliament. Lady Holland on one occasion took him into her own drawing-room to see her pictures, which included thirty by Stothard, all on subjects from Lord Byron's poems. "Yes," said her ladyship, "poor Lord Byron sent them to me a short time before the separation. I sent them back, and told him that, if he gave them away, he ought to give them to Lady Byron. But he said that he would not, and that if I did not take them the bailiffs would, and that they would be lost in the wreck." Samuel Rogers promised to be there to meet Macaulay, "in order to give him an insight into the ways of that house," and of its imperious mistress, whose pride and rudeness must have been simply intolerable to ordinary mortals. Rogers was the great oracle of the Holland House circle—a sort of non-resident premier. To some members of the literary world who had not the privilege of joining in the charming circle at Holland House, the sense of their exclusion seemed to find vent in some shape or form. Theodore Hook would appear to be one of these, for about the year 1819, among other experiments, he tried to set up a tiny magazine of his own—the *Arcadian*—published, we believe, at a shilling; but we know not how many numbers of it were issued before the publisher lost heart. One number contained a lengthy ballad of provoking pungency, satirising Holland House in very severe terms.

Some excellent remarks *àpropos* of Holland House gatherings and its associations may here be abridged from Mr. J. Fisher Murray's "Environs of London," in which a scholar who had the *entrée* of that hospitable mansion writes, at once prophetically and pathetically, as follows:—"Yet a few years, and these shades and these structures may follow their illustrious masters. The wonderful city which, ancient and gigantic as it is, still continues to grow, as a young town of logwood by a water-privilege in Michigan, may soon dispense with those turrets and gardens which are associated with so much that is interesting and noble; with the courtly magnificence of Rich, with the loves of Ormond, with the councils of Cromwell, with the death of Addison. The time is coming when, perhaps, a few old men, the last survivors of our generation, will seek in vain, amid new streets and squares, and railway stations, for the site of that dwelling which in their youth was the favourite resort of wits and beauties, of painters and poets, of scholars, philosophers, and statesmen; they will remember, with strange tenderness, many objects familiar to them—the avenue and terrace, the busts and the paintings, the carvings, the grotesque gilding, and the enigmatical mottoes. With peculiar tenderness they will recall that venerable chamber in which all the antique gravity of a college library was so singularly blended with all that female grace and wit could devise to embellish a drawing-room. They will recollect, not unmoved, those shelves loaded with the varied learning of many lands and many ages; those portraits in which were preserved the features of the best and wisest Englishmen of two generations. They will recollect how many men who have guided the politics of Europe, who have moved great assemblies by reason and eloquence, who have put life into bronze or canvas, or who have left to posterity things so written that society will not willingly let them die, were there mixed with all that was lovely and gayest in the society of the most splendid of modern capitals. . . . They will remember the singular character, too, which belonged to that circle; in which every talent and accomplishment, every art and science, had its place. They will remember how the last Parliamentary debate was discussed in one corner, and the last comedy of Scribe in another; while Wilkie gazed in admiration on Reynolds's 'Baretti;' while Mackintosh turned over Thomas Aquinas to verify a quotation; while Talleyrand related his conversation with Barras at the Luxembourg, or his ride with Lannes over the field of Austerlitz. They will remember, above all, the grace and the kindness—far more admirable than grace—with which the princely hospitality of that ancient mansion was dispensed; they will remember the venerable and benignant countenance of him who bade them welcome there; they will remember that temper which thirty years of sickness, of lameness, and of confinement served only to make sweeter; and, above all, that frank politeness which at once relieved all the embarrassment of the most timid author or artist who found himself for the first time among ambassadors and earls. They will remember, finally, that in the last lines which he traced he expressed his joy that he had done nothing unworthy of the friend of Fox and of Grey; and they will have reason to feel a similar joy if, in looking back on many troubled years of life, they cannot accuse themselves of having done anything unworthy of men who were honoured by the friendship of Lord Holland."

Mr. Rush, in his "Court of London," tells us a good story of a little incident which happened in the drawing-room here after dinner. Advancing towards Sir Philip Francis, Mr. Rogers asked permission to put a question to him. Francis, no doubt, guessed what was coming, for everybody at the time was asking, "Who is Junius?" and many persons were even then more than disposed to identify him with the author of the "Letters" which were published under that signature, and were exciting the nation. Francis, who was an irritable man, shut him fairly up with the words, "At your peril, sir!" On this, Rogers quietly turned away, observing that if Francis was not "Junius," at all events he was "Brutus." It is not a little singular, if the letters were not written by Francis, that they ceased to appear after the very day on which Francis quitted the shores of England for India, and that Garrick, who was in the secret, prophesied a day or two before that they were about to cease.

On the death of his uncle, Charles James Fox, Lord Holland was introduced into the Cabinet as Lord Privy Seal; but the strength of the Whig portion of the Government had then departed, and the only measure worthy of notice in which his lordship co-operated after his accession to office was the Bill for the Abolition of the Slave Trade. He took an active part in the multifarious debates upon the Catholic question, the Regency Bill, &c.; and when the Bill to legalise the detention of Napoleon as a prisoner of war was before the House of Lords, Lord Holland raised his voice against it, and, until death relieved the prisoner, he never ceased to deprecate what he deemed the unwarrantable conduct towards him of the British Government and its agents.

Lord Holland died in October, 1840, after an illness of only two days' duration. Mr. T. Raikes, in notifying the occurrence in his "Diary," remarks:—"Flahault had been staying at Holland House while he was in England, and left him in good health on Tuesday. He arrived here yesterday morning, and to-day receives the account of his death. Lord Holland was in the Cabinet, and held the lucrative post of Chancellor of the Duchy of Lancaster; he was sixty-seven. When I went to Eton he was the head of the school, and was the first prepositor that gave me my liberty. He was a mild, amiable man, ruled by his wife. She was a Miss Vassall, with a large fortune, who eloped with him from her first husband, Sir Godfrey Webster; she is a great politician, and affects the *esprit fort.* They kept a hospitable house, and received all the wits of the day." The following lines were written by Lord Holland on the morning of the day when his last illness commenced, and were found after his death on his dressing-room table:—

"Nephew of Fox and friend of Grey,
Sufficient for my fame,
If those who knew me best shall say
I tarnished neither name."

Mr. Raikes also adds:—"Mrs. Damer writes me that the new Lord Holland inherits an estate of £6,000 per annum, on which there is an enormous debt. Holland House is left to Lady Holland, who will not live there." "Lord Holland," says Mr. Peter Cunningham, "called on Lord Lansdowne a little before his death, and showed him his epitaph of his own composing. 'Here lies Henry Vassall Fox, Lord Holland, &c., who was drowned while sitting in his elbow-chair.' He died in this house, in his elbow-chair, of water in the chest."

The following is a character of Lord Holland, written by a friend :—" The benignant, the accomplished Lord Holland is no more; the last and best of the Whigs of the old school, the long-tried friend of civil and religious liberty, has closed a life which has been an ornament and a bulwark of the Liberal cause. He was one of England's worthies in the pristine sense of the word; and a more finished example of the steady statesman, the urbane gentleman, and the accomplished scholar, never existed. Lord Holland's was a fine mind, and a fine mind in perpetual exercise of the most healthful kind. It was observed of him that he was never found without a good book in his hand. His understanding was thoroughly masculine, his taste of a delicacy approaching perhaps to a fault. His opinions he maintained earnestly and energetically, but with a rare, a beautiful candour. Nothing was proscribed with him. As of old, the meanest wayfarers used to be received hospitably, lest angels should be turned away; so Lord Holland seemed to have a hearing for every argument, lest a truth should be shut out from his mind. The charm of his conversation will never be forgotten by those who have enjoyed it. His mind was full of anecdote, which was always introduced with the most felicitous appositeness, and exquisitely narrated.

"Lord Holland had lived with all the most distinguished and eminent men of the last forty years; but his knowledge of the greatest, the most eloquent, the most witty, or the most learned, had not indisposed him to appreciate merits and talents of a less great order. He was a friend of merit wherever it could be found, and knew how to value and to encourage it in all its degrees.

HOLLAND HOUSE, FROM THE NORTH.

"None ever enjoyed life more than Lord Holland, or enjoyed it more intellectually, and none contributed more largely to the enjoyment of others. He possessed the sunshine of the breast, and no one could approach him without feeling its genial influence. Lord Holland was a wit, without a particle of ill nature, and a man of learning, without a taint of pedantry. His apprehension of anything good was unfailing; nothing worth observing and remarking ever escaped him. The void which Lord Holland has left will never be filled; a golden link with the genius of the last age is broken and gone. The fine intellect, whose light burned at the shrine of freedom, is extinguished. An influence the most propitious to the peace, so precious to the world's best interests, is lost when the need of it is great indeed."

GRAND STAIRCASE, HOLLAND HOUSE.

Lord Holland was succeeded in his title and estates by his only son, Henry Edward, who was some time the British Minister at the Court of Tuscany. He died at Naples in 1859, when the barony became extinct. From that time, down to the year 1874, it was always a matter of apprehension that a day would sooner or later come when, as prophesied by Sir Walter Scott, Holland House must become a thing of the past, and be swept away in order to make room for new lines of streets and villas between Kensington and Notting Hill. In the above year, however, this feeling was quieted by the rumour that Lady Holland, the widow of the last lord, had disposed of the reversion of the house, by sale, to the Earl of Ilchester, who, it was stated, had expressed his intention of keeping the mansion in its integrity. Lord Ilchester's name is Fox-Strangways, and it is the latter name that has been assumed by his branch of the family, the first Lord Holland and the first Lord Ilchester, as stated above, having been brothers. Lord Macaulay, in writing of Holland House, says it "can boast of a greater number of inmates distinguished in political and literary history than any other private dwelling in England." In the lifetime of the third Lord Holland it was the meeting-place of the Whig party; and his liberal hospitality made it, as Lord Brougham tells us, "the resort not only of the most interesting persons composing English society, literary, philosophical, and political, but also to all belonging to those classes who ever visited this country from abroad."

With the death of the third Lord Holland, the glories of Holland House may be said to have passed away, although the building has been occupied as an occasional residence by the widow of the last lord since his death in 1859; and an air of solitude seems indeed to have gathered round the old mansion. A custom was observed for many years, till a recent date, of firing off a cannon at eleven o'clock every night; this custom originated, we believe, through a burglary which was once attempted here.

Several spots in the grounds round the house have acquired celebrity in connection with some name or circumstance. Of these we may note the part lying to the west, towards the Addison Road, which formerly went by the name of "the Moats," where the duel between Captain Best and the notorious Lord Camelford took place, early in the present century. The exact spot is supposed to have been the site of the older mansion belonging to the De Veres. The quarrel between Lord Camelford and Mr. Best, of which we have spoken in our accounts of New Bond Street and Conduit Street,* was on account of a friend of Lord Camelford, a lady of the name of Symons, and it occurred at the "Prince of Wales's" coffee-house in Conduit Street. The duel was fought on the following day (March 7, 1804), and Lord Camelford was killed. Although there really was no adequate cause for a quarrel, the eccentric nobleman would persist in fighting Mr. Best, because the latter was deemed the best shot in England, and that "to have made an apology would have exposed his lordship's courage to suspicion." The parties met on the ground about eight o'clock in the morning, and having taken up their position, Lord Camelford gave the first shot, which missed his antagonist, when Mr. Best fired, and lodged the contents of his weapon in his lordship's body. He immediately fell, and calling his adversary to him, seized him by the hand, and exclaimed, "I am a dead man! you have killed me; but I freely forgive you." He repeated several times that he was the sole aggressor. He was conveyed to a house close at hand, and a surgeon soon arrived from Kensington, and immediately pronounced the wound mortal. Upon the spot where the duel was fought the late Lord Holland set up an "expiatory classical altar," which, however, was removed a few years ago. With the passion for eccentricity which had characterised him, Lord Camelford had directed that he should be buried in a lonely spot on an island in Switzerland, which had interested him during his travels; his wishes, however, were not complied with, for his body was interred in the vaults of St. Anne's Church, Soho, where it still remains.* "This very spot," the Princess Marie Lichstenstein tells us, "was, a few years ago, the scene of merry parties, where the Duke and Duchess d'Aumale used to fish with the late Lord Holland." At the back of the mansion is a broad expanse of greensward, dotted here and there with stately elms; and here, in an alcove facing the west, is inscribed the couplet that we have given as a motto to this chapter, and which was put up by the late Lord Holland in honour of Mr. Rogers. Here is also a copy of verses by Mr. Luttrell, expressing his inability to emulate the poet. The undulating grounds on this side of the house are terminated by a row of mansions built on the fringe of the estate; and the eastern side is bounded by a rustic lane, in part overhung with trees. Close by the western side of the house are small gardens, laid out in both the ancient and modern styles, the work of the late Lady Holland, the former of them being a fitting accompaniment to the old house. Here are evergreens clipped into all sorts of fantastic forms, together with fountains and terraces befitting the associations of the place. In one of these gardens, says Leigh Hunt, was raised the first specimen of the dahlia, which the late Lord Holland is understood to have brought from Spain; in another, on a pedestal, is a colossal bust of Napoleon, by a pupil of Canova. Engraved on the pedestal is a quotation from Homer's "Odyssey," which may be thus rendered in English:—

"The hero is not dead, but breathes the air
In lands beyond the deep:
Some island sea-begirded, where
Harsh men the prisoner keep."

The Highland and Scottish Societies' gatherings, with their characteristic sports and pastimes, were held in these grounds for many years.

The grounds around the house are rich in oaks, plane-trees, and stately cedars, whose dark foliage sets off the features of the old mansion. Of the grounds in front of the house, there is a tradition that Cromwell and Ireton conferred there, "as a place in which they could not be overheard." Leigh Hunt, in his "Old Court Suburb," observes

* See Vol. IV., pp. 302, 323.

* See Vol. III., p. 182.

that, "whatever the subject of their conference may have been, they could not have objected to being seen, for there were neither walls, nor even trees, we believe, at that time in front of the house, as there are now; and," he adds, "we may fancy royalists riding by, on their road to Brentford, where the king's forces were defeated, and trembling to see the two grim republicans laying their heads together."

Near Holland House, in Nightingale Lane, stands a small mansion, called Little Holland House, where Mrs. Inchbald once spent a few days with its occupant, a Mrs. Bubb; here, too, lived and died Miss Fox, sister of the late Lord Holland.

Facing the Uxbridge Road at the extreme end, at the north-west corner of the grounds of Holland House, there was a smaller mansion, with a "pleasaunce" garden and lawn, of about seven acres, which for many years was owned and tenanted by a natural son of Lord Holland—General Fox, the celebrated numismatist, some time M.P. for Stroud, and Secretary to the Ordnance Board, who married Lady Mary Fitzclarence. The grounds, however, were sold in 1875 for building purposes, and the house was soon after pulled down.

At the western extremity of the parish of Kensington, on the road towards Hammersmith, were the nursery-grounds of Messrs. Lee. These grounds, says Leigh Hunt, "have been known in the parish books, under the title of the Vineyard, ever since the time of William the Conqueror. Wine, described as a sort of burgundy, was actually made and sold in them as late as the middle of the last century. James Lee, the founder of the present firm who own the grounds, was the author of one of the earliest treatises on botany, and a correspondent of Linnæus." In Faulkner's "History of Kensington," published in 1820, we read that the nursery-grounds round this neighbourhood covered no less than 124 acres, and that they belonged to eight different proprietors.

CHAPTER XV.

NOTTING HILL AND BAYSWATER.

The Old Turnpike Gate—Derivation of the Name of Notting Hill—The Manor of Notting or Nutting Barns—Present Aspect of Notting Hill—Old Inns and Taverns—Gallows Close—The Road where Lord Holland drew up his Forces previous to the Battle of Brentford—Kensington Gravel Pits—Tradesmen's Tokens—A Favourite Locality for Artists and Laundresses—Appearance of the District at the Beginning of the Present Century—Reservoirs of the Grand Junction Waterworks Company—Ladbroke Square and Grove—Kensington Park Gardens—St John's Church—Notting Hill Farm—Norland Square—Orme Square—Bayswater House, the Residence of Fauntleroy, the Forger—St. Petersburgh Place—The Hippodrome—St. Stephen's Church—Portobello Farm—The Convent of the Little Sisters of the Poor—Bayswater—The Cultivation of Watercresses—An Ancient Conduit—Public Tea Gardens—Sir John Hill, the Botanist—Craven House—Craven Road, and Craven Hill Gardens—The Pest-house Fields—Upton Farm—The Toxophilite Society—Westbourne Grove and Terrace—The Residence of John Sadleir, the Fraudulent M.P.—Lancaster Gate—The Pioneer of Tramways—Queen Charlotte's Lying-in Hospital—Death of Dr. Adam Clarke—The Burial-ground of St. George's, Hanover Square.

As soon as ever we quit the precincts of Kensington proper, and cross the Uxbridge Road, we become painfully conscious of a change. We have left the "Old Court Suburb," and find ourselves in one that is neither "old" nor "court-like." The roadway, with its small shops on either side, is narrow and unattractive, and the dwellings are not old enough to have a history or to afford shelter for an anecdote. About the centre of this thoroughfare, at the spot whence omnibuses are continually starting on the journey eastward towards the City, stood, till about the year 1860, a small and rather picturesque turnpike-gate, which commanded not only the road towards Notting Hill and Shepherd's Bush, but also that which branches off to the north and north-east in the direction of the Grove of Westbourne. What rural ideas and pictures arise before our mental eye as we mention Notting—possibly Nutting—Hill, and the Shepherd's Bush and Westbourne Grove! We fear that the nuts, and the shepherds, and the nightingales which, so lately as the reign of William IV., sang sweetly here in the summer nights, are now, each and all, things of the past.

Notting Hill is said to derive its name from a manor in Kensington called "Knotting-Bernes," or "Knutting-Barnes," sometimes written "Notting," or "Nutting-barns"—so, at least, writes Lysons, in his "Environs of London." He adds that the property belonged formerly to the De Veres, Earls of Oxford (which would naturally be the case, as it formed part of Kensington parish and manor); and subsequently to Lord Burleigh, who, as we have already seen, lived at Brompton Hall, not very far from the neighbourhood of Kensington. In Robins' "History of Paddington," we read that the "manor of Noting barons, *alias* Kensington, then 'Nutting Barns,' afterwards called

'Knotting-barns,' in Stockdale's new map of the country round London, 1790; 'Knolton Barn,' now 'Notting-barns,' was carved out of the original manor of 'Chenesitun.'" From an inquisition taken at Westminster, in the reign of Henry VIII., it appears that "the manor called Notingbarons, *alias* Kensington, in the parish of Paddington, was held of the Abbot of Westminster as of his manor of Paddington by fealty and twenty-two shillings rent;" but since the time of the Reformation "Notting-barns" seems to have been considered a part of Kensington. Notting Barns Manor was held successively by the De Veres, and by Robert Fenroper, Alderman of London, who exchanged with King Henry VIII. It was afterwards granted to Pawlet, Earl of Wiltshire, from whom it passed to Lord Burghley. The manor was next held by the Copes, Andersons, and Darbys, and in 1820 it was owned by Sir William Talbot. Down to a very recent period, much of the district through which we are about to pass bore rather a bad character for thieves and housebreakers, and was somewhat noted for its piggeries and potteries; but these have all been swept away by the advancing tide of bricks and mortar. The "potteries" are still kept in remembrance by Pottery Lane, in which is the Roman Catholic Church of St. Francis of Assisi, referred to in a previous chapter. The ground about Notting Hill lies high, and the soil is a stiff clay, while that of Kensington proper is chiefly sand and gravel; but in reality, Notting Hill forms part and parcel of Kensington itself, which stretches away some distance northward in the direction of Kensal Green. "The principal street," writes Faulkner, in 1820, "runs along the high road for about three furlongs. The village enjoys an excellent air and beautiful prospects on the north, and lying in the direct road for Uxbridge and Oxford, it is enlivened every hour by the passage of mail-coaches, stages, and wagons."

The neighbourhood has become, of late years, a favourite residence for artists and sculptors, among whom may be reckoned Mr. J. Philip, Mr. Watts, Mr. Holman Hunt, and also Mr. William Theed. On either side of a narrow lane leading from Campden Hill towards Holland House is a nest of mansions, each standing in its own grounds, known as the "Dukery." Among its present and late occupants are the Dukes of Argyll and Rutland, the Dowager Duchess of Bedford, and Lords Airlie and Macaulay.

Cornelius Wood, a celebrated soldier of fortune, characterised in the *Tatler* under the name of "Silvio," died here in 1711. As in most of the suburbs of London which lay along the main roads, so here the various inns and taverns would appear to have shown by their signs a tendency to the sports of the road, for within a short distance we find "The Black Lion," "The Swan," "The Feathers," "The Nag's Head," "The Horse and Groom," and "The Coach and Horses," many of which, no doubt, were, half a century ago, the resorts of highwaymen when they had done a little bit of business on the Uxbridge or the Harrow Road, and which, if their mute walls could speak, might tell many a tale of coaches robbed, and the plunder shared between the "knights of the road" and obliging landlords.

The parish extends along the Uxbridge Road as far as Shepherd's Bush. On the left of the road was a piece of waste ground, known till recently as "Gallows Close," so called from the fact of two men having been executed here for a highway robbery in 1748. The gallows, or part of it, remained till about 1800. The ancient highway from London to Turnham Green is said by Faulkner, in his "History of Kensington" (1820), to have passed by Tyburn to the Gravel Pits, and to have branched off to the left at Shepherd's Bush, through a field, at the western extremity of which (he adds) the road is still visible, though now entirely impassable from the overhanging branches of the trees on both sides of the road, and from having become a deep slough in the neighbourhood of Pallenswick Green. This was the road where the Earl of Holland drew up his forces previous to the Battle of Brentford, as related in "Clarendon's History of the Rebellion." But we must not travel too far afield.

We have already spoken of Kensington Gravel Pits. This must be understood as a vague name for an undefined district, lying partly to the north and partly to the south of the Uxbridge Road; indeed, the greater part was on the north side: this is evident from the fact that the house belonging to Lord Craven, at Craven Hill, which was borrowed by Queen Anne as a nursery for her children, is mentioned by contemporary writers as being "situated at Kensington Gravel Pits." Several local tradesmen's tokens, dated in 1660-70, at the Gravel Pits, are engraved by Faulkner. Since the disappearance of the actual gravel pits, their name seems to have been superseded by the joint influence of the new streets on Notting Hill and in Bayswater. Leigh Hunt, in his "Old Court Suburb," says:—"Readers may call to mind a remnant of one of the pits, existing but a few years ago, to the north of the Palace in Kensington Gardens, and adding greatly to their picturesque look thereabouts. A pleasant poetical tradition was connected with it, of which we shall have something further to say.

Now, the Gravel Pits were the fashionable suburb resort of invalids, from the times of William and Anne to the close of the last century. Their 'country air,' as it was called, seems to have been preferred, not only to that of Essex, but to that of Kent. Garth, in his 'Dispensary,' makes an apothecary say that sooner than a change shall take place, from making the poor pay for medicine to giving it them gratis—

"'Alps shall sink to vales,
And leeches in our glasses turn to whales;
Alleys at Wapping furnish us with new modes,
And Monmouth Street Versailles' riding hoods;
The rich to th' Hundreds in pale crowds repair,
And change "the Gravel Pits" for Kentish air.'"

The spot, in fact, has long been held in high repute for the salubrity of the air, and in the last generation it had become a noted place for the residence of artists. The neighbourhood, too, has long been a favourite haunt and home of laundresses; and no wonder, for Faulkner, in his "History of Kensington," speaks of an overflowing spring on the Norland House Estate as "peculiarly soft, and adapted to washing," the same water being "leased to three persons, who pay each seven shillings a week for it, and retail it about the neighbourhood at a halfpenny a pail."

These were really gravel pits half a century ago, and the inequality of the surface bore testimony to the fact. Sir A. Calcott's house was in a hollow, artificially made, and his garden was commanded from above by that of his next-door neighbour, Mr. Thomas Webster, then a rising artist, but who retired from the Royal Academy in 1876. Faulkner thus writes in his "History of Kensington," published in 1820:—"The valley on the north is laid down with grass, and the whole of this district appears to have undergone but little alteration, in respect to culture and division of the land, for several ages. Although the distance from London is scarcely three miles, yet the traveller might imagine himself to be embosomed in the most sequestered parts of the country, for nothing is heard to interrupt the course of his meditations but the notes of the lark, the linnet, or the nightingale. In the midst of these meadows stands the Manor House of Notting Barns, now occupied by William Smith, Esq., of Hammersmith. It is an ancient brick building, surrounded by spacious barns and other out-houses; the public road to Kensal Green passes through the farm-yard." How altered the appearance of the neighbourhood at the end of half a century!

It is much to be lamented by the lovers of rural scenery that here, as indeed on every side of London, acres which, only half a century ago, were still nursery-grounds and market-gardens, have been forced to give place to railways and their approaches, and to the building of suburban towns. To use the words of a writer in the *Cornhill Magazine* in 1866:—"The growth of London has gradually pushed the market-gardener into the country; and now, instead of sending up his produce by his own wagon, he trusts it to the railway, and is often thrown into a market fever by a late delivery. To compensate him, however, for the altered state of the times, he often sells his crops, like a merchant upon 'Change, without the trouble of bringing more than a few hand-samples in his pockets. He is nearly seventy years of age, though he looks scarce fifty, and can remember the time when there were 10,000 acres of ground under cultivation for vegetables within four miles of Charing Cross, besides about 3,000 more acres planted with fruit to supply the London consumption. He has lived to see the Deptford and Bermondsey gardens sadly curtailed; the Hoxton and Hackney gardens covered with houses; the Essex plantations pushed further off; and the Brompton and Kensington nurseries—the home of vegetables for centuries—dug up, and sown with International Exhibition temples, and Italian Gardens, that will never grow a pea or send a single cauliflower to market. He has lived to see Guernsey and Jersey, Cornwall, the Scilly Isles, Holland, Belgium, and even Portugal, with many other still more distant places, competing with the remote outskirts of London, and has been staggered by seeing the market supplied with choice early peas from such an unexpected quarter as French Algeria."

Building operations would seem to have commenced about this neighbourhood, on either side of the main road, in the early part of the present century. Much later, about the year 1857, a portion of the north margin of Holland Park, abutting upon the roadway, and extending from Holland Lane to Addison Road, was cut off and laid out for building purposes, and two rows of mansions, with large gardens before them, have been erected.

Close by, on the top of Campden Hill, but separated from the main road by Notting Hill Square and Grove, are the reservoirs and engine-house of the Grand Junction Waterworks Company. The chief works in connection with this company are situated on the north bank of the Thames, a little above Kew Bridge. The water is taken by a large conduit pipe from the middle of the river to the works on the shore, where it is pumped into filtering reservoirs, &c., and then supplied to the town. In connection with the works at Kew is a stand-pipe, upwards of 200 feet in height, by which the water is conveyed through the main pipes into the districts to be supplied. The main which brings the water to Campden Hill is between six and seven miles in length, and the reservoir here is capable of containing 6,000,000 gallons. The tall brick shaft of the works here forms a conspicuous object on every side of Notting Hill. In 1811 a company was formed, who availed themselves of the powers granted by a clause in the Grand Junction Canal Company's Act, for supplying water brought by the canal from the rivers Colne and Brent, and from a large reservoir supplied by land drainage in the north-western part of Middlesex. These waters were represented to be much superior to that of the Thames; but experience disappointed the hopes of the projectors: the water was found not only to be bad in quality, but deficient in quantity also; and after various vain expedients to remedy the evils, the company, which had taken the name of the "Grand Junction Waterworks Company," resorted to the Thames, taking their supply from a point near Chelsea Hospital. Adjoining the Waterworks is a lofty castellated building in the Gothic style, called Tower Crecy, erected by Mr. Page, the architect of Westminster Bridge, in honour of the Black Prince, whose emblems adorn the exterior in all its stages. It is said that the holder of the lease of the house is bound to hoist on its summit a flag on the anniversary of the Battle of Crecy. Between Holland Park and the Waterworks are some detached mansions—Aubrey House and others. One of these was the site of some medicinal wells which were of repute in the last century.

HOUSE AT CRAVEN HILL IN 1760.

On the north side of Notting Hill is Ladbroke Square—so called after the name of the family who took it on a building lease—and which, for style in the houses and the general appearance of the central enclosure, falls but little short of some of the more aristocratic squares of the West-end. The west end of the Square is crossed by Ladbroke Grove, which extends northward as far as Kensal New Town. On the north side of the Square are Kensington Park Gardens, a name given to a goodly row of houses overlooking the Square. The handsome modern Gothic, or Early English, church of St. John, not far off, in Lansdowne Crescent, dates from the year 1845. It is cruciform in plan, with an elegant spire rising from the intersection of the nave and chancel. This church stands on what was "Notting Hill Farm," when Faulkner wrote in 1820, a lonely hill commanding extensive views, owing to the absence of woods.

erected about 1815, called St. Petersburg Place, Moscow Road, Coburg Place, &c. These names commemorate the visit of the Allied Sovereigns, in 1814. In the centre of Petersburg Place, Mr. Orme erected in 1818 a private chapel, to serve as a chapel of ease to Paddington. It appears to have been the first private speculation of the kind in the suburbs, and not to have been built till the growth of the population rendered it necessary.

NOTTING BARN FARM, 1830.

Norland Square perpetuates the name of Norland House, a small but well-wooded estate, which, in the reign of William IV., belonged to one of the Drummonds, the bankers, of Charing Cross. Many of the new streets about Notting Hill were built between the years 1850 and 1860.

Orme Square, which abuts upon the Uxbridge Road, overlooking Kensington Gardens, is named after a Mr. Orme, formerly a printseller in Bond Street, who purchased a considerable space of ground lying to the west of Craven Hill, upon which the Square is built. Bayswater House, an isolated mansion in the Bayswater Road, between Lancaster Gate and Orme Square, was the residence of Fauntleroy, the forger. A new range of buildings, to the north-east of Orme Square, was

Much of the ground about this neighbourhood, before it was cut up into streets, terraces, crescents, &c.—indeed, as lately as the time when Queen Victoria ascended the throne—was the scene of an establishment which enjoyed some popularity while it lasted—namely, the Hippodrome; but so brief is fame, that although it was flourishing at the above period, it had become almost forgotten after a lapse of twenty years, and its site clean blotted out. For much of the following sketch of the Hippodrome in all its novelty and pride, we are indebted to the *Sporting Magazine* for 1837:—

"Making the *cours aristocratique* of Routine (*alias* Rotten) Row, you pass out at Cumberland Gate, and then trot on to Bayswater. Thence you arrive at the Kensington Gravel Pits, and descending where on the left stands the terrace of Notting Hill, find opposite the large wooden gates of a recent structure. Entering these, I was by no means prepared for what opened upon me. Here, without figure of speech, was the most perfect race-course that I had ever seen. Conceive, almost within the bills of mortality, an enclosure some two miles and a half in circuit, commanding from its centre a view as spacious and enchanting as that from Richmond Hill (?), and where almost the only thing that you can *not* see is London. Around this, on the extreme circle, next to the lofty fence by which it is protected, ... is constructed, or rather laid out—for the leaps are natural fences—the steeplechase course of two miles and a quarter. Within this, divided by a slight trench, and from the space appropriated to carriages and equestrians by strong and handsome posts all the way round, is the race-course, less probably than a furlong in circuit. Then comes the enclosure for those who ride or drive as aforesaid; and lastly, the middle, occupied by a hill, from which every yard of the running is commanded, besides miles of country on every side beyond it, and exclusively reserved for foot people. I could hardly credit what I saw. Here was, almost at our doors, a racing emporium more extensive and attractive than Ascot or Epsom, with ten times the accommodation of either, and where carriages are charged for admission at three-fourths less. This great national undertaking is the sole result of individual enterprise, being effected by the industry and liberality of a gentleman by the name of Whyte. . . . This is an enterprise which must prosper; it is without a competitor, and it is open to the fertilization of many sources of profit. As a site for horse exercise, can any riding-house compare with it? For females, it is without the danger or exposure of the parks; as a training-ground for the turf or the field it cannot be exceeded; and its character cannot be better summed up than by describing it as a necessary of London life, of the absolute need of which we were not aware until the possession of it taught us its permanent value."

The earliest mention of the Hippodrome in the *Racing Calendar* is to be found in the volume for 1837, when two races were run, the one for fifty and the other for a hundred sovereigns—three horses starting for one, and four for the other.

"At the close of the reign of William IV.," says Mr. Blaine, in his "Rural Sports," "an attempt was made to establish a regular series of race meetings, and also a training locality within two miles of the metropolis. To this intent a large portion of land was treated for and engaged close to Notting Hill. Here were erected stabling and boxes for about seventy-five race-horses, with every convenience for a training establishment; a very good race-course also was formed, and numerous stakes were run for on it in 1838. But, unfortunately, the proprietors overlooked one circumstance at once fatal to the Hippodrome, as the establishment was named: the soil was a deep, strong clay, so that the training-ground could be used by horses only at particular periods of the year. This was a difficulty not to be got over, and as a race-course the Hippodrome soon closed its short career, doubtless with a heavy loss to the proprietors."

It would appear, from other channels of sporting information, that the first public day was given on Saturday, the 3rd of June, 1837, and that it naturally drew together as brilliant an assembly as ever met together in London. "On account of its vicinity to town, every refreshment was provided at a rate for which those who had been used to the terrible extortions elsewhere would hardly have been prepared. Splendid equipages occupied the circle allotted to them, while gay marquees, with all their flaunting accompaniments, covered the hall, filled with all the good things of this life, and iced champagne, which can hardly be called a mortal beverage. The racing was for plates of fifty and 100 sovereigns, with moderate entrances, given by the proprietors. The £100 plate was won by Mr. Wickham's 'Pincher,' and the steeplechase by Mr. Elmore's 'Lottery,' ridden by Mason. There was a second meeting appointed for Monday and Tuesday, the 19th and 20th of the same month, but the former day alone 'came off,' the other day's racing being postponed on account of the death of King William."

A writer in the *Sporting Magazine*, who signs himself "Juan," remarks:—"As a place of fashionable resort, it certainly opened under promising auspices, the stewards being Lord Chesterfield and Count D'Orsay. Another year, I cannot doubt, is destined to see it rank among the most favourite and favoured of all the metropolitan rendezvous, both for public and for private recreation. Unquestionably, of the varieties of the present season none has put forward such a claim to popularity and patronage as the 'Hippodrome.'" But the defect, which we have already mentioned, in the subsoil was irremediable; and after four years of a very chequered and struggling career, its last public meeting was held in June, 1841. At this date the land along its southern and eastern sides was beginning to be in demand for building purposes, and so pieces were sliced off to form those streets and thoroughfares which lie to the north of Westbourne Grove and south of the Great Western Railway. A large portion of the riding ground, however, was still kept laid down in turf—rather of a coarse kind, it must be owned; and some hedges were preserved, over which dashing young ladies would ride their chargers as lately as the year 1852. But in the course of the next five or six years the green sward, and the green trees, and the green hedges were all swept away, and on the spot selected by the "Di Vernons" and "pretty horse-breakers" for their trial-jumps now stands St. Stephen's Church.

Portobello Farm was marked in the maps of the neighbourhood as lately as 1830: it was named by its then owner at the time of the capture of that city by Admiral Vernon. It then stood in the midst of open fields, in which the cows and sheep grazed and pigs were fed. In what is now Portobello Road, skirting the eastern end of Ladbroke Square, stands a convent of the Little Sisters of the Poor. The "sisters" themselves feed off the scraps left by the paupers whom they support by going round to the doors of London houses for broken victuals. Upwards of a hundred poor persons are daily supported by the "sisters" in this benevolent manner. The head-quarters of this charity are at Hammersmith, where the chief institution will be described in its proper place. There was a pretty walk this way across to Kensal Green till about 1850-60.

The splendid new town of Bayswater, close by, which has joined North Kensington and Shepherd's Bush on to London, had no existence during the first few years of Queen Victoria, when "Hopwood's Nursery Ground" and the Victoria Gardens —so famed for running-matches and other sporting meetings—faced the dull brick wall which effectually shut out the green glades and leafy avenues of Kensington Gardens from the view of passengers along the Bayswater Road. Bayswater is a vague name for the district extending from the Gravel Pits to the north-west corner of Hyde Park. Lord Chesterfield, in one of his poems, has praised the healthiness of the situation, though, probably, he was too fond of the town to walk often so far in the direction of the open country. The whole district of streets, squares, terraces, and crescents sprung into existence in the course of about ten years—between 1839 and 1849. Bayswater was noted of old for its springs, reservoirs, and conduits, supplying the greater part of the City of London with water. With regard to the origin of the name of Bayswater, the following particulars from the disclosures made in a trial at Westminster, as summarised by a writer in the first volume of *Notes and Queries*, help to elucidate the question:—"The Dean and Chapter of Westminster are possessed of the manor of Westbourne Green, in the parish of Paddington, parcel of the possessions of the extinct Abbey of Westminster. It must have belonged to the Abbey when *Domesday* was compiled; for, although neither Westbourne nor Knightsbridge (also a manor of the same house) is specially named in that survey, yet we know, from a later record of the time of Edward I., that both of those manors were members, or constituent hamlets, of the *ville* of Westminster, which is mentioned in *Domesday* among the lands of the Abbey. The most considerable tenant under the abbot in this *ville* was *Bainiardus*, probably the same Norman associate of the Conqueror who is called Baignardus and Bainardus in other parts of the survey, and who gave his name to Baynard's Castle. The descent of the land held by him under the abbot cannot be clearly traced, but his name long remained attached to part of it; and as late as the year 1653 a parliamentary grant of the Abbey or Chapter lands to Foxcrafte and another, describes 'the common field at Paddington' as being 'near to a place commonly called *Baynard's Watering*.' In 1720, the lands of the Dean and Chapter in the same common field are described, in a terrier of the Chapter, to be in the occupation of Alexander Bond, of *Bear's Watering*, in the same parish of Paddington. The common field referred to is the well-known piece of garden-ground lying between Craven Hill and the Uxbridge Road, called also *Bayswater Field*. We may, therefore, fairly conclude that this portion of ground, always remarkable for its springs of excellent water, once supplied water to Baynard, his household, or his cattle; that the memory of his name was preserved in the neighbourhood for six centuries; and that his 'watering-place' now figures on the outside of certain omnibuses, in the streets of London, under the modern name of 'Bayswater.'"

The running streams and gravelly soil of this neighbourhood were at one time highly favourable for the growth of watercress, of which, as lately as the year 1825, there were several cultivators here, as in other places in the vicinity of London. The cultivation of watercress is said to have been first attempted, at the commencement of the present century, by a Mr. Bradbury, near Gravesend. Gerarde, the herbalist, says that eating watercresses restores the "wonted bloom to the cheeks of young ladies." Perhaps that is one reason why that plant is so popular.

On a slanting grassy bank, about a hundred yards from the back of the line of dwelling-houses now bearing the name of Craven Hill, stood, down to about the year 1820, an ancient stone-built conduit-house, whence the water-supply was conveyed by pipes underground into the City. Conduit Passage and Spring Street, both near at hand, thence derive their designation. The conduit was constructed and kept up by the Corporation of London, "to preserve a large spring of pure water, which rose at the spot, and was formerly conveyed by leaden pipes (cast in Holland) to Cheapside and Cornhill." "It was," says a writer in the *City Press*, "one of the most ancient springs in the vicinity of London, and, being situate in a manor once belonging to the Sanford family, and subsequently to the Earl of Craven, was granted to the citizens by one Gilbert Sanford in the twenty-first year of the reign of Henry III., A.D. 1236." Some reference is made to it in Lysons' "Environs of London," where it is stated that the water, "conveyed by brick drains, supplies the houses in and about Bond Street, which stand upon the City lands." Lysons further states that "the springs at this place lie near the surface, and the water is very fine." One of the principal reservoirs here, of which the Serpentine received the overplus, was situated where Trinity Church now stands, at the corner of Gloucester Gardens, Bishop's Road, not far from the "Royal Oak" tavern. In the *Saturday Magazine* for May 18th, 1844, there is an illustration of the Conduit-head at Bayswater, and in the article which accompanies it, the writer thus observes:—"The sources of the various conduits of London, formerly kept with so much care, have for the most part entirely disappeared. That at Paddington, however, still exists, though probably not in its original form; and Mr. Matthews says that, up to a recent period, it afforded a plentiful supply of water to some houses in Oxford Street. The conduit, or spring, is situate in a garden about half a mile to the west of the Edgware Road, and at the same distance from Bayswater, within two hundred or three hundred yards of the Grand Junction Water Company's reservoirs. It is covered by a circular building in good condition, and some of the pipes continue in a sound state, although several centuries have elapsed since they were laid down. From the same source, about a century ago, the palace at Kensington received a part of its supply, which was effected by the aid of a water-wheel placed at Bayswater Bridge; but on the establishment of the Chelsea Waterworks, it became useless, and was removed."

There is also in the illustrated edition of Pennant's "London," in the British Museum, a print of this conduit as it appeared in the year 1798, of which a copy is given on page 186. The aqueduct itself was "round, and cased thick with stone, and in the upper spiral part they lapped over each other, tile-like, and were fastened together with iron cramps to the brickwork, thick within. It was of a regular circumference, from the pediment or base about eight feet, and then spread up to the point, and was capped with a ball. Its height, about twenty feet, had four air-lets, resembling windows, with a door next the garden, plated with iron plates, over which, in an oblong square, was cut, 'REP. ANNO 1632'; in another part were the City arms, with the date, 1782." The water, we are told, was constantly issuing from under the door, through a wooden pipe, at the rate of thirty gallons an hour, and took its course under the bridge into Kensington Gardens. When this water was let to the proprietors of Chelsea Waterworks, a stipulation was made that the basin therein should be kept full. This spring also supplied the basin in Hyde Park, whence, as we have already seen, it was conveyed by a water-wheel, "at Hyde Park wall, near Knightsbridge chapel," on to the Thames at Pimlico. It also took a subterraneous course into the City, "whose name and arms it bore," and whose property it was, and to whom now, no doubt, the land belongs all round about whereupon it was built. The water-course to the City was formerly denoted by stones above ground, laid along through the fields; and in the burying-ground of St. George, Hanover Square, which abuts upon the Bayswater Road, was once a brick well and several stones, marked with the City arms, and the date of 1773. There was also a well against the shop, 254, Oxford Street, with the City arms, inscribed "1772." In the centre of the "conduit-field" there was a very curious antique stone, much mutilated, which pointed out the rise of the spring. There were also two other mark-stones, almost hid in the earth, near to the conduit. When the Craven Hill estate was parcelled out for building purposes, the stone conduit-house was pulled down, and the stream was led either into the main sewer or into the river Serpentine, which rises much farther up in a north-easterly direction, and now rushes, occasionally with great impetus, under the centre of the roadway in Kensington Garden Terrace, and, crossing the Bayswater Road, enters Kensington Gardens where the fountains are.

Apropos of the ancient streams in this locality, it may be added that it is said there was in the olden days very good fishing in the trout stream which ran from Notting Hill Manor towards Hay

Hill, Berkeley Square, taking its course through Brook Street, Grosvenor Square, which was built on the high banks of the said stream, where it ceased to blend with the Tye. We know that as early as the reign of Henry III. there were six fountains in this locality from which water was supplied to the City by means of pipes.

In Lambert's "London and its Environs," published in 1805, we read :—"Bayswater is a hamlet to Paddington, about a mile from London, on the Uxbridge Road. Its public tea-gardens formerly belonged to the celebrated Sir John Hill, who here cultivated the medicinal plants from which he prepared his essences, tinctures, &c." Sir John Hill was the son of a clergyman, born about 1716, and bred as an apothecary. He was employed by Lord Petre and the Duke of Richmond in the arrangement of their botanic gardens in Essex and Sussex; and by their assistance he executed a scheme of travelling over several parts of the kingdom, to collect the most rare plants, accounts of which he published by subscription. But this proved a failure, and showed that he was in advance of his time. His "Vegetable System" extends over twenty-six folio volumes! and for this he was rewarded by a Swedish order of knighthood from the king of that country. It appears that, for a time at least, Sir John Hill, though little better than a charlatan and an empiric, enjoyed the reputation of a great and learned botanist. He was at one time a second-rate actor, and he made an unsuccessful attempt to obtain admission into the Royal Society. Garrick's epigram on him is well known, and has often been quoted :—

> "For physic and farces his equal there scarce is;
> His farces are physic; his physic a farce is."

Among the medicines produced by Sir John Hill were his "Water-dock Essence" and his "Balm of Honey." These gardens are now covered by the long range of mansions called Lancaster Gate. They were originally known as the "Physic Garden," and were opened as a place of amusement towards the close of the last century. They were still in existence as gardens as late as 1854, though no longer frequented by pleasure-seekers of the upper classes. It is not a little singular that the gardens at Bayswater are not even mentioned by name, in the article on "Old Suburban Tea Gardens," in Chambers' "Book of Days." Faulkner, writing in 1820, says that within the last few years Bayswater has increased to a "popular neighbourhood."

Craven House, which gave its name to Craven Hill, above mentioned, became the residence of Lord Craven's family some time before 1700, on their removal from Drury Lane. It was borrowed (as stated above) by Queen Anne, as a nursery for her son, the little Duke of Gloucester, before she engaged Campden House, where we have already seen her.

Craven Hill is now called Craven Road, the inequality of it having been levelled by filling up the low ground where a small brook once crossed it from north to south. The houses in Craven Road and Craven Hill Gardens stand on the site of a field which was given about the year 1720 in exchange for the "Pest-field," near Golden Square, already mentioned; and it may be the reverse of comforting to the inhabitants to know that, under an old agreement between Lord Craven and the parochial authorities, the plot of ground in question may be taken for the purpose of a burial-ground, in case London should ever again be visited with the plague; unless, indeed, this liability has been done away with by the Act which enforces extra-mural interments. This land was not used during the cholera of 1849; and at the present time, as we have shown above, a grand London square, called Craven Gardens, alone indicates the site of the Pest-house fields. The property, which belonged in former times to one Jane Upton, and was called Upton Farm, was purchased by the trustees of this charity-estate for £1,570.

In 1821 the Toxophilite Society rented about four acres of ground here, between Sussex Gardens and the Bayswater Road, just opposite the point where Hyde Park and Kensington Gardens meet; they formed then part of quite a rural district, the ground shelving down somewhat steeply on the west to a little brook. A pavilion was erected here for the use of the members, and we are told that "there was space for three pairs of targets, with a range of about 200 yards." The Society held these grounds until 1834, when they removed to their present gardens in the Regent's Park. The exact site of these grounds is preserved in the name of the Archery Tavern in Bathurst Street, leading to Sussex Square.

In the fields a little to the north of Craven Hill, towards Westbourne Green, was the cottage (see page 147) where the Princess of Wales used to throw off the restraints of royal etiquette in the company of her intimate friends.

The district lying between Kensington Gardens and Paddington, a little to the north of Bayswater, was known, till the reign of George IV., as Westbourne Green, and was quite a leafy retreat at the time of that king's accession. That portion of the district lying to the north of Westbourne Grove and Bishop's Road will be best dealt with in our chapter on Paddington; but with regard to Westbourne Grove itself, we may state that, as lately as 1852, this thoroughfare, which now consists almost entirely of attractive shops, was a quiet street, consisting of detached cottages, with gardens in front. At the end nearest Paddington was an open nursery garden, rich in dahlias, geraniums, &c.

Oxford Square and Norfolk Square, may be rapidly passed over. Each and all of these places can boast of goodly mansions, interspersed with gardens and enclosures filled with trees and shrubs; but the whole district is of too modern growth to have a history.

THE BAYSWATER CONDUIT IN 1798. (*From Pennant.*)

Westbourne Terrace, which unites Bishop's Road with Craven Road, is so called from the West Bourne, a small brook running from Kilburn between Paddington and Bayswater, and passing into the Serpentine. It was built in 1847–52.

Sussex Gardens and Sussex Square, Pembridge Square and Crescent, Talbot and Leinster Squares, Hyde Park Gardens and Hyde Park Square, Cleveland Square and Queen's Road and Gardens, Southwick Crescent and Place are named after Southwick Park, Hampshire, the property of the Thistlethwayte family, formerly joint-lessees of the Paddington Manor.

In Gloucester Square, Westbourne Terrace, at No. 11, lived John Sadleir, the fraudulent M.P., who committed suicide on Hampstead Heath in February, 1856.

A splendid new city of palaces, Lancaster Gate,

NOTTING HILL IN 1750.

&c., sprung up between 1860 and 1870, on the site of Hopwood's Nursery Grounds and the Victoria Tea Gardens, which we have mentioned above.

About the year 1861, we may here remark, a novelty, in the way of street railways, was introduced in the Bayswater Road, by Mr. George F. Train, who was at least the pioneer of a useful invention. Permission had been given by the Commissioners of Highways for Mr. Train to lay down the rails for his new conveyance, and the event was inaugurated by a public banquet at St. James's Hall. Notwithstanding the coldness with which the project was at first received, the plan has since been carried out in various parts of London in the tramways.

In the autumn of 1832, when the cholera was spreading death far and wide throughout the land, Dr. Adam Clarke, the author of a well-known Commentary on the Bible, here fell a victim to that fatal malady. He was engaged to preach at Bayswater on Sunday, the 26th of August, and on the Saturday before he was conveyed there in a friend's chaise. He was cheerful on the road, but was tired with his journey and listless in the evening; and when a gentleman asked him to preach a charity sermon for him and fix the day, he replied, "I am not well; I cannot fix a time; I must first see what God is about to do with me." He retired to bed early, not without some of those symptoms that indicated the approach of this awful disease, but which do not appear to have excited any suspicions in himself or in his friends. He rose in the morning ill, and wanting to get home; but before arrangements could be made for his removal, he had sunk into his chair—that icy coldness, by which the complaint is characterised, had come on, and when the medical men arrived, they pronounced it a clear case of cholera. His wife and most of his children, short as the summons was, gathered about him—he had ever been the most affectionate of husbands and parents—and his looks indicated great satisfaction when he saw them; but he was now nearly speechless. "Am I blue?" however, he said to his son—a question indicating his knowledge of the malady under which he was sinking; and without any effort of nature to rally, he breathed his last.

On the north side of the Bayswater Road, about a quarter of a mile from the site of Tyburn Turnpike, is a dreary burial-ground, of about an acre, with a chapel of the plainest description, belonging to the parish of St. George, Hanover Square. In this burial-ground was deposited, in 1768, the body of Laurence Sterne, the author of "Tristram Shandy," who had died in poverty at his lodgings in Bond Street, as we have already stated. But the body was afterwards taken up by some of the "resurrection men," and sent to Cambridge to the professor of anatomy for dissection. Such, at all events, is the story told by Sir J. Prior, in his "Life of Malone." His grave here is marked by a plain upright stone, with an epitaph clumsily expressed, "a perpetual memorial of the bad taste of his brother masons."

Among other eminent persons buried here were Mr. J. T. Smith, the author of "The Book for a Rainy Day," and many other antiquarian works on London; Mrs. Radcliffe, the author of "The Mysteries of Udolpho;" and last, not least, General Sir Thomas Picton, who fell at Waterloo; but in 1859 his body was removed, and re-interred in St. Paul's Cathedral.

CHAPTER XVI.

TYBURN AND TYBURNIA.

"The three-square stilt at Tyburn."—*Old Saying.*

Derivation of the Name of Tyburn—Earliest Executions on this Spot—Sir Roger Bolinbroke, the Conjuror—Elizabeth Barton, the "Holy Maid of Kent"—Execution of Roman Catholics—Morocco Men—Mrs. Turner, the Poisoner, and Inventor of the Yellow Starched Ruffs and Cuffs—Resuscitation of a Criminal after Execution—Colonel Blood—Jack Sheppard and Jonathan Wild—Mrs. Catherine Hayes—"Clever Tom Clinch"—"Execution Day"—The Execution of Lord Ferrers—The Rev. Mr. Hackman—Dr. Dodd—The Last Act of a Highwayman's Life—"Sixteen-string Jack"—McLean, the "Fashionable Highwayman"—Claude Duval—John Twyn, an Offending Printer—John Haynes, and his Resuscitation after Hanging—Ryland, the Forger—An Unlucky Jest—"Jack Ketch"—Tyburn Tickets—Hogarth's "Tom Idle"—The Gallows and its Surroundings—The Story of the Penance of Queen Henrietta Maria—An Anecdote about George III.—The Site of Tyburn Tree—The Tyburn Pew-opener—Tyburnia—Connaught Place—The Princess Charlotte and the Prince of Orange—The Residence of Mr. T. Assheton-Smith, and of Haydon the Painter.

TYBURNIA, which of late years has become almost, if not quite, as fashionable and aristocratic as Belgravia, is the district lying between Edgware Road and Westbourne and Gloucester Terrace and Craven Hill, the south side of which is bounded by the Bayswater Road, and may be said to have sprung into existence only since the reign of William IV.

The little river Tyburn, or Tybourn, whence the district derives its name, consisted of two arms, one of which, as already stated, crossed Oxford Street, near Stratford Place; while the other, further to the west, followed nearly the course of the present Westbourne Terrace and the Serpentine. Five hundred years ago, or less, it was a pleasant brook enough, with rows of elms growing on its banks. These trees were a place of execution in those days; and Roger de Mortimer, the paramour of Queen Eleanor, widow of Edward II., was dragged thither on a hurdle, and hung and quartered, his body being exposed there for several days. Elm's Lane, Bayswater, now swept away, preserved down to our own time the memory of these fatal elms, which are to be regarded as the original "Tyburn Trees." It was at a subsequent time that the place of execution was removed nearer to London, the corner of the Edgware Road. Here it became a fixture for centuries; here many notable and many notorious persons have "died in their shoes," to use a favourite cant expression. Here suffered the "Holy Maid of Kent;" Mrs. Turner, the poisoner, and the inventor of the starched ruff which adorns so many portraits of fair ladies of other days; Felton, the assassin of the Duke of Buckingham; a batch of the parliamentary regicides; some dozens of Roman Catholic priests, condemned as "traitors;" a long line of illustrious highwaymen, such as Jack Sheppard and Jonathan Wild; Lord Ferrers, the murderer of his steward; Dr. Dodd, for forgery; and last, not least, Mother Brownrigg, the same

> "Who whipped three female 'prentices to death,
> And hid them in the coal-hole."

An absurd derivation of the name has been suggested, as though it was from the words "tie" and "burn," though some countenance is given to the derivation by the fact that traitors were strung or "tied" up first, and afterwards "burnt." But the real origin is from the little brook, or burn, which ran by the spot, as above mentioned.

The gallows were removed hither (as we have seen) from opposite to St. Giles's Pound; but there had been occasional executions here earlier: for instance, it is upon record that Judge Tressilian and Nicholas Brembre, or Brambre, were hung here in A.D. 1388. Mr. Dobré was at great pains to discover the record of an earlier execution here, but failed.

The complete history of the neighbourhood of "Tyburn Tree" has still to be written, though the materials are far from scanty; for between the Reformation and the reign of George III., few years elapsed in which Roman Catholic priests, and even laymen, were not sent thither to suffer, nominally as "traitors," but in reality because they were the adherents of a proscribed and persecuted faith, and refused, at the bidding of an earthly sovereign, to abandon their belief in the Pope as the spiritual head of Christendom. Here, too, during the same period, almost as many men of a different stamp paid the last penalty of the law for violating other enactments—highwaymen, robbers, forgers, and murderers. The highwaymen generally went to the scaffold merrily and jauntily, as men who had all their lives faced the chance of a violent death, and were not afraid to meet it at Tyburn. As they passed along the streets in the fatal cart, gaily dressed in their best clothes, young women in the crowd would present them with nosegays, and in the eyes of the assembled multitudes their deaths were regarded as almost as glorious as those of the Roman Catholic "confessors" were esteemed by their co-religionists.

Our readers will not, of course, forget the lines in the song of "Macheath," in the *Beggar's Opera*, which thus refer to Tyburn:—

> "Since laws were made for every degree,
> To curb vice in others as well as in me,
> I wonder we ha'nt better company
> 'Neath Tyburn Tree."

One of the earliest executions on this spot was that of "Sir Roger Bolinbroke, the conjuror" (A.D. 1440), who suffered for high treason, in conjunction with the Duchess of Gloucester, as recorded by Shakespeare.* From the Harleian MSS., No. 585, we learn his fate in detail. On the same day on which he was condemned at Guildhall, he was drawn from the Tower to Tyburn, and there hanged, beheaded, and quartered, his head being set up on London Bridge, and his four quarters being disposed of in like manner at Hereford, Oxford, York, and Cambridge.

Here was executed, in the fifteenth century, Fisher, a skinner, already mentioned† by us as the man who released Sir John Oldcastle when a prisoner in the Tower.

Here, in 1534, were executed Elizabeth Barton, the so-called "Holy Maid of Kent," who had prophesied the speedy death of Henry VIII.; several of her supporters suffered with her.

Here, too, a few years later, suffered Sir Thomas Percy, Aske, D'Arcy, Bigod, Sir John Bulmer, and the Abbot of Jewaux, for the share they had taken in a foreign pilgrimage and in a last desperate effort to restore the Catholic religion in England.

* See *Henry VI.*, part ii., act 1, sc. 2. † See Vol. II., p. 65.

Tyburn is mentioned by Holinshed, who writes of a certain "false servant" that, being convicted of felony in court of assize, he was judged to be hanged, "and so *was at Tyburn.*"

To enumerate the names of all who suffered the "extreme penalty of the law" at Tyburn would be a difficult, and, indeed, a needless task. Among those who went thither to end their days, however, were not only murderers, highwaymen, and traitors, but also housebreakers, sheep-stealers, and forgers; the penalty of death, however, was not confined to them, but was made to include even some of the loose and disreputable hangers-on of the demoralising State lottery-offices, known as "Morocco men," for going about the country with red morocco pocket-books, in which they entered the names of the victims whom they gulled.

Here was executed Mrs. Turner, the poisoner, for complicity with the Countess of Somerset in the murder of Sir Thomas Overbury, an event which formed one of the episodes in the corrupt reign of James I. "Mrs. Turner's execution," says John Timbs, in his "Romance of London," "excited immense interest. She was a woman of great beauty, and had much affected the fashion of the day. Her sentence was to be 'hang'd at Tiburn in her yellow Tinny Ruff and Cuff, she being the first inventor and wearer of that horrid garb.' The ruff and cuff were got up with *yellow starch*, and in passing her sentence, Lord Chief Justice Coke told her that she had been guilty of all the seven deadly sins, and declared that as she was the inventor of the yellow-starched ruffs and cuffs, so he hoped that she would be the last by whom they would be worn. He accordingly ordered that she should be hanged in the gear she had made so fashionable. The execution attracted an immense crowd to Tyburn, and many persons of quality, ladies as well as gentlemen, in their coaches. Mrs. Turner had dressed herself specially for her execution: her face was highly rouged, and she wore a cobweb lawn ruff, yellow-starched. An account, printed next day, states that 'her hands were bound with a black silk ribbon, as she desired; and a black veil, which she wore upon her head, being pulled over her face by the executioners, the cart was driven away, and she left hanging, in whom there was no motion at all perceived.' She made a very penitent end. As if to ensure the condemnation of yellow starch, the hangman had his hands and cuffs of yellow, 'which,' says Sir S. D'Ewes, 'made many after that day, of either sex, to forbear the use of that coloured starch, till it at last grew generally to be detested and disused.'"

Following in the wake of Mrs. Turner, came Southwell, the "sweet versifier;" Felton, the assassin of the Duke of Buckingham; and John Smith, the burglar, of Queen Anne's time. In connection with this last-named execution, even the gallows may be said to have its romantic side; for we read in Chambers' "Book of Days" that a reprieve came after Smith had been suspended for a quarter of an hour. He was taken down, bled, and *revived.*

We have already mentioned Colonel Blood's bold attempt to seize the Duke of Ormonde in St. James's Street.* He also endeavoured to complete his act of highway violence by hanging his victim by open force at Tyburn; but, happily for the duke, he did not succeed in the attempt.

We next come to the names of two others who have become famous through the agency of cheap literature—Jack Sheppard, the notorious housebreaker, and Jonathan Wild, the "thief and thief-taker." Of the early life of the first-named culprit we have already spoken in our account of Wych Street, St. Clement Danes;† and for his various exploits in Newgate we must refer our readers to our account of that prison.‡ The whole career of crime as practised by this vagabond carpenter has been strikingly told by Mr. Harrison Ainsworth, in his romance of "Jack Sheppard;" and his portrait, as he appeared in the condemned cell at Newgate, was painted by Sir James Thornhill, and sold by thousands as a mezzo-tint engraving. Jonathan Wild's particular sphere of action lay in the trade of the restoration of stolen property, which he carried on for many years through a secret confederacy with all the regular thieves, burglars, and highwaymen of the metropolis, whose depredations he prompted and directed. His success received some check by an Act of Parliament passed in 1717, by which persons convicted of receiving or buying goods, knowing them to have been stolen, were made liable to a long term of transportation. Wild, however, managed to elude this new law; but he was at last convicted, under a clause which had been enacted with a particular view to Wild's proceedings—such as trafficking in stolen goods, and dividing the money with felons. His execution took place at Tyburn, in May, 1725. At his trial he had a printed paper handed to the jury, entitled, "A list of persons discovered, apprehended, and convicted of several robberies on the highway, and also for burglary and housebreaking, and also for returning from transportation: by Jonathan Wild." It contained the names of thirty-five robbers, twenty-two housebreakers, and ten

* See Vol. IV., p. 166. † See Vol. III., p. 34. ‡ See Vol. II., p. 459.

returned convicts, whom he had been instrumental in getting hanged before he found the tables turned against himself.

Among the hundreds of murderers hung at Tyburn, few were more notorious than Catharine Hayes, who was executed in 1726. She and her husband lived in Tyburn Road, now called Oxford Street, but, not being contented with her spouse, she engaged two assassins, Wood and Billings, to make him drunk, and then aid her in dispatching him. They did so, and chopped up the body, carrying the head in a pail to the Horseferry at Westminster, where they threw it into the Thames, the other portion being secreted about a pond in Marylebone Fields. The head being found and identified, search was made for the rest of the body, and this being discovered, the other murderers were hung near the spot where Upper Wimpole Street now stands. Mrs. Hayes was reserved to suffer at Tyburn, blazing fagots being placed under her. The murder, as might be imagined, caused a great sensation when it became known, and is constantly mentioned in the publications of the time.

The following lines, from Swift's "Tom Clinch going to be Hanged," give a picture of the grim cavalcade wending its way from Newgate to Tyburn, in 1727:—

> "As clever Tom Clinch, while the rabble was bawling,
> Rode stately through Holborn to die in his calling,
> He stopped at the 'George' for a bottle of sack,
> And promised to pay for it—when he came back.
> His waistcoat, and stockings, and breeches were white,
> His cap had a new cherry-ribbon to tie 't;
> And the maids to the doors and the balconies ran,
> And cried 'Lack-a-day! he's a proper young man!'"

"Execution-day," as it was termed, must have been a carnival of frequent occurrence. Horace Walpole says that in the year 1752 no less than seventeen persons were executed at Tyburn in a batch. One of the most memorable executions that took place here was on the 5th of May, 1760, when that eccentric nobleman, Lawrence, third Earl Ferrers, met his fate for the murder of his steward, a Mr. John Johnson. The scene of the tragedy was his lordship's seat of Staunton Harold, near Ashby-de-la-Zouche, and the deed itself was deliberately planned and carried out. The career of Lord Ferrers for many years previously had been one of the grossest dissipation, and had resulted in his estates becoming seriously involved. The Court of Chancery ordered that the rents due to him should be paid to a receiver, the nomination of the said receiver being left to his lordship, who hoped to find in that person a pliant tool, who would take things easily and let him have his own way. The person whom Lord Ferrers so appointed was none other than Mr. Johnson, who had been in the service of his lordship's family, as steward, for many years. But he soon found out that he had got a different man to deal with than he had expected; and, accordingly, from that time, he conceived an inveterate hatred towards him, on account of the opposition which he offered to his desires and whims, and he finally resolved to "move heaven and earth" to obtain his revenge. Lord Ferrers' household at that time consisted of a Mrs. C——, who acted as housekeeper, her four daughters, and five domestic servants; and Mr. Johnson's farm-house, the Mount, was about a mile distant from the mansion, across the park. On Sunday, the 13th of January, in the year 1760, Lord Ferrers called on Mr. Johnson, and, after some discourse, arranged for another meeting, to take place at Staunton on the following Friday, at three o'clock. The Friday came round, and Johnson was true to his appointment. Shortly before that hour, his lordship had desired Mrs. C—— to take the children out for a walk, and the two men-servants he had contrived to get out of the way on different pretexts, so that when Johnson arrived there was no one in the house except his lordship and the three maid-servants. On the arrival of Mr. Johnson he was at once admitted into his lordship's private sitting-room. "They had sat together, talking on various matters, for some ten minutes or more, when the earl got up, walked to the door, and locked it. He next desired Johnson at once to settle some disputed account; then, rising higher in his demands, ordered him, as he valued his life, to sign a paper which he had drawn up, and which was a confession of his (Johnson's) villany. Johnson expostulated and refused, as an honest man would refuse, to sign his name to any such document. The earl then drew from his pocket a loaded pistol, and bade him kneel down, for that his last hour was come. Johnson bent one knee, but the earl insisted on his kneeling on both his knees. He did so, and Lord Ferrers at once fired. The ball entered his body below the rib, but it did not do its fell work instantaneously. Though mortally wounded, the poor fellow had strength to rise and to call loudly for assistance. The earl at first coolly prepared as though he would discharge the other pistol, so as to put his victim out of misery; but, suddenly moved with remorse, he unlocked the door and called for the servants, who, on hearing the discharge of the pistol, had run, in fear and trembling, to the wash-house, not knowing whether his lordship would not take it into his head to send a bullet through their bodies also. He called them once and again, desired one to fetch a surgeon, and another to help the wounded man into a bed. It was clear, however, that Johnson had not many hours to live; and, as he desired to see his children before he died, the earl ordered that they should be summoned from the farm. Miss Johnson came speedily, and found her father apparently in the agonies of death, and Lord Ferrers standing by the bedside, and attempting to stanch the blood that flowed from the wound." During the night, by a clever *ruse*, Johnson was removed to his own house, where he lingered only a few hours, dying early the next morning. The coroner's jury returned a verdict of "wilful murder" against Lord Ferrers, who was at once lodged in Leicester Gaol. About a fortnight afterwards, we are told, he was brought up to London in his own landau, drawn by six horses, under a strong guard, and he was "dressed like a jockey, in a close riding frock, jacked boots and cap, and a plain shirt." Arraigned before the House of Lords, he was at once committed to the Tower, and two months later was again brought up for trial at the bar of the House of Peers. His trial lasted nearly three days, and resulted in his being sentenced to be "hanged by the neck until he was dead;" but, "in consideration of his rank," a few days' extension of time was allowed before the sentence was carried into effect, and also he was permitted to be hanged with a silken instead of a hempen rope. Lord Ferrers, to use the slang expression of the sporting world, "died game." To the last he had respect to his rank, and, declining to journey to Tyburn in a cart, went slowly and stately thither in his own landau, again drawn by six horses. In this, dressed in his wedding suit, he rode as calmly to the gallows as the handsomest highwayman of his day, and went through the performance there with as little unnecessary affectation as though, like many a "gentleman of the road," he had looked to such an end as "the appropriate and inevitable conclusion of his career." It may be added that the landau in which Lord Ferrers rode to Tyburn was never used again, but was left to rot away and fall to pieces in a coach-house at Acton. His lordship's body found a grave at old St. Pancras Church.

THE PLACE OF EXECUTION, TYBURN, IN 1750.

In our account of Covent Garden, in a previous

volume,* we have spoken at some length of the murder of Miss Reay by the Rev. Mr. Hackman. Boswell was present at Hackman's trial at the Old Bailey, and further, after his condemnation and sentence, attended him in his coach to Tyburn, in company with a sheriff's officer. Selwyn, who, like Boswell, was fond of seeing executions, was not present on this occasion; but his friend, the Earl of Carlisle, attended, in order "to give some account of Hackman's behaviour." This he did, to the following effect:—"The poor man behaved with great fortitude; no appearances of fear were to be perceived, but very evident signs of contrition and repentance. He was long at his prayers; and when he flung down his handkerchief as the sign for the cart to move on, Jack Ketch, instead of instantly whipping on the horse, jumped on the other side of him to snatch up the handkerchief, lest he should lose his rights. He then returned to the head of the cart, and Jehu'd him out of the world."

In 1777, Dr. Dodd, in company with another felon, made his exit from the world at Tyburn Tree. The two were drawn in an open cart from Newgate to Tyburn, the execution being attended by an immense crowd. In apprehension of an attempt to rescue the criminal, twenty thousand men were ordered to be reviewed in Hyde Park during the execution, which, however, "though attended by an unequalled concourse of people, passed off with the utmost tranquillity." "Upon the whole," writes a friend of George Selwyn, who was present, "the piece was not very full of events. The doctor, to all appearance, was rendered perfectly stupid from despair. His hat was flapped all round and pulled over his eyes, which were never directed to any object around, nor ever raised, except now and then lifted up in the course of his prayers. He came in a coach, and a very heavy shower of rain fell just upon his entering the cart, and another just at his putting on his nightcap. During the shower an umbrella was held over his head, which Gilly Williams, who was present, observed was quite unnecessary, as the doctor was going to a place where he might be dried. . . . The executioner took both the doctor's hat and wig off at the same time. Why he put on his wig again I do not know, but he did; and the doctor took off his wig

EXECUTION OF LORD FERRERS AT TYBURN. (*From an Old Print of the Period.*)

* See Vol. III., p. 261.

a second time, and tied on a nightcap, which did not fit him; but whether he stretched that or took another, I could not perceive. He then put on his nightcap himself, and upon his taking it, he certainly had a smile on his countenance; and very soon afterwards there was an end of all his hopes and fears on this side of the grave. He never moved from the place he first took in the cart; seemed absorbed in prayer, and utterly dejected, without any other signs of animation but in praying. I stayed till he was cut down and put into the hearse. The body was hurried to the house of Davies, an undertaker in Goodge Street, Tottenham Court Road, where it was placed in a hot bath, and every exertion made to restore life, but in vain." We have already given some particulars of the life of Dr. Dodd, and of the crime for which he suffered;* it only remains to add that Dr. Johnson made eloquent and strenuous exertions with his pen to get the capital sentence remitted, but in vain. "The malevolence of men and their good nature," wrote Horace Walpole, "displayed themselves in their different characters against Dodd. His character appeared so bad to Dr. Newton, Bishop of Bristol, that he said, 'I am sorry for Dr. Dodd.' Being asked why, he replied, 'Because he is to be hanged for the least crime he ever committed.'"

The fondness which many minds feel (or rather felt) for these melancholy sights is thus discussed by Boswell and Dr. Johnson:—"I mentioned to him that I had seen the execution of several convicts at Tyburn† two days before, and that none of them seemed to be under any concern. *Johnson:* 'Most of them, sir, have never thought at all.' *Boswell:* 'But is not the fear of death natural to man?' *Johnson:* 'So much so, sir, that the whole of life is but keeping away the thoughts of it.' He then, in a low and earnest tone, talked of his meditating upon the awful hour of his own dissolution, and in what manner he should conduct himself upon that occasion. 'I know not,' said he, 'whether I should wish to have a friend by me, or have it all between God and myself.'

"Talking of our feeling for the distresses of others —*Johnson:* 'Why, sir, there is much noise made about it, but it is greatly exaggerated. No, sir, we have a certain degree of feeling to prompt us to do good; more than that Providence does not intend. It would be misery to no purpose.' *Boswell:* 'But suppose now, sir, that one of your intimate friends were apprehended for an offence for which he might be hanged.' *Johnson:* 'I should do what I could to bail him, and give him any other assistance; but if he were once fairly hanged, I should not suffer.' *Boswell:* 'Would you eat your dinner that day, sir?' *Johnson:* 'Yes, sir; and eat it as if he were eating with me. Why, there's Baretti, who is to be tried for his life to-morrow; friends have risen up for him on every side, yet if he should be hanged, none of them would eat a slice of pudding the less. Sir, that sympathetic feeling goes a very little way in depressing the mind.'" ‡

Tyburn Tree was the usual end of the "highwayman," as people in the days of Queen Anne and the Georges euphemistically called the robber and assassin of the king's high road. "Alas!" writes Thackeray, "there always came a day in the life of that warrior when it was the fashion to accompany him as he passed, without his black mask, and with a nosegay in his hand, accompanied by halberdiers, and attended by the sheriff, in a carriage without springs, and a clergyman jolting beside him, to a spot close by Cumberland Gate and the Marble Arch, where a stone still records that 'here Tyburn turnpike stood.' What a change in a century; nay, in a few years! Within a few yards of that gate the fields began: the fields of his exploits, behind the hedges of which he lurked and robbed. A great and wealthy city has grown over those meadows. Were a man brought to die thereon, the windows would be closed, and the inhabitants would keep their houses in sickening horror. A hundred years ago people crowded there to see the last act of a highwayman's life, and made jokes on it. Swift laughed at him, grimly advising him to provide a holland shirt and white cap, crowned with a crimson or black ribbon, for his exit, to mount the cart cheerfully, shake hands with the hangman, and so farewell; or Gay wrote the most delightful ballads, and then made merry over his hero."

Among those who suffered here the penalty of their crimes as highwaymen was the notorious "Sixteen-string Jack," who is said by Dr. Johnson to have "towered above the common mark" in his own line as much as Gray did in poetry. He was remarkable for foppery in his dress, and, as Boswell tells us, derived his name from a bunch of sixteen strings which he wore at the knees of his breeches. John Rann, for such was this malefactor's real name, was executed here in November, 1774, for robbing Dr. Bell, the chaplain to the Princess Amelia, in Gunnersbury Lane.

* See page 47, *ante*.

† Six unhappy men were executed at Tyburn on Wednesday, the 18th (*one* day before). It was one of the irregularities of Mr. Boswell's mind to be passionately fond of seeing these melancholy spectacles. Indeed, he avows and defends it (in the *Hypochondriac*, No. 68, *London Mag.*, 1783) as a *natural* and irresistible impulse.—CROKER.

‡ Boswell's "Life of Johnson."

"Rann was a smart fellow, and a great favourite with a certain description of ladies; he had been coachman to the Earl of Sandwich, when his lordship resided in the south-east corner house of Bedford Row. It was pretty generally reported that the *sixteen strings* worn by this freebooter at his knees were in allusion to the number of times he had been tried and acquitted. However, he was caught at last; and J. T. Smith records his being led, when a boy, by his father's playfellow, Joseph Nollekens, to the end of John Street, to see the notorious terror of the king's highway, Rann, pass on his way to execution. The malefactor's coat was a bright pea-green; he had an immense nosegay, which he had received from the hand of one of the frail sisterhood, whose practice it was in those days to present flowers to their favourites from the steps of St. Sepulchre's Church, as the last token of what they called their attachment to the condemned, whose worldly accounts were generally brought to a close at Tyburn, in consequence of their associating with abandoned characters. Such is Mr. Smith's account of the procession of the hero to Tyburn; and Nollekens assured Smith, had his father-in-law, Mr. Justice Welsch, been high constable, they could have walked all the way to Tyburn by the side of the cart." The "sixteen strings" which this freebooter wore at his knees were, in reality, to the initiated at least, a covert allusion to the number of times that he had been tried and acquitted. Fortunately for the Boswell illustrators, there is an etched portrait of "Sixteen-string Jack;" for, thief though he was, he had the honour of being recorded by Dr. Johnson. A correspondent of Hone's "Year-Book," published in 1832, states that he well remembered seeing "Sixteen-string Jack" taken in the cart to Tyburn.

It was, in fact, at Tyburn that most of the highwaymen of the last century—of whom Captain Macheath was another example, and whose exploits were so well known on Hounslow Heath, at Finchley, and on the Great North Road—closed their career.

"The species of gentleman highwayman," observes Mr. James Hannay, "no longer exists to frighten the traveller, and does no greater harm than put you to sleep in the pages of a novel. A gentleman can now roll through the country in his travelling-carriage without any fear of being robbed by a gallant horseman, summoning him to surrender with the air of a courtier, and pocketing his money with a quotation from Horace. The last of these heroes long ago died on that greatest of all 'trees of liberty,' the tree of Tyburn; and his only representative now-a-days is the common footpad—a vulgar fellow—who knocks you down, and rifles you when you are insensible."

Another notorious character who was hanged here about the middle of the last century was McLean, the "fashionable highwayman," of whom Walpole thus writes:—"One night, in the beginning of November, 1749, as I was returning from Holland House by moonlight, about ten o'clock, I was attacked by two highwaymen in Hyde Park, and the pistol of one of them going off accidentally, raised the skin under my eye, left some marks of shot in my face, and stunned me. The ball went through the top of the chariot, and if I had sat an inch nearer to the left side, must have gone through my head." One of these highwaymen was McLean. He also attacked and robbed Lord Eglinton, Sir Thomas Robinson, Mrs. Talbot, and many others. He carried off a blunderbuss belonging to the old Scotch earl. McLean was at one time a grocer in Welbeck Street, but having the misfortune to lose his wife, he gave up business and took to the road, having as a companion, one Plunket, a journeyman apothecary. McLean was captured in the autumn of 1750, by selling a laced waistcoat to a pawnbroker in Monmouth Street, who happened to carry it to the very man who had just sold the lace. Walpole tells us "there were a wardrobe of clothes, three-and-twenty purses, and the celebrated blunderbuss found at his lodgings, besides a famous kept mistress." Soame Jenyns, in his poem entitled "The Modern Fine Lady," written in the year this "fashionable highwayman" came to grief, writes—

> "She weeps if but a handsome thief is hung."

To which is appended this note:—"Some of the brightest eyes were at this time in tears for one McLean, condemned for robbery on the highway."

Even a cursory account of Tyburn would be incomplete without mention of one more highwayman, who here paid the penalty of his offences on the triangular gallows. This was Claude Duval, who was, perhaps, even more famous than McLean. He made Holloway the chief scene of predatory exploits. In Lower Holloway his name was long kept in remembrance by Duval's Lane, which, curiously enough, as John Timbs tells us in his "Romance of London," "was previously called Devil's Lane, and more anciently Tolentone Lane." Macaulay, in his "History of England," says that Claude Duval "took to the road, and became captain of a formidable gang;" adding that "it is related how, at the head of his troop, he stopped a lady's coach, in which there was a booty of four hundred pounds; how he took only one hundred, and suffered the fair owner to ransom the rest by dancing a coranto with him on the heath." This celebrated exploit has been made the subject of one of Mr. Frith's remarkable pictures, and has been engraved. Duval was arrested at the "Hole-in-the-Wall," a noted house near Covent Garden, and he was executed in January, 1669, in the twenty-seventh year of his age. It is on record how that, "after *lying in state* at the Tangier Tavern, in St. Giles's, he was buried in the middle aisle of St. Paul's, Covent Garden, his funeral being attended with flambeaux and a numerous train of mourners, 'to the great grief of the women.'"

Tyburn, it may be added, has also some other associations, being connected with the history of newspapers and the liberty of the press. At the Restoration the latter had almost ceased to exist, and the press had not only to make itself heard through the small voice of a "Licencer," but to regulate its proceedings by Act of Parliament. In 1663 a Tyburn audience was assembled to witness the execution of a troublesome printer. He was named John Twyn, and had carried on his business in Cloth Fair, near to Milton's hiding-place, when he had "fall'n on evil days." Twyn was accused of having printed some seditious work bearing on the arguments often urged against the Commonwealth, "that the execution of judgment and justice is as well the people's as the magistrates' duty; and if the magistrates pervert judgment, the people are bound by the law of God to execute judgment without them and upon them." Roger L'Estrange was the "licencer" who had hunted up this offending printer; and Chief Justice Hyde sentenced him to be "drawn on a hurdle to Tyburn, and there hanged by the neck;" and, being alive, that he should be cut down, and his body mutilated in a way which decency forbids the mention of; that his entrails should afterwards be taken out, "and, you still living, the same to be burnt before your eyes; your head to be cut off, and your head and quarters to be disposed of at the pleasure of the King's Majesty." It is fortunate for the law, as well as for offenders, that such merciful and upright judges have ceased to exist.

In 1782, the year preceding that which witnessed the last executions at Tyburn, the dead body of one John Haynes, a professional thief and housebreaker, who, in consequence, had finished here his career, was taken, as a "subject" for dissection, to the residence of Sir William Blizard. The body, we are told, showed signs of life, and Sir William perfected its recovery. Anxious to know the sensations which John Haynes had experienced at the moment of his suspension, the surgeon questioned the thief earnestly upon the subject. The only answer he could obtain was as follows:—"The last thing I recollect was going up Holborn Hill in a cart. I thought then that I was in a beautiful green field; and that is all I remember till I found myself in your honour's dissecting-room." It is worthy of record that the last criminal executed here was one Ryland, who was hung for forgery in 1783; after which the gallows were taken down about London in order to concentrate the executions at Newgate and Horsemonger Lane.

Many good stories are told about Tyburn; among others, the following:—"A celebrated wit one evening was walking along a lane near Oxford Road, as it was then called, when he was accosted by a shabby-looking fellow, who asked him the way to Tyburn. The gentleman, being fond of a jest, answered, 'Why, you have only to rob the first person you meet, and you will find the way there easily.' The fellow thanked him, and pulled out and presented a pistol, threatening to blow his brains out if he did not give up his purse. The wit was forced to comply, and lost his money and his jest at once."

Before leaving the subject of the "gallows," a word or two about "Jack Ketch" and his office may not be out of place. The origin of the name "Jack Ketch," as applied to the public executioner, is thus explained in Lloyd's MS. Collection of English Pedigrees in the British Museum. We give it for what it is worth. "The Manor of Tyburn," writes Mr. Lloyd, "where felons were for a long time executed, was formerly held by Richard Jacquett, from whence we have the name Jack Ketch as a corruption." But the work of the executioner was sufficiently artistic to admit of degrees of skill. Thus Dryden remarks:—"A man may be capable (as Jack Ketch's wife said of her servant) of a plain piece of work, a bare hanging; but to make a malefactor die sweetly was only belonging to her husband."

The earliest hangman whose name has descended to us, if we may trust the authority of that accomplished antiquary, the late Dr. Rimbault, is one Bull, who is mentioned in his public capacity in Gabriel Harvey's tract against Nash, called "Pierce's Supererogation" (1593). Bull was succeeded by the more celebrated Derrick, who cut off the head of the unfortunate Earl of Essex in 1601. In Dekker's "Bellman of London," printed in 1608, under the article "Prigging Law," are the following notices of this worthy:—"For he rides his circuit with the devil, and Derrick must be his host, and Tiburne the land at which he will light." "At the gallows, where I leave them, as to the haven at which they must all cast anchor, if Derrick's cables do but hold." Again, at the end of his "Wonderful Year," is this passage:—"But by these tricks imagining that many thousands have been turned wrongfully off the ladder of life; and praying that Derrick or his successors may live to do those a good turn that have done so to others. *Hic finis Priami!* Here is an end of an old song." Derrick held his unenviable post for nearly half a century; and from him was named the temporary crane formed on board ship for unloading and general hoisting purposes, by lashing one spar to another, gibbet fashion. The next hangman was the notorious Gregory Brandon, who, as the story goes, by a *ruse* played upon Garter King-at-Arms, had a grant of arms confirmed to him, and was thereby "made a gentleman," which the mob in a joke soon elevated into esquire, "a title by which he was known for the rest of his life, and which was afterwards transferred to his successors in office." He had frequently acted as a substitute for Derrick; and had become so popular that the gallows was sometimes called by his Christian name, as may be seen in the following lines:—

> "This trembles under the Black Rod, and he
> Doth fear his fate from the *Gregorian* tree."

Gregory Brandon was succeeded by his son Richard, who seems to have claimed the gallows by inheritance. This Richard Brandon, as we have shown in a previous volume, has the credit of being the executioner of Charles I.* "Squire" Dun was the next common hangman, and he in turn was succeeded by the veritable Jack Ketch, who was the executioner of Lord William Russell and the Duke of Monmouth. Macaulay, in his account of the death of the latter, says: "He then accosted John Ketch, the executioner, a wretch who had butchered many brave and noble victims, and whose name has, during a century and a half, been vulgarly given to all who have succeeded him in his odious office. 'Here,' said the duke, 'are six guineas for you. Do not hack me as you did my Lord Russell. I have heard that you struck him three or four times. My servant will give you some gold if you do the work well.'" This notable functionary does not seem to have had a very easy time of it; at all events, in 1678, a broadside was published, entitled "The Plotter's Ballad: being Jack Ketch's incomparable receipt for the cure of traytorous recusants." In the same year appeared a quarto tract: "The Tyburn Ghost; or, Strange Downfal of the Gallows: a most true Relation how the famous Triple Tree, near Paddington, was pluckt up by the roots, and demolisht by certain Evil Spirits; with Jack Ketch's Lamentation for the Loss of his Shop, 1678." In the next year was produced "Squire Ketch's Declaration concerning his late Confinement in the Queen's Bench and Marshalsea, whereby his hopeful harvest was liked to have been blasted." Two years later we find him at Oxford:—"Aug. 31, 1681. Wednesday, at 11, Stephen College suffered death by hanging in the Castle Yard, Oxon, and when he hanged about half an hour was cut down by *Catch*, or *Ketch*, and quartered under the gallows." † The name of Ketch is often mentioned, in the lampoons of the day, along with that of the infamous Judge Jeffreys, as his brother in crime. One poet writes:—

> "While Jeffreys on the bench, Ketch on the gibbet sits."

He is also mentioned by D'Urfey, in his humorous poem, entitled "Butler's Ghost," published in 1682; and in the following year he is thus mentioned in the epilogue to Dryden and Lee's "Duke of Guise:"—

> "Lenitives, he says, suit best with our condition;
> Jack Ketch, says I, 's an excellent physician."

For the following scrap of antiquarian lore respecting the interesting locality of which we treat, our readers are indebted to "honest" John Timbs:—"Formerly, when a person prosecuted another for any offence, and the prisoner was executed at Tyburn, the prosecutor was presented with a 'Tyburn Ticket,' which exempted him and its future holders from having to serve on juries. This privilege was not repealed till the sixth year of the reign of George IV."

The following is said to be the reason why Tyburn was chosen as the place of execution and burial of traitors:—The parishioners of St. Sepulchre's, near Newgate, were not over-well pleased that the bodies of those malefactors who had suffered the last penalty of the law should be buried amongst them; in proof, it may be mentioned, on the authority of a letter from Fleetwood to Lord Burghley, that they "would not suffer a traytor's corpes to be layed in the earthe where theire parents, wyeffs, chyldren, kynred, maisters, and old naighboures did rest: and so his carcas was returned to the buryall ground neere to Tyborne."

The gallows at Tyburn was triangular in plan, having three legs to stand on, and appears to have been a permanent erection. From the number of criminals hanged there, it would indeed seem to have been useless to have taken it down after each execution. We may learn, from a sermon preached

* See Vol. III., p. 350.

† "A'Wood's Life," by Dr. Bliss, 1848.

by good Bishop Horne, towards the close of the eighteenth century, that it was no uncommon thing to see scores of felons executed here. Taylor, the Water Poet, in "The Praise and Virtue of a Jayle and Jaylers" (1623), gives these lines:—

"I have heard sundry men ofttimes dispute,
Of trees that in one yeare will twice beare fruit;
But if a man note Tyburn, 'twill appeare
That that's a tree that bears twelve times a yeare."

CONNAUGHT PLACE.

Again, in Dr. Johnson's "London" (a poem), we read:—

"Scarce can our fields—such crowds at Tyburn die—
With hemp the gallows and the fleet supply."

Then there is a parody on Gray's "Elegy," in which we read—

"Yet e'en these humble vices to correct,
Old Tyburn lifts his triple front on high."

In Shirley's play of *The Wedding*, published in 1629, an execution at Tyburn is thus depicted: —"*Rawbone:* I do imagine myself apprehended already; now the constable is carrying me to Newgate; now, now, I'm in the Sessions House, in the dock; now I'm called; 'Not guilty, my lord.' The jury has found the indictment, *billa vera.* Now, now, comes my sentence. Now I'm in the cart, riding up Holborn in a two-wheeled chariot, with a guard of halberdiers. 'There goes a proper fellow,' says one; 'Good people, pray for me.' Now I'm at the three wooden stilts. Hey! now I feel my toes hang i' the cart; now 'tis drawn away; now, now, now!—I'm gone!"

At Tyburn, upon the restoration of monarchy, was performed the farce of dragging Sir Henry Mildmay, Wallop, and some other members of the regicide party, to the fatal tree, with halters round their necks. Miles Corbet, the regicide also, having been arrested on the Continent, was brought to London, dragged through the streets hither, and executed.

Evelyn, in his "Diary," under date January 30, 1661, the first anniversary of the murder of Charles I. since the Restoration, writes:—"The carcases of those rebels, Cromwell, Bradshaw, the judge who condemned his Majesty, and Ireton (son-in-law to the Usurper), were dragged out of their superb tombs in Westminster among the kings to Tyburn, and hanged on the gallows there from nine in the morning till six at night, and then buried under that fatal and ignominious monument in a deep pit, thousands who had seen

THE IDLE APPRENTICE EXECUTED AT TYBURN (*After Hogarth's Print.*)

them in all their pride being spectators." How far this "deep pit" can be regarded as really the last resting-place of Cromwell's body may be inferred from what we have already written on the subject, in our account of Red Lion Square, Holborn.*

In the "New View of London," published in 1708, no mention is made of either Oxford or Uxbridge Road, but the thoroughfare is entered as Tyburn Road. It is thus described as lying "between St. Giles' Pound, east, and the lane leading to the Gallows, west, 350 yards in length." The writer adds:—"This street has its name as being the next street to Tyburn, the place for execution of all such malefactors, generally speaking, as have committed acts worthy of death within the City and Liberties of London and County of Middlesex. I have known, he continues, "nineteen executed at one sessions, though these are held about eight times a year; but this is near twenty years ago." He then congratulates the nation on the decrease in the number of executions of late, which he ascribes to improvements in the law, and to the efforts of societies for the reformation of manners; and ends by telling a story of a man who revived, after being cut down off the gallows, in 1705.

Tyburn, it need scarcely be added, figures constantly in the caricatures of Hogarth. Thus, in his "Industry and Idleness," "Tom Idle" goes to Tyburn in a cart with a coffin in it, whilst the other apprentice, Francis Goodchild, drives to the Mansion House, as Lord Mayor of London, with footmen and sword-bearer, the King and the Court looking on from a balcony in St. Paul's Churchyard, and smiling approval. In Hogarth's print of Tyburn Tree, the hangman is represented coolly smoking his pipe, as he reclines by the gibbet, in full view of the hills of Hampstead and Highgate. "Could Tom Idle's ghost have made its appearance in 1847," asks Thackeray, in his "Humourists," "what changes would have been remarked by that astonished escaped criminal! Over that road which the hangman used to travel constantly, and the Oxford stage twice a week, go ten thousand carriages every day; over yonder road, by which Dick Turpin fled to Windsor, and Squire Western journeyed into town, when he came to take up his quarters at the Hercules Pillars on the outskirts of London, what a rush of civilisation and order flows now! What armies of gentlemen with umbrellas march to banks, and chambers, and counting-houses! What regiments of nursery-maids and pretty infantry; what peaceful processions of policemen; what light broughams and what gay carriages; what swarms of busy apprentices and artificers, riding on omnibus-roofs, pass daily and hourly! Tom Idle's times are quite changed; many of the institutions are gone into disuse which were admired in his day. There's more pity and kindness, and a better chance for poor Tom's successors now than at that simpler period, when Fielding hanged him and Hogarth drew him."

* See Vol. IV., p. 546.

Tyburn also figures in one of Hogarth's pictures of "Marriage à la Mode," where Counsellor Silvertongue pays the last penalty of the law for sending a certain noble earl out of the world before his time. In Hogarth's hands, no doubt, Tyburn was usefully employed, both

"To point a moral and adorn a tale."

But Tyburn has witnessed other scenes besides those of which we have spoken above. The story of Queen Henrietta Maria doing penance here is thus told by Mr. S. W. Gardiner, in his "History of England under the Duke of Buckingham and Charles I.:"—"It was after a long day spent in attendance on the devotions of her Church at the Chapel at St. James's that the young queen of Charles I. strolled out, with her ladies, to breathe the fresh evening air in St. James's Park. By-and-by she found her way into Hyde Park, and by accident or design directed her steps towards Tyburn. In her position it was quite natural that she should bethink herself of those who had suffered there as martyrs for the faith which she had come to England to support. What wonder if her heart beat more quickly, and if some prayer for strength to bear her weary lot rose to her lips? A week or two probably passed away before the tale reached Charles, exaggerated in its passage through the mouths of men. . . . The Queen of England, he was told, had been conducted on a pilgrimage to offer prayer to dead traitors, who had suffered the just reward of their crimes. The cup of his displeasure was now full; . . . those who had brought her to this should no longer remain in England. . . . On July 31 the king and queen dined together at Whitehall. After dinner he conducted her to his private apartments, locked the door on her attendants, and told her that her servants must go." Meanwhile, Conway was taking measures for the removal of her ladies to Somerset House. "As soon as the young queen perceived what was being done she flew to the window and dashed to pieces the glass, that her voice might be heard by those who were bidding her adieu for the last time; and Charles, it is said, dragged her back into the room, with her hands bleeding from the energy with which she clung to the bars." As we have already stated, in our account of Somerset House,* no time was lost in sending off the queen's French attendants to their native country.

It is more probable that the act on the part of her Majesty was a voluntary one; for, although pious and devout, the queen was not at all a person to be led blindly at the will of any confessor. However, in the illustrated edition of Pennant's "London," in the British Museum, there is to be seen a copy of a rare German print, purporting to be a representation of the scene. At a short distance off is the confessor's carriage, drawn by six horses; in the coach is seated the confessor himself, and a page, with a lighted candle or torch, is standing at the door. The fact is certainly recorded in a cotemporary document published in the first series of "Original Letters," edited by Sir Henry Ellis; but as the language used is of the most rabid and foul-mouthed kind—the confessor being styled "Luciferian," and the details of the affair styled "ridiculous," "absurd," "beggarly"—we may reasonably entertain a doubt whether it was not a "mare's-nest." In all probability the story was concocted by some Titus Oates of the day. The letter in question, which purports to be "from Mr. Pory to Mr. Joseph Mead," contains the following expressions:—"No longer agone then upon St. James *his day last*, those hypocritical dogges made the pore Queen to walke a foot (some add barefoot) from her house at St. James to the gallowes at Tyborne, *thereby to honour the Saint of the day* in visiting that holy place where so many martyrs (forsooth) had shed their bloud in defense of the Catholique cause. . . . Yea, they have made her to go barefoot, to spin, to eat her meat out of tryne (wooden) dishes, to waite at the table and serve her servants, with many other ridiculous and absurd penances. It was, certainly, 'high time' that this French train should be dismissed; and packed off they were ('contumaciously refusing to go') in coaches, carts, and barges, to Gravesend."

If it be true that old George III. took such an interest in the welfare of those condemned to die upon the gallows as he is represented to have done in an anecdote which was at one time freely circulated, his time must have been pretty well occupied by devotional exercises. The anecdote in question, albeit highly honourable to his sense of public duty, is mentioned on the authority of Stevenson, the American envoy in London. Some extraordinary occurrence having called a French statesman to the palace as late as two o'clock in the morning, he found the king in his cabinet, examining the case of a prisoner condemned to execution. The envoy afterwards ascertained that the king keeps a register, recording the name of every person capitally condemned, the decision, and its reasons. Frequently, in the still hours of the night, he performs the task of investigating those cases, and adds to the record the circumstances which had influenced his decision. The envoy probably did not know that the great and good George III. had pursued nearly the same practice fifty years before, weighed the evidence with the deepest anxiety, and generally shut himself up in his cabinet at Windsor (it was presumed in prayer) during the hour appointed for the execution in London.

The exact spot on which the fatal Tyburn Tree was erected has been often discussed by antiquaries. It would appear, however, to be identified with the site of the house in the south-east corner of Connaught Square, formerly numbered 49; for in the lease granted by the Bishop of London, to whom the property belongs, this fact is particularly mentioned. A writer in *The Antiquary*, in October, 1873, says, with reference to this subject:—"I was born within 100 yards of the exact spot on which the gallows stood, and my uncle took up the stones on which the uprights were placed. The following is his statement to me, and the circumstance of his telling it:—In 1810, when Connaught Place was being built, he was employed on the works, and for many years lived at the corner of Bryanston Street and the Edgware Road, nearly opposite Connaught Mews. My father, a master carpenter, worked for several years in Connaught Place, and on one occasion he employed his brother, I think in the year 1834; at all events, we had just left No. 6, the residence of Sir Charles Coote. It was at this time I said to my uncle, 'Now you are here, tell me where the gallows stood;' to which he replied, 'Opposite here, where the staves are.' I thereupon crossed over, and drove a brass-headed nail into the exact spot he indicated. On reaching home, I told my mother of the occurrence, and asked if it were correct. She said it was so, for she remembered the posts standing when she was a child. This might be about the year 1800; and, as she was born in Bryanston Street, I believe she stated what she knew to be a fact. I well remember Connaught Square being built, and I also recollect a low house standing at the corner of the Uxbridge Road, close to No. 1, Connaught Place (Arklow House), and that, on the removal of this house,

* See Vol. III., p. 91.

quantities of human bones were found. I saw them carted away by Mr. Nicholls, contractor, of Adams' Mews. He removed Tyburn toll-house in 1829. From what I have been told by old inhabitants that were born in the neighbourhood, probably about 1750, I have every reason to believe that the space from the toll-house to Frederick Mews was used as a place of execution, and the bodies buried adjacent, for I have seen the remains disinterred when the square and adjoining streets were being built."

Smith, in his "History of St. Marylebone," states that "the gallows were for many years a standing fixture on a small eminence at the corner of the Edgware Road, near the turnpike, on the identical spot where a toll-house was subsequently erected by the Uxbridge Road Trust. Beneath this place are supposed to lie the bones of Bradshaw, Ireton, and other regicides, which were taken from their graves after the Restoration, and buried under the gallows. The gallows itself subsequently consisted of two uprights and a cross-beam, erected on the morning of execution across the Edgware Road, opposite the house at the corner of Upper Bryanston Street and the Edgware Road, wherein the gallows was deposited after being used; this house had curious iron balconies to the windows of the first and second floors, where the sheriffs sat to witness the executions. After the place of execution was changed to Newgate, in 1783, the gallows was bought by a carpenter, and made into stands for beer-butts in the cellars of the 'Carpenters' Arms' public-house, hard by."

"Around the gibbet," says Mr. Timbs, in his "Curiosities of London," "were erected open galleries, like a race-course stand, wherein seats were let to spectators at executions: the key of one of them was kept by Mammy Douglas, 'the Tyburn pew-opener.' In 1758, when Dr. Henesey was to have been executed for treason, the prices of seats rose to 2s. and 2s. 6d.; but the doctor being 'most provokingly reprieved,' a riot ensued, and most of the seats were destroyed."

The name of "Tyburn," thus mixed up with the saddest portions of our national history, and associated with ideas of villany and crime, very naturally smelt anything but sweet in the nose of the metropolis; and it was not until the city grew in bulk so tremendously that it threatened to burst its swathing bands, that the region around the old gallows, now known as "Tyburnia," came to be built upon, and inhabited by the upper classes of society.

It is recorded by Mr. Percy Fitzgerald, in his sketch of Charles Townshend, that his eccentric mother, Audrey, Lady Townshend, who so long "entertained" at her house in Whitehall, was one day rallied by her friends on taking a short lease of "a villa at Tyburn." "Oh," replied the witty woman, "you see it is a neighbourhood of which I could never tire, for my neighbours are being hanged every week; so we are always changing!" It was this same lady who, on being asked if it was true that Whitfield had recanted, answered, "No, madam; but I know he has canted;" and who sarcastically remarked of the royal family, who took a fancy to go to all public shows and suppers, that it was "the cheapest family to see, and the dearest to keep, of any that had ever been seen."

Mr. G. A. Sala hits the right nail on the head, in his "Gaslight and Daylight," when he remarks that while the region of the Grosvenors is the place for the "swells of the peerage, those of blue blood and the strawberry-leaves," Tyburnia suits admirably "the nobility of yesterday, your mushroom aristocrats, millionaires, ex-lord mayors, and people of that sort;" and he also pithily adds, "Tyburn is gone: I am not such an old fogey as to remember *that*, nor so staunch a conservative as to regret it now that it is gone."

"Tyburnia" proper, as we may call the city which sprang up between the Edgware Road and Westbourne Terrace, in the reign of William IV., consists of squares, terraces, and rows of stately mansions, which now rival in elegance her more southern sister, "Belgravia." Oxford and Cambridge Terraces, which run from the Edgware Road to the southern end of Westbourne Terrace, with Oxford and Cambridge Squares to the south of them, will long keep in remembrance the munificence of Lady Margaret, Countess of Richmond, as the founder of divinity professorships in our two great and ancient universities.

The Rev. J. Richardson, referring to the days of the Regency, writes thus in his "Recollections," published in 1856:—"The northern boundary of the old metropolis, then called Oxford Road, terminated abruptly at the entrance of the Park, where now stands the triumphal arch lately removed from Buckingham Palace. The now fashionable district which forms one side of the Bayswater Road, and occupies the angle between that road and Paddington, was, in the eyes of all respectable people, a locality to be avoided. Ragged fields stretched over scores of acres of ground; and the ominous name of Tyburn frightened, not, indeed, those whom it ought to have deterred, but those who either assumed a character for decency, or really possessed one. In fact, this part was a blank in the improvements of London for years after other suburbs had been built upon; and it was not until comparatively a recent date that the tea-gardens, and other similar low haunts of debauchery, gave way to the elegant and stately buildings with which it is now covered." It is impossible not to recognise these places of amusement in the portrait which Charles Dickens gives us, in his "Sketches by Boz," of the typical London tea-gardens, with their snug boxes and alcoves; the men and women, boys and girls, sweethearts and married folk, babies in arms and children in chaises, the pipes and the shrimps, the cigars and the periwinkles, the tea and tobacco, are each and all described with a skill almost equal to that of a photographer. To the particular "Sketch" entitled "London Recreations" we must refer our readers for all further details. As we have shown in the preceding chapter, the last of the tea-gardens—covering what is now Lancaster Gate—did not disappear until about 1855.

At Connaught House, Connaught Place, close by the Edgware Road, the unfortunate Caroline, Princess of Wales, took up her residence when banished from the Palace; and hither came the Princess Charlotte in a hackney-coach, when she quarrelled with her father and left Warwick House, as we have stated in our account of that place.* The young princess, as she advanced towards womanhood, became more and more intractable and wilful. In the end, the Regent and his Ministers thought the best step would be to find her a husband; and the youthful Prince of Orange was suggested as the most eligible. He was by birth a Protestant; he had been educated at Oxford, and had served in Spain with credit; but the self-willed young lady refused him—in a word, "turned up her nose" at him. Every opportunity was given to him to make himself agreeable to the future heiress of the English throne; but either his capacities and acquirements were of a low order, or the princess had proposed to herself quite another standard of excellence as her *beau ideal.* She simply said "she did not like Oranges in any shape;" and though her royal papa stormed, and bishops reasoned with her, her resolution remained unshaken. The public admired her pluck and firmness, and her refusal to be sold into matrimony like a common chattel. She was a princess, but she was also a true-hearted woman, and she felt that she must really love the man whom she should wed, if she would escape the unhappiness which had darkened the married life of her parents. The fortunate individual who pleased her taste was not long in appearing; and her marriage with Prince Leopold of Saxe-Coburg was solemnised, ere long, with her father's consent, and with the hearty good wishes of the people. The Prince himself, then a humble cadet of a petty German house, was travelling in England; he met the Princess Charlotte at one of the many mansions of the aristocracy, and he soon obtained an interest in her affections, and also the consent of the Prince Regent, who was probably glad enough to get his intractable daughter off his hands at any price. Leopold at that time was one of the noblest-looking young princes in Europe. Tall and princely in his bearing, and fascinating in his manners, a brave soldier, and an accomplished courtier, he was worthy to win such a prize. They were married on May 2nd, 1816. Alas! within a little more than a year the great bell of St. Paul's was tolled to announce to a sorrowing people the death of the princess in giving birth to a dead infant!

The sale of the effects of the Princess of Wales, at Connaught House, took place in October, 1814. The name of the mansion was at a later date changed to Arklow House; the latter, like the former, being one of the titles inherent in the royal family. The late Duke of Sussex was also Baron of Arklow. Sir Augustus D'Este, son of the Duke of Sussex, lived here for some time subsequently. It is now the town residence of Mr. A. Beresford-Hope.

At No. 13 in Hyde Park Square, lived that specimen of a fine old English gentleman, Mr. T. Assheton-Smith, whose name is so well known among Masters of Hounds. A glass apartment on the roof of this house, after his death, was magnified, by the fears of the servant-girls in the neighbourhood, into the abode of a ghost; and the ghost—or, at all events, the alarm—was only suppressed by editors "writing it down" in the London newspapers.

In concluding this chapter, we may remark that the whole neighbourhood is of too recent a growth to have many historical reminiscences. Haydon, the painter, it is true, lived for some time in Burwood Place, close by Connaught Square, and there he died by his own hand in 1846. We shall have more to say about him when we come to Paddington.

* See Vol. IV., p. 82.

PADDINGTON CANAL, 1820.

CHAPTER XVII.

PADDINGTON.

"And the Bishop's lands, too, what of them? I'll warrant you'll not find better acres anywhere than those which once belonged to his lordship."—*Boz.*

Rustic Appearance of Paddington at the Commencement of this Century—Intellectual Condition of the Inhabitants—Gradual Increase of the Population—The Manor of Paddington—The Feast of Abbot Walter, of Westminster—The Prior of St. Bartholomew's and his Brethren—Dr. Sheldon's Claim of the Manor—The Old Parish Church—Hogarth's Marriage—Building of the New Parish Church—A Curious Custom—Poorness of the Living—The Burial-ground—Noted Persons buried here—Life of Haydon, the Painter—Dr. Geddes—The New Church of St. James—Holy Trinity Church—All Saints' Church—The House of the Notorious Richard Brothers—Old Public-houses—Old Paddington Green—The Vestry Hall—The Residences of Thomas Uwins, R.A., and Wyatt, the Sculptor—Eminent Residents—The Princess Charlotte and her Governess—Paddington House—"Jack-in-the-Green"—Westbourne Place—Westbourne Green—Desborough Place—Westbourne Farm, the Residence of Mrs. Siddons—The Lock Hospital and Asylum—St. Mary's Hospital—Paddington Provident Dispensary—The Dudley-Stuart Home—"The Boatman's Chapel"—Queen's Park—Old Almshouses—Grand Junction Canal—The Western Water-Works—Imperial Gas Company—Kensal Green Cemetery—Eminent Persons buried here—Great Western Railway Terminus.

PADDINGTON, or Padynton, as the name of the place is often spelled in old documents, down to the end of the last century was a pleasant little rural spot, scarcely a mile to the north-west of the Tyburn turnpike, upon the Harrow Road. Indeed, it would seem to have preserved its rustic character even to a later date; for it is amusing to read without a smile the grave expressions in which Priscilla Wakefield describes, in 1814, a visit to this then remote and rustic village—a journey which now occupies about three minutes by the Underground Railway:—"From Kensington we journeyed northward to Paddington, a village situated on the Edgware Road, about a mile from London. In our way thither we passed the Lying-in Hospital at Bayswater, patronised by the queen." The place is described by Lambert, in his "History and Survey of London and its Environs," at the commencement of the present century, as "a village situated upon the Edgware Road, about a mile from London"—a description which, perhaps, was not wholly untrue even at the accession of Queen Victoria; in fact, until its selection as the terminus of the Great Western Railway caused it to be fairly absorbed into the great metropolis.

The parish, being so rural, and so very thinly

populated, was, doubtless, far behind its "courtly" sister suburb of Kensington in mental and intellectual progress; so that, perhaps, there may be little or no exaggeration in the remarks of Mr. Robins, in his "History of Paddington," when he remarks:—"Although the people of Paddington lived at so short a distance from the two rich cathedral marts of London and Westminster, they made apparently no greater advances in civilisation for many centuries than did those who lived in the most remote village in the English 'shires.' The few people who lived here were wholly agricultural, and they owed every useful lesson of their lives much more to their own intelligence and observation than to any instruction given them by those who were paid to be their teachers." But if "the schoolmaster" was not "abroad," and if the education given in the parish church and other public buildings was deficient, it is a consolation to learn, from the same authority, that the defect was supplied, in some measure, at least, by the ale-houses in which debating clubs were established. A correspondent of Hone's "Year-Book," in 1832, remarks of Paddington as well as Bayswater, that they were both quite rural spots within his own remembrance, little as they then deserved the name. What would this writer have said if he could have looked forward to their condition in the year of grace 1876?

THE PADDINGTON CANAL, 1840.

Its population seems to have been always scanty. As the earliest parish register goes back no further than 1701, we are driven to draw our inferences from the Subsidy Rolls. Probably, in the reign of Henry VIII., the entire population did not exceed a hundred, and at the accession of James II. it had risen, according to the same calculation, to only a little over three hundred. Even as lately as the year 1795 the hamlet appears to have contained only 341 houses, which, allowing five souls to a house, would give a population of about 1,700. Indeed, so small and insignificant did the village continue down to our own times, that George Canning instituted a witty comparison between a great and a small premier, when he uttered the *mot*:—

"As London to Paddington
So is Pitt to Addington."

The old stone indicating the first mile from Tyburn turnpike towards Harrow still remains in the road. In 1798, when Cary published his "Road Book," there were ten "stages" running every day from London to Paddington. William Robins, in his work on Paddington, already quoted, which was published in the year 1853, says:—"A city of palaces has sprung up here within twenty years. A road of iron, with steeds of steam, brings into the centre of this city, and takes from it in one year, a greater number of living beings than could be found in all England a few years ago; while the whole of London can be traversed in half the time it took to reach Holborn Bars at the beginning of this century, when the road was in the hands of Mr. Miles, his pair-horse coach, and his redoubtable boy," long the only appointed agents of communication between Paddington and the City. The fares were 2s. and 3s.; the journey, we are told, took more than three hours; and to beguile the time at resting-places, "Miles's Boy" told tales and played upon the fiddle. Charles Knight also tells us that "at the beginning of the present century only one stage-coach ran from the then suburban village of Paddington to the City, and that it was never filled!"

A map of London, published so lately as 1823, exhibits Paddington as quite distinct from the metropolis, which has the Edgware Road as its western boundary. A rivulet is marked as running from north to south through Westbourne Green, parallel with Craven Place; and Westbourne House is marked with the name of its resident owner, Mr. Cockerell, just like a country manor house fifty miles from London; while half a mile further are two isolated farms, named Portobello and Notting Barns respectively. The present parish includes in its area a portion of Kensington Gardens.

How little known to the inhabitants of the great metropolis this suburb was in the middle of the last century may be inferred from the silence of "honest" John Stow, and even of Strype, who, in treating of London, make no mention of Paddington. Indeed, though they devote a chapter of "The Circuit Walk," which concludes the "Survey of London," to Kensington, Hammersmith, Fulham, and Marylebone, we do not find any mention of the names of Paddington or Bayswater; the only hint in that direction being an entry of "Lisham" (*i.e.* Lisson) "Grove" in the index as "near Paddington." The whole neighbourhood, indeed, is passed entirely *sub silentio* by Evelyn and Pepys; it is not mentioned by name by Horace Walpole; and, though so near to Tyburn, it is apparently ignored by Dr. Johnson and Boswell. It may be inferred that even Mrs. Montagu scarcely ever drove so far out into the western wilds. Charles Dickens and George A. Sala, too, say but little about it. It is clear, then, that we must go to other sources for any antiquarian notes on this neighbourhood, or for anecdotes about its inhabitants.

Paddington is not mentioned in the "Domesday Book;" and it is probable that in the Conqueror's time the whole site was part of the great forest of Middlesex, of which small portions only appear to have been at any time the property of the Crown. The district, nevertheless, was, in remote times, a part of the extensive parish of St. Margaret's, Westminster, as appears from the fact that its church was for a century or two, if not longer, a sort of chapel of ease, subject to the Rector or Vicar of St. Margaret's, as, indeed, it continued to be down to the dissolution of monasteries, under Henry VIII., when the manor of Paddington was given to the newly-founded see of Westminster. The manor of Paddington was given in 1191, by the Abbot Walter, to the Convent of St. Peter's, Westminster; and from the close of the thirteenth century the whole of the temporalities of the district, such as the "rent of land and the young of animals," were devoted to charity. We read that, in 1439, a "head of water at Paddyngton" was granted to the Lord Mayor and citizens of London, and to their successors, by the Abbot of Westminster. On the abolition of the see of Westminster, shortly after its establishment, Edward VI. gave this manor to Ridley, Bishop of London, and his successors. It will be observed that the names of many of the streets around Paddington, especially to the north, perpetuate the names of several successive Bishops of London, such as Randolph, Howley, Blomfield, and Porteus. "Crescents and Colonnades," writes Hone in his "Table-Book," in 1827, "are planned by the architect to the Bishop of London on the ground belonging to the see near Bayswater."

The above-mentioned abbot of Westminster, Walter, appears to have purchased the interest in the soil here from two brothers, who were called respectively Richard and William de Padinton; and on his death the manor of Paddington was assigned to the almoner for the celebration of his anniversary, when a solemn feast was to be held. The almoner for the time being was directed to find for the convent "fine manchets, cakes, crumpets, cracknells, and wafers, and a gallon of wine for each friar, with three good pittances, or doles, with good ale in abundance at every table, and in the presence of the whole brotherhood; in the same manner as upon other occasions the cellarer is bound to find beer at the usual feasts or anniversaries, in the great tankard of five quarts."

Maitland, in his "History of London," tells us that, in 1439, "the Abbot of Westminster granted to Robert Large, the mayor, and citizens of London, and their successors, one head of water, containing twenty-six perches in length and one in breadth, together with all its springs in the manor of Paddington; in consideration of which grant the City is for ever to pay to the said abbot and his successors, at the feast of St. Peter, two peppercorns. But if the intended work should happen to draw the water from the ancient wells in the manor of Hida, then the aforesaid grant to cease and become entirely void." Mr. Robins, in his "Paddington, Past and Present," remarks that, "although the abbots at length, and by slow degrees, acquired to themselves and their house, either with or without the sanction of the Crown, both spiritual and temporal dominion over these places, we must not imagine that all the tenements in Westbourn and Paddington had been by this time transferred by the devout and the timid to their safe keeping; for besides the few small holders, who obstinately preferred their hereditary rights to works of charity or devotion, there is good reason to believe that the ancient family of De Veres held a considerable tract of land in this parish down to 1461."

The high road at Paddington must have presented an amusing spectacle in the year 1523, when the Prior of St. Bartholomew's and all his brethren, with the lay brethren, and an array of wagons and boats upon trucks, went along through Paddington towards Harrow, where they had resolved to remain for two months, till the fatal day should have passed on which it was foretold that the Thames should suddenly rise and wash away half London!

During the Commonwealth "the manor of Paddington, wth ye appurten'ces," was sold to one Thomas Browne, for the sum of three thousand nine hundred and fifty-eight pounds, seventeen shillings, and four pence; but when Dr. Sheldon was appointed to the bishopric of London, after the Restoration, he claimed the manor and also the rectory. Sheldon's relatives, it is stated, received the profits of the manor and rectory for nearly eighty years.

"In the middle of the last century," says John Timbs, in his "Curiosities of London," "nearly the whole of Paddington had become grazing-land, upwards of 1,100 acres; and the occupiers of the bishop's estate kept here hundreds of cows."

Robins, in his work on this parish, writes:—"The fact of Paddington, in Surrey, or 'Padendene,' as it was called, being mentioned in the Conqueror's survey, while Paddington, in Middlesex, was not noticed, inclines me to believe the *dene* or *den*, in Surrey, was the original mark of the Pœdings; and that the smaller enclosure in Middlesex was at first peopled and cultivated by a migration of a portion of that family from the *den*, when it had become inconveniently full. . . . At what period this migration happened," he adds, "it is impossible to say; but there is very little doubt that the first settlement was made near the bourn, or brook, which ran through the forest." This brook, of which we have already had occasion to speak in a previous chapter, was, at the beginning of this century, a favourite resort for anglers.

There is extant a curious etching of the old parish church of Paddington, dated 1750. It stood about eighty yards to the north of the present edifice, and its site may still be seen among the tombs, which were ranged inside and outside of it. It was a plain, neat building, of one aisle, consisting of only a nave, and with a bell-turret and spire at the west end, not unlike the type of the country churches of Sussex, and its picturesqueness was heightened by the dark foliage of an ancient yew-tree.

This church was built by Sir Joseph Sheldon and Daniel Sheldon, to whom the manor was leased by Sheldon, Bishop of London, and afterwards Archbishop of Canterbury, in the reign of Charles II., and it replaced a more ancient church, which had become "old and ruinous," and which was taken down about the year 1678.

In this second church, which was dedicated to St. James, were married, on the 23rd of March, 1729, Hogarth and Jane Thornhill, the daughter of Sir James Thornhill; the marriage, it is said, was a runaway match, carried out much against the will of the bride's father.

Mr. J. T. Smith, the antiquary, states that the walls of the demolished church were adorned with several texts from Scripture, in accordance with the instructions of Queen Elizabeth:—

"And many a holy text around she strews
To teach the rustic moralist to die."

In 1788 an Act was passed for rebuilding the parish church and enlarging the churchyard, and accordingly St. Mary's Church, on the Green, was erected. The preamble of the Act tells us that its predecessor "is a very ancient structure, and in such a decayed state that it cannot be effectually repaired, but must be taken down and rebuilt; besides which, the same is so small, that one-fourth of the present inhabitants within the said parish cannot assemble therein for divine worship. The new church was built partly by subscription and partly by assessment of the inhabitants.

A print of the church, in the *European Magazine* for January, 1793, shows the building exactly in its present state; but on the other side of the road, opposite to the south entrance, is a large pond, in which stakes and rails stand up after the most rural fashion. The village stocks, too, are represented in this engraving. So much admired was this church at the time when it was built, and so picturesque an object it is said to have been, "particularly from the Oxford, Edgware, and Harrow Roads," that almost all the periodicals of the day noticed it. The following description of the building, given in the *European Magazine*, was doubtless correct at the time it was written:—"It is seated on an eminence, finely embosomed in venerable elms. Its figure is composed of a square of about fifty feet. The centres, on each side of the square, are projecting parallelograms, which give recesses for an altar, a vestry, and two staircases. The roof terminates with a cupola and vane. On each of the sides is a door: that facing the south is decorated with a portico, composed of the Tuscan and Doric orders, having niches on the sides. The west has an arched window, under which is a circular portico of four columns, agreeable to the former composition." The church, in fact, is a nondescript building, though it pretends to be erected after a Greek model.

The old and present churches are described (with illustrations) in the supplement to the *Gentleman's Magazine* for 1795. The writer of the description says that the monuments in the former building were transferred to a light vault under the new one.

Lysons mentions the custom of loaves being thrown from the church tower to be scrambled for—a remnant, no doubt, of the old Easter "largess;" and Priscilla Wakefield, in her "Perambulations of London" (1814), writes—"The strange custom is observed, on the Sunday before Christmas Day, of throwing bread from the church steeple, to be scrambled for by the populace, in consequence of a gift from two maiden ladies." Under date of Tuesday, December 21, 1736, the *Grub Street Journal* gives the following account of the "Bread and Cheese Charity:"—"On Sunday, after divine service, was performed the annual ceremony of throwing bread and cheese out of Paddington Church steeple among the spectators, and giving them ale. The custom was established by two women, who purchased five acres of land to the above use, in commemoration of the particular charity whereby they had been relieved when in extreme necessity." It is almost needless to add that this custom has long since been allowed to fall into disuse.

The living of Paddington is said to have been formerly so small that it was a difficult task for the bishop to find anybody to discharge its duties. In fact, it would appear that during the Tudor and early Stuart reigns, the parson of Paddington did not come up even to the standard of Goldsmith's model—

"Passing rich on forty pounds a year;"

for as late as the year 1626 its value was just ten pounds a year. Yet even its poverty had its advantages; for when Bishop Aylmer's enemies, among other charges, accused him of ordaining his porter, the fact was admitted, but justified on the ground that the man was of honest life and conversation, and proved to be an earnest and zealous pastor, by the scantiness of the stipend which he was content to receive, and less than he had actually received in a lay capacity.

In the new burial-ground rest the remains of William Collins, R.A., the painter of "As Happy as a King," who died in 1847, at the age of fifty-nine; of Banks, the Royal Academician, the sculptor, who was buried here in 1805, at the age of seventy; and of George Barret, one of the founders of the Society of Painters in Water-Colours, who died in 1842. Here, too, are buried the celebrated singers, Antonio Sapio and Antonio Zarra; and at least one centenarian, John Hubbard, who is recorded on his tomb as having been born in 1554, and having died in 1665, at the ripe age of one hundred and eleven. Here, too, lies buried George Bushnell, the clever but vain and fantastic sculptor, to whom we owe the statues on Temple Bar, and who executed those of Charles I., Charles II., and Sir Thomas Gresham for the first Royal Exchange. In after life he embarked in several mad schemes, which nearly ruined him; among other "crazes" of his, which are recorded, is an attempt to build a model of the Trojan horse in wood and stucco; the head was large enough to hold twelve men and a table, and the eyes served as windows. It cost £500, and was demolished by a storm of wind; and no entreaty could induce him to put the monster together again. He died in 1701.

Mrs. Siddons and Benjamin Robert Haydon, the painter, lie quite at the northern end of the burial-ground, not far apart; their monuments are simple and plain; that of Haydon bears upon it a quotation from *King Lear*, in allusion to his life of fretful disappointment; that of Mrs. Siddons is a flat stone, surrounded with a plain iron railing. We shall have more to say of Mrs. Siddons when we come to Upper Baker Street. With reference to Haydon, of whose last abode in Burwood Place we have spoken in the preceding chapter, we may state that he was the son of a bookseller, and was born at Plymouth in 1786. He came to London at the age of eighteen to seek his fortune—at all events, to make his way as a painter—bringing little with him except introductions to Northcote and Opie, the Royal Academicians. His career was eccentric and fitful; at one time he basked in the sunshine of public favour, and then again lost it, and with it, what was worse, he lost heart. From time to time he exhibited historical pictures at the Egyptian Hall, and had the mortification of seeing them eclipsed by the most common-place sights which drew crowds together, whilst his pictures were neglected. The slight, added to the pressure of debt, was more than poor Haydon could stand, and on the 22nd of June he died in his own studio, by his own hand, in front of one of his historical paintings. "Thus died poor Haydon," says his biographer, "in the sixty-first year of his age, after forty-two years of struggles, strivings, conflicts, successes, imprisonments, appeals to ministers, to Parliament, to patrons, to the public, self-illusions, and bitter disappointments." His first picture was exhibited in 1807; the subject of it, "Joseph and Mary resting with our Saviour after a Day's Journey on the Road to Egypt." It was sold; and the next year he exhibited the celebrated "Dentatus," which he considered badly hung by the Royal Academicians, and forthwith proceeded to make enemies of those forty potentates of art—a most imprudent step for so young an artist to take. Lord Mulgrave bought "Dentatus;" and in the following year it obtained the prize at the British Institution, and soon became very popular. The "Judgment of Solomon" appeared next; but during its progress Haydon's resources failed, and the directors of the British Institution voted him a present of one hundred guineas. Previous to this the artist had for some time devoted ten or twelve hours a day to the study of the Elgin marbles, which had just arrived in England; and he wrote and talked about them so enthusiastically and eloquently that he mainly contributed to their being purchased for the nation. He went, accompanied by Wilkie, to Paris in 1814, to study at the Louvre, and on his return commenced his largest work, "Christ entering into Jerusalem." This picture was exhibited in 1820, both in London and the provinces, to visitors at a shilling each, and he gained a considerable sum by it. It was considered a triumph of modern art. But, with all his acknowledged powers, Haydon mistook or disdained to follow the more certain path to fame and fortune. While his more successful brethren were engaged on cabinet pictures, his works were on too large a scale to be hung in private rooms; hence, the orders he obtained were comparatively few, and he became embarrassed.

In 1827, Haydon gave the following melancholy account of the fate of his great pictures:—"My 'Judgment of Solomon' is rolled up in a warehouse in the Borough! My 'Entry into Jerusalem,' once graced by the enthusiasm of the rank and beauty of the three kingdoms, is doubled up in a back room in Holborn! My 'Lazarus' is in an upholsterer's shop in Mount Street! and my 'Crucifixion' is in a hay-loft in Lisson Grove!"

In 1832, Haydon painted at Paddington his great picture of the "Reform Banquet;" and here most of the leading Whigs—Macaulay, among others—gave him sittings.

Few diaries are more sad than that which Haydon kept, and which accumulated to twenty-six large MS. volumes. At one time he mourned over the absence of wealthy patrons for his pictures; at another, of some real or fancied slight he had received from other painters; while in his entries repeated reference was made to debts, creditors, insolvencies, applications to friends for loans—in fact, despondency marked every line.

And now the time arrived when his cup of bitterness overflowed. One great and honourable ambition he had cherished—to illustrate the walls of the new Houses of Parliament with historical pictures; but this professional eminence was denied to him, and the rejection of his cartoon by the Royal Commission was the death-blow to his hopes. He would have borne up had he but realised the hope of painting one of the frescoes, or been cheered under his disappointment by popular support!

Such was the mental condition of the unhappy

painter in the early part of the year 1846, when the so-called "General Tom Thumb" came to England. Haydon had then just finished a large picture, on which he had long been engaged, "The Banishment of Aristides." He hoped by it to redeem his fallen fortunes, and to relieve himself of some of his debts, by exhibiting the picture in London. He engaged a room in the Egyptian Hall, under the same roof where "Tom Thumb" was attracting crowds, and sent out invitations to several distinguished persons and critics to attend a private view. The following entry in his diary on April 4th showed how acutely the poor man felt his comparative want of success:—"Opened; rain hard; only Jerrold, Baring, Fox Maule, and Hobhouse came. Rain would not have kept them away twenty-six years ago. Comparison:—

"1st day of 'Christ entering Jerusalem,' 1820 .. £19 16 0
1st day of 'Banishment of Aristides,' 1846 .. 1 1 6
I trust in God, Amen!"

Shortly afterwards Haydon wrote—and we can readily imagine the spirit in which he jotted down the lines—"They rush by thousands to see Tom Thumb. They push, they fight, they scream, they faint, they cry 'Help!' and 'Murder!' They see my bills and caravan, but do not read them; their eyes are on them, but their sense is gone. It is an insanity, a *furor*, a dream, of which I would not have believed England could have been guilty."

Mr. Cyrus Redding thus speaks, in his "Fifty Years' Reminiscences," of Paddington Green and its churchyard in the year 1806:—"At such times I crossed Paddington Green, and the new part of the churchyard, since thickly encumbered with memorials of the dead. There were then only three or four tombstones to be seen in that part. One nearest the iron palisades was placed by Lord Petre in memory of an excellent man and scholar, Dr. Geddes. He was the author of a new translation of some part of the Holy Scriptures. The Catholics and High Church Protestants did not approve of his conduct, because, in place of vindicating the authority of their churches in matters of religion, he supported the right of private judgment. His stone I saw in perfect preservation but a few years ago, in the same place as at first. It must have been designedly removed. Perhaps the epitaph displeased some strait-laced official. I will repeat it from memory, though I am not certain I am correct to a word.

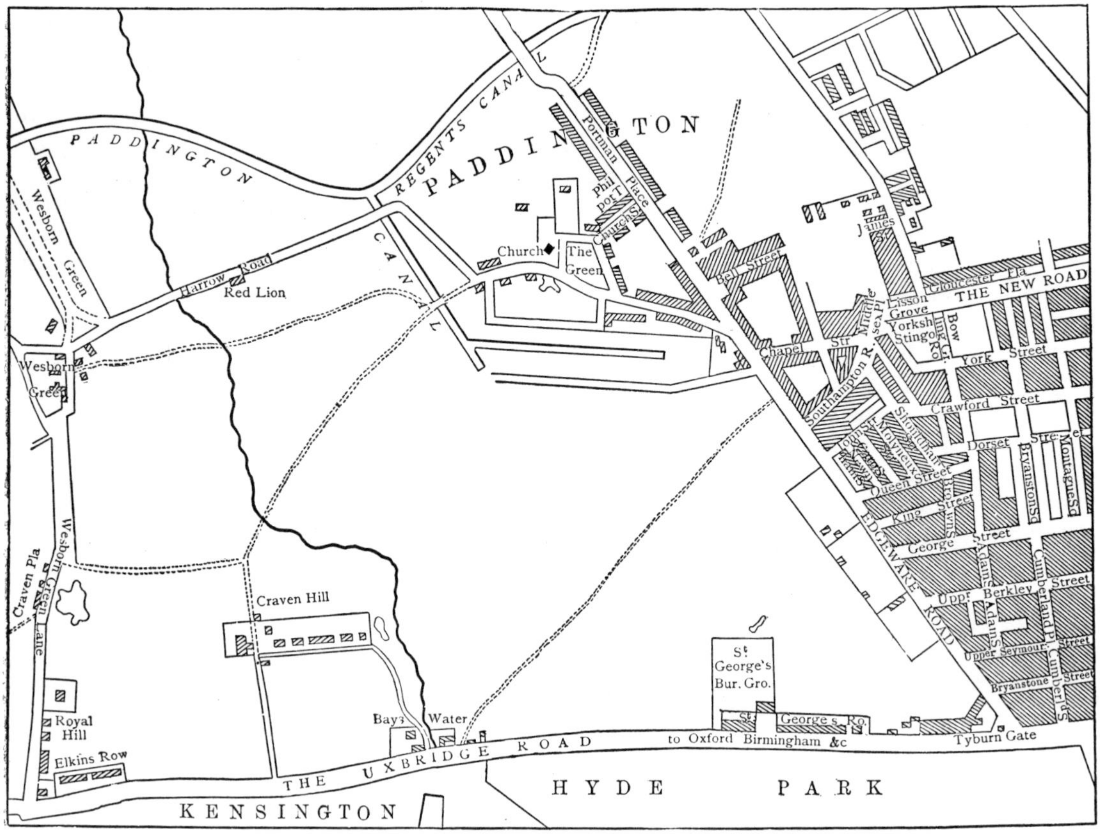

MAP OF PADDINGTON, IN 1815.

PADDINGTON GREEN IN 1750. (*From a Drawing in Mr. Crace's Collection.*)

'Christian is my name, Catholic my surname. If I cannot greet thee as a disciple of Jesus, still I should love thee as my fellow-man.'"

The Church of St. Mary ceased to be the parish church of Paddington in 1845, when it was superseded by the new Church of St. James, at the west end of Oxford and Cambridge Terraces, and the south end of Westbourne Terrace. "By these means," says the Report of 1840, "accommodation will be provided for 4,000 persons, or including Bayswater Chapel, which may hereafter be made a parochial chapel, for more than 5,000 persons, in a parish supposed to contain 20,000 souls." The edifice, we are informed, was originally designed for a secular building, but was altered to suit the "taste of the times." In 1844-46 was built a new church, in the elaborate Gothic style, dedicated to the Holy Trinity, in Gloucester Gardens, Bishop's Road. It is a large church, capable of accommodating nearly 1,600 worshippers, and is built in the "Perpendicular" style of architecture, from the designs of Mr. Cundy. It has a very richly crocketed spire and pinnacled tower, upwards of 200 feet high, and a beautiful stained glass window in the chancel. The crypt is said to be on a level with the roofs of the houses in Belgrave Square. This fabric is the "pet church of Paddington," and its "fair proportions and elegance of form" were said in those days to be "pleasing to the eye of all who admire the architectural art." The building cost nearly £20,000. In 1847, All Saints' Church was erected in Cambridge Place, at the end of Star Street. It occupies a portion of the site of the old Grand Junction Waterworks' reservoir.

There is an ancient house still standing at the right-hand corner of Old Church Street, going from Paddington Green. The uppermost storey of the building slightly overhangs the lower one, and the ground surrounding the house has been so raised that a descent of a step has to be made on going into it. In this house, which was for some time a disagreeable-looking butcher's shop, and now serves as the office of the district surveyor, lived formerly the religious fanatic, Richard Brothers, who is said to have represented himself to be the "Nephew of God, and His prophet and preacher." His grave is in St. John's Wood Churchyard, appropriately opposite that of Joanna Southcott.

Paddington has long been noted for its old public-houses. In the etching above referred to is represented, apparently about a hundred yards to the south-west of the church, a large and lofty building, presumably an inn, as a large sign-board projects into the street in front. This there can be little difficulty in identifying with the "Dudley Arms," in Dudley Grove, Harrow Road, or, at all events, with its predecessor on the same spot. At the corner of Old Church Street and the Edgware Road is the "Wheatsheaf" Tavern. There is an engraving extant of this old tavern, which represents it as a lowly, thatched, roadside hostelry; and, notwithstanding the visits of Ben Jonson, tradition says the house bore no very good repute, as both that and the old "Pack-horse," in the Harrow Road, were the favourite resorts of the masked and mounted gentlemen who made the Uxbridge and Edgware Roads perilous to travellers down to the close of the last century.

The "White Lion," another old tavern in the Edgware Road, dates from 1524, "the year when hops were first imported." George Morland is said to have been the painter of the sign of the "White Lion," which used to hang in front of this tavern, where he used to carouse, along with his friends Ibbetson and Rathbone. At the "Red Lion," near the Harrow Road, tradition says that Shakespeare acted as a strolling player; another "Red Lion," formerly near the Harrow Road bridge over the bourn, is described in an "inquisition" dated as far back as the reign of Edward VI.

As recently as 1840, the year of the opening of the Great Western Railway, a wide and open space of land in this vicinity was occupied by market and nursery gardens, and the red-tiled weather-boarded cottages of labourers and laundresses. Eight or ten years later, the appearance of the district was entirely changed: terraces and squares of fine houses had risen up in every direction west of the bourn; but the approaches to it from the Edgware Road, whether by Praed Street or the Harrow Road, were very deplorable. They are not much better even now; but as the grimy-looking houses at the entrance to the Harrow Road are in the course of removal, some improvement will eventually be brought about. We are informed, by a resident of some years' standing, that "anything more disgraceful than the appearance of the portion that remained of old Paddington Green it is impossible to imagine; all the refuse of the neighbourhood was heaped upon it, and the hollows filled with stagnant water, which made the place horrible to every sense. It was the play-ground of idle boys, and children uncared-for and squalid, who spent the day in fighting, swearing, shouting, crying, and throwing stones, so as to make the passing-by as dangerous as it was disagreeable. On all Sundays, and, in summer time, on week-day evenings, two or three self-constituted preachers, whose doctrines were as extraordinary as their English, were wont to establish themselves there, and rant and vociferate even louder than the boys; and, not unfrequently, a bold Freethinker stood up in opposition to them to propagate his reckless creed."

In 1865 the ground was at last enclosed and ornamentally laid out, and in the summer of the next year it was thrown open to the public. How great the improvement to the neighbourhood can be known only to those who saw it in the days of its degradation. The fine old houses skirting the further side of the Green put on a renovated appearance, and rents rose immediately; and now, instead of squalor and unruliness, decently-dressed people and children daily enjoy the grassy lawns, and flower-beds, and seats beside the gravel paths, and order and neatness reign there. The poor, too, are not excluded.

The Vestry Hall is another improvement of the last ten years; and the building of St. Mary Magdalene's Church another.

On Paddington Green was for some years the residence of Thomas Uwins, R.A., and here he painted his picture of "The Little Girl in the Brigand's Hat," so well known to us by the engraver's art. Here, too, was the studio of Wyatt, in which was moulded the equestrian statue of the Duke of Wellington, so long at Hyde Park Corner. The Rev. J. Richardson records, in his amusing "Recollections," the fact that twelve gentlemen sat down to a repast in the interior of the horse, like the Greeks in the belly of the Trojan horse, in imitation of Virgil's Æneid.

Literature and art have been represented among the inhabitants of this neighbourhood. Robert Browning has lived for some time in Warwick Crescent; and the venerable Chevalier de Chatelain, who has done useful work in translating various poems, and also Shakespeare's works, into French, resides next door to him, at Castelnau Lodge. At one time Mr. Babbage was resident here; and close by the canal lived the great line-engraver, Henry Robinson. George Colman, too, died here; he was buried, as already mentioned, at Kensington.* The Princess Charlotte was an occasional visitor at Dudley House, Paddington Green. The fields about there were pleasant places for a country ramble, even at the beginning of the present century. The author of the "Old City" writes:—"On a September day in 1807, I was walking on the banks of the Grand Junction Canal, at Paddington, and then quite in the country, when a plain private carriage drew up. Two ladies, one very young, and the other of middle age, got out, and commenced promenading. It was the Princess Charlotte and her governess, the Duchess of Northumberland, I think. They were both in plain morning dress, and evidently sought to avoid notice. The princess, tall and stout for her age (she was then eleven), wore a white muslin frock, and a straw bonnet, crossed by a plain white satin riband. The waist of the frock, according to the ugly fashion of the time, was placed high up under her arms, much as may be seen in her more mature portrait by Sir Thomas Lawrence. Her forehead was broad and rather high, her face full, and her nose prominent, but not disagreeably so. She might have been styled pleasing, but she had no pretensions to beauty; and she was more womanly than is usual with girls of the same age. She frequently asked questions of her elder companion, and the tones of her voice were soft and musical. Once, apparently forgetting her studied school-step, she was breaking into a run, but the duchess checked her by a look, and the decorous step was resumed. For a few minutes she escaped notice, but the instant that her rank was known, importunate promenaders began to throng about, and soon obliged her and the duchess to beat a retreat to the carriage." It is satisfactory to find that the fathers and grandfathers of the present generation were quite as ill-mannered and vulgar as the Englishmen and Englishwomen who "mobbed" Queen Adelaide when she paid a visit to the palm-house at Kew, or intruded their gaze upon Queen Victoria at Brighton, on her accession to the throne, and so drove her from the place. Dudley House is kept in remembrance by the "Dudley Arms" Tavern and Dudley Grove, in the Harrow Road.

At the close of the last century, Mrs. Hutchins and Mr. Samuel Pepys Cockerell were the two principal residents in Westbourne Green; and Paddington Green boasted John Chamberlain and John Symonds amongst its inhabitants.

Paddington House is described, at the commencement of the present century, as "a handsome brick edifice, on the east side of the Green." It is said to have been built by a certain Mr. Dennis Chirac, who, having made a fortune as jeweller to Queen Anne, chose late in life to retire here into the country. Having long since been converted into shops, it was pulled down in 1876.

Hone, in his "Every-Day Book," mentions Paddington as one of the suburbs of London which formerly were enlivened by the "Jack in the Green on May Day." "The last specimens of the 'Jacks in the Green' that I remember," he writes, in 1827, "were at the Paddington May-dance, near the 'Yorkshire Stingo,' about twenty years ago, whence, as I heard, they diverged to Bayswater,

* See *ante*, p. 129.

Kentish Town, and the adjoining neighbourhood. A 'Jack o' the Green' always carried a long walking-stick with floral wreaths; he whisked it about in the dance, and afterwards walked with it in high estate, like a Lord Mayor's footman." We have already mentioned the May-pole in our account of the Strand.*

> "It was a pleasant sight to see
> A little village company
> Drawn out upon the first of May
> To have their annual holyday:
> The pole hung round with garlands gay,
> The young ones footing it away;
> The aged cheering their old souls
> With recollections and their bowls,
> Or, on the mirth and dancing failing,
> Then ofttimes told old tales re-taleing."—*Hone.*

Westbourne Place, situated close to the Green, was the residence, successively, of Isaac Ware (the architect, and editor of Palladio's works); of Sir William Yorke, Chief Justice of the Court of Common Pleas; of J. Coulson, Esq.; of Mr. Samuel Pepys Cockerell; and, lastly, of the veteran Peninsular General, Lord Hill, who here entertained William IV. and Queen Adelaide. In the *Universal Magazine* for September, 1793, appears the following notice of the mansion and its surroundings:—"Westbourne Place, the handsome villa of Jukes Coulson, Esq., an eminent anchor-smith in Thames Street, London, is situated at Westbourne Green, one mile and a half from Tyburn Turnpike, and three-quarters of a mile from the new church at Paddington. This green is one of those beautifully rural spots for which that parish, although contiguous to the metropolis, is distinguished. The house is situated on a rising ground, which commands a pleasing view of Hampstead and Highgate; the village of Paddington, with the elegant new church, produces a pretty effect when viewed from hence; and as no part of London can be seen, a person disposed to enjoy the pleasures of rural retirement might here forget his proximity to the 'busy hum of men.' The house was built by Mr. Isaac Ware, who quitted the ignoble profession of a chimney-sweeper, and commencing the man of science and taste, was employed in building many houses, and distinguished himself, moreover, by some books on the subject of architecture. The gardens and pleasure-grounds are laid out with great taste; and close to Mr. Coulson's elegant mansion is a farm-house, which is occupied as an occasional country residence by the Most Noble George Grenville Nugent, Marquis of Buckingham."

Hughson, who published his "History of London and its Neighbourhood" in 1809, and who, by the way, does not appear to have had a single subscriber for his work in this neighbourhood, writes of Westbourne Green, that "it is one of those beautifully rural spots for which Paddington is distinguished. It occupies rising ground, and commands a lovely view of Hampstead and Highgate, with the distant city. An important mansion, called Westbourne Place, is situated here, built by that born architect, Isaac Ware, the editor of Palladio's works, who, originally a sweep, became conspicuous as a student of art and science, and the proprietor of the estate of Westbourne Green." Mr. Coulson inhabited Westbourne Place when Hughson wrote. At that time this house and gardens must have occupied the ground on which the Lock Hospital stands; this institution remaining at Grosvenor Place till 1842. "In the reign of William IV.," writes the Rev. J. Richardson, in his "Recollections," "this spot was really what its name implied," a green. It was not built over till long into the reign of Queen Victoria.

Desborough Place, a small row of the houses to be seen on the south-west side of the Harrow Road, before reaching the Lock Hospital, adjoins an old mansion, now partly pulled down, called Desborough House, after John Desborough, or Disbrowe, the brother-in-law of the "Lord Protector Cromwell"—that "ploughman Desborough," as Oliver would often style him, half in jest and half in earnest.

There is a discrepancy between Robins and Mr. Peter Cunningham as to the whereabouts of Mrs. Siddons' residence in Paddington, the one placing her in Desborough Lodge, the other in a house and grounds levelled to make room for the Great Western Railway; but Incledon, the singer, describes a visit to the great *tragedienne*, at her villa on "Westbourne Green," which was situated at the top of the Harrow Road, close to the Lock Hospital, and where formerly several genteel houses stood; but now only the name remains.

Westbourne Farm—for so, as we have stated previously, Mrs. Siddons' cottage was called—was standing down to about the year 1860, when it was demolished to make room for a row of shops and houses. It was a little retired house in a garden, screened with poplars and other trees, resembling a modest rural vicarage. This was at one time the residence of Madame Vestris; but, before her, Mrs. Siddons liked to withdraw here from the noise and din of London. The following amusing description of the place is said to be from the pen of her husband:—

* See Vol. III., p. 87.

"ON MRS. SIDDONS' COTTAGE AT WESTBOURNE.

"Would you I'd Westbourne Farm describe?
I'll do it, then, and free from gall;
For sure it would be sin to gibe
A thing so pretty and so small.

"A poplar-walk, if you have strength,
Will take a minute's time to step it;
Nay, certes 'tis of such a length
'Twould almost tire a frog to leap it.

"But when the pleasure-ground is seen,
Then what a burst comes on the view!
Its level walk, its shaven green,
For which a razor's stroke would do.

"Now, pray be cautious when you enter,
And curb your strides with much expansion;
Three paces take you to the centre;
Three more, you're close against the mansion.

"The mansion, cottage, house, or hut—
Call't what you will—has room within
To lodge the King of Lilliput,
But not his court nor yet his queen.

"The kitchen-garden, true to keeping,
Has length, and breadth, and width in plenty;
A snail, if fairly set a-creeping,
Could scarce go round while you told twenty.

"Perhaps you'll cry, on hearing this,
'What, everything so very small!'
No; she that made it what it is
Has greatness that makes up for all."

The great actress was certainly living here in 1806, and the following year, for Cyrus Redding thus mentions her abode, in his "Fifty Years' Recollections:"—"I did not slumber in bed, often rising at four o'clock, walking to Manchester Square, calling up a friend there, and then going into the country to an inn near Mrs. Siddons' villa, a little on the town side of Kensal Green, but then far in the green fields. We breakfasted together. I returned to Gough Square, sometimes before my fellow-lodger had left his bed, and generally before ten o'clock; thus I gained six hours on the day."

The Lock Hospital and Asylum, which stand on the opposite side of the Harrow Road, derive their name from the "Loke," or "Lock," in Kent Street, Southwark, an ancient hospital for lepers. The name may have been derived, as suggested by a writer in *Notes and Queries*, from the old French word *loques*, "rags"—referring to the linen rags applied to sores; but with more probability it comes, as Archer is inclined to believe, in his "Vestigia," from the Saxon *log* or *loc*, equivalent to "shut," or "closed," in reference to the isolated condition of the leper.

This hospital was founded in 1746, and the asylum about forty years later, mainly by the efforts of the Rev. Thomas Scott, the well-known Biblical commentator; and it is mentioned in Strype's edition of "Stow," in 1765, as being "at Pimlico." It was removed hither from Grosvenor Place* in 1842. A chapel has been attached to it since 1764. In 1849 its authorities were able to double the number of patients and penitents, through the help of the late Duke of Cambridge, who issued an autograph appeal on behalf of the charity. This establishment is in reality a branch of the Lock Hospital, and is intended for the reception of females only; the branch for males is situated in Dean Street, Soho. From the published report, we learn that since the foundation of the asylum, the institution has been the means of giving the advantages of domestic training to about three thousand females. During the year 1875, no less than fifty young women were fitted for service, nearly all of whom have given satisfactory proof of real amendment by their conduct in their situations; whilst of those sent out in previous years, many have earned the reward given by the committee of the institution for remaining twelve months in the same situation; several have been restored to friends; whilst others have testified to the great change that has been effected in them by contributing from their scanty earnings to the support of the institution, which has rescued them from a life of misery. The buildings here cover a large extent of ground, and the gardens surrounding them are well planted with trees and shrubs.

Although not in the immediate vicinity of the Lock Hospital, it may not be altogether out of place here to speak of one or two other institutions, devoted to charitable purposes, which exist in the parish. St. Mary's Hospital, originally styled the Marylebone and Paddington Hospital, stands in Cambridge Place, on a site which once formed the reservoir of the Grand Junction Waterworks, between the Great Western Railway Terminus and the Harrow Road, in the centre of a crowded neighbourhood. The first stone was laid by the Prince Consort, in June, 1845, and the first ward was opened in 1850. It is built of red brick, with stone dressings, and was erected from the designs of Mr. Thomas Hopper and Mr. J. H. Wyatt. The building will accommodate 180 beds, and in its construction the greatest attention was paid to the ventilation and warming. Twelve hundred cubic feet of space, at least, is allotted to each bed. This is the only general hospital for an extensive and populous district of the metropolis, and its doors are ever open for the relief of the sick and maimed.

* See p. 14, *ante*.

It receives annually, as in-patients, about 1,800 cases of serious accident or disease, and as out-patients and casualties about 20,000. All poor persons applying for relief for accident or disease of extreme urgency, are admissible, after due examination, without any letter of recommendation. The laws of the institution provide that there shall be "a chaplain, who is required to be in full orders in the Church of England; and, in addition to the ordinary duties of his office in ministering to is responsible to the board for his good conduct." The laws, it may be added, are framed in the most liberal spirit towards the medical profession. "The medical committee consists of the ten principal medical officers in the various departments of the hospital for the time being, and ten medical governors of the charity who do not hold any office in the hospital or hospital school, elected annually. All legally qualified medical and surgical practitioners, being governors, are eligible to be

MRS. SIDDONS' HOUSE AT WESTBOURNE GREEN, 1800.

the spiritual wants of the inmates of the hospital, he is to be the principal of the collegiate establishment." The staff of the hospital, according to the original report, consists of three physicians, three assistant physicians, three surgeons, three assistant surgeons, a physician-accoucheur, a surgeon-accoucheur, an ophthalmic surgeon, and an aural surgeon. The laws of the hospital provide for four resident medical officers, all of whom are to be fully qualified medical practitioners.

"In the Hospital Medical School and Medical Collegiate Establishment the determination of the course of education, the rules and regulations for the government and conduct of the pupils, and the appointment of all lecturers and teachers, is vested, under the advice of the medical committee, in the governors at large; and every pupil of the school members of this committee; and legally qualified medical and surgical practitioners, whether governors or not, are at liberty, on a proper introduction, to attend the practice of the hospital. The medical governors are also at liberty to attend all lectures delivered by the teachers in the hospital school; and if residing within half a mile of the hospital, they are entitled to be summoned to all important operations, on paying a trifling contribution towards the expense of summoning. Thus the medical profession at large has every opportunity to form its opinion of the principles and practice taught in the hospital, an efficient voice in the management of the medical affairs of the institution, and a direct influence in the system of education to be adopted in the hospital school, of which their own sons or private pupils might be members."

PADDINGTON CHURCH: 1750 AND 1805.

St. Mary's Hospital, being without endowment, is supported entirely by the voluntary contributions and donations of the public at large; and when the number of patients annually relieved is taken into consideration, it is easy to imagine that the expenses of the institution are very great, amounting as they do to something like £10,000 annually. Within a short distance of St. Mary's is another charitable institution, the Paddington Provident Dispensary, which dates its career of usefulness from the year 1838. Upwards of 7,000 persons are relieved here during the course of the year. Another very useful charity in the neighbourhood is the Dudley Stuart "Home for the Houseless," in Market Street, close by. Here a temporary home is afforded to destitute and houseless persons of good character, and means are adopted for restoring them to their position in life.

There is a chapel in the Harrow Road, on the south side, at the entrance to Paddington Green; it is for the use of the Irvingites, or members of the Apostolic Church; and among those set apart for the use of other denominations is one called "The Boatman's Chapel," which stands on ground leased to the Grand Junction Canal Company. "This place of worship," Mr. Robins tells us, in his book on Paddington, "was constructed out of a stable and coach-house, at the expense of a few pious individuals, who saw how much the poor boatmen wanted the advantages which accrue from religious instruction, and how little likely they were to get it in a parish-church, which could not hold one-fourth part of the settled inhabitants. This little place of worship is in connection with 'Paddington Chapel'—a place of worship belonging to the Independents."

The formation of the Great Western Railway caused a slight diversion of the Harrow Road, which was carried by a bridge over the canal, and so round by what is now Blomfield Terrace to Westbourne Green. It is on record that John Lyon, the founder of Harrow School, left forty acres of land in the parish of Marylebone, and another plot at Kilburn, for the purpose of repairing the roads between London, Harrow, and Edgware; and now the rents of Hamilton Terrace, Abercorn Place, &c., are applied to the purpose.

The road, at a little distance from London, was a dangerous one, being infested by footpads as recently as the year 1827, when Mr. Allardin, a respectable veterinary surgeon, residing at Lisson Grove, was made to dismount from his horse, robbed, and brutally ill-treated, about a mile from Paddington Green.

On the north side of the Harrow Road, a short distance beyond the Lock Hospital, a model town has sprung up within the last few years, under the auspices of the Artisans', Labourers', and General Dwellings Company. Queen's Park—for so this batch of dwellings is called—occupies a site about eighty acres in extent, and the houses are designed to accommodate no less than 16,000 persons. This model city has now its own public lecture-hall and institute, its co-operative stores, its coal-depôt, dairy-farm, baths and wash-houses, and other buildings. It is the intention of the promoters of the company that there shall be no public-house on the estate; while, at the same time, every opportunity will be taken to promote and develop temperance principles by the formation of temperance societies and "bands of hope;" and reading-rooms, discussion clubs, libraries, and other substitutes for "the house round the corner," will be a marked feature. This certainly is a sign of improvement from the state of things which existed a quarter of a century ago; for, apart from the public establishments to which we have referred above, there were no places for rational amusement—unless, indeed, we consider such places as the "Flora Tea-gardens," and "Bott's Bowling-green," to come under this designation. "In that region of the parish, still devoted to bull-dogs and pet spaniels," writes Mr. Robins in 1853, "the bodies of broken-down carriages, old wheels, rusty grates, and old copper boilers, little gardens, and low miserable sheds, there is an establishment which boasts of having the truly attractive glass, in which, 'for the small charge of two-pence, any young lady may behold her future husband.' But although such attractions as these exist, the youths who live on the celebrated Paddington estate have not to thank the lords of the soil for setting apart any portion of it for their physical improvement. In Paddington there is no public gymnasium; there is now no village-green worthy of the name; the young are not trained to use their motive powers to the best advantage; there are no public baths. And when, on the establishment of the baths and wash-houses in Marylebone, the governing body in Paddington was solicited to join in that useful work, that good offer was rejected, and the people of Marylebone were permitted to carry out that necessary and useful undertaking by themselves." In 1874, however, any difficulties that may have existed with reference to the above subject were surmounted, and some extensive baths and wash-houses were erected in the Queen's Road, at a cost, inclusive of land, of about £40,000.

In the Harrow Road, on a portion of what had been Paddington Green, stood, till about 1860, the oldest charitable building in the parish; it was a block of small almshouses, said to have been built in 1714. It afforded shelter for sixteen poor old women belonging to the parish, who were supported there out of the poor-rates. The inmates, doubtless, felt themselves more "at home" here than they would do if compelled to take up their quarters in the great parish poor-house, which is situated on a portion of the land once known as "The Upper Readings," purchased by the Bishop of London and the trustees of the Paddington estate, immediately to the west of the Lock Hospital. In the end, however, the almshouses were swept away in the course of parochial improvements.

Running westward through the parish, almost in a line with the Harrow Road, is the Paddington and Grand Junction Canal. The success of the Duke of Bridgewater's canal between Liverpool and Manchester led to the passing of an Act of Parliament, in 1795, for the formation of the Paddington Canal, which was opened for traffic on the 1st of June, 1801, when the first barge arrived, with passengers from Uxbridge, at the Paddington basin. There were public rejoicings, and all the north-western suburb was *en fête* in honour of the occasion. Bells were rung, flags were hung out, and cannon were fired; and one enthusiastic Paddingtonian had good reason to remember the day, for the gun which he was firing burst and shattered his arm. But the Grand Junction Canal Company were so elated at the thought of the public benefit which they had bestowed on the country, that they took a classical motto from Horace:—

"Æquè pauperibus prodest, locupletibus æquè."

In 1853, Mr. Robins, in his work above referred to, writes:—"The glory of the first public company which shed its influence over Paddington has, in a great measure, departed; the shares of the Grand Junction Canal Company are below par, though the traffic on this silent highway to Paddington is still considerable; and the cheap trips into the country offered by its means during the summer months are beginning to be highly appreciated by the people, who are pent in close lanes and alleys; and I have no doubt the shareholders' dividends would not be diminished by a more liberal attention to this want. If every one had their right," continues the writer, "I am told there would be a wharf adjoining this canal, open free of cost to the people of Paddington for loading and unloading goods. It is certain that the old road to Harrow was never leased to the Grand Junction Canal Company; but a wharf, upwards of one hundred feet wide, now exists in a portion of that road; and, as I am informed, the rent of this wharf is not received by the parish." At its first opening, passenger boats went about five times a week from Paddington to Uxbridge; and the wharves at Paddington presented for some years a most animated and busy appearance, on account of the quantity of goods warehoused there for transit to and from the metropolis, causing the growth of an industrious population around them. But this was only a brief gleam of prosperity, for when the Regent's Canal was opened, the goods were conveyed by barges straight to the north and eastern suburbs, and the wharfage-ground at Paddington suffered a great deterioration in consequence.

In 1812 the Regent's Canal was commenced. This undertaking, which was completed and opened in 1820, begins at Paddington, and passing under the Edgware Road, Maida Hill, and St. John's Wood, by a tunnel 372 yards in length, opens into a basin near the "Jew's Harp;" thence the canal passes on to Camden Town and Islington, and then by a tunnel into the City Road, by Kingsland and Hackney, and so on to Stepney Fields and Limehouse, where it joins the Thames. In its course through London there are no less than twelve locks and about forty bridges. "On the banks of the canal," says Mr. John Timbs, "the immense heaps of dust and ashes, once towering above the house-tops, are said to have been worth £10,000 a heap."

At the western extremity of the parish an artesian well was formed, to which the name of "The Western Water-works" was given. The water from this well supplied the houses which were built on that clayey district; the West Middlesex and Grand Junction Water-works Companies supplying the other parts of this parish.

In 1824 gas was first introduced into the parish, on the establishment of the Imperial Gas Company. Up to this time, during the long winter evenings, the muddy roads which led to the cottages on the Paddington estate were in total darkness, unless the "parish lantern" chanced to offer its acceptable light. The parish surveyors, in a report to the vestry on the state of these cottages, in 1816, say —"We cannot refrain from thus recording our expression of regret that the ground-landlords should be so inordinate in their demands; the effect of which is, the buildings are ill-calculated to afford shelter from the inclemency of the weather, and the want of drainage and consequent damp produce disease, filth, and wretchedness." The cottages here referred to, which were for many years so prominent a feature in the parish, and so much sought after by the poor, as a sort of "country retreat," were, at the beginning of this century, the generators of "disease, filth, and wretchedness."

As a proof of the poverty-stricken character of the inhabitants of Paddington, it may be stated that a wretched hovel here was, in 18[illegible]3, the scene of the death of a well-known beggar at the West End, and that upwards of £200 was found hoarded up in his chests—a sum which was claimed by a female partner of his trade. Among his effects was a paper in which were recorded the various profits which he had made in different parts of London by begging—a most interesting and curious document, and one well worthy of the attention of the Society for the Suppression of Mendicity.

"The transition state from an agricultural village to the fashionable Tyburnia," writes Mr. Robins, "was no very agreeable time for the majority of those who lived in Paddington. When the cottages were swept away, and the heavy poor-rates which they had entailed were diminished, new burdens sprang up, scarcely less grievous. Rents became enormous; the Highway, Watching, and Lighting Rates were excessive; and these were rendered more oppressive, on account of those who received the greatest benefit from the causes which necessitated the greater expenditure not bearing their just share of this local taxation."

On the north-west side of the parish is Kensal New Town, with its appendage of Kensal Green. In his work already quoted, Mr. Robins writes:—"Kensell, or Kensale, comes, as I take it, from King's-field. In the Harleian MS. (No. 606, f. 46 b.), the Green of this name is called Kellsell, and Kingefelde. In Mary's reign, we perceive by this document also that 'the Green Lane,' and 'Kingefelde Green,' were the same place. And as 'the Green Lanes' still exist—in name—we may ascertain with something like accuracy the situation of this field, or green, which formerly belonged to the king." Here is the best known of the London cemeteries. It occupies a considerable space of ground between the Grand Junction Canal and the North-Western Railway, and has its entrance lodge and gateway in the Harrow Road. The necessity of providing cemeteries out of town, though not as yet enforced by Parliament, was felt so keenly, that a company was formed in 1832, and fifty-six acres of ground at Kensal Green—then two miles distant from the metropolis—were purchased, laid out, and planted. And no sooner was the cemetery opened than the boon was eagerly embraced by the public, and marble obelisks and urns began to rise among the cypresses in all the variety which heathen and classical allusions could suggest. In the course of the next five years other cemetery companies were formed at Highgate, Norwood, Nunhead, &c., and now we have in the suburbs of London some ten or twelve humble rivals of the Père la Chaise of Paris. The Bishop of London, however, opposed in Parliament the Bill for the formation of these new cemeteries; and one of his archdeacons, a City rector, wrote a pamphlet or a charge to prove that City churchyards were rather healthy than otherwise! After overcoming all sorts of difficulties, the cemetery here was laid out on the principle of Père la Chaise. The principal entrance is a noble erection of the Doric order, one wing of which forms the office, and the other the residence of the superintendent. Against the northern boundary wall, and parallel with the Episcopal Chapel, is a small colonnade, and beneath this are the old or original catacombs. Every space in these vaults has been long since occupied, but the same care, it may be remarked, is nevertheless observable, on the part of the company, to preserve them in that orderly condition which is observable in the more recent interments. The extensive colonnades and chambers for the erection of tablets to the memory of persons whose remains are resting in the catacombs below, are spots where the visitor to the cemetery may find an almost endless number of subjects for meditation. The names of statesmen, soldiers, poets, and philosophers, are inscribed side by side on the sculptured slabs which adorn the walls. In a notice of it, printed in 1839, Kensal Green Cemetery is described as "a flourishing concern; the original £25 shares being already at £52." Here are buried the Duke of Sussex, Sydney Smith, Sir W. Beatty (Nelson's surgeon), Sir Anthony Carlisle, Dr. Valpy, Anne Scott and Sophia Lockhart, daughter of Sir Walter Scott and John Hugh Lockhart, his grandson, the "Hugh Little-John" of the "Tales of a Grandfather;" Thomas Hood, Liston, Ducrow, Madame Vestris; Calcott, Daniell, and Mulready, the painters; William C. Macready, Allan Cunningham, J. C. Loudon, William Makepeace Thackeray, Shirley Brooks, John Leech, the well-known comic artist; John Cassell, and many other men of mark; indeed, Kensal Green may now be called the "God's Acre" of London celebrities, a character, however, which it divides to some extent with Norwood, Highgate, and Nunhead Cemeteries. The Princess Sophia also is buried here. Why his Royal Highness the Duke of Sussex chose this spot for his last resting-place is told by Mr. Mark Boyd, in his "Social Sketches:"—"At the funeral of William IV. there was so much of delay and confusion, and so many questions of etiquette and precedence broke out, that the duke remarked to a friend, 'This is intolerable. Now, recollect what I say to you. If I should die before I return to Kensington, see I am not buried at Windsor; as I would not be buried there after this fashion for all the world.'" It was at first proposed that Thackeray should be buried in the Temple Church, where lie the ashes of Goldsmith, whom he so tenderly censured in his "Lectures on the Humorists;" but after consultation with his relatives, it was deemed better that he should be laid to rest with his own family at Kensal Green. Accordingly, on December 30th, 1863, a bright, balmy day, almost like spring, Thackeray was here consigned to his last rest, being followed to the grave by his friends Dickens, A. Trollope, Mark Lemon, Theodore Martin, G. H. Lewes, Robert Bell, Millais, Robert Browning, George Cruickshank, John Leech, and Shirley Brooks.

Leigh Hunt, too, lies buried here. His grave was for years without a stone, or any other distinguishing mark, until, through the advocacy of Mr. Samuel Carter Hall, in the columns of the *Art Journal*, a subscription was set on foot, and in 1874–75 a monument was erected to the poet's memory. We may mention also the names of George Dyer, the historian of Cambridge; Thomas Barnes, the "Thunderer" of the *Times;* Dr. Birkbeck, the founder of Mechanics' Institutions; John Murray, the publisher; and the famous George Robins, the auctioneer, of whom we have already spoken in our account of Covent Garden. The following lines, though of a mock-heroic character, which have been handed down respecting him, serve to show that he was regarded in his day as a typical personage:—

"High in a hall, by curious listeners fill'd,
Sat one whose soul seem'd steeped in poësy;
So bland his diction, it was plain he will'd
His hearers all should prize as high as he
The gorgeous works of art there plac'd around.
The statues by the Phidian chisel wrought:
Endymion, whom Dian lov'd distraught;
Dian herself, Laocöon serpent-bound;
The pictures touch'd by Titian and Vandyke,
With rainbow pencils, in the which did vie
Fair form and colour for the mastery;
Warm'd his discourse till ear ne'er heard the like.
'Who is that eloquent man?' I asked one near.
'That, sir? that's Mr. Robins, auctioneer.'"

Besides those whose names we have mentioned, there are also buried here the Right Hon. Joseph Planta, Sir George Murray, Sir Edward Hyde East, Sir John Sinclair, Chief Justice Tindal, the Marquis of Thomond, the Bishops of St. David's (Dr. Jenkinson) and Quebec (Dr. Stewart), and a very large number of the aristocracy.

The practice of burying the dead in cities is of necessity injurious to the public health; and it is strange that, in a city like London, where no expense has been spared in promoting sanitary measures, it should so long have been permitted and tolerated. It was a custom of very early antiquity to attach burying-grounds to Christian churches, though both the Jews of old and the heathen Romans buried their dead in caves and tombs by the road-side, as shown by the constant inscription of "Siste Viator," instead of "Sacred to the Memory of." But when streets and whole towns grew up around these consecrated spots, the public convenience and decency could not fail to suggest the expediency of having the depositories of the dead at a distance from the dwellings of the living. Accordingly, most Continental cities have their cemeteries in the suburbs; but the servile adherence of our people to ancient customs, even when shown to be bad, kept up this loathsome practice in the midst of our dense population until some twenty years after the accession of Queen Victoria, when many of the City churches, and some at the West End also, were little better than charnel-houses; and their dead increased in numbers so rapidly that one sexton started the question whether he might not refuse to admit an iron coffin into a church or churchyard, because in that case the deceased took a fee-simple in the ground, which ought to be granted him only for a term of years! It is perhaps a matter of complaint that it has never entered into the contemplation of the Legislature, or even of an individual, to form a general and extensive cemetery in the suburbs of the metropolis.

Although perhaps not actually within the limits of Paddington, we may add that a plot of ground on the west side of the cemetery, nearer Willesden, was, about the year 1860, secured by the Roman Catholics of London as a place of burial. Among the earliest who were interred here was Cardinal Wiseman, who, as we have already stated,* died at his residence in York Place, Baker Street, in February, 1865. The body of the cardinal was taken first to the chapel of St. Mary, Moorfields, where part of the service was celebrated, after which the funeral *cortége*, of considerable length and imposing appearance, passed on its way hither, through the streets of London.

Beyond the cemetery there is but little of interest to note in this part of Paddington. An old tavern once stood here, called "The Plough," of which Faulkner, in 1820, says:—"It has been

* See Vol. IV., p. 422.

built upwards of three hundred years. The timber and joists, being of oak, are still in good preservation." George Morland, the painter, was much pleased with this then sequestered and quiet place, and spent much of his time here towards the close of his life, surrounded by those rustic scenes which his pencil has so faithfully and so ably delineated. In the same neighbourhood, apparently, resided Robert Cromwell, a near relative of Oliver, the

THE "PLOUGH" AT KENSAL GREEN, 1820. (*See page* 221.)

Protector. At all events, in the register of burials at Kensington, under date 1691, is an entry of "Cromwell," the "reputed" son of Robert Cromwell, of Kensal Green, and of Jane Saville, his servant.

In the matter of education, it is only within the last few years that Paddington appears to have made much progress. A Sunday-school, in connection with the parish church, was established here during the last century; but it was not till the beginning of this that any public means of instruction existed for the children of the poor on weekdays. Lysons, in his "Environs of London," tells us that "a charity-school for thirty boys and thirty girls was established in the parish in 1802," and that it was "supported by voluntary contributions, and the collections at an annual charity-sermon." This public day-school for poor children was one of the first established in the outskirts of London. The building, which was capable of accommodating only one hundred children, was erected on land said to have been given by Bishop Compton. In 1822, new school-rooms were built on a part of Paddington Green, on a spot which was formerly known as the "town pool." Since the above period, in consequence of the altered condition of Paddington, the parish has gone on increasing in the number of its schools, so that now it may doubtless claim to be on as good a footing as any other parish in the metropolis. A large Board School was opened in the neighbourhood of the Edgware Road in 1874-5.

We have already mentioned the naming of some of the streets and terraces after various bishops of London; one or two others, however, still remain to be spoken of. For instance, Tichborne Street, a turning out of the Edgware Road, although not built so far back as the reign of Henry VIII., reminds us of one "Nicholas Tychborne, gent., husband of the second daughter and co-heir of Alderman Fenroper;" and of "Alderman Tichbourn," one of Cromwell's peers and King Charles's judges.

Praed Street preserves the memory of a banker of that name, one of the first directors of the Grand Junction Canal Company. This street connects Edgware Road with the Great Western Railway Terminus and Hotel. The latter is a magnificent building, and was one of the first constructed on the "monster" principle in connection with the railway terminus, with which it has communication by a covered passage. The edifice in itself comprises five separate floors, containing in all upwards of one hundred and fifty rooms, the chief of which are large and lofty, and beautifully ornamented; the designs generally, in the Louis Quatorze style, were executed by Mr. Philip Hardwick, R.A., and the pediment upon the front is surmounted by a piece of allegorical sculpture. The Great Western Railway line, which communicates with the west and extreme south-west of England, is situated close to and below the level of the terminal wharf of the Paddington branch of the Grand Junction Canal. The Act of incorporation, under which this line was formed, was passed in the year 1835; and it was intended to connect the seaport of Bristol and the great towns of the south-west with London. The original estimate for the construction of the railway was £2,500,000, or about £39,000 a mile. The line was constructed on that known as the "broad gauge," and the engineer was Mr. I. K. Brunel, son of Isambard Brunel. This estimate, however, was largely exceeded, the directors accounting for it by stating "that it is accounted for by the intended junction with the Birmingham line at Acton." In 1838 the railway was open only to Maidenhead; to Twyford in 1839; in the following year to Faringdon Road; and in 1841 it was completed to Bristol. It was at first proposed that this line should be connected with the London and Birmingham Railway at Kensal Green; but some obstacles having arisen to the satisfactory arrangement of this plan between the two companies, the intention was ultimately abandoned, and the Great Western Railway had an independent terminus erected here. To effect this it was necessary to construct about two and a-half miles of additional railway, while the total distance to be travelled would be lessened by about three miles. The Box Tunnel, on this line, is upwards of 3,000 yards

KENSAL GREEN CEMETERY. (*See page* 221.)

in length. The various lines and branches now included in the Great Western system comprehend about 2,000 miles of railway.

The station itself, which, with its numerous departure and arrival platforms, offices, engine-sheds, and workshops, covers several acres of ground, is built close up to the hotel. Its chief feature, from an architectural point of view, is its triple-spanned roof of glass and iron, which, having been erected shortly after the Great Exhibition of 1851, may be said to have been one of the first adaptations of that principle of construction upon a gigantic scale; and it is almost needless to add that it has since been copied, more or less exactly, at almost all the large railway stations of the metropolis. The length of this building of glass is 263 yards, its breadth is 93 yards, and the central span of the roof is no less than 70 feet in height.

As an instance of the improvement made in travelling since the days of George I., we may mention that, whereas in 1725 the stage-coach journey from London to Exeter occupied four long summer days, the express train on the Great Western Railway now accomplishes the distance in little more than four hours. In those good old days, as we learn from letters still preserved in families of the west country, the passengers were roused each morning at two o'clock, started at three, dined at ten, and finished their day's journey at three in the afternoon!

CHAPTER XVIII.

UNDERGROUND LONDON: ITS RAILWAYS, SUBWAYS, AND SEWERS.

"Thus far into the bowels of the land
Have I rode on."

Proposal of a Scheme for Underground Railways—Difficulties and Oppositions it had to encounter—Commencement of the Undertaking—Irruption of the Fleet Ditch—Opening of the Metropolitan Railway—Influx of Bills to Parliament for the Formation of other Underground Lines—Adoption of the "Inner Circle" Plan—Description of the Metropolitan Railway and its Stations—The "Nursery-maids' Walk"—A Great Triumph of Engineering Skill—Extension of the Line from Moorgate Street—The East London Railway—Engines and Carriages, and Mode of Lighting—Signalling—Ventilation of the Tunnel—Description of the Metropolitan District Railway—Workmen's Trains—The Water Supply and Drainage of London—Subways for Gas, Sewage, and other Purposes.

As we are now at Paddington, which is the common centre of three railways, and, in a certain sense, was the birth-place of the Great Western and the Metropolitan lines, it may be well to descend the steps which lead to one of the platforms of the latter company, and to ask our readers to accompany us, mentally, of course, in a "journey underground."

The overcrowding of the London streets, and the consequent difficulty and danger of locomotion, had been for many years a theme of constant agitation in the metropolis. Numberless plans were propounded for the relief of the over-gorged ways in connection with the vehicular circulation of the streets. New lines of streets were formed, and fresh channels of communication were opened; but all to little purpose. The crowd of omnibuses, cabs, and vehicles of all descriptions in our main thoroughfares remained as dense and impassable as ever. At length it was proposed to relieve the traffic of the streets by subterranean means; and in the end a scheme was propounded "to encircle the metropolis with a tunnel, which was to be in communication with all the railway termini—whether northern, or eastern, or western, north-western, or south-western—and so be able to convey passengers from whatever part of the country they might come to whatever quarter of the town they might desire to visit, without forcing them to traverse the streets in order to arrive there."

"Such a scheme," writes a well-known author, "though it has proved one of the most successful of modern times, met with the same difficulties and oppositions that every new project has to encounter. Hosts of objections were raised; all manner of imaginary evils were prophesied; and Mr. Charles Pearson, like George Stephenson before him, had to stand in that pillory to which all public men are condemned, and to be pelted with the missiles which ignorance and prejudice can always find ready to their hands. The project was regarded with the same contempt as the first proposal to light our streets with gas; it was the scheme of a 'wild visionary:' and as Sir Humphrey Davy had said that it would require a mound of earth as large as Primrose Hill to weigh down the gasometers of the proposed new gas-works, before London could be safely illuminated by the destructive distillation of coal, so learned engineers were not wanting to foretell how the projected tunnel must necessarily fall in from the mere weight of the traffic in the streets above; and how the adjacent houses would be not only shaken to their foundation by the vibration caused by the engines, but the families residing in them would be one and all poisoned by the sulphurous exhalations from the fuel with which the boilers were heated."

After years of hard work and agitation, confidence in the undertaking at length gained ground, and the scheme was set on foot about the year 1860. The Great Western Railway, with the view of obtaining access for their traffic to the City, came forward with £200,000 as a subscription to the enterprise; while the Corporation of the City of London, finding that the new lines of streets were comparatively useless as a means of draining off the vehicles from the main thoroughfares, also agreed to subscribe a similar sum to ensure the accomplishment of the object. Up to this time the shares in the undertaking had been at a low discount; and the low price, indeed, continued even after both the City and the Great Western Company had subscribed. The shares gradually attained higher prices as the prospects of opening the line increased; but after the opening they rose so rapidly as to promise an enormous return to the promoters.

From a *brochure*, entitled "The Metropolitan Railway," published in 1865, we learn that "during the construction of the Underground line, the meandering stream of the Fleet ditch had to be crossed at least three times, before its cloacinal flood was diverted from its previous course. Bell-mouthed tunnels had to be made, so as to bring two subterranean borings into one; and stations, which were merely enormous cellars built deep underground, had to be illuminated by the light of day. Moreover, new forms of engines and carriages had to be designed—engines which would evolve neither smoke nor steam, and carriages which could be lighted by gas, so that the usual unpleasant atmosphere and obscurity of railway tunnels might be avoided. Further, it was necessary to devise a special system of signals in connection with the line, upon which it was intended that train after train should succeed one another, with but a few minutes' intervals, throughout the day." In spite of a variety of difficulties, including an irruption of the Fleet ditch in the neighbourhood of King's Cross, the permanent way was opened for passenger traffic from Paddington to Farringdon Street on the 10th of January, 1863. It was calculated that over 30,000 persons were carried over the line in the course of the day. Indeed, the desire to travel by this line on the opening day was more than the directors had provided for, and from nine o'clock in the morning till past midday it was impossible to obtain a place in the up or Cityward line at any of the mid-stations. In the evening the tide turned, and the crowd at the Farringdon Street station was as great as at the doors of a theatre on the first night of some popular performer. At first the directors of the Great Western undertook the management of the line, but such differences soon arose between the two companies that, some seven months afterwards, the Great Western directors gave notice that in two months they would cease to continue their carriages upon it, and on the 1st of August following they reduced the notice as to their secession from the management of the line to ten days. In the short interval left to the Metropolitan Company to undertake the conduct of the traffic, engines and carriages had to be hired from what other railway companies were able and willing to supply them. Accordingly, on the 10th of August, 1863, the Metropolitan Company commenced working the line themselves, and have since continued to do so. "The traffic, indeed, by the Underground Railway," says the writer of the above-mentioned work, "is of so special and peculiar a character as to cause it to differ totally from all other railways, and to make it require a distinct management. The attention of the authorities in connection with large systems of railways is devoted chiefly to what is called the 'long-traffic' element; whereas, the Metropolitan—being essentially a 'short-traffic' line, and the numbers carried upon it being so great, as well as the trains so numerous throughout the day—needs an amount of care and continual supervision in its working, which could not possibly be given by the officers of those lines where trains are in the habit of succeeding one another at comparatively lengthened intervals. It is, therefore, much to the public advantage that the Underground Railway should be worked by the company itself, and that an organised staff of officials should be specially trained and maintained for the duty."

So great was the success of the Metropolitan Railway, from the very day of its inauguration, that in the next session of Parliament there was such an influx of bills for the proposed formation of railway lines in connection with the new form of transit in the metropolis, that it was found that "nearly one-half of the City itself would have to be demolished if the majority of the plans were carried out, and that almost every open space of ground or square in the heart of the metropolis would have to be given up for the erection of some terminus, with its screaming and hissing locomotives. The consequence was that a Committee of the two Houses was formed to take the whole of the metropolitan schemes into consideration, as well as to determine what general plan should be adopted, in order to unite together the various threads of the railway lines converging towards the capital, and forming the principal fibres of that great web of iron highways which had been spun over the country since the opening of the Liverpool and Manchester line in 1830. Accordingly, after deliberating for some time upon the matter, the Legislature came to the determination to adopt what is now known as the 'inner circle' plan of Mr. Fowler (the engineer of the line of which we are treating), and to recommend the carrying out of an 'outer circle' also."

On the first opening of the Underground Railway the line extended only from Bishop's Road, Paddington, to Farringdon Street; and in the course of a twelvemonth the number of passengers by it amounted to nearly 9,500,000, or, in round numbers, more than three times the entire population of the capital; but this number was almost doubled in the course of two years. Since the extension of the line, which we shall presently notice, the number of passengers who have availed themselves of this means of transit has amounted to nearly fifty millions annually.

The number of trains running upon this line is about 350 on week days, and 200 on Sundays; and they travel at intervals of five to ten minutes, between the hours of 5.15 a.m. up to midnight.

The original terminal point of this railway, as we have stated above, was at Bishop's Road. The station here adjoins the terminus of the Great Western line, and there is a covered way for passengers leading from the one station to the other. Between Bishop's Road and Edgware Road the Underground Line, being extended westward, now takes a semi-circular sweep round the western extremity of London, by way of Notting Hill Gate, Kensington, Sloane Square, and Westminster, and so on by a tunnel along the Victoria Embankment to Blackfriars and the Mansion House Station in Cannon Street.

Passing eastward from Bishop's Road, the line, in the course of half a mile, reaches the Edgware Road Station, where are workshops for the repair of the company's engines and carriages. Unlike most of the stations on this route, that at Edgware Road has the advantage of being open and above ground. From Edgware Road another half-mile or so of tunnel eastward brings the passenger to the Baker Street Station. The entrances to this station are in Baker Street, on either side of the Marylebone Road, broad flights of stairs leading down to the platforms; this part of the station, with the line itself, being immediately under the roadway. Great ingenuity is displayed in the construction of this station, for although so deep underground, it enjoys the advantage of daylight, which is made to glance down from the roadway above through long shafts lined with white glazed tiles. From Baker Street a branch line of the Underground Railway conveys passengers northward, by St. John's Wood, Marlborough Road, and the Swiss Cottage Stations, within a few minutes' walk of the breezy heights of Hampstead, and so on by Kilburn and Brondesbury to Harrow.

Resuming our course towards the City, the next station from Baker Street, which is reached through another tunnel about half a mile long, is at Portland Road, near the top of Portland Place. This is at what is called the "summit-level" of the line, and two large circular openings have been constructed over the line for the purpose of ventilation. Smaller openings for the ventilation of the tunnel have been made between other stations. Large numbers are conveyed to this station, on their way to the Regent's Park and the Zoological Gardens. "It is a peculiarity of this district," says the author above quoted, "that, between the semi-circular enclosure of Park Crescent and the quadrangular space within Park Square, a tunnel under the New Road has been for a long time in existence, as a means of uniting the two enclosures. This was familiarly known as the 'Nursery-maids' Walk,' and was the means by which the children of the residents in Park Crescent could avail themselves of the extra accommodation afforded them by the enclosure of Park Square; and such was the resistance offered by the inhabitants of this part to the progress of the railway, that ascending and descending gradients, to the extent of 1 in 100, had to be introduced, so as to carry the line under this subterranean thoroughfare, for the benefit of the nursery-maids and children of this highly-genteel neighbourhood."

From Portland Road the line is continued, by a tunnel rather under half a mile long, to Gower Street. The station here is very similar in construction to that of Baker Street, being originally lighted by the reflection afforded by white glazed tiles from the roadway above. Since its construction, however, it has been opened up very much to the upper air with very decided advantage both to its light and ventilation. This is a convenient outlet for the country immigrants arriving at the Euston Square Station of the London and North-Western Railway; and it is also available for those residing in the densely-populated district of Tottenham Court Road. A tunnel, three-quarters of a mile in length, next brings the passenger to King's Cross Station, which is one of the finest in point of construction of any on the line; the roof especially is worthy of notice, for the length and proportion of its span. Within the station itself, the up and down lines from the Great Northern and Midland Railway enter the King's Cross Station, and thence to Farringdon Road pass through a separate tunnel running parallel with the Metropolitan line. In the formation of this second tunnel immense engineering difficulties had to be met, and were successfully accomplished, the union of the two tunnels being effected upon the "bell-mouth" principle, similar to that between Edgware Road and Bishop's Road. The Midland Railway, as we shall hereafter see, when we come to Camden Town, was carried out by a triumph of engineering skill, under the Grand Junction Canal. Shortly before reaching King's Cross, the great Fleet sewer crosses both the junction lines; and during the construction of the aqueduct through which it was ultimately to pass, it was necessary that the sewage should not be interrupted for a moment; moreover, in addition to the difficulties connected with such a work, it may be stated that the whole of the sewage had to be conducted under the roadway; it now passes through an immense wrought-iron tube, some dozen feet in diameter, bedded in brickwork.

The line, on leaving King's Cross, takes a curve in a southerly direction, and shortly afterwards passes under the Fleet ditch a second time, by a short piece of tunnelling, and then, after passing through an open cutting, and another tunnel about half a mile in length, the line passes under a bridge, which serves as a viaduct to Ray Street, Clerkenwell, and carries the traffic over the railway. Once more the line passes under the Fleet ditch; the contents of this, which is within the station-yard of Farringdon Road, are conveyed across the line in one span in a capacious wrought-iron tube, and in the formation of the line at this point considerable difficulty was experienced in consequence of the sewer on two or three different occasions bursting its bounds, and thereby greatly impeding the progress of the work. Close by this sewer is another bridge for carrying the traffic over the railway; it is constructed mainly of iron, and was built in 1875-6, in order to form part of the new direct thoroughfare which connects Oxford Street with Old Street, St. Luke's.

It should be stated here that shortly before emerging into the light of day at Farringdon Street, the tunnel of the Midland and Great Northern lines is made to dive from north-east to south-west under that of the Metropolitan, which here is some thirty feet below the surface, revealing the fact that "even in the lowest depths there is a lower still," and displaying one of the greatest triumphs of the engineers' art to be seen in the neighbourhood of London. This gigantic "tunnel under another tunnel" was carried into effect without the stoppage of a single train on the Metropolitan Railway. The illustration on page 229 represents the passage of a Metropolitan train over the Great Northern and Midland lines near Farringdon Road Station.

Farringdon Road Station is very spacious, and, with the goods depôt of the Great Northern Railway, cover a large space of ground between the main road and Turnmill Street. This station was at first the utmost limit of the line Citywards; but by degrees the railway has been gradually extended eastward, the intention of the Metropolitan being ultimately to form a connection with the other end at the Mansion House Station. After leaving Farringdon Road the line passes, by means of a short tunnel, under the Metropolitan Meat Market at Smithfield, and then, after once more coming into daylight, enters the large and well-built station of Aldersgate Street, the lines being duplicated. Here there is a junction of the main line with that of the London, Chatham, and Dover Railway, which passes under Smithfield, then on under Holborn Viaduct, and so on to Ludgate Hill in its way southward. From Aldersgate Street, the Metropolitan Railway continues by a short tunnel and an open cutting on to Moorgate Street, which was for some time the farthest extent of the line in this direction. In 1875 the line was continued to Liverpool Street, where it forms a junction with the Great Eastern Railway. Since then it has been extended to Aldgate, and thence to the Tower. After passing under Finsbury Circus towards Bishopsgate Station in Liverpool Street, the railway tunnel is carried between the chapel of St. Mary's, Moorfields, and Finsbury Chapel, and in the construction of this portion of the line considerable engineering difficulties had to be surmounted.

In the meantime, other subterranean works in connection with the modern system of locomotion had been going on further eastward; and by this means the northern and south-eastern hemispheres of London, so to speak, have been banded together by the iron girdle of the East London Railway, which, passing on through Whitechapel and Shadwell, and then through the old Thames Tunnel to Rotherhithe and Deptford Road, terminates at New Cross, where it joins the Brighton line.

Throughout the whole length of the various

systems of Underground Railways, it may be safely asserted that the works are signal instances of modern engineering skill and ingenuity. The rails on the Metropolitan Line were originally laid on the mixed-gauge principle, the rails themselves having steeled surfaces given to them; but these being found to be not of a very durable character, were gradually replaced with others of solid steel, which, although much more costly to lay down, have been found to be more lasting, and consequently cheaper in the end. Within the last few years, the broad-gauge rails have been taken up, and only the narrow-gauge is now used.

So far as the engines and carriages are concerned, but little need be said here. The former are fine, powerful machines, specially designed by Mr. Fowler, the engineer-in chief; and they are arranged either to exhaust the steam through the chimney in the ordinary way, or else to condense it in tanks which are placed on either side of the engine, and contain 1,000 gallons of water—a supply sufficient for the double journey. The carriages are extremely large and roomy vehicles, the united bodies being no less than forty feet long. The first-class carriages are luxuriously fitted up, and are constructed to carry sixty passengers; whilst the second and third classes carry as many as eighty persons respectively, and very frequently more. The mode of lighting the carriages is by gas, which is carried in long india-rubber bags, within wooden boxes, arranged on the tops of the carriages, and extending from one end to the other of each set of vehicles composing the train. "These gas bags," says the writer of the work above referred to, "are weighted on the top, and, as the weights descend, an indicator, at the side of each box, points either to E or F, to show how near the india-rubber reservoirs are to being either *empty* or *full*. The jets in the carriages are supplied by means of a gas-pipe in communication with the bags on the roofs, and extending from the back of the vehicles themselves, while along the lower part of each portion of the train runs the 'main,' as it were, by which the bags are replenished from the gasometers established at either end of the line. The gasholders are kept charged with supplies from the neighbouring gas-works, and are so heavily weighted that the elastic bags along the top of the carriages can be filled (by means of 'hydrants' and flexible tubes in connection with the gas-holders) in the short space of two or three minutes. The light thus afforded to the passengers is so bright

TRIAL-TRIP ON THE UNDERGROUND RAILWAY, 1863. (*See page* 225.)

as to utterly remove all sense of travelling underground, and entirely dissipate that nervousness which the semi-obscurity of ordinary oil-lighted railway carriages gives to the sensitive during their transit through the tunnels on other lines."

From the rapid rate at which the trains are dis-

ENTRANCE TO THE CLERKENWELL TUNNEL FROM FARRINGDON STREET. (*See page* 227.)

patched one after the other on this line, it will be readily conceived that the system of signalling must be one of the greatest exactitude in order to ensure perfect safety. The system, however, is so simple, and at the same time so certain, as "to require no exercise of skill on the part of the signal-man, but rather to bring the official working them down to the level of the unerring machine upon which he has to operate." The following extract from the *Railway News* gives all that need be said on this subject:—

"We will suppose," says the writer of a clever article upon "Underground Signals," in the publication before mentioned, "the signal-man to be at Baker Street; on the down line he will have possession of the line to the Edgware Road Station, on the up line possession of the length to Portland Road Station. In the front of each dial there is an opening, in which appears, as the case may be, the words 'Line clear' on a white ground, or, 'Train on line,' on a red ground. Below this are two keys, one red and one white, having over them corresponding words to those which appear in the opening on the face of the telegraph dial. Press the white key, and the words 'Line clear' are shown on the instruments; press the red key, and the words 'Train on line' appear. There is no movement of needles to the one side or the other, which may be liable to be mistaken; there is no sound of a bell, which may be misunderstood. The needle of the dial does not point to a communication which it wishes to make, but it carries on its back the actual message, and presents it to the sight of the person for whom it is intended.

"Let us see how this system is carried into actual practice. A passenger train is about to start from Edgware Road on the up-line. The signal-man presses down a key, which rings a bell at Baker Street to call attention. This bell has a conducting wire, entirely separated from that connected with the signalling instruments, so that no mistake can occur in the transmission of signals. The beats on the bell are made to describe the approaching train, whether it be a Metropolitan, Great Western, or Great Northern one. Having thus called attention, he presses down the red key, and at Baker Street is instantly shown the signal 'Train on line.' Baker Street replies by repeating the beats on the bell, and pegs down the key which corresponds to the signal shown. Edgware Road puts the signal to 'Danger,' to prevent any up-line train from following, and Baker Street keeps the signal pegged down until the train has not only reached him, but has actually passed out of the station. After the train has left Baker Street it is signalled on to Portland Road, just as it had previously been sent on from the Edgware Road. The Baker Street sends back to Edgware Road three beats on his bell, re-pegs his red key, presses down a white key, which shows 'Line clear.' The signal is acknowledged, the white key pegged down by the signal-man at Edgware Road, who thus takes possession of the line up to Baker Street. When the train has left Portland Road Station, Baker Street is signalled to, just as Edgware Road had been, and the up-line is clear to the next station. And so the work goes on from station to station throughout the day, and trains may run with safety at intervals of two minutes, whereas, without these signals, it would not have been possible to run more frequently than every quarter of an hour."

The question of ventilation of the Underground Railway gave rise to considerable discussion at the time of the formation of the line, and, indeed, long afterwards, and various means were adopted by which that "vexed question" could be set at rest. Instead of the coal used on ordinary lines the company have used coke made from the best and finest Durham coal, and burnt in the ovens for a very long time, in order to deprive it of every trace of sulphur and other objectionable exhalations. We have already seen how that the engines are specially constructed to exhaust the steam during the transit of the trains. By these means the engines may be said to "hold their breath," as it were, whilst travelling through these lower regions, and thus little or no foul sulphurous fumes are evolved from the chimney, nor waste steam discharged. One part of the line, nevertheless, from some cause or other, remained in which the foul air continued to cause annoyance and discomfort to passengers. This extended from the Portland Road to the Gower Street Station. Between these stations the arch of the railway tunnel is crossed nearly at right angles by the tube of the old Pneumatic Despatch Company. In a lucky moment the "happy thought" arose that this tube might be made subservient towards the removal of the foul air in the tunnel beneath, and the more efficient ventilation of the railway in its immediate vicinity. In 1874 this idea was most successfully worked out and practically applied in a very ingenious manner to the desired purpose by Mr. De Wylde, the engineer to the Pneumatic Despatch Company, who was materially assisted in his labours by Mr. Tomlinson, the engineer of the Metropolitan line.

From the above description of the Underground Railway, it will be at once perceived that there is scarcely any part of London or any of its outlying districts which cannot now be reached by rail, and by trains that are arriving and departing every few minutes. The Metropolitan Railway is, indeed, a mighty underground undertaking, by which, in half an hour, the heart of the City is reached with comfort and safety from Hammersmith or Notting Hill, Kensington or Brompton, and nearly all round London. Travelling seems to have reached its climax, when what was half a day's journey twenty years ago is done now in a quarter of an hour—for it requires but some such interval of time as that between shaking hands with friends in parting at the Mansion House, and doing the same with others on meeting in Camden Town. The Metropolitan Railway service appears to be capable of almost indefinite extension. There are now six companies which are exclusively devoted to the metropolitan railway traffic—the Metropolitan, the Metropolitan District, the Metropolitan and St. John's Wood, the North London, the East London, and the London, Chatham, and Dover.

The "District Railway" owns nearly half of the whole line, and has the advantage, in one respect; its portion of the stations being all open to the daylight, and the tunnels not so frequent. Its terminal station, the "Mansion House," within a few minutes' walk of the Exchange, the Bank, St. Paul's Cathedral, and the heart of the City, is a handsome, light, commodious building, spanned with an iron and glass roof. The space is necessarily somewhat cramped in a spot where land is said to be more valuable than anywhere else in the world. There are only three lines of rails, and the same number of platforms; but although, from 8 a.m. to 8 p.m., thirteen trains run in and out every hour, this is found sufficient accommodation, even when there is an unusual pressure of business; and occasionally three trains have entered the station, discharged their passengers, been re-filled, and supplied with gas, in six minutes.

On leaving the Mansion House Station, the line passes westward along under Queen Victoria Street, to Blackfriars Bridge, where there is a station, which, although the platforms are considerably below the level of the outer roadway, is open to the light of day. In the neighbourhood of Blackfriars Bridge, the railway is crossed by a tramroad for the conveyance of coals from the river to the works of the City Gas Company; and nearly at the same point the subway of the Embankment rises to the surface. The low-level sewer crosses obliquely beneath the railway; and the Fleet Ditch also crosses beneath it at right angles, previous to joining the low-level sewer. The "Fleet" formerly opened and discharged its contents into the river under the first arch of the bridge.

At various points of the railway sewers pass beneath it to enter the low-level main sewer; and the summits of these sewers, as originally constructed, would rise somewhat above the permanent way. It was, of course, impossible to lower them, and the difficulty was surmounted by giving a depressed shape to portions that pass under the line. The original sewers presented elliptical sections, with the major axis vertical, and the new portions have their major axis horizontal. In this way the necessary area is preserved, and the line is only so far interfered with that the sleepers are carried over the sewers on a bridge of iron plates. The railway itself is drained by a barrel-drain along the "six-foot" space, and this drain is carried below each sewer and back to its former level by four rectangular bends. The original opening of the Fleet Ditch was immediately to the westward of Blackfriars Bridge, and under the management of the Board of Works its new opening has been made beneath the bridge. Beneath the station it was found necessary, at the construction of the works, to lower the level and contract the area of the diversion of the Fleet which had to be made, by which it emptied its contents into the river on the east side of the bridge; for this purpose another diversion was made to the eastward of the first, leaving it to the north, and re-entering it at the south of the station. When this was completed, the portion of the first diversion that passed under the station was converted into a barrel-drain by iron tubing seven feet in diameter; and then the second diversion was closed. The low-level sewer at first passed beneath the barrel-drain, but was eventually connected with the Fleet channel, so as to relieve the latter of some portion of the contents. The tramroad to the City gas-works passes under the roadway of the Embankment, and over the railway; and the subway of the Embankment is also carried over the railway. Close by Blackfriars Station, in Earl Street, nearly equal difficulties were encountered on a smaller scale, from the number of gas-pipes, water-pipes, and other channels that crossed the line near together, and at all possible levels. These pipes, however, have all been re-arranged in a regular and orderly manner. The difficulty of finding room for all these requirements was extreme, as may well be imagined.

A short piece of tunneling along the Victoria Embankment brings us to the Temple Station, which is the nearest outlet for the eastern parts of the Strand. Within the precincts of the Temple, as a precautionary measure against the interruption of legal studies by noise and vibration, the sleepers rest upon a layer of tan, six inches in thickness, placed immediately below the ballast. This plan had already been adopted, with good results, in the neighbourhood of Westminster Abbey, and the Benchers of the Temple made its employment one of the conditions of their approval of the line.

The Embankment, beneath which the line passes on by Somerset House and Charing Cross (where there is another station) to Westminster Bridge, is, we need hardly say, one of the most successful pieces of engineering skill which this country has ever produced; but it was not effected without considerable risk and danger to surrounding property; indeed, owing to the undermining of the foundation of King's College, which adjoins Somerset House, the roof of the hall gave way, and fears were at one time entertained as to the safety of the building. Besides the railway tunnel there are other immense subways passing along it, some of which serve the purposes of the main drainage, the low-level sewer of the northern system, as we have already shown, passing this way in its course from Pimlico towards the east of London. The railway also passes under the first arch of Waterloo Bridge. For some portion of the distance between Charing

Cross and Westminster Bridge the line is covered in by iron girders, placed obliquely, and connected by brickwork; this was so arranged in order to support a garden attached to the offices of the Board of Control.

The distance from Blackfriars Station to Westminster Bridge Station is 2,200 yards, and the stations are very nearly equidistant. Instead of the semi-circular arched roof usually found in other tunnels, that in the Embankment is flat, formed of transverse iron girders placed about eight feet apart, with shallow brick arches between them, and supported on brick walls, about fourteen feet in height, the south of which is in contact with the concrete of the Embankment.

At Westminster there is a branch tunnel or subway which passes under the roadway at the foot of the bridge to the Houses of Parliament. In the construction of the tunnel between Westminster Bridge and the St. James's Park Stations, great difficulties presented themselves from the irregular nature of the soil, but these were in the end surmounted; and in the course of the excavations at this point quantities of bones of animals—supposed to be those of the mammoth and other antediluvian animals—were unearthed. Another difficulty arose from the fear of the excavations weakening the foundations of the Abbey. The line passes almost close under the walls of St. Margaret's Church and Westminster Abbey, and emerges into daylight close by Queen Anne's Gate, near the St. James's Park Station. The next station is Victoria, which is situated close to that of the Brighton and the London, Chatham, and Dover Railways. Leaving this station the line proceeds, by a short tunnel, under Eccleston and Ebury Streets, Pimlico, to Sloane Square, where there is a large and commodious station. A few minutes' ride next brings us to South Kensington Station, which, with its far-stretching roof of iron and glass, is light and open. Here we may be said to have got clear of "underground London," for although the line passes on for some distance before it reaches Paddington, which we made our starting point, a considerable portion of it is open to the light of day. The stations passed before arriving at Praed Street, Paddington, are the Gloucester Road (whence there are branches to West Brompton, Addison Road, and Hammersmith); High Street, Kensington; Notting Hill Gate; Queen's Road, Bayswater.

One feature of the Metropolitan and of the District Railway is the facility which it gives to working men who, through the demolition of small dwelling-houses in London, or from other circumstances, may have taken up their abode in the western suburbs. When the Metropolitan Company obtained their extension to Moorgate Street, the Act of Parliament—obtained mainly through the instrumentality of the late Lord Derby—imposed upon them the condition that *one* train daily should run *to* the City in the morning, and one train *from* the City at night, "for the convenience of workmen living in the environs," and that the fares should be one penny for each single journey by such trains. The experiment was tried before the formation of the line between Farringdon Road and Moorgate Street; and in one of the trains so run, the author of the *brochure* quoted from above thus gives us his experiences of the class of men he met with:—

"Our object was to ride in the train with the workmen themselves, and to hear from them what benefits they derived from the institution. Early as was the hour, we found the platform all of a bustle with men, many of whom had bass baskets in their hands, or tin flagons, or basins done up in red handkerchiefs. Some few carried large saws under their arms, and beneath the overcoat of others one could just see a little bit of the flannel jacket worn by carpenters, whilst some were habited in the grey and clay-stained fustian peculiar to ground labourers. There was but little time for the arrangement of plans with the general manager ere the whistle screamed, and we were thrust into a third-class compartment, which we found nearly filled with plasterers, joiners, and labourers.

"The subject of our mission was soon opened. All present agreed that the cheap and early trains were a great benefit to the operative classes. The labourer assured us that he saved at least two shillings a week by them in the matter of rent only. He lived at Notting Hill, and would have to walk six miles to and from his work every day if it were not for the convenience of the railway. He had two rooms now, almost in the open country, for the same price as he would have to pay for one in some close court in the heart of London, besides what he saved in medicine for his wife and family. A plasterer, who had to go all the way to Dockhead to his work, who was a fellow-passenger, took up the matter, and said that 'it was impossible to reckon up how much workmen gained by what is called the Workmen's Trains, especially if you took into account the saving in shoe-leather, the gain in health and strength, and the advantage it was for men to go to their work fresh and unfatigued by a long walk at the commencement of the day.' The plasterer, too, was great on the *moral* effects (it is astonishing how working men delight in the morality of a question), and urged, with some force, that the best thing in connection with such institutions was.

that it enabled operatives to have different sleeping-rooms for themselves and their young children.

"As the train stopped at Edgware Road, Baker Street, Portland Road, and, indeed, every other station, fresh crowds were waiting on the platform, ready to avail themselves of it; and when we reached Gower Street, we and the manager got into another carriage, so as to be able to consult as many working men as possible on the matter. Here we found a butcher on his way to the meat-market, a newsvendor going to fetch his morning papers, and others connected with the building trade. We spoke to a carpenter in a grey slouch hat, and with the brass top of his foot-rule just peeping out of the side pocket of his trousers. He was one of those strange growling and grumbling characters so often met with among the working classes. For his part, he didn't see that working men were in any way gainers by the cheap trains, as it cost them 1s. a week for travelling. All he knew was, that he paid about the same rent out at Paddington as when he lived in Clerkenwell; for landlords were landlords, all the world over. If a man did save 1s. a week, what was it? Only a pint of beer a day. Besides, the company hadn't kept faith with the public; they had made grand speeches in Parliament about the great benefits they were going to confer on the working classes by giving them penny trains, and directly they got their bill passed, by such humbug, they began by charging them twopence. What was a working man to save upon that, he should like to know?

"'Come, come, mate,' said another workman, 'fair's fair. Just think of what these here trains save you at night after your work's over. If a man gets home tired after his day's labour, he is inclined to be quarrelsome with his missus and the children, and this leads to all kinds of noises, and ends in his going off to the public for a little bit of quiet; while if he gets a ride home, and has a good rest after he has knocked off for the day, I can tell you he is as pleasant a fellow again over his supper. Besides, if a chap's on piece-work, as I am, it makes a good bit of difference in his earnings at the week's end, whether he goes to his work fagged with walking a long way to it, or comes fresh to it after a ride.'

"On our way to Farringdon Street we passed the early down-train; and this, we could just see, was full of costermongers coming from the Saturday morning's market. At a later part of the same day we travelled from the City to Bishop's Road, in company with other men returning from their work. Many of these lived out at Silver Street, Notting Hill. One man in particular was very communicative, and delighted to go into all the details of what he saved by being able to live in the suburbs. 'He had a six-roomed house, with a kitchen,' he said, 'and for this he paid £28 the year, rent and taxes. He let off four rooms for 8s. the week, so that he stood at about 3s. a week rent for himself, and for the same accommodation as he had now he would have to pay from 6s. to 6s. 6d. the week in some wretched dog-hole in town.' He certainly found that things were very dear out at Kensington, where he lived; but this made hardly any difference to him, for he did all his marketing at Newgate Market after his work was over, early on the Saturday. 'See here, sir,' said he, spreading open the bass-basket on his knee, 'there's a prime bit of ribs of beef for the young ones to pitch into to-morrow. I gave 7½d. the pound for it, and where I hang out it would have cost me 10d. or 11d. There ain't so much difference in vegetables, and bread's pretty well the same price everywhere. It's mostly people in the building trade as comes up by these trains to the heavy jobs in the City. No one can say what benefit the trains are to men like us. Why, I've made seven and a half days this week, and if it wasn't for the convenience of them, I shouldn't have done six.'"

So much for the Underground Railway. This, however, although a very gigantic work, is but a fraction, so to speak, of the intricate and almost inexplicable labyrinth of arteries and sinews that go to make up the great body of "Underground London." Mr. Charles Knight, in his "London," has pithily remarked:—"Could we imagine that this great capital of capitals should ever be what Babylon is—its very site forgotten—one could not but almost envy the delight with which the antiquaries of that future time would hear of some discovery of a *London below the soil* still remaining. We can fancy we see the progress of the excavators from one part to another of the mighty but, for a while, inexplicable labyrinth, till the whole was cleared open to the daylight, and the vast system lay bare before them, revealing, in the clearest language, the magnitude and splendour of the place to which it had belonged, the skill and enterprise of the people. Let us reflect for a moment upon what this system accomplishes. Do we want water in our houses? We turn a small instrument, and the limpid stream from the springs of Hertfordshire, or of Hampstead Heath, or from the river Thames, comes flowing, as it were by magic, into our vessels. Do we wish to get rid of it when no longer serviceable? The trouble is no greater; in an instant it is on its way through the silent depths. Do we wish for an artificial day? Through that same mysterious channel comes steaming up into every corner of our chambers, counting-houses, or shops, the subtle air which waits but our bidding to become—light! The tales which amuse our childhood have no greater marvels than these." Yet, as the very nature of a system of underground communication prevents it from being one of the shows of the metropolis, we seldom think of it; unless, indeed, when passing through the streets we at times come across an open sewer that has been laid bare for repairs or some other purpose; or when we see an artisan at work in repairing a breach in a telegraph wire, when the fibrous substance which forms the means of transmitting the electrical communication is lying gathered up in coils from its receptacle beneath the pavement. The sewage, the gas and water supply, and the electric telegraph, then, are the matters which we have to consider in the present chapter.

The Fleet Ditch, of which we have given an account in a previous volume,* was for centuries the principal channel for conveying the sewage of the metropolis into the Thames. Its commencement was from springs on the southern slopes of the ridge of Hampstead and Highgate Hills; and in its course towards the Thames at Blackfriars it received the drainage of parts of Hampstead and Highgate, of all Kentish Town, Camden Town, and Somers Town, of parts of Islington, Clerkenwell, and St. Sepulchre, and nearly all that part of the Holborn division lying south of the Euston Road, from Paddington to the City. The private drains from each house entered the main sewer in all cases about two feet from its level; and these drains carried off every description of refuse, with the exception of such as was conveyed away by the London dustman. Scientific experiments were made to discover the best and most economical mode of cleansing the sewers, the deposit at the bottom of which averaged one and a-half inches yearly, and an ingenious apparatus was invented for using water in flushes, by which the sewers were effectually scoured. "The water used for forming a head was contracted for with the water companies, and amounted to about 20,000 hogsheads yearly. When a sewer was to be cleansed, the water was backed up, and when let off, it cleansed the sewer to an extent proportionate to the quantity of head-water, the fall of the sewer, and the depth of the deposit. The breaking-up of streets to cleanse the sewers, when their contents were deposited on the surface, was avoided by means of a flushing apparatus. Under the old system, the deposit accumulated at the bottom of the sewer, until the private drains leading into it became choked; and it was only from the complaints arising from this circumstance that the Commissioners of Sewers became aware of the state of the main drain, and that smaller drains, connected with the main sewer, were generally choked also."

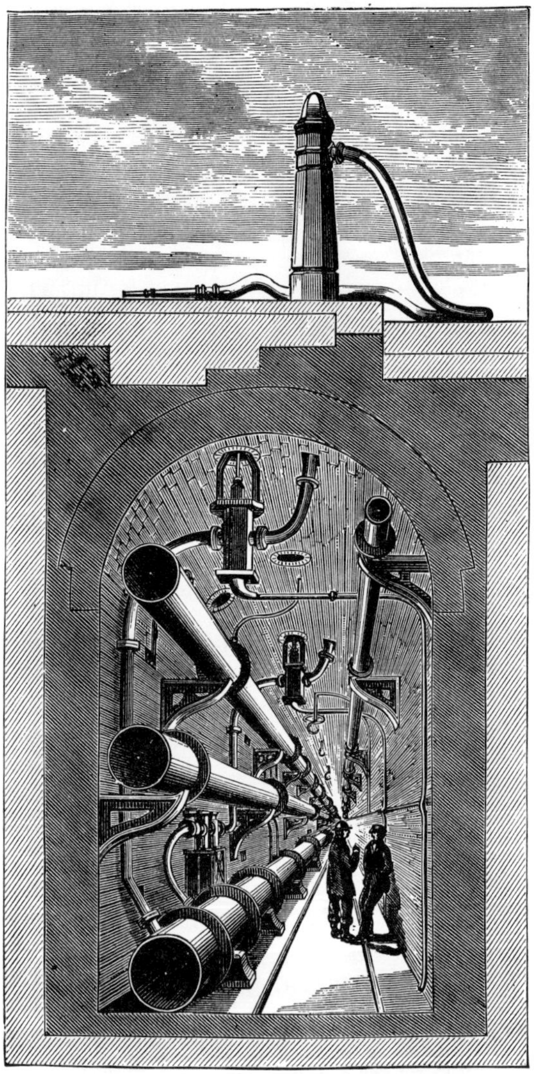

INTERIOR OF SUBWAY, HOLBORN VIADUCT.
From Mr. Haywood's Report. (*See page* 239.)

In 1847, the eight boards of commissioners—comprising those for the City, Westminster, Holborn and Finsbury, Tower Hamlets, Poplar and Blackwall, Surrey and Kent, Greenwich and St. Katherine's—were superseded by one commission, termed "The Metropolitan Commissioners

* See Vol. II., pp. 416—423.

SECTION OF THE HOLBORN VIADUCT, SHOWING THE SUBWAYS.

Taken by Permission from Mr. Haywood's Report. (*See page* 239.)

of Sewers," whose members were nominated by the Government, and during the nine succeeding years six new and differently-constituted commissions were successively appointed; but throughout this period they appear to have been unable to mature and carry out works of any magnitude with the view of remedying the evils arising from the sewage flowing into the Thames. In 1854, Mr. Bazalgette, the chief engineer to the Commissioners of Sewers, was directed to prepare a scheme of intercepting sewers, intended to effect the main drainage of London, and Mr. Haywood was associated with him for the northern portion. These plans remained under consideration until the formation of the Metropolitan Board of Works, two years later, when fresh plans for the drainage of the metropolis were drawn up by Mr. (afterwards Sir Joseph) Bazalgette. After some further delay, these plans were eventually adopted, and the works were commenced in 1859. The chief object sought to be attained by the main drainage works was the interception of the sewage, so as to divert it from the river near London. New lines of sewers were accordingly constructed, laid at right angles to those already existing, and a little below their levels, so as to intercept their contents and convey them to outfalls about fourteen miles below London Bridge. These outfalls are situated at Barking Creek, in Essex, and at Crossness Point, in Erith Marshes. As large a proportion of the sewage as practicable is by this means carried away by gravitation into the salt water, and for the remainder a constant discharge is effected by pumping with powerful engines and machinery. At the outlets the sewage is received into reservoirs, situate on the banks of the Thames, and placed at such a level as will enable them to discharge into the river at or about the time of high water. By this arrangement the sewage is not only at once diluted by the large volume of salt water in the Thames at high water, but is also carried by the ebb tide to a point in the river some twenty-six miles below London Bridge, and the possibility of its return by the following tide within the metropolitan area is by this means effectually prevented.

The drainage of London on the north side of the Thames is effected by three lines of sewers, the High Level, the Middle Level, and the Low Level. The first of these commences by a junction with the old Fleet sewer, at the foot of Hampstead Hill, and passes through Upper Holloway, Stoke Newington, and Hackney Wick, to Abbey Mills pumping-station, near Plaistow; the second commences at Bayswater, and skirting Hyde Park, passes along Oxford Street, High Holborn, and by the railway-station in Farringdon Road, and Old Street Road, and joins the High Level sewer at Old Ford; whilst the Low Level sewer, with its branches, extends from Chiswick and Acton to Abbey Mills, passing on its way by Chelsea and Pimlico, where we have already noticed the large pumping-station,* and so on by the Houses of Parliament, and along the Victoria Embankment. From the pumping-station at Abbey Mills the drainage is conveyed across Plaistow Marshes by the outfall sewer to the reservoir at Barking Creek. On the south side of the Thames the intercepting sewers extend from Upper Norwood, Clapham, and Putney, in three main lines, to Deptford, where they unite, and thence pass on through Charlton and Woolwich, and across Plumstead Marsh to the pumping-house and reservoir at Crossness Point.

It need hardly be mentioned that during the formation of this vast net-work of sewers—comprising, as it does on the whole, something over 1,300 miles—a large number of ancient remains of animals, coins, and curiosities, were found; they consisted chiefly of the bones of elephants, whales, and horns of deer and oxen, with some flint implements of war, and human skulls, stone and leaden coffins, and a number of Roman coins.

It must not, however, be supposed that the various railway tunnels are all, or nearly all, the wonders of subterranean London, for the arrangements for supplying the metropolis with gas and water, and for carrying off the drainage from the streets and dwellings of the entire metropolis, are equally wonderful; and as these present a *terra incognita* to most readers of the educated classes, they may well claim a brief notice here.

Any one who has seen London at night from some elevation in the neighbourhood—say Hampstead Heath, or Sydenham Hill—will readily understand how minute, as well as extensive, must be the network of pipes overspreading its soil a few feet below the surface, to afford an unfailing supply of gas to illuminate such a vast space as is spread out before him. Thirty years after the general introduction of gas for the lighting of the metropolis—which took place in 1814—there were no less than eighteen public gas-works in London and its immediate vicinity, and twelve public gas-works companies; the capital employed in works, pipes, tanks, gas-holders, apparatus, &c., amounted to the sum of £2,800,000, and the yearly revenue derived represented nearly £500,000. 180,000

* See p. 41, *ante*.

tons of coal were annually used in the making of gas; 1,460,000,000 cubic feet of gas were made in the year; 134,300 private burners were supplied to about 400,000 customers; there were 30,400 public or street consumers—about 2,650 of these were in the City of London; 380 lamp-lighters were employed; 176 gas-holders, several of which were double ones, capable of storing 5,500,000 cubic feet; 890 tons of coal were used in the retorts in the shortest day, in twenty-four hours; 7,120,000 cubic feet of gas were used in the longest night (say 24th of December); and about 2,500 persons were employed in the metropolis alone in this branch of manufacture. Between the years 1822 and 1827 the consumption of gas was nearly doubled; and within the next ten years it was again nearly doubled; and since 1837 these figures must be trebled. Since 1841, when the above statistics were taken, many of the gas companies have amalgamated; and in 1872 their number was reduced to nine, a number which has since been slightly increased. One advantage of the amalgamation of the different companies is that the consumer's interests are more effectually provided for, and that the gas is supplied at a lower price and better in quality.

In a previous chapter we have spoken of the pipes that were laid from the conduit at Bayswater * in order to supply the City with water. We learn from Stow that this arrangement dated from the time of Henry III., when—"the river of the Wells, the running water of Walbrook, the bourns, and other the fresh water that were in and about the City, being in process of time, by encroachment for buildings, and otherwise heightening of grounds, utterly decayed, and the number of the citizens mightily increased, they were forced to seek sweet waters abroad"—at the request of the king, powers were "granted to the citizens and to their successors by one Gilbert Sanford, to convey water from the town of Tyburn, by pipes of lead, into the City." Besides the conduits which were set up in Cheapside, Leadenhall, Fleet Street, and other public places, "bosses" of water were also provided in different parts, which, like the conduits, in some places drew their supply from the Thames. The conduits and water-heads, as we have already had occasion to show, used to be regularly visited in former times by the Lord Mayor "and many worshipful persons, and divers of the masters and wardens of the twelve companies." During these early days the water had to be brought from the conduits to the dwellings of the inhabitants in pitchers or other vessels. It was not until 1582 that any great mechanical power or skill was applied in providing London with water; in that year, however, Peter Morris, a Dutchman, made at London Bridge a "most artificial forcier," by which water was conveyed into the houses. We are told how that, on the Lord Mayor and Aldermen going to view the works in operation, Morris, to show the efficiency of his machine, caused the water to be thrown over St. Magnus' Church. The water-works at the bridge were famous for a long time as one of the sights of London. In 1594 water-works of a similar kind were erected near Broken Wharf, which supplied the houses in West Cheap and around St. Paul's, as far as Fleet Street. This was all that was accomplished in the way of supplying London with water up to the appearance of Hugh Middleton, "citizen and goldsmith," upon the scene, early in the reign of James I. It seems that power had been granted by Elizabeth for cutting and conveying a river from any part of Middlesex or Hertfordshire to the City of London, with a limitation of ten years' time for the accomplishment of the work; but the man to accomplish it was not forthcoming. James I. confirmed the grant; and then it was that Middleton came forward with the offer of his wealth, skill, and energy. After long search and deliberation two springs rising in Hertfordshire were fixed upon, and in 1608 the work was actually commenced. Of the difficulties and obstacles with which the worthy "citizen and goldsmith" met in the accomplishment of his self-imposed task, and also of the "New River," which he formed, we have spoken in our account of Islington.*

When London, however, mustered beyond a million of inhabitants, even the "New River" failed to give an adequate supply of water to the mouths and the houses which required it, and other companies were formed for the purpose of supplying different parts of the great metropolis, and the Chelsea and other water-works were started by various companies in succession. Of some of these we have already made mention.

In 1833-4, the quantity of water *daily* supplied by the eight different water companies of London was upwards of 21,000,000 imperial gallons. By far the greatest portion of this was drawn from the Thames, a small quantity from the springs and ponds of Highgate and Hampstead, and the rest from the River Lea and the New River. The capital expended on the works of these companies then amounted to more than £3,000,000, and their

* See p. 183, *ante*.

* See Vol. II., p. 266.

gross rental to nearly £300,000. The number of houses or buildings supplied by them was nearly 200,000, each of which had an average supply of about 180 gallons, at a cost, also, on the average, of about 30s. yearly. It is not easy to ascertain the capital now sunk in the water-supply of the metropolis. But in 1876 the average daily supply of the following eight companies—Chelsea, East London, Grand Junction, Kent, Lambeth, New River, Southwark and Lambeth, and West Middlesex—was rather more than 120,000,000 gallons, upwards of 60,000,000 being taken from the Thames, and the rest from other sources. The Thames supply is drawn from various points, extending up the river as far as Hampton and Ditton; the rest comes to Londoners from the River Lea, and from the chalk-wells in the neighbourhood of Crayford, Chislehurst, Bromley, and Dartford, in Kent. The net-work of pipes underground to convey the water to almost every house in London, must indeed be something surprising; and it presents a striking contrast to the state of things which must have existed when the ancient conduits were the only sources of supply.

From the Report of the Examiner appointed by Government to test the purity of our water, as published by him in September, 1876, it appears that the number of miles of streets which contain mains constantly charged, and upon which hydrants for fire purposes could at once be fixed, is 667. The total number of hydrants erected at the above date was 4,211, of which 2,695 were for private purposes, 541 for street watering, 500 for public use, and 475 for Government establishments. Of the average daily supply of water in the metropolis one-fifth was delivered for other than domestic purposes. There are 398 acres of reservoirs with available capacity for the subsidence and storage of 1,041,550,000 gallons of unfiltered water, and covered reservoirs capable of storing 106,187,000 gallons of filtered water within the radius prescribed.

From an analytical report, made by Dr. Frankland, of the state of the Thames water supplied to the metropolis during the month of October, 1876, we learn that, taking unity to represent the amount of organic impurity (on this occasion) in a given volume of the Kent Company's water, the proportional amount in an equal volume of water supplied by each of the other metropolitan companies was as follows:—New River, 0·9; East London, 2·4; West Middlesex, 2·8; Grand Junction, 3·3; Lambeth, 4·1; Chelsea, 4·2; and Southwark, 4·5. The water delivered by the five companies drawing their supply exclusively from the Thames, compared with that delivered in August and September, showed a marked deterioration in quality, the proportion of contamination with organic matter in solution having increased. The West Middlesex Company delivered the best of the Thames waters. The sample of the Southwark Company's water was "slightly turbid from insufficient filtration, and contained moving organisms." The other samples of Thames water were, however, clear and transparent. The water supplied by the New River and the East London Companies was much superior in quality to that drawn from the Thames; indeed, the New River water, in chemical purity, is said to surpass even the deep well water delivered by the Kent Company, which rises in the chalk hills about Crayford.

Previous to the completion of the Main Drainage works, the system of drainage that had been adopted in London for several years gave an amount of sewerage almost equal in extent to the length of every street, lane, and alley in the metropolis. On the north side of the Thames there were about fifty main sewers, measuring upwards of a hundred miles; about twenty of equal magnitude, extending some sixty miles, were on the south side of the river. Add to these the private sewers, turnings, alleys, subways, &c., the mileage of sewerage might have been found of sufficient length to reach from London to Constantinople. Through these secret channels rolled the refuse of London, in a black, murky flood, here and there changing its temperature and its colour, as chemical dye-works, sugar-bakers, tallow-melters, and slaughterers added their tributary streams to the pestiferous rolling river. About 31,650,000,000 gallons of this liquid was poured yearly into the Thames, in its course through London, and even this enormous quantity has only partially drained the great city, leaving some parts of it totally undrained for eight hours out of every twelve. The river of filth struggling through its dark channel sometimes rose to a height of five feet, but generally from two to three. The system of "flushing" the sewers, which we have already described, tends greatly to purify them; and by means of the artificial waterfalls thus secured much of the filth is swept away which would otherwise never be removed; and then, again, the sewers are better ventilated by the introduction of iron gratings, down which the daylight faintly struggles. Consequently, those whose business leads them to descend into the sewers are not now, as they formerly were, exposed to great risk of health and life.

Another important feature of "Underground London" is its "subways." These are among the latest advances which have been made in engineering skill, and have resulted from the peculiar formation of some of the new streets, where, the roadway being of a higher level than formerly, owing to its construction upon arches, an opportunity has been seized upon for their erection. Mr. Haywood, in his Report on the Holborn Valley Improvement (1869), says:—"The public advantage resulting from the construction of subways has long been acknowledged; but, at the same time, it is well known that the Gas and Water Companies showed at first considerable hesitation in using subways; and in the case of those of Southwark Street, constructed under the direction of the Metropolitan Board of Works, it was not until the Board succeeded in obtaining an Act of Parliament that the respective companies placed their pipes in such subways."

In a previous volume* we have given a general account of Holborn Viaduct, and of the improvement effected in the surrounding locality by the wholesale demolition of small and crowded houses, and the formation of new, broad, open streets; but we may here say something on a part of that mighty undertaking, which, from its being below the surface of the roadway, is passed over unseen and unthought-of by the majority of individuals who cross over the Viaduct. The work of construction extended from Fetter Lane to Newgate Street, between which points the new surfaces of the Viaduct and roads, as compared with the former lines of thoroughfare, may be thus summarised:—At Hatton Garden, and in front of the tower of St. Sepulchre's Church, the street surface is now three feet higher than formerly; at Shoe Lane it is upwards of twenty-four feet; and at Farringdon Street Bridge there is a difference of more than thirty-two feet.

From Fetter Lane to the Viaduct Circus, the width of Holborn varies from 86 feet to 107 feet; the Viaduct, from the Circus at its western end to Giltspur Street at its eastern end, is 1,285 feet long and 80 feet wide, the carriage-way being 50 feet and the two footpaths each 15 feet in width. The centre of the Viaduct is formed of a series of large arches, and on both sides are subways for gas, water, and telegraph pipes, and vaults for the use of the houses. At the western end, between Fetter Lane and the Circus, and at the eastern end, from Snow Hill to Giltspur Street, the new levels were made by filling up the ground removed from the excavations for the foundations of the Viaduct. Between Snow Hill and the Circus, the central portions of the Viaduct are formed of a series of arches, similar to those employed in railway viaducts; each arch is twenty-one feet in span, and forty-five feet in width, and the series is interrupted only by the three bridges which had to be erected on the line of the Viaduct—namely, one over Shoe Lane, another over Farringdon Street, and a third over the London, Chatham, and Dover Railway. A line of carriage-way, upwards of ten feet in width, is left throughout the whole length of these vaults, and entrances to them are provided from Farringdon Street and Shoe Lane. The vaults, which are immediately adjacent to Farringdon Street and Shoe Lane, are lighted by windows looking on to those streets, and can be used for office purposes by those having possession of them; arrangements are also made by which access can be given to each separate compartment, arch, or vault, by forming a passage-way, *beneath* the subways and *over* the sewers, from the houses on either side of the Viaduct, so that the vaults can either be let singly or in a group, as may be expedient. Each vault is ventilated on to the surface of the roadway by iron gratings, and in the spandrils are lines of pipes, through which the water is conveyed into the sewers below.

The "subways" extend along the Viaduct beneath the pavement on either side, and between the larger vaults above described, and the vaults of the houses on the outer sides of the Viaduct. They are for the most part seven feet wide, and rather more than eleven feet high, and their coverings are formed of semi-circular arches in brickwork. The internal faces of the subways are of white brick, and the floors are of Yorkshire stone landings, built into the walls on each side, and laid with inclinations nearly the same as those of the surface of the Viaduct. On the sides next to the central vaults are channels cut in the landings, and at intervals of twenty-four feet are openings, covered with bell-traps, which communicate with the sewers beneath. Immediately above these trapped openings to the sewers are iron pipes, which connect with the drain-pipes in the spandrils of the central vaults, and convey the water which may leak through from the street surface into the sewer; by means of these trapped openings, the rain water which falls into the subways through the ventilators in the footways, and the water used in washing the subways, escapes into the sewers.

Owing to the difference between the old and new levels, and to the three bridges on the line of the Viaduct, the subways necessarily vary in design at about every eighty feet of their length; they are carried over the London, Chatham, and Dover Railway by an iron construction; on both sides

* See Vol. II., pp. 501-2.

of Farringdon Street Bridge they are connected with the Farringdon Street level by vertical shafts, which terminate close to their entrances in Farringdon Street; at Shoe Lane they descend by shafts, and are carried beneath that street, and are there eight feet high and seven feet wide, formed with brick sides, stone floors, and iron coverings. The entrances to the subways at Farringdon Street are by large iron gates, eight feet wide, and varying from twelve feet to fifteen feet in height; in their rear are wooden doors, which can be closed as occasion may require. There are also entrances, closed by iron doors, with open gratings over them, in Shoe Lane; and at the eastern and western ends of the Viaduct there are openings, very similar in character to those ordinarily used over the entrances to the sewers, but larger, beneath which are flights of steps for the entry of workmen; means are also provided by which pipes of large size can be lowered into or taken out of the subways.

The ventilation of the subways is effected by shafts rising from the crowns of the arches, terminating by large open gratings, let into the pavements; secondly, also, by circular flues, which start from the crowns of the arches, and, passing over the house vaults, are carried up in the party walls of the houses, and terminate at the roofs; and thirdly, by openings in the crowns of the arches connecting with the lamp-posts on the public way, the lower part of each post being perforated to afford ventilation. The length of subway on the southern side of the Viaduct, between Farringdon Street and Shoe Lane, is lighted by gratings, filled in with glass lenses, placed at intervals of forty feet, which render it sufficiently light by day for the purposes of inspection and work; the others have no daylight, excepting that obtained through the ventilating gratings in the footways, but provision is made for artificial lighting throughout the whole lines of subways by burners suspended from the crowns of the arches, and connected with the gas mains in the subways. To afford a supply of gas and water to the houses, square iron tubes are built into the walls, between the subways and the house vaults, through which the service-pipes, after being connected with the mains, are passed. The provision made in the subways for carrying the gas, water, and other pipes, consists of chairs and brackets, which are either let into the stone floor or project from the walls.

KING'S CROSS UNDERGROUND STATION IN 1868. (*See page* 227.)

SECTION OF THE THAMES EMBANKMENT, 1867. (*See page* 232.)

Showing (1) The Subway. (2) The Low-Level Sewer. (3) The Metropolitan District Railway. (4) The Pneumatic Railway.

As we learn from Mr. Haywood's Report, to which we are indebted for much of the information here given, it is some years since subways were first constructed in various parts of London and elsewhere, and pipes of various character have been laid in one or other of them; but the Viaduct subways were the first in which gas, water, and telegraph pipes, with all the appliances necessary to a complete system, were placed in one and the same subway. The subways of the Viaduct have been on several occasions lighted up with gas and exhibited to the public; workmen have executed repairs, and performed their ordinary work in them; and no special precautions have been found necessary as regards the use of lights or fires, no explosions have taken place, nor has such contraction or expansion of pipes resulted from the variations of temperature, as materially to affect either the gas or water supply; and the system may be said to be successful.

Another important feature of "Underground London" which we have not mentioned is the Electric Telegraph. The old Electric Telegraph Company, which for many years carried out the entire system of telegraphy in England, formerly had its head-quarters in Lothbury, in the heart of the City, and, as such, became the originators of that particular portion in the works of "Underground London" to which we have already incidentally referred. The company was incorporated by Act of Parliament in 1846, and immediately on its incorporation became the possessor, by purchase, of all the patents previously granted to Sir W. Fothergill Cooke and Sir Charles Wheatstone, the inventors or the introducers of the electric system of telegraphy into England. "As these patents gave the company an exclusive right to the use of those essential principles on which all electric telegraphs are based, we may attribute much of the subsequent success of the undertaking to the possession of this important right." In an interesting article in *Once a Week*, in the year 1861, entitled "The Nervous System of the Metropolis," by the late Dr. Wynter, we read that—"It is anticipated that for a considerable time the new telegraph will be principally confined to the use of public offices and places of business. Thus the principal public offices are already connected by its wires; and, if we might be permitted the ugly comparison, the Chief Commissioner of Police at Scotland Yard, spider-like, sits in the centre of a web co-extensive with the metropolis, and is made instantly sensible of any disturbance that may take place at any point. The Queen's Printer, again, has for years sent his messages by one of these telegraphs between the House of Commons and his printing-office near Fleet Street. The different docks are put *en rapport* with each other, and it will be especially applicable to all large manufacturing establishments requiring central offices in the City. Thus, the Isle of Dogs and Bow Common, the grand centres of manufacturing energy, are practically brought next door to offices in the centre of the City." About the year 1864, the business of the Electric Telegraph Company was taken in hand by the Government, and transferred to the Post Office; since the erection of the new General Post Office, this department has had its head-quarters in St. Martin's-le-Grand, as we have already stated when describing that locality.*

Whilst we are on the subject of Underground London, it may be desirable here to place on record the fact of the establishment of a Pneumatic Despatch Company about the year 1868. Its head-quarters were in High Holborn, near the Little Turnstile, and its object was the rapid transmission of letters, newspapers, and small packages of goods, by tubes laid under the street, and worked by pneumatic agency. These tubes were laid between the office and the Euston Square Station, and also between Holborn and the General Post Office; but the scheme was "in advance of the age," and it failed to answer; there was not enough demand for its services to make it "pay" commercially; and so, after about eighteen months of trial, it was abandoned. The traffic in the tube was worked by alternate atmospheric pressure and suction, the carriers, containing mails and parcels, being by turns propelled to and drawn from Euston Square by the pneumatic apparatus at the Holborn station of the company. The same process was, of course, followed with regard to the length of tube between Holborn and the General Post Office. Taking advantage of the proximity of the tube to the tunnel of the Metropolitan Railway in the vicinity of Gower Street, and of the fact that air had to be drawn into the tube after every carrier that was sucked—so to speak—from Euston to Holborn, it was determined to open a communication between tube and tunnel, and to utilise the exhausting power of the pneumatic machinery for ventilating this portion of the Metropolitan Railway, and, as we have stated above, this was ultimately accomplished. The tubes are still *in situ*, and the scheme, doubtless, only sleeps for a time, to be revived when London is ripe for its services.

---

* See Vol. II., pp. 215-16.

CHAPTER XIX.

KILBURN AND ST. JOHN'S WOOD.

"Shall you prolong the midnight ball
With costly supper at Vaux Hall,
And yet prohibit earlier suppers
At *Kilburn*, Sadler's Wells, or Kuper's?
Are these less innocent in fact,
Or only made so by the act?"

Rural Aspect of Kilburn in Former Times—Maida Vale—Derivation of the Name of Kilburn—The Old Road to Kilburn—Godwin, the Hermit of Kilburn—The Priory—Extracts from the Inventory of the Priory—The Sisterhood of St. Peter's—St. Augustine's Church—Kilburn Wells and Tea-gardens—The "Bell" Tavern—A Legend of Kilburn—The Roman Catholic Chapel—George Brummell's liking for Plum Cake—Oliver Goldsmith's Suburban Quarters—Lausanne Cottage—St. John's Wood—Babington the Conspirator—Sir Edwin Landseer—Thomas Landseer—George Osbaldiston and other Residents in St. John's Wood—Lord's Cricket Ground—The "Eyre Arms" Tavern—Charitable Institutions—Roman Catholic Chapel of Our Lady—St. Mark's Church—St. John's Wood Chapel and Burial-ground—Richard Brothers and Joanna Southcott.

SUCH has been the growth of London in this north-westerly direction, within the last half-century, as we have shown in our chapter on Paddington, and such the progress of bricks and mortar in swallowing up all that was once green and sylvan in this quiet suburb of the metropolis, that the "village of Kilburn," which within the last fifty years was still famous for its tea-gardens and its mineral spring, has almost become completely absorbed into that vast and "still increasing" City, and in a very short space of time all its old landmarks will have been swept away. Kilburn, or Kilbourne, as the name was sometimes written, is said to be "a hamlet in the parish of Hampstead, and Holborn division of the hundred of Ossulston." This, however, is not quite correct, as only one side of the hamlet is in the parish of Hampstead, the remaining part (or that to the south-west of the Edgware Road) lying in the parish of Willesden. In old books on the suburbs, the place is spoken of as being "about two miles from London, on the road to Edgware." Time was, probably in the reign of "bluff King Hal," when the little rural village numbered only some twenty or so of houses, all nestling round a small chapel and priory, the memory of which is still kept up in "Abbey Road" and "Priory Road." Now, however, the block of houses known collectively as Kilburn has invaded no less than four parishes—Hampstead and Willesden, to which, as we have shown, it legitimately belongs, and also Marylebone and Paddington. The district, including the locality now known as St. John's Wood, lies mainly on the north side of the Harrow Road, and stretches away from Kensal Green to Regent's Park and Primrose Hill, and may be said to be divided into two parts by the broad thoroughfare of Maida Vale, as that part of the Edgware Road is called which passes through it. Maida Vale, we may add, is so called after the famous battle of Maida, which was fought in 1806.

Like Tybourne and Mary-le-Bourne, so Kilbourne also took its name from the little "bourne," or brook, of which we have already spoken as rising on the southern slope of the Hampstead uplands. It found its way from the slope of West End, Hampstead, towards Bayswater, and thence passing under the Uxbridge Road, fed the Serpentine in Hyde Park. The brook, however, has long since disappeared from view, having been arched over, and made to do duty as a sewer.

The road to Kilburn in the days of the Regency, writes the Rev. J. Richardson in his "Recollections," was "such a road as now is to be seen only twenty miles out of town." Any one going a mile northward from the end of Oxford Street, found himself among fields, farm-houses, and such-like rural scenes.

It would seem that the land here, as part of "Padyngton," appertained to the manor of Knightsbridge, which, as we have seen, in its turn was subject to the Abbey at Westminster. We read, therefore, that it was not without the consent of the "chapter and council" that one Godwin, or Goodwyne, a hermit at Kilburn, gave his hermitage to three nuns—"the holy virgins of St. John the Baptist, at Kilburn, to pray for the repose of King Edward, the founder of the Abbey, and for the souls of all their brethren and benefactors." On this occasion the Abbot of Westminster not only confirmed the grant, but augmented it with lands at "Cnightbriga," or "Knyghtsbrigg" (Knightsbridge), and a rent of thirty shillings. The exact spot on which the priory stood is now known only by tradition. Lambert, in his "History and Survey of London and its Environs," in 1805, remarks:—"There are now no remains of this building; but the site of it is very distinguishable in the Abbey Field, near the tea-drinking house called Kilburn Wells." This, it would appear, must have been as nearly as possible at the top of what is now St. George's Terrace, close to the station of the London and North-Western Railway, on its northern side; for when the railway was widened, about the year 1850, the labourers came here upon its foundations, and discovered, not only coins, but tessellated tiles, several curious keys of a Gothic pattern, and the clapper of a bell, together with human bones, denoting the presence of a small cemetery.

This priory was the successor of the hermitage founded here by Godwin. The spot which he chose for his hermitage or cell was on the banks of the little "bourne" already mentioned, and it came to be called indifferently Keeleburne, or Coldburne, or Caleburn, in an age when few could spell or read, and fewer still could write. To this little cell might perhaps have been applied the lines of Spenser's "Faery Queen :"—

"A little lowly hermitage it was,
Down in a dale, hard by a forest side;
Far from resort of people, that did pass
In traveill to and froe; a little wyde
There was an holy chappell edifyde;
Wherein the hermit dewly wont to say
His holy things, each morne and eventyde;
Thereby a christall streame did gently play,
Which from a sacred fountaine welled forth alway."

Godwin, in course of time, it appears, gave over and granted his hermitage and the adjoining fields to the abbot and monks of Westminster, "as an alms for the redemption of the entire convent of the brethren," under the same terms and conditions as those under which one of the Saxon kings had long before granted the manor of "Hamstede" to the same church. The little cell at Kilburn, however, was destined to undergo another transfer in the lifetime of Godwin, and, indeed, at his request; for we next read that, with the consent of Gilbert, the then Bishop of London, the brethren of St. Peter's, at Westminster, made it over to a sisterhood of three nuns, named Christina, Gunilde, and Emma, all of them, as the story goes, ex-maids of honour to Queen Matilda, or Maud, consort of Henry I. The hermitage, therefore, was changed into a convent of the order of St. Benedict, Godwin himself undertaking the performance of the duties of chaplain and warden.

Soon after the death of Godwin a dispute arose between the Abbot of Westminster and the Bishop of London as to the spiritual jurisdiction over the convent; the difference, however, was at length adjusted in favour of the former, on consideration that from its foundation the "Cell of Keleburn" belonged to their church. Notwithstanding that the dispute was so adjusted, the litigation was subsequently revived by Bishop Roger Nigel, and continued by his successor, who at last agreed to a compromise, under which the abbot "presented" the warden, and the bishop "admitted" him to his office.

But little is known of the history of the convent from this time to the dissolution of religious houses under Henry VIII., except that, during the reign of Edward III., the good nuns were specially exempted from the payment of taxes to the Crown, on account of the dilapidated state of their little house, and of the necessity under which they lay of relieving the wants of many poor wayfarers, and especially of pilgrims bound for St. Alban's shrine. As soon as the fiat of "bluff King Hal" had gone forth for the dissolution of all the lesser religious houses in 1536, we find that the "Nonnerie of Kilnborne" was surrendered to the commissioners, when, doubtless, its gentle sisters were thrown out upon the world to beg their bread, instead of doling it out to the poor and suffering. At that time the priory was returned as of the value of £74 7s. 11d., and it passed into the hands of the rapacious king, who exchanged its lands with the Prior of the Hospital of St. John of Jerusalem, at Clerkenwell, for his manor of Paris Garden, which lay across the Thames, in Southwark.

But ten years later, the greater monasteries shared the fate of the lesser houses, and along with the Priory of St. John, that of Kilburn was transferred to the hands of a favoured courtier, the Earl of Warwick. From his family the estate passed, through an intermediate owner, to the Earl of Devonshire, and in the early part of the present century to one of the Howards; from them it came to the Uptons, its present owners, by one of whom the Church of St. Mary, at Kilburn, has been erected on a site adjoining the ancient chapel. It is said that the Abbey Farm comprised about forty-five acres, including the land covered by the priory out-buildings.

In Park's "History of Hampstead" there is a view of the old priory, which never could have been one of very imposing appearance. The edifice, it may be added, was dedicated jointly to "The Blessed Virgin Mary and St. John the Baptist," the latter of whom is depicted on the conventual seal as clothed in his garment of camels' hair.

From an "inventory" taken on the 11th day of May, in the year of the surrender of the house to the king, it appears that the buildings of the priory consisted of "the hall, the chamber next the church, the middle chamber between that and the prioress's chamber, the prioress's chamber, the buttery, pantry, and cellar, inner chamber to the prioress's chamber, the chamber between the latter and the hall, the kitchen, the larder-house, the brewhouse and bakehouse, the three chambers for the chaplain and the hinds or husbandmen, the confessor's chamber, and the church." A few extracts from the above-mentioned inventory will serve to show that, in spite of all the changes worked in our domestic arrangements, in those far-off days, on the whole, the chamber furniture did not differ very materially from that of our own. Thus we read in the middle chamber:—

"It'm: 2 bedsteddes of bordes, viij*d.* It'm: 1 fetherbedd, v*s.*, 2 matteres, xv*d.*, 2 old cov'lettes, xx*d.*, 3 wollen blankettes, viij*d.* It'm: a syller of old steyned worke, iiij*d.* It'm: 2 peces of old hangings, paynted, x*d.*"

The following is the list of books—not very numerous, it must be owned—of which his Majesty was not ashamed to rob his defenceless female subjects:—

"It'm: 2 bookes of *Legenda Aurea*, the one in prynt, and other written, both Englishe, viij*d.* It'm: 2 mas bookes, one old writen, and the oder prynt, xx*d.* It'm: 4 p'cessions, in p'chement, iij*s.*, and paper, x*d.* It'm: 2 chestes wt div'se bookes p'teinynge to the chirche, bokes of no value. It'm: 2 legendes, viij*d*; the one in p'chment, and thoder on paper."

With regard to church furniture and vestments the nuns would seem to have been better off; for besides altar-cloths, curtains, hangings, copes, chalices, &c., we find the following articles mentioned in the inventory:—

"It'm: a relique of the *holy crosse*, closed in silver, and guilt, sett wt counterfeyte stones and perls, worth iij*s.* iiij*d.* It'm: a cross wt certain other reliques plated wt silver gilded, ij*s.* iiij*d.* It'm: a case to kepe in reliques, plated and gilt, v*d.* It'm: a clocke, v*s.*"

It may be added that the orchard and cemetery were valued at "xx*s.* by the yere," and "one horse of the coller of black," at 5*s.* Anne Browne, the last prioress, was probably a member of the noble house of Lord Montagu.

Mr. Wood, in his "Ecclesiastical Antiquities of London," mentions a tradition, which may or may not be true, that the nuns of Kilburn enjoyed the privilege of having seats in the triforium in Westminster Abbey.

Not far from the site of the old priory, a "Home" has been established, called the "Sisterhood of St. Peter's." It was founded by a Mr. and Mrs. Lancaster, to carry out by united effort the work of missionaries and nurses amongst the poor. The establishment, which was formerly at Brompton, consists of a lady superior, four sisters, and a limited number of serving-sisters. Besides the more spiritual object of the sisterhood, it undertakes the special care of a large number of sick people, who are received from the hospitals, and nursed until restored to health.

In Kilburn Park Road, near Edgware Road Station, is the Church of St. Augustine, one of the finest ecclesiastical structures in London, and, with the exception of St. Paul's and Westminster Abbey, by far the largest. The church, which at present has sittings for about 1,000 worshippers, is in the "First Pointed" style of Gothic architecture, and was commenced in 1872 from the designs of Mr. Pearson. The sisterhood of St. Peter above mentioned assist in the district in nursing the sick and in mission work; then there are "Sisters of the Church" for the education of the poor, and also a "Guild," with several branches. In May, 1876, the foundation-stone of the nave of this church was laid.

After the Reformation the reminiscences of Kilburn are secular rather than religious, leading us in the direction of suburban pleasure-grounds and "the gardens," and mineral waters. In fact, before the end of the sixteenth century, and even perhaps earlier, near a mineral spring which bubbled up not far from the spot where the nuns had knelt in prayer, and had relieved the beggars and the poor out of their slender store, there arose a rural house, known to the holiday folks of London as the "Kilburn Wells." The well is still to be seen adjoining a cottage at the corner of the Station Road, on some premises belonging to the London and North-Western Railway. The water rises about twelve feet below the surface, and is enclosed in a brick reservoir of about five feet in diameter, surmounted by a cupola. The key-stone of the arch over the doorway bears the date 1714. The water collected in this reservoir is usually about five or six feet in depth, though in a dry summer it is shallower; and it is said that its purgative qualities are increased as its bulk diminishes. These wells, in fact, were once famous for their saline and purgative waters. A writer in the *Kilburn Almanack* observes:—"Upon a recent visit we found about five feet six inches of water in the well, and the water very clear and bright, with little or no sediment at the bottom; probably the water has been as high as it now is ever since the roadway parted it from the 'Bell' Tea Gardens, not having been so much used lately as of old." "Is it not strange," asks Mr. W. Harrison Ainsworth, "that, in these water-drinking times, the wells of Hampstead and Kilburn should not come again into vogue?"

The house with grounds contiguous to the well was formerly a place of amusement, and would appear to have borne a tolerably good character for respectability, if we may judge from the "Dialogue between a Master and his Servant," by Richard Owen Cambridge, in imitation of Horace, and published in 1752, which we quote as a motto to this chapter.

The following prospectus of the "Wells," now superseded by the "Bell" Tavern, taken from the *Public Advertiser* of July 17th, 1773, we here give *in extenso* :—

"KILBURN WELLS, NEAR PADDINGTON.—The waters are now in the utmost perfection; the gardens enlarged and greatly improved; the house and offices re-painted and beautified in the most elegant manner. The whole is now open for the reception of the public, the great room being particularly adapted to the use and amusement of the politest companies. Fit either for music, dancing, or entertainments. This happy spot is equally celebrated for its rural situation, extensive prospects, and the acknowledged efficacy of its waters; is most delightfully situated on the site of the once famous Abbey of Kilburn, on the Edgware Road, at an easy distance, being but a morning's walk, from the metropolis, two miles from Oxford Street; the footway from the Mary-bone across the fields still nearer. A plentiful larder is always provided, together with the best of wines and other liquors. Breakfasting and hot loaves. A printed account of the waters, as drawn up by an eminent physician, is given gratis at the Wells."

THE "BELL INN," KILBURN, 1750.

The "Bell" Tavern, we may add, dates from about the year 1600. The following "Legend of Kilburn" we condense from Mr. John Timbs' "Romance of London:"—"There is a curious traditionary relation connected with Kilburn Priory, which, however, is not traceable to any authentic source. The legend states that, at a place called St. John's Wood, near Kilburn, there was a stone of a dark red colour, showing the stain of the blood of Sir Gervaise de Morton, or de Mortoune, which flowed upon it some centuries ago. The story runs that Stephen de Morton, being enamoured of his brother's wife, frequently insulted her by the open avowal of his passion, which at length she threatened to make known to her husband; and that, to prevent this being done, Stephen resolved to waylay his brother and kill him. This he effected by seizing him in a narrow lane and stabbing him in the back; whereupon he fell upon a projecting rock and dyed it with his blood. In his expiring moments Sir Gervaise, recognising his brother in the assassin, upbraided him with his cruelty, adding, 'This stone shall be thy death-bed.' Stephen returned to Kilburn, and his brother's wife still refusing to listen to his criminal proposals, he confined her in a dungeon, and strove to forget his many crimes by a dissolute enjoyment of his wealth and power. Oppressed, however, by a troubled conscience, he determined upon submitting to a religious penance; and so, ordering his brother's remains to be removed to Kilburn, he gave directions for their re-interment in a handsome mausoleum, erected with stone brought from the quarry hard by where the murderous deed was committed. The identical stone on which his murdered brother had breathed his last thus came too for his tomb, and the legend adds that as soon as the eye of the murderer rested upon it blood began to issue from it. Struck with horror at the sight, the murderer hastened to the Bishop of London, and making a full confession of his guilt, he demised his property to the Priory at Kilburn, in the hope thereby of making atonement. But all in vain; for in spite of having thus endeavoured to compensate his guilt by a deed of charity and mortification, he was seized upon by such feelings of remorse and grief as quickly hurried him to his grave."

THE PRIORY, KILBURN, 1750.

Whether there is any truth or not in this story we are not prepared to say; but, at all events, it wears about it the air of probability, and it is told here, as they say, "just for what it is worth." We may add, however, that just three hundred and thirty years after the surrender of the old chapel and priory to Henry VIII., a new Roman Catholic chapel and monastery was founded on a spot hard by, in Quex Road, by the Fathers known as the "Oblates of Mary." The first stone was laid in 1866, and the chapel opened two years later.

A writer in the *Mirror*, in 1824, expresses his regret that, on re-visiting Kilburn after a long absence, he has found it grown from the little rural hamlet, which he remembered it, into a town, with its own chapel and its own coaches!

The Rev. J. Richardson, in his amusing "Recol

lections," states that one of its residents at the beginning of the present century was a lady of some means, the owner of a villa here, who used to entertain George Brummell too hospitably when he was a boy at school; and that one day the future "Beau," having stuffed himself almost to bursting, broke out into a flood of tears, regretting that his stomach would not stretch any further so as to hold more plum-cake. In 1826, "Brondesbury House, near Kilburn," figures in the Blue Book as the country seat of Sir Coutts Trotter, whose town-house was in Grosvenor Square.

Within the last few years, the growth of London in this direction has been rapid and continuous: long rows of terraces, streets, and villas having sprung up in all directions. Two or three railway-stations have been built within the limits of Kilburn and Brondesbury, and churches, chapels, schools, a town hall, and other public buildings have been erected. Of the churches, the only one calling for special mention is St. Augustine's, a large red-brick Gothic structure, which has become noted for its ritualistic or "high church" services.

As to the rest of Kilburn, there is little to be said beyond mentioning the tradition, long fondly cherished in the neighbourhood, that Oliver Goldsmith wrote his comedy, *She Stoops to Conquer*, and his *Deserted Village*, whilst lodging in a house which stood on the spot now occupied by "Goldsmith's Place." The tradition, however, may have no other foundation than the fact that Boswell in his "Life of Johnson" tells us that Goldsmith had "taken lodgings at a farmer's house. . . . on the Edgware Road," adding that "He said he believed the farmer's family thought him an odd character, similar to that in which the *Spectator* appeared to his landlady and her children—he was *The Gentleman*." The house here referred to, however, is in Hyde Lane, "near the village of Hyde, looking towards Hendon."

Opposite to the entrance of Willesden Lane formerly stood a quaint-looking old building, mainly of wood, with high-pointed roofs, now known as Lausanne Cottage, but which was said to have been used as a hunting-box, or as a kennel for his favourite spaniels, by King Charles II. In one of the rooms there was to be seen a fine old carved mantel-piece, probably as old as the reign of James I.

St. John's Wood, to which we now pass, was so called after its former possessors, the Priors of St. John of Jerusalem. It is now a thickly-peopled suburban district, which has gradually grown up around the western boundaries of the Regent's Park, enclosing the then rural and retired cricket-ground which had been formed there by Mr. Thomas Lord in 1780, of which we shall have more to say presently.

According to Mr. Wood's "Ecclesiastical Antiquities of London," it was originally called "Great St. John's Wood," near Marylebone Park, to distinguish it from Little St. John's Wood, at Highbury.

Here, as tradition says, Babington and his comrades in his conspiracy to murder Lord Burghley, in the reign of Elizabeth, sought refuge. Many of the houses in the neighbourhood are detached or semi-detached, and in most of the principal thoroughfares they are shut in from the roadway by brick walls and gardens; and altogether the place has an air of quietude and seclusion, and, as might almost be expected, has long been a favourite abode of the members of the literary and artistic professions.

In St. John's Wood Road—which connects Maida Hill with the Regent's Park—was the residence of the late Sir Edwin Landseer, and here the renowned painter spent much of his life. He arranged the construction of the house so as to suit his own tastes, and to afford him the most favourable facilities for pursuing the art to which he was so devoted. In his studio here many of his most celebrated works were executed. The house is situated on the south side of the main road, between Grove Road and Cunningham Place, and, with the grounds belonging to it, occupies an area of about two acres. Sir Edwin Landseer was the youngest son of John Landseer, A.R.A., some time Associate Engraver to the Royal Academy, and was born in 1802. He excelled in the painting of animals while still a boy, and became a student of the Academy in 1816. Among the best known of his numerous pictures are the following:—"A Highland Breakfast," "The Twa Dogs," "There's no Place like Home," "Comical Dogs," "War" and "Peace," "Bolton Abbey in the Olden Time," "The Duke of Wellington, accompanied by his Daughter-in-law, visiting the Field of Waterloo," "Deer-stalking," "Windsor Park," and "Man Proposes, but God Disposes." One of his latest designs was that for the lions at the base of the Nelson Monument, Trafalgar Square. In 1866 he was elected President of the Royal Academy, but he declined to serve. He died here in 1873, and his remains were interred in St. Paul's Cathedral.

At No. 30, South Bank, lived Thomas Landseer, the elder brother of Sir Edwin. He occupied for many years a distinguished place as an engraver, and constantly exhibited his engravings at the Royal Academy. In 1860-61 he added to his previous reputation by his finely-executed plate of Rosa Bonheur's "Horse Fair."

Cyrus Redding lived in Hill Road; Mr. J. A. St. John, too, was a resident in St. John's Wood; as also was Douglas Jerrold, who lived close to Kilburn Priory. Charles Knight (for a short time) resided in Maida Vale; and a certain Lord de Ros, who closed his inglorious career in 1839, lived at No. 4, Grove Road. In the Grove Road, too, in 1866, died Mr. George Osbaldiston, the sporting squire. He was born at Hutton Bushell, in Yorkshire, but losing his father when only six years of age, he went to reside with his mother, at Bath, where he received his first lessons in riding, from Dash, the celebrated teacher of the last century. He subsequently entered at Brasenose College, Oxford, and, while still an undergraduate here, commenced his career as master of hounds, with a pack which he purchased from the Earl of Jersey. The entire career of Mr. Osbaldiston, as a master of hounds, lasted during a period of thirty-five years. He further became famous as a most bold and daring rider of steeplechases, in which he had no superior, and is said to have never been beaten. His celebrated 200-mile match took place at Newmarket, in November, 1831. "Squire Osbaldiston," as he was familiarly called, was creditably known upon the turf, and, in fact, in every branch of field sports.

Another noted resident in St. John's Wood was M. Soyer, with whose name, in connection with the culinary art, we have already made our readers acquainted, in our accounts of the Reform Club and Kensington Gore.* He died in August, 1858, after a short illness, at 15, Marlborough Road. M. Soyer, who was of French extraction, had been for many years known as a culinary benefactor to the public, and more particularly during the war with Russia, a few years before his death; his success in ameliorating the condition, in a culinary view, of the army in the Crimea, was well known to all. Subsequent to his return to England he prepared a new dietary for military hospitals, as well as for Government emigrants, both of which were adopted by the authorities. He was also the author of "The Gastronomic Regenerator," a cookery-book for the upper classes; "Pantropheon, or History of Food;" "Shilling Cookery," and "A Culinary Campaign," which gives a vivid description of the Crimean war.

On the north side of St. John's Wood Road is Lord's Cricket Ground, a spot that has become famous in the annals of the manly and invigorating game of cricket. The ground is some six or seven acres in extent, and on it are erected permanent "stands"—after the fashion of those on race-courses—where visitors can sit and witness the matches that are here played. The present ground superseded the space now covered by Dorset Square, which had served for some years as the "old Marylebone" ground.

At the end of the last century men played cricket in summer at the old Artillery Ground, in Finsbury, in the days when they skated on Moorfields in the winter, and shot snipes in Belgravia. At the old Artillery Ground, so large was the attendance, and so heavy were the stakes, that a writer in an old newspaper complains of the idleness of the City apprentices in consequence, and of the unblushing way in which the laws against gaming were broken, matches being advertised for £500, or even £1,000 a side. Indeed, in 1750, an action was tried in the King's Bench for the sum of £50, being a bet laid and won on a game of cricket—Kent *v.* England.

But at this time cricket was deemed a vulgar game. Robert Southey states the fact, and quotes No. 132 of the *Connoisseur*, dated 1756, where we are introduced to one Mr. Tony Bumper "drinking purl in the morning, eating black-puddings at Bartholomew Fair, boxing with Buckhorse (the most celebrated of the old pugilists), and also as frequently engaged at the Artillery Ground with Faukner and Dingate at cricket, and considered as good a bat as either of the Bennets."

One who reads with all the curiosity and interest of a cricketer will pick up little notices, which, when put together, throw light on the early history of the game, and show its spread, and how early it had taken root in the land; for instance, in Smith's 'Life of Nollekens," we are told that Alderman Boydell, the etcher and printseller, had many shops, but that the best was the sign of "The Cricket Bat," in Duke's Court, St. Martin's Lane. This was in 1750. Again, in one of the caricatures of 1770, in Mr. Wright's collection, Lord Sandwich is represented with a bat in his hand, in allusion to his fondness for cricket; but it is a curved piece of wood, more like a modern golf club. A bat also is placed satirically in the hand of a cricket-loving lady, in a print of 1778—"Miss Wicket," with her friend, "Miss Trigger"—fast ladies both, no doubt, in their day. In 1706, William Goldwin, an "old king's man," published in *Musæ Juveniles* a poem called "Certamen Pilæ," or "The Cricket Match." "A ram and bat, 9*d.*," figures as one of the ten extras in an Eton boy's school-bill, as far back as 1688.

When the game grew "genteel," men of position aspired to better company than the City apprentices,

* See Vol. IV., p. 149, and p. 122, *ante*.

and founded a club in White Conduit Fields. But hard indeed it were in these days to pitch good wickets within view of the Foundling Hospital. So Thomas Lord then came upon the stage—a canny lad from the north country—who, after waiting on Lords Darnley and Winchilsea, Sir Horace Mann, the Duke of Dorset, and others of their contemporaries in the White Conduit Fields Club, speculated in a ground of his own, where now, as we have stated above, is Dorset Square, the original "Lord's." This was in 1780. It was on this ground that the club, taking the name of the Marylebone Cricket Club, brought the game to perfection.

In a map of London published in 1802, the site of Dorset Square is marked as "The Cricket Ground," probably implying that it was the only public ground then devoted to that sport in the neighbourhood of London.

On the present ground is annually fought the "great batting match," as it is called, between Harrow and Eton. The two Universities of Oxford and Cambridge, likewise, here enter into friendly rivalry, some months after their perhaps more exciting contest on the River Thames. Here, too, nearly all the great cricket matches of the metropolitan clubs and southern counties of England are played.

Apropos of Lord's Cricket Ground, we may add that there is nothing in which a more visible improvement has taken place than in our sports. The prize-ring and bear-garden, dog-fighting and rat-killing, are things of the past; but our glorious boat-races, in which we are the first in the world; cricket, in which we have no rivals; and athletic sports—running, jumping the hurdles—in which we have reached to the highest perfection. The Duke of Wellington attributed a great deal of his success in war to the athletic exercises which Englishmen had practised in peace. The steady nerve, quick eye, and command of every muscle, exercised considerable power in the battle-field. On the Continent these games are almost unknown, and the biggest Frenchman or Prussian is the veriest baby in the hands of an Englishman in any physical display. We attribute a good deal of the temperance which characterises this age of ours to the growth of those sports; for the intemperate man, shattered in nerves and dim of eye, has no chance in such noble pastimes.

Much of the land in and about St. John's Wood belongs to the family of Eyre, whose estate adjoins those of Lord Portman and the Duke of Portland; their name is kept fresh in remembrance by the sign given to a tavern of some note in the Finchley Road, called the "Eyre Arms." The grounds belonging to this house were occasionally the scene of balloon ascents in the early days of aëronautics. One of the latest was the ascent of Mr. Hampton here on the 7th of June, 1839.

In the rear of the inn is a large concert-room, which is often used for balls, bazaars, public lectures, &c.; and on the opposite side of the way is the St. John's Wood Athenæum, which serves as a club for the residents of the neighbourhood.

Close by, in Circus Road, the Emperor Napoleon lived for some time during his sojourn in England; and in Ordnance Road, between St. John's Wood and the west side of Primrose HIll, are some barracks, generally occupied by a regiment of the Line or of the Guards.

Among the various charitable and provident institutions here is the Ladies' Home, which was founded in 1859, in Abbey Road. It affords board, lodging, and medical attendance to ladies of limited income, each paying from 16s. to 14s. per week. In the St. John's Wood Road are the girls' schools belonging to the Clergy Orphan and Widow Corporation. The objects of this institution, which was established in 1749, are to clothe, educate, and maintain the poor orphans of clergymen. This charity is one of the most extensive in the kingdom, and has greatly assisted the orphans of a large number of clergymen in beginning life. The boys' school in connection with the institution is at Canterbury.

Another old and useful institution is the School of Industry for Female Orphans, which was established in 1786, in Grove Road. The school will accommodate about eighty girls, but it has rarely, if ever, mustered above fifty at one time, the number being restricted by the funds. Board, clothing, and education is here given to girls who have lost both parents.

At the top of the Avenue Road, close to the Swiss Cottage, is the School for the Blind, founded in 1838, and erected from the designs of a Mr. Kendal. It will accommodate about 100 inmates, male and female. The school was established for the purpose of imparting secular knowledge and the fundamental doctrines of Christianity, and teaching the blind to read by means of embossed or raised print. A portion of the pupils are received free; others pay a small sum half-yearly. The course of instruction given in the school, it may be added, is as complete as it well could be, and is fitted, in so far as that is possible, to enable the pupils, despite their sorrowful deprivation, to earn their own livelihood, and to take their place of usefulness and honour in the work of life, side by side with those who possess all the inestimable advantages of sight. In the industrial department, the work among the boys consists chiefly of basket-making and chair-caning; amongst the girls, of chair-caning, knitting, and bead-work. Of the progress made by the pupils generally, Mr. Charles Richards, the literary examiner, made the following encouraging remarks in his annual report to the committee of the institution, in May, 1876:—Speaking of the boys, he says, "The difficulty in learning to write to one who is unable to see a copy is evident; but by means of embossed letters, &c., the difficulty has been so far overcome that many of the boys are able to write very creditably. I was somewhat surprised to find that those who had been at the school a few months only were able to read very fairly. The reading of the others would compare favourably with that of boys of their age who have the advantage of sight. . . . Arithmetic is worked on boards with movable type, and necessarily takes more time than if worked with slate and pencil. Some have advanced as far as the extraction of square and cube roots. All the examples were correctly worked, and I consider this part of the examination to have been very satisfactory. . . . In history, geography, grammar, and religious knowledge, I was altogether satisfied. The answers were given readily, and showed an intelligent knowledge of the subjects." Of the instruction of the girls in this department Mr. Richards' report is equally satisfactory, and he concludes by saying that he "cannot speak too highly of the excellent discipline in both schools, the principle of government being love rather than severity."

The Roman Catholic Chapel in Grove Road is a large Gothic structure, built about the year 1836, through the munificence of two maiden ladies of the name of Gallini, whose father, an Italian refugee, had settled in London, and having taught dancing to sundry members of the royal family, became Sir John Gallini.* So noble and generous was their gift esteemed that they were rewarded with a magnificent testimonial from the Roman Catholic ladies of England, presented by the hands of the Princess Donna Isabella Maria of Portugal. The chapel was one of the early works of Mr. J. J. Scoles, and is a rather poor reproduction of some of the features of the Lady Chapel in St. Saviour's Church, Southwark. It is a cruciform structure, in the "Early English" style, and it consists of a nave, chancel, and side aisles; the wings on each side have been converted into dwelling-houses, one of them serving as a residence for the clergy. The windows of the chapel are "lancets," after the fashion of the twelfth or early part of the thirteenth century, and are filled with stained glass, principally as memorial windows.

Hamilton Terrace and the surrounding streets commemorate, by their names, the governors and other authorities of Harrow School in the last generation. Aberdeen Place, Abercorn Place, Cunningham Place, Northwick Terrace, &c., at all events, serve to show that the foundation of the honest yeoman of Preston, John Lyon, is not in danger of being forgotten or useless.

In Hamilton Terrace is the large Church of St. Mark's. It was built in 1847, in the Gothic style of architecture, from the designs of Messrs. Cundy.

At the junction of the Finchley and St. John's Wood Roads, close by the station on the Underground Railway, is the St. John's Wood Chapel, with its burial-ground, in which a few individuals of note have been buried; and among them the impostors, Richard Brothers and Joanna Southcott. Of the former of these two characters we have spoken in our account of Paddington.* Joanna Southcott was a native of Devonshire, and was born about the middle of the last century. In her youth she lived as a domestic servant, chiefly in Exeter, and having joined the Methodists, became acquainted with a man named Sanderson, who laid claim to the spirit of prophecy, a pretension in which she herself ultimately indulged. In 1792, she declared herself to be the woman driven into the wilderness, the subject of the prophecy in the 12th chapter of the Book of Revelation. She gave forth predictions in prose and doggerel rhyme, in which she related the denunciation of judgments on the surrounding nations, and promised a speedy approach of the Millennium. In the course of her "mission," as she called it, she employed a boy, who pretended to see visions, and attempted, instead of writing, to adjust them on the walls of her chapel, "the House of God." A schism took place among her followers, one of whom, named Carpenter, took possession of the place, and wrote against her: not denying her mission, but asserting that she had exceeded it. Although very illiterate, she wrote numerous letters and pamphlets, which were published, and found many purchasers. One of her productions was called "The Book of Wonders." She also issued to her followers sealed papers, which she termed her "seals," and which, she assured them, would

* See Vol. IV., p. 318.

* See p. 212, *ante*.

protect them from the judgments of God, both in this and the other world, assuring them final salvation. Strange as it may seem, thousands of persons received these with implicit confidence, and among them were a few men and women of good education and a respectable position in society. In course of time Joanna is said to have imagined herself to have the usual symptoms of pregnancy, and announced that she was to give birth, at midnight, on the 19th of October, 1814, to a second "Shiloh," or Prince of Peace, miraculously conceived, she being then more than sixty years of age. The infatuation of her followers was such that they received this announcement with devout reverence, prepared an expensive cradle, and spent considerable sums, in order that all might be suitable for so great and interesting an occasion. The expected birth did not take place; but on the 27th of December, 1814, the woman died, at her house in Manchester Street.* On a post-mortem examination, it was found that the appearance of pregnancy which had deceived others, and perhaps herself, was due to dropsy. Her followers, however, were not to be undeceived, and for some time continued to believe that she would rise again from her "trance," and appear as the mother of the promised Shiloh.

LORD'S GROUND IN 1837. (*See page* 249.)

Mr. James Grant writes thus, in his "Travels in Town," published in 1839:—"Many persons will be surprised when they are informed that Joanna Southcott has still her followers in London. I cannot state with certainty what their number is, but I have reason to believe it is 200 or 300 at least. They meet together on Sundays, but I have not been able to discover the exact place; but I know they are most numerous in the parishes of St. Luke and Shoreditch. I lately met one of their preachers, or 'prophets,' and had some conversation with him. He was evidently a man of education, and strenuously maintained the Divine mission of Joanna. When I asked him how he got over the non-fulfilment of the promise, or rather the assurance, which she made to her 50,000 followers that she would rise from the dead on the third day, his answer was that the expression 'three days' was not to be taken in a literal sense, but as denoting three certain periods of time. Two of these periods, he said, had

* See Vol. IV., p. 425.

already passed, and the third would expire in 1842, in which year he held it to be as certain that the prophetess would arise from her grave, and give birth to 'Shiloh,' as that he was then a living man!" More than thirty years have passed away since these words were written, and the grave of Joanna Southcott has never yet given up the dead bones which rest in it.

Some passages in Joanna's "prophecies" are of rather a practical character, if the following may be taken as a specimen:—"I am the Lord thy God and Master. Tell I——— to pay thee five pounds for expenses of thy coming up to London; and he must give thee twenty pounds to relieve the perplexity of thy handmaid and thee, that your thoughts may be free to serve me, the Lord, in the care of my Shiloh." The Lord is made to inform his people somewhere, anxious to go to meet the Shiloh at Manchester, that travelling by the new cut is not expensive. On her death-bed, poor Joanna is reported to have said:—"If I have been misled, it has been by some spirit, good or evil." In her last hours, Joanna was attended by Ann Underwood, her secretary; Mr. Tozer, who was called her high-priest; Colonel Harwood, and some other persons of property; and so determined were many of her followers to be deceived, that neither death nor dissection could convince them of their error. Her remains were first removed to an undertaker's in Oxford Street, whence they were taken secretly for interment in this cemetery. A tablet to her memory contains these lines:—

"While through all thy wondrous days,
Heaven and earth enraptured gazed;
While vain sages think they know
Secrets thou alone canst show;
Time alone will tell what hour
Thou 'lt appear to 'greater' power."

SABINEUS.

THE "EYRE ARMS" IN 1820.

About three years after the death of Joanna Southcott, a party of her disciples, conceiving themselves directed by God to proclaim the coming of the Shiloh on earth, marched in procession through Temple Bar, and the leader sounded a brazen trumpet, and proclaimed the coming of Shiloh, the Prince of Peace; while his wife shouted, "Wo! wo! to the inhabitants of the earth, because of the coming of Shiloh!" The crowds pelted the fanatics with mud, some disturbance ensued, and some of the disciples had to answer for their conduct before a magistrate.

CHAPTER XX.

MARYLEBONE, NORTH: ITS HISTORICAL ASSOCIATIONS.

"Suburban villas, highway-side retreats,
That dread th' encroachment of our growing streets,
Tight boxes, neatly sash'd, and in a blaze
With all a July sun's collected rays,
Delight the citizen, who, gasping there,
Breathes clouds of dust, and calls it country air."—*Cowper.*

North Bank and South Bank—Rural Aspect of the Neighbourhood Half a Century Ago—Marylebone Park—Taverns and Tea-gardens—The "Queen's Head and Artichoke"—The "Harp"—The "Farthing Pie House"—The "Yorkshire Stingo"—The Introduction of London Omnibuses by Mr. Shillibeer—Marylebone Baths and Washhouses—Queen Charlotte's Lying-in Hospital—The New Road—The Paddington Stage-Coach—A Proposed Boulevard round the Outskirts of London—Dangers of the Road—Lisson Grove—The Philological School—A Favourite Locality for Artists—John Martin, R.A.—Chapel Street—Leigh Hunt—Church Street—The Royal Alfred Theatre—Metropolitan Music-Hall—Portman Market—Blandford Square—The Convent of the Sisters of Mercy—Michael Faraday as a Bookbinder—Harewood Square—Dorset Square—The Original "Lord's" Cricket-Ground—Upper Baker Street—Mrs. Siddons' Residence—The Notorious Richard Brothers—Invention of the "Tilbury."

THE district through which we are now about to pass lies between Edgware Road and Regent's Park, and the St. John's Wood Road and Marylebone Road. At the beginning of the century, Cowper's lines quoted above might, perhaps, have been more applicable to it than now; but even to this day they are not altogether out of place when applied to those parts lying to the north of Lisson Grove, more especially towards the Park Road, and to the villas known respectively as North Bank and South Bank, the gardens of which slope down towards the Regent's Canal, which passes between them. Here we have "trim gardens," lawns, and shrubs; towering spires, banks clothed with flowers; indeed, all the elegances of the town and all the beauties of the country are at this spot happily commingled.

Of the early history of Marylebone, and of that portion of the parish lying on the south side of the Marylebone Road, we have already spoken;* but we may add here that at the beginning of the eighteenth century the place was a small village, quite surrounded by fields, and nearly a mile distant from any part of the great metropolis. Indeed, down to a much later date—namely, about 1820—we have seen an oil-painting, by John Glover, of Primrose Hill and the ornamental water in the Regent's Park, taken from near the top of Upper Baker Street or Clarence Gate, in the front of which are a party of haymakers, sketched from life, and there are only three houses dotted about near the then new parish church of Marylebone. Indeed, at the commencement of the present century Marylebone was a suburban retreat, amid "green fields and babbling brooks." A considerable extent of ground on the north side of what is now called the Marylebone Road, and comprising besides nearly the whole of what is now Regent's Park, was at one time known as Marylebone Park, and was of course attached to the old Manor House, which we have already described.† A reminiscence of the Manor House, with its garden, park, and environs, as they stood in the time of Queen Elizabeth, when her Majesty here entertained the Russian ambassadors with a stag hunt in the said park, is preserved in a drawing made by Gasselin in 1700, and re-published by Mr. J. T. Smith in 1800. Marylebone Park Farm and its cow-sheds, which covered the rising ground almost as far northward as Le Notre's Canal, has now become metamorphosed into a rural city. From 1786 to 1792, the additions and improvements in this neighbourhood were carried into effect in quick succession. Almost all of the Duke of Portland's property in Marylebone, except one farm, was let at that period on building leases, and the new buildings in the north-west part of the parish increased with equal rapidity. The large estates at Lisson Grove, in process of time, all became extensively and, in many instances, tastefully built upon.

A correspondent of "Hone's Year-Book" writes, in 1832, with an almost touching tenderness about "Marylebone Park," the memory of which name has long since passed away, confessing that it "holds in his affections a far dearer place than its more splendid but less rural successor"—referring, of course, to the Regent's Park. This, too, is the romantic district through which Mr. Charles Dickens, in the person of his "Uncommercial Traveller," must have descried at a distance in the course of his "various solitary rambles," which he professes to have "taken northward for his retirement," the West-end out of season, "along

* See Vol. IV., p. 428 *et seq.*

† See Vol. IV., p. 429.

the awful perspectives of Wimpole Street, Harley Street, and similar frowning districts."

But the district in former times was made attractive for the pent-up Londoner by its public tea-gardens and bowered taverns. Of the last-named we may mention the "Queen's Head and Artichoke," which stood near what is now the southern end of Albany Street, not far from Trinity Church. "At the beginning of this century," says Mr. Jacob Larwood, in his "History of Sign-boards," "when Marylebone consisted of 'green fields, babbling brooks,' and pleasant suburban retreats, there was a small but picturesque house of public entertainment, yclept the 'Queen's Head and Artichoke,' situated 'in a lane nearly opposite Portland Road, and about 500 yards from the road that leads from Paddington to Finsbury'—now Albany Street. Its attractions chiefly consisted in a long skittle and 'bumble-puppy' ground, shadowy bowers, and abundance of cream, tea, cakes, and other creature comforts. The only memorial now remaining of the original house is an engraving in the *Gentleman's Magazine* for November, 1819. The queen was Queen Elizabeth, and the house was reported to have been built by one of her gardeners: whence the strange combination on the sign."

Mr. Larwood tells us an anecdote about some other public gardens in this neighbourhood, which is equally new to most readers, and interesting to the topographer and the biographer. "There was," he remarks, "in former times, a house of amusement called the 'Jew's Harp,' with bowery tea-gardens and thickly-foliaged snuggeries, near what now is the top of Portland Place. Mr. Onslow, the Speaker of the House of Commons in the reign of George II., used to resort thither in plain attire when able to escape from his chair of office, and, sitting in the chimney-corner, to join in the humours of the other guests and customers. This he continued to do for some time, until one day he unfortunately happened to be recognised by the landlord, as he was riding, or rather driving, in his carriage of state down to the Houses of Parliament; and, in consequence, he found, on the occasion of his next visit, that his *incognito* had been betrayed. This broke the charm—for him, at least; and, like the fairies in the legend, he 'never returned there any more again from that day.'" From Ben Jonson's play, *The Devil's an Ass*, act i., scene 1, it appears that it was formerly the custom to keep in taverns a fool, who, for the edification of customers, used to sit on a stool and play the Jew's harp, or some other humble instrument. The Jew's harp, we may add, was an instrument formerly called *jeu trompe*, *i.e.*, toy-trumpet. There was another tavern, with tea-gardens, bearing the same sign at Islington, down to the end of last century.

Mr. J. T. Smith, in his "Book for a Rainy Day," under date of 1772, gives us the following graphic sketch of this locality at that period:—"My dear mother's declining state of health," he writes, "urged my father to consult Dr. Armstrong, who recommended her to rise early and take milk at the cow-house. I was her companion then; and I well remember that, after we had passed Portland Chapel, there were fields all the way on either side. The highway was irregular, with here and there a bank of separation; and that when we had crossed the New Road, there was a turnstile* at the entrance of a meadow, leading to a little old public-house, the sign of the 'Queen's Head and Artichoke;' it was much weather-beaten, though, perhaps, once a tolerably good portrait of Queen Elizabeth. . . . A little beyond a nest of small houses contiguous was another turnstile, opening also into fields, over which we walked to the 'Jew's Harp House Tavern and Tea-Gardens.' It consisted of a large upper room, ascended by an outside staircase, for the accommodation of the company on ball nights; and in this room large parties dined. At the south front of these premises was a large semi-circular enclosure with boxes for tea and ale-drinkers, guarded by deal-board soldiers between every box, painted in proper colours. In the centre of this opening were tables and seats placed for the smokers. On the eastern side of the house there was a trapball-ground; the western side served for a tennis-hall; there were also public and private skittle-grounds. Behind this tavern were several small tenements, with a pretty good portion of ground to each. On the south of the tea-gardens a number of summer-houses and gardens, fitted up in the truest cockney taste; for on many of these castellated edifices wooden cannons were placed; and at the entrance of each domain, of about the twentieth part of an acre, the old inscription of 'Steel-traps and spring-guns *all over* these grounds,' with an 'N.B.—Dogs trespassing, will be shot.' In these rural retreats the tenant was usually seen on Sunday evening in a bright scarlet waistcoat, ruffled shirt, and silver shoe-buckles, comfortably taking his tea with his family, honouring a Seven-Dial friend with a nod on his peregrination to the famed Wells of Kilburn. William's Farm, the extent of my mother's walk, stood at about a quarter of a mile south; and I remember that the room in which she sat to take

* Called, in an early plan which I have since seen, "The White House."

the milk was called 'Queen Elizabeth's Kitchen,' and that there was some stained glass in the windows."

At the top of Portland Place, close to the station on the Metropolitan Railway, stands the "Green Man" tavern. It occupies the site of the old "Farthing Pie House"—a sign not uncommon in the suburbs in the early part of the eighteenth century—of which we have already given an illustration.*

Farther westward along the Marylebone Road, nearly opposite Chapel Street and the entrance to Lisson Grove, is a house bearing the well-known sign of the "Yorkshire Stingo." This tavern is memorable as the house from which the first pair of London omnibuses were started, July 4th, 1829, by the introducer of that conveyance into London, Mr. John Shillibeer, having already, for several months, been adopted in the streets of Paris. They were drawn by three horses abreast, and were such a novelty, that the neighbours used to come out from their houses in order to see them start. They ran to the Bank and back, and were constructed to carry twenty-two passengers, all inside; the fare was a shilling, or sixpence for half the distance, a sum which included the luxury of the use of a newspaper. It is said that the first conductors were the two sons of a British naval officer. It was not till several years afterwards that the outside of omnibuses was made available for passengers, and the "knife-board" along the roof is quite a modern invention. Mr. Shillibeer is widely known in connection with the funeral carriages which bear his name; but the benefits which he conferred on *living* inside passengers as well ought not to be forgotten. There is "nothing new, however, under the sun," and the omnibus is little more than a modification or improvement of the old Greenwich stage of the time of George IV.

Nearly adjoining the "Yorkshire Stingo" on the east are the Baths and Washhouses for the parish of Marylebone, to which we have already had occasion to allude, in our account of Paddington.† These baths and washhouses were among the first of the kind erected in the metropolis; the building, which is a fine structure, was erected from the designs of Mr. Eales. As we learn from Weale's work on "London," these institutions, which have within the last twenty years rapidly increased in London as well as in the country, originated in a public meeting held at the Mansion House, in 1844, when a large subscription was raised to build an establishment to serve as a model for others which it was anticipated would be erected, when it had been proved that the receipts, at the very low rate of charge contemplated, would be sufficient to cover the expenses, and gradually to repay the capital invested. The committee then appointed partially completed the model establishment in Goulston Square, Whitechapel, in 1847, and opened forty baths to the public, the demand for which by the working classes has established beyond doubt the soundness of the principles which actuated the committee; and such was the attention attracted to the subject by its proceedings, that the Government, at the suggestion and instigation of the late Rev. Sir Henry Dukinfield, Bart., the then Rector of St. Martin's-in-the-Fields, induced Parliament to pass an Act to enable boroughs and parishes to raise money on the security of the rates, for the purpose of building baths and washhouses in all parts of the country.

Near the "Yorkshire Stingo" is Queen Charlotte's Lying-in Hospital, originally established at Bayswater, as we have already stated.

The New Road, connecting the corner of Lisson Grove with the village of Islington, was formed in 1757, not without great opposition from the Duke of Bedford, who succeeded in obtaining the insertion of a clause in the Act forbidding any buildings being erected within fifty feet of either side of the roadway. This accounts for the long gardens which extend in front of the rows of houses on either side, many of which have been converted into stonemasons' yards, though some few have been built upon. This thoroughfare was called the New Road, a name which it retained for a century, when the eastern portion was named the Euston Road, and the western part the Marylebone Road. This road, at the commencement of the present century, was the route taken by the Paddington stage-coach, which travelled twice a day to the City and back. Hone, in his "Year-Book," tells us that "it was driven by the proprietor, or rather, dragged tediously along the clayey road from Paddington to the City in the morning, performing its journey in about two hours and a half, 'quick time!' It returned to Paddington in the evening within three hours from its leaving the City; and this was deemed 'fair time,' considering the necessity for precaution against the accidents of night travelling." In order to explain the length of time occupied by the "Paddington stage" on its way into the City, it should be stated that, after winding its way slowly through the miry ruts of the Marylebone Road, New Road, and Gray's Inn Road, it waited an hour or so at the "Blue Posts," Holborn Bars. The route to the Bank by way of the City Road was as

* See Vol. IV., p. 432. † See *ante*, p. 218.

yet a thing unthought of; and the driver of the Hampstead or Paddington stage who first achieved that daring feat was regarded with admiration somewhat akin to that bestowed on the man who first "doubled the Cape" on his way to India.

This allusion to the Paddington stages is curious, in the preface to the *Penny Magazine*, in 1832:—"In a book upon the poor, published in 1673, called 'The Grand Concern of England Explained,' we find the following singular proposal:—'That the multitude of stage-coaches and caravans, now travelling upon the roads, may all, or most of them, be suppressed, especially those within forty, fifty, or sixty miles of London.' The evil of the stage-coaches is somewhat difficult to be perceived at the present day; but this ingenious author had no doubt whatever on the matter, 'for,' says he, 'will any man keep a horse for himself, and another for his man, all the year, for to ride one or two journeys, that at pleasure, when he hath occasion, can step to any place where his business lies, for two, three, or four shillings, if within twenty miles of London, and so proportionably into any part of England?' We laugh at the lamentation over the evil of stage-coaches, because we daily see or experience the benefits of the thousands of public conveyances carrying forward the personal intercourse of a busy population, and equally useful whether they run from Paddington to the Bank, or from the General Post Office to Edinburgh."

Mr. Loudoun, as far back as the reign of George IV., proposed the formation of a promenade or boulevard round what were then the outskirts of London, by combining the New Road westwards along this course to Hyde Park, thence crossing the Serpentine, and coming out opposite Sloane Street; then along this road and part of the King's Road to Vauxhall Bridge, and thence across Lambeth and Southwark to Blackheath, and through Greenwich Park, and on a high viaduct across the Thames; so by the City Road back to the New Road. The "northern boulevard," which it was intended to have planted with trees, was to have been extended westwards from the "Yorkshire Stingo" down the centre of Oxford and Cambridge Terraces; but difficulties intervened, and the road was never carried out according to the original design. Had this great work been carried out in its entirety, it is possible that the outlying districts of London might have been better protected from the depredations of footpads and highwaymen, which at one time would seem to have been the rule rather than the exception. That Marylebone, in the middle of the last century, was one of the worst neighbourhoods in this respect, numerous records will prove. We have already mentioned some instances in our account of Marylebone Gardens;* and we may add that we read in the papers of the time that "on the 23rd of July, 1763, one Richard Watson, tollman of Marylebone Turnpike, was found barbarously murdered in his toll-house; upon which, and some attempts made on other toll-houses, the trustees of the turnpikes have come to a resolution to increase the number of the toll-gatherers, and furnish them with arms, enjoining them not to keep any money at the toll-bars after eight o'clock at night."

Lisson—or, more properly, Lileston—Grove, occupying the site of what was once Lisson Green, is thus mentioned by Lysons, in his "Environs of London:"—"The manor of Lilestone, containing five hides (now Lisson Green, in the parish of Marylebone), is mentioned in Doomsday-book among the lands of Ossulston Hundred, given in alms. . . . . This manor became the property of the priory of St. John of Jerusalem; on the suppression of which it was granted, anno 1548, to Thomas Heneage and Lord Willoughby, who conveyed it in the same year to Edward, Duke of Somerset. On his attainder it reverted to the Crown, and was granted, anno 1564, to Edward Downing, who conveyed it the same year to John Milner, Esq., then lessee under the Crown. After the death of his descendant, John Milner, Esq., anno 1753, it passed under his will to William Lloyd, Esq. The manor of Lisson Green (being then the property of Captain Lloyd, of the Guards) was sold in lots, anno 1792. The largest lot, containing the site of the manor, was purchased by John Harcourt, Esq., M.P."

In Marylebone Road, at the corner of Lisson Grove, is the Philological School, a handsome Gothic building, of red brick, with stone dressings. It was founded in 1792, and is now in union with King's College. Education is here afforded, almost free of cost, to a certain number of boys, the sons of professional gentlemen, who have suffered under the blows of fortune.

At a lonely public-house at the corner of this street, the tradition is that foot-travellers, at the end of the last century, used to collect their forces and examine their fire-arms before attempting the dangerous crossing of "Lisson Fields."

As the streets about were few, and the space to the north was an open field, Lisson Grove was a favourite neighbourhood for artists, especially on account of the excellence of the light. Not far off, along the New Road, lived John Martin, R.A.,

* See Vol. IV., p. 435.

the painter of the "Deluge," the "Destruction of Babylon," and other sacred subjects, so familiar to most persons by the aid of the engraver's art. "Martin's pictures," says Dr. Waagen, "unite in a high degree the three qualities which the English require above all in works of art—effect; a fanciful invention, inclining to melancholy; and topographical historic truth." And at the hospitable table of a great lover of art, in Chapel Street, would assemble a goodly band of actual and future associates and members of the Royal Academy, the immediate predecessors of Landseer.

At one time this street contained a chapel of ease, which gave its name to the street, and of which the late Rev. Basil Woodd was the minister. The street connects the Edgware Road and Paddington with the New Road. In it are the Metropolitan Railway Company's Store Departments, and also the Locomotive Carriage and Permanent Way Departments, as we have already mentioned.

Leigh Hunt, the gossiping chronicler of the "Old Court Suburb," was for some time a resident in this neighbourhood. "When Leigh Hunt resided in the New Road," says Cyrus Redding, in his "Fifty Years' Recollections," "I spent many an evening with him, pleasant, informing, and varied by conversation on subjects that chance brought up, or association introduced stealthily."

In the *Post Boy* of January 1, 1711–12, mention is made of the "Two White Balls," as the sign of a school at Marylebone, in which "Latin, French, Mathematics, &c., were taught." The notice adds that "in the same house there lives a clergyman, who teaches to write well in three days!" The locality at one time had about it an air of quietude and seclusion; but of late years a number of small streets have sprung up in the neighbourhood of the Edgware Road and Lisson Grove, and altogether it has now become, for the most part, poor and squalid; yet it is certain that this parish is by no means the poorest in London, and by no means the worst in general sanitary arrangements of the houses of the poor. Yet even here there were till lately, and it is to be feared there still are, many houses which are not "fit for human habitation." Dr. Whitmore, the medical officer of the Board of Health for the parish, in his report in 1874, draws a terrible picture of the existing dwellings of the poor in that locality, showing the necessity of still more stringent powers than are possessed by the

THE "QUEEN'S HEAD AND ARTICHOKE."

Artisans and Labourers' Dwellings Act, in order to compel the owners of such disgraceful property to do their duty by their tenants. Dr. Whitmore draws attention more especially to several tenements in Marylebone. "One of these," he then remarks, "contains nineteen rooms, which would appear to have been originally constructed with especial disregard to order in arrangement, uniformity, and convenience. Every part of this miserable abode is in a ruinous and dilapidated condition: the flooring of the rooms and staircases is worn into holes, and broken away; the plaster is crumbling from the walls; the roofs let in the wind and rain; the drains are very defective; and the general aspect of the place is one of extreme wretchedness. The number of persons living in this house is forty-seven." He adds that his first impulse was to condemn the house as unfit for human habitation, but that he hesitated to do so, fearing to drive the poor inhabitants into rooms more foul and squalid still. It will scarcely, we imagine, be believed by our grandchildren that such things could have happened in the thirty-eighth year of Queen Victoria's reign in so wealthy a district as this.

In Church Street, which connects the Grove and Edgware Roads, is the Royal Alfred Theatre. This place of amusement is celebrated for its sensational dramas and cheap prices. It was first opened in 1842, as a "penny theatre," under the name of the "Marylebone." It was enlarged in 1854 to hold 2,000 persons; and more recently the name has been altered to the "Royal Alfred." Many of Shakespeare's plays have been performed here. Close by, on the west side of the Edgware Road, another large establishment, where entertainment is nightly provided, is the Metropolitan Music Hall. In Church Street, between Carlisle and Salisbury Streets, is Portman Market, which was established many years ago for the sale of hay and straw, and also for butter, poultry, butchers' meat, and other provisions. It is largely frequented by the inhabitants of the surrounding streets of the artisan class.

LISSON GREEN IN THE EIGHTEENTH CENTURY.

On the east side of Lisson Grove we find ourselves once more among the "squares," but they are of modern growth, and consist, for the most part, of middle-class residences. They are named respectively Blandford Square, Harewood Square, and Dorset Square. In Blandford Square is the

Convent of the Sisters of Mercy, dedicated to St. Edward. This foundation owes its existence to the exertions of the late Rev. John Hearne, of the Sardinian Chapel, in Lincoln's Inn Fields, and his brother, the Rev. Edward Hearne, of Warwick Street Chapel. The community was established in 1844, and for a few years carried on their works of charity in the neighbourhood of Queen Square, Bloomsbury, where the convent was first founded. Their chief duties while there, as we learn from the "Catholic Hand-book," were the visitation of the sick poor and the instruction of adults. But possessing no means of carrying out the other objects of the institute—namely, the "education of poor children," and the "protection of distressed women of good character," they became desirous of building a convent, with schools and a House of Mercy attached to it. In 1849, the ground on which the present Convent of St. Edward stands was selected as an eligible site for the building required; and the sisters having opened a subscription-list and obtained sufficient funds to begin with, the erection was commenced early in the following year, from the designs of Mr. Gilbert Blount. In 1851, the community removed from Queen Square to their present home. School-rooms have since been erected in connection with the convent; and in 1853 the "House of Mercy," dedicated to "Our Blessed Lady and St. Joseph," was erected, at the expense of Mr. Pagliano. This house is for the admission and protection of young women of good character, who are intended for service, or who may be for a time out of employment. Girls of fourteen or fifteen usually remain here for two years, till trained for service; and those who have already been in service till they are provided by the sisters with suitable situations. While in the house, they are employed in needlework, housework, washing, ironing, &c. There is an extensive laundry attached to the House of Mercy, and the profits arising therefrom are the principal support of this institution.

In Blandford Street, Dorset Square, Michael Faraday, as we have already stated in our notice of the Royal Institution in Albemarle Street,* was apprenticed to a bookbinder, named Ribeau, in a small way of business. Faraday was placed here by his friends when only nine years of age, and continued in the occupation till he was twenty-one. The circumstances that occasioned Faraday to exchange the work-room of the binder for the laboratory of the chemist have been thus forcibly related :—

"Ned Magrath, formerly secretary to the Athenæum, happening, many years ago, to enter the shop of Ribeau, observed one of the bucks of the paper bonnet zealously studying a book he ought to have been binding. He approached; it was a volume of the old *Britannica*, open at 'Electricity.' He entered into talk with the journeyman, and was astonished to find in him a self-taught chemist, of no slender pretensions. He presented him with a set of tickets for Davy's lectures at the Royal Institution: and daily thereafter might the nondescript be seen perched, pen in hand, and his eyes starting out of his head, just over the clock opposite the chair. At last the course terminated; but Faraday's spirit had received a new impulse, which nothing but dire necessity could have restrained; and from that he was saved by the promptitude with which, on his forwarding a modest outline of his history, with the notes he had made of these lectures, to Davy, that great and good man rushed to the assistance of kindred genius. Sir Humphrey immediately appointed him an assistant in the laboratory; and after two or three years had passed, he found Faraday qualified to act as his secretary." His career in after life we have already narrated.

In Harewood Square lived, for the last thirty or forty years, the self-taught sculptor, John Graham Lough, and here he died in 1876. Sir George Hayter, many years serjeant-painter to the Queen, and "painter of miniatures and portraits" to the Princess Charlotte and to the King of the Belgians, was for many years a resident in this square, and subsequently in Blandford Square. Sir George Hayter is perhaps best known as the author of the appendix to the "Hortus Ericæus Woburnensis," on the classification of colours. He subsequently removed into the Marylebone Road, and there died, at an advanced age, in January, 1871.

Dorset Square, as we have shown in the previous chapter, covers the site of what, in former times, was a noted cricket-field; and its present name is said to have been given to it "after the great patron of cricket, the Duke of Dorset." In our account of Lord's Cricket-ground* we have entered at some length into the history of the game of cricket; but as this spot was the original "Lord's," it may not be out of place to make here a few additional remarks. Cricket made a great start about the year 1774; and Sir Horace Mann, who had promoted the game in Kent, and the Duke of Dorset and Lord Tankerville, who seem to have been the leaders of the Surrey and Hants Elevens, conjointly

* See Vol. IV., p. 297.

* See p. 249, *ante*.

with other noblemen and gentlemen, formed a committee, under the presidency of Sir William Draper. They met at the "Star and Garter," in Pall Mall, and laid down the first rules of cricket, which very rules form the basis of the laws of cricket of this day. The Marylebone Club first played their matches at "Lord's," when it occupied this site. It would be superfluous to say anything about the Marylebone Club, as the rules of this club are the only rules recognised as authentic throughout the world, wherever cricket is played.

Eastward of this square, and connecting the Park Road with Marylebone Road, is Upper Baker Street. In the last house on the eastern side of this street lived the tragic muse, Mrs. Siddons, as we are informed by a medallion lately placed on its front. The house contains a few memorials of the great actress; and among them, on the staircase, is a small side window of painted glass, designed and put up by her: it contains medallion portraits of Shakespeare, Milton, Spenser, Cowley, and Dryden. The dining and drawing-rooms, and also what was the music-room, have bow windows looking north, and commanding a view across the park to Hampstead. It is worthy of remark that, when the houses of Cornwall Terrace were about to be brought close up to the gate of the park, Mrs. Siddons appealed to the Prince Regent, who kindly gave orders that her country view should be spared. The house, which is still unchanged in its internal arrangements, is now used as the estate office of the Portman property.

Of her acting when in her prime, Cyrus Redding thus writes, in his "Fifty Years' Recollections": —"My very first sight of Mrs. Siddons was in "Queen Catherine." Never did I behold anything more striking than the acting of that wonderful woman; for, no heroine off the boards, she was the ideal of heroic majesty in her personations. I have seen real kings and queens, for the most part ordinary people, and some not very dignified, but in Siddons there was the poetry of royalty, all that hedges round the ideal of majesty—the ideal of those wonderful creations of genius, which rise far beyond the common images exhibited in the world's dim spot. It was difficult to credit that her acting was an illusion. She placed the spectator in the presence of the original; she identified herself with heroic life; she transferred every sense of the spectator into the scenic reality, and made him cast all extraneous things aside. At such times, the crowded and dense audience scarcely breathed; the painted scenery seemed to become one, and live with the character before it. Venice, Rome were there, not their representations. Another moment, and there was no object seen but that wonderful woman, because even the clever adjuncts vanished as if of too little moment to engross attention. If her acting were not genius, it was the nearest thing to it upon record. In 'Lady Macbeth' she made the beholders shiver; a thrill of horror seemed to run through the house; the audience—thousands in number, for every seat was filled, even the galleries—the audience was fear-stricken. A sorcerer seemed to have hushed the breathing of the spectators into the inactivity of fear, as if it were the real fact that all were on the verge of some terrible catastrophe." Some one remarked once to Mrs. Siddons that applause was necessary to actors, as it gave them confidence. "More," replied the actress; "it gives us breath. It is that we live on."

We learn from "Musical and Theatrical Anecdotes," that Mrs. Siddons, in the meridian of her glory, received £1,000 for eighty nights (*i.e.*, about £12 per night). Mrs. Jordan's salary, in her meridian, amounted to thirty guineas per week. John Kemble, when actor and manager at Covent Garden, was paid £36 per week; Miss O'Neill, £25 per week; George Cook, £20; Lewis, £20, as actor and manager. Edwin, the best buffo and burletta singer that ever trod the English stage, only £14 per week.

Mrs. Siddons' father, we are told, had always forbidden her to marry an actor, but, of course—like a true woman—she chose a member of the old gentleman's company, whom she secretly wedded. When Roger Kemble heard of it, he was furious. "Have I not," he exclaimed, "dared you to marry a player?" The lady replied, with downcast eyes, that she had not disobeyed. "What! madam, have you not allied yourself to about the worst performer in my company?" "Exactly so," murmured the timid bride; "nobody can call him an actor."

"I remember Mrs. Siddons," says Campbell, in his life of that lady, "describing to me the scene of her probation on the Edinburgh boards with no small humour. 'The grave attention of my Scottish countrymen, and their canny reservation of praise till they are sure it is deserved,' she said, had well-nigh worn out her patience. She had been used to speak to animated clay, but she now felt as if she had been speaking to stones. Successive flashes of her elocution, that had always been sure to electrify the south, fell in vain on those northern flints. At last, as I well remember, she told me she coiled up her powers to the most emphatic possible utterance of one passage, having previously vowed in her heart that, if this could not touch the Scotch, she would never again cross the Tweed. When it was finished, she paused, and looked to the audience. The deep silence was broken only by a single voice exclaiming, 'That's no bad!' This ludicrous parsimony of praise convulsed the Edinburgh audience with laughter. But the laugh was followed by such thunders of applause, that, amidst her stunned and nervous agitation, she was not without fears of the galleries coming down."

Mrs. Siddons retired from the stage in the zenith of her fame, in June, 1812, after appearing for the last time in her favourite character of "Lady Macbeth." She appeared, however, again on two or three particular occasions between that time and 1817, and also gave, about the same time, a course of public readings from Shakespeare at the Argyll Rooms.

By her will, which was made in 1815, Mrs. Siddons left her "leasehold house in Upper Baker Street" to her daughter Cecilia, together with her "carriages, horses, plate, pictures, books, wine, and furniture, and all the money in the house and at the banker's." She also left to her, and to her son George, the inkstand made from a portion of the mulberry-tree planted by Shakespeare, and the pair of gloves worn by the bard himself, which were given to her by Mrs. Garrick. Mrs. Siddons herself, as stated above, lies buried in Paddington Churchyard.

In this same street lived for some years Richard Brothers, who, during the years 1792–4, had much disturbed the minds of the credulous by his "prophecies." He had been a lieutenant in the navy. Among other extravagances promulgated by this man, he styled himself the "Nephew of God;" he predicted the destruction of all sovereigns, the downfall of the naval power of Great Britain, and the restoration of the Jews, who, under him as their prince and deliverer, were to be re-seated at Jerusalem; all these things were to be accomplished by the year 1798. In the meantime, however, as might be expected, Mr. Brothers was removed to a private madhouse, where he remained till 1806, when he was discharged by the authority of the Lord Chancellor, Lord Erskine. He died at his residence in this street in 1824, and was buried at St. John's Wood Cemetery, as already stated.

A little beyond the top of Upper Baker Street, on the way to St. John's Wood, is the warehouse of Messrs. Tilbury for storing furniture, &c. The name of Tilbury is and will long be known in London on account of the fashionable carriage invented by the Messrs. Tilburys' grandfather in the days of the Regency, and called a Tilbury, which was succeeded by the Stanhope. Each had its day, and both have been largely superseded by the modern cabriolet, though every now and then the light and airy Tilbury re-asserts its existence in the London parks.

CHAPTER XXI.

THE REGENT'S PARK: THE ZOOLOGICAL GARDENS, &c.

"What a dainty life the milkmaid leads,
When o'er these flowery meads
She dabbles in the dew,
And sings to her cow,
And feels not the pain
Of love or disdain.
She sleeps in the night, though she toils all the day,
And merrily passeth her time away."—*Old Play.*

Rural Character of the Site in Former Times—A Royal Hunting-ground—The Original Estate Disparked—Purchased from the Property of the Duke of Portland—Commencement of the Present Park—The Park thrown open to the Public—Proposed Palace for the Prince Regent—Description of the Grounds and Ornamental Waters—The Broad Walk—Italian Gardens and Lady Burdett-Coutts' Drinking-Fountain—The Sunday Afternoon Band—Terraces and Villas—Lord Hertford and the Giants from St. Dunstan's Church—Mr. Bishop's Observatory—Explosion on the Regent's Canal—The Baptist College—Mr. James Silk Buckingham—Ugo Foscolo—Park Square—Sir Peter Laurie a Resident here—The Diorama—The Building turned into a Baptist Chapel—The Colosseum—The Great Panorama of London—The "Glaciarium"—The Cyclorama of Lisbon—St. Katharine's College—The Adult Orphan Institution—Chester Terrace and Chester Place—Mrs. Fitzherbert's Villa—The Grounds of the Toxophilite Society—The Royal Botanical Society—The Zoological Gardens.

"AMONG the magnificent ornaments of our metropolis commenced under the auspices of his present Majesty, while Regent," we read in "Time's Telescope" for March, 1825, "the Regent's Park ranks high in point of utility as well as beauty, and is an invaluable addition to the comforts and the pleasures of those who reside in the north-west quarter of London. It is no small praise to the Commissioners of Woods and Forests to say that this park is under their especial direction; and although, from the various difficulties they have necessarily encountered, they have not been enabled to carry into execution every part of their intended plan, they have done enough to entitle them to the lasting thanks of a grateful public. A *park*, like a *city*, is not made *in a day;* and to posterity it must be left fully to appreciate the merits of those who designed and superintended this delightful metropolitan improvement."

As we have stated in the previous chapter, this park was formed out of part of the extensive tract of pasture land called Marylebone Park Fields, which, down to the commencement of the present century, had about them all the elements of rustic life; indeed, the locality seems to have been but little altered then to what it was two centuries previously; for in *Tottenham Court*, a comedy by Thomas Nabbs, in 1638, is a scene in Marylebone Park, in which is introduced a milkmaid, whose song, which we quote as a motto to this chapter, testifies to the rural character of the place.

In the reign of James I. the manor of Marylebone was granted to Edward Forest; the king, however, reserved the park in his own hands, and here he entertained foreign ambassadors with a day's hunting, as Queen Elizabeth had done before him. In the Board of Works accounts for 1582 there is the entry of a payment "for making of two new standings in Marebone and Hide Parkes for the Queene's Majestie and the noblemen of Fraunce to see the huntinge." In 1646, Charles I. granted Marylebone Park to Sir George Strode and John Wandesforde, by letters patent, as security for a debt of £2,318 11s. 9d., due to them for supplying the king with arms and ammunition. After the death of Charles no attention was paid to the claims of these gentlemen, but the park was sold by the Parliament to John Spencer, on behalf of Colonel Harrison's regiment of dragoons, on whom it was settled for their pay. At this time, the deer and much of the timber having been sold, Marylebone Park was disparked, and it was never again stocked with deer. At the Restoration, Sir George Strode and Mr. Wandesforde were reinstated in their possession of the Marylebone Park, which they held till their debt was discharged, except the great lodge, or palace, as it was sometimes called, and sixty acres of land which had been granted to Sir William Clarke, secretary to the Lord General (Monk) the Duke of Albemarle. A compensation was also made to John Carey for the loss of his situation as ranger, which he had held before the Protectorate.

After both park and manor had been "disparked" by Cromwell, the land was held on lease, for various terms, by different noblemen and gentlemen in succession; the last who held it in this way being the Duke of Portland, whose lease expired in 1811.

The present park was commenced in 1812, from the designs of Mr. Nash, the architect, who had lately finished Regent Street; and for several years the site, we are told, presented "a most extraordinary scene of digging, excavating, burning, and building, and seemed more like a work of general destruction than anything else." Indeed, it took such a long time to lay out and build, that Hughson, in his "Walks through London," published in 1817, speaks of it as "not likely to receive a speedy completion," though it was already "one of the greatest Sunday promenades about the town." By degrees, however, the elements of confusion and chaos were cleared away; and in the year 1838, when the park was thrown open, Nash's grand design received the admiration of the public. It was at first proposed to build a large palace for the Prince Regent (after whom the park is named) in the centre, but this plan was not entertained, or, if entertained, it was speedily abandoned. It was, likewise, at first intended, as we have already stated, to connect the park with Carlton House; and this design, though never realised in its full extent, gave birth to Regent Street.*

The park is over 400 acres in extent, and is nearly circular in form. It is crossed from north to south by a noble road, bordered with trees, known as the Broad Walk, and is traversed in every direction to all points of the compass by wide gravel paths, furnished with seats at short intervals. Around the park runs an agreeable drive nearly two miles long; and an inner drive, in the form of a circle, encloses the Botanic Gardens—which, it is stated, was the site reserved by Mr. Nash for the proposed palace of the Prince Regent—adjoining which is the garden belonging to the Toxophilite Society. When the park was laid out, much expense was saved by the building of terraces round the enclosure, and by letting some part of the land to certain gentlemen who were willing to build villas for themselves within the grounds on long leases. These, and the gardens of the Royal Botanic Society and the Zoological Society, do not injure the general effect, but rather add to the beauty of the place. The full extent of this park, which is decidedly one of the finest in London, is nowhere seen, in consequence of the public road crossing it towards the south end, and the Inner Circle being taken out of it. And besides the Inner Circle, the gardens of the Zoological

* Vol. IV., p. 250.

FARM IN THE REGENT'S PARK, 1750.

Society cover a large portion on the north side. The ornamental water in this park is superior to that of St. James's; and that part of the ground where it is situated is in all respects the most interesting. "The water itself," says the author of Weale's "London and its Vicinity Exhibited" (1851), "is of a good form, with its terminations well covered, and several fine islands, which are well clothed with trees. It lies also in the midst of some villas and terraces, from which it receives additional beauty. It is on the south side of the park. Some noble weeping willows are placed along its southern margin. Three light suspension bridges, two of which carry the walk across an island at the western end of the lake, are neat and elegant, but the close wire fence at their sides sadly interferes with the beauty of their form. These bridges are made principally of strong wire rods. It is to be regretted that the material which came out of the lake at the time of its formation has been thrown into such an unmeaning and unartistic heap on the north side; although the trees which have been placed upon it in some measure relieve its heaviness. Here, perhaps, more than anywhere else, a good mass of shrubs, as undergrowth, would have been of the greatest assistance. Passing along the western road from Portland Place to the Inner Circle, there is a very picturesque and pleasing nook of water on the right, where the value of a tangled mass of shrubs for clothing the banks will be very conspicuously seen." Here are a number of aquatic birds, almost rivalling those already mentioned in St. James's Park. They build and rear their young freely in the bays and islands. The ornamental water consists of a large lake, with three widely-diverging bays or inlets, and it is a favourite resort of skaters in the winter season. At that time, whenever the ice will bear, notwithstanding the throng of fashionables, there may be seen here a large number of the working, and even of the vagabond classes, pursuing their favourite recreation with perhaps more spirit than elegance. In the winter of 1866-7 a terrible accident occurred in one portion of the ornamental waters; a large field of ice gave way suddenly, and upwards of 200 persons were immersed. Forty were drowned; and the lake was afterwards cleared out, and the water reduced in depth. Boats, of late years, are allowed to be let for amusement here, and during the pleasant

THE HOLME, REGENT'S PARK.

evenings of summer a very agreeable scene is here presented. The banks of the lake and its three armlets during the summer months form a most agreeable and picturesque promenade, and in fine weather they are at all times crowded with idlers and juveniles, to whom this park, from its central situation, is conveniently accessible. Between the water and the top of the long walk lies a broad open space on the slope of a hill facing the west. "Perhaps," says the author above quoted, "as the area is intersected with several walks, it may be a little too bare, and might possibly be improved by a few small groups of trees or thorns; but in parks of this description, such a breadth of grass glade, especially on the face of a hill that does not front any cold quarter, is of immense value, both for airiness and effect. It will only want some scattered groups of trees along the edge of the slope, near the summit, to form a foreground to any view that may be attainable from the top of the hill, and also to get a broken horizontal line when looking up the slope of the hill from the bottom. The space we are speaking of is by no means favourably circumstanced in the latter respect, as the hill is crowned by the fourfold avenue of the long walk, which presents an exceedingly flat and unbroken surface line." The Brothers Percy, in 1823, call it one of the greatest ornaments of the metropolis, "around which noble terraces are springing up as if by magic." Walker thus writes in "The Original" in 1835: "The beauties of the Regent's Park, both as to buildings and grounds, seem like the effect of magic when contrasted with the recent remembrance of the quagmire of filth and the cow-sheds and wretched dwellings of which they now occupy the place." It was thought, indeed, so magnificent at the time of its completion and opening to the public, that a panoramic view of it was published on five large sheets.

Of late years the surface has been, in common with that of the other metropolitan parks, considerably improved. It has been thoroughly drained, so that the dampness of the clayey soil is greatly obviated. A portion of the central avenue has had its sides opened, and laid out as elegant Italian gardens, which are well supplied with flowers, and kept in order with the greatest taste; and more recently some enclosed portions of the park have been thrown open.

At the upper end of this long walk, opposite the principal entrance to the Zoological Gardens, stands a handsome drinking-fountain, presented, in 1871, by Lady Burdett-Coutts. It is of granite, marble, and bronze, with statuary and carving, and is surmounted with a cluster of lamps, with jets of water springing up from the basins. The architect was Mr. Darbishire.

Taken as a whole, the Regent's Park is more like the demesne of an English nobleman than the breathing-ground of the denizens of a great city, being well wooded and adorned with trees, many of them of ancient growth, and standing in ranks, avenues, or clusters picturesquely grouped. It is, however, situated too far from the Court and the Houses of Parliament ever to be fashionable in the best sense of the word; but still it is much frequented by those of the higher professional classes who wish to unite the enjoyments of town life with fresh air and the sight of green leaves. The nightingale still is often heard here.

Thirty or forty years ago it was remarked, and with some show of justice, that foreigners are perfectly surprised when they contrast the splendour of our streets and public edifices with the waste and dreary appearance of our parks; but such a remark would certainly not hold good now, though we are not even yet as well off as we might be.

The park is always full, but on Sundays and holidays it really swarms with pleasure-seekers, who find in its trees, grass, and flowers a very fair substitute for the fields of the country. During the summer months a band plays on Sunday afternoons on the green-sward by the side of the long avenue, and is the means of attracting thousands of the working classes thither. Still, the numbers that are now to be found there are not unexampled in the same place, for it is on record that 50,000 persons have been at one time in the Marylebone fields on a fine Sunday evening to hear the preaching of Whitefield.

On entering the park at York Gate, which is opposite Marylebone Church, will be noticed a fine range of buildings, called Ulster Terrace, extending some distance to the right; on the left is a similar range, named Cornwall Terrace; and further on are Clarence Place, Sussex Place, and Hanover Terrace—all bearing names connected with royalty. Though differing in architectural style, the mansions comprised in these several "places" and "terraces" have a corresponding uniformity of design, consisting of a centre and wings, with porticoes, piazzas, and pediments, adorned with columns of various orders. Sussex Place is crowned with singular gourd-like cupolas. Hanover Terrace, unlike Cornwall and the other terraces, is somewhat raised from the level of the road, and fronted by a shrubbery, through which is a carriage-drive. The general effect of the terrace is pleasing, and the pediments, supported on an arched rustic basement by fluted Doric columns, are full of richness and chaste design, the centre representing an emblematical group of the arts and sciences, the two ends being occupied with antique devices, and the three surmounted with figures of the Muses. The frieze is also light and simple elegant. The terrace was built from the designs of Mr. Nash. Altogether, Hanover Terrace may be considered as one of the finest works of the neighbourhood, and at one time it was an object of special admiration.

"The architectural spirit which has arisen in London since the late peace, and ramified from thence to every city and town of the empire, will present an era in our domestic history." Such is the opinion of a writer in Brande's *Quarterly Journal*, in 1827; and he goes on to describe the new erections in the Regent's Park as the "dawning of a new and better taste, and, in comparison with that which preceded it, a just subject of national exultation." Of the general merits of these erections, the same author further says:—"Regent's Park and its circumjacent buildings promise, in few years, to afford something like an equipoise to the boasted *Palace-group* of Paris. If the plan already acted upon is steadily pursued, it will present a union of rural and architectural beauty on a scale of greater magnificence than can be found in any other place. The variety is here in the detached groups, and not as formerly in the individual dwellings, by which all unity and grandeur of effect was, of course, annihilated. These groups, undoubtedly, will not always bear the eye of a severe critic, but altogether they exhibit, perhaps, as much beauty as can easily be introduced into a collection of dwelling-houses of moderate size. Great care has been taken to give something of a classical air to every composition; and with this object, the deformity of *door-cases* has been in most cases excluded, and the entrances made from behind. The Doric and Ionic orders have been chiefly employed; but the Corinthian, and even the Tuscan, are occasionally introduced. One of these groups is finished with domes; but this is an attempt at magnificence which, on so small a scale, is not deserving of imitation."

It must not, however, be supposed that all the various terraces of the Regent's Park front the green-sward of the park. For instance, Kent Terrace, so named after the father of her present Majesty, faces Alpha Road and St. John's Wood, a little above the top of Upper Baker Street. Here, at No. 5, the genial and kindly humourist, Shirley Brooks, the life and soul of *Punch* almost from its commencement, and the successor of Mark Lemon in its editorial chair, spent the last few years of his life, and there he died in February, 1874. He was buried at Kensal Green: may the turf lie light upon his grave!

Most of the mansions to which we have referred above are situated in or near what is called the Outer Circle, a carriage-drive which, for nearly two miles in extent, encloses the whole area of the park; while some of them are in the park itself, their beautiful private gardens forming part of the enclosed land. Among the most remarkable of these noble edifices are The Holme, nearly central in the park-land, built by Burton, the architect; St. John's Lodge, long the residence of Sir Isaac Lyon Goldsmid; and St. Dunstan's Villa. As we mentioned in our account of Fleet Street, when old St. Dunstan's Church was pulled down, the clock was sold by auction, and bought by Lord Hertford, for whom Mr. Decimus Burton erected St. Dunstan's Villa here. In the grounds of this villa the old clock was put up, with its automaton giants striking the hours and the quarters; and it is still to be seen there in full working order, performing the same duties as of old in Fleet Street, as may be seen in our illustration.* The clock and figures were put up in old St. Dunstan's Church in 1671, the "two figures, or boys with poleaxes," being made to strike the quarters. The clock had a large gilt dial overhanging the street, and above it two figures of savages, life-size, carved in wood, standing beneath a pediment, each having in his right hand a club, with which he struck the quarters upon a suspended bell, moving his head at the same time. To see the men strike was very attractive, and opposite St. Dunstan's Church was a famous field for pickpockets, who took advantage of the gaping crowd. When the old church was taken down, in 1830, Lord Hertford attended the second sale of the materials, and purchased the clock, bells, and figures for £210, and placed them in the grounds of his new villa here. In the year 1855, after the death of the Marquis of Hertford, the "costly effects" of St. Dunstan's Villa were brought to the hammer of the auctioneer. In a notice of the sale which appeared in the newspapers of the time, it is stated that "the interior of this building is somewhat grotesque and irregular, it having been erected at enormous expense and by instalments, for the sole purpose of entertaining the late marquis's numerous friends." The sale consisted of the furniture and effects, a few valuable pictures, antique sculptures, Florentine bronzes, &c.

South Villa, which is situated between the Inner Circle and the ornamental water, was for many years the residence of Mr. Bishop, whose observa-

* See Vol. I., p. 49.

tory here, erected in 1836, under the management successively of the late Rev. W. R. Dawes and Mr. J. R. Hind, gained great distinction by the discovery of asteroids and variable stars. Mr. Hind was previously an assistant in the Royal Observatory at Greenwich, and almost immediately after undertaking the management of Mr. Bishop's observatory, in 1844, he applied himself diligently to the discovery of the small planets revolving in orbits between Mars and Jupiter. The first four of this series of asteroids, which now amount to more than 160, were discovered in the first seven years of the present century; no further discoveries were made till 1845, when the detection of the fifth by M. Hencke induced Mr. Hind to prosecute his researches in this particular field of astronomy. Between the years 1847 and 1854 Mr. Hind's labours were rewarded by the discovery of no less than ten. In order to accomplish this work, it was necessary to construct charts of that portion of the heavens where the planets are usually found, and the accuracy required in mapping down the positions of minute stars in this region led to the discovery of these small planets. This observatory was a few years ago removed to Twickenham.

Proceeding onwards, in the direction of North Gate, by St. Dunstan's Villa, we cross a bridge under which passes the Regent's Canal; on each side is a foot-path, with a beautiful margin of trees. Outside the North Gate is the extensive district of St. John's Wood, of which we have already treated, and likewise Primrose Hill, of which we shall speak presently.

This portion of the park was the scene of a deplorable accident, on the 2nd of October, 1874, by which three lives were lost. In the early morning, shortly before five o'clock, five barges laden with merchandise, and among the rest a large quantity of combustibles, were being towed by a steam-tug along the canal. The head of the little flotilla had just passed under the North Bridge when a terrific explosion occurred, which shook nearly the whole of London, and blew the stout iron bridge into atoms, shattering the lodge-house to pieces, and causing considerable damage to the surrounding property. The bridge has since been rebuilt on almost precisely the same plan.

Holford House, a mansion of large extent and rare magnificence a little to the north of St. Dunstan's Villa, has since the decease of its wealthy proprietor been transformed into a training college for ministers of the Baptist denomination. The college was founded at Stepney in 1810, but transplanted hither in 1856.

We must now mention some of the chief inhabitants of the park. In Hanover Lodge lived for some time old Lord Dundonald. At 26, Sussex Place, lived for several years Mr. William Crockford, the proprietor of the club in St. James's Street which bore his name; and No. 11, Cornwall Terrace was long the residence of Mr. James Silk Buckingham, some time M.P. for Sheffield, and the most restless and indefatigable of literary toilers. Not many months previous to his death, Mr. Buckingham commenced an "Autobiography," which promised to be exceedingly voluminous. The portion published sufficed to show that the career of the author had been singularly chequered and adventurous. In his early days, he went to sea in a humble capacity. He afterwards became connected with journalism in India, travelled over the greater part of the world, and, returning to England, acquired some fame as a lecturer, and grew conspicuous by his connection with various philanthropic schemes, many of which, however, were looked upon as impracticable. In 1832 he was elected M.P. for Sheffield, and he continued to represent that constituency until the dissolution in 1837. His connection with the British and Foreign Institute, and the ridicule with which many of his proceedings were visited by *Punch*, were for a long time matters of public notoriety.

Another resident in Regent's Park in its early days was Ugo Foscolo, the Italian exile and poet, who built for himself a house, which he furnished sumptuously and with exquisite taste; but he had not occupied it long when it was seized by his creditors. His poetic genius rendered him utterly unpunctual and impracticable. He used to say to his friends, "Rich or poor, I will live and die like a gentleman, on a clean bed, surrounded by Venus and Apollo, and the Graces, and the busts of great men, among flowers and with music breathing around me; . . . and since I must be buried in England, I am happy in having got for the remainder of my life a cottage, independent of neighbours, open to the air of heaven, and surrounded by shrubs and flowers, among which I will build a small dwelling for my corpse, under a beautiful plane-tree from the East, which I mean to cultivate till the last day of my existence." Poor poet! "man proposes, but God disposes." Within a few months his cottage and all its belongings came to the hammer, and his memory has passed away from the Regent's Park. He died at Turnham Green in 1827, and was buried at Chiswick.

At the south-eastern corner of the park, opposite to the northern end of Portland Place, is Park Square. Its site was, in 1817, when Hughson wrote his "Walks through London," an open field, with a rustic gate; and the southern side of the road, where Park Crescent now stands, was much in the same condition. The houses, built in almost open country, were finished so slowly and found so few ready to take them, that for a long time it seemed doubtful whether the formation of the Regent's Park would not have to be abandoned. "The works have been so long," writes Hughson, "in this half-built state that grass has grown on the top of the walls, reaching in some places higher than the kitchen windows!" Park Square, as we have already stated,* occupies the site of what was originally intended as part of a large circus, which was to have closed the northern end of Portland Place; only one half, however, was erected, and that, as we have observed, is now called Park Crescent. The square consists of two rows of houses, elongated upon the extremities of the crescent, and separated from the Marylebone Road, from the park, and from each other by a spacious quadrangular area, laid out with ornamental pleasure grounds. Extending from the crescent to the enclosed area of the square, under the roadway, is the underground passage or tunnel, called the "Nursery-maids' Walk," of which we have spoken in a former chapter.† In 1826, Park Square was completed, and just beginning to be occupied. At No. 7 lived for many years the amiable and eccentric alderman, Sir Peter Laurie. He was the son of a small agriculturist, and came from Scotland to London to push his fortunes as a poor boy. He at first filled a clerk's place in a saddler's counting-house, and having married the daughter of his employer, set up on his own account as a merchant. He became ultimately head of the firm of Laurie and Marner, the great coach-builders of Oxford Street, and Lord Mayor of London. He died in 1861.‡

On the east side of Park Square stands the building formerly known as the Diorama. It was built by Messrs. Morgan and Pugin, architects, and was opened in 1823. It was erected for the purpose of exhibiting two dioramic views which had been previously shown in Paris by the originators, MM. Bouton and Daguerre; the latter, the inventor of the Daguerreotype, died in 1851. The pictures were changed two or three times every year; they were suspended in separate rooms, and a circular room, containing the spectators, was turned round, "much like an eye in its socket," to admit the view of each alternately. The pictures were eighty feet in length and forty feet in height, painted in solid and in transparency, and arranged so as to exhibit changes of light and shade and a variety of natural phenomena, the spectators being kept in comparative darkness, while the picture received a concentrated light from a ground-glass roof. The interior of Canterbury Cathedral, the first picture exhibited, is said to have been a triumph of architectural painting; the companion picture, the Valley of Sarnen, was equally admirable in its atmospheric effects. On one day (Easter-Monday, 1824) the receipts exceeded £200. Although the speculation was artistically successful, it did not answer commercially. In 1848, the building and ground in the rear, with the machinery and pictures, were sold; and the property, with sixteen pictures, rolled on large cylinders, subsequently realised only £3,000, not a third of the original cost of the Diorama, which was built and opened in the space of four months. The building was purchased by Sir S. Morton Peto in 1852, and turned by him into a Baptist chapel, its first minister being the Rev. Dr. Landels.

About two hundred yards to the north, and overlooking the park, stood, till 1875, the Colosseum, which was at one time a magazine of artistic and mechanical wonders, well known not only to Londoners, but to sight-seeing strangers from far and near who visited the metropolis; indeed, for many years it enjoyed a celebrity of its own as a place of amusement, with attractions for "country cousins," such as panoramas of London, Rome, Paris, and other cities, dioramas, dissolving views, grottoes, conservatories, a Gothic aviary, Temple of Theseus, &c. It was, perhaps, badly named, for, though "colossal" in its size, it bore no resemblance, physically or æsthetically, to that magnificent ruin, the Coliseum at Rome, and consequently could not fail to raise expectations which it disappointed afterwards. This, and the absence of an underground railway to make it easily accessible, ruined its popularity. The Colosseum itself was originally planned by Mr. Horner, a land surveyor, and was begun in 1824 from the designs of Decimus Burton, Messrs. Grissell and Peto being the contractors. Together with the conservatories and garden adjoining, it occupied about an acre. It was a heavy nondescript building, polygonal in form, and surmounted by an immense dome or cupola of glass, by which alone it was lighted. In the principal or western front, towards the Regent's Park, was a grand portico, with large fluted columns, of the Doric order, supporting a bold pediment. "The whole," writes Mr. Baker in his "Pictorial Handbook of London," "resembles rather a miniature of the Pantheon at Rome, except that the portico is Doric, with only six columns, said to be full-sized models of those of the Pantheon at Athens. The

* See Vol. IV., p. 450. † See p. 226, *ante*.
‡ See Vol. I., p. 413.

stripping off the plaster showed up the sham grandeur of the denuded remnant; and the prostitution of the place to a mere show-room, exceeding the bounds of a burlesque, failed to hit the taste of the public, and brought the place to grief."

On the canvas walls of the interior, for many years from and after 1829, was exhibited perhaps the most popular of all panoramas, "London," one of the first objects which country cousins were taken to see in the days of our youth. It was painted from sketches taken by Mr. Horner himself in a temporary wooden cabin or "crow's nest" erected in 1821 on the summit of the cross of St. Paul's, as we have stated in a previous volume.* The view of the picture was obtained from two galleries, one above the other, intended to correspond with the two galleries in the dome of the Cathedral. The ascent to these galleries was by spiral staircases, built on the outside of what may be termed a huge central shaft. In the inside of this was a chamber, capable of containing ten or twelve persons at a time, called the "Ascending Room." This was hoisted by invisible machinery to the level of the two galleries already mentioned. The ceiling of the picture was formed by an inner dome. "The painting of this panorama," says Mr. Timbs, in his "Curiosities of London," "was a marvel of art. It covered upwards of 46,000 square feet, or more than an acre of canvas. The dome on which the sky was painted was thirty feet greater than that of St. Paul's in diameter, and the circumference of the horizon from the point of view nearly 130 miles. Except the dome of St. Paul's, there was (at that time at least) no painted surface in Great Britain to compare with it in magnitude. . . . It is inferred that Sir James Thornhill, in painting the interior of the dome of St. Paul's, used the scaffolding which had been employed for its construction, and his designs comprised twelve several compartments, each distinct in itself. Not so this panorama of London, which, as one subject, required unity, harmony, and accuracy of linear and aërial perspective. The perpendicular canvas and the concave ceiling of stucco were not to be seen by or even known to the spectator, on whom a veritable illusion was intended to be practised; and the combination of a vertical and horizontal surface, though used, was not to be detected. After

OLD BRIDGE OVER THE LAKE, REGENT'S PARK, IN 1817.

* See Vol. I., p. 255.

THE COLOSSEUM IN 1827. (*Front to the Regent's Park.*)

THE PANORAMA OF LONDON. (*See page* 269.)

the sketches were completed upon 2,000 sheets of large paper, and the building finished, no person could be found to paint the picture in a sufficiently short period, and many artists were consequently employed upon it. At last, by the use of platforms slung by ropes, with baskets for conveying the colours, temporary bridges, and other ingenious contrivances, the painting was executed, but in the particular style, taste, and notions of each artist; to reconcile which, and to bring them to form one vast whole, was a novel, intricate, and delicate task which several persons tried, but without effect. At length, Mr. E. T. Parris, possessing an accurate knowledge of mechanics and perspective and practical execution in painting, combined with great enthusiasm and perseverance, accomplished the labour, principally with his own hands, standing in a wooden box or cradle suspended from cross poles, and lifted, as required, by ropes. The panorama, thus completed, was viewed from a gallery with a projecting framework beneath it, in exact imitation of the outer dome of St. Paul's, so as to produce the illusion that the spectator was actually standing at that altitude, the perspective and light and shade of the campanile towers above the western front being admirably managed. There was above this another staircase, leading to an upper gallery, the view from which was intended to represent the view from the cross at the top of St. Paul's." It has been said, with some truth, that of all the panoramic pictures that ever were painted in the world, of the proudest cities formed and inhabited by the human race, the view of London contained in the Colosseum was the most pre-eminent, exhibiting as it did, at one view, "to the eye and to the mind the dwellings of near a million and a half of human beings, a countless succession of churches, bridges, halls, theatres, and mansions; a forest of floating masts, and the manifold pursuits, occupations, and powers of its ever-active, ever-changing inhabitants."

This panorama, though opened early in 1829, retained its popularity so long that in 1845 it was re-painted by Mr. Parris, when a second exhibition—the same, of course, *mutatis mutandis*—"London by Night," was exhibited in front of the other. It was illuminated in such a way as to produce the illusion of a moonlight night, with the lamps in the shops, on the bridges, &c., and the rays of the moon falling on the rippling river. In 1848, the Panorama of Paris, painted by Danson, of the same size as the night view of London, was exhibited there, the localities made famous by the then recent Revolution being brought out into prominence. In 1850 both of these exhibitions gave way to a panorama of the Lake of Thun, in Switzerland; but in the following year—that of the first Great Exhibition—the old panorama re-asserted its claim on the public attention, and was reproduced with great success.

These gigantic pictures, however, were by no means the only, though they were the principal, features of the Colosseum in the days of its celebrity. It contained a sculpture gallery, called the "Glyptothec," two large conservatories of glass, and a Swiss *chalet*, with mountain scenery and real water running through it, the execution of Mr. Horner, the original designer of the building. In 1834, there was exhibited here a very fine collection of animals and other curiosities from Southern and Central Africa, which created a great sensation by their novelty, and formed one of the attractions of the season. It has often been said that there is nothing new under the sun; but it may sound novel and strange to many readers to learn, on the authority of the "Chronicles of the Seasons," published in 1844, that the experiment of a skating-hall, with boards for ice, and with skates on wheels, was tried here forty years before either "rinks" or Plimpton's patent skates were heard of. The author of that book writes: "As the exercise of skating can be enjoyed in this country only for a short period in the winter, and sometimes not for many years together near our large towns, an attempt has been made to supply a substitute by which persons might glide rapidly over any level surface, though not with so much facility as upon ice. This contrivance, which . . . . emanated from a Mr. Tyers, consists of the woodwork of a common skate, or something nearly like it; but instead of a steel support at the bottom, having a single row of little wheels placed behind one another, the body of the skater being carried forward by the rolling of the wheels, instead of by the sliding of the iron. We have seen these skates used with much facility on a boarded floor. . . . . A more successful plan still has been adopted by an ingenious inventor, who has furnished the lovers of skating in the metropolis with a fine sheet of artificial ice. It was at first exhibited at the Colosseum, in the Regent's Park, but was afterwards removed to a building where a more spacious area could be opened for the purpose. The place is decorated with scenery representing snowy mountains, and in summer it presents, with its parties of skaters, a strange contrast to the actual state of things out of doors." The "glaciarium," or "skating-rink" of real ice, was the invention of the late Mr. Bradwell, the chief machinist of Covent Garden Theatre, who was himself the inventor of the ice, and first tried *it* at the theatre. "At first," says a writer in the *Athenæum*, "the surface was hard and polished, and bore skating well; but the amateurs complained it would not enable them to cut a figure like real ice, so next year Bradwell invented an ice which cut well with the skate. The affair was on too small a scale to pay in those days." We have already mentioned this early attempt to make a skating-rink in summer in our account of Madame Tussaud's Exhibition, in Baker Street.* In spite of all this ingenuity, the projector failed, and the building passed, by sale, into other hands. The Colosseum was soon afterwards altered, with the exception of the panorama, and sundry additions and improvements were made to enhance its attractions. An entrance made on the east from Albany Street, a Gothic aviary, sundry pieces of rock scenery, and models of the ruins of the arch of Titus, the temples of Vesta and Theseus, as well as other classical subjects, a stalactite cavern, &c., were among the most important. In 1848, there was added a sort of theatre, highly decorated with reproductions of bacchanalian groups, some of Raphael's cartoons, &c. "Upon the stage," says John Timbs, "passed the Cyclorama of Lisbon, representing with terrible minuteness the terrible scenes which marked the earthquake of 1755." This exhibition was very popular for a time, and Dr. Bachhoffner added to its attractiveness by his lectures and other exhibitions. In the end, however, perhaps for the reasons we have stated above, the number of visitors dwindled, and the exhibition was closed.

The Colosseum was put up to auction by Messrs. Winstanley in 1855, but no bid was made which reached the "reserve price," £20,000, about a tenth of the sum which had been up to that time expended upon it. The building afterwards passed into several hands, and ultimately it was purchased by a small number of gentlemen, with the idea of erecting there a grand hotel; but this idea was abandoned. Subsequently the lease was purchased by a Mr. Bird, and the walls were levelled to the ground, as stated above. On its site a number of private residences have been erected.

Not far to the north of the Colosseum stands the modern Collegiate Church of St. Katharine's, once part of a royal hospital and religious foundation, established on the eastern side of the Tower of London, by Matilda, the queen consort of King Stephen. On the destruction of the former establishment in 1825, to make room for the St. Katharine's Docks, this building was erected from the designs of Mr. Ambrose Poynter, and completed in 1828. It is a Gothic structure, of yellow brick, consisting of a chapel, six residences for pensioners, and a detached residence for the master. The chapel is in the florid Gothic style, and is a poor imitation of the chapel of King's College, Cambridge; it has two octagonal towers, with a large window of perpendicular tracery, above which are the royal arms and those of the college; it has, moreover, a pulpit of wood, a gift to the church from Sir Julius Cæsar. Here, too, is the tomb of John Holland, Duke of Exeter (who fought in France in the wars of Henry VI., and who died in the year 1447), which was also removed hither from the old church of St. Katharine at Tower Hill. It is an altar-tomb, and on it rest the effigies of the duke and his two wives, under a rich canopy. On the dwellings of the chaplains the arms of the college are repeated, encircled with the motto, "Elianora fundavit," with the royal arms to correspond. The same arms are also carved on the two lodges, and are encircled with the inscriptions, "Fundavit Mathilda, 1548," and "In hoc situ restitit, 1828." In the centre of the court-yard is a conduit for the supply of the hospital. The west end of the chapel immediately faces the park road, on the opposite side of which stands the house of the master, whose office is in the gift of the Queen Consort for the time being, if there is one—if not, of the Crown. The present hospital was built with the money awarded as compensation for the removal of the old hospital, situated on the east of the Tower of London, described by us previously,† and whose homely buildings and cloisters are described by Stow as holding more inhabitants than some cities in England. Of the foundation of this hospital and its history, down to the time of its removal hither, we have already spoken; but we may add here something concerning the inmates of the hospital. Under the charter and statutes granted by Philippa, queen of Edward III., the brethren were to wear "a strait coat," and over that a black mantle, with "the sign of the holy Katharine." Green clothes or those entirely red, or any striped clothes, "as tending to dissoluteness," were not to be used. The clerks were to have shaven crowns. The curfew-bell was to ring home at night the brethren and sisters. The queen contributed to the rebuilding of the collegiate church in 1340, and her husband there founded a chantry for the repose of her soul. The hospital still remains under queenly patronage, and the mastership is a valuable sinecure. The revenues of the ancient hospital were directed

* See Vol. IV., p. 421.

† See Vol. II., pp. 117, 118.

to the maintenance of "six poor bachelors and six poor spinsters."

The community now consists of a master and three brethren, all bound by the charter to be priests, three sisters, and twenty bedesmen, and alike the number of bedeswomen, their chief duties being regular celebration and attendance at divine service, and works of charity and almsgiving among the poor, as examples of good Christian life and conversation. Conformably with these pious instructions we find that the master is a layman of quality who resides near St. James's Palace; that the three brethren have houses and occupations elsewhere, one at a time being "in residence" for a few months in the year; that the sisters "do not in general reside;" that the bedesmen and bedeswomen "have no residence," and though "still called by their ancient style, have no duties to perform," beyond receiving their annual dole of £10 a-piece; that the charity to the poor consists in the maintenance of a school containing as many as thirty-six boys and eighteen girls; and that the income of the community amounts to about £7,000, which, by better management, might be raised to £10,000 or £11,000. The chaplains hold country livings together with their appointments, which are practically fellowships without the restriction of celibacy.

During the last century a MS. register-book of the monastery of Christ Church, or the Holy Trinity within Aldgate—on the ground of which monastery Queen Matilda had founded her hospital—contained many interesting particulars about the connection of these two houses. Queen Eleanor, it seems, was not content that the government of a house, the patronage of which was in her gift, should remain in the hands of the Austin Canons. Both at Westminster and before the Lord Mayor she was defeated in her suit to obtain the entire control of this ecclesiastical foundation. But afterwards, at her request, a visitation was held by the Bishop of London, who cajoled the monks into surrendering their right by a threat of the king's displeasure if they continued to assert them. At length then, in her widowhood, the old queen was enabled to carry out her project, and she certainly founded an establishment which might have worked well down to the present day with no essential changes in its constitution. To her foundation were subsequently added various benefactions of chapelries, &c., and Edward II. presented, in 1309, the advowson, still held by the chapter, of Kingsthorpe, Northampton, with its belongings. The various chaplaincies have lapsed at some period unknown, probably at the Reformation, when the whole house was threatened with dissolution, together with the other monasteries of the kingdom, and was only rescued through the fact that, the patronage being in the hands of the queen consort. Anne Boleyn thought it worth while to induce her royal master to continue this source of influence to her and her successors.

In the reign of Elizabeth, and with the queen herself, began the first abuse of this institution. Up to that period the master had always been a priest, and held a position similar to that of a dean at the head of his chapter. The Crown, however, to whom the appointment on this occasion lapsed through default of a queen consort, contravened the old statutes, and, by a writ of *non-obstante*, placed Thomas Wilson, Doctor of Laws, in this ecclesiastical post, in which he ought, according to the charter of Queen Philippa (a special benefactress), to perform all priestly offices. This layman not only was incapacitated from carrying out the original intentions of the foundresses, but endeavoured in every possible way to enrich himself at the expense of the corporation. He surrendered the charter of Henry VI., on which foundation the hospital had hitherto rested, and in lieu thereof received one from the queen—one which remains in force to the present day. In this latter charter an important omission was made of all mention of the fair hitherto held by this hospital on Tower Hill for twenty-one days. This fair was now granted to the Corporation of the City of London, who paid to this generous master the sum of £466 13s. 4d., a slight fee which went into his own private purse.

At this hospital, for ages, the queens consort had appointed their chaplains, their ladies of the bed-chamber, or other dependants, to posts where in their old age they might perform many useful offices to the poor around them, and in return for which they might receive a decent maintenance. There were plenty of duties, and the pay was tolerably good. Besides, foreign chaplains, or chaplains attached to foreign queens, would be the very men to understand best of all the language and customs of the seafaring men and foreigners who in each reign would come in greatest numbers from the country where the queen consort had passed her youth, and would settle down in this free precinct (both ecclesiastical and civil courts belonging to the hospital), just outside the City walls, where they would be entirely free from the exactions of the City merchants, ever jealous of outsiders. This institution, therefore, was remarkably well adapted for the locality in which it was placed. But in the reign of George IV., about the year 1824, an attempt was made, and, as we have seen, with success, to remove this venerable hospital from its ancient site, and to demolish its church, a fine edifice of Perpendicular architecture. At first a strong opposition was made by the inhabitants, but eventually the influence of the moneyed shareholders carried their point, and the king, nothing loth to adorn the park which was to commemorate his earlier administration, sanctioned its withdrawal to the north-west of London, where no precinct was assigned to it, where there was no necessity for such a mission-house, and no opening for its proper working and development.

There was at St. Katharine's a "fraternity of the guild of our glorious Saviour Christ Jesus, and of the Blessed Virgin and Martyr St. Barbara." The beadroll runs as follows:—"First, ye shall pray especially for the good estate of our sovereign lord and most Christian and excellent prince King Henry VIII. and Queen Catherine, founders of the said guild and gracious brotherhood, and brother and sister of the same. And for the good estate of the French Queen's Grace, Mary, sister to our said sovereign lord, and sister of the said guild. Also, ye shall pray for the good estate of Thomas Wolsey, of the title of St. Cecilia of Rome, priest, cardinal, and *legatus a latere* to our Holy Father the Pope, Archbishop of York, and Chancellor of England, brother of the said guild. Also for the good estate of the Duke of Buckingham and my lady his wife; also for the good estate of the Duke of Norfolk and my lady his wife; the Duke of Suffolk; also for my Lord Marquis; for the Earl of Shrewsbury; the Earl of Northumberland; the Earl of Surrey; my Lord Hastings; and for all their ladies, brethren and sisters of the same. Also for Sir Richard Chomley, knt.; Sir William Compton, knt.; Sir William Skevington, knt.; Sir John Digby, knt., &c.; and for all their ladies, brethren and sisters of the same, that be alive, and for the souls of them that be dead; and for the masters and wardens of the same guild, and the warden collector of the same. And for the more special grace, every man of your charity say a Paternoster and an Ave. And God save the king, the master, and the wardens, and all the brethren and sisters of the same."

Of the eminent Masters of St. Katharine's Hospital, prior to its removal hither, we have already spoken. Sir Herbert Taylor, G.C.B., held the office at the time of the change. He had served with the Duke of York during the whole of the campaign in Holland; he was for some time private secretary to George III.; and in 1812 he was nominated one of the trustees of the king's private property; and soon after (in consequence of the Regency), private secretary to the Queen, a post which he afterwards held under William IV. and Queen Adelaide. He was appointed to the post of Master of St. Katharine's in 1818, and retained it till his death, in 1839. The next appointment was made by the late Queen Dowager, during the reign of Queen Victoria. When there is a queen consort a queen dowager loses her patronage.

Between the site of the old Colosseum and Park Square, on the north of St. Andrew's Place, is the Adult Orphan Institution, which was established in 1820. The object of this institution is the education as governesses of the orphan daughters of clergymen and of naval and military officers. The number of inmates is generally about thirty, and the income is about £4,000 annually, but it is dependent mainly on voluntary contributions.

In Chester Terrace the eminent architect, Professor Cockerell, R.A., spent the last ten years of his life, and he died here in 1863. We have already mentioned him in our account of St. Paul's Cathedral.* He was for some years Professor of Architecture in the Royal Academy, but, late in life, withdrew from active professional practice. His merits as an architect received the highest testimony of approbation by his election, in 1860, as President of the Institute of British Architects. In 1862, he resigned his position as R.A., and became one of the first of the "honorary retired Academicans." Professor Cockerell published, late in life, a large folio work, descriptive of the Temples of Jupiter and Apollo, in Ægina and the Peloponnesus, which many years before he had explored in company with Lord Byron.

In Chester Place, which is also on the east side of the Park, Charles Dickens had a house for a few months in 1847, and there was born his son, Sydney Smith Dickens, who became a lieutenant in the navy, and died at sea soon after his father. Dickens had previously lived in Osnaburgh Terrace, which is close by, though only for a few weeks, in the summer of 1844, before he started for Italy, having let his house in Devonshire Terrace.

The villa of Mrs. Fitzherbert, the wife of George Prince of Wales (afterwards George IV.), stands on the north side of the Park, in the neighbourhood of Primrose Hill, facing the canal at North Gate. It now bears the name of Stockleigh House, and has been occupied by several different families in succession. The villa was severely injured by the gunpowder explosion on the canal, of which we have spoken above.

---

* See Vol. I., p. 260.

As we have now travelled round the circuit of the Park, it is time that we should give a brief account of its hitherto unexplored interior, which is intersected by a road known as the Inner Circle. We enter this Inner Circle at the south, opposite Marylebone Church, and pass over a bridge across the ornamental water. On the right hand are the grounds of the Toxophilite Society, nearly adjoining those of the Royal Botanical Society, which reach back almost to the centre of the Park. We will speak of both of these in turn.

ST. KATHARINE'S HOSPITAL. (*See page* 273.)

In 1781, as we have stated in a previous volume,* the survivors of the "old Finsbury Archers" established the Toxophilite Society in the gardens at the back of Leicester House, then in Leicester Fields, it is stated, principally through Sir Ashton Lever, who, as we have already mentioned, showed his museum there. The society then held their meetings in Bloomsbury Fields, behind the present site of Gower Street. Some twenty-five years later they removed on "target days" to Highbury Barn, and from thence to Bayswater, where we found them again.† In 1834 they took up their quarters here, where they have a rustic lodge, and between five and six acres of ground. The members of the society meet every Friday during the spring and summer, and many prizes are shot for during the season. They possess the original silver badge of the old Finsbury Archers. Strutt, in his "Sports and Pastimes," says: "There is no art more conspicuous for the high degree of perfection to which it has been carried in this kingdom than that of archery. With our ancestors it had a double purpose to answer, that of a means of destruction in war, and an object of amusement in time of peace. The skill of the English, however, has always been proverbial; their many and glorious victories are their best eulogiums. By the Saxons, or Danes, though well acquainted with the use of the bow, it was used principally for pastime, or for the purpose of procuring food, in times anterior to the Conquest. Under the Normans, who used their bow as a military weapon, the practice of archery was much improved, and generally diffused throughout the kingdom; it was, in the age of chivalry, considered an essential part of the education of a young man who wished to distinguish himself."

* See Vol. III., p. 177. † See p. 185, *ante*.

Notwithstanding the advantages of the practice of archery, it seems to have been neglected, even when the glory of the English archers was at its greatest height, in the reign of Edward III., for we find a letter from that monarch to the sheriffs of London, declaring that the skill in shooting with arrows was almost totally laid aside for the pursuit of various useless and unlawful games; he therefore commands them to prevent such idle practices within the City and liberties of London, and to see that the leisure time upon holidays was spent in recreations with bows and arrows. In the fifth year of Edward IV., an ordinance was made, commanding every Englishman and Irishman dwelling in England to have a long bow of his own height; the Act directs that butts should be made in every township, at which the inhabitants were to shoot up and down upon all feast days, under the penalty of one halfpenny for every time they omitted to perform this exercise. In the sixteenth century we find heavy complaints of the disuse of the long bow, especially in the vicinity of London. Stow attributes this to the enclosures made near the metropolis, by which means the citizens were deprived of room sufficient or proper for the purpose. In the reign of Henry VIII., three several Acts were made for promoting the practice of shooting with the long bow; yet, notwithstanding the interference of the Legislature in its favour, archery gradually declined, and at the end of the seventeenth century was nearly, if not altogether, discontinued.

An author in the time of Queen Elizabeth informs us that it was necessary the archer should have a *bracer*, or close sleeve, to lace upon the left arm; this bracer was to be made of materials sufficiently rigid to prevent any folds that might impede the bow-string when loosed from the hand; to this was to be added a shooting glove, for the protection of the fingers. The bow, he tells us, ought to be made of well-seasoned wood, and formed with great exactness, tapering from the middle towards each end. Bows were sometimes made of brazil, of elm, of ash, and several other woods, but yew was held in most esteem. With regard to the bow-string, the author was undecided which to prefer; he would, therefore, leave the choice to the string-maker. A thin string casts the arrow farther, a thick string gives greater certainty. For the arrow, he says, there are three essential parts—the *stile*, or wand, the *feathers*, and the *head*.

THE BOTANICAL GARDENS, REGENT'S PARK. (*See page* 279.)

The stile was not always made of the same sort of wood, but varied as occasion required to suit the different manners of shooting practised by the archers. Our author then gives some instruction as to the management of the bow, and first recommends a graceful attitude.

Another writer says:—"The shooter should stand fairly and upright with his body, his left foot at a convenient distance before his right, holding the bow by the middle, with his left arm stretched out, and with the three first fingers and the thumb of the right hand upon the lower part of the arrow affixed to the string of the bow. Secondly, a proper attention should be paid to the notching, that is, the application of the notch at the bottom of the arrow to the bow-string; the notch of the arrow should rest between the fore-finger and the middle finger of the right hand. Thirdly, the proper drawing of the bow-string is to be attended to. In ancient times the right hand was brought to the right pap, but at present it is elevated to the right ear; the latter method is to be preferred. The shaft of the arrow below the feathers ought to be rested upon the knuckle of the fore-finger of the left hand, the arrow to be drawn to the head, and not held too long in that situation, but neatly and smartly discharged, without any hanging upon the string."

We must not judge of the merits of ancient bowmen from the practice of archery in the present day. There are no such distances now assigned for the *marks* as we find mentioned in old historians or old poetical legends; nor such precision even at short lengths in the direction of the arrow.

"The stranger he made no mickle ado,
But he bent a right good bow,
And the fattest of all the herd he slew,
Forty good yards him fro;
'Well shot! well shot!' quoth Robin Hood, &c."
Old Ballad.

Few, if any, of the modern archers in long shooting reach four hundred yards, or in shooting at a mark exceed eighty or a hundred. It must be borne in mind, however, that archery is now followed only for amusement, and as a delightful and healthful exercise for both sexes.

Strutt observes:—"I remember, about four or five years back, at a meeting of the Society of Archers, in their ground near Bedford Square, the Turkish Ambassador paid them a visit, and complained that the enclosure was by no means sufficiently extensive for a long shot; he therefore went into the adjacent fields to show his dexterity, where I saw him shoot several arrows more than double the length of the archery ground, and his longest shot fell upwards of 480 yards from his standing. The bow he used was much shorter than that used by the English archers, and his arrows were of the bolt kind, with round heads made of wood."

"This delightful amusement," says a writer in "Colburn's Kalendar of Amusements for 1840," "is becoming almost as popular amongst us as it was with our forefathers. It decidedly is the most graceful game that can be practised, permitting the utmost exertion of skill and address, and, from bygone glorious associations, recommending itself instantly to every lover of pleasure. The ancient festival of 'Robin Hood and May-game' was so much in repute in the reign of the eighth Harry, that he and his nobles would frequently appear as Robin and his merry men, dressed in Kendal green, with hoods and hosen. In an ancient drama called *The Play of Robin*, 'very proper to be played in May Game,' a friar, surnamed Tuck, forms one of the principal characters. He comes to the forest in search of the bold Robin, with full intent to fight with him, but is prevailed upon to change his intention and to become chaplain to Mayde Marian. The character of Marian was generally represented by a boy; it, however, appears, from an entry in a list of the expenses of the play at Kingston-upon-Thames, that it was twice performed there by a female, who for each year's services received the sum of one shilling!"

The presence of ladies at the gatherings of the Toxophilite Society having largely increased, about 1839, the meetings began to be wound up by balls, which grew to formidable dimensions, and threatened to eclipse the object of the society; accordingly, they were given up, and instead was established a "Ladies' Day," annually on the 5th of July, on which the fair "archeresses" of England—so called in the records of the society, be it observed—compete for silver bugles, bracelets, and other prizes. The average number of ladies who join in the shooting on these occasions is between fifty and sixty. The late Prince Consort and the Prince of Wales have successively been patrons of this society, whose meetings are among the pleasantest gatherings of the London season. In due course of time, though contrary to the spirit, if not to the letter, of the rules of the society, croquet became legitimised on these days. In 1869 the grounds were turned to a novel use in winter, by being laid down as a skating-rink. In the grounds is a pavilion, called the Hall, for the use of the society, tastefully adorned with stags' heads and antlers and the armorial bearings of members. The silver cups, badges, and other treasures of the society, we may add, are worth inspection.

The Royal Botanic Society, whose gardens and ornamental grounds, as we have stated, adjoin those of the Toxophilite Society, was established in 1839, under the Duke of Richmond, and having among its supporters the most eminent botanists and scientific men in the metropolis. Meetings for the reading of papers and the discussion of subjects connected with botany, or its adaptation to the arts, form a very prominent part of the operations of the society. The grounds, which are about eighteen acres in extent, allow of excellent opportunity for display; between 4,000 and 5,000 species of hardy herbaceous plants, trees, and shrubs flourish in the open air, and in the glass-houses about 3,000 species and varieties. The grounds were laid out by Mr. Robert Marnock, the designer and former curator of Sheffield Botanic Gardens, assisted by Mr. Decimus Burton as architect. In May, June, and July, floral exhibitions take place here, when nearly 3,000 medals are distributed, the value of them ranging between fifteen shillings and twenty pounds. About £1,000 is annually spent by the society in the encouragement, acclimatization, and growth of rare plants.

This garden, as we have stated above, occupies the spot said to have been reserved for a palace for the Prince Regent. It was for some time used as a nursery-garden by a Mr. Jenkins, and from this circumstance derived the advantage of having a number of ornamental trees, some of which are of respectable growth, already existing upon it when it was taken by the Royal Botanic Society. The numerous specimens of weeping ash, the large weeping elms, and many of the more common trees on the south-western side of the garden, are among the older tenants of the place. Although situated as it were in London, this garden does not suffer much from the smoke incident to the metropolis; and being in the midst of Regent's Park, with the ground falling away from it on most sides, while conspicuous hills and swells rise in the distance, this place is made, by a wise treatment of the boundary, to appear twice as large as it really is; for, from the middle of the garden, the fences are scarcely at all seen, and much of the plantations blending with those outside, and with the surrounding country, great indefiniteness of view is procured.

"In a landscape point of view," says the author of Weale's "London" (1851), "we may safely affirm that Mr. Marnock has been particularly happy in the arrangement and planting of this garden. As a whole, the avowedly ornamental parts are probably superior to anything of the kind in the neighbourhood of the metropolis. Much has been attempted, especially in the variation of the surface of the ground, and almost all that has been proposed is fully and well achieved. We would particularly point out the clever manner in which the boundary fence is got rid of on the northern and north-western sides, as seen from the middle of the garden; the beautiful changes in the surface of the ground, and the grouping of the masses of plants, in the same quarter; the artistic manner in which the rockery is formed, out of such bad materials, and the picturesque disposal of the plants upon it; and the treatment of the large mound, from which so many and such excellent views of the garden and country are obtained. . . . . Entering by the principal gate, not far from York Gate," continues the writer, "the first thing deserving of notice is the very agreeable and effective manner in which the entrance is screened from the gardens, and the gardens from the public gaze. This is not done by large close gates and heavy masonry, but by a living screen of ivy, planted in boxes, and supported by an invisible fence. There are, in fact, two screens: one close to the outside fence, opposite the centre of the principal walk, and having an entrance-gate on either side of it; and the other several feet farther in, extending across the sides of the walk, and only leaving an opening in the centre. By keeping the ivy in boxes, it does not interfere with the continuity of the gravel walk, and has a neater appearance, and can, we suppose, be taken away altogether, if required. At any rate, it has a temporary look, which is of some consequence to the effect. These screens are from six to eight feet high. In a small lodge at the side, visitors enter their names, and produce the orders of the Fellows of the Society, which are necessary for seeing the gardens." After passing through the screen above described, we find ourselves on a broad, bold walk, at the end of which, on a slightly-raised platform, is the great conservatory. Before passing up this central walk, we will make the circuit of the grounds, starting by a pathway on the right-hand side. The ascent of a large mound is one of the first things that commands attention. "Directly the visitor sets upon this walk he will perceive that an entire change of character has been contemplated. Instead of the highly-artificial features of the broad walk opposite the entrance, we are here introduced to an obvious imitation of nature. The surface of the ground is kept rough, and covered only with undressed grass—such, we mean, as is only occasionally and not regularly mown; the direction of the walks is irregular, or brokenly zigzag, and their sides ragged; the plants and trees are mostly of a wild character, such as furze, broom, ivy, privet, clematis, thorns, mountain ash, &c., and these are clustered together in tangled masses. . . . In the very midst of a highly-cultivated scene, which is overlooked at almost every step, and adjoining a compartment in which the most formal systematic arrangement is adopted in beds, and almost within the limits of the great metropolis itself, such an introduction of the rougher and less cultivated features of nature is assuredly to be deprecated. Several platforms on the face of the mound, and especially one at the summit, afford the most beautiful views of Regent's Park and its villas, Primrose and other neighbouring hills, and the more distant country. On a clear day, and the wind south-west, west, or north-west, these landscapes are truly delightful. There is a mixture of wood, grass, mansion, and general undulation, which is singularly refreshing so near London, and which abundantly exhibits the foresight that has been displayed in the formation of this mound. Unquestionably, when the atmosphere is at all favourable, the ascent of the mound is one of the greatest attractions of the garden to a lover of landscape beauties. . . . Descending the mound on its eastern side, a small lake, out of which the material for raising the mound was procured, is seen to stretch along its base, and to form several sinuous arms. Like the mound itself, an air of wildness is thrown around this lake, which is increased by the quantity of sedgy plants on its margins, and the common-looking dwarf willows which abound near its western end. In this lake, and in some of the small strips of water by which it is prolonged towards the east, an unusually complete collection of hardy water-plants will be found, and these are planted without any appearance of art, so as to harmonise with the entire scene. There is a rustic bridge over one arm of the lake, which, being simple and without pretension, is quite in character with the neighbouring objects. Between the lake and the boundary fence, in a little nook formed on purpose for them, the various hardy ferns and Equiseta are cultivated. The plants of the former are put among masses of fused brick, placed more with reference to their use in affording a position for growing ferns than for their picturesque effect. This corner is," in fact, adds the writer, "altogether an episode to the general scene, and does not form a part of it.

"On a border near these ferns, and extending along the south side of the lake, are several interesting collections, illustrative of one of the society's objects, which is to show, in a special compartment, the hardy plants remarkable for their uses in various branches of manufacture. Commencing at the western end of this border, we find, first, the plants which afford tanning materials; the *Rhus cotinus* and *coriaria*, the Scotch fir, the larch, and the oak, are among these. Next in order are the plants whose fibre is used for chip plat, comprising *Salix alba*, the Lombardy poplar, &c. Then follow the plants whose fibre is adapted for weaving, cordage, &c.; the *Spartium junceum*, flax and hemp, rank in this class. The plants used in making baskets, or matting, &c., next occur, and embrace the lime and osier among others. Grasses of different kinds then illustrate the plants whose straw is used for plaiting. The cork-tree and *Populus nigra* furnish examples of plants whose bark yields cork. A collection of plants whose parts furnish materials for dyeing finishes the series. Altogether, this is a very instructive border, and all the objects are labelled under the respective heads here given, so that they may be readily referred to.

"A large herbaceous garden adjoins the lake at its eastern end, and the plants are here arranged in beds, according to the natural system, the species of each order being assigned to one bed. Of course, the beds will thus vary greatly in size. Three or four crescent-shaped hedges are placed here and there across this garden, partly for shelter, but principally to act as divisions to the larger groups of natural orders. These hedges separate the garden into the great natural divisions, and each of the compartments they form is again sub-divided into orders by walks four feet in width, the sub-orders being indicated by division-walks of two feet in width. The inquiries of the student are thus greatly aided, and he is enabled to carry away a much clearer impression of the natural system than can be had from books. This is an excellent place for ascertaining what are the best and most showy herbaceous border flowers. Further on, in the same direction, is a garden assigned entirely to British plants, disposed, in conformity with the Linnæan system, in long beds, with alleys between. In this division will be seen how very ornamental are some of the plants to which our soil gives birth; and the less informed will be surprised to find that many of their garden favourites are the natural products of some part or other of our own country. A well-stocked 'medical garden' terminates this chain of scientific collections, and is more pleasing than the other two, on account of the plants being much more varied. The arrangement of this tribe is founded on the natural system, and the plants are in narrow beds, which take a spiral form. Near the medical garden are the plant-houses, pits, and reserve-ground, in which all the plants are grown for stocking the conservatory, flower-beds, borders, &c. The plant-houses are constructed in a very simple manner, with a path down the centre, flat shelves or stages at the sides, the hot-water pipes under the stages, near the walls, the lights resting on the side-walls, and *all fixed*, with ventilators, in the shape of small sashes, here and there along the top of the larger lights, on both sides of the centre. One of these houses, which is used for orchids, has no means of ventilation at all, except at the end, over the door, where there is a small sash capable of being opened. With proper shading it is found, both here and elsewhere, that orchids very seldom require fresh air. One of the span-roofed houses is almost wholly occupied with a cistern containing the great *Victoria regia*, *Nymphæa cærulea*, and other aquatics. From the reserve-ground a few steps lead to the large conservatory, which is more appropriately termed the 'winter-garden.' At the eastern end of this conservatory, and in a corresponding place at the other end, there is a large vase placed on the gravel; and along the front of the conservatory, at the edge of the terrace, are several more vases, of a handsomer kind. The conservatory, which is of large dimensions, is of the very lightest description, built wholly of iron and glass. The front is simply adorned with a kind of pilaster, composed of ground glass, neatly figured, which gives a little relief, without obstructing the light. The central flattish dome has an ornamental kind of crown, which helps to break the outline. The roof is, for the most part, composed of a series of large ridges, the sides of these being of an inverted sort of keel shape, and a transverse ridge extending along the principal front from either side of the domical portion. The warming of the building is effected by means of hot water circulating in cast-iron pipes, placed in brick chambers under the surface of the floor, and by a continuous iron tank, eighteen inches wide and six inches deep, placed in a brick chamber around the building. The heated air escapes by perforated castings level with the floor, and air-ducts communicate with the chambers containing the pipes and tank, bringing air to be heated from parts of the house most remote from the heating surface. Ventilation is provided by means of sashes made to slide on the roof, and worked simultaneously by means of simple machinery, and at the ends of the house and in the front by casements hung on pivots. The conservatory is capable of accommodating 2,000 visitors, and it was erected at a cost of about £7,000."

The gardens are open every week-day, from nine till sunset, and on Sundays after two o'clock; and we need hardly add that during the summer, and in the height of the London "season," its pleasant pathways and rustic walks form very agreeable promenades and lounges for the "upper ten thousand," and especially on fête-days.

Leaving the gardens by the gate on the eastern side, and passing for a short distance along Chester Road, we enter the "broad walk" of the Park, and proceeding northward, find ourselves at the entrance to the Zoological Gardens. These gardens, it need hardly be stated, are the chief attraction of Regent's Park to the thousands who flock to London during the holiday seasons. Here, as almost all the world knows, is collected the most comprehensive assemblage of animated nature in the whole kingdom, perhaps in the whole world. Here the different animals and tribes of animals, instead of being confined in wooden cages, and bandied about the country in travelling menageries, are surrounded by the very circumstances which attend them in their wild state, as far as that is possible, and thus they live, and thrive, and multiply almost as freely and certainly as in their native homes. The denizens of this unrivalled spot must be numbered by thousands, and they embrace not only all that roam the forest and the desert, and cleave the air, but some others that dwell in the caverns of the deep. The gardens, as we have stated above, are on the north-west side of the Park, and are about seventeen acres in extent. They are divided into two parts by the "Outer Circle" or carriage-drive, which passes through them elliptically, each part being appropriately connected by a short tunnel. The north entrance to the gardens is in this road. A straight principal walk passes through the gardens at an oblique angle from the main entrance in the Broad Walk, and leads by a flight of steps over the roof of one of the larger menageries, this roof being balustraded at the sides, and forming a large terrace-platform, from which a large part of the gardens, and also of the Park, may be viewed. The sides of the walk leading to this terrace are bordered by small flower-beds, backed by shrubs. The rest of the garden is laid out in the most irregular manner possible, so as to obtain a greater number and variety of walks. Several of the structures appropriated to the different animals are picturesque and pleasing examples of the rustic style; and in different parts of the gardens are sheets of water, some of them containing miniature islands, wherein the various species of water-fowl disport themselves. The northern division of the gardens is connected with the other part by a tunnel, which passes under the roadway. The ground in this part of the garden is on the slope of the banks of the canal, and constitutes a pleasant and shady walk during the summer months. The museum, the giraffes, the huge hippopotamus, the elephants, &c., are in this direction; but of these, and some of the other animals, we shall speak more in detail presently.

The Zoological Society of London, to which these gardens belong, and of which we have spoken in our notice of Hanover Square,* was instituted in 1826, under the auspices of Sir Humphrey Davy, Sir Stamford Raffles, and other eminent individuals, "for the advancement of zoology, and the introduction and exhibition of subjects of the animal kingdom, alive or in a state of preservation." The collection of animals first established here in 1828 was soon after swelled by the royal collection in the Tower of London, of which we have spoken in a previous volume,† the remains of which were transferred hither in 1834. The collection in the Tower is said to have grown out of a group of three leopards, presented by the Emperor Frederick II., the greatest zoologist of his day, to Henry III., in allusion to the three leopards which then adorned the royal shield of England, but which have since been exchanged for lions, as were also their living representatives. A full account of the Zoological Society and its living treasures, in the first few years of their occupation of its present abode, will be found in "The Gardens and Menagerie of the Zoological Society delineated," printed by Whittingham at the Chiswick Press. During the period which has elapsed since the opening of the gardens a very large number of species of mammalia and birds has been obtained, either by bequest or by purchase, detailed lists of which are to be found in the successive annual reports of the society. To these there were added, in 1849, a collection of reptiles, which has afforded great facilities to the scientific observers of this class of animals, and, more recently, a collection of fishes and of the lower aquatic animals, both marine and fresh-water, which has given rise to many interesting discoveries in their habits and economy.

ENTRANCE TO THE ZOOLOGICAL GARDENS IN 1840.

That part of the menagerie over which is the terrace of which we have spoken above was formerly called the house of the "great carnivora." Here were exhibited, in dens, the lions, tigers, leopards, jaguars, panthers, &c.; but at the com-

* See Vol. IV., p. 316. † See Vol. II., p. 88.

mencement of 1876 they were removed to more spacious and comfortable quarters in a new "lion house," which is situated a little farther to the south, not far from the ponds set apart for the seals and sea-lions. The noble beasts made the journey, not in a sort of quiet and sober procession, and as they are seen in pictures of Bacchus and his attendant train, but in closed boxes, with slipped sides, into which they were tempted by the sight of some extra slices of meat. This done, they were transported on trucks, in a most unroyal and ignoble manner, to the new abode, where the closed box was placed against the front bars of the new den, into which they were only too glad to make their way. The new "lion house" is excellently constructed and well warmed; and far more persons are now able to watch its inmates dine at four o'clock on Sunday afternoons in "the season" than was the case before this change was made.

THE MONKEY-HOUSE.

A writer in a work called "Colburn's Calendar of Amusements," published in the year 1840, tells the following story, which shows the king of beasts in an amiable light:—"The lion in the collection of the Zoological Gardens was brought, with his lioness, from Tunis, and, as the keeper informed us, they lived most lovingly together. Their dens were separated only by an iron railing, sufficiently low to allow of their jumping over. One day, as the lioness was amusing herself with leaping from one den to the other, whilst her lord looked on, apparently highly delighted with her gaiety, she unfortunately struck her foot against the top of the railing, and was precipitated backwards; the fall proved fatal, for, upon examination, it was found she had broken her spine. The grief of her partner was excessive, and, although it did not show itself with the same violence as in a previous instance, it proved equally fatal: a deep melancholy took possession of him, and he pined to death in a few weeks." The writer tells us that these lions, during the voyage, behaved with so much suavity and good humour, that they were allowed the freedom of the ship, coming and going whithersoever it pleased them, and being on terms of friendship with all on board. When the vessel reached port, numerous visitors arrived, and, as these were confined to the male sex, the lions continued the same genteel behaviour; but no sooner had several ladies set foot on the deck of the vessel than they took to flight, and, hiding themselves in some corner of the ship, showed the most extraordinary symptoms of fear and antipathy at the sight of the new comers.

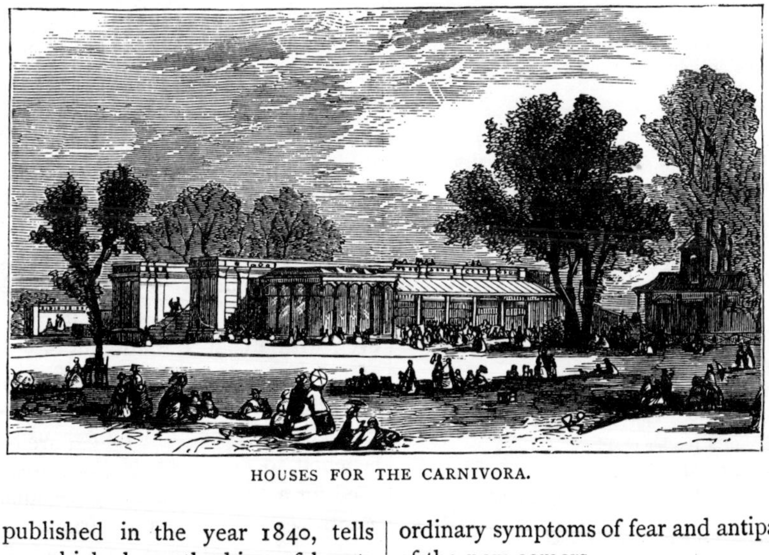

HOUSES FOR THE CARNIVORA.

Occasionally the menagerie has been fortunate enough to obtain a specimen of the African chimpanzee—the nearest approach of the monkey tribe to humanity—but in each case it has been only for a short time, the climate of England proving too cold for their lungs. The first specimen, which was brought to England in 1836, caused quite as great a *furore* as did the arrival of the first hippopotamus, and all London society rushed to "leave its cards" on the "little stranger;" so that there was hardly an exaggeration in the words of a poem, by Theodore Hook, in *Blackwood*:—

"The folks in town are nearly wild
To go and see the monkey-child,
In Gardens of Zoology,
Whose proper name is Chimpanzee.
To keep this baby free from hurt,
He's dressed in a cap and a Guernsey shirt;
They've got him a nurse, and he sits on her knee,
And she calls him her Tommy Chimpanzee."

The Tory poet then describes, in graphic colours, imaginary visits paid to the chimpanzee by Lord Melbourne, Lord John Russell, Lord Palmerston, Lord Glenelg, the Speaker, and the other ministers of State—

"Lord John came up the other day,
Attended by a lady gay,
'Oh, dear!' he cried, 'how like Lord T.!
I can't bear to look at this chimpanzee.'
The lady said, with a tender smile
Fit all his sorrows to beguile,
'Oh, never mind, Lord John: to me
You are not in the least like a chimpanzee!'

"Glenelg mooned up to see the brute,
Of distant climes the rarest fruit,
And said to the keeper, 'Stir him up for me:
He seems but an indolent chimpanzee.'
Says the keeper, 'My lord, his is a snug berth—
He never does nothing whatever on earth;
But his brother Bob, who is over the sea,
Is a much more sprightly chimpanzee.'

"The Speaker next, to make him stare,
Proceeded, dressed as he is in the chair;
When Tommy saw him, such a scream raised he
As had never been heard from a chimpanzee.
'What's the matter, Mr. Keeper?' the Speaker cried.
'Why, really, Mr. Speaker,' the man replied,
'I hope no offence, but I think that he
Takes you for the late Mrs. Chimpanzee.'

"Lord Palmerston, just turning grey,
Came up to gaze, and turned away,
And said, 'There's nothing here to see;
He's but a baby chimpanzee!'
'No,' said the keeper, 'my lord,' and smiled,
'Our Tom is but a tender child;
But if he live to be fifty-three,
He'll make a most Cupid-like chimpanzee.'

"Lord Melbourne cantered on his hack
To get a peep at Tommy's back;
He said to the keeper, he wanted to see
The tail of this wonderful chimpanzee.
'He's got no tail,' said the keeper, 'my lord.'
'You don't mean that! upon my word,
If he does without a *tail* he's superior to me,'
Said Melbourne, and bowed to the chimpanzee."

The poet ends by a suggestion that perhaps the Ministry itself might do well to give place to so clever a creature:—

"For if the King—God bless his heart—
Resolve to play a patriot's part,
And seek to mend his Ministry,
No doubt he'll send for the chimpanzee."

Three other specimens of the chimpanzee have been exhibited here since then, but they have never suceeeded in obtaining the attention which was bestowed on their predecessor; the last died in 1875.

The most important block of buildings in the gardens are those which contain the collection of the larger animals, such as the hippopotamus, the giraffe, and the elephants, &c. The fact of hippopotami having been on many occasions exhibited by the Emperors of Rome in the great displays of wild beasts which were presented to the people in the circus, was a sufficient proof that the animal could be transported from its haunts in the Nile with success. And, therefore, although 1,500 years had elapsed since the last recorded instance of this kind, the Council of the Zoological Society, in the year 1849, undertook, with considerable confidence, the operation of carrying one from Upper Egypt, all attempts to obtain it on the west coast having proved futile. By the influence of the Hon. C. A. Murray, then Agent and Consul-General at Cairo, his Highness the Viceroy, Abbas Pasha, was induced to give orders that this object should be effected; and in the month of July in that year a party of hunters, specially organised for the purpose, succeeded in capturing a calf of some three days' old on the island of Obaysch, in the White Nile. When found in the reedy covert to which the mother had confided him, the hippopotamus, who now weighs at least four tons, was of such small dimensions that the chief huntsman took him up in his arms to carry him to the boat from which his men had landed. Covered, however, with a coat of slime, more slippery than that of any fish, the calf glided from his grasp, and struggled to regain the safe recesses of the river. Quicker than he, the hunter used the gaff-hook fastened to his spear, of the same model as that used for a like purpose at the mouth of the Nile 3,000 years before, and struck him on the side, and safely held him. From Obaysch, many hundred miles above Cairo, the hippopotamus travelled down in charge of the hunters and a company of infantry, who finally landed him at the British Agency in the month of November, 1849, and in May of the following year he was landed on English soil. A special train conveyed him to London, every station yielding up its wondering crowd to look upon the monster as he passed—fruitlessly, for they only saw the Arab keeper, who then attended him night and day, and who, for want of air, was constrained to put his head out through the roof. The excitement created by the arrival of the hippopotamus was immense; the number of visitors to the gardens suddenly rose from 168,895 in 1849 to 360,402 in 1850; and the population of London thus attracted to the establishment as suddenly discovered that it contained an unrivalled collection of the most interesting and instructive character, in which, if, as often happened, they failed to see the hippopotamus, they still had the rhinoceros and a vast number of other objects to occupy them, which were scarcely, if at all, less attractive.

The hippopotamus, which thus became a household word, for many years continued to be a prime favourite with the public; and the arrival of his mate, the more juvenile "Adhela," in 1853, did not diminish his attraction.

Professor Owen published a report on the new acquisition, which formed so great an attraction. Macaulay writes thus of him in 1849:—"I have seen the hippopotamus, both asleep and awake; and I can assure you that, asleep or awake, he is the ugliest of the works of God."

It may be added that two hippopotami have been born in the gardens: the first died, and is to be seen stuffed, in the rear of the giraffe house; the second, who is called "Guy Fawkes," was born on the 5th of November, 1874.

The first living giraffe which appeared in this country was transmitted to George IV., in 1827, by Mohammed Ali, Viceroy of Egypt. It lived, however, only a few months in the menagerie at Windsor. Seven years afterwards, the Council of the Zoological Society succeeded in obtaining four specimens from Khordofan, where they were captured by M. Thibaut. This acquisition cost the society upwards of £2,300, including £1,000 for steamboat passage; and the female produced six fawns here between 1840 and 1851.

The reptile-house was fitted up in 1849. The creatures are placed in large plate-glass cases; here are pythons and rattlesnakes, and a variety of other species, some of which have produced their young in the gardens. Several years ago some serpents were exhibited which were taught to dance. This, however, was nothing new, as the same thing was exhibited in 1778 by a foreigner at "Bartlemy Fair." On one occasion a keeper in the gardens was killed by the bite of a *cobra di Capello*, a large Indian serpent; and some years ago a large boa-constrictor swallowed a blanket, and disgorged it about a month afterwards.

The collection of bears is said to be one of the largest ever made; and the bear-pit has always been a centre of attraction, especially for juveniles, in order to see the grizzly monsters climb the "ragged staff" and catch the biscuits and other edibles that are thrown to them; but the most attractive feature of the gardens, however, in the eyes of children, is the monkey-house, in which there are three large cages full of spider-monkeys, ring-tailed, black-fronted, and white-handed lemurs, dog-faced baboons, apes, the sacred monkey of the Hindoos, and other species. Their frolics in summer, and on a fine warm sunny day in winter, cause the pathways round the cages to be crowded with visitors, watching their ever-varying antics, and occasionally mischievous tricks. It would be well for many a lady's bonnet if its wearer had never approached too near to the bars of the cage of these light-fingered gentry. But every winter makes sad havoc in their numbers, as few of the specimens survive more than a couple of years; dying mostly of consumption or from lung disease, in spite of the admirable arrangements for warming their house. The orang-utan, named "Darby," brought from Borneo in 1851, was the finest specimen of his class that had, up to that time, been seen in Europe; he is stated to have been "very intelligent, and as docile as a child."

Then, again, the elephants are never forgotten, and a ride on the back of one of these monsters, as he paces slowly round his paddock, is a sight as pleasing to adults as it is enjoyable for the young. Usually there are three or four elephants here, either Asiatic or African. With these animals the Council of the Society has been somewhat unfortunate: in 1847, died here the great Indian elephant, "Jack," after having been in the gardens sixteen years; one died in 1875, and another, about the same time, broke the end off the proboscis of its trunk. In 1881–2 no little excitement was aroused by the sale of one of the elephants, "Jumbo," to Mr. Barnum, the American showman.

Adjoining the stable is a tank of water, of a depth nearly equal to the height of a full-grown elephant, in which they bathe on warm summer afternoons. Although every means has been tried to induce the breeding of elephants here, it has, so far, met with no success whatever.

Another great attraction of the gardens is the seal-pond, in which three or four of these "monsters of the deep" may be seen daily playing their gambols, just as on the shores of South Wales or of Brittany. They are most attached and obedient to the keeper—a rough-hewn French coast-guardman, who, when he feeds them publicly, makes them perform all sorts of amusing feats—climbing chairs, &c.

The parrot-house, in the northern section of the gardens, is well worthy of a visit, containing, as it does, every variety of the painted inhabitants of the woods of South America and Australia. The screaming and screeching of these not very tuneful songsters, when they are heard in chorus, may reconcile us to the dull plumage of our native birds, and teach us that there is a law of compensation not only for human beings, but for the beasts of the field and the fowls of the air.

The obituary of the gardens for the year 1873, which we make as a sample for that of most years, included not only a rhinoceros and the little hippopotamus already mentioned, but a seal, an ostrich, and the old and venerable lion "Nero," who died peacefully and quietly, not of any disease, but of sheer age. We might add that, if inquests were held on the bodies of beasts, it would have been the duty of a jury to bring in a verdict of "Wilful murder" against the British public in the case of the seal and the ostrich, the former of which was killed by swallowing a bag of nuts thrown to it by some schoolboys, without cracking the shells; while the latter was shown, upon dissection, to have met its end by twenty-one penny pieces which it could not digest, although it was an ostrich.

The climate, it is true, has something to do, at times, with the longevity of the animals: for instance, some fine white oxen from Italy, the gift of Count Cavour, are now all dead, reminding the classical reader of the well-known line of Virgil—

> "Hinc albi, Clitumne, greges, et maxima taurus
> Victima."

Some huge white oxen from India, however, now in the gardens, thrive well and multiply.

During the year above mentioned (1873) the list of new arrivals comprised upwards of 1,000 entries, including births, purchases, donations, exchanges, and "deposits." Among these was a handsome lioness, which was purchased in Dublin, and which, shortly after reaching Regent's Park, presented her new masters with a litter of four cubs.

It should be added that at intervals a "duplicate list" of animals is issued and circulated by the secretary of the society; one of such lists now before us (dated September, 1872) includes a large variety of specimens, ranging from the Indian elephant (offered at £450) down to ring-necked and crested paroquets, at 15s. and 10s., and a common heron at 10s. The books kept daily at the office of the society contain not only the list of "arrivals" and "departures," but also a record of the temperature in the various "houses" in the gardens, and what would be called an "*æger* list"—namely, a list of such birds, beasts, and fishes as require medical attendance. In one corner of the gardens, not easily found by chance visitors, is a small and unobtrusive dissecting-room, where the carcases of such animals as die from natural causes are made subservient to the purposes of anatomical science.

In 1875 an extensive addition was made to the gardens, by inclosing about four acres of land on the north side of the canal, which is crossed by a bridge, thus enabling the society to open an additional entrance in the Outer Circle of the Park, nearly opposite the foot of Primrose Hill.

In these gardens were lodged, in a temporary building, the collection of beasts and birds brought back by the Prince of Wales from India, in 1876, including several tiger cubs, goats, sheep, dwarf oxen, and dwarf elephants, as well as several varieties of the pheasant tribe.

We may add, in conclusion, that Regent's Park is, and must be, at a disadvantage when compared with the other places of fashionable resort in London; and although crowds of the *bon ton* flock to the *fêtes* at the Botanical Gardens, and lounge away their Sunday afternoons at "the Zoo" in the season, yet it never will or can become really "the fashion," as the tide sets steadily in a south-west direction.

"The Regent's Park, above all," writes the Vicomte d'Arlingcourt, in his account of a visit to England in 1844, "is a scene of enchantment, where we might fancy ourselves surrounded by the quiet charms of a smiling landscape, or in the delightful garden of a magnificent country house, if we did not see on every side a countless number of mansions, adorned with colonnades, porticoes, pediments, and statues, which transport us back to London; but London is not here, as it is on the banks of the Thames, the gloomy commercial city. Its appearance has entirely changed. Purified from its smoke and dirt, and decked with costly splendour, it has become the perfumed abode of the aristocracy. No artisans' dwellings are to be seen here: nothing less than the habitations of princes."

CHAPTER XXII.

PRIMROSE HILL AND CHALK FARM.

"—— templa serena,
Despicere unde queas alios."—*Lucretius,* ii.

Situation of Primrose Hill, and its Appearance in Bygone Times—Barrow Hill and the West Middlesex Waterworks—The Manor of Chalcot—Murder of Sir Edmund Berry Godfrey—Duel between Ugo Foscolo and Graham—Primrose Hill purchased by the Crown, and made a Park for the People—The Tunnel through the Hill—Fireworks in Celebration of the Peace in 1856—The Shakespeare Oak—Lady Byron's Residence—Chalk Farm—Duels fought there—The Wrestling Club of Cumberland and Westmoreland—The Eccentric Lord Coleraine—The Old Chalk Farm Tavern—The Railway Station—Pickford's Goods Depôt—The Boys' Home—The "York and Albany" Tavern—Gloucester Gate—Albany Street—The Guards' Barracks—Park Village East—Cumberland Market—Munster Square—Osnaburgh Street—Sir Goldsworthy Gurney—The "Queen's Head and Artichoke"—Trinity Church.

As the Green Park forms a sort of supplement and appendage to St. James's Park, so does Primrose Hill to the Regent's Park: it has the character of a "park for the people," and its associations are the reverse of aristocratic. The hill lies on the north side of the park, and its name still bears testimony to its rural and retired situation, when its sides were covered with brushwood and an undergrowth of early spring flowers. Going back to the time of the Roman settlers, we find that when they planted their colony on the banks of the Thames and founded London, most part of the northern district consisted of a large forest filled with wolves and other wild animals. Early in the thirteenth century the forest of Middlesex was disafforested, but although portions were cleared, St. John's Wood, as we have already seen, remained sufficiently dense in Queen Elizabeth's reign to afford shelter and concealment to Babington, the conspirator, and his associates. At that time, however, the slopes of Primrose Hill were used as meadow land, and were probably in the mind of writers who allude to the many "haicockes in July at Pancredge" (St. Pancras), as a thing known to everybody. This district dates back to very early times, if we may accept the name of Barrow Hill—formerly Greenberry Hill—which lies on its western side, as evidence that it was once the scene of a battle and place of sepulture for the slain. There was formerly a Barrow Farm, and Barrow Hill itself is now occupied by the reservoir of the West Middlesex Waterworks. The name survives in Barrow Hill Place and Road.

MEDAL TO COMMEMORATE THE MURDER OF GODFREY.

"The definite history of the place," says a writer in the *Builder*, "dates from the time when 'sundry devout men of London' gave to the Leper Hospital of St. James (afterwards St. James's Palace) four hides of land in the field of Westminster, and eighty acres of land and wood in Hendon, Chalcot, and Hampstead. Edward I. confirmed these gifts, but in course of time dissensions arose between the convent and the Abbey of Westminster, which Henry VI. brought to an end by giving the custody of the hospital into the hands of the provost and fellows of his newly-founded college of Eton, and with it the before-mentioned acres. In the twenty-third year of Henry VIII.'s reign the hospital was surrendered to the king, who turned it into a manor-house. The property of Chalcot and its neighbourhood was probably of little value, and no doubt the Eton authorities had not much difficulty in getting it into their own hands again."

More than two centuries pass away, farmhouses are built, and the manor of Chalcot is divided into Upper and Lower, which are described as the Chalcots. Towards the close of the year 1678 the eyes of all England were directed towards this retired and lonely spot, for there had been discovered the dead body of Sir Edmund Berry

Godfrey, of whose murder we have already spoken in our account of Somerset House.* The hill at that time doubtless was famous for the primroses that grew upon it; and although the fields around were used for grazing, the place, covered as it was with brambles, was inaccessible, and wonder was excited as to the means by which the body came there. The name of the victim has been variously written: Macaulay, in common with many others, calls him Edmundsbury Godfrey, whilst by some it is written Edmund Berry Godfrey. On a monument in the cloister of Westminster Abbey to the memory of a brother of Sir Edmund, the knight is designated as Edmundus Berry Godfrey; but the late Mr. J. G. Nichols went still further, and brought forward as his authority Sir Edmund's father. The following is an extract from the diary of Thomas Godfrey, of Lidd, Kent:—"My wife was delivered of another son the 23rd December, 1621, who was christened the 13th January, being Sunday. His godfathers were my cousin, John Berrie, his other godfather my faithful loving friend and my neighbour sometime in Grub Street, Mr. Edmund Harrison, the king's embroiderer. . . . They named my son Edmund Berrie, the one's name, and the other's Christian name."

It has been suggested that the confusion has arisen partly from the likeness of the name to that of the celebrated town in Suffolk, and partly from the infrequent use at that time of two Christian names. Sir Edmund was a rich timber merchant, and lived at the river end of Northumberland Street, in the Strand. He was Justice of the Peace for the Court quarter of town, and was so active in the performance of his duties, that during the time of the Great Plague, in 1664-5, upon the refusal of his men to enter a pest-house in order to bring out a culprit who had furnished a large number of shops with at least 1,000 winding-sheets stolen from the dead, he ventured in alone and brought the wretch to justice. He was knighted for his conduct during the plague, and Bishop Burnet says that he was esteemed the best justice of the peace in England. At the time of his death he was entering upon the great design of taking up all beggars, and putting them to work.

He is said to have been a zealous Protestant and Church of England man, but not forward to

PRIMROSE HILL IN 1780.

* See Vol. III., p. 92.

execute the laws against the Nonconformists, and to have somehow got mixed up in the so-called Popish plot. We are told that he grew apprehensive and reserved, and assured Burnet that "he believed he should be knocked on the head," yet he took no care of himself, and went about alone. One day he was seen, about one o'clock, near St. Clement's Church but was never heard of again until his body was found in a ditch on the south not coming near 500 yards of the place." Burnet was one of those who went to the White House, and he describes what he saw as follows:—"His sword was thrust through him; but no blood was on his clothes or about him. His shoes were clean. His money was in his pocket, but nothing was about his neck, and a mark was round it about an inch broad, which showed how he was strangled. His breast was likewise all over marked with

OLD CHALK FARM IN 1730.

side of Primrose Hill, about two fields distant from the White House, or Lower Chalcot farmhouse, whither the corpse was taken, and where it lay for two days, being seen by large multitudes. From the "White House" the body of Sir Edmund was conveyed back to London, to be buried in St. Martin's Churchyard, having first "lain in state for two days at the Bridewell Hospital." The spot on which the corpse was found is thus described in a publication of the period:—"As to the place, it was in a ditch on the south side of Primrose Hill, surrounded with divers closes, fenced in with high mounds and ditches; no road near, only some deep dirty lanes, made for the convenience of driving cows, and such like cattle, in and out of the grounds; and those very lanes bruises, and his neck was broken. There were many drops of white waxlights on his breeches, which he never used himself; and since only persons of quality and priests use those lights, this made all people conclude in whose hands he must have been." Four medals were struck to commemorate his death, on one of which he was represented as walking with a broken neck and a sword in his body. On the reverse of this medal St. Denis is shown bearing his head in his hand. Underneath is the following inscription:—

"Godfrey walks up hill after he is dead;
Denis walks down hill carrying his head."

A great procession, consisting of eight knights, all the aldermen of the city of London, and seventy-two clergymen, accompanied the body to the grave in St. Martin's Church, and a portrait of Sir Edmund was placed in the vestry-room. The press now teemed with pamphlets on the subject. In one, the murder was charged to the Earl of Danby; in another, Garnet's ghost addressing the Jesuits is made to show the greatest delight in the horrors of the plot. Wishes are expressed—

> "That the whole nation with one neck might grow,
> To be slic'd off, and you to give the blow."

The nation thus roused to a state of frenzy, thirsted for revenge, and Somerset House, as we have mentioned, then the residence of Queen Catherine of Braganza, consort of Charles II., was fixed upon as the scene of the murder. Three persons—namely, Robert Green, cushion-man of the queen's chapel; Lawrence Hill, servant to Dr. Godden, treasurer of the chapel; and Henry Berry, porter at Somerset House—were tried for the crime on the 10th of February, 1679, when the infamous witnesses, Oates, Prance, and Bedloe, declared "that he (Godfrey) was waylaid, and inveigled into the palace, under the pretence of keeping the peace between two servants who were fighting in the yard; that he was there strangled, his neck broke, and his own sword run through his body; that he was kept four days before they ventured to remove him; at length his corpse was carried in a sedan-chair to Soho, and then on a horse to Primrose Hill." In spite of the abandoned character of the witnesses and the irreconcilable testimony they gave, the jury found all the prisoners guilty, and Lord Chief Justice Scroggs said he should have found the same verdict had he been one of the jury. The three men, all declaring their innocence to the last, were executed, and the law had its victims; but from that day to this the murder of Godfrey has remained an unsolved mystery. It was pointed out in a printed letter to Prance, 1681, that his story of Hill carrying the body before him on horseback could not be true on account of the condition of the district; and it was further stated that it would have been "impossible for any man on horseback, with a dead corpse before him, at midnight to approach, unless gaps were made in the mounds, as the constable and his assistants found from experience when they came on horseback thither." It has been a popular belief that Greenberry Hill, mentioned above, took its origin from the names of the three supposed murderers, but it is doubtful whether this was the case; and Narcissus Luttrell, in his contemporary "Diary," remarks on the singular coincidence of the names of Green, Berry, and Hill with the old designation of the hill. The name has long since been changed to Barrow Hill, thus assisting to bury in obscurity, if not in oblivion, the awful fate of a man who lived and died guiltless of any crime, except the strict execution of his duty.

On the western side of Primrose Hill is another and a smaller eminence, the summit of which has been, beyond the memory of man, bare of all vegetable substance. "The popular tradition is," observes a writer in the *Mirror*, "that there two brothers, enamoured of the same lady, met to decide by arms to whom she should belong. Ridiculous idea! that a woman's heart would consent to receive a master from the point of a sword, or trust its hopes of happiness to the hired arbitration of a trigger! Both died at the same time, each by the weapon of his adversary!" Here, too, about the year 1813, Ugo Foscolo fought a duel—happily, bloodless—with Graham, the editor of the *Literary Museum*.

In 1827, the provost and fellows of Eton began to see that their property would soon become valuable, and they obtained an Act of Parliament (7 Geo. IV., c. 25, private), enabling them to grant leases of lands in the parishes of Hampstead and Marylebone. Soon after the accession of Queen Victoria, endeavours were made to obtain Primrose Hill for the Crown, and a public act was passed (5 and 6 Vict., c. 78), for effecting an exchange between Her Majesty and the provost and college of Eton. By this act Eton College received certain property at Eton, and gave up all their rights in the Hill. In the schedules setting forth the particulars of the transfer we read of Shepherd's Hill, Square Field, Bluehouse Field, and Rugmere Close, all in the vicinity of Primrose Hill. The Eton property is now largely built upon, and the appropriate names of Eton, College, King Henry's, Provost, Fellows', Oppidans', and Merton Roads, all on the north, south, and east of the Hill, mark its position.

It may be added here that the North-Western Railway, entering a tunnel at Chalk Farm, passes under Primrose Hill, emerging again between St. John's Wood and Kilburn. This tunnel, which runs in a parallel direction with a portion of the Adelaide Road, is nearly 3,500 feet in length, and was made in 1834. It was for many years considered one of the greatest triumphs of engineering skill in the neighbourhood of the metropolis; in fact, it was the largest work of the kind carried out by any engineers up to that time. It passes through 1,100 yards of stiff London clay, "the most unmanageable and treacherous of all materials." Within the last few years another tunnel has been constructed for the main line traffic.

There is little more to be said about Primrose Hill in the way of history. On May 29, 1856, fireworks were exhibited here in celebration of the peace, as well as in Hyde, Green, and Victoria Parks. In 1864, under the auspices of a committee, an oak was planted by Mr. Phelps, the tragedian, on the south side of the hill, to commemorate the tercentenary of Shakespeare. Improvements have been made here at various times. Thus, fifty acres at the foot of the hill were enclosed and laid out as a park; appliances for gymnastics were erected near the Albert Road; and later in time, lamps were placed in the park and over the brow of the hill. These have a particularly pretty effect when lighted up at night. Few places are more appreciated by the popular pleasure-seeker on Easter and Whit Mondays than Primrose Hill, which is often so crowded that at a distance it seems as if one could walk upon the heads of the people congregated there. The summit is 206 feet above Trinity high-water mark of the Thames, and an exceedingly fine view can be obtained from it on a clear day. The hill was a place of meeting for many years, for popular demonstrations, &c., before Hyde Park was chosen. It is said that on the morning of the frightful gunpowder explosion on the Regent's Canal, of which we have spoken in the preceding chapter, an artist was waiting there to watch the rising of the sun, and to see London gradually awake. He saw and heard more than he expected. We may add that this spot is now entirely hemmed in by houses on all sides, but we hope that the prophecy of Mother Shipton—that when London shall surround Primrose Hill the streets of the metropolis will run with blood—may not be fulfilled, in our day at least.

With a certain class of poets, akin to those of the "Lake" School, it became the fashion to exalt the London suburbs as paragons of beauty. The Alps were nothing to Primrose Hill, and the elms which then crowned its summit were as the cedars of Lebanon to the ready writer. Highgate outvied Parnassus, buttercups and dandelions outshone the exotics of southern climes. New phrases were coined even for the cow-keepers of the district; and, to use Cyrus Redding's phrase, "the peak of Hampstead became as famous in their view as Chimborazo to that of Humboldt." Professor Wilson, it may be remembered, lashed this school rather severely in *Blackwood*, on account of its tendency to magnify trifles.

In St. George's Terrace, in the house nearest to the eastern slope of Primrose Hill, died, in 1860, Lady Byron, the widow of the poet. The marriage was, no doubt, ill-assorted, and could never have been a happy one. But, abused and maligned as she was in life, it is a pleasure to quote here the words of the Hon. Amelia Murray in her "Recollections:"—"She was traduced and misunderstood; one of those pure spirits little valued by the world, though worshipped by those who knew her well. Her friendship was the chief blessing of my earliest years, and her loss can never be replaced."

A house in St. James's Terrace, at the corner of the Park and Primrose Hill, was the residence for many years of Mr. Hepworth Dixon, the editor of the *Athenæum*, and author of "Her Majesty's Tower," "New America," &c.

Burnet describes Primrose Hill as "about a mile out of town, near St. Pancras Church." Such a description might answer in Burnet's time, when St. Pancras Church was the only landmark of importance in the neighbourhood, and they were separated merely by fields and cultivated grounds; but now a perfect city of houses has grown up between them. In fact, only a century ago the old church of St. Pancras was so very rural that it was only enclosed by a low and very old hand-railing, which in some parts was covered with docks and nettles. Whitefield's Chapel, in Tottenham Court Road; Montagu House, Great Russell Street; Bedford House, Bloomsbury Square; and Baltimore House, situated where Russell Square is now built, could all be seen from the churchyard. By this time the White House had become a tavern and tea-gardens for the benefit of ruralisers, and was known as Chalk Farm. This name is a corruption from Chalcot, and its transitional form can be seen in Rocque's map of London (1746), where England's Lane, Haverstock Hill, is marked as Upper Chalk House Lane. The old manor-house of Upper Chalcot still remains in England's Lane on Haverstock Hill, and the site of Lower Chalcot is indicated by Chalk Farm and Chalcot Terrace. The etymology of Chalk Farm is evidently a contraction or vulgar abridgment of Chalcot Farm, and has nothing whatever to do with the nature of the soil, as may perhaps by some people be supposed; there being no chalk in the neighbourhood, the whole district resting on London clay. The next point in the history of Chalk Farm is its selection as the scene of frequent duels. It was particularly suitable for the purpose, as it was near town, and at the same time quite secluded. Before the Regent's Park was planned, Marylebone Fields were looked upon as quite a wilderness, and few Londoners strolled as far northwards as Primrose Hill. Chalk Farm for some years, indeed, as a place for "affairs of honour," even rivalled in popularity Wimbledon

Common, where the Duke of York fought Colonel Lennox in 1789; Battersea Fields, where the Duke of Wellington met face to face with the Earl of Winchilsea, in 1829; and Putney Heath, where Pitt met Tierney in 1798, and Castlereagh and Canning exchanged shots in 1809. "Then there was Chalk Farm," writes Mr. S. Palmer, in his "History of St. Pancras," "which was better known latterly as the favourite place for discontented men to meet in order to settle their differences with the pistol, as if gunpowder were the stronger argument, and a steady aim the best logic. This absurd custom is now dying out, and it is quite possible in the present day for a man to be a man of honour and yet decline to risk his own more valuable life against a man who values his at nothing." One of the earliest duels on record as having taken place at Chalk Farm was that between Captain Hervey Aston and Lieutenant Fitzgerald, in the summer of 1790, a lady, as usual, being in the case. Fitzgerald had the first fire, and shot Aston through the neck; he, however, recovered, but was shot in another duel a few years later. In April, 1803, Lieutenant-Colonel Montgomery and Captain Macnamara met near Chalk Farm to settle, by force of arms, a dispute which had occurred between them in Hyde Park. The quarrel arose out of the fact that the dog of the one "officer and gentleman" had snarled and growled at the dog of the other. The dog's growl, however, was terribly avenged in the sequel, for the colonel was killed and the captain severely wounded. Captain Macnamara was tried for murder at the Old Bailey, but although the judge summed up for manslaughter, the jury returned a verdict of "Not guilty." Three years later, an encounter took place here between "Tom" Moore and Francis Jeffrey; but, fortunately, although the principals were in earnest, the affair came to an abrupt termination by the arrival of the police officers before the signal for firing was given. It was stated at the time that the pistols were loaded with only blank cartridges. This little matter gave rise to an epigram which ended—

> "They only fire ball-cartridge at reviews."

Byron alludes to this report in his "English Bards and Scotch Reviewers:"—

> "Health to great Jeffrey! Heaven preserve his life,
> To flourish on the fertile shores of Fife,
> And guard it sacred in its future wars,
> Since authors sometimes seek the field of Mars!
>
> "Can none remember that eventful day,
> That ever glorious, almost fatal, fray,
> When Little's leadless pistol met his eye,
> And Bow Street myrmidons stood laughing by?"

Moore, who wrote a long account of this "affair of honour," has described the spot where the would-be duellists met as "screened on one side by large trees." He also induced Byron to add to his lines a note, to the effect that the pistol was actually loaded. Moore, it is stated, borrowed his pistols from a brother poet, who sent the Bow Street officers to prevent the two little men from killing each other. Here is Moore's narrative of this hostile meeting as recorded in his diary:—

"I must have slept pretty well; for Hume, I remember, had to wake me in the morning; and the chaise being in readiness, we set off for Chalk Farm. Hume had also taken the precaution of providing a surgeon to be within call. On reaching the ground we found Jeffrey and his party already arrived. I say his party, for although Horner only was with him, there were, as we afterwards found, two or three of his attached friends (and no man, I believe, could ever boast of a greater number) who, in their anxiety for his safety, had accompanied him, and were hovering about the spot. And then was it that, for the first time, my excellent friend Jeffrey and I met face to face. He was standing with the bag, which contained the pistols, in his hand, while Horner was looking anxiously around. It was agreed that the spot where we found them, which was screened on one side by large trees, would be as good for our purpose as any we could select; and Horner, after expressing some anxiety respecting some men whom he had seen suspiciously hovering about, but who now appeared to have departed, retired with Hume behind the trees, for the purpose of loading the pistols, leaving Jeffrey and myself together. All this had occupied but a very few minutes. We, of course, had bowed to each other at meeting; but the first words I recollect to have passed between us was Jeffrey's saying, on our being left together, 'What a beautiful morning it is!'—'Yes,' I answered, with a slight smile, 'a morning made for better purposes;' to which his only response was a sort of assenting sigh. As our assistants were not, any more than ourselves, very expert at warlike matters, they were rather slow in their proceedings; and as Jeffrey and I walked up and down together, we came once in sight of their operations; upon which I related to him, as rather *apropos* to the purpose, that Billy Egan, the Irish barrister, once said, when, as he was sauntering about in like manner while the pistols were loading, his antagonist, a fiery little fellow, called out to him angrily to keep his ground. 'Don't make yourself unaisy, my dear fellow,' said Egan; 'sure, isn't it bad enough to take the dose, without being by at the mixing up?' Jeffrey had scarcely time to smile at this story, when our two friends, issuing from behind the trees, placed us at our respective posts (the distance, I suppose, having been previously measured by them), and put the pistols into our hands. They then retired to a little distance; the pistols were on both sides raised, and we waited but the signal to fire, when some police officers, whose approach none of us had noticed, and who were within a second of being too late, rushed out from a hedge behind Jeffrey; and one of them, striking at Jeffrey's pistol with his staff, knocked it to some distance into the field, while another running over to me, took possession also of mine. We were then replaced in our respective carriages, and conveyed crest-fallen to Bow Street." It is known that Moore and Jeffrey afterwards became cordial friends.

In January, 1818, a fatal duel was fought at Chalk Farm between Theodore O'Callaghan and Lieutenant Bailey; and in February, 1821, it was the scene of an encounter between John Scott, the avowed editor of the *London Magazine*, and Mr. Christie, a friend of Lockhart, the supposed contributor to *Blackwood's Magazine*, which grew out of some articles in the *London*, reflecting on the management of *Blackwood*. Mr. Scott was severely wounded, and he was conveyed from the battle-field on a shutter to the Chalk Farm Tavern, where he lingered for a little more than a fortnight. Mr. Christie, together with Mr. Trail and Mr. Patmore, who acted as seconds, were tried at the Old Bailey, on the charge of murder, but Mr. Patmore did not surrender to take his trial. Lord Chief Justice Abbot summed up the evidence with much feeling, and in the end the jury returned a verdict of "Not Guilty." By this time, so great had been the inroads made upon this retired spot by the erection of houses, that even if duelling had not been put down by the voice of society and "strong arm of the law," the duellists, from and after that date, would have been forced to seek another place of meeting.

It deserves to be mentioned to the credit of William Hone, author of the "Year Book," "Table Book," &c., that he was among the first persons who had the courage to try and write down by banter and jest, as well as by serious argument, the system of duelling, as foolish and unchristian. Here is one of his *jeux d'esprit*, entitled "An Answer to a Challenge," which arose out of a squabble between two lawyers at Andover in 1826:—

"I am honoured this day, sir, with challenges two,
The first from friend L——, and the second from you.
As the one is to fight and the other to dine,
I accept *his* engagement, and *yours* must decline.
Now in giving this pref'rence I trust you'll admit
I have acted with prudence, and done what was fit;
Since encountering him, and my weapon a knife,
There is some little chance of preserving my life,
Whilst a bullet from you, sir, might take it away,
And the maxim, you know, is to live while you may."

We all know that a jest will sometimes succeed where a sermon fails; but jests and sermons appear to have been equally fruitless in their attacks on this silly practice, as it survived for at least three or four years into the reign of Victoria.

But the old tavern at Chalk Farm has other reminiscences besides those which associate it with the many duels fought in its neighbourhood. From the year 1834 to 1838—at which time the fields attached to it were called "Mr. Bowden's Grounds"—there used to be held the annual matches of the Wrestling Club of Cumberland and Westmoreland. These sports had previously been held in various places in the suburbs—on Kennington Common, at Chelsea, and at the Eyre Arms, St. John's Wood; they were subsequently held, at various dates, at Highbury Barn, at Copenhagen House, at Hornsey Wood House, at Cremorne Gardens, and at Hackney Wick. Since 1864, however, these sports have been among the attractions of the New Agricultural Hall, at Islington. They have always been, and, strange to say, are still, celebrated on Good Friday. The chief and most noted wrestlers are "North Country" men, though the prizes are mostly open to all comers, and the Cornish wrestlers are almost equally celebrated. They are under the management of a committee with a president, a secretary, and other officers, and the money collected at their yearly gatherings has often, perhaps generally, been handed over to one or other of our metropolitan charities. Although such sports have been held in London periodically for upwards of a century, it was not till the year 1824 that a society was actually founded for the purpose of encouraging those wrestling matches for which the natives of Cumberland and Westmoreland have been so famed from time out of mind, and the celebration of which in London has, no doubt, had the merit of keeping up old friendships and connections which would otherwise have been dropped. This society has at various times received encouragement from such men as the late Earl of Lonsdale and Professor Wilson; and it will be remembered that Charles Dickens has described a wrestling match in *Household Words*, having drawn his picture from what he saw when present at a field-day at Windermere. Those who object to such games should remember that wrestling formed one of the series of five contests which made up the "pentathlon" at the old Olympic games of Greece. A full account of these matches will be found in a small work called "Wrestliana."

As lately as 1846 Charles Dickens alludes to "the bowers for reading and smoking scattered about the tea-gardens at Chalk Farm" as still in existence, comparing them with those in his then Swiss residence at Lausanne. But in another decade they were already things of the past.

In the neighbourhood of Chalk Farm, in 1824, George Hanger, the eccentric Lord Coleraine, breathed his last. His death is thus recorded in the pages of the *Gentleman's Magazine* for that year:—"March 31. Died, of a convulsive fit, at his residence, near the Regent's Park, aged seventy-three, the Right Hon. George Hanger, fourth Lord Coleraine, of Coleraine, Co. Londonderry, in the Peerage of Ireland, and a major-general in the army; better known by the title of Colonel Hanger, or the familiar appellation of 'George Hanger.'" Such is the curt and brief manner in which Mr. "Sylvanus Urban" records the decease of a nobleman who had played in his day a conspicuous part among the early boon companions of George Prince of Wales, of whom he was wittily said to be not the constant *Hanger*, but the constant "Hanger on." Like Lord Rochester and Lord Camelford before him, he lived a life not very creditable to a member of "the upper ten

TRINITY CHURCH, ALBANY STREET. (*See page* 300.)

SIR RICHARD STEELE'S HOUSE, HAVERSTOCK HILL.

thousand"—fighting duels, and selling coals on commission, and spending a year or two occasionally within "the rules" of the King's Bench or the Marshalsea prison. He died lamented and regretted by none, or, at all events, by few of his contemporaries; and the extinction of his title, which was caused by his death, could scarcely be said to have been lamented, or to have created in the Irish peerage any gap or void which it was difficult to fill up.

The old Chalk Farm Tavern, which had witnessed so many duels in its day, stood in what is now called Regent's Park Road, on the north side, about half-way between the foot of Primrose Hill and the North London Railway Station. It was rather a picturesque old house, with a veranda running along outside, from which the visitors looked down into some pleasant gardens. "This house," writes Mr. Samuel Palmer, in his "History of St. Pancras," "has long been known as a place of public entertainment, similar in character to the 'Adam and Eve' and 'Bagnigge Wells.' From its proximity to Hampstead, it was the usual resort of holiday-folk on their return from the Heath. Being on the incline of Primrose Hill, the terrace in front of the house was very often crowded to inconvenience, the prospect being charming and the air invigorating. Semi-theatrical entertainments were at times provided for the visitors, whilst at other times balls, promenades, masquerades, wrestling-matches, and even prize-fights and other brutal sports were offered for their amusement. These latter sports, singularly enough, were principally the amusements for the Sunday. The fatal issue of one such encounter, between John Stone and Joseph Parker, resulting in a trial, and ultimately in a verdict of manslaughter against the survivor and the seconds on both sides, aided in a great measure to suppress this brutal exhibition." Mr. Palmer, however, omits to tell us the date of this occurrence.

About the year 1853 it was pulled down, to make way for a modern and more pretentious hotel, which now occupies its site. On the opposite side of the way, even to a more recent date, were some tea-gardens and pleasure-grounds, where there were occasional displays of fireworks on summer evenings; but these also have given way to the steady advance of bricks and mortar. Indeed, the growth of London in this direction has been steadily going on for many years, for as far back as 1832 a correspondent of Hone's "Year Book" writes: "The Hampstead Road and the once beautiful fields leading to and surrounding Chalk Farm have not escaped the profanation of the builders' craft." Indeed, one does not feel at all inclined to agree with the sentiment expressed by Mr. Parkle, in the "Uncommercial Traveller" of Charles Dickens, that "London is so small." We should rather say, it is so large. He complains, "What is a man to do? . . . . If you go west, you come to Hounslow. If you go east, you come to Bow. If you go south, there's Brixton or Norwood. If you go north, you can't get rid of Barnet!" We must own that our impression is rather in the opposite direction, and that, go which way we will, we can never get rid of the monotony of the streets of the metropolis.

Fairs in old times were held in this neighbourhood, much to the delight, no doubt, of the lads and lasses living at Hampstead, Highgate, and St. Pancras. But of late these fairs have dwindled away to nothing. "Chalk Farm Fair," writes G. A. Sala, in "Gaslight and Daylight" in 1860, "is a melancholy mockery of merriment;" and we believe it is now a matter of history.

The Chalk Farm Railway Station, at which we have now arrived, has become a great centre of passenger and goods traffic; it is joined by the large goods station of Messrs. Pickford, covering several acres to the south, and reaching half-way to the "York and Albany." The station here was for many years the termination of the North London Railway, and in the end the line became joined on to the North-Western line to Birmingham and Liverpool. The railway station premises run for nearly a quarter of a mile along Chalk Farm Road, with ranges of coal-sheds and depôts for warehousing goods. Close by, at the foot of Haverstock Hill, is the Adelaide Hotel, so named after the consort of King William IV. On Haverstock Hill stood, till recently, a house said to have been occupied by Steele. The circular building which projects into the Chalk Farm Road near the Adelaide Hotel was built to accommodate the locomotive engines in the early days of the London and Birmingham Railway. It is about 120 feet in diameter, and has in its centre a turn-table, by means of which the engines can be shifted to the up and down lines, and to the various sidings. Externally, the building is not very attractive, but its interior is light, the arched roof being supported on graceful iron pillars.

At the end of Regent's Park Road, close by Chalk Farm Railway Station, is an institution which has achieved a large amount of good in its own especial field of action. The Boys' Home, for such the institution in question is called, was originally established in 1858 in the Euston Road, for the prevention of crime, arresting the destitute child in danger of falling into a criminal life, and training him, by God's blessing, to honest industry; a work which, as experience has shown, can only be successfully done by such voluntary agency. It is, in fact, an industrial school for the training and maintenance, by their own labour, of destitute boys not convicted of crime. Owing, however, to the Midland Railway Company requiring the site of the "home" in the Euston Road for their new terminus, in 1865 new premises were secured here, consisting of three unfinished houses and a yard, which were taken on a ninety-nine years' lease from the governors of Eton College, to whom the property belongs. The applications for admission soon became so numerous—about 300 in a year—that it was determined to increase the numbers. The school and the workshops, which were subsequently built, will enable 100 boys to work, instead of fifty as at first provided for.

The boys are lodged in separate houses, holding about twenty-five boys in each, in ordinary bed-rooms; each boy is provided with his own bed, each room under the charge of a monitor, and each house under the direct control of the master or matron living in it, who endeavour to become the true parents of these poor lads, to guide them no less by affection than by firm discipline, to establish a happy "family" feeling, and to attract their once ragged and disorderly pupils by the force of kindly teaching and good example. The late Lady Truro, daughter of the Duke of Sussex, in 1866 left a bequest to the institution, by which the committee of management have been enabled to extend the "home," by adding to it another house; and a chapel was likewise built for their accommodation, by a generous donor, in 1864. This chapel has since germinated, through the generosity of the provost and fellows of Eton College, into a handsome new church—St. Mary's, at the north-eastern corner of Primrose Hill.

The institution itself is called not a school but a "home," and in every sense of the word it is a home. "I call a home," once said Mr. "Tom" Hughes, when pleading for this very institution, "a place in which you will find sympathy. It must be a place in which the great bond of love which binds all the world together comes out and is recognised. This is the very first condition. . . . The second condition which I understand as essential to a home is that you shall have there order and discipline. . . . The third law of the world is that it is a world of work; 'he that will not work, neither shall he eat.' . . . There is one other condition, as I understand the matter, without which there can be no true and righteous home, and that condition is economy. In God's natural world there is no waste whatever, and it is His world in which we are. We are under His laws, and ought to study His methods of administering them."

The boys accommodated in the Home are all lodged there, fed and clothed, and receive instruction in various trades—carpentry, brushmaking, tailoring, shoemaking, &c. A large quantity of firewood is cut on the premises, and delivered to customers, and several boys are employed by private families in the neighbourhood in cleaning knives and shoes. The amount of the industrial work done in the Home is highly satisfactory. The products of the labour of the boys and their teachers—clothes, shoes and boots, brushes of every kind, carpentry and firewood—are sold, and contribute to the general funds of the institution; yet a large expenditure, chiefly caused by the extreme youth of many of the boys, is annually necessary to enable the managers to continue and extend their useful exertions.

Children of all ages are admitted, ranging from six or seven up to fourteen or fifteen; and it may be mentioned that there is a branch at East Barnet for training still younger children. An ants' nest could not display more activity and life than may be witnessed here among the youths who have been rescued from the streets. At first, the restraint, gentle as it is, is frequently irksome to the little urchin, and he plots to run away, and now and then he succeeds. However, he soon returns of his accord, or is brought back, and after a very short interval, becomes steady and reconciled to the happiness of the Home. Indeed, he soon becomes proud of it—proud of being associated with it, proud of his work, proud of his learning, proud of the self-respect which the very character of the Home inspires. All this, there can be no doubt, is brought about by the kindness which he experiences from all around him; and so, instead of being abased by mischievous companions, or the angry words of elders, he feels himself raised at once in the social scale. There is a school, too, to which he goes, and an excellent schoolmaster to guide his thoughts in the right direction. "In all his labours," observes a writer in *Once a Week*, "he is taught patience, and soon understands that, if his progress be slow at first, it will eventually become more rapid. Scriptural or moral mottoes are placed in every room, so that his eye hourly feeds his heart with sound counsel. To avoid monotony and tediousness, his tasks are frequently diversified, and he is taught either a musical instrument or singing. Indeed, the band of this juvenile institution acquits itself very creditably. In the school-room is a harmonium, usually presided over by the teacher, whose performances naturally excite the delight of these civilised British Bedouins."

As we have intimated above, various trades are taught, and, when fit, the boys are put out into real life as may suit each. With all these young men a constant intercourse is kept up after they have left the Home by letters and visits, and a register of all cases is kept at the Home by which the history of every one from his admittance can be traced. To show the class of boys rescued, the particulars of one or two cases will suffice:—

G. L., aged ten years, but looking much younger, was received on the 22nd of August, 1862. This poor boy was described in the paper sent to the Home from the office of the Reformatory and Refuge Union, as "awfully filthy and neglected," and was stated to have been in the casual-ward of several workhouses for single nights. He was in a sad condition when he entered the Home—shoeless, dirty and tattered, footsore and hungry. The boy's father was a clown in some itinerant show, and had deserted his mother. The mother, who was of anything but good character, wandered to London, where the child was found destitute in the streets. The case coming strictly within the operation of the "Industrial Schools' Act," the boy was sent to the Home by the presiding magistrate of the Thames Police Court.

J. P., aged fourteen, was a message-boy at the barracks, Liverpool. Believing him to be an orphan, the soldiers persuaded him to conceal himself on board a ship bound with troops to Gibraltar, from which place, by similar means, he contrived to find his way to China. When at Hong Kong he was allowed to ship as second-class boy on board H.M. line-of-battle ship *Calcutta*, in which, a few days after, he met with so severe an accident by scalding, that he was removed to the hospital-ship stationed at Hong Kong. His life was despaired of, and for nearly a year he suffered from the effects of this disaster. Recovering in some degree from this accident, he was shipped in a man-of-war for England, and landed at Portsmouth, discharged from the navy only half-cured and destitute. He was indebted to the active benevolence of a chaplain of the navy for his admission into the Boys' Home, where, by the assistance of good living, a comfortable and cheerful home, and good medical help, he soon became a healthy boy again. He recently re-visited the Home as an able-bodied seaman, with a good character.

Ragged schools have done great things for this destitute class, but to the Boys' Home we look for really and permanently raising a lad out of the slough of depravity, and landing him safely and firmly on the rock of honest industry.

It may be stated here that the boys admitted to the Home are chosen by joint vote of the Committee on account of their extreme destitution and want. Those who have neither parent alive stand the first chance of admission, those who have lost their father stand next, and those who have lost their mother are last on the roll of candidates. Many of them, however, never knew that they ever had either father or mother, or a home of any kind whatsoever.

The latest report of Her Majesty's inspector states:—"My inspection of the school this day has given me much satisfaction. I have found all in good order. The boys look healthy and cheerful. They appear to be managed with good sense and good judgment. They have passed a very creditable examination. The dictation and arithmetic of the upper classes were above the average. The school appears to be doing its work well, with most encouraging results."

It is not intended that the Boys' Home should be dependent upon alms; the object of the promoters is to make it self-supporting. But whilst the grass is growing, we all know the steed may starve. Yet such need not be the case if the public would buy the brushes, book-stands, work-tables, &c., made by the boys' hands, and employ the little fellows themselves in carpenters' jobs, and in cleaning boots and shoes in the neighbourhood.

Passing from the Boys' Home by the Gloucester Road, a short walk brings us to the "York and Albany Hotel," which is pleasantly situated, overlooking the north-eastern corner of the Regent's Park. The house, which has at the back some extensive tea-gardens, forms the starting-point of a line of omnibuses to the west and south of London. It may be mentioned here that the bridge over the Regent's Canal, between the "York and Albany" and Gloucester Gate, having been long considered too narrow and ill-constructed to suit the requirements of the present day, the Metropolitan Board of Works in the end decided upon rebuilding it upon a much larger scale, at a cost of about £20,000. It is surmounted by groups of statuary, and now forms a very handsome approach and entrance to the Regent's Park on the eastern side.

In Regent's Park Terrace, close by Gloucester Gate, Louis Kossuth, the Hungarian patriot, was living in 1859.

Albany Street, like the hotel above mentioned, takes its name from royalty—the late Duke of York having been Duke of Albany as well; it extends from this point to the Marylebone Road, near the top of Portland Place, and close to the south-east entrance of the Regent's Park. At the top of this street, almost facing the east window of the chapel of St. Katherine's Hospital, are spacious barracks, which are constantly used, in turn with others, by a regiment of the Guards. Together with the drill-ground and the various outbuildings, they occupy no less than seven or eight acres. To the north of this lies Park Village East, a collection of detached villas, built in a rustic style; and close by is the basin of an arm of the Regent's Canal.

At the end of the canal basin is Cumberland Market, or, as it is sometimes called, Regent's Park Market. It was established for the sale of hay, straw, and other articles, removed, in the reign of George IV., from the Haymarket, as already stated by us,* between Piccadilly and Pall Mall; but it has never been very largely attended.

Munster Square, as a poor group of houses built round a plot of market ground close by is called, derives its name from one of the inferior titles inherent in the Crown; and the reader will remember that William IV. created his eldest natural son, Colonel Fitzclarence, a peer, by the title of the Earl of Munster.

In Osnaburgh Street—which, by the way, is likewise named after a member of the royal family, the late Duke of York having also been "Bishop of Osnaburgh," in the kingdom of Hanover—is the St. Saviour's Hospital. Here tumours and cancerous growths are treated in such a manner as to dispense with the use of the knife. In this street, too, is another institution for the exercise of charity and benevolence; it is called the St. Saviour's Home and Hospital for the Sisters of Charity.

In Albany Street the late Sir Goldsworthy Gurney was practising as a medical man about the year 1825, employing his spare time in making practical experiments, more especially in manufacturing a steam-carriage, which, under many difficulties, he perfected sufficiently to make a journey along the high road to Bath, in July, 1829, two months before the successful efforts of George Stephenson in the North to solve the question of steam conveyance. Miss Gurney thus describes the difficulties under which her father laboured before carrying out his invention:—"Our house was in Argyle Street, Regent Street, where my father was in practice as a medical man, at the same time making experiments of all sorts; and his steam-carriage was begun at that house, but a manufactory was soon taken, and he found it necessary to be there and to have his family with him. We occupied rooms which were probably intended for Sir William Adams, a celebrated oculist, for whom this building was erected as an eye infirmary, in Albany Street. . . . . From a window of my room I looked into the yard where my father was constructing his steam-carriage. The intense combustion caused by the steam-blast, and the consequent increase of high-pressure steam force acting on the jet, created such a tremendous current or draught of air up the chimney that it was something terrific to see or to hear. The workmen would sometimes throw things into the fire as the carriage passed round the yard—large pieces of slate or sheet-iron—which would dart up the chimney like a shot, falling occasionally nearer to the men than was safe, and my father would have to check their enthusiasm. The roaring sound, too, sometimes was astounding. Many difficulties had to be overcome, which occupied years before 1827. The noise had to be got rid of, or it would have frightened horses, and the heat had to be insulated, or it might have burnt up the whole vehicle. The steam machinery was at first contrived to be in the passenger-carriage itself, as the turnpike tolls would have been double for two vehicles. My father was forcibly reminded of this fact, for there was then a turnpike-gate immediately outside the manufactory. This gate was first on the south side of the doors, and the steam-carriage was often exercised in the Regent's Park barrack-yard; then the gate was moved just a few yards to the north, between the doors and the barracks. But perhaps the greatest difficulty—next to that of prejudice, which was strong against all machinery in those days—was to control the immense power of the steam and to guide the carriage. It would go round the factory yard more like a thing flying than running, and my father was often in imminent peril while making his experiments. He, however, at last brought the carriage completely under control, and it was perfected. One was built to carry the machinery, the driver, and stoker only, and to draw another carriage after it. My father could guide it, turn it, or back it easily; he could set it going or stop it instantly, up hill or down; it frequently went to Hampstead, Highgate, Edgware, Barnet, Stanmore, and its rate could be maintained at twenty miles an hour, though this speed could only be indulged in where the road was straight and wide, and the way clearly

* See Vol. IV., p. 217.

to be seen. I never heard of any accident or injury to any one with it, except in the fray at Melksham, on the noted journey to Bath, when the fair people set upon it, burnt their fingers, threw stones, and wounded poor Martyn, the stoker. The steam-carriage returned from Bath to the Hounslow Barracks—eighty-four miles—stoppages for fire and water included, in nine hours and twenty minutes, or at the rate, when running, of fourteen miles an hour. This journey from London to Bath, the first ever maintained with speed by any steam locomotive, was made in July, 1829, on the common turnpike road, in the face of the public, and two months before the trial at Rainhill."

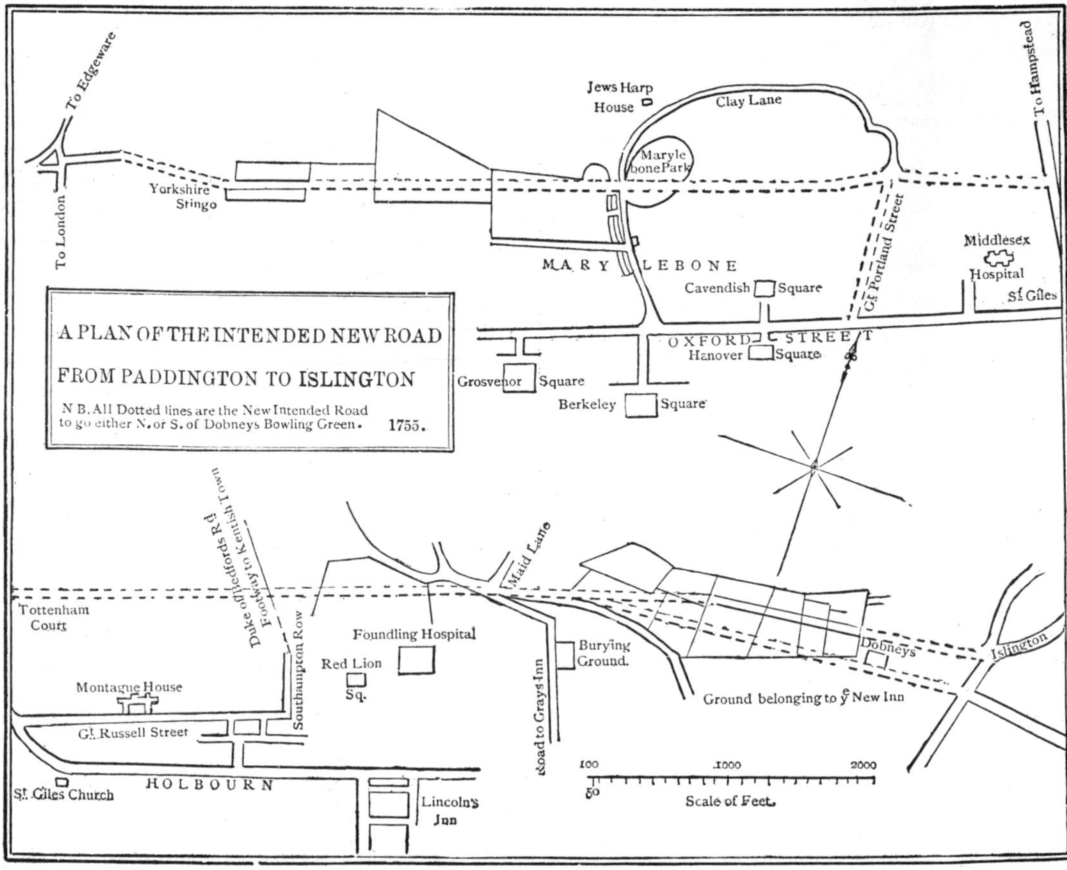

GROUND PLAN OF NEW ROAD FROM ISLINGTON TO EDGWARE ROAD (1755).

At the south end of this street, with Osnaburgh Street on its east side, is Trinity Church, which was built from the designs of Sir John Soane. The principal front consists of a portico of four columns of the Ionic order, approached by a small flight of steps; on each side is a long window, divided into two heights by a stone transum (panelled). Each of the windows is filled with ornamental iron-work, for the purpose of ventilating the vaults or catacombs. The flank of the church has a central projection, occupied by antæ, and six insulated Ionic columns; the windows in the inter-columns are in the same style as those in front; the whole is surmounted by a balustrade. The tower is in two heights; the lower part has eight columns of the Corinthian order, after the temple of Vesta at Tivoli. These columns, with their stylobatæ and entablature, project, and give a very extraordinary relief in the perspective view of the building. The upper part consists of a circular peristyle of six columns, the example apparently taken from the portico of the octagon tower of Andronicus Cyrrhestes, or tower of the winds, from the summit of which rises a conical dome, surmounted by the vane. The more minute detail may be seen by the engraving (page 294). The prevailing ornament is the Grecian fret. The Rev. Dr. Chandler, late Dean of Chichester, was for many years rector of this church, in which he was succeeded by Dean Elliot, and he again by the Rev. William Cadman.

CAMDEN TOWN, FROM THE HAMPSTEAD ROAD. MARYLEBONE, 1780. (*See page* 305.)

CHAPTER XXIII.

EUSTON ROAD, HAMPSTEAD ROAD, AND THE ADJACENT NEIGHBOURHOOD.

"Not many weeks ago it was not so,
But Pleasures had their passage to and fro,
Which way soever from our Gates I went,
I lately did behold with much content,
The Fields bestrew'd with people all about;
Some paceing homeward and some passing out;
Some by the Bancks of Thame their pleasure taking,
Some Sulli-bibs among the milk-maids making;
With musique some upon the waters rowing;
Some to the adjoining Hamlets going,
And Hogsdone, Islington, and Tothnam (*sic*) Court,
For Cakes and Cream had then no small resort."—*Britain's Remembrancer.*

Pastoral Character of the Locality in the Last Century—The Euston Road—Statuary-yards—The "Adam and Eve" Tavern—Its Tea-gardens and its Cakes and Creams—A "Strange and Wonderful Fruit"—Hogarth's Picture of the "March of the Guards to Finchley"—The "Paddington Drag"—A Miniature Menagerie—A Spring-water Bath—Eden Street—Hampstead Road—The "Sol's Arms" Tavern—David Wilkie's Residence—Granby Street—Mornington Crescent—Charles Dickens' School-days—Clarkson Stanfield—George Cruikshank—The "Old King's Head" Tavern—Tolmer's Square—Drummond Street—St. James's Church—St. Pancras Female Charity School—The Original Distillery of "Old Tom"—Bedford New Town—Ampthill Square—The "Infant Roscius"—Harrington Square.

THERE was, till the reign of William IV., a rustic character which invested the outskirts of London between King's Cross and St. John's Wood. But, thanks to the progress of the demon of bricks and mortar, the once rural tea-gardens have been made in every suburb of London to give way to the modern gin-palace with its flaring gas and its other attractions. Chambers draws out this "change for the worse" in his "Book of Days:"—"Readers of our old dramatic literature may be amused with the rustic character which invests the (then) residents of the outskirts of Old London comprehended between King's Cross and St. John's Wood, as they are depicted by Swift in the *Tale of a Tub.* The action of the drama takes place in St. Pancras Fields, the country near Kentish Town, Tottenham

Court, and Marylebone. The *dramatis personæ*," continues Mr. Chambers, "seem as innocent of London as if they were inhabitants of Berkshire, and talk a broad country dialect. This northern side of London preserved its pastoral character until a comparatively recent time, it not being very long since some of the marks used by the Finsbury archers of the days of Charles II. remained in the Shepherd and Shepherdess Fields between the Regent's Canal and Islington. . . . The *prætorium* of a Roman camp was visible where now stands Barnsbury Terrace; the remains of another, as described by Stukely, were situated opposite old St. Pancras Church, and herds of cows grazed near where now stands the Euston Square Terminus of our North-Western Railway, but which then was Rhode's Farm. At the commencement of the present century the country was open from the back of the British Museum to Kentish Town; the New Road from Battle Bridge to Tottenham (Court Road) was considered unsafe after dark; and parties used to collect at stated points to take the chance of the escort of the watchman in his half-hourly round." In 1707 there were no streets west of Tottenham Court Road; and one cluster of houses only, besides the "Spring Water House" nearly half a century later, at which time what is now the Euston Road was part of an expanse of verdant fields.

In the reign of George IV., as Mr. Samuel Palmer writes in his "History of St. Pancras," "the rural lanes, hedgeside roads, and lovely fields made Camden Town the constant resort of those who, busily engaged during the day in the bustle of . . . London, sought its quietude and fresh air to re-invigorate their spirits. Then the old 'Mother Red Cap' was the evening resort of worn-out Londoners, and many a happy evening was spent in the green fields round about the old wayside house by the children of the poorer classes. At that time the Dairy, at the junction of the Hampstead and Kentish Town Roads, was a rural cottage, furnished with forms and benches for the pedestrians to rest upon the road-side, whilst its master and mistress served out milk fresh from the cow to all who came." In fact, as we have already noticed in our account of Bloomsbury Square and other places, down to the close of the last or even the beginning of the present century, all this neighbourhood was open country; so that, after all, Thackeray was not far wide of the mark when he put these words into the mouth of Mr. St. John in "Esmond:"—"'Why, Bloomsbury is the very height of the *mode!* 'Tis *rus in urbe;* you have gardens all the way to Hampstead, and palaces round about you—Southampton House and Montagu House.' 'Where you wretches go and fight duels,' cries Mrs. Steele."

But it is time for us to be again on our perambulation. Leaving Trinity Church, we now make our way eastward along the Euston Road, as far as the junction of the Tottenham Court and the Hampstead Roads. The Euston Road—formerly called the New Road—was at the time of its formation, about the middle of the last century, the boundary-line for limiting the "ruinous rage for building" on the north side of the town. It was made by virtue of an Act of Parliament passed in the reign of George II. (1756), after a most violent contest with the Duke of Bedford, who opposed its construction on the ground of its approaching too near to Bedford House, the duke's town mansion. The Duke of Grafton, on the other hand, strenuously supported it, and after a fierce legal battle it was ultimately decided that the road should be formed.

In the *Gentleman's Magazine* for 1755 there is a "ground plan" of the New Road, from Islington to Edgware Road, showing the then state of the ground (and the names of the proprietors thereof) between Oxford Street and the New Road. The Act of Parliament for the formation of this great thoroughfare, as we have already had occasion to observe, directs that no building should be erected "within fifty feet of the New Road." In Gwynn's "London Improved," published about the beginning of this century, it is stated that "the present mean appearance of the backs of the houses and *hovels* have rendered this approach to the capital a scene of confusion and deformity, extremely unbecoming the character of a great and opulent city." Down to a comparatively recent date, Mr. Gwynn's remarks would have applied very aptly to that quarter of a mile of the New Road which lies between Gower Street North, where the old Westgate Turnpike formerly stood, and the eastern entrance to the Regent's Park. Here the road was narrow, and perpetually obstructed by wagons, &c., that might be unloading at the various timber and stone yards, which occupied the ground that an Act of Parliament had ordered should be "used only for gardens." "The intention of this judicious clause," says the author of a work on London about half a century ago, "was, no doubt, to preserve light, air, and cheerfulness, so highly necessary to a great leading thoroughfare. Such it has hitherto been, and with increasing respectability, excepting at the point I am about to mention—many great improvements have taken place, such as the Regent's Park and Crescent, the new Pancras Church and Euston Square, &c.

With these useful and even splendid works upon the same line of road, it becomes a matter of surprise that the distance between Westgate Turnpike, at the crossing of Gower Street North, up to the Regent's Park, should not only remain without any reformation, but that buildings, workmens' huts, sheds, smoky chimneys, and all manner of nuisances, should be allowed not only to continue, but to increase daily close to the road.

"In proceeding from the City westward," continues the writer, "a fine line of road, and noble footpaths on each side, are found until, on arriving near Tottenham Court Road, both appear to terminate abruptly, and the road is faced and its regularity destroyed by the projection of a range of low buildings and hovels, converted, or now converting, into small houses, close to the highway, which, strange to say, is much narrowed, at a point where, from the increased traffic caused by the crossing of the road to Hampstead, a considerable increase of width is doubly requisite. But here the houses project about ten feet, and nearly close up the footpath; and this being one of the stations for the Paddington coaches to stop at, it becomes a service of no small danger to drive through the very small opening that is left for the public to pass through. A few yards farther, on both sides of the road, are ranges of stone-yards, with the incessant music of sawing, chipping, and hacking stone, grinding chisels, and sharpening of saws; cow-yards, picturesque stacks of timber, building materials, and dead walls. Another angle turned, and the traveller emerges again from the region of smoke, stone-dust, and mud, and traversing some hazardous passages, pounces at once into the magnificent Crescent of Regent's Park, wondering at the utter lack of public taste, which could allow such a combination of nuisances to exist, and even increase, in the immediate neighbourhood of this great public improvement, and along the only road leading to it from the city of London." In course of time, the desired improvement was effected, and that part of the road to which we have specially referred was widened by the removal of some of the obtruding houses, and the thoroughfare made as nearly as possible of one uniform width all along, with the exception of the hundred yards immediately to the west and east of the "Adam and Eve," where the Euston Road is crossed by the junction of the Hampstead and Tottenham Court Roads. Just as Piccadilly was a hundred years ago, so the 200 or 250 yards of roadway lying between Park Crescent and the Hampstead Road is, or was down to a comparatively recent date, one of the dullest and dreariest of thoroughfares. It is just possible, however, that more lions' and stags' heads, and other heraldic devices for decorating the park-gates of noble lords and "county families" in the country, have proceeded of late years from the various statuary-yards which adorn the southern side of the Euston Road than from all the rest of the metropolis put together. These statuary-yards are really the backs of houses in Warren Street, which we have already described in a previous volume.* It may be added here that the houses in Euston Road, opposite the sculptors' yards, were till recently known as "Quickset Row," thus preserving some trace of the former rurality of the place.

As we have stated in a previous chapter, the Metropolitan Railway Company have laid their railway entirely under the Euston Road from end to end. To carry out that great undertaking, the road was, at great expense, torn completely up. After constructing the railway at a considerable depth, the company re-made the roadway, and now it is one of the finest roads in London.

At the corner of the Euston Road and the Hampstead Road stands a public-house which perpetuates the sign of an older tavern of some repute, yclept "The Adam and Eve," which was once noted for its tea-gardens. Of this house we have already given an illustration.†

Hone, in his "Year Book," identifies this tavern with the site of the old Manor of Toten Hall, a lordship belonging to the deans of St. Paul's as far back as the time of the Norman Conquest. Under the earlier Stuarts it passed into the hands of the Crown, and was leased to the Fitzroys, Lords Southampton, in the early part of the reign of George III. Near it was another ancient house called King John's Palace. "Whether that monarch ever really resided there," remarks Mr. Palmer, in his "History of St. Pancras," "it is now impossible to ascertain, but tradition states that it was known as *the Palace*, and the houses on the site being called 'Palace Row' supports the tradition." Opposite to it, nearly on the site of what now is Tolmer's Square, was a reservoir of the New River Company, surrounded with a grove of trees; this was not removed till about 1860. The "Adam and Eve," even as late as 1832, was quite a rural inn, only one storey in height; and Mr. Hone tells us that he remembered it when it stood quite alone, "with spacious gardens at the side and in the rear, a fore-court with large timber trees, and tables and benches for out-door customers. In the gardens were fruit-trees," he adds,

* See Vol. IV., p. 476. † See Vol. IV., p. 475.

"and bowers and arbours for tea-drinking parties. In the rear there were no houses at all; now there is a town." At that time the "Adam and Eve" tea-gardens were resorted to by thousands, as the end of a short walk into the country; and the trees were allowed to grow and expand naturally, unrestricted by art or fashion. Richardson, in 1819, said that the place had long been celebrated as a tea-garden; there was an organ in the long-room, and the company was generally respectable, till the end of the last century, "when," as Mr. Larwood tells us in his "History of Sign-boards," "highwaymen, footpads, pickpockets, and low women beginning to take a fancy to it, the magistrates interfered. The organ was banished, and the gardens were dug up for the foundation of Eden Street." In these gardens Lunardi came down after his unsuccessful balloon ascent from the Artillery Ground, in May, 1783.

The "Adam and Eve" was celebrated for its cakes and cream, which were esteemed a very luxury by the rural excursionists; and George Wither, in his "Britain's Remembrancer," published in 1628, doubtless refers to the tea-gardens attached to this tavern, when he speaks of the cakes and cream at "Tothnam Court," in the lines quoted as a motto to this chapter. Gay thus poetically, but scarcely with exaggeration at the time, alludes to this, addressing his friend and patron, Pulteney:—

> "When the sweet-breathing spring unfolds the buds,
> Love flies the dusty town for shady woods?
> Then Tottenham Fields with roving beauty swarm."

Broome, another poet of the seventeenth century, in his "New Academy," published in 1658, thus writes:—"When shall we walk to *Tottenham Court*, or crosse o'er the water; or take a coach to Kensington, or Paddington, or to some one or other of the City outleaps, for an afternoon?"

An advertisement in the public journals in September, 1718, tells us how that "there is a strange and wonderful fruit growing at the 'Adam and Eve,' at Tottenham Court, called a Calabath (? calabash), which is five feet and a half round, where any person may see the same gratis."

The "Adam and Eve," as Mr. Larwood tells us, in his work quoted above, "is a very common sign of old, as well as at the present time. Our first parents were constant *dramatis personæ* in the mediæval mysteries and pageants, on which occasions, with the *naïveté* of those times, Eve used to come on the stage exactly in the same costume as she appeared to Adam before the Fall.*" Hogarth has represented the "Adam and Eve" in his well-known picture of "The March of the Guards to Finchley." Upon the sign-board of the house is inscribed "Tottenham Court Nursery," in allusion to Broughton's Amphitheatre for Boxing erected in this place. The pugilistic encounters were carried out upon an uncovered stage in a yard open to the high road. The great professor's advertisement, announcing the attractions of his "Nursery," is somewhat amusing:—

From the *Gymnasium* at *Tottenham Court*, on *Thursday next, at Twelve o'clock, will begin:*

A Lecture on Manhood, or Gymnastic Physiology, wherein the whole Theory and Practice of the Art of Boxing will be fully explained by various Operators on the Animal Œconomy and the Principles of Championism, illustrated by proper Experiments on the Solids and Fluids of the Body; together with the True Method of investigating the Nature of the Blows, Stops, Cross-buttocks, &c., incident to Combatants. The whole leading to the most successful Method of beating a Man deaf, dumb, lame, and blind.

By THOMAS SMALLWOOD, A.M.,
Gymnasiast of St. Giles's,
and
THOMAS DIMMOCK, A.M.,
Athleta of Southwark
(Both Fellows of the *Athletic Society*).

*** The Syllabus or Compendium for the use of Students in Athleticks, referring to Matters explained in this Lecture, may be had of Mr. Professor Broughton, at the "Crown," in Market Lane, where proper instructions in the Art and Practice of Boxing are delivered without Loss of Eye or Limb to the Student.

The "Adam and Eve" was, we need hardly add, a favourite resort for the Londoner of the last century; and its arbours and alcoves, commanding the open road to the north, became the snug quarters for a friendly pipe and glass. The reader, therefore, will "not be surprised" to read that such a hero as "George Barnwell," in the "Rejected Addresses" of the Brothers Smith—

> "Determined to be quite the crack, O!
> Would lounge at the 'Adam and Eve,'
> And call for his gin and tobacco."

We learn something of the rural appearance of the neighbourhood of the "Adam and Eve," at the beginning of the last century, from the following advertisement, which appeared in the *Postman*, Dec. 30, 1708:—"At Tottenham Court, near St. Giles's, and within less than a mile of London, a very good Farm House, with outhouses and above seventy acres of extraordinary good pastures and meadows, with all conveniences proper for a cowman, are to be let, together or in parcels, and there is dung ready to lay on. Enquire further at Mr. Bolton's, at the sign of the 'Crown,' in Tottenham Court aforesaid, or at 'Landon's Coffee House,' over against Somerset House, Strand."

* This statement is made on the authority of Hone, in his "Ancient Mysteries." Doubts, however, have been expressed as to the accuracy of his data upon this particular subject.

In the year 1800 the road from Whitefield's Chapel hither was lined on either side with the hawthorn hedge, and then the "Adam and Eve" tea-gardens were the constant resort of thousands of Londoners; particularly at the time of Tottenham Fair, of which we have spoken in a previous volume;* and when, after its suppression, it was followed by its more innocent one called "Gooseberry Fair." At that period there was only one conveyance between Paddington and the City, which was called the "Paddington Drag," and which stopped at this tavern door as it passed to take up passengers. It performed the journey, as the notice-paper said, "in two hours and a half *quick time.*" The same distance is now accomplished *under* this road by the Metropolitan Railway in about a quarter of an hour.

At one time (long before the establishment of the Zoological Gardens), the "Adam and Eve" owned a sort of miniature menagerie, "when it could boast of a monkey, a heron, some wild fowl, some parrots, with a small pond for gold-fish." As late as July, 1796, the general Court-Baron of the Lord of the Manor of Tatenhall was held at this tavern by order of William Birch, who was at that time steward, dating his notice from Dean Street, Soho. There were also near to this tavern some celebrated baths, of which we find in an old paper of 1785 the following advertisement:—

"Cold Bath, in the New Road, Tottenham Court Road, near the 'Adam and Eve' Tea Gardens, is now in fine order for the reception of ladies and gentlemen. This bath is supplied from as fine a spring as any in the kingdom, which runs continually through it, and is replete with every accommodation for bathing, situate in the *midst* of a pleasant garden. This water hath been remarkably serviceable to people subject to lowness of spirits and nervous disorders. For purity of air and water, with *an agreeable walk* to it, an exercise so much recommended by the faculty, this Bath is second to none."

It is worth noticing, perhaps, as an appendage to the "Adam and Eve," that the first street to the north of that tavern, in the Hampstead Road, is called Eden Street, though it bears at present—whatever it may have done heretofore—few signs or marks of Paradise.

The Hampstead Road is a broad thoroughfare, which runs hence northwards in a direct line with Tottenham Court Road, connecting it with High Street, Camden Town, and so with both Hampstead and Kentish Town and Highgate. The road is traversed by tramways, and has altogether a business-like aspect.

The streets on the west side (with the exception of the first—Eden Street—which occupies part of the site of the old "Adam and Eve" tea-gardens) are mostly named after Christian names in the family of the owner of the land, such as Henry, Charles, Frederick, William, Robert, and Edward Streets. At the corner of Charles Street (formerly Sol's Row) is the "Sol's Arms," which is immortalised by Dickens in "Bleak House." It derives its name from the Sol's Society, an institution which was conducted somewhat upon the principles of freemasonry. They used to hold their meetings at the "Queen of Bohemia's Head," in Drury Lane; but on the pulling down of that house the society was dissolved. In Sol's Row, David Wilkie, the artist, resided for some time, and there painted his "Blind Fiddler." We found him afterwards in the more fashionable suburb of Kensington.† Each of the above-mentioned streets cross at right angles a broader and more important thoroughfare, called Stanhope Street, which runs parallel with the Hampstead Road.

The remaining streets on this side of the Hampstead Road bear more ambitious designations: one is called Rutland Street, the next is Granby Street, and the thoroughfare is terminated by Mornington Crescent, which connects the road with High Street, Camden Town. Granby Street commemorates the most popular of English generals, the "Marquis" of that name; and the name Mornington, no doubt, was given to the crescent out of compliment to the Earl of Mornington, Governor-General of India, the brother of the Duke of Wellington, and afterwards better known as the Marquis of Wellesley. At the corner of Granby Street is a Congregational Chapel, which, however, does not require further notice.

We are told by Mr. J. Forster, in his "Life of Charles Dickens," that after his release from the drudgery of the blacking warehouse at Hungerford Stairs, when about twelve years old, the boy who became afterwards "Boz" was sent to a school, kept by a Welshman named Jones, in the Hampstead Road, close to the corner of Mornington Place and Granby Street; but the schoolroom has long since disappeared, having been "sliced off" at a later date to make room for the London and Birmingham Railway. It was ambitiously styled Wellington House Academy, and there are many allusions to it to be found in his minor writings; there is also a paper among his pieces,

* See Vol. IV., p. 477.

† See *ante*, p. 134.

reprinted from *Household Words*, of October 11, 1851, which purports to describe it in detail. The school is also of interest, as having supplied some of the lighter traits of Salem House in "David Copperfield." At this time "Boz" was living with his parents, in "a small street leading out of Seymour Street, north of Mr. Judkin's Chapel." Whilst here he would ramble, in childish sport and fun, over the "Field of the Forty Footsteps," scenes to which he would often allude with pleasure in after life. Even at this time he was a great devourer of the light magazine literature, and, along with his school-fellows, got up a miniature theatre, on the boards of which they would perform such pieces as *The Miller and his Men.* On another occasion they would act the part of mendicants, and go up as "poor boys" to ladies in the streets, and ask for coppers—laughing heartily when they got a refusal. Verily, even at that early age, in his case the child was father of the man.

In the house close to Mornington Crescent the veteran artist, Mr. George Cruikshank, resided for many years, having succeeded in it another artist, whose name stands even higher in the annals of art—namely, Mr. Clarkson Stanfield, R.A. Born at Sunderland, towards the close of the last century, Clarkson Stanfield "had the sea for his first art academy," and continued to make the sea the principal theme of his art studies through life. At an early age he determined to be a sailor, and, curiously enough, joined the same ship in which Douglas Jerrold was serving as a midshipman; and it is told that the officers having got up a play young Stanfield painted the scenery, while Jerrold acted as stage-manager. When he quitted the service he accepted an engagement as scene-painter at the old Royalty Theatre, near Wellclose Square, which was then noted as a sailors' theatre, and in course of time transferred his services to Drury Lane Theatre. In 1827 he exhibited, at the British Institution, his first large picture, "Wreckers off Fort Rouge;" and from that time he produced a large number of works. He was elected an Associate of the Royal Academy in 1832, and became a Royal Academician three years later. He died in 1867, at Hampstead, where we shall have more to say about his later and more finished works.

H. W. BETTY. *The Infant Roscius.* (*See page* 309.)

Of George Cruikshank we may remark that his artistic productions were for the most part confined

TURNPIKE IN THE HAMPSTEAD ROAD, AND ST. JAMES'S CHURCH, IN 1820. (*See page* 308.)

to illustrating periodicals and other works of popular literature. The son of a water-colour draughtsman and caricaturist, he had an hereditary claim to some artistic gifts, the humorous turn of which he began to develop at a very early age. Among Mr. Cruikshank's best-known etchings are those in "Sketches by Boz," "Oliver Twist," "Jack Sheppard," "The Tower of London," "Windsor Castle," &c. In 1842 appeared the first number of "Cruikshank's Omnibus," the letter-press of which was edited by Leman Blanchard. From the first this artist had shown a strong vein of virtuous reproof in his treatment of intoxication and its accompanying vices: some instances of this tendency are to be found in his "Sunday in London," "The Gin Juggernaut," "The Gin Trap," and more especially in his series of eight prints entitled "The Bottle." These also brought the artist into direct personal connection with the leaders of the temperance movement. He moreover, himself became a convert to their doctrines, and was for many years one of the ablest advocates of the temperance cause. Late in life Mr. Cruikshank turned his attention to oil-painting, and contributed to the exhibitions of the Royal Academy and the British Institution; among his latest productions in oil is a large picture called "The Worship of Bacchus," which was exhibited to the Queen at Windsor Castle in 1863. The whole of Mr. Cruikshank's etchings, extending over a period of more than seventy years, and illustrating the fashions, tastes, follies, and frivolities of four reigns, including the Regency, were purchased, in 1876, by the managers of the Royal Aquarium, at Westminster, and were placed in their picture-gallery. Mr. Cruikshank's talents were not confined merely to painting or etching, but he possessed no little dramatic taste, and often took part in amateur performances at the public theatres for benevolent purposes. He died in 1878.

We must now retrace our steps to the Euston Road, in order to deal with the east side of the Hampstead Road. The "Old King's Head," at the corner opposite to the "Adam and Eve," has long presented an awkward break in the uniform width of the Euston Road, by projecting some feet beyond its neighbours, and so narrowing the thoroughfare. At the time of the formation of the "Underground Railway" it was considered that there was at last a chance of its removal. Such, however, was not the case; for the owner not being satisfied with the amount of compensation which was offered by the railway company, who, by the way, offered to rebuild the house, but setting it at the same time farther back, the latter got over the difficulty by running their tunnel under the house, which their engineer supported on huge posts of timber during the process, thus dispensing with its removal. To the north of this tavern much of the land facing Eden Street was not built upon down to about the year 1860. Here were large waterworks and a reservoir, sheltered by a grove of trees. The site is now covered by Tolmer's Square, a small square, the centre of which is occupied by a handsome Gothic Nonconformist chapel, with a tall spire.

Drummond Street, the next turning northward, extends along by the principal front of Euston Square Railway Terminus. This street crosses George Street, which forms a direct line of communication from Gower Street to the Hampstead Road. Between George Street and Cardington Street is St. James's Church, formerly a chapel of ease to the mother church of St. James's, Piccadilly. It is a large brick building, and has a large, dreary, and ill-kept burial-ground attached to it. Here lie George Morland, the painter, who died in 1804; John Hoppner, the portrait-painter, who died in 1810; Admiral Lord Gardner, the hero of Port l'Orient, and the friend of Howe, Bridport, and Nelson; and, without a memorial, Lord George Gordon, the mad leader of the Anti-Catholic Riots in 1780, who died a prisoner in Newgate in 1793, having become a Jew before his death! One of the best-known vicars of this church was the Rev. Henry Stebbing, author of the "History of the Reformation," "History of the Christian Church," "History of Chivalry and the Crusades," and "Lives of the Italian Poets." He died in 1883. Close by are the St. Pancras Female Charity School and the Temperance Hospital.

It may interest some of our readers who do not advocate strict temperance principles to hear that the celebrated article now called "Old Tom" or "Jackey" was originally distilled at Carre's Brewery (formerly Deady and Hanley's distillery), in the Hampstead Road.

We are now once more upon Russell property, as is testified by the names of several of the streets and squares round about; indeed, a considerable part of the district is called Bedford New Town.

Ampthill Square, which we have now reached, and which is in reality not a square, but a triangle, is so named after Ampthill Park, in Bedfordshire, formerly the seat of the Earls of Upper Ossory, but afterwards the property of the ducal house of Bedford, to whom the land about this part belongs. The south-west corner of the square is crossed by a deep cutting, through which passes the North-Western Railway, spanned by a level bridge. At his residence in this square, died, in September, 1874, at a good old age, Henry West Betty, better known as the "infant Roscius," more than seventy years after he had first appeared on the boards, under Rich, at Covent Garden, and had "taken the town by storm." He was born on the 13th of September, 1791, and having made his *début* before a provincial audience at Belfast, he first appeared as a "star" at Covent Garden, December 1, 1803, as "Selim," in *Barbarossa*. He is said to have cleared in his first season upwards of £17,000. When quite young he retired and left the stage, but afterwards, being induced to come back, he was unsuccessful, and found that the public taste is a fickle jade. He was a great favourite with many ladies of fashion and title, and the Duke of Clarence, it is said, used to show his partiality for the boy, by driving him home from the theatre in his own private royal carriage—a thing in itself enough to turn a boy's head. The mania for the "young Roscius" is one of the earlier "Reminiscences" of the veteran Mr. Planché; and an account of him will be found in Timbs' "English Eccentrics."

Harrington Square—which, however, is a square in name alone, seeing that it faces only two sides of a triangular plot of ground, facing Mornington Crescent—adjoins Ampthill Square on the north, and ends close to the corner of the High Street, Camden Town. It is so called after the Earl of Harrington, one of whose daughters married the seventh Duke of Bedford.

CHAPTER XXIV.

CAMDEN TOWN AND KENTISH TOWN.

"Vix rure urbem dignoscere possis."

Camden Town—Statue of Richard Cobden—Oakley Square—The "Bedford Arms"—The Royal Park Theatre—The "Mother Red Cap"—The "Mother Shipton"—The Alderney Dairy—The Grand Junction Canal—Bayham Street, and its Former Inhabitants—Camden Road—Camden Town Railway Station—The Tailors' Almshouses—St. Pancras Almshouses—Maitland Park—The Orphan Working School—The Dominican Monastery—Gospel Oak—St. Martin's Church—Kentish Town: its Buildings and its Residents—Great College Street—The Royal Veterinary College—Pratt Street—St. Stephen's Church—Sir Henry Bishop—Agar Town.

Camden Town, says Mr. Peter Cunningham, "was so called (but indirectly) after William Camden, author of the 'Britannia.' Charles Pratt, Attorney-General and Lord Chancellor in the reign of George III., created, in 1765, Baron Camden of Camden Place, in Kent, derived his title from his seat at Chislehurst, in Kent, formerly the residence of William Camden, the historian. His lordship, who died in 1794, married the daughter and co-heir of Nicholas Jeffreys, Esq., son and heir of Sir Geoffery Jeffreys, of Brecknock; and his lordship's eldest son was created, in 1812, Earl of Brecknock and Marquis Camden. Lord Camden's second title was Viscount Bayham; and all these names, Pratt, Jeffreys, Brecknock, and Bayham, may be found in Camden Town."

Camden Town, we may here remark, was commenced towards the close of the last century, Lord Camden having, in the year 1791, let out the ground on leases for building 1,400 houses. The houses in Camden Road and Square have perhaps the most aristocratic appearance of any in the district. The High Street, which originally consisted of a row of small shops with one floor above, and trim gardens in their fronts, separated by hedges of privet, have within the last few years been for the most part either rebuilt or enlarged, and are now on a par with the other business parts of London; and on Saturday evenings the upper part of the street, thronged as it is with stalls of itinerant vendors of the necessaries of daily life, and with the dwellers in the surrounding districts, presents to an ordinary spectator all the attributes of a market place.

At the lower end of High Street, facing Eversholt Street, is a marble statue of Richard Cobden, which was erected by subscription in the year 1863. The statue, which stands in a conspicuous position, is rather above life-size, and is placed upon a granite pedestal of two stages, about twelve feet high, the plinth of which is simply inscribed "Cobden. The Corn-Laws Repealed, June, 1846." The great politician is represented in a standing attitude, as if delivering an address in the House of Commons. He is attired in the ordinary dress of a gentleman of the present day, and holds in one hand a Parliamentary roll. The sculptor's name was Wills. Born at Dunford, in Sussex, in the year 1804, Cobden was brought up as a lad to business, and served behind a counter in a large establishment at Manchester. About the year 1840 he helped to found the Anti-Corn Law League, whose efforts in less than ten years' time set aside the restrictions imposed by the old Corn

Laws on the importation of foreign grain, and eventually secured to the country the advantages of free trade. He was offered, but refused, all honours and offices; but he represented Stockport, the West Riding, and Rochdale from 1841 down to his death, in 1865.

Oakley Square, which lies on the east side of Eversholt Street and Harrington Square, is so called after Oakley House, one of the seats of the ducal owner, near Bedford. In this square is St. Matthew's Church, a large and handsome Gothic building, with a lofty tower and spire. It was erected in 1854, from the designs of Mr. J. Johnson, F.R.S., and is capable of seating upwards of 1,200 persons.

The "Bedford Arms," in Grove Street, on the west side of the High Street, has been a tavern of some note in its day. Formerly, the tea-gardens attached to the house were occasionally the scene of balloon ascents. The *Morning Chronicle* of July 5, 1824, contains an account of an aërial voyage made from these gardens by a Mr. Rossiter and another gentleman. The ascent took place shortly after five o'clock, and the balloon alighted safely in Havering Park, two miles from Romford, in Essex. The two aëronauts, having been provided with a post-coach, returned at once to Camden Town, and arrived at the "Bedford Arms" about half-past ten o'clock. On the 14th of June, 1825, as we learn from the *Morning Herald*, Mr. Graham took a trip into the aërial regions from these grounds, accompanied by two ladies. Their ascent was witnessed by a large concourse of spectators; and after a pleasant voyage of nearly an hour, they alighted at Feltham, near Hounslow. Of late years the "Bedford Arms" has added the attractions of a music-hall, called "The Bedford."

In Park Street, which connects Camden Town with the north-east corner of Regent's Park, stood the Park Theatre, a place of dramatic entertainment, originally opened in 1873, under the name of the Alexandra Theatre. The theatre was burnt down in 1881, and its site is now occupied as stabling by an omnibus company.

From a manuscript list of inns in this neighbourhood about the year 1830, we find that in Camden Town at that time there were the "Mother Red Cap," the "Mother Black Cap," the "Laurel Tree," the "Britannia," the "Camden Arms," the "Bedford Arms," the "Southampton Arms," the "Wheatsheaf," the "Hope and Anchor," and the "Elephant and Castle." The two first-named of these houses were, and are still, rival establishments at the northern, or upper, end of the High Street. The "Mother Black Cap" stands within a few doors of the corner of Park Street.

The "Mother Red Cap," observes Mr. J. T. Smith, in his "Book for a Rainy Day," was in former times a house of no small terror to travellers. "It has been stated," he adds, "that 'Mother Red Cap' was the 'Mother Damnable' of Kentish Town in early days, and that it was at her house that the notorious 'Moll Cut-purse,' the highway woman of Oliver Cromwell's days, dismounted, and frequently lodged." The old house was taken down, and another rebuilt on its site, with the former sign, about the year 1850. This, again, in its turn, was removed; and a third house, in the modern style, and of still greater pretensions, was built on the same site some quarter of a century afterwards.

Great doubts have been entertained as to the real history of the semi-mythic personage whose name stands on the sign-board of this inn. It has been stated that the original Mother Red Cap was a follower of the army under Marlborough, in the reign of Queen Anne; but this idea is negatived by the existence of a rude copper coin, or token, dated 1667, and mentioning in its inscription, "Mother Read Cap's (*sic*) in Holl(o)way." Further arguments in refutation of this idea will be found in the *Monthly Magazine* for 1812. Again, some writers have attempted to identify her with the renowned Eleanor Rumming, of Leatherhead, in Surrey, who lived under Henry VIII. This noted alewife is mentioned by Skelton, the poet laureate of Henry VIII., as having lived

"In a certain stead,
Beside Leatherhead."

She was, he assures us, one of the most frightful of her sex, being

"——ugly of cheer,
Her face all bowsy,
Wondrously wrinkled,
Her een bleared,
And she grey-haired."

The portrait of Eleanor on the frontispiece of an original edition of the "Tunning of Eleanor Rumming," by Skelton, will satisfy the reader that her description is no exaggeration.

Perhaps there may be more of truth in the following "biographical sketch" of the original Mother Red Cap, which we now quote from Mr. Palmer's work on "St. Pancras, and its History," above referred to:—"This singular character, known as 'Mother Damnable,' is also called 'Mother Red Cap,' and sometimes 'The Shrew of Kentish Town.' Her father's name was Jacob Bingham, by trade a brickmaker in the neighbourhood of Kentish Town. He enlisted in the army, and went with it to Scotland, where he married a Scotch pedlar's daughter. They had one daughter, this 'Mother Damnable.' This daughter they named Jinney. Her father, on leaving the army, took again to his old trade of brickmaking, occasionally travelling with his wife and child as a pedlar. When the girl had reached her sixteenth year, she had a child by one Coulter, who was better known as Gipsey George. This man lived no one knew how; but he was a great trouble to the magistrates. Jinney and Coulter after this lived together; but being brought into trouble for stealing a sheep from some lands near Holloway, Coulter was sent to Newgate, tried at the Old Bailey, and hung at Tyburn. Jinney then associated with one Darby; but this union produced a cat-and-dog life, for Darby was constantly drunk; so Jinney and her mother consulted together, Darby was suddenly missed, and no one knew whither he went. About this time her parents were carried before the justices for practising the black art, and therewith causing the death of a maiden, for which they were both hung. Jinney then associated herself with one Pitcher, though who or what he was, never was known; but after a time his body was found crouched up in the oven, burnt to a cinder. Jinney was tried for the murder, but acquitted, because one of her associates proved he had 'often got into the oven to hide himself from her tongue.' Jinney was now a 'lone woman,' for her former companions were afraid of her. She was scarcely ever seen, or if she were, it was at nightfall, under the hedges or in the lanes; but how she subsisted was a miracle to her neighbours. It happened during the troubles of the Commonwealth, that a man, sorely pressed by his pursuers, got into her house by the back door, and begged on his knees for a night's lodging. He was haggard in his countenance, and full of trouble. He offered Jinney money, of which he had plenty, and she gave him a lodging. This man, it is said, lived with her many years, during which time she wanted for nothing, though hard words and sometimes blows were heard from her cottage. The man at length died, and an inquest was held on the body; but though every one thought him poisoned, no proof could be found, and so she again escaped harmless. After this Jinney never wanted money, as the cottage she lived in was her own, built on waste land by her father. Years thus passed, Jinney using her foul tongue against every one, and the rabble in return baiting her as if she were a wild beast. The occasion of this arose principally from Jinney being reputed a practiser of the black art—a very witch. She was resorted to by numbers as a fortune-teller and healer of strange diseases; and when any mishap occurred, then the old crone was set upon by the mob and hooted without mercy. The old, ill-favoured creature would at such times lean out of her hatch-door, with a grotesque red cap on her head. She had a large broad nose, heavy shaggy eyebrows, sunken eyes, and lank and leathern cheeks; her forehead wrinkled, her mouth wide, and her looks sullen and unmoved. On her shoulders was thrown a dark grey striped frieze, with black patches, which looked at a distance like flying bats. Suddenly she would let her huge black cat jump upon the hatch by her side, when the mob instantly retreated from a superstitious dread of the double foe.

"The extraordinary death of this singular character is given in an old pamphlet:—'Hundreds of men, women, and children were witnesses of the devil entering her house in his very appearance and state, and that, although his return was narrowly watched for, he was not seen again; and that Mother Damnable was found dead on the following morning, sitting before the fire-place, holding a crutch over it, with a tea-pot full of herbs, drugs, and liquid, part of which being given to the cat, the hair fell off in two hours, and the cat soon after died; that the body was stiff when found, and that the undertaker was obliged to break her limbs before he could place them in the coffin, and that the justices have put men in possession of the house to examine its contents.'

"Such is the history of this strange being, whose name will ever be associated with Camden Town, and whose reminiscence will ever be revived by the old wayside house which, built on the site of the old beldame's cottage, wears her head as the sign of the tavern."

The figure of Mother Red Cap, as it was represented on the sign, exhibited that venerable lady—whether she was ale-wife or witch—with a tall extinguisher-shaped hat, not unlike that ascribed to Mother Shipton; and it is not a little remarkable that two inns bearing the names of these semi-mythical ladies exist within half a mile of each other.

Although the tavern bearing the sign of "Mother Shipton" is thus far off, at the corner of Malden Road, near Chalk Farm, some account of the other weird woman may not be altogether out of place here. "The prophecies of Mother Shipton," writes Dr. C. Mackay, in his "Memoirs of Extraordinary Popular Delusions," "are still believed in many of the rural districts of England. In cottages and in servants' halls her reputation is still great; and she rules, the most popular of British prophets, among all the uneducated or half educated portion of the community. She is generally supposed to have been born at Knaresborough, in the reign of Henry VII., and to have 'sold her soul to the devil' for the power of foretelling future events. Though during her lifetime she was looked upon as a witch, yet she escaped the usual witches' fate, and died peaceably in her bed at an extreme old age, near Clifton, in Yorkshire. A stone is said to have been erected to her memory in the churchyard of the place, with the following epitaph:—

"'Here lies she who never lied,
Whose skill often has been tried;
Her prophecies shall still survive,
And ever keep her name alive.'"

"Never a day passed," says her traditionary biography, "wherein she did not relate something remarkable, and that required the most serious consideration. People flocked to her from far and near, her fame was so great. They went to her of all sorts, both old and young, rich and poor, especially young maidens, to be resolved of their doubts concerning things to come; and all returned wonderfully satisfied in the explanations that she gave to their questions." Among the rest, Dr. Mackay tells us, who went to her was the Abbot of Beverley, to whom she foretold the suppression of the monasteries by Henry VIII., his marriage with Anne Boleyn, the fires for heretics in Smithfield, the death of Cardinal Wolsey, and the execution of Mary Queen of Scots. She also foretold the accession of James I. to the English throne, adding that with him—

"From the cold north
Every evil shall come forth.

THE OLD "MOTHER RED CAP," IN 1746. (*See page* 310.)

On a subsequent visit, she is said to have uttered another prophecy, which, perhaps, may be realised during the present century:—

"'The time shall come when seas of blood
Shall mingle with a greater flood:
Great noise shall there be heard; great shouts and cries,
And seas shall thunder louder than the skies;
Then shall three lions fight with three, and bring
Joy to a people, honour to a king.
That fiery year as soon as o'er
Peace shall then be as before;
Plenty shall everywhere be found,
And men with swords shall plough the ground.'"

The craven heart of James I. was not less disturbed than that of his masculine predecessor, Elizabeth, by the prophecy of the weird-woman, Mother Shipton, that—

> "Before the good folk of this kingdom be undone,
> Shall Highgate Hill stand in the midst of London."

It is the wont of superficial writers to say that James despised this and other prophecies of the like kind; but it is a fact that under him all sorts of legal enactments were passed which forbade any further additions to London in the way of building. Though these enactments were defied to a very great extent, yet no doubt they helped for many a long day to keep the metropolis within very manageable limits down to the time of the Great Fire of 1666

We learn from the *Morning Post*, of 1776, that the open space opposite the "Mother Red Cap" was at one time intended to have been made a second Tyburn. "Orders have been given from the Secretary of State's office that the criminals capitally convicted at the Old Bailey shall in

THE ASSEMBLY ROOMS, KENTISH TOWN, 1750.

future be executed at the cross road near the 'Mother Red Cap' inn, the half-way house to Hampstead, and that no galleries, scaffolds, or other temporary stages be built near the place."

At the beginning of the present century the "Mother Red Cap" was a constant resort for many a Londoner who desired to inhale the fresh air, and enjoy the quiet of the country, for at that time the old tavern—which, by the way, was also known as the half-way house to Highgate and

Hampstead—stood almost in the open fields, and was approached on different sides by green lanes and hedgeside roads. At that time, too, the dairy over the way, at the corner of the Chalk Farm, or Hampstead, and the Kentish Town Roads was not the fashionable establishment it afterwards became, but partook more of the character of "milk fair," as noticed by us in our account of Spring Gardens,* for there were forms for the pedestrians to rest on, and the good folk served out milk fresh from the cow to all who came.

The Grand Junction Canal, after leaving the Regent's Park, passes through Camden Town. It is spanned on the Chalk Farm Road by a fine bridge of cast iron. A little farther to the east it crosses the Midland Railway, or rather the latter is carried under it. This work was effected by a triumph of engineering skill almost unparalleled. The waters of the canal are drained off every year for exactly seven days, in order to clear its bed; during this period sc strong a force of men was put upon it that between one Saturday and the next a tunnel was dug under the canal, and bricked and roofed over before the water was sent back into its channel.

Running parallel with High Street, on its eastern side, is Bayham Street, which is worthy of notice, as having been the first home of Charles Dickens in London, when he came up thither from Chatham with his parents in the year 1821; and here he took his first impressions of that struggling poverty which is nowhere more vividly shown than in the commoner streets of an ordinary London suburb. It is thus described in Forster's Life of Dickens:—"Bayham Street was then about the poorest part of the London suburbs, and the house was a mean, small tenement, with a wretched little garden abutting on a squalid court. Here was no place for new acquaintances for him; no boys were near with whom he might hope to become in any way familiar. A washerwoman lived next door, and a Bow Street officer lived over the way. Many times has he spoken to me of this, and how he seemed at once to fall into a solitary condition apart from all other boys of his own age, and to sink at home into a neglected state which had always been quite unaccountable to him. 'As I thought,' he said, very bitterly, on one occasion, 'in the little back garret in Bayham Street, of all that I had lost in losing Chatham, what would I have given (if I had anything to give) to have been sent back to any other school, and to have been taught something anywhere!' He was at another school already, not knowing it. The self-education forced upon him was teaching him, all unconsciously as yet, what, for the future that awaited him, it most behoved him to know."

An old inhabitant of this neighbourhood, and one who likewise spent his early childhood in this very street, questioned the accuracy of the above narrative, in a letter to the *Daily Telegraph.* The writer, who signed himself "F. M.," remarked:—"Fifty years ago Camden Town, like some other London suburbs, was but a village. Bayham Street had grass struggling through the newly-paved road. There were not more than some twenty or, at most, thirty newly-erected houses in it. These were occupied by, No. 1, Mr. Lever, the builder of the houses; No. 2, Mr. Engelheart, a then celebrated engraver; No. 3, a Captain Blake; No. 4, a retired linendraper, one of the old school; No. 5, by my father and his family; No. 6, by a retired diamond merchant, two of whose sons have made their mark, one as an artist and another as the author of 'True to the Core.' At No. 7 lived a retired hairdresser, who, like most others there, had a lease of his house. In another lived a Regent Street jeweller; and so I could enumerate the inhabitants of this squalid neighbourhood. When Charles Dickens lived there it must have been about the year 1822; and if he lived over the way, the description given by his biographer of its character is a perfect caricature of a quiet street in what was then but a village. I was then a boy of some six years of age, and, to my childish apprehension, it was a country village. Mr. Lever's field was at the back of the principal row of houses, in which haymaking was enjoyed in its season, and it was, indeed, a beautiful walk across the fields to Copenhagen House. Camden Road then was not. The village watchman's box was at one end of the street by the 'Red Cap' tea-garden. Old Lorimer, who lived in Queen Street—then with gardens and a field in front of but one row of houses—was the only constable. Occasionally robberies of articles in the out-houses caused some consternation, but gas had not then arrived to enlighten the darkness of this squalid neighbourhood."

The above account of Bayham Street and its residents was supplemented by two other letters in the *Daily Telegraph*, which we take the liberty of quoting. In the first, which was signed "C. L. G.," the writer says: "As a boy I was a constant visitor at one of the houses occupied by the late Mr. Holl, the celebrated engraver, the father of Mr. Frank Holl, and of the late William Holl, engravers, and of Mr. Henry Holl, the actor and novelist. Mr. Charles Rolls, another artist of note, in addition

* See Vol. IV., p. 76.

to Mr. Engelhart, and to Mr. Henry Selous, the painter, and Mr. Angelo Selous, the dramatic author, resided in Bayham Street. The private theatricals at the late Mr. Holl's residence will not be forgotten, as all the gentlemen just named took parts therein, as also another actor, who is no more, Mr. Benjamin Holl. The houses in Bayham Street were small, but the locality half a century since was regarded as a suburb of London. Fields had to be crossed to reach it, on which the best houses of Camden Town have been since erected. The description of Bayham Street by the late Charles Dickens must have been prompted by personal privations. What a romance he could have created out of the house occupied by Mr. Holl, where was concealed for months young Watson, who was implicated in the treasonable attempt for which his father and Thistlewood were tried and acquitted—the latter not taking warning by his escape on that occasion, for he afterwards concocted the Cato Street conspiracy, for which he was executed at Newgate. Young Watson shot a gunmaker in Snow Hill, for which his comrade Cashman, the sailor, was hanged. Mr. Holl was a Reformer in days when it was looked upon as treason to differ from the Government. He gave shelter to young Watson, having been on intimate terms with his father, Dr. Watson. Mr. Holl contrived the escape to America of Watson, junior, disguising him as a Quaker. Bayham Street was occupied by men of advanced political opinions, some of whom lived to see their notions realised."

In the other letter referred to, which appeared with the initials of "E. P. H.," we get a different account of Bayham Street. The writer remarks:—"I have a perfect recollection of Bayham Street thirty years ago, and took a stroll up it this morning to see if I could trace the house to which Mr. Forster refers. On entering the street from Crowndale Road I literally rubbed my eyes with astonishment. There is a public-house at the corner, the sign of which is the 'Hope and Anchor.' When last I noticed it the name over the door was 'Barker,' now it is 'Dickens.' Who shall say that this is not a world of strange coincidences when a Dickens comes to Bayham Street to live just at the time when we get the record of a greater Dickens having once trotted round the corner where that public-house stands? 'F. M.' seems to me to be in error about Bayham Street having been so respectable many years since. The block of houses to which he refers was at one end; then came fields; and, lower down towards the Old St. Pancras Road, a lot of small houses or cottages with gardens in front, in one of which I presume the parents of Charles Dickens to have resided. There are still two houses remaining, near Pratt Street, which I remember as being old houses twenty-five years ago."

Camden Road is a broad thoroughfare, running north-east from the top of High Street to Holloway. At the top of this road is the Camden Town Athenæum, an institution which has been established to meet the intellectual requirements of this district. The building, which was erected in 1871, is Italian in style, and was built from the designs of Mr. F. R. Meeson. Externally the edifice is of brick, with red brick plinth, string-courses, cornices, &c., and the enrichments are of red terra-cotta. The building consists of a large hall, suitable for lectures and other entertainments, a reading-room, library, &c.

At the junction of Camden Road and Great College Street is the Camden Town Station of the North London Railway, near which the line branches off to Gospel Oak and Hampstead, forming a junction with the London and North-Western Line at Willesden, and with the West London Railway at Kensington Station.

Not far from the Chalk Farm station, at the foot of the slope of Haverstock Hill, near the entrance to Maitland Park, are the Tailors' Almshouses, consisting of six residences and a small chapel, built in red brick and stone in the Gothic style, and standing in the middle of a garden of about an acre and a half. They were founded and built in 1837–42, by the late Mr. J. Stulz, of Clifford Street, Hanover Square, for the support of aged tailors of every nation in the world, irrespective of creed. Each pensioner, besides his rooms, receives £20 a year, in addition to coals and candles.

A few steps farther northwards brings us to the almshouses for the parish of St. Pancras. They were founded in 1850, by Mr. Donald Fraser, M.D., for decayed and aged parishioners. The buildings consist of a row of ornamental cottages, with pointed roofs, and red-brick facings; they are separated from the roadway by a light stone wall and a spacious and well-kept lawn.

The grounds of the above institutions abut upon Maitland Park, where there is another edifice devoted to charitable purposes—viz., the Orphan Working School, which was originally established in the east end of London, as far back as the year 1758, but was removed here when it had nearly completed a century of existence. Here orphans and other necessitous children are clothed, educated, and wholly maintained, from seven years of age until they are about fourteen or fifteen; and the number of children usually in the school is about 400. At the age of fourteen the boys are apprenticed, and the girls, who are all trained for domestic service, remain for a year or two longer. The annual income of this institution is about £10,000, the larger half being derived from voluntary contributions. On leaving the school, outfits are provided for the children, in money value—to the boys of £5, to the girls of £3 3s.; and to encourage them to keep the situations which are provided for them, annual rewards are given, from 5s. to 21s., depending upon the length of service, for the seven years after they leave the school. The education imparted is unsectarian, and of a thoroughly practical character, fitting the children for useful positions in life. Many of the former pupils, it may be added, are governors and liberal supporters of the charity.

The Dominican Monastery, close by, stands at the foot of the hill which ascends to Hampstead. Its first stone was laid by Cardinal Wiseman, in the presence of nearly all his clergy, in August, 1863, and the building was opened two years later. It is in the Early English style, with a lofty bell and clock tower. The buildings surround a quadrangle, and have altogether an imposing appearance The church, which was consecrated in 1883, is built of brick, with stone dressings, columns, and arches. It is erected according to the prevalent type of the larger Dominican churches. Attached to the monastery is a plot of ground, which the monks themselves are employed in cultivating. This monastery is a branch of the Order of St. Dominic, whose head-quarters in this country are at Woodchester, near Stroud, in Gloucestershire. St. Dominic, the founder of this Order, is known to history as the author of the devotion called the Rosary. His feast day is kept on the 4th day of August. He was of the noble family of Guzman, and was born in Old Castile in 1170. He conducted the preaching crusade against the Albigenses in the south of France, and dying in 1221, was canonised about twelve years later by Pope Gregory IX. His monks, called the "Black Friars" from the colour of their dress, were numerous in almost all the west of Europe, and in England and Scotland, and especially at Paris and Oxford, where they held the chairs of theology. It is to the honour of this Order that it produced the great doctor of theology, St. Thomas Aquinas; and Chambers tells us that, in spite of its losses at the time of the Reformation, the Order in the eighteenth century could boast of possessing a thousand monasteries and convents, divided into forty-five provinces, who all revered St. Dominic as their founder.

From the neighbourhood of the Dominican monastery and Gospel Oak a thoroughfare named Fleet Road leads away north-west to Hampstead. It is named after the Fleet rivulet, which till lately ran behind the houses, through green fields, in its way townwards, but it is now nearly dry, and what water passes down it in winter finds its way into a sewer. We shall have occasion to mention the Fleet River again, when we come to St. Pancras.

The Gospel Oak Fields, a little to the east of the monastery, are now built over with numerous streets, crescents, and circuses. The Midland Railway emerges from the Haverstock Hill tunnel in the middle of these streets, about half a mile to the west of the Kentish Town station.

In these fields a rural fair, called "Gospel Oak Fair," was held as lately as 1857. There are many "Gospel Oaks" in various parts of this country. Mr. John Timbs, in his "Things not Generally Known," tells us that these Gospel oaks are traditionally said to have been so called in consequence of its having been the practice in ancient times to read aloud, under a tree which grew on the parish boundary line, a portion of the Gospel, on the annual "beating of the bounds" on Ascension Day. These trees may have been, in some instances, even Druidical, and under such "leafy tabernacles" the first Christian missionaries of St. Augustine may have preached. The popular, though mistaken, idea is, that these trees were so called because the parishioners were in the habit of assembling there at the era of the Reformation in order to read the Bible aloud. Herrick thus alludes to the real derivation of the term in the 502nd of his "Hesperides:"—

> "Dearest, bury me
> Under that holy oak, or gospel-tree,
> Where, though thou see'st not, thou mayst think upon
> Me when thou yearly go'st in procession."

The pagan practice of worshipping the gods in woods and trees continued for many centuries, till the introduction of Christianity; and the missionaries did not disdain to adopt every means to raise Christian worship to higher authority than that of paganism by acting upon the senses of the heathens to whom they preached.

Beneath one of the trees in the Gospel Oak Fields, of which we are now speaking, Whitefield, the Methodist, and companion of Wesley, is said to have preached to crowded audiences of the working classes.

Close by, in Dale Road, so named after the late poet, Canon Dale, some time Vicar of St. Pancras, is the Church of St. Martin, a Gothic structure in the Decorated style with a lofty tower, and a fine peal of bells. It was erected and endowed about the year 1866, by Mr. John Derby Allcroft, who also built a handsome parsonage and schools adjoining it.

"At the foot of the Hampstead hills," writes Mr. Larwood, in his "History of Sign-boards," "the noisiest and most objectionable public-house in the district bears the significant sign of the 'Gospel Oak.' It is the favourite resort of navvies and quarrelsome shoemakers, and took its name, not from any inclination to piety on the part of its landlord, but from an old oak-tree in the neighbourhood, at the boundary line of Hampstead and St. Pancras parishes—a relic of the once usual custom of reading a portion of the Gospel under certain trees in the parish perambulations equivalent to 'beating the bounds.'" "The boundaries of the parish of Wolverhampton," says Shaw, in his "History of Staffordshire," "are thus in many points marked out by what are called 'Gospel Trees.'" The old "Gospel Oak" at Kentish Town was not removed, we may add, till it had given its name to the surrounding fields, to a group of small houses (Oak Village), and to a chapel, and a railway station, as well as to the public-house mentioned above.

Kentish Town, which lies on the east side of Gospel Oak, and is approached from the "Mother Red Cap," at Camden Town, by a direct road called the Kentish Town Road, is described in gazetteers, &c., as "a hamlet and chapelry in the parish of St. Pancras, in the Holborn division of the hundred of Ossulston." The place is mentioned in Domesday Book as a manor belonging to the Canons of St. Paul's; and it gives title to the Prebendary of Cantelows (or Kentish Town), who is Lord of the Manor, and holds a court-leet and court-baron. Moll, in his "History of Middlesex," on noticing this hamlet, states: "You may, from Hampstead, see in the vale between it and London a village, vulgarly called Kentish Town, which we mention chiefly by reason of the corruption of the name, the true one being Cantilupe Town, of which that ancient family were originally the owners. They were men of great account in the reigns of King John, Henry III., and Edward I. Walter de Cantilupe was Bishop of Worcester, 1236 to 1266, and Thomas de Cantilupe was Bishop of Hereford, 1275 to 1282. Thomas was canonised for a saint in the thirty-fourth year of Edward's reign; the inheritance at length devolving upon the sisters, the very name became extinct." The place itself is named, not after Kent, as might be possibly imagined, seeing that Lord Camden's property lies mainly in that county, but after that manor in the hundred of Ossulston, known as Kantelowes or Kentelowes, which appears sometimes to have been called Kentestown. In this, doubtless, we must seek the origin of Ken* (now commonly called Caen) Wood, the seat of Lord Mansfield, between Hampstead and Highgate. We may, however, add that the thoroughfare now known as Gray's Inn Road is stated to have led northwards to a "pleasant rural suburb, variously named Ken-edge Town and Kauntelows," in which we can discern the origin of its present name.

The situation of Kentish Town is pleasant and healthy; and it is described by Thornton, in his "Survey of London," 1780, as "a village on the road to Highgate, where people take furnished lodgings in the summer, especially those afflicted with consumption and other disorders."

That old gossip, Horace Walpole, who probably never went so far afield from the metropolis as the place of which he writes, tells his friend, Sir Horace Mann, in 1791: "Lord Camden has just let ground at Kentish Town for building fourteen hundred houses; nor do I wonder, nor does he wonder. There will soon be one street from London . . . to every village ten miles round." The place is described by the author of "Select Views of London and its Environs," published in 1804, as "a very respectable village between Highgate and London, containing several handsome houses, and particularly an elegant seat built by the late Gregory Bateman, Esq., and intended as a kind of miniature of Wanstead House, in Essex." The limits of the village, we may add, have within the last few years been considerably extended by the erection of new streets and ranges of handsome houses, so that altogether the place is now one of considerable importance. It can now boast of having two railway stations, in addition to two or three others on its borders, besides a line of tramway, and a service of omnibuses connecting it with Fleet Street, the West End, Charing Cross, and other parts of the metropolis.

Kentish Town was inhabited long before Somers Town or Camden Town were in existence. It is not certain that there was a chapel here earlier than the reign of Elizabeth; and little or nothing is known in detail concerning it. Norden refers to a chapel of ease as existing in his time in this village, as he says, speaking of the old parish church, "Folks from the hamlet of Kennistonne now and then visit it, but not often, *having a chapele of their owne.*" And the chapel (now converted into a church, and known as Holy Trinity) was

* The word appears also in Kensington, see *ante*, p. 118.

erected by Wyatt in 1783—a dark age for church architecture—but has since been rendered more suitable for Christian worship, having been enlarged about the year 1850, and altered to the Early Decorated style, from the designs of Mr. Bartholomew. It has two lofty steeples, and a large painted window at the eastern end; the altar recess has some elaborate carved work. In this church is buried Grignion, the engraver.

In 1841, at which time the population of Kentish Town numbered upwards of 10,000, there was only one place of worship belonging to the Established Church; the erection of a new church was proposed and erected upon the estate of Brookfield, the greater part of which is in the hamlet of Kentish Town, and the remainder in the adjoining chapelry of Highgate. The building is erected in the Early English style, and has a fine tall spire; some of the windows are enriched with painted glass. The site of the church was given by the proprietor of the ground whereon it stands, Lady Burdett-Coutts gave the peal of bells, and other grants were made towards the fabric.

In 1848 a large Congregational chapel was built here, in the ecclesiastical style of architecture of the fifteenth century. It has several richly-traceried windows filled with stained glass, including a splendid wheel-window fifteen feet in diameter. Messrs. Hodge and Butler were the architects.

In Fortess Place is the Roman Catholic Chapel of St. Mary. A mission chapel was built in the Highgate Road in 1847, and a schoolroom attached to it. In 1854 the chapel was, however, closed by order of the diocesan, and from that time for several months the Passionist Fathers from The Hyde served the place. In 1855 a piece of freehold ground was purchased (funds being provided by Cardinal Wiseman), and three cottages which stood upon the land were converted into a temporary chapel, capable of accommodating about 200 persons. The new church, which is in the Gothic style, has since been erected in its place.

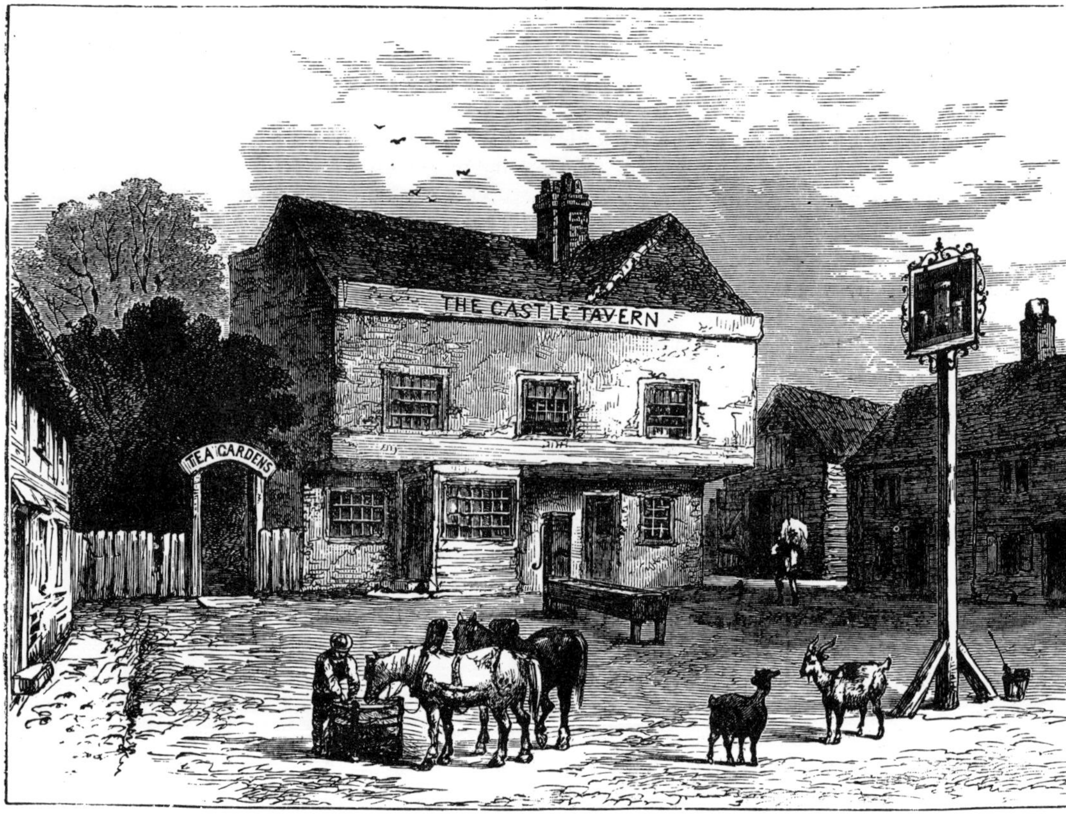

THE "CASTLE" TAVERN, KENTISH TOWN ROAD, IN 1800. (*See page* 321.)

The historical memorabilia of Kentish Town, we need scarcely remark, are comparatively very scanty. We are told how that William Bruges, Garter King-at-Arms in the reign of Henry V., had a country-house here, at which he entertained the German Emperor, Sigismund, who visited England in 1416, to promote a negotiation for peace with France. This is literally all the figure that it acts

GENERAL VIEW OF OLD KENTISH TOWN, 1820.

in history down to quite recent times, when we incidentally learn that the Prince Regent was nearly meeting with a serious accident here, in December, 1813, through a dense fog, which would not yield even to royalty. On his way to pay a visit to the Marquis of Salisbury, at Hatfield House, Herts, the Prince was obliged to return to Carlton House, after one of his outriders had fallen into a ditch at the entrance of Kentish Town, which at that time was not lit with gas, and probably not even with oil.

The road through this district, however, even when no fog prevailed, does not seem to have been very safe for wayfarers after dark, in former times, if we may judge from the numerous notices of outrages which appear in the papers of the times, of which the following may be taken as a sample:—

The *London Courant*, August 8, 1751, contains the following:—"On Sunday night, August 5th, 1751, as Mr. Rainsforth and his daughter, of Clare Street, Clare Market, were returning home through Kentish Town, about eight o'clock, they were attacked by three footpads, and after being brutally ill-used, Mr. R. was robbed of his watch and money."

A few years later, the following paragraph appeared in the *Morning Chronicle* (January 9, 1773): —"On Thursday night some villains robbed the Kentish Town stage, and stripped the passengers of their money, watches, and buckles. In the hurry they spared the pockets of Mr. Corbyn, the druggist; but he, content to have neighbours' fare, called out to one of the rogues, 'Stop, friend! you have forgot to take my money.'"

The result of these continual outrages was that the inhabitants of the district resolved upon adopting some means for their protection, as was notified by the following announcement in the newspapers: —"The inhabitants of Kentish Town, and other places between there and London, have entered into a voluntary subscription for the support of a guard or patrol to protect foot-passengers to and from each place during the winter season (that is to say) from to-morrow, being old Michaelmas Day, to old Lady Day next, in the following manner, viz.:—That a guard of two men, well armed, will set out to-morrow, at six o'clock in the evening, from Mr. Lander's, the 'Bull,' in Kentish Town, and go from thence to Mr. Gould's, the 'Coach and Horses,' facing the Foundling Hospital gate, in Red Lion Street, London; and at seven will return from thence back to the 'Bull;' at eight will set out again from the 'Bull' to the 'Coach and Horses,' and at nine will return from thence to the 'Bull' again; and will so continue to do every evening during the said winter season, from which places, at the above hours, all passengers will be conducted without fee or reward."

Kentish Town, in the middle of the last century, could boast of its Assembly Rooms, at which the balls were sufficiently attractive to draw persons from all parts of the neighbourhood of London. In fact, it became a second "Almack's"*—in its way, of course. It was a large wooden building, and stood at the angle of the main road, where the Highgate and Holloway Roads meet, and on gala nights it was lighted up with numberless lamps. In 1788 the house was taken by a person named Wood, who issued the following advertisement:—"Thomas Wood begs leave to inform his friends and the publick in general, that he has laid in a choice assortment of wines, spirits, and liquors, together with mild ales and cyder of the best quality, all of which he is *determined* to sell on the most *valuable* terms. Dinners for public societies or private parties dressed on the shortest notice. Tea, coffee, &c., morning and evening. A good trap-ball ground, skittle ground, pleasant summer-house, extensive garden, and every other accommodation for the convenience of those who may think proper to *make an excursion* to the above house during the summer months. A good ordinary on Sundays at two o'clock."

By the side of the roadway, facing the old Assembly Rooms, was an elm-tree, beneath whose spreading branches was an oval-shaped marble-topped table, the edge of which was surrounded with the following inscription:—"Posuit A.D. 1725 in Memoriam Sanitatis Restauratæ ROBERTUS WRIGHT, Gent." The old tree was struck by lightning in 1849.

A little farther from town, in or about the year 1858, some gardens were opened as a place of public amusement on the Highgate Road, near the foot of Highgate Rise. But the place was not very respectably conducted, and after a run of about a year the gardens were closed, the magistrates refusing a spirit licence to the proprietor, a Mr. Weston, the owner of a music-hall in Holborn.

In 1833 races were held at Kentish Town, the particulars of which, as they appeared in the *Daily Postboy*, are reprinted in Mr. Palmer's "History of St. Pancras." These races in their day drew as much attention as did Epsom then, but all memory of them has long passed away. There was also at one time established here a society or club, known as "The Corporation of Kentish Town," an institution, there is little doubt, much on a par with

* See Vol. IV., p. 197.

that which we have already described as existing at "The Harp," in Russell Street, Covent Garden, which is denominated "The Corporation of the City of Lushington." * The club is referred to in the following announcements which appear in the newspapers of the period :—

The Officers and Aldermen of the Corporation of Kentish Town are desired to attend the next day of meeting, at Two o'clock, at Brother Legg's, the "Parrot," in Green Arbour Court, in the Little Old Baily, in order to pay a visit to the Corporation of Stroud Green, now held at the "Hole in the Wall" at Islington; and from thence to return in the evening to Brother Lamb's in Little Shear Lane, near Temple Bar, to which house the said Corporation have adjourned for the winter season.

By order of the Court,
T. L., *Recorder*.
October 1, 1754.

CORPORATION OF KENTISH TOWN, 1756.

GENTLEMEN,

Your Company is desired to meet the past Mayors, Sheriffs, and Aldermen of this Corporation, the ensuing Court Day, at Mr. Thomas Baker's, the "Green Dragon," in Fleet Street, precisely at Two o'clock, in order to go in a body to Mr. Peter Brabant's, the "Roman Eagle," in Church Street, Deptford, to pay a visit to our Right Worshipful Mayor who now resides in that town.

By order of the Court,
J. J., *Recorder*.

The Company of the Aldermen of Stroud Green, the Loyal Regiment of British Hussars, and the Brethren of the Most Antient and Noble Order of Bucks, will be esteem'd a great favour.

The "Castle" Tavern, in Kentish Town Road, stands upon the site of an older house bearing the same sign, which had the reputation—true or false—of dating its origin from the time of King John. The front of the old building had the familiar and picturesque projecting storeys, supported originally by a narrow pier at the side of a bolder one. The interior of one of the rooms had a fireplace of stone, carved with a flattened arch of the Tudor style, with the spandrils enriched with a rose and a leaf-shaped ornament terminating in a snake's tail. This fireplace had been for years hidden from view by a coat of plaster. It is possible that, in their ignorance of Gothic architecture, the good people of Kentish Town ascribed a Tudor arch to the early part of the thirteenth century.

Another old building at Kentish Town was the Emanuel Hospital, an establishment for the reception of the blind, which was burnt down in 1779. The house had been purchased by a Mr. Lowe, who was one of the chief promoters of the charity, and who took every possible method to forward the establishment and procure subscriptions. He was entrusted with the management of the design, and the receipt of subscriptions, which flowed in largely; and he insured the house for £4,000. Circumstances having occurred to show that the destruction of the building was not caused by accident, suspicion fastened upon Mr. Lowe; but before he could be secured and brought to justice, he put an end to his life by poison.

Among the "worthies" of Kentish Town we may mention Dr. William Stukeley, the celebrated antiquary, who formerly lived here. We shall have occasion to mention him again when we reach St. Pancras. He was called by his friends "the Arch-Druid," and over the door of his villa a friend caused to be written the following lines :—

"Me dulcis saturet quies,
Obscuro positus loco,
Leni perfruar otio,
Chyndonax Druida."

These lines may be thus translated:—

"Oh, may this rural solitude receive
And contemplation all its pleasures give
The Druid priest."

The word "Chyndonax" is an allusion to an urn of glass so inscribed in France, in which the doctor believed were contained the ashes of an Arch-Druid of that name, whose portrait forms the frontispiece to his work on Stonehenge. Dr. Stukeley's reputation, however, as an antiquary is not great at the present day, as he has been proved by Mr. B. B. Woodward, in the *Gentleman's Magazine*, to have been equally credulous and superficial.

Here, too, lived an eccentric old bachelor and miser, Mr. John Little, at whose sudden death, intestate, in 1798, about £37,000 of property, 173 pairs of breeches, and 180 old wigs were found in a miserably furnished apartment which he allowed no one to enter. These and his wealth all passed to a brother whom he had discarded, and whom he had meant to disinherit had not death prevented him.

It is generally said that Charles Mathews the elder was a resident in Kentish Town; but his home, Ivy Cottage, was in Millfield Lane, in the hamlet of Brookfield, of which, as well as of St. Anne's Church, Brookfield, it will be more convenient to treat in our notice of Highgate. At present we have no intention to climb the breezy "northern heights of London."

At No. 8, in Lower Craven Place, lived, for some time, Douglas Jerrold. He afterwards removed to Kilburn, where he died in June, 1857.†

* See Vol. III., p. 279.

† See *ante*, p. 249.

One of the peculiarities of this district, and one which it retained down to a very recent date, was its slate pavement. It certainly, on fine days, looked very clean, and was pleasant to the tread; but in wet and frosty weather it became slippery and dangerous in the extreme. It has now been superseded by the ordinary pavement of stone-flags.

During the last few years the green fields which fringed one side of the road at Kentish Town have passed away, and unbroken lines of streets connect it with the Holloway Road. Many new churches and chapels have been erected, and the once rural village now forms, like Camden and Somers Town, but a portion of the great metropolis.

Great College Street, by which we return to the eastern side of Camden Town, in the direction of old St. Pancras Church, is so named from the Royal Veterinary College, which covers a large space of ground on its eastern side. This institution was established in 1791, with the view of promoting a reformation in that particular branch of veterinary science called "farriery," by the formation of a school, in which the anatomical structure of quadrupeds of all kinds, horses, cattle, sheep, dogs, &c., the diseases to which they are subject, and the remedies proper to be applied, should be investigated and regularly taught. Of the foundation of this institution we gather the following particulars from the *Monthly Register* of 1802:—"To the agricultural societies in different parts of this kingdom the public is greatly indebted. It will be matter of surprise to men of thought, that the improvements in the veterinary art, instead of originating with the military establishment to which it is so important for the benefit of the cavalry, has been chiefly promoted by an obscure association at Odiham, in Hampshire, which entertain the design of sending two young men of talents into France, to become students in this new profession. Monsieur St. Bel, in the year 1788, was driven from that country, either from his own pecuniary embarrassments, or by the internal disorganisation which then prevailed. He offered his services to this society, in consequence of which the college was instituted, and he was nominated to superintend it, and some noblemen and gentlemen of the highest rank and consideration in the country were appointed as managers of the undertaking. Monsieur St. Bel, possessing, however, many excellent qualities, was not precisely suited to his situation; his private difficulties impeded his public exertions. In 1792, to ascertain his ability to discharge the duties of his situation, he was examined by Sir George Baker and several other physicians and surgeons, and was considered competent to his duties. Whether these gentlemen comparing the merits of Monsieur St. Bel with the ordinary farriers, imagined consummate skill in the profession not necessary to the success of this new enterprise, we will not determine; but it is certain, however ingenious he might be in shoeing and in the inferior branches, with the pharmaceutic art, or that which respects the healing the diseases of the animal, he was wholly unacquainted. In August, 1793, Monsieur St. Bel died, and it is probable that the fatal event was accelerated by the disappointment he felt at the ill success of the establishment he conducted.

"In the time of Monsieur St. Bel a house was taken at Pancras for the purposes of the institution. Since his decease the professorship has devolved to Mr. Coleman, and a handsome theatre has been prepared, with a museum and dissecting rooms for the use of the pupils, and for their examination; and for other purposes a medical committee has been appointed, comprising Dr. Fordyce, Dr. Bailie, Dr Babington, Dr. Relp, Mr. Cline, Mr. Abernethy, Mr. A. Cooper, Mr. Home, and Mr. Houlstone.

"In consequence of the new regulations pupils are admitted for the sum of twenty guineas, and they are accommodated in the college with board or otherwise, according to their own convenience. For this sum they see the practice of the college, and by the liberality of the medical committee are admitted to the lectures of those who compose it gratis; and in the army the veterinary surgeons are advanced to the rank of commissioned officers, by which condescension of the commander-in-chief the regiments of English cavalry have, for the first time, obtained the assistance of gentlemen educated in a way to discharge the important duties of their situations."

The Duke of Northumberland was the first president of the college. A school for the instruction of pupils in veterinary science is carried on under the direction of a duly-qualified professor; and diseased horses are admitted upon certain terms into the infirmary. Such is thought to be the national importance of this institution, that Parliament has liberally afforded aid when the state of the college's finances rendered a supply essential.

Lectures are delivered daily in the theatre of the college during the session, which commences in October and ends in May; to these only students are admitted. The fee for pupils is twenty-five guineas, which entitles them to attend the lectures and general practical instructions of the college until they shall have passed their examination. On Tuesday evenings there are discussions on various subjects connected with the veterinary art. The buildings are of plain brick, and have an extensive frontage to the street, within which they stretch back to the distance of more than 200 yards. The theatre for dissections and lectures is judiciously planned; and in a large contiguous apartment are numerous anatomical illustrations. The infirmary will hold about sixty horses. There is likewise a forge, for the shoeing of horses on the most approved principles, and several paddocks are attached to the institution.

Not far from the Veterinary College lived, in 1802, Mr. Andrew Wilson, a gentleman who is described as "of the Stereotype Office," and who took out a patent for the process of stereotyping. He was not, however, the original inventor of the stereotypic art, nor was he destined to be the man who should revive it practically or perfect it. As early as the year 1711, a Dutchman, Van der Mey, introduced a process for consolidating types after they had been set up, by soldering them together at the back; and it is asserted that the process, as we now understand it, was practised in 1725 by William Gedd, or Gedde, of Edinburgh, who endeavoured to apply it to the printing of Bibles for the University of Cambridge. It is well known that the process was, half a century later or more, carried out into common use by the then Lord Stanhope, at his private printing-press at Chevening, in Kent.

Pratt Street, as we have already stated, is so called after the family name of Lord Camden. This is one of the principal streets in Camden Town, and connects Great College Street with the High Street. In it is the burial-ground for the parish of St. Martin's-in-the-Fields, together with a chapel and residence for the officiating clergyman. The site formed originally two fields, called Upper Meadow and Upper Brook Meadow, and was purchased from the Earl of Camden and Dr. Hamilton, Prebendary of Canteloes, in accordance with the provisions of an Act of Parliament passed for that purpose, and the cemetery was laid out and consecrated by the Bishop of London in 1805. Here lies buried Charles Dibdin, the author of most of the best of our naval songs. Charles Knight speaks of him, somewhat sarcastically, it must be owned, as a man who, "had he rendered a tithe of the services actually performed by him to the naval strength of his country under the name of a 'Captain R.N.' instead of as a writer, he would have died a wealthy peer instead of drawing his last breath in poverty."

St. Stephen's Church, in this street, with its adjoining parsonage and schools, covering several acres, is a large and commodious structure, in the Grecian style. It was built about the year 1836.

Among the residents in Camden Town in former times, besides those we have named, was the veteran composer, Sir Henry Rowley Bishop—the last who wrote English music in a distinctive national style, carrying the traditions of Purcell, Arne, Boyce, &c., far on into the present century. Born towards the close of the last century, he had as his early instructor Signor Bianchi. In 1806 he composed the music for a ballet performed at Covent Garden Theatre, and shortly afterwards commenced to write regularly for the stage. From 1810 to 1824 he held the post of musical director at Covent Garden, and subsequently became a director of the Concerts of Ancient Music. He received the honour of knighthood in 1842, but it was a barren honour; and in spite of a knighthood and the Professorship of Music at Oxford, added to the more solid rewards of successful authorship, his last days were spent in comparative poverty. Such are the rewards held out in this country to professional eminence! In every house where music, and more especially vocal music, is welcome, the name of Sir Henry Bishop has long been, and must long remain, a household word. Who has not been soothed by the melody of "Blow, gentle gales," charmed by the measures of "Lo! here the gentle lark," enlivened by the animated strains of "Foresters, sound the cheerful horn," or touched by the sadder music of "The winds whistle cold?" Who has not been haunted by the insinuating tones of "Tell me, my heart," "Bid me discourse," or "Where the wind blows," which Rossini, the minstrel of the South, loved so well? Who has not felt sympathy with "As it fell upon a day, in the merry month of May," or admired that masterpiece of glee and chorus, "The chough and the crow," or been moved to jollity at some convivial feast by "Mynheer von Dunck," the most original and genial of comic glees? Sir Henry Bishop died in 1855, at his residence in Cambridge Street, Edgware Road.

As we pass down Great College Street, we have on our left, stretching away towards Islington, a sort of "No man's land," formerly known as Agar Town, and filling up a part of the interval between the Midland and the Great Northern Railway, of which we shall have more to say in a future chapter. On our right, too, down to a comparatively recent date, the character of the locality was not much better; indeed, the whole of the neighbourhood which lay—and part of which still lies—between Clarendon Square and the Brill and St. Pancras Road, would answer to the description of what Charles Dickens, in his "Uncommercial Traveller," calls a "shy neighbourhood," abounding in bird and birdcage shops, costermongers' shops, old rag and bottle shops, donkeys, barrows, dirty fowls, &c., and with the inevitable gin-shop at every corner. "The very dogs of shy neighbourhoods usually betray a slinking consciousness of being in poor circumstances," is one of the appropriate remarks of "Boz;" and another is to the same effect—"Nothing in shy neighbourhoods perplexes me more than the bad company which birds keep. Foreign birds often get into good society, but British birds are inseparable from low associates."

THE ROYAL VETERINARY COLLEGE, 1825. (*See page* 322.)

CHAPTER XXV.

ST. PANCRAS.

"The rev'rend spire of ancient Pancras view,
To ancient Pancras pay the rev'rence due;
Christ's sacred altar there first Britain saw,
And gazed, and worshipp'd with an holy awe,
Whilst pitying Heaven diffused a saving ray,
And heathen darkness changed to Christian day."—*Anon.*

Biographical Sketch of St. Pancras—Churches bearing his Name—Corruption of the Name—The Neighbourhood of St. Pancras in Former Times—Population of the Parish—Ancient Manors—Desolate Condition of the Locality in the Sixteenth Century—Notices of the Manors in Domesday Book and Early Surveys—The Fleet River and its Occasional Floods—The "Elephant and Castle" Tavern—The Workhouse—The Vestry—Old St. Pancras Church and its Antiquarian Associations—Celebrated Persons interred in the Churchyard—Ned Ward's Will—Father O'Leary—Chatterton's Visit to the Churchyard—Mary Wollstoncraft Godwin—Roman Catholic Burials—St. Giles's Burial-ground and the Midland Railway—Wholesale Desecration of the Graveyards—The "Adam and Eve" Tavern and Tea-gardens—St. Pancras Wells—Antiquities of the Parish—Extensive Demolition of Houses for the Midland Railway.

BEFORE venturing to set foot in either of the "shy" localities to which we have referred at the close of the previous chapter, it would, perhaps, be as well to say something about the parish of St. Pancras generally—the mother parish, of which Camden, Kentish, Agar, and Somers Towns may be said to be, in a certain sense, the offspring, or, at all events, members. It is pleasant, at length, after so many chapters descriptive of a district which is thoroughly modern, to find ourselves at a spot which actually has its annals, and in which the biographical element blends itself with the topographical. One can scarcely help feeling weary after reading accounts of parishes and vicinities which have about them nothing of past interest beyond tea-gardens and road-side inns; and therefore we welcome our return at St. Pancras into a region of history, where the memorials of past celebrities abound. In fact, it must be owned that the whole of the district through which we have travelled since we quitted Kensington, and crossed the Uxbridge Road, is extremely void of interest, as, indeed, is nearly the whole of the north-western district of London, a geographical entity which we owe to Sir Rowland Hill and the authorities of the General Post-Office.

St. Pancras, after whom this district is named, was a young Phrygian nobleman who suffered martyrdom at Rome under the Emperor Diocletian for his adherence to the Christian faith; he became a favourite saint in England. The Priory of Lewes, in Sussex, was dedicated to his honour; and besides the church around which this particular district grew up, there are at least eight other churches in England dedicated to this saint, and several in Italy—one in Rome, of which we read that mass is said in it constantly for the repose of the souls of the bodies buried here. The parish of St. Pancras contains two churches dedicated to the saint—the new parish church, of which we shall speak when we come to Euston Square; and the ancient or Old St. Pancras, in St. Pancras Road. Of the other churches in England dedicated to this saint, we may mention one in the City—St. Pancras, Soper Lane, now incorporated with St. Mary-le-Bow; Pancransweek, Devon; Widdecome-in-the-Moor, Devon; Exeter; Chichester; Coldred, in Kent; Alton Pancras, Dorset; Arlington, Sussex; and Wroot, in Lincolnshire.

THE FLEET RIVER, NEAR ST. PANCRAS, 1825.

In consequence of the early age at which he suffered for the faith, St. Pancras was subsequently regarded as the patron saint of children. "There was then," as Chambers remarks in his "Book of Days," "a certain fitness in dedicating to him the first church in a country which owed its conversion to three children"—alluding, of course, to the fair children whom Gregory saw in the streets of Rome, the sight of whom had moved the Pope to send St. Augustine hither. "But there was also another and closer link which connected the first church built in England by St. Augustine with St. Pancras, for," adds Mr. Chambers, "the much-loved monastery on the Cœlian Mount, which Gregory had founded, and of which Augustine was prior, had been erected on the very estate which had belonged anciently to the family of Pancras." The festival of St. Pancras is kept, in the Roman Catholic Church, on the 12th of May, under which day his biography will be found in the "Lives of the Saints," by Alban Butler, who tells us that he suffered martyrdom at the early age of fourteen, at Rome, in the year 304. After being beheaded for the faith, he was buried in the cemetery of Calepodius, which subsequently took his name. His relics are spoken of by Gregory the Great. St. Gregory of Tours calls him the Avenger of Perjuries, and tells us that God openly punished false oaths made before his relics. The church at Rome dedicated to the saint, of which we have spoken above, stands on the spot where he is said to have suffered; in this church his body is still kept. "England and Italy, France and Spain abound," adds Alban Butler, "in churches bearing his name, in most of which relics of the saint were kept and shown in the ages before the Reformation. The first church consecrated by St. Augustine at Canterbury is said by Mr. Baring Gould, in his "Lives of the Saints," to have been dedicated to St. Pancras. In art, St. Pancras is always represented as a boy, with a sword uplifted in one hand and a palm-branch in the other; and it may be added that the seal of the parish represents the saint with similar emblems. There is a magnificent brass of Prior Nelond, at Cowfold, in Sussex, where St. Pancras is represented with a youthful countenance, holding a book and a palm-branch, and treading on a strange figure, supposed to be intended to symbolise his triumphs over the arch-enemy of mankind, in allusion to the etymology of the saint's name. The saint figures in Alfred Tennyson's poem of "Harold," where William Duke of Normandy exclaims—

> "Lay thou thy hand upon this golden pall;
> Behold the jewel of St. Pancratius
> Woven into the gold. Swear thou on this."

That the name, like most others in bygone days, did not escape corruption, may be seen from the way in which it is written, even towards the close of the last century. In Goldsmith's "Citizen of the World" (published in 1794), is a semi-humorous description of a journey hither, by way of Islington, in which the author thus speaks of the name of the place:—"From hence [*i.e.*, from Islington] I parted with reluctance to Pancras, as it is written, or Pancridge, as it is pronounced; but which should be both pronounced and written Pangrace. This emendation I will venture *meo arbitrio:* πᾶν, in the Greek language, signifies *all;* which, added to the English word *grace*, maketh *all grace*, or Pangrace: and, indeed, this is a very proper appellation to a place of so much sanctity, as Pangrace is universally esteemed. However this be, if you except the parish church and its fine bells, there is little in Pangrace worth the attention of the curious observer." We fear that the derivation proposed for Pancras must be regarded as utterly absurd.

Many of our readers will remember, and others will thank us for reminding them, that the scene of a great part of the *Tale of a Tub*, by Swift, is laid in the fields about "Pankridge." Totten Court is there represented as a country mansion isolated from all other buildings; it is pretended that a robbery is committed "in the ways over the country," between Kentish Town and Hampstead Heath, and the warrant for the apprehension of the robber is issued by a "Marribone" justice of the peace.

Again, we find the name spelt as above by George Wither, in his "Britain's Remembrancer" (1628):—

> "Those who did never travel till of late
> Half way to Pankridge from the city gate."

In proof of the rural character of the district some three centuries ago, it may be well to quote the words of the actor Nash, in his greetings to Kemp in the time of Elizabeth: "As many allhailes to thy person as there be haicockes in July at Pancredge" (*sic*).

Even so lately as the commencement of the reign of George III., fields, with uninterrupted views of the country, led from Bagnigge Wells northwards towards St. Pancras, where another well and public tea-gardens invited strollers within its sanitary premises. It seems strange to learn that the way between this place and London was particularly unsafe to pedestrians after dark, and that robberies between this spot and Gray's Inn Lane, and also between the latter and the "Jew's Harp" Tavern, of which we have spoken in a previous chapter, were common in the last century.

St. Pancras is often said to be the most populous parish in the metropolis, if taken in its full extent as including "a third of the hamlet of Highgate, with the other hamlets of Battle Bridge, Camden

Town, Kentish Town, Somers Town, all Tottenham Court Road, and the streets east and north of Cleveland Street and Rathbone Place," besides—if we may trust Lysons—part of a house in Queen Square. Mr. John Timbs, in his "Curiosities of London," speaks of St. Pancras as "the largest parish in Middlesex," being no less than "eighteen miles in circumference;" and he also says it is the most populous parish in the metropolis. Mr. Palmer, however, in his history of the parish, published in 1870, says that "its population is estimated, at the present day, at a little over a quarter of a million, its number being only exceeded of all the metropolitan parishes by the neighbouring one of Marylebone." He adds that it is computed to contain 2,700 square acres of land, and that its circuit is twenty-one miles. From the "Diary" of the vestry for the year 1876-7 we learn that the area of the parish is 2,672 statute acres. The population of St. Pancras parish in 1881 amounted to 236,209, and the number of inhabited houses to 24,655. There are 278 Parliamentary and municipal boroughs in England and Wales, exclusive of the metropolis, and only five of these—viz., Liverpool, Manchester, Birmingham, Leeds, and Sheffield—contain a larger population; and there are twenty-two counties with a less population in each than St. Pancras.

There are four ancient prebendal manors in the parish, namely, Pancras; Cantlowes, or Kentish Town; Tothill, or Tottenham Court; and Ruggemure, or Rugmere. The holder of the prebendal stall of St. Pancras in St. Paul's Cathedral was also, *ex officio*, the "Confessarius" of the Bishop of London. Among those who have held this post may be enumerated the learned Dr. Lancelot Andrews, afterwards Bishop of Winchester—of whom we shall have more to say when we come to his tomb in St. Saviour's, Southwark; Dr. Sherlock, and Archdeacon Paley; and in more modern times, Canon Dale.

The church had attached to it about seventy acres of land, which were let in 1641 for £10, and nearly two hundred years later, being leased to a Mr. William Agar, formed the site of Agar Town, as mentioned in the previous chapter. Norden thought the church "not to yield in antiquitie to Paules in London:" in his "Speculum Britanniæ" he describes it as "all alone, utterly forsaken, old, and weather-beaten."

Brewer, in his "London and Middlesex," says: "When a visitation of the church of Pancras was made in the year 1251, there were only forty houses in the parish." The desolate situation of the village, in the latter part of the sixteenth century, is emphatically described by Norden in his work above mentioned. After noticing the solitary condition of the church, he says: "Yet about the structure have bin manie buildings, now decaied, leaving poore Pancrast without companie or comfort." In some manuscript additions to his work, the same writer has the following observations:—"Although this place be, as it were, forsaken of all, and true men seldom frequent the same, but upon deveyne occasions, yet it is visayed by thieves, who assemble not there to pray, but to waite for prayer; and many fall into their handes, clothed, that are glad when they are escaped naked. Walk not there too late."

As lately as the year 1745, there were only two or three houses near the church, and twenty years later the population of the parish was under six hundred. At the first census taken in the present century it had risen to more than 35,000, and in 1861 it stood at very little under 200,000. There has, however, been a decrease since that time on account of the extensive clearances made for the terminus of the Midland Railway, of which we shall speak presently.

Pancras is mentioned in "Domesday Book," where it is stated that "the land of this manor is of one caracute, and employs one plough. On the estate are twenty-four men, who pay a rent of thirty shillings per annum." The next notice which we find of this manor is its sale, on the demise of Lady Ferrers, in 1375, to Sir Robert Knowles; and in 1381 of its reversion, which belonged to the Crown, to the prior of the house of Carthusian Monks of the Holy Salutation. After the dissolution of the monasteries it came into the possession of Lord Somers, in the hands of whose descendants the principal portion of it—Somers Town—now remains.

Of the manor of Cantelows, or Kennestoune (now, as we have already seen, called Kentish Town), it is recorded in the above-mentioned survey that it is held by the Canons of St. Paul's, and that it comprises four miles of land. The entry states that "there is plenty of timber in the hedgerows, good pasture for cattle, a running brook, and two 20d. rents. Four villeins, together with seven bordars, hold this land under the Canons of St. Paul's at forty shillings a year rent. In King Edward's time it was raised to sixty shillings."

In the reign of Henry IV., Henry Bruges, Garter King-at-Arms, had a mansion in this manor, where on one occasion he entertained the German Emperor, Sigismund, during his visit to this country. The building, which stood near the old Episcopal

Chapel, was said to have been erected by the two brothers, Walter and Thomas de Cantelupe, during the reign of King John. According to a survey made during the Commonwealth, this manor contained 210 acres of land. The manor-house was then sold to one Richard Hill, a merchant of London, and the manor to Richard Utber, a draper. At the Restoration they were ejected, and the original lessees reinstated; but again in 1670 the manor changed hands, the father of Alderman Sir Jeffreys Jeffreys (uncle of the notorious Judge Jeffreys) becoming proprietor. By the intermarriage of Earl Camden with a member of that family, it is now the property of that nobleman's descendants. The estate is held subject to a reserved rent of £20, paid annually to the Prebendary of St. Paul's. Formerly the monks of Waltham Abbey held an estate in this manor, called by them Cane Lond, now Caen Wood, valued at thirteen pounds. It is said by antiquaries to be the remains of the ancient forest of Middlesex. Of this part of the manor we shall have to speak when we come to Hampstead.

The manor of Tottenham Court, or Totten Hall—in "Domesday" Tothele, where it is valued at £5 a year—was kept in the prebendary's hands till the fourteenth century; but in 1343 John de Caleton was the lessee, and, after the lease had come to the Crown, it was granted in 1661 in satisfaction of a debt, and became the property, shortly after, of the ducal family of Fitzroy, one of whose scions, Lord Southampton, is the present possessor.

The manor of Ruggemere is mentioned in the survey of the parish taken in 1251, as shown in the records of the Dean and Chapter of St. Paul's. "Its exact situation," says Mr. Palmer, "is not now known. Very possibly," he continues, "at the breaking up of the monasteries it reverted to the Crown, and was granted by bluff Harry to some Court favourite. The property of the Bedford family was acquired in a great measure from that monarch's hands. It is, therefore, very probable that the manor of Ruggemere consisted of all that land lying at the south-east of the parish, no portion of that district lying in either of the other manors."

The village church stood pretty nearly in the centre of the parish, which, with the lands about Somers Town, included the estates of the Skinners' Company, of the Duke of Bedford, and of Mr. "Councillor" Agar. The land which the parish comprises forms part of what is called the London Basin, the deposits of which are aqueous, and belong to the Eocene period.

In a previous chapter we have spoken of the Fleet River, which used to flow through this parish. Hone, in his "Table Book," 1827, thus describes it as winding its sluggish course through Camden Town and St. Pancras in its way to King's Cross:—"The River Fleet at its source in a field on the land side of the Hampstead Ponds is merely a sedgy ditchling, scarcely half a step across, and winds its way along, with little increase of depth, by the road from the 'Mother Red Cap' to Kentish Town, beneath which road it passes through the pastures to Camden Town; in one of these pastures the canal running through the tunnel at Pentonville to the City Road is conveyed over it by an arch. From this place its width increases till it reaches towards the west side of the road leading from Pancras workhouse to Kentish Town. In the rear of the houses on that side of the road it becomes a brook, washing the edge of the garden in front of the premises late the stereotype foundry and printing-office of Mr. Andrew Wilson, which stand back from the road; and, cascading down behind the lower road-side houses, it reaches the 'Elephant and Castle,' in front of which it tunnels to Battle Bridge."

Tradition would carry the navigation of the Fleet River far higher up than Holborn Bridge, which has been stated in a previous part* of this work as the utmost limit to which it was navigable, since it relates, say the Brothers Percy, in their "London," that "an anchor was found in this brook at Pancras wash, where the road branches off to Somers Town." But they do not give a date or other particulars. Down to a very late date, even to the year in which the Metropolitan Railway was constructed, the Fleet River was subject to floods on the occasion of a sudden downfall of rain, when the Hampstead and Highgate ponds would overflow.

One of the most considerable overflows occurred in January, 1809. "At this period, when the snow was lying very deep," says a local chronicler, "a rapid thaw came on, and the arches not affording a sufficient passage for the increased current, the whole space between Pancras Church, Somers Town, and the bottom of the hill at Pentonville, was in a short time covered with water. The flood rose to a height of three feet from the middle of the highway; the lower rooms of all the houses within that space were completely inundated, and the inhabitants suffered considerable damage in their goods and furniture, which many of them had not time to remove. Two cart-horses were

* See Vol. II., p. 418.

drowned, and for several days persons were obliged to be conveyed to and from their houses, and receive their provisions, &c., in at their windows by means of carts."

Again, in 1818, there was a very alarming flood at Battle Bridge, which lies at the southern end of Pancras Road, of which the following account appears in the newspapers of that date:—"In consequence of the quantity of rain that fell on Friday night, the river Fleet overflowed near Battle Bridge, where the water was soon several feet high, and ran into the lower apartments of every house from the 'Northumberland Arms' tea-gardens to the Small-pox Hospital, Somers Town, being a distance of about a mile. The torrent then forced its way into Field Street and Lyon Place, which are inhabited by poor people, and entered the kitchens, carrying with it everything that came within its reach. In the confusion, many persons in attempting to get through the water fell into the Fleet, but were most providentially saved. In the house of a person named Creek, the water forced itself into a room inhabited by a poor man and his family, and before they could be alarmed, their bed was floating about in near seven feet of water. They were, by the prompt conduct of the neighbours and night officers, got out safe. Damage to the extent of several thousand pounds was occasioned by the catastrophe."

Much, however, as we may lament the metamorphosis of a clear running stream into a filthy sewer, the Fleet brook did the Londoner good service. It afforded the best of natural drainage for a large extent north of the metropolis, and its level was so situated as to render it capable of carrying off the contents of a vast number of side drains which ran into it. "There still remain, however," writes Mr. Palmer, "a few yards visible in the parish where the brook runs in its native state. At the back of the Grove, in the Kentish Town Road, is a rill of water, one of the little arms of the Fleet, which is yet clear and untainted. Another arm is at the bottom of the field at the back of the 'Bull and Last' Inn, over which is a little wooden bridge leading to the cemetery."

The "Elephant and Castle," above referred to, is one of the oldest taverns in the parish of St. Pancras. It is situated in King's Road, near the workhouse, and is said to have derived its name from the discovery of the remains of an elephant which was made in its vicinity more than a century ago. King's Road lies at the back of the Veterinary College, and unites with the St. Pancras Road at the southern end of Great College Street. At the junction of these roads are the Workhouse and the Vestry Hall. The former building was erected in 1809, at a cost of about £30,000. It has, however, since then been very much enlarged, and is now more than double its original size. It often contains 1,200 inmates, a number equal to the population of many large rural villages. It has not, however, always been well officered. For instance, in 1874, a Parliamentary return stated that out of 407 children admitted into the workhouse during the previous twelvemonth eighty-nine had died, showing a death-rate of 215 per 1,000 per annum!

The St. Pancras Guardians have wisely severed their pauper children from the associations of the workhouse by establishing their schools in the country at Hanwell. In connection with the workhouse a large infirmary has been erected on Highgate Hill, whither the sick inmates have been removed from the old and ill-ventilated quarters.

The Vestry of St. Pancras formerly had no settled place of meeting, but met at various taverns in the parish. The present Vestry Hall was erected in 1847. The architect was Mr. Bond, the then surveyor of the parish, and Mr. Cooper the builder. Mr. Palmer, in his work already referred to, mentions a tradition that the architect, in making the plans for the building, omitted the stairs by which the first-floor was to be reached, and that he afterwards made up the defect by placing the present ugly steps outside.

On the north-east side of Pancras Road, near the Vestry Hall, is the old church of St. Pancras. This ancient and diminutive edifice was, with the exception of a chapel of ease at Kentish Town, now St. John the Baptist's, the only ecclesiastical building the parish could boast of till the middle of the last century. It is not known with certainty when the present structure was erected, but its date is fixed about the year 1350; there was, however, a building upon the same spot long before that date; for in the records belonging to the Dean and Chapter of St. Paul's, in which there is noticed a visitation made to this church in the year 1251, it states that "it had a very small tower, a little belfry, a good stone font for baptisms, and a small marble stone to carry the pax."

Norden, whose remarks on the condition of the church in the reign of Queen Elizabeth we have quoted above, states that "folks from the hamlet of Kennistonne now and then visit it, but not often, having a chapele of their own. When, however, they have a corpse to be interred, they are forced to leave the same within this forsyken church or churchyard, where it resteth as secure against the day of resurrection as if it laie in stately

St. Paule's." Norden's account implies that where the church is situated was then one of the least frequented and desolate spots in the vicinity of the metropolis.

A writer in the *Gentleman's Magazine*, for July, 1749, in the lines quoted as a motto to this chapter, states that—

"Christ's sacred altar *here* first Britain saw."

Other antiquaries inform us that the original establishment of a church on this site was in early Saxon times; and Maximilian Misson, in writing of St. John Lateran at Rome, says, "This is the head and mother of all Christian churches, if you except that of St. Pancras under Highgate, near London."

In the last century Divine service was performed in St. Pancras Church only on the first Sunday in every month, and at all other times in the chapel of ease at Kentish Town, it being thought that the few people who lived near the church could go up to London to pray, while that at Kentish Town was more suited for the country folk, and this custom continued down to within the present century. The earliest date that we meet with in the registry of marriages and baptisms is 1660, and in that of burials 1668. The earlier registers have long since perished.

In the table of benefactions to the parish it is stated that certain lands, fee-simple, copyhold of inheritance, held of the manors of Tottenhall Court and of Cantelows, "were given by some person or persons unknown, for and to the use and benefit of this parish, for the needful and necessary repair of the parish church and the chapel, as the said parish in vestry should from time to time direct; and that these lands were, by custom of the said manors, and for the form of law, to be held in the names of eight trustees who were elected by the inhabitants of the said parish in vestry assembled."

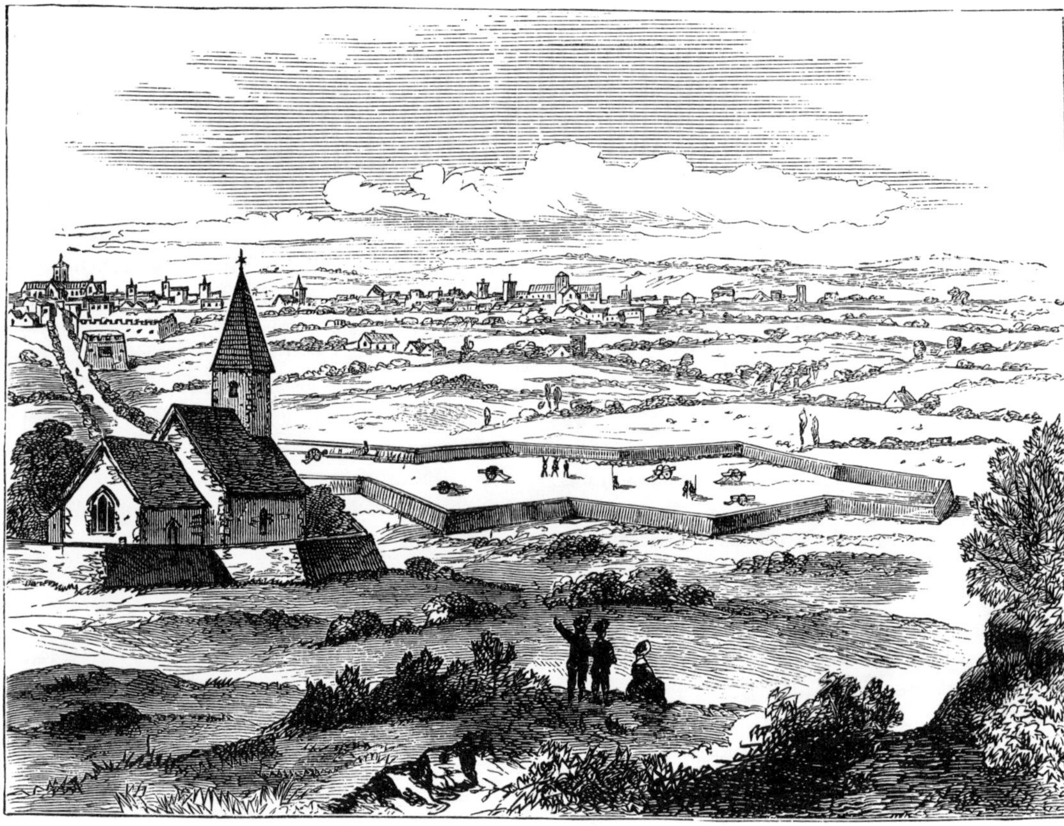

FORTIFICATIONS OF OLD ST. PANCRAS.

There are four parcels of land, the rents and profits of which have been immemorially applied towards the repair of the parish church and the chapel at Kentish Town. By reason of this application a church-rate in former times was considered unnecessary, and whenever the disbursements of the churchwardens exceeded their receipts, the parishioners always preferred to reimburse them out of the poor-rate rather than make a church-rate.

From the survey of church livings taken by order

ST. PANCRAS CHURCH IN 1820. (*From an Original Sketch.*)

of Parliament in 1650, it appears that these lands were disposed of as follows, by Sir Robert Payne, Knight, Peter Benson, and others, feoffees in trust, by licence granted them from the lord of the manors of Tottenhall and Cantlows Court:—"To wit, in consideration of fifty-four pounds to them in hand, paid by Mr. Richard Gwalter, they did, by lease dated the 1st June, 9th Charles I. (A.D. 1633), demise unto the said Richard Gwalter four acres of the said land for twenty-one years, at twopence a year rent. And in consideration of £27 in hand, paid by the said Richard Gwalter, they did, by another lease, dated 2nd August in the year aforesaid, demise unto the said Richard Gwalter two acres of the said land for the term aforesaid for the like rent. There was also (A.D. 1650), a lease dated 20th June, 9th Charles I., unto Thomas Ive (deceased), of seventeen acres of the said land for twenty-one years at £17 a year rent; the remainder of which was assigned unto Peter Benson, and was then in his possession."

The money received by way of premium on the granting of the before-mentioned leases to Richard Gwalter in the year 1633, was expended in the rebuilding of Kentish Town Chapel, of which we have spoken in the preceding chapter. The site seems to have been originally the property of Sir William Hewitt, who was a landowner in this parish in the reign of Charles I. It appears by a statement of Randolph Yearwood, vicar of St. Pancras, dated 1673, that the parish did not buy the site, nor take a lease of it, but that they paid a noble per annum to the Hewitts to be permitted to have the use of it.

In 1656, Colonel Gower, Mr. George Pryer, and Major John Bill were feoffees of the revenue belonging to the parish church of St. Pancras. The land belonging to the rectory was subsequently leased by various persons, when, in 1794, it was vested in a Mr. Swinnerton, of the "White Hart" Inn, Colebrook, and then passed into the hands of Mr. Agar, who, as we have already stated, gave a notoriety to the spot by granting short building leases, which created Agar Town and its miserable surroundings, till the whole was cleared by the Midland Railway Company, who are now the owners of a large part of this once prebendal manor.

The family of Eve or Ive, mentioned above, is of great antiquity in the parish of St. Pancras. In 1457 Henry VI. granted permission to Thomas Ive to enclose a portion of the highway adjoining to his mansion at Kentish Town. In 1483 Richard Ive was appointed Clerk of the Crown in Chancery in as full a manner as John de Tamworth and Geoffrey Martyn in the time of Edward III., and Thomas Ive in the time of Edward IV. enjoyed the same office. In the old parish church is an altar-tomb of Purbeck marble with a canopy, being an elliptical arch ornamented with quatrefoils, which in better days had small brasses at the back, with three figures or groups, with labels from each, and the figure of the Trinity, and three shields of arms above them. This monument was to the memory of Robert Eve, and Lawrentia his sister, son and daughter of Francis and Thomas Eve, Clerk of the Crown, in the reign of Edward IV. Weever, in his work on "Funeral Monuments," informs us that when he saw it the "portraitures" and the following words remained:—

> "Holy Trinitie, one God, have mercy on us.
> Hic jacent Robertus Eve et Lawrentia soror eius, filia Francisci Eve filii
> Thome Eve clerici corone cancellarie Anglie . . . . .
> Quorum . . . . . ."

When Mr. J. T. Smith, as a boy, made an expedition to this church as one of a sketching party, in 1777, he describes it as quite a rural place, in some parts entirely covered with docks and nettles, enclosed only by a low hand-rail, and commanding extensive views of open country in every direction, not only to Hampstead, Highgate, and Islington, but also to Holborn and St. Giles's, almost the only building which met the eye in that direction being Whitefield's Chapel in Tottenham Court Road, and old Montagu House.

The first mention, apparently, that has been found to be made of the church of St. Pancras occurs in the year 1183, but it does not appear whether it then was or was not a recent erection. William de Belmeis, who had been possessed of the prebend of Pancras, within which the church stood, had conveyed the tithes thereof to the canons of St. Paul's; which conveyance was, in that year, confirmed by Gilbert, Bishop of London. The church tithes, &c., were, not long after, granted by the dean and chapter to the hospital within their cathedral, founded by Henry de Northampton, they reserving to themselves one mark per annum. In 1327 the rectory was valued at thirteen marks per annum. In 1441 the advowson, tenths, rents, and profits of the church were demised to Walter Sherington, canon residentiary, for ten marks per annum; and in like manner the rectory continued to be from time to time leased, chiefly to canons of the church. At the suppression, the dean and chapter became re-possessed of the rectory, which has from that period been demised in the manner customary with church property, subject to a reserved rent of £13 6*s.* 8*d.*

The old church formerly consisted of a nave and chancel, built of stones and flint, and a low tower with a bell-shaped roof. It has been several times repaired, and the most recent of the restorations has taken away—externally, at least—all traces of its antiquity. In 1847–8 it was enlarged by taking the space occupied by the old square tower into the body of the church, and a spire was placed on the south side. The west end, which was lengthened, has an enriched Norman porch, and a wheel window in the gable above, which, together with the chancel windows, are filled with stained glass. The old monuments have been restored and placed as nearly as possible in their original positions. On the north wall, opposite the baptistery, is the early Tudor marble Purbeck memorial which Weever, in his "Funeral Monuments," ascribes to the ancient family of Gray, of Gray's Inn. The recesses for brasses are there, but neither arms nor date are remaining. A marble tablet, with palette and pencils, the memorial of Samuel Cooper, a celebrated miniature-painter, who died in 1672, is placed on the south-east interior wall. The church still consists only of a nave and chancel, without side aisles. Heavy beams support the roof, and upon those over the chancel and the western gallery are written in illuminated scrolls various sentences from Scripture, such as "I am the Way, the Truth, and the Life;" "He that cometh unto Me I will in no wise cast out," &c. There is a very elegant stained-glass window over the altar, and on either side of the nave are pointed windows of plain glass. The walls are exceedingly thick, and will, no doubt, last for ages. A narrow strip of oaken gallery runs above the nave, affording accommodation for only two rows of seats. It is approached by a single circular staircase in the southern tower, and its diminutive size is in keeping with the other parts of the building.

We may state here that, after his execution at Tyburn, the body of Lawrence Earl Ferrers was taken down and carried to this church, where it was laid under the belfry tower in a grave fourteen feet deep, no doubt for fear lest the popular indignation should violate his place of burial.

During the removal of parts of the church, while the additions and alterations were being made, several relics of antiquity connected with the old structure were discovered. Among others were the following:—An Early-English piscina and some sedilia, found on the removal of some heavy wainscoting on the south side of the chancel, the mouldings of the sedilia retaining vestiges of red colouring, with which they had formerly been tinted. A Norman altar-stone, in which appeared the usual decoration, namely, five crosses, typical of the five wounds of our Lord. The key-stone of the south porch, containing the letters H.R.T.P.C. incised, arranged one within the members of the other, after the manner of a monogram; these letters are apparently contemporary with the Norman moulding beneath. Part of a series of niches in chiselled brick was likewise discovered. These had been concealed by a sufficient coating of plaster, but were discovered in the first instance on the removal of some of the stonework in the exterior of the chancel. That operation being suspended, and the interior plastering being removed, the upper niche was discovered perfect, with mouldings and spandrils sharply chiselled in brick, but the impost being of stone, coloured so as to resemble the former. The back of the niche was in plaster likewise tinted and lined so as to correspond with the brick. Below this had been a double niche divided by a mullion, the principal part of which, however, was destroyed by the above-mentioned removal of the materials from without. These decorations were on the south side of the east window in the chancel, and had probably contained effigies. There was no corresponding appearance on the north side.

A curious view of the old church, somewhat idealised, representing it as a cruciform structure with a central bell-turret or campanile, was published in 1800, by Messrs. Laurie and Whittle, of Fleet Street; but if it represents any real structure, it must be that of a much earlier date. In this print there are near it three rural and isolated cottages, and a few young elm or plane trees complete the scene.

There is a tradition that this church was the last in or about London in which mass was said at the time of the Reformation, and that this was the cause of the singular fondness which the old Roman Catholic families had for burying their dead in the adjoining churchyard, where the cross and every variety of Catholic inscriptions may be seen on the tombs. It is, however, mentioned in "Windham's Diary," that while Dr. Johnson was airing one day with Dr. Brocklesby, in passing and returning by St. Pancras Church, he fell into prayer, and mentioned, upon Dr. Brocklesby inquiring why the Catholics selected that spot for their burial place, that some Catholics in Queen Elizabeth's time had been burnt there. This would, of course, give additional interest to the sacred spot.

In this churchyard were buried, amongst many others, Abraham Woodhead, a Roman Catholic controversialist, who died in 1678; Obadiah Walker, writer against Luther, 1699; John Ernest Grabe, editor of the Alexandrian Septuagint, 1711; Jeremy Collier, nonjuring bishop, and castigator of the stage, 1726; Edward Walpole, translator of Sannazarius, 1740; James Leoni, architect, 1746; Simon Francis Ravenet, engraver, and Peter Van Bleeck, portrait-painter, 1764; Abraham Langford, auctioneer and dramatist, 1774; Stephen Paxton, musician, 1787; Timothy Cunningham, author of the "Law Dictionary," 1789; Michael John Baptist, Baron de Wenzel, oculist, 1790; Mary Wollstonecraft Godwin, author of "Rights of Women," 1797, with a square monumental pillar with a willow-tree on each side; the Bishop of St. Pol de Leon, 1806; John Walker, author of the "Pronouncing Dictionary," 1807; Tiberius Cavallo, the Neapolitan philosopher, 1809; the Chevalier d'Eon, political writer, 1810; J. P. Malcolm, historian of London, 1815; the Rev. William Tooke, translator of Lucian, 1820; and Governor Wall.

Among the eccentric characters who lie buried here is William Woollett, the landscape and historical engraver, known by his masterly plates of Wilson's pictures and his battle-pieces; his portrait, by Stuart, is in the National Gallery. He lived in Green Street, Leicester Square; and whenever he had finished an engraving, he commemorated the event by firing a cannon on the roof of his house. He died in 1785, and sixty years after his death his gravestone was restored by the Graphic Society.

Another eccentric individual whose ashes repose beneath the shade of Old St. Pancras Church, is the celebrated "Ned" Ward, the author of the "London Spy," and other well-known works. He was buried here in 1731. The following lines were written by him shortly before his death:—

"MY LAST WILL.

"In the name of God, the King of kings,
Whose glory fills the mighty space;
Creator of all worldly things,
And giver of both time and place:
To Him I do resign my breath
And that immortal soul He gave me,
Sincerely hoping after death
The merits of His Son will save me.
Oh, bury not my peaceful corpse
In Cripplegate, where discord dwells,
And wrangling parties jangle worse
Than alley scolds or Sunday's bells.
To good St. Pancras' holy ground
I dedicate my lifeless clay
Till the last trumpet's joyful sound
Shall raise me to eternal day.
No costly funeral prepare,
'Twixt sun and sun I only crave
A hearse and one black coach, to bear
My wife and children to my grave.
My wife I do appoint the sole
Executrix of this my Will,
And set my hand unto the scrole,
In hopes the same she will fulfil.

"Made under a dangerous illness, and signed this 24th of June, 1731. "EDW. WARD."

Here, too, is buried Pasquale de Paoli, the hero of Corsica, who died April 5th, 1807, at the age of eighty-two. The early part of his life he devoted to the cause of liberty, which he nobly maintained against Genoese and French tyranny, and was hailed as the "Father of his country." Being obliged to withdraw from Corsica by the superior force of his enemies, he was received under the protection of George III., and found a hearty and cordial welcome from the citizens of London. A bust, with an inscription to his memory, is erected in the south aisle of Westminster Abbey.

The best known to fame of the many Roman Catholic priests, not mentioned above, who have been interred here, was "Father O'Leary," the eloquent preacher, and "amiable friar of the Order of St. Francis," who died in 1802. His tomb was restored by subscription among the poor Irish in 1842–3. Many amusing anecdotes are related concerning this witty divine:—"I wish, Reverend Father," once said Curran to Father O'Leary, "that you were St. Peter, and had the keys of heaven, because then you could let me in." "By my honour and conscience," replied O'Leary, "it would be better for you that I had the keys of the other place, for then I could let you out." Again, a Protestant gentleman told him that whilst willing to accept the rest of the Roman Catholic creed, he could not believe in purgatory. "Ah, my good friend," replied the priest, "you may go further and fare worse!"

Here, in 1811, was buried Sidhy Effendi, the Turkish minister to this country. A newspaper of the time thus describes his interment:—"On arriving at the ground, the body was taken out of a white deal shell which contained it, and, according to the Mahometan custom, was wrapped in rich robes and thrown into the grave; immediately afterwards a large stone, nearly the size of the body, was laid upon it; and after some other Mahometan ceremonies had been gone through, the attendants left the ground. The procession on its way to the churchyard galloped nearly all the way. The grave was dug in an obscure corner of the churchyard."

Besides the graves of famous men in Old St. Pancras churchyard, this old-fashioned nook has other and interesting memories associated with it. A curious story is told which connects the unhappy and highly gifted Chatterton with this place. One day, whilst looking over the epitaphs in this churchyard, he was so deep sunk in thought as he walked on, and not perceiving a grave just dug, he tumbled into it. His friend observing his situation, ran to his assistance, and, as he helped him out, told him, in a jocular manner, he was happy in assisting at the resurrection of Genius. Poor Chatterton smiled, and taking his companion by the arm, replied, "My dear friend, I feel the sting of a speedy dissolution; I have been at war with the grave for some time, and find it is not so easy to vanquish it as I imagined—we can find an asylum to hide from every creditor but that!" His friend endeavoured to divert his thoughts from the gloomy reflection; but what will not melancholy and adversity combined subjugate? In three days after the neglected and disconsolate youth put an end to his miseries by poison.*

A more affecting incident, perhaps, might have been witnessed here, when Shelley, the poet, met Mary, the daughter of William Godwin, and in hot and choking words told her the story of his wrongs and wretchedness. This girl, afterwards the wife of the poet, has been thus described by Mrs. Cowden Clarke: "Very, very fair was this lady, Mary Wollstonecraft Godwin, with her well-shaped golden-haired head almost always a little bent and drooping, her marble-white shoulders and arms statuesquely visible in the perfectly plain black velvet dress, which the customs of that time allowed to be cut low, and which her own taste adopted; her thoughtful, earnest eyes, her short upper lip and intellectually curved mouth, with a certain close-compressed and decisive expression while she listened, and a relaxation into fuller redness and mobility when speaking; her exquisitely-formed, white, dimpled, small hands, with rosy palms, and plumply commencing fingers, that tapered into tips as delicate and slender as those in a Vandyke portrait, all remain palpably present to memory. Another peculiarity in Mrs. Shelley's hand was its singular flexibility, which permitted her bending the fingers back so as almost to approach the portion of her arm above her wrist. She once did this smilingly and repeatedly, to amuse the girl who was noting its whiteness and pliancy, and who now, as an old woman, records its remarkable beauty." Many are the verses written by Shelley to Mary Godwin, the dedication to "The Revolt of Islam" being among the most impassioned; but the following will suffice as a specimen:—

"They say that thou wert lovely from thy birth,
Of glorious parents, thou aspiring child.
I wonder not—for one they left the earth
Whose life was like a setting planet mild,
Which clothed thee in the radiance undefiled
Of its departing glory; still her fame
Shines on thee, thro' the tempests dark and wild
Which shake these latter days; and thou canst claim
The shelter, from thy sire, of an immortal name.

* * * * * *

"Truth's deathless voice pauses among mankind;
If there must be no response to my cry,
If men must rise and stamp with fury blind
On his pure name who loves them, thou and I,
Sweet friend! can look from our tranquillity,
Like lamps into the world's tempestuous night;
Two tranquil stars, while clouds are passing by
Which wrap them from the foundering seaman's sight,
That burn from year to year with unextinguished light."

Mrs. Shelley's passion for her husband was exalted and beautiful:—"'Gentle, brave, and generous,' he described the poet in 'Alastor;' such he was himself, beyond any man I have ever known. To these admirable qualities was added his genius. He had but one defect, which was his leaving his life incomplete by an early death. Oh, that the serener hopes of maturity, the happier contentment of mid life, had descended on his dear head."

Among the quaint epitaphs in this old churchyard, we may be pardoned for printing the following, as it is now nearly illegible:—

"Underneath this stone doth lye
The body of Mr. Humpherie
Jones, who was of late
By Trade a plate-
Worker in Barbicanne;
Well known to be a good manne
By all his Friends and Neighbours too,
And paid every bodie their due.
He died in the year 1737,
August 10th, aged 80; his soule, we hope, 's in
Heaven."

A good epigram, by an unknown hand, thus commemorates this depository of the dead:—

"Through Pancras Churchyard as two tailors were walking,
Of trade, news, and politics earnestly talking,
Says one, 'These fine rains, Thomas,' looking around,
'Will bring things all charmingly out of the ground.'
'Marry, Heaven forbid,' said the other, 'for here
I buried two wives without shedding a tear.'"

In 1803 a large portion of the ground adjoining the old churchyard was appropriated as a cemetery for the parish of St. Giles's-in-the-Fields; and in it was buried, among other celebrities, the eminent architect, Sir John Soane, and also his wife and son, whose death, in all probability, caused Sir John to make the country his heir, and to found,

* See Vol. II., p. 547.

as a public institution, the museum which bears his name in Lincoln's Inn Fields, and which we have already described.

In 1862 the Midland Railway Company, wishing to connect their line of railway in Bedfordshire with the metropolis, obtained an Act of Parliament, entitled the "St. Giles's-in-the-Fields Glebe Act." It was so called because this new line, in its course through the north-western part of London, would cross a portion of the above-mentioned burial-ground, which immediately adjoins the more famous one of St. Pancras. In one section of the above Act it is stated that "the rector and his successors, at his or their expense, shall maintain the disused burial-ground in decent order as an open space for ever, and subject to the same rights and liabilities in all respects as if it were a churchyard; and make the necessary repair of the walls and other fences of the disused burial-ground; and he or they respectively shall be the person or persons from time to time legally chargeable for the costs and expenses of and incident to any such maintenance and repair, any Act or Acts of Parliament to the contrary notwithstanding, provided that the rector and his successors, from time to time, respectively shall not interfere with, or wilfully permit injury to be done to, any vault, grave, tablet, monument, or tombstone, either in the disused burial-ground, or in or under the chapel."

ST. PANCRAS WELLS AND CHURCH IN 1700. *From an Old Print.* (*See page* 339.)

In the following year the same railway company obtained further powers from the Legislature (who offered little or no opposition) to take a corner of the St. Pancras Churchyard for part of their main line, ostensibly for the purpose of erecting a pier for the viaduct which crosses the entire yard, and which, from being constructed on arches, would be the means of allowing trains to be constantly flying past the very windows of the church, and at the same time to be rumbling over the tombs of the hallowed dead. The only reason for taking this corner was because it was supposed by the engineer of the railway company "not to have been used for interment, there being no tombstone or any superficial indication of the fact." This, it was maintained, would appear as if the railway company had not made those minute inquiries into the matter which they should have done, when they urged such a reason as an excuse for their acts; as if otherwise they could not have failed to have learned from the parish authorities that the whole extent of both the churchyard and burial-ground were filled with dead bodies, including this very corner, upon which, at that time, the sexton's house stood.

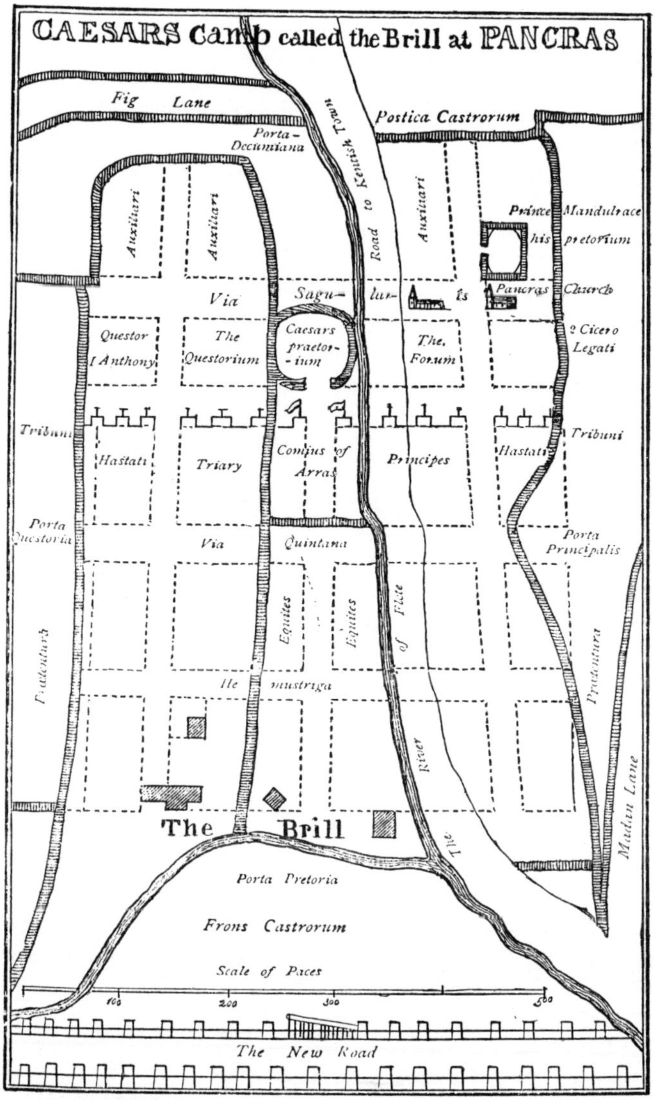

DR. STUKELEY'S PLAN OF THE CAMP AT ST. PANCRAS. (*See page* 340.)

In 1864, not content with the powers they had obtained in 1862 and 1863, the railway company asked for fresh powers—namely, to take the old church and the whole of the graveyard attached thereto as being part of the land required, in order to effect a junction between the main line and the Metropolitan Railway at the King's Cross Station; but this modest request was refused, and no further power was conceded to the company than to cross the entire breadth of the St. Pancras burial-ground by a tunnel. The roof of this tunnel was not to come within twelve feet of the present surface of the burial-ground, although it is stated that "the ground is so crowded with dead that hundreds of bodies are buried to a depth of twenty-four feet in the older part of the ground." It may be stated here that, in 1848, when the church was being altered, it was found necessary to take in a piece of the churchyard to admit of the enlargement of the building; and while making the excavations which were necessary, it was discovered that at depths varying from eight to twelve feet the clay was laden with fœtid decomposition and filthy water from the surrounding ground, and that masses of coffins were packed one upon the other in rows, with scarcely any intervening ground.

In 1866 the railway company commenced their operations against the St. Giles's burial-ground; but immediately upon the discovery, through the works of the contractor, that bodies were buried there, application was made to the Secretary of State for the Home Department, as also to the solicitors and engineer of the company; and an undertaking was obtained that the works should be stopped, and the exposed places decently covered, until an order could be obtained for the proper removal of the remains. Upon this discovery becoming known, a loud outburst of indignation was raised by the parishioners, especially those living in the immediate neighbourhood, and who, consequently, were most affected thereby. They very justly considered that a "horrible desecration of the dead" had taken place, and such as ought not to be tolerated, or even justified, by any Act of Parliament. They accordingly decided that the matter should be made as public as possible, and that it should be brought prominently to the notice of the authorities in view to putting a stop to the proceedings of the railway company.

In the House of Commons the attention of the Government was twice called by a member to the proceedings of the railway company; and the consequent inquiry into the facts of the case would, it was fondly hoped, protect this sacred spot from profanation. But alas! that hope was a vain one. The company in their turn appeared to have given up the making of the tunnel; but in the end the railway was carried across it: many tombs and many bodies were displaced, and the authorities of the parish availed themselves of the opportunity to enlarge and improve the place, and convert it into a public recreation-ground. The old disused burial-ground was accordingly laid out as a garden, and a memorial erected to record the many eminent persons buried all around. This memorial was built at the cost of Lady Burdett-Coutts, and the grounds were opened to the public in 1877.

The new Cemetery of St. Pancras, eighty-seven acres in extent, was opened in 1854. It is situated on the Horse Shoe Farm, at Finchley, about four miles from London, and two miles from the northern boundary of the parish. It was the first extra-mural parish burial-ground made for the metropolis.

Close by the old church of St. Pancras it would appear that there was formerly another "Adam and Eve" tavern—a rival, possibly, to that which we have already noticed at the corner of the Hampstead and Euston Roads. The site of the old "Adam and Eve" tea-gardens, in St. Pancras Road, is now occupied by Eve Terrace, and a portion of the burial-ground for St. Giles's-in-the-Fields, of which we have spoken already. The tavern originally had attached to it some extensive pleasure-grounds, which were the common resort of holiday-folk and pleasure-seekers. The following advertisements appear in the newspapers at the commencement of this century:—

ADAM AND EVE TAVERN, ADJOINING ST. PANCRAS CHURCHYARD

G. Swinnerton, jun., and Co., proprietors, have greatly improved the same by laying out the gardens in an elegant manner, improving the walks with arbours, flowers, shrubs, &c., and the long room (capable of dining any company) with paintings, &c. The delightfulness of its situation, and the enchanting prospects, may justly be esteemed the most agreeable retreat in the vicinity of the metropolis. They therefore solicit the favour of annual dinners, &c., and will exert their best endeavours to render every part of the entertainment as satisfactory as possible. The proprietors have likewise, at a great expense, fitted out a squadron of frigates, which, from a love to their country, they wish they could render capable of acting against the natural enemies of Great Britain, which must give additional pleasure to every well-wisher to his country. They therefore hope for the company of all those who have the welfare of their country at heart, and those in particular who are of a mechanical turn, as in the above the possibility of a retrograde motion is fully evinced.

The Gardens at the Adam and Eve, St. Pancras Church, are opened for this season, which are genteel and rural. Coffee, tea, and hot loaves every day; where likewise cows are kept for making syllabubs: neat wines and all sorts of fine ales. Near which gardens is a field pleasantly situated for trap-ball playing. Mr. Lambert returns those gentlemen thanks who favoured him with their bean-feasts last season, and hopes for the continuance of their future favours, which will ever be most gratefully acknowledged by, gentlemen, your most obedient humble servant, GEO. LAMBERT.

☞ Dinners dressed on the shortest notice; there is also a long room which will accommodate 100 persons.

All those who love trap-ball to Lambert's repair,
Leave the smoke of the town, and enjoy the fresh air.

Apropos of this place of rural retirement for the citizen of years long gone by, as a place to which he could escape from the din and turmoil of the great Babel of London, we may be pardoned for quoting the words of the facetious Tom Brown, in his "London Walks:"—"It was the wont of the good citizens," he says, "to rise betimes on Sunday mornings, and, with their wives and children under their arms, sally forth to brush the cobwebs from their brains, and the smoke from their lungs, by a trip into the country. Having no cheap excursions by boat and rail to relieve the groaning of the metropolis for twelve hours of a few of its labouring thousands, the immediate neighbourhood of London naturally became the breathing space and pleasure-ground of the lieges to whom time and shillings were equally valuable. Then it was that Sadler's and Bagnigge Wells, the Conduit, Marylebone Gardens, the Gun (at Pimlico), Copenhagen House, Jack Straw's Castle, the Spaniards and Highbury Barn, first opened their hospitable portals, and offered to the dusty, thirsty, hungry, and perspiring pleasure-seeker rest and refreshment—shilling ordinaries—to which, by the way, a known good appetite would not be admitted under eighteenpence. Bowling-greens, where the players, preferring elegance, appeared in their shirt-sleeves and shaven heads, their wigs and long-skirted coats being picturesquely distributed on the adjacent hedges, under the guard of their three-cornered hats and Malacca canes. Hollands, punch, claret, drawn from the wood at three-and-sixpence a quart; skittles and quoits, accompanied, of course, with pipes and tobacco, offered their fascinations to the male customers; while the ladies and juveniles were beguiled with cakes and ale, tea and shrimps, strawberries and cream, syllabubs and junkets, swings and mazes, lovers' walks and woodbine bowers."

St. Pancras had formerly its mineral springs, which were much resorted to. Near the churchyard, in the yard of a house, is, or was till recently, the once celebrated St. Pancras Wells, or Spa, the waters of which are said to have been of a slightly cathartic nature. The gardens of the Spa were very extensive, and laid out with long straight walks, which were used as a promenade by the visitors. In the bills issued by the proprietors it was stated that the quality of its waters was "surprisingly successful in curing the most obstinate cases of scurvy, king's evil, leprosy, and all other breakings out of the skin." The following advertisement, dated 13th February, 1729, thus alludes to the Spa:—

To be Lett, at Pancras, a large House, commonly called Pancridge Wells, with a Garden, Stable, and other conveniences. Inquire, &c.

Another advertisement, which appeared forty years later, states that—

St. Pancras Wells Waters are in the greatest perfection, and highly recommended by the most eminent physicians in the kingdom. To prevent mistakes, St. Pancras Wells is on that side the churchyard towards London; the house and gardens of which are as genteel and rural as any round this metropolis; the best of tea, coffee, and hot loaves, every day, may always be depended on, with neat wines, curious punch, Dorchester, Marlborough, and Ringwood beers; Burton, Yorkshire, and other fine ales, and cyder; and also cows kept to accommodate ladies and gentlemen with new milk and cream, and syllabubs in the greatest perfection. The proprietor returns his unfeigned thanks to those societies of gentlemen who have honoured him with their country feasts, and humbly hopes a continuance of their favours, which will greatly oblige their most obedient servant, JOHN ARMSTRONG.

Note.—Two long rooms will dine two hundred compleatly. June 10, 1769.

Apart from its tea-gardens and mineral springs, St. Pancras has in its time possessed a building devoted to the Muses, for we learn that at a private amateur theatre in Pancras Street, Mr. J. R. Planché made some of his earliest appearances on a stage.

The "village" of St. Pancras, too, has not been without its oddities; for such, we presume, must have been one Harry Dimsdale, or, as he was called, Sir Harry, the mock "Mayor of Garratt,"* who was a well-known character, some years since, at all the public-houses in the parish. According to Mr. Palmer, in his "History of St. Pancras," "he was a poor diminutive creature, deformed, and half an idiot. He was by profession a muffin-seller. The watermen at the hackney-coach stands throughout the parish used to torment him sadly; almost every day poor Harry was persecuted, and frequently so roughly used by them that he often shed tears. Death released poor Harry from his persecutors in the year 1811." There are several portraits of him in existence.

Inter alia, St. Pancras has the honour of having given birth to the imaginary "Emmanuel Jennings," who figures in the "Rejected Addresses" in the imitation of Crabbe—

"In Holywell Street, St. Pancras, he was bred,
Facing the pump, and near the 'Granby's Head.'"

Before proceeding to describe Somers Town in detail, we may state that the vivid imagination of Dr. Stukeley, whose utter untrustworthiness as an antiquary is shown by the late Mr. B. B. Woodward in the *Gentleman's Magazine* for 1866, not only discovered the remains of a veritable Roman camp here (called the Brill), but drew it out on

* See Vol. VI., p. 486.

paper, in minute detail, showing even the stables of the horse soldiers. Dr. Stukeley affirmed that the old church of St. Pancras covered part of the encampment, the outline and plan of which he gave in the "Itinerarium Curiosum," as far back as 1758; but notwithstanding that his opinion has been strongly condemned by more trustworthy antiquaries and topographers, the supposition of Dr. Stukeley may derive some confirmation from the fact that in 1842 a stone was found at King's Cross or Battle Bridge, bearing on it the words LEG. XX. (Legio Vicesima), one of those Roman legions which we know from Tacitus to have formed part of the army under Suetonius. It may further be mentioned that the spot known for so many centuries as Battle Bridge, and the traditional scene of a fierce battle between the Britons and the Romans, corresponds very closely to the description of the battle-field as still extant in the pages of the 14th book of the "Annals" of Tacitus. We learn from a writer in *Notes and Queries* (No. 230), that during the Civil War a fortification was erected at the Brill Farm, near Old St. Pancras Church, where, some hundred and twenty years later, Somers Town was built. A view of it, published in 1642, is engraved on page 336.

We may add, in concluding this chapter, that the desecration of the St. Pancras churchyard, of which we have spoken above, was as nothing compared to the demolition of the hundreds of houses of the poorer working classes in Agar Town and Somers Town, occasioned by the extension of the Midland Railway. The extent of this clean sweep was, and is still, comparatively unknown, and has caused a very considerable portion of St. Pancras parish to be effaced from the map of London. Perhaps no part of London or its neighbourhood has undergone such rapid and extensive transformation. It will, perhaps, be said that in the long run the vicinity has benefited in every way; but it is to be feared that in the process of improvement the weakest have been thrust rather rudely to the wall.

CHAPTER XXVI.

SOMERS TOWN AND EUSTON SQUARE.

"Quis novus hic nostris successit sedibus hospes?"—*Virgil, "Æn."*

Gradual Rise and Decline of Somers Town—The Place largely Colonised by Foreigners—A Modern Miracle—Skinner Street—The Brill—A Wholesale Clearance of Dwelling-houses—Ossulston Street—Charlton Street—The "Coffee House"—Clarendon Square and the Polygon—Mary Wollstoncraft Godwin—The Chapel of St. Aloysius—The Abbé Carron—The Rev. John Nerinckx—Seymour Street—The Railway Clearing House—The Euston Day Schools—St. Mary's Episcopal Chapel—Drummond Street—The Railway Benevolent Institution—The London and North-Western Railway Terminus—Euston Square—Dr. Wolcot (Peter Pindar)—The Euston Road—Gower Street—Sir George Rose and Jack Bannister—New St. Pancras Church—The Rev. Thomas Dale—Woburn Place.

DOWN to about the close of the last century, the locality now known as Somers Town—or, in other words, the whole of the triangular space between the Hampstead, Pancras, and Euston Roads—was almost exclusively pastoral; and with the exception of a few straggling houses near the "Mother Red Cap," at Camden Town, and also a few round about the old church of St. Pancras, there was nothing to intercept the view of the Hampstead uplands from Queen's Square and the Foundling Hospital. An interesting account of the gradual rise and decline of this district is given in the *Gentleman's Magazine* for 1813, wherein the writer says:—"Commencing at Southampton Row, near Holborn, is an excellent private road, belonging to the Duke of Bedford, and the fields along the road are intersected with paths in various directions. The pleasantness of the situation, and the temptation offered by the New Road, induced some people to build on the land, and the Somers places, east and west, arose; a few low buildings near the Duke's road (now near the 'Lord Nelson') first made their appearance, accompanied by others of the same description; and after a while Somers Town was planned. Mr. Jacob Leroux became the principal landowner under Lord Somers. The former built a handsome house for himself, and various streets were named from the title of the noble lord (Somers); a chapel was opened, and a polygon began in a square. Everything seemed to prosper favourably, when some unforeseen cause arose which checked the fervour of building, and many carcases of houses were sold for less than the value of the building materials. In the meantime gradual advances were made on the north side of the New Road (now the Euston Road), from Tottenham Court Road, and, finally, the buildings on the south side reached the line of Gower Street. Somewhat lower, and nearer to Battle Bridge, there was a long grove of stunted trees, which never seemed to thrive; and on the site of the Bedford Nursery a pavilion was erected, in which Her Royal Highness the Duchess of York gave away colours to a volunteer regiment. The interval between Southampton Place and Somers Town was soon one vast brick-field. On the death of Mr. Leroux," continues the writer, "and the large property being submitted to the hammer, numbers of small houses were sold for less than £150, at rents of £20 per annum each. The value of money decreasing at this time, from thirty to forty guineas were demanded as rents for these paltry habitations; hence everybody who could obtain the means became a builder: carpenters, retired publicans, leather workers, haymakers, &c., each contrived to raise his house or houses, and every street was lengthened in its turn. The barracks for the Life Guards, in Charlton Street, became a very diminutive square, and now we really find several of these streets approaching the old Pancras Road. The Company of Skinners, who own thirty acres of land, perceiving these projectors succeed in covering the north side of the New Road from Somers Place to Battle Bridge, and that the street named from them has reached the 'Brill Tavern,' have offered the ground to Mr. Burton to build upon, and it is now covered by Judd Street, Tonbridge Place, and a new chapel for some description of Dissenters or other." Mr. Burton, as we have previously stated, was the builder, not only of the houses covering the land belonging to the Skinners' Company, but also of Russell Square, Bedford Place, &c.*

At the end of the last century this district, rents being cheap, was largely colonised by foreign artisans, mostly from France, who were driven on our shores by the events of the Reign of Terror and the first French Revolution. Indeed, it became nearly as great a home of industry as Clerkenwell and Soho. It may be added that, as the neighbourhood of Manchester and Portman Squares formed the head-quarters of the *emigrés* of the wealthier class who were thrown on our shores by the waves of the first French Revolution, so the exiles of the poorer class found their way to St. Pancras, and settled down around Somers Town, where they opened a Catholic chapel, at first in Charlton Street, Clarendon Square, and subsequently in the square itself. Of this church, which is dedicated to St. Aloysius, we shall have more to say presently.

"Somers Town," wrote the Brothers Percy in 1823, "has now no other division from the rest of the metropolis but a road, and Kentish and Camden Towns will soon be closely connected with it." During the ten subsequent years we find that great strides had been made in the progress of building in Somers Town, for a correspondent of Hone's "Year Book," in 1832, tells us that, though it had then become little better than another arm to the "Monster Briareus" of London, he remembered it as "isolated and sunny, when he first haunted it as a boy."

Under the heading of "A Miracle at Somers Town," Hone, in his "Every-day Book," tells the following laughable tale:—"Mr. ——, a middle-aged gentleman who had long been afflicted by various disorders, and especially by the gout, had so far recovered from a severe attack of the latter complaint, that he was enabled to stand, yet with so little advantage, that he could not walk more than fifty yards, and it took him nearly an hour to perform that distance. While thus enfeebled by suffering, and safely creeping in great difficulty, on a sunny day, along a footpath by the side of a field near Somers Town, he was alarmed by loud cries intermingled with the screams of many voices behind him. From his infirmity he could only turn very slowly round, and then, to his astonishment, he saw, within a yard of his coat-tail, the horns of a mad bullock—when, to the equal astonishment of its pursuers, this unhappy gentleman instantly leaped the fence, and, overcome by terror, continued to run with amazing celerity nearly the whole distance of the field, while the animal kept its own course along the road. The gentleman, who had thus miraculously recovered the use of his legs, retained his power of speed until he reached his own house, where he related the miraculous circumstance; nor did his quickly restored faculty of walking abate until it ceased with his life several years afterwards. This miraculous cure," adds Mr. Hone, "can be attested by his surviving relatives."

Skinner Street, where we now resume our perambulation, lies in the south-east corner of Somers Town, and connects the Euston Road with Brill Row; this street is so called after the Skinners' Company, who, as above stated, own a great part of this district. The company hold the land on behalf of their grammar school, at Tonbridge, in Kent. The property, which was originally known as the Sandhills Estate, and was comparatively worthless three centuries ago, was bequeathed by Sir Andrew Judd, Lord Mayor of London, in 1558, to endow the said school;† hence the nomenclature of the streets in this neighbourhood—Judd

* See Vol. IV., p. 576.

† See Vol. IV., p 576.

Street, Skinner Street, Tonbridge Place, &c. The property now brings in a regular income of several thousands a year.

Brill Row, at the northern end of Skinner Street, together with the "Brill" tavern close by, are nearly all that remains of the locality once familiarly known by that name, which was nothing more nor less than a range of narrow streets crossing each other at right angles, and full of costermongers' shops and barrows, but which were swept away during the formation of the Midland Railway Terminus.

Dr. Stukeley derives the name of the "Brill" as a contraction from Burgh Hill, a Saxon name for a place on an elevated site; but surely that derivation will scarcely apply here, as it certainly does not lie as high as the land on its eastern or western side. The place on a Sunday morning was thus facetiously described by a writer in the *Illustrated News of the World*, just before the time of its demolition:—"The 'Brill' is situated between Euston Square and the station of the Great Northern Railway, and is a place of great attraction to thousands who inhabit Somers, Camden, and Kentish Towns. Though bearing the name of a well-known fish, our early riser will most probably find that the Somers 'Brill' claims no special relationship to the scaly tribe. . . Here is the 'Brill' tavern, and how it came to have this name would, no doubt, be as interesting as to know the origin of the names given to other public-houses. Some landlord of old may have had a particular liking for this fish, or may have been fortunate in procuring a super-excellent cook who could satisfy the most fastidious appetite of the most fastidious customer by placing before him a superior dish. Very likely some local antiquarian could tell us all about it and much else. He could tell us, no doubt, when, and under what circumstances, this north-west suburb of London itself was so named from the noble family of Somers; that this very 'Brill' was known in days gone by as Cæsar's Camp, and for this latter statement might quote as an authority the distinguished and well-known Dr. Stukeley himself. The oldest inhabitant could also talk with great volubility respecting the site on which Somers Town now stands—how, some sixty or seventy or more years ago, it was a piece of wild common or barren brick-field, whither resorted on Sundays the bird-fanciers and many of the

THE "BRILL," SOMERS TOWN, IN 17.0.

THE POLYGON, SOMERS TOWN, IN 1850. *From an Original Sketch.* (*See page* 345.)

'roughs' from London to witness dog-fights, bull-baiting, and other rude sports, now happily unknown in the locality. This 'oldest inhabitant' would most probably contrast the dark ages of Somers Town with its present enlightened and civilised days, and conclude an animated harangue with the words—'Nobody would believe that here, where I can now purchase tea, coffee, beef, everything I want, on a Sunday morning, that such barbarous practices were followed while bishops and divines were preaching in St. Paul's, St. Pancras, and in all the churches and chapels around on the Divine obligation of the Sunday; nobody would believe such a thing now.'

"As the philanthropic or curious visitor enters Skinner Street, about eleven o'clock some bright Sunday morning, his ears will be greeted, not by the barking of dogs and the roaring of infuriated bulls, as of old, but by the unnaturally loud cries of men, women, boys, and girls, anxious to sell edibles and drinkables—in fact, everything which a hard-working man or poor sempstress is supposed to need in order to keep body and soul together. The various so-called necessaries of life have here their special advocates. The well-known 'buy, buy, buy,' has, at the 'Brill,' a peculiar shrillness of tone, passing often into a scream—and well it may, for the meat is all ticketed at 4½d. per pound. Here the female purchasers are not generally styled 'ladies,' but 'women,' and somewhat after this fashion—'This is the sort of cabbage, or meat, or potatoes to buy, women;' and each salesman seems to think that his success depends upon the loudness of his cry. . . . The purchasers not only come from all parts of Somers Town itself to this spot on a Sunday morning, but from Camden Town, Holloway, Hampstead, and Highgate, and even from distances of five and six miles. The leading impression made by the moving scene is that of great activity and an 'eye to business.' Every one at the 'Brill,' as a rule, comes there on a Sunday morning for a definite purpose. The women come to buy meat, fish, vegetables, and crockery; and the men, chiefly 'navigators,' as they are termed, come to purchase boots, boot-laces, blouses, trousers, coats, caps, and other articles of wearing apparel.

"Altogether, at the Brill matters are carried on in a business-like way. The salesmen, many of them young boys, are too intent on selling, and the purchasers too intent on buying, to warrant the supposition that they derive much spiritual benefit from the preachers of all persuasions and of no persuasions who frequent the neighbourhood. The most ardent, and apparently the most successful, of the street preachers are those who occupy posts in the immediate vicinity, and 'hold forth' in familiar strains on the advantages of teetotalism, and the evil consequences following intemperance."

Although, as we have stated, a large portion of the houses in this locality have been swept away, some few remain. Of these we may take as a specimen, Chapel Street, in which the same attractions as those above mentioned are still held out, especially on Saturday evenings and Sunday mornings.

"On inquiry," says the writer above quoted, "it will be found that this market is in every way a very profitable concern, both to those who expose their goods for sale and those who own the property in the surrounding neighbourhood. The small paltry-looking houses, with a front shop, and very restricted accommodation, yield a yearly rental of from £60 to £80 per annum. It is not likely, therefore, everything considered, that either the owners of the property, the proprietors of the shops and stalls, or the purchasers themselves, who have special advantages given them, will take the initiative in abolishing the Sunday morning Brill trade. Whatever is done in this direction must be brought to bear *ab extra;* wages must be paid earlier in the week, facilities afforded to the poorer classes for purchasing in the cheapest markets, and other changes, which in due course the philanthropic and humane will bring about when they once know the actual state of things, and recognise the necessity of abolishing Sunday trading altogether."

The fourteen acres of land taken by the Midland Railway Company were covered with dwellings occupied by poor people, and the whole of this population were driven out of their old homes and compelled to seek fresh accommodation elsewhere: most of them migrated to Kentish Town and the Gospel Oak Fields, already mentioned above.

Ossulston Street, the next turning westward from Skinner Street, keeps in remembrance the name of the ancient hundred of Ossulston, a geographical division which still, as in the days of our Saxon ancestors, embraces a great part of the north-western districts of London, but is now forgotten, though it furnishes the Earl of Tankerville with his second title.

Passing still further along the Euston Road, we arrive at Charlton Street. In this street is a public-house called the "Coffee House." The name seems inappropriate now, but is not really so, for in early times it really was what that name imports—the only coffee-house in the neighbourhood. "Early in the last century Somers Town was a delightful and rural suburb, with fields and flower-gardens. A short distance down the hill," writes

Mr. Larwood, "were the then famous Bagnigge Wells, and close by the remains of Totten Hall, with the 'Adam and Eve' tea-gardens, and the so-called King John's Palace. Many foreign Protestant refugees had taken up their residence in this suburb on account of the retirement it afforded, and the low rents asked for small houses. At this time the Coffee-House was a popular place of resort, much frequented by the foreigners of the neighbourhood as well as by the pleasure-seeking cockney from the distant city. There were near at hand other public-houses and places of entertainment, but the speciality of this establishment was its coffee. As the traffic increased, it became a posting-house, uniting the business of an inn with the profits of a tea-garden. Gradually the demand for coffee fell off, and that for malt and spirituous liquors increased. At present the gardens are all built over, and the old gateway forms part of the modern bar; but there are in the neighbourhood aged persons who remember Sunday-school excursions." The house was burnt down in 1880, but soon rebuilt.

Charlton Street terminates in the south-east corner of Clarendon Square, which, as stated above, occupies the site formerly covered by the barracks of the Life Guards. This is somewhat irregular in its plan as a square, inasmuch as in its centre is inscribed a circle of houses, called the Polygon. In this square lived Scriven, the engraver, and near him De Wilde, the best pictorial annalist of our national style, and from whose pencil came all the portraits illustrating Bell's edition of the "English Theatre," so highly praised by T. F. Dibdin, in his "Library Companion." Indeed, as late as the year 1832, Somers Town was full of artists, if we may trust Hone's "Year Book," which appeals, in proof of the statement, to the Royal Academy catalogues. Their names, however, as well as their memories, have passed away along with the houses which they formerly inhabited.

In the Polygon lived Mary Wollstoncraft, after her marriage with William Godwin. She was the author of the "Vindication of the Rights of Women." Here Godwin wrote his "Political Justice" and some of his other works. "The Polygon," observes Mr. Peter Cunningham, "now enclosed by the dirty neighbourhood of Clarendon Square, was, when Godwin lived in it, a new row of houses, pleasantly seated near fields and nursery gardens." Mary Wollstoncraft (Godwin) here died in childbed in 1797; her infant grew to womanhood, and, as we have stated in the previous chapter, became the wife of the poet Shelley.

On one side of the square stands the Roman Catholic Chapel of St. Aloysius, founded in 1808, by the Abbé Carron, for the use of the French refugees who settled in the neighbourhood. For more than half a century the Rev. J. Nerinckx officiated here, and as a memorial of his unremitting attention to his charge, a handsome monumental tablet was erected in 1857. It is nearly seven feet high, of Gothic design, carved in Caen stone, and richly ornamented. It is placed immediately outside the railings of the sanctuary, and is inscribed "In memory of the Venerable and Saintly John Nerinckx, born at Nenore, in Belgium, August, 1776: Pastor of the Church of St. Aloysius, Somers Town, and Founder of the schools attached to the same; who after Fifty-four Years of Faithful Service in the Priesthood, was called to his Lord on the 21st of December, 1855. On his soul Sweet Jesus have Mercy." With the reverend gentleman's life the history of this "mission" is closely united. He joined the Abbé Carron in January, 1800, having succeeded in escaping from Cayenne, where he had been sent by the French Republicans; and he was ordained in the chapel in Charlton Street by the emigrant Bishop of Avranches.

In the *Gentleman's Magazine* for 1813, Mr. J. T. Malcolm, in speaking of the founder of this church, says:—"The Abbé Carron is a gentleman who does his native country honour. He resides in the house lately occupied by the builder Leroux, and presides over four schools—for young ladies, poor girls, young gentlemen, and poor boys. A dormitory, bakehouse, &c., are situated between his house and the emigrant Catholic chapel, recently built, which contains a monument to the Princess of Condé; further on is the school for the poor girls, and at the back of the whole are convenient buildings for the above purposes, and a large garden. The general voice of the place is in the Abbé's favour; and he has been of incalculable service to his distressed fellow-sufferers, who are enthusiastic in his praise."

On the return of the Abbé Carron to France, in 1815, Mr. Nerinckx succeeded to this charge, which he held for the long space of time already mentioned, and it was he who erected the schools now occupied by the nuns of the Order of the Faithful Companions of Jesus. The church underwent considerable repairs and alterations in the year 1850, the altar and sanctuary being decorated in an elaborate arabesque style. The projecting pillars on either side of the altar are embellished with paintings, in compartments, representing the blessed Virgin and our Saviour, and St. Aloysius and St. Philomena. Besides the monument above mentioned, there are also in this church monuments to the Abbé Carron and the Bishop of St. Pol; the busts are said to be faithful likenesses.

On the west side of Clarendon Square is Seymour Street, which, with Crawley and Eversholt Streets, forms a continuous thoroughfare between the north-east corner of Euston Square and Camden Town, and the other northern suburbs. In this street is the Railway Clearing House. It was established in 1842, for the mutual use of the several railway companies. It is regulated by an Act of Parliament which was passed in 1850. The following description of its scope and operations is condensed from Charles Knight's "Cyclopedia of London:—" Many of our readers may have seen in Seymour Street, close to the Euston Square, an office doorway inscribed with the name of the 'Railway Clearing House;' the history of this establishment is full of instruction in connection with our railway system. When the various lines of railway became connected from end to end, it was absolutely necessary to devise some means of combined operation, to prevent passengers from being shifted from one train to another when they left one company's territory and entered upon that of another. Again, all the formalities of booking, weighing, loading, packing, and conveying goods, and of booking and conveying passengers, if they had to be observed and gone through afresh by every company for the same goods and the same passengers, would entail a great deal of needless work as well as ruinous delays and charges; indeed, the large traffic, and especially the through traffic, would be almost paralysed. To remedy this evil a remarkable and successful scheme was adopted, even in the early days of railroad travelling, based on the 'clearing-house' system of the London bankers. A sort of imaginary company is formed, called the Clearing House, to which all the railways stand related as debtors and creditors, and which manages all the cross accounts and fragments from one company to another. . . . Passengers all pay their respective fares to the company from whose station they start; but the goods toll may be paid at either end of the journey, according to circumstances. The Clearing House has to calculate how large a share is due to each company respectively, according to the mileage run, for each passenger, parcel, and ton of goods, according to the rates of charge decided on by the said companies. Most of the companies provide locomotives, carriages, wagons, and trucks; and as all these may run on any of the lines according to arrangements, the Clearing House has to determine how much each company is entitled to charge for the use of such rolling-stock as is thus employed. There is thus a double account, every company charging all the rest for the use of every mile of its rails; and the Clearing House has to work out these complicated sums, and to determine the exact ratios day by day. The booking company pays all the Government duty on each passenger's fare, and this matter has also to be adjusted by other companies over whose lines the same train runs. A *black* ink return is forwarded from every station to the Clearing House every day, stating the amount of booking, moneys received, goods sent, &c., while a *red* ink return daily states the amount of goods arrived and received; and the Clearing House has to square up these accounts. The sum total of all the black accounts ought to agree with that of the red; and if this agreement does not appear, the Clearing House has to seek out the cause of the discrepancy and set it straight. All the tickets and cheques are likewise sent in hither, and these ought to agree exactly with the amount of moneys received. There are agents of the Clearing House at every junction and every important station; and the system pursued is so rigorous that the daily history, so to speak, of every locomotive and carriage can be traced." The Clearing House, it may be added, enters into a monthly settlement with all the various companies, and its managers are elected by the companies interested in its working.

Some idea of the extent of the work accomplished at the Railway Clearing House may be gathered from the fact that in 1842, the first year of its establishment, the number of companies which were parties to it was forty-nine, whereas in 1883 they amounted to seventy-five; that in the first-mentioned year the approximate number of stations was 887, but that these amounted in 1883 to 7,000; the approximate number of miles of railway open being over 16,000, as against 3,633 in 1849; and that the gross revenue adjusted, which was at first £1,691,720, is now nearly £18,000,000. The *employés* of the Clearing House have formed amongst themselves a Literary Society, of over a thousand members, with a library of nearly 14,000 volumes, and various other useful societies.

In this street are the Euston Day Schools, built by the London and North-Western Railway Company, about the year 1850. The number of boys and girls on the books is usually about 400, mostly the children of railway *employés*.

St. Mary's Episcopal Chapel is in this street. The building was erected from the designs of Messrs. Inwood: it is constructed of brick, with stone dressings, and in plan approaches nearly to a square. According to a critical writer in the *Gentleman's Magazine*, it is "perhaps the completest specimen of 'Carpenter's Gothic' ever witnessed, the church at Mitcham only excepted." It is said to have cost £15,000 (!), though it seats only 1,500 persons. In this street was formerly a chapel of ease to St. Pancras. It was a gloomy building, erected in 1787, and called Bethel Chapel; it afterwards belonged to the Baptists.

Drummond Street, which we now enter, unites Seymour Street with the Hampstead Road. At No. 57 in this street, a house which was formerly used as the Railway Clearing House, are now the offices of the Railway Benevolent Institution. This association was established in 1859, for the purpose of allowing grants and pensions of from £10 to £25 to disabled railway servants and widows of deceased members, and to educate their orphan children. The income, which in 1860 was only £1,168, has now (1883) risen to £28,658. Its members, who are composed of the officers and working staff of nearly all the chief railways in the United Kingdom, are now upwards of 80,000, and its object, as shown above, is to provide for these individuals, when left in necessitous circumstances. There is also a "casualty fund," the tables of which show that 2,454 individuals (in other words, one in thirty of all the subscribers) were relieved during the year 1883, when injured by accidents. The institution is under the patronage of the Queen, the Prince of Wales, the Dukes of Sutherland, Buckingham, &c., and of the principal railway directors. The contributions of the railway *employés* are supplemented by about 10,000 of the public at large. The subscription is 10s. 6d. for officers yearly, and for servants 2d. a week. The sum of £2,000 is now set apart yearly for the relief of distressed *non-members* who may meet with accidents in the performance of their duties and the widows of those who are killed. There is also an orphanage in Derby which belongs to this excellent Institution.

In this street is the principal entrance to the London and North-Western Railway Terminus. The station itself occupies a surface of about twelve acres, in which the operations necessary for the dispatch and reception of nearly one hundred trains per day are carried on with so little noise, confusion, or semblance of bustle, that it would almost seem that these complicated arrangements acted of their own accord. The entrance to the station is through a gateway beneath a lofty and apparently meaningless Doric temple—for it seems placed without reference to the court-yard it leads to—in the centre line of Euston Square. This arch, which cost, it is said, £30,000, and stands where, judging by the analogy of other railway termini, we should have expected to see a modern hotel, was erected from a design by Mr. Hardwick; and although handsome in itself, and possibly one of the largest porticoes in the world, it nevertheless falls far short in grandeur to the *Arc de Triomphe* in Paris. Some of the blocks of stone used in its construction weighed thirteen tons. Facing this entrance is a large, massive, plain range of buildings containing the offices, waiting-rooms, and board and meeting-rooms of the company.

"As Melrose should be seen by the fair moonlight," writes Mr. Samuel Sidney, in his "Rides on Railways," in 1851, "so Euston, to be viewed to advantage, should be visited by the grey light of a summer or spring morning, about a quarter to six o'clock, three-quarters of an hour before the starting of the parliamentary train, which every railway, under a wise legislative enactment, is compelled to run 'once a day from each extremity, with covered carriages, stopping at every station, travelling at a rate of not less than fifteen miles an hour, at a charge of one penny per mile.' We say wise, because the competition of the railway for goods, as well as passengers, drove off the road not only all the coaches, on which, when light-loaded, footsore travellers got an occasional lift, but all the variety of vans and broad-wheeled wagons which afforded a slow but cheap conveyance between our principal towns. At the hour mentioned, the railway passenger-yard is vacant, silent, and as spotlessly clean as a Dutchman's kitchen; nothing is to be seen but a tall soldier-like policeman in green, on watch under the wooden shed, and a few sparrows industriously yet vainly trying to get a breakfast from between the closely-packed paving-stones. How different from the fat debauched-looking sparrows who throve upon the dirt and waste of the old coach-yards! It is so still, so open; the tall columns of the portico entrance look down on you so grimly; the fronts of the booking-offices, in their garment of clean stucco, look so primly respectable that you cannot help feeling ashamed of yourself—feeling as uncomfortable as when you have called too early on an economically genteel couple, and been shown into a handsome drawing-room, on a frosty day, without a fire. You cannot think of entering into a gossip with the railway guardian, for you remember that 'sentinels on duty are not allowed to talk'—except to nursery-maids."

Passengers pass firstly into an immense and beautiful hall, on either side of which are entrances to the booking-offices. The hall was designed by Mr. P. C. Hardwick; it is about 140 feet in length by sixty in breadth, and between seventy and eighty feet high. A light and elegant gallery runs round three sides of the hall, guarded by bronze railings, on a level with the board-room, which is reached by a noble flight of thirty steps, surmounted by a range of Doric columns, the sculptured groups being emblematical of the progress of industry and science. Prominent in the hall is Baily's colossal statue in marble of George Stephenson, "the father of railways." Above the staircase and around the galleries are offices for the chief managers. In the angles of the hall, about fifty feet from the floor, are allegorical figures in relief, representing the counties travelled by the several railways of which this station is the terminus. The total length of platform for this terminus is upwards of a mile, and it is divided into three arrival and two departure platforms.

"The booking-offices," says Mr. Weale, in his "London," "are very fine specimens of architecture, but the waiting-rooms are far from corresponding with them in magnificence. Indeed," he adds, "the habits of our travelling public are not such as to require much accommodation in the intervals during which they wait for the departure of the trains. At foreign railway stations passengers are not allowed to go upon the platform until just before the time for departure. In England the practice is to allow the public access to all parts of the station devoted to the dispatch of the trains, and consequently it is found that they prefer walking about the platforms with their friends until the last moment. A very social result, perhaps; but the presence of so many strangers must sadly interfere with the execution of the duties of the company's servants."

ENTRANCE TO EUSTON SQUARE STATION. (*See page* 347.)

The extensions, branch lines, and the immense number of country lines which communicate with the London and North-Western Railway are so numerous, that it is, perhaps, impossible to say precisely the number of miles over which passengers are booked here. Originally the departure platforms for the main line adjoined the waiting-rooms on the east side of the great hall, and those for the midland counties on the west side; but the gradual opening up of new lines of railway and branches has somewhat altered this arrangement. There are several spare rails under the same roof.

upon which the carriages are examined, cleaned, and arranged for departure; and at the end of the platform is a series of turn-tables, by means of which the carriages can be easily transferred from one set of rails to another. The whole of the operations connected with the reception and the dispatch of the trains are thus carried on under a shed of immense superficial extent; some idea of its size may be gathered from Sir Francis Head's amusing and instructive book called "Stokers and Pokers." It is said that there are not less than 8,980 square yards of plate glass in the skylights only. We may mention here that the roof of the range of building on the west side of the platform remains in its original condition; but that on the east side has been considerably heightened by means of a novel and ingenious contrivance by which the roof was raised bodily, without having to be taken to pieces and rebuilt.

On the west of the lines leading from the station are the workshops where the carriage repairs for the London end of the line are effected; they are very extensive, and, of course, fitted up with the very best appliances. The line between Euston Station and Camden Town is principally carried in an open cutting about twenty feet below the level of the neighbouring streets. The works were executed in the London clay, and, although neatly carried out, it was afterwards found necessary, on account of the great width of the railway at this point, to consolidate the retaining walls by a series of immense cast-iron struts, which cause that portion of the line in the neighbourhood of Camden Town to resemble an open tunnel.

NEW ST. PANCRAS CHURCH. (*See page* 353.)

It will be remembered that, when in 1831-2 the London and Birmingham Railway (as this line was originally called) was first projected, the metropolitan terminus was at Chalk Farm, near the north-east corner of Regent's Park. It was not until 1835 that a bill was brought into Parliament, and carried after great opposition, for bringing this terminus as near to London as what was then termed "Euston Grove." Up to the year 1845, for fear of frightening the horses in the streets, the locomotive engines came no nearer to London than Chalk Farm, where the engine was detached from the train, and from thence to Euston Station the carriages were attached to an endless rope moved by a stationary engine at the Chalk Farm end of the line.

In 1845 a scheme was set on foot for converting a part of the bed of the Regent's Canal into an extension of the North-Western Railway, so as to bring the terminus nearer to the City. Indeed, it was proposed to carry it as far as Farringdon Street, but the opposition offered to the plan was so strong that it had to be abandoned, and it was reserved for other companies to carry out that great desideratum subsequently.

The Lost Luggage Office at the Euston Station is not the least important feature of this monster establishment. "If," writes Charles Knight, "a passenger has lost any of his luggage, there is an office where he can apply respecting it; if a railway porter finds luggage left in a carriage without an owner, there is a room where it is deposited, and the company spares no pains in affording facilities for the recovery of the lost property." Yet it is surprising how much luggage is left at various stations and never called for. In one apartment such articles are kept for two months, ticketed and numbered; if not re-claimed within that time, they are transferred to a large vaulted chamber, where they are placed in different apartments classified as to their character. If not claimed within two years, they are sold by public auction, and a pretty miscellaneous sale a railway auction is, consisting of coats, shawls, hats, caps, rugs, walking-sticks, umbrellas, parasols, opera-glasses, gloves, ladies' scent-bottles, boxes of pills and other patent medicines, hair-dyes, and other articles.

Sir Francis Head, in his "Stokers and Pokers," gives a lively and graphic picture of what he saw on paying a visit to this chamber:—"One compartment is choke full of men's hats, another of parasols, umbrellas, and sticks of every possible description. One would think that all the ladies' reticules in the world were deposited in a third. How many smelling-bottles. how many embroidered pocket-handkerchiefs, how many little musty eatables and comfortable drinkables, how many little bills, important little notes, and other very small secrets each may have contained, we felt that we would not for the world have tried to ascertain. One gentleman had left behind him a pair of leather hunting breeches, another his boot-jack. A soldier of the 22nd Regiment had left behind him his knapsack containing his 'kit.' Another soldier of the 10th, poor fellow! had forgotten his scarlet regimental coat. Some cripple, probably overjoyed at the sight of his family, had left behind him his crutches. But what astonished us most of all was that some honest Scotchman, probably in the ecstasy of seeing among the crowd the face of his faithful Jenny, had actually left behind him the best portion of his bag-pipes. Some little time ago the superintendent, in breaking open, previous to a general sale, a locked hat-box which had lain in this dungeon for two years, found in it, under the hat, £65 in Bank of England notes, with one or two private letters, which enabled him to restore the money to the owner, who, it turned out, was so positive that he left his hat-box at an hotel in Birmingham that he made no inquiry for it at the railway office."

Again, the Parcel Office, which is on the western side of the departure platform, is scarcely less interesting; and here, too, we are indebted to Charles Knight for a sketch of its interior working: "The superintendent has within view two offices or compartments, the one laden with parcels which are about to be dispatched, and the other with parcels which have arrived by train. In the daytime the down parcels are dispatched in the break-carriages of the passenger trains, while at night a train of locked-up vans is dispatched. When the parcels are about to be thus sent, a porter calls out the name of the party to whom it is addressed, its weight, and how much (if anything) has been paid upon it. One clerk enters these particulars in a ledger, another clerk writes out a label; a porter pastes this label on to the packet, which is forthwith dispatched, with others, to the van or carriage." All this is done with extraordinary quickness, the result of daily experience.

It should be mentioned here that this was the first really long line of railway from London that was opened for passenger traffic. The line was opened throughout between London and Birmingham on the 17th of September, 1838. At that time the journey to Birmingham took five and a-half hours, being an average rate of about twenty miles an hour; in 1777, the coach was twenty-seven hours on the road!

The daily working details of the London and

North-Western Railway at the Euston Station were graphically sketched many years ago by the late Sir Francis Head, in an article on "Railways in General" in the *Quarterly Review*, and which was subsequently enlarged and re-published in the small volume above mentioned, entitled "Stokers and Pokers." Although written in a rattling and gossiping style, it contained many amusing and instructive details relating to the permanent way, rolling stock, goods and passenger trains, signals, telegraphs, accidents, &c., which are still more or less true in fact, and applicable, *mutatis mutandis*, to other lines beside this.

"Euston, including its dependency, Camden Station," says Mr. Sidney, in his "Rides on Railways," (1851), "is the greatest railway port in England, or indeed in the world. It is the principal gate through which flows and re-flows the traffic of a line which has cost more than twenty-two millions sterling; which annually earns more than two millions and a half for the conveyance of passengers, and merchandise, and live stock; and which directly employs more than ten thousand servants, besides the tens of thousands to whom, in mills or mines, in iron-works, in steam-boats and coasters, it gives indirect employment. What London is to the world, Euston is to Great Britain; there is no part of the country to which railway communication has extended, with the exception of the Dover and Southampton lines, which may not be reached by railway conveyance from Euston station."

Euston Square, which we now enter on the north side from the front of the station, between the Victoria and Euston Hotels, dates from about the year 1813. It is named after the Fitzroys, Dukes of Grafton, Earls of Euston, and Lords Southampton, who are the ground landlords, and it occupies a considerable portion of what was formerly known as Montgomery's Nursery Gardens. Dr. Wolcot, who wrote and published numerous poems under the cognomen of "Peter Pindar," resided for some years, at the latter end of his life, in a small house in these gardens, the site of which John Timbs identifies with the north side of the square. Here he dwelt in a secluded, cheerless manner, being blind, with only a female servant to attend him; occasionally visited by some of his old friends, and visiting them in return. One of his most frequent visitors was John (commonly called Jack) Taylor, editor of *The Sun*. This gentleman, author of "Monsieur Tonson," &c., was a most inveterate and reckless punster, and often teased Peter by some pointless ones, which provoked the caustic remarks of the old poet. At one of these visits, on taking leave, Taylor exclaimed, pointing to Peter's head and rusty wig, "Adieu! I leave thee without hope, for I see *Old Scratch* has thee in his claws."

Mr. C. Redding tells us, in his "Fifty Years' Recollections," that Dr. Wolcot's house, though now built in among streets near Euston Square, was in his time standing alone in a gardener's ground, called "Montgomery's Nursery." Beyond its enclosure were the open fields. "The poet," adds Mr. Redding, "loved the smell of flowers, and the fresh air of the place. No one can imagine either flowers or fresh air on that spot now. I never pass the house but I stop and look at it. The front is unchanged, though completely built in. I cannot but think of the many pleasant hours I passed there. George Hanger used to drop in there occasionally, when I first came to town. He died in 1824, an eccentric, genuine in his oddities, but he had no taste for the fine arts, like Wolcot. Both were humourists, but of a different character. He would not be called Lord Coleraine, when the title ultimately came to him, but 'plain George Hanger, sir, if you please.' He used also to go and smoke a pipe occasionally at the 'Sol's Arms' in the Hampstead Road in the evening, where, in consideration of his rank, a large arm-chair was placed for him every evening by the fire." We have already mentioned him in our account of Chalk Farm.*

Of Dr. Wolcot, Mr. Cyrus Redding tells the following anecdote:—"Speaking of Dr. Johnson, Wolcot said that everybody appeared in awe of him, nor was he himself an exception. He determined to try what Johnson would say in the way of contradiction. I laid a trap for him. 'I think, doctor,' I observed, 'that picture of Sir Joshua's is one of the best he ever painted,' naming the work. 'I differ from you, sir; I think it one of his worst.' Wolcot made no other attempt at conversation. The picture was really one of Sir Joshua's best. 'Traps are good things,' said Wolcot, 'to bring out character. The idea of a discussion with Johnson never entered my head. I had too great an apprehension of his powers of conversation to attempt disputing with the giant of the day.'"

Mr. Redding gives us the following sketch of the "inner life" of this eccentric writer:—"He sat always in a room facing the south. Behind the door stood a square pianoforte, on which there generally lay his favourite Cremona violin; on the left, a mahogany table with writing-materials. Every-

* See *ante*, p. 294.

thing was in perfect order, and the doctor knew where to put his hand upon it without aid. Facing him, over the mantelpiece, hung a fine landscape by Richard Wilson, and two of Bone's exquisite enamels, presents from that artist, who, being a Cornishman and a native of Truro, was indebted to the doctor for some valuable and influential introductions on making his *début* in town. In other parts of the room, under glass, there were suspended a number of the doctor's crayon drawings, most of them scenes in the vicinity of Fowey, which place stands in the midst of picturesque scenery. In writing, except a few lines hap-hazard, the doctor was obliged to employ an amanuensis, of which he complained. Of all his acquisitions music alone remained to him unaltered. 'He could still,' he said, 'strum the piano and play the fiddle'—what resources should he have had without these attainments, he observed. He even composed light airs for amusement. These things were more in the way of resource than many other people possessed. They were great comforts. 'You have seen something of life in your time. See and learn all you can more. You will fall back upon it when you grow old—an old fool is an inexcusable fool to himself and others—store up all; our acquirements are, perhaps, most useful when we become old.'"

Wolcot, as is well known, lavished much of his satire on George III. A lady at a dinner-party, who was one of that king's greatest admirers, once asked him if he felt no pricks of conscience for having so grievously held up to scorn and contempt so excellent a sovereign, and whether he was not a most "disloyal subject?" "I have not thought about that, madam," was the doctor's reply; "but I know the king has been a deuced good 'subject' for me." The loyal lady was annoyed and petrified.

When he was dying he expressed a wish "to lie as near as possible to the bones of old Hudibras Butler." He had his desire gratified, for he was buried, as we have told the reader,* at St. Paul's, Covent Garden.

Dr. Wolcot's verses, when he was in the zenith of his powers, would command a ready sale of from 20,000 to 30,000 copies. Though they were full of gross attacks on George III., they were great favourites with the Regent and the Carlton House circle; and the doctor despised his patron accordingly. He was offered a pension by the ministers on condition of his writing them up, but he declined the offer, saying, "Peter can do without a pension." We may add that Opie, the painter, in the early part of his career, was an inmate of Dr. Wolcot's house; it is said, at first in a somewhat menial capacity.

Strutt tells us, in his book on "Sports and Pastimes," that in the fields about here parties of Irishmen used to meet, about the year 1775, and play at "hurling to goals." Instead of throwing the ball with the hand, they used a kind of bat, differing, however, apparently, from that employed in cricket.

The Euston Road, which, as we have already stated, was formerly called the New Road, passes through the centre of the square, on its way to Pentonville and Islington. It is strange that it should have preserved its original name of the "New Road" for above a century. It was projected in 1754–5, as it is traced in the map prefixed to the edition of Stow's "Survey of London," published in the former year; and the *Public Advertiser*, of Feb. 20, 1756, enumerates at length the advantages which were thought likely to accrue to the public from its formation. Horace Walpole himself, who does not often travel so far afield from his favourite haunts about Piccadilly and St. James's Street, thus mentions it in one of his letters to General Conway, a month later: "A new road through Paddington (to the City) has been projected, to avoid the stones. The Duke of Bedford, who is never in town in the summer, objects to the dust it will make behind Bedford House, and to some buildings proposed (no doubt, in the rear of his gardens), though if he were in town he is too short-sighted to see the prospect." An opening in the central enclosure of Euston Square, on the north side of the road, leads directly up to the entrance to the North-Western Railway Station, and by the side of this opening is placed a colossal bronze statue of Robert Stephenson, the great railway engineer; it stands upon a granite pedestal. Along this route, which still was really "the New Road," the body of Queen Caroline was conveyed, after her death in 1821, *en route* for Harwich and the Continent. "I saw her funeral as it passed along," writes Lady Clementina Davies, in her "Recollections of Society." "It was followed by a multitude of people. On the coffin-lid was the inscription, dictated by herself, 'Caroline of Brunswick, the murdered Queen of England.' This inscription caused some ecclesiastical authorities to refuse it shelter on its way for embarkation; but Sergeant Wilde (afterwards Lord Truro), and the late Dr. Lushington accompanied the remains of their royal client to their place of final repose."

In the south-west corner of the square is Gower

* See Vol. III., p. 256.

Street, the lower end of which, adjoining Bedford Square, we have noticed in the preceding volume.* Among the residents in the upper part of it was "Jack" Bannister, the actor, as already mentioned. Sir George Rose, not less known for his wit and vivacity than for those talents which he displayed as a lawyer, was a near neighbour of Bannister, living on the opposite side of the street. One day, as he was walking, he was hailed by Bannister, who said, "Stop a moment, Sir George, and I will go over to you." "No," said the good-humoured punster, "I never made you *cross* yet, and I will not begin now." He joined the valetudinarian, and held a short conversation, and immediately after his return home, wrote—

On meeting the Young Veteran toddling up Gower Street, when he told me he was seventy.

"With seventy years upon his back
Still is my honest friend young Jack,
Nor spirits checked, nor fancy slack,
But fresh as any daisy.
Though time has knocked his *stumps* about,
He cannot bowl his temper out,
And all the Bannister is stout,
Although the *steps* be crazy."

This good-natured *jeu d'esprit*, we may here remark, was left by its author almost immediately afterwards at Bannister's door.

A chapel at the north end of this street, within a few yards of the Euston Road, was at one time the head-quarters of open and avowed Antinomian doctrines.

No. 40, Upper Gower Street was for many years the residence of that most powerful landscape painter, Peter de Wint, the effect of whose broad and masterly touch throws nearly every other artist, excepting Turner, into the shade. At No. 15 lived and died Francis Douce, the antiquary. In 1822 Charles Dickens as a boy was living with his parents for a short time in this street, but the place has no reminiscences of his early youth, as the future "Boz" was employed during that time as a drudge in the blacking warehouse at Hungerford Stairs.

Three or four well-built streets running out of the south side of Euston Square, lead into Gordon and Tavistock Squares, which we have already dealt with, when describing the adjacent neighbourhood, in the previous volume.†

At the south-east corner of the square stands the New Church of St. Pancras. The foundation-stone was laid by the Duke of York in July, 1819, and the church was consecrated by the Bishop of London in April, 1822. The model of the edifice is after the ancient temple of Erectheus, at Athens; and this church is said to have been the first place of Christian worship erected in Great Britain in the strict Grecian style. Mr. William Inwood was the architect. The steeple, upwards of 160 feet in height, is from an Athenian model, the Temple of the Winds, built by Pericles; it is, however, surmounted by a cross in lieu of the Triton and his wand, the symbols of the winds, in the original. The western front of the church, of which we give an engraving on page 349, has a fine portico of six columns, with richly-sculptured capitals. Towards the east end are lateral porticoes, each supported by colossal female statues on a plinth, in which are entrances to the catacombs beneath the church; each of the figures bears an ewer in one hand, and rests the other on an inverted torch, the emblem of death. These figures are composed of terra-cotta, formed in pieces, and cemented round cast-iron pillars, which in reality support the entablatures. The eastern end of the church differs from the ancient temple in having a semi-circular, or apsidal, termination, round which, and along the side walls, are terra-cotta imitations of Greek tiles. The interior of the new church is in keeping with its exterior. Above the communion-table are some *verd antique* scagliola marble columns, copied from the Temple of Minerva. The pulpit and reading-desk are made of the celebrated Fairlop Oak, which stood in Hainault Forest, in Essex, and gave its name to the fair at Easter-tide long held under its branches. Gilpin mentions this tree in his "Forest Scenery." "The tradition of the country," he says, "traces it half way up the Christian era." The tree was blown down in 1820. When the new church was erected in the New Road the fields to the north were quite open; and we have seen a print showing the unfinished edifice rising out of a surrounding desert of brick-fields.

Of the several vicars of St. Pancras, since this new church was built, none, perhaps, have been more popular than the Rev. Thomas Dale, who afterwards became Canon of St. Paul's, and subsequently, for a very few months, Dean of Rochester. The son of well-to-do parents, he was born in Pentonville, then almost a country village, at the close of the last century. Losing both his parents when quite a child, he was placed by his friends in Christ's Hospital, and in due course he found his way to Cambridge. In 1818, while still an under-graduate, he published "The Widow of Nain, and other Poems," which were well received by the public, and ran through several editions. On leaving Cambridge, Mr. Dale employed himself

* See Vol. IV., p. 567.

† See Vol. IV., pp. 572-3.

for a time in taking pupils, and was soon appointed to the incumbency of St. Matthew's Chapel, Denmark Hill, Camberwell. In 1835 Sir Robert Peel conferred upon him the vicarage of St. Bride's, Fleet Street, and here he became extremely popular as a preacher. In 1843 he accepted a canonry of St. Paul's, which was vacated by the death of Canon Tate. Three years later he resigned St. Bride's, on accepting the larger and more important living of St. Pancras, which he held for more than fourteen years. Already—namely from 1840 to 1849—he had held what is known as the "Golden Lectureship" at St. Margaret's, Lothbury. He accepted this lectureship not so much for the emolument (though that was considerable), as to break up the evils connected with it. The principal source from which the income was derived was the rent of a notoriously bad but licensed house near Temple Bar. This evil, so great a blot on the lectureship, he determined to root out, and therefore he not only refused to renew the lease, but turned out the tenants, keeping the house empty and himself with a greatly reduced income, until he could find a respectable person willing to take it.

Mr. Dale was succeeded in the living of St. Pancras by the Rev. William Weldon Champneys, grandson of a former vicar of this parish. Born at Camden Town in 1807, he was ordained in 1831, and having held one or two curacies in Oxford, became afterwards rector of Whitechapel, where he continued till his appointment to this vicarage, in 1860. He succeeded Canon Dale in the canonry vacated by him in St. Paul's Cathedral, and in 1868 he was nominated to the Deanery of Lichfield, which he held till his decease. His son, the Rev. Weldon Champneys, succeeded him. From 1869 till 1877 the Vicarage was held by Dr. Thorold, now Bishop of Rochester, who was succeeded by Canon Spence.

GATEWAY OF THE FOUNDLING HOSPITAL. (*See page* 356.)

From St. Pancras Church, a walk of a few minutes, in a southward direction, by way of Woburn Place and Tavistock Square, brings us once more to Guilford Street, the southern boundary of the parish of St. Pancras. The Foundling Hospital, which stands on the north side of this street, but just within the limits of the parish of which we have been treating, having been unavoidably passed by in our previous perambulation in this neighbourhood, will form the subject of the following chapter.

FRONT OF THE FOUNDLING HOSPITAL. (*See page* 356.)

CHAPTER XXVII.

THE FOUNDLING HOSPITAL AND NEIGHBOURHOOD.

"The helpless young that kiss no mother's hand
She gives in public families to live,
A sight to gladden Heaven."—*Thomson.*

Establishment of the Hospital by Captain Coram in Hatton Garden—Its Removal to Lamb's Conduit Fields—Parliamentary Grant to the Hospital—Wholesale Admission of Children—Tokens for the Identification of Children deposited in the Hospital—Withdrawal of the Parliamentary Grant—Rules and Regulations—Form of Petition for the Admission of Children—Baptism of the Infants—Wet-nurses—Education of the Children—Expenditure of the Establishment—Extracts from the Report of the Royal Commission—Origin of the Royal Academy of Arts—Hogarth's Liberality to the Institution—His "March of the Guards to Finchley Common"—The Picture Gallery—The Chapel—Handel's Benefactions to the Hospital—Lamb's Conduit Fields—Biographical Notice of Captain Coram—Hunter Street—A Domestic Episode in High Life—Tonbridge Chapel—The British College of Health.

THIS quaint and dull old-fashioned looking building, which reminds us of the early days of the last century, stands on the north side of Guilford Street, and forms part of the south-eastern boundary of the parish of St. Pancras. It is constructed of brick, with stone dressings, and consists mainly of a centre and wings, with a large open space before it for the exercise of the children, and extensive gardens at the back. These gardens, including the court in front, which is laid down in turf, cover some acres. The hospital was first established by royal charter, granted in 1739 to Thomas Coram (master of a trading vessel), for the reception, maintenance, and education of exposed and deserted young children, after the example of similar institutions in France, Holland, and other Christian countries. The first intention of Captain Coram, however, was modified after his death, because it was feared that the hospital would prove in practice only an encouragement of vice, if illegitimate children were admitted as long as there was room, without any restriction; and the restrictions imposed so far diminished the applications, that in a few cases the doors were thrown open for the reception of some legitimate children of soldiers.

In the petition which Coram makes for a charter, backed by "a memorial signed by twenty-one ladies of quality and distinction," he recites that, "no expedient has been found out for preventing the frequent murders of poor infants at their birth, or for suppressing the custom of exposing them to perish in the streets, or putting them out to nurses" (*i.e.*, persons trading in the same manner as the baby-farmers of more recent times), "who, undertaking to bring them up for small sums, suffered them to starve, or, if permitted to live, either turned them out to beg or steal, or hired them out to persons, by whom they were trained up in that way of living, and sometimes blinded or maimed, in order to move pity, and thereby become fitter instruments of gain to their employers." In order to redress this shameful grievance, the memorialists express their willingness to erect and support a hospital for all helpless children as may be brought to it, "in order that they may be made good servants, or, when qualified, be disposed of to the sea or land services of His Majesty the King."

The governors first opened a house for "foundlings" in Hatton Garden, in 1740–1; any person bringing a child, rang the bell at the inner door, and waited to hear if the infant was returned from disease or at once received; no questions whatever were to be asked as to the parentage of the child, or whence it was brought; and when the full number of children had been taken in, a notice of "The house is full" was affixed over the door. Often, we are told, there were 100 children offered, when only twenty could be admitted; riots ensued, and thenceforth the mothers balloted for the admission of their little ones by drawing balls out of a bag.

It was not until some years after the granting of the charter that the governors thought of building the present hospital. Fresh air is as necessary for children as for plants; and so the governors, wandering round the then suburbs in search of some healthy spot whereunto they could transfer their tender "nurslings," found it in the balmy meads of Lamb's Conduit Fields, then far away out in the green pastures, five minutes' walk from Holborn. The governors bought fifty-five acres of these fields from the Earl of Salisbury, for £5,500; in fact, the governors bought the whole estate, not because they required it, but because the earl, its owner, would not sell any fractional part of it. As London increased, the city approached this property; and in course of time a considerable part of the estate—indeed, all that was not actually absorbed in the hospital and its contiguous grounds—became covered with squares and streets of houses, the ground-rents producing an annual income equal to the purchase-money. The new building was at once commenced, the west wing being completed first, the east wing afterwards; the chapel, connecting the two, was finished last. The edifice was built from the designs of Jacobson.

The children, 600 in number, were removed hither in 1754, when the expenses of the establishment amounted to something very considerably above the income. The governors, nevertheless, who had long been desirous of making it a Foundling Hospital on the largest scale, found in the known favourable inclinations of the king towards them an excellent opportunity for pushing their scheme. London was not then a sufficient field for their exertions, and they accordingly applied to Parliament, who voted them £10,000, and sanctioned the general admission of children, the establishment of county hospitals, &c.

A basket was hung at the gate of the hospital in London in which the children were deposited, the persons who brought them ringing a bell to give notice to the officers in attendance. In order to forward the "little innocents" up from the country, a branch of the carrying trade was established, and babies arrived in London in increasing numbers from the most distant parts of the country. Large prices were, in some instances, paid for their conveyance, a fact which more than hints at the position of the parents; and as the carriage was prepaid, there was a strong inducement on the part of the carriers to get rid of their burthens on the way. Many of the infants were drowned; all of them were neglected, and that, in the large majority of cases, was equal to their death. It was publicly asserted in the House of Commons that one man, having the charge of five infants in baskets—they appeared to have been packed like so many sucking-pigs—and happening to get drunk on his journey, lay asleep all night on a common, and in the morning three out of the five were found dead. Many other instances of negligence on the part of carriers, resulting in the death of infants entrusted to them for carriage to London, are on record. Even the clothing in which the children were dressed was often stolen on the way, and the babes were deposited in the basket just as they were born. It is reported that a foundling who lived to become a worthy banker in the north of England, but who was received into the hospital at this time, being in after life anxious to make some inquiry into his origin, applied at the hospital, when all the information he could obtain from this source was that it appeared on the books of the establishment that he was put into the basket at the gate naked.

On the first day of this general reception of infants, June 2nd, 1756, no less than 117 children were deposited in the basket. The easy manner in which the children were thus disposed of led naturally to suspicion, on the part of neighbours, that they had not been fairly dealt with; and a person was actually tried for infanticide, and would have been hung, were it not that he was able to prove that the crime was committed by the carrier. In order to secure the parents against any such suspicion, in 1757 a notice was issued by the governors to the effect, that all persons bringing children should leave some token by which, in case any certificate should be wanted, it might be found out whether such child had been taken into the hospital or not. From that date all the children received had some token attached to their person, and in course of time a goodly collection of these was accumulated. Dr. Wynter, in an article on this subject in the *Shilling Magazine*, enumerates several of these tokens, which are still preserved in the hospital. Here are a few of them:—"Coins of an ancient date seem to have been the favourite articles used for this purpose, but there are many things of a more curious nature. A playing card—the ace of hearts—with a dolorous piece of verse written upon it; a ring with two hearts in garnets, broken in half, and then tied together; three or four padlocks, intended, we suppose, as emblems of security; a nut; an ivory fish; an anchor; a gold locket; a lottery ticket. Sometimes a piece of brass, either in the shape of a heart or a crescent moon, was used as a distinguishing mark, generally engraved with some little verse or legend. Thus one has these words upon it, '*In amore hæc sunt vitia;*' another has this bit of doggerel:—

"'You have my heart;
Though we must part.'

Again, a third has engraved upon it a hand holding a heart. Whilst we were musing over these curious mementoes of the past, the obliging secretary of the hospital brought us a large book, evidently bulged out with enclosures between its leaves: this proved to be a still more curious recollection of the past, as it enclosed little pieces of work, or some article of dress worked by the mother as a token, with some appeal for kind treatment attached. In many cases the token was a finely-worked cap, quaintly fashioned in the mode of the time; sometimes it was a fine piece of lace. We remarked a book-marker worked in beads, with the words, 'Cruel separation;' and again, a fine piece of ribbon, which the mother had evidently taken from her own person. All of these tokens in the book indicated that the maternal parents were of the better class—many of them that they were of the best class." Now these tokens are no longer wanted. The letters of the alphabet and figures are prosaically made to supply their place.

Before the use of tokens was insisted upon, the only means of identification open to the governors was the style in which the infant was dressed. Some of the entries show that "the quality" were by no means above taking advantage of the hospital. Thus under date 1741, on the very opening of the institution, we find the following record:—"A male child, about a fortnight old, very neatly dressed; a fine holland cap, with a cambric border, white corded dimity sleeves, the shirt ruffled with cambric." Again, "A male child, a week old; a holland cap with a plain border, edged biggin and forehead cloth, diaper bib, shaped and flounced dimity mantle, and another holland one; Indian dimity sleeves turned up with stitched holland, damask waist-coat, holland ruffled shirt." This poor baby of a week old must have exhibited a remarkable appearance. Doubtless these costly dresses were used with the idea that special care would be taken of the wearers; but this was a vain hope: the offspring of the drab and of the best "quality" stood on an equal footing inside the Foundling gates; and possibly in after years their faces—that invariable indication of breed—proved their only distinguishing mark.

Besides the tokens, letters were occasionally deposited in the basket with the child; some of these were impudent attempts upon the credulity of the governors. Thus, one had the following doggerel lines affixed to its clothes:—

> "Pray use me well, and you shall find
> My father will not prove unkind
> Unto that nurse who's my protector,
> Because he is a benefactor."

In less than four years, while this indiscriminate admission lasted, and until Parliament, appalled at the consequences, withdrew the grant, no less than nearly 15,000 babes were received into the hospital; but out of this number only 4,400 lived to be apprenticed, this "massacre of the innocents" having been effected at a cost to the nation of £500,000. After the withdrawal of the Government grant, the governors were left to their own resources, to recruit their now empty exchequer; and this they did by the very notable plan of taking in all children that offered, accompanied by a hundred-pound note, no questions being asked, and no clue to their parents being sought. As none but the wealthy could deposit children at the gates of the hospital on such terms, it is obvious that this was nothing less than a premium upon pure profligacy in the well-to-do classes. This system lasted, nevertheless, for upwards of forty years—in fact, till the year 1801; and of all the children so received, no sign of their "belongings" is left behind.

The present plan of admitting children dates from the abolition of these hundred-pound infants. The regulations are very curious, and apparently rather capricious. Thus, the committee will not receive a child that is more than a year old, nor the child of a footman or of a domestic servant, nor any child whose father can be compelled to maintain it. When, however, the father dies, or goes to the "diggings," or enlists as a soldier, the child is eligible. The mother's moral character must be generally good, and the child must be the result of her "first fault;" and she must show that, if relieved of the incumbrance of her child, she can shift to another part of the town or country, where her "fault" will be unknown. The first step to be taken by the mother is to obtain a printed form of petition; when this is done a day is appointed for her examination, when, if she prevaricates in any of her statements, her application is rejected, and many otherwise eligible cases are dismissed on this ground.

The following is the printed form of petition:—

THE PETITION OF (*name*) OF (*place of abode*)

HUMBLY SHEWETH—

That your petitioner is a (*widow or spinster*, ( ) years of age, and was on the ( ) day of ( ) delivered of a (*male or female*) child, which is wholly dependent on your petitioner for its support, being deserted by the father. That (*father's name*) is the father of the said child, and was, when your petitioner became acquainted with him, a (*his trade*), at (*residence when the acquaintance began*), and your petitioner last saw him on the ( ) day of ( ), and believes he is now (*what is become of him*). Your petitioner therefore humbly prays that you will be pleased to receive the said child into the aforesaid hospital.

The instructions appended to this printed form state that no money is ever received for the admission of children, nor any fee or perquisite taken by any officer of the hospital. It may be added that no recommendation is necessary to the success of a petitioner's claim.

The mother is obliged to attend before the board and tell her story, and inquiries are afterwards set on foot in as secret a manner as possible to verify her statement. The object of the charity is not only to save the life of the child, but to hide the shame of the mother, by giving her time to retrieve her faults. The world is but too prone to be hard upon poor women who have "made a slip" of this nature; and but too often their own sex affix a kind of moral ticket-of-leave to them, which effectually prevents their regaining their position. Under the contumely and the desperation to which such treatment reduces them, the poor creature sometimes sacrifices not only her own life, but also that of the unhappy child.

Immediately the infant is received into the house, it is baptised. Of old, contributions were laid upon every name illustrious in the arts and sciences. When these were exhausted, all our naval heroes were pressed into the service; then our famous poets once more—in name, at least—walked the earth. The Miltons, Drydens, and Shakespeares that flourished within the walls of the Foundling in the last century must have made it a perfect Walhalla. Let no man flatter himself that he is descended from our famous bards upon the strength of a mere name, however uncommon, lest some spiteful genealogist should run him to earth at the end of Lamb's Conduit Street.

In the *Gentleman's Magazine*, under date 29th March, 1741, occurs this entry: "The orphans received into the hospital were baptised there, some nobility of the first rank standing godfathers and godmothers. The first male was named Thomas Coram, and the first female Eunice Coram, after the first founder of that charity and his wife. The most robust boys, being designed for the sea-service, were named Drake, Norris, Blake, &c., after our most famous admirals." Thus, when the Foundling was first opened, noble lords and ladies stood sponsors to the little ones, and gave them their own names. As these foundlings grew up, however, more than one laid claim to a more tender relationship than was altogether convenient. Now-a-days, it is thought best to fall back upon the Brown, Jones, and Robinson class of names of ordinary life to be found in the Directory. The governors, however, act in a perfectly impartial manner in this respect. A list of names is made out beforehand, and as the children arrive they are fitted to them in regular order. As soon as they are baptised they are dispatched into the country, where wet-nurses have been provided for them. Within a distance of twenty miles, in Kent and Surrey, there are always about 200 of these foundlings at nurse. Every child has its name sewn up in its frock, and also a distinguishing mark hung round its neck by a chain, which the nurse is enjoined to see is always in its place. These children are regularly inspected by a medical man, and the greatest care is taken that due nourishment is afforded to the babes. When the nurse cannot do this, a certain amount of milk is required to be given. The foster-children, whilst at nurse, are under the observation of visitors in the neighbourhood. When Hogarth lived at Chiswick, he and his wife took charge of a certain number of these little ones; and it is pleasant to read the faded accounts in the handwriting of the great painter, in which he shows that the interest he took in the charity was of the most intimate kind; that he not only enriched it with the gifts of his pencil, as we shall presently show, but also with his tender solicitude for the foundlings who could make him no return for the care with which he watched over them. The foster-children, as a rule, are very well taken care of; a large per-centage, indeed, surviving the maladies of childhood, which they certainly would not have done, under the peculiar circumstances of their birth, inside the walls of the asylum.

"Though mothers may abandon their children to the tender mercies of a public company," says a writer in *Chambers' Journal*, "they cannot do so without pain. The court-room of the Foundling has probably witnessed as painful scenes as any chamber in Great Britain; and again, when the children, at five years old, are brought up to London, and separated from their foster-mothers, these scenes are renewed. Even the foster-fathers are sometimes found to be greatly affected by the parting, while the grief of their wives is excessive; and the children themselves so pine after their supposed parents, that they are humoured by holidays and treats for a day or two after their arrival, in order to mitigate the change. In very many cases the solicitude of the foster-mothers does not cease with their charge of the little ones, as they frequently call to inquire after them, and they, in return, look upon them as their parents."

The education which the children receive at the Foundling is confined to reading, writing, and arithmetic, and they are also taught part-singing. At fifteen the boys and girls are apprenticed, the boys to tradesmen, and the girls to private families as domestic servants; and we hear that, as a rule, both turn out very well. The governors make a very strict inquiry into the characters of those wishing to receive them before they are permitted to have an apprentice, and they desire to be furnished with regular reports as to the conduct of their wards. Whilst the term of their apprenticeship lasts, the governors continue their careful watch over them; and when they are out of their time, means are afforded the boys of setting out in life as artisans: whilst the girls are, if well behaved, entitled to a marriage portion. It will be remembered that Thomas Day, the eccentric author of "Sandford and Merton," selected from the Foundling Hospital one of the two girls whom he resolved to bring up and educate, in the hope that she would prove a model wife; but both, it is needless to add, turned out failures. Even at the termination of apprenticeship all connection with the hospital does not necessarily cease, as many of the children return to it as their home when in necessity, and, if well behaved, they are never denied assistance. Some of the children, crippled and helpless, remain for their whole lives as pensioners upon the bounty of the institution. It is stated by Hone, in his "Year Book," that for the plan adopted in rearing the children here, the hospital was largely indebted to Sir Hans Sloane. An economical kitchen, ingeniously fitted up for the institution by Count Rumford, is described at some length in the "Annual Register" for 1798.

INTERIOR OF THE CHAPEL OF THE FOUNDLING HOSPITAL. (*See page* 363.)

The whole expenditure of the establishment in town and country, for the year ending December, 1882, amounted to £13,105 0s. 4d., which—after deducting the expenses with reference to apprentices, and a few other miscellaneous accounts—divided by the average number of children on the establishment in that year, namely, 497, gave an average cost of £19 10s. per head.

The girls and the boys in the hospital are pretty equally divided. Owing to the liberal support afforded to the Benevolent Fund, the design of which is to relieve the hospital altogether from the burden of adults, the number of late years has been reduced.

It appears from the report of the Royal Commission, instituted in 1869, to inquire into the working of this charity, that, though the infants received into the hospital are never again seen by their mothers (save in peculiar cases), a species of intercourse with them is still permitted. Mothers are allowed to come every Monday and ask after their children's health, but are allowed no further information. On an average, about eight women per week avail themselves of this privilege, and there have been some who attend regularly every fortnight. Even when application is made by mothers for the return of their child, the request is frequently refused. When they are apprenticed no intercourse is permitted between them, unless master and mistress, as well as parent and child, approve of it; nor when he has attained maturity, unless the child as well as the mother demand it. Thus a woman, who was married from the hospital, and had borne seven children, once requested to know her parents, on the ground that "there was money belonging to her," and her application was refused. But in November of the same year the name of a certain foundling was revealed upon the application of a solicitor, and his setting forth that money had been invested for its use by the dead mother. The governors granted this request upon the ground that the mother herself had disclosed the secret, which they were otherwise bound to keep inviolable. Again, in 1833, a foundling, seventy-six years of age, was permitted, for certain good reasons, to become acquainted with his own preserve its identification during its subsequent abode in the hospital, since the children appear in chapel twice on Sunday, and dine in public on that day, which gives opportunities of seeing them from time to time, and preserving the recollection of their features. In these attempts at discovery, however, mistakes are often committed, and attention lavished on the wrong child; instances have even occurred of mothers coming in mourning attire

THE SMALL-POX HOSPITAL, KING'S CROSS, IN 1800. (*See page* 366.)

name, though, as may be imagined, not with his parent. "It is a wise child in the Foundling who knows even its own mother."

The stratagems resorted to by women to identify their children, and to assure themselves of their well-being, are often singularly touching. Sometimes notes are found attached to the infant's garments, beseeching the nurse to tell the mother her name and residence, that the latter may visit her child during its stay in the country; and they have been even known to follow on foot the van which conveys their little one to its new home. They will also attend the baptism in the chapel, in the hope of hearing the name conferred upon the infant; for, if they succeed in identifying the child during its stay at nurse, they can always

to the hospital, to return thanks for the kindness bestowed upon their deceased offspring, only to be informed that they are alive and well. One exception to the rule of non-intercourse is related, where a medical attendant certified that the sanity of one unhappy woman might be affected unless she was allowed to see her child.

Another piece of information afforded by the Commission, and this, perhaps, the saddest of all, is that "twice or thrice in the year the boys are permitted to take an excursion to Primrose Hill; but at other times (except when sent on errands), and the girls *at all times*, are kept within the hospital walls." This confinement, it is asserted, so affects their growth, that few of either sex attain to the average height of men and women.

George III. on more than one occasion testified in a marked and substantial manner the interest which he took in the institution, and on the 21st of June, 1799, his Majesty, accompanied by the Queen, the Prince of Wales, the Duke of Clarence, and five of the princesses, visited the hospital in state.

That Tenterden Steeple was the cause of the Goodwin Sands does not seem at all more strange than that the Foundling Hospital should have been in some sense the parent of the Royal Academy of Arts. Yet such was the case. Not long after the incorporation of the society, the present building was erected, as we have mentioned; but as its funds were not available for its decoration, many of the chief artists of the day generously gave pictures from their own easels for the decoration of its several apartments. In course of time these came to be shown to the public on application, and a small sum being charged for admission, they took their place among the sights of the metropolis. Ultimately they proved so attractive that their success suggested a combined exhibition of the works of artists. This, as we have stated,* first took shape in the rooms of the Society of Arts in the Adelphi, from which, again, the Royal Academy took its idea. Thus, within the walls of the Foundling the curious visitor may see the state of British art in the era immediately preceding the extension of the patronage of George III. to Benjamin West.

Among the earliest "governors and guardians" of this charity we find the name of William Hogarth, who liberally gave his time, his labour, and his money towards aiding the benevolent design of his friend, Captain Coram. His first artistic aid was the designing and drawing of a head-piece to a power of attorney drawn for collecting subscriptions in support of the institution; and he next presented to the governors an engraved plate of Captain Coram's portrait.

The list of the early artistic friends and supporters of the newly-formed society includes the sculptor Rysbrach; Hayman, the embellisher of Vauxhall Gardens; Hudson, Highmore, Allan Ramsay, and Richard Wilson, the prince of English landscape-painters of that age. They often met together at the hospital, and thus advanced the charity and the arts at the same time; for the exhibition of their donations in the shape of paintings drew a daily crowd of visitors in splendid carriages and gilt sedan chairs, so that to pay a visit to the Foundling became one of the fashionable morning lounges in the reign of George II. The straight flat ground in front of the building formed the chief promenade; and brocaded silk, gold-headed canes, and laced three-cornered hats formed a gay and constant assembly in "Lamb's Conduit Fields," when they were fields indeed.

Some very interesting memoranda of the artists whose works adorn the Foundling, with a *catalogue raisonnée* of the pictures which they presented, will be found in Mr. Brownlow's "Memoranda or Chronicles of the Hospital." Among the pictures are "The Charter House," by Gainsborough; a portrait of Handel, by Sir Godfrey Kneller; and three works of Hogarth, namely, "The March to Finchley," "Moses brought to Pharaoh's Daughter," and the original portrait of Captain Coram.

As we have already shown, Hogarth took a pride and pleasure in this institution. Writing about himself, he remarks that the portrait which he presented with the greatest pleasure, and on which he spent the greatest pains, was that of Captain Coram, which hangs in the gallery of the hospital; and in allusion to the detraction from which he had suffered as an artist, he adds, "If I am such a wretched artist as my enemies assert, it is somewhat strange that this, which was one of the first that I painted the size of life, should stand the test of twenty years' competition, and be generally thought the best portrait in the place, notwithstanding the first painters in the kingdom exerted all their talents to vie with it." The portrait, we may add here, was engraved by McArdell, who resided at the "Golden Ball," in Henrietta Street, Covent Garden, and whose engraved portraits were pronounced by so good a judge as Sir Joshua Reynolds, "sufficient to immortalise their author."

The "March to Finchley," which adorns the secretary's room, like several of his other works, was disposed of by Hogarth by way of lottery. There were above 1,840 chances subscribed for out of 2,000; the rest were given by the painter to the Foundling Hospital, and on the same night on which the drawing took place, the picture was delivered to the governors of that institution. There is, however, some little doubt as to how it came into their hands, for it is said by some that the "prize" ticket was among those bestowed on the hospital; others—an anonymous writer in the *Gentleman's Magazine*, for instance—says that a *lady* was the holder of the fortunate ticket, for which she had subscribed with the view of presenting the picture to the governors. The writer adds, however, that a kind and prudish friend having suggested that a door would be opened for scandal if one of the female sex should make such a present, it was handed back to Hogarth on condition that he

* See Vol. III., p. 107.

should give it in his own name. Our readers may believe which version of the story they please.

Another good story is told about this picture. When Hogarth had finished his print of "The March of the Guards to Finchley," he proposed dedicating it to the king, and for that purpose went to court to be introduced. Previous to his Majesty's appearance, Hogarth was spied by some of the courtiers, who, guessing his business, begged to have a peep. He complied, and received much laughter and commendation. Soon after, the king entered the drawing-room, when Hogarth presented his print; but no sooner had the monarch thrown his eyes upon it, than he exclaimed—"Dendermons and death! you Hogarth; what you mean to abuse my soldier for?" In vain the other pleaded his attachment to the army in general, and that this was only a laugh at the expense of the dissolute and idle. His Majesty could not be convinced, till the late Lord Ligonier told him, "He was sure Mr. Hogarth did not mean to pay any disrespect to the army." This, however, but half pacified him; for, holding up the print hastily, he carelessly handed it to one of the lords in waiting, and desired him to let the artist have two guineas. Hogarth took the money, as the etiquette and practice of courts is not to refuse anything, but dedicated his piece to the King of Prussia.

The council-room adjoining is decorated with four large subjects from Holy Scripture, including the "Finding of Moses," and with eight medallion sketches of the chief London and suburban hospitals—St. Thomas's, St. Bartholomew's, Chelsea, Greenwich, &c.—in the middle of the last century.

In a corridor beyond hangs a fine portrait of Lord Chief Justice Wilmot. An inner room, formerly used as a hall, and now converted into a gallery, contains, besides the portrait of the founder, Captain Coram, spoken of above, the "Murder of the Innocents," by Raffaelle; the "Worthies of England," by James Northcote, R.A.; and fine portraits of George II., Lords Dartmouth and Macclesfield, Dr. Mead, Prince Hoare, Jacobson (the architect), and other friends of the hospital. The recesses in the windows are filled with glass cases containing autographs of the kings and queens of England from Henry VIII. downwards, as also of Hogarth, Sir Joshua Reynolds, Benjamin West, Captain Coram, Sir W. Sidney Smith, the Duke of Wellington, Charles Dickens, &c.

The chapel has, ever since the days of Handel, been celebrated for the attractiveness of the musical part of the services on Sundays, when its doors are open to the public; and readers of Thackeray's ballad of Eliza Davis and the false deluding sailor will remember how Policeman X., whom she let into her master's house in Guilford Street, refers to that unfashionable locality by the following reminder for his West-end friends:—

"P'raps you know the Fondling Chapel,
Where the little children sings?
Lord! I like to hear, on Sundays,
Them there pretty little things!"

Those who have attended the Foundling Hospital chapel must have been charmed with the beautiful effect of the fresh young voices swelling from the pyramid of little ones ranged on each side, and towering to the topmost pipes of the great organ (the gift of Handel), the girls in their quaint costume and high mob-caps, the boys in their very ugly uniform.

Among the principal benefactors to the hospital Handel stands among the foremost. Here, in this chapel, he frequently performed his oratorio of the *Messiah*, the score of which he left by will to this institution. Lysons, in his "Environs of London," remarks: "When that great master presided there, at his own oratorios, it was generally crowded; and as he engaged most of the performers to contribute their assistance gratis, the profits to the charity were very considerable, and in some instances approached nearly to £1,000."

The following is a copy of the announcement of Handel's performance of the *Messiah* for the benefit of the charity:—

Hospital for the Maintenance and Education of Exposed and Deserted Young Children, in Lamb's Conduit Fields, April 18, 1750.

George Frederick Handel, Esq., having presented this Hospital with a very fine organ for the chapel thereof, and repeated his offer of assistance to promote this charity,* on Tuesday, the first day of May, 1750, at twelve o'clock at noon, Mr. Handel will open the said organ, and the sacred oratorio called *Messiah* will be performed under his direction. Tickets for this performance are ready to be delivered by the Steward at the Hospital, at "Batson's" Coffee House, in Cornhill; and "White's" Chocolate House, in St. James's Street, at half-a-guinea each. N.B. There will be no collection. By order of the general Committee.

HARMAN VERELST, *Secretary.*

The concourse of visitors on this occasion was so great, that the performance of the oratorio was repeated a fortnight afterwards. In the course of the following twenty years the *Messiah* was several times performed here, and the entire proceeds, which were added to the funds of the hospital, amounted to no less a sum than £10,299. Some of the announcements of these performances read curious now-a-days. We take the following from the

* Allusion is here made to a performance which Handel had given on the 27th of May, 1749, for the benefit of this institution.

General Advertiser of the 17th of May, 1751:—"Yesterday the oratorio of *Messiah* was performed at the Foundling Hospital to a very numerous and splendid audience, and a voluntary on the organ was played by Mr. Handel, which met with universal applause." The *Gentleman's Magazine*, in giving an account of this performance, thus observes: "There were above five hundred coaches, besides chairs, and the tickets amounted to above seven hundred guineas." For the oratorio, in 1752, the number of tickets taken was 1,200, at half-a-guinea each; and in the following year the sum realised by the sale of tickets was 925 guineas. The performance on this occasion is thus noticed by the *Public Advertiser* of the 2nd of May, 1753:—"Yesterday the sacred oratorio called *Messiah* was performed in the chapel at the Foundling Hospital, under the direction of the inimitable composer thereof, George Frederick Handel, Esq., who in the organ concerto played himself a voluntary on the fine organ he gave to that chapel."

In Schœlcher's "Life of Handel" we are told that the great musician in a manner divided his "property" in the *Messiah* with the Foundling Hospital; he gave the institution a copy of the score, and promised to come and conduct it every year for the benefit of the good work. This gift was the occasion of an episode in which may be perceived the choleric humour of the worthy donor. The administrators of the hospital, being desirous of investing his intentions with a legal form, prepared a petition to Parliament, which terminated in the following manner:—"That in order to raise a further sum for the benefit of the said charity, George Frederick Handel, Esq., hath been charitably pleased to give to this corporation a composition of music called 'The Oratorio of *The Messiah*,' composed by him; the said George Frederick Handel reserving to himself only the liberty of performing the same for his own benefit during his life. And whereas the said benefaction cannot be secured to the sole use of your petitioners, except by the authority of Parliament, your petitioners therefore humbly pray that leave may be given to bring in a bill for the purpose aforesaid." When one of the governors waited upon the musician with this form of petition, he soon saw that the committee of the hospital had built on a wrong foundation, for Handel, bursting into a rage, exclaimed, "De Devil! for vat sal de Foundling put mein oratorio in de Parlement! De devil! mein music sal not go to de Parlement." The petition went no further; but Handel did not the less fulfil the pious engagement which he had contracted.

The organ still in use in the chapel is the same that was presented by Handel, and the altar-piece, "Christ Blessing Little Children," is considered as one of West's finest productions. About the year 1872 the chapel was considerably enlarged and improved. The hospital, in fact, has not been without other friends also, for we are told how that a black merchant, a native of Calcutta, named Omichand, towards the end of the last century, left a legacy of £5,000, the interest of which is shared between this institution and the Magdalen Hospital. Captain Coram himself, the founder of the hospital, lies buried in a vault beneath the chapel, as also does Lord Tenterden, the chief justice, who died in 1832. It was suggested that Handel should be interred near the grave of the founder, but this idea was overruled, and the remains of the great musician found a resting-place in Westminster Abbey. It may be added that Laurence Sterne preached in this chapel in 1761, and that in more recent times Sydney Smith occupied the pulpit.

Whilst, as we have said, some 200 of the children on the books of the hospital are laying in a stock of health in the cottages and amid the orchards of Surrey and Kent, the rest are to be seen within the walls of this building, in itself one of the most open and healthful spots in the metropolis. It is true it does not stand, as of old, in the centre of Lamb's Conduit "Fields," for the town has crept up and devoured the latter; but it will be observed that the squares that flank the institution on either hand have no houses on the sides next to the hospital, and that consequently these large enclosures act as supplementary lungs to the ample gardens and grounds of the institution itself. Nevertheless, the governors at the end of the last century let off enough of their land for building purposes to bring in upwards of £5,500 per annum, or as much as they originally gave for the fee-simple of the whole estate to the Earl of Salisbury. As the land was let upon building leases of ninety-nine years, large house property will fall into the hands of the charity in the course of a few years from the present time; possibly by that period, if not before, the Foundling Hospital will be transplanted to the green country, as the Charterhouse School has already been, and possibly Westminster School will be; for why, it has been asked, should we keep young children in the midst of a smoky town when cheaper and better air can be provided for them in fields far away, and brighter than were even the Lamb's Conduit Fields of old? We should not dream of planting a nursery-ground in the metropolis from choice; and children, it should be remembered, flourish just as ill as roses in contaminated air. When this institution is removed to "fresh fields and pastures new," the sale of their land for building purposes will probably bring in upwards of £50,000 a year, and the charity will possess the means of vastly increasing the field of its usefulness.

At the gates of the hospital, facing Lamb's Conduit Street, there is a statue of Captain Thomas Coram, by W. Calder Marshall. The following short notice of the founder of this institution, from the "Biographical Dictionary," may not be out of place here:—"Captain Coram was born about 1668, bred to the sea, and spent the first part of his life as master of a vessel trading to the colonies. While he resided in that part of our metropolis which is the common residence of sea-faring people, business often obliged him to come early into the City and return late, when he had frequent occasions of seeing young children exposed, through the indigence or cruelty of their parents. This excited his compassion so far, that he projected the Foundling Hospital, in which humane design he laboured seventeen years, and at last by his sole application obtained the royal charter for it. He was highly instrumental in promoting another good design—viz., the procuring a bounty upon naval stores imported from the colonies; and was eminently concerned in setting on foot the colonies of Georgia and Nova Scotia. His last charitable design, which he lived to make some progress in, but not to complete, was a scheme for uniting the Indians in North America more closely to the British interest, by an establishment for the education of Indian girls. Indeed, he spent a great part of his life in serving the public, and with so total a disregard to his private interest, that towards the latter part of it he was himself supported by the voluntary subscriptions of public-spirited persons, at the head of whom was the truly amiable and benevolent Frederick Prince of Wales. This singular and memorable man died at his lodgings near Leicester Square, March 29th, 1751, in his eighty-fourth year; and was interred, pursuant to his desire, in the vault under the chapel of the Foundling Hospital, where his memory is recorded in a suitable inscription."

Readers of the works of Charles Dickens will scarcely need to be reminded how in the opening scene of "No Thoroughfare," the postern gate of the Foundling Hospital opens, and Sally steps out and asks, with all a mother's affection, what name "they have give to her poor baby." Nor will they forget, in the next scene, how, whilst the foundling children are at dinner after service, a veiled lady walking round the table, asks, on the sly, which is Walter Wilding; or how, further on in the story, Bintrey asks "whether Joey Ladle is to take a share in Handel, Mozart, Haydn," &c., as "Mr. Wilding knows by heart all the choruses to the anthems in the Foundling Hospital collection;" and how, in the issue, it turns out that Mr. Wilding, the wine merchant, was that very child for whom "Sally" had asked so tenderly.

The "Boat," an isolated tavern in the open fields at the back of the Foundling, doubtless commemorated the time when boats and barges came up the Fleet River as far as Battle Bridge. It formed the head-quarters of the rioters and incendiaries who aided and abetted Lord George Gordon in his anti-Popish riots in 1780.

Behind the Foundling Hospital, in a line with Judd Street, of which we have already spoken, is Hunter Street. At No. 2 for many years lived the lady who called herself the Marchioness Townshend. She was a daughter of Mr. William Dunn Gardner, of Chatteris, in the Isle of Ely, and in 1807 was married to Lord Chartley, afterwards Marquis Townshend, who died in 1855, leaving no family. The story of her married life is thus narrated in Hardwicke's "Annual Biography:"—"Shortly after the marriage, Lord Chartley separated from his wife, a proceeding which the lady endeavoured to set aside by a suit in the Ecclesiastical Courts. These courts, however, are proverbially slow in their proceedings, and while her suit was pending, she eloped from her father's house with a Mr. John Margetts, a brewer of St. Ives, with whom she lived, in this street and other places, down to his death in 1842, calling herself at one time Mrs. Margetts and at other times the Marchioness Townshend. During this time she had by Mr. Margetts a family of sons and daughters, the former of whom were sent to Westminster School, first in the name of Margetts, and afterwards under the names of Lord A. and B. Townshend. The eldest son was actually returned to Parliament in 1841, as Earl of Leicester, by the electors of Bodmin, who fondly imagined that they had secured as their representative the eldest son of a live marquis, and one who would hereafter prove a powerful patron of their interests in the House of Lords. At this time, Lord Charles Townshend, next brother to the marquis, and then heir presumptive to the title, presented a petition to the Crown and to the House of Lords, entreating that the children of Lady Townshend by Mr. Margetts might be declared illegitimate. The petition was referred to a committee of privilege, who, after hearing the evidence of a considerable number of witnesses, reported their opinion in favour of a bill to that effect. A bill accordingly was introduced 'for declaring the issue of Lady Townshend illegitimate,' and it passed the House of Lords, by a large majority, in May, 1843. If it had not been for this procedure on the part of Lord Charles Townshend, which was rendered more difficult by the forced residence of the marquis abroad (for he had never taken his seat in the House of Peers, nor had he been in England since his accession to the title, nor seen his wife since her elopement), the marquisate of Townshend, with the noble estates of Raynham, in Norfolk, and the castle at Tamworth, would have passed to a spurious and supposititious race, the children of a brewer at St. Ives. After the death of the marquis, in December, 1855, his disconsolate wife, having remained a widow for nearly a fortnight, was married by special licence to a Mr. John Laidler, an assistant to a linendraper at the west end of London."

In the Euston Road, near the end of Judd Street, is Tonbridge Chapel, a place of worship for Dissenters of the Congregationalist denomination, dating from about the year 1812. Close to Tonbridge Chapel, opposite to the former site of the Small-Pox Hospital, and facing the terminus of the Midland Railway, stands the British College of Health. It was erected in 1828, for the manufacture and sale of a vegetable pill, by Mr. James Morison, a gentleman of Scottish extraction, who began his career as a merchant at Riga, and subsequently in the West Indies. Ill health compelled him, however, to leave so hot a climate, and in 1814 he settled at Bordeaux. Finding no relief from the course of treatment carried out by his physicians, he at length decided on a method of his own. "From such men as Culpeper, and others of the old medico-herbalists, he sought advice, and his adventitious career was crowned with success. He found in the gardens of Nature (what his physicians could not find from minerals and from poisons) that alleviation of his disease which ultimately led to his complete recovery. Stimulated by this knowledge, his philanthropy was excited, and he decided to benefit others as he himself had been benefited. This was the origin of his founding the British College of Health." The world-wide fame which Morison's pills speedily attained, as well as the common sale attendant thereon, excited first the astonishment, then the jealousy, and afterwards

COUNCILLOR AGAR'S HOUSE, SOMERS TOWN, IN 1830. (*See page* 369.)

FRONT OF ST. PANCRAS STATION AND HOTEL. (*See page* 371.)

the malice of the regular practitioners. Action after action was commenced against the proprietor for the sale of "so poisonous an article;" but falling to the ground, they only assisted in still further extending his fame and sale, until his very name became a "household word," which no other medicine has obtained either before or since. Its notoriety was such that *Punch* of those days continually referred to it. On Morison's death, in the year 1856, a memorial was erected in front of his establishment in the Euston Road by a penny subscription; "no person was allowed to give more than one penny, and no one was to subscribe but those who had derived some benefit from the Hygeist's medicine." The memorial consists of a granite pedestal, surmounted by the British lion, and on the sides of the pedestal are various poetical quotations and remarks.

CHAPTER XXVIII.

AGAR TOWN, AND THE MIDLAND RAILWAY.

Origin of the Midland Railway—Agar Town as it was—A Good Clearance—Underground Operations for the Construction of the Midland Railway and Terminus—Re-interment of a Roman Catholic Dignitary—The Midland Railway—Mr. William Agar—Tom Sayers, the Pugilist—The English "Connemara"—A Monster Hotel—The Midland Terminus: Vast Size of the Roof of the Station—A Railway Goods Bank—The Imperial Gas Works—York Road.

THE Midland Railway, unlike most other long lines, was commenced, not in London, but in the provinces, having been originated in 1832 at a village inn on the borders of Leicestershire and Nottinghamshire, in the necessities of a few coal-owners—not of the richest and most influential class. It has, however, gradually found its way from the provinces into London, and has spread out its paths of iron, like a net-work, north and south, east and west, through half the counties of England, till they stretch from the Severn to the Humber, from the Wash to the Mersey, from the Thames to the Solway Firth. Its construction has cost fifty millions of money, bringing in an income of five millions a year; and it has before it an almost unlimited future. We do not intend here to attempt an account of the entire Midland line; but as we have already given some details about the London and North-Western line in our account of Euston Square, so our description of St. Pancras will not be complete without a few particulars about this railway. When this line was brought into London, in 1866, it wrought a mighty revolution in the neighbourhood where we now are. "For its passenger station alone it swept away a church and seven streets of three thousand houses," writes Mr. F. Williams, in his "History of the Midland Railway: a Narrative of Modern Enterprise." "Old St. Pancras churchyard was invaded, and Agar Town almost demolished. Yet those who knew this district at that time have no regret at the change. Time was when the wealthy owner of a large estate had lived here in his mansion; but after his departure the place became a very 'abomination of desolation.' In its centre was what was termed La Belle Isle, a dreary and unsavoury locality, abandoned to mountains of refuse from the metropolitan dust-bins, strewn with decaying vegetables and foul-smelling fragments of what once had been fish, or occupied by knackers'-yards and manure-making, bone-boiling, and soap-manufacturing works, and smoke-belching potteries and brick-kilns. At the broken doors of mutilated houses canaries still sang, and dogs lay basking in the sun, as if to remind one of the vast colonies of bird-fanciers and dog-fanciers who formerly made Agar Town their abode; and from these dwellings came out wretched creatures in rags and dirt, and searched amid the far-extending refuse for the filthy treasure by the aid of which they eked out a miserable livelihood; whilst over the whole neighbourhood the gas-works poured forth their mephitic vapours, and the canal gave forth its rheumatic dampness, extracting in return some of the more poisonous ingredients in the atmosphere, and spreading them upon the surface of the water in a thick scum of various and ominous hues. Such was Agar Town before the Midland Railway came into the midst of it."

The above sketch is slightly—but only slightly—overdrawn; for the canal still flows where it did, and it is known that gas-works, though unsightly, are not really unhealthy neighbours. Be this, however, as it may, a mighty clearance of houses was made, and a population equal to that of ten small boroughs was swept away, as the first step towards a new order of things. The neighbourhood for many months presented the appearance of an utter chaos, with mounds of earth, the *débris* of houses and tunnels in the course of being dug. By the side of the Euston Road, close under the front of the Midland Railway Hotel, was dug a large trench in which was built a tunnel for the use of the Metropolitan Company whenever it shall need to double its present traffic-lines. Further to the north came sweeping round another large cutting in which was to be made the actual junction of the Metropolitan and the Midland lines. "So vast, indeed, were these subterranean operations," writes Mr. Williams, "that the St. Pancras Station became like an iceberg, the greater portion of it being below the surface; indeed, remarkable as is the engineering skill displayed in the large building which towers so majestically above all its neighbours, it is as nothing compared with the works concealed below ground. For right underneath the monster railway station are two other separate constructions, one above the other, none the less wonderful because they will never see the light of day, but are irrevocably doomed

'To waste their sweetness on the desert air.'"

These works are the Underground Railway and the Fleet Sewer, while the branch of the Metropolitan that joins the Midland not only crosses it at the southern extremity, but thence runs up under the western side of the station, to re-cross at its northern end to the eastern side, where it gradually rises to its junction about a mile down the line.

Of the difficulty experienced in carrying the railway through the graveyard of Old St. Pancras Church, and also through that of St. Giles's parish which adjoins it, without any unavoidable disturbance of the dead, we have spoken in a previous chapter; * but we may add here, that, though every precaution was taken by the agents of the Midland Railway Company, a most serio-comic incident occurred during the process. The company had purchased a new piece of ground in which to re-inter the human remains discovered in the part which they required. Among them was the corpse of a high dignitary of the Roman Catholic Church in France. Orders were received for the transshipment of the remains to his native land, and the delicate work of exhuming the corpse was entrusted to some clever gravediggers. On opening the ground they were surprised to find the bones, not of one man, but of several. Three skulls and three sets of bones were yielded up by the soil in which they had lain mouldering. The difficulty was how to identify the bones of a French ecclesiastic amid so many. After much discussion, the shrewdest of the gravediggers suggested that, as he was a foreigner, the darkest-coloured skull must be his. Acting upon this idea, the blackest bones were sorted and put together, until the requisite number of lefts and rights were obtained. These were reverently screwed up in a new coffin, conveyed to France, and buried again with all the "pomp and circumstance" of the Roman Catholic Church.

Shortly after passing the churchyard of Old St. Pancras the line crosses the Regent's Canal, and then passes under the North London Railway, which is carried above it by a bridge of three arches. "Their construction," Mr. Jackson tells us, "was a matter of no ordinary difficulty on account of the ceaseless traffic on the line overhead; it was, however, accomplished without the interruption of a single hour." The Midland line is here joined by the branch which comes up from the Metropolitan at King's Cross, as mentioned above. The lines actually converge near the Camden covered-way; but the transfer of passengers usually takes place at Kentish Town Station, half a mile farther from the London Terminus. At Kentish Town a line branches off to Holloway and Tottenham, while the main line is carried by a long tunnel under Haverstock Hill, whence, emerging into open daylight, the trains run on to Hendon and St. Albans, and thence northwards through the "midland" counties.

We have spoken above of the great clearance of houses which was effected in this locality by the formation of the Midland Railway. The district, which is—or was—known as Agar Town, consisted mostly of small tenements of the lowest class, named after one Mr. William Agar—or, as he was commonly called, "Councillor Agar," an eccentric and miserly lawyer—to whom the site was let on a short lease for building purposes, about the year 1840.

Twenty years later the fee-simple of the greater part of this locality was transferred by the Ecclesiastical Commissioners, to whom it had reverted, to the Midland Railway Company for a considerable sum, and most of the houses have been swept away to form ale and coal stores and other warehouses in connection with the terminus of the Midland Railway, about which we shall speak presently. Much of the vacant ground not required for the company's use has been laid out for building warehouses, and has raised, as it were, another town in the place of this already overcrowded neighbourhood.

It can hardly be expected that such a district as this can have any historical associations worth recording; but still the place has not been without its "celebrities," for here lived for many years the

* See *ante*, p. 336.

well-known pugilist, Tom Sayers. His notoriety arose from his accepting the challenge of Heenan, the American champion, in 1860, to fight for the champion belt of the world. Sayers was comparatively small in stature, whilst Heenan was much above the ordinary height; and it is said that when Sayers met his monster opponent for the first time he felt a little daunted. The fight, nevertheless, came off, and in the first round Sayers's right arm was broken; but still, with this fractured limb, he continued the encounter for some time, and in the end, if he did not obtain the victory, he made it a drawn battle, and received with Heenan the honour of a double belt. Henceforth Tom Sayers was everywhere greeted as a hero; and at the Stock Exchange a purse of £1,000 was handed to him for his "gallant conduct," on the understanding that he at once retired from the Ring. For a time Sayers was the topic of general conversation; but he did not long survive his triumph, if such it may be called. He died soon afterwards from pulmonary consumption, and was buried, with considerable ceremony, in the Highgate Cemetery, his profile and a portrait of his dog being the only memorials on his tombstone to mark the place of his interment.

If the Midland Railway had conferred no other benefit on London and Londoners, our thanks would be due to it for having cleared away the whole, or nearly the whole, of the above-mentioned miserable district of mud and hovels, and given us something better to look upon. So dreary and dirty indeed was the place—though its creation was only of so recent date—that it was styled by Charles Dickens our "English Connemara." It was mainly occupied by costermongers, and by dog and bird fanciers.

Having made these general remarks about the line, and of the site which it occupies, we will proceed with a few details concerning the station and the "grand hotel" which adjoins it. The latter building, which abuts upon the Euston Road, facing Judd Street, was opened in 1873, and completed in the spring of 1876. It was erected from the designs of Sir Gilbert Scott, and is constructed chiefly of red brick, with dressings of Bath stone, in the most ornate style of Gothic art. It must be owned that towering as it does into mid air, it is a most beautiful structure; indeed, to quote the words of the "Tourist's Guide," "it stands without a rival in the hotel line, for palatial beauty, comfort, and convenience." The style of architecture is a combination of various mediæval features, the inspection of which recall to mind the Lombardic and Venetian brick Gothic or Gothic-Italian types, while the critical eye of the student will observe touches of Milan and other Italian terra-cotta buildings, interlaced with good reproductions of details from Winchester and Salisbury Cathedrals, Westminster Abbey, &c.; while in the interior and exterior may be seen the ornaments of Amiens, Laon, and other French edifices, which, though a conglomerate, must have required great pains and skill to properly harmonise in order to produce so attractive a result. The designs of the interior, as well as the apartments (some of which are embellished with almost regal splendour), were the production of Sir Gilbert Scott, afterwards assisted by Mr. Sang. The colouring is rich and almost faultlessly pleasing and harmonious, producing a marked mediæval character. The ceiling of the reading-room glows in an atmosphere of gold and colour, yet free and graceful in its figures and ornaments, designed by Mr. Sang. The large and magnificent coffee-room, the "grand saloon," together with the adjoining "state" and reception rooms, probably have no equal in point of design or finish in any building of the kind; while the corridors and staircases throughout are all decorated in a rich style, at once tasteful and beautiful.

A broad terraced carriage-drive, 400 feet in length, separates the hotel from the roadway, and leads by various entrances to the building and archways to the station. Altogether, the hotel has a frontage of about 600 feet; and it is very lofty, consisting of seven storeys, including attics in the sloping roofs. At the south-east corner of the building is a clock-tower 240 feet high, nearly forty feet higher than the Monument at London Bridge. There are bedrooms for upwards of 500 guests, all most luxuriously furnished; and a uniformly mild temperature is maintained in all seasons. The cost of the hotel, with its fittings and furniture, is said to have been not less than half a million pounds sterling. The whole of the arrangements for conducting the business of the hotel, it need hardly be added, are most complete. There are speaking-tubes, electric bells, lifts, and dust-shafts; and an apparatus for the extinction of fire is laid on at every floor. In the basement are spacious and extensive cellars, and a laundry; and it may be added that the whole of the washing and drying is done by steam power.

It was found necessary to raise the level of the terminus about fifteen feet higher than the Euston Road, in order to secure good gradients and proper levels for some of the suburban stations. The space underneath was then utilised as a cellarage for the Burton and other ale traffic, and thus the entire station may be said, seriously as well as jestingly, to rest on a substratum of beer. The roof of part of the cellarage forms the flooring of the terminus and platform of the station, and is so constructed as to bear the immense weight of many locomotive engines at the same time.

The roof is of glass, supported by huge iron girders, "not unlike lobster's claws, from which the shorter nippers have been broken," and forming a Gothic arch, not resting on piers, but embedded in the ground. It is 100 feet high, 700 feet in length, and its width about 240 feet. The span of the roof covers four platforms, eleven lines of rails, and a cab-stand twenty-five feet wide; altogether the station occupies a site of nearly ten acres. There are twenty-five principal ribs in the roof, and the weight of each is about fifty tons. The very scaffolding, by the help of which the roof was raised into its position, contained eight miles of massive timber, 1,000 tons in weight, besides about 25,000 cubic feet of wood, and eighty tons of ironwork. No other roof of so vast a span has been attempted. It is double the width of the Agricultural Hall at Islington, and ten yards wider than the two arches of the neighbouring terminus of the Great Northern Railway, which, when first built, were considered a triumph of engineering skill. Some idea may be formed of the vast expanse of the roof of the Midland Terminus when we state that it contains no less than two acres and a half of glass. The gigantic main ribs cost a thousand pounds apiece. These and the other interior portions of the framework are painted a sky-blue, and by this means the roof is made to look particularly light and airy. We may add that in the station and its approaches were absorbed about sixty millions of bricks, nine thousand tons of iron, and eighty thousand cubic feet of dressed stone. The consulting engineer was Mr. Barlow.

The opening of the St. Pancras Station in the year 1868, and its connection with the Metropolitan and other lines, gave the Midland Company, for the first time, a London terminus. Up to this period the Midland trains travelled on the Great Northern line from King's Cross as far as Hitchin, and thence by a branch line to Bedford and other portions of the Midland Railway system.

At the Midland Railway Goods Station alone some 1,300 men are employed, and at the Coal Depôt in York Road, close by, there are from 150 to 200 coal porters and carters. From the "Report of the London City Mission," which gives an account of the work that is being done by the society's agents among the labourers employed here, we quote the following description of a "Goods Bank:"—"The 'Goods Banks,' as they are called, are three in number. But does the reader know what a 'Goods Bank' is? Let me attempt a description. Suppose a building of adequate length to receive a tolerably long goods train, and about sixty or eighty feet wide, with a platform raised just high enough to load a cart at, or to unload a train of trucks without the toil of raising the goods. Fancy this platform running the whole length of the edifice, and more than half its width, packed up with every conceivable sort of merchandise, with little passages between leading to the carts, trucks, and various parts of the platform. Then imagine these carts, trucks, and passages all alive with men, some in uniform, some without, some with caps that tell you they are foremen, &c., and all variously employed. Here is a string of them, with handbarrows loaded; there another with the same articles empty; here are men at the cranes raising the goods to the height required, while there are men receiving them; then, again, over there are the officials with long papers in their hands, that make you wonder where all that writing is done, and how they manage to get rid of the goods described on them. But just look around on the goods. You will no longer wonder that Webster's Dictionary is such a thick volume, but rather stand wondering where the English language gets names from to describe the multiplicity of articles before you, and you go away with a much better idea of the intelligence of the railway official who knows how to describe the items in such a miscellaneous collection. Amongst this endless array I have seen sewing machines, reaping machines, pianos, harmoniums, holly and mistletoe, bags and sacks that you could not imagine what was inside, and bags and sacks that from their peculiar colour and odour, as well as from the appearance of the men handling them, you know at once to be soot. On one occasion an official said to me, 'Do you smell anything particular this morning?' On my replying negatively, he said, 'We have just had a large arrival of cats' meat in a bad condition;' and I learnt that this article sometimes came up by tons from Scotland—our friends out north being too canny to waste anything. At another time I saw the dead carcase of a horse swinging high in the air, as it was about to be delivered to a waiting cart or van. But," adds the missionary, "this terrible bustle of business makes the 'Bank' in itself an unfavourable place for religious work."

Between the Midland and the Great Northern lines a large space of ground is covered partly by the Imperial Gas Works, and partly by a coal depôt and the Great Northern Railway Goods Depôt. On the east side of these various centres of industry runs northwards the road which forms the boundary between the parishes of St. Pancras and Islington. This thoroughfare, as we have stated in a previous volume,* was, till recently, called Maiden Lane, and it is one of the most ancient roads in the north of London. The historian Camden says, "It was opened to the public in the year 1300, and was then the principal road for all travellers proceeding to Highgate and the north." It was formerly called "Longwich Lane," and was generally kept in such a dirty, disreputable state as to be almost impassable in winter, and was so often complained of that the Bishop of London was induced to lay out a new road to Highgate Hill, so that a carrier might get to the north by avoiding Longwich Lane. But of this we shall have more to say when we reach Highgate.

"The old and anciente highwaye to High Barnet, from Gray's Inn and Clerkenwell," writes John Norden, in his "Speculum Britanniæ," "was through a lane to the east of Pancras Church, called Longwich Lane, from whence, leaving Highgate on the west, it passed through Tallingdon Lane, and so on to Crouche Ende, thence through Hornsey Great Park to Muswell Hill, Coanie Hatch, Fryene Barnete, and so on to Whetstone. This anciente waye, by reason of the deepness and dirtieness of the passage in the winter season, was refused by wayfaring men, carriers, and travellers, in regard, whereof, it is agreed between the Bishop of London and the countrie, that a new waye shall be laide forthe through Bishop's Park, beginning at Highgate Hill, to leade directe to Whetstone, for which a certain tole should be paid to the Bishop, and for that purpose has a gate been erected on the hill, that through the same all travellers should pass, and be the more aptly staide for the tole."

Before quitting Maiden Lane, we may here mention the fact that for some few months previous to the erection of the Great Northern Terminus at King's Cross, which occupies the site of the Small-pox Hospital, the trains of that company started from a temporary station in Maiden Lane.

From King's Cross as far as Camden Road this thoroughfare was some years ago named York Road,

THE DUST-HEAPS, SOMERS TOWN, IN 1836. (*See page* 368.)

* See Vol. II., p. 276.

on account of the contiguity of the London and York (now the Great Northern) Railway; and from the "Brecknock Arms," at the north-east corner of Camden Town, to the foot of Highgate Hill, it was, a few years ago, re-named the Brecknock Road, by order of the Metropolitan Board of Works. By this road we will now proceed leisurely on our way northwards.

"THE SEVEN SISTERS" IN 1830. (*See page* 380.)

CHAPTER XXIX.

HOLLOWAY.

"Boreales visere terras."—*Tibullus.*

The Work of an Amiable Hermit—Copenhagen Fields—The New Cattle Market—Our Meat Supply—The "Brecknock Arms" Tavern—Duel between Colonel Fawcett and Lieutenant Munro—The City Prison—The Camden Town Athenæum—The New Jerusalem Church—Holloway Congregational Chapel—Seven Sisters' Road—Holloway Hall—The Old "Half Moon" and "Mother Red Cap" Taverns—St. Saviour's Hospital and Refuge for Women and Children—St. John's Church—The "Archway" Tavern—Dangers of the Roads—Descendants of the Poet Milton—The Lazar House—The Small-pox Hospital—Whittington's Stone—Whittington's Almshouses—Benefactions of Sir Richard Whittington.

In a previous part of this work, whilst speaking of the limits of the old Manor of Highbury,* we touched slightly upon that district lying to the west of the Hornsey and Holloway Roads, known respectively as Upper and Lower Holloway; but many other interesting details not mentioned on that occasion still remain to be told.

Holloway is a hamlet which belonged originally to the parish of Islington; and it received its name from being situated in the "hollow way" or low-land valley between that place and Highgate. It is said that the soil in this part being a stiff clay, that part of the road from Highgate to Islington which passes through Holloway was made with gravel excavated on the top of Highgate Hill by an amiable hermit, who had taken up his abode there. "A two-handed charity," quaintly remarks old Fuller, "providing water on the hill, where it was

* See Vol. II., p. 273.

wanting, and cleanness in the valley, which before, especially in winter, was passed with great difficulty." It is stated in the *Ambulator* that the last "hermit" of Highgate was one William Forte, who lived in the reign of Henry VIII. But of this hermit and his work we shall have more to say on a future occasion.

A large portion of Holloway, lying between the York Road and Caledonian Road, was formerly known as the Copenhagen Fields—once the resort of Cockney lovers, Cockney sportsmen, and Cockney agitators. Of the past history of this place, including the noted Copenhagen House, which stood here, we have already spoken in the chapter above referred to;* but it remains to be added that about the year 1852 much of the ground hereabouts, to the extent of some seventy acres, was taken by the Corporation of London, in accordance with the provisions of an Act of Parliament passed in the above year, as a site for the new cattle-market, which was to supersede the old market at Smithfield. The new market was planned, and the various buildings connected with it erected, from the designs of Mr. J. B. Bunning, the architect to the City of London, at a cost of nearly £500,000.

The question of the removal of the cattle-market from its old quarters, almost in the heart of the City, to a more strictly suburban locality had long been under consideration; and its absolute removal in the end became almost a matter of sheer necessity, not only on account of the inconvenience in transacting business, but from the danger arising through the driving of cattle along the crowded streets of London. As we have mentioned in a previous volume,† so far back as 1836 a cattle-market was established at Islington, but its career seems to have been but of brief duration. The situation of this establishment was, perhaps, considered the best that could have been chosen for its purpose, lying open, as it did, to most of the great roads from the northern and eastern counties, from which the chief supply of cattle and sheep to the London market is derived, and communicating conveniently, by means of the New or City Road, with the greater part of the town, without driving through the heart of it, than any other would have done. As we have intimated, however, this market does not seem to have met with the success which was anticipated, and the old market was carried on with unabated vigour in the crowded pens of Smithfield Bars. Latterly, however, the nuisance engendered by the dirt and crowd, and the rush of horned cattle through the neighbouring streets, had become so intolerable, that the matter was taken in hand by the Corporation of London, and after considerable opposition from persons with "vested interests," the New Cattle Market was laid out, as we have stated above, at Copenhagen Fields, and it was opened by the Prince Consort in person, in June, 1855.

As regards the site, it was thought by many at the time that the market should have been placed at a greater distance from the City; but it is, nevertheless, a great improvement upon old Smithfield. In our account of Pentonville, in the volume above referred to, we have given a few details of the new cattle-market at Copenhagen Fields, but we may be pardoned for giving a more detailed description here. It forms an irregular quadrangle, and is all that could be desired in its architectural and general design. All the plans for drainage, so far as place is concerned, are said to be excellent; the space for the various animals is ample; water, &c., is conveniently at hand; and so good is the opportunity for general inspection, that much of the cruelty which was so justly a matter of complaint when the cattle market was held in Smithfield is avoided.

The open area of the market is partitioned off into divisions for the reception of all sorts of live stock, and is inclosed by metal railings, well worthy of notice for their artistic merit; indeed, ornament is not despised in the midst of all these very practical arrangements, for in those parts appropriated to cattle, sheep, &c., each central rail is ornamented with characteristic casts of the heads of oxen, sheep, pigs, &c., designed and modelled by Bell, the sculptor. In the centre of the inclosure is a lofty clock-tower, from which the bell gives notice of the commencement and close of the market; and around the base of this tower is a sort of rotunda—a twelve-sided structure—in which are the branch offices of several banks, railway companies, salesmen, telegraph companies, shops for the sale of chemicals, &c. This edifice is commonly called the Bank Building. The clerk of the market has also his office here, where, with the aid of his assistants, he is busily engaged in registering the receipts and delivery of animals. On ascending to the belfry, in the centre of the enclosure, and looking down, the geometrical arrangement of the pens and sheds presents a curious and agreeable appearance, and it will be at once seen that nearly all round the market space has been reserved for extension—a necessary consideration, when it is borne in mind that in half a century hence the population of the

* See Vol. II., p. 275. † See Vol. II., p. 282.

metropolis, if it goes on increasing at the rate of progress which it has shown since the formation of the market, may perhaps be doubled. The open space mentioned above will accommodate about 7,000 cattle, 42,000 sheep, and a proportionate number of calves and pigs; and the different pens and sheds, which run at right angles, are lettered and numbered. The departments for calves and pigs are covered in above by light, partially-glazed roofs, supported on iron columns, which serve at the same time as water-drains. At the four corners of the principal area of the market are taverns of large size, with stabling, &c., adjoining; and on the north side, standing upon part of the vacant space belonging to the market, is a neat red-brick building, ornamentally constructed, which serves as the Drovers' Institute. On the south and west sides are extensive "lairs" for the reception of such live stock as may not have been disposed of on market-days, or which may have arrived too soon. There are also store-houses for hay, corn, and other provender, and a small space for a dead-meat market. On the east side a large space of ground has been covered in with long ranges of slaughter-houses or *abattoirs*, constructed on the principle so generally exemplified in foreign cities. These buildings are very spacious, thoroughly ventilated, and supplied with water, machinery, and every other necessary convenience. By the erection of these *abattoirs*, the unpleasant practice of driving the cattle through the crowded streets of the metropolis has in a great measure been avoided; while the inconvenient and unsanitary practice of slaughtering animals in back slums and alleys, and in the midst of a large population, has now become almost a thing of the past.

Close to the market are stations for the reception of cattle from the lines of the Great Northern, the London and North-Western, and other railways, so that animals can be brought directly into the market by railway from almost all parts of the kingdom. This, indeed, is a great advantage upon the old system of bringing cattle to the metropolitan market, for it must be remembered that in former times it took five or six weeks to drive oxen and sheep from the north of Scotland to London, whereas they can now be brought from the same distance at far less cost—taking their condition, &c., into consideration—by train, in about a couple of days. Indeed, since the time when the market was first established here, there have been great changes in respect of the supply of animal food for the population of the metropolis. "Then," as we have already had occasion to observe, "most of the beasts and sheep converted into meat for sale in the shops of London butchers were brought to London alive, and then slaughtered by the retailers. With the development of our railway system, and the additions to the great main lines by extensions which brought them into the business parts of the metropolis, the dead-meat traffic from the provinces exhibited year by year a heavier tonnage." Most of the large meat salesmen of London are now represented in the shambles at the Cattle Market, and a considerable quantity of the cattle for metropolitan consumption is killed here almost as soon as it arrives: some, it is true, is still slaughtered in different parts of London, whilst others have to take a long journey before they become "food for the use of man."

Of late years, it is asserted, enormous strides have been made in the improvement of our cattle. The old big-boned stock has now been, in a great measure, replaced by the smaller, more symmetrical, but nevertheless greater meat-carrying, animal; consequently, in a large number of beasts offered now, the actual weight of meat is in reality much in excess of what it would have been a few years back; and not only that, but the quality is so much better that waste is reduced to a minimum. The year 1876 saw the introduction of a novel feature in the cattle trade, and one which it behoves the home breeders to watch narrowly if they do not wish to fall behind in the race. Consumers must have hailed with satisfaction the opening up of a new source of supply. America has now entered the field, and judging from the success which has attended the initiation of the scheme, she may be considered to have definitely and permanently taken up a position to compete with our graziers for the supply of live stock to the British public. Healthy competition is to be encouraged, as it must have the natural effect of stimulating us to fresh exertions, and if the large amount of success which has already attended us is to be taken as a fair criterion of our powers, possibly in the near future the general excellence of our cattle will be so advanced as to greatly excel all previous shows. Year by year cattle-rearing is becoming more and more of a science. Greater judgment is required in the selection of animals for breeding purposes, and increased care is necessary in their management. Well-bred and well-fed stock is now so plentiful that a second-rate animal stands no chance in the market. To expedite sales, good quality and condition must be guaranteed. The Americans are to be praised for the manner in which they placed so many good beasts in our market, apparently but little distressed with their long voyage. But this, perhaps, is a digression.

The market-days here are Mondays and Thursdays for cattle, sheep, and pigs, and Fridays for horses, donkeys, goats, &c.; but the great market of the year is that which is held a week or two before Christmas, when the sale of fat stock for consumption at the festive season takes place. The number of beasts exhibited for sale at Old Smithfield Market in 1844 was about 5,700; in 1854, the last year in which it was held there, it had reached upwards of 6,100. In the first Christmas market at Copenhagen Fields, the number of beasts offered for sale was 7,000; in 1863, as many as 10,300 were shown, which was almost double the number brought to market in 1868. Since the latter year the numbers have ranged from 6,300 to 7,600.

At a short distance from the north-west corner of the market, and standing at the corner of the Camden and Brecknock Roads, is the well-known tavern bearing the sign of the "Brecknock Arms," a sign which keeps in remembrance the second title of the Marquis Camden. In former times it vied with its near neighbour, the "White House," at Chalk Farm, as a rendezvous for the lovers of athletic exercises, in the shape of single-stick and wrestling matches, &c. The house stands on the very borders of Camden Town and Holloway; it is an attractive building, and at one time had some pleasant tea-gardens attached to it. In the summer of 1843, when it stood almost alone in the road, the place acquired considerable notoriety from a fatal duel which was fought there between Colonel Fawcett and Lieutenant Munro, in which the former was killed. The record of this duel possesses a twofold interest, from the fact of its being probably the last—certainly the last fatal one—that was ever fought in England, and also that the principal actors in it were not only brother officers, but also brothers-in-law—at all events, they had married two sisters. The origin of the quarrel was a hasty expression used by Colonel Fawcett respecting some family differences, which led his adversary, Lieutenant Munro, to send him a challenge. The duel came off early in the morning of Saturday, July 1, in a field in Maiden Lane (now Brecknock Road), adjoining the rifle-ground belonging to the "Brecknock." The colonel on being brought, dangerously wounded, to this inn, was refused admittance; so he was taken to the "Camden Arms," where he died on the following Monday. The coroner's jury on the inquest returned a verdict of wilful murder, not only against Lieutenant Munro, but against the seconds also. The latter, however, were acquitted, and Munro evaded the hands of justice by seeking refuge abroad; but four years afterwards he surrendered to take his trial at the Old Bailey. He was found guilty of wilful murder, and sentence of death was recorded against him. He was strongly recommended to mercy, and his sentence was afterwards commuted to twelve months' imprisonment.

At the top of Camden Road, at its junction with Holloway, stands the City Prison, or House of Correction for male and female prisoners sentenced at the Central Criminal Court, the Mansion House, or Guildhall Justice Rooms. It is also the Queen's and Debtors' Prison for London and Middlesex. This prison had its origin in the old Giltspur Street Compter, of which we have already given some particulars;* and on the demolition of the Whitecross Street Prison a few years later, the debtors confined there were removed hither. It was built in 1850, on land originally purchased by the Corporation as a cemetery, during the first visitation of the cholera in 1832, and it covers about ten acres. Its boundary walls are nearly twenty feet in height, and erected as it is in the castellated style, and standing on a conspicuous eminence, it presents a rather imposing appearance. It has some strongly fortified gateways, and is embattled throughout the extent of its radiating wings, which are six in number. The prisoners are employed in various ways, and the discipline is a mixture of the separate and associated systems. The architect of the building was Mr. J. B. Bunning, and the cost of its erection was about £105,000. It is fire-proof throughout; it is ventilated by a shaft nearly 150 feet high, and is supplied with water from an artesian well which is carried down into the chalk upwards of 300 feet. On either side of the gate-house are picturesque buildings of red brick with stone dressings, which serve as residences for the governor of the prison and the chaplain. The gateway tower itself is an imposing structure; like the main portion of the prison, it is embattled, and reminds one of the entrance to some grand old mediæval castle. Above the entrance gateway are the dwelling-rooms of the chief warder. In the rear of the gate-house is a spacious court-yard, on the farther side of which is the Gothic arched doorway of the prison. This part of the edifice is particularly grand and massive, having been built after a model of the principal front of Warwick Castle. On either side of the window above the doorway large painted griffins appear to be doing duty as sentinels, and over the door are some

* See Vol. II., p. 486.

bold machicolations. Stretching away to the right and left of the entrance are lofty wings; the former is used for female prisoners, and the latter for debtors, or rather—since imprisonment for debt has been abolished—for those persons who may be committed for contempt of court, non-payment of fines, &c. This wing was at first occupied by juvenile offenders, and at times as many as eighty or one hundred have been confined there at once; but such has been the diminution in crime of late years, owing to the establishment of reformatories and industrial schools, that the number is now very considerably diminished, rarely exceeding ten or twelve at one time.

Passing through the doorway, the visitor enters a spacious and lofty hall, or reception-room for prisoners, whence a broad flight of steps leads to a balcony at one end, and so on to a long corridor extending back to that part of the prison containing the cells. On the left of the hall is a room into which prisoners are first taken to be weighed, to be duly and properly described in a large book kept for that purpose, and to have their warrants of commitment checked. Here, too, are kept photographs of all the prisoners confined here, with all the details of the crimes duly set down to their account; these, combined with the entries in the book above mentioned, would doubtless furnish ample material for a biographical memoir of many a well-known criminal. These records are kept posted up, upon the "double-entry principle," in a ledger and also in a day-book; all particulars concerning the various prisoners—such as their names, ages, height, weight, colour of hair and eyes, and any peculiarity or malformation of their limbs—are duly set down in writing, so that little or no difficulty is experienced by those whose duty it is to keep these accounts, in finding out whether any criminal has been previously convicted, although he may have assumed a different name from that by which he (or she) was previously known. This mode of keeping accounts of offenders against the law was, in a great measure, brought to its present state of simple perfection by Mr. Agar, the chief warder of the prison, an official who, having risen to that position after many years' experience in the various details of prison-life, in the execution of his duty, while enforcing strict discipline, has at the same time endeavoured to blend the reformatory and industrial principles laid down by his superior officers, and to whom we are indebted for much of the information here given while acting as our *cicerone*. On either side of the corridor mentioned above are the various offices for the governor and the chief warder; also the doctor's room, the aldermen's committee-room, and the visitors' room. This last-mentioned apartment is divided in the centre by two partitions, the outer side of each being further subdivided into a series of small compartments. These compartments have an open aperture, facing each other, about six inches by twelve, and guarded by wire-work, through which the conversation is carried on between the prisoner and the visitor; in the intervening space between the two partitions a warder is on duty during the visiting time.

At the end of the corridor, a doorway leads at once into the centre of the prison. From this point the four principal wings radiate; they are lettered A, B, C, and D respectively. That on the left, which lies parallel with the "debtors' wing" mentioned above, is set apart for prisoners who have never before been convicted; in the next are confined, as far as practicable, tradesmen, mechanics, and persons who have hitherto filled a respectable position in life; the third wing is devoted to the reception of criminals who may have been convicted for petty offences; and the last, or D wing, serves as the receptacle for known old offenders. These wings are three storeys in height, and light iron galleries run round three sides of each, from which the cells are reached. For criminals there are 349 cells, 289 for males and 60 for females; and for "debtors" there are 60 cells, and four day-rooms. Provisions are raised to the different floors by lifts in the central hall. Each cell is about twelve feet long by seven feet wide, and is well lighted, warmed, and ventilated; and each is provided with every necessary for the convenience of its inmate. The chapel is a large and convenient apartment above the offices; it is so arranged that prisoners of each class, while they can see and be seen by the chaplain, cannot see one another; the male prisoners being arranged on a deep gallery, in four groups, as above distinguished, whilst the females are placed in a sort of transept on the north side of the communion-table, hid from the sight of their fellow-prisoners by a high partition, but, at the same time, able to see the clergyman, whose reading-desk is placed in the centre of a gallery on the east side of the chapel, the "debtors" having accommodation in a similar way on the south side; in the eastern gallery are seats for the governor, the chief warder, and other officers.

At the ends of the four wings above mentioned are the various work-rooms for mat-making, tailoring, shoemaking, and other trades, also the school, infirmaries, treadwheel, and dark cells. The whole of the water supply for the prison is pumped from the well above mentioned by the aid of the treadwheel. Brickmaking is largely carried on by the prisoners in the grounds at the rear. There are sufficient means for enforcing hard labour, according to the numbers sentenced; and prisoners are at all times under supervision. Prisoners are allowed to participate in the profits of their labour if they perform any over and above their task-work. This system, it is affirmed, makes the prisoners more industrious and attentive, prevents breaches of discipline, and enables them to earn their living on discharge. As we learn from the published report of the Commissioners of Prisons, issued in 1883, the average daily number of criminals in custody during the year was 680. The greatest number in the prison at any one time during the year was 759, and the least number during the same period was 593, the prisoners being exclusively males.

Holloway Prison was taken over by Government, on the Prisons' Act of 1877 coming into force. The prison is partially self-supporting, a considerable sum being realised annually by the employment of prisoners on such work as mat-making, brick-making, oakum-picking, shoe-making, tailoring, and other branches of industry. The hours of labour for the prisoners are from half-past five in the morning till eight in the evening, out of which time one hour is set aside for exercise, another hour for service in the chapel, and two hours for meals.

Since the passing of the above-mentioned Act, a new system of accounts has come into operation throughout the prisons generally. The perfecting of the whole system of the accounting machinery in so extensive a scheme must necessarily be a work of time and experience. At the suggestion of the Accounts Committee, a variety of changes have from time to time been introduced, having for their object, on the one hand, the improvement of the means of check, and, on the other, the abolition of all unnecessary detail. The total ordinary expenditure of Holloway Prison, including salaries to all officers, &c., is about £11,000, and the average annual cost per prisoner, without allowing for earnings of labour, is about £35.

Great danger, from a sanitary point of view, having arisen from the exceedingly dirty condition of a large number of the prisoners on their reception, the subject has been fully considered by the Commissioners of Prisons; and from their

CLAUDE DUVAL'S HOUSE, IN 1825. (*See page* 381.)

HIGHGATE, FROM UPPER HOLLOWAY. (*From Chatelain,* 1745.)

Report, above referred to, it is satisfactory to learn that steps are taken to remedy the evil, and that the clothing in which prisoners are received is disinfected by exposure to heat in a hot-air chamber, or stove, for the purpose of being thoroughly cleansed and purified; if it is found "utterly vile" it is destroyed, and other clothing is furnished to the prisoner on leaving.

With such a population as that which this place contains, it can hardly be supposed that the rules and regulations of the prison are not sometimes broken, or that the warders and other officials have at times some very refractory characters to deal with. That this is the case the reader may conclude on learning that during the year above mentioned recourse was had to irons and handcuffs in seven cases among the male criminals for prison offences; that eighty males and one female had to be placed in the solitary or dark cells; and 1,435 males and one female had to undergo punishment in the shape of a stoppage of diet.

"On several occasions," observes the writer on Prison Discipline in "Chambers' Encyclopædia," "grave abuses have been exposed by Parliamentary inquiries and otherwise, in the practice of prison discipline in this country. The exertions of John Howard, Mrs. Fry, and other investigators, awakened in the public mind the question, whether any practice in which the public interest was so much involved should be left to something like mere chance—to the negligence of local authorities, and the personal disposition of gaolers. The tendency lately has been to regulate prison discipline with extreme care. The public sometimes complain that too much pains is bestowed on it—that criminals are not worthy of having clean, well-ventilated apartments, wholesome food, skilful medical attendance, industrial training, and education, as they now have in this country. There are many arguments in favour of criminals being so treated, and the objections urged against such treatment are held, by those who are best acquainted with the subject, to be invalid; for it has never been maintained by any one that a course of crime has been commenced and pursued for the purpose of enjoying the advantages of imprisonment. Perhaps those who chiefly promoted the several prominent systems expected from them greater results in the shape of the reformation of criminals than any that have been obtained. If they have been disappointed in this, it can, at all events, be said that any prison in the now recognised system is no longer like the older prisons—an institution in which the young criminals advance into the rank of proficients, and the old improve each other's skill by mutual communication. The system now received is that of separation, so far as it is practicable. Two other systems were tried—the silent system and the solitary system. The former imposed entire silence among the prisoners even when assembled together; the latter endeavoured to accomplish their complete isolation from sight of or communication with their race. By the separate system, the criminals are prohibited from communicating with each other; but they are visited by various persons with whom intercourse is more likely to elevate than to debase—as chaplains, teachers, Scripture-readers, the superior officers of the prison, and those who have the external control over it."

It may be interesting to learn that the moral welfare of the inmates receives the greatest attention. A Bible, prayer-book, and hymn-book are placed at the disposal of every prisoner, besides books from the prison library. Two services are held in the chapel every Sunday, and one on Good Friday and Christmas Day; and prayers are read daily to the prisoners by the chaplain, who gives an address on Wednesdays and Fridays always, and frequently on other days a short exhortation. Prisoners not belonging to the Established Church have the privilege of being visited by ministers of their several communions. Uneducated male prisoners receive two hours' secular instruction weekly, in classes; and in special cases, individual instruction in their cells. The females receive four hours' instruction weekly in class, and have lessons in their cells also.

Opposite the gates of the City Prison, standing at the junction of Park Road and Camden Road, is the Camden Town Athenæum. This building, which was erected in 1871, we have described in a former chapter.*

Adjoining the above building, in the Camden Road, is the New Jerusalem Church, a handsome Gothic edifice, with a lofty spire; and at the eastern end of the road, at its junction with the Caledonian and Holloway Roads, stands the Holloway Congregational Chapel.

On the north-east side of the Holloway Road, and forming a continuation of Camden and Park Roads, is the Seven Sisters' Road, which leads to Finsbury Park, and so on to Tottenham, leaving the Holloway reservoir of the New River Company on the right side of the road. The "Seven Sisters" was the sign of an old public-house at Tottenham, in the front of which were planted seven elms in a circle, with a walnut-tree in the middle. They

* See *ante*, p. 315.

were upwards of 500 years old, and the tradition ran that a martyr had been burnt on the spot where they stood. The trees were more recently to be seen at the entrance of the village from Page Green; and when they died off, a few years ago, they were replaced by others. But we shall have more to say about them when we reach Tottenham. At a short distance beyond the Seven Sisters' Road is Holloway Hall, a large but plain modern edifice, used for concerts, lectures, and similar entertainments.

Passing northward along the Holloway Road, having on our left side Tufnell Park, Dartmouth Park, and other estates now being rapidly covered with buildings, and named after their respective ground-landlords, we next wend our way through Upper Holloway, a place, as we have shown in a previous volume,* at one time noted for its cheese-cakes.

The old "Half Moon" and the "Mother Red Cap" taverns, of which we have spoken in the volume referred to, have both been modernised, or, for the most part, rebuilt. The former house was struck by lightning about the year 1846. A view of the old tavern appears in the *Builder* of that date.

In Alfred Terrace, near the Upper Holloway station on the Midland Railway, is one of the numerous charitable institutions that abound in this neighbourhood, namely, St. Saviour's Hospital and Refuge for Women and Children. It was founded in 1864 for the purpose of rescuing young women from a life of sin, and providing a refuge for those fallen ones about to become mothers, as well as a home for their children; it is said to be the only institution of its kind. The hospital is wholly dependent on voluntary contributions. During the year ending March, 1876, 250 cases were relieved, the average number in the institution being seventy.

On the left-hand side of the road, just beyond the railway station, and near the foot of Highgate Hill, stands St. John's Church, a large brick building of the "Perpendicular" style of architecture, erected in 1828 from the designs of Sir Charles Barry. The church was one of those built under the auspices of the late Dr. Wilson, some time Vicar of Islington, and afterwards Bishop of Calcutta.

At the foot of Highgate Hill, and in the angle formed by its junction with the Archway Road, stands the Archway Tavern, a house which has long been used as the starting-point for the various lines of omnibuses, and more recently for the cars of the various tramway lines which run from that point.

In this neighbourhood, in former times, were the residences of a few families of distinction; notably among them were the Blounts, of whom we have already spoken. Howitt, in his "Northern Heights of London," says that "in Nelson's time there were some old houses which appeared to have belonged to persons of eminence, on the north side of the road at Upper Holloway. In one of them, which became the 'Crown' public-house, and which has long disappeared, there was a tradition that Cromwell had lived. Nelson doubts Cromwell ever having a house there, but thinks he might have visited his friend, Sir Arthur Haselrigge, who, undoubtedly, had a residence in Islington, as appears by the following entry in the journals of the House of Commons, May 21, 1664-5:—'Sir Arthur Haselrigge, by command of the House, related the circumstance of an assault made on him by the Earl of Stamford, and Henry Polton and Mathew Patsall, his servants, in the highway leading from Perpoole Lane, Clerkenwell, as he was peaceably riding from the House of Commons to his house in Islington, by striking him with a drawn sword, and other offensive instruments, and was enjoined to keep the peace, and not to send or receive a challenge.'"

Of the dangers of the roads, particularly in the northern suburbs, in the last century, we have already had occasion more than once to speak. Claude Duval, the dashing highwayman, as we have intimated in our account of Tyburn,† made Holloway one of the chief scenes of his predatory exploits. Of the house supposed to have been occupied by him in this neighbourhood we have spoken in our notice of the Hornsey Road.‡ Duval's Lane, branching from Holloway, within our grandfathers' memory, was so notoriously infested with highwaymen that few people would venture to peep into it even in mid-day. Another highwayman who infested Holloway and the back lanes of Islington, in the early part of the last century, was none other than the noted "Dick" Turpin. On the 22nd of May, 1737, he here robbed several persons in their coaches and chaises. One of the gentlemen so stopped signified to him that he had reigned a long time. Turpin replied, "'Tis no matter for that, I am not afraid of being taken by you; therefore, don't stand hesitating, but give me the gold."

It may be added that Holloway shares with

* See Vol. II., p. 274.

† See *ante*, p. 195.

‡ See Vol. II., p. 275.

Hornsey, Finchley, and Kentish Town the benefits of Sir Roger Cholmeley's benefaction as founder of the Grammar School at Highgate.

There is but little else to record in the way of historical memorabilia so far as Holloway is concerned. One fact, however, of some little literary interest must not be passed over by us here, for in Holloway there were living, as recently as the year 1735, Mary and Catherine Milton, the nieces of the poet, daughters of his brother, Sir Christopher. A note in Hazlitt's edition of Johnson's "Lives of the Poets" tells us that "at that time these ladies possessed a degree of health and strength as enabled them on Sundays and Prayer Days to walk a mile up the steep hill to Highgate Chapel. One of them was ninety-two at the time of her death. The parentage of these ladies," he adds, "was known to few persons, and their names were corrupted into 'Melton.'" We have incidentally mentioned, in a former part of this work,* another relative, and, indeed, a descendant of the poet, Elizabeth, daughter of the poet's daughter Deborah, who, having married Thomas Foster, a weaver in Spitalfields, kept "a petty grocer's or chandler's shop" in Holloway. She knew, however, little of her grandfather, and that little was not good; for she was chiefly eloquent on the poet's harshness towards his daughters, and his refusal to have them taught to write. In 1750 *Comus* was played for her benefit, which realised £130. Dr. Johnson wrote the prologue, which was spoken by Garrick himself, and Tonson was among the contributors. With this addition to their store she and her husband removed to Islington; and this is said to have been the greatest pecuniary benefit which Milton's family ever derived from his service of the Muses.

One of the oldest institutions at the foot of Highgate Hill, just where it slopes quietly down into Holloway, was a lazar-house, or hospital for lepers. The building stood as nearly as possible on the site of Salisbury Road, which was laid out about the year 1852. Stowe, in speaking of "leprous people and lazar-houses," enumerates certain lazar-houses "built without the city some good distance; to wit, the Lock without Southwark, in Kent Street; one other betwixt the Miles-end and Stratford, near Bow; one other at Kingsland, betwixt Shoreditch and Stoke Newington; and another at Knightsbridge, west from Charing Cross." There were, however, at least three or four others round London—namely, at Hammersmith, Finchley, and Ilford. Of that at Knightsbridge we have spoken in a former chapter.† The chapel of the hospital at Kingsland was pulled down in 1846. Stow, who rightly distinguishes between those lazar-houses provided for patients "without the city," and institutions not exclusively devoted to the purposes of the citizens, confines his notice to the first-named four: "These four," he says, "I have noted to be erected for the receipt of leprous people *sent out of the city*." But these houses were not wholly limited to sufferers from that disease. The accounts of St. Bartholomew's Hospital, about the middle of the sixteenth century, contain items of expenses incurred for the removal of general patients to all of them, including "this lazar-house at Holloway," the prevalence of leprosy having then considerably diminished. Leprosy was "the linenless disease." "This phrase," remarks Mr. W. Howitt, in his "Northern Heights of London," "denotes the true cause of leprosy—the wearing of woollen garments next the skin; for through the habit of not having these garments regularly changed and washed, but wearing them till saturated with perspiration, the skin becomes diseased. On the introduction of linen and more frequent washing this loathsome disease rapidly disappeared."

This house was, in one sense, a royal foundation, as we gather some particulars of it from Stow's remarks. He says, "Finally, I read that one William Pole, yeoman of the crown to King Edward IV., being stricken with a leprosy, was also desirous to build an hospital to the honour of God and St. Anthony, for the relief and harbouring of such leprous persons as were destitute in the kingdom, to the end they should not be offensive to others in their passing to and fro: for the which cause Edward IV. did by his charter, dated the [24th day of February, 1473, in the] twelfth of his reign, give unto the said William for ever a certain parcel of his land lying in his highway of Highgate and Holloway, within the county of Middlesex, containing sixty feet in length and thirty-four in breadth." The intention of William Pole was carried into effect; for, four years afterwards (1477), we find that the king gave and granted to Robert Wilson, who, although described in the grant as a saddler of London, yet appears to have been a disabled soldier, and to have served in the Wars of the Roses, and also to have been afflicted with leprosy: "The new lazar-house at Hygate, which we lately caused to be constructed by William Pole, not long since one of the yeomen of our crown, now deceased, to have and to hold the same

* See Vol. II., p. 268.

† See *ante*, p. 23.

house, with the appurtenances, of our gift and of our almoign, to the same Robert Wylson, for the term of his life, without any matter or account therefor to us to be yielded or paid." The next grant that occurs is in the fifth year of the reign of Henry VII., when John Gymnar and Katharine his wife have conferred upon them the "keepership (*custodiam*) of a certain hospital, with a certain chapel of St. Anthony, being between Highgate and Holwey (*sic*), in our county of Middlesex, to have and to enjoy the same keepership to the aforesaid John and Katharine during their lives, and the longest liver of them." No allusion to leprosy appears in this record, nor is the hospital even styled a lazar-house; from which it may be inferred that this dreadful disease was then declining, or else that it was designed to subserve more general purposes. We meet with no further records of appointments to this hospital till far into the reign of Henry VIII., when we find one under the Privy Seal, whereby one Simon Guyer had a grant for life of the "Spytyl Howse of Holowey, Middlesex." Perhaps, it has been suggested, the poverty of the institution, coupled with the decline of leprosy, may have rendered the appointment of little worth. That the institution was in some respects supported by "voluntary contributions," or offerings at the chapel of St. Anthony, is evidenced by a bequest in the will of William Cloudesley, of Islington, dated 13th of January, 1517: "Item, I bequeath to the poor lazars of Hyegate, to pray for me by name in their *bede role*, 6s. 8d."

A contributor to the *Gentleman's Magazine*, writing on the subject, remarks that in the reign of Queen Elizabeth the appointment to this hospital, if we may judge from the formality and length of the grant, was considered an object of emolument; for on the 23rd of March, 1565, the queen, "in consideration of his services in the wars of her progenitors, and in consideration of his age, gave and granted to William Storye, the governance (*gubernationem*) of our hospital or almshouse at Highgate, in our county of Middlesex, commonly called the poorhouse or hospital of Highgate, within the parish of Islington, with all its rights, members, and appurtenances, and also the keepership and governance of all the poor persons, from time to time in the same house being, to have, hold, and enjoy the keepership and governance of the hospital or house aforesaid, and of the paupers aforesaid, during his natural life, without account, or yielding, or paying any other thing therefor to us, our heirs or successors. Provided always, that the afore-named William Storye during his natural life shall find and provide for all the poor persons in the house aforesaid, from time to time being, victuals as other governors or keepers of the hospital or house aforesaid heretofore have from time to time been accustomed to do, and that he will repair, sustain, and maintain the said house in all necessary reparations so often as need or occasion shall require." From this it appears that the hospital had lost its character as a leper-house, as well as its religious associations; for the Reformation must have swept away Saint Anthony and all his belongings long before the date of the above appointment. However, in common parlance, it still retained its name of the "spittle-house" as well as that of a common poor-house; and, as late as 1605, an inmate (presumedly an infant) is described as "a lazar of our spital," in the parish register of St. Mary, at Islington, from the pages of which it may be gathered that the inmates of this institution were, at the end of the sixteenth and commencement of the seventeenth century, such as were subsequently provided for in parish workhouses. The keeper, ruler, or governor, was also commonly called the "guide," being in fact some person of medical education, or one whose previous pursuits may have qualified him for undertaking the duties of such a charge. Here are a few of the entries in the parish register of St. Mary, Islington, above referred to, some of which are curious:—

Thomas Patton was buried from the Spittle howse, the 24th Jan. 1582.

Ralph Buxton was buried from the Spitle howse on the 30 of October 1583.

Joane Bristowe, from the pore howse at Higate, was buried the 1 Oct. 1583.

William Storye, Gwyder of ye pore-howse, at Upper Holloway, was buried the 30th day of March, ao 1584.

Jerome Tedder was buried from the same howse the 23rd March 1584.

A pore man, from Spitle howse at Upper Holloway, was buried ye 15 June, 1584.

A dome child, from the Spittle howse at Upper Holloway, was buried the 30th July, 1576.

Anne, the daughter of Thomas Watson, guyde of the Spitle howse at Higate, was buried the 5th day of Sept. 1593.

A crisom childe from the Spittle howse was buried the 4th day of May, 1593.

Three children from the Spittle howse, sonnes of Arthur Hull, 13 Sept. 1603.

Anne Symonds from the Spittle howse, bd. 13 Sept. 1603.

Jerome Coxe, the Innocente, was buried from the Spitle howse, 15 Sept. 1603.

Elizabeth ——, a childe putt to the Spittle howse by Mr. Struggs the butcher, was buried the 5th day of October 1603.

Elizabeth Slatewell, lazer of our Spitle, was baptised at the Spittle the thirde day of Sept. 1605.

After Storey's death, in March, 1584, a similar

grant and appointment passed the great seal (July 14) in favour of John Randall, to whom, in consideration of his infirmity, was granted the keepership in precisely the same form; and about five years later he received a second grant and appointment in the same words as the former, but with the addition of "all and singular orchards, gardens, lands, tenements, meadows, pastures, and hereditaments whatsoever to the same almshouse belonging or appertaining, and together with the same house heretofore used, letten, or granted, or as part, parcel, or member of the said almshouse heretofore being, with all other rights, members," &c. With a proviso that if he should at any time abuse his keepership, or the poor persons aforesaid, or should not demean himself properly, the appointment should be void.

THE ROMAN ROAD, TUFNELL PARK, IN 1838.

In due course, the time came when all property of the Crown was carefully surveyed and sold to the best bidder; and, therefore, among them the old "Lazar House" passed into private hands. By deed of indenture enrolled in Chancery, in 1653, and made between William Steele, Esq., Recorder of London, Thomas Coke, William Bosserville, and others, being persons entrusted by an Act of Parliament with "the sale of all the manors and lands heretofore belonging to the late king of England, or queen, or prince," of the one part, and Ralph Harrison, Esq., of London, of the other part, it was witnessed, that in consideration of £130 10s. paid by the said Ralph Harrison, "they bargained and sold to him all that messuage or tenement, with the appurtenances, commonly called or known by the name of the 'Spittle House,' situate and being near the roadway leading from London, between Highgate and Holloway, within the parish of Islington, in the county of Middlesex; and all the houses, outhouses, yards, gardens, yard and curtilage, to the same belonging, or in any wise appertaining, containing in the whole by estimation two roods, be the same more or less, of the possessions of Charles Stuart, late King of England, and of the yearly value of nine pounds."

It is somewhat singular that after a lapse of two or three centuries another institution for dealing with a malady very similar in its loathsomeness to the leprosy should have been established almost upon the site of the old Lazar House; but so it is. About the year 1860 the Small-pox and Vaccination Hospital was removed hither from King's Cross, where, as we have already seen, it had previously stood upon the site now occupied by the Great Northern Railway Station.* On page 361 will be found an engraving of the original edifice at King's Cross previous to its demolition in the year 1850, or thereabouts. The present hospital is an attractive building standing upon its own grounds, slightly receding from the roadside, in Whittington Place. The institution was originally founded in 1746, "to receive and treat medically persons suffering from small-pox, and to vaccinate others." At present upwards of 200 in-patients are received each year, and 300 persons vaccinated; but in times when the small-pox is prevalent in the metropolis the resources of this hospital are taxed on a far larger scale.

WHITTINGTON'S STONE IN 1820. (*From an Original Sketch.*)

At the foot of the steep road which leads up Highgate Hill, almost in front of the site of the old Lazar House, and at the corner of Salisbury Road is a public-house rejoicing in the sign of the "Whittington Stone," the stone itself being at the edge of the pavement in front. The stone, an upright block about three feet high, resting upon a circular slab of stone, is enclosed by an iron railing painted and gilt, from which springs four uprights bearing a lamp. Upon the stone is the following inscription:—

* See Vol II., p. 278.

Whittington Stone.
Sir
Richard Whittington,
Thrice Lord Mayor
of London.
1397. Richard II.
1406. Henry IV.
1420. Henry V.
Sheriff in 1393.
This stone was restored,
The railing fixed, and lamp erected,
A.D. 1869.

It marks the spot on which, as we are told, stood the mile-stone at which the poor boy, Dick Whittington, is said to have rested when he listened to the peal of Bow Bells, and heard them, or fancied that he heard them, say—

"Turn again, Whittington,
Lord Mayor of London town."

It is stated in the *Ambulator* that the original stone, being broken in two pieces, was removed hence to the corner of Queen's Head Lane, in Lower Street, and placed against the posts to serve as curb-stones. A correspondent in the *Gentleman's Magazine*, for September, 1824, alluding to the story of Whittington, observes, "A stone at the foot of Highgate Hill was supposed to have been placed there by him, on the spot where he had heard Bow bells. It had a pavement around it of about eighteen feet in circumference. This stone remained till about 1795, when one S——, who was a parish officer of Islington, had it removed and sawn in two, and placed the halves on each side of Queen's Head Lane, in the Lower Street, Islington. The pavement he converted to his own use, and with it paved the yard of the 'Blue Last' public-house (now the 'Marlborough Head'), Islington." Whereupon, it is added, some of the parishioners expressing their dissatisfaction, Mr. Finch, a mason, was employed to place another stone in its stead, on which the inscription "Whittington's Stone" was cut. Another correspondent of the above-mentioned work also observed, "Some land, I have always been told, lying on the left-hand side on ascending the hill, and probably just behind the stone, is held on the tenure of keeping the stone in repair; and when the officious interference of S—— removed the *stone and pavement surrounding it*, a new one was immediately placed there of *smaller dimensions*, though it was never known by whom." "The substituted stone of 1795," writes a subsequent correspondent of Sylvanus Urban, "in fact, consisted of three stones, namely, the stone called Whittington's, and the two bases that were placed in order to keep the Whittington stone upright, and to render it as much in conformity with the ancient stone as circumstances would allow; but that this second Whittington stone was removed in May, 1821, by order of the churchwardens of St. Mary, at Islington, at a cost of £10 13s. 8d., when the present battered memorial was set up at the point where it now stands, and till this last summer it stood at the edge of the causeway or raised footpath in a bend of that side of the road, which evidently owed its irregular form from the room occupied by the preceding Whittington's Stone; but a straight pavement being now made, the stone at present stands between that and the site of the ancient curved causeway—in fact, between the footpath and the field, instead of fronting the high road as before. I may here mention that this field, in the ancient Court Rolls of the manor of St. Mary, Clerkenwell, is styled the Lazarett Field, and the Lazarcot Field, although in later documents it has obtained the name of the Blockhorse Field, an appellation evidently derived from the use to which the stone had been applied." *

In the year 1745 a print was published, from a drawing by Chatelain, in which the observations of the writer quoted above, showing a traditional connection between the field and the stone, are, to a certain extent, borne out. The engraving is a view of Highgate from Upper Holloway,† taken from a point a little below the place where Whittington's Stone stands, or stood, in which the stone appears as the base or plinth of a cross, with part of the pillar still remaining; and it has been suggested that what was formerly called Whittington's Stone was nothing else than a way-side cross in front of the chapel of St. Anthony, erected for the purpose of attracting the notice of the traveller to the unhappy objects of the hospital, and as a means of soliciting the alms of the charitable, and consequently erected long after the time when Whittington flourished. Considering that, according to a note of Mr. W. J. Thoms, in his edition of Stow's "London" (1842), the earliest narrative of Whittington's road-side adventure is to be found in a work published as late as 1612 (Johnson's "Crown Garland of Roses"), and that the existence of what served for a way-side seat can in every probability be shown to have been commenced long after Whittington had ended his prosperous days, we are afraid that we must dismiss not only the story of the "cat," but also the very pretty legend which shows the favourite hero of our childhood as making his escape from the drudgery to

* See *Gentleman's Magazine*, December, 1852.
† See *ante*, p. 379.

which he had been consigned in the house of the rich London merchant, Fitzwarren, and resting by the way-side cross at Holloway. Of Whittington's birth and parentage, of his benefactions to the City, and how he was *four* times Lord Mayor of London, we have already spoken in our chapter on "famous Lord Mayors;"* but as Holloway is so closely associated with him, not only from the popular legend above referred to, but also from the alms-houses or college which bear his name, to pass him over without any further mention would be like putting on the stage the play of *Hamlet* and at the same time omitting the character of the Prince of Denmark. We will therefore narrate what Grafton says about him, as quoted in Keightley's "Tales and Popular Fictions:"—"This year [1406] a worthy citizen of London, named Richard Whittington, mercer and alderman, was elected mayor of the said city, and bore that office three times. This worshipful man so bestowed his goods and substance to the honour of God, to the relief of the poor, and to the benefit of the common-weal, that he hath right well deserved to be registered in the book of fame. First, he erected one house, a church, in London, to be a house of prayer, and named the same after his own name, Whittington College, and so it remaineth to this day; and in the said church, beside certain priests and clerks, he placed a number of poor aged men and women, and builded for them houses and lodgings, and allowed unto them wood, coal, cloth, and weekly money, to their great relief and comfort. This man, also, at his own cost, builded the gate of London called Newgate, in the year of our Lord, 1422, which before was a most ugly and loathsome prison. He also builded more than half of Saint Bartholomew's Hospital, in West Smithfield, in London. Also he builded, of hard-stone, the beautiful library in the Grey Friars, in London, now called Christ's Hospital, standing in the north part of the cloister thereof, where in the walls his arms are graven in stone. He also builded, for the ease of the mayor of London, and his brethren, and of the worshipful citizens, at the solemn days of their assembly, a chapel adjoining to the Guildhall; to the intent they should ever, before they entered into any of their affairs, first go into the chapel, and, by prayer, call upon God for His assistance. And in the end, joining on the south side of the chapel, he builded for the City a library of stone, for the custody of their records and other books. He also builded a great part of the east end of Guildhall, beside many other good works that I know not. But among all others I will show unto you one very notable, which I received credibly by a writing of his own hand, which also he willed to be fixed as a schedule to his last will and testament. He willed and commanded his executors, as they would answer before God at the day of the resurrection of all flesh, that if they found any debtor of his that ought to him any money, if he were not, in their consciences, well worth *three times as much*, and also out of the debt of other men, and well able to pay, that then they should never demand it, for he clearly forgave it, and that they should put no man in suit for any debt due to him. *Look upon this, ye aldermen, for it is a glorious glass!*"

Stow informs us that Richard Whittington rebuilt the parish church of St. Michael Royal, and made a college of St. Spirit and St. Mary, with an almshouse, called God's House or Hospital, for thirteen poor men, who were to pray for the good estate of Richard Whittington, and of Alice his wife, their founders; and for Sir William Whittington, knight, and Dame Joan his wife; and for Hugh Fitzwarren, and Dame Malde his wife, the fathers and mothers of the said Richard Whittington, and Alice his wife; for King Richard the Second, Thomas of Woodstock, &c. Hence it clearly follows that Sir Richard Whittington never could have been a poor bare-legged boy; for it is here plainly stated that his father was a knight, no mean distinction in those days. Yet in every popular account of Whittington, he is said to have been born in very humble circumstances. This erroneous idea has evidently been owing to the popular legend of him and his cat, and it shows how fiction will occasionally drive Truth out of her domain. Such, then, is the real history of this renowned Lord Mayor; but tradition, we know, tells a very different tale. In the words of Whitehead in the "Legends of London:"—

"The music told him in the chime
That Whittington must 'turn again,'
And by good fortune high should climb,
And as the city's magnate reign.

"The boy, by listening, fancy-led,
Quickly arose from off the stone,
And proudly raised his hand and head,
While thus his fortunes were made known.

"'Thrice, thrice Lord Mayor,' the bells repeat,
'Then turn again yet, Whittington:'
Thus was it still—the fond deceit
Beguiled his fancy on and on.

"And 'Whittington, then turn again,'
He saw the city spires afar,
And through a cloud of hovering rain
He saw there shone one lonely star

* See Vol. I., p. 398.

"He hastened home, that rustic bell
Lulled him to sleep upon that night;
The pastoral dream, remembered well,
Lifted his hopes to high delight."

"In the whole of the legendary history," observes a writer in the *Saturday Magazine*, "there does not appear to be one single word of truth further than this—that the maiden name of Lady Whittington was Alice Fitzwarren. It would be extremely interesting to ascertain the exact age of the legend. Neither Grafton nor Holinshed, who copies him, says anything of the legendary history of Sir Richard; but the legend itself, as we now have it, must have been current in the reign of Elizabeth, for in the prologue to a play, written about 1613, the citizen says:—'Why could you not be contented, as well as others, with the legend of Whittington? or the life and death of Sir Thomas Gresham, with the building of the Royal Exchange? or the story of Queen Eleanor, with the rearing of London Bridge upon woolsacks?' The word *legend* in this case would seem to indicate the story of the cat; and we cannot, therefore, well assign it a later date than the sixteenth century. . . . . Whittington's cat," continues the writer above quoted, "has not escaped the shrewdness of those persons who have a wonderful inclination to discover a groundwork of historical truth in popular legends, for in some popular 'History of England,' the story has been *explained*, as it is called; and two or three country newspapers have copied the explanation with evident delight. Sir Richard Whittington was, it seems, the owner of a *ship* named the *Cat*, by his traffic in which he acquired the greater part of his wealth. It is not, however, quite clear that our worthy mercer was directly engaged in foreign traffic."

A few yards before the traveller reaches the Whittington Stone the road separates into two branches, of which the right-hand one is a modern cutting, known as the Archway Road, from its passing under Highgate Archway, of which we shall speak presently. On the right hand of this road, but within the limits of Upper Holloway, is situated Sir Richard Whittington's College, or almshouse, originally founded in the parish of St. Michael Paternoster, London, by the celebrated Lord Mayor,* who, in 1421, left the residue of his estate for the foundation and endowment of almshouses for thirteen poor people under the control of the Mercers' Company. William Howitt, in his "Northern Heights of London," thus relates the story of the foundation of these almshouses:—"The Mercers' Company having in hand £6,600 from the estates of Sir Richard Whittington, in 1822, commenced establishing a set of almshouses for twenty-four single women not having individually property to the amount of £30 a year. They receive a yearly stipend of £30 each, besides other gifts, with medical attendance and nurses in time of illness. At first the establishment was proposed to be erected on the main road up Highgate Hill, near to the Whittington's Stone; but the ground not being procurable, they built it in the Archway Road instead, but still near to the stone which commemorates the name of the founder. This is a much better situation, however, on account of its greater openness and retirement. The buildings are Gothic, of one storey, forming three sides of a quadrangle, having the area open to the road. In the centre of the main building is a chapel or oratory for the reading of daily prayers. The establishment has its tutor, or master, its matrons, nurses, gardener, gate-keeper, &c. It is a remarkably pleasant object viewed from the road, with its area embellished by a shrubbery and sloping lawn." The remarks of Mr. Howitt in censure of the "miserable philosophy, falsely called utilitarian," which would discourage the erection of such homes and retreats for our aged poor, are such as can be cordially endorsed by any one who has a heart to feel for the sufferings of others.

The high road in this neighbourhood, and the fields on either side, leading up the slopes of Highgate, must have presented a strange sight during the "great fire" of London, for John Evelyn tells us, in his "Diary," that many of the poorer citizens who had lost their all and their homes in the conflagration, encamped hereabouts. "I then went," he writes, under date Sept. 7th, 1666, "towards Islington and Highgate, where one might have seen some 200,000 people, of all ranks and degrees, dispersed and lying along by their heaps of what they could save from the fire, deploring their loss; and yet ready to perish for hunger and destitution, yet not asking one penny for relief, which to me seemed a stranger sight than any I had yet beheld."

The houses on the road which leads from the "Archway" Tavern up to Highgate are poor and mean, and inhabited by more than a fair proportion of laundresses and rag-shop keepers. But in the parts which lie off the road are many comfortable mansions, belonging, for the most part, to retired citizens. Few of them, however, are old enough to have a history.

---

* See Vol. II., p. 26.

CHAPTER XXX.

HIGHGATE.

"The sister hills that skirt Augusta's plain."—*Thomson's "Seasons."*

Population of Highgate at the Commencement of the Century—The Heights of Highgate—The Old Roadway—Erection of the Gate—Healthiness of the Locality—Growth of London Northwards—Highgate Hill—Roman Catholic Schools—St. Joseph's Retreat—"Father Ignatius"—The "Black Dog" Tavern—Highgate Infirmary—The "Old Crown" Tavern and Tea-gardens—Winchester Hall—Hornsey Lane—Highgate Archway—The Archway Road—The "Woodman" Tavern—The Alexandra Orphanage for Infants—Asylum of the Aged Pilgrims' Friend Society—Lauderdale House—Anecdote of Nell Gwynne—The Duchess of St. Albans—Andrew Marvell's Cottage—Cromwell House—Convalescent Hospital for Sick Children—Arundel House—The Flight of Arabella Stuart—Death of Lord Bacon—Fairseat, the Residence of Sir Sydney Waterlow.

HIGHGATE, though now it has gradually come to be recognised as a parish, is the name of a district, or hamlet, embracing sundry outlying portions of Hornsey, Islington, and St. Pancras; and it is treated as such not only by older writers, but by Lysons, in his "Environs of London." It must, however, have been an important hamlet of the parish, for the Parliamentary Return of the Population in 1801 assigns to Highgate no less than 299 out of the 429 inhabited houses in Hornsey.

It may well be styled one of the "northern heights" of London, for its summit is about 350 feet above the level of the Thames, or twenty-five feet higher than Hampstead Heath; and—passing into the region of poetry—Garth has suggested that the heights of Highgate might put in a claim to rivalry with the mountain in Greece which was the fabled haunt of the Muses—

"Or Highgate Hill with lofty Pindus vie."

We have already seen* that the old highway between London and Barnet ran from the east end of St. Pancras Church, and thence to Crouch End, leaving Highgate considerably to the left; but in 1386, or thereabouts, the Bishop of London consented, on account of the "deepnesse and dirtie" passage of that way, to allow a new road to be carried through his park at Highgate, at the same time imposing a toll on all carts, wagons, and pack-horses; and that for this purpose there was erected on the top of the hill the gate which for five hundred years has given its name to the locality. In fact, until the fourteenth century there would seem to have been no public road at all over the top of Highgate Hill into the midland and northern counties.

The great northern road was, no doubt, very largely frequented in the Middle Ages, because it was the only means of access to the shrine of St. Alban, which from the Saxon days was a constant object of pilgrimage. The road at that time, however, did not lie over the top of Highgate Hill, but wound round its eastern slope, by way of Crouch End and Muswell Hill; but we have reason to believe that the country hereabouts through which it passed was densely covered with forest-trees and brushwood, and was the home and haunt of all sorts of "beasts and game," among which Fitzjames enumerates "stags, bucks, boars, and wild bulls;" to which "wolves" also must be added, if Matthew Paris is to be believed, who states that owing to such beasts of prey the good pilgrims were often in imminent danger of their lives and property.

Norden tells us, in his "Speculum Britanniæ," that "the name is said to be derived from the High Gate, or Gate on the Hill, there having been from time immemorial the toll-gate of the Bishop of London on the summit. . . . . It is a hill over which is a passage, and at the top of the said hill is a gate through which all manner of passengers have their way; so the place taketh the name of the High Gate on the hill, which gate was erected at the alteration of the way which is on the east of Highgate. When the way was turned over the said hill to lead through the park of the Bishop of London, as it now doth, there was in regard thereof a tole raised upon such as passed that way with carriages. And for that no passenger should escape without paying tole, by reason of the wideness of the way, this gate was raised, through which, of necessity, all travellers pass." The road here described, no doubt, as Mr. Prickett suggests, in his "History of Highgate," formed a junction with the northern private road between the bishop's palace and the common at Finchley. Other writers, including Mr. James Thorne, F.S.A., in his "Handbook of the Environs of London," suggest that the name denotes simply the high road or passage, the word "gate" being used almost in the same sense as the "gatt" or "gate" of our eastern counties, and preserved in Danish in the Cattе*gatt*.

The gateway, which thus gave its name to the place, is described by Mr. Prickett, in his work above mentioned, as having been built, not at the

* See *ante*, p. 372.

side of the road, but across it, as an arch; and he tells us that it extended from the gate-house on the west side of the road to the old burying-ground on the east. "The rooms," he adds, "were approached by a staircase in the eastern buttress;" but they do not seem to have been of a very imposing character, as immediately before the removal of the gateway in 1769 they were occupied by a laundress. The cause of the removal of the arch was the fact of its crown being so low that even moderately laden stage-wagons could not pass under it; but whenever it was found that the wagon would not pass under the archway, the latter was taken round through a yard in the rear of the "Gate House Tavern," on the site afterwards covered by the Assembly Rooms. It may be added here that there was a corresponding gate at the other end of the episcopal demesne, at the "Spaniards," just at the north-east end of Hampstead Heath.

THE GATE-HOUSE, HIGHGATE, IN 1820. (*From an Original Sketch.*)

The newly-made way, no doubt, soon became the leading thoroughfare to the North of England, for we read that it was by way of Highgate that, in the reign of Mary, her sister, the Princess Elizabeth, was brought up to London from Ashridge, in Hertfordshire, to be imprisoned in the Tower.

Norden, whom we have quoted above, bears testimony to the healthiness of this locality. He writes: "Upon this hill is most pleasant dwelling, yet not so pleasant as healthful; for the expert inhabitants there report that divers who have long been visited by sickness not curable by 'physicke have in a short time repaired their health by that sweet salutary air." Indeed, the place is still proverbially healthy, and therefore has been chosen from time immemorial as the site of hospitals and other charitable institutions. It is worthy of note that Defoe, in his "History of the Plague," records not a single death from that fearful visitation having happened here, though it extended its ravages into and beyond the northern suburbs, and even as far as Watford and St. Albans; and his silence is corroborated by the fact that during the continuance of the plague only sixteen deaths are recorded in the register. Convalescent hospitals and infirmaries abound here in plenty; the earliest —except the Lazar House already mentioned—being a hospital for children, established on Highgate Hill in 1665.

HIGHGATE ARCHWAY GATE AND TAVERN IN 1825. (*From an Original Sketch.*)

So continuous are the lines of streets and roads between London and Highgate that the latter may now be reckoned quite as much a part of the great metropolis as Kensington or Chelsea. Indeed, not only have the prophetic lines of Mother Shipton, already quoted,* been to a certain extent verified, but the same, in a great measure, may be said of another curious prophecy, which appears in a collection of epigrams written by Thomas Freeman, a native of Gloucester, and published in 1614, under the title of "Rub and a Great Cast." The lines are headed "London Progresse," and run as follows:—

"Why how now Babell, whilt thou build?
The old Holborne, Charing-Cross, the Strand,
Are going to St. Giles'-in-the-Fields:
St. Katerine, she takes Wapping by the hand,
And Hogsdon will to Hy-gate ere 't be long.
London has got a great way from the streame;
I think she means to go to Islington,
To eat a dish of strawberries and creame.
The City's sure in progresse, I surmise,
Or going to revell it in some disorder
Without the walls, without the liberties,
Where she neede feare nor Mayor nor Recorder.
Well, say she do, 'twere pretty, yet 'tis pity,
A Middlesex Bailiff should arrest the citty."
Brayley's "Londiniana."

The whole of the above prediction may be said to be accomplished, with the exception of the union of Hoxton with Highgate; but even that is in a rapid course of fulfilment. This extension of "modern Babylon" has, no doubt, in a great measure been mainly brought about by the easy means of transit northwards by the various lines of railway running thitherward. Perhaps no line has felt so rapidly the increase of the suburban traffic as the Great Northern. "There was a time, indeed," says the *North Londoner*, "when, in common with all the leading railway companies, it rather threw cold water upon it. It has now at least 4,000 season-ticket holders, and trains call at Holloway and Finsbury Park almost continuously during the working hours of the day, and every train is crowded with passengers. Speculative builders have been very busy in the north of London, which was till lately regarded by them as a *terra incognita*. Highgate Hill was an insurmountable difficulty. Nor did the Archway Road, which at the time of its construction was held to be the eighth wonder of the world, do much to remove it. A heavy toll most materially interfered with the traffic, and thus the north of London was almost as free, and airy, and untrodden as it was when the Gunpowder Plot conspirators (we merely quote a local tradition) stood on the hill between Hampstead and Highgate to witness the speedy exit to the upper regions of the British Solomon and his Parliament; or as when Dick Turpin, from his far-famed oak on Finchley Common, an oak which still defies the battle and the breeze, was in the habit, immortalised by Dickens, of accosting the passing traveller, and by means of a couple of balls in his saddle prevailing on him to stop. A fatal blow was dealt to this state of things by the connection of the Great Northern with the Underground Railway. All at once London discovered that there were no more salubrious breezes, no greener fields, no more picturesque landscapes, no more stately trees than could be shown in the district of country bounded by Highgate Hill on one side and Barnet on the other. The green lanes of Hornsey and Southgate ceased to be such. The lucky landowner who had purchased his lands at sixty or seventy pounds an acre sold them at a thousand pounds an acre. Ancient mansions, where City aldermen had lived, where lord mayors had dined, where even monarchs had deigned to shine, were pulled down; broad parks were cut up into building lots; and instead we have semi-detached villas—much better, as a rule, to look at than to live in—advertised as being in the most healthy of all neighbourhoods, and within half an hour's ride of the City."

From Holloway the transition to Highgate, morally speaking, is very easy, though the actual ascent of the hill which leads up to its breezy heights is tolerably steep, in spite of the causeway, the handy-work of the amiable hermit whom we have mentioned in the previous chapter. We must accordingly commence it, starting from "Dick Whittington's Stone."

On both sides our road is fringed by small cottages, some standing in dreary and unkempt gardens, and mostly belonging to laundresses and small shopkeepers. Norden says that the maker of the causeway was not only a hermit, but "poor and infirm;" and Dr. Fuller writes that it was a double benefit, "providing water on the hill, where it was wanting, and cleanness in the valley, which before, especially in winter, was passed with great difficulty." And to come to a far more recent time, that of the reign of Queen Anne, we find it stated, so lately as 1714, in a preamble of an Act for erecting turnpikes and making other improvements on the roads about Islington, Highgate, &c., that the highways were very ruinous and almost impassable for the space of five months in the year. It may be added here that the hill is a

* See *ante*, p. 313.

mass of London clay, crowned with a layer of sand and gravel.

Ascending the hill, we pass, at some distance up on the left-hand side, the Roman Catholic schools for boys and girls, belonging to the Passionist Community. The schools are spacious buildings of light-coloured brick, with ornamental string-courses, &c.; and the porch is surmounted by a turret rising high above the roof. Higher up the hill, and standing at the corner of Dartmouth Park Hill—which, by the way, is a continuation of the York and Brecknock Roads, which we have noticed in the preceding chapter, and like them, was till very recently known as Maiden Lane—is a large monastic establishment, called St. Joseph's Retreat. It occupies the site of a house formerly known as the "Black Dog Inn," and the grounds which adjoined it, enclosing altogether an area of about six or seven acres. Mr. Howitt, in his "Northern Heights of London," published in 1869, says: "Of late years the Catholics have established a large chapel and house for priests on the hill descending towards Holloway, by the entrance to Maiden Lane, under the name of St. Joseph's Retreat. The greater part of the priests there being foreign, and with a predominance of Italians, speaks pretty plainly of its origin in the Propaganda; and it seems to have succeeded greatly, its chapel being generally crowded, especially by the Irish living in Upper Holloway. For many years the Roman Catholic Church has instituted a system of perpetual prayer, which is carried on by priests and nuns, whose especial office it is to pray for the conversion of England; and the strange tendency evinced, especially amongst the established clergy, towards a reversal of the Reformation, looks as though these ceaseless prayers were in course of being answered."

The first superior of this monastery was the Hon. and Rev. George Spencer, brother of the Lord Althorp of Reform celebrity, and himself formerly a beneficed clergyman of the Church of England, but who had thrown up his preferment on becoming convinced of the claims of the Roman Catholic Church. He had been educated at Eton and at Cambridge, and as the brother of a cabinet minister he enjoyed the fairest prospects of advancement in his profession; but these he abandoned in order to assume the cowl and coarse gown and open sandals of a Passionist, and adopted instead of his hereditary title the name of "Father Ignatius." He died in 1864. The author of the "Life of Father Ignatius" writes shortly before his death:—"In 1858 we procured the place in Highgate now known as St. Joseph's Retreat. Providence guided us to a most suitable position. Our rule prescribes that our houses shall be outside the town, and yet near enough for us to be of service in it. Highgate is wonderfully adapted to all the requisitions of our rule and constitution. Situated on the brow of a hill, it is far enough from the din and noise of London to be comparatively free from its turmoil, and yet sufficiently near for its citizens to come to our church. The grounds are enclosed by trees; a hospital at one end and two roads meeting at the other promise a freedom from intrusion and a continuance of the solitude which we now enjoy."

The new monastery, designed by Mr. Francis W. Tasker, and erected in 1875–6, was solemnly blessed and opened in the latter year by Cardinal Manning. It forms three sides of a square, and is built in a broad Italian style, after the fashion of the monastic buildings of the Romagna and of Central Italy. The walls are faced with white Suffolk bricks with stone dressings, and the roofs, which project in a remarkable manner, are covered with large Italian tiles. The building contains guests' rooms, a choir or private chapel for the "religious," a community-room, library, refectory, kitchen and kitchen-offices, and infirmary, with forty "cells" or rooms for the monks. The chapel is on the north side of the monastery, and adjoining it is a room for the meeting of the members of religious brotherhoods or confraternities connected with the Passionist order.

We have stated above that the Retreat occupies the site of the "Black Dog" tavern; and we may add here that the dog, in one of its various kinds, has always been a common sign in England, and of all dogs the "Black Dog" would appear to have been the favourite; possibly, it has been suggested, because it means the English terrier, a dog who once "had his day" among us, just as the Scotch terriers and the pugs have now. The "Black Dog" here may have been chosen on account of his being the constant companion of the drovers who frequented this house. But it is also possible that the "Black Dog" may have been of a more poetical character, and have derived its name, as Mr. Larwood suggests in his "History of Sign-boards," from "the canine spectre that still frightens the ignorant and fearful in our rural districts, just as the 'Dun Cow' and the Lambton 'Worm' were the terror of the people in the Midland counties and the North of England in former times."

Be this as it may, the Passionist fathers now own not only the old "Black Dog" and its out-premises, but the adjoining property, a private house and grounds, and on the conjoined properties have constructed a monastery and chapel in which all traces of the "Black Dog" will be thoroughly "exorcised" in the course of time, if, indeed, that has not been done already.

It should be explained that while the St. Joseph's Retreat enjoys a long frontage on the west side of Highgate Hill, it is bounded in the rear by the steep and narrow lane mentioned above. On the right-hand side, as we go down the lane, is the Highgate Infirmary, a large modern building, of nondescript architecture, affiliated to one of the large London parishes. It was originally constructed as the infirmary of the St. Pancras Union. The foundation-stone was laid, in the year 1869, by Sir William H. Wyatt, chairman of the Board of Guardians, and at the close of the following year the management of the building was transferred to the Board of Managers of the Central London Sick Asylum District, representing the following unions and parishes :—St. Pancras, St. Giles-in-the-Fields, St. George's, Bloomsbury, Strand Union, and Westminster Union. The building, which covers a large space of ground, commands, at the back, extensive views over the fields—or what is left of them unbuilt upon—in the direction of Kentish Town and Paddington. It was erected from the designs of Messrs. Giles and Biven, and forms a square, the north side of which is occupied by the governor's house and offices, the principal entrance, &c.

On the east side of Highgate Hill, opposite the Passionist Monastery, is the "Old Crown" public-house, with its tea-gardens. The grounds, which are cut up into arbours, are not very extensive, and, notwithstanding its sign, the building has altogether a modern appearance. It is a favourite resort for London holiday-makers.

Close by the grounds of the above establishment is a narrow thoroughfare, running in an eastward direction, known as Hornsey Lane, an ancient cross-road, forming, in this place, the boundary line of Islington parish.

At the opposite corner of the lane, and adjoining the grounds of Cromwell House, stands a large, old-fashioned, red-brick mansion, called Winchester Hall, for what reason, however, it will puzzle the antiquary to explain.

Along Hornsey Lane we now pass on our way to the famous Highgate Archway. This structure, at the time of its erection in 1813, was considered an engineering triumph, though it is insignificant enough by the side of more recent constructions. It is simply a bridge carried over a roadway, which, as we have already stated, strikes off on the right at the foot of Highgate Hill, and which was formed in order to avoid the steepness of the hill itself.

In cutting this road various fossil remains were found, consisting of shells, crabs, and lobsters, the teeth and vertebræ of sharks and other fish, thus proving that there was a time when the hill held a far lower level, or else that the whole valley of the Thames was one large arm of the sea. The construction of this roadway cost something like £13,000, which was, perhaps, rather a large sum, seeing that its length is only a little more than a mile.

Previous to the formation of the roadway and the erection of the arch, a scheme was projected to construct a tunnel through the London clay at Highgate Hill, for the purpose of making a more easy communication between Holloway and Finchley. The attempt, however, failed, and the result was the construction of the open cutting which forms the present Highgate Archway Road. The failure appears to have arisen, in a great measure, from the want of experience on the part of the engineers who had charge of the work, more especially as they had such very difficult and heavy ground to work in as the London clay. The tunnel was nearly completed when it fell in with a terrific crash, in April, 1812, fortunately before the workmen had commenced their labour for the day. The idea of forming the tunnel, therefore, was ultimately abandoned, and the present arch constructed in its stead. The toll which was levied upon passengers along this road was of its kind unique, for not only was a toll levied upon the drivers of horses and vehicles, but one penny was also levied upon foot passengers; sixpence was the toll upon every horse drawing. When the subject of tolls was before the House of Commons in 1861, the "Holyhead Road Act" was passed, and in this the Highgate Archway Road was included. It is not an ordinary turnpike-road, belonging, in fact, to a company. The company in 1861 owed the Consolidated Fund Loans £13,000; but by the Holyhead Road Act the debt and arrear of interest were compounded for a payment of £9,000, in instalments spread over fifteen years. Then the tolls were to cease, and this happy time having at length come round, the year 1876 saw Highgate freed from the impost. Within the previous twelve years more than one hundred turnpike-gates had been removed from the thoroughfares of the metropolis; and before many years are passed we may expect to see all the toll-gates in our suburbs superseded.

The archway thrown across this thoroughfare is about thirty-six feet high, and eighteen feet in width. It is formed of stone, flanked with substantial brick-work, and surmounted by three semi-arches, carrying a bridge sufficiently wide to allow of the transit of two carriages abreast. An open stone balustrade ranges along the top. The only useful purpose attained by the construction of this archway is the continuation of Hornsey Lane. It is recorded on a brass plate, fixed to the southern entrance to the structure, that the foundation-stone was laid by Edward Smith, Esq., on the 31st of October, 1812; and above the arch is cut in Roman capitals the following inscription:—"GEO. AVG. FRED. WALLIÆ. PR. REGIS. SCEPTRA. GERENTE." The archway presents itself as a pleasing object to the traveller either leaving or entering London by this road; and from the pathway of the bridge on a clear day is obtained an excellent view of the surrounding country, and of many buildings in the metropolis, among which St. Paul's Cathedral stands finely displayed.

At the top of the Archway Road, where it is cut by Southwood Lane, is the "Woodman" Inn, a favourite resort for Londoners. The "Woodman" is a common sign in rural villages, but not often to be met with so near to a large city. The sign-board is almost always a representation of Barker's picture, and evidently suggested by Cowper's charming description of a winter's morning in "The Task." The sign-board at Highgate formed, and possibly forms, no exception to the rule.

On the slope of the hill, and turning out of the Hornsey Lane, a little to the east of the archway, is Hazelville Road. In this road are two very useful charitable institutions, places for the reception of the two extremes of the great human family—namely, of infancy and old age. The first hospital, which we pass on our left in descending the hill, is a neat and unostentatious red-brick building, called the Alexandra Orphanage for Infants. It was founded in 1864, and is a branch of the Orphan Working School at Haverstock Hill, which we have already noticed.* The other building referred to stands nearer to the foot of the hill, and covers a large space of ground. This is the asylum of the Aged Pilgrims' Friend Society; an institution established in 1807 for giving life pensions of five, seven, and ten guineas per annum to the aged Christian poor of either sex, and of every denomination, who are not under three-score years of age. The present asylum, which was opened in 1871, forms three sides of a quadrangle, and, as originally constructed, consisted of a centre and two wings, which afforded one room and a small scullery for each of the eighty inmates, besides committee-rooms, warden and matron's rooms, a laundry, and a beautiful chapel; but in 1876 the two wings were lengthened, thus giving space for forty additional rooms. The buildings are of two storeys, with the chapel in the centre of the north side; the south side, which was originally unbuilt upon, has now in the centre a large hall in which lectures and addresses are sometimes given, and festive gatherings among the aged inmates take place. The hall is connected with the wings of the building on either side by a covered pathway. The spacious central enclosure, owing to the steepness of the ground, forms two or three grassy slopes and terraces, connected with each other by flights of steps.

Since the foundation of this institution, in 1807, it has been the means of relieving upwards of 3,600 aged persons, and has distributed amongst them the sum of upwards of £116,900. The total number of the recipients of the charity in 1876 was 1,038, and the annual sum expended in pensions alone is upwards of £6,200. The pensioners are each provided with a comfortable home, together with a sufficient supply of coals, with medical attendance when sick, and other comforts. One of the earliest and best friends of this institution was Mr. John Box, of Northampton Square, who, in addition to many other gifts, bequeathed a sum of £12,000 towards the funds for the new building.

Retracing our steps to the top of Highgate Hill, the first building which we notice, on our left, is Lauderdale House, now the Convalescent Home to St. Bartholomew's Hospital. The house, said to have been erected about the middle of the seventeenth century, was formerly the residence of the Earls of Lauderdale, and at one time the home of Nell Gwynne. It has about it nothing in the way of architectural details to attract the attention of the passer-by. A high wall and iron gates, with a garden on either side of the stone pathway to the door, separate it from the high road. It has two fronts—one facing the highway, and the other looking down south-eastward towards Holloway. It has on each front a very simple pediment, and has been stuccoed, probably in very recent times. The upper storey on the side of the house overlooking the garden projects somewhat from the lower, and is supported by a row of columns. Much of the old gardens remain, though doubtless considerably altered from what they were when "poor Nelly" occupied the mansion. "Those who remember this house some years since," writes Mr. Prickett, in his "History of Highgate," "describe the internal arrangements as bearing testimony to its antiquity; indeed, the entrance-hall, which is pro-

* See *ante*, p. 315.

bably still in its primitive state, the delightful terrace on the southern side, and the walls of the garden, thoroughly testify to the remnants of ancient days."

This house is supposed to have been built about the time of the restoration of Charles II., "one of whose most active and detestable ministers Lauderdale was from first to last," says William Howitt, in his "Northern Heights of London." "Nay," he continues, "we are assured that he was a prominent man, even in the reign of Charles I., in Scotland, being then a Covenanter, and one of those who sold Charles I. to the English army. He turned round completely under Charles II., and became one of the most frightful persecutors of the Covenanters that existed, he and Archbishop Sharpe going hand-in-hand in their diabolical cruelties. He was not only an English minister, a leading one of the celebrated Cabal Administration, but Lord-Deputy of Scotland, where nothing could surpass his cruelty but his rapacity. Lord Macaulay draws this portrait of him: 'Lauderdale, the tyrant deputy of Scotland at this period, loud and coarse both in mirth and anger, was, perhaps, under the outward show of boisterous frankness, the most dishonest man in the whole Cabal. He was accused of being deeply concerned in the sale of Charles I. to the English Parliament, and was, therefore, in the estimation of good Cavaliers, a traitor of a worse description than those who sat in the High Court of Justice. He often talked with noisy jocularity of the days when he was a canter and a rebel. He was now the chief instrument employed by the court in the work of forcing episcopacy on his reluctant countrymen; nor did he in that cause shrink from the unsparing use of the sword, the halter, and the boot. Yet those who knew him knew that thirty years had made no change in his real sentiments; that he still hated the memory of Charles I., and that he still preferred the Presbyterian form of government to any other.' If we add to this picture Carlyle's additional touch of 'his big red head,' we have a sufficient idea of this monster of a man as he was at that time at work in Scotland with his renegade comrade, Archbishop Sharpe, with their racks, thumbscrews, and iron boot in which they used to crush the legs of their victims with wedges, so vividly described by Sir Walter Scott in 'Old Mortality' and in the 'Tales of a Grandfather;' whilst their general, Turner, was pursuing the

LAUDERDALE HOUSE, IN 1820.

flying Covenanters to the mountains and morasses with fire and sword." To complete his military despotism, as any reader of English history will know, Lauderdale got an Act passed in Scotland for the raising of an army there which the king should have the right to march to any part of his dominions; his design being, as Bishop Burnet stated at the bar of the House of Commons, to have "an army of Scotch to keep down the English, and an army of Irish to keep down the Scotch." "When Lauderdale was in Scotland on this devil's business," continues Mr. Howitt, "no doubt his indulgent master used to borrow his house at Highgate for one of his troop of mistresses; and thus it was that we find pretty Nelly Gwynne flourishing directly under the nose of the indignant patriot Marvell. If Charles had picked his whole harem, however, he could not have found one of his ladies less obnoxious than 'poor Nelly.' As for Lucy Walters, the mother of the Duke of Monmouth, she was dead. Lady Castlemaine, Duchess of Cleveland, the mother of the Dukes of Grafton, was a bold and fiery dame that kept even the king in constant hot water. Madame de Querouaille, created Duchess of Portland, mother of the Dukes of Richmond, was the spy of Louis XIV. of France, sent expressly to keep Charles to his obedience, and for this service Louis gave her a French title and estate. Moll Davis, the rope-dancer, the mother of the Radclyffes, had lost her influence, and Miss Stewart had got married. Of all the tribe Nelly was the best; and yet Marvell launched some very sharp arrows at her. He describes Charles as he might be seen walking in the Lauderdale gardens as—

> 'Of a tall stature and of sable hue,
> Much like the son of Kish, that lofty grew;'

and Nelly, as 'that wench of orange and oyster,' in allusion to her original calling; for she commenced life by selling oysters about the streets, and then oranges at the theatres."

MARVELL'S HOUSE, 1825.

In our account of Pall Mall we have spoken at some length of Nell Gwynne's career at Court,* but a little of her history still remains to be told. Though of the lowest extraction, "her beauty, wit, and extreme good nature," writes the author above quoted, "seem to have made her friends amongst

* See Vol. IV., p. 126.

the actors; and her figure and loveliness raised her to the stage. There she attracted the dissolute monarch's attention by a merely ludicrous circumstance. At another theatre an actor had been introduced as 'Pistol' in a hat of extravagant dimensions. As this caused much merriment, Dryden caused Nelly to appear in a hat as large as a coach-wheel. The audience was vastly diverted, and the fancy of the king, who was present, was taken at once. But as she was already the mistress of Lord Buckhurst, Charles had to compound with him for the transfer of Nelly by an earldom, making him Earl of Middlesex. Nelly soon won the ascendancy among the mistresses of the king,

'Who never said a foolish thing,
And never did a wise one.'

"Though extremely gay and witty, poor Nell Gwynne seems never to have shown any hauteur in her elevation, nor any avarice, a prominent vice in some of her rivals. On the contrary, she made no secret of condemning her peculiar position, and was always ready to do a good action. Charles never endowed her with the wealth and titles that he lavished on other women, probably because she did not worry him; but on his death-bed his conscience pricked him for his neglect, and he said, 'Don't let poor Nelly starve!' a frail security against starvation for a king's mistress in a new court.

"The circumstance which connects her memory with Lauderdale House is the tradition that, as the king delayed to confer a title on her child, as he had done on the eldest son of others of his mistresses, she one day held the infant out of an upper window of Lauderdale House, and said, 'Unless you do something for your son, here he goes!' threatening to let him fall to the ground. On this Charles replied, 'Stop, Nelly; save the Earl of Burford!' Whether these words were said exactly as related or not, at all events, the story is very like one of Nell's lively sallies; and the child was created Earl of Burford, and afterwards Duke of St. Albans." An exquisite portrait of Nell Gwynne, by Sir Peter Lely, is in the National Portrait Gallery.

This story, it will be seen, differs somewhat from the version we have told in the volume above referred to, but the reader is at liberty to choose which he pleases as being the more reliable; perhaps the one is as truthful as the other. It is rather a curious coincidence that on the western slope of Highgate, a few years ago, lived a certain Duchess of St. Albans, the wife of one of Nell's descendants, who had also begun life, like her, as an actress. This was Miss Harriet Mellon, who married firstly Mr. Thomas Coutts, the banker, and who, after his death, became the wife of William Aubrey de Vere, ninth Duke of St. Albans. Of this lady we have spoken in our account of Piccadilly.* "Like Nelly," remarks Mr. Howitt, "she had, whether actress or duchess, a noble nature; and the inhabitants of Highgate still bear in memory her deeds of charity, as well as her splendid *fêtes* to royalty, in some of which, they say, she hired all the birds of the bird-dealers in London, and fixing their cages in the trees, made her grounds one great orchestra of Nature's music."

Lauderdale House of late years has been occupied as a private dwelling, and was for some time the residence of the first Lord Westbury before he reached the woolsack. In 1872 the house was converted to its present use, having been made over by its then owner, Sir Sydney Waterlow, to the governors of St. Bartholomew's Hospital for the purposes of a convalescent hospital, and it was opened in the above year as such by the Prince and Princess of Wales. The building contains beds for thirty-four patients. In its external appearance it is very slightly changed from what it must have been in the days of Lord Lauderdale and Nell Gwynne.

The house formerly occupied by Andrew Marvell, the poet and patriot, as we have intimated above, adjoins the grounds of Lauderdale House, on the north side. The house—or cottage, for it was scarcely anything more—was small, and, like Andrew Marvell himself, very unpretentious. It was built mainly of timber and plaster; and with its bay window, latticed doorway, and gabled roof, had about it all the attributes of the picturesque. In front were some old trees, and a convenient porch led to the door, in which its owner doubtless used to sit and look forth upon the road. Most of the old windows had been modernised, and other alterations had been made which the exigencies of tenancy had rendered necessary since Marvell's days; and in the end a large part of the building itself was demolished, all that remains being a few fragments of the lower portion of the walls, now profusely overgrown with ivy, and the stone steps leading up to the door. Of Andrew Marvell himself we have already had occasion to speak in our notices of the Strand and of St. Giles's Church.†

Mr. Samuel Carter Hall, in his "Pilgrimages to English Shrines," published in the year 1850, thus describes his visit to this interesting spot:—"We know nothing more invigorating than to breast the

* See Vol. IV., p. 280. † See Vol. III., pp. 64, 202.

breeze up a hill, with the bright clear sky above, and the crisp ground under foot. The wind of March is as pure champagne to a healthy constitution; and let mountain-men laugh as they will at Highgate Hill, it is no ordinary labour to climb it, and look down upon London from its height. Here, then, are we, once more, opposite the house where lived the satirist, the poet, and the incorruptible patriot. . . . The dwelling is evidently inhabited; the curtains in the deep windows as white as they were when we visited it some years previous to the visit concerning which we now write; and the garden is as neat as when in those days we asked permission to see the house, and we were answered by an elderly servant, who took in our message. An old gentleman came into the hall, invited us in, and presented us to his wife, a lady of more than middle age, and of that species of beauty depending upon expression, which it is not in the power of time to wither, because it is of the spirit rather than of the flesh; we also remembered a green parrot, in a fine cage, that talked a great deal, and was the only thing which seemed out of place in the house. We had been treated with much courtesy; and, emboldened by the memory of that kindness, we now again ascended the stone steps, unlatched the little gate, and knocked.

"Again we were received courteously and kindly by the lady whom we had formerly seen here; and again she blandly offered to show us the house. We went up a little winding stair, and into several neat, clean bedrooms, where everything was so old-fashioned that you could fancy Andrew Marvell was still its master.

"'Look out here,' said the old lady; 'here's a view! They say this was Andrew Marvell's closet where he wrote *sense;* but when he wrote *poetry*, he used to sit below in his garden. I have heard there is a private way under the road to Cromwell House opposite; but surely that could not be necessary. So good a man would not want to work in the dark; for he was a true lover of his country, and a brave man. My husband used to say that the patriots of those times were not like the patriots now; that then they acted for their country, now they talk about it! Alas! the days are passed when you could tell an Englishman from every other man, even by his gait, keeping the middle of the road, and straight on, as one who knew himself, and made others know him. I am sure a party of Roundheads, in their sober coats, high hats, and heavy boots, would have walked up Highgate Hill to visit Master Andrew Marvell with a different air from the young men of our own time—or of *their* own time, I should say—for *my* time is past, and *yours* is passing.'

"That was quite true; but there is no reason, we thought, why we should not look cheerfully towards the future, and pray that it may be a bright world for others, if not for ourselves; the greater our enjoyment in the contemplation of the happiness of our fellow-creatures, the nearer we approach to God.

"It was too damp for the old lady to venture into the garden; and, sweet and gentle as she was, both in mind and manner, we were glad to be alone. How pretty and peaceful the house looks from this spot. The snowdrops were quite up, and the yellow and purple tips of the crocuses were bursting through the ground in all directions. This, then, was the garden the poet loved so well, and to which he alludes so charmingly in his poem, where the nymph complains of the death of her fawn:—

> "'I have a garden of my own,
> But so with roses overgrown
> And lilies, that you would it guess
> To be a little wilderness.'

The garden seems in nothing changed; in fact, the entire appearance of the place is what it was in those glorious days when inhabited by the truest and the most unflinching patriot that ever sprang from the sterling stuff that Englishmen were made of in those wonder-working times. The genius of Andrew Marvell was as varied as it was remarkable; not only was he a tender and exquisite poet, but entitled to stand *facile princeps* as an incorruptible patriot, the best of controversialists, and the leading prose wit of England. We have always considered his as the first of the 'sprightly runnings' of that brilliant stream of wit, which will carry with it to the latest posterity the names of Swift, Steele, and Addison. Before Marvell's time, to be witty was to be strained, forced, and conceited; from him—whose memory consecrates that cottage—wit came sparkling forth, untouched by baser metal. It was worthy of him; its main feature was an open clearness. Detraction or jealousy cast no stain upon it; he turned aside, in the midst of an exalted panegyric to Oliver Cromwell, to say the finest things that ever were said of Charles I.

"Beneath Italian skies his immortal friendship with Milton seems to have commenced; it was of rapid growth, but was soon firmly established; they were, in many ways, kindred spirits, and their hopes for the after-destinies of England were alike. In 1653 Marvell returned to England, and during the eventful years that followed we can find no record of his strong and earnest thoughts, as they worked upwards into the arena of public life. One glorious fact we know, and all who honour virtue must feel its force, that in an age when wealth was never wanting to the unscrupulous, Marvell, a member of the popular and successful party, continued poor. Many of those years he is certain to have passed—

> "Under the destiny severe
> Of Fairfax, and the starry Vere,'

in the humble capacity of tutor of languages to their daughters. It was most likely during this period that he inhabited the cottage at Highgate, opposite to the house in which lived part of the family of Cromwell."

In 1657 he was introduced by Milton to Bradshaw, and shortly after became assistant-secretary, along with Milton, in the service of the Protector. After he had occupied this post for some time, he was chosen by the burgesses of his native town, Hull, as their representative in Parliament. "Whether under Cromwell or Charles," writes the author of the work quoted above, "he acted with such thorough honesty of purpose, and gave such satisfaction to his constituents, that they allowed him a handsome pension all the time he continued to represent them, which was till the day of his death."

Opposite the door of Marvell's house was the residence of General Ireton and his wife Bridget, the eldest daughter of Oliver Cromwell. The house, now the Convalescent Hospital for Sick Children, still bears the name of Cromwell House, and is thus described in Prickett's "History of Highgate:" "Cromwell House is supposed to have been built by the Protector, whose name it bears, about the year 1630, as a residence for General Ireton, who married his daughter, and was one of the commanders of his army; it is, however, said to have been the residence of Oliver Cromwell himself; but no mention is made, either in history or in his biography, of his having ever actually lived at Highgate. Tradition states there was a subterraneous passage from this house to the mansion house, which stood where the new church now stands, but of its reality no proof has hitherto been adduced. Cromwell House was evidently built and internally ornamented in accordance with the taste of its military occupant. The staircase, which is of handsome proportions, is richly decorated with oaken carved figures, supposed to have been those of persons in the general's army in their costume, and the balustrades are filled in with devices emblematical of warfare. On the ceiling of the drawing-room are the arms of General Ireton; this, and the ceilings of the other principal apartments, are enriched in conformity with the fashion of those days. The proportions of the noble rooms, as well as the brickwork in front, well deserve the notice and study of the antiquarian and the architect. From the platform on the top of the mansion may be seen a perfect panorama of the surrounding country."

The staircase above described is a remarkably striking and elegant specimen of internal decoration, broad and noble in its proportions; indeed, the woodwork of the house generally is everywhere equally bold and massive. There are some ceilings in the first storey which are in rich plaster-work, ornamented with the arms of Ireton, together with mouldings of fruit and flowers. The series of figures which stand upon the newels of the staircase are ten in number; they are about a foot in height, and represent the different soldiers of the Cromwellian army, from the fifer and drummer to the captain. It is stated that there were originally twelve of these figures, and that the missing two represented Cromwell and Ireton. In 1865, at which time Cromwell House was occupied as a boarding-school, the building was partially destroyed by fire, but it did not injure the staircase, or anything of historical interest. The building was thoroughly restored, and now presents much the same appearance that it did before. The front of the house is rather low, being only of two storeys, finished by a parapet, so that the roof, which is thrown backwards, adds but little to its elevation. It is of a solid and compact bright-red brickwork, and has a narrow cornice or entablature running the whole length of the front over each row of windows. Its doorway is arched, and faced with a portal of painted wood, in good keeping with the building. In front is a gateway, with solid square pillars surmounted by stone globes. At the lower end a lofty archway admits to the rear of the building. The mass of the mansion running backwards is extensive, and behind lies a portion, at least, of its ancient gardens and pleasure-grounds.

Ireton, one of the staunchest and bravest of Cromwell's generals, was a native of Attenborough, in Nottinghamshire, and, as stated above, married Bridget, the eldest daughter of Cromwell, who, after Ireton's death, became the wife of General Fleetwood. Ireton commanded the left wing of Cromwell's army at the battle of Naseby. He was constantly with the Protector when he was in treaty with King Charles, at Hampton Court, in 1647, and in the following year sat on the trial of the king, and voted heartily for his death. Morrice, in his "Life of Lord Orrery," declares that "Cromwell himself related that in 1647, at the time they were endeavouring to accommodate matters with the king, Ireton and he were informed that a scheme was laid for their destruction, and that they might convince themselves of it by intercepting a secret messenger of the king's, who would sleep that night at the 'Blue Boar,' in Holborn, and who carried his dispatches sewed up in the skirt of his saddle. Cromwell and Ireton, disguised as troopers, waited that evening, seized the saddle, and found letters of the king's to the queen in France, confirming all that they had heard. From that hour, convinced of Charles's incurable treachery, they resolved on his death." Clarendon describes Ireton as taciturn, reserved, and uncommunicative, and as being "never diverted from any resolution he had taken." Such was the son-in-law for whom this old mansion was built. There is a portrait of Ireton by Walker, in the National Portrait Gallery. It was formerly in the Lenthall collection.

In 1869, Cromwell House was taken as a convalescent establishment in connection with the Hospital for Sick Children, in Great Ormond Street, of which we have already spoken.* Fifty-two beds are here provided for the little ones on leaving the hospital. The number of admissions to the Convalescent Hospital, as we learn from the printed report of the committee of management, amounts annually to about 400, and the testimony of the medical officers who attend at Cromwell House, in reference to the progress of the children under treatment there, is of a most satisfactory character. The spacious play-ground attached to the house presents an attractive picture on fine days, when nearly all the children are out of doors at sport.

A little higher up the hill, or bank, as it is called, than Cromwell House, once stood Arundel House, the suburban residence of the Earls of Arundel. A few scattered remains of the old mansion and its garden-walls still exist. "Its site," says Mr. Howitt, in his "Northern Heights of London," "is now occupied by some modern houses, but its position may be known by its abutting on an old house, called Exeter House, probably also from its being once the abode of the Earls of Exeter; of this, however, there seems to be no record. It is not until towards the middle of the reign of James I. that we hear of the Earl of Arundel having a house at Highgate. When Norden wrote his 'Survey of Middlesex,' in 1596, the principal mansion was thus mentioned:—'Upon this hill is a most pleasant dwelling, yet not so pleasant as healthful, for the expert inhabitants there report that divers that have long been visited with sickness, not curable by physick, have in a short time repaired their health by that sweete salutarie air. At this place, —— Cornwalleys, Esquire, hath a very faire house, from which he may with great delight behold the stateley citie of London, Westminster, Greenwich, the famous river Thames, and the country towards the south very farre.' . . But the question here is, was the house of the Cornwallis family on what is called the Bank that which became the property of the Earl of Arundel? Lysons has remarked that there is in the Harleian Manuscripts a letter of Sir Thomas Cornwallis, dated 'Hygat, 16 July, 1587.' Sir Thomas, who was Treasurer of Calais, and Comptroller of the Household to Queen Mary, had been knighted as early as 1548, so that the Mr. Cornwallis mentioned by Norden in 1596, was doubtless his son William, who had taken up his residence there, while Sir Thomas had retired to his mansion at Brome, in Suffolk. It is said that this house at Highgate was visited by Queen Elizabeth in June, 1589. At all events, it is on record that the bell-ringers of St. Margaret's, Westminster, were paid 6d. on the 11th of June, when the Queen's Majesty came from Highgate.†

"It is certain, however, that James I., the year after his accession, visited the Cornwallises here. On May 1, 1604, the house was the scene of a splendid royal feast. Ben Jonson was employed to compose his dramatic interlude of *The Penates* for a private entertainment of the king and queen, given on Monday morning by Sir William Cornwallis, at his house at Highgate; and Sir Basil Brooke, of Madeley, in Shropshire, was knighted there at the same time. At the end of the same year, Sir Thomas Cornwallis died at his house at Brome—namely, on the 24th of December—aged eighty-five; and a writer in the *Gentleman's Magazine* for 1828 says that 'it is most probable that Sir William then removed to reside in the Suffolk mansion, as we hear no more of his family in Highgate. This residence, it is clear, from what has been already stated, had been the principal mansion in the place; and as we find the Earl of Arundel occupying a house of a similar description a few years later, whilst we have no information of his having erected one for himself, there appears reason to presume that it was the same mansion.'"

Arundel House numbers amongst its historical

* See Vol. IV., p. 560.

† Nichols's "Progresses of Queen Elizabeth," vol. iii., p. 30.

associations two very different and yet very interesting events: the flight from it of Arabella Stuart, in the reign of James I., and the death of the great Chancellor Bacon in the same reign, about fifteen years afterwards. The story of the early life of Arabella Stuart, and how she was held in dread by King James, is told by Mr. Howitt at some length in his work above mentioned, but it will be sufficient for our purpose to extract that portion of the narrative which has special reference to Arundel House:—

"James might have permitted Lady Arabella to marry, and dismissed his fears; but then, instead of a poor pusillanimous creature, he must have been a magnanimous one. She was dependent on the Crown for fortune, and the pension allowed her was miserably paid. Under these circumstances she met with an admirer of her early youth, William Seymour, second son of Lord Beauchamp, the eldest son of the Earl of Hertford. Their juvenile attachment was renewed, and the news of it flew to James, and greatly alarmed him. Seymour,

STAIRCASE OF CROMWELL HOUSE, 1876.

VIEW IN HIGHGATE CEMETERY.

on his side, was descended from Henry VII., and there were people who thought his claim better than James's, for Henry VIII. had settled the descent, in case of failure of his own issue, on his youngest sister, Mary, and her line, which was that of the Seymours. James fiercely reprimanded Seymour for presuming to ally himself with royal blood, though Seymour's was as royal as his own, and forbade them, on their allegiance, to contract a marriage without his permission. But Love laughed at James, as it is said to do at locksmiths, and in 1610 it was discovered that they were really married. James committed Seymour to the Tower, and Arabella to the custody of Sir Thomas Parry, in Lambeth; but not thinking her safe there, he determined to send her to Durham, in charge of the bishop of that see. Refusing to comply with this arbitrary and unjustifiable order, she was suddenly seized by officers in her bed, and was carried thus, shrieking and resisting, to the Thames, and rowed some distance up the river. She was then put into a carriage, and conveyed forcibly as far as Barnet. But by this time her agitation of mind had brought on a fever, and a physician called in declared that her life must be sacrificed by any attempt to carry her farther. After some demur, James consented to her being brought back as far as Highgate. The account says that she was conveyed to the house of a Mr. Conyers; tradition asserts this house to be that now called Arundel House. Probably it belonged to a Mr. Conyers before it became the property of the Earl of Arundel, whose it was when Lord Bacon was its guest, fifteen years afterwards. Lady Arabella had leave to stay here a month, and this term was extended to two months, which she made use of to establish a correspondence with her husband in the Tower, and to plan a scheme for their mutual escape. This plan was put into effect on June 3, 1611, the very day that the Bishop of Durham had set out northward to prepare for her reception."

How the Lady Arabella made her way, disguised as a man, down to Gravesend, where she expected to find her husband on board a French vessel, which was in waiting to receive them—how the captain, growing impatient, put to sea before Seymour's arrival; and how the latter engaged a collier, and was conveyed safe to Flanders—are all matters of history. Poor Arabella, as we read, was not so fortunate as her husband; for no sooner had the escape of the two prisoners become known than there was a fearful bustle and alarm at Court. A number of vessels of war dropped hastily down the Thames in pursuit, and another put out of the Downs. The latter intercepted the boat carrying Lady Arabella in the Calais roads, and after a sharp struggle the Frenchman struck, and gave up the fugitive. The poor distracted Arabella was carried back to London and committed to the Tower, exclaiming that she could bear her own fate, could she but be sure of the safety of her husband. Her grief and despair soon deprived her of her senses, and after a captivity of four years she died in the Tower, on September 27, 1615. Seymour, who was permitted to return to England after his wife's death, did not die till 1660, nearly half a century after the above romantic adventure.

Mr. Thorne, in his "Environs of London," states that it was from the house of Mr. Thomas Conyers, at East Barnet, that the Lady Arabella made her escape, and not from Arundel House, as generally stated by biographers and topographers; but the latter tradition is too firmly grounded at Highgate to be lost sight of here.

Of the death of Lord Bacon, which occurred at Arundel House in April, 1626, the following particulars are given by John Aubrey:—"The cause of his lordship's death," he writes, "was trying an experiment, as he was takeing the aire in the coach with Dr. Witherborne, a Scotch man, physitian to the king. Towards Highgate snow lay on the ground, and it came into my lord's thoughts why flesh might not be preserved in snow as in salt. They were resolved they would try the experiment. Presently they alighted out of the coach, and went into a poore woman's house at the bottome of Highgate Hill, and bought a hen, and made the woman exenterate it [take out the entrails], and then stuffed the bodie with snow, and my lord did help to doe it himself. The snow so chilled him that he immediately fell so ill, that he could not return to his lodgings (I suppose then at Gray's Inn), but went to the Earl of Arundel's house, at Highgate, where they put him into a good bed, warmed with a panne, but it was a dampe bed, that had not been layn in for about a yeare before, which gave him such a colde, that in two or three dayes, as I remember, he (Hobbes) told me he died of suffocation."

Bacon was attended in his last illness by his near relative, Sir Julius Cæsar, the Master of the Rolls, who was then grown so old that he was said to be "kept alive beyond Nature's course by the prayers of the many poor whom he daily relieved." At the dictation of the great ex-chancellor Sir Julius Cæsar wrote the following letter to Lord Arundel:—

"My very good Lord,—I was likely to have had the fortune of Caius Plinius the elder, who lost his life by trying an experiment about the burning of the mountain Vesuvius. For I also was desirous to try an experiment or two touching the conservation and induration of bodies. For the experiment itself, it succeeded remarkably well; but in the journey between Highgate and London I was taken with a fit of casting, as I know not whether it was the stone, or some surfeit, or cold, or, indeed, a touch of them all three. But when I came to your lordship's house, I was not able to go back, and therefore was forced to take up my lodging here, where your housekeeper is very careful and diligent about me, which I assure myself your lordship will not only pardon towards him, but think the better of him for it. For, indeed, your lordship's house was happy to me; and I kiss your noble hands for the welcome which I am sure you give me to it."

This letter shows that at the moment when he dictated it Bacon did not suppose himself to be on his death-bed; but he must have died in the arms of his friend, Sir Julius Cæsar, very shortly after the epistle was penned.

Arundel House was originally a mansion in the Elizabethan style, with spacious windows commanding a magnificent view of the surrounding country. It was partially pulled down in the year 1825, but the present building still bears the name, and the walls which are left standing of the old house bear evidences of great antiquity.

On the opposite side of the roadway, and adjoining the remains of Andrew Marvell's cottage, is Fairseat, the residence of Sir Sydney Waterlow, Treasurer of St. Bartholomew's Hospital, whose gift of Lauderdale House to that institution we have mentioned above. Sir Sydney Waterlow was Lord Mayor of London in 1872–3; he was representative of the county of Dumfries in the House of Commons, in 1868–9; and in 1874 he was returned as one of the members for the borough of Maidstone. His mansion here was named after that of his late father-in-law, Mr. William Hickson, of Fairseat, Wrotham, Kent.

At the back of Sir Sydney Waterlow's house, and covering a greater part of the slope of the hill looking towards Kentish Town, is Highgate Cemetery, of which we shall give a description in the following chapter.

We find but very scanty mention of this neighbourhood (and, indeed, of all the northern suburbs) in the Diaries of Pepys and Evelyn. The former, however, incidentally states, under date January, 1660–1, that Highgate was for two or three days the head-quarters of sundry "fanatiques at least 500 strong," who raised the standard of rebellion, avowing a belief that "the Lord Jesus would come here and reign presently." They appear to have routed the king's life-guards and train-bands, and to have killed twenty persons, before they were captured and their outbreak suppressed. Again, Pepys mentions the fact that on the 4th of August, 1664, he and a friend went to see a play at "the King's House," one of the best actors of which, named Clun, had been waylaid, and killed in a ditch by the roadside between Kentish Town and Highgate. The following day the little secretary and his cousin Joyce, mounted upon two horses which had been lent them for this purpose by Sir W. Warren, rode out of town towards Highgate, to inspect the scene of the murder.

CHAPTER XXXI.

HIGHGATE (*continued*).

"They bury their dead in the fairest suburb of the city."

Swaine's Lane—Traitors' Hill, or Parliament Hill—St. Anne's Church, Brookfield—Dr. Coysh—Highgate Cemetery—Arrangement of the Grounds—The Catacombs—A Stroll among the Tombs—Eminent Persons buried here—Stray Notes on Cemeteries—Sir William Ashurst's Mansion—Charles Mathews, the Actor—Anecdotes of Mathews—Ivy Cottage—Holly Lodge, the Residence of Lady Burdett-Coutts—Holly Village—Highgate Ponds—The "Fox and Crown" Public house—West Hill Lodge—The Hermitage.

Leaving the main street of Highgate by Dartmouth Park Road, of which we have made mention in the preceding chapter, and passing in a southwest direction, we find ourselves at the entrance of a narrow thoroughfare called Swaine's Lane (formerly Swine's Lane), which branches off from the Highgate Road just on the outskirts of Kentish Town. This lane runs along the base of that part of Highgate which was formerly known by the name of Traitors' Hill, from being the rendezvous, real or reputed, of the associates of Guy Fawkes. It is traditionally stated that it was upon this spot that the conspirators anxiously awaited the expected explosion on the 5th of November, 1605. It was called also Parliament Hill. "The more common tradition," says Mr. Thorne, "is that it was called Parliament Hill, from the Parliamentary generals having planted cannon on it for the defence of London." To the left of Swaine's Lane stands St. Anne's Church, Brookfield, a large and handsome edifice erected by a Miss Barnett to the memory of her brother. The fine peal of bells in the tower was the gift of Miss (since Lady) Burdett-Coutts. In Swaine's Lane lived the celebrated medical practitioner, Dr. Coysh, as is certified by the following memorandum from the Court Rolls of the Manor of Cantelowes:—"These very ancient copyhold premises were formerly in the possession and occupation of Dr. Elisha Coysh, who, at the time that the plague of London prevailed, in the year 1665–6, was very famed in his medical practice and advice in cases of that dreadful malady, and was much resorted to at this his copyhold residence (modernly called Swaine's Lane) formerly called Swine's Lane, Highgate." The house in which he resided has long since been pulled down, but a portion of the ancient garden wall is standing.

Passing up Swaine's Lane, we soon arrive at the entrance to Highgate Cemetery. This is a showy composition, in the pointed or Old English style; for the most part machicolated, and flanked with turrets and octagonal buttresses, pierced with windows or panelled, the former capped with cupolas and finials, and the latter surmounted with pinnacles and finials. In the centre is a Tudor-arched gateway, above which is an apartment, lighted at each end by a bay window; the roof terminating with two bold pointed gables, bearing in its centre an octangular bell-tower of two storeys, enriched with pinnacles, and surmounted with a cupola and finial. The right wing contains the lodge and clerk's office; and the left wing is appropriated as a chapel, the windows being filled with stained glass. The cemetery covered originally about twenty acres of ground on the southern slope of the hill, between the east and west bays; but a further extension has since been made, as we shall presently show. This cemetery possesses many natural beauties which are not enjoyed by any other rival of Père la Chaise in or out of London. The beauty of the situation would naturally lead to the supposition that it had been previously a park or garden of some nobleman; and such, indeed, we find to be the case, for in Mr. Prickett's "History of Highgate" it is stated that it comprises part of the grounds belonging to the mansion of Sir William Ashurst. The irregularity of the ground, here rising into a terrace, and there sinking into a valley, together with its many winding paths and its avenues of dark shrubs and evergreen trees, combine to impart to this hallowed spot a particularly charming effect.

The ground is the property of the London Cemetery Company, which was incorporated by Act of Parliament in 1839; and the cemetery itself was one of the first which was actually established by the Burial Act of 1835, which "rung the death-knell of intramural interments." The London Cemetery Company were among the early promoters of that reform which, as we have stated in our account of Kensal Green Cemetery,* was so long needed. It was founded by Mr. Stephen Geary, who also acted as architect to the Company, and who was buried here in 1854.

By the artist-like arrangement of the landscape gardener, Mr. Ramsey, the grounds are so disposed that they have the appearance of being twice their actual size; this effect is produced by circuitous roads, winding about the acclivity, and making the ascent more gradual. Besides the carriage road, the footpaths in all directions encircle the numerous plantations and flower-beds. On the left of the entrance is the chapel, a spacious and lofty building, well adapted and fitted up for its solemn purpose. The absence of all unnecessary ornament produces an effect of appropriate simplicity. A bier stands at the western end, which can be lowered through an aperture in the floor by hydraulic pressure. The object of this bier is to convey the coffin to a subterranean passage below, at the termination of the service in the chapel, so as to facilitate its conveyance to the new ground on the opposite side of the lane; for it may be here stated that the original ground being now fully occupied, an addition to the cemetery has been made, and this too is now being rapidly filled up. On leaving the chapel we pass by the lodge of the superintendent, and ascend a flight of broad stone steps which lead up towards the higher and more distant parts of the grounds. About half way up the hill, the roads gradually descend again to the entrance of a tunnel or passage, called the Egyptian Avenue. The angular aperture at the entrance of this avenue, with its heavy cornice, is embellished with the winged serpent and other Oriental ornaments; the Egyptian pillars and the well-proportioned obelisks that rise gracefully on each side of the entrance recall to the imagination the sepulchral temples at Thebes described by Belzoni. The group around this entrance is one of the most artistic points in the cemetery. The solemn grandeur of this portion of the cemetery is much heightened by the gloomy appearance of the avenue, which is one hundred feet long; but, as the road leading through it is a gentle ascent, the perspective effect makes it appear a much greater length. There are numerous square apartments, lined with stone, on each side

* See *ante*, p. 220.

of the avenue; these sepulchres are furnished with stone shelves, rising one above the other on three sides of the sepulchre, capable of containing twelve coffins, in addition to those which could be placed upon the floor. The doors of the sepulchres are of cast iron; they are ornamented with a funeral device of an inverted torch. At the termination of the avenue is a circular road five hundred feet in circumference; on each side of the road are sepulchres similar to those already described; the inner circle forms a large building, flat at the top, which is planted with flowers and shrubs; from the midst rises the magnificent cedar of Lebanon. The avenue, the sepulchres in the circles, with the elegant flights of steps leading to the upper ground of the cemetery, form a mass of building in the Egyptian style of architecture that, for extent and grandeur, is perhaps unequalled.

The lower parts of the grounds are striking, from their beauty of situation and tasteful arrangement; but the view of the upper plantations, on ascending from the sepulchre, is still more so. Here we have an architectural display of another character: a long range of catacombs, entered by Gothic doorways, and ornamented with buttresses, the whole surmounted with an elegant pierced parapet. Above the catacombs is a noble terrace, which communicates with the centre ground by an inclined plane and a flight of steps. The view from this terrace on a clear day is extensive and beautiful: the foreground is formed by the cemetery gardens, and the pleasure grounds of the suburban villas, beyond which are seen the spires, domes, and towers of the great metropolis, backed by the graceful sweep of the Surrey hills.

The Gothic Church of St. Michael at the summit of the hill, with its lofty spire rising from amid the surrounding trees, forms a prominent and interesting feature in the background as the cemetery is viewed from Swaine's Lane. On the upper terrace above-mentioned is the long range of Gothic catacombs, immediately beneath this church, presenting one of the most ingenious points of design in the architectural arrangement of the cemetery, of which the church appears to be an integral part, though such is not the case. We may here remark, *en passant*, that catacombs are found in most parts of the world. The catacombs of Rome, at a short distance from the city, are very extensive, and have evidently been used as burying places and as places of worship. The catacombs of Naples are cut under the hill called Corpo di Monte; the entrance into them is rendered horrible by a vast heap of skulls and bones, the remains of the victims of a plague which desolated Naples in the sixteenth century. At Palermo and at Syracuse there are similar recesses. In the island of Malta catacombs are found at Città Vecchia cut into the rock in which that old town stands. They occur again in the Greek islands of the Archipelago. At Milo there is a mountain completely honeycombed with them. In Egypt they occur in all parts of the country where there is rock; and in Peru, and in some other parts of South America, catacombs have been discovered.

"Many names familiar to London ears," writes the author of "Northern Heights," "present themselves on the tombs as you wander through this city of decomposition; and some of considerable distinction. The French have found their Montmartre or Père la Chaise; Germans, their Friedhof; and natives of countries still more distant lie scattered here and there. Perhaps no tomb has ever, as already stated, attracted so many thousand visitors as that of Tom Sayers, bearing on it his own portrait and that of his dog.* Wombwell, with his lion standing over him, as if to say, 'Well, he kept me cramped up for many years in his vans, but I have got him safe under my paw at last,' was, in its newness, a thing of much note; but it never had a charm for the pugnacious populace of London like the tomb of the great boxer."

It would be impossible, and indeed superfluous, to give here anything like a complete list of the various personages who have been buried in this cemetery; but a few of the most important may be mentioned.

Here reposes Michael Faraday, the celebrated chemist and philosopher,† already mentioned by us in our account of the Royal Institution, and of North Marylebone. He died in August, 1857, and, being a Sandemanian of the mystic school, he was laid in his grave without any service, not even a prayer or a hymn. H. Crabb Robinson, the friend of Coleridge, Goethe, Wordsworth, Lamb, Flaxman, and Clarkson, and the author of a most interesting Diary, who died in February, 1867, aged ninety-one, was here interred. Here, too, lie Mr. and Mrs. John Dickens, the father and mother of Charles Dickens, together with the latter's little daughter Dora. Sir John Gurney, a Baron of the Court of Exchequer, was buried here in 1845. Sir Thomas Joshua Platt, also a Baron of the same Court, who died in 1862, lies here; here too repose the remains of Judge Payne, and those of John Singleton Copley, Lord Lyndhurst, thrice Lord Chancellor of Great Britain, who was buried here in 1863.‡ Admiral Lord Radstock was interred here in 1857.

Of the artists buried in Highgate Cemetery, we

* See *ante*, p. 370. † See Vol. IV, p. 297, and *ante*, p. 260.
‡ See Vol. IV., p. 322.

may mention Charles Turner, A.R.A., who died in 1857; Alfred Edward Chalon, who died in 1860, brother of the more celebrated John James Chalon, who also was buried here in 1854. He was a native of Geneva, and achieved his greatest reputation as a portrait painter in water colours, and that mostly by his sketches of courtly and well-born ladies. Charles Joseph Hullmandel, the lithographic artist, was interred here in 1850. Sir William Ross, whom Sir Thomas Lawrence declared to be the first miniature painter of his day, and who died at an advanced age in 1860, lies buried here. Near to the upper entrance gate lie the remains of Mrs. Bartholomew, an artist of some note, the wife of Mr. Valentine Bartholomew, the celebrated flower painter, who also rests here. Two other Royal Academicians, Abraham Cooper and George Jones, lie buried here; the former died in 1868, and the latter in the following year.

Among persons of literary note whose remains are interred here we may notice Mr. Alaric A. Watts, editor of the "Literary Souvenir;" Pierce Egan, author of "Life in London," "Boxiana," "Life of an Actor," &c., the veteran historian of the ring, and sporting journalist; Mr. Samuel Lucas, managing proprietor of the *Morning Star;* Mr. W. J. Pinks, the Clerkenwell antiquary; Mr. James Kennedy, M.R.C.S., author of a "History of the Cholera," &c.; Mr. Joseph Guy, author of "Guy's Geography;" "George Eliot," the novelist; and Mr. George B. Sowerby, the naturalist, author of "The Genera of Recent and Fossil Shells." Here, too, is buried the Rev. Frederick Maurice, the Founder and Principal of the Working Men's College in Great Ormond Street, of which we have spoken in a previous volume;* and also the Rev. Dr. Hamilton, a well-known author, and the successor of the great Edward Irving.

CROMWELL HOUSE, HIGHGATE. (*See page* 400.)

Of the miscellaneous interments we may mention those of Mr. John Vandenhoff, the actor; Lillywhite, the well-known cricketer, whose marble monument, erected by the members of the Marylebone Cricket Club, is carved with a wicket struck by a ball, representing the great cricketer as "bowled out;" of Colonel Stodare, the famous conjuror; and Atcheler, the horse-slaughterer, or knacker, to the Queen, whose tomb is marked by a rudely-carved horse, to show, it may be supposed, his fondness for his profession.

* See Vol. IV., p. 560.

As an appendage to an account of Highgate Cemetery, which appeared in the *Mirror*, shortly after these grounds were laid out, the writer thus observes :—"The most ancient cemetery we are acquainted with, and perhaps the largest in the world, is that of Memphis; and of all the ancient burial places, no one conforms so nearly to modern ideas of cemeteries as that of Arles. In the early ages of Christianity the cemeteries were established without the cities, and upon the high roads, and dead bodies were prohibited from being brought into the churches; but this was afterwards abrogated by the Emperor Leo. The early Christians celebrated their religious rites in the cemeteries, upon the tombs of their martyrs. It was also in cemeteries that they built the first churches, of which the subterranean parts were catacombs. Naples and Pisa have cemeteries, which may be regarded as models, not only for good order and conveniency, but for the cultivation of the arts and the interest of humanity. That in Naples is composed of a large enclosure, having three hundred and sixty-five openings or sepulchres, answering to the days of the year, symmetrically arranged. The *campo-santo* or cemetery of Pisa is on every account worthy of attention. As a work of art, it is one of the first in which the classical style of architecture began to be revived in modern Europe. It was constructed by John of Pisa, being projected by Ubaldo, archbishop of Pisa, in 1200. The length of this cemetery is about 490 feet, its width 170, height 60, and its form rectangular. It contains fifty ships' freights of earth from Jerusalem, brought hither in 1288. The whole of the edifice is constructed of white marble. The galleries are ornamented with various specimens of early painting. Fine antique sarcophagi ornament the whole circumference, raised upon consoles, and placed upon a surbase, breast high. The Turks plant odoriferous shrubs in their cemeteries, which spread a salubrious fragrance, and purify the air. This custom is practised also in the Middlebourg and Society Islands."

IVY COTTAGE, HIGHGATE, 1825. (*See page* 411.)

Cemeteries, or public burial-grounds planted and laid out as gardens, around the metropolis, are a novelty of our time, although they were suggested just after the Great Fire in 1666, when Evelyn regretted that advantage had not been taken of that calamity to rid the city of its old burial places, and establish a necropolis without the walls. He deplores that "the churchyards had not been banished to the north walls of the city, where a grated inclosure, of competent breadth, for a mile in length, might have served for a universal cemetery to all the parishes, distinguished by the like separations, and with ample walks of trees; the walks adorned with monuments, inscriptions, and titles, apt for contemplation and memory of the defunct, and that wise and excellent law of the Twelve Tables restored and renewed."

As we have intimated above, Highgate was once important enough to possess a "Mansion House," the grounds of which now serve as a part of the cemetery. The house itself stood at the top of the hill, as nearly as possible on the site now occupied by St. Michael's Church. The mansion was built by Sir William Ashurst, Lord Mayor of London in 1694, and, as may be imagined from its situation, commanded a most delightful prospect over the county for many miles on the one side, and an extensive view of the metropolis on the other. The chestnut staircase is said to have been executed from a design by Inigo Jones; some of the rooms were hung with tapestry, and the chief doorway was richly carved. The extensive pleasure grounds are said to have been laid out with considerable taste. The house was for some years occupied by Sir Alan Chambre, one of the Justices of the Common Pleas, and he was almost the last person who used it as a private residence. It was taken down in 1830. The stone doorway, with the coat of arms, has been placed as an entry to a house in the High Street; and some other armorial bearings, carved in wood, which once adorned the mansion, found a depository in the house of a local antiquary.

In Millfield Lane, in the hamlet of Brookfield, not far west from the spot where now stands St. Anne's Church, was the suburban retreat of Charles Mathews, the comedian, to which we have briefly referred in our notice of Kentish Town.* This celebrated humourist was the son of a well-known theological bookseller in the Strand, and was born in 1776. He used to relate, in his own amusing way, that he had ascertained from his nurse that he was "a long, lanky, scraggy child, very good tempered, with a face that could by no means be called regular in features; in fact," she said, she "used to laugh frequently at the oddity of his countenance." He received his education at Merchant Taylor's School, where the peculiar manners of three brothers, schoolfellows, incited his first attempts at mimicry, and which he afterwards embodied in one of his "entertainments." He could just remember Macklin, the centenarian actor, on whom he called when quite a young man, in order to ask his advice as to going on the stage. The old man, though he had then seen his hundredth birthday, frightened him so much that he was glad to beat a retreat.

In 1803 Mathews first appeared on the London stage in Cumberland's *Jew*. From this time the fame of the comedian was fully established; "never had broad humour been better represented." In 1818 he first resolved on giving an "entertainment" by himself, and in that year first announced himself "At Home" at the English Opera House. His success was signal, and such as to induce the managers of Old Drury and Covent Garden to attempt to interdict the performances; but in this they failed.

His "At Home," as we learn from Crabb Robinson's "Diary," was very popular in 1822, when he represented Curran, Wilkes, and other statesmen of the reign of George III. His imitation of Lord Ellenborough, indeed, is stated to have been so remarkable, that he was rebuked for the perfection with which he practised his art. In 1819 and three following years he resumed these profitable labours in the "Trip to Paris," "Country Cousins," &c. These "entertainments" have been given in almost every theatre in the United Kingdom. His last appearance in the regular drama was in *Hamlet*, when Mr. Young took leave of the stage, in 1832.

Charles Mathews' sense of humour, however, was so strong, that he was unable to restrain himself at any time from comic speeches. It is said that his residence at the foot of Highgate Hill was so situated that the wind when high blew with great violence on the house, and at times very much alarmed Mrs. Mathews. "One night, after they had retired to rest," as the story is told by Mr. Palmer, in his "History of St. Pancras," "Mrs. Mathews was awakened by one of these sudden gales, which she bore for some time in silence; at last, dreadfully frightened, she awoke her husband, saying, 'Don't you hear the wind, Charley? Oh, dear, what shall I do?' 'Do?' said the only partially-awakened humourist; 'open the window, and give it a peppermint lozenge; that is the best thing for the wind.' At another time, and when on his death-bed, his attendant gave him in

* See *ante*, p. 321.

mistake, instead of his medicine, some ink from a phial which stood in its place. On discovering his error he exclaimed, 'Good heavens, Mathews, I have given you ink!' 'Never, ne-ver mind, my boy, ne-ver mind,' said the mimic, 'I'll—I'll swallow——bit—bit—of blotting-paper.' Fun was in him by nature, and to the last he could not be serious."

Charles Mathews has been styled "the Hogarth of the English stage." His pleasant thatched cottage here, which looked down on Kentish Town, and commanded a distant view of London, was, as he was wont to say, his "Tusculum." It rose, not unlike a country vicarage, in the midst of green lawns and flower-beds, and was adorned externally with trellis-work fancifully wreathed and overgrown with jasmine and honeysuckles. In the interior of this retired homestead was collected a more interesting museum of dramatic curiosities than ever was gathered together by the industry of one man. Here he would show to his friends, with pride and pleasure, relics of Garrick—a lock of his hair, the garter worn by him in *Richard III.*; and also his collection of theatrical engravings, autographs, and portraits now in the Garrick Club.*

"A merrier man,
Within the limit of becoming mirth,
I never spent an hour's talk withal.
His eye begat occasion for his wit,
For every object that the one did catch
The other turned to a mirth-moving jest."

Charles Mathews, whose wit and versatility were proverbial, died at Devonport, June 27th, 1835, immediately after his return from America. Mrs. Charles Mathews wrote her husband's memoirs after his decease.

A view of Ivy Cottage, as the residence of Charles Mathews was called, is given by Mr. Smith, in his "Historical and Literary Curiosities." With it is a ground-plan, showing the apartments devoted to his theatrical picture-gallery, and the arrangement of his portraits, now in the possession of the Garrick Club. Among the treasures of the house also was the casket made out of Shakespeare's mulberry-tree at Stratford-on-Avon, in which the freedom of that town was presented to Garrick, on the occasion of his jubilee, in 1769. A sketch of this is also given in the same volume.

Holly Lodge, the residence of Lady Burdett-Coutts, stands in its own extensive grounds on Highgate Rise, overlooking Brookfield Church, Millfield Lane, and the famous Highgate Ponds, which lie at the foot of the south-western slope of the hill. The house—formerly called Hollybush Lodge—was purchased by Mr. Thomas Coutts, the well-known banker, of whom we have spoken in our account of Piccadilly,† and it was bequeathed by him, with his immense property, to his widow, who afterwards married the Duke of St. Albans. On her decease, in 1837, it was left, with the great bulk of her fortune, amounting to nearly £2,000,000, to Miss Angela Burdett, a daughter of Sir Francis Burdett, the popular M.P. for Westminster, who thereupon assumed the additional name of Coutts. As we have intimated in the chapter above referred to, the extensive power of benefiting society and her fellow-creatures, which devolved upon her with this bequest, was not lost sight of by its possessor, and her charities are known to have been most extensive. Amongst the chief of these have been the endowment of a bishopric at Adelaide, in South Australia, and another at Victoria, in British Columbia; also the foundation and endowment of a handsome church and schools in Westminster in 1847, and the erection of a church at Carlisle in 1864. Besides the above, she has been also a large contributor to a variety of religious and charitable institutions in London—churches, schools, reformatories, penitentiaries, drinking-fountains, Columbia Market, model lodging-houses, &c. Miss Burdett-Coutts also exercised her pen, as well as her purse, in mitigating and relieving dumb animals and the feathered tribe from the suffering to which they are often subjected, having written largely against cruelty to dumb creatures. In recognition of her large-heartedness she was, in the year 1871, raised to the peerage as Baroness Burdett-Coutts.

Holly Village, of which we have already spoken, stands on the southern side of the pleasure-grounds of Holly Lodge. It was built about the year 1845 by Lady Burdett-Coutts, as homes for families of the upper middle class. They comprise a group of about ten cottages, erected to add picturesque and ornamental features to the surroundings of Holly Lodge, and are surrounded by trim and well-kept gardens. They were also intended, in the first instance, to provide cottage accommodation of a superior description for the workpeople on the estate; this idea, however, was abandoned, and the houses are now occupied by a higher class in the social scale. The whole village has been erected with an amount of care and finish such as is seldom bestowed on work of this description, or even work of a much more pretentious kind. Some of the houses are single, and some comprise

* See Vol. III., p. 263.

† See Vol. IV., p. 280.

two dwellings. They are built of yellow, white, and moulded brick, some with stone dressings. Although bearing a general resemblance, and in one or two instances arranged as corresponding pairs, they all differ more or less in form, and considerably in the details. All of them have a quiet elegance that is very uncommon in buildings of their class. The entrance is rather elaborately adorned with two carved statues of females, holding a lamb and a dove; and there is some pretty carving elsewhere. Mr. Darbishire was the architect of this model village.

The ponds mentioned above are on the estate of the Earl of Mansfield, and lie below Caen Wood, in the fields leading from Highgate Road to Hampstead, between Charles Mathews' house and Traitors' Hill. In the summer season they are the resort of thousands of Londoners, whilst the boys fish in them for tadpoles and sticklebats, or sail miniature boats on their surface. The ponds are very deep, and many a poor fellow has been drowned in them, some by accident, and more, it is to be feared, by suicide. About the year 1869 these ponds were leased to the Hampstead Waterworks Company, which has since become incorporated with the New River Company. These ponds, for a long time, supplied a considerable portion of the parish with water.

Nearly on the brow of the West Hill, a little above the house and grounds of Lady Burdett-Coutts, as we ascend towards the Grove and the town, we notice a roadside inn, of a retired and sequestered aspect, rejoicing in the name of the "Fox and Crown." It bears, however, on its front the royal arms, conspicuously painted, with a notice to the effect that "this coat of arms is a grant from Queen Victoria, for services rendered to Her Majesty when in danger travelling down this hill," and dated a few days after her accession. Some accident, it appears, happened to one of the wheels of the royal carriage, and the landlord had the good luck to stop the horses, and send for a wheelwright to set matters straight, accommodating Her Majesty with a seat in his house whilst the repairs were being executed. The event, if it did not turn the head of Boniface, brought him no luck, for he died heart-broken, the only advantage which he reaped from the adventure being, it is said, the right of setting up the lion and unicorn with the crown.

On West Hill, immediately below the "Fox and Crown," stands a rustic house, at right angles to the road, called West Hill Lodge. This was occupied for many years by William and Mary Howitt, who wrote here many of the books by which their names will be hereafter remembered. Of these we may mention "The Ruined Castles and Abbeys of Great Britain and Ireland," the "Illustrated History of England," "History of the Supernatural in all Ages and Nations," "Visits to Remarkable Places, Old Halls, and Battle Fields;" and last, not least, the "Northern Heights of London." Another residence on West Hill, a little above the entrance to Millfield Lane, was called the Hermitage, of which the Howitts were the last occupants. It stood enclosed by tall trees, and adjoining it was a still smaller tenement, which was said to be the "real and original Hermitage." It is thus described by Mr. Howitt:—"It consisted only of one small low room, with a chamber over it, reached by an outside rustic gallery. The whole of this hermitage was covered with ivy, evidently of a very ancient growth, as shown by the largeness of its stems and boughs, and the prodigality of its foliage. In fact, it looked like one great mass of ivy. What was the origin of the place, or why it acquired the name of the Hermitage, does not appear; but being its last tenant, I found that its succession of inhabitants had been a numerous one, and that it was connected with some curious histories. Some dark tragedies had occurred there. One of its tenants was a Sir Wallis Porter, who was an associate of the Prince Regent. Here the Prince used to come frequently to gamble with Sir Wallis. This hermitage, hidden by the tall surrounding trees, chiefly umbrageous elms, and by the huge ivy growth, seemed a place well concealed for the orgies carried on within it. The ceiling of the room which they used was painted with naked figures in the French style, and there they could both play as deeply and carouse as jovially as they pleased. But the end of Sir Wallis was that of many another gamester and wassailer. Probably his princely companion, and *his* companions, both drained the purse as well as the cellar of Sir Wallis, for he put an end to his existence there, as reported, by shooting himself.

"There was a pleasanter legend of Lord Nelson, when a boy, being once there, and climbing a very tall ash-tree by the roadside, which therefore went by the name of 'Nelson's tree,' till it went the way of all trees—to the timber-yard. It was reported, too, that Fauntleroy, the forger, when the officers of justice were in quest of him, concealed himself for a time at this hermitage." The old Hermitage, however, with its quaint buildings, its secluded lawn, and its towering trees, disappeared about the year 1860, and on its site a terrace of houses has been erected

CHAPTER XXXII.

HIGHGATE (*continued*).

"—— Many to the steep of Highgate hie;
Ask, ye Bœotian shades! the reason why?
'Tis to the worship of the solemn Horn,
Grasped in the holy hand of Mystery,
In whose dread name both men and maids are sworn,
And consecrate the oath with draught and dance till morn." —*Byron.*

Charles Knight—Sir John Wollaston—The Custom of "Swearing on the Horns"—Mr. Mark Boyd's Reminiscence of this Curious Ceremonial—A Poetical Version of the Proceedings—Old Taverns at Highgate—The "Angel Inn"—The Sunday Ordinary—A Touching Story—The Chapel and School of Highgate—Tomb of Coleridge, the Poet—Sir Roger Cholmeley, the Founder of the Grammar School—Southwood Lane—The Almshouses—Park House—St. Michael's Church—Tablet erected to Coleridge—Fitzroy House—Mrs. Caroline Chisholm—Dr. Sacheverel—Dorchester House—Coleridge's Residence—The Grove—Anecdote of Hogarth—Sir John Hawkins' House—A Proclamation in the Time of Henry VIII.—North Hill—The "Bull Inn."

RETURNING once more to the main street of the village—"this romantic rather than picturesque village," as Crabb Robinson calls it in his "Diary"—we resume our perambulation, starting from Arundel House, of which we have given an account in an earlier chapter.*

A small house close by the site of Arundel House was for many years the residence of Mr. Charles Knight, whose name is well known in connection with popular literature.

A little to the north of this house, but standing back from the high road, was the mansion of Sir John Wollaston, the founder of some almshouses in Southwood Lane, which we shall presently notice. Sir John Wollaston, we may here remark, was at one time Lord Mayor of London, and held several appointments of trust in the City. He died in the year 1658, and was buried in the old chapel of Highgate.

The main street of the village, although so near to London, has about it that appearance of quietude and sleepiness which one is accustomed to meet with in villages miles away from the busy metropolis; and like most other villages, the number of its public-houses, as compared with other places of business, is somewhat remarkable. In 1826 there were, in Highgate, no less than nineteen licensed taverns, of which Hone, in his "Every-day Book," gives the signs. In former times a curious old custom prevailed at these public-houses, which has been the means of giving a little gentle merriment to many generations of the citizens of London, but is now only remembered as a thing of the past. It was a sort of burlesque performance, presided over by "mine host," in which the visitor, whoever he might be, was expected to take an oath, which was duly administered to him, and was familiarly called "swearing on the horns." "No one," writes Mr. Samuel Palmer, "ever hears of this hamlet without at once referring to it:—

'It's a custom at Highgate, that all who go through,
Must be sworn on the horns, sir; and so, sir, must you.
Bring the horns, shut the door; now, sir, take off your hat,
When you come here again, don't forget to mind *that.*'

A few years ago it was usual all over the kingdom to ask, 'Have you been sworn at Highgate?' And if any person in conversation laid an emphasis more than usual on the demonstrative pronoun *that*, it was sure to elicit the inquiry. Some sixty years ago upwards of eighty stage-coaches would stop every day at the 'Red Lion' inn, and out of every five passengers three were sworn. So soon as the coach drew up at the inn-door most pressing invitations would be given to the company to alight, and after as many as possible could be collected in the parlour, the landlord would introduce the Highgate oath. A little artifice easily led to the detection of the uninitiated, and as soon as the fact was ascertained the horns were brought in. There were generally sufficient of the initiated to induce compliance with those who had not yet passed through the ordeal. The horns were fixed on a pole five feet in height, and placed upright on the ground before the person who was to be sworn. The neophyte was then required to take off his hat, which all present having also done, the landlord, in a bold voice, began the ceremony. It commenced by the landlord saying—

'Upstanding and uncovered: silence. Take notice what I now say to you, for *that* is the first word of the oath; mind *that!* You must acknowledge me to be your adopted father, I must acknowledge you to be my adopted son. If you do not call me father, you forfeit a bottle of wine; if I do not call you son, I forfeit the same. And now, my good son, if you are travelling through this village of Highgate, and you have no money in your pocket, go call for a bottle of wine at any house you may think proper to enter, and book it to your father's score. If you have any friends with you, you may treat them as well; but if you have money of your own, you must pay for it yourself; for you must not say you

* See *ante*, p. 501.

have no money when you have; neither must you convey your money out of your own pocket into that of your friend's pocket, for I shall search them as well as you, and if I find that you or they have any money, you forfeit a bottle of wine for trying to cheat and cozen your old father. You must not eat brown bread while you can get white, unless you like brown the best; nor must you drink small beer when you can get strong, unless you like small the best; you must not kiss the maid while you can kiss the mistress, unless you like the maid best; but sooner than lose a good chance, you may kiss them both. And now, my good son, 'I have now to acquaint you with your privileges as a freeman of Highgate. If at any time you are going through the hamlet, and want to rest yourself, and you see a pig lying in a ditch, you are quite at liberty to kick her out and take her place; but if you see three lying together, you must only kick out the middle one, and lie between the two; so God save the king!'" These last liberties, however, are, according to Mr. Larwood, a later

THE "OLD CROWN INN," HIGHGATE, IN 1830. (*See page* 418.)

I wish you a safe journey through Highgate and this life. I charge you, my good son, that if you know any in this company who have not taken this oath, you must cause them to take it, or make each of them forfeit a bottle of wine; for if you fail to do so, you will forfeit one yourself. So now, my son, God bless you; kiss the horns, or a pretty girl if you see one here, which you like best, and so be free of Highgate.'

If a female were in the room, she was, of course, saluted; if not, the horns were to be kissed, but the option was not allowed formerly. The peculiarity of the oath was in the pronoun *that*, which generally resulted in victimising the strangers of some bottles of wine. So soon as the salutation was over, and the wine drank, the landlord, addressing himself to the newly-made son, said,

addition to the oath, introduced by a facetious blacksmith, who at one time kept the "Coach and Horses."

Mr. Mark Boyd describes at length, in his "Social Gleanings," the whole of the process to which it appears that he and his brother were subjected one fine Sunday half a century ago, and to which they submitted with all the less reluctance because they learnt that Lord Bryon and several other distinguished personages had been sworn there before them. He relates the initiatory steps of ordering a bottle of the Boniface's best port, and another of sherry, "which the landlord took care should be excellent in honour of so grave a ceremonial, and for which he did not omit to charge

VIEWS IN HIGHGATE.

accordingly." He goes on to describe how "the landlord and his waiter then retired to prepare for the imposing ceremony, and in ten minutes a thundering knock at the door announced the approach of the officials. In marched, with all solemnity, the swearer-in, dressed in a black gown with bands, and wearing a mask and a wig; his clerk also in a black gown, carrying the horns fixed on a pole in one hand, and in the other a large book, from which the oath was to be read. The landlord then proclaimed, in a loud voice, "Upstanding and uncovered. Take notice what now I say to you, &c.," and so proceeded to administer the oath *verbatim*, as above. "The custom," adds Mr. Boyd, "has now fallen into disuse; but at the 'Gate House Tavern,' some months ago (1875), whilst the waiter was administering to me an excellent luncheon, I mentioned that, were the landlord to revive the custom, many of the present generation would extremely enjoy the fun in which their ancestors had indulged, and none more than our 'American cousins.' 'Moreover,' said I to the waiter, 'where you now make five shillings you would pocket ten; and if your landlord provided as good port and sherry as formerly, he would sell two bottles for one.'" In spite, however, of Mr. Boyd's specious argument, and even the example of Lord Byron, we believe that the landlord has not at present ventured on reviving this absurdity, even in this age of "revivals" of various kinds. In fact, if the truth must be told, he takes no interest in the historic past, and does not care to be questioned about the ceremony.

The following is one version, among several, of an old initiation song which was used on these occasions in one of the Highgate inns, which either "kept a poet," or had a host who was fond of rhyming. We take it from Robert Bell's "Ballads and Songs of the Peasantry of England;" the author states that it was supplied to him by a very old man, who had been an ostler at Highgate. "The old man," adds Mr. Bell, "told him that it was not often used of late years, as 'there was no landlord that could sing, and gentlemen preferred the speech.' He also owned that the lines were not always alike, some saying them one way and some another, some making them long, while others cut them short:"—

Enter Landlord, *dressed in a black gown and bands, and wearing an antique-fashioned wig; followed by the Clerk of the Court, also in appropriate costume, and carrying the register book and the horns.*

Landlord. Do you wish to be sworn at Highgate?
Candidate. I do, father.
Clerk. Amen.

The Landlord then says or sings as follows:

Silence! O yes! you are my son!
Full to your old father turn, sir;
This is an oath you may take as you run,
So lay your hand thus on the horn, sir.

[*Here the Candidate places his right hand on the horn.*

You shall not spend with cheaters or cozens your life,
Nor waste it on profligate beauty;
And when you are wedded, be kind to your wife,
And true to all petticoat duty.

[*The Candidate says "I will," and kisses the horns, in obedience to the Clerk, who exclaims, in a loud and solemn tone, "Kiss the horns, sir."*

And while you thus solemnly swear to be kind,
And shield and protect from disaster,
This part of the oath, you must bear it in mind,
That you and not she is the master.

[*Clerk: "Kiss the horns again, sir."*

You shall pledge no man first when a woman is near,
For 'tis neither proper nor right, sir;
Nor, unless you prefer it, drink small for strong beer,
Nor eat brown bread when you can get white, sir.

[*Clerk: "Kiss the horns again, sir."*

You shall never drink brandy when wine you can get,
Say when good port or sherry is handy,
Unless that your taste on strong spirit is set,
In which case you may, sir, drink brandy.

[*Clerk: "Kiss the horns again, sir."*

To kiss the fair maid when the mistress is kind
Remember that you must be loth, sir;
But if the maid's fairest, your oath does not bind,
Or you may, if you like it, kiss both, sir.

[*Clerk: "Kiss the horns again, sir."*

Should you ever return, take this oath here again,
Like a man of good sense, leal and true, sir;
And be sure to bring with you some more merry men,
That they on the horn may swear too, sir.

Landlord. Now, sir, if you please, sign your name in that book; and if you can't write, then make your mark, and the Clerk of the Court will attest it.

[*Here one of the above requests is complied with.*

Landlord. You will now please to pay half-a-crown for court fees, and what you please to the Clerk.

The necessary ceremony being thus gone through, the business terminates by the Landlord saying "God bless the King (or Queen) and the Lord of the Manor," to which the Clerk responds, "Amen, amen!" N.B. The court fees are always returned in wine, spirits, or porter, of which the Landlord and the Clerk are invited to partake.

It will now be seen what is the meaning of the old proverb as applied to a knowing fellow:—"He has been sworn at Highgate." The words are applicable to a person who is well acquainted with good things, and who takes care to help himself to the best of all.

Grose speaks of this whimsical ceremony at some length in his "Classical Dictionary of the

Vulgar Tongue," published in 1785, and it is clear from what he says that even in his day the ceremony was very ancient. Hone's "Year Book" contains also a full account of the ceremony, as it was performed in the early part of the present century at the "Fox," or (as it was then styled) "The Fox under the Hill," an inn already mentioned by us. Hone does not throw much light on the origin of the practice, which, doubtless, is as old as the Reformation, and was originally intended as a parody on the admission of neophytes into religious guilds and confraternities by the clergy of the Catholic Church.

Grose, being a shallow antiquary, apparently regarded it as a piece of comparatively modern tomfoolery, got up by some landlord "for the good of the house." A correspondent, however, subsequently points out the antiquity of the custom, and sends a copy of the initiation song, which varies, however, considerably from our version above.

It may be added that Grose was in error on another score, as Mr. Robert Bell observes, when he supposed that the ceremony was confined to the lower orders; for both when he wrote, and in subsequent times, the oath, absurd as it is, has often been taken by persons of rank and education too. An inspection of the register-books, had any still existed, would doubtless have shown that those who have kissed the mystic horn at Highgate have belonged to all ranks of society, and that among them the scholars of Harrow have always been conspicuous—led on, no doubt, like so many sheep, by the example of their bellwether, Lord Byron. When, however, the stage-coaches ceased to pass through Highgate, the custom gradually declined, and appears to have been kept up at only three inns, respectively called "The Original House," the "Old Original House," and the "Real Old Original House." Mr. Bell, writing about the year 1860, says: "Two of the above houses have latterly ceased to hold courts, and the custom is now confined to the 'Fox under the Hill,' where the rite is celebrated with every attention to ancient forms. ceremonies, and costume, and for a fee which, in deference to modern notions of economy, is only one shilling."

The old crier of Highgate is said still to keep a gown and wig ready to swear in any persons who may wish to go through the ceremony; for the swearer-in, whoever he might or may be, generally wore a black gown, mask, and wig, and had with him a person to act as clerk and bearer of the horns.

Of course there was room for a luxuriance of comicality, according to the wit of the imposer of the oath, and the simplicity of the oath-taker; and, as might be expected, the ceremony was not a dry one. Scarcely ever did a stage-coach stop at a Highgate tavern in those days, without a few of the passengers being initiated amidst the laughter of the rest, the landlord usually acting as high priest on the occasion, while a waiter or an ostler would perform the duty of clerk, and sing out "Amen" at all the proper places.

Although some ten or dozen pairs of horns are religiously kept in as many of the chief inns in Highgate, where they pass along with the house in the inventory from one landlord to his successor; yet, singularly enough, none of the register books in which the neophytes were wont to inscribe their names after taking the oath, are now known to exist. Their loss is much to be regretted, as in all probability, as we have above intimated, an inspection of them would have shown that many persons otherwise celebrated for wisdom made fools of themselves at least once in their lives. It appears, however, from an article in the *Penny Magazine*, published in 1832, that even then the ceremony had been abandoned by all respectable members of society.

The origin of this singular custom is variously accounted for. One is that it was devised by a landlord who had lost his licence, and who used it to cover the sale of his liquors. Another, and more probable one, is, that "Highgate being the nearest spot to London where cattle rested on their way from the North to Smithfield for sale, many graziers put up at the 'Gate House' for the night. These men formed a kind of fraternity, and generally endeavoured to secure the inn for their exclusive accommodation on certain days. Finding, however, they had no power to exclude strangers, who, like themselves, were travelling on business, these men formed themselves into a sort of club, and made it imperative on all who wished to join them to take a certain oath, and bringing an ox to the door, compelled them either to kiss its horns, or to quit their company."

The house of greatest dignity and largest accommodation was the "Gate House," so called from the original building having been connected with a gate which here crossed the road, and from which, as we have already stated, the name of the village is understood to have been derived.

The old "Gate House Inn" still stands, though the droll ceremony which we have described has fallen into disuse for more than a quarter of a century. In the hall of the inn, however, are still to be seen a gigantic pair of mounted horns, the same, it is affirmed, which were used in the administration of the Highgate oath.

In Hone's time the principal inn, the "Gate House," had stag-horns, as had also the "Mitre," the "Green Dragon," the "Bell," the "Rose and Crown," the "Bull," the "Wrestlers," the "Lord Nelson," the "Duke of Wellington," the "Crown," and the "Duke's Head." Bullocks' horns were used at the "Red Lion" and "Sun," and rams-horns at the "Coach and Horses," the "Castle," the "Red Lion," the "Coopers' Arms," the "Fox and Hounds," the "Flask," and the "Angel." At each of the above houses the horns were mounted on a stick, to serve in the mock ceremonial when required.

In some cases there was also a pair of mounted horns over the door of the house, as designed to give the chance passengers the assurance that the merry ceremonial was practised there; and Mr. Thorne states that at *one* inn in Highgate the horns are still to be seen on the outside of the house. It is acknowledged that there were great differences in the ceremonial at different houses, some landlords having much greater command of wit than others.

In the good old days, "when George III. was king," societies and corporations, and groups of workpeople, who were admitting a new member or associate, would come out in a body to Highgate, to have him duly sworn upon the "horns," and to enjoy an afternoon's merrymaking at his expense.

The only historical fact which has been preserved regarding this singular custom, is that a song embodying the burlesque oath was introduced in a pantomime at the Haymarket Theatre in 1742.

If we can put faith in Byron—in the lines quoted as a motto to this chapter—parties of young people, under (it is to be hoped) proper superintendence, would dance away the night after an initiation at the "Horns." It may be added that similar customs prevailed in other places besides Highgate, such as at Ware, at the "Griffin" at Hoddesdon, and other villages.

The "Angel Inn," on the crest of the hill, just opposite the old village forge, is remarkable for its antiquity, dating probably from before the era of the Reformation. It is one of the few hostelries now standing which are built wholly of wood. Doubtless it was originally the "Salutation" Inn; and when, at the Reformation, the Virgin Mary was struck out of the signboard, the Angel remained, and so became the sign.

Whilst on the subject of taverns and houses of public entertainment, it may not be out of place to speak of the celebrated "Sunday ordinary, at one shilling per head," at one of the Highgate inns, to which in former times the London citizens flocked in great numbers. A curious print, representing some of the characters who frequented this ordinary, was published by Harrison and Co., towards the close of the last century. Mr. Palmer, in his "History of St. Pancras," tells the following touching story in connection with this ordinary:—"A constant visitor at this *table d'hôte* was accustomed to take considerable notice of a very attractive young girl who waited at table, and from passing observations drew her at length to become the partner of his Sunday evening rambles. After some time he made known his passion to the object of his affection, and was accepted. He informed her that his occupation would detain him from her all the week, but that he should dine at home on Sunday, and leave regularly on the Monday morning. He would invest in her own name and for her exclusive use £2,000 in the Three per Cent. Consols on their marriage; but she was not to seek to discover who he was or what he did, for should she once discover it he would never return to her again. Strange as were the terms, she acquiesced, and was married, and everything went on for a long time amicably and comfortably. At length her woman's nature could hold out no longer; she must at all hazards discover her husband's secret. She tried to suppress the desire, for she really loved him; but Eve-like, she could resist no longer; and therefore on his leaving her as usual one Monday morning, she disguised herself as well as she could, and followed him from Highgate to London, when he entered a low coffee-shop, from whence after a while he issued—yes, *her husband*—in the meanest possible dress, and with a broom began to sweep the crossing near Charing Cross. This was more than she could bear; she made herself known, and reviled him for his deceit. After an angry discussion she saw her husband return to the coffee-shop, again dress himself in his gentlemanly attire, and bidding her farewell, depart, no more to return. Grieved and annoyed, she returned to Highgate; his marriage bestowment maintained her in comfort, but it left her solitary and alone."

Close by the old gate, at the summit of the hill, and opposite the tavern now known as the "Gate House," stood, till the year 1833, the chapel and school of Highgate, which dated their origin from the sixteenth century, as the following minute records:—"M^{dum} that the fyrst stone of the Chapell and free Scoole at Higate was leyd the 3rd day of

Julye 1576, and the same Chapell and Scoole was finished in Sept[r] 1578." There had, however, been a chapel on this spot from at least the fourteenth century; for, in the year 1386, Bishop Braybroke gave "to William Lichfield, a poor hermit, oppressed by age and infirmity, the office of keeping our chapel of Highgate, by our park of Haringey, and the house annexed to the said chapel, hitherto accustomed to be kept by other poor hermits." This institution is noticed by Newcourt, in his "Repertorium," but he had met with one other, by which Bishop Stokesley, in 1531, "gave the chapel, then called the chapel of St. Michael, in the parish of Hornesey, to William Forte, with the messuage, garden, and orchard, and their appurtenances, with all tenths, offerings, profits, advantages, and emoluments whatever." "Regarding these hermits," writes Mr. J. Gough Nichols, in the *Gentleman's Magazine*, "we have this further information, or rather tradition, related by the proto-topographer of Middlesex: 'Where now (1596) the Schole standeth was a hermytage, and the hermyte caused to be made the causway* betweene Highgate and Islington, and the gravell was bad from the top of Highgate hill, where is now a standinge ponde of water. There is adjoining unto the schole a chapple for the ease of that part of the countrey, for that they are within the parish of Pancras, which is distant thence neere two miles.'"

Hughson, in his "History of London," tells us that, though the site of the hermitage in ancient times is idealised, little is known about it. Nor is this wonderful, for does not the poet write—

> "Far in a wild, remote from public view,
> From youth to age a reverend hermit grew?"

The chapel itself, for some reason or other, was granted by Bishop Grindal, in 1565, to the newly-founded grammar-school of Sir Roger Cholmeley, together with certain houses, edifices, gardens, and orchards, and also two acres of pasture abutting on the king's highway.

The edifice was a singular, dull, and heavy nondescript sort of building of brick and stone. It consisted of a nave, chancel, two aisles, and galleries, together with a low square embattled tower at the western end, flanked on either side by a porch with a semicircular-headed doorway. Above the lowest window of the tower, between the two doorways, was a stone bearing the following inscription:—

"Sir Roger Cholmeley knt, L[d] chiefe baron of y[e] exchequer, and after that L[d] chiefe justice of the king's bench, did institvte and erect at his own charges this publiqve and free gramer schole; and procvred the same to be established and confirmed by the letters patents of queen Elizabeth, her endowinge the same with yearly maintaynance; which schoole Edwyn Sandys L[d] bishop of London enlarged an[o] D'ni 1565 by the addition of this chapel for divine service and by other endowments of pietie and devotion. Since which the said chappel hath been enlarged by the pietie and bounty of divers hon[ble] and worthy personages. This inscription was renewed anno D'ni 1668 by the governors of the said schoole."

From the above inscription some doubts were raised as to the exact date of the erection of the chapel; and about the year 1822, when the new church was first projected, a warm controversy sprung up respecting it. The main subject of the dispute, however, was the right of property in the chapel, whether it was vested entirely in the governors of the school, or shared by the inhabitants. "The truth appears to have been," writes Mr. Nichols, "that the chapel was actually the property of the charity, as well by grant from the Bishop of London, the ancient patron of the hermitage, as by letters patent from the Crown, and also by transfer from a third party, who had procured a grant of it from the queen as a suppressed religious foundation; that for the first century and a half the inhabitants had been allowed to have seats gratuitously; and that about the year 1723 the pews had been converted into a source of income for the school."

With regard to the association of the name of Bishop Sandys with the date 1565, one error is manifest, for he was not Bishop of London until 1570. Newcourt perceived the incoherency, and in copying the substance of the inscription into his "Repertorium," he altered the year *suo periculo* to 1570. A searching examination which the records of the school have since undergone, has disclosed that the correct date is either 1575 or 1576; for it was in the former year that the rebuilding was projected; and in the latter, when it had not far proceeded, Bishop Sandys was translated to the see of York. The alteration of the date was probably accidentally made when the inscription was re-cut.

One portion of the old chapel had a very extraordinary appearance; for small round windows were placed directly over the round-headed long ones, not unlike the letter *i* and its dot. These round windows originally lighted three rooms belonging to the master's house, which, down to near the close of the last century, stood over the body of the chapel. The edifice had undergone four

* See *ante*, p. 392.

THE OLD CHAPEL, HIGHGATE, 1830. (*See page* 418.)

several repairs and enlargements between the years 1616 and 1772, and also, probably, another when the inscription was renewed in 1668. The repairs in 1720 seem to have been important, as they incurred an expense of more than £1,000, of which sum £700 were contributed by Mr. Edward Paunce-fort, treasurer to the charity, and the balance by the inhabitants of Highgate. Again, in 1772, the body of the chapel was, in a great measure, rebuilt; and it was then that its ceiling was raised by the removal of the three rooms above mentioned. Within the chapel was a monument to William Platt, Esq. (the founder of some fellowships in St. John's College, Cambridge), who died in 1637; also a monument to the memory of Dr. Lewis Atterbury (brother of the celebrated bishop), who was preacher here. This monument, on the chapel being pulled down for the erection of the present church of St. Michael, was removed to Hornsey Church, of which Dr. Atterbury had been vicar. Sir Francis Pemberton, Chief Justice in the reign of Charles II., who died at his residence in Highgate, was buried in the old chapel; as also was Sir John Wollaston, the founder of the almshouses in Southwood Lane. On the demolition of the chapel, several of the monuments and tablets were removed to the new church. The chapel enjoyed some celebrity and popular favour in the reign of Queen Anne and George I., when it was the only place of worship in a rather extensive neighbourhood, and was consequently a centre of attraction to persons of all classes, who, after service was over, used to promenade the terraced sides of the Green. One of its ministers was the Rev. Henry Felton, D.D., well known as the author of a learned "Dissertation on the Classics," and sometime Principal of St. Edmund's Hall, Oxford.

Becoming inadequate to the accommodation of the inhabitants of the neighbourhood, and part passing into a state of dilapidation, it was taken down in 1833. The area of the chapel for many years formed the burial-ground for the hamlet; and till 1866 it remained much in its original condition. In it stood, among other tombs, that of Samuel Taylor Coleridge, the poet and philosopher, who during the latter period of his life resided at Highgate, and where he died in 1834. The tomb itself is now to be seen in the resuscitated chapel of the Grammar School.

Lord Chief Justice of England, about the year of Christ 1564: the pencion (*sic*) of the master is uncertaine; there is no usher, and the schole is now in the disposition of six governors, or feoffees. Where now the schole standeth was a hermitage, and the hermit made the causeway between Highgate and Islington." From the same authority we learn that Sir Roger Cholmeley "instituted and erected the schole" at his owne charges, obtaining a confirmation by letters patent from Queen

DORCHESTER HOUSE, 1700. (*See page* 424.)

Sir Roger Cholmeley, the founder of the Grammar School, and the great benefactor of Highgate, was in high favour under Henry VII., who bestowed on him the manor of Hampstead. He held the post of Chief Justice under Mary; but was committed to the Tower for drawing up the will of Edward VI., in which he disinherited his sisters. He spent his declining years in literary retirement at "Hornsey"—probably at no great distance from the school which he had founded—and died in 1565.

We meet with the following description of the school and its situation in Norden's "Speculum Britanniæ:"—"At this place is a free school built of brick, by Sir R. Cholmeley, knight, some time

Elizabeth, who was always ready to welcome and encourage such improvements, and may be supposed to have taken a personal interest in one which lay so close to her own royal chase and hunting ground. It appears, from Norden, that the chapel was added in order to enlarge the school; but how this addition was calculated to effect such an end does not appear, unless the pew-rents or endowment of the chaplain were added to the salary of the schoolmaster, and this, as we have shown above, really seems to have been the case.

It is perhaps worthy of note that Mr. Carter, who was master of the school during the civil wars, was ejected and treated with great cruelty by the

Puritans. Walker, in his "Sufferings of the Clergy," says that he was "turned out of the house with his family whilst his wife was in labour, and that she was delivered in the church porch." Another fact to be recorded is that Master Nicholas Rowe, the poet and Shakespearian commentator, was a scholar here.

It would appear from the "Account of Public Charities," published in 1828, that the forty boys in the school were then taught no classics, and that, although the "reader" of the chapel was charged with their education, the latter performed his duty by deputy, and that his deputy was the sexton! It is somewhat sarcastically added by the compilers of the "Account," that "this forms the only instance we have met of the conversion of a grammar foundation into a school of English literature!" This school, it may be added, has several scholarships and exhibitions for boys who are proceeding to the universities, and has for some years held a high place among the leading grammar schools of the second class, under Dr. Dyne and his successor. It now numbers upwards of two hundred scholars. The school has attached to it a cricket and football field of about ten acres, on the north side of the road leading to Caen Wood and Hampstead Heath. The ground was in great part paid for by donations of friends of the school, and an annual payment added to the boys' fees. A pavilion also was erected by the donations of "old boys." On this ground the croquet tournament of all England was held in 1869. The original school buildings, as erected by Cholmeley, disappeared many years ago. A new school-house was erected in 1819, but this having at length become inadequate for the wants of the pupils, it was, at the tercentenary of the school which was celebrated in June, 1865, determined to raise new buildings. The old school was accordingly taken down in 1866, and rebuilt from the design of Mr. F. Cockerell. It is now a handsome Gothic structure of red brick, with stone dressings, and has attached to it a handsome chapel in a similar style of architecture, and a spacious library, school-room, and class-rooms. The chapel, built in remembrance of Mr. George Abraham Crawley, a governor of the school, was the gift of his widow and family; the expense incurred in the erection of the library was mostly paid for by funds raised by former scholars.

Southwood Lane is the name of a narrow and irregular road which runs in a south-easterly direction across from the back of Sir R. Cholmeley's school to the "Woodman," and leads thence to Muswell Hill. In this lane, in the year 1658, Sir John Wollaston founded six almshouses, which he devised, with their appurtenances, to the governors of the Free School, "in trust for the use of six poor alms people, men and women, of honest life and conversation, inhabitants of Hornsey and Highgate." In 1722 the almshouses were doubled in number and rebuilt, as a stone over the entrance informs us, at the expense of Mr. Edward Pauncefort, who likewise founded and endowed a charity-school for girls. The school, however, appears, through some neglect, to have lost much of the endowment designed for it by the founder. The Baptist chapel in this lane is one of the oldest buildings in the parish, having been founded as a Presbyterian chapel as far back as 1662. In course of time the Unitarians settled here, when the chapel had among its ministers David Williams, the "High Priest of Nature," and founder of the Literary Fund, of which we have spoken in our notice of Bloomsbury Square.* Dr. Barbauld and Dr. Alexander Crombie were also ministers here. Early in the present century the chapel passed into the hands of the Baptists.

On the north side of the lane stands a large modern brick mansion known as Park House. The Asylum for Idiots was founded here in 1847, by Dr. Andrew Reed; but about eight years later was transplanted to more spacious buildings at Earlswood, near Red Hill, in Surrey. In 1863, Park House was purchased, and converted into the London Diocesan Penitentiary.

The new Church of St. Michael stands at some little distance from the site of the old chapel, on the summit of the hill, overlooking the cemetery on the one side and Highgate Grove on the other; and, as we have stated in the preceding chapter, it occupies the site of the old mansion built by Sir William Ashurst, who was Lord Mayor of London in 1694. It is a poor and ugly sham Gothic structure, though the spire looks well from a distance. It was built from the designs of Mr. Lewis Vulliamy, and was thought to be a wonderful triumph of ecclesiastical art when it was consecrated in 1832. At the end overlooking the cemetery is a magnificent stained-glass window, representing the Saviour and the apostles, the gift of the Rev. C. Mayo, many years preacher in the old chapel. It was executed in Rome. The border contains several coats of arms from the windows of the old chapel. There are a few interesting monuments removed hither from the former edifice; but that which is most worthy of notice is a tablet erected to the memory of Cole-

* See Vol. IV., p. 543.

ridge, of whose tomb we have spoken above. It bears the following inscription :—

Sacred to the memory of
SAMUEL TAYLOR COLERIDGE,
Poet, Philosopher, Theologian.
This truly great and good man resided for
The last nineteen years of his life
In this Hamlet.
He quitted "the body of his death,"
July 25th, 1834,
In the sixty-second year of his age.
Of his profound learning and discursive genius
His literary works are an imperishable record.
To his private worth,
His social and Christian virtues,
JAMES AND ANN GILLMAN,
The friends with whom he resided
During the above period, dedicate this tablet.
Under the pressure of a long
And most painful disease
His disposition was unalterably sweet and angelic.
He was an ever-enduring, ever-loving friend,
The gentlest and kindest teacher,
The most engaging home companion.

"O framed for calmer times and nobler hearts,
O studious poet, eloquent for truth!
Philosopher, contemning wealth and death,
Yet docile, child-like, full of life and love."

Here,
On this monumental stone thy friends inscribe thy worth.

Reader! for the world mourn.
A Light has passed away from the earth!
But for this pious and exalted Christian
"Rejoice, and again I say unto you, Rejoice!"

Ubi
Thesaurus
ibi
Cor.

S. T. C.

Besides the celebrities whose names we have already mentioned, Highgate has been the home of many others. Lord Southampton had a mansion here, called Fitzroy House, which was situated in Fitzroy Park, adjoining Caen Wood. It was built about the year 1780, and is said to have been a handsome square brick building. Lord Southampton was the Lord of the Manor of Tottenhall, or Tottenham Court, in whose family it still remains. In the rooms of the mansion were portraits of Henry, the first Duke of Grafton; George, Earl of Euston; and Charles, Duke of Grafton. The Duke of Buckingham resided at Fitzroy House in 1811. In 1828 the mansion was taken down, and the park sub-divided and improved by the erection of several elegant villas.

Mrs. Caroline Chisholm has lived at Highgate, on the Hill, for some years. A native of Wootton, in Northamptonshire, she was born about the year 1810. Her father, Mr. William Jones, was a man of most philanthropic character, which his daughter inherited from him. The energy of her character was exercised for the benefit of the needy of her own neighbourhood, until her marriage with Captain Alexander Chisholm, of the Indian army, removed her to a more extended sphere of usefulness. The name of Mrs. Chisholm will be best remembered as the champion of the cause of emigration in various social phases, when grievances of any kind required to be redressed. Among her efforts in this direction may be mentioned the consigning of two shiploads of children from various workhouses to their parents in Australia at the expense of the Government. A similar success attended her efforts on behalf of convicts' wives, who had been promised free transmission, in certain cases of meritorious behaviour on the part of their husbands. Her greatest achievement, however, was the establishment of the Female Colonisation Loan Society, for the promotion of female emigration.

In 1724, died at his house in the Grove, Dr. Henry Sacheverel,* the great leader of the Tory party in the factions of 1709. He was a bigoted High Churchman, and his sermons were the brands to set the Established Church on fire. For expressions in his writings he was impeached and brought to the bar of the House; but far from disowning his writings, he gloried in what he had done. His trial lasted three weeks, and excluded all other public business for the time, when his sermons were voted scandalous and seditious libels. The queen was present as a private spectator. His sentence prohibited him from preaching for three years, and his sermons were ordered to be burnt by the common hangman. The following anecdote is recorded :—A portrait of this divine, with the initials S. T. P. attached to his name (signifying *Sanctæ Theologiæ Professor*), was hanging up in a shop window, where some persons looking at it, asked the meaning of the affix, when Thomas Bradbury, the Nonconformist minister, hearing the inquiry, and catching a glimpse of the print in passing, put his head among them, and adroitly said, "Stupid, Troublesome Puppy," and passed on.

Sir Richard Baker, author of the "Chronicles" which bear his name, died at his residence in Highgate at the commencement of the seventeenth century; as also did Sir Thomas Cornwallis, a man who had acquired considerable eminence in the reigns of Edward VI. and Queen Mary. Here lived Sir Henry Blunt, one of the earliest travellers

* See Vol. II., p. 512.

in Turkey, and also Sir John Pettus, a distinguished mineralogist. The great Arbuthnott seems also to have been at one time a resident here, for it appears from a chance expression in one of Dean Swift's letters, that he was obliged to quit Highgate by the *res angusta domi.*

Dorchester House, a large mansion of note here, was formerly the seat of Henry Marquis of Dorchester, and was used in the middle of the last century as a ladies' hospital. Part of Grove Row covers the site of this house, which was devoted by its owner, William Blake, a draper of Covent Garden, to a most excellent charity, the failure of which is deeply to be lamented, as its only fault appears to have been that it was in advance of the selfish age which witnessed its birth. The mansion bore the name of its former owner, the Marquis of Dorchester, from whom Blake purchased it early in the reign of Charles II., for £5,000—all that he possessed—with the intention of establishing it as a school or hospital for forty fatherless boys and girls. "The boys were to be taught the arts of painting, gardening, casting accounts, and navigation, or put out to some good handicraft trade. The girls were to learn to read, write, sew, starch, raise paste, and make dresses, so as to be fitted for any kind of service, thus anticipating the orphan working schools of our own time. When he sunk his money in this purchase, he hoped, and no doubt believed, that the benevolence of the wealthy would furnish the means for its support. But here he was doomed to disappointment." Far from being so fortunate as Franke of Halle, or the Curé d'Ars, or Müller of Bristol, he found charity much colder than he expected. Having exhausted his own resources, he made earnest appeals to the titled personages and city ladies of London, but in vain. For some time, indeed, his generous establishment struggled on. In 1667 there were maintained and educated in it thirty-six poor boys, dressed in a costume of blue and yellow—not unlike that of the boys of Christ's Hospital. It still existed in 1675, but it cannot be traced later than 1688, or about twenty years. In order to describe and recommend the institution which lay so near to his heart, Blake wrote and published a curious book, called "Silver Drops; or, Serious Things." It is written in a most eccentric style. He speaks of the place as meant "at first only for a summer recess from London, which, having that great and noble city, with its numerous childhood, under view, gave first thought to him of such a design." Mr. Howitt infers from the style, which is "almost insane," and from the "nobility of soul struggling through it," the piety and spirituality, the desire to have the boys taught the art of painting, and finally from the name of William Blake, that the "strange and good" founder must have been the grandfather or great-grandfather of the "eccentric but inspired writer-artist" of the same name, whom we have already mentioned more than once in our account of the neighbourhood of Oxford Street, and whose father is known to have been a hosier in Carnaby Market, not far from Covent Garden. A view of the mansion is engraved in Lysons' "Environs," and in the *Gentleman's Magazine,** and also in William Howitt's "Northern Heights of London."

Part of the site of Dorchester House is now also covered by Pemberton Row, in which, says Mr. Prickett in his "History of Highgate," a part of the materials of the old building seem to have been utilised; for "on examining the elevation of Dorchester House with Pemberton Row, a remarkable similitude will appear in the character and style of the pedimented dormers, cornices, and heavy roofs." Among the early occupants of the houses erected after the removal of Dorchester House, was Sir Francis Pemberton, a distinguished judge of the seventeenth century. Sir Henry Chauncy gives a very high character of him in his "History of Hertfordshire," and there is a portrait of him among the "Council of the Seven Bishops." The row of houses has since borne his name.

Dorchester House itself stood on the west side of the Grove or Green, and the house occupied by Mr. Gillman, the surgeon, who had Coleridge as his inmate, stands on another portion of its site. Charles Lamb and Henry Crabb Robinson were frequent visitors of Coleridge whilst he was living here; in the "Diary" of the latter, under date of July, 1816, we read:—"I walked to Becher's, and he accompanied me to Mr. Gillman's, an apothecary at Highgate, with whom Coleridge is now staying. He seems already to have profited by his abstinence from opium, for I never saw him look so well." Mr. Thorne, in his "Environs of London," describes the house in which Coleridge lived as "the third house in the Grove, facing the church, a roomy, respectable, brick dwelling, with a good garden behind, and a grand look-out Londonwards. In front of the house is a grove of stately elms, beneath which the poet used to pace in meditative mood, discoursing in unmeaning monologue to some earnest listener like Irving or Hare, or an older friend, like Wordsworth or Lamb. The house remains almost unaltered; the elms, too, are there," but, he adds, "some Vandal has deprived

* See *Gentleman's Magazine*, Vol. LXX., Part II., p. 721.

them of their heads." It was in his walks about Highgate that Coleridge one day met Keats. He thus describes him:—"A loose, slack, and not well-dressed youth met me in a lane near Highgate. It was Keats. He was introduced to me, and stayed a minute or so. After he had left us a little way, he ran back and said, 'Let me carry away the memory, Mr. Coleridge, of having pressed your hand.' 'There is death in that hand,' I said, when Keats was gone; yet this was, I believe, before the consumption showed itself distinctly.'"

Coleridge was called by De Quincey "the largest and most spacious intellect, the subtlest and most comprehensive that has yet existed among men;" and Walter Savage Landor admits the truth of the statement with a reserve in favour of only Shakespeare and Milton. Charles Lamb calls him "metaphysician, bard, and magician in one." If he had written nothing but the "Ancient Mariner," his name would have lived as long as English literature itself, though Southey denounces it as "the clumsiest attempted German sublimity that he ever saw." It was after a visit to Coleridge, at Highgate, in all probability, that Shelley thus wrote of him:—

"You will see Coleridge: him who sits obscure
In the exceeding lustre, and the pure
Intense irradiation of a mind
Which, with its own internal lustre blind,
Flags wearily through darkness and despair,
A cloud-encircled meteor of the air,
A hooded eagle among blinking owls."

Almost everybody knows the general outline of the story of the wasted life of Coleridge. How in early manhood he enlisted into the 15th Light Dragoons, but was released from the uncongenial life he had chosen by friends who accidentally detected his knowledge of Greek and Latin; how even when he had gained a name and a position as an essayist, he refused a handsome salary for regular literary work, declaring that he "would not give up the pleasure of lazily reading old folio columns for a thousand a year," and that "he considered any money beyond three hundred and fifty pounds a year a real evil." But this lazy reading of folios led, in his case, to confirmed idleness, an indolent resolution to gratify the mind and sense, at the cost of duty. "Degenerating into an opium-eater, and a mere purposeless theoriser, Coleridge wasted his time, talents, and health, and came, in his old age, to depend on the charity of others, and at last died; all his friends and many others besides regretted that he had done so little worthy of his genius."

Before he died Coleridge composed for himself the following epitaph, most striking for its simplicity and humility:—

"Stop, Christian passer-by! stop, child of God!
And read with gentle breast. Beneath the sod
A poet lies, or that which once seemed he;
Oh, lift a thought in prayer for S. T. C.!
That he who many a year, with toil of breath,
Found death in life, may here find life in death;
Mercy for praise—to be forgiven for fame.
He asked and hoped through Christ. Do thou the same."

Highgate Green, or Grove, is situated on the summit of West Hill, opposite St. Michael's Church. Until within a few years ago, when the Green was completely enclosed with dwarf iron railings, and planted with shrubs by a committee of the inhabitants, aided by the assistance of the vestry of St. Pancras, it was an open space, having several seats placed for the convenience of those who were weary. The green was formerly a favourite resort of the London folk, as it afforded space for recreation or dancing. Almost in the centre of this Green stands the "Flask" Inn, which was formerly one of the head-quarters of revellers at Highgate, as was its namesake at Hampstead.

In a comedy, published in 1601, entitled *Jack Drum's Entertainment*, on the introduction of the Whitsun morris dance, the following song is given in connection with the hostelry:—

"Skip it, and frisk it nimbly, nimbly!
Tickle it, tickle it lustily!
Strike up the tabour,
For the wenches' favour,
Tickle it, tickle it lustily!
Let us be seen on Highgate Green,
To dance for the honour of Holloway;
Since we are come hither,
Let's spare for no leather,
To dance for the honour of Holloway."

The following story is told connecting Hogarth's name with this Green:—"During his apprenticeship he made an excursion to this favourite spot with three of his companions. The weather being sultry, they went into a public-house on the Green, where they had not been long, before a quarrel arose between two persons in the same room, when, one of the disputants having struck his opponent with a quart pot he had in his hand, and cut him very much, causing him to make a most hideous grin, the humourist could not refrain from taking out his pencil and sketching one of the most ludicrous scenes imaginable, and what rendered it the more valuable was that it exhibited the exact likenesses of all present." The "public-house" here mentioned, no doubt, was the "Flask."

A large part of the Green was formerly a pond, which was fringed on one side, at least, by farm buildings. Once a year, at fair-time, its surface was covered—if tradition speaks the truth—with little sailing vessels, which made the place quite gay with an annual regatta.

It is perhaps worthy of a note, by the way, that this village, or hamlet, was not unrepresented at the "Tournament of Tottenham"—real or imaginary—recorded by Warton, in his "History of Poetry," for we read that among those who repaired to it, either as spectators, or to bear a part in the lists, were

"——all the men of that country—
Of Iseldon (Islington), of Hygate, and of Hakenay."

Church House, on the Green, close by the entrance to Swaine's Lane, was, in the middle of the last century, the abode of Sir John Hawkins, author of a "History of Music," of whom we have spoken in our account of Westminster.* At the time when Sir John Hawkins lived here, the roads were very badly kept; indeed, so difficult was the ascent of Highgate Hill that the worthy knight always rode to the Sessions House, Hicks's Hall, in a carriage drawn by four horses. Pepys tells us how that Lord Brouncker found it necessary to put six horses into his coach in order to climb Highgate Hill. The capacious coach-house and stables belonging to the house now serve as the lecture-hall and offices of the Highgate Literary Institute.

Prior to the construction of the roadway over the hill, the whole of this district was only known as a portion of Hornsey, and was for the greater part covered with the woods of Hornsey and Haringey Park; indeed, it is affirmed that it originally formed part of the Forest of Middlesex, wherein King Henry VIII. indulged in the sports of the chase, as may be seen by the following proclamation issued by him in 1546:—

HORNSEY WOOD HOUSE, 1800. (*See page* 430.)

PROCLAMATION.

Yt noe person interrupt the Kinges game of partridge or pheasant—Rex majori et vicecomitibus London. Vobis mandamus, &c.

Forasmuch as the King's most Royale Majestie is much desirous of having the game of hare, partridge, pheasant, and heron, preserved in and about his manour at Westminster for his disport and pastime; that is to saye, from his said Palace toe our Ladye of Oke, toe Highgate and Hamsted Heathe, to be preserved for his owne pleasure and recreation; his Royale Highnesse doth straightway charge and commandeth all and singular of his subjects, of what estate and condition soev' they be, not toe attempt toe hunte, or hawke, or kill anie of the said games within the precincts of Hamsted, as they tender his favour and wolvde eschewe the imprisonment of theyre bodies and further punishment, at his majestie's will and pleasure.

* See Vol. IV., p. 34.

HORNSEY CHURCH IN 1750. *From a Contemporary Print.* (*See page* 432.)

Teste meipso apud Westm. vij. die Julij anno tercesimo septimo Henrici octavi 1546.

Of Hornsey Wood itself, the chief portion left is Bishop's Wood, extending nearly all the way from Highgate to Hampstead; a smaller fragment, known as Highgate Wood, lies on the north side of Southwood Lane, near the "Woodman" Tavern, but this was much cut up in forming the Highgate and Edgware Railway; another piece, somewhat less encroached upon, lies at the end of Wood Lane.

North Hill, as the broad roadway north of the "Gate House" is called, is cut through what was once part of the Great Park or bishop's land, and joins the main road about half a mile beyond Southwood Lane. The road may be said to form part of the village of Highgate, for its sides are almost wholly occupied by villas and rows of cottages, among which are several public-houses, including the "Red Lion," one of the principal coaching houses of former times, and one where the largest number of persons were "sworn on the horns," as stated above.

The "Bull Inn," on the descent of the Great North Road towards Finchley, is worthy of note as one of the many such residences of the eccentric painter, George Morland, to whom we have frequently alluded. It is recorded that he would stand for hours before this hostelry, with a pipe in his mouth, bandying jests and jokes with the drivers of all the coaches which travelled by this route to Yorkshire and the North.

We may observe, in conclusion, that, in the opinion of many persons, Highgate does not possess the same variety of situations and prospects as Hampstead, nor is it so large and populous a place; but its prospects to the south and east are superior to those in the same direction from Hampstead.

CHAPTER XXXIII.

HORNSEY.

"To vie with all the beaux and belles,
Away they whip to Hornsey Wells."
Spirit of the Public Journals, 1814.

Etymology of Hornsey—Its Situation and Gradual Growth—The Manor of Hornsey—Lodge Hill—The Bishops' Park—Historical Memorabilia—The New River—Hornsey Wood and "Hornsey Wood House"—An Incident in the Life of Crabbe—Finsbury Park—Appearance of this District at the Commencement of the Present Century—Mount Pleasant—Hornsey Church—The Grave of Samuel Rogers, Author of "The Pleasures of Memory"—A Nervous Man—Lalla Rookh Cottage—Thomas Moore—Muswell Hill—The Alexandra Palace and Park—Neighbourhood of Muswell Hill, as seen from its Summit—Noted Residents at Hornsey—Crouch End.

As we have in the preceding chapters been dealing with Highgate—which, by the way, was originally but a hamlet situated within the limits of Hornsey—it is but natural that we should here say something of the mother parish. This once rural, but now suburban village, then, lies about two miles to the north-east from the top of Highgate Hill, whence it is approached either by Hornsey Lane or by Southwood Lane.

The etymology of this locality must be sought for in its more ancient appellation. From the thirteenth to the sixteenth century public records call it "Haringea," "Haringhea," or "Haringey." About Queen Elizabeth's time it was usually called "Harnsey," or, as some will have it, says Norden, "Hornsey." Lysons, indulging in a little pleasantry, observes that "if anything is to be gathered relating to its etymology, it must be sought for in its more ancient appellation, *Har*-ringe, the meadow of hares." In "Crosby's Gazetteer," 1816, Hornsey is described as "a pleasant village situated in a low valley five miles from London, through which the New River flows. This place is a favourite resort of the good citizens of London." Hornsey and London since that time have approached much nearer to each other, and it appears probable that before long it will form a portion of the metropolis. The opening of the Alexandra Park doubtless tended strongly to stretch London considerably in the direction of Hornsey. The citizens of London, instead of making it a place of occasional resort, have made it a place of residence. Crosby continues:—"In its vicinity is a small coppice, known by the name of Hornsey Wood. The Hornsey Wood House is a famous house of entertainment." Both the Wood and the "Wood House" have been swept away, and the sites have been taken into Finsbury Park. In 1818, as we learn from advertisements of the time, "coaches go daily from the 'White Bear,' Aldersgate Street, at eleven in the morning; in the afternoon at seven, in the winter, and at four and eight in the summer." Such, however, have been the changes brought about by the whirligig of time, that now, during the day, there are railway trains to and from London and various parts of Hornsey to the number of upwards of fifty each way.

The Manor of Hornsey has belonged to the Bishops of London from a time antecedent to the Norman Conquest; and in the centuries immediately following that event, those prelates had a residence here long before they owned a palace on the banks of the Thames at Fulham. Mr. Prickett has shown pretty conclusively, in his "History of Highgate," that the site of this residence is to be looked for in the centre of Hornsey Great Park, about half a mile to the north-west of the "High Gate."

Norden, in his "Speculum Britanniæ," thus describes it:—"There is a hill or fort in Hornsey Park, called Lodge Hill, for that thereon stood some time a lodge, when the park was replenished with deer; but it seemeth by the foundation that it was rather a castle than a 'lodge;' for the hill is trenched with two deep ditches, now old and overgrown with bushes; the rubble thereof, as brick, tile, and Cornish slate, are in heaps yet to be seen; the which ruins are of great antiquity, as may appear by the oaks at this day standing, above a hundred years' growth, upon the very foundations of the building." Lysons, writing at the close of the last century, says that "the greater part of it is now covered with a copse, but the remains of a moat or ditch are still to be seen in an adjoining field." Lysons adds a remark to the effect that "Bishop Aylmer's house at Hornsey, the burning of which put him to 200 marks expense, must have been upon another site." When the bishop's lands were sold, the Manor of Hornsey passed into the hands of Sir John Wollaston, of whom we have spoken in the previous chapter; he held it till his death, in 1658, after which his widow enjoyed it till the Restoration. Mr. Prickett adds, that in his time (1842) the form of the moat which surrounded it was still visible, and that it covered seventy yards square. He writes, "The site of the castle is still uneven, and bears the traces of former foundation; it is somewhat higher than the ground outside the trenches. The portion of the moat which still remains consists of a spring constantly running, and is now used as a watering-place for cattle."

It is almost needless to say here that the park of the Bishops of London must have been originally a portion of the great forest of Middlesex, which we have mentioned in our account of Primrose Hill (page 287). It occupied a somewhat irregular triangle, the base of which would extend from Highgate to Hampstead, while its apex reached nearly to Finchley northwards. In fact, a great portion of it still remains as forest-land, though regarded as a part of Caen Wood.

Hornsey Park is not altogether without its scraps of history, for it is said to have been the place where, in the year 1386, the Duke of Gloucester, the Earls of Arundel, Warwick, and other noblemen, assembled in a hostile manner, and marched thence to London to oppose Richard II., and to compel him to dismiss his two favourite ministers—the Earl of Suffolk and Robert Duke of Ireland—from his councils.

As we learn from Stow's "Annals," the Lodge in Hornsey Park, then the residence of the Duke of Gloucester, was, in the reign of Henry VI., the scene of the reputed witchcraft in which Eleanor Duchess of Gloucester was concerned; for here the learned Robert Bolingbroke, an astrologer, and Thomas Southwell, a canon of St. Stephen's, are alleged to have "endeavoured to consume the king's person by necromantic art," Southwell having said masses over the instruments which were to be used for that purpose. Bolingbroke was executed as a traitor at Tyburn; Southwell died in the Tower; whilst the Duchess had to do penance in the public streets, an incident which Shakespeare has rendered familiar to his readers in the second part of the play of *Henry VI.*

Once more, when the ill-fated and short-lived Edward V. was brought to London, after his father's death, under the escort of his uncle, Richard of Gloucester, he was here met by the Lord Mayor and 500 citizens of London. Hall, in his "Chronicles," quaintly tells us that, "When the kynge approached neere the cytee, Edmonde Shawe, goldsmythe, then Mayre of the cytie, with the Aldermenne and shreves [sheriffs] in skarlet, and five hundreth commoners in murraye, receyved his grace reverently at Harnesay Parke, and so conveighed him to the cytie, where he entered the fourth day of May, in the fyrst and last yere of his reigne."

Henry VII., on his return from a victory in Scotland, was likewise here met by the Lord Mayor and citizens of London, and conducted on his progress to the City in like manner.

Miss Jane Porter states, in her "Scottish Chiefs," that "the remains of Wallace were secretly removed and deposited temporarily in the chapel of Hornsey Lodge; and that Robert Bruce was concealed at Lodge Hill, in the garb of a Carmelite, when Gloucester sent him a pair of spurs, as an intimation that he must depart with all speed;" but it should be added that neither Lysons nor Prickett, in his history of the place, mentions these facts, so that possibly they are somewhat apocryphal.

Few villages near London have retained so rural a character down to quite recent times as that of Hornsey; this may perhaps be accounted for by the fact that both the high north road and the thoroughfare leading to Cambridge leave the place untouched. "The surrounding country," writes the author of the "Beauties of England and Wales," "is rendered attractive by soft ranges of hills; and the New River, which winds in a tortuous progress through the parish, is at many points a desirable auxiliary of the picturesque." Hone, in the second volume of his "Every-day Book," gives an engraving of "The New River at Hornsey," the spot represented being the garden of the "Three Compasses" inn. "But," says Mr. Thorne, in his "Environs of London," "the New River would now be sought for there in vain; its course was diverted, and this portion filled up with the vestigia of a London cemetery."

"About a mile nearer to London than Hornsey," observes the *Ambulator*, in 1774, "is a coppice of young trees called Hornsey Wood, at the entrance of which is a public-house, to which great numbers of persons resort from the City."

"Hornsey Wood House," for such was the name of this place of entertainment, stood on the summit of some rising ground on the eastern side of the parish. It was originally a small roadside public-house, with two or three wide-spreading oaks before it, beneath the shade of which the weary wayfarer could rest and refresh himself. The wood itself, immediately contiguous to the house, for some time shared with Chalk Farm the honour of affording a theatre for cockney duellists. The building was just beyond the "Sluice House," so celebrated for its eel-pies in the last generation. Anglers and other visitors could pass to it through an upland meadow along a straight gravel-walk anglewise. It was a good, plain, brown-brick, respectable, modern, London-looking building. Within the entrance, to the left, was a light and spacious room of ample accommodation and dimensions, of which more care seems to have been taken than of its fine leather folding screen in ruins, which Mr. Hone, in his "Every-day Book," speaks of as "an unseemly sight for him who respects old requisites for their former beauty and convenience." "It still bears," he further tells us, "some remains of a spirited painting spread all over its leaves, to represent the amusements and humours of a fair in the low countries. At the top of a pole, which may have been the village May-pole, is a monkey with a cat on his back; then there is a sturdy bear-ward in scarlet, with a wooden leg, exhibiting Mr. Bruin; an old woman telling fortunes to the rustics; a showman's drummer on the stage before a booth beating up for spectators to the performance within, which the show-cloth represents to be a dancer on the tight-rope; a well-set-out stall of toys, with a woman displaying their attractions; besides other really interesting 'bits' of a crowded scene, depicted by no mean hand, especially a group coming from a church in the distance, apparently a wedding procession, the females well looking and well dressed, wearing ribbons and scarfs below their waists in festoons. The destruction of this really interesting screen, by worse than careless keeping, is much to be lamented. This ruin of art is within a ruin of nature. 'Hornsey Tavern' and its grounds have displaced a romantic portion of the wood, the remains of which, however, skirt a large and pleasant piece of water formed at considerable expense. To this water, which is well stored with fish, anglers resort with better prospects of success than to the New River; the walk round it, and the prospect from its banks, are very agreeable."

With advancing years, the old tavern became more and more frequented, and in the end it was altered and enlarged, the grounds laid out as tea-gardens, and the large lake formed, which was much frequented by cockney anglers. For some time previous to the demolition of the house, in 1866, the grounds were used for pigeon-shooting by a gun-club section of the "upper ten thousand;" but it was soon superseded as such by the attractions of the "Welsh Harp" and of "Hurlingham." Hone, in the first volume of his "Every-day Book" (1826), speaks thus of the old house and its successor:—"The *old* 'Hornsey Wood House' well became its situation; it was embowered, and seemed a part of the wood. Two sisters, a Mrs. Lloyd and a Mrs. Collier, kept the house; they were ancient women, large in size, and usually sat before their door on a seat fixed between two venerable oaks, wherein swarms of bees hived themselves. Here the venerable and cheerful dames tasted many a refreshing cup with their good-natured customers, and told tales of bygone days, till, in very old age, one of them passed to her grave, and the other followed in a few months afterwards. Each died regretted by the frequenters of the rural dwelling, which was soon afterwards pulled down, and the oaks felled, to make room for the present roomy and more fashionable building. To those who were acquainted with it in its former rusticity, when it was an unassuming 'calm retreat,' it is, indeed, an altered spot. To produce the alteration, a sum of £10,000 was expended by the present proprietor; and 'Hornsey Wood Tavern' is now a well-frequented house. The pleasantness of its situation is a great attraction in fine weather." The lake was used not merely for fishing, but also for boating, which was largely indulged in during the summer months. Indeed, the attractions of the place seem to have been so great as to inspire the mind of the prosaic antiquary, Mr. Hone, who commemorates it in the following sentimental lines:—

> "A house of entertainment—in a place
> So rural, that it almost doth deface
> The lovely scene; for like a beauty-spot
> Upon a charming cheek that needs it not,
> So 'Hornsey Tavern' seems to me. And yet,
> Though nature be forgotten, to forget
> The artificial wants of the forgetters
> Is setting up oneself to be their betters.
> This is unwise; for they are passing wise
> Who have no eyes for scenery, and despise
> Persons like me, who sometimes have sensations
> Through too much sight, and fall in contemplations,
> Which, as cold waters cramp and drown a swimmer,
> Chill and o'erwhelm me. Pleasant is that glimmer
> Whereby trees *seem* but wood. The men who know
> No qualities but forms and axes, go
> Through life for happy people. They are so."

We are told in the "Life of Crabbe," by his son, that Hornsey Wood was one of the favourite haunts of the poet when he first came to London, and that he would often spend whole afternoons here in searching for plants and insects. "On one occasion," writes his son, "he had walked further than usual into the country, and felt himself too much exhausted to return to town. He could not afford to give himself any refreshment at a public-house, and much less to pay for a lodging; so he sheltered himself upon a hay-mow, beguiled the evening with Tibullus, and when he could read no longer, slept there till the morning."

Hornsey Wood House was pulled down in 1866, at which time the tea-gardens and grounds became absorbed in the so-called Finsbury Park, a large triangular space, some 120 acres in extent, laid out with ornamental walks and flower-gardens. It was opened by Sir John Thwaites, under the auspices of the Metropolitan Board of Works, in 1869, as a public recreation-ground and promenade for the working classes. Why the place is called "Finsbury" Park it would be difficult for us to say, seeing that it lies some miles away from Finsbury, the districts of Holloway, Islington, and Hoxton intervening, and that the site has always been known as Hornsey Wood. It ought to be styled, in common honesty, Hornsey Park.

The *Illustrated London News*, in noticing the opening of the park in 1869, says:—"The Act sanctioning the formation of this park was passed so far back as 1857. The site is what was formerly known as Hornsey Wood, which is associated with many interesting events in the history of North London. It commands a view of Wood Green, Highgate, the Green Lanes, and other suburban retreats. The ground has a gentle southern slope, from Highgate on the west and towards Stoke Newington on the east; and is skirted on the south by the Seven Sisters Road and on the east by the Green Lanes. The Great Northern Railway bounds it by a cutting and embankment on the western side, and latterly the London, Edgware, and Highgate Railway has been made with a station adjoining the park. There are several pleasant walks and drives, and in the centre of the park a trench has been cut, into which water will be brought from the New River, and in this way a pretty artificial lake will be added to the other attractions. The cost of the freehold land was about £472 per acre. The funds were principally raised by a loan, in 1864, of £50,000, at 4½ per cent., for thirty years, and £43,000 borrowed on debenture in 1868."

The lake above mentioned is an oblong piece of water surrounded by pleasant walks, and in parts shaded by trees, and in it are one or two islands well covered with young trees, which give to the lake somewhat the appearance of the "ornamental waters" in St. James's Park, a similitude borne out by the number of ducks and other water-fowl disporting themselves on its surface.

The Seven Sisters Road, skirting the south side of Finsbury Park, was constructed in 1832, prior to which time there was no thoroughfare through Holloway and Hornsey to Tottenham.

In a map of the suburbs of London in 1823, "Duval's Lane" is shown as running from Lower Holloway towards Crouch End, with scarcely a house on either side. A small and crooked road, marked Hem Lane, with "Duval's House" at the corner, leads also through fields towards "Hornsey Wood House," and so into the Green Lanes—all being open country. The now populous district of Crouch End appears here as a small group of private residences. Between the "Wood House" and Crouch End is Stroud Green, around which are five or six rustic cottages. On the other side of the "Wood House" is the "Sluice House," where privileged persons and customers of "mine host" went to fish in the New River and to sup upon eels, for which that place was famous, as stated above. Upper Holloway itself figures in this map as a very small collection of houses belonging apparently to private residents.

A pretty walk from Finsbury Park to Hornsey Church in fine dry weather is by the pathway running in a northerly direction over Mount Pleasant, a somewhat steep hill, from which some pleasant views are to be obtained of the surrounding country, embracing Highgate, the Alexandra Palace, Epping Forest, Tottenham Church, and the valley of the river Lea. The summit of Mount Pleasant is upwards of 200 feet above the level of the river; and its eastern end, from its peculiar shape, has been called the Northern Hog's Back.

The parish church of Hornsey lies, at some little distance from the village, in a valley near the Hornsey Station on the Great Northern Railway, and its tower forms a conspicuous object in the view from the neighbouring uplands. With the exception of the tower, the present fabric is comparatively modern, dating only from about the year 1833; it is built of brick, and is of Gothic architecture. Its predecessor, which was pulled down in 1832, is stated by Norden and Camden to have been built with stones taken from the ruins of the palace of the Bishops of London, about the year 1500. The *Ambulator*, in 1774, describes the church as "a poor, irregular building, said to have been built out of the ruins of an ancient castle." The tower, which is now profusely covered with ivy, is built of a reddish sandstone, and is embattled, with a newel turret rising above the north-west corner. On the western face of the tower are

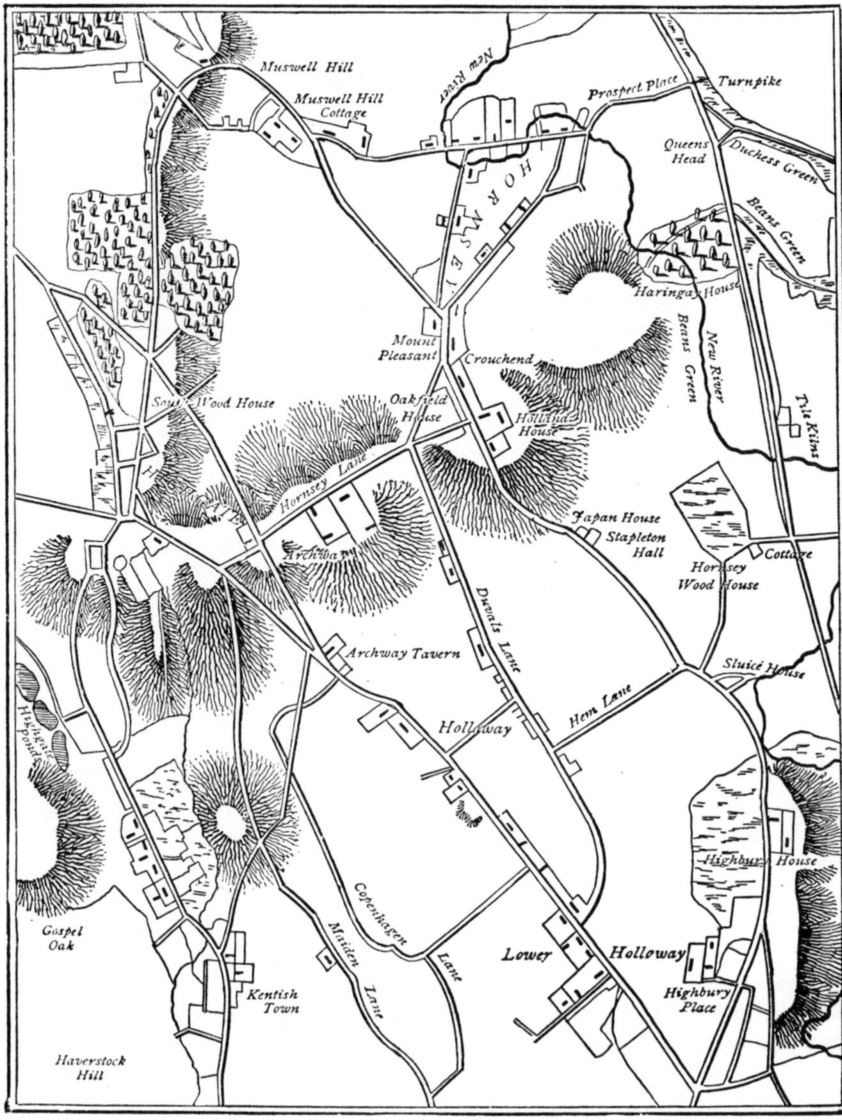

MAP OF HORNSEY AND NEIGHBOURHOOD IN 1819.

sculptured two winged angels, bearing the arms of Savage and Warham, successively Bishops of London, the former of whom came to the see in 1497. It is probable that both of these prelates were contributors to the fabric. Some of the windows of the present church are filled with stained glass, and among the monuments are a few preserved from the older building. Among these is a large mural slab, on which are engraved the kneeling figures of a man, two females, and a boy; the dress appears to be of the latter part of the sixteenth century, and the monument was erected to the memory of George Rey, of Highgate. A Corinthian column, surmounted with armorial bearings, commemorates Dr. Lewis Atterbury (brother of the celebrated bishop), some time rector of the parish, who died in 1731. This monument was brought hither on the demolition of the old chapel at Highgate, where, as we have stated in a previous chapter, Dr. Atterbury was for many years preacher. Samuel Buckley, the editor of *Thuanus*, who died in 1741, is commemorated by a monument; as also is "Master Richard Candish [Cavendish], of Suffolk, Esq." An inscription in verse upon the latter monument informs us that "this memorial was promised and made by Margaret, Countess of Cōberland, 1601."

THE ALEXANDRA PALACE, 1876. (*See page* 435.)

The churchyard is sheltered by rows of tall elms, which impart to it an air of retirement and seclusion. Here, amongst other tombs, on the northern side of the church, is that of the poet Rogers, of whom we have spoken in our account of St. James's

Place.* It is an altar-tomb, resting on a high base, and surrounded by an iron railing. The following are the inscriptions on the face of the tomb :—" In this vault lie the remains of Henry Rogers, Esq., of Highbury Terrace; died December 25, 1832, aged 58. Also of Sarah Rogers, of the Regent's Park, sister of the above; died January 29, 1855, aged 82. Also of Samuel Rogers, author of the 'Pleasures of Memory,' brother of the above-named Henry and Sarah Rogers; born at Newington Green, July 30, 1763, died at St. James's Place, Westminster, December 18, 1855." Near the south-east corner of the churchyard an upright stone marks the grave of Anne Jane Barbara, the youngest daughter of Thomas Moore, the poet.

Amongst the rectors of Hornsey there have been a few who have become known beyond the circle of the parish. Of these we may mention Thomas Westfield, who resigned the living in 1637, afterwards Bishop of Bristol, and who is described as "the most nervous of men." His biographer says that "he never, though almost fifty years a preacher, went up into the pulpit but he trembled; and never preached before the king but once, and then he fainted." "Yet he was held in such esteem by all parties," writes Mr. Howitt in his "Northern Heights of London," "that on May 13, 1643, the committee for sequestrating the estates of delinquents, being informed that his tenants refused to pay his rents as Bishop of Bristol, speedily compelled them, and granted him a safe conduct for his journey to Bristol with his family, being a man of great learning and merit, and advanced in years. His successor at Hornsey, Thomas Lant, did not meet with quite such agreeable treatment. He was turned out of his living and house with great cruelty by the Puritans, who would not allow him even to procure a place of retirement. Samuel Bendy, rector in 1659, petitioned the committee, setting forth that his income was only £92, out of which he had to pay £16 to the wife and children of the late incumbent. The committee made him recompense." The Rev. William Cole, the Cambridge antiquary, and the friend and correspondent of Horace Walpole, held the rectory for about a year in the middle of the last century.

At the end of the lane running west from the church, and at the foot of Muswell Hill, is Lalla Rookh Cottage, where Moore was residing in 1817 when he wrote, or, at all events, when he published, the poem bearing the title of "Lalla Rookh," for which, as we learn from his "Life," he received £3,000 from Messrs. Longmans, the publishers. In this house his youngest daughter died, as above stated.

A native of Dublin and a son of Roman Catholic parents, Moore came over to England when still young to push his fortunes in the world of literature, and became the poet laureate of Holland House and of the Whig party. During his latter years he occupied Sloperton Cottage, a small house adjoining Lord Lansdowne's park at Bowood, near Calne, in Wiltshire, where he died in 1852, at the age of seventy-three. Lord Russell claims for Moore the first place among our lyric poets, but few will be willing to allow his superiority to Robert Burns, though he was certainly the English Beranger. He was probably the best hand at improvised song-writing on the common topics of every-day life, but he had no real depth of feeling. A refined, voluptuous, and natural character, equally frank and gay, he passed, after all, a somewhat butterfly existence, and has left behind him but little that will last except his "Irish Melodies."

Continuing along the pleasant lane westward from Lalla Rookh Cottage, we come to Muswell Hill, a place which has now become familiar to Londoners—and, probably, to the majority of readers—from the fact that its summit and sides are for the most part occupied by the Alexandra Palace and Park, which covers altogether an area of about five hundred acres. Before venturing to give a description of this place of amusement, or a narrative of its unfortunate career, we may be pardoned for saying a few words about the hill whereon it is situated.

Muswell Hill, then, we may observe, derives its name from a famous well on the top of the hill, where formerly the fraternity of St. John of Jerusalem, in Clerkenwell, had their dairy, with a large farm adjacent. Here they built a chapel for the benefit of some nuns, in which they fixed the image of Our Lady of Muswell. These nuns had the sole management of the dairy; and it is singular that the said well and farm do, at this time, belong to the parish of St. James, Clerkenwell. The water of this spring was then deemed a miraculous cure for scrofulous and cutaneous disorders; and, as tradition says, a king of Scotland—whose name, by the way, does not transpire—being afflicted with a painful malady, made a pilgrimage hither, and was perfectly cured. At any rate, the spring was much resorted to, and became an object of pilgrimage in the Middle Ages; indeed, for some considerable time there was a great throng of pilgrims to the shrine of Our Lady, who came laden with their offerings and buoyed up with their hopes from all parts of the country.

* See Vol. IV., pp. 172—175.

Lysons, writing in 1795, remarks that "the well still remains; but," he somewhat naïvely adds, "it is not famed, as I find, for any extraordinary virtues." Muswell farmhouse, with the site of the chapel, together with the manor of Muswell, was alienated in 1546 by William Cowper to William Goldynge, and, after a few other changes of ownership, passed into the hands of the Rowes, in whose possession it continued at the end of the seventeenth century. It soon afterwards came into the family of Pulteney; and, according to Lysons, on the death of Lady Bath, devolved, under Sir William Pulteney's will, on the Earl of Darlington. Muswell Hill, it may be added, was in former times called also Pinsenhall Hill.

Shortly after the close of the second International Exhibition (that of 1862) at South Kensington, it was resolved to erect on this spot a place of popular entertainment for the working classes of northern London, which should rival the Crystal Palace at Sydenham. To the great mass of people in the north of London the Crystal Palace, except on great occasions and great attractions, is so distant as to be almost inaccessible; and it is reported, as was proved by railway returns, it is mainly the south London population which keeps up the great building "over the water." There seemed no valid reason, therefore, why the north of London, with at least three times the number of inhabitants, should not be able to support a Crystal Palace of its own. It was considered, moreover, that the Alexandra Palace—for such the building was to be named, in honour of the Princess Alexandra—would not be dependent on support from local influences. The rare beauty of its site, which probably has not its equal anywhere round London, together with the special attractions in the building, would be sure to make it a universal favourite with both the north and south of the metropolis.

With regard to the palace itself, it was decided to purchase some portion of the materials of the International Exhibition, and with them to erect the building on the summit of Muswell Hill, in the same manner as the originators of its prototype at Sydenham had purchased for that purpose the materials of the Great Exhibition of 1851. The new palace, therefore, was almost entirely built out of the materials of the Great Exhibition of 1862, but totally altered and improved in their re-construction. It had only one of the noble domes in the centre transept, with two less lofty octagon towers at either end. It had one main nave, exclusive of the entrances, about 900 feet long, and three cross transepts of about 400 feet each. The building was beautifully decorated in the Renaissance style; and round the eight columns which supported the great central dome were ranged groups of statuary surrounded by flowers. Behind this ornamental walk were placed the cases for the exhibitors, mixed, as in the nave itself, with flowers and statuary. Then there were a variety of courts—such as the glass court, china court, furniture court, courts for French goods, courts for American, Indian, Italian—in short, all the courts which we are accustomed to find in a regular exhibition. At the north end of the centre transept was built a splendid organ by Willis, decorated in a style to be in harmony with its surroundings, and in front of this was the orchestra. A large concert-room was in another part of the building. Then there was a theatre capable of holding 2,000 spectators, and having a stage as large as that of Drury Lane Theatre.

During the progress of the building, sundry stoppages and hindrances arose from various causes; and in the grounds great difficulty was at times experienced through the subsidence of the soil; indeed, to use the words of one of the contractor's foremen, the hills round Muswell had during one winter "been slipping about like anything." Strange as such a statement may seem, it is literally true. The hills, it is asserted, had been moving in all sorts of directions. They are mostly of gravel, but resting, at about twenty feet deep, on a two-feet seam of soapy clay, which, when the superincumbent mass was thoroughly penetrated by the constant rain, allowed it to slip. Fortunately, the Alexandra Palace was so deeply moored in its foundations that it never shifted or showed the slightest signs of any subsidence or yielding in any direction; yet a very formidable landslip took place close by it, and in one night between three and four acres slipped quietly down a few feet. Another hill came forward as much as three inches in a single night, but beyond this landslip none of the hills round the palace have moved to any material extent, except where the viaduct for the railway crosses over a small valley just before arriving at the palace.

After a delay of some six or seven years beyond the first appointed time, the palace and grounds being all but completed, the place was opened to the public on the 24th of May, 1873. The proceedings, though not graced by the presence of royalty, were as successful an inauguration of a national institution as could possibly have been expected. The opening was inaugurated by a grand concert, presided over by Sir Michael Costa, in which some of the leading singers of the day took part. But, alas! about mid-day on the 9th of June the whole building fell a prey to the flames, and all that was left was a melancholy and gutted ruin. The fire originated at the base of the great dome, where some workmen had been employed in "repairing the roof," and had, possibly, let some lighted tobacco fall into a crevice. During the brief period the palace was open (fourteen days only) it was visited by as many as 124,124 persons, and its success was no longer doubtful. Thus encouraged, the directors resolved at once to rebuild the palace, and in its re-construction they availed themselves of the experience so dearly purchased, particularly with reference to arrangements for protection from fire.

The new building, which was opened on the 1st of May, 1875, occupies an area of about seven acres, and is constructed in the most substantial manner. It contains the grand hall, capable of seating 12,000 visitors and an orchestra of 2,000; the Italian garden, a spacious court in which are asphalte paths, flower-beds, and a fine fountain; also the concert-room, which has been erected on the best known acoustic principles, and will seat 3,500 visitors. The conservatory is surmounted by a glass dome, and in close proximity are two spacious halls for the exhibition of works of art; also the corridor for displaying ornamental works. The reading-room is a very comfortable apartment, and near thereto are the modern Moorish house and an Egyptian villa. The theatre is of the most perfect kind, and will seat more than 3,000 persons. The exhibition department is divided into two parts, the space occupied being 204 feet by 106 feet. The bazaar department is 213 feet by 140 feet. The frontage of the stalls is upwards of 3,000 feet, and they are so arranged as to give the greatest facility of access to visitors and purchasers. The picture-galleries are on the northern side of the building, and comprise six fine, large, well-lighted rooms. The refreshment department is of the most complete and extensive character, including spacious grill and coffee rooms, two banqueting rooms, drawing, billiard, and smoke rooms, and private rooms for large or small parties, and the grand dining saloon, which will accommodate as many as 1,000 persons at table. For the efficient supply of this vast establishment, the plan of the basement is considered to be the most perfect as well as the most extensive of its kind ever yet seen. Also, within the building, are numerous private offices for manager and clerks, and a spacious board-room.

The park is richly timbered, and of a pleasingly undulated surface, intersected by broad carriage drives, and there are several ornamental lakes of great beauty in connection with the surrounding scenery; a number of Swiss chalets and other rustic buildings, also horticultural gardens, with extensive ranges of glass houses. At the foot of the hill on which the palace stands there is a racecourse upwards of a mile in length, and the grand stand is one of the handsomest and most substantial buildings of its kind in this country. There is also a trotting ring on the American principle, and, in connection therewith, an extensive range of stabling for several hundred horses, thus rendering the property well adapted for horse and agricultural shows; and a grand stand and paddock. The cricket-ground is ten acres in extent, with two pavilions, and every convenience for cricketers. There is also a Japanese village, comprising a temple, a residence, and a bazaar. In the bazaar articles of Japanese work were offered for sale. A circus for equestrian performances was likewise erected in the grounds, together with a spacious banqueting hall, an open-air swimming-bath, and other novel features. Besides all these attractions, there is a charming and secluded nook in the grounds, called the Grove, bordering on the Highgate Road. In a house here, Thrale, the brewer, is reported to have lived, and to have had among his guests the great lexicographer of the Georgian era, as is testified to this day by a pathway shaded by trees, called Dr. Johnson's Walk. The Grove has been described by an able writer as "a wild natural garden, clothed with the utmost beauty to which the luxuriance of our northern vegetation can attain. On one side a low, thick hedge of holly, pillared by noble oaks, flanks a great terrace-walk, commanding a noble view over a slope which descends rapidly from the prickly barrier. Very few such oaks are to be found within this island: lofty, sturdy, and well-grown trees, not marked by the hollow boles and distorted limbs of extreme old age, but in the very prime of vegetable manhood. Turning at right angles, at the end of this semi-avenue, the walk skirts a rapid descent, clothed with turf of that silky fineness which denotes long and careful garden culture, and set with a labyrinth of trees, each one of which is a study in itself. A noble cedar of Lebanon rises in a group of spires like a foreshortened Gothic cathedral. A holly, which, from its perfect and unusual symmetry, deceives the eye as to size, and looks like a sapling close at hand, has a bole of some fifteen feet girth, rising for twenty-four feet before it breaks into branches. Farther on, the walk is bordered by laurel hedges, and overlooks a wide sweep of country, undulated, wooded, and studded by many a spiry steeple to the north; and here we meet with an elm, standing alone on the turf, as perfect in its giant symmetry as the holly we have just admired. Then, perhaps, the monarch of all, we come upon a gigantic chestnut, which seems as if, like the trees once in the Garden of Eden, no touch of iron had ever fallen upon its limbs." Notwithstanding all these varied attractions, the Alexandra Palace has never yet answered the expectations of its promoters, and has more than once been offered for sale by auction and withdrawn, the offers falling far short of the value put upon the property by its owners.

The view from the top of the hill on which the palace stands is, perhaps, unrivalled for beauty within many miles of London. At our feet, looking northwards, is Southgate, of which Leigh Hunt wrote that it was a pleasure to be born in so sweet a village, cradled, not only in the lap of Nature, which he loved, but in the midst of the truly English scenery which he loved beyond all other. "Middlesex is," he adds, "a scene of greenery and nestling villages, and Southgate is a prime specimen of Middlesex. It is a place lying out of the way of innovation, and therefore it has the pure sweet air of antiquity about it." And the remark is true, with a few exceptions, of all the towns and villages of this district. Look along the line of railway that branches off at Wood Green, and you will see the Enfield where Keats grew to be a poet, and where Charles Lamb died. Look a little to the left, and there is Colney Hatch Asylum, with its two thousand inmates. A little farther on lies Hadley Wood, a lovely spot for a picnic; and there rises the grey tower of Barnet Church, reminding you of the battle of Barnet, fought but a little farther on. A little on our left is Finchley Common, where they still show us Grimaldi's Cottage and Dick Turpin's Oak. If we look over Wood Green, now a town, but a short time back a wild common, we see in the far distance Tottenham and Edmonton, and what remains of Epping Forest. Hornsey, with its ivy tower, is just beneath; to our right is Highgate; and a little farther on is Hampstead Heath.

Johnson's friend, Topham Beauclerc, it may be added, lived for some time on Muswell Hill; and Sir Robert Walpole, it is asserted, also resided at one time in this locality. Boswell is silent as to the connection of the former with this place, and for the residence of Sir Robert Walpole here we have only a local tradition.

Among its inhabitants during the last century was Lawrence, the "mad" Earl Ferrers, who lodged here for some months previous to committing the murder of his steward, for which he was executed at Tyburn.* His conduct even whilst here was most eccentric, and such as might fairly have consigned him to a lunatic asylum. He mixed with the lowest company, would drink coffee out of the spout of a kettle, mix his porter with mud, and shave one side of his face. He threatened more than once to "do for" his landlady, and on another occasion he violently broke open on a Sunday the stable where his horse was locked up, knocking down with his fist the ostler's wife when she asked him to wait a few minutes while her husband brought the key.

Another resident at Hornsey in former times was the learned John Lightfoot, the commentator, who selected this spot in order that he might have access to the library at Sion College. Lightfoot, who was born at the beginning of the seventeenth century, is stated to have published his first work, entitled "Erubhim; or, Miscellanies Christian and Judaical," in 1629, the next year after settling at Hornsey. He was a strong promoter of the Polyglott Bible, and at the Restoration was appointed one of the assistants at the Savoy Conference. In 1675 he became Vice-Chancellor of the University of Cambridge.

Crouch End, which lies to the south-west of the village, is connected with the Highgate Archway Road by the sloping lands of Hornsey Rise. Stroud Green, of which we have spoken in our account of the manor of Highbury,† is in this district; and although it is fast being encroached upon by the demon of bricks and mortar, it has still some few shady lanes and "bits" of rural scenery left. On rising ground on the south side of Crouch End stands Christ Church, one of the district churches of Hornsey. It was built in 1863, from the designs of Mr. A. W. Blomfield, and is a neat edifice, in the Gothic style of architecture. The church was enlarged about ten years later, when a tower and spire were added. St. Luke's Church, Hornsey Rise, built in 1861, from the designs of Mr. A. D. Gough, is a respectable common-place modern Gothic building; and consists of a nave with side aisles, transepts, and chancel with side chapels.

At the beginning of 1877 a handsome Gothic church was consecrated here; it is dedicated to the Holy Innocents, and stands near the railway station. This church was the third which had been built during the incumbency of Canon Harvey, in which period Hornsey has grown from a mere village into a town of some 10,000 inhabitants.

* See *ante*, p. 192.

† See Vol. II., p. 275.

THE VALE OF HEALTH. (*See page* 457.)

CHAPTER XXXIV.

HAMPSTEAD.—CAEN WOOD AND NORTH END.

"When the sweet-breathing spring unfolds the buds,
Love flies the dusty town for shady woods;
Then Tottenham fields with roving beauty swarm,
And Hampstead halls the City virgins warm."—*Gay.*

The Etymology and Early History of Hampstead—"Hot Gospellers"—The Hollow Tree—An Inland Watering-place—Caen Wood Towers—Dufferin Lodge—Origin of the Name of Caen (or Ken) Wood—Thomas Venner and the Fifth Monarchy Men—Caen Wood House and Grounds—Lord Mansfield—The House saved from a Riotous Attack by a Clever Ruse—Visit of William IV.—Highgate and Hampstead Ponds—The Fleet River—Bishop's Wood—The "Spaniards"—New Georgia—Erskine House—The Great Lord Erskine—Heath House—The Firs—North End—Lord Chatham's Gloomy Retirement—Wildwood House—Jackson, the Highwayman—Akenside—William Blake, the Artist and Poet—Coventry Patmore—Miss Meteyard—Sir T. Fowell Buxton—The "Bull and Bush."

In commencing this chapter we may observe that there are two ways by which the pedestrian can reach Hampstead from Highgate—namely, by the road branching off at the "Gate House" and running along the brow of the hill past the "Spaniards," and so on to the Heath; and also by the pleasant footpath which skirts the grounds of Caen Wood on its southern side. This pathway branches off from Millfield Lane, nearly opposite the grounds of Lady Burdett-Coutts, and passing by the well-known Highgate Ponds, winds its course over the gently undulating meadows and uplands which extend westward to the slope of the hill leading up to Hampstead Heath; the pathway itself terminating close by the ponds of Hampstead, of which, together with the charming spot close by, called the Vale of Health, we shall have more to say presently. For our part, we shall take the first-named route; but before setting out on our perambulation, it will be well, perhaps, to say a few words about Hampstead in general.

Starting, then, with the name, we may observe that the etymology of Hampstead is evidently derived from the Saxon "ham" or *home*, and "stede" or *place*. The modern form of the word "homestead" is still in common use for the family residence, or more generally for a farmhouse, surrounded by barns and other out-buildings. "Homestead," too, according to the ingenious Mr. Lysons, is the true etymology of the name. "Hame" is

CAEN WOOD, LORD MANSFIELD'S HOUSE, IN 1785. (*See page* 441.)

the well-known Scotch form for "home;" and the syllable "ham" is preserved in "hamlet," and, as a termination, in innumerable names of places in this country. West Ham, Birming-ham, Old-ham, and many others immediately suggest themselves; and we can easily reckon a dozen Hamptons, in which the first syllable has a similar origin to that of Hampstead; while, under the modern German form, *heim*, we meet with it in Blenheim. There are two Hampsteads in Berkshire, besides Hemel Hempstead in Hertfordshire. The name, then, of the solitary Saxon farm was applied in the course of years to the village or town which gradually surrounded it and at length took its place. Who the hardy Saxon was who first made a clearing in this elevated part of the thick Middlesex forest, we know not; but we have record that this wood afforded pannage or pasturage for a hundred head of swine, which fed on the chestnuts, beech-nuts, and acorns. In 986 King Ethelred granted the manor of Hamstede to the Abbot of Westminster; and this grant was confirmed by Edward the Confessor, with additional privileges. We are told by Mr. Park, in his "History of Hampstead," that in early times it was a little chapelry, dependent on the mother church of Hendon, which was itself an incumbency in the gift of the abbot and monks of the convent of St. Peter in Westminster. To this day the Dean and Chapter of Westminster own a considerable quantity of land in the parish, whence they draw a considerable income, owing to the increased and increasing value of property. Before the Reformation, it is clear that the Rector of Hendon was himself responsible for the cost of the keep of "a separate capellane," or chaplain to serve "the chapell of the Blessed Virgin at Hamsted;" this, however, was not a very heavy cost, for the stipend of an assistant curate at that day was only from six to eight marks a year; and in the reign of Edward VI., the curacy of Hampstead itself, as we learn casually from a Chancery roll, was valued at £10 per annum. It is not at all clear when the benefice of Hampstead was separated from that of Hendon, but the ties of the one must have been separated from those of the other before the year 1598, when the churchwardens of Hampstead were for the first time summoned to the Bishop of London's visitation, a fact which looks like the commencement of a parochial settlement. It is probable that the correct date is 1560, as the register of baptisms, marriages, and burials commences in that year.

In the reign of Edward VI. the manor and advowson of Hampstead were granted by the young king to Sir Thomas Wroth, Knt., from whose family they passed, about seventy years later, by purchase, to Sir Baptist Hickes, afterwards Viscount Campden, whose descendant Baptist, third Earl of Gainsborough, alienated them to Sir W. Langhorne, Bart., in 1707. They passed from the Langhornes by descent through the hands of three females, to the family of the present patron, Sir Spencer Maryon-Wilson, Bart., of Charlton House, Kent.

At the time of the dissolution, Hampstead, it appears, was a very small village, inhabited chiefly by washerwomen, and for the next 150 years its history is almost a blank. In the Puritan times the "Hot Gospellers," as they were nicknamed, often preached under the shade of an enormous elm, which was certainly a great curiosity, its trunk having been occupied by some virtuoso unrecorded in local history, who constructed a winding staircase of forty-two steps within the hollow, and built an octagonal tower on the summit, thirty-four feet in circumference, and capable of holding twenty persons. The height from the ground to the base of the turret was thirty-three feet, and there were sixteen side lights. There is a curious etching, by Hollar, of this "Hollow Tree at Hampstead." The exact locality of this tree is a matter of doubt. The copy of the etching in the royal collection at Windsor forms part of a "broadside" at the foot of which is printed "To be given or sold on the hollow tree at Hampstead." One Robert Codrington, a poetical student, and afterwards a Puritan, inspired by the tree, wrote an elaborate poem, in which he says,

> "In less room, I find,
> With all his trusty knights, King Arthur dined."

Hampstead is now nearly joined to London by rows of villas and terraces; but within the memory of the present generation it was separated from town by a broad belt of pleasant fields. Eighty or a hundred years ago it was a rural village, adorned with many fine mansions, whither retired, in search of health or recreation, some of the most eminent men of the age. The beauty of its fields is celebrated by the author of "Suburban Sonnets" in Hone's "Table Book:"

> "Hampstead, I doubly venerate thy name,"

for it seems it was here that the writer first became imbued with the feeling of love and with the spirit of poetry.

It is the fashion to undervalue the suburbs of London; and several clever writers, proud of their mountains and their lakes, have a smile of contempt ready for us when we talk of our "upland hamlets," our fertile valleys, and our broad river. The fact is that the suburbs of London are beautiful as compared with the suburbs of other great cities. But so long as the breezy heath, and its smooth velvet turf, sloping away to the north and east, remain unbuilt upon, Hampstead will never cease to be the favourite haunt and home of poets, painters, and artists, which it has been for the last century or more. There still attaches to the older part of the town a certain stately air of dignified respectability, in the red-brick spacious mansions; and the parish church, though really not old as churches count age, with its spacious churchyard, bears record of many whose names are familiar to us all.

Hampstead, it has been observed, is in every respect a watering-place—except in there being no sea there. With that important drawback, it possesses all the necessary attributes: it has its donkeys, its bath-chairs, its fashionable esplanade, its sand and sandpits, its chalybeate spring, its "eligible" houses "to be let furnished," its more humble "apartments," its "Vale of Health," where "parties" can be supplied with "hot water for tea," at various prices, from twopence to fourpence per head; its fancy stationers' shop, with the proper supply of dolls, novels, and illustrated note paper; its old church and its new church; its chapel of ease; its flagstaff—ready to "dip" its colours to steamers, which, from the nature of the case, can never appear in the offing; its photographic pavilion, with portraits "in this style" (a style which would effectually prevent any sensible person from entering the place of execution); its country walks and rides; its residents, so exclusive; its troops of visitors; its boys, fishing for tadpoles with crooked pins in the (freshwater) ponds; its tribes of healthy children with their nurses and nursemaids;—in fact, it has all that can make the heart glad, and place Hampstead on the list of sea-bathing places, with the trifling omission mentioned above.

With these remarks, we will once more take up our staff and proceed.

Leaving Highgate by the turning westward close by the "Gate House," and passing by the Grove, we make our way along the high road which connects the village with Hampstead. The old way being narrow, and nearly impassable, a new and more direct road was made, affording a splendid panoramic view of vast extent. In the formation of the new road, too, its course in one or two parts was slightly altered. On the slope of the hill to the left, and standing on ground which originally formed a portion of Fitzroy Park, is Caen Wood Towers, till lately the residence of Mr. Edward Brooke, the patentee of the magenta and other dyes. The building occupies part of the site of Dufferin Lodge, formerly the seat of Lord Dufferin, which was pulled down in 1869. The present house, which was completed in 1872, from the designs of Messrs. Salomons and Jones, is built of red brick with stone dressings; and with its bay windows, gables, and massive towers, stands out prominently amid the surrounding trees.

Pursuing our course along the Hampstead road, we reach the principal entrance to the estate of Caen (or Ken) Wood, the seat of the Earl of Mansfield. Though generally regarded as part and parcel of Hampstead, the estate lies just within the boundary of the parish of St. Pancras, and was part of the manor of Cantelows. It is said by antiquaries to form a part of the remains of the ancient forest of Middlesex. Lysons is of opinion that the wood and the neighbouring hamlet of Kentish Town (anciently Kentestoune) were both named after some very remote possessor. There was, he says, a Dean of St. Paul's named Reginald de "Kentewode," and "the alteration from Kentwode to Kenwood is by no means unlikely to happen." Mr. Howitt looks for the origin of the syllable in the word "Ken," a view. As, however, we have stated in previous chapters,* the word Caen may, perhaps, be an equivalent to "Kaen" or Ken, which lies at the root of *Ken*tish Town, *Ken*sington, &c.

The earliest mention of the place, remarks Mr. Prickett, in his "History of Highgate," appears in Neale's "History of the Puritans," where it is spoken of as affording shelter for a short time to Venner and his associates—the "Fifth monarchy men." In the outbreak of the "Fifth monarchy men," under Thomas Venner, the cooper of Coleman Street, in January, 1661, these fanatics having fought one engagement with the "Train-bands," and expecting another struggle next day, took shelter for a night in Caen Wood, where some of them were taken prisoners next morning, and the rest were dispersed. As probably few or none of them were killed, the spot where the encounter took place cannot now be identified by any discovery of bodies hastily buried, as is commonly the case in the neighbourhood of battle-fields.

From the first volume of "Selected Views in London and its Environs," published in 1804, we glean the following particulars of this demesne:—"Caen Wood, the beautiful seat of the Earl of Mansfield, is situated on a fine eminence between Hampstead and Highgate, and its extensive

* See *ante*, pp. 118, 317.

grounds contribute in no small degree to enrich the neighbouring scenery. These, with the wood which gives name to them, contain about forty acres, and are laid out with great taste. On the right of the garden front of the house (which is a very noble mansion) is a hanging wood of tall spreading trees, mostly beeches; and on the left the rising hills are planted with trees, that produce a pleasing effect. These, with a sweet shrubbery immediately before the front, and a serpentine piece of water, render the whole a very enlivening (*sic*) scene. The enclosed fields adjoining to the pleasure-grounds contain about thirty acres more. Hornsey great woods, held by the Earl of Mansfield under the Bishop of London, join this estate on the north, and have lately been added to the enclosure."

Mr. Howitt, in his "Northern Heights," gives the following interesting particulars about Caen Wood and House:—"Caen House," he writes, "is a large and massive building of yellow stone, impressive from its bulk and its commanding situation, rather than from its architecture, which is that of Robert Adam, who was very fashionable in the early part of the reign of George III. Caen Wood House has two fronts, one facing the north, with projecting wings; the other facing the south, extending along a noble terrace, and has its façade elongated by a one-storeyed wing at each side. The basement storey of the main body of the house is of rustic work, surmounted by a pediment supported by Ionic pilasters, the columns of the wings being of the same order. Within, Adam, as was usual with him, was more successful than without. The rooms are spacious, lofty, and finely proportioned. They contain a few good paintings, among which are some of Claude's; a portrait of Pope, the poet, with whom the first earl was very intimate; and a full-length one of the great law lord himself, as well as a bust of him by Nollekens. The park in front, of fifty acres, is arranged to give a feeling of seclusion in a spot so near to London. The ground descends to some sheets of water forming a continuation of the Highgate Ponds, lying amid trees; and a belt of fine, well-grown wood cuts off the broad open view of the metropolis. Here you have all the sylvan seclusion of a remote country mansion; and charming walks, said to be nearly two miles in extent, conduct you round the park, and through the woods, where stand some trees of huge growth and grandeur, especially cedars of Lebanon and beeches. A good deal of this planting, especially some fine cedars yet near the house, was done under the direction of the first lord himself. A custom is kept up here which smacks of the old feudal times. Every morning, when the night-watchman goes off duty, at six o'clock, he fires a gun, and immediately three long winds are given on a horn to call the servants, gardeners, and labourers to their employment. The horn is blown again at breakfast and dinner hours, and at six in the evening for their dismissal.

"This charming place had been in the hands of a succession of proprietors. In 1661 it was the property of a Mr. John Bill, who married a Lady Pelham, supposed to be the widow of Sir Thomas Pelham, and a daughter of Sir Henry Vane. It must afterwards have belonged to one Dale, an upholsterer, who, as Mackay, in his 'Tour through England,' says, 'had bought it out of the 'Bubbles' —*i.e.*, the South Sea affair. This was in 1720. This Mr. Dale, unlike the majority of speculators, must have been a fortunate one. It then became the property of the Dukes of Argyll; and the great and good Duke John, whom Sir Walter Scott introduces so nobly in the scene with Jeanie Deans and Queen Caroline in 'The Heart of Midlothian,' who had lived in the reigns of Anne and Georges I. and II., and who had fought bravely at Ramillies, Malplaquet, and Oudenarde, and who afterwards beat the rebel Earl of Mar and drove the Pretender from Scotland, resided here when called to London. The property was then devised by the Duke of Argyll to his nephew John, third Earl of Bute, who is only too well remembered in the opening of the reign of George III. for his unpopularity as a minister* of the Crown.

"Lord Bute married the only daughter of the celebrated Lady Mary Wortley Montagu, who, of course, resided much here as Countess of Bute. It is observed that in Lady Mary's letters to her daughter, she always spells the name of the place 'Caen.' The earlier possessors spelt it 'Ken,' and it is curious, too, that though in the patent of the earldom granted to Lord Mansfield it is spelt 'Caen,' Lord Mansfield himself, in his letters, to the end of his life spelt it 'Ken.'

"The Earl of Bute sold Caen Wood, in 1755, to Lord Mansfield, who, on his death, devised it, as an appendage of the title, to his nephew (and successor in the earldom of Mansfield), Lord Stormont, whose descendants now possess it. Lady Mary Wortley Montagu's daughter brought Lord Bute seven sons and six daughters, so at that time the house and grounds of Caen Wood resounded with life enough. It is now very little occupied, its proprietor being much fonder of Scone Palace, his Scotch residence."

---

* See Vol. IV., p. 88

Among the trees mentioned above are four fine cedars, planted in the reign of George II.; they are now upwards of a hundred feet in height.

Mr. Thorne, in his "Handbook of the Environs of London," says that among the treasures that are preserved here, are "the charred and stained relics saved from the fire made of Lord Mansfield's books, by the Gordon rioters, in 1780."

Coleridge, in one of his letters to Mr. H. C. Robinson, speaks of being "driven in Mr. Gillman's gig to Caen Wood, and its delicious groves and valleys—the finest in England; in fact, a cathedral aisle of giant lime-trees, and Pope's favourite composition walk when staying with the Earl of Mansfield." As, however, Pope died at Twickenham, in 1744, and Lord Mansfield did not come into possession of Caen Wood until ten or eleven years after Pope's death, it is clear that there must be some discrepancy here.

Although born in Scotland, Lord Mansfield seems to have turned his back upon his native country at a very early age; indeed, Dr. Johnson, if we may believe Boswell, "would not allow Scotland to derive any credit from Lord Mansfield, for he was educated in England; much," he would say, "may be made of a Scotchman, if he be caught young."

In our account of Bloomsbury Square,* we have spoken of the burning of Lord Mansfield's house, and of the escape of his lordship and Lady Mansfield. Maddened by this and many other unchecked excesses, the word of command was given "to Ken Wood," the rioters evidently intending that this mansion should share a similar fate. "The routes of the rabble," writes Mr. Prickett, in his work above quoted, "were through Highgate and Hampstead, to the 'Spaniards' Tavern,' kept at the time by a person named Giles Thomas. He quickly learnt their object, and with a coolness and promptitude which did him great credit, persuaded the rioters to refresh themselves thoroughly before commencing the work of devastation; he threw his house open, and even his cellars for their entertainment, but secretly dispatched a messenger to the barracks for a detachment of the Horse Guards, which, arriving through Millfield Farm Lane, intercepted the approach northward, and opportunely presented a bold front to the rebels, who by that time had congregated in the road which then passed within a few paces of the mansion. Whilst some of the rioters were being regaled at the 'Spaniards,' others were liberally supplied with strong ale from the cellars of Ken Wood House, out of tubs placed on the roadside. Mr. William Wetherell, also, who attended the family, happened to be on the spot, and, with great resolution and presence of mind, addressed the mob, and induced many to adjourn to the 'Spaniards' for a short period. The liquors, the excitement, and the infatuation soon overcame the exhausted condition of the rabble, who, in proportion to the time thus gained by the troops, had become doubly disqualified for concerted mischief; for, great as were their numbers, their daring was not equal to the comparatively small display of military, which, the leading rioters felt, would show them no mercy; they instantly abandoned their intentions, and returned to the metropolis in as much disorder as they quitted it."

* See Vol. IV., p. 539.

In 1835, King William IV., accompanied by several members of the royal family, the Duke of Wellington, and many of the leading nobility, paid a visit to Caen Wood. A grand entertainment was given by Lord Mansfield on the occasion, and a triumphal arch was erected on Hampstead Heath, under which the king received an address from his loyal subjects.

In the lower part of Lord Mansfield's grounds are several large ponds, of which we have spoken in our account of Highgate; four of these are within the demesne of Caen Wood, and the other three are in the fields lying in the hollow below Fitzroy Park and Millfield Lane, as we have stated previously. The three outside Caen Wood are known as the Highgate Ponds. The stream which feeds the seven extensive and well-known ponds, and gave its origin to the Hampstead Waterworks, takes its rise in a meadow on the Manor Farm at Highgate, and forms a spacious lake in Caen Wood Park, whence it approaches Hampstead, and so flows on to Camden Town and London. Its waters are of a chalybeate character, as has been ascertained from the circumstance of a large variety of petrifactions having been met with in its channel, more especially in the immediate vicinity of its source. The mineral properties of this streamlet are of a ferruginous nature, its medicinal virtues are of a tonic character, and are said to be efficacious in cases of nervous debility.

In the summer season these ponds are the resort of thousands of Londoners, more especially the possessors of aquariums, for the sake of water-beetles "and other interesting abominations," whilst the boys fish in them for tadpoles and sticklebats, or sail miniature boats on their surface.

Half a mile farther to the south-west are the other large sheets of water, known as the Hampstead Ponds, which form great centres of attraction to the visitors to the heath. These ponds, we need scarcely add, are familiar to the readers of "Pickwick," the origin of the "tittlebats" or "sticklebacks" in them being among the subjects on which at least one learned paper had been read before the Pickwick Club. It is a matter of interest to record that the originator of these ponds was no other person than Paterson, the founder of the Bank of England.

Westminster was authorised to search for springs on the heath, and conveyed water from them to his manor of Hendon. From some cause or other, as Mr. Lysons tells us, the water company and the people of Hampstead fell into disputes about what the Americans call their "water privileges," and the inhabitants amongst themselves even proceeded to law about the year 1700. Park found that the present ponds existed in the seventeenth century,

HIGHGATE PONDS.

The Fleet River, or the River of Wells, of which we have spoken in a previous chapter,* had its rise in this locality. This river, we are told, was the same as the Langbourne, which flowed through London and gave its name to a ward of the City. It was called the Fleet River down to the commencement of the present century.

The authorities of the City of London, remarks Mr. Howitt, in his "Northern Heights," were prohibited by their Act of Henry VIII. from interfering with the spring at the foot of the hill of Hampstead Heath, which, he says, "was closed in with brick for the use and convenience of the inhabitants of Hampstead." At the same time the Bishop of

* See *ante*, p. 328.

being mentioned amongst the copyholds—the upper pond on the heath stated to contain three roods, thirty perches; the lower pond one acre, one rood, thirty-four perches. The pond in the Vale of Health was added in 1777. "The ponds," he adds, "have been fatal to many incautious bathers, owing to the sudden shelving of their sides." In the Vale of Health are visible, or were till recently, two rows of wooden posts, which, it has been suggested, might be the remains of a bridge either leading across the water, or to some aquatic pleasure-house built upon it.

On the north side of Hampstead Lane, facing the entrance to Caen Wood House, is Bishop's Wood. This wood, with one farther to the north called Mutton Wood, and another to the west known as Wild Wood, was, as we have already shown, a portion of the great wood attached to the estate and castle of the Bishop of London, at Highgate.* In 1755 it was purchased by Lord Mansfield, and left as a wild copse; it has since been strictly preserved as a cover for game.

The "Spaniards," a well-known tavern by the roadside, just as it emerges upon Hampstead Heath, stands on the site of a small lodge once occupied by the keeper of the park gate—the toll-gate at the Hampstead entrance to the Bishop of London's lands, of which we have already spoken. It is said by some writers to have derived its name from the fact of its having been once inhabited by a family connected with the Spanish embassy, and by others from its having been taken by a Spaniard, and converted into a house of entertainment. The Spanish Ambassador to King James I. wrote whilst residing here, complaining that he and his suite had not seen very much of the sun in England. Later on, its gardens were "improved and beautifully ornamented" by a Mr. William Staples, who, "out of a wild and thorny wood full of hills, valleys, and sand-pits, hath now made pleasant grass and gravel walks, with a mount, from the elevation whereof the beholder hath a prospect of Hanslope steeple, in Northamptonshire, within eight miles of Northampton; of Langdon Hills, in Essex, full sixty miles east; of Banstead Downs, in Surrey, south; of Shooter's Hill, Kent, south-east; Red Hill, Surrey, south-west; and of Windsor Castle, Berkshire, to the west. These walks and plats this gentleman hath embellished with a great many curious figures, depicted with pebble-stones of various colours." Such is the description of the "Spaniards" in a MS. account of the place, quoted by Park, in "History of Hampstead," and by Prickett, in his "History of Highgate;" but the statement must be received with caution, for certainly no resident of Hampstead, so far as we can learn, has ever been able to descry the steeple of Hanslope, or of any other church, in Northamptonshire. "The 'Spaniards,'" says Mr. Thorne, "still has its garden and its bowling-green; but the curious figures are gone, and so has (is) the mound, and with it the larger part of the prospect, partly, perhaps, owing to the growth of the neighbouring trees, and the erection of two or

THE "SPANIARDS," HAMPSTEAD HEATH.

* See *ante*, p. 389.

three large houses between it and the Heath." It was the brave landlord of this inn who, as we have said before, saved Caen Wood House from being wrecked by the mob during the Gordon riots. As we have stated above, he detained the mob here by a *ruse* till the military arrived. Curiously enough, the "Spaniards" is not mentioned in Mr. Larwood's otherwise exhaustive "History of Signboards," in connection, at all events, with Hampstead.

Another place of entertainment in this neighbourhood in former times, though now quite forgotten, was a cottage, with gardens attached to it, which rejoiced in the name of New Georgia. It has been identified with Turner's Wood, now enclosed in Lord Mansfield's grounds, opposite the western lodge of Caen Wood. From the same MS. from which the above description of the "Spaniards" was taken, we learn that "here the owner showeth you several little rooms, and numerous contrivances of his own to divert the beholder; and here, the gentleman is put in the pillory, and the ladies are obliged to kiss him, with such other oddities; the building is irregular and low, of wood, and the ground and wilderness is laid out in a romantic taste." Among the "numerous contrivances" was a chair which sank into the ground on a person sitting in it. In 1748, these singular grounds, like "Spring Gardens,"* were interspersed with representations of various reptiles, so connected with mechanism, as to make efforts of attack upon parties who unsuspectingly trod upon a board or spring. It is not improbable that the consequences of those frights to the ladies caused the disuse and decay of New Georgia, for about the year 1770 this species of mechanism seems to have been entirely discontinued.

The house next to the "Spaniards," and close by the entrance of Hampstead Heath, is called Erskine House, as having been the residence of the famous advocate, but less famous chancellor, Thomas Lord Erskine. The building is a plain white house, with a long portico opening upon the roadway. Of the house itself but little is seen from the road, excepting one end; a high wall shuts in what little garden it has on that side, and another high wall shuts out from observation the spacious gardens and grounds formerly belonging to it on the opposite side of the road. The house itself, says Mr. Howitt, is "simply a bald, square mass, shouldered up again by another house at its back. We see, however, the tall windows of its large drawing-room on the second floor, commanding a splendid view over Caen Wood and some part of Highgate. Yet this was the house inhabited by Thomas Lord Erskine, contemporary with both the law lords, his neighbours, Mansfield and Loughborough. Here he converted the place from a spot of no account into a very charming residence, laying out, with great enthusiasm, its grounds, and so planting it with bays and laurels, that he called it Evergreen Hill. He is said also to have planted with his own hand the extraordinary broad holly hedge separating his kitchen-garden from the Heath, opposite to the Fir-tree Avenue." The garden on the opposite side of the road was connected with the house by a subterranean passage. This garden, however, has long been taken into Lord Mansfield's estate.

Lord Erskine's account of his residence, where Edmund Burke was a frequent visitor, is too amusing to be omitted here. It is told by Mr. Rush, in his "Court of London:"—"When we got to Mr. Trotter's, Lord Erskine kept up his sprightly vein at table. 'I believe,' said our host, 'the soil is not the best in that part of Hampstead where your seat is.' 'No; very bad,' he replied, 'for although my grandfather was buried there as an earl near a hundred years ago, what has sprouted up from it since but a mere baron?' He alluded, of course, to his own title. He mentioned, however, a fact which went to show that although the soil yielded no increase in titles of nobility, it did in other things; for in his description he referred to a chestnut-tree upon it, which, when he first went to live there, was bought by his gardener for sixpence, but now yielded him thirty pounds a year."

"Here," says Mr. Howitt, "during the intervals of his arduous professional labour, Lord Erskine was zealously engaged in planning and carrying out his improvements. With his old gardener, John Barnett, he took his spade, and schemed and dug, and planted and transplanted; and no one who has not tried it can tell the immense refreshment derived from such an active diversion of otherwise exhausting trains of thought. To men compelled to spend long days in crowded, ill-ventilated courts, the health and spirits given by such tastes is incalculable. No doubt, from these occupations Erskine returned with tenfold vigour of body and mind to his pleadings, and to his parliamentary conflicts." Lord Erskine, at one time, contemplated cutting down a renowned group of elm-trees, nine in number, which flourished in all their picturesque beauty near his mansion; but the great lawyer thought better of his purpose, and the trees were spared. Cowper commemorated their escape, in a poem, in which we find that the Muses (sym-

* See Vol. IV., p. 77.

pathising, perhaps, with the number nine) interfered:—

> "Erskine (they cried) at our command
> Disarms his sacrilegious hand;
> Whilst yonder castle [Windsor] towers sublime,
> These elms shall brave the threats of Time."

In the same poem the poet of the "Task" refers to another performance of the Muses in the same locality, in relation to another great lawyer, the first Earl of Mansfield:—

> "When Murray deign'd to rove
> Beneath Caen Wood's sequester'd grove,
> They wander'd oft, when all was still,
> With him and Pope, on Hampstead Hill."

Lord Erskine's first rise in his profession, as he himself told Samuel Rogers, was due to an accident—the fact that he was suddenly called upon to defend Captain Baillie, in a matter of contention between himself and the authorities of Greenwich Hospital. His astonishing eloquence and energy, joined to the right being on his side, gained the day; and the all but briefless barrister went home that night with sixty-seven retaining fees in his pocket.

From an account by Sir Samuel Romilly, quoted by Mr. Howitt, we see not only what sort of men frequented his house in those days, but also the nature of Erskine's curious hobbies:—"Here he gave gay parties, of which he was the life, by his good humour and whimsicalities. I dined there one day, at what might be called a great Opposition dinner. The party consisted of the Duke of Norfolk, Lord Grenville, Lord Grey, Lord Holland, Lord Ellenborough, Lord Lauderdale, Lord Henry Petty, Thomas Grenville, Pigot, Adam, Edward Morris, Lord Erskine's son-in-law, and myself. If the most malignant enemies of Erskine had been present, they would have admitted that nothing could be more innocent than the conversation which passed. Politics were hardly mentioned. Amid the light and trifling topics of conversation after dinner, it may be worth while to mention one, as it strongly characterises Lord Erskine. He had always felt and expressed a great sympathy for animals. He has talked for years of a bill he was to bring into Parliament to prevent cruelty to them. He has always had several favourite animals to which he has been much attached, and of whom all his acquaintances have a number of anecdotes to relate. He had a favourite dog, which he used to bring, when he was at the bar, to all his consultations; another favourite dog, which, at the time he was Lord Chancellor, he himself rescued in the street from some boys who were about to kill it, under pretence of its being mad. A favourite goose, which followed him whenever he walked about his grounds; a favourite macaw; and other dumb favourites without number. He told us now, that he had two favourite leeches. He had been blooded by them when he was dangerously ill at Portsmouth; they had saved his life, and he had brought them with him to town—had ever since kept them in a glass—had himself every day given them fresh water, and formed a friendship for them. He said he was sure they knew him, and were grateful to him. He had given them the names of Howe and Clive, the celebrated surgeons, their dispositions being quite different. He went and fetched them for us to see; but without the vivacity, the tones, the details and gestures of Lord Erskine, it would be impossible to give an idea of this singular scene." *Apropos* of Lord Erskine's consideration for dumb animals, Twiss in his "Life of Eldon," tells the following anecdote concerning his lordship:—"On one occasion, in the neighbourhood of Hampstead Heath, a ruffianly driver was pummelling a miserable bare-boned hack horse. Lord Erskine's sympathy provoked him to a smart remonstrance. 'Why,' said the fellow, 'it's my own; mayn't I use it as I please?' and as he spoke, he discharged a fresh shower of blows on the raw back of the beast. Lord Erskine, excessively irritated, laid his walking-stick sharply over the shoulders of the offender, who, crouching and grumbling, asked what business he had to touch him with his stick. 'Why,' replied Erskine, to whom the opportunity of a joke was irresistible, 'it is my own; mayn't I use it as I please?'"

His lordship's witty sallies, indeed, rendered his society particularly enjoyable, and doubtless would have filled a volume of *Punch*. Of those which are on record, we cannot do more than quote one or two.

On one occasion, when Captain Parry remarked that "when frozen up in the Arctic regions they lived much on seals," "Yes," observed the ex-chancellor, "and very good living too, *if you keep them long enough!*" Being invited to attend the ministerial fish dinner at Greenwich when he was chancellor, "To be sure," he replied, "what would your dinner be without the *Great Seal?*"

Mr. Howitt, in his notice of this place, says:—"On the staircase of the house possessed by Lord Erskine, and the copyhold of which he transferred to Lord Mansfield, there is a window of stained glass, in which are emblazoned Lord Erskine's arms, with the baron's coronet, and the motto which he assumed, 'Trial by Jury.' The tunnel under the road, which connected the premises with the pleasure-grounds on the other side, is now built up, Lord Mansfield having resumed the grounds on his side. Baron (Chief Justice) Tindal at one time lived in this house."

Heath House, the residence next to that of Lord Erskine, and overlooking the Heath, was successively the abode of Mr. Edward Cox, the author of some poems, published at the beginning of this century; and of Sir Edward Parry, the Arctic voyager.

The next house, called The Firs, was built by a Mr. Turner, a tobacconist of Fleet Street, who planted the avenue of Scotch firs, which so largely contribute to the beauty of this part of the Heath. Mr. Turner also made the roadway across the Heath, from The Firs to the pleasant hamlet of North End and Golder's Green, on the slope of the hill looking towards Hendon, whither we now proceed.

A large house on the eastern slope of the hill leading from Hampstead to North End and Hendon, is that in which the great Lord Chatham lived for some time in gloomy retirement in 1767. It is now called Wildwood House, but formerly bore the name of North End House. The grounds extend up the hill, as far as the clump of Scotch firs, where the roads divide; and in the highest part of the gardens is a summer-house surmounted by a dome. Recently the house has undergone considerable alteration, having been raised a storey, besides having had other additions made to it; but some part at least of its interior remains unaltered. Mr. Howitt, in his "Northern Heights," says:—"The small room, or rather closet, in which Chatham shut himself up during his singular affliction—on the third storey—still remains in the same condition. Its position from the outside may be known by an oriel window looking towards Finchley. The opening in the wall from the staircase to the room still remains, through which the unhappy man received his meals or anything else conveyed to him. It is an opening of, perhaps, eighteen inches square, having a door on each side of the wall. The door within had a padlock which still hangs upon it. When anything was conveyed to him, a knock was made on the outer door, and the articles placed in the recess. When he heard the outer door again closed, the invalid opened the inner door, took what was there, again closed and locked it. When the dishes or other articles were returned, the same process was observed, so that no one could possibly catch a glimpse of him, nor need there be any exchange of words." It may be added that in making the alterations above mentioned, the condition of the room occupied by Lord Chatham was as little interfered with as possible; and even in the boards of the floor the marks caused by his lordship's wheeled chair are well preserved. In this house, in more recent times, lived Mr. Tagart, the minister of Little Portland Street Unitarian Chapel, and author of "Locke's Writings and Philosophy," "Sketches of the Reformers," &c.

On the opposite side of the road towards Hendon, over against the summer-house mentioned above, an elm-tree marks the spot where formerly stood a gibbet, on which was suspended the body of Jackson, a highwayman, for murdering Henry Miller on or near this spot, in May, 1673. "In 1674 was published," says Park, in his "History of Hampstead," "Jackson's Recantation; or, the Life and Death of the notorious Highwayman now hanging in chains at Hampstead," &c. Park adds that he was told that the post of this gibbet was in his time (1818) remaining as a mantel-tree over the fire-place in the kitchen of the "Castle" public-house on the Heath. One of the two trees between which the gibbet stood was blown down not many years ago. Hampstead, we may add, was a well-known place for highwaymen, who waylaid persons returning from the Wells as they rode or drove down Haverstock Hill, or across the Heath, and towards Finchley. We are told in the "Cabinet of Curiosities," published by Limbird in 1822, that Lord Kenyon referred to a case in which a highwayman had the audacity to file a bill before a Court of Equity to compel his partner to account to him for a half-share of his plunder, in which it was expressly stated that the plaintiff and his partner, one Joseph Williams, continued their joint dealings together in several places—viz., at "Bagshot, in Surrey; at Salisbury, in Wiltshire; at Hampstead, in Middlesex, and elsewhere, to the amount of £2,000 and upwards." It is satisfactory to learn that the insolent plaintiff was afterwards executed, and one of his solicitors transported for being concerned in a robbery.

Golder's Hill, at North End, was the residence of Mark Akenside, the author of "Pleasures of the Imagination." The son of a butcher at Newcastle-on-Tyne, he was born at that place in 1721, and was educated at the grammar-school of that town. He afterwards went to Edinburgh, in order to qualify himself for the ministry; but preferring the study of physic, he took his degree of M.D. in 1744, by royal mandate from the University of Cambridge. In that same year he produced the poem above mentioned, and it was well received. In the following year he published his first collection of odes. His life was uneventful. He practised as a physician with but indifferent success, first at

Northampton, afterwards in Hampstead, and finally in London. At length, just as bright prospects were opening upon him, he was carried off by an attack of fever, in 1770. He was a man of great learning, and of high character and morality; he lies buried, as we have seen,* in the Church of St. James, Piccadilly. His house stood on the site of that now occupied by Sir Spencer Wells.

At a farmhouse close by, just on the edge of the Heath, William Blake, the artist and poet, used to lodge. Linnell, the painter, frequently occupied the house during the summer months. Mr. Coventry Patmore, too, lived for some time at North End; Mrs. Craik, the novelist (formerly Miss Dinah Muloch), likewise formerly resided here, in the house afterwards occupied by Miss Meteyard, the authoress of the "Life of Joshua Wedgwood" and other antiquarian works. Collins' Farm, at North End, has often been painted. It is the subject of a picture by Stuart, exhibited in 1830. The large house on the right of the avenue, descending from the Heath, was for some time the residence of Sir T. Fowell Buxton, whose name became associated with those of Clarkson, Wilberforce, and other kindred spirits, in effecting the abolition of slavery and the emancipation of the slaves throughout the colonial possessions of the British empire.

The "Bull and Bush," a well-known public-house in North End, was, it is said, the frequent resort of Addison and his friends. The house has attached to it some pleasant tea-gardens, in which some of the curiously constructed bowers and arbours are still to be seen.

CHAPTER XXXV.

HAMPSTEAD (*continued*).—THE HEATH AND THE "UPPER FLASK."

"It is a goodly sight through the clear air,
From Hampstead's healthy height, to see at once
England's vast capital in fair expanse—
Towers, belfries, lengthen'd streets, and structures fair.
St. Paul's high dome amidst the vassal bands
Of neighbouring spires a regal chieftain stands;
And over fields of ridgy roofs appear,
With distance softly tinted, side by side
In kindred grace, like twain of sisters dear,
The Towers of Westminster, her Abbey's pride.

Joanna Baillie.

The View from the Heath—Attempted Encroachments by the Lord of the Manor—His Examination before a Committee of the House of Commons—Purchase of the Heath by the Metropolitan Board of Works as a Public Recreation-ground—The Donkeys and Donkey-drivers—Historic Memorabilia—Mr. Hoare's House, and Crabbe's Visits there—The Hampstead Coaches in Former Times—Dickens' Partiality for Hampstead Heath—Jack Straw's Castle—The Race-course—Suicide of John Sadlèir, M.P.—The Vale of Health—John Keats, Leigh Hunt, and Shelley—Hampstead Heath a Favourite Resort for Artists—Judge's Walk, or King's Bench Avenue—The "Upper Flask"—Sir Richard Steele and the Kit-Kat Club—"Clarissa Harlowe."

THE great attractions of Hampstead, as we have endeavoured to show at the commencement of the preceding chapter, are its breezy heath, which has long been a favourite resort not only of cockney holiday folk, but also of artists and poets, and its choice beauties of scenery, to which no mere description can do justice. Standing upon the broad roadway which crosses the Heath, in continuation of the road by the "Spaniards," and leading to the upper part of the town, the visitor will be at a loss whether to admire most the pleasing undulations of the sandy soil, scooped out into a thousand cavities and pits, or the long avenues of limes, or the dark fir-trees and beeches which fringe it on the north—of which we have already spoken—or the gay and careless laughter of the merry crowds who are gambolling on the velvet-like turf, or riding donkeys along the steep ridge which reaches towards Caen Wood. It is probably Hampstead Heath to which Thompson alludes when he writes in his "Seasons:"—

"Or I ascend
Some eminence, Augusta, in thy plains,
And see the country far diffused around,
One boundless bush."

Indeed, few, if any, places in the neighbourhood of the metropolis can compare with its range of scenery, or show an equally "boundless bush." As Richardson puts into the mouth of Clarissa Harlowe: "Now, I own that Hampstead Heath affords very pretty and very extensive prospects; but it is not the wide world neither."

In addition to the charming landscape immediately around us, teeming with varied and picturesque attractions, the view is more extensive, perhaps, than that commanded by any other spot of only

* See Vol. IV., p. 256.

equal elevation in the kingdom; for from the broad roadway where we are now standing—which, by the way, seems to be artificially raised along the ridge of the hill—we get a fine view of St. Paul's, with the long line of Surrey Hills in the background extending to Leith Hill, the grand stand on Epsom race-course, and St. Martha's Hill, near Guildford. Standing nearly on a level with the top of its cross, we have the whole of the eastern metropolis spread out at our feet, and the eye follows the line of the river Thames, as it winds its way onwards, nearly down to Gravesend. Dr. Preston, in a lecture on Hampstead, very graphically describes how, throwing himself mentally back five hundred years, he commands from its high ground a distant view of London:—"I am alone in the midst of a wood or forest, and I cannot see around me for the thickness of the wood. Neither roads nor bridle-paths are to be seen; so I climb one of the tallest of the oaks, and survey the landscape at leisure. The City of London rises clear and distinct before me to the south, for I am at least three hundred feet above the level of its river banks, and no coal is burnt within its walls to thicken and blacken the atmosphere. I can just distinguish the Tower, and the walls ranging from Bishopsgate to Cripplegate, Aldersgate, and Ludgate. Outside the City gates, however, all is open country, except a group of cottages round the Priory, at Kilburn." And then he describes how London stands on a group of smaller hills, intersected by brooks and water-courses, as we have already seen in detail.*

JACK STRAW'S CASTLE.

The northern side of the Heath is particularly wild and charming; and the groups of elms and fir-trees, combined with the broken nature of the sandy and gravelly soil, add greatly to the picturesque beauty of the foreground. Looking in this direction, or somewhat to the north-west, the background of the view is formed by the dark sides of Harrow hill; nor is water altogether wanting to lend its aid to the picture, for from certain points the lake at Kingsbury at times gleams out like a sheet of burnished silver in the mid-distance.

From this description it is obvious that a stranger climbing to the top of Hampstead Hill on a bright summer morning, before the air is darkened with the smoke of a single fire, and looking down on the vast expanse of London to his left and to

* See Vol. I., p. 434; Vol. II., p. 416.

HAMPSTEAD HEATH IN 1840. *From a Drawing by Constable.* (*See page* 454.)

his right, stretching away for miles along the bosom of the Thames valley from Greenwich and Woolwich up to Kew and even Richmond, with its towers, spires, and roofs all crowded before him as in a panorama, they, with pride and enthusiasm, may well exclaim, with the essayist, "Yonder is the metropolis of the empire, the abode of the arts and of science, as well as the emporium of trade and commerce; the glory of England, and the wonder of the world."

Turning from poetry to prose, however, we may observe that the Heath, "the region of all suburban ruralities," as it has been called, originally covered a space of ground about five hundred acres in extent; but by the gradual growth of the neighbouring town of Hampstead and of the surrounding hamlets, and also by occasional enclosures which have been made by the lord of the manor, and by the occupiers of villas on its frontiers, it has been shorn of nearly half its dimensions. These encroachments, though unlawful at the time when made, have become legalised by lapse of years. As an "open space" or common for the free use of the Londoners, its fate was for some time very uncertain. About the year 1831 an attempt was made by the lord of the manor, Sir Thomas Wilson, to build on the Heath, near the Vale of Health; but he was forced to desist. A new road and a bridge, and a range of villas was designed and commenced, traces of which are still to be seen on the side of the hill rising from the Vale of Health towards the south front of Lord Mansfield's park. Sir Thomas Wilson made another attempt at enclosing the Heath, near "Jack Straw's Castle," in more recent years, but was forced again to desist by a decree of the Court of Chancery, to which the residents appealed. Indeed, numerous attempts were made by successive lords of the manor to beguile Parliament into sanctioning their natural desire for power of enclosure; but, fortunately, so great was the outcry raised by the general voice of the people, through the press, that all further encroachment was stayed.

How far Sir Thomas Wilson considered himself justified in his attempted enclosures of the Heath, and the consequent shutting out of the holiday folk from their ancient recreation-ground, may be gathered from his answers before the "Select Committee appointed to inquire into the Open Spaces of the Metropolis." The extract is from the Report of the Select Committee; the catechised is Sir Thomas Wilson:—

Are you aware that many thousands of people frequent Hampstead Heath on holidays?—They go there on holidays.

Have you ever treated them as trespassers?—When there are *fêtes*, and people go up there to amuse themselves, they pay an acknowledgment.

Have you not treated pedestrians as trespassers?—No; I do not know that I have. It is unenclosed land, and I could only bring an action for trespass, and should probably get one penny for damages.

You have never treated the public as trespassers?—Some people imagine that they go to Hampstead Heath to play games, but it could not be done. Part of the heath is a bog, and there are cases of horses and cows having been smothered there.

But people go there and amuse themselves?—Just as they do in Greenwich Park, but they have no right in Greenwich Park.

You have never treated people as trespassers?—No. Are they treated as trespassers in Greenwich Park?

Do you claim the right of enclosing the whole of the Heath, leaving no part for public games?—If I were to enclose the whole of it, it would be for those only who are injured to find fault with me.

Would you sell Hampstead Heath?—I have never dreamt of anything of the kind; but if the public chose to prevent me, or to make any bargain that I am not to enclose it, they must pay the value of what they take from me.

Do you consider Hampstead Heath private property?—Yes.

To be paid for at the same rate as private land adjoining?—Yes.

Do you concede that the inhabitants in the neighbourhood have rights on the Heath?—There are presentments in the Court Rolls to show that they have none.

Sir Thomas Wilson valued the Heath at two and a half millions of money for building purposes; and such might, perhaps, have been its market value if actually laid out for building. But the law restricted his rights, and his successor was glad to sell them for less than a twentieth part of the sum.

The Metropolitan Commons Act, procured in 1866 by the Right Hon. William Cowper, then Chief Commissioner of the Board of Works, secured the Heath from further enclosure; and in 1870, the manor having passed to a new lord, the Metropolitan Board of Works were enabled to purchase the manorial rights for the sum of £45,000, and thus to secure the Heath in perpetuity for public use. Prior to this exchange of ownership, the surface of the Heath had for several years been largely denuded of the sand and gravel of which it was composed, the result being that several of the hillocks and lesser elevations had been partially levelled, deep pits had been scooped out, trees in some parts undermined, and their gnarled roots left exposed above the surface of the ground to the action of the wind and rain. But since the Board of Works has taken the Heath under its fostering care, the barren sand has become in many places re-clothed with verdure, and the wild tract of land is again resuming its original appearance, gay and bright with purple heather and golden furze blossom.

Apart from an occasional sham fight on its slopes on a volunteer field day, the Heath is now left to the sole use of the people as a place of common resort and recreation, where they can breathe the fresh air, and indulge in cricket, and in such rural pastimes as may be provided for them by the troops of donkeys and donkey-boys who congregate on these breezy heights. Indeed, "Hampstead," as the modern poet says, "is the place to ruralise;" it is also, it may be added, especially at Whitsuntide, the place to indulge in a sort of equestrian exercise. Decked out with white saddle-cloths, frisking away over the sunny heath, and perhaps occasionally pitching some unlucky rider into a shallow sand-pit, the donkeys, we need hardly say, are, to the juvenile portion of the visitors at least, the chief source of amusement. By the male sex the horse is principally affected; the women and children are content with donkeys. The horse of Hampstead Heath has peculiar marks of his own. His coat is of the roughest, for he knows little about curry-combs, and passes his nights—at any rate, during the summer months—under the canopy of heaven. For his own sake it is to be hoped that he has not often a tender mouth, when we consider the sort of fellows who mount him, and how mercilessly they jerk at the reins. The Hampstead Heath horse is a creature of extremes. He is either to be seen flying at full gallop, urged along by kicks, and shouts, and blows; or if left to himself, he shambles slowly forwards, being usually afflicted in one or more of his legs with some equine infirmity. As for the donkeys, they are much like their brethren everywhere in a country where the donkey is despised and mismanaged. They are much more comfortable to ride when homeward than outward bound. The sullen crawl of the "outward-bound" donkey—his perpetual endeavours to turn round, and his craving after roadside vegetation—are, as may be well imagined, varied at intervals by the onslaughts of the donkey-man, who, with a shower of blows, a string of guttural oaths, and a hoarse "kim up," stimulates the unlucky beast into a spasmodic gallop of two minutes' duration, during which time the equestrian powers of the rider are severely tested. It may be here stated that whatever may have been the torture to which the poor animals were subjected in bygone days, there is at least a possibility of their being more tenderly dealt with hereafter, seeing that the "donkey-boys" are now under the control of the authorities who rule the Heath, and that any undue severity practised by them may end in a suspension or withdrawal of their licence.

We get some little insight into the character and amusements of the company usually brought together here at the commencement of the last century, in a comedy called *Hampstead Heath*, which was produced at Drury Lane Theatre in 1706. The following extract will serve our purpose:—

Act I., Sc. 1. Scene, Hampstead.

Smart. Hampstead for a while assumes the day; the lively season o' the year, the shining crowd assembled at this time, and the noble situation of the place, give us the nearest show of Paradise.

Bloom. London now, indeed, has but a melancholy aspect, and a sweet rural spot seems an adjournment o' the nation where business is laid fast asleep, variety of diversions feast our fickle fancies, and every man wears a face of pleasure. The cards fly, the bowl runs, the dice rattle, some lose their money with ease and negligence, and others are well pleased to pocket it. But what fine ladies does the place afford?

Smart. Assemblies so near the town give us a sample of each degree. We have court ladies that are all air and no dress, city ladies all dress and no air, and country dames with broad brown faces like a Stepney bun; besides an endless number of Fleet Street semptresses that dance minuets in their furbeloe scarfs and cloaths hung as loose about them as their reputations. . . .

Enter *Driver.*

Smart. Mr. Deputy Driver, stock jobber, state botcher, and terror of strolling strumpets, and chief beggar hunter, come to visit Hampstead.

Driver. And d'you think me so very shallow, captain, to leave the good of the nation and getting money to muddle it away here 'mongst fops, fiddlers, and furbeloes, where ev'ry thing's as dear as freeholders' votes, and a greater imposition than a Dutch reckoning? I am come hither, but it is to ferret out a frisking wife o' mine, one o' the giddy multitude that's rambled up to this ridiculous assembly.

That this exhilarating subject has not altogether lost its hold on the play-going public may be inferred when we state that *Happy Hampstead* was the title of a comedy or farce produced at the Royalty Theatre in the year 1877.

On fine Sundays and Mondays, and on Bank Holidays, we need hardly add, the Heath is alive with swarms of visitors; and it is estimated that on a bright and sunny Whit-Monday as many as 50,000 people have been here brought together. Writing on this subject in the "Northern Heights of London," Mr. Howitt observes: "Recent times have seen Sunday dissipation re-asserting itself, by the erection of a monster public-house with a lofty tower and flag, to attract the attention of Sunday strollers on the Heath. Of all places, this raised its Tower of Babel bulk in that formerly quiet and favourite spot, the Vale of Health. That suitable refreshments should be attainable to the numerous visitors of the Heath on Sundays and holidays is quite right and reasonable; but that taps and gin-palaces on a Titanic scale should be licensed, where people resort ostensibly for fresh air, relaxation, and exercise, is the certain mode of turning all such advantages into popular curses, and converting the very bosom of nature into a hotbed of demoralisation and crime. Any one who has witnessed the condition of the enormous crowds who flock to the Heath on summer Sundays, as they return in the evening, needs no argument on the subject."

Hampstead Heath has very few historical associations, like Blackheath; but there is one which, though it savours of poetry and romance, must not be omitted here. Our readers will not have forgotten the lines in Macaulay's ballad of "The Armada," in which are described the beacons which announced to the outlying parts of England the arrival of the Spanish Armada off Plymouth; how

> "High on bleak Hampstead's swarthy moor they started for the North."

It is, of course, quite possible that Hampstead Heath may have been used for telegraphic purposes, but there is no actual record of the fact.

Like Blackheath, however, and, indeed, most of the other bleak and open spaces in the neighbourhood of London, Hampstead Heath has its recollection of highwaymen, of their depredations, and of their executions, as we have mentioned in the previous chapter. In a poem published at the close of the seventeenth century, called "The Triennial Mayor; or, The New Raparees," we read—

> "As often upon Hampstead Heath
> We've seen a felon, long since put to death,
> Hang, crackling in the sun his parchment skin,
> Which to his ear had shrivelled up his chin."

Mr. Howitt, in his "Northern Heights," says that "one of the earliest and most curious facts in history connected with Hampstead Heath is that stated by Matthew of Paris, or rather by Roger of Wendover, from whom he borrows it, that so lately as in the thirteenth century it was the resort of wolves, and was as dangerous to cross on that account at night, as it was for ages afterwards, and, in fact, almost down to our own times, for highwaymen."

Down to the commencement of the last century, when that honour was transferred to Brentford as more central, the elections of knights of the shire for Middlesex were held on Hampstead Heath, as we learn from some notices which appear in the *True Protestant Mercury*, for March 2–5, 1681, the *Flying Post* for October 19–22, 1695, and for November 9–12, of the same year.

The poet Crabbe was a frequent visitor at the hospitable residence of Mr. Samuel Hoare, on the Heath. Campbell writes: "The last time I saw Crabbe was when I dined with him at the house of Mr. Hoare, at Hampstead. He very kindly came to the coach to see me off, and I never pass that spot on the top of Hampstead Heath without thinking of him." The mansion is called "The Hill," and was the seat of Mr. Samuel Hoare, the banker. Here used to congregate the great poets of the age, Rogers, Wordsworth, Coleridge, Campbell, Lucy Aikin, Mrs. Marcet, and Agnes and Joanna Baillie; whilst the centre of the gathering was the poet Crabbe. In the "Life of the Rev. George Crabbe," by his son, we read: "During his first and second visits to London my father spent a good deal of his time beneath the hospitable roof of the late Samuel Hoare, Esq., on Hampstead Heath. He owed his introduction to this respectable family to his friend Mr. Bowles, and the author of the delightful 'Excursions in the West,' Mr. Warner; and though Mr. Hoare was an invalid, and little disposed to form new connections, he was so much gratified with Mr. Crabbe's manners and conversation, that their acquaintance grew into an affectionate and lasting intimacy. Mr. Crabbe, in subsequent years, made Hampstead his head-quarters on his spring visits, and only repaired thence occasionally to the brilliant circles of the metropolis."

At the commencement of the century, if we may trust Mr. Chambers's assertion in his "Book of Days," Hampstead and Highgate could be reached only by "short stages" (*i.e.*, stage-coaches), going twice a day; and a journey thither once or twice in the summer time was the farthest and most ambitious expedition of a cockney's year. Both villages then abounded with inns, with large gardens in their rear, overlooking the pleasant country fields towards Harrow, or the extensive and more open land towards St. Albans or towards the valley of the Thames. The "Spaniards" and "Jack Straw's Castle" still remain as samples of these old "rural delights." The features of the latter place, as they existed more than a century since, have been preserved by Chatelaine in a small engraving executed by him about the year 1745. The formal arrangement of the trees and turf, in humble imitation of the Dutch taste introduced by William III., and exhibited on a larger scale at Hampton Court and Kensington Palace, may be noted in this humbler garden.

To Hampstead Heath, as every reader of his "Life" is aware, Charles Dickens was extremely partial, and he constantly turned his suburban walks in this direction. He writes to Mr. John Forster: "You don't feel disposed, do you, to muffle yourself up, and start off with me for a good brisk walk over Hampstead Heath? I know a good house there where we can have a red-hot chop for dinner and a glass of good wine." "This note," adds Forster, "led to our first experience of 'Jack Straw's Castle,' memorable for many happy meetings in coming years."

Passing into "Jack Straw's Castle," we find the usual number of visitors who have come up in Hansoms to enjoy the view, to dine off its modern fare, and to lounge about its gardens. The inn, or hotel, is not by any means an ancient one, and it would be difficult to find out any connection between the present hostelry and the rebellion which may, or may not, have given to it a name. The following is all that we could glean from an old magazine which lay upon the table at which we sat and dined when we last visited it, and it is to be feared that the statement is not to be taken wholly "for gospel:"—"Jack Straw, who was second in command to Wat Tyler, was probably entrusted with the insurgent division which immortalised itself by burning the Priory of St. John of Jerusalem, thence striking off to Highbury, where they destroyed the house of Sir Robert Hales, and afterwards encamping on Hampstead heights. 'Jack Straw,' whose 'castle' consisted of a mere hovel, or a hole in the hill-side, was to have been king of one of the English counties—probably of Middlesex; and his name alone of all the rioters associated itself with a local habitation, as his celebrated confession showed the rude but still not unorganised intentions of the insurgents to seize the king, and, having him amongst them, to raise the entire country."

This noted hostelry has long been a famous place for public and private dinner-parties and suppers, and its gardens and grounds for alfresco entertainments. In the "Cabinet of Curiosities," published by Limbird in 1822, we find the following lines "on 'Jack Straw's Castle' being repaired:"—

"With best of food—of beer and wines,
Here may you pass a merry day;
So shall mine host, while Phœbus shines,
Instead of straw make good his hay."

The western part of the Heath, behind "Jack Straw's Castle," would appear to have been used in former times as the Hampstead race-course long before the "Derby" or "Ascot" had been established in the popular favour. The races, however, do not appear to have been very highly patronised, if we may judge from the fact that at the September meeting, 1732, one race only was run, and that for the very modest stake of ten guineas. "Three horses started," says the *Daily Courant* of that period; "one was distanced the first heat, and one was drawn; Mr. Bullock's 'Merry Gentleman' won, but was obliged to go the course the second heat alone." We learn from Park's "History of Hampstead" that the races "drew together so much low company, that they were put down on account of the mischief that resulted from them." The very existence of a race-course on Hampstead is now quite forgotten; and the uneven character of the ground, which has been much excavated for gravel and sand, is such as would render a visitor almost disposed to doubt whether such could ever have been the case.

On the greensward behind "Jack Straw's Castle," on Sunday morning, February 17, 1856, was found the dead body of John Sadleir, the fraudulent M.P. for Sligo. The corpse was lying in a hollow on the sloping ground, with the feet very near to a pool of water; beside it was a small phial which had contained essential oil of almonds, and also a silver cream-jug from which he had taken the fatal draught. In his pocket, among other things, was found a piece of paper on which was written "John Sadleir, Gloucester Square, Hyde Park." In 1848, as we learn from his memoir in the *Gentleman's Magazine*, Mr. Sadleir became chairman of the London and County Joint Stock Banking Company, and for several years he presided over that body with great ability. Shortly before his death, he vacated the chair; and though still a director, he ceased to take an active part in its business. He continued to be a principal manager of the affairs of the Tipperary Bank, and he was chairman of the Royal Swedish Railway Company, in which it appeared that, out of 79,925 shares issued, he got into his own possession 48,245; besides which he dishonestly fabricated a large quantity of duplicate shares, of which he had appropriated 19,700. Among other enterprises in which Mr. Sadleir was also actively engaged, were the Grand Junction Railway of France, the Rome and Frascati Railway, a Swiss railway, and the East Kent line. He had dealt largely in the lands sold in the Encumbered Estates Court in Ireland, and in several instances had forged conveyances of such lands, in order to raise money upon them. The catastrophe was brought about by Messrs. Glyn, the London agents of the Tipperary Bank, returning its drafts as "not provided for," a step which was followed a day or two after by the Bank of Ireland. On the day preceding that on which his body was discovered on Hampstead Heath, Sadleir wrote to Mr. Robert Keating, M.P. for Waterford (another director of the Tipperary Bank), a letter, intended to be posthumous, commencing thus:—

"Dear Robert,—To what infamy have I come

step by step—heaping crime upon crime; and now I find myself the author of numberless crimes of a diabolical character, and the cause of ruin, and misery, and disgrace to thousands—aye, tens of thousands! Oh, how I feel for those on whom this ruin must fall! I could bear all punishment, but I could never bear to witness the sufferings of those on whom I have brought this ruin. It must be better that I should not live."

One of the Dublin newspapers—the *Nation*—speaking of this unexampled swindler, thus expresses itself: "He was a man desperate by nature, and in all his designs his character, his objects, his very fate, seemed written in that sallow face, wrinkled with multifarious intrigue—cold, callous, and cunning—instinct with an unscrupulous audacity, and an easy and wily energy. How he contrived and continued to deceive men to the last, and to stave off so securely the evidences of his infamies, until now, that they all seem exploding together over his dead body, is a marvel and a mystery."

"Hampstead," says Mr. Thorne, in his "Environs of London," "is an awkward place for a suicide to select. The lord of the manor possesses very extensive rights, among them being that of deodand, and is, therefore, in the case of a person who commits suicide within the manor, entitled as heir to 'the whole of the goods and chattels of the deceased, of every kind, with the exception of his estate of inheritance, in the event of the jury returning a verdict of *felo de se*.' Sadleir's goods and chattels were already lost or forfeited; but the cream-jug was claimed and received by the lord as an acknowledgment of his right, and then returned." As "deodands" have been since abolished by Act of Parliament, such a claim could not arise again.

THE "UPPER FLASK," ABOUT 1800. (*See page* 459.)

John Sadleir, we need hardly remind the reader of Charles Dickens's works, figures in "Little Dorritt" as Mr. Merdle. "I shaped Mr. Merdle himself," writes Dickens, "out of that gracious rascality."

In Hardwicke's "Annual Biography" for 1857 we read thus: "Strange as it may sound, there are not wanting those who believe (in spite of the identification of the corpse by the coroner, Mr. Wakley, who had formerly sat in Parliament with him), that, after all, John Sadleir did not commit suicide, but simply played the trick so well known in history and in romance, of a pretended death and a supposititious corpse. These persons believe that he is still alive and in America."

Immediately at our feet, as we look down in the hollow towards the east, from the broad road in front of "Jack Straw's Castle," is the Vale of Health, with its large modern hotel, and its ponds glistening in the sunshine beyond. We wish that it could be added that this hotel forms any ornament to the scene: for down to very recent years this Vale of Health presented a sight at once picturesque and pleasant. "In front of a row of cottages," writes Mr. Howitt, "and under the shade of willows, were set out long tables for tea, where many hundreds, at a trifling cost, partook of a homely and exhilarating refreshment. There families could take their own tea and bread and butter, and have water boiled for them, and table accommodation found for them, for a few pence; but then came this great tavern, with its towers and battlements, and cast them literally and practically into the shade. It was, however, really gratifying to see that the more imposing and dangerous place of entertainment never could compete with the more primitive tea-tables, nor banish the homely and happy groups of families, children, and humble friends."

An "old inhabitant" of Hampstead writes thus in 1876:—"A plot of land lately enclosed in the Vale of Health is classic ground. In a picturesque cottage, with its pretty balcony environed with creepers, and a tall *arbor vitæ* almost overtopping its roof, lived for some time Leigh Hunt. Here Byron and Shelley visited him; and when this cottage from age was obliged to be pulled down, there was still in the parlour window a pane of glass on which Byron had written these lines of Cowper—

"'Oh for a lodge in some vast wilderness,
Some boundless contiguity of shade,
Where rumour of oppression and deceit,
Of unsuccessful or successful war,
Shall never reach me more.'"

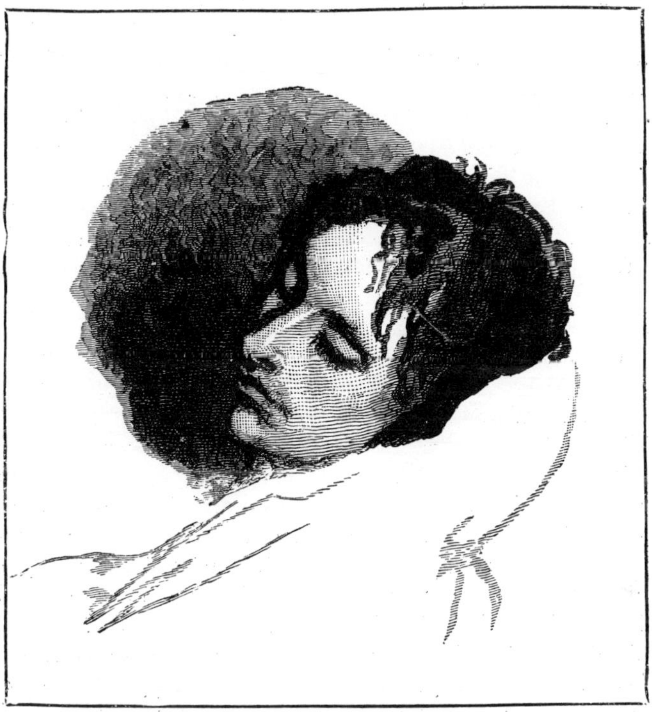

JOHN KEATS. *Copied by permission from the Sketch taken by Mr. Severn.* (*See page* 458.)

It may be well to note here the fact that on this site South Villa now stands.

Cyrus Redding, in his "Recollections," thus writes, in 1850:—"I visited him (Leigh Hunt) in the Vale of Health at Hampstead, where there was always a heartiness that tempted confidence, and with much imaginativeness, much skimming of literature, and a light culling of its wild flowers, criticism without envy, and opinions free of insincerity. Leigh Hunt yet survives, or I might be tempted to proceed to many details, which would infringe the rule I have made for myself in the mention of but few who are still spared from a day of our literature, the similar of which is hardly likely soon, if ever, to recur again." Leigh Hunt died at the house of a friend at Putney, in 1859.

The "Cockney poets," Keats, Shelley, Leigh

Hunt, and their friends, loved Hampstead. Coleridge, who lived many years at Highgate, was no stranger to "The Spaniards" or the "Vale of Health," with its toy-like cluster of cottages in the little hollow where we are gazing down. Keats (whom the author of "Childe Harold" styled, in his Ravenna letter to the elder Disraeli, "a tadpole of the lakes," but to whom he made the *amende honorable* by a magnificent compliment a year later) was residing in lodgings at Hampstead when he felt the first symptoms of the deadly consumption which shortly afterwards laid the most fervid genius of this century in the Protestant burying-ground at Rome.

The name of John Keats has many associations with Hampstead. At Leigh Hunt's house Keats wrote one of his finest sonnets, and in a beautiful spot between Millfield Lane and Lord Mansfield's house, as we have already narrated, occurred that one short interview between Keats and Coleridge, in which the latter said that death was in the hand of the former after they had parted. These words soon proved true. In a recent volume of the *Gentleman's Magazine* there is a very interesting passage touching the author of "The Eve of St. Agnes." "I see," says Miss Sabilla Novello, "that Sylvanus Urban declares himself an unmeasured admirer of Keats; I therefore enclose for your acceptance the photograph of a sketch made of him, on his death-bed, by his friend Joseph Severn, in whose diary at that epoch are written, under the sketch, these words: '28th January, 3 o'clock, morning—Drawn to keep me awake. A deadly sweat was on him all this night.' I feel you will be interested by the drawing." The sketch is, indeed, a most touching memento of the youth who, having his lot cast in the golden age of modern English poetry, left us some of the finest, and purest, and most perfect poetry in the language, and died at twenty-five. So excellent a work is this little picture, and so accurately does it suggest the conditions under which it was drawn, that no doubt the time will come when it will be regarded as the best personal relic of the author of "Endymion." Severn's portrait of Keats, taken at Hampstead, is in the National Portrait Gallery; and hard by, in the South Kensington Museum, Severn's merits as an artist may be seen in his poetic transcription of Ariel on the bat's back.

Connected with Keats's illness and death may be mentioned two incidents that for the living reader contain a mournful and a striking interest. Among the earliest friends of Keats were Haydon, the painter, and Shelley, the poet. When Keats was first smitten, Haydon visited the sufferer, who had written to his old friend, requesting him to see him before he set out for Italy. Haydon describes in his journal the powerful impression which the visit made upon him—"the very colouring of the scene struck forcibly on the painter's imagination. The white curtains, the white sheets, the white shirt, and the white skin of his friend, all contrasted with the bright hectic flush on his cheek, and heightened the sinister effect; he went away, hardly hoping." And he who hardly hoped for another, what extent of hope had he for himself? From the poet's bed to the painter's studio is but a bound for the curious and eager mind. Keats, pitied and struck down by the hand of disease, lies in paradise compared with the spectacle that comes before us—genius weltering in its blood, self-destroyed because neglected. Pass we to another vision! Amongst the indignant declaimers against the unjust sentence which criticism had passed on Keats, Shelley stood foremost. What added poignancy to indignation was the settled but unfounded conviction that the death of the youth had been mainly occasioned by wanton persecution. Anger found relief in song. "Adonais: an Elegy on the Death of John Keats," is among the most impassioned of Shelley's verses. Give heed to the preface:—"John Keats died at Rome of a consumption in his twenty-fourth year, on the — of ——, 1821, and was buried in the romantic and lovely cemetery of the Protestants in that city, under the pyramid which is the tomb of Cestius, and the massy walls and towers, now mouldering and desolate, which formed the circuit of ancient Rome. The cemetery is an open space among the ruins, covered in winter with violets and daisies. *It might make one in love with death to think that one should be buried in so sweet a place.*" Reader, carry the accents in your ear, and accompany us to Leghorn. A few months only have elapsed. Shelley is on the shore. Keats no longer lives, but you will see that Shelley has not forgotten him. He sets sail for the Gulf of Lerici, where he has his temporary home; he never reaches it. A body is washed ashore at Via Reggio. If the features are not to be recognised, there can be no doubt of the man who carries in his bosom the volume containing "Lamia" and "Hyperion." The body of Shelley is burned, but the remains are carried——whither? You will know by the description, "The cemetery is an open space among the ruins, covered in winter with violets and daisies. *It might make one in love with death to think that one should be buried in so sweet a place.*" There he lies! Keats and he, the mourner and the mourned, almost touch each other!

All the later years of Keats's life, until his departure for Rome, were passed at Hampstead, and here all his finest poetry was written. Leigh Hunt says:—"The poem with which his first volume begins was suggested to him on a delightful summer day, as he stood by the gate which leads from the battery on Hampstead Heath into a field by Caen Wood; and the last poem, the one on 'Sleep and Poetry,' was occasioned by his sleeping in the Vale of Health." There are, perhaps, few spots in the neighbourhood of Hampstead more likely to have suggested the following lines to the sensitive mind of poor Keats than the high ground overlooking the Vale of Health:—

"To one who has been long in city pent
'Tis very sweet to look into the fair
And open space of heaven—to breathe a prayer
Full in the smile of the blue firmament.
Who is more happy when, with heart's content,
Fatigued he sinks into some pleasant lair
Of wavy grass, and reads a debonair
And gentle tale of love and languishment?
Returning home at evening with an ear
Catching the notes of Philomel—an eye
Watching the sailing cloudlets' bright career,
He mourns that day so soon has glided by,
E'en like the passage of an angel's tear,
That falls through the clear ether silently."

No wonder that great painters as well as poets have loved this spot, and made it hallowed ground. Romney, Morland, Haydon, Constable, Collins, Blake, Linnell, Herbert, and Clarkson Stanfield have all in their turn either lived in Hampstead, or, at the least, frequented it, studying, as artists and poets only can, the glorious "sunset effects" and wondrous contrasts of light and shade which are to be seen here far better than anywhere else within five miles of St. Paul's or Charing Cross.

Linnell, the painter of the "Eve of the Deluge" and the "Return of Ulysses," made frequently his abode at a cottage beyond the Heath, between North End and the "Spaniards." To this quiet nook very often resorted, on Sunday afternoons, his friend William Blake, that "dreamer of dreams and seer of visions," and John Varley, artist and astrologer, who were as strange a pair as ever trod this earth.

Goldsmith, who loved to walk here, describes the view from the top of the hill as finer than anything he had seen in his wanderings abroad; and yet he wrote "The Traveller," and had visited the sunny south.

Between the Heath and the western side of the town is a double row of noble lime-trees, the gravel path under which is "still called the Judge's Walk, or King's Bench Avenue." The story is, that when the plague was raging in London, the sittings of the Courts of Law were transferred for a time from Westminster to Hampstead, and that the Heath was tenanted by gentlemen of the wig and gown, who were forced to sleep under canvas, like so many rifle volunteers, because there was no accommodation to be had for love or money in the village. But we do not guarantee the tradition as well founded.

Making our way towards the village of Hampstead, but before actually quitting the Heath, we pass on our left, at the corner of Heath Mount and East Heath Road, the house which marks the spot on which, in former times, stood the "Upper Flask" tavern, celebrated by Richardson, in his novel of "Clarissa Harlowe." A view of the old house, formerly the rendezvous of Pope, Steele, and others, and subsequently the residence of George Steevens, the commentator on Shakespeare, will be found in Mr. Smith's "Historical and Literary Curiosities."

The "Upper Flask" was at one time called the "Upper Bowling-green House," from its possessing a very good bowling-green. We have given an engraving of it on page 456.

When the Kit-Kat Club was in its glory, its members were accustomed to transfer their meetings in the summer time to this tavern, whose walls—if walls have ears—must have listened to some rare and racy conversation. We have already spoken at some length of the doings of this celebrated club in a previous volume.* In 1712, Steele, most genial of wits and most tender of humorists, found it necessary to quit London for a time. As usual, the duns were upon him, and his "darling Prue" had been, we may suppose, a little more unreasonably jealous than usual. He left London in haste, and took the house at Hampstead in which Sir Charles Sedley had recently died. Thither would come Mr. Pope or Dr. Arbuthnot in a coach to carry the eminent moralist off to the cheerful meetings of the Kit-Kat at the "Flask." How Sir Richard returned we are not told, but there is some reason to fear that the coach was even more necessary at the end of the evening than at its beginning. These meetings, however, did not last long. We shall have more to say of Sir Richard Steele when we reach Haverstock Hill.

Mr. Howitt, in his "Northern Heights of London," gives a view of the house as it appeared when that work was published (1869). The author states that the members of the Kit-Kat Club used "to sip their ale under the old mulberry-tree, which

* See Vol. I., p. 70.

still flourishes, though now bound together by iron bands, and showing signs of great age," in the garden adjoining. Sir Richard Blackmore, in his poem, "The Kit-Kats," thus commemorates the summer gatherings of the club at this house:—

"Or when, Apollo-like, thou'st pleased to lead
Thy sons to feast on Hampstead's airy head:
Hampstead, that, towering in superior sky,
Now with Parnassus does in honour vie."

Since that time the house has been much altered, and additions have been made to it. One Samuel Stanton, a vintner, who came into possession of it near the beginning of the last century, was probably the last person who used it as a tavern. In 1750 it passed from his nephew and successor, "Samuel Stanton, gentleman," to his niece, Lady Charlotte Rich, sister of Mary, Countess of Warwick; a few years later George Steevens, the annotator of Shakespeare, bought the house, and lived there till his death, in 1800.

Steevens is stated to have been a fine classical scholar, and celebrated for his brilliant wit and smart repartee in conversation, in which he was "lively, varied, and eloquent," so that one of his acquaintances said that he regarded him as a speaking Hogarth. He possessed a handsome fortune, which he managed, says his biographer, "with discretion, and was enabled to gratify his wishes, which he did without any regard to expense, in forming his distinguished collections of classical learning, literary antiquity, and the arts connected with it. . . . . He possessed all the grace of exterior accomplishment, acquired when civility and politeness were the characteristics of a gentleman. He received the first part of his education at Kingston-upon-Thames; he went thence to Eton, and was afterwards a fellow-commoner of King's College, Cambridge. He also accepted a commission in the Essex militia, on its first establishment. The latter years of his life he chiefly spent at Hampstead in retirement, and seldom mixed in society except in booksellers' shops, or the Shakespeare Gallery, or the morning conversations of Sir Joseph Banks."

"Steevens," says Cradock, in his "Memoirs," "was the most indefatigable man I had ever met with. He would absolutely set out from his house at Hampstead, with the patrol, and walk to London before daylight, call up his barber in Devereux Court, at whose shop he dressed, and when fully accoutred for the day, generally resorted to the house of his friend Hamilton, the well-known editor and printer of the *Critical Review*."

Steevens, it is stated, added considerably to the house. It was subsequently occupied for many years by Mr. Thomas Sheppard, M.P. for Frome, and afterwards by Mrs. Raikes, a relative of Mr. Thomas Raikes, to whose "Journal" we have frequently referred in these pages. On her death the house passed into the hands of a Mr. Lister. The old house is still kept in remembrance by a double row of elms in front of it, forming a shady grove.

With the interest attached to the place through the pages of "Clarissa Harlowe," it would be wrong not to make more than a passing allusion to it. We will, therefore, summarise from the work those portions having special reference to the "Upper Flask" and its surroundings:—

Richardson represents the fashionable villain Lovelace as inducing Clarissa—whom he had managed, under promise of marriage, to lure away from her family—to take a drive with him in company with two of the women of the sponging-house into which he had decoyed her. Lovelace, afterwards writing to his friend Belford, says:—"The coach carried us to Hampstead, to Highgate, to Muswell Hill; back to Hampstead, to the 'Upper Flask.' There, in compliment to the nymphs, my beloved consented to alight and take a little repast; then home early by Kentish Town." Clarissa no sooner discovers the nature of the vile place into which Lovelace has brought her, than she at once sets about endeavouring to effect her escape. By one of Lovelace's accomplices she is tracked to a hackney coach, and from her directions to the driver it is at once made clear that Hampstead is her destination. The fellow then disguises himself, and making his way thither, discovers her at the "Upper Flask," which fact he communicates to Lovelace in the following words: —"If your honner come to the 'Upper Flax,' I will be in site (sight) all day about the 'Tapphouse' on the Hethe." Lovelace pursues his victim in all haste, and arrives at the "Upper Flask," but only to find that she had been there, but had since taken up her abode somewhere in the neighbourhood. We next find Lovelace writing from the "Upper Flask:"—"I am now here, and have been this hour and a half. What an industrious spirit have I." But all that he could learn with any certainty respecting the runaway was, that "the Hampstead coach, when the dear fugitive came to it, had but two passengers in it; but she made the fellow go off directly, paying for the vacant places. The two passengers directing the coachman to set them down at the 'Upper Flask,' she bid them set her down there also."

Clarissa has in the meantime taken up her abode in the lodging-house of a Mrs. Moore, as she herself tells us in one of her epistles:—"I am at present at one Mrs. Moore's, at Hampstead. My heart misgave me at coming to this village, because I had been here with him more than once; but the coach hither was such a convenience that I knew not what to do better." She, however, is not allowed to rest quietly here, but is soon surrounded by Lovelace's tools and spies. She attempts to escape, and, making her way to the window, exclaims to the landlady—"'Let me look out! Whither does that path lead to? Is there no probability of getting a coach? Cannot I steal to a neighbouring house, where I may be concealed till I can get quite away? Oh, help me, help me, ladies, or I am ruined!' Then, pausing, she asks—'Is that the way to Hendon? Is Hendon a private place? The Hampstead coach, I am told, will carry passengers thither?'" Richardson writes: "She, indeed, went on towards Hendon, passing by the sign of the 'Castle' on the Heath; then stopping, looked about her, and turned down the valley before her. Then, turning her face towards London, she seemed, by the motion of her handkerchief to her eyes, to weep; repenting (who knows?) the rash step that she had taken, and wishing herself back again. . . . Then, continuing on a few paces, she stopped again, and, as if disliking her road, again seeming to weep, directed her course back towards Hampstead."

Hannah More bears testimony to the fact that, when she was young, "Clarissa" and "Sir Charles Grandison" were the favourite reading in any English household. And her testimony to their excellence is striking. She writes: "Whatever objection may be made to them in certain respects, they contain more maxims of virtue, and more sound moral principle, than half the books called 'moral.'"

At the end of a century, Macaulay tells us that the merits of "Clarissa Harlowe" were still felt and acknowledged. On one occasion he said to Thackeray: "If you have once thoroughly entered on 'Clarissa,' and are infected by it, you can't leave it. When I was in India, I passed one hot season at the hills, and there were the governor-general, and the secretary of the Government, and the commander-in-chief, and their wives. I had 'Clarissa' with me; and as soon as they began to read it, the whole station was in a passion of excitement about Miss Harlowe and the scoundrel Lovelace. The governor's wife seized the book, and the secretary waited for it, and the chief justice could not read it for tears. He acted the whole scene as he paced up and down the Athenæum Library; I daresay he could have spoken pages of the book."

The following is the testimony of R. B. Haydon to the merits of "Clarissa Harlowe" as a work of fiction:—"I was never so moved by a work of genius as by *Othello*, except by 'Clarissa Harlowe.' I read seventeen hours a day at 'Clarissa,' and held up the book so long, leaning on my elbows in an arm-chair, that I stopped the circulation, and could not move. When Lovelace writes, 'Dear Belton, it is all over, and Clarissa lives,' I got up in a fury, and wept like an infant, and cursed Lovelace till I was exhausted. This is the triumph of genius over the imagination and heart of the readers."

Richardson, by all accounts, was one of the vainest of men, and loved to talk of nothing so well as his own writings. It must be owned, however, that he had something to be vain and proud about when he wrote "Clarissa Harlowe," which at once established itself as a classic on the bookshelves of every gentleman and lady throughout England.

"The great author," writes Thackeray, in his "Virginians," "was accustomed to be adored—a gentler wind never puffed mortal vanity; enraptured spinsters flung tea-leaves round him, and incensed him with the coffee-pot. Matrons kissed the slippers they had worked for him. There was a halo of virtue round his nightcap."

So great is the popularity of the author of "Pamela," "Clarissa," and "Sir Charles Grandison," that foreigners of distinction have been known to visit Hampstead, and to inquire with curiosity and wonder for the "Flask Walk," so distinguished as a scene in "Clarissa's" history, just as travellers visit the rocks of Mellerie, in order to view the localities with which they have already been familiarised in Rousseau's tale of passion. The "Lower Flask" tavern, in Flask Walk, is mentioned in "Clarissa Harlowe" as a place where second-rate persons are to be found occasionally in a swinish condition. The "Flask Inn," rebuilt in 1873, is still here, and so is Flask Walk, but both are only ghosts of their former selves!

CHAPTER XXXVI.

HAMPSTEAD (*continued*).—THE TOWN.

"A steeple issuing from a leafy rise,
With balmy fields in front, and sloping green,
Dear Hampstead, is thy southern face serene,
Silently smiling on approaching eyes.
Within, thine ever-shifting looks surprise,
Streets, hills, and dells, trees overhead now seen,
Now down below, with smoking roofs between—
A village revelling in varieties.
Then northward, what a range—with heath and pond,
Nature's own ground; woods that let mansions through,
And cottaged vales, with pillowy fields beyond,
And clumps of darkening pines, and prospects blue,
And that clear path through all, where daily meet
Cool cheeks, and brilliant eyes, and morn-elastic feet."—*Leigh Hunt.*

Description of the Town—Heath Street—The Baptist Chapel—Whitefield's Preaching at Hampstead—The Public Library—Romney, the Painter—The "Hollybush"—The Assembly Rooms—Agnes and Joanna Baillie—The Clock House—Branch Hill Lodge—The Fire Brigade Station—The "Lower Flask Inn"—Flask Walk—Fairs held there—The Militia Barracks—Mrs. Tennyson—Christ Church—The Wells—Concerts and Balls—Irregular Marriages—The Raffling Shops—Well Walk—John Constable—John Keats—Geological Formation of the Northern Heights.

THE town of Hampstead is built on the slope of the hill leading up to the Heath, as Mr. Thorne, in his "Environs" styles it, "in an odd, sidelong, tortuous, irregular, and unconnected fashion. There are," he adds, "the fairly-broad winding High Street, and other good streets and lanes,

THE OLD WELL WALK, HAMPSTEAD, ABOUT 1750. (*See page* 467.)

lined with large old brick houses, within high-walled enclosures, over which lean ancient trees, and alongside them houses small and large, without a scrap of garden, and only a very little dingy yard; narrow and dirty byways, courts, and passages, with steep flights of steps, and mean and crowded tenements; fragments of open green spaces, and again streets and lanes bordered with shady elms and limes. On the whole, however, the pleasanter and sylvan character prevails, especially west of the main street. The trees along the streets and lanes are the most characteristic and redeeming feature of the village. Hampstead was long ago 'the place of groves,' and it retains its early distinction. It is the most sylvan of suburban villages." Besides these avenues or groves, almost every part of "old Hampstead" is distinguished by rows of trees, of either lime or elm, planted along the broad footpaths in true boulevard fashion. Mr. Howitt, in his "Northern Heights," in writing on this subject, says: "Its old narrow roads winding under tall trees, are continually conducting to fresh and secluded places, that seem hidden from the world, and would lead you to suppose yourselves far away from London, and in some especially old-fashioned and old-world part of the country. Extensive old and lofty walls enclose the large old brick houses and grounds of what were once the great merchants' and nobles' of London; and ever and anon you are reminded of people and things which lead your recollection back to the neighbouring capital and its intruding histories."

Like Tunbridge Wells and other fashionable resorts of the same kind, Hampstead was not without its inducements for the "wealthy, the idle, and sickly," who flocked thither; and "houses of entertainment and dissipation started up on all sides." The taverns had their "long-rooms" and assembly-rooms for concerts, balls, and card parties; and attached to them were tea-gardens and bowling-greens. On the Heath races were held, as we have stated in the previous chapter; fairs were held in the Flask Walk, and the Well Walk and Church Row became the fashionable promenades of the place. But to proceed.

Leaving the Lower or East Heath, with its pleasant pathways overlooking the Vale of Health, the "ponds," and the distant slopes of Highgate behind us, we descend Heath Mount and Heath Street, and so make our way into the town. On our left, as we proceed down the hill, we pass the Baptist Chapel which was built for the Rev. William Brock, about the year 1862. It is a good substantial edifice, and its two towers are noticeable features in its architecture. This fabric, or rather its predecessor on the same site, is not without its historical reminiscences. "The Independent congregation at Hampstead," says Mr. Howitt, "is supposed to owe its origin to the preaching of Whitefield there in 1739, who, in his journal of May 17, of that year, says, 'Preached, after several invitations thither, at Hampstead Heath, about five miles from London. The audience was of the politer sort, and I preached very near the horse course, which gave me occasion to speak home to the souls concerning our spiritual race. Most were attentive, but some mocked. Thus the Word of God is either a savour of life unto life, or of death unto death.' The congregation experienced its share of the persecutions of those times. The earliest mention of the chapel is 1775." It was some time leased by Selina, Countess of Huntingdon, who relinquished her right in 1782. The present fabric is called Heath Street Chapel.

In a house on the west side of High Street is the Hampstead Public Library. After undergoing many vicissitudes of fortune, this institution seems to have taken a new lease of life with the commencement of 1880.

On our right, between the High Street and the Heath, lived—from 1797 to 1799, George Romney, the famous painter. He removed hither from his residence in Cavendish Square.* He took great pains in constructing for himself a country house, between the "Hollybush Inn" and the Heath, with a studio adjoining. He did not derive, however, any great pleasure from his investment, for he entered the house when it was still wet, and he never enjoyed a day of good health afterwards. Allan Cunningham, in his "Lives of British Painters," says that Romney had resolved to withdraw to the pure air and retirement of Hampstead "to paint the vast historical conceptions for which all this travail had been undergone, and imagined that a new hour of glory was come;" but after a few months—a little more than a year—finding his health growing worse and worse, he made up his mind to return back to the wife whom more than a quarter of a century before he had deserted, and who nursed him carefully till his death. The great artist's studio was subsequently converted into the Assembly Rooms. These rooms were erected on the principle of a tontine; but all sorts of legal difficulties arose, and no one knows who is now the rightful owner. Here for many years—1820 to 1860—were held, at first every month, and subsequently every quarter of a year, *conversazioni*, to which

* See Vol. IV., p. 446.

the resident artistic and literary celebrities used to lend all sorts of works of art to enliven the winter evenings. The cessation of these pleasant gatherings was much regretted. About 1868 an attempt was made to revive these gatherings by means of a succession of lectures during the winter, but these also came to an end after the second season.

The "Hollybush" is not at all an uncommon sign in England, and as it is generally found near to a church, we may conclude that it points back to the ancient custom—now so generally revived amongst us—of decking our houses with evergreens at Christmas. It is said that this custom is as old as the times of the Druids.

The sisters Agnes and Joanna Baillie lived in the central house of a terrace consisting of three mansions facing the Assembly Rooms at the back of the "Hollybush Inn." The house is now called Bolton House, and is next door but one to Windmill Hill, a name which points to the fact of a windmill having stood there at one time. Joanna Baillie, who is well known for her "Plays on the Passions," enjoyed no small fame as a poetess, and was the author of several plays, which were praised by Sir Walter Scott. *Basil* and *De Montfort*, however, were the only tragedies of Miss Joanna Baillie that were performed on the London stage, though *The Family Secret* was brought out with some success at the Edinburgh Theatre.

In Mr. H. Crabbe Robinson's "Diary," under date of May, 1812, we find the following particulars of this amiable and accomplished lady:—"Joined Wordsworth in the Oxford Road (*i.e.*, Oxford Street); we then got into the fields, and walked to Hampstead. . . . We met Miss Joanna Baillie, and accompanied her home. She is small in figure, and her gait is mean and shuffling; but her manners are those of a well-bred lady. She has none of the unpleasant airs too common to literary ladies. Her conversation is sensible. She possesses apparently considerable information, is prompt without being forward, and has a fixed judgment of her own, without any disposition to force it on others. Wordsworth said of her with warmth, 'If I had to present to a foreigner any one as a model of an English gentlewoman, it would be Joanna Baillie.'"

Indeed, according to the testimony of all those who knew her, Joanna Baillie was a plain, simple, homely, unpretending woman, who made no effort to dazzle others, and was not easily dazzled by others. She loved her home, and she and her sister contrived to make that home for many years a centre of all that was good, as well as intellectual.

"I believe," says Miss Sedgwick, an American lady, "of all my pleasures here, dear J. will most envy me that of seeing Joanna Baillie, and of seeing her repeatedly at her home—the best point of view for all best women. She lives on Hampstead Hill, a few miles from town, in a modest house, with Miss Agnes Baillie, her only sister, a kindly and agreeable person. Miss Baillie—I write this for J., for women always like to know how one another look and dress—Miss Baillie has a well-preserved appearance: her face has nothing of the vexed or sorrowful expression that is often so deeply stamped by a long experience of life. It indicates a strong mind, great sensibility, and the benevolence that, I believe, always proceeds from it if the mental constitution be a sound one, as it eminently is in Miss Baillie's case. She has a pleasing figure, what we call lady-like—that is, delicate, erect, and graceful; not the large-boned, muscular frame of most English women. She wears her own gray hair—a general fashion, by the way, here, which I wish we elderly ladies of America may have the courage and the taste to imitate; and she wears the prettiest of brown silk gowns and bonnets, fitting the *beau-ideal* of an old lady—an ideal she might inspire, if it has no pre-existence. You would, of course, expect her to be free from pedantry and all modes of affectation; but I think you would be surprised to find yourself forgetting, in a domestic and confiding feeling, that you were talking with the woman whose name is best established among the female writers of her country; in short, forgetting everything but that you were in the society of a most charming private gentlewoman."

The *Quarterly Review* also gives her the credit of having borne a most tasteful and effective, though subordinate part, in that entire and wonderful revolution of the public taste in works of imagination and in literature generally, which contrasts this century with the latter half of the last. "Unversed in the ancient languages and literature, and by no means accomplished in those of her own age, or even of her own country, this remarkable woman owed it, partly to the simplicity of her Scottish education, partly to the influence of the better part of Burns's poetry, but chiefly to the spontaneous action of her own powerful genius, that she was able at once, and apparently without effort, to come forth the mistress of a masculine style of thought and diction, which constituted then, as it constitutes now, the characteristic merit of her writings, and which contributed most beneficially to the already commenced reformation of the literary principles of the century."

We learn from Lockhart's "Life," that Sir

Walter Scott, too, on being asked whether among poets born north of the Tweed he preferred Burns or Campbell, gave no direct answer, but said, "If you wish to speak of a real poet, Joanna Baillie is now the highest genius of our country." In fact, Scott was one of her most ardent admirers. Mentioning in a letter at the time his own "House of Aspen," he says, "The 'Plays of the Passions' have put me entirely out of conceit with my Germanised brat." His esteem of the talents of the author led, in Miss Baillie's case, as in that of Miss Edgeworth and others, to Scott's acquaintance and friendship with the woman. The cordial and agreeable intimacy between Miss Baillie and Scott, which ceased but with the life of the latter, dates from his introduction to her at Hampstead, in 1806, by the translator and poet, Sotheby. Joanna Baillie herself, many years afterwards, described the interview to a friend as one of the most remarkable events of her life. She, from that period of their first acquaintance, became a continual correspondent of the mighty minstrel; and some of the most entertaining letters he ever wrote are addressed to her. The author of the "Man of Feeling" was also her friend. The prologue to the play of *The Family Legend* was written by Scott, the epilogue by Mackenzie. Joanna Baillie was honoured also from Lord Byron with the remark that she was the only woman who could write a tragedy.

When her "Plays on the Passions" were first published, they appeared without a name, and great was the speculation of the public as to who the author could be. Mrs. Piozzi stood almost single-handed in maintaining that they were the work of a woman; and she tells us, what is in itself a proof of the faulty taste and judgment of her age, that no sooner was their authorship owned by "an unknown girl" than the work fell so much in value as to become almost unsaleable.

William Howitt, who knew her in her Hampstead home, calls her a "powerful dramatic writer," a "graceful and witty lyrist," and a "sweet and gentle woman." Miss Berry says that her tragedies were highly appreciated by that connoisseur of literature and art, Sir George Beaumont, who sent them to Charles James Fox, and that the latter was in such raptures about them that he wrote a critique of five pages upon the subject.

Miss Lucy Aikin has preserved a few traits of her character, having been acquainted with her through meeting her at Mr. Barbauld's house. She was shy and reserved to a degree, for the "repression of all emotions, even the most gentle and the most honourable to human nature, seems to have been the constant lesson taught by her parents in her Presbyterian home." The first thing which drew upon Joanna the admiring notice of Hampstead society was the devoted assiduity of her attention to her mother, then blind as well as aged, and whom she attended day and night. But this part of her duty came at length to its natural termination; and the secret of her authorship having been at length permitted to transpire, she was no longer privileged to sit in the shade, shuffling off upon others her own fair share of conversation. Latterly her discourse flowed freely enough; but even then it was less on books than on real life and the aspects of rural nature that she loved to talk. "Her genius," writes Miss Aikin, "had shrouded itself under so thick a veil of silent reserve, that its existence seems scarcely to have been ever suspected beyond the domestic circle when the 'Plays on the Passions' burst upon the world. The dedication of the volume to Dr. Baillie gave a hint in what quarter the author was to be sought; but the person chiefly suspected was the accomplished widow of his uncle, John Hunter. Of Joanna, at all events, no one dreamed on this occasion. She and her sister—I well remember the scene—arrived on a morning call at Mr. Barbauld's; my aunt immediately introduced the topic of the anonymous tragedies, and gave utterance to her admiration with that generous delight in the manifestation of kindred genius which always distinguished her. But not even the sudden delight of such praise, so given, would seduce our Scottish damsel into self-betrayal. The faithful sister rushed forward, as we afterwards recollected, to bear the brunt, while the unsuspected author of the 'Plays' lay snugly wrapt up in the asylum of her taciturnity."

Miss Aikin remarks that in spite of her long residence in the neighbourhood of London, Joanna Baillie retained her Scotch predilections to the last. She died in 1851, at the age of ninety, carrying with her to the grave the love, reverence, and regrets of all who had enjoyed her society.

Hard by the house of Joanna Baillie is an old mansion named Fenton House, but generally known as "The Clock House," from a clock which adorned its front, though now superseded by a sundial; the house is chiefly remarkable for its heavy high-pitched roof, not unlike that of many a château in Normandy. It now belongs to a member of Lord Mansfield's family.

The large red-brick house, on the left in ascending from Hollybush Hill towards the Heath, is called Branch Hill Lodge. It was in part rebuilt about the year 1745 for Sir Thomas Clark, Master of the Rolls. The house was afterwards the residence of Lord Chancellor Macclesfield, and subsequently, among others, of Lord Loughborough, before his removal to Rosslyn House, where we shall presently speak of him again. At the close of the last century it was purchased of Colonel Parker, a younger son of Lord Macclesfield, by Sir Thomas Neave, who, as Lysons states in his "Environs of London," here had "a very large and most valuable collection of painted glass, a great part of which was procured from various convents on the Continent, immediately after the French Revolution."

At the junction of Heath and High Street is the Fire Brigade Station, an attractive building of coloured bricks, with a lofty watch tower and clock, erected by public subscription in 1870; it commands a view over a large extent of country. Mr. G. Vulliamy was the architect.

On the east slope of the hill, and covering the ground on our left as we descend Heath Street and the High Street, lies that portion of the town which may fairly lay claim to being called "Old Hampstead." Our approach to this once fashionable quarter is by a narrow passage out of the High Street, which brings us at once to the "Lower Flask Tavern," which we have incidentally mentioned at the close of the previous chapter.

The "Flask" is a very appropriate, and therefore a very common, sign to mark a house devoted to the service of topers. There was a celebrated "Flask" in Pimlico; and the "Upper" and "Lower Flasks" at Hampstead are historical.

Flask Walk, which runs eastward from the tavern, is a long straggling thoroughfare, in part planted with trees along the edge of the broad pavement. In the triangular space near the end—now a pleasant grass-plat—an annual fair was formerly held. It was noted for its riotous character; conducted as it was much on the same principle as the celebrated "Bartlemy Fair" in Smithfield. An advertisement on the cover of the original edition of the *Spectator* is as follows:—"This is to give notice, that Hampstead Fair is to be kept upon the Lower Flask Tavern Walk, on Friday, the first of August, and holds (*i.e.*, lasts) for four days." Formerly the Flask Walk was open to the High Street, and was shaded throughout with fine trees; many of these, however, are now gone, and small houses have taken their place. In Flask Walk were formerly the parish stocks. Not long ago some busy-bodies wanted to change the name of the thoroughfare, but common sense ruled otherwise.

One of the chief sources of the Fleet, as we have already stated, was in Hampstead; it rose in a spring nearly under the walls of Gardnor House, at the east end of Flask Walk, and within a hundred yards westward of the old Wells. At the junction of Flask Walk and Well Walk, and nearly opposite the "Wells Tavern," are the Middlesex Militia Barracks, a spacious brick building, partly formed out of an old mansion, called Burgh House, two projecting wings having been added. The barracks was built in 1863, from the designs of Mr. Henry Pownall.

In a house at the corner of Flask Row, opposite to the Militia Barracks, the mother of the poet Tennyson spent the last years of her life; and here she died about the year 1861. It is almost needless to add that up to that date Alfred Tennyson was a constant visitor at Hampstead, and was frequently to be seen strolling on the Heath wrapped up in thought, though he mixed little with Hampstead society. Mrs. Tennyson lies buried in Highgate Cemetery.

Close by this spot, on the sloping ground leading up to Squire's Mount, is one of the many religious edifices of the town, Christ Church, a large Perpendicular building, with a lofty spire, which serves as a landmark for miles around; this church was built in 1852. In the same neighbourhood is the new workhouse, a large and well-built structure of brick and stone, together with the other parochial offices.

Both Flask Walk and Well Walk have an air of fading gentility about them, and, like many of the other streets and lanes in the village, they are planted with rows of shady limes or elms, which every year, however, are becoming fewer and fewer.

Well Walk (which connects Flask Walk with the lower portion of East Heath) and the "Wells Tavern" still serve to keep in remembrance the famous "wells," which commanded an open view across the green fields towards Highgate.

In the days of the early celebrity of its "waters," Hampstead must have rivalled Tunbridge Wells and Epsom; and its Well Walk in the morning, with all its gay company of gentlemen in laced ruffles and powdered wigs, and of ladies in hoops of monstrous size, must have reminded one of the Mall in St. James's Park, or the gardens of Kensington Palace. At the time when London was surrounded by "spas" and "wells"—when the citizens resorted to Bagnigge Wells in the morning, to Sadlers' Wells and the White Conduit in the evening, and to Tunbridge Wells, Bath, and Cheltenham in the summer and autumn—the springs of Hampstead were in great repute, and they were, no doubt, exceedingly beneficial to people whose principal complaints were those of idleness, dissipation, and frivolity. A local physician wrote a long account of these valuable waters, describing them in terms of extravagant hyperbole, and lauding their virtues to the skies. The analysis which he publishes is, however, a curious practical comment on his rapturous enthusiasm. As a matter of fact, the water was and is simply exceedingly pure spring water, with a faint trace of earthy salts such as those of iron, magnesia, and lime. The total amount of solid matter is but seven grains to the gallon—about as much as is to be found in the water of the Kent Company, and about a fourth of the quantity held in solution by the water of the companies which derive their supply from the Thames. Other physicians were to be found who were as ready as he of Hampstead to trumpet the merits of the spa. Says one of them, "It is a stimulant diuretic, very beneficial in chronic diseases arising from languor of the circulation, general debility of the system, or laxity of the solids, or in all cases where tonics and gentle stimulants are required, and in cutaneous affections. The season for drinking it is from April to the end of October."

The "Wells," we need hardly say, formed one of the leading features of Hampstead in its palmy days. As far back as the year 1698 they are spoken of by the name of "The Wells;" and two years later it is ordered by the authorities of the Manor Court, "that the spring lyeing by the purging wells be forthwith brot to the toune of Hamsted, at the parish charge, and y[t] y[e] money profitts arising thereout be applied tow[rds] easing the Poor Rates hereafter to be made." It was not long before they came into fashion and general use.

THE OLD CLOCK HOUSE, 1780. (*See page* 466.)

The *Postman* of April, 1700, announces that "the chalybeate waters of Hampstead, being of the same nature, and equal in virtue, with Tunbridge Wells, are sold by Mr. R. Philps, apothecary, at the "Eagle and Child," in Fleet Street, every morning, at threepence per flask, and conveyed to persons at their own houses for one penny more. [N.B.—The flask to be returned daily.]"

Early in the eighteenth century we meet with advertisements to the effect that the mineral waters from the wells at Hampstead might be obtained from the "lessee," who lived "at the 'Black Posts,' in King Street, near Guildhall." They are also to be had at ten or twelve other houses in London, including "Sam's Coffee-house, near Ludgate, and the 'Sugar Loaf,' at Charing Cross."

In 1734, Mr. John Soame, M.D., published some directions for drinking the Hampstead waters, which he designated the "Inexhaustible Fountain of Health." In this work the worthy doctor placed on record some "experiments of the Hampstead waters, and histories of cures." Hampstead has long been celebrated for the choice medicinal herbs growing abundantly in its fields and hedgerows; and Dr. Soame in his pamphlet tells us how that "the Apothecaries Company very seldom miss coming to Hampstead every spring, and here have their herbalising feast. I have heard them say," he adds, "that they have found a greater variety of curious and useful plants near and about Hampstead than in any other place."

For the first ten or twelve years of the last century the Wells seem to have been in full favour, for at that time dancing and music were added to the attractions of the place. In the *Postman*, of August 14-16, 1701, it is announced that "At Hampstead Wells, on Monday next, being the 18th of this instant August, will be performed a Consort (*sic*) of both vocal and instrumental musick, with some particular performance of both kinds, by the best masters, to begin at 10 o'clock precisely. Tickets will be delivered at the said Wells for 1s. per ticket; and Dancing in the afternoon for 6d. per ticket, to be delivered as before." In September the following advertisement appeared:—"In the Great Room at Hampstead Wells, on Monday

KEATS' SEAT, OLD WELL WALK.

next, being the 15th instant, exactly at 11 o'clock forenoon, will be performed a Consort of vocal and instrumental musick, by the best masters; and, at the request of several gentlemen, Jemmy Bowen will perform several songs, and particular performances on the violin by 2 several masters. Tickets to be had at the Wells, and at Stephen's Coffee-house in King Street, Bloomsbury, at 1s. each ticket. There will be Dancing in the afternoon, as usual." In 1702, the *London Post*, for May 5, has this advertisement:—"Hampstead Consort. In the Great Room of Hampstead Wells, on Monday next, the 11th instant, will be performed a Consort of vocal and instrumental musick by the best masters, with particular entertainments on the violin by Mr. Dean, beginning exactly at 11 o'clock, rain or fair. To continue every Monday, at the same place and time, during the season of drinking the waters. Tickets to be had at Stephen's Coffee-house, in Bloomsbury, and at the Wells (by reason the room is very large) at one shilling each ticket. There will be dancing in the afternoon as usual." The *Postboy*, of May 8-10, 1707, informs "all persons that have occasion to drink the Hampstead mineral waters, that the Wells will be open on Monday next, with very good music for dancing all day long, and to continue every Monday during the season;" and it further adds that "there is all needful accommodation for water-drinkers of both sex (*sic*), and all other entertainments for good eating and drinking, and a very pleasant bowling-green, with convenience of coach-horses; and very good stables for fine horses, with good attendance; and a farther accommodation of a stage-coach and chariot from the Wells at any time in the evening or morning." No. 201 of the *Tatler*, July 22, 1710, contains the following announcement:—"A Consort of Musick will be performed in the Great Room at Hampstead this present Saturday, the 22nd instant, at the desire of the gentlemen and ladies living in and near Hampstead, by the best masters. Several of the Opera songs by a girl of nine years, a scholar of Mr. Tenoe's, who never performed in public but once at York Buildings with very good success. To begin exactly at five, for the conveniency of gentlemen's returning. Tickets to be had only at the Wells, at 2s. and 6d. each. For the benefit of Mr. Tenoe."

Gay, author of the "Fables" and the *Beggar's Opera*, drank of the waters and rambled about the Heath in 1727, and was cured of the colic; but his friend, Dr. Arbuthnot, had less success a few years afterwards, perhaps from medical want of faith. While he was staying there, Pope used to visit him; and then it probably was that the worthy doctor enjoyed those meetings with Pope's friend, Murray, which Cowper celebrated.

In more than one novel, written about the middle of the last century, we are treated with some remarks upon the visitors to the Wells at Hampstead, where we get a glimpse of the vulgar cockneyism which had succeeded to the witty flirtations of the fine ladies and gentlemen of fifty years previously. One author tells us how Madame Duval, rouged and decked in all the colours of the rainbow, danced a minuet; how "Beau Smith" pestered the pensive Evelina, who was thinking only of the accomplished and uncomfortably perfect Lord Orville, and much annoyed at the vulgar impertinence of the young men who begged the favour of "hopping a dance with her." Of the Long Room our author says: "The room seems very well named, for I believe it would be difficult to find any other epithet which might with propriety distinguish it, as it is without ornament, elegance, or any sort of singularity, and merely to be marked by its length." This building was used for many years previous to 1850 as a chapel of ease to the parish church; and a few years later was fitted up as the drill-room for the Hampstead (3rd Middlesex) Volunteers.

Nor is this all that we have to say about the Wells. From an advertisement in the *Postboy*, April 18, 1710, it appears that Hampstead rivalled for a time Mayfair* and the Fleet† in the practice of performing "irregular" marriages, and that the "Wells" even enjoyed sufficient popularity to have a chapel of their own.

"As there are many weddings at Zion Chapel, Hampstead," we read, "five shillings only is required for all the church fees of any couple that are married there, provided they bring with them a licence or certificate according to the Act of Parliament. Two sermons are continued to be preached in the said chapel every Sunday; and the place will be given to any clergyman that is willing to accept of it, if he is approved of."

The lessee at this time was one Howell, who was commonly spoken of as "the Welsh ambassador," and under his management irregular marriages were frequently celebrated. The advertisements of the period show pretty plainly what was the nature of the proceedings here. One notice which appeared in 1711 announced that those who go to be married must carry with them licences or dispensations, a formality which we may readily imagine was not unfrequently dispensed with. In *Read's Weekly Journal*, September 8,

* See Vol. IV., p. 347. † See Vol. II., p. 411.

1716, it is announced that "Sion Chapel, at Hampstead, being a private and pleasure place, many persons of the best fashion have lately been married there. Now, as a minister is obliged constantly to attend, this is to give notice that all persons upon bringing a licence, and who shall have their wedding dinner in the gardens, may be married in that said chapel without giving any fee or reward whatsoever; and such as do not keep their wedding dinner at the gardens, only five shillings will be demanded of them for all fees."

The exact site of this chapel is no longer known, but in all probability it adjoined the Wells, and belonged to the keeper of the adjoining tavern. There can be little doubt that it was a capital speculation before the trade in such matters was spoiled, a century or so ago, by the introduction of the "Private Marriage Act," so cruelly introduced by Lord Hardwicke.

This being the condition of the place, we need not be surprised to learn that its popularity with certain classes was unbounded. In fact, so much was Hampstead the rage at the beginning of the last century, that in the comedy of *Hampstead Heath*, above referred to we find one of the characters, "Arabella," the wife of a citizen, thus telling us what she thinks of the place:—

"Well, this Hampstead 's a charming place, to dance all night at the Wells, and be treated at Mother Huff's; to have presents made one at the raffling shops, and then take a walk in Caen Wood with a man of wit. But to be five or six miles from one's husband!—marriage were a happy state could one be always five or six miles from one's husband."

This, we need scarcely remark, is a sentiment very congenial with the morals—or rather want of morals—which marked the age. The "Mother Huff" referred to so admiringly by the lady, was better known in the gossiping literature of the time by the even less euphonious name of "Mother Damnable." As we have seen in a previous chapter,* she appears to have been a person of accommodating disposition, who fixed her modest abode near the junction of the roads leading to Hampstead and through Kentish Town to Highgate, and made herself useful and agreeable to such modish ladies as Arabella and her witty friend.

The "raffling shops," also alluded to, are mentioned in the *Tatler*, in which Mr. Isaac Bickerstaffe, otherwise Sir Richard Steele, the "Christian hero," thought fit, as censor of public morals, to call attention to them. Writing in August, 1709, he says:—"I am diverted from my train of discourse by letters from Hampstead, which give me an account there is a late institution there under the name of a Raffling Shop, which is (it seems) secretly supported by a person who is a deep practitioner in the law, and out of tenderness of conscience has, under the name of his maid Sisly, set up this easier way of conveyancing and alienating estates from one family to another."

The Wells continued to be more or less a place of resort for invalids, real and imaginary, down to the early part of the present century, when their fame was revived for a time by Mr. Thomas Goodwin, a medical practitioner of the place, who had made the discovery that the Hampstead waters were possessed of two kinds of saline qualities, answering to the springs of Cheltenham and Harrogate; but the tide of popular favour seems to have flowed in another direction, after the visit of George III. and his Court to Cheltenham, and Hampstead soon became deserted by its fashionable loungers, notwithstanding the efforts of the doctors, who missed their guineas, and those of the proprietors of the ball-rooms and the raffling-shops, to resuscitate its fame. Dr. Soame complained that the royal family visited the wells at Islington, then achieving a temporary popularity, and neglected Hampstead; and he also seized the opportunity of levelling his shafts at the habit of tea-drinking, then a comparatively modern innovation. "I hope," he says, "that the inordinate drinking of tea will be retrenched, which, if continued, must bring a thousand ills upon us, and generations after us—the next generation may be in stature more like pigmies than men and women." What would Dr. Soame have said could he have lived to see the members of the Middlesex Rifle Volunteers, every fine fellow of which corps drinks tea every day, performing feats of prowess and agility while skirmishing among the furze-bushes and gravel-pits of his beloved Hampstead?

But no amount of appeal or puff direct could make Hampstead what it was in its aristocratic days. The wells and ball-rooms remained, and were well attended, but by another class. Their prestige was gone, and the world of fashion resigned them to the London aborigines dwelling east of Temple Bar. The waters of Hampstead are no longer taken medicinally, and their former celebrity is now only remembered in the name of the charming little grove called Well Walk, which leads from Flask Walk towards the eastern side of the Heath, and where there has been set up, as though in mockery of the past, a modern drinking-fountain.

Well Walk was in former times the fashionable

* See *ante*, p. 310.

morning lounge for the visitor to the "Wells;" and here the gallants of the period could enjoy the fresh air in the shade of the tall lime-trees, which still remain along the edge of the raised pathway. In Well Walk, between the "Long Room" and the "Wells Tavern," lived and died John Constable, the painter. Like Gainsborough and Crome, Constable always proved himself a heartfelt lover of an English homestead. "I love," he said, "every stile, and stump, and lane in the village; as long as I am able to hold a brush I shall never cease to paint them." "The Cornfield or Country Lane" and "The Valley Farm," both in the National Gallery, may have suggested to Leslie the following passage:—"There is a place," says this most sympathetic of critics on simply English art, "among our painters which Turner left unoccupied, and which neither Wilson, Gainsborough, Cozens, nor Girtin so completely filled as Constable. He was the most genuine painter of English cultivated scenery, leaving untouched its mountains and its lakes." His tomb in the old churchyard records that he was "many years an inhabitant of this parish." He died in 1837. Mrs. Barbauld, too, at one time, lived in Well Walk, where she was visited, not only by literary folks, but by men of high scientific attainments, such as Josiah Wedgwood. She afterwards lived at the foot of Rosslyn Hill, where we shall presently have more to say concerning her.

It was in Well Walk that John Keats wrote both his "Endymion" and his "Eve of St. Agnes;" and it was probably after hearing the nightingale in the adjoining gardens that he wrote those well-known stanzas, in which he apostrophises "The light-winged Dryad of the trees."

Hone, in his "Table Book," writes of this place: "Winding south from the Lower Heath, there is a charming little grove in Well Walk, with a bench at the end, whereon I last saw poor Keats, the poet of the 'Pot of Basil,' sitting and sobbing his dying breath into a handkerchief—glancing parting looks towards the quiet landscape he had delighted in so much—musing as in his 'Ode to a Nightingale.'"

Samuel Taylor Coleridge would sometimes come over across the green fields, by way of Millfield Lane, from Highgate, to have a chat with Keats on his seat at the end of Well Walk; and when he last shook hands with him here, he turned to Leigh Hunt, and whispered, "There is death in that hand." And such was too truly the case; for John Keats was in a consumption; and he went abroad very soon afterwards, to die beneath the sunny skies of Italy.

"And wilt thou ponder on the silent grave
Of broken-hearted Keats, whom still we love
To image sleeping where the willows wave
By Memory's fount, deep in the Muses' grove;
Shaded, enshrouded, where no steps intrude,
But peace is granted him; his dearest boon;
And while he sleeps, with night-time tears bedew'd,
'Endymion' still is watched by his enamoured moon."

The copyhold property in the rear of Well Walk belongs to the trustees of the Wells Charity, who are bound to devote its proceeds to apprenticing children, natives of Hampstead, under a scheme lately approved by the Court of Chancery.

Although it has not been attempted in these columns to enter into details respecting the geological structure of the localities which we have described, yet we ought not to omit to mention, with respect to Highgate and Hampstead, a few facts of interest to those who have the least taste for that branch of science.

It is well known to most readers that the whole of London lies on a substratum of chalk formation, which is covered by a higher stratum of a stiff bluish clay. On this again, there is every reason to believe, there once lay a covering of gravel and sand, which in the course of long ages has been washed away by the action of water, at a time when, probably, the whole valley of the Thames was an arm of the sea.

The "Northern Heights" of Highgate and Hampstead, if their formation is considered in detail, throw considerable light on this statement. Their summits exhibit a top coating or "cap" of gravel and sand, which, by some chance or other, has not been so swept away, but has maintained its position unchanged. This gravel and sand rest on an undersoil of a soft and spongy nature, from which issue springs of water, which appear to be squeezed out of the sides of the hills by the weight of the superincumbent mass.

These spongy soils gradually die away into a blue clay from thirty to five hundred feet in depth, in which, both at Hampstead and at Highgate, a variety of fossils have been found, proving the existence here of plants, trees, and animals akin to, but still differing from, those of our own age and latitude; some of these are of a marine and estuarine aquatic nature, showing that a sea must at one time have washed the sides of the heights that we have been climbing. As an instance in point, it may be mentioned that, in 1876, in boring a well through the clay at the brewery in High Street, the workmen came upon a fine specimen of the nautilus. Other marine shells of a smaller kind have been constantly dug up in the same stratum about these parts.

CHAPTER XXXVII.

HAMPSTEAD (*continued*).—ITS LITERARY ASSOCIATIONS, &c.

"Well, this Hampstead 's a charming place."—*Old Play.*

Church Row—Fashionable Frequenters of "the Row" in the Last Century—Dr. Sherlock—Dr. John Arbuthnot—Dr. Anthony Askew—Dr. George Sewell—The Rev. Rochmont Barbauld—Mr. J. Park—Miss Lucy Aikin—Reformatory Schools—John Rogers Herbert—Henry Fuseli—Hannah Lightfoot—Charles Dickens—Charles Knight—An Artistic Gift rejected by Hampstead—The Parish Church—Repairs and Alterations in the Building—Eminent Incumbents—The Graves of Joanna Baillie, Sir James Mackintosh, John Constable, Lord Erskine, and Others—St. Mary's Roman Catholic Chapel—Grove Lodge and Montagu Grove—The Old Workhouse.

Retracing our steps to the High Street, and passing up a narrow lane on the west side, called Church Lane, we find ourselves in Church Row. Here, and almost only here, the hand of the "improver" and "restorer" has not been at work; the projecting hooded doorways of the days of Queen Anne still frown over the entrances of the red-bricked houses on our right and left, just as they did in the days "when George III. was king;" and the whole street has an air of quiet, homely, and venerable respectability which we can scarcely see elsewhere. Long may it remain in *statu quo*, this venerable relic of the days when the fashionable crowd—the "quality"—gentlemen with powdered wigs and gold-headed canes, and ladies in farthingales and "hoops of wondrous size"—used to make "the Row" their evening parade, after drinking the waters at the chalybeate spring, which, as we have just seen, still flows so invitingly on the other side of the High Street. Like Flask Walk and Well Walk, and some other thoroughfares which we have mentioned, Church Row—and, indeed, the High Street also—could in former times boast of its row of lime-trees growing down the centre of the roadway. Those in the High Street, save one, disappeared long ago; and of those in Church Row one solitary lime remains as a memento of the past. It may not be out of place to add here that the sedan-chairs continued in use in Hampstead longer than in any other part of London; indeed, it was no farther back than the early part of the present century that they were superseded by the donkey-carriages, which may still be seen driven along the quiet thoroughfares. Till comparatively recent times, too, the link-extinguishers of former days remained *in situ* by the doors of most of the houses in Church Row, although their use had been long ago set aside by the introduction of gas.

Among the frequenters of Church Row at the beginning of the last century doubtless might have been seen Dr. William Sherlock, Dean of St. Paul's and Master of the Temple, and also Dr. Arbuthnot, the witty physician, and friend of Swift, Gay, and Pope. The former, at all events, died at Hampstead, in June, 1707, at the age of sixty-six. He was induced by his wife, somewhat reluctantly, to submit to William and Mary. Walking with his spouse, he was pointed at by a bookseller, who said, "There goes Dr. Sherlock with his reasons for taking the oaths on his arm." Dr. Sherlock was the author of a "Practical Treatise on Death." He was buried in St. Paul's Cathedral.

Dr. John Arbuthnot, of whom we have already spoken in our account of Dover Street, Piccadilly,* was for some time a resident at Hampstead. He was eminent as a wit and man of letters, even among the choice spirits of the reign of Queen Anne. Soon after coming to England from Scotland, the place of his birth, he went to practise as a physician at Dorchester, but the salubrity of the air was unfriendly to his success, and he took horse for London. A neighbour, meeting him on full gallop, asked him where he was going. "To leave your confounded place, where I can neither live nor die." His wit and pleasantry sometimes assisted his prescriptions, and in some cases superseded the necessity of prescribing. Queen Anne and her consort appointed him their physician; the Royal Society elected him a member, and the College of Physicians followed. "He gained the admiration of Swift, Pope, and Gay," writes Hone in his "Year Book," "and with them he wrote and laughed. No man had more friends, or fewer enemies; yet he did not want energy of character; he diverged from the laughter-loving mood to tear away the mask from the infamous 'Charitable Corporation.' He could do all things well but walk. His health declined, while his mind remained sound to the last. He long wished for death to release him from a complication of disorders, and declared himself tired with 'keeping so much bad company.' A few weeks before his decease he wrote, 'I am as well as a man can be who is gasping for breath, and has a house full of men and women unprovided for.' . . . Dr. Arbuthnot was a man of great humanity and benevolence. Swift said to Pope, 'Oh that the world had but a

* See Vol. IV., p. 292.

dozen Arbuthnots in it; if so, I would burn my travels.' Pope no less passionately lamented him, and said of him, 'He was a man of humour, whose mind seemed to be always pregnant with comic ideas.' Arbuthnot was, indeed, seldom serious, except in his attacks upon great enormities, and then his pen was masterly. The condemnation of the play of *Three Hours after Marriage*, written by him, Pope, and Gay, was published by Wilkes, in his prologue to the *Sultaness*:—

> 'Such were the wags who boldly did adventure
> To club a farce by tripartite indenture;
> But let them share their dividend of praise,
> And wear their own fool's cap instead of bays.'

Arbuthnot simply retorted, in 'Gulliver Decyphered.' Satire was his chief weapon, but the wound he inflicted on folly soon healed; he was always playful, unless he added weight to keenness for the chastisement of crime."

OLD HOUSES IN CHURCH ROW.

To the above names of the frequenters of Church Row may be added that of Dr. Johnson, during his sojourn at Frognal, just round by the western end of the church, whose "ivy-mantled tower" forms a pleasing termination to the bottom of Church Row.

Another distinguished physician who resided for some time at Hampstead, and who, doubtless, might have been seen mixing with the fashionable throng in Church Row, was Dr. Anthony Askew, who died here in 1774. He practised originally at

CHURCH ROW, HAMPSTEAD, IN 1750.

Cambridge, but seems to have been introduced to London, and zealously recommended there, by the celebrated Dr. Mead. Dr. Askew was chiefly noted for his collection of classical works, which were sold at his death. Nichols says that his collection of Greek and Latin works was "one of the best, rarest, and most valuable ever sold in Great Britain."

Dr. George Sewell, an intimate friend of Pope and Arbuthnot, had lodgings in Hampstead, where he died in 1725. He contributed largely to the supplemental volumes of the *Tatler* and *Spectator*, and wrote the principal part of a translation of Ovid's "Metamorphoses." His principal work, however, was the tragedy of *Sir Walter Raleigh*, which was produced at the Duke's Theatre, in Lincoln's Inn Fields.

John Wylde, Lord Chief Baron of the Exchequer during the civil war, spent the last few years of his life in retirement at Hampstead, and died about ten years after the Restoration.

The Rev. Rochmont Barbauld—a well-known Unitarian minister at Hampstead at the close of the last century—resided in Church Row, where he had a few pupils. Hampstead at that time was deemed almost inaccessible. In a diary kept by Mr. Barbauld, he frequently speaks of being prevented from going to town by the state of the roads. Mrs. Barbauld resided in Hampstead long after her husband's death, but chiefly on Rosslyn Hill; we shall have more to say of her on reaching that place.

Mr. J. Park, the author of the "History of Hampstead," most excellent as a man and as an antiquary, lived in Church Row; he died in June, 1833. The work associated with his name was published before Mr. Park came of age, and in closing the preface, which is dated November 30, 1813, Mr. Park remarked, "The severer studies of an arduous profession now call upon me to bid a final adieu to those literary blandishments which have beguiled my youthful days." To this resolution he firmly adhered; but afterwards committed to the care of Mr. Nichols, the well-known antiquary, to whom we have frequently had occasion to refer, some additional documents, which were printed as an appendix, in 1818. Mr. Park became a barrister-at-law of Lincoln's Inn, and two years before his death he was appointed Professor of Law and Jurisprudence at King's College, London.

Another literary name, long associated with Hampstead, is that of Miss Lucy Aikin, niece of Mrs. Barbauld, and the author of "Memories of the Court of Queen Elizabeth," &c. On the death of her father, Dr. Aikin, which happened at Stoke Newington, in December, 1822, she took up her abode in Church Row, to be near her aunt, Mrs. Barbauld. Her mother accompanied her, and spent here her declining years, and died here in 1830. She had been brought up among the descendants of the old Puritans, and afterwards lived much among the disciples and fellow-workers of Price and Priestley and Dr. Enfield—all Unitarians, or men of the broadest views in that direction. Her only, or at all events her chief, publication whilst living here was her "Memoir of Addison," which appeared in 1843. She quitted Hampstead in the next year, to reside first in London and afterwards at Wimbledon, but returned to it some seven or eight years later, and spent the last twelve years of her life in the house of Mr. P. H. Le Breton, who had married her niece. Late in life she wrote in one of her letters, "I am all but a prisoner to my house and little garden." She died here in January, 1864, in her eighty-third year, and her grave in the old churchyard is next to that of her great friend, Joanna Baillie. "To Hampstead," writes Mr. Le Breton, in his preface to her "Memoirs," "Lucy Aikin was much attached, and her return to it gave her much pleasure, as many dear relatives and friends lived there. The vicinity of Hampstead to the metropolis afforded, at the same time, the opportunity of intercourse with a more varied society. She enjoyed with a keen relish, and thoroughly appreciated, the company of literary men and of eminent politicians and lawyers, with whom she delighted to discuss questions of interest. With almost every distinguished writer of this period she was acquainted, and of many of them notices will be found in her correspondence." Miss Harriet Martineau was among her numerous friends and visitors here.

The Hampstead of 1830–40 is thus portrayed by Miss Lucy Aikin, in one of her charming letters to Dr. Channing:—"Several circumstances render society here peculiarly easy and pleasant; in many respects the place unites the advantages and escapes the evils both of London and provincial towns. It is near enough (to London) to allow its inhabitants to partake in the society, the amusements, and the accommodations of the capital as freely as ever the dissipated could desire; whilst it affords pure air, lovely scenery, and retired and beautiful walks. Because every one here is supposed to have a London set of friends, neighbours do not think it necessary, as in the provinces, to force their acquaintance upon you; of local society you may have much, little, or none, as you please; and with a little, which is very good, you may associate on the easiest terms. Then the summer brings an influx of Londoners, who are often genteel and agreeable people, and pleasingly vary the scene. Such is Hampstead." And such, to a certain extent, it may be added, is Hampstead in the present day; for as yet it is quite distinct from the great metropolis, and has quite a character of its own.

The Hampstead Reformatory School for Girls, founded in 1857, occupied a large-sized house in Church Row, down to the close of 1876, when the establishment was removed to Heathfield House, near "Jack Straw's Castle." This institution is certified under the Reformatory Schools Act of 1866; and the inmates, numbering on an average about a hundred, receive an excellent education. Their former home is still devoted to reformatory purposes, being occupied by girls from the Field Lane Refuge on Saffron Hill. The large old-fashioned house at the corner of Church Row and Church Lane is devoted to a similar purpose, though its inmates are somewhat older.

This quarter of Hampstead, in fact, seems to have had particular attractions for authors and artists. Here, or close at hand, lived Henry Fuseli, R.A., of whom we quote the following extract from the "Mitchell Manuscripts" in the British Museum. The letter is from Mr. Murdock, of Hampstead, to a friend at Berlin, dated Hampstead, 12th June, 1764:—"I like Fuseli very much; he comes out to see us at times, and is just now gone from this with your letter to A. Ramsay, and another from me. He is of himself disposed to all possible economy; but to be decently lodged and fed, in a decent family, cannot be for less than three shillings a day, which he pays. He might, according to Miller's wish, live a little cheaper; but then he must have been lodged in some garret, where nobody could have found their way, and must have been thrown into ale-houses and eating-houses, with company every way unsuitable, or, indeed, insupportable to a stranger of any taste, especially as the common people are of late brutalised. Some time hence, I hope, he may do something for himself; his talent at grouping figures and his faculty of execution being really surprising."

Another eminent artist, in more recent times an inhabitant of Church Row, was John Rogers Herbert. He was for some years head-master of the School of Design at Somerset House, and in 1846 was selected to paint one of the frescoes in the vestibule of the Houses of Parliament. He was afterwards commissioned to paint a series of nine subjects, illustrating "Human Justice," for the peers' robing-room. Mr. Herbert was elected a Royal Academician in 1846. His works since 1840, when he embraced the Roman Catholic faith, have assumed a character in accordance with his religious convictions. Of these we may mention his "Introduction of Christianity into Great Britain," "Sir Thomas More and his Daughter observing from their Prison Window the Monks going to Execution," "St. John the Baptist reproving Herod," and "The Virgin Mary." This last-mentioned picture was painted for the Queen in 1860. Sundry other Royal Academicians and artists have likewise been residents here, besides the artists whose names we have enumerated.

Among the residents at Hampstead, in the middle of the last century, was Hannah Lightfoot, the fair Quakeress who is said to have captivated the heart of George III.;* and here she made her will in 1767–8, signing it "Hannah Regina," recommending "my two sons and daughter to the kind protection of their royal father, my husband, His Majesty George III."

Another resident here was Mr. Hamond, one of the literary friends of Mr. H. Crabbe Robinson. The latter writes in his "Diary," under date August, 1812: "A delightful day. The pleasantest walk by far I have had this summer. The very rising from one's bed at Hamond's house is enjoyment worth going to Hampstead over night to partake of. The morning scene from his back rooms is extremely beautiful." And then he describes his walk past the "Spaniards," and down some fields opposite Ken Wood, and so across Finchley to Colney Hatch and Southgate.

Mr. J. Forster, in his "Life of Charles Dickens," speaks several times of his almost daily "fore-gatherings" here, in the early period of his literary life, with Maclise, Stanfield, David Roberts, and other literary friends.

At Hampstead the elder Mr. Dickens resided during part of the time whilst his son was at school in Mornington Place, but the exact house is not known. Charles Knight, the well-known author and publisher, was a resident at Hampstead from 1865 to 1871. Mr. Knight died at Addlestone, in Surrey, in 1873, aged eighty-one. The whole of his long and honourable career was devoted to the cause of popular literature, of which he was one of the earliest and most accomplished advocates. We have already mentioned him as living at Highgate. Among the numerous works which he published or edited were the "Penny Magazine," the "Library of Entertaining Knowledge," the "Pictorial History of England," "London Pictorially Illustrated," the "Land we Live in," the "English

* See Vol. IV., p. 207.

Cyclopædia," and the "Popular History of England." At Hampstead his venerable, but genial and pleasant, face and snow-white locks were familiar to rich and poor, old and young. Here, surrounded by his books and a small but attached circle of literary friends, he spent his declining years, busying himself chiefly with two genial retrospective works—his "Shadows of the Old Booksellers," and "Passages of a Working Life," as he modestly termed his autobiography, and occasionally contributing a stray paper or two to the literature of the day.

We have mentioned Hampstead as a place which for many a long year has been a favourite home and resort of artists. As a proof of this fact, it may be mentioned that the survivor of the brothers Chalon, the eminent painters, about the year 1860 proposed to bestow on Hampstead the whole of his own and his brother's drawings on condition of the inhabitants building a gallery for their reception, and paying the salary of a custodian until his own decease. The lord of the manor, in order to forward the arrangement, offered to give a freehold site upon the Heath, just opposite to the "Upper Flask;" but there was not enough public spirit or taste in the residents to raise the sum required to meet the benefaction; the gift consequently lapsed, and the arrangement fell through.

The old parish church of Hampstead, as we have stated above, stands at the bottom of Church Row, and its green coating of ivy contrasts pleasingly with the red brick and tiled houses on either hand as we approach it. The building seems to have exercised a strange fascination over the artistic mind of the day, for a proposal to pull it down and rebuild it was received a short time ago with a perfect shout of disapproval. It is true that the church is most picturesquely situated, and that the distant view of the spire as it peeps from the mass of variegated foliage which adorns the churchyard is exceedingly pretty; but there is no reason why another church built on the same site should not be even more pleasing. The body of the church is ugly, awkward, and inconvenient in no common degree; the tower is mean, and the spire a shabby minaret, without grace or beauty of any kind. Nor has the structure the merit of antiquity. It dates only from 1747, when church architecture was at its lowest ebb, and it was designed with a wilful disregard of all true principles. The soil being sandy, and the position the side of a steep hill, it was necessary to lay the walls upon timber. In process of time the timber—it is hardly necessary to say—rotted away, and there has been a series of somewhat alarming settlements. The church had hardly been finished a dozen years when it was found necessary to pull down and rebuild the tower and spire. As a reason, we are told that the mason had proved a rogue, and had used Purbeck instead of Portland stone. The fact probably was that the foundations had given way, as it appears has been the case on more than one occasion since. In 1772 the church was subjected to a general repair and ornamentation after the usual churchwarden's fashion, but it has always been insecure and uncomfortable.

As we have stated in a previous chapter, Hampstead, before the Reformation, was only a chapelry in, and dependent on, the mother church of Hendon, and it was only after the dissolution of the monasteries that it came to be formed into a separate parish, the advowson of the living being appended to the lordship of the manor.

In 1549 the lord of the manor presented to the living for the first time; but it was not till a much later date that the vicar and churchwardens of Hampstead put in an appearance at the bishop's visitation; and, indeed, it was only in the year 1588 that the incumbent acknowledged himself as bound to apply to the bishop for his licence in order to officiate. The old chapel of St. Mary, which in the pre-Reformation times had been "served" on Sundays and other holy days by the monks from Westminster, or by a chaplain from Hendon, was a quaint and unpretending edifice, consisting of a nave and low side-aisles, surmounted by a wooden belfry. There is a very scarce print of it by Hollar, which was republished by Park in his "History of Hampstead," now a rare and valuable book. Park tells us that in the early part of the eighteenth century, having been "patched up as long as it would last, and being at length quite worn out," as well as too small to accommodate the inhabitants of Hampstead, the former church was taken down in 1745, and that the present edifice was finished two years later. It is a mistake, therefore, to speak of it as dating from the reign of Queen Anne, for it has nothing about it older than the second George. Before undertaking the work of rebuilding their church, the good people of Hampstead applied to Parliament for aid, but apparently without success, for shortly afterwards they raised by subscription the sum of £3,000 for the purpose; and this not being sufficient, they had recourse to a measure of very doubtful legality, in order to "raise the wind;" for they entered into a sort of joint-stock combination, by which it was agreed that several persons who contributed £20 and upwards should be elected trustees, and that those who subscribed £50 and upwards should have the first choice of seats and pews, which should become heirlooms in their families, though not to be alienated by purchase, but should be distributed to other benefactors of the church by the lord of the manor, the vicar, and the trustees; and in the main this principle still holds good, in spite of all efforts to put an end to such arrangements. It then contained pew-room for 550 persons, exclusive of benches; but further accommodation has since been made on several occasions by the addition of transepts and by other expedients. The church is described by Park as "a neat but ill-designed brick building, in the common style of modern churches, except that, contrary to all custom, the belfry and tower are at the east end, behind the chancel." No doubt the motive for this arrangement was economy, as the ground slopes down abruptly at the west end, and had the tower been placed there it would have been necessary to lay deeper foundations; and another inducement, no doubt, was the wish to create an imposing effect as the parishioners approached their church by the road from the High Street. The total cost of this unsightly structure—for such it really is externally—was between four and five thousand pounds, to which nearly half as much more must be added for repairing the ravages of the dry rot five years later, and for pulling down and rebuilding in 1759 the greater part of the steeple, owing to the knavery of the mason, who, as stated above, had used Purbeck instead of Portland stone as agreed by the contract. The present insignificant copper spire was added in 1784.

Park, who wrote at the commencement of this century, observed, in words which are as true now as then, that "considerable settlements are appearing at the east end, owing to the weight of the tower." The church, we may add, is still under the management of a body of local trustees, who direct the repairs and alterations, and receive and administer the pew rents for the benefit of the incumbent. In 1874-5 the parishioners of Hampstead were engaged in a keen controversy as to whether the church should be "rebuilt" or "restored," mainly through the threatened subsidence of the tower; and matters even went so far that the trustees appointed Mr. F. P. Cockerell as their architect, and that he supplied designs for the two-fold purpose; but here the matter seems to have rested for a time, when it was finally decided that the church should be enlarged by the addition of a chancel at the western end, sundry alterations being made in the interior arrangements at the same time, and the tower being underpinned and strengthened.

And yet it must be owned that the church itself looks well, and even imposing, when seen from a distance, especially from the south. The following interesting sketch of the parish church appears in the *Sunday at Home* for July, 1876:—"From Primrose Hill a full view is obtained of the outline of the fine ridge to the north on which rest the suburbs of Highgate and Hampstead. The steeples of Highgate Church and of Christ's Church, Hampstead, are conspicuous marks in the landscape, while St. John's Church, or, as it is commonly called, old Hampstead Church, may be dimly descried amid a clustering group of trees. Proceeding by the Finchley Road to the old church, and taking the ascending pathway through the fields, a stranger would confront before he was aware the object of his quest, which he would find to be a brick-built and substantial, though a plain and unpretentious building in the Italian style. The belfry and tower are placed in the east end, behind the chancel, contrary to the usual method of church architecture. The advantage, however, is gained, that the handsomest part of the building is brought prominently into view and faces the village, while the clinging ivy covering almost the whole front removes to some extent the prosaic character of the brickwork, and lends an air of antiquity and a certain poetic charm to the sacred edifice, much in keeping with the beauty of the situation and with the decayed memorials of the surrounding burying-ground. The still older church—smaller but more picturesque—occupied the site of the existing building. It had been patched up as long as it would last; but becoming at length quite worn out from inevitable decay, and besides being too small to accommodate the increased population, it was pulled down. The new building was finished in 1747, at a cost of between £4,000 and £5,000, and was consecrated by Dr. Gilbert, Bishop of Llandaff, by commission from the Bishop of London, on the 8th of October of that year; it was dedicated to St. John."

Of the various clergymen who have held the incumbency of Hampstead, since the living passed into the hands of the lord of the manor, there have been some few whose names have become known beyond the circle of their parishioners. Of these we may mention the Rev. Robert Warren, D.D., who was an able, learned, and pious minister, and a man of mark among the clergy of his day. He preached repeatedly before the Lord Mayor of London, and was the author of several works of practical devotion, which in their time were popular, and ran through numerous editions. The general pious character of Dr. Warren's writings may be learned from the title of one of his most successful books, originally published in the year 1720, "The Daily Self-Examinant, or an Earnest Perswasion to the duty of Self-Examination; with Devout Prayers, Meditations, Directions, and Ejaculations for a Holy Life and Happy Death." Dr. Warren broke a lance with Bishop Hoadley on the nature of the sacrament, and, in his "Impartial Churchman," published an earnest and affectionate in it:—"It is my positive and express will that all my sermons, letters, and papers whatever, which are now in a deal box directed to Dr. Forester (his chaplain), and now standing in my library at Hampstead, be burnt, without being read by any, as soon as may be after my decease."

Samuel Butler and Dr. Secker, afterwards Archbishop of Canterbury, were both the sons of Dissenters, and were schoolfellows together at the

VANE HOUSE, IN 1800.

address to Protestant dissenters. He died in 1740; his son, Langhorne, was nominated his successor. Unlike to the father, the son does not appear to have been addicted to authorship; his only publication is a sermon on a text from the Book of Proverbs. During the incumbency of Langhorne Warren, the celebrated Dr. Butler, Bishop of Durham, resided at Hampstead, in the house built, and for a time occupied, by Sir Harry Vane—the house, indeed, from which the latter was taken to the Tower, where he was executed in 1662.

One of the witnesses to the bishop's will is the Rev. Langhorne Warren; the will was made at Hampstead, and bears date 25th of April, 1752. The following is one of the directions contained

Dissenting academy of Mr. Jones, at Tewkesbury, where, in the impressible days of their boyhood, was contracted that warm friendship which lasted through life between these eminent men. Secker, when in residence as Dean of St. Paul's, was constantly in the society of the author of the "Analogy" at Hampstead, and, it is said, dined with him every day. "A friend of mine, since deceased, told me," says the Rev. John Newton, "that when he was a young man he once dined with the late Dr. Butler, at that time Bishop of Durham, and though the guest was a man of fortune, and the interview by appointment, the provision was no more than a joint of meat and a pudding. The bishop apologised for his plain fare by saying that it was his way of living; that he had been long disgusted with the fashionable expense of time and money in entertainments, and was determined that it should receive no countenance from his example."

When his health was fast failing, Dr. Butler left Hampstead for Clifton. Afterwards he went to Bath, to try the effect of the waters of that place. Dr. Forester thus writes from Bath to Secker, then Bishop of Oxford, on the 4th of June, 1752:—"My lord, I have barely strength and spirits to inform your lordship that my good lord was brought hither, in a very weak state, yesterday, in hopes of receiving some benefit from the waters." On the 16th of the same month Dr. Butler died. He was buried in the cathedral of Bristol, where two monuments have been erected to his memory.

Ten years after the death of the great bishop, died his friend Langhorne Warren, curate of Hampstead, who, in his turn, was succeeded by his son Erasmus. This gentleman lived until 1806; so that for nearly a century the perpetual curacy of Hampstead was held by the Warren family. Mr. Warren's two assistant curates, the Rev. Charles Grant, and the Rev. Samuel White, in turn succeeded to the incumbency. Dr. White dying in 1841, was succeeded by the Rev. Thomas Ainger, under whose incumbency the parish was subdivided into ecclesiastical districts, for which five new churches were erected. Mr. Ainger was succeeded by the Rev. Charlton Lane, one of the professors in Gresham College; and he by the Rev. Sherard Burnaby.

Able and zealous clergymen connected with the churches which have sprung up of late years efficiently sustain the cause of the Church of England in Hampstead. Of these we would mention the name of the Rev. E. H. Bickersteth, the vicar of Christ Church. Mr. Bickersteth is besides favourably known in the world of letters, both as a poet and an essayist.

The amiable and accomplished Joanna Baillie, of whom we have already spoken, was scrupulously regular in her attendance on divine service in the parish church. She died on the 23rd of February, 1851; her grave may readily be found among the other memorials of the dead in the burying-ground adjoining the edifice. One other grave there will specially attract the visitor—it is that of Sir James Mackintosh, the brilliant lawyer

ROSSLYN HOUSE. (*See page* 488.)

and historian, who died in May, 1832. Mackintosh was a man of great powers and intellectual ability, and was President of the Board of Control under Earl Grey.

In a previous chapter (page 149) we have mentioned Sir Thomas Fowell Buxton in the midst of his benevolent labours residing at North End. In his "Memoirs" we find a letter from him to Sir James Mackintosh, whose mind was then engaged on the questions of the criminal law and colonial reform, inviting him to lend a full, hearty, and unreserved co-operation in the cause of the West Indian slaves. The death of Sir James Mackintosh, after a long illness, was really occasioned by a piece of chicken sticking in his throat when at dinner. He was nearly strangled, and though the meat was dislodged at the time, his health suffered ever afterwards.

Sir James Mackintosh is praised by all his cotemporaries for his wonderful stores of information, his philanthropy, his amiability, and great powers of conversation. Lord Russell tells us that he was "the ablest, the most brilliant, and the best-informed" of all those whose conversational talents are mentioned by Tommy Moore, who often came from Muswell Hill to meet him at the hospitable table of the Longmans on the Green Hill. He is thus portrayed in the "New Whig Guide:"—

"—— Mackintosh strives to unite
The grave and the gay, the profound and polite,
And piques himself much that the ladies should say
How well Scottish strength softens down in Bombay!
He frequents the assembly, the supper, the ball,
The *philosophe beau* of unlovable Staël;
Affects to talk French in his hoarse Highland note,
And gurgles Italian half-way down his throat.
His gait is a shuffle, his smile is a leer,
His converse is quaint, his civility queer;
In short, to all grace and deportment a rebel,
At best he is but a half-polished Scotch pebble."

This beautiful churchyard, perhaps one of the loveliest in England, and one of which it may be said with truth that "it would make one in love with death to think that he should be buried in so sweet a spot," is crowded with other tombs which bear distinguished names. Among them are those of John Constable, the artist; of Lord Erskine; of Harrison, who discovered the mode of ascertaining the longitude; and of the sweet-voiced Incledon, "the most wonderful nature-taught singer this country has ever produced." Not the least interesting of the graves is that of an old lady from St. Giles's parish, who was the solitary victim in Hampstead to the visitation of the cholera in 1849. The story is extant, and written in very choice English in the reports of the medical officer of the Privy Council. She had, it seems, lived in the parish of St. Giles, and having drank of the water from the church pump, fondly imagined that no other could be so good. When, therefore, her husband died, and she retired upon a modest competency to the northern suburb, she arranged with the conductor of an omnibus to bring her a jar of it daily. She drank of it and of it only, and never tired of praising its excellences: The sparkle which she found so attractive was, however, but a form of death; the water was literally loaded with sewage gas and with the phosphates which had filtered through the earth from the churchyard close by. It was, as it were, a matter of course that she should die, but she did not die in vain. The history of her case has been of a value to medical science which few can over-estimate. Had the old lady known much of local history, she would, perhaps, have pinned her faith to the waters of Hampstead, and perhaps have been living at the present time. Among other notabilities preserved in local memories as resting here is Miss West, better known as "Jenny Diver," the most accomplished lady pickpocket of her age, who died here in 1783, leaving £3,000, the fruits of her industry, to her two children, one of whom was born in Bridewell. This desultory gossip leads us to curious associations; but the grave, like misery, makes us acquainted with strange bedfellows; and the ashes of poor Jenny lie peacefully enough with those of better people.

The old churchyard covers about three acres, and lies chiefly on the south of the church. A little higher up on the slope of the hill is the new or upper churchyard, one end of which abuts upon Church Row. It is not quite so large as the other, and was consecrated in 1812.

At the northern extremity of this churchyard stands the little Roman Catholic chapel of St. Mary's, its western front conspicuously decorated with a handsome statue of the Virgin and the Divine Child in a niche. It was built in 1815–16 by the exertions of the Abbé Morel, one of those French *emigrés* whom the waves of the first French Revolution threw upon our shores. For many years the abbé lived in Hampstead, teaching his native language; his gains he laid by in order to found the mission and chapel, in which he rests beneath a handsome altar-tomb. Before the consecration of the chapel by the "Vicar Apostolic" of the London district in 1816, the abbé used to say mass over a stable in Rosslyn Park, and afterwards at Oriel House, at the upper end of Church Row. He died in 1851. In the interior of the chapel are some fine sacred pictures.

Grove Lodge and Montagu Grove, near here, are places worthy of mention, the former as having been at one time the residence of Sir Gilbert Scott, the architect; and the latter as the residence of Mr. Edward Montagu, the first patron of the Hampstead Sunday School. Concerning this gentleman, the *European Magazine* for June, 1788, tells the following anecdote:—"June 10. This morning Lord Mansfield sent a servant from Caen Lodge, to Mr. Montagu, the Master in Chancery, Frognal Grove, near Hampstead, requesting that gentleman's company to dinner. The answer returned was that 'Mr. Montagu had come home the preceding evening from London ill, and remained then indisposed.' The messenger returned back, pressing Mr. Montagu's attendance on his lordship, who had some material business to communicate, upon which Mr. Montagu replied, 'He would wait on the earl in the afternoon.' At five the master went to Caen Wood Lodge, where he was introduced to Earl Mansfield, who was alone. 'I sent for you, sir,' said his lordship, 'to receive, as well officially as my acquaintance and friend, the resignation of my office; and, in order to save trouble, I have caused the instrument to be prepared, as you here see.' He then introduced the paper, which, after Mr. Montagu had perused, and found proper, the earl signed. The master underwrote it, and afterwards dispatched it to the Lord Chancellor's house, who laid it before the king." Montagu Grove was afterwards the residence of Chief Baron Richards.

Opposite Montagu Grove, on some sloping ground leading towards Mount Vernon, and now occupied as a garden, it is said that the workhouse of Hampstead formerly stood. The old house, as depicted in Park's "Hampstead," was a picturesque building, with projecting wings, gabled roof, and bay windows. Here, before it became the parish poorhouse, Colley Cibber used to meet his friends, Booth and Wilkes, the actors, to concert plans for their dramatic campaigns.

CHAPTER XXXVIII.

HAMPSTEAD (*continued*).—ROSSLYN HILL, &c.

"Hæ latebræ dulces, et jam, si credis, amœnæ."—*Horace.*

Sailors' Orphan Girls' School and Home—Clarkson Stanfield—The Residence of the Longmans—Vane House, now the Soldiers' Daughters' Home—Bishop Butler—The "Red Lion" Inn—The Chicken House—Queen Elizabeth's House—Carlisle House—The Presbyterian Chapel—Mr. and Mrs. Barbauld—Rosslyn House—Lord Loughborough—Belsize Lane—Downshire Hill—Hampstead Green—Sir Rowland Hill—Sir Francis Palgrave—Kenmore House and the Rev. Edward Irving—St. Stephen's Church—The "George" Inn—The Hampstead Waterworks—Pond Street—The New Spa—The Small-pox Hospital—The Hampstead Town Hall—The "Load of Hay"—Sir Richard Steele's Cottage—Nancy Dawson—Moll King's House—Tunnels made under Rosslyn and Haverstock Hills.

RETRACING our steps through Church Row on our way towards Rosslyn Hill—which is a continuation of the High Street towards London—we notice on our right, at the corner of Greenhill Road and Church Lane, a large and handsome brick building, with slightly projecting wings, gables, and a cupola turret. This is the Sailors' Orphan Girls' School and Home, which was originally established in 1829, in Frognal House, on the west side of the parish church. The present building was erected in 1869, from the designs of Mr. Ellis. The objects of the institution are the "maintenance, clothing, and education of orphan daughters of sailors and marines, and the providing of a home for them after leaving, when out of situations." The number of inmates is about one hundred, and the children look healthy and cheerful. Its annual income averages about £2,000. This institution was opened by Prince Arthur, now Duke of Connaught, in whose honour the road between it and the Greenhill is named Prince Arthur's Road.

On the Greenhill, close by the Wesleyan chapel, and where Prince Arthur's Road opens into the High Street, stands a venerable house, once the home of Clarkson Stanfield, the artist, till lately used as a branch of the Consumptive Hospital. It is now a school, and named Stanfield House. A native of Sunderland, and born about the end of the last century, Clarkson Stanfield, as we have stated in a previous chapter,* commenced life as a sailor. He, however, soon abandoned the sea for the more congenial pursuit of a scene-painter, having accepted an engagement at an east-end theatre, whence he soon after migrated to Drury Lane. His familiarity with the mysteries of the deep enabled him to surpass most other painters of sea-pieces. Among his early works, not already mentioned by us, were his "View near Chalons-sur-Saône," and "Mount St. Michael," painted for the Senior United Service Club. Among his more

* See *ante*, p. 306.

important later works we may mention his "Castle of Ischia," the "Day after the Wreck," "French Troops crossing the Magra," "Wind against Tide," and "The *Victory* towed into Gibraltar after the Battle of Trafalgar. Great as was Mr. Stanfield's knowledge of the sea, he comparatively seldom painted it in a storm. Throughout his industry was almost as remarkable as his genius. As a scene-painter he had the means of doing much towards advancing the taste of the English public for landscape art. For many years he taught the public from the stage—the pit and the gallery to admire landscape art, and the boxes to become connoisseurs; and he decorated the theatre with works so beautiful, that we can but regret the frail material of which they were constructed, and the necessity for "new and gorgeous effects," and "magnificent novelties," which caused the artist's works to be carried away. It was not the public only whom Stanfield delighted, and awakened, and educated into admiration—the members of his own profession were as enthusiastic as the rest of the world in recognising and applauding his magnificent imagination and skill. Mr. J. T. Smith, in his "Book for a Rainy Day," says, "Mr. Stanfield's easel pictures adorn the cabinets of some of our first collectors, and are, like those of Callcott, Constable, Turner, Collins, and Arnold, much admired by the now numerous publishers of little works, who unquestionably produce specimens of the powers of England's engravers, which immeasurably out-distance the efforts of all other countries." Clarkson Stanfield died in 1867 at his residence in Belsize Park, a few months after removing from his long-cherished home.

Another large old red-brick house, just below that formerly occupied by Clarkson Stanfield, for many years the home of the Longmans, and the place of reunion for the Moores, Scotts, Russells, and other clients and friends of that firm, has been swept away to make room for the chapel mentioned above. The cedars which stood on the lawn are still left, and so also are some of the ornamental evergreens; the rookery and grounds adjoining are appropriated to sundry new Italian villas. The rooks, who for successive generations had built their nests in these grounds for the best part of a century, frightened at the operations of the builders, flew away a few years since, and, strangely, migrated to a small grove half a mile nearer to London, at the corner of Belsize Lane.

A little below the Greenhill, on the same side of the High Street, is Vane House; this edifice stands a short distance back from the road, with a gravelled court in front of it. Though almost wholly rebuilt of late years, it is still called by the name of its predecessor, and it is occupied as the Soldiers' Daughters' Home. Vane House was originally a large square building, standing in its own ample grounds. In Park's time—that is, at the beginning of the present century—the house had been considerably modernised in some parts, but it still retained enough of the antique hue to make it a very interesting object. The entrance at the back, with the carved staircase, remained in their original condition. In the upper storey one very large room had been divided into a number of smaller apartments, running along the whole back front of the house. The old mansion, when inhabited by Sir Harry Vane, probably received and welcomed within its walls such men as Cromwell, Milton, Pym, Fairfax, Hampden, and Algernon Sidney; and from its doors its master was carried off by order of Charles II. to the executioner's block on Tower Hill. The house was afterwards owned and occupied by Bishop Butler, who is said to have written here some portions of his masterly work, "The Analogy between Natural and Revealed Religion." The Soldiers' Daughters' Home was instituted in 1855, in connection with the Central Association for the Relief of the Wives and Children of Soldiers on Service in the Crimea, and, as the report tells us, "for the maintenance, clothing, and education of the daughters of soldiers, whether orphans or not." This "Home" is one of the most popular among the various charitable institutions in the metropolis. The present buildings, which are spacious, substantial, and well adapted to their purpose, were erected in 1858, from the designs of Mr. Munt, and they have since been enlarged. The "Home" was inaugurated under the auspices of the late Prince Consort, and has ever since been under the patronage of royalty, including Her Majesty, the Prince of Wales, the Duke of Cambridge, and others. The annual *fête* on behalf of the institution, held in the charming grounds of the "Home," is attended by the *élite* of fashion, and has always been quite a gala day at Hampstead. In 1874 the committee of the institution unanimously resolved to add three girls to the number of admissions into the Home by election, to be called the "Gold Coast Scholars," one from each of the regiments serving in the African war, as a tribute to the gallantry and self-sacrifice displayed by the troops employed under Sir Garnet Wolseley during the campaign in Ashantee. A fourth scholar from the Royal Marines has since been added. The Regimental Scholarships' Fund, established in 1864, was then very liberally responded to, but the contributions have since fluctuated greatly. These contributions are all funded; and when they accumulate to a sufficient sum, according to the age of the girl, and to the scale of payment in force, enable regiments to nominate a scholar for direct admission into the Home independently of election. The average number of girls in the institution is about 150, but there is accommodation for 200 when the income is sufficient for their maintenance.

Still on our right, half way down the steep descent of Rosslyn Hill, on the site now occupied by the police-station, stood formerly the "Red Lion Inn," a wooden house of great antiquity, probably dating from the fourteenth century. The "Red Lion" is so common a sign as to need no other remark except that it probably was put up in allusion to the marriage of John of Gaunt, Duke of Lancaster, with Constance, daughter of Don Pedro, King of Leon and Castile. But this house is worthy of special note, as it was held on lease from the Dean and Chapter of Westminster, on condition of its "Boniface" supplying a truss of hay for the horse of the "mass- priest," who came up from the Abbey to celebrate divine service at Hampstead on Sundays and the greater saints' days, in the Chapel of St. Mary, on the site of which now stands the parish church. Although the inn is gone, its name remains in "Red Lion Hill," as Rosslyn Hill is usually called among the working classes.

On the opposite side of the road, but a trifle lower down the hill, may be seen what little now remains of a noted old building, called the Chicken House, which Mr. Park, in his "History of Hampstead," says that local tradition designates as "an appendage to royalty." In this work it is stated that there was nothing remarkable in the interior of the house, except some painted glass, well executed, representing Our Saviour in the arms of Simeon, and (in another window) small portraits of King James and the Duke of Buckingham, under the former of which was the following inscription: "Icy dans cette chambre coucha nostre Roy Iaques, premier le nom. Le 25 Aoust, 1619." This glass afterwards formed part of the collection of Sir Thomas Neave, at Branch Hill Lodge, which we have already mentioned. Originally it was a low brick building in the farm-house style, and of ordinary appearance. The side which abutted upon the roadway is now hid by houses and small shops; the only view of the building, therefore, is obtained by passing up a narrow passage from the street. The old building is now cut up into small tenements, inhabited by several families.

Gale, the antiquary, died at the Chicken House in 1754; he lies buried in the churchyard. In the Chicken House Lord Mansfield is stated to have lodged before he purchased Caen Wood. "But at that time, no doubt," says Mr. Howitt in his "Northern Heights," "the Chicken House had an ample garden, and overlooked the open country, for it is described as being at the entrance of Hampstead." In 1766, not many years after Lord Mansfield and his legal friends had ceased to resort hither for the purposes of "relaxation from the fatigues of their profession," the place seems to have sadly degenerated, for we are told that it had become a rendezvous of thieves and vagabonds.

Near to the Chicken House there used to stand another building, commonly known as "Queen Elizabeth's House;" its architecture, however, was of too late a date to warrant such a name, though the tradition was current that the "Virgin Queen" once spent a night there. It was subsequently occupied by some nuns, who changed its name to "St. Elizabeth's Home."

Close by the Chicken House stood, till 1875–6, a fine mansion in its own grounds, known as Carlisle House. It was the property of, or at all events occupied by, a gallant admiral, at the close of the last century; and it is a tradition in Hampstead that Lord Nelson, when in the zenith of his fame, was often a guest within its walls. The house has been pulled down, and the site utilised for building purposes.

Adjoining is the site of the Presbyterian chapel. This edifice was constructed as the successor of another chapel which is supposed to have been established in the reign of Charles II., by one of the ejected ministers whose lives are recorded by Dr. Calamy. The first Presbyterian minister was Mr. Thomas Woodcock, son of a learned divine of the same name, who had been ejected, and cousin to Milton's second wife. Zechariah Merrell, who was minister in the reign of Queen Anne, wrote the exposition of the First Epistle of Peter, in continuation of Matthew Henry's "Commentary." He died in 1732. The Rev. Mr. Barbauld, of whom we have spoken above, in our account of Church Row, was a minister here. On his leaving the congregation it ceased to be Presbyterian. The cause of Presbyterianism has, however, within the last twenty-five years been resuscitated at Hampstead. For about ten years, and until his failing health compelled him to desist, the Rev. James D. Burns preached at Hampstead to the congregation known as English Presbyterians. He was the author of "The Vision of Prophecy," and other poems. The original Presbyterian chapel is supposed to have been removed in 1736, and the chapel which superseded it was rebuilt in 1828. This, in turn, gave way to the present building, which was completed in 1862, and is one of the ugliest of modern ecclesiastical structures.

Mr. Barbauld officiated in the old Presbyterian chapel from 1785 till the commencement of this century, when he removed to Newington Green. He was a native of Germany, and died in the year 1808. His widow, who resided for many years in a house on the west side of Rosslyn Hill, was the celebrated Mrs. Anna Letitia Barbauld, and sister of Dr. John Aikin, the distinguished author and physician. The eldest child and only daughter of Dr. John Aikin, and of Jane, his wife, daughter of the Rev. John Jennings, she was born at the village of Kibworth Harcourt, in Leicestershire. Shortly after their marriage, Mr. and Mrs. Barbauld settled at Palgrave, in Suffolk, where Mr. Barbauld was a Dissenting minister, and kept a school. At first all seemed prosperous. In addition to Lord Denman, Sir William Gell, Dr. Sayers, and William Taylor, of Norwich, were amongst the pupils of the Palgrave school. Here also Mrs. Barbauld wrote her "Early Lessons" and "Hymns in Prose." Their winter vacation was always spent in London, where they had the *entrée* into good society. After eleven years of teaching, Mrs. Barbauld and her husband left Palgrave, and ultimately planted themselves in Hampstead. Here Mrs. Barbauld found many excellent friends—Miss Joanna Baillie and others. One of Mrs. Barbauld's occasional guests at Hampstead was Samuel Rogers, the poet. Mr. H. Crabb Robinson's "Diary" contains several interesting entries concerning this lady. "In 1805, at Hackney," writes Crabb Robinson, "I saw repeatedly Miss Wakefield, a charming girl. And one day, at a party, when Mrs. Barbauld had been the subject of conversation, and I had spoken of her in enthusiastic terms, Miss Wakefield came to me and said, 'Would you like to know Mrs. Barbauld?' I exclaimed, 'You might as well

SIR RICHARD STEELE. (*See page* 491.)

VIEW FROM "MOLL KING'S HOUSE," HAMPSTEAD, IN 1760.

ask me whether I should like to know the angel Gabriel!' Said she, 'Mrs. Barbauld is much more accessible. I will introduce you to her nephew.' She then called to Charles Aikin, whom she soon after married. And he said, 'I dine every Sunday with my uncle and aunt at Stoke Newington, and I am expected always to bring a friend with me. Two knives and forks are laid for me. Will you go with me next Sunday?' Gladly acceding to the proposal, I had the good fortune to make myself agreeable, and soon became intimate in the house.

"Mr. Barbauld had a slim figure, a weazen face, and a shrill voice. He talked a great deal, and was fond of dwelling on controversial points of religion. He was by no means destitute of ability, though the afflictive disease was lurking in him which in a few years broke out, and, as is well known, caused a sad termination to his life.

"Mrs. Barbauld bore the remains of great personal beauty. She had a brilliant complexion, light hair, blue eyes, a small elegant figure, and her manners were very agreeable, with something of the generation then departing. Mrs. Barbauld is so well known by her prose writings, that it is needless for me to attempt to characterise her here. Her excellence lay in the soundness and acuteness of her understanding, and in the perfection of her taste. In the estimation of Wordsworth she was the first of our literary women, and he was not bribed to this judgment by any especial congeniality of feeling, or by concurrence in speculative opinions."

Wordsworth, like Rogers, greatly admired Mrs. Barbauld's "Address to Life," written in extreme old age. "Repeat me that stanza by Mrs. Barbauld," he said to Robinson, one day at Rydal; the latter did so, and Wordsworth made him repeat it again. "And," as Robinson tells us, "so he learned it by heart. He was at the time walking in his sitting-room, with his hands behind him; and I heard him mutter to himself, 'I am not in the habit of grudging people their good things, but I wish I had written those lines:—

> 'Life! we've been long together,
> Through pleasant and through cloudy weather:
> 'Tis hard to part when friends are dear,
> Perhaps 'twill cost a sigh, a tear:
> Then steal away, give little warning;
> Choose thine own time;
> Say not good night, but in some brighter clime
> Bid me good morning.'"

Mrs. Barbauld incurred great reproach by writing a poem entitled "1811." It is in heroic rhyme, and prophesies that on some future day a traveller from the antipodes will, from a broken arch of Blackfriars Bridge, contemplate the ruins of St. Paul's! "This," remarks Mr. Robinson, "was written more in sorrow than in anger; but there was a disheartening and even gloomy tone, which even I, with all my love for her, could not quite excuse. It provoked a very coarse review in the *Quarterly*, which many years afterwards Murray told me he was more ashamed of than any other article that had appeared in the *Review*." Mrs. Barbauld spent the last few years of her life at Stoke Newington, where we shall again have occasion to speak of her.

A little lower down the hill, and on the same side of the way, stands Rosslyn House, formerly the property of Alexander Wedderburn, first Earl of Rosslyn, better known, perhaps, by his former title of Lord Loughborough, which he took on being appointed Lord Chancellor in the year 1795. Before purchasing this mansion, Lord Loughborough, as we have stated in a previous chapter, resided at Branch Hill Lodge, higher up in the town, on the verge of the Heath. Rosslyn House—or as it was originally called, Shelford Lodge—at that time, and long after, stood alone amidst the green fields, commanding an extensive view over the distant country. It was surrounded by its gardens, groves, and fields, with no house nearer to it than the village of Hampstead above and Belsize House below.

Lysons states that the mansion was for many years "in the occupation of the Cary family," and that it was held under the Church of Westminster. It has been supposed that it was built by a family of the name of Shelford, who, being Catholics, planted the great avenue leading to it in the form of a cross, the head being towards the east, and leading direct to the high road. "But," says Mr. Howitt, "this is very doubtful. The celebrated Lord Chesterfield," he adds, "is said to have lived here some years, when he held the lease of the manor of Belsize, of which it was a part; and more probably his ancestors gave it the name from Shelford Manor, their seat in Nottinghamshire;" for the Earls of Chesterfield held the estate of Belsize from 1683 down to early in the present century, when the land was cut up in lots, and sold for building purposes. Mr. Howitt tells us that "when Lord Rosslyn purchased the place, he added a large oval room, thirty-four feet long, on the west side, with a spacious room over it. These rooms, of a form then much in vogue, whilst they contributed greatly to the pleasantness of the house, disguised the original design of it, which was on the plan of what the French call a *maison* or *château à quatre tourelles*, four-square, with a high mansard roof in the centre, and a square turret at each corner, with pyramidal roof. Notwithstanding various other alterations by Lord Rosslyn and his successors, part of this original structure is still visible, including two at least of the turrets."

Here Lord Loughborough used to entertain the Prince of Wales and the leaders of the Whig party, including Fox, Sheridan, and Burke, with other distinguished personages of opposite politics, such as Pitt, Windham, and the Duke of Portland. "Junius" was not among his friends, as may be guessed from the fact of his describing him as "Wedderburn the wary, who has something about him which even treachery cannot trust."

Whilst holding a subordinate legal office, he fomented the war against America by furiously attacking the colonists to such an extent that Benjamin Franklin swore that he would never forgive the insults that he heaped upon his countrymen. Lord Loughborough was much disliked, and, to speak the honest truth, despised also, by Lord Thurlow. The fact is that he was rather a turncoat, and played fast and loose with both parties.

"Lord Loughborough," says Mr. Howitt in his "Northern Heights of London," "was one of that group of great lawyers who, about the same time, planted themselves on the heights of Hampstead, but with very different characters and aims—Mansfield, Loughborough, and Erskine. Lord Loughborough was, in simple fact, a legal adventurer of consummate powers, which he unscrupulously and unblushingly employed for the purposes of his own soaring and successful ambition." From the time of his promotion to the Lord Chancellorship—the grand aim of his ambition—he seems to have given way fully to his unbounded love of making a great figure on the public stage. "His style of living," says Lord Campbell, "was most splendid. Ever indifferent about money, instead of showing mean contrivances to save a shilling, he spent the whole of his official income in official splendour. Though himself very temperate, his banquets were princely; he maintained an immense retinue of servants, and, not dreaming that his successor would walk through the mud to Westminster, sending the Great Seal thither in a hackney coach, he never stirred about without his two splendid carriages, exactly alike, drawn by the most beautiful horses, one for himself, and another for his attendants. Though of low stature and slender frame, his features were well chiselled, his countenance was marked by strong lines of intelligence, his eye was piercing, his appearance was dignified, and his manners were noble."

In 1801 the Great Seal passed from his hands to those of Lord Eldon. "After this," writes Mr. Howitt, "his influence wholly declined. He seemed to retain only the ambition of being about the person of the king, and he hired a villa at Baylis, near Slough, to be near the Court; yet so little confidence had he inspired in George III., with all his assiduous attentions, that when the news of his death was brought to the monarch, who had seen him the day before—for he went off in a fit of gout in the stomach—the king cautiously asked if the news were really true; and being answered that it was, said, as if with a sense of relief, 'Then he has not left a greater knave behind him in my dominions!'"

Lord Brougham, in his "Historical Sketches," gives his own estimate of Lord Rosslyn's character, which is equally severe. He describes him as a "man of shining but superficial talents, supported by no fixed principles, embellished by no feat of patriotism, nor made memorable by any monuments of national utility; whose life being at length closed in the disappointment of mean and unworthy desires, and amidst universal neglect, left behind it no claim to the respect or gratitude of mankind, though it may have excited the admiration or envy of the contemporary vulgar."

After Lord Rosslyn's death the house passed through several hands. It was first of all inhabited by Mr. Robert Milligan, the projector of the West India Docks, and afterwards successively by Sir Francis Freeling, secretary of the General Post Office, by Admiral Sir Moore Disney, and by the Earl of Galloway. The place subsequently fell into the hands of a speculative builder, who, happily, failed before the old mansion was destroyed or all the old trees were cut down, though it was shorn of much of its beauty. The house still stands, though much altered externally and internally, and deprived of most of its grounds. The estate was cut up for building purposes about 1860–5, and is intersected by roads named after Lords Thurlow, Mansfield, Lyndhurst, Eldon, and other great legal luminaries. For some four years before the above-mentioned period the house had been used as a cradle for the Soldiers' Daughters' Home. In 1860 Prince Albert led the children up the hill to their new home, which, as we have already stated, occupies the site of old Vane House. In 1861 the mansion was purchased by Mr. Charles H. L. Woodd, a descendant of John Evelyn, and of Dr. Basil Woodd, Chancellor of Rochester, who fought under Charles I. at the battle of Edge Hill. In the course of alterations and repairs, which this gentleman has had effected, several coins of Elizabeth, Charles II., and William III. were found under the flooring. "Upon the old panellings, when the canvas covering was removed," Mr. Howitt tells us, "were seen the words written, 'To-morrow last day of Holidays!!! 1769.' At first it was supposed that Lord Chesterfield's son, to whom the 'Letters' were addressed, might have inscribed this pathetic sentence; but the date shuts out the possibility. Lord Chesterfield died in 1773, and this his only son five years before him."

The main body of the avenue still exists, and amongst its trees are some very fine Spanish chestnuts; they are supposed to have been planted about the close of the reign of Queen Elizabeth.

On the south side of Rosslyn House there is a narrow thoroughfare called Belsize Lane, which, down to about the year 1860, had a truly rural appearance, its sides being in part bordered by hedge-rows, and overhung by tall and flourishing trees. Part of these trees and hedgerows still remain. In it, too, was a turnpike gate, which stood close to the farm-house which still stands about the centre. The Queen was driving up this lane on one occasion to look at Rosslyn House, with the idea of taking it as a nursery for the royal children. A little girl, left in charge of the gate, refused to allow Her Majesty to pass. The Queen turned back, according to one account; according to another, she was much amused, and one of her equerries advanced the money necessary to satisfy the toll; but however that may have been, Her Majesty did not become the owner or the tenant of Rosslyn House.

At the foot of Rosslyn Hill, on the left, next to Pilgrim's Lane, is Downshire Hill, so called after one of the ministers in Lord North's cabinet, Lord Hillsborough, afterwards first Marquis of Downshire. At the foot of Downshire Hill, where John Street branches off, stands a plain heavy structure, which has long served as a chapel of ease to Hampstead, and known as St. John's Chapel.

Hampstead Green, as the triangular spot at the junction of Belsize Lane and Haverstock Hill was called till it was appropriated as the site for St. Stephen's new church, has many literary associations. In one of the largest houses at the southern end, now called Bartram's, Sir Rowland Hill, the philanthropic deviser of our penny post system, spent the declining years of his useful and valuable life. Born of yeoman parents, at Kidderminster, in December, 1796, in early life he became a schoolmaster, and, together with his brothers, he established the large private school which for more than half a century has flourished at Bruce Castle, Tottenham. It was he who showed forcibly the abuses and wastefulness of the old system of high-priced postage, and it is to him that the middle classes of this country mainly owe the introduction of the penny post, which superseded that system in 1840, as well as the improvements of the Money-Order Office, and the use of postage-stamps. His next public benefit was the establishment of cheap excursion trains on our railways on Saturdays, Sundays, and Mondays, an experiment first made when Sir Rowland Hill was chairman of the Brighton Railway Company. In 1854 he was recalled to assist in the Control of the General Post Office, first as Assistant Joint-Secretary, and afterwards as Chief Secretary. He was rewarded for his great public services by a knighthood, with the Order of the Bath, Civil Division, coupled with a pension on his retirement. But the reward which he valued the most was the sum of £13,000 which was presented to him, and which was largely contributed from the pence of the poor. In 1876, when he was upwards of eighty, it was resolved to erect in his honour a public statue at Kidderminster, where he was born. The veteran philanthropist was a man who never spared himself from hard work, and as a schoolmaster, as a postal reformer, as an officer of "my Lords of the Treasury," as a railway reformer, and as a social reformer, he did good work in his day. He died here in 1879.

Next door to Sir Rowland Hill lived Sir Francis Palgrave, the historian of the Norman Conquest, &c. He was of Jewish extraction, and at an early age became connected with the Office of Public Records, of which he became the Deputy Keeper in 1838. His name is well known as the author of the "History of the Norman Conquest," "Calendars of the Treasury of the Exchequer," and of many antiquarian essays, and also of a work of a lighter character, the "Merchant and the Friar." Two of his sons, who spent their childhood here, have since attained to eminence—Mr. Francis T. Palgrave, of the Privy Council Educational Department, as a poet and art-critic; and Mr. William Gifford Palgrave, as an Eastern traveller, and the author of the best work that has been published of late years on Arabia.

Kenmore House, a little lower down, has attached to it a large room originally built for the Rev. Edward Irving, who would here occasionally manifest to his followers the proofs of his power of speaking in the "unknown tongues."

St. Stephen's Church, mentioned above, was built in 1870, from the designs of Mr. S. S. Teulon. It is of the early semi-French style of architecture, of very irregular outline, and unusually rich in external ornament. Altogether, the church has a very handsome and picturesque appearance. In the lofty campanile tower there is a beautiful peal of bells and a magnificent carillon, the gift of an inhabitant of the place.

The "George" Inn, on Hampstead Green, once a quaint old roadside public-house, is now resplendent with gas-lamps, and all the other accessories of a modern hotel. Close by this hotel is the church belonging to the religious community known as the Sisters of Providence; their house, formerly Bartram's Park, was the residence of Lord S. G. Osborne.

Hampstead Green, at the lower or eastern end, gradually dies away, and is lost in Pond Street, which leads to the bottom of the five or six ponds on the Lower Heath. Pond Street has been, at various times, the temporary home and haunt of many a painter and poet. Leigh Hunt at one time lived in lodgings here; John Keats occupied, at the same date, a house near the bottom of John Street, immediately in the rear, almost facing the ponds. Among the more recent residents of Pond Street may be enumerated Mr. George Clarkson Stanfield, who inherits much of his father's talent, and Mr. Charles E. Mudie, the founder of the great lending library in New Oxford Street.

Near one of the lower ponds on the East Heath, nearly opposite the bottom of Downshire Hill and John Street, is a singular octagonal dome-crowned building, built about the reign of Queen Anne; it is connected with the Hampstead Water-works, and forms a picturesque object to the stranger as he approaches Hampstead from Fleet Road and Gospel Oak.

At the commencement of the present century another mineral spring was discovered on the clay soil, between the bottom of Pond Street and the lower end of the Heath. It was called the "New Spa," and is so marked on a map which appears in a small work published in 1804 by a local practitioner, Thomas Goodwin, M.D., and a Fellow of the College of Surgeons, under the title of "An Account of the Neutral Saline Waters lately discovered at Hampstead." The work includes an essay on the importance of bathing in general, and an analysis of the newly-found waters; but the New Spa never displaced or superseded the older "Wells" near Flask Walk; and its memory and all traces of its site have perished, though, no doubt, its existence caused the erection of so many modern houses at the foot of the slope of Pond Street.

Close to Hampstead Green, on the eastern slope looking down upon Fleet Road and Gospel Oak, is an irregular structure, which at the first view resembles barracks hastily thrown up, or a camp of wooden huts. This structure was first raised under the authority of the Metropolitan Asylums Board, as a temporary Fever Hospital, about the year 1867; it has since been used for the accommodation of pauper lunatics; and in 1876–7 it was appropriated to patients suffering from an outbreak of small-pox, very much to the discomfort and annoyance of the residents of Hampstead, who petitioned Parliament for its removal, but in vain. Its location here, in the midst of a population like that of Hampstead, and close to two thoroughfares which during the summer are crowded by pleasure-seekers, cannot be too strongly censured, as tending sadly to depreciate the value of property around the entire neighbourhood.

On the right of Haverstock Hill the visitor can scarcely fail to remark a fine old avenue of elms, which, as we shall see presently, once formed the approach to Belsize House. At the corner of this avenue is a drinking-fountain, most conveniently placed for the weary foot-passenger as he ascends the hill; and close by it stands a handsome Town Hall, in red brick and stone, in the Italian style, erected in 1876–7, at the cost of £10,000. It is used for the meetings of the Hampstead Liberal Club, and of the Hampstead Parliament.

Lower down the road, on the opposite side of the way, and just by the top of the somewhat sharp hill, is the "Load of Hay," which occupies the place of a much older inn, bearing witness to the once rural character of the place. Its tea-garden used to be a favourite resort of visitors on their way to Hampstead Heath, who wished to break the long and tedious walk. The entrance to the gardens was guarded by two painted grenadiers—flat boards cut into shape and painted—the customary custodians of the suburban tea-gardens of former times. The house itself was a picturesque wooden structure until about the year 1870, when, shorn of most of its garden, and built closely round with villas, it degenerated into a mere suburban gin-palace.

On the opposite side of the road were the poplars that stood before the gate of Sir Richard Steele's cottage, over the site of which Londoners now drive in cabs and carriages along Steele's Road. A view of Sir Richard Steele's cottage on Haverstock Hill, standing in the midst of green fields, and apparently without even a road in front of it, from a drawing taken in 1809, is to be found in Smith's "Historical and Literary Curiosities," and it is also shown in our illustration above, on p. 295. It may be interesting to know that it was much the same in outward appearance until its demolition, about the year 1869, though close in front of it ran the road to Hampstead, from which it was sheltered by the row of tall poplars alluded to above.

Sir Richard Steele was living on Haverstock Hill in June, 1712, as shown by the date of a letter republished in *fac-simile* in Smith's "Historical and Literary Curiosities." "I am at a solitude," he writes, "an house between Hampstead and London, where Sir Charles Sedley died. This circumstance set me thinking and ruminating upon the employment in which men of wit exercise themselves. It was said of Sir Charles, who breathed his last in a room in this house—

'Sedley had that prevailing, gentle art
Which can with a resistless charm impart
The loosest wishes to the chastest heart:
Raise such a conflict, kindle such a fire,
Between declining virtue and desire,
Till the poor vanquished maid dissolves away
In dreams all night, in sighs and tears all day.'

This was a happy talent to a man about town, but I dare say, without presuming to make uncharitable conjectures on the author's present condition, he would rather have had it said of him that he prayed—

'O thou my voice inspire
Who touched Isaiah's hallowed lips with fire.'"

Nichols somewhat unkindly suggests that there "were too many pecuniary reasons for the temporary solitude" in which Steele resided here.

We have already spoken at some length of Sir Richard Steele in our account of Bury Street, St. James's,* but still something remains to be told about him. "The life of Steele," writes his biographer, "was not that of a retired scholar; hence his moral character becomes all the more instructive. He was one of those whose hearts are the dupes of their imaginations, and who are hurried through life by the most despotic volition. He always preferred his caprices to his interests; or, according to his own notion, very ingenious, but not a little absurd, 'he was always of the humour of preferring the state of his mind to that of his fortune.' The result of this principle of moral conduct was, that a man of the most admirable qualities was perpetually acting like a fool, and,

BELSIZE HOUSE IN 1800.

* See Vol. IV., p. 202.

with a warm attachment to virtue, was the frailest of human beings." The editor of the "Biographia Dramatica" says: "Sir Richard retired to a small house on Haverstock Hill, on the road to Hampstead. . . . Here Mr. Pope, and other members of the Kit-Cat Club, which during the summer was held at the 'Upper Flask,' on Hampstead Heath, used to call on him, and take him in their carriages to the place of rendezvous." Dr. Garth, smiled on Steele for a time, and we next hear of him as having taken a house in Bloomsbury Square, where Lady Steele set up that coach which landed its master in so many difficulties. No mention, apparently, is to be found of Steele's residence at Haverstock Hill in Mr. Montgomery's work on "Sir Richard Steele and his Contemporaries." In the *Monthly Magazine*, Sir Richard Phillips tells us that in his time Steele's house had

SHEPHERD'S WELL IN 1820. (*See page* 500.)

too, was a frequent visitor here. He was a member of the Kit-Cat Club, and notorious for his indolence. One night, when sitting at the "Upper Flask," he accidentally betrayed the fact that he had half-a-dozen patients waiting to see him, and Steele, who sat next him, asked him, in a tone of banter, why he did not get up at once and visit them. "Oh, it's no great matter," replied Garth; "for one-half of them have got such bad constitutions that all the doctors in the world can't save them, and the others such good ones that all the doctors could not possibly kill them."

Here Steele spent the summer days of 1712, in the company of many of his "Spectators," returning generally to town at night, and to the society of his wife, who, as we have stated, at that time had lodgings in Bury Street. Fortune seems to have been "converted into two small ornamental cottages for citizens' sleeping boxes. . . . Opposite to it," he adds, "the famous 'Mother' or 'Moll' King built three substantial houses; and in a small villa behind them resided her favourite pupil, Nancy Dawson. An apartment in the cottage was called the Philosopher's Room, probably the same in which Steele used to write. In Hogarth's 'March to Finchley' this cottage and Mother King's house are seen in the distance . . . Coeval with the *Spectator* and *Tatler*, this cottage must have been a delightful retreat, as at that time there were not a score of buildings between it and Oxford Street and Montagu and Bloomsbury Houses. Now continuous rows of streets extend from London to this spot."

Steele's cottage was a low plain building, and

the only ornament was a scroll over the central window. It was pulled down in 1867. The site of the house and its garden is marked by a row of houses, called Steele's Terrace, and the "Sir Richard Steele" tavern. A house, very near to Steele's, was tenanted by an author and a wit of not dissimilar character. When Gay, who had lost his entire fortune in the South Sea Bubble, showed symptoms of insanity, he was placed by his friends in retirement here. The kindly attentions of sundry physicians, who visited him without fee or reward, sufficed to restore his mental equilibrium even without the aid of the famous Hampstead waters.

Nancy Dawson died at her residence here in May, 1767. Of this memorable character Mr. John Timbs writes thus in his "Romance of London:"—"Nancy Dawson, the famous hornpipe dancer of Covent Garden Theatre, in the last century, when a girl, set up the skittles at a tavern in High Street, Marylebone. She next, according to Sir William Musgrove's 'Adversaria,' in the British Museum, became the wife of a publican near Kelso, on the borders of Scotland. She became so popular a dancer that every verse of a song in praise of her declared the poet to be dying in love for Nancy Dawson, and its tune is as lively as that of 'Sir Roger de Coverley.' In 1760 she transferred her services from Covent Garden Theatre to the other house. On the 23rd of September, in that year, the *Beggar's Opera* was performed at Drury Lane, when the play-bill thus announced her: 'In Act 3, a hornpipe by Miss Dawson, her first appearance here.' It seems that she was engaged to oppose Mrs. Vernon in the same exhibition at the rival house; and there is a full-length print of her in that character. There is also a portrait of her in the Garrick Club collection." She lies buried behind the Foundling Hospital, in the ground belonging to St. George the Martyr, where there is a tomb-stone to her memory, simply stating, "Here lies Nancy Dawson."

Both Rosslyn and Haverstock Hills, it may here be stated, have had tunnels carried through them at a very heavy cost, owing to the fact that the soil hereabouts is a stiff and wet clay. The northernmost tunnel connects the Hampstead Heath station with the Finchley Road station on the branch of the North London Railway which leads to Kew and Richmond. The other tunnel, which is one mile long, with four lines of rails, passes nearly under the Fever Hospital, and was made by the Midland Railway in 1862–3.

CHAPTER XXXIX.

HAMPSTEAD (*continued*).—BELSIZE AND FROGNAL.

"Estates are landscapes gazed upon awhile,
Then advertised, and auctioneered away."

Grant of the Manor of Belsize to Westminster Abbey—Belsize Avenue—Old Belsize House—The Family of Waad—Lord Wotton—Pepys' Account of the Gardens of Belsize—The House attacked by Highway Robbers—A Zealous Protestant—Belsize converted into a Place of Public Amusement, and becomes an "Academy" for Dissipation and Lewdness—The House again becomes a Private Residence—The Right Hon. Spencer Perceval—Demolition of the House—The Murder of Mr. James Delarue—St. Peter's Church—Belsize Square—New College—The Shepherds' or Conduit Fields—Shepherds' Well—Leigh Hunt, Shelley, and Keats—Fitzjohn's Avenue—Finchley Road—Frognal Priory and Memory-Corner Thompson—Dr. Johnson and other Residents at Frognal—Oak Hill Park—Upper Terrace—West End—Rural Festivities—The Cemetery—Child's Hill—Concluding Remarks on Hampstead.

On our right, as we descend Haverstock Hill, lies the now populous district of South Hampstead, or Belsize Park. It is approached on the eastern side through the beautiful avenue of elms mentioned at the close of the preceding chapter; on the west it nearly joins the "Swiss Cottage," which, as we have seen, stands at the farthest point of St. John's Wood.

It is traditionally stated that the manor of Belsize had belonged to the Dean and Chapter of Westminster from the reign of King Edgar, nearly a century before the Conquest; but it is on actual record that in the reign of Edward II. the Crown made a formal grant to Westminster Abbey of the manor of Belsize, then described as consisting of a house and 284 acres of land, on condition of the monks finding a chaplain to celebrate mass daily for the repose of the souls of Edmund, Earl of Lancaster, and of Blanche, his wife. This earl was a grandson of Henry III.; he had taken up arms against Edward, but was captured and beheaded. His name survives still in Lancaster Road.

About 1870 the Dean and Chapter of Westminster gave up the fine avenue above-mentioned, called Belsize Avenue, to the parish of Hampstead, on condition of the vestry planting new trees as the old ones failed. A row of villas is now built on the north side, and at the south-east corner, as stated above, a new town-hall for Hampstead was erected in 1876–7.

At the lower end of the avenue stood, till very recently, a house which, a century ago, enjoyed a celebrity akin to that of the Vauxhall of our own time, but which at an earlier period had a history of its own. An engraving of the house soon after this date will be found in Lysons' "Environs of London," from which it is reproduced in Charles Knight's "Pictorial History of England." It stood near the site of what is now St. Peter's Church, facing the avenue above mentioned, at right angles.

Upon the dissolution of the monasteries one Armigel Wade, or Waad, who had been clerk to the Council under Henry VIII. and Edward VI., and who is known as the British Columbus, obtained a lease of "Old Belsize"—for so this house was called—for a term of two lives. He thereupon retired to Belsize House, where he ended his days in 1568. There was a monument erected to his memory in the old parish church of Hampstead. His son, Sir William Waad, made Lieutenant of the Tower, and knighted by James I., also lived at Belsize and died in 1623. Sir William had married, as his second wife, a daughter of Sir Thomas Wotton, who, surviving as his widow, got the lease of the house and estate renewed to her for two more lives, at a yearly rental of £19 2s. 10d., exclusive of ten loads of hay and five quarters of oats payable to Westminster. She left Belsize to her son, Charles Henry de Kirkhaven, by her first husband; and he, on account of his mother's lineage, was created a peer of the realm, as Lord Wotton, by Charles II., and made this place his residence.

That old gossip, Pepys, thus speaks of it in his "Diary," under date August 17, 1668: "To Hampstead, to speak with the attorney-general, whom we met in the fields, by his old rout and house. And after a little talk about our business, went and saw the Lord Wotton's house and garden, which is wonderful fine: too good for the house the gardens are, being, indeed, the most noble that ever I saw, and such brave orange and lemon trees."

The gardens, indeed, were quite fine enough to offer temptations to thieves and robbers, for soon after this date we find that an attack was made upon the place. In the *True Protestant Mercury* of October 15—19, 1681, we read—"London, October 18. Last night, eleven or twelve highway robbers came on horseback to the house of Lord Wotton, at Hampstead, and attempted to enter therein, breaking down part of the wall and the gate; but there being four or five within the house, they very courageously fired several musquets and a blunderbuss upon the thieves, which gave the alarm to one of the lord's tenants, a farmer, that dwelt not far off, who thereupon went immediately into the town and raised the inhabitants, who, going towards the house, which was about half a mile off, it is thought the robbers hearing thereof, and withal finding the business difficult, they all made their escape. It is judged they had notice of my lord's absence from his house, and likewise of a great booty which was therein, which put them upon this desperate attempt."

On Lord Wotton's death the Belsize estate fell to the hands of his half-brother, Lord Chesterfield. The latter, however, did not care to live there, but sold his interest in the place, and the house remained for some time unoccupied. In the reign of George I., however, we find Belsize in the hands of a retired "sea-coal" merchant, named Povey, to whom the then French ambassador, the Duc d'Aumont, offered the (at that time) immense rental of £1,000 a year on a repairing lease. It transpired that the duke wanted the place because it contained or had attached to it a private chapel. On this the coal-merchant refused to carry out the bargain, on the ground that he "would not have his chapel desecrated by Popery." For this piece of Protestant zeal he hoped that he would have been applauded by the magistrates; his surprise, therefore, must have been great when, instead of praise, he received from the Privy Council a reprimand, as being an "enemy to the king." It is recorded that when the Prince of Wales (afterwards George II.) came soon afterwards to see the house, Povey addressed to him a letter, informing his royal highness of these particulars, but the prince never condescended to vouchsafe him a reply. Povey, we may add, made himself notorious in his day by the publication of sundry pamphlets exposing the evil practices of Government agencies. He also took to himself great credit as a patriot for having refused to let his mansion to the French ambassador, and modestly put in a claim for some reimbursement from the nation, for having "kept the Romish host" from being offered in Hampstead, at a cost to himself of one thousand pounds. Our readers will hardly need to be told that Mr. Povey got no thanks for his pains, any more than he did shortly afterwards for his equally disinterested offer of his house and chapel for the use of his Royal Highness the Prince of Wales, "for a place of recess or constant residence." Not obtaining an answer to his impertinent intrusion, he seems to have turned Belsize to good account pecuniarily, and perhaps, at the same time, to have "paid out" his neighbours for their coolness to him, by allowing it to be opened as a place of fashionable amusement.

For a period of about forty years—in fact, during the reigns of George I. and George II.—Belsize ceased to be occupied as a private residence, being opened by a Welshman of the name of Howell as a place of public amusement, and sank apparently down into a second-rate house of refreshments and gambling. In the park, which was said to be a mile in circumference, were exhibited foot-races, athletic sports, and sometimes deer-hunts and fox-hunts: and it is said that one diversion occasionally was a race between men and women in wooden shoes. Upon the whole, it is to be feared that Belsize was not as respectably conducted as it might have been and ought to have been; the consequence was that its customers fell off, and in the end it was shut up.

The newspapers of the period announce that the house was opened as a place of public entertainment "with an uncommon solemnity of music and dancing." It is somewhat amusing to note that the advertisements wind up with an assurance that for the benefit of visitors timid about highwaymen "twelve stout fellows completely armed patrol between Belsize and London." Notwithstanding that the house had been the residence of the lord of the manor, better company (we are told) came to it in its fallen estate than before. A year or two after it was opened to the public grievous complaints were made by the people of Hampstead of the multitude of coaches which invaded their rural solitude. The numbers were often as many as two or three hundred in a single night. We glean from Park's "History of Hampstead" the following particulars concerning Belsize House as a place of amusement:—"Of Belsize House, as the mansion of a manorial district in the parish of Hampstead, I have already spoken; it is introduced again here as a place formerly of considerable notoriety for public diversions. The following extracts will give some idea of the nature and character of these amusements, and indicate that it was the prototype of Vauxhall, Ranelagh, and many other more modern establishments:—'Whereas that the ancient and noble house near Hampstead, commonly called Bellasis-house, is now taken and fitted up for the entertainment of gentlemen and ladies during the whole summer season, the same will be opened with an uncommon solemnity of music and dancing. This undertaking will exceed all of the kind that has hitherto been known near London, commencing every day at six in the morning, and continuing till eight at night, all persons being privileged to admittance without necessity of expense,' &c., &c.—*Mist's Journal*, April 16, 1720.

"A hand-bill of the amusements at Belsize (formerly in the possession of Dr. Combe), which has a print of the old mansion-house prefixed, announces Belsize to be open for the season (no date), 'the park, wilderness, and garden being wonderfully improved and filled with variety of birds, which compose a most melodious and delightful harmony. Persons inclined to walk and divert themselves, may breakfast on tea and coffee as cheap as at their own chambers. Twelve stout fellows, completely armed, to patrole between Belsize and London,' &c., &c. 'Last Saturday their Royal Highnesses the Prince and Princess of Wales dined at Belsize-house, near Hampstead, attended by several persons of quality, where they were entertained with the diversion of hunting, and such other as the place afforded, with which they seemed well pleased, and at their departure were very liberal to the servants.'—*Read's Journal*, July 15, 1721.

"In the same journal, September 9, 1721, is an account of his Excellency the Welsh ambassador giving a plate of six guineas to be run for by eleven footmen. The Welsh ambassador appears to have been the nickname of one Howell, who kept the house.

"'The Court of Justices, at the general quarter sessions at Hickes's-hall, have ordered the high-constable of Holborn division to issue his precepts to the petty constables and headboroughs of the parish of Hampstead, to prevent all unlawful gaming, riots, &c., at Belsize-house and the Great Room at Hampstead.'—*St. James's Journal*, May 24, 1722.

"'On Monday last the appearance of nobility and gentry at Belsize was so great that they reckoned between three and four hundred coaches, at which time a wild deer was hunted down and killed in the park before the company, which gave near three hours' diversion.'—*Ibid.*, June 7, 1722."

In 1722 was published, in an octavo volume, "'Belsize House,' a satire, exposing, 1. The Fops and Beaux who daily frequent that academy. 2. The characters of the women who make this an exchange for assignations. 3. The buffoonery of the Welsh ambassador. 4. The humours of his customers in their several apartments, &c. By a Serious Person of Quality." The volume, however, is of little real value, except as a somewhat coarse sketch of the manners of the age.

According to this poetical sarcasm, Belsize was an *academy* for dissipation and lewdness, to a degree that would scarcely be tolerated in the present times, and that would be a scandal in any; but some allowance must probably be made for the jaundiced vision of the caustic writer. We find in it the following brief description of the house:—

"This house, which is a nuisance to the land,
Doth near a park and handsome garden stand,
Fronting the road, betwixt a range of trees,
Which is perfumed with a Hampstead breeze;
And on each side the gate 's a grenadier,
Howe'er, they cannot speak, think, see, nor hear;
But why they 're posted there no mortal knows,
Unless it be to fright jackdaws and crows;
For rooks they cannot scare, who there resort,
To make of most unthoughtful bubbles sport."

The grounds and gardens of Belsize continued open as late as the year 1745, when foot-races were advertised there. In the course of the next generation, however, a great change would seem to have come over the place; at all events, in the "Ambulator," (1774), we read: "Belsize is situated on the south-west side of Hampstead Hill, Middlesex, and was a fine seat belonging to the Lord Wotton, and afterwards to the Earl of Chesterfield; but in the year 1720 it was converted into a place of polite entertainment, particularly for music, dancing, and play, when it was much frequented, on account of its neighbourhood to London, but since that time it has been suffered to run to ruin."

After the lapse of many years, during which little or nothing is recorded of its history, Belsize came again to be occupied as a private residence, and among its other tenants was the Right Hon. Spencer Perceval, afterwards Prime Minister, who lived here for about ten years before taking office as Chancellor of the Exchequer, namely, from 1798 to 1807. Mr. Perceval was the second son of the Earl of Egmont. Having first applied himself to the study of the law, he entered Parliament, in 1796, as member for Northampton, and under Mr. Addington's administration, in 1801, was appointed Solicitor-General. Next year he became Attorney-General, attaining also great distinction as a Parliamentary debater. On the fall of the Duke of Portland's Administration, in 1809, Mr. Perceval was appointed First Lord of the Treasury and Chancellor of the Exchequer, and he was still in office when he was assassinated by Bellingham, in the lobby of the House of Commons, in 1812.* A portrait of Mr. Perceval, painted by Joseph, from a mask taken after death by Nollekens, is to be seen in the National Portrait Gallery.

In more recent times Belsize House was occupied by a Roman Catholic family named Wright, who were bankers in London. The old house, originally a large but plain Elizabethan mansion, with central tower and slightly projecting wings, was remodelled during the reign of Charles II., and subsequently again considerably altered. Its park, less than a century ago, was a real park, somewhat like that which encompasses Holland House, at Kensington. It was surrounded by a solid wall, which skirted the south side of a lane leading from the wood of the Knights of St. John towards Hampstead.

Belsize seems, on the whole, to have been rather an unlucky place. The mansion was pulled down about the year 1852, and the bricks of the house and of the park wall were used to make the roads which now traverse the estate, and to form the site of the handsome villa residences which now form Belsize Park; and at the present time all that is left to remind the visitor of the past glories of the spot is the noble avenue of elms which, as we have stated, once formed its principal approach.

On the 21st of February, 1845, Mr. James Delarue, a teacher of music, was murdered by a young man named Hocker, close by the corner of Belsize Park, in the narrow lane leading from Chalk Farm to Hampstead. The lane, at that time, as may be imagined, was very solitary, seeing that, with the exception of Belsize House, there were no houses near the spot. The crime was perpetrated about seven o'clock in the evening. Cries of "murder" were heard by a person who happened to be passing at the time, and on an alarm being given, the body of the murdered man was quickly discovered. Hocker, it seems, had in the meanwhile gone to the "Swiss Tavern," and there called for brandy and water; but on the arrival of the police and others, Hocker too appeared on the spot, inquired what was amiss, and, taking the dead man's hand, felt his pulse and pronounced him dead, and gave some bystanders money to help carry the corpse away. Mr. Howitt, in noticing this tragedy in his "Northern Heights," says, "The murder was afterwards clearly traced to Hocker, the cause of it being jealousy and revenge, so far as it appeared, for his being supplanted by Delarue in the affections of a young woman of Hampstead. On the trial Hocker read a paper endeavouring to throw the charge of the murder on a friend, whose name, of course, he did not disclose, and added an improbable story of the manner in which his clothes had become stained with blood. The reading of this paper only impressed the court and the crowd of spectators with an idea of Hocker's excessive hypocrisy and cold-bloodedness. He was convicted and executed." Miss Lucy Aikin alludes to

* See Vol. III., p. 530.

this murder of Delarue in one of her letters to a friend: "I rather congratulate myself on not being in Church Row during the delightful excitement of this murder and the inquest, which appear to have had so many charms for the million. . . . . But I think the event will give me a kind of a dislike to Belsize Lane, which hitherto I used to think the pleasantest way from us to you."

We have stated above that the manor of Belsize belongs to the Dean and Chapter of Westminster; we may add here that "Buckland" Crescent and "Stanley" Gardens, which now form part of the estate, are named after deans of that collegiate establishment, and that St. Peter's Church is so dedicated after St. Peter's Abbey itself. It is a neat cruciform building, in the Decorated style of architecture, with side aisle and tower, and was erected in 1860.

In Belsize Square lived for some time, and there died in 1875, Henry Malden, M.A., formerly Fellow of Trinity College, Cambridge, and for forty-five years Professor of Greek in University College, London. The son of a surgeon at Putney, he was born in the year 1800, and was educated at Trinity College, Cambridge, where he was elected to a Craven Scholarship, together with the late Lord Macaulay. Whilst at Cambridge, he contributed to *Knight's Quarterly Magazine*, and wrote a poem entitled "Evening," which was published in a volume of poems edited by Joanna Baillie. In 1834 he published a small work on the "Origin of Universities and Academical Degrees," which was written as an introduction to the Report of the Argument before the Privy Council in support of the application of the University of London for a charter empowering it to grant degrees.

FROGNAL PRIORY. (*See page* 501.)

On the western side of the Belsize estate, at the angle of the Finchley and Belsize Roads, stands New College, a substantial-looking stone-built edifice, erected about the year 1853, as a place of training for young men for the ministry of the Independent persuasion. Not far from it, at the top of Avenue Road, is a handsome Gothic Chapel belonging also to the Nonconformists, and known as New College Chapel.

Down till very recently, Hampstead was separated from Belsize Park, Kilburn, Portland Town, &c., by a broad belt of green meadows, known as the Shepherds' or Conduit Fields, across which ran

POND STREET, HAMPSTEAD, IN 1750.

a pleasant pathway sloping up to the south-western corner of the village, and terminating near Church Row. On the eastern side of these fields is an old well or conduit, called the Shepherd's Well, where visitors in former times used to be supplied with a glass of the clearest and purest water. This conduit is probably of very ancient date. The spring formerly served not only visitors but also the dwellers in Hampstead with water, and poor people used to fetch it and sell it by the bucket. There used to be an arch over the conduit, and rails stood round it; but since Hampstead has been supplied by the New River Company the conduit has become neglected, and the spring is covered over.

Towards the close of the last century, Lord Loughborough, who, as we have seen, was then living close by, desired to stop the inhabitants from obtaining the water, by enclosing the well, or otherwise cutting off all communication with it; but so great was the popular indignation, that an appeal was made to the Courts of Law, when a decision was very wisely given in the people's favour, and so the well remained in constant use till our own times. In this we are reminded of

> "Some village Hampden that, with dauntless breast,
> The little tyrant of the fields withstood;"

but who the "village Hampden" was on this occasion is not recorded by local tradition.

From Hone's "Table Book" (1827) we glean the following particulars concerning this well:—"The arch, embedded above and around by the green turf, forms a conduit-head to a beautiful spring; the specific gravity of the fluid, which yields several tons a day, is little more than that of distilled water. Hampstead abounds in other springs, but they are mostly impregnated with mineral substances. The water of 'Shepherd's Well,' therefore, is in continual request; and those who cannot otherwise obtain it are supplied through a few of the villagers, who make a scanty living by carrying it to houses for a penny a pailful. There is no carriage-way to the spot, and these poor things have much hard work for a very little money. . . . The water of Shepherd's Well is remarkable for not being subject to freeze. There is another spring sometimes resorted to near Kilburn; but this and the ponds in the Vale of Health are the ordinary sources of public supply to Hampstead. The chief inconvenience of habitations in this delightful village is the inadequate distribution of good water. Occasional visitants, for the sake of health, frequently sustain considerable injury by the insalubrity of private springs, and charge upon the fluid they breathe the mischief they derive from the fluid they drink. The localities of the place afford almost every variety of aspect and temperature that invalids require; and a constant sufficiency of wholesome water might be easily obtained by a few simple arrangements." It may be well to add, however, that the want of good water is not among the requirements of Hampstead at the present day; and also that what Lord Loughborough was unable to effect in the way of stopping the supply of water from this spring, was partially accomplished about the years 1860–70, through the excavation of tunnels under the hill on the side of which it stands, when the spring became almost dried up.

The fields which we have now before us are those over which Leigh Hunt so much delighted to ramble, and which, no doubt, he found far more pleasant than the interior of Newgate, in which he had been immured for calling the Prince of Wales "a fat Adonis." In these fields Hunt would often meet with the genial company of his fellow-poets. Shelley would walk hither from his lodgings in Pond Street, and Keats would turn up from Well Walk. Here the three friends once frightened an old lady terribly: they thought themselves quite alone, and Shelley, throwing himself into attitude, began to spout the lines—

> "Come, brothers, let us sit upon the ground,
> And tell sad stories of the deaths of kings."

The old lady made off as quick as her feet could carry her, and told her friends that she had met in the fields three dangerous characters, who, she was quite sure, were either madmen, or republicans, or actors! It was the view of Hampstead from these fields that suggested to the mind of Leigh Hunt the following lines, descriptive of their beauties, and which are well worthy to appear among his various poems on the scenery of this neighbourhood:—

> "A turret looking o'er a leafy vine,
> With hedgerow styles in front, and sloping green,
> Sweet Hampstead, is thy southward look serene;
> And such thou welcomest approaching eyes.
> To me a double charm is in thy skies
> From her meek spirit, oft in fancy seen
> Blessing the twilight with her placid mien."

In 1874–5 it was proposed by some of the inhabitants of Hampstead to purchase a portion of these grassy slopes, and to devote them to public use, in the shape of a "park" for the working classes of the neighbourhood; but the plan was brought to an abrupt termination by some speculative builders, by whom the greater part of the ground was bought and laid out for building purposes, a broad roadway, called Fitzjohn's Avenue, being made at the same time across their centre, thus connecting the town of Hampstead with St. John's Wood, Kilburn, and the west end of London. It is not a little singular that just a hundred years previously—namely, in 1776—the construction of a new road was proposed from Portman Square to Alsopp's Farm, across the fields, and on through a part of Belsize, to the foot of Hampstead Town.

In these fields and in those lying between the southern terrace of the churchyard and the lower portions of Frognal, rise two or three springs, which form the sources of the brook which we have already seen trickling through Kilburn, and by Westbourne Green down to Bayswater, where it forms the head of the Serpentine river.

Leaving the Conduit Fields and Fitzjohn's Avenue on our right, and making our way down College Lane by some neat school-buildings, which have been lately erected there, we emerge upon the Finchley Road, close by the "North Star" tavern, whence a short walk along the road, with pleasant fields and hedgerows on either hand, brings us to the western part of the village of Hampstead. On our way along the Finchley Road we pass, on our right, the large, new, and handsome church of the Holy Trinity; and on our left, the Finchley Road stations on the Midland and North London Railways, which here again emerge into daylight, after passing through tunnels, as already stated, under the Belsize and Rosslyn estates. A footpath, cut diagonally across a sloping meadow, between some venerable oaks, takes us from the main road, behind Frognal Priory, to West End Lane, a narrow carriage-way connecting the Finchley Road with the village of Hampstead. This lane is still in parts overhung at the sides by elms and quickset hedges, and has about it some of that quiet air of rusticity which Constable so delighted in painting.

Frognal, as the neighbourhood of the western slope of Hampstead is called, is still, happily, a "beautiful and suburban village," just as it is described by the Rev. J. Richardson in his amusing "Recollections." He writes: "The view from the upper part of this locality is one of the finest in England [he should have said in the neighbourhood of London]. The late Dr. White, who held some years back the living of Hampstead, and also that of Nettlebed, in Oxfordshire, used to affirm that on a clear day, with the aid of a good telescope, he could discern the windmill at Nettlebed from his garden at Frognal, the distance between the two places being about thirty-five miles in a direct line."

This neighbourhood is full of gentlemen's seats and villas, standing in their own grounds. On our right, as we ascend the hill, we pass the site on which, from the close of the last century down to the year 1876, stood a curious building—an absurd specimen of modern antiquity—in the gingerbread Gothic style, a not very successful imitation of Horace Walpole's Strawberry Hill, pretentiously styled Frognal Priory. Mr. Howitt, in his "Northern Heights," published in 1869, gives the following particulars of the eccentric house, and its still more eccentric owner:—"This house, now hastening fast to ruin, was built by a Mr. Thompson, best known by the name of 'Memory Thompson,' or, as stated by others, as 'Memory-Corner Thompson.' This Mr. Thompson built the house on a lease of twenty years, subject to a fine to the lord of the manor. He appears to have been an auctioneer and public-house broker, who grew rich, and, having a peculiar taste in architecture and old furniture, built this house in an old English style, approaching the Elizabethan. That the house, though now ruinous, is of modern date, is also witnessed by the trees around it being common poplar, evidently planted to run up quickly. Thompson is said to have belonged to a club of auctioneers or brokers, which met once a week; and at one of these meetings, boasting that he had a better memory than any man living, he offered to prove it by stating the name and business of every person who kept a corner shop in the City, or, as others have it, the name, number, and business of every person who kept a shop in Cheapside. The former statement is the one most received, and is the more probable, because Thompson, being a public-house broker, was no doubt familiar with all these corner-haunting drink-houses. Having maintained his boast, he was thence called 'Memory,' or 'Memory-Corner Thompson;' but his general cognomen was the first. Thompson not only asserted that he built his house on the site of an ancient priory, continuing down to the Dissolution, and inhabited as a suburban house by Cardinal Wolsey, but, as an auctioneer, he had the opportunity of collecting old furniture, pieces of carving in wood, ebony, ivory, &c. With these he filled his house, dignifying his furniture (some of which had been made up from fragments) as having belonged to Cardinal Wolsey, to Queen Elizabeth, the Queen of Scots, and other historical magnates. On the marriage of Queen Victoria, he offered for sale a huge old bedstead, as Queen Elizabeth's, with chairs to match, to Her Majesty, but the queen declined it. It is said, however, to have been purchased by Government, and to be somewhere in one of the palaces. This bedstead, and the chairs possibly, had some authentic character, as he built a wing of his house especially for their reception. Thompson had an ostensibly magnificent library, containing, to all appearance, most valuable works of all kinds; but, on examination, they proved to be only pasteboard bound up and labelled as books. The windows of the chief room were of stained glass, casting 'a dim, religious light.' And this great warehouse of articles of furniture, of real and manufactured antiquity, of coins, china, and articles of *virtu*, became so great a show place, that people flocked far and near to see it. This greatly flattered Thompson, who excluded no one of tolerable appearance, nor restricted visitors to stated hours. It is said that, in his ostentation, he used to leave five-guinea gold pieces about on the window seats." But this last statement is mythical. The best, and indeed the only good portion of the house, was the porch, a handsome and massive structure, in the ornamented Jacobean style, and which had formed the entrance of some one of the many timber mansions still to be found in Cheshire and in other remote counties, and which Thompson had "picked up" as a bargain in one of his business tours. It was surmounted with the armorial bearings of the family to whom it had belonged, and was often sketched by artists. After his death, at the age of eighty years, a sale of his goods and chattels took place; but the principal part of his wealth descended to his niece, who married Barnard Gregory, the proprietor of the notorious *Satirist*. Gregory, it seems, on the death of his wife, did not pay the customary fine to the lord of the manor, and Sir Thomas Wilson recovered possession by an injunction, intending to remove the offices of the manor thither. From a fear, however, of the appearance of some heir of Thompson after he had repaired it, which was at one time a possibility, Sir Thomas left it *in statu quo ante;* and the house having gone rapidly to decay and ruin, was, in the end, wholly demolished. A few trees, forming a sort of grove, and the remains of a small lodge-house, now profusely overgrown with ivy, are all that is left to mark the site of the singular edifice heretofore known as Frognal Priory.

In a cottage close by the entrance to the Priory, as we have stated in a previous chapter, Dr. Johnson stayed for a time as a visitor; and here Boswell tells us that he wrote his "Town," and busied himself during a summer with his essay on the "Vanity of Human Riches." It is not a little singular, however, that neither of these poems bear much trace of the inspiration of the Hampstead Muses. The fact is that the burly doctor preferred society to scenery, and with the winter returned to Fleet Street, and presented himself once more amongst his friends, in whose company he felt, we may be sure, much more at home than amidst the breezes of Hampstead, and whose conversation gave him more gratification than the songs of her nightingales. Park says the house at which Dr. Johnson used to lodge was "the last in Frognal southward, occupied in his (Park's) time by Benjamin Charles Stephenson, Esq., F.S.A." The house has been rebuilt, or, at all events, remodelled since that date.

At Frognal lived also Mr. Thomas William Carr, some time solicitor of the Excise, whose house was the centre of literary *réunions*. Here, Crabb Robinson tells us in his "Diary," he met Wordsworth, Sir Humphrey Davy, Joanna Baillie, and some other persons of note. One of Mr. Carr's daughters married Sir Robert M. Rolfe, afterwards Lord Chancellor Cranworth.

Frognal Hall, standing close to the western end of the church, was formerly the residence of Mr. Isaac Ware,* the architect, and author of "A Complete Body of Architecture," and of a translation of "Palladio on the Fine Arts," &c. Although Mr. Ware found a patron in the great Lord Burlington, he is stated to have died at his house near Kensington Gravel Pits in "depressed circumstances." A French family, named Guyons, occupied the hall after Ware quitted it; and it was subsequently the residence of Lord Alvanley, Master of the Rolls, and some time Chief Justice of the Court of Common Pleas. After passing through one or two other hands, Frognal Hall became the residence of Mr. Julius Talbot Airey. It has now been turned into a Roman Catholic boarding-school. The adjoining seat, that of Miss Sulivan, is known as Frognal Mansion, and was originally the manor house of this district. A part of the manorial rights attached to this property consists of a private road leading past the north side of the parish church, with a private toll-gate, which even royalty cannot pass without payment of the customary toll. It is nearly the only toll-gate now remaining in all the suburbs of London.

It was probably in the upper part of Frognal that Cyrus Redding for some time resided; at all events, it was in a lodging on the western slope of the hill, as he tells us himself, that he began in 1858 his "Fifty Years' Recollections, Literary and

* See *ante*, p. 214.

Personal." His windows commanded a charming and extensive view. He writes picturesquely:—"Before me palatial Windsor is seen rising proudly in the distance. The spire of Harrow, like a burial obelisk, ascending in another direction, brings before the glass of memory eminent names with which it is associated—Parr, Byron, Peel, and others, no longer of the quick, but the dead. The hills of Surrey southward blend their faint grey outline with the remoter heaven. The middle landscape slumbers in beauty; clouds roll heavily and sluggishly along, with here and there a break permitting the glory of the superior region to shine obliquely through, in strong contrast to the shadowy face of things beneath."

To the west of Frognal there is some rising ground, which the late Mr. Sheffield Neave laid out for the erection of about twelve handsome houses, called Oak Hill Park. One of these has been frequently occupied during the summer months by Miss Florence Nightingale. Near the entrance of this park is a house which was occupied for many years as the Sailors' Orphan Girls' Home, before the transfer of that institution to its new buildings between Church Row and Greenhill, and Prince Arthur's Road. To the north of Frognal is the Upper Terrace, which screens this portion of Hampstead from the bleak winds that blow across the Heath. In this terrace a house known as the "Priory" was the residence of the eminent sculptor and Royal Academician, Mr. J. H. Foley. In another house in this terrace lived Mr. Magrath, one of the founders, and during its earlier years the secretary, of the Athenæum Club.

Half a mile westward, beyond Frognal, lies West End, a group of houses surrounding an open space which is still a village green. This used to be the scene of a fair held annually in July; but the fair was suppressed about the year 1820 on account of the disorderly conduct of its frequenters. There is extant in the British Museum a curious handbill, dated 1708, and entitled "The Hampstead Fair Rambler; or, The World's Going quite Mad. To the tune of 'Brother Soldier, dost hear of the News?' London, printed for J. Bland, near Holborn, 1708." From this it is clear that, like most rural and suburban fairs, it was remarkable chiefly for its swings, roundabouts, penny trumpets, spiced gingerbread, and halfpenny rattles. Occasionally, however, its proceedings were varied; under date July 2, 1744, we read: "This is to give notice that the Fair will be kept on Wednesday, Thursday, and Friday next, in a pleasant, shady walk, in the middle of the town. On Wednesday a pig will be turned loose, and he that takes it up by the tail and throws it over his head shall have it. To pay twopence entrance, and no less than twelve to enter. On Thursday, a match will be run by two men, a hundred yards, in two sacks, for a large sum. And to encourage the sport, the landlord of the inn will give a pair of gloves, to be run for by six men, the winner to have them. And on Friday, a hat, value ten shillings, will be run for by men twelve times round the green; to pay one shilling entrance; no less than four to start. As many as will may enter, and the second man to have all the money above four."

This, doubtless, was the *locale* of the scenes mentioned in the public prints of June, 1786:—"On Whit Tuesday was celebrated, near Hendon, in Middlesex, a burlesque imitation of the Olympic Games. One prize was a gold-laced hat, to be grinned for by six candidates, who were placed on a platform with horses' collars to grin through. Over their heads was written '*detur tetriori*'—'The ugliest grinner shall be the winner.' Each party had to grin for five minutes by himself, and then all the other candidates joined in a grand chorus of distortion. The prize was carried by a porter to a vinegar-merchant, though he was accused by his competitors of foul play, for rinsing his mouth with verjuice. The sports were concluded by a hog with his tail shaved and soaped being let loose among some ten or twelve peasants, any one of whom that could seize him by the *queue* and throw him across his own shoulders was to keep him as a prize. The animal, after running for some miles about the neighbourhood of the Heath, so tired his pursuers, that they at last gave up the chase in despair. We are told that on this occasion a prodigious concourse of people attended, among whom were the Tripoline Ambassador, and several other persons of distinction and quality."

The Rev. Mr. Richardson, in his amusing "Recollections," states that as lately as 1819 the fair was attended by about two hundred "roughs" from London, who assaulted the men and the women with brutal violence, cutting their clothes from their backs. The Hampstead magistrates were obliged to call the aid of special constables in order to suppress the riot. This riot, however, had one good effect, as it helped to pave the way for the introduction of the new police by Sir Robert Peel. There is a tradition that the last Maypole in the neighbourhood stood on this green. A good sketch of a dance round a country Maypole will be found in Hone's "Every-Day Book," under "May-day."

West End, for the most part, lies low, and the houses are but poor second and third-rate cottages; and there is a public-house bearing the sign of the "Cock and Hoop." Here is a small Gothic structure, forming at once a village school and a chapel of ease for the parish.

A new cemetery for the parish of Hampstead was formed on the north of West End in 1876; it covers twenty acres of ground, and is picturesquely laid out; and close by is a reservoir belonging to the Grand Junction Waterworks Company.

A little farther on the road to Hendon is an outlying district of Hampstead parish, known as Child's Hill, consisting almost wholly of cottages, dotted irregularly around two or three cross-roads. Here a small district church was erected about the year 1850; it is a Gothic edifice, consisting of a nave and chancel, with a small bell-turret. The road, here branching off to the right, will take the tourist through a pleasant lane to the north-west corner of the Heath, where the gorse and furze bloom in all their native beauty. Following this road, and leaving on his right Telegraph Hill—the site of a semaphore half a century ago—he will find himself once more at the back of "Jack Straw's Castle," whence a short walk will take him back into the centre of Hampstead.

Having thus far made our survey of the parish of Hampstead, little remains to be said. The place, as we have endeavoured to show, has long been considered healthy and salubrious, and, therefore, has been the frequent resort of invalids for the benefit of the air. From the formal reports of the medical officer of health for Hampstead, issued yearly, we learn that the death-rate of late years has varied from 14 to 16 in a thousand—a very low rate of mortality, it must be owned, though not quite so low as it stood in the year 1875, when Dr. Lord gave to the parish, in allusion to its lofty and salubrious situation, the name of *Mons Salutis*.

The parish extends over upwards of 2,000 acres of land, of which, as we have stated, between 200 and 300 are waste. In 1801 there were 691 inhabited houses in the parish, and the number of families occupying them was 953; and the total number of the inhabitants was 4,343. In 1851 the population had grown to 12,000. Ten years later it had increased to 19,000; in 1865 it had reached 22,000; and at the present time (1884) its numbers may be estimated at nearly 50,000.

On more than one occasion, when silly prophets and astrologers have alarmed the inhabitants of London by rumours of approaching earthquakes, and tides that should swallow up its citizens, the high ground of Hampstead and Highgate has afforded to the crowds in their alarm a place of refuge and safety. An amusing description of, at all events, two such instances will be found in Dr. Mackay's "Memoirs of Extraordinary Popular Delusions," in the chapter devoted to the subject of "Modern Prophecies." It may sound not a little strange when we tell our readers that one of these unreasoning panics occurred so lately as the first year of the reign of George III. It is only fair to add that a slight shock of an earthquake had been felt in London a month before, but so slight, that it did no harm, beyond throwing down one or two tottering stacks of chimneys.

Apropos of the gradual extension of the limits of the metropolis, of which we have already more than once had occasion to speak, we cannot do better, in concluding this part of our perambulations, than to quote the following lines of Mr. Thomas Miller, in his "Picturesque Sketches of London." "Twelve miles," he writes, "would scarcely exceed the almost unbroken line of buildings which extends from Blackwall to far beyond Chelsea, where street still joins to street in apparently endless succession. And yet all around this vast city lie miles of the most beautiful rural scenery. Highgate, Hornsey, and Hampstead, on the Middlesex side, hilly, wooded, and watered; and facing these, the vast range called the Hog's Back, which hems in the far-distant Surrey side from beyond Norwood; . . . . whilst the valleys on both sides of the river are filled with pleasant fields, parks, and green, winding lanes. Were London to extend five miles farther every way, it would still be hemmed in with some of the most beautiful country scenery in England; and the lowness of the fares, together with the rapidity of railway travelling, would render as nothing this extent of streets."

COLUMBIA MARKET, HACKNEY. (*See page* 506.)

CHAPTER XL.

THE NORTH-EASTERN SUBURBS.—HAGGERSTON, HACKNEY, &c.

"Oppidum rure commistum."—*Tacitus.*

Appearance of Haggerston in the Last Century—Cambridge Heath—Nova Scotia Gardens—Columbia Buildings—Columbia Market—The "New" Burial-ground of St. Leonard's, Shoreditch—Halley, the Astronomer—Nichols Square—St. Chad's Church—St. Mary's Church—Brunswick Square Almshouses—Mutton Lane—The "Cat and Mutton" Tavern—London Fields—The Hackney Bun-house—Goldsmiths' Row—The Goldsmiths' Almshouses—The North-Eastern Hospital for Sick Children—The Orphan Asylum, Bonner's Road—City of London Hospital for Diseases of the Chest—Bonner's Hall—Bishop Bonner's Fields—Botany Bay—Victoria Park—The East-enders' Fondness for Flowers—Amateur Yachting—The Jews' Burial-ground—The French Hospital—The Church of St. John of Jerusalem—The Etymology of "Hackney."

HAVING in the preceding chapters devoted our attention to the north-western part of London, we now take up fresh ground, and begin anew with the north-eastern districts, which, although not so extensive as the ground over which we have travelled since starting from Belgravia and Pimlico, will doubtless be found to contain much that may prove interesting to the general reader.

Taking our stand close by the north-easternmost point described in the previous parts of this work—namely, by St. Leonard's Church, Shoreditch*—we have on our left the districts of Hoxton and Islington, and on our right that of Bethnal Green. Stretching away in an easterly direction is the Hackney Road, which divides these last-named districts from that of Haggerston.

In Rocque's map of Hackney, published in 1745, the Hackney Road appears entirely unbuilt upon, with the exception of a couple of houses at the corner of the roadway leading to the hamlet of Agostone (now Haggerston), and a small cluster of dwellings and a roadside public-house called the "Nag's Head," at the bottom of a narrow thoroughfare called Mutton Lane, which passes through the fields in the north, by the front of the Goldsmiths' Almshouses, of which we shall have more to say presently. The greater part of the lane itself is now called Goldsmiths' Row. At the eastern end of the Hackney Road, Cambridge Heath is marked as a large triangular space, the apex of

* See Vol. II., p. 195.

which terminates close by Coats's Lane, Bethnal Green. From Cambridge Heath the roadway trends to the north by Mare (or Meare) Street, on the east side of London Fields, forming the principal roadway through the town of Hackney.

At a short distance eastward of Shoreditch Church, on our right hand as we pass along the Hackney Road, and therefore within the limits of the parish of Bethnal Green, the eye is struck by Columbia Square and Market, the tall roofs of which rise against the sky, reminding us of the Houses of Parliament, though on a smaller scale. They were erected in 1869, from the designs of Mr. H. A. Darbishire. On the site now occupied by the market and a few of the surrounding buildings existed till very recently a foul colony of squalor and misery, consisting of wretched low tenements—or, more correctly speaking, hovels—and still more wretched inhabitants; the locality bore the name of Nova Scotia Gardens, and it abounded in pestilential drains and dust heaps. Nova Scotia Gardens and its surroundings, in fact, were formerly one of the most poverty-stricken quarters of the whole East-end, and, doubtless, one of those spots to which Charles Dickens refers in his "Uncommercial Traveller," when he draws attention to the fact that while the poor rate in St. George's, Hanover Square, stands at sevenpence in the pound, there are districts in these eastern slums where it stands at five shillings and sixpence. By the benevolence of Lady Burdett-Coutts, whose charity and will to benefit the poor of London we have already had occasion to remark upon in our account of Highgate,* the whole of this seat of foulness and disease was cleared away, and in its place four large blocks of model lodging-houses, forming a square called Columbia Buildings, have been erected, and are occupied by an orderly and well-behaved section of the working-class population of the district. Contiguous to the square stands the Market, which was also established by the same benevolent lady for the convenience of the neighbourhood. The market covers about two acres of ground, and the buildings, which are principally constructed of brick, with stone dressings, are very elaborately ornamented with carved work, in the shape of medallions and armorial bearings. The market-place forms three sides of a square, having an arcade opening on the central area through Gothic arches. Tables for the various commodities which may be brought to the market for sale, occupy the centre of the quadrangular space, and are partly covered in by a light roof. The chief feature of the building, which occupies the whole of the eastern side of the quadrangle, is a large and lofty Gothic hall. The exterior of this edifice is particularly rich in ornamentation. The basement is lighted by a range of small pointed windows, above which is an ornamental string-course. The hall itself, which is reached by a short flight of steps, is lighted by seven large pointed windows on each side, with others still larger at either end; the buttresses between the windows terminate in elaborate pinnacles; in fact, the whole building, including the louvre in the centre of the roof, and the tall clock-tower, bristles with crocketed pinnacles and foliated finials.

* See *ante*, p. 411.

Whether the building is too ornate, or whatever may be the cause, it is not for us to say; but, at all events, as a place of business in the way designed by its noble founder, Columbia Market for many years proved a comparative failure. Scarcely any of the shops which open upon the arcades were occupied; indeed, very little in the way of business was ever carried on there. In 1877, it was re-opened as a market for American meat, but the attempt proved ineffectual. It afterwards, however, became established as a fish depôt, to which, in January, 1884, a vegetable market was added.

On the opposite side of the Hackney Road, facing the entrance to Columbia Square, is the "new" burial-ground belonging to St. Leonard's, Shoreditch. This has been long disused, and within the last few years the grave-mounds have been levelled, the place being made to serve as a recreation-ground for the children in the neighbourhood.

Haggerston, on our left, at one time an outlying hamlet in the parish of St. Leonard's, Shoreditch, is mentioned in "Domesday Book" under the name of Hergotestane. It is now an extensive district, stretching away from the north side of the Hackney Road to Dalston, and from the Kingsland Road on the west to London Fields, and is crowded with factories and with the residences of the artisan class. In the seventeenth century the hamlet contained only a few houses, designed for country retirement. The celebrated astronomer, Halley, was born and resided here, though the house which he occupied is not known. He died in 1741, and lies buried in the churchyard of Lee, Kent.

Nichols Square, which we pass on our left, keeps in remembrance the name of Mr. John Nichols, F.S.A., the well-known antiquary, and "the Dugdale of the present age." Mr. Nichols was the author of "Literary Anecdotes of the Eighteenth

Century," the "History of the County of Leicester," "Progresses and Processions of Queen Elizabeth," &c., and was many years editor of the *Gentleman's Magazine* in its palmy days. He was a native of the adjoining parish of Islington, where he chiefly resided. He died in 1826, and was succeeded in his property in this neighbourhood by his son, Mr. John Bowyer Nichols, who shortly afterwards became proprietor of the *Gentleman's Magazine.* This gentleman died at Ealing in 1863. The Messrs. Nichols have been for many years printers to the two Houses of Parliament.

In the north-east corner of Nichols Square stands St. Chad's Church. It is a large red-brick edifice, with an apsidal eastern end, and comprises nave and aisles, transepts, and chancel, with a dwarf spire at the intersection. The transepts are lighted by large wheel windows, and the body of the fabric by narrow Gothic pointed windows. The church was built about 1865. It is noted for its "High Church" or ritualistic services.

St. Mary's Church, in Brunswick Square, close by, was built in 1830, but considerably altered in 1862. It is of Gothic architecture, and, externally, is chiefly remarkable for the lofty tower at the western end. The organ, which was originally in St. George's Chapel, Windsor, was built by Father Smith. It has been within the last few years much enlarged by Willis.

The parish of Haggerston contains a Church Association, of which all the communicants are members, and each member is required to do some work for the cause of the Established Church.

On the west side of Brunswick Square is a row of almshouses, of neat and picturesque appearance. These almshouses, belonging to the parish of Shoreditch, were founded in 1836, and stood originally on the south side of the Hackney Road, but were rebuilt on this site on the demolition of the houses, in order to make room for the approaches to Columbia Square, &c.

Passing eastward, by the Imperial Gas-works, we arrive at Goldsmiths' Row, which, as stated above, was formerly known as Mutton Lane, a name still given to that part of the thoroughfare bordering upon the southern extremity of London Fields, where stands a noted public-house, rejoicing in the sign of the "Cat and Mutton." Affixed to the house are two sign-boards, which are rather curious; they have upon them the following doggrel lines:—

> "Pray, Puss, do not tare,
> Because the mutton is so rare."
>
> "Pray, Puss, do not claw,
> Because the Mutton is so raw."

The open space in front, known as London Fields, and extending over several acres, has within the last few years been taken in hand by the Board of Works, and has had its surface levelled, and, where necessary, sown with fresh grass; it is crossed by numerous paths, and in part planted with trees. The spot has been for ages the resort of the dwellers in the neighbourhood for the purposes of recreation, and from the neighbouring tavern and its associations had in process of time become better known as the "Cat and Mutton" fields.

Strype tells us that the Bishop of London held demesnes in Hackney as far back as the time of Edward I., in the nineteenth year of whose reign (A.D. 1290) the right of free warren in this parish was granted to Richard de Gravesend, who then held the see; and from an "inquisition" in the same reign, it is clear that a yeoman named Duckett held lands here under the bishop, who in his turn held them from the king as his superior. There are, or were, several manors within the parish of Hackney; the principal of these is termed the "Lord's-hold," and was attached to the bishopric of London until the year 1550, when it was surrendered to the Crown by Bishop Ridley, whose memory is kept up in connection with this locality by the name of Ridley, given to a roadway on the north side of Dalston Lane.

In the short thoroughfare connecting the London Fields with Goldsmiths' Row there is a shop which in bygone times was almost as much noted for its "Hackney Buns" as the well-known Bun-house at Chelsea was for that particular kind of pastry about which we have already spoken.*

Goldsmiths' Row extends from the canal bridge, near the south-west corner of London Fields, to the Hackney Road. The thoroughfare is very narrow, and in parts consists of very inferior shops and tenements. On the west side, about half way down, stand a row of almshouses belonging to the Goldsmiths' Company. They were founded in 1703, by a Mr. Morrell, for six poor almsmen belonging to the above-mentioned company, each of whom has a pension of £21 per annum. On the opposite side, near the corner of the Hackney Road, are some new buildings in connection with the North-Eastern Hospital for Sick Children, which was founded in 1867, in the Hackney Road. The new buildings were inaugurated a few years ago by the Princess Louise. The institution was established, as its name implies, for the purpose of affording medical relief to sick children; and about

* See *ante*, p. 69.

10,000 patients are annually relieved here. Patients are admitted free, on the production of a subscriber's ticket; otherwise a small fee is paid by out-patients and in-patients.

At the eastern end of Hackney Road formerly stood the Cambridge Heath turnpike gate, which was removed a few years ago, when tolls upon the metropolitan highways were abolished; its site is now marked by an obelisk set up in the centre of the roadway. From this point, Mare Street, of which we shall have more to say presently, branches off to the left; Cambridge Road, on our right, leads past the Bethnal Green Museum, and so on to the Whitechapel Road and Mile End. Prospect Place, which extends eastward from the Hackney Road, and its continuation, Bishop's Road, leads direct to the principal entrance to Victoria Park.

On the east side of Bonner's Road, which here branches off to the right, leading to Old Ford Road, stands an Orphan Asylum, or Home for outcast children; and also the City of London Hospital for Diseases of the Chest. The latter edifice is a large and well-proportioned building of red brick, consisting of a centre and wings, in the Queen Anne style, and was constructed from the designs of Mr. Ordish. It has a central campanile, and a small Gothic chapel on the north side, connected with the main building by a covered corridor. The hospital, which was opened by Prince Albert in 1848, for "the relief of indigent persons afflicted with consumption and other diseases of the chest," was first of all located in Liverpool Street, Finsbury, and by the end of the year 1849 about 900 patients were relieved. Since its removal to the neighbourhood of Victoria Park its accommodation has vastly increased, so that in the year 1883 about 800 in-patients and 15,000 out-patients had experienced the benefits of this most excellent charity. The hospital stands upon a large triangular plot of ground, surrounded by a light iron railing; and the grounds are laid out in grass plats, and flower-beds, and are well planted with shrubs and trees. Some of the latter are the remains of an avenue formerly extending from the Old Ford Lane to the principal entrance of Bonner's Hall, which stood on the east side of where the hospital now stands. The old building is traditionally said to have been the residence of Bishop Bonner, and certainly to have been his property. The surrounding land down to a comparatively recent date was known as Bishop Bonner's Fields, names which are now preserved in the two roads above mentioned. The site of Bishop Bonner's Hall was occupied by some private buildings in the early part of the present century; and Bishop Bonner's Hall Farm, a curious old-fashioned structure of plaster and brickwork, stood near what is now the western entrance to Victoria Park down to about the year 1850.

In this neighbourhood, at the time of the formation of Victoria Park, was swept away a wretched village of hovels, formerly known as "Botany Bay," from so many of its inhabitants being sent to "another place" bearing that name.

By the side of the park gates is a picturesque lodge-house of the Elizabethan character, built from the designs of Mr. Pennethorne; it is constructed chiefly of red bricks, and has a lofty tower and porch. The ground now forming Victoria Park was purchased by the Government with the proceeds of the sale of York (now Stafford) House,* St. James's, in pursuance of an Act of Parliament passed in 1840 for that purpose. It is bounded on the south-east by Sir George Duckett's Canal—a branch cut from the Regent's Canal, near Bonner's Hall Farm, crossing the Grove Road, and communicating with the river Lea, near Old Ford; on the north-east by Old Ford Lane, or Wick Lane; on the north-west by Grove Street and lands belonging to Sir John Cass's charity and to St. Thomas's Hospital; and on the west by the Regent's Canal.

Victoria Park is nearly 300 acres in extent, with avenues which one day with an ampler growth will be really superb, a lake, or chain of lakes, on which adventurous spirits daily learn to "tug the labouring oar," and such a pleasant arrangement of walks, shrubberies, green turf, gay flowers, and shady trees, that if the place were situated in the western suburbs, it would, perhaps, become the resort of the *élite* of fashion. On an island upon one of the lakes is a two-storeyed Chinese pagoda, which, with the trees and foliage surrounding it, has a pretty effect. Here, as in the West-end parks, floriculture has been greatly extended of late; and through the summer months, its variegated parterres are aglow with flowers of every hue, making altogether a glorious show. Among the large foliage plants which have found their way here, may be remarked, on one sheltered slope, a group of *Ficus elastica*, the india-rubber tree, and close by is a specimen of the *Yucca gloriosa*, which has the more popular name of "Adam's needle," the tradition probably being that one of its pointed leaves helped to make the fig-leaf apron. Tropical plants of different varieties are to be found in the snug nooks and recesses which abound here. As to the flowering plants, such as the geranium, calceolaria, verbena, lobelia, &c., reliance is placed

* See Vol. IV., p. 122.

chiefly upon masses of colour instead of the narrow bands adopted in the other parks. In the Regent's Park, as we have already seen,* great skill has been shown in grouping and composition; there is an attempt in landscape-gardening at something of the effects of landscape painting, using Nature's own colours, with the ground for canvas. In Hyde Park the red line of geraniums between Stanhope Gate and Grosvenor Gate is as well known among gardeners as the "thin red line" at Balaclava among soldiers. But in Victoria Park the old gardening tactics prevail; for the most part, masses of colour are brought to bear upon the eye in oval, round, and square; and with a wide area of turf in which to manœuvre our floral forces, these tactics are probably the most effective that could be adopted. More ingenious designs, however, are not wanting. Near the ornamental water, a pretty effect is produced by scrolls of purple verbena enclosed by the white-leaved *Cerastium tomentosum*, looking like amethysts set in silver. In another part of the park this design is reversed, and the blue lobelia is made a frame for a central pattern of the same delicate silvery foliage plant, lit up by an occasional patch of scarlet, with a background of dahlias and evergreens. Elsewhere we come upon a fanciful figure which, after some study, resolves itself into an outstretched butterfly of enormous size, with wings as vividly coloured as those of any that fly in the sun. For borderings the *Amaranthus melancholicus* and the usual foliage plants of small growth are employed.

In fine weather, when the band plays, over 100,000 persons are frequently collected in this park. The people are orderly, most of them being of the humbler class, and their appreciation of the flowers is quite as keen as that of the frequenters of the West-end parks. Some of the dwellers in the East-end have a great fondness for flowers, and contrive somehow or other, in the most unlikely places, to rear very choice varieties. In small, wretched-looking yards, where little air and only the mid-day sun can penetrate, may be seen patches of garden, evidently tended with uncommon care, and yielding to their cultivators a fair reward in fragrance and in blossom. In some places may be descried bits of broken glass and a framework which just holds together, doing duty as a greenhouse; and in this triumph of patience and ingenuity the poor artisan spends much of his leisure, happy when he can make up a birthday bouquet for some friend or relation. The flowers in the neighbouring park, with their novel grouping and striking contrasts of colour, are, of course, a continual source of pleasure for these struggling artisans, and gladden many a moment when, perhaps, work is not too plentiful, and home thoughts are not very happy. In Victoria Park the plants and flowers are labelled in letters which he who walks may read without need of getting over fence or bordering. This is not always the case in the other parks, where the labels, from dirt or the smallness of the characters, are often practically illegible. One of the lakes is devoted to miniature yacht sailing. This amusement seems almost confined to East London; and here on a summer evening, when a capful of wind is to be had, the surface of the lake is whitened by some forty or fifty toy boats and yachts, of all rigs and sizes, while here and there a miniature steamboat is puffing and panting. There is even a yacht-club, whose members compete with their toy-yachts for silver cups and other prizes. The expense of keeping up a yacht here is not considerable, and the whole squadron may be laid up until wanted in a boat-house provided for the purpose. But the matches and trials of these tiny crafts are a special attraction of the park, and draw together every evening hundreds of people. Bathing, too, is largely indulged in during the summer. Ample space is available for cricket, and in the two gymnasia candidates for swinging, jumping, and climbing appear to be never wanting.

In one open part of the grounds stands a very handsome drinking-fountain, surrounded by parterres of flowers. It was erected by Lady Burdett-Coutts, whose care for the social welfare of the poor of London, and particularly in the East-end districts, we have already had occasion to mention. In the part devoted to cricket and such like sports, some of the semi octagonal recesses, which afforded shelter for foot-passengers on old Westminster Bridge,† have been re-erected, and serve as alcoves.

On the north side of Victoria Park is a large plot of ground, which since the end of the last century has been used as a burial-place for the Jewish community, belonging to the Hamburg synagogue.

Making our way through Grove Street, we reach the south-west corner of Hackney Common. Close by this point stands the French Hospital, a large and ornamental building of dark red brick, with stone dressings, which presents a pleasing contrast to the foliage of the trees which surround it. The institution was established as far back as 1708, for

* See *ante*, p. 266.

† See Vol. III., p. 299.

the "support of poor French Protestants and their descendants."

A short walk through Lammas Road and Groombridge Road, which skirt the western side of the Common, brings us to Grove Street, by the end of King Edward Road, where stands the large and handsome church of St. John of Jerusalem, the parish church of the recently-formed district of South Hackney. The church, which is built of Kentish rag-stone, is in the best Pointed style of the thirteenth and fourteenth centuries, and was erected in 1846 from the designs of Mr. E. C. Hakewell, to supersede a church erected in Well Street early in the present century. The plan of the edifice is cruciform, with a tower and spire of equal height, together rising nearly 200 feet; the latter has graceful lights and broaches, and the four Evangelists beneath canopies at the four angles. The nave has side aisles, with flying buttresses to the clerestory; each transept is lit by a magnificent window, about thirty feet high, and the choir has an apse with seven lancet windows. The principal entrance, at the western end, is through a screen of open arches. The roof, of open work, is very lofty, and has massive arched and foliated ribs; the chancel has a stone roof, and the walls of the apse are painted and diapered—red with fleur-de-lis, and blue powdered with stars. All the windows are filled with painted, stained, or richly-diapered glass. The tower has a fine peal of eight bells.

HACKNEY, LOOKING TOWARDS THE CHURCH, 1840.

Before proceeding with a description of the old town of Hackney, upon which we are now entering, we may remark that it has been suggested, and with considerable probability, that the name of the place is derived from "Hacon's ey," or the island which some Danish chief named Hacon had, in the mild method prevalent among the warriors of fifteen hundred years ago, appropriated to himself. But authentic history is silent upon the point; and, indeed, almost the earliest record we find of the place is that the Knights Templars held the manor, which afterwards became the property of their rivals, the Knights of St. John of Jerusalem. Of late years the parish has been styled by the name of St. John at Hackney, as though it belonged to the fraternity of the Knights of St. John of Jerusalem, who had, as it is said, a mansion and other possessions in the parish; but from ancient records preserved in the Tower

BITS OF OLD HACKNEY.

1 Brook House, 1765. 2 Barber's Barn, 1750. 3. Shore Place, 1730.

of London it is found to be written, *Ecclesia Parochialis S. Augustini de Hackney*. The Temple Mills, in Hackney Marshes, even now preserve the memory of the priestly warriors of the Templar order.

In the reign of Henry III., when the first mention of the place occurs as a village, it is called Hackenaye, and Hacquenye; and in a patent of Edward IV., granting the manors of Stepney and Hackney to Thomas Lord Wentworth, it is styled Hackeney, otherwise Hackney. "The parish, no doubt," says Dr. Robinson, "derived its appellation from circumstances of no common nature, but what they were it is at this time difficult to conjecture; and no one will venture to assert that it received its name from the Teutonic or Welsh language, as some have supposed."

We may conclude this chapter by remarking that Dr. Robinson, in his "History and Antiquities of Hackney," describes it as an ancient, extensive, and populous village, "situated on the west side of the river Lea, about two miles and a half from the City of London, within the division of the Tower Hamlets, in the hundred of Ossulston, in the county of Middlesex." "In former times," he adds, "many noblemen, gentlemen, and others, of the first rank and consequence, had their country seats in this village, on account of its pleasant and healthy situation." In the parish of Hackney are comprised the nominal hamlets of Clapton (Upper and Lower), Homerton, Dalston, Shacklewell, the greater part of Kingsland, and that part of Stoke Newington which lies on the eastern side of the high road to Tottenham; but modern Hackney, considered as an assemblage of dwellings, is quite united to Homerton and Lower Clapton, on the east and north, and also by rows of buildings on the west to the parish of St. Leonard, Shoreditch.

CHAPTER XLI.

THE NORTH-EASTERN SUBURBS.—HACKNEY (*continued*).

"I had a parcel of as honest religious girls about me as ever pious matron had under her tuition at a Hackney boarding-school."
Tom Brown: Madam Cresswell to Moll Quarles.

Hackney in the Last Century—Its Gradual Growth—Well Street—Hackney College—Monger's Almshouses—The Residence of Dr. Frampton—St. John's Priory—St. John's Church—Mare Street—Hackney a Great Centre of Nonconformity—The Roman Catholic Church of St. John the Baptist—The "Flying Horse" Tavern—Elizabeth Fry's Refuge—Dr. Spurstowe's Almshouses—Hackney Town Hall—The New Line of the Great Eastern Railway—John Milton's Visits to Hackney—Barber's Barn—Loddidge's Nursery—Watercress-beds—The Gravel-pit Meeting House—The Church House—The Parish Church—The "Three Cranes"—The Old Church Tower—The Churchyard—The New Church of St. John—The Black and White House—Boarding Schools for Young Ladies—Sutton Place—The "Mermaid" Tavern—"Ward's Corner"—The Templars' House—Brooke House—Noted Residents at Hackney—Homerton—The City of London Union—Lower Clapton—John Howard, the Prison Reformer—The London Orphan Asylum—Salvation Army Barracks and Congress Hall—The Asylum for Deaf and Dumb Females—Concluding Remarks on Hackney.

In treating of this parish we have no Pepys or Boswell to guide or interest us, and to gossip with us over this neighbourhood, and to furnish us with stores of anecdote; but, fortunately, we have the assistance of Strype, who, in his edition of Stow's "London," includes Hackney in his "Circuit Walk on the North of London." He styles it a "pleasant and healthful town, where divers nobles in former times had their country seats," enumerating among its residents an Earl of Northumberland, a Countess of Warwick, and a Lord Brooke. Still, the houses and their walks, for the most part, have no stories connected with them, *carent quia vate sacro*, and the whole district supplies us but scanty materials, historical, topographical, and biographical, as compared with St. Pancras or Hampstead.

Hackney is described in the "Ambulator," in 1774, as "a very large and populous village, on the north of London, inhabited by such numbers of merchants and wealthy persons, that it is said there are near a hundred gentlemen's coaches kept." The writer enumerates its several hamlets, viz., "Clapton on the north, Dorleston [Dalston] and Shacklewell on the west; and on the east, Homerton, leading to Hackney Marshes."

There is still an old-fashioned air about Hackney itself; but Dalston has thrown out lines of commonplace villas across the fields and orchards on the south-west; Clapton has developed itself on the north; Victoria Park has initiated a new town on the south; a busy railway station stands near the tower of the old church, of which we shall speak presently; and down in the Marshes are now large hives of manufacturing industry.

The town (if considered independently of its hamlets), down to a comparatively recent date, consisted chiefly of four streets, termed Church Street, Mare (or Meare) Street, Grove Street, and Well Street; but such has been the growth of the place during the past half century that large numbers of other streets and terraces have sprung up in all directions, on land which hitherto had served as the gardens attached to the mansions of the nobility and City merchants, or as nursery grounds, market gardens, and even watercress-beds. The population of Hackney, too, which at the commencement of this century was about equal to that of a good-sized country village, had, according to the census returns for 1881, reached something like 400,000; and the place, since 1868, has enjoyed the privilege of Parliamentary representation.

From Grove Street, incidentally mentioned near the close of the preceding chapter, we pass into Well Street, which winds somewhat circuitously to the west, where it unites with Mare Street. Hackney College, which we notice on our left immediately on entering Well Street, was founded in 1803 with the object of preparing students for the Congregational ministry, and of granting votes in support of chapels. The average number of students in the college is about twenty, and the annual receipts about £1,500. At the close of the last century there was a college for Dissenters established at Lower Clapton, to which Dr. Rees, Dr. Priestley, and his scarcely less renowned Unitarian coadjutor, Mr. Belsham, and Gilbert Wakefield were attached; but it was broken up in 1797, owing to the bad conduct of some of the students. The well-known college at Homerton was established about the latter part of the seventeenth century. Dr. Pye Smith, the great geologist, whose conclusions anticipated some of the views of Mr. Goodwin in his "Mosaic Cosmogony," was for many years the principal of the seminary; and many eminent ministers of the Nonconformist bodies there received their education.

In Well Street are almshouses for six aged and poor men, founded by Henry Monger in 1669.

Farther on, on the right, a large old-fashioned mansion may be observed, although it is now cut up into tenements, and the lower part converted into shops. This was once the residence of the celebrated Dr. Frampton, whose memory is preserved in the locality in the name of Frampton Park Road.

The residence of the Knights of St. John existed till a very recent period, under the name of the Priory, in Well Street. In 1352 the Prior of St. John disposed of the mansion, then called Beaulieu, to John Blaunch and Nicholas Shordych. In Stow's time it bore the name of Shoreditch Place,* since shortened into Shore Place and Shore Road. The Priory, within the memory of the present generation, was a strange-looking brick building, divided into small tenements, and inhabited by chimney-sweeps and others of kindred calling.

A chapel of ease, dedicated to St. John, in this street, was consecrated in 1810 by Bishop Randolph, and endowed as a district parish church for South Hackney. In 1846 it was superseded by the new parish church, which we have already described.

Mare Street, as we have already stated, commences at the eastern end of the Hackney Road, and forms the main thoroughfare through the centre of the town. Throughout its entire length it is well sprinkled with the remains of dwellings of the wealthy classes of society, who formerly inhabited this now unfashionable quarter of London. Here, too, the number of religious edifices, of all denominations, is somewhat remarkable, and in some cases the buildings are fine specimens of ecclesiastical architecture.

Hackney has altogether upwards of twenty places of worship for Dissenters; it has, in fact, long been renowned as a great centre of Nonconformity, and some eminent Dissenting divines have preached there. Dr. Bates, the learned author of the "Harmony of the Divine Attributes," died there in 1679. Matthew Henry, the compiler of the well-known "Commentary" on the Bible, preached at Hackney between 1710 and 1714. Robert Fleming, the author of "The Rise and Fall of the Papacy," died at Hackney on the 24th of May, 1716. His prophecies were believed to have been fulfilled in 1794; and in 1848, when a second revolution occurred in Paris, Fleming's book was eagerly sought for, and reprinted, and read by thousands.

The Presbyterian Dissenters' Chapel was established in this street early in the seventeenth century. Here Philip Nye and Adoniram Byfield, two eminent Puritan divines, preached in 1636. The old meeting-house has been taken down, and a new one built on the opposite side of the street, and occupied by Independents.

On the east side of Mare Street, near King Edward Road, stands the Roman Catholic Church of St. John the Baptist, which was built about the year 1848, from the designs of Mr. Wardell. It is built in the decorated Gothic style, and comprises nave, chancel, aisles, and sacristy. The rood-screen and altar are elaborately carved, and some of the windows are filled with painted glass. In 1856 a brass plate was placed in the chancel, over the grave of the founder and first rector, the Rev. J. Leucona, who died in 1855. Mr. Leucona was a Spanish Catholic missionary, and the author of a

* See Vol. II., p. 194.

few published works, among them a pamphlet in reply to some of the writings of Dr. Pusey.

On the west side of this street, near the narrow lane leading into London Fields, stands a very old public-house, bearing the sign of the "Flying Horse." It is a large, rambling house, of two storeys, and consists of a centre and two wings. It is traditionally said to have been one of the old posting-houses of the time of "Queen Bess," on the old road to Cambridge and Newmarket.

Farther to the north, one of a row of old mansions with small gardens before them, has a large board displayed upon its front inscribed with the words "Elizabeth Fry's Refuge." This institution was founded in the year 1849, for the purpose of providing temporary homes for female criminals on their release from prison.

Hackney has always been remarkable for the number of its charitable institutions: besides those which we have already mentioned, and others which we have still to notice, are some almshouses for widows near Mare Street, founded by Dr. Spurstowe, who died in the reign of Charles II.

The Town Hall, which stands in The Grove, is a modern structure, having been erected only a few years ago to supersede an older and less commodious building farther on, near the old parish church. The edifice, with its noble portico, and its ample supply of windows—for, like Hardwick Hall, it might almost be said to have "more windows than wall"—presents a striking contrast to many of the quaint old buildings which surround it. Notwithstanding the grand appearance of the building externally, and the thousands of pounds spent in its erection, the interior does not seem to have given that satisfaction to the parishioners which they were led to expect, and the accommodation, or rather, the want of accommodation in some of the rooms which the edifice affords, was such as to serve as a bone of contention among them for some considerable time after its erection.

Running parallel with Mare Street, on the west side, and overlooking the London Fields, is the new line of the Great Eastern Railway, from which, at the Hackney Downs station, a line branches off on the left to Enfield. In the construction of this railway several old houses were swept away, among them an ancient mansion which had long been used as a private lunatic asylum, and another which, with its gardens, covered a large space of ground, and was formerly used as a hospital by the Honourable East India Company.

To the Tower House, at the corner of London Lane, which connects Mare Street with London Fields and the railway station, often came an illustrious Parliamentarian, no other than John Milton; for there he wooed his second wife, the daughter of Captain Woodcock, who lived here.

On the east side of Mare Street, and covering the ground now occupied by St. Thomas's Place, once stood an ancient edifice known as Barber's Barn, or Barbour Berns, which dated from about the end of the sixteenth century. It was in the Elizabethan style of architecture, with pediments, bay-windows, and an entrance porch, and contained numerous rooms. It is said to have been the residence of John Okey, the regicide. He is reported to have been originally a drayman and stoker in a brewery at Islington, but having entered the Parliamentary army, to have risen to become one of Cromwell's generals. He sat in judgment on Charles I., and was the sixth who signed the warrant for the king's execution. About the middle of the last century Barber's Barn, with its grounds and some adjoining land, passed into the possession of one John Busch, who formed a large nursery ground on the estate. Mr. Loudon, in his *Gardeners' Magazine*, says that Catharine II., Empress of Russia, "finding that she could have nothing done to her mind, determined to have a person from England to lay out her garden." Busch was the person engaged to go out to Russia for this purpose. In 1771 he disposed of his nursery at Hackney to Messrs. Loddige, who ranked with the most eminent florists and nurserymen of their time. Indeed, the name of the Loddige family has been known for nearly a century in the horticultural and botanical world; and few persons who take an interest in gardening and flowers can fail to recognise the names of Conrad Loddige and his sons, of Hackney, as the authors of the "Botanical Cabinet," published in twenty large quarto volumes during the Regency and the subsequent reign of George IV. They had here extensive greenhouses, and also hothouses which were heated by steam. The ancient house having become the property of Mr. Conrad Loddige, was taken down many years ago, and Loddige's Terrace, together with some residences called St. Thomas's Place, were built on its site. A few houses in Well Street occupy the other portion of the former gardens.

In 1787 Mr. Loddige removed from what was called Busch's Nursery, and formed another nursery on some grounds which he purchased from the governors of St. Thomas's Hospital; these grounds had until then been open fields, and he enclosed them towards the north with a brick wall. The last vestiges of Loddige's gardens disappeared about the year 1860, when some of the plants were transferred to the Crystal Palace at Sydenham.

Hackney, it may be added, was celebrated till a comparatively recent date for its market gardens, and even for its watercress beds. A large watercress garden was in existence until 1860, and perhaps even more recently, only a few yards to the south of the North London Railway Station.

In Paradise Place, at the end of Paragon Road, stands the New Gravel-pit Meeting House, "Sacred to One God the Father." The chapel was built on what was formerly Paradise Fields. The old Gravel-pit Meeting House, where Dr. Price and Dr. Priestley were formerly ministers, and which dates its erection from the early part of the last century, stands at a short distance to the east. Dr. Priestley preached his farewell sermon in the old chapel in 1794, previous to his departure for America.

At a short distance northward from the new Town Hall, Mare Street is spanned by the North London Railway. Near this spot, on the east side of the street, and close by the entrance to the churchyard, was standing, in Lysons' time or at the end of the last century, an ancient building, thus described in the chantry-roll at the Augmentation Office, which bears date the first year of the reign of Edward I.:—"A tenement buylded by the parishioners, called the Churche Howse, that they might mete together and comen of matters as well for the kyng's business as for the churche and parishe, worth 20s. per an." It appeared by an inscription, remaining on the front towards the street, that it was built in the year 1520, when Christopher Urswick was rector. The house was for many years, in the last century, used as a free school, but in its latter years it seems to have reverted again to its original purpose. The site was afterwards occupied by a more modern Town Hall, which is still standing, but which, as we have already seen, has since been superseded by the new building in Mare Street.

If we may follow the statements of Stow and Strype, Hackney was, as far back as the close of the thirteenth century, a distinct parish, with a rector and also a vicar, and a church dedicated to St. Augustine; but the Knights of St. John of Jerusalem having obtained possession of a mill and other possessions in the parish formerly held by the Knights Templars, the appellation of the church came to be changed from St. Augustine to St. John. In the reign of Edward III. this church, in lieu of that of Bishop's Stortford, in Hertfordshire, was annexed to the precentorship of St. Paul's Cathedral. In confirmation of the assertion that the church was dedicated to St. Augustine, it may be added that a statue of that saint, erected in it as lately as the reign of Henry VIII., is mentioned in the will of Christopher Urswick, rector, and also Dean of Windsor.

This old church, then, of which the tower alone now remains, though dedicated to St. Augustine, has for many years been known as St. John's Church. Newport, in his "Repertorium," speaking of Hackney Church, says:—"The church has of late years gone by the name of St. John of Jerusalem at Hackney, as if dedicated to St. John, which I take to be a mistake; because I find that Arthur Wood, in December, 1509, instituted to the vicarage of St. Augustin at Hackney—to which saint, I rather believe, that church had been dedicated—no presentation having been made by the name of St. John of Jerusalem at Hackney till after the restoration of King Charles II. One — Heron, Esq., is taken by some to be the founder of it, by his arms engraven upon every pillar, which is a *chevron ermine between three herons;* but I rather think that he was a very great benefactor to the new building or repairing of the church, for which reason his arms (are) upon every pillar; and in the north aisle thereof, in a tomb of white freestone, without any inscription, his body lies."

In the Cottonian Library there is a volume relating to the Knights Templars, in which mention is made of St. Augustine's at Hackney, and of the lands and rents there which belonged to that order, including a mill which was known as Temple Mill. It appears that these, after the suppression of the Templar order, passed into the hands of the Knights of St. John, whose influence in and upon the parish was so great, that the very dedication of the church to St. Augustine was forgotten.

There is in the Tower records a patent or licence to one Henry Sharp, the "parson" of St. Augustine's at Hackney, to erect in his church a "Guild of the Holy Trinity and of the Glorious Virgin Mary;" in whose honour, therefore, doubtless a light was kept constantly burning before an altar in an aisle or side chapel. This guild, or "perpetual fraternity," was to consist of "two guardians or brethren, and sisters, of the same parish, and of others who, from their devotion, will be of the same fraternity."

It is impossible to fix the date of erection of the *first* church of St. Augustine at Hackney. It appears to have been taken down and rebuilt in the early part of the sixteenth century; and "it is probable," says Dr. Robinson, in his "History of Hackney," "that Sir Thomas Heron, who was master of the jewel house to King Henry VIII., and Christopher Urswick (then rector) were the principal benefactors to its re-erection; for besides the arms above-mentioned, the same arms occurred on one side of the chancel window, and on the other side the arms of Urswick." The conjecture that some member of the Heron family had at least something to do with the rebuilding of the fabric, receives a certain amount of support or confirmation from a tradition that the house called the "Three Cranes," nearly opposite, was the first public-house in the parish, and that it was built for the accommodation of the workmen whilst they were erecting the church: it is said to have had originally the sign of "The Herons." The ancient church of St. Augustine was taken down towards the close of the last century, except the old tower, which, as we have stated, still remains. It is of Gothic architecture, and contains a peal of eight bells. From an account of the old church printed in the *Gentleman's Magazine* for April, 1796, we learn that its exterior, in its latter days, was "an incomprehensible jumble of dissonant repairs, without a trace of the original building remaining, except the windows of part of it." There were two side aisles, and the pillars, twelve in number, are described as being "remarkably strong, good, and well-proportioned, and the arches pointed." The galleries, of which there were several, seem to have been erected at different periods, and did not reach, as is usual, from one end to the other of the church, nor extend to the pillars which divided the aisles; and one of the galleries appeared as if it "were hung to the roof by iron hooks." Along the frieze of the organ gallery there was an inscription, setting forth that the church was repaired in 1720; and above, in the panels, were three pictures, "drawn with much taste and freedom in black and white, though very slight;" the subjects were, the Miraculous Draught of Fishes, Christ in the Storm at Sea, and Elijah fed by Ravens.

HACKNEY CHURCH, 1750.

A view of the old church, taken in 1806, shortly before its removal, will be found in a work on the suburbs of London, entitled, "Ecclesiastical Topography," published in 1811, anonymously. The writer describes it as having been a large irregular building, with few traces remaining of the original structure, except the windows; and, to do the writer justice, it must be owned that never was a fine mediæval church more ruthlessly and tastelessly perverted into a chaos of confusion. "The nave and the tower," he adds, "may probably be referred to the middle of the fourteenth century. The sepulchral inscriptions were extremely numerous, but fortunately most of these are preserved in Strype's additions to Stow, and others in Weever's 'Funeral Monuments,' and in Lysons' 'Environs of London.'"

The parish of Hackney in former times had among its vicars many men who attained some eminence in the ecclesiastical world. Among them were Cardinal Gauselinus, who flourished about 1320; David Doulben, afterwards Bishop of Bangor; Gilbert Sheldon, afterwards Archbishop of Canterbury; and William Spurstowe, a well-known divine among the Nonconformists, and mentioned in the well-known definition of the name "Smectymnus."

"If any are ignorant who this Smectymnus is,
*S*tephen *M*arshall,
*E*dmund *C*alamy,
*T*homas *Y*oung, } can tell you."
*M*atthew *N*ewcomen,
*W*illiam *S*purstowe,

The old church, before its demolition, was extremely rich in monuments and brasses, most of which have now altogether disappeared, whilst some few have been preserved and fixed against the new church of St. John. Among many other members of the nobility buried here were Henry Lord Percy, Earl of Northumberland, who died in this town in 1537, and of whom we shall have more to say presently. The funeral service over his remains was performed by the Bishop of St. Asaph and the Abbot of Stratford.

Alice Ryder, who died in 1517, was commemorated by her "portraiture in brass, with a milk-pail upon her head." She appears to have been a milkwoman, who, having obtained great wealth by selling milk in the City, was a great benefactress to the church. The following was her epitaph:—

"For the Sowl of Alice Ryder, of your Charite,
Say a Pater-noster, and an Ave . . . 1517."

Besides the tower mentioned above, the Rowe Chapel, which was built in the reign of James I., and attached to the south side of the church, also remained after the demolition of the body of the fabric, and is still standing. This chapel or mausoleum was founded by Sir Henry Rowe, of Shacklewell, as a place of interment for his family. The Rowes possessed some property at Muswell Hill, in the parish of Hornsey, and the family became extinct in the male line in the person of Anthony Rowe, of Muswell Hill, who was buried

THE BLACK AND WHITE HOUSE, 1800. (*See page* 519.)

here in 1704. He left some daughters, co-heirs, one of whom married an ancestor of the Marquis of Downshire, in the possession of whose descendants the Rowe Chapel has continued. Among the freeholders of Hackney, the Marquis of Downshire is mentioned as possessing "a freehold, fifteen feet square, in the old church yard;" this refers, of course, to the above-mentioned burial-place of the Rowes, and it is added that it "descended to the marquis as an heir-loom." A monument against the interior south wall of the mausoleum is inscribed with the following quaint epitaph :—

"Here (under fine of Adam's first defection)
Rests in hope of happie resurrection,
Sir Henry Rowe (sonne of Sir Thomas Rowe,
And of Dame Mary, his deare yoke-fellowe,
Knight and right worthy), as his father late
Lord Maior of London, with his vertuous Mate
Dame Susan (his twice fifteen yeres and seeven),
Their issue five (surviving of eleven),
Four named here, in these four names forepast,
The fifth is found, if eccho sound the last,
Sad Orphanes all, but most their heir (most debtor)
Who built them this, but in his heart a better.
Quam pie obiit Anno Salutis 1612
die Novembris 12, Ætatis 68."

It is worthy of mention that John Strype, the antiquary, to whom we owe so much of the retrospective portions of this work, was lecturer at this church for thirty-six years, and died in 1737, at the great age of ninety-four.

The reason why the tower of the old church was permitted to remain was that the eight bells were believed to be too heavy for the tower of the new building; and as the parishioners were unwilling to lose their peal, it was decided that they should retain their original position, but some years later they were moved to the new church, where they still remain. So there stand the weather-beaten old tower and the little Rowe Chapel, a few paces farther to the east, amidst the graves of the ancient inhabitants of Hackney, among which a winding path leads to the more modern church, in which are preserved some of the tombs and carved work of the older edifice. It is recorded that on the 27th of September, 1731, a sailor slid down on a rope from the top of the church steeple, with a streamer in each hand.

The old burial-ground has many walks through it, most of which are public thoroughfares, and occupied by the hurrying and thoughtless passengers. "Its numerous paths, all concentrating towards the sacred edifice," says Dr. Robinson, writing about forty years ago, "are lined with lofty trees, and in the summer season the vastly peopled city of the dead seems one beautiful verdant canopy stretching over the peaceful ashes of the 'forefathers of the hamlet.' Great taste has been displayed in planting Hackney churchyard with so many fine trees, but amongst them the yew-tree, with its sombre foliage, is nowhere to be found. Every visitor to this burial-ground must be struck with the curious and solitary appearance of the old square grey tower, rearing its lofty walls, a singular relic of the ancient church of which nothing but this building now remains. We can only guess at the edifice, which must, in times long since passed away, have extended its aisles and raised its sacred oriel for the devotions of our ancestors. The marble tombs which once must have filled the edifice with 'hoar antiquity,' and the 'storied urn and animated bust,' which once told of the honoured dead, seem all swept away by the hand of oblivion—obscuring the humble and the great—yet Time, as if willing to spare us some resemblance of the older days, left only this old grey tower, as a conspicuous monument, which, by its lonely desolation, tells so forcibly of the terrible power which, by one fell swoop, has eradicated all besides. The bells whose music once cheered or soothed the ears of those who have now for some centuries slept the sleep of death around its enduring walls, still remain and retain their vigorous tones in the same elevated chamber where they have swung from the time of our Edwards and Henries. This tower must have sent forth its loud clamorous notes in the passing of many a royal progress, when banners and knights and ladies gay, 'in purple and pall,' have circled past, or when the proud and mitred abbot, with princely train, passed to and fro from his princely abbey."

The new church of St. John, which stands at a short distance to the north-east of the old tower, was built at the close of the last century, and is constructed chiefly of brick, in the "late classical" style of architecture. The plan, though pretending to be cruciform, is really an unsightly square; the projecting face of the elevation of each front is finished by a triangular pediment, the cornice of which receives and terminates the covering of the roof. There are five entrances, each of which opens to a spacious vestibule, like that of a theatre or a town-hall. The principal entrance is on the north, and is protected by a semi-circular Ionic portico of Portland stone. The interior of the church is plain and utterly unecclesiastical, and is surmounted by a vaulted and stuccoed ceiling—certainly no improvement on the structure which it was built to supersede. Some of the windows are enriched with coloured glass, and that over the communion-table is painted with a design illustrative of the Scriptural verse, "Let there be light," &c.

Near the church, on the west side, formerly stood an ancient mansion called the "Black and White House." It appears to have been built in the year 1578 by a citizen of London, whose arms, with those of the Merchant Adventurers and the Russian Company, appeared over the chimney in one of the principal rooms, and also in the windows of the great parlour; other armorial bearings also occurred in some of the windows. In the seventeenth century the house was the residence of the Vyner family, and the building was enlarged and considerably repaired in 1662 by Sir Thomas Vyner. At the close of the last century, when it was pulled down, it had been for many years used as a boarding-school for girls.

Hackney in former times seems to have been noted for its boarding-schools for young ladies. In the *Tatler*, No. 83, there is this reference to them:—"For the publication of this discourse, I wait only for subscriptions from the undergraduates of each university, and the young ladies in the boarding-schools at Hackney." Again, "Don Diego," in Wycherly's *Gentleman's Dancing Master*, makes this remark:—"If she be not married to-morrow (which I am to consider of), she will dance a corant in twice or thrice teaching more; will she not? for 'tis but a twelvemonth since she came from Hackney School." Shadwell also, in *The Humourists*, makes "Striker" (a haberdasher's wife) give vent to the following ejaculation:—"Good, Mistress Gig-em-bob! your breeding! ha! I am sure my husband married me from Hackney School, where there was a number of substantial citizens' daughters. Your breeding!" These three quotations we owe to Mr. Peter Cunningham.

At Hackney Downs are large Middle Class Schools founded by the Grocer's Company under the sanction of the Charity Commissioners.

Sutton Place, on the south-east side of the churchyard, reminds us of a great and good man, whose latter days were passed at Hackney; for at his house here died, on the 12th of December, 1611, Thomas Sutton, the worthy and benevolent founder of the hospital and school of the Charterhouse, of whom we have already spoken at some length in a previous part of this work.*

Close by the "Three Cranes," in Mare Street, stood, till recently, another ancient hostelry, called the "Mermaid," which in its time was noted for its tea-gardens and its assembly-room. Modern shops have now taken the place of the old tavern, and its gardens have been covered with rows of private houses.

* See Vol. II., p. 303—0.

At the upper end of Mare Street, close by Dalston Lane, in a large house which remained standing till comparatively recently, and known as "Ward's Corner," lived in the last century a man who was noted for his great wealth and insatiable avarice—the famous and infamous John Ward, member of Parliament, pilloried to all posterity in two stinging lines by Pope, who linked him with the infamous Colonel Francis Chartres, and a kindred worthy, Waters:—

> "Given to the fool, the mad, the vain, the evil,
> To Ward, to Waters, Chartres, and the devil."

John Ward was prosecuted by the Duchess of Buckingham for forgery, and being convicted, expelled the House of Commons, and stood in the pillory in March, 1727. He was suspected of joining in a conveyance with Sir John Blunt to secrete £50,000 of that director's estate, forfeited to the South Sea Company by Act of Parliament. The company recovered the £50,000 against Ward; but he set up prior conveyances of his real estate to his brother and son, and concealed all his personal, which was computed to be £150,000. These conveyances being also set aside by a bill in Chancery, Ward was imprisoned, and amused himself in confinement by giving poison to cats and dogs, in order that he might watch their dying agonies. To sum up the worth of this gentleman at the several eras of his life: at his standing in the pillory he was worth above £200,000; at his commitment to prison he was worth £150,000; but has been so far diminished in his reputation as to be thought a worse man by fifty or sixty thousand. After his death, a most characteristic prayer was found among his papers. The old sinner did not pray for forgiveness of his sins, but in this fashion:—"O Lord, Thou knowest I have nine estates in the City of London, and likewise that I have lately purchased an estate in fee-simple in the county of Essex. I beseech Thee to preserve the two counties of Middlesex and Essex from fire and earthquake; and as I have a mortgage in Hertfordshire, I beg of Thee likewise to have an eye of compassion on that county; and for the rest of the counties Thou mayest deal with them as Thou art pleased." He then prays for the bank, that his debtors may be all good men; and for the death of a profligate young man, whose reversion he had bought—"as Thou hast said the days of the wicked are but short"—against thieves, and for honest servants.

Tradition says that an old building close by the spot, nearly opposite Dalston Lane, which was not completely pulled down till 1825, was the Templars' House. It may have occupied the site, but could scarcely have been the identical edifice; for it was built with projecting bays, in what is called the Renaissance style. About the middle of the last century it was a public-house, the "Blue Posts;" afterwards it was known as "Bob's Hall," and the road between the churchyard and Clapton Square was styled Bob's Hall Lane.

On the south side of the road to Clapton formerly stood a mansion called "Brooke House," and at one time the "King's House," the manor-house of the manor termed King's Hold. It is said to have belonged originally to the Knights Templars; and after the dissolution of the order to have been granted, in common with other possessions, to the monastery of St. John of Jerusalem. On the dissolution of the latter order the estate appears to have been granted to Henry, Earl of Northumberland, who possibly died here, since he was buried, as we have seen, at Hackney. This earl was the person employed, in conjunction with Sir Walter Walsh, to arrest Cardinal Wolsey at his house at Cawood. He had, as every reader of English history knows, been, in his youthful days, a lover of Anne Boleyn (then one of the maids of honour to Queen Catherine), but withdrew his suit in consequence of the interference of his father, who had been purposely made acquainted with the king's partiality to that lady. When the inconstant monarch's affection for Anne Boleyn (then his queen) began to decline, a supposed pre-contract with the Earl of Northumberland was made the pretence for a divorce, though the earl, in a letter to Secretary Cromwell (dated Newington Green, May 13th, 1537), denied the existence of any such contract in the most solemn manner. "Henry, Earl of Northumberland, died," says the account of his funeral in the Heralds' College, "at his manor of Hackney, now the King's House, between two and three in the morning, on the 29th of June, 1537; 29 Hen. VIII." The earl, as we have stated above, was buried in the old church close by. The estate afterwards reverted to the Crown, and was granted by Edward VI., in 1547, to William Herbert, Earl of Pembroke. The house occupied by Lord Pembroke is described in the particulars for the grant of the manor, as "a fayre house, all of brick, with a fayre hall and parlour, a large gallery, a proper chapel, and a proper gallery to laye books in," &c. It is also stated to be "situated near the London road," and to be "enclosed on the back side with a great and broad ditch."

A few years later it was purchased by Sir Henry Carey, Lord Hunsdon, who again conveyed it, in 1583, to Sir Rowland Hayward. It was subsequently possessed by Fulke Greville (afterwards Lord Brooke) and by Sir George Vyner. Under date of May 8, 1654, John Evelyn, in his "Diary," gives us the following note of a visit he paid to this place:—"I went to Hackney," he writes, "to see my Lady Brooke's garden, which was one of the neatest and most celebrated in England; the house well furnish'd, but a despicable building."

At the end of the seventeenth century this manor became part of the Tyssen property, of which we shall have occasion to speak more fully hereafter.

When Lord Brooke sold the manor of King's Hold, he reserved the mansion, which, it is stated, continued vested in his family, and at the commencement of this century was the property of the Earl of Warwick. The author of the "Beauties of England and Wales," writing in 1816, says: "This house has experienced considerable alterations, but large portions of the ancient edifice have been preserved. These consist principally of a quadrangle, with internal galleries, those on the north and south sides being 174 feet in length. On the ceiling of the south gallery are the arms of Lord Hunsdon, with those of his lady, and the crests of both families frequently repeated. The arms of Lord Hunsdon are likewise remaining on the ceiling of a room connected with this gallery. It is therefore probable that the greater part of the house was rebuilt by this nobleman during the short period for which he held the manor, a term of no longer duration than from 1578 to 1583. The other divisions of this extensive building are of various but more modern dates." At the time when the above description was written, the house seems to have been occupied as a private lunatic asylum.

Several of the nobility and wealthy gentry, indeed, appear to have chosen Hackney for a residence. There is a record of a visit to Hackney by Queen Elizabeth, but to whom is not certain, in 1591. The son and daughter of her dancing chancellor, Sir Christopher Hatton, were both married in Hackney Church, so that he, too, probably lived here. Vere, Earl of Oxford, the soldier and poet, who accompanied Leicester on his expedition to Holland, who supplied ships to oppose the Armada, and sat on the trials of Mary Queen of Scots and the Earls of Arundel, Essex, and Southampton, was, in his latter days, a resident of Hackney. It is also said that Rose Herbert, a lady of noble family, and one of the nuns who at the Reformation were turned adrift upon the world from the Convent of Godstow, near Oxford, died here towards the end of Elizabeth's reign, in a state of destitution, at the age of ninety-six.

Early in the seventeenth century, George Lord Zouch, a noted man in his day, and Lord Warden of the Cinque Ports, had a house at Hackney, where he amused himself with experimental gardening. He died there, and was buried in a small chapel adjoining his house. Ben Jonson, who was his intimate friend, discovered that there was a hole in the wall affording communication between the last resting-place of Lord Zouch and the wine-cellar, and thereupon vented this impromptu :—

"Wherever I die, let this be my fate,
To lye by my good Lord Zouch,
That when I am dry, to the tap I may hye,
And so back again to my couch."

Owen Rowe, one of those who sat as "judges" at the trial of King Charles, died and was buried at Hackney, in 1660.

Another memorable inhabitant of Hackney at this time was Susanna Prewick, or Perwick, a young musical phenomenon, whose death, at the age of twenty-five, in 1661, was celebrated in some lengthy poems, chiefly commendatory of her personal graces. We have no means of judging of her musical powers, which created an extraordinary sensation at the time ; but it is gratifying to know that—

"All vain, conceited affectation
Was unto her abomination.
With body she ne'er sat ascue,
Or mouth awry, as others do."

Dr. Thomas Wood, Bishop of Lichfield, who died in 1692, was a native of Hackney.

Defoe, who at one time lived at Stoke Newington, in all probability also was a resident here ; for in 1701 his daughter Sophia was baptised in Hackney Church ; and in 1724, an infant son, named Daniel, after his distinguished father, was buried in the same church.

Eastward of Hackney churchyard lies Homerton, which, together with Lower Clapton, may be said to form part of the town of itself. Hackney Union is here situated in High Street.

In 1843 a college was founded close by, for the purpose of giving unsectarian religious training to young men and women who wish to become teachers in Government-aided schools.

Homerton was noted in the last and early part of the present century for its academy for the education of young men designed for Dissenting ministers. The late Dr. John Pye Smith was some time divinity tutor here.

A row of almshouses in the village, termed the Widows' Retreat, has upon the front of a small chapel in the centre, the following inscription :—"For the Glory of God, and the comfort of twelve widows of Dissenting Ministers, this retreat was erected and endowed by Samuel Robinson, A.D. 1812."

Homerton High Street leads direct to Hackney Marsh, where, says the "Ambulator" of 1774, "there have been discovered within the last few years the remains of a great causeway of stone, which, by the Roman coins found there, would appear to have been one of the famous highways made by the Romans." The Marsh Road, too, leads straight on to Temple Mills, of which we have already had occasion to make mention.

The City of London Union covers a large space of ground to the north-east of Hackney churchyard, abutting upon Templar Road. Northward lies the rapidly extending hamlet of Lower Clapton. Here, in a curious old house, which was pulled down many years ago, was born, in the year 1727, John Howard, the future prison reformer and philanthropist. The house had been the "country residence" of John Howard's father, who was an upholsterer in London ; and it descended to the son, who sold it in 1785. In an article in the *Mirror* in 1826, this house, so interesting to humanity, is said to have been "taken down some years ago." Much of Howard's early life seems to have been passed here ; and his education, which was rather imperfect, was gained among one of the Dissenting sects, of which his father was a member. On the death of his father he was apprenticed to a wholesale grocer in the City. On quitting business he indulged in a tour through France and Italy. He subsequently, for the benefit of his health, took lodgings at Stoke Newington. We shall have more to say about him on reaching that place. The old house at Clapton where Howard was born is said to have been built in the early part of the last century ; it had large bay-windows, a pedimented roof, numerous and well-proportioned rooms, and a large garden. The site of the house was afterwards covered by Laura Place, and its memory is now kept up by the name of Howard Villas, which has been given to some houses lately erected on the opposite side of the road. A view of the house in which Howard was born will be found in "Smith's Historical and Literary Curiosities," and also in the seventh volume of the *Mirror*.

At no great distance from the site of Howard's old house, but on the west side of the road, was a school, known by the name of Hackney School, which had flourished for upwards of a century on the same spot. This academy was long under the direction of the Newcome family. "It was celebrated," says Mr. Lysons, "for the excellence of the dramatic performances exhibited every third year by the scholars. In these dramas Dr. Benjamin Hoadly, author of the *Suspicious Husband*, and his brother, Dr. John Hoadly, a dramatic writer also, who were both educated at this school, formerly distinguished themselves."

In 1813, the London Orphan Asylum was instituted at Lower Clapton; but about the year 1870 its inmates were removed to new buildings erected at Watford, in Hertfordshire. The building here, which consisted of a centre, with a spacious portico and wings, together with the outlying grounds, was bought in 1882, for about £23,000, by the Salvation Army, and converted into a "Barrack and Congress Hall." What was once an extensive lawn in front of the building is now covered with houses.

Dr. Robinson, in his "History of Hackney," says that on the west side of the road, nearly opposite the Congress Hall, stood an old house, which many years ago was known by a very vulgar appellation, from the circumstance of the person who built it having made a considerable fortune by manufacturing and selling sundry articles of bed-room ware adorned with the head of Dr. Sacheverell. "The date of its erection is not exactly known; but it probably was after the year 1710, because the trial of Sacheverell did not take place till the February or March of that year. . . There are at the present time (1842)," he adds, "two urns with flowers, surmounting the gate-piers at the entrance." The building was subsequently converted into an Asylum for Deaf and Dumb Females.

HOWARD'S HOUSE, AT CLAPTON, ABOUT 1800. (*See page* 521.)

Among the historical characters connected with this place whom we have not already named, was Major André, hanged by Washington as a spy; he was born at Clapton. He was originally intended for a merchant; but being disappointed in love for Honora Sneyd (the friend of Anna Seward), who became afterwards the mother-in-law of Miss Maria Edgeworth, he entered the army, and ultimately met with the fate above mentioned.

To go back a little into the reign of antiquity, we may remark that, though far removed from the crowded city, and generally considered a salubrious spot, Hackney suffered much from visitations of the plague, which in 1593 carried off 42 persons; in

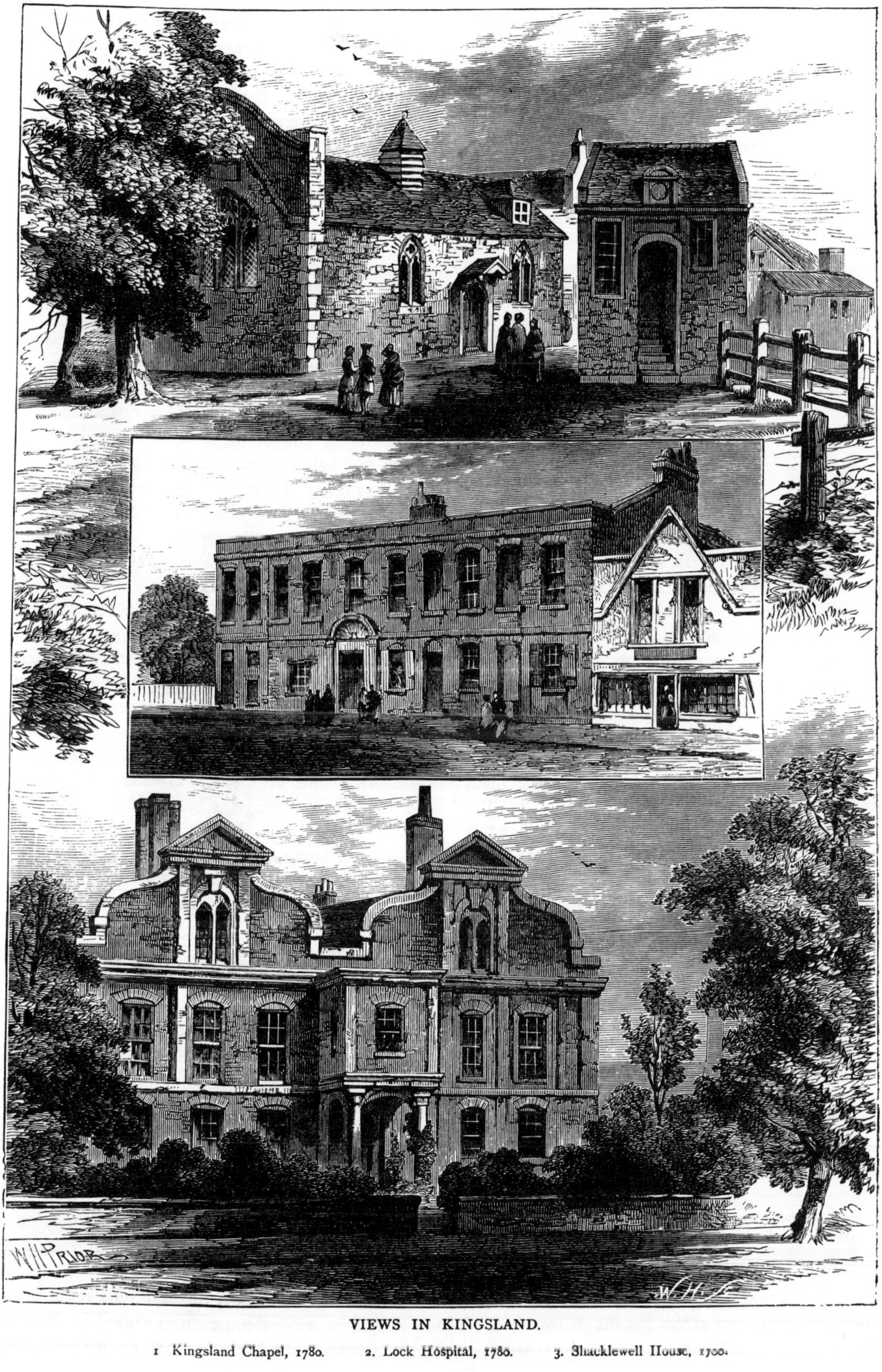

VIEWS IN KINGSLAND.

1 Kingsland Chapel, 1780. 2. Lock Hospital, 1780. 3. Shacklewell House, 1700.

1603, 269; in 1625, 170; and in the terrible year 1665, as many as 225.

In the early part of the eighteenth century Hackney was much infested by robbers, which rendered travelling after dark very insecure. The roads between London and this rural suburb were then lonely and unprotected; and it was not until January, 1756, that lamps were placed between Shoreditch and Hackney, and patrols, armed with guns and bayonets, placed on the road. In the Marshes towards Hackney Wick were low public-houses, the haunt of highwaymen and their Dulcineas. Dick Turpin was a constant guest at the "White House," or "Tyler's Ferry," near Joe Sowter's cock-pit, at Temple Mills; and few police-officers were bold enough to approach the spot.

Maitland, in his "History of London," says, "The village of Hackney being anciently celebrated for the numerous seats of the nobility and gentry, occasioned a mighty resort thither of persons of all conditions from the City of London, whereby so great a number of horses were daily hired in the City on that account, that at length all horses to be let received the common appellation of 'Hackney horses;' which denomination has since communicated itself both to public coaches and chairs; and though this place at present be deserted by the nobility, yet it so greatly abounds with merchants and persons of distinction, that it excels all other villages in the kingdom, and probably on earth, in the riches and opulence of its inhabitants, as may be judged from the great number of persons who keep coaches there." But it is to be feared that in this matter Maitland is not to be trusted; for though it has often been supposed, and occasionally assumed even by well-informed writers, that as Sedan-chairs and Bath-chairs were named from the places where they were first respectively used, so the village of Hackney has had the honour of giving the name to those hackney carriages which were the immediate forerunners of the London cabriolet, it is simply a fact that the word "hackney" may be traced to the Dutch, French, Spanish, and Italian languages. In our own tongue it is at least as old as Chaucer and Froissart, who borrowed it from the French *haquenée*, a slow-paced nag. At all events, in Chaucer's "Romaunt of the Rose," we find the phrase thus used:—

> "Dame Richesse on her hand gan lede
> A yonge man full of semely hede,
> That she best loved of any thing,
> His lust was much in householdyng;
> In clothyng was he full fetyse,
> And loved wel to have horse of prise;
> He wende to have reproved be
> Of thrifte or murdre, if that be
> Had in his stable an *hackenay*."

Froissart, in one of his Chronicles, says, "The knights are well horsed, and the common people and others on litell *hakeneys* and geldyngs." The word subsequently acquired the meaning of "let for hire," and was soon applied to other matters than horses. In *Love's Labour's Lost* Shakespeare says, "Your love, perhaps, is a hacknie." In "Hudibras" we meet with "a broom, the nag and hackney of a Lapland hag." Pope calls himself "a hackney scribbler." Addison and Steele, in the *Spectator* and *Tatler*, speak of "driving in a hack," and our readers surely remember the hackney coach in which Sir Roger de Coverley went to Westminster Abbey. Hogarth gave the expressive name of "Kate Hackabout" to the poor harlot whose progress he depicted. Cowper, in the "Task," uses "hackneyed" as a passive verb; and Churchill employs it as an adjective. So there are authorities enough for the meaning of "hackney;" and the pleasant village, now the centre of a suburban town, must, we fear, be deprived of the honour of having invented hackney coaches.

CHAPTER XLII.

HOXTON, KINGSLAND, DALSTON, &c.

"Dalston, or Shacklewell, or some other suburban retreat northerly."—*C. Lamb, "Essays of Elia."*

Kingsland Road—Harmer's Almshouses—Gefferey's Almshouses—The Almshouses of the Framework Knitters—Shoreditch Workhouse—St. Columba's Church—Hoxton—"Pimlico"—Discovery of a Medicinal Spring—Charles Square—Aske's Hospital—Balmes, or Baumes House—The Practising Ground of the Artillery Company—De Beauvoir Town—The Tyssen Family—St. Peter's Church, De Beauvoir Square—The Roman Catholic Church of Our Lady and St. Joseph—Ball's Pond—Kingsland—A Hospital for Lepers—Dalston—The Refuge for Destitute Females—The German Hospital—Shacklewell.

HERE, it is true, we have no historian or old annalist to guide our steps, for the district had no entity of its own till quite a recent date, and it is not old enough to have a history. Its records are the annals of a "quiet neighbourhood." Beyond an occasional remark, too, we can glean nothing of interest about the neighbourhood from the pages of Strype, Maitland, or honest John Stow;

> "The quaint and antique Stow, whose words alone
> Seem letter'd records graven upon stone."

These close-lying suburbs—which we scarcely know whether to reckon as parts and parcels of the great metropolis or not—have been wittily defined by Mr. G. O. Trevelyan, in his "Life of Lord Macaulay," as "places which, as regards the company and the way of living, are little else than sections of London removed into a purer air." And so rapidly is London growing year by year that even Mr. Trevelyan's words will soon prove out of date, so far as regards purity of air.

This district is approached from the City by Bishopsgate Street and the broad and open thoroughfare called Kingsland Road, which runs northward from the end of Old Street Road, diverging at Shoreditch Church from the road by which we have travelled towards Hackney.

On the east side of the road we pass several almshouses. The first of these belong to the Drapers' Company, and are known as Harmer's Almshouses. The buildings, which were erected in 1713, have a somewhat picturesque appearance, and afford homes for twelve single men and women. Gefferey's Almshouses and Charity, in the gift of the Ironmongers' Company, are situated close to the above; these were founded in 1703, for the purpose of providing homes and pensions for a certain number of poor persons. Next we have the almshouses belonging to the Framework Knitters' Company. These were established in the early part of the last century as homes, &c., for twelve poor freemen and widows of the above-mentioned company.

The only buildings worthy of mention in the Kingsland Road, which we pass on the west side on our way northward, are the Workhouse of the parish of Shoreditch, and St. Columba's Church. The latter building, a large and lofty red-brick edifice, with a clergy house adjoining, was built about the year 1868 from the designs of Mr. P. Brooks; and the services in the church are conducted on "Ritualistic" principles.

Hoxton, which lies on the west side of the Kingsland Road, and north of Old Street Road, now included in Shoreditch parish, was formerly, as we have stated in the previous chapter, reckoned as part of Hackney. The locality in bygone times acquired a certain celebrity from a noted tavern or ale-house, called "Pimlico," which existed there; it is referred to by Ben Jonson, Dodsley, and others in plays of the seventeenth century. The name of "Pimlico" is kept in remembrance by Pimlico Walk, near the junction of the New North Road and Pitfield Street. The origin of the name of Hoxton is somewhat involved in obscurity. The place was formerly sometimes called Hogsdon, as we have already seen;* and Hog Lane, in Norton Folgate, close by, would lead to the inference that it was so named in consequence of the number of hogs that might have been reared there; but this seems doubtful, for in the "Domesday" record we find the name of the place entered as Hocheston, and in a lease of the time of Edward III. it is mentioned as Hoggeston. Stow, in 1598, describes the place as "a large street with houses on both sides;" but it has long since lost all pretensions to a rural or retired character. A medicinal spring was discovered at Hoxton in the seventeenth century, on digging the cellar for a house near Charles Square; but it does not appear to have attained any eminence or reputation. In Charles Square lived the Rev. John Newton, Cowper's friend and correspondent, many years rector of St. Mary Woolnoth, in Lombard Street, and who died in 1807. Peter Cunningham, in his "Handbook of London" (1850), speaks of the house of Oliver, third Lord St. John of Bletsoe, who died in 1618, as still standing.

Hoxton has long been noted for the number of its charitable institutions, among which Aske's Hospital, at the upper end of Pitfield Street, held a prominent place. It consisted of some almshouses and schools, founded by Robert Aske, an alderman of London, and a member of the Haberdashers' Company, in 1688, as homes for twenty poor freemen of that company, and for the education of 220 sons of freemen. The buildings were extensive, and had in front a piazza upwards of 300 feet in length. The chapel was consecrated by Archbishop Tillotson in 1695. In 1875–6 the almshouses were removed, and a large middle-class school, called Aske's Haberdashers' School, now occupies the site.

Hoxton in former times boasted of at least one mansion of some importance; this was Balmes House—termed in old writings Bawmes, or Baulmes. In the early part of the seventeenth century the old house was rebuilt on a scale of great magnificence by Sir George Whitmore, who was Lord Mayor of London, and a considerable sufferer for his loyalty to Charles I. The mansion was purchased about fifty years afterwards by Richard de Beauvoir, a Guernsey gentleman, who lived there in great style. Foreigners visited the

* See ante, p. 39.

mansion as one of the sights of London; and it was noticed as a memorable show place in French and German works on architecture and landscape gardening. At the end of the last century it was surrounded by a moat spanned by drawbridges, and there were beautiful gardens, watered by streams from Canonbury Fields. But Time worked strange changes in Baumes; and in the end the "old house at Hoxton"—a melancholy high-roofed dingy building, enclosed by high walls—came to be a private lunatic asylum, of which Charles Lamb was once, and his sister Mary more than once, an inmate. Some few years ago the building was pulled down; but Whitmore Bridge preserves the memory of the hospitable alderman of the Stuart days, and the smart De Beauvoir Town, near at hand, is a handsome memorial of his successor in the splendour of Baumes.

The fields near the old building appear to have been formerly used by the Artillery Company as a place of exercise; and the "Baumes March" is said to have been "a favourite exercise at arms." A melancholy interest attaches to the fields hereabouts, from the fact that it was in one of them that Ben Jonson killed in a duel Gabriel Spenser, the player.*

Nearly all the land round this part belongs to the Tyssen and De Beauvoir families, after whom and their connections and alliances, streets, squares, and terraces are named in almost endless succession. One district, indeed, is collectively named De Beauvoir Town.

The Tyssens were formerly merchants at Flushing, in Holland, but about the reign of James II. they settled in London and became naturalised subjects. Like many other City merchants at that time, they seem to have fixed their abode at Hackney and Shacklewell, and several of them were buried in Hackney Church. Francis Tyssen, of Shacklewell, married Rachel, the youngest daughter of Richard de Beauvoir, of Guernsey, and subsequently of Baumes, as mentioned above; and on his death, in 1717, he was buried at Hackney "with great funeral pomp" by his brother merchants, who had resolved to do honour to his memory. His body lay in state in Goldsmiths' Hall (from which we may infer that he was very rich indeed), surrounded by a magnificent display of plate, gold and silver sconces and trophies. Then the corpse was borne to Hackney Church with a great procession of horse and footmen, and such an abundant following, that the Earl of Suffolk, deputy Earl-Marshal, became alarmed for the funeral privileges of people of quality, and published a notice in the *Gazette* to the effect that the display "far exceeded the quality of the deceased, being only a private gentleman," and that "funerals of ignoble persons should not be set forth with such trophies of honour as belong only to the peers and gentles of the realm." The funeral must really have been a grand affair, for it cost £2,000, a large sum in those days. Three days after Tyssen was laid in the grave with so much pomp, his widow was confined of a son, the heir to the large property. This his only son, Francis John Tyssen, lord of the manor of Hackney, died in 1781, leaving a daughter, who subsequently conveyed the property by marriage to the Amhursts, of Rochester. At the close of the last century, through failure of male heirs, the property passed, by marriage of an heiress, to Mr. William George Daniel, of Foley House, Kent, and Westbrook, Dorset, who thereupon assumed, by royal sign-manual, the surname and arms of Tyssen. His eldest son, who inherited the manor of Hackney, took the additional name of Amhurst, a name given to one of the principal thoroughfares connecting the main street of Hackney with the high road at Stoke Newington.

De Beauvoir Town is that part of this neighbourhood lying on the north side of Hoxton, stretching away from the Regent's Canal on the south to Ball's Pond Road on the north, and from Kingsland Road on the east to the New North Road and Canonbury on the west. Its centre is formed by De Beauvoir Square, which is surrounded by a number of small streets and terraces. St. Peter's Church, in the south-west corner of the square, is a pseudo-Gothic edifice, and was erected about the year 1830.

In Tottenham Road, near the Kingsland main road, is the Roman Catholic church of Our Lady and St. Joseph, which was solemnly opened in the year 1856 by the late Cardinal Wiseman. The presbytery, which adjoins the church, fronts the Culford Road. The church is a spacious brick edifice. It was originally built for manufacturing purposes, but was converted to its present use under the direction of Mr. Wardell. Externally, the building has not much pretensions to beauty or ecclesiastical architecture. It is, however, spacious, and will accommodate about six hundred worshippers. The division of the chancel from the body of the church is formed by a flight of steps of considerable elevation, and on each side is a screened enclosure—the one used for the organ-chamber and choir, and the other for the sacristy. At the western ends of these enclosures are the side altars. The high altar is arranged with

* See Vol. II., p. 195

baldachino, reredos, and frontal; and the roof of the chancel is divided into panels of a blue ground, relieved with sacred monograms. Underneath the church are spacious and convenient schools.

The north end of the De Beauvoir and Culford Roads is crossed at right angles by Ball's Pond Road, which connects Kingsland Road and Dalston Lane with Essex Road, Islington.

Ball's Pond was originally a small hamlet belonging to the parish of Islington, and abutting upon the Newington Road. It consisted of only a few houses and gardens, and received its name from one John Ball, whose memory is preserved on a penny token, as the keeper of a house of entertainment called the "Salutation," or more commonly the "Boarded House," at this place about the middle of the seventeenth century. The inscription on the token is as follows: "John Ball, at the Boarded House, neere Newington Green: his Penny;" and the sign is depicted upon the coin by the representation of two gentlemen saluting each other. The place was formerly famous for the exercise of bull-baiting and other brutal sports, and was much resorted to by the lower orders of society from all parts of the metropolis. There was, near this spot, a large pond, which by the frequenters of the place became coupled with the name of "mine host." This pond was used, doubtless, like that which we have mentioned in our account of May Fair,* for duck-hunting and other such cruel and unmanly sports.

When the citizens of London used to take lodgings for the summer at Islington for the sake of its pure and healthy air, the district all around us must have consisted of open fields, and nothing met the eye between Hoxton and Stoke Newington. The fields were doubtless used by the Finsbury archers when Hoxton got too hot, or rather too populous, to hold them; and probably within this present century a stray toxophilite may have been seen hereabouts stringing his bow, and dreaming of the days that were past.

In passing through Ball's Pond we have the New River on our left, not, however, any longer, as it used to be, open to the view, and reflecting the sky as in a mirror, but stealing along, like the mole, underground, being arched over in order to keep its stream clean and pure, and free from the smuts and other impurities from which it would be difficult to purify it by all the filtration in the world.

Kingsland lies to the north of the Regent's Canal, which, after leaving the Regent's Park and Camden Town, is carried by a tunnel under the high ground of Islington, and passes hence through Hackney to Mile End, and so into the Thames at Limehouse. It probably derived its name from the royal residence on Stoke Newington Green, of which we shall have more to say presently. The fields adjoining being occupied by royalty for the chase, came conventionally to be styled the "King's lands"—hence Kingsland.

We get a glimpse of the pastoral scenery that at one time lay between London and Kingsland in the "Diary" of the inimitable Pepys. Under date of May 12th, 1667, he writes:—"Walked over the fields to Kingsland and back again; a walk, I think, I have not taken these twenty years; but puts me in mind of my boy's time, when I boarded at Kingsland, and used to shoot with my bow and arrow in these fields."

This, and the whole neighbourhood with which we are now concerned, must at one time have been part and parcel of the great northern forest of Middlesex, if there be truth in what Lord Lyttelton tells us on the authority of an old chronicler of the reign of Henry II., that the citizens of London once had a chace or forest which extended from Hounsditch nearly twelve miles north. The last part of this large forest was Enfield Chace, the farthest portion from town; and if it all once belonged to the people, it would be interesting to find out how it passed into the hands of the sovereign.

Kingsland is a chapelry partly in Hackney and partly in Islington parish. It is described by the "Ambulator," in 1774, as a hamlet of the parish of Islington, lying between Hoxton and Clapton. It consists chiefly of rows of houses, extending in a somewhat monotonous series along the road from London to Stamford Hill.

Lewis, in his "Topographical Dictionary" (1835), writes: "Here are brick-fields, and some part of the ground is occupied by nurserymen and market-gardens. Previously to the middle of the fifteenth century there was at Kingsland a hospital for lepers, which, after the Reformation, became annexed to St. Bartholomew's Hospital, and was used as a sort of out-ward to that institution."

This hospital appears to have been established at a very early period; for, as we learn from Strype's "Survey of London," as far back as the year 1437, "John Pope, citizen and barber, gave by will to the Masters and Governors of the House of Lepers, called *Le Lokes*, at Kingeslond without London, an annual rent of 6s. 8d. issuing out of certain shops, situate in Shirborne Lane, toward the sustentation of the said House at

* See Vol. IV., p. 352.

Kingeslond, for ever." It appears from the records of St. Bartholomew's Hospital, that soon after the establishment of that charity in the reign of Henry VIII., certain Lock, or Lazar, Hospitals were opened in situations remote from the City, for the reception of peculiar patients; and the ancient house for lepers at Kingsland was converted into one of these receptacles. It was afterwards rebuilt on a larger and more commodious plan. A substantial edifice of brick, formerly appropriated to the use of the diseased, having over the door the arms of St. Bartholomew's Hospital, remained standing here down to the commencement of the present century.

This hospital was anciently called the "Loke," or "Lock."* The greater part of the building was burnt down in the middle of the last century, but was subsequently rebuilt. The structure joined a little old chapel, which escaped the fire.

A writer in *Notes and Queries* states that "a sundial on the premises formerly bore this inscription, significant of sin and sorrow: 'Post voluptatem misericordia.'" Prior to its alienation from the mother hospital, the house had a communication with the chapel, so contrived that the patients might take part in the service without seeing or being seen by the congregation. It may be mentioned here that there was a similar arrangement in the Lock Chapel, Grosvenor Place. In 1761 the patients were removed from Kingsland, and the site of the establishment was let out on building leases, though the chapel itself was suffered to stand, and to be used as a proprietary chapel. It was a small edifice in the Early English style of Gothic architecture, with pointed windows and a bell turret. It was in the patronage of the Governors of St. Bartholomew's Hospital, and the endowment was very insignificant. The chapel, it should be added, was removed in the reign of William IV., in order to make room for building private residences. The chapel adjoined the turnpike at the south-eastern corner of the road leading to Ball's Pond, and was, perhaps, coeval with the first establishment of the house for lepers on this spot. The lower part of the structure, in its latter years, was so much hidden by the accumulation of earth on the outside, that the floor of the area was full three feet below the surface of the highway.

BALMES HOUSE IN 1750. (*See page* 525.)

* See *ante*, pp. 214 and 215.

Dalston, or Dorlston, as it was spelt formerly, is usually regarded as a hamlet of Hackney parish; it properly designates the houses on either side of the road leading from Kingsland and Ball's Pond to Hackney, called Dalston Lane; but has gradually come to be applied to the whole neighbouring locality.

The district, which is still styled Dorlston, is curtly described in the "Amulator" (1774) as "a small but pleasant village near Hackney, to which parish it belongs;" and it is spoken of by Lambert, in his "History and Survey of London and its Environs," published in 1806, as "a small hamlet adjoining Hackney, which has nothing remarkable but its nursery grounds." Some of these grounds were still cultivated as lately as 1860; but now the "demon of bricks and mortar" has fairly possessed the neighbourhood, and a crowded railway junction, with constant trains, covers the once rural spot; indeed, Dalston has lately become an important suburb, on account of its railway junction. Of late years, too, large numbers of streets and terraces have sprung up in this neighbourhood; even the small open space known as Kingsland Green is now (January, 1884,) doomed to become a "thing of the past," so that the place is now one of the most populous districts in the suburbs of London.

The old manor-house at Dalston is now used as the Refuge for Destitute Females, which was instituted in 1805, with the view of reforming female criminals, and training them for domestic service. The Refuge was founded under the auspices of Zachary Macaulay, William Wilberforce, Stephen Lushington, Samuel Hoare, Thomas Fowell Buxton, and other leading philanthropists of that day. The sight of a poor destitute boy sitting on a door-step, just discharged from prison homeless and friendless, first kindled the spark of compassion which resulted in the foundation of this time-honoured charity, which was first opened in the month of June, 1805, at Cupar's Bridge, Lambeth. In 1811 the establishment was removed to the Hackney Road. The male branch, in 1815, was transferred to Hoxton, although the females continued in the former locality. The institution for boys was discontinued altogether in 1849, ten years after the incorporation of the society (1 & 2 Vic., cap. 71), on account of Government retrenchments, and about the same time the females were removed to the present commodious and desirable premises at

THE MANOR-HOUSE, DALSTON.

the Manor House, Dalston. Another charitable institution, in Dalston Lane, is the German Hospital, which was erected in 1845. It is a handsome building of red brick, capable of affording relief to a considerable number of patients. It was established for the benefit of Germans suffering from disease, and also of English in cases of accidents. The total number of persons annually relieved is about 12,000. There are in London, principally at the East-end, about 30,000 Germans, chiefly of the working classes, and occupied as sugar-bakers, skin-dressers, and skin-dyers.

Shacklewell, on the north side of Dalston Lane, is said to have been named after some springs or wells which were of high repute in former days, but the very site of which is now forgotten. It is a hamlet to the parish of Hackney lying on the east side of the Stoke Newington Road, and covering a triangular plot of ground, the north-east side of which is bounded by Amhurst Road and Hackney Downs. The old manor-house originally belonged to the family of Heron, and is worthy of mention, as having been the abode of Cecilia, the daughter of the great Sir Thomas More, who married George Heron, "of Shacklewell." Her husband becoming involved in the ruin of his father-in-law, and her only son dying in infancy, the family became extinct. The estate then passed into other hands, and in 1700 was sold to Mr. Francis Tyssen, by its then owner, a gentleman named Rowe, who, it is said, late in life was forced to apply for relief to the parish in which he had once owned a manor.

CHAPTER XLIII.

STOKE NEWINGTON.

"I like the neighbourhood, too, the ancient places
That bring back the past ages to the eye,
Filling the gap of centuries—the traces
Mouldering beneath your head that lie!"
Adam and Eve, a Margate Story.

Stoke Newington in the Last Century—The Old Roman Road, called Ermine Street—Beaumont and Fletcher's Reference to May-day Doings at Newington In the Olden Times—Mildmay Park—The Village Green—Mildmay House—Remains of the King's House—King Henry's Walk—St. Jude's Church and the Conference Hall—Bishop's Place—The Residence of Samuel Rogers, the Poet—James Burgh's Academy—Mary Wollstonecraft Godwin—St. Matthias' Church—The New and Old Parish Churches—Sir John Hartopp and his Family—Queen Elizabeth's Walk—The Old Rectory House—The Green Lanes—Church Street—The House of Isaac D'Israeli—The School of Edgar Allan Poe—John Howard, the Prison Reformer—Sandford House—Defoe Street—Defoe's House—The Mansion of the Old Earls of Essex—The Manor House—Fleetwood Road—The Old "Rose and Crown"—The Residence of Dr. John Aikin and Mrs. Barbauld—The "Three Crowns"—The Reservoirs of the New River Company—Remarks on the Gradual Extension of London.

We are now about to traverse another of the northern suburbs of London, but one which it would not be possible to include among the "northern heights" of the great metropolis. We shall find ourselves in far less romantic scenery than that which we have so lately seen at Highgate and Hampstead, but still the neighbourhood now before us is not deficient in interest; at all events, to those who in their youth have strolled along the banks of the Lea, rod in hand, or mused in its meadows over the pleasant pages of Izaak Walton; or to those who remember the legend of Johnny Gilpin and his ride to Edmonton, as told by Cowper; or who rejoice in the "Essays of Elia" and the other desultory writings of Charles Lamb. To such persons, and doubtless they may be counted by millions, even the full straight level road which leads from Dalston and Kingsland, through Stoke Newington, and Stamford Hill, and Tottenham, to Edmonton, can scarcely be wholly devoid of interest and of pleasant reminiscences. There is also another section of the community to whom this part of the northern suburbs of London will always be a welcome subject; we mean the Nonconformist portion of the religious world, in whose eyes the cemetery of Abney Park is scarcely less sacred than that of Bunhill Fields.

Stoke Newington is described in the "Ambulator" (1774) as "a pleasant village near Islington, where a great number of the citizens of London have built houses, and rendered it extremely populous, more like a large flourishing town than a village. The church," adds the writer, "is a small low Gothic building, belonging to the Dean and Chapter of St. Paul's. . . . . Behind the church is a pleasant grove of tall trees, where the inhabitants resort for the benefit of shade and a wholesome air."

"Our village," writes the Rev. Thomas Jackson, the rector, "was once called Neweton Canonicorum, in order to distinguish it from all other Stokes, Newtowns, and Newingtowns in the world, and especially from its rival on the south of the Thames, Newington Butts; and it was so called doubtless because the manor was given by Athelstan or by Edward the Confessor to the canons of St. Paul's."

The name of the village carries us back to the Saxon times, denoting the new village or town built on the borders of a wood. We may remind the reader that our land is full of Stokes, and that wherever there is a Stoke we may be sure that there was once a wood. Newington, indeed, appears formerly to have been situated in a wood, which was part of the great Middlesex forest already mentioned by us. At the time when King Charles was beheaded there were still seventy-seven acres of woodland in the parish. The timber of Stoke Newington probably helped to build again that London which had perished in the Great Fire of 1666, and possibly at an earlier date it furnished fagots for the fires lit at Smithfield alternately by the Protestants and the Catholics.

The old Roman road, known as the Ermine or Irmin Street, ran northwards through Stoke Newington to Enfield, though its exact route is a subject of debate. Mr. Jackson, in his "Lecture on Stoke Newington," says:—"One boundary of our Saxon manor is the Irmin Street, one of the central highways which our forefathers dedicated to the Hero-god, the illustrious War-man, or Man of Hosts, as his name literally means—that Herman or Arminius, the mighty Cheruscan, who fought the fight of Winfield on the Weser, who turned back the tide of Roman invasion, routing Varus and his legions, and delivering Germany from Italian despotism—a hero truly national, the benefactor and relative of us all. Coming a little down the stream of time, I find Newington Manor among the first of religious endowments in this country. . . . I find the rents and profits of our lands, the fruits of the fields that we daily tread, supporting the men who chanted at the funeral of Edward the Confessor, and assisted at the coronation of William the Norman."

We read of Stoke Newington in the plays of the seventeenth century as a place of pleasant conviviality. Thus Beaumont and Fletcher, in the *Knight of the Burning Pestle*, first published in 1613, introduce Ralph, dressed as a king of the May, who thus speaks:—

"London, to thee I do present this merry month of May;
Let each true subject be content to hear me what I say.
* * * * * * * *
March out and show your willing minds by twenty and by twenty,
To Hogsdon (Hoxton) or to Newington, where ale and cakes are plenty."

Soon afterwards Stoke Newington appears, by the testimony of some historians, to have become conspicuous for its Puritanism, through the influence, probably, of the Pophams and the Fleetwoods, and afterwards through the worthy family of Abney, who had purchased the manor.

The parish is described in Lewis's "Topographical Dictionary" (1835), as consisting principally of one long street, extending from Kingsland Road to Stamford Hill, on the high road from London to Cambridge, and containing at that time a population of nearly 3,500 souls. The eastern side of this street is actually in the parish of Hackney, and from the western side, near the centre of it, branches off a street, called Church Street, leading to the parish church and the Green Lanes.

From the western end of Ball's Pond Road, a thoroughfare called Mildmay Park—a good roadway lined on either side by private residences—leads direct to Newington Green. This place, says the "Ambulator" just a century ago, "consists of a handsome square of considerable extent, surrounded by houses which are in general well built; before each side is a row of trees, and an extensive grass-plat in the middle." The green is still adorned with lofty elms, has an old-world appearance, and forms really a handsome, though somewhat irregular square. It is situated partly in the parish of Newington, and partly in that of Islington, and is principally inhabited by merchants and private families.

In the "Beauties of England and Wales" (1816), we read of an old dwelling situated here, called Mildmay House, then a boarding-school for young ladies. It is said to have been, in the reign of Charles I., the property of Sir Henry Mildmay, who had acquired the estate by marriage with the daughter and heiress of William Halliday, an alderman of London. On one of the chimney-pieces appeared the arms of Halliday; and the ceilings contained the arms of England, with the initials of King James, and medallions of Hector, Alexander, &c. Mildmay Park Road, mentioned above, was so named from this house.

On the southern side of the green is an old mansion, now divided into two, which is traditionally said to have been at one time a residence of Henry VIII., when his Majesty wished to divert himself with the pleasures of the chase, which about three centuries ago extended northerly hence to Haringay and Enfield. On the ceiling of the principal room in the house are to be seen the armorial bearings and royal monogram of James I. This room contains a very fine and lofty carved mantelpiece of the "Jacobean" style, not unlike that in the Governor's Room at the

Charterhouse. Most of the rooms have also their walls handsomely panelled in oak. It is probable that this residence caused the adjoining fields to the south to be called the King's Land—now abridged into Kingsland.

At the north-west corner of the green there formerly stood a large building, called Bishop's Place; it is said to have been the residence of Percy, Earl of Northumberland, when he wrote the memorable letter disclaiming any matrimonial contract between himself and Queen Anne Boleyn, referred to in our account of Hackney Church, and which was dated from Newington Green the 13th of May, in the 28th year of Henry VIII. "This house," writes the author of the "Beauties of England and Wales," "was popularly reported to have been occupied by Henry VIII. for the convenience of his irregular amours. The tradition is supported chiefly by the circumstance of a pleasant winding path, which leads to the turnpike road by Ball's Pond, bearing the name of 'King Henry's Walk.'" Mr. Jackson, in his "Lecture on Stoke Newington," thus muses on this old mansion in connection with Bluff King Hal:—"Let us imagine that we see him, blunt, big, and sturdy, with his feet wide apart, and his chin already doubling, sallying forth with a crowd of obsequious attendants from the house afterwards called Mildmay House, or from that just mentioned, to disport himself in the woodlands of Newington. Is Catharine of Arragon his queen, or the hapless Anne, of the swan-like neck, or Jane Seymour, who died so young? Is he plotting the death of a wife, or of his chancellor? Look at him as represented in the portraits of Holbein. His eye good-natured; his mouth indicative of an iron and unscrupulous will; his brow strong in intellectual vigour; his whole physiognomy sensual and selfish. Can you not suppose that you meet him in some of our by-lanes wondering at the changes which have passed upon the London of the sixteenth century, or musing on the suspicions which he entertained respecting a contract of marriage presumed to have been made between the Earl of Northumberland and Anne Boleyn previous to her marriage with the king. Poor earl! he writes to Lord Cromwell from his house on Newington Green a letter of such abject earnestness, that one would imagine his neck already felt the halter, or his eye caught the cold gleam of the executioner's axe, while he denies with the greatest solemnity the fact of any such contract."

In King Henry's Walk, at the corner of Queen Margaret's Grove, and near the North London Railway, stands St. Jude's Church, a large edifice of the "late Decorated" style of architecture, built in 1855 from the designs of Mr. A. D. Gough. It was enlarged, and indeed almost reconstructed, in 1871. In connection with this church, but situated in Mildmay Park, near Newington Green, is a large building known as the Conference Hall.

Dr. Robinson, in his "History of Stoke Newington," describes Bishop's Place as having been a quadrangular building of wood and plaster, and as having had a square court in the centre, with communications to the various apartments all round by means of small doors opening from one room into another. The house, prior to its demolition, had been for many years divided into a number of small tenements, occupied by poor people. When the house was taken down, some parts of the old wainscot were found to be richly gilt, and ornamented with paintings, but well-nigh obliterated from the effects of time.

Newington Green, in its time, seems to have had among its residents many members of the nobility and of the world of letters. An old house on the western side, not far from that above described, was for many years the residence of Samuel Rogers, the poet. The building, which was considerably altered in appearance by its subsequent owners, was pulled down about 1879 to make room for shops. The hall, mentioned by Rogers in his "Pleasures of Memory," and the little room on the first floor in which he used to sit and write, together with the three rooms on the ground floor, facing the south and the sunny garden, remained unchanged. But the hall became lined with modern canvas, spread over the old panelling, and had lost its venerable appearance. The plane-tree, under which the poet would sit and entertain his friends in summer evenings, also flourished; but the greater part of the little paddock in the rear had disappeared, and a new street was carried across the poet's garden, destroying a part of the mushroom-beds which he cultivated with such care and pride. Though nearly a quarter of a century had passed since Samuel Rogers was its master, the house bore to the end tokens of his former presence; and it required no great stretch of imagination to picture the venerable face and figure of the author of "The Pleasures of Memory" seated in his arm-chair here among his books and his friends.

Although the poem is stated by the author to refer to "an obscure village," there can be little doubt in the minds of those who read the "Pleasures of Memory" with attention, that many of the opening lines reflect the old house at Stoke Newington:—

"Mark yon old mansion frowning through the trees.
* * * * * * *
As jars the hinge what sullen echoes call!
Oh! haste, unfold the hospitable hall!
That hall where once in antiquated state
The chair of justice held the grave debate;
Now stained with dews, with cobwebs darkly hung,
Oft has its roof with peals of rapture rung,
When round yon ample board in one degree
We sweetened every meal with social glee.
* * * * * * *
Ye household deities, whose guardian eye
Marked each pure thought, ere registered on high,
Still, still ye walk the consecrated ground,
And breathe the soul of Inspiration round.
* * * * * * *
As o'er the dusky furniture I bend,
Each chair awakes the feelings of a friend.
The storied arras, source of fond delight,
With old achievement charms the wildered sight.
* * * * * * *
That massive beam, with curious carvings wrought,
Whence the caged linnet soothed my pensive thought;
Those muskets, cased with venerable rust,
Those once-loved forms, still breathing through their dust;
Still from the frame, in mould gigantic cast,
Starting to life—all whisper of the past.
As through the garden's desert paths I rove,
What fond illusions swarm in every grove.
* * * * * * *
Childhood's lov'd group revisits every scene,
The tangled wood-walk and the tufted green;
Indulgent memory wakes, and lo! they live,
Clothed with far softer hues than light can give."

A writer in the *Mirror* (1824), in giving his "Recollections of Newington Green," says that it is memorable for having been the residence of persons of distinguished talents. An academy, which was some years since pulled down, formerly (1747) belonged to the celebrated James Burgh, which he supported with great reputation to himself and benefit to his scholars for nineteen years. He was the author of "The Dignity of Human Nature," "Thoughts on Education," "A Warning to Dram-drinkers," &c. Its last master was Dr. James Lindsay, who suddenly expired at Dr. Williams's Library, Red Cross Street, whilst advocating the cause of public education. He was long pastor of the Dissenting meeting-house upon the green, whose pulpit had been occupied by Dr. Price, Dr. Towers, &c. On this spot, too, at one time, resided Mary Wollstonecraft Godwin, of whom we have already spoken in our account of St. Pancras.*

The handsome church of St. Matthias, so noted for its "ritualistic" services, is situated at the end of Howard Road, between the green and the main road. It was consecrated about the year 1854. It is a large Gothic edifice, and was built from the designs of Mr. W. Butterfield.

From Newington Green a short walk by way of Albion Road brings us near to the western end of Church Street, mentioned above, where stands the new parish church, dedicated to St. Mary. It is a very spacious and handsome structure, consisting of nave, side aisles, chancel, choir, and transepts, in the Early Decorated style, and was built from the designs of Sir G. Gilbert Scott. The interior is enriched with an elaborate reredos, representing the "Last Supper;" and the capitals of the pillars of the nave are sculptured with varieties of English foliage in bold relief. Some of the windows are filled with painted glass, and the organ and the pulpit are both much admired. The church was consecrated in 1858, and is complete except the tower and spire.

It stands on the south of the road directly facing the former parish church, which is still allowed to remain as hitherto, though practically reduced to the second rank of a chapel of ease to the daughter edifice. The old parish church is a low-roofed structure. It was erected, in the place of a still older edifice, by William Patten, the lessee of the manor in 1563, which date appears over the south doorway. The building has since been repeatedly enlarged, and a spire added. It is small and unattractive, especially in its interior, where are to be seen a variety of specimens of the square family pews, now almost obsolete. It was enlarged and "beautified" about the year 1829 by Sir Charles Barry, and was one of his first and poorest attempts in the Gothic style. The only part of the structure that can boast of antiquity is the south aisle, which contains the manorial pew, where it is said that the Princess Elizabeth was an occasional worshipper during the reign of her sister Mary, during the stolen visits which she paid to Newington from Hatfield House.

In the chancel is a fine mural monument to Mrs. Sutton, who was married first to a Mr. Dudley, and whose second husband was Thomas Sutton, the founder of Charterhouse School and Hospital.† It was restored some years ago by a subscription among the gentlemen who had been educated at the Charterhouse. The Rev. Dr. Gaskin, a former rector, lies in a vault on the north side of the church. Fearing that his body might be removed from its grave after his death, he was buried, by his own desire, not here, but in St. Gabriel's, Fenchurch Street. When that church was taken down in order to carry out improve-

* See *ante*, p. 335.

† See Vol. II., p. 383.

ments in the City, his coffin was removed hither by the care of his successor in the rectory, the Rev. Thomas Jackson, and consigned to what it may be hoped will prove his last resting-place.

The churchyard, which is planted with evergreens, is full of family tombs; few of them, however, possess any antiquarian interest. Near the southern entrance, where once probably stood a "lych-gate," a square tomb covers the remains of whom we have already mentioned† as having endeavoured to improve the Strand on the west side of Temple Bar. His son and his daughter also are recorded on his monument. The former was killed in India, and the latter was burnt to death whilst performing some filial attention by her father's sick bed. Bridget, the daughter of Oliver Cromwell, and wife of General Fleetwood, lies buried beneath the church.

STOKE NEWINGTON CHURCH, 1750.

Mrs. Barbauld and of her brother, Dr. Aikin, whom we have already mentioned in our account of Hampstead.* At the extreme south-west corner is the grave of some of the Wilberforces, members of the family of the eminent philanthropist † who lies in Westminster Abbey. Had not a public funeral been voted to him, in all probability, he would himself have been laid to rest in this quiet and peaceful spot. On the south of the chancel is the family grave of Wilberforce's friend and fellow-worker in the cause of the slave, Mr. James Stephen, a Master in Chancery, the father of the late Right Honourable Sir James Stephen.

In the churchyard lies buried Alderman Pickett,

The parish church has many monuments and memorials of the family of Sir John Hartopp, who were at one time residents at Stoke Newington. Among the rest is this curious entry in the register, relative to the wife of Sir John:—"1711, Dame Elizabeth Hartopp was buried in woollen the 26th day of November, according to an Act of Parliament made on that behalf; attested before Mr. Gostling, minor canon of St. Paul's, London." And again, relative to another member of the family:—"My lady Hartopp was buried in a velvet coffin, September 22, 1730, in the church." The dame Elizabeth, who was buried in woollen, was the daughter of General Fleetwood, who married

* See *ante*, p. 476. † See *ante*, p. 95.

† See Vol. III., p. 10.

VIEWS IN STOKE NEWINGTON.

1. Rogers' House, 1877. 2. Fleetwood House, 1750. 3. St. Mary's Rectory. 4 St. Mary's New Church. 5. New River at Stoke Newington. 6. Queen Elizabeth's Walk, 1800. 7. Old Gateway.

Bridget, one of Oliver Cromwell's children; and the education of her son was entrusted to the learned and pious Dr. Watts, of whom we shall have more to say presently. The Rev. Dr. Stoughton, in his "Shades and Echoes of Old London," says:—"Dame Hartopp has been sometimes regarded as the offspring of Bridget, and consequently as the Protector's granddaughter; and if that view of her lineage were correct, then the youth to whom Watts became tutor would be no other than a great-grandson of the strong-willed man who, without a crown, swayed a sceptre over three old kingdoms." But Noble, in his "Memoirs of the Protectoral House," shows, as we think satisfactorily, that Elizabeth, who was married to Sir John Hartopp, was a daughter of Fleetwood by his first wife, Frances Smith. Still, as the Hartopps would be intimately connected with the Cromwells, the family traditions of the latter would be familiar to the former, and stories of Oliver and his son-in-law would often be told in the dining-hall and the gardens of Sir John at Newington.

Near the old church, on the northern side of it, is a walk between trees, still called Queen Elizabeth's Walk; and as some justification of the name, it may be added that Newington was the abode of her Majesty's favourite, Robert Dudley, Earl of Leicester, and of his contemporary, Edward Vere, Earl of Oxford.

On the south side of the road, between the two churches, stood formerly a picturesque old rectory-house, mostly built of wood, with a curious gable projecting into the street, over the pavement. The south and west sides of the house and its garden were bounded by a moat, which is now filled up, the present rectory being built upon its site. The ribs and back-bone of the old rectory-house were evidently part and parcel of large forest trees; and where oak was not used in its construction, its place was supplied by other hard and vigorous timber, equally heavy and durable.

On the western side of the parish there is a large but rather winding road, running northwards, popularly known as the "Green Lanes," and leading, by way of Wood Green and Winchmore Hill, to Enfield. This is rather a sporting neighbourhood, and the road is largely used for trotting matches by farmers, butchers, and other tradesfolk, a fact which does not contribute to the quiet or comfort of the residents. The Green Lanes dispute with Stoke Newington Road the claim to be considered the old Saxon Ermine Street mentioned above. At this point commences a narrow and slightly-winding thoroughfare, called Church Street, which, passing eastward, leads us into the straight and wide road from Dalston to Stamford Hill. It was evidently once a rural lane, and was probably used more by farmers' wagons than by gentlemen's carriages. It is fringed, however, on both sides with a long series of private dwelling-houses, most of them red-bricked mansions of the date of Queen Anne and George I., with projecting summits to the doorways, and screened from the street by iron railings of varied and handsome designs, not unlike those still to be seen in the older parts of Kensington, Chelsea, Hampstead, and Highgate. One of the first houses on the northern side of the way, now a ladies' school, was the home of Mr. Isaac D'Israeli, the author of the "Curiosities of Literature," before he settled down in Bloomsbury Square. A large white house near it was the scene of the school-days of the eccentric and gifted poet, Edgar Allan Poe, who in his writings ascribes much of the romantic element in his character to the fact of having been sent as a boy to a place so abounding in old associations. Edgar Poe (born at Baltimore in January, 1811) was adopted as a child by a Mr. Allan, a rich gentleman who had no children of his own. Mr. Allan brought him to England, and placed the spoiled child, then a witty, and beautiful, and precocious boy, at school in Church Street. He remained here five years, but returned to the United States in 1822.

A tall red house on the same side of the way, now embodied in Church Row, was the house where John Howard lodged when he married the widow lady who kept it, as we have mentioned in our account of Lower Clapton.* Here he studied his first essays in philanthropy. "The delicate state of his health required better and more attentive nursing than he found where he first lodged, so he removed into apartments under the roof of one Mrs. Sarah Lowne, a widow possessed of a little property, residing in Church Street, who devoted her time to the care and comfort of the young invalid, who was only twenty-five, while she was fifty-two. From being his nurse, she became his wife. She died in 1755, and lies buried in St. Mary's, Whitechapel." It is on record that Mr. Howard was a constant worshipper in the old Independent chapel here. After the death of the nurse whom he thus strangely endeavoured to reward, Mr. Howard married into a respectable family of Cambridgeshire. His second wife, however, died soon after she had given birth to a son. In the course of a voyage to Lisbon Mr. Howard had the misfortune to be captured, and was lodged in France as a prisoner of war. The sufferings

* See *ante*, p. 521.

which he was now compelled to witness are supposed to have operated with such force on his mind as to lead to those indefatigable exertions for the redress of abuses in prisons which speedily produced such important effects throughout the greater part of Europe. Mr. Howard died, in the year 1790, at one of the Russian settlements on the Black Sea, the victim of a malignant fever, which he had caught in visiting some prisoners. A monument to his memory was erected in 1876 at Kherson.

On the south side of the street, a similar house, with lofty windows and a handsome entrance doorway, was the home of the eccentric Thomas Day, the author of "Sandford and Merton." It is now styled Sandford House.

A few yards farther to the east, on the same side of the way, we come to Defoe Street. This was formed in 1875, by the demolition of the house in which Defoe resided, and in which he is reputed to have written "Robinson Crusoe." It is said to have been remarkable for the number of its doors, and for the massive locks and bolts with which they were secured. The house itself was a gloomy and irregular pile of red brick, apparently of the reign of Queen Anne. It had thick walls and deep window seats, with curious panelling and cupboards in the recesses. Here, besides writing that matchless story with which his name is associated, Defoe plotted as a politician; and here he set in order the materials on which were founded the union between England and Scotland. Hence he was carried a prisoner to Newgate in 1713. A native of Cripplegate, he had been educated at an academy on Newington Green, kept by Charles Morton. "Robinson Crusoe" was published in April, 1719, in which year the rolls of the manor of Stoke Newington mention Defoe as a resident in Church Street.

Close by, and on the same side of the street, stands a portion, though only a fragment, of the mansion of the old Earls of Essex, dating perhaps from the reign of Elizabeth. On the same side of the street, but considerably more to the east, stood a house which at the beginning of the last century was a large hotel or tavern, with gardens and pleasure-grounds, which formed a favourite resort for newly-married couples to spend their honeymoon, in the days when there were no railways to whirl them off on the wings of steam to Brighton, Hastings, or the Isle of Wight. It was afterwards converted into two private houses, one of which contained a spacious apartment that had formerly been the assembly-room of the tavern.

On the opposite, or northern, side of Church Street, is a dwelling called, though incorrectly, the Manor House, in the grounds of which is a curious archway of brick, which must formerly have been the entrance to a large and important residence. It is probably of the fifteenth or sixteenth century. It is now filled up with modern bricks; but the hinges on which its huge doors once swung are still to be seen *in situ*. Little or nothing appears to be known about its history. Mr. Lewis, in his "Dictionary" quoted above, says that "the ancient manor-house is particularly worthy of notice; but," curiously enough, he adds, "a brick gateway, with a pointed arch on the northern side of Church Street, is the only part now standing of the buildings belonging to the old manor-house."

The same ancient tradition which connects Henry VIII. with the southern portion of Stoke Newington, tells us that Queen Elizabeth visited the manor-house in Church Street; and a pleasant grove of elms, close by the old church, as mentioned above, once the "mall" of the parish, still retains the name of "Queen Elizabeth's Walk." But when did the "maiden" queen make Stoke Newington her abode? Was it in her childhood, her girlhood, or her early womanhood? We know that a branch of the Dudleys, Earls of Essex, lived here after Elizabeth had come to the throne, but there is no proof of their having been here at an earlier date. Mr. Jackson tells us that the story current in the village in the last century was that, some time in Mary's reign, "probably when the house of the French Ambassador Noailles was the rendezvous of the discontented of every description, and when the princess herself was the hope of the Protestants, exasperated by persecution, she was brought by her friends to the secluded manor-house, embosomed in trees, as to a secure asylum, where she might communicate with her friends, and be ready for any political emergency. They tell us that an ancient brick tower stood in the early part of the last century near the mansion, and that a staircase was remembered leading to the identical spot where the princess was concealed." But even Mr. Jackson, with all his poetic antiquarianism, is unable to confirm the tradition. Church Row, we may add, stands on the site of the old manor-house and grounds.

Fleetwood Road, a little to the east of this, still commemorates the residence of Fleetwood, the Parliamentarian general.

About a hundred yards farther to the east we come to some handsome and lofty iron gates, behind which are some fine cedars of Lebanon and other tall evergreens. These were the front entrance of Sir Thomas Abney's mansion, of which we shall have more to say presently, as well as of its owners.

The old "Rose and Crown" tavern stood at the corner of a road leading out of Church Street in a southward direction. The old tavern retained its ancient appearance until early in the present century, when it was pulled down, and a new house erected on its site, which was enlarged and brought forward in a line with the adjoining houses; previous to which the old house stood back some feet from the footpath. Robinson, in his history of the parish, gives an illustration of the tavern as it appeared in 1806. Upon the sign-post is shown a pair of horns, similar to those which we have described in our account of Highgate.*

Near the middle of Church Street are two houses, nearly opposite to one another, which have had some distinguished residents; that on the north side was Dr. John Aikin's; his sister, Mrs. Barbauld, lived on the south, in a small private residence, now converted into a jeweller's shop. In Dr. Aikin's house the "Winter Evening Conversations" were written. Dr. Aikin died in December, 1822. Crabb Robinson writes of him that "he had for some years sunk into imbecility after a youth and middle age of great activity. He was in his better days a man of talent of the highest personal worth—in fact, one of the 'salt of the earth.'" Mrs. Barbauld was a resident here both before and after her living at Hampstead. She is frequently mentioned in H. Crabb Robinson's "Diary," from which we cull the following characteristic entries:—

"1816—*11th Feb.*—I walked to Newington, and dined with Mrs. Barbauld. As usual, we were very comfortable. Mrs. Barbauld can keep up a lively argumentative conversation as well as any one I know; and at her advanced age (she is turned of seventy), she is certainly the best specimen of female Presbyterian society in the country. N.B.—Anthony Robinson requested me to inquire whether she thought the doctrine of Universal Restoration scriptural. She said she thought we must bring to the interpretation of the Scriptures a very liberal notion of the beneficence of the Deity to find the doctrine there."

Here is a picture of her five years afterwards:—"1821—*21st Jan.*—Went to Mrs. Barbauld's. She was in good spirits, but she is now the confirmed old lady. Independently of her fine understanding and literary reputation, she would be interesting. Her white locks, fair and unwrinkled skin, brilliant starched linen, and rich silk gown, make her a fit object for a painter. Her conversation is lively, her remarks judicious and always pertinent."

About four years subsequently Robinson writes:—"1824—*4th Nov.*—Walked to Newington. Mrs. Barbauld was going out, but she stayed a short time with me. The old lady is much shrunk in appearance, and is declining in strength. She is but the shade of her former self, but a venerable shade. She is eighty-one years of age, but she retains her cheerfulness, and seems not afraid of death. She has a serene hope and quiet faith—delightful qualities at all times, and in old age peculiarly enviable."

Four months afterwards, on the 9th of March, 1825, she died, after a few days' serious illness. At the end of the same year we find Robinson making this entry:—"*27th Dec.*—At Royston. This morning I read to the young folks Mrs. Barbauld's 'Legacy.' This delightful book has in it some of the sweetest things I ever read. 'The King in his Castle' and 'True Magicians' are perfect allegories, in her best style. Some didactic pieces are also delightful."

Among other distinguished residents and personages connected with Stoke Newington, whose names we have not already mentioned, were Adam Anderson, author of the "History of Commerce," and Archbishop Tillotson.

The "Three Crowns," at the junction of Church Street and the main road, commemorates the spot where James I.—in whom the three crowns were first united—stayed to bait his horses, after meeting the Lord Mayor and aldermen at the top of Stamford Hill.

The western side of the High Road, as far as Stamford Hill, formed, till recently, part of the original parish of Hackney; but the latter has been sub-divided, and West Hackney and Stamford Hill have been made independent ecclesiastical districts. The latter was formerly a private and proprietary chapel of ease, but it was purchased by a subscription among the residents, enlarged, and consecrated.

About half a mile to the north, between Stoke Newington and the Seven Sisters' Road, at the entrance of the Green Lanes, are the large reservoirs in which the New River Company filter their water before it is brought into London. We have already sketched the history of this river in our account of Islington,† but for the following particulars, which ought to have a place here, we are indebted to the "Life of Sir Hugh Middleton," in Mr. Charles

* See *ante*, p. 418.

† See Vol. II., pp. 266, 267.

Knight's *Penny Cyclopædia*:—"The fall of the New River is three feet per mile, which gives a velocity of about two miles an hour. The average width is about twenty-one feet, and the average depth about four feet in the centre; so that, taking it at about half that depth, there is a section of forty-two square feet of water flowing into London at the rate of two miles an hour. At the sluice, near Highbury, the river is dammed back to the height of twenty inches, and at Enfield to two feet four inches; and there are three or four more such interruptions for the purpose of checking the current . . . The New River is occasionally rendered dirty, especially in winter, by drainage from the land and villages along its course; and the company has been at a great expense in order to purify the water before it is delivered to the inhabitants of London. For this purpose two large settling reservoirs were formed in 1832 at Stoke Newington, under the direction of Mr. Mylne, the company's engineer. The water here covers an area of thirty-eight acres, more than twenty feet deep in some parts, and twelve feet on an average throughout. The water of the New River can be turned into the upper reservoir, where it settles, and it is then drawn off by a steam-engine, and poured into the lower reservoir, where another settlement takes place, and the water is then turned again once more into the channel of the river. Bathing in the New River is entirely prohibited; and men called 'walksmen' mow the bed of the river every week in order to keep down the growth of weeds, which are stopped by gratings placed at intervals, where the weeds are regularly removed."

We may conclude this chapter with an apt quotation from the Rev. T. Jackson's "Lecture on Stoke Newington:"—"It is said that in North America the line of civilisation stretches farther and farther into the west at the rate of about fifteen miles a year. The modest backwoodsman who now stands on the frontier of civilised life, finds himself a twelvemonth hence within its boundary. The progress of London—the Babylon and Nineveh of modern times—is scarcely less remarkable, if less rapid. There are persons yet living (1855) who remember the erection of Finsbury Square, upon what was then the northern limit of the great town. Others have heard their fathers speak of the wall in front of Old Bedlam, and of the cherry-trees that grew in Broad Street and London Wall. Now the south of Stoke Newington may be regarded as within the capital. The meadows and cornfields of Kingsland are no more; they are covered with lines of busy and well-inhabited streets. The tide of population is scarcely arrested by the uplands of Highbury Hill, once the seat of a Roman summer camp, and threatens to invade the quiet hill-top of Crouch End. When will our green fields be finally absorbed? when will Lordship Road be covered with villas, to be, as time rolls on, gradually deteriorated, till they are joined by intervening houses and broken into shops?"

CHAPTER XLIV.

STOKE NEWINGTON (*continued*), AND STAMFORD HILL.

"Si monumenta quæris, circumspice."

Abney House—Sir Thomas and Lady Abney—The Visit of Dr. Isaac Watts to Abney House—His Library and Study—The Death of Dr. Watts—Sale of Abney Park, and the Formation of the Cemetery—Abney House converted into a School—Monument of Isaac Watts—The Mound and Grotto in the Cemetery—Distinguished Personages buried here—Stamford Hill—Meeting of King James and the Lord Mayor at Stamford Hill—The River Lea—Izaak Walton and the "Complete Angler."

In the foregoing chapter we have briefly referred to the mansion of Sir Thomas Abney, the entrance to which was on the north side of Church Street. It was a large square substantial red-brick building with stone quoins, and dated its erection from the close of the seventeenth century. The roof was flat, with a balustrade around it; and it had a central turret, which commanded an extensive prospect of the surrounding country. The iron entrance-gates, which still remain, are richly ornamented with carved work of fruit and flowers. The principal rooms of the house were all large and stately, and the walls were lined with oak wainscoting. On the first floor an apartment termed the "painted chamber" was finished in a costly manner, and might be considered an interesting specimen of the taste of the age in which it was arranged. The mouldings were gilt, and the whole of the panels on the sides were painted with subjects taken from the works of Ovid. On the window-shutters were some pictorial decorations—strangely contrasting with the above heathenish embellishments—in the form of emblems of grief and death, and mingled with the arms of Gunston and Abney, and intended, doubtless, to honour their memory; these were supposed to have been added by the pencil of Dr. Isaac Watts himself, who was an artist as well as poet and divine, and who, as we shall presently see, found in this mansion an asylum for upwards of six-and-thirty years.

THE OLD RECTORY, STOKE NEWINGTON, IN 1858. (*See page* 536.)

The building, with its "old brick front, its old brick wall, and its old iron gate, all redolent of the times of William III. and Queen Anne," was commenced about the year 1690, by a Mr. Gunston, who at that time had purchased considerable property at Stoke Newington. He died, however, before the house was completely finished; an event which drew forth a funeral poem from the pen of Dr. Watts, in which, not content with the calling on "the buildings to weep," he writes—

"Mourn, ye young gardens, ye *unfinished gates!*"

The mansion now became the property and residence of Sir Thomas and Lady Abney, who, with their family, of which Dr. Watts may be considered a member, took up their abode here.

Sir Thomas Abney was a member of the Fishmongers' Company, and a distinguished Nonconformist. He was knighted by William III., and served the office of Lord Mayor in 1700. He is celebrated for the costliness of his procession on the occasion of entering on the mayoralty, as may be seen in detail in Mr. J. G. Nichols' "London Pageants." We are told how that "a person rode before the cavalcade in armour, with a dagger in his hand, representing Sir William Walworth, the head of the rebel Wat Tyler being carried on a pole before him." "Sir Thomas," as John Timbs informs us, "was not more distinguished by his hospitality than by his personal piety. Neither business nor pleasure ever interrupted his observance of public and private domestic worship. Upon the evening of the day that he entered on the office of Lord Mayor, without any notice he withdrew from the public assembly at Guildhall after supper, went back to his house, there performed his devotions, and then returned back to his company."

Isaac Watts began to preach at the age of twenty-three, while living under the roof of Sir John and Lady Hartopp at Stoke Newington, where, as we have seen in the preceding chapter, he was engaged as tutor. He was soon afterwards invited to assist Dr. Chauncey, of whose congregation in Mark Lane Sir John Hartopp was a member; subsequently, on the retirement of the old pastor, Watts was induced—though somewhat reluctantly, owing to ill health—to undertake the charge, in. March, 1702. Ten years later, a nervous disease had so grown upon him that he was compelled to suspend his public labours, and abandon the length of exactly thirty years.' 'Sir,' added Lady Abney, in words which contained infinitely more than mere compliment, 'what you have termed a long thirty years' visit, I consider as the shortest visit my family ever received.'"

Stoke Newington thus became Dr. Watts's home; and here, and at Theobalds, where Sir Thomas Abney had a favourite summer retreat, he wrote most of those "Divine and Moral Songs" with

ABNEY HOUSE, 1845.

exercise of his ministry. In the meantime the congregation had removed from Mark Lane to a chapel in Bury Street, where Sir Thomas Abney and his amiable lady were members. They had become devoted friends to the poet and divine. "Watts, being lonely—a bachelor in the midst of his sad affliction—the Abneys invited him to come and stay with them for a few weeks' change. He did so. One day, long afterwards, the Countess of Huntingdon called upon the invalid. 'Madam,' said he, 'your ladyship is come to see me on a very remarkable day.' 'Why so remarkable?' she asked. 'This day thirty years I came hither to the house of my good friend Sir Thomas Abney, intending to spend but one single week under his friendly roof, and I have extended my visit to the

which his name is so closely associated. Old Sir Thomas Abney died in 1722, upwards of fourscore years old; but Watts continued to reside at Abney Park with Lady Abney and her daughter until his own death. "Here," writes Dr. Stoughton, "he enjoyed the uninterrupted demonstrations of the truest friendship. Here, without any care of his own, he had everything which could contribute to the enjoyment of life, and favour the unwearied pursuit of his studies. Here he dwelt in a family which, for piety, order, harmony, and every virtue, was a house of God. Here he had the privilege of a country recess—the fragrant bower, the spreading lawn, the flowery garden, and other advantages—to soothe his mind and aid his restoration to health, to yield him, whenever he chose them, the most grateful intervals from his laborious studies, and enable him to return to them with redoubled vigour and delight."

Watts was chaplain to the household of the good old knight; and morning and evening he led the devotions, and on Sunday night preached to the family. The doctor's study in Lady Abney's house at Stoke Newington was the local centre of his existence. From it he at times diverged only to return to it again with a deeper feeling of home attachment. Mrs. S. Carter Hall, in her "Pilgrimages to English Shrines," describing her visit to this mansion, after speaking of the library, says, "We followed our conductor to the top of the house, where, in a turret upon the roof, many of Dr. Watts's literary and religious works were composed. We sat upon the seamed bench, rough and worn, the very bench upon which he sat by daylight and moonlight—poet, logician, and Christian teacher. The chamber upon whose walls hung the parting breath of this benevolent man might well be an object of the deepest interest to all who follow, however humbly, the faith of Jesus. We were told of a little child who, knowing every hymn he had written, was taken into his room, having some vague but happy idea that she should meet him there. Learning, as she eagerly looked round, that the author of 'Watts's Hymns' was dead, she burst into bitter tears, which did not cease while she remained in the house. Many of his works are said to have been produced in this room, which, though small, was lofty and pleasant."

Here is a picture of the doctor's study and its learned occupant, as drawn by Dr. Stoughton, in his "Shades and Echoes of Old London:"—"Here are some lines from Horace, hung up in a frame outside the door, denouncing the faithless friend. Within, the shelves are loaded with a goodly array of books—poetical, philosophical, historical, theological, and critical. Where there are no shelves, there are prints of noted persons, chiefly divines. A lofty panel covers the fireplace, with inscriptions from Horace on either side: the one, where the portraits are numerous, indicating that the space is filled up by shades of the departed; the other, where they are fewer, soliciting additions to the illustrious group. The classical fancifulness of all this indicates the scholar and the poet; but the avocations of the worthy occupant of this literary retreat indicate those noble purposes, those high Christian aims, of which all else in his character and habits were ornamental adjuncts. There he sits at his writing table, enveloped in a scholarly robe, small in figure, and sickly in complexion; the forehead not so broad and high as we might expect, limited somewhat by the wig that crowns and borders it; the features large and marked, the eyes clear and burning."

"Isaac Watts," observes the Rev. T. Jackson, in his lecture on Stoke Newington, "adopted substantially the fatal errors of Arius." This accusation may or may not be true; but as Dr. Stoughton remarks, "without trimming, without temporising, he was quiet and without bustle; without boasting or parade, he did his own business—the work that God had given him. And now no church repudiates him; Nonconformity cannot monopolise him. His eulogium is pronounced by Samuel Johnson and Robert Southey, as well as by Josiah Conder; and whilst his monument looks down on Dissenting graves in Abney Park, his effigy reposes beneath the consecrated roof of Westminster Abbey." Dr. Watts died at Abney Park, surrounded by his friends, on the 24th of November, 1748; and his remains were interred in Bunhill Fields.

Miss Abney, the daughter of Sir Thomas Abney, ordered by her will that on her death the estate of Abney Park should be sold and the proceeds given to the poor, and distributed among charities. It was accordingly sold, and the purchase money of the new owner, whose name was Eade, was devoted to the execution of her intentions.

The mansion, after having been for many years used as a college for the instruction of youths of the Wesleyan Society, was pulled down in 1845, the park and garden-grounds having, four or five years previously, been converted into a cemetery. Many of the fine old cedars and yews that adorn the cemetery flourished here during the lifetime of Dr. Watts, who, it is said, wrote much of his poetry beneath their shade, and upon the mound consecrated by his name, and which, a vague tradition tells us, covers the ashes of no less a personage than Oliver Cromwell. We have already had occasion, more than once, to record some of the traditions concerning Cromwell's supposed resting-place.* That his body received but a mock funeral at Westminster, and was really peaceably reposing elsewhere, is said to have been a favourite belief with his partisans; and General Fleetwood's residence at Stoke Newington, the circumstance of his marriage with Bridget, the eldest daughter of the "Lord High Protector," and widow of General Ireton, and the fact that he was a very distinguished character during the Protectorate of his father-in-law—may easily have led to the tradition above mentioned, however unfounded. A large portion of Abney Park, ranging from the magnificent

* See Vol. III., pp. 437, 539; Vol. IV., p. 546.

cedar of Lebanon, in the part of the grounds once called the Wilderness, and stretching away to the north extremity, where the mound is placed, and all the land eastward of that line, extending as far as the principal entrance to the cemetery, was, during the Commonwealth, and after the Restoration, the property of General Fleetwood, of whose house we have spoken in the previous chapter.

Abney Park Cemetery covers in all about thirty acres of ground, and was opened in 1840. It is full of monuments of men whom time will not let die. A cenotaph monument and statue to the memory of Dr. Isaac Watts rises conspicuously above other mementoes of the departed, connecting the place with his name, and exciting the visitor to some recollections of his works and virtues. Mrs. S. C. Hall, writing in 1850, says:—"The trees and the avenues, preserved with a most delicate respect to the memory of the poet, are so well kept, there is such an air of solemnity and peace and positive 'beauty' in the arrangement of the whole, that if spirits were permitted to visit the earth, we might hope to meet his shade amid his once favourite haunts. There is nothing to offend us in such receptacles for the perishing dust of humanity, but everything to soothe and harmonise the feelings of the past and present. A statue in pure and simple character of this high-priest of charity stands (we are told) upon the 'exact spot' where the house stood; but we think it has been placed rather farther back than was the dwelling." The inscription upon the pedestal of the statue, which was executed by Mr. E. H. Baily, R.A., and "erected by public subscription, September, 1845," is as follows:—

"In memory of Isaac Watts, D.D., and in testimony of the high and lasting esteem in which his character and writings are held in the great Christian community by whom the English language is spoken. Of his Psalms and Hymns, it may be predicted in his own words:—

'Ages unborn will make his songs
The joy and labour of their tongues.'

He was born at Southampton, July 17th, 1674, and died November 24th, 1748, after a residence of thirty-six years in the mansion of Sir Thomas Abney, Bart., then standing in these grounds."

Dr. Johnson wrote of him:—"Few men have left behind such purity of character, or such monuments of laborious piety; he has provided instruction for all ages, from those who are lisping their first lessons to the enlightened readers of Malebranche and Locke. He has left neither corporeal nor spiritual nature unexamined; he has taught the Art of Reasoning and the Science of the Stars; such he was, as every Christian Church would rejoice to have adopted."

The "mound," too, which we have mentioned above, whence the poet loved to overlook the green and fertile country—for London at that time had not escaped from Shoreditch—is walled in, fenced round, and guarded as a sanctuary. It is in the north-east corner of the grounds.

As a cemetery, Abney Park has some natural features of great beauty and interest. It is remarkable for its fine old trees, amongst which there is a splendid cedar of Lebanon of two centuries' growth. It contains also a beautiful arboretum, formed with great taste. The buildings are bold and effective, though of limited extent; and what is wanting in costliness has been more than compensated by the skill of the architect, Mr. W. Hosking, who has here shown how much may be effected by "that true simplicity which results from a few carefully-studied and well-finished features." Near the centre of the grounds stands a neat brick-built chapel, of Gothic architecture, the tower of which is surmounted by a tapering spire. The ground is (using the words of the proprietors) "a General Cemetery for the City of London, and its eastern and north-eastern suburbs, which shall be open to all classes of the community, and to all denominations of Christians, without restraint in forms." There is, therefore, no separating line in this cemetery between the parts appropriated to members of the Church of England and to Dissenters. The greater part of the ground is thickly studded with tombs and monuments, most of which are remarkable for simplicity, and many of the graves are enriched with flowers or other touching emblems of the grief of sorrowing friends of the departed. Unlike Kensal Green and other cemeteries which we have visited in the course of our perambulation round London, Abney Park cannot boast of containing the ashes of many who have distinguished themselves "by flood and field;" but a large number of those who achieved distinction in more peaceable walks of life have here found a resting-place. Among them we may mention the Rev. Dr. Fletcher, of Finsbury, "the Children's Friend;" the Rev. Andrew Reed, D.D., the philanthropic founder of many orphan asylums and other public charities, who died in 1862; the Rev. Dr. Fletcher, of Stepney; Dr. John Campbell; the Rev. Thomas Binney, one of the most prominent leaders of the Independent connexion, and for many years minister at the Weigh-house Chapel, Fish Street Hill; the Rev. Dr. Pye Smith; Dr. Archer; and last, not least, Mr. Braidwood, who was many years chief of the London Fire Brigade, and who lost his life during the great fire in Tooley Street, in June, 1861.

Passing northward, after leaving the cemetery gates, we soon arrive at Stamford Hill, a gentle eminence on the main road. The old Cambridge Road, which we have mentioned as passing through Hackney by way of Mare Street, after continuing its course through Lower and Upper Clapton, joins the new road, by which we are now proceeding, at the summit of the hill. Both sides of the road, as we pass up the hill, are occupied by rows of houses and detached villas, many of them of an elegant character, that almost force upon the recollection the lines of Cowper—

> "Suburban villas, highway side retreats,
> That dread th' encroachment of our growing streets.
> Tight boxes, neatly sashed, and in a blaze
> With all a July's sun's collected rays,
> Delight the citizen, who, gasping there,
> Breathes clouds of dust and calls it country air."

So much may the neighbourhood now be considered part of London, that the road itself is traversed by tram-cars, which run between the City and the top of Stamford Hill. On our right we pass a new Congregational Chapel, a large Gothic structure, the tall spire of which forms a prominent object for some distance round.

On reaching the summit of the hill, where the two roads meet as above mentioned, an entirely different scene presents itself, and we begin to feel that we have reached almost the limits of our journey in this direction. Green fields, trees, and hedge-rows now burst upon the view; and winding away to the north-east the road leads on towards the village of Tottenham, whither we will presently direct our steps. Before proceeding thither, however, we will give a glance back over the ground we have wandered; and conjure up to our imagination the sweeping change which must have taken place within the last three or four centuries, when London was walled in on every side, and all away to the north was fields—"Moor Felde," "Smeeth Felde," and the like—and forest land, through which passed the lonely road, called "Hermen [or Ermine] Strete," of which we have spoken in the previous chapter, after emerging from "Creple Gate," on its way by Stoke Newington, to St. Albans and the north. The swampy nature of the ground, too, in some parts is still indicated by the name of Finsbury (*Fensbury*); but all this, as we have seen, has long been built upon, and "Moorfields are fields no more."

As Mr. Matthew Browne writes in "Chaucer's England," we must "either be at a great distance from London or must possess a very lively imagination to conceive of the English capital as a place of gardens, such as it was in the time of the Plantagenets. Within my own memory, the area within which roses will not grow in the metropolis has been widening and widening in the most odious manner, and in every direction. The great brick-giant marches out towards the fields, and the roses fly before him; and you have to go nearly out of the sound of 'Big Ben' to see gardens no sweeter and gayer than lay under the shadow of St. Paul's and the Savoy Palace in the days of John of Gaunt."

In the reign of King James, Stamford Hill was crowned with a grove of trees, and its eastern declivity was overgrown with brushwood. The whole country on the Essex side was marshy as far as Epping Forest, some three miles distant. Through a swampy vale on the right the river Lea, so dear to the angler, took its slow and silent course, while through a green valley on the left flowed the New River.

In Mr. Harrison Ainsworth's romance of the "Star Chamber" is a graphic and spirited, though somewhat sensational, sketch of the view looking towards London from this elevated spot at the above period:—"Arrived at the summit of the hill commanding such extensively charming views, Jocelyn halted and looked back with wonder at the vast and populous city he had just quitted, now spread out before him in all its splendour and beauty. In his eyes it seemed already overgrown, though it had not attained a tithe of its present proportions; but he could only judge according to his opportunity, and was unable to foresee its future magnitude. But if London has waxed in size, wealth, and population during the last two centuries and a half, it has lost nearly all the peculiar features of beauty which distinguished it up to that time, and made it so attractive to Jocelyn's eyes. The diversified and picturesque architecture of its ancient habitations, as yet undisturbed by the innovations of the Italian and Dutch schools, and brought to full perfection in the latter part of the reign of Elizabeth, gave the whole city a characteristic and fanciful appearance. Old towers, old belfries, old crosses, slender spires innumerable, rose up amid a world of quaint gables and angular roofs. Storey above storey sprang those curious dwellings, irregular, yet homogeneous; dear to the painter's and the poet's eye; elaborate in ornament, grotesque in design, well suited to the climate, and admirably adapted to the wants and comforts of the inhabitants; picturesque like the age itself, like its costume, its manners, its literature. . . . Another advantage in those days must not be forgotten. The canopy of smoke overhanging the vast modern Babel, and oftentimes obscuring even the light of the sun itself, did not dim the beauties of the ancient city—sea-coal being but little used in comparison with wood, of which there was then abundance, as at this time in the capital of France. Thus the atmosphere was clearer and lighter, and served as a finer medium to reveal objects which would now be lost at a quarter the distance.

"Fair, sparkling, and clearly defined, then rose up Old London before Jocelyn's gaze. Girded round with grey walls, defended by battlements, and approached by lofty gates, four of which—to wit, Cripplegate, Moorgate, Bishopsgate, and Aldgate—were visible from where he stood; it riveted attention from its immense congregation of roofs, spires, pinnacles, and vanes, all glittering in the sunshine; while in the midst of all, and pre-eminent above all, towered one gigantic pile—the glorious Gothic cathedral. Far on the east, and beyond the city walls, though surrounded by its own mural defences, was seen the frowning Tower of London—part fortress and part prison—a structure never viewed in those days without terror, being the scene of so many passing tragedies. Looking westward, and rapidly surveying the gardens and pleasant suburban villages lying on the north of the Strand, the young man's gaze settled for a moment on Charing Cross—the elaborately-carved memorial to his queen Eleanor, erected by Edward I., and then ranging over the palace of Whitehall and its two gates, Westminster Abbey—more beautiful without its towers than with them—it became fixed upon Westminster Hall; for there, in one of its chambers, the ceiling of which was adorned with gilded stars, were held the councils of that terrible tribunal which had robbed him of his inheritance, and now threatened him with deprivation of liberty and mutilation of person. A shudder crossed him as he thought of the Star-Chamber, and he turned his gaze elsewhere, trying to bring the whole glorious city within his ken.

"A splendid view, indeed! Well might King James himself exclaim, when standing, not many years previously, on the very spot where Jocelyn now stood, and looking upon London for the first time since his accession to the throne of England—well might he exclaim in rapturous accents, as he gazed on the magnificence of his capital, 'At last the richest jewel in a monarch's crown is mine!'"

However much the above description of the view from Stamford Hill may be overdrawn, and whether Jocelyn could descry the cross at Charing from this spot or not, there is at least some foundation for the exclamation which Mr. Harrison Ainsworth has put into the mouth of King James; for it is on record how that on the 7th of May, 1603, his Majesty was here met by the Lord Mayor and aldermen on his first public entry into London after his accession.

The river Lea, which flows at the distance of from one to two miles on our right, all the way from Kingsland, and which here makes its nearest approach to the road that we are travelling, divides the county of Middlesex from that of Essex, as far to the north as Waltham Abbey. Its course on the whole is due south, though somewhat winding, and here and there it divides its water into two or three separate channels, and then re-unites them. Nearly all along its course there is a broad belt of meadow and marsh land on one side of the river, or on both, which is used as pasturage for cattle. The Lea itself, after sweeping past Chingford, Stratford, and Bow, falls into the Thames close by the Victoria Dock. This river in former times was deemed one of considerable importance, as the means of supply in conveying corn, meal, and malt to the metropolis; so much so, in fact, that in the reign of Edward IV. an Act of Parliament was passed for improving the navigation. It has, too, an historical interest, for Drayton, in his "Polyolbion," tells us how that—

"The old Lea brags of the Danish blood."

It is said in Lambarde's "Dictionarium Topographicum" that "it hath of longe tyme borne vessels from London twenty miles towards its head: for in the tyme of King Ælfrede, the Danes entered Leymouthe and fortified at a place adjoyning this river twenty miles from London, where by fortune Kinge Alfred passinge by espied that the channel of the river might be in such sorte weakened, that they should want water to return with their shippes; he caused therefore the water to be abated by two great trenches, and settinge the Londoners upon them he made them batteil, wherein they lost four of their captaines, and a great number of their common souldiers, the rest flyinge into the castell which they had built. Not long after they were so pressed that they forsoke all and left their shippes as a prey to the Londoners; which, breakinge some and burninge other, conveyed the rest to London." He adds that this castle, though it might seem to be Hertford, was on another part of the river's bank; but where it stood is not clearly defined, and must always remain a moot point. Other authors, however, confirm in the main the leading statement of Lambarde, namely, Sir William Dugdale in his "History of the Embanking and Draining the Fens," and Sir John Spelman in his "Life of Alfred the Great." A perusal of the latter work will leave the honest reader in very little doubt but that these trenches are the very same that now branch off from the river between the Temple Mills and Old Ford, and crossing the Essex Road near Stratford, enter the Thames together with the main stream of the Lea.

On those channels of the Lea which are not used for the purposes of navigation there are corn and paper mills, near which are the favourite resorts for the disciples of Izaak Walton's "gentle craft." At many places the fishing is strictly preserved, and admission to these pleasant spots is obtained only by the "silver key" of a yearly subscription. There is a tranquillising influence in such spots, which harmonise best with minds formed as those of John Scott, the Quaker poet of Amwell, and of the author of the "Complete Angler." In fact, Scott has paid his tribute to Izaak Walton, who

> "Oft our fair haunts explored; upon Lea's shore
> Beneath some green tree oft his angle laid,
> His sport suspending to admire their charms."

"Honest Izaak" has been immortalised by his literary labours, which were mainly of a biographical character; but his best known production is the "Complete Angler, or Contemplative Man's Recreation."* This appeared in 1653, and has gone through numerous editions. The motto to the first edition was, "Simon Peter said, I go a fishing; and they said, We also go with thee;" but it was cancelled in subsequent editions. This "pleasant curiosity of fish and fishing," writes his amiable biographer, "is a series of dialogues—no long 'and watery discourse,' but truly a rich entertainment—quaint, humorous, and cheerful, abounding in happy touches of wit and raillery, practical wisdom, sagacious reflections, and snatches of poetry and song. While his lectures on his art are so clear and so curious, his digressions are ever most amusing."

DR. WATTS' MONUMENT, ABNEY PARK CEMETERY.

While he continued in London, his favourite recreation was angling, in which he was the greatest proficient in his time; and indeed so great were his skill and experience in the art that there is

* See Vol. II., p. 233.

VIEWS ON THE RIVER LEA.

1. Ferry House. 2. Tottenham Church from Lea River. 3. Tumbling Weir. 4. Fishing Cottage 5. Tottenham Lock.

scarce any writer on the subject since his time who has not made the rules and practice of Walton his very foundation. It is therefore with the greatest propriety that Langbaine, in his "Lives of the English Dramatic Poets," calls him "the common father of all anglers." The river that he seems mostly to have frequented for this purpose was the Lea, which has its source above Ware, in Hertfordshire, and falls into the Thames, as we have seen, a little below Blackwall; unless we suppose that the vicinity of the New River to the place of his habitation might sometimes tempt him out with his friends—honest Nat and R. Roe, whose loss he so pathetically deplores in his preface of the "Complete Angler"—to "spend an afternoon there." In the above work, the kindness of old Izaak's nature often peeps out, as when he tells his friend and disciple or scholar who had caught his first chub, "it is a good beginning of your art to offer your first fruits to the poor, who will thank both you and God for it." "He was no ascetic, for he liked 'the barley-wine, the good liquor that our honest forefathers did use to drink of,' and he loved such mirth 'as did not make friends ashamed to look on one another the next morning.' His humour is sometimes quite comic, as when, after instructing his listener and companion in the art of impaling a frog upon a hook, and securing the upper part of its leg by one loop to the arming wire, he naïvely adds, 'In so doing, use him as if you love him.'"

According to Izaak Walton, the river Lea affords fine sport to the angler, not only in perch, chub, pike, barbel, dace, roach, gudgeon, and other common fish, but also in trout. He speaks of the Lea meadows as flowery above the average, and even of the milkmaids of the neighbourhood as prettier and more charming than their sisters in other parts; but in this last respect he probably mixed up too much of the poet with the philosopher. His serene heart, in fact, is ever going out in admiration of the clear stream in its shallows, pools, and flowery banks; the shady trees, the odorous honeysuckle, the green pastures, the disporting of the lambs, the hum of the bee, the clouds and sky, and the song of the linnet and the lark, the blackbird and thrush. "The book," writes its reviewer, "will ever be a favourite with all 'that love virtue and angling,' as did its author, who was at peace with himself and all creation excepting otters." Yet, in spite of this, Byron could write of Walton reproachfully in the following couplet—

> "That quaint old cruel coxcomb in his gullet
> Should have a hook and a small trout to pull it."

Rennie, in one of his notes on the "Complete Angler," tells a good story anent this river. An old river Lea angler being daily seen in one particular spot hereabouts, a brother angler conceived that the place must be the resort of abundance of fish, and therefore commenced his operations there one summer morning before daybreak. The usual attendant of the place arrived some hours after, and threw in his line. After a long silence, the first-comer remarked that he was out of luck, not having caught a single fish in this hole, which he had noticed to be such a favourite with his brother of the rod. "Sir," replied the old stager, "I confess that long custom has made me very partial to the spot; but as for fish, I assure you that here I have angled regularly for forty years, and have never had a bite as yet!"

The "Jolly Anglers" inn, at Lea Bridge, a little to the east of Upper Clapton, is of itself sufficient to indicate that the stream hereabouts is largely frequented by the lovers of Walton's "gentle art." It is also, during the summer months, much frequented for the purposes of bathing and boating, and the number of fatal accidents arising from the unskilful management of small craft by youths who can neither row nor swim is lamentably great.

CHAPTER XLV.

TOTTENHAM.

"It will not be long ere we shall be at Tottenham High Cross; and when we come thither, I will make you some requital of your pains."—*Izaak Walton.*

The Division of the Parish into Wards—Extent and Boundaries of the Parish—Early History of Tottenham—The Manor owned by King David Bruce of Scotland—Other Owners of the Manor—The Village of Tottenham—The Hermitage and Chapel of St. Anne—The "Seven Sisters"—The Village Green—The High Cross—The River Lea at Tottenham—Bleak Hall—Old Almshouses—The "George and Vulture"—The Roman Catholic Chapel of St. Francis de Sales—Bruce Castle—The Parish Church—The Chapel and Well of St. Loy—Bishop's Well—White Hart Lane—Wood Green—Tottenham Wood—Concluding Remarks.

We descend the sloping ground to the north of Stamford Hill, and following the roadway—the river Lea running parallel with our course through the green fields on our right—we soon enter the village of Tottenham. This village, or, as it is generally called, Tottenham High Cross, is described at some length in the "Ambulator" (1774). It is stated that "the present Duke of Northumberland and the late Lord Coleraine had seats here; and there are also a great number of pretty houses belonging to the citizens of London."

The parish of Tottenham is very extensive, or, at all events, was so, until sundry ecclesiastical districts were formed out of it. It was divided into four "wards," thus enumerated in the "Ambulator:"—"1. Nether Ward, in which stands the parsonage and vicarage; 2. Middle Ward, comprehending Church End and Marsh Street; 3. High Cross Ward, containing the hall, the mill, Page Green, and the High Cross; 4. Wood Green Ward, which comprehends all the rest of the parish, and is considerably bigger than the three other wards put together."

Bedwell, in his "History of Tottenham," describes the parish as being nearly fifteen miles in circumference. "It is divided," he writes, "on the east, from Walthamstow, in Essex, by the river Lea; on the north it meets the parish of Edmonton; on the west it is bounded by Hornsey and Friern-Barnet; and on the south by Hackney and Stoke Newington. The western division is watered by the circuitous progress of the New River; and a little brook, termed the Mosell, which rises at Muswell Hill, passes through the village, and shortly unites with a branch of the Lea."

The first that we hear of Tottenham is in the reign of Edward the Confessor, when it formed part of the possessions of Waltheof, Earl of Huntingdon. He took a prominent part in opposing the Norman invasion, but not long after he joined William, and married Judith, the niece of that king. From that time until his death, although he professed to be on William's side, still he was continually intriguing with the English, and a few years after his marriage he was betrayed by his wife and beheaded. Judith, however, was allowed to keep the manor of Tottenham, or, as it was then called, Toteham, on condition that she should pay to the king every year the value of five hides, equal to about 100 Norman shillings. There is a curious old record in the Domesday Book which mentions this fact, and also that the land consisted of ten carucates, or ploughlands. A carucate is estimated at about 240 acres, and thus the whole estate would be 2,400 acres. The value of the land, including a wood for 500 hogs and a weir worth 3s., amounted to £25 15s. and three ounces of gold. After the death of Judith the manor passed to her daughter Maud, who married a Norman noble, Simon de St. Liz. He died in the reign of Henry I., leaving a son Simon, from whom the king took away the estate and gave it to David, the son of Malcolm III., King of Scotland, who then married Simon's mother Maud. Their son Henry, their grandson Malcolm, and their great-grandson William the Lion, held it until the last joined Prince Henry against his father, Henry II., who ejected William, and restored it to its rightful owner Simon; but after his death the king gave it back to William, and he to his brother David, who then took the title of Earl of Huntingdon. On his death the manor probably fell to the share of his second daughter Isabel, who married the father of Robert Bruce, the competitor with John Baliol for the crown of Scotland, and afterwards king. It was he who made Tottenham his place of residence, and, as we shall presently see, gave the house the name of Bruce Castle, or rather, as it was then called, Le Bruses. On his revolt from Edward I. his property in England was forfeited, and came into the hands of the Crown. After this the manor was split up among different persons, to whom the king gave it in return for some service or other, but it appears that it never went down to the descendants of the owner, but always reverted to the Crown after his death. In the reign of Henry VI. we find that there were several lesser manors, which went by the following names:—Bruce's, Pembroke's, Mocking's, and Dawbeney's. These were named from their owners, and were held on condition that whenever the king went to war in person the owner should furnish him with a pair of silver spurs gilt.

David Bruce, King of Scotland, having thus become possessed of this manor and church, the latter, after it had belonged to the Earls of Northumberland and Chester, was given to the monastery of the Trinity, in London; but King Henry VIII. granted it to William, Lord Howard of Effingham, who being afterwards attainted, it again reverted to the king, who thereupon granted it to the Dean and Chapter of St. Paul's, to whom it still belongs.

In the "Beauties of England and Wales" it is stated that the manor of Tottenham, after having been held for several generations by three distinct families—and called respectively by the names of the manor of Bruses (or Bruce), the manor of Baliols, and the manor of Pembrokes—was in the reign of Edward I. given to William Dawbeny, "in consideration of his military services." King Henry VIII. gave the whole estate to Sir William Compton, groom of his bedchamber, who entertained at Bruce Castle the king and his sister Margaret, the wife of James IV., King of Scotland, who made Tottenham their place of meeting when the Scottish queen came up from the North. The manors thus united have, it is stated, ever since that time passed through the same hands. Early in the seventeenth century they were purchased by Hugh, second Lord Coleraine, from whom they descended to his next brother, the third lord, who compiled an essay towards a "History of Tottenham." His lordship's family name of Hanger may perhaps be still commemorated here by the name of Hanger Lane, though there is another possible derivation of the term from the hanging woods which fringed it. On the death of the third Lord Coleraine, the manor of Tottenham did not devolve upon his eccentric brother, the fourth and last lord, of whom we have already spoken in our account of Chalk Farm,* but were bequeathed to a natural daughter of the third lord; but as the lady was an alien, the estates were escheated to the Crown. The lady, however, having married Mr. James Townsend, an alderman of London, the lands were subsequently granted to that gentleman, and have since changed hands by sale on several occasions.

At Tottenham the first ambassador from the "Emperor of Cathair, Muscovia, and Russeland," who had been wrecked on the coast of Scotland, was met in 1556 by a splendid procession of the members of the Russia Company, then lately founded for carrying on traffic with that country.

The main street of the village of Tottenham is formed of good houses, irregularly built, along each side of the great northern road, with a few smaller streets branching off at right angles on either hand. The situation is unpleasingly flat, and the buildings for the most part straggling and unequal, yet partaking little of a rural character. On the east side of High Street, and at a short distance southward from the Cross, stood formerly the Hermitage and Chapel of St. Anne. It was a small square building, constructed chiefly of brick, and had a narrow strip of ground annexed to it, stretching away along by the highway southward from the building to the "Seven Sisters." The "Hermitage" was a cell dependent on the Monastery of the Holy Trinity in London, and its site is now covered by the "Bull" public-house; whilst on the strip of ground mentioned above a row of houses has been erected called Grove Place.

The "Seven Sisters," as we have already remarked,† is the sign given to two public-houses at Tottenham. In front of that at Page Green, near the entrance of the village, were planted seven elms in a circle, with a walnut-tree in the middle. Of these trees we have given an illustration, when describing the Seven Sisters' Road, which was named after them. It was traditionally asserted that a martyr had been burnt on the spot where the trees were originally planted more than five hundred years ago; but the tradition wants verification.

The centre of Tottenham is occupied by a large triangular enclosure, called the Green. Mr. Harrison Ainsworth, from whose romance of the "Star Chamber" we have quoted in the previous chapter, introduces to our notice some of the rustic scenes which may have been witnessed here at the period at which the plot of his story is laid. The following are some of his remarks:—

"Long before Jocelyn and his companion reached Tottenham, they were made aware, by the ringing of bells from its old ivy-grown church tower, and by other joyful sounds, that some festival was taking place there; and the nature of the festival was at once revealed as they entered the long straggling street, then, as now, constituting the chief part of the pretty little village, and beheld a large assemblage of country folk, in holiday attire, wending their way towards the Green for the purpose of setting up a May-pole upon it, and making the welkin ring with their gladsome shouts. All the youths and maidens of Tottenham and its vicinity, it appeared, had risen before daybreak that morning, and sallied forth into the woods to cut green boughs and gather wild flowers for the ceremonial. At the same time they selected and hewed down a tall, straight tree—the tallest and straightest they could find; and, stripping off its branches, placed it on a wain, and dragged it to the village with the help of an immense team of oxen, numbering as many as forty yoke. Each ox had a garland of flowers fastened to the tip of its horns; and the tall spar itself was twined round with ropes of daffodils, bluebells, cowslips, primroses, and other early flowers, while its summit was surmounted with a floral crown, and festooned with garlands, various-coloured ribands, kerchiefs, and streamers. The foremost yokes of oxen had bells hung round their necks, which they shook as they moved along, adding their blithe melody to the general hilarious sounds. When the festive throng reached the village, all its inhabitants—male and female, old and young—rushed forth to greet them; and such as were able to leave their dwellings for a short while joined in the procession, at the head of which, of course, was borne the May-pole. After it came a band of young men, armed with the necessary implements for planting the

* See *ante*, p. 294.

† See *ante*, pp. 380, 381.

shaft in the ground; and after them a troop of maidens, bearing bundles of rushes. Next came the minstrels, playing merrily on tabor, fife, sackbut, rebec, and tambourine. Then followed the Queen of the May, walking by herself—a rustic beauty, hight Gillian Greenford—fancifully and prettily arrayed for the occasion, and attended, at a little distance, by Robin Hood, Maid Marian, Friar Tuck, the hobby-horse, and a band of morris-dancers. Then came the crowd, pell-mell, laughing, shouting, and huzzaing—most of the young men and women bearing green branches of birch and other trees in their hands.

"The spot selected for the May-pole," he adds, "was a piece of greensward in the centre of the village, surrounded by picturesque habitations, and having on one side of it the ancient cross. The latter, however, was but the remnant of the antique structure, the cross having been robbed of its upper angular bar, and otherwise mutilated, at the time of the Reformation, and it was now nothing more than a high wooden pillar, partly cased with lead to protect it from the weather, and supported by four great spurs."

On the eastern side of the street, not far from the centre of the village, and close by the north-east angle of the Green, stands the high cross, whence this particular "ward" or division of the parish receives its second name. The structure forms a very interesting feature in the antiquities of Tottenham. Lysons, in his "Environs of London," states that "the hie crosse" is mentioned in a Court Roll, dated 1456; and Norden, in his "Speculum Britanniæ" (1593–1620), says, "Tottenham High Cross was a hamlet belonging to Tottenham, and hath this adjunct High Cross of a wooden cross there lately raised on a little mound of earth." Bedwell, in his history of the parish, written in 1631, describes the appearance of the cross some fifty years previously as "a columne of wood, covered with a square sheet of leade to shoote the water off every way, underset by four spurres." He adds: "There hath been a cross here of long continuance, even so long as since that decree was made by the Church that every parish should in places most frequented set up a cross, but whether it were such at the first as afterwards it is manifest it was I much doubt of, for that it hath been of an extraordinary height, and from thence the towne gained the addition of *alta crucis*."* Notwithstanding the preservatives spoken of by Bedwell, the cross speedily afterwards sank to decay, for at the commencement of the seventeenth century, Dean Wood, who had a residence close by, "built a plain octangular cross of brick, which," says Mr. Brewer, in the "Beauties of England and Wales" (1816), "yet remains, but has recently experienced considerable alteration. In consequence of a subscription among some of the inhabitants of Tottenham," he adds, "a complete covering of stucco was bestowed in 1809, and at the same time various embellishments, of the character usually termed Gothic, were introduced. These are in the style which prevailed in the Tudor era, and it is to be regretted that the date at which the alterations were effected is not placed in a conspicuous situation. On each face of the octagon is a shield with one of the letters composing the word *Totenham* in the old character." It is perhaps even still more a matter of regret that the "restoration" of the cross was not postponed for half a century, until the public had become a little more enlightened as to the principles of Gothic architecture. In that case it would not probably have been covered with a composition of stucco, but conscientiously renewed in Bath stone.

Bedwell, in speaking of the "Eleanor crosses," does not venture to assert that this is one of the series, but remarks that "it was against the corps should come thro' the towne re-edified and peradventure raised higher."

It will be remembered by the reader of Izaak Walton's "Complete Angler" how, in the opening scene, "Piscator" cries out to his friends "Venator" and "Auceps," who are on their way to the "Thatched House," in Hodsden, "You are well overtaken, gentlemen. A good morning to you. I have stretched my legs up Tottenham Hill to overtake you, hoping your business may occasion you towards Ware;" and how "Auceps," in reply, agrees to bear him company as far as Theobalds, at Cheshunt. In fact, the long street of Tottenham is the direct road not only to Theobalds, but to Enfield and Edmonton, and so on to Ware and Hatfield.

On reaching Tottenham Cross, "Piscator" thus addresses his fellows, "Venator" and the "Scholar:" "And pray let us now rest ourselves in this sweet shady arbour, which Nature herself has woven with her own fine fingers; it is such a contexture of woodbines, sweet-briars, jessamine, and myrtle, and so interwoven as will secure us both from the sun's violent heat and from the approaching shower. And being sat down, I will requite a part of your courtesies with a bottle of sack, milk, oranges, and sugar, which, all put together, make a drink like

* "A Brief Description of the Towne of Tottenham High Cross, in Middlesex, together with an historical narrative of such memorable things as are there to be seen and observed; collected, digested, and written by William Bedwell, Pastor of the parish, 1631."

nectar—indeed, too good for anybody but us anglers. And so, master, here is a full glass to you of that liquor; and when you have pledged me, I will repeat the verses which I promised you." It is to be feared that the "Piscator" of the present day would find this pretty picture of sweet shady arbours, overgrown with jessamine, sweetbriars, and myrtle, to say the least, a little overdrawn.

Almost every illustrated edition of the "Complete Angler" has an engraving of a fishery and ferry here, called "Bower Banks;" and no wonder, for the river Lea, as it flows by Tottenham, is very charming, especially in its old course about the Mill. The author of "Rambles by Rivers" thus sketches the scene at this point:—"An old pollard willow, with an angler under its shadow—a few cows, perhaps, standing in the water, and enjoying with philosophic quiescence the cooling luxury—perchance a punt in the middle of the river—a bright blue sky overhead, reflected with a softened lustre in the clear stream—an abundance of yellow water-lilies at our feet, and the low banks decked with all gay flowers—these are the materials of the picture; and he who has not his heart gladdened as he gazes on them, has yet to learn that there are things in heaven and earth not dreamt of in his philosophy. Walton was not one of these:

TOTTENHAM HIGH CROSS, 1820.

'The meanest flow'ret of the vale,
The simplest note that swells the gale,
The common sun, the air, the skies,
To him *were* opening Paradise.'

And only such as, in a measure, can participate in these feelings and sympathies are fitted to wander along Izaak Walton's Lea."

A short distance farther up the stream, at a place called Cook's Ferry, stood Bleak Hall, the house fixed upon as being the one to which "Piscator" took his scholar, and which was then "an honest ale-house, where might be found a cleanly room, lavender in the windows, and twenty ballads stuck about the wall; with a hostess both cleanly, and handsome, and civil." The old house has long been swept away; a portion of it, however, remained standing down into the present century. It consisted of a kitchen, with a room over it (ascended by a staircase on the outside), called the "fisherman's locker," from its having been used as a locker for their tackle. If not the actual place to which Izaak Walton refers, it must long have been a well-known hostel for Lea fishermen. The evidence appears to tell against its identity as the Bleak Hall of old Izaak, but local tradition was, and is, very strong in its favour. The Lea, we need scarcely add, is the only river, next to the Thames, that is engrafted in the affections of the Londoner.

BRUCE CASTLE.

In 1596, an almshouse was founded in the High Street of Tottenham by one Zanchero, a Spaniard, the first confectioner ever known in this kingdom. Near to the Cross there is another row of almshouses, founded by a Mr. Nicholas Richardson, and which date their erection from the early part of the last century.

The "George and Vulture" tavern, in the high road, nearly opposite Bruce Grove, occupies the site of a much older inn, which was frequented by the Londoners in early times for the purpose of recreation. It is mentioned in the "Search after Claret," as far back as the reign of William III., but was probably far older. Its charms are thus described in a newspaper paragraph, immortalised by Mr. Larwood in his "History of Sign-boards:"

> "If lur'd to roam in summer hours,
> Your thought inclines tow'rd Totnam bowers,
> Here end your airing tour, and rest
> Where Cole invites each friendly guest.
> Intent on signs, the prying eye
> The 'George and Vulture' will descry:
> Here the kind landlord glad attends
> To wellcome all his cheerfull Friends,
> Who, leaving City smoke, delight
> To range where vision's scenes invite.

The spacious garden, verdant field,
Pleasures beyond expression yield;
The Angler here to sport inclined,
In his Canal may pastime find.
Next, racy Wine and home-brew'd Ale
The nicest palates may regale;
Nectarious Punch—and (cleanly grac'd)
A Larder stor'd for every taste.
The cautious Fair may sip with glee
The freshest Coffee, finest Tea.
Let none the outward *Vulture* fear;
No *Vulture* host inhabits here:
If too well us'd ye deem ye—then
Then take your revenge, and come again."

On the western side of the chief street, near White Hart Lane, stands in a retired situation, as though retreating from the public gaze, the Roman Catholic Chapel of St. Francis de Sales. It is a small and unpretending structure, in the style of the Dissenting chapels of half a century ago, about forty feet in length by thirty. It was erected by the late Baroness de Montesquieu in 1826–7, on a site purchased by her for that purpose, and was solemnly opened by Bishop Poynter, in the May of the latter year, previous to which time the Roman Catholics here had been content with the use of a room in the house of the resident priest. For more than a century Tottenham and Edmonton have been noted for the number of poor lodging-houses in which lived the Irish labourers who worked in the fields and market gardens around this part. On the outbreak of the first French Revolution their number was increased by an influx of emigrants from the north of France, who brought with them much skilled industry, but more poverty. It was not, therefore, till about 1793 that any regular provision was made in Tottenham for their religious wants. In that year the Abbé Cheireux, afterwards Bishop of Boston, in the United States, and subsequently Archbishop of Bordeaux, and a cardinal, being employed as tutor in a Protestant family in Tottenham, obtained the use of a room in Queen Street, Tottenham Terrace, in order to minister to the spiritual needs of both the Irish and the French poor. On his departure for America, the Abbé Cheireux handed over his charge to another French *emigré* priest, and eventually, about the year 1805, the Abbé Le Tethier erected a modest chapel-house and still more modest presbytery in the same street. This, however, became alienated, through debt or other causes, and the Roman Catholics were left without a chapel or chaplain from the year 1818 down to the time when the present structure was built by the Baroness de Montesquieu, as mentioned above. In 1871, some nuns of the Servite order settled down in a house in Hanger Lane, at the southern end of Tottenham, where they have opened a school and a chapel.

Westward of the main street, near Bruce Grove Station on the branch line of the Great Eastern Railway, is Bruce Castle, which has long been used as a private school. The mansion was rebuilt in the latter part of the seventeenth century, and is a good specimen of Elizabethan domestic architecture. The structure, as stated above, takes its name from a castellated mansion, the residence of Robert Bruce the elder, father of the Scottish king of that name, which in ancient times occupied this site. The original building is said to have been erected by Earl Waltheof, who married Judith, niece to William the Conqueror, who gave him for her portions the earldoms of Northumberland and Huntingdon. Their only daughter, Maud, after the death of her first husband, married David I., King of Scotland, and being heiress of Huntingdon, had in her own right, as appended to that honour, "the manor of Tottenham, in Middlesex." Through her these possessions descended to Robert Bruce, brother of William III., King of Scotland. Bruce contended for the throne of Scotland with John Baliol, who was ultimately adjudged heir to the crown. Upon this adjudication Robert Bruce retired to England, and, settling on his grandfather's estate at Tottenham, repaired the castle, and acquiring an adjacent manor, named it and the castle Bruce. In the reign of Henry VIII. the property, as we have already had occasion to remark, was granted to Sir William Compton, then groom of the king's bedchamber.

It is recorded that, in 1516, Henry VIII. here met his sister Margaret, Queen of Scots. Dr. Robinson, in his "History of Tottenham," says: "It is probable that Sir William Compton rebuilt the house soon after he became possessed of the manor in 1514, and that it was finished to receive the royal guests in 1516, for on the Saturday after Ascension Day in that year King Henry VIII. met his sister, Margaret Queen of Scots, at 'Maister Compton's house, beside Totnam!'" The next royal visitor was Queen Elizabeth, who became the guest of Margaret's grandson, Henry, Lord Compton, so that it would seem that the daughter of the Queen of Scots had married the heir of the Comptons. A passage in Robinson, referring to Queen Elizabeth's visit to Henry, Lord Compton, would seem to throw some doubt on his earlier statement that Sir William Compton rebuilt the house, for in it he observes, "The style of the building, which is of that period—namely, 1578—seems to justify the conjecture that the house was built by Henry, Lord Compton;" but it receives additional strength from the following passage from Lord Coleraine's MS. :—"In respect to its great antiquity more than conveniency, I keep the old brick tower in good repair, although I am not able to discover the founder thereof; and among the other anticaglia of this place I range Sir William Compton's coat of armes, which I took out of the old porch when I raised the tower in the front of the house." It appears, therefore, as if Lord Coleraine's evidence goes to confirm the first statement of Robinson. The coat of arms he referred to is believed to be that which is now affixed on the north side of the house, above the windows of one of the class-rooms.

Among the "Burghley papers" in the British Museum there is a curious letter, which was written by the Marquis of Winchester to Sir W. Cecil, afterwards Lord Burghley. It seems to refer to the occasion of some visit of Queen Elizabeth to Henry, Lord Compton. The following is a copy of it :—

"After my hartie commendacions with like thanks to you for your letter of libertie given me for the repaire of Mr. Compton's House at Totenham, in order as well for the Queene's Highness, as for the owner, which I shall gladlie do. And because my Ladie of Pembroke hereth that th' Officers take the loppes and toppes of the Trees that be felled for reparations for their fees, which indeede ought not to be, and that resteth in your order, and then the wood may be feld to the profit of the reparation, yet the Woodwarde had neede to have something for his labour; and if yt shall please my Ladie to send one honest man to your feodarie and me, he shall see all the tymber that shall be taken, and howe it shalbe employed, and if my Ladie will the house still unrepaired, mynding a better House to be built upon the ground, You and I shall be well content therewith: for that you and I shall do ys for the Quene's honor and Mr. Compton's profitt, otherwise You and I meane not to do any thing, and herein knowe my Lord's pleasure and write to me againe I pray you in that matter, and I shall yelde myself to all that shall be thought for the best. So fare you well. Written this Xth of November 1563.

"Your loving friend

"WINCHESTER.

"To my loving friend
Sir William Cecil Knight
Principall Secretary to the Quene's Matie."

The Comptons seem to have held the estate until 1630, when the last Compton died. The next owners were the Hares of Norfolk, but how they got possession of it we are not able to discover. Certain it is that Bedwell, in his book entitled "A Breef Description of Tottenham High-crosse" (written in 1631), mentions that Hugh Hare, who was created Lord Coleraine in 1625, was then in possession of the whole estate. This Hugh Hare was a great favourite of Charles I., who created him an Irish baron when he was only nineteen years of age. On the breaking out of the Civil War, he supplied the king with money and gave up his seat at Longford, in Wiltshire, for a royal garrison. But this was afterwards taken and plundered by the Roundheads, and his other estates were sequestered. However, soon after the Restoration they were all restored. His son, grandson, and great-grandson all held the estate. The last married Miss Rose Duplessis, the daughter of a French clergyman, by whom he had a daughter, Rose. On his death in 1749 a question arose, as we have shown above, as to whether his wife, the first Rose, ought not to forfeit the estate, since she was an alien; and in 1755 the cause was finally determined in favour of the heirs at law. The estate having thus reverted to the Crown, a grant of it was obtained by Mr. Chauncey Townsend, for his son James, who married Miss Duplessis. By her he had a son, James Hare Townsend, who in 1789 had to sell a great part of the estate to pay off his father's debts. It passed through the hands of various owners, and in 1827 was bought by Mr. (afterwards Sir Rowland) Hill, of whom we have already spoken in our account of Hampstead.* Six years later the Messrs. Hill finally removed hither from Hazelwood, near Birmingham, where their school had been first established.

It is utterly impossible to tell how many houses have been in succession built on these grounds, but there must have been three at least, if not more. It is probable that they were not all built on exactly the site where the present house stands, but on some other spot near. This supposition is corroborated by the fact that very frequently when drains are dug at some depth old brick foundations and walls are found. For instance, a few years ago, when the well was being repaired, three or four feet below the surface, the workmen came upon the top of a wall, which extended to the depth of about twelve feet. Near the bottom of this wall a silver coin of the beginning of King Henry VIII.'s reign was found, and on the side of the wall, not so deep down, a gilt button, probably of the time of Queen Anne.

There is no mention of any castle in the Domesday Book at the time when the estate was in the

* See *ante*, p. 490.

possession of Earl Waltheof; nor, indeed, do we find any record of a house until the reign of Edward II. But if Bruce lived here—and he must have done so, or how would the place have received the name?—there must have been a house for him to live in, and therefore we may fairly conjecture that there was a castle at that time. As we mentioned above, the house was rebuilt in the reign of Henry VIII. In the "Antiquities of Tottenham" we find that there formerly hung over the chimney-piece in one of the parlours a picture, which exhibited two other towers, besides the one which is still left. Lord Coleraine says that the house was either rebuilt or new-fronted by the Hare family a little before the Revolution. We suppose that the middle part was only the thickness of the refectory, which was then the entrance-hall; for a few years ago, when a part of the wainscoting of the inner wall in one of the class-rooms was taken down, there were found on the wall inside some dead stalks of a vine or other creeping plant, clearly proving that that had been once the outside wall. But we can find no mention of the other part having been added. The room which is now called the porch-room used to be the porch, and from it a passage led straight through the house into the pleasure-grounds beyond. There used formerly to be a west wing of the house, but it was pulled down, together with the stables and coach-house, about sixty years ago, by Mr. Ede, the then owner. The east wing was added by Alderman Townsend, and in it, tradition says, John Wilkes has been often entertained.

A very peculiar custom prevailed here, the origin of which is not known. At the burial of any of the family the corpse was not suffered to be carried through the gate, but an opening was made in the wall nearest to the church, through which the corpse and mourners passed into the churchyard. "There are still," says Dr. Robinson, "the appearance of several apertures which have been bricked up, and among them is that through which passed the corpse of Mr. James Townsend, the last that was carried from the castle to the mausoleum of the Coleraine family. This aperture has been recently opened, and a Gothic door is now fixed in the place."

Although still called a castle, the building now presents none of the features usually associated with such structures; it is constructed of brick, with stone dressings, and is altogether a spacious edifice. It consists chiefly of a centre, with projecting wings. The old entrance-hall in the centre—the doorway of which has been blocked up, the hall itself being converted into a small sitting-room—is surmounted by a large square tower, surrounded by two external galleries, and crowned by an octagonal turret. The rooms throughout the house are exceptionally good, the boys' dormitories being all lofty and well ventilated. The walls of the dining-room are wainscoted to the ceiling, and are hung with a large number of engraved portraits of old divines and other ancient worthies; and to add to the effect, and to give the place a somewhat baronial character, above the portraits are placed several pairs of spreading antlers. The school-room in itself is a large and lofty apartment at the north-west corner of the house. The school and grounds occupy upwards of twenty acres. The grounds are laid out in the style of a park, in which are some very fine trees; and they include a cricket-ground and a field for football. There is also an old-fashioned walled kitchen-garden, comprising about two acres, near to which is an excellent infirmary for such of the boys as may require medical treatment, entirely detached from the school buildings. A detached tower, of red brick, which covers a deep well—now disused and filled up—is the only surviving relic of the previous edifice which was built by the Comptons early in the sixteenth century. This structure is now used as a larder. A fresh well has been dug close by. In Hone's "Year-Book" there is an engraving of Bruce Castle, reproduced from a view taken in 1686, from which it appears that the main portion of the building has been considerably altered since that time. Among the pictures that adorn the walls of the principal staircase, too, is an oil painting showing the castle as it appeared in the early part of the last century. In this view the upper part of the central portion of the house on either side of the tower is terminated by a gable with one window in each. These gables have now entirely disappeared, the front of the house having been carried up to the level of the top of the gable, and two false windows inserted.

Having been for fifty years managed by Sir Rowland Hill and his family, Bruce Castle School changed hands in 1877. The average number of pupils in the school is about seventy. On Sunday mornings the whole of the pupils attend the service in the parish church, which is close by the north-west corner of the ground, and on Sunday evenings divine service is conducted by the head-master of the school in the house. The pupils have daily access to a well-selected library, containing nearly 3,000 volumes. With reference to the rise and subsequent growth of this library, we may state that it was first started about the commencement of the present century by Mr. Thomas W. Hill, the father of Sir Rowland Hill, and that it was for two or three years so small that it was kept in a master's desk. When the school was removed to Hazelwood, the library was taken there and added to occasionally by the head-master, until 1817, when a school fund was started, part of which was spent every year in new books. Former members of the school used also sometimes to send a book or two, and thus the library kept increasing slowly year by year. In 1827 rewards were first given to those boys who passed a successful examination in books of an instructive nature, and from that time the reading of those books has formed here a part of nearly every boy's education. When, in 1827, the school was first started at Bruce Castle, Mr. Rowland Hill began to form the present library, and when, six years later, the Messrs. Hill finally removed, as we have stated above, to Tottenham, they brought with them a part of the Hazelwood library.

We may add, in conclusion, that the pupils at this school, as a rule, are preparing for the universities, the public schools, or professional life. While very accessible from London, Bruce Castle has all the advantages of the country, and few schools have better in-door and out-door arrangements for the health and comfort of their pupils.

In Bruce Grove, near the Castle, are the Sailmaker's Almshouses, comprising some forty or more neat brick-built dwellings. They were erected in the year 1869, and are in the gift of the Drapers' Company.

The parish church of All Hallows, which stands at a short distance north of Bruce Castle, and is bounded by the little river called the Mosel on the west, north, and east, is an ancient building, in the Gothic or pointed style, and the chief parts may perhaps be ascribed to the fourteenth century. It has at the west end a square embattled tower, of red brick, picturesquely covered with dark ivy of many years' growth.

This tower was supposed by Lord Coleraine to have been more lofty than it was at the time he wrote his history of the parish, for after speaking of the upper windows, he adds: "And as the steeple seems to have been heretofore considerably more lofty, so upon the middle of the outside top of it there stood of old a long cross of wood, covered with lead, fastened into the centre of the roof so strongly as that it was a signification of some cause why the town mark and the parish had the sign of a high cross, which defied all its enemies from Henry VIII.'s days till the unhappy civil wars, when the violent zeal of some cunning Parliamentarians blew up some rascally fellows to set about the pulling down of this cross, which they did with such great difficulty and hazard as that they repented their foolish attempt long afterwards, one breaking his leg and the rest never thriving after the fact, and leaving a stump for the grafting another cross upon it, as a token of their rashness in reformation." It is indeed somewhat remarkable that this cross on the church tower should have escaped the zeal of the early reformers, considering the ado that was made about "superstitious" images and crosses in the latter part of the reign of Henry VIII., and the general destruction of such objects.

From the statement made by Lord Coleraine that the steeple of Tottenham Church was before his time "more lofty," many persons have fallen into the mistake of supposing the extra height to have been beyond its present height. Such a view, however, is at variance with the true sense of his lordship's statement, which describes the windows which had been sunk as the upper windows of the tower, within which the bells (which had not at that time, 1693, been re-cast) undoubtedly hung.

It is very probable that the upper portion of the tower was at one time covered with one of those pyramidal roofs or dwarf kind of steeples peculiar to some of the ancient church towers, upon the apex of which roof or steeple the cross referred to by Lord Coleraine might originally have stood, and which he might fairly describe as being "fastened into the centre of the roof." This steeple might have become out of repair, owing to the treatment it had received by the rebels, and, with its "stump," have been removed lest another cross might afterwards be grafted upon it. Its appearance would then warrant the statement made by Lord Coleraine that it seemed to have been "more lofty." All the old doorways and window-openings in the tower are in the plain pointed style, as is also the massive and well-formed arch which opens from the tower into the church on the east side. The style of this arch, although similar to that of the arches in the nave, differs considerably from them in its mouldings.

On the south side of the church is a large porch, built of brick, with stone dressings. Lord Coleraine, in his account of the parish, noticed above, says, with reference to this porch:—"Long since the building of the great door there has bin an edifice joyned to it, not as a twin, but as a younger brother to the church; therefore I suppose the old porch to this church, being so small or decayed, might by the charity of some great and well-minded person be taken down, and the present large fabrick set up in its stead." The same writer supposes the porch to be "not older than Henry VII.'s time," and states that he had heard that it was built by a widow lady, whom he believes was Joan Gedney, "who was lady of some of the manors before they fell to the Comptons, or by one of the Comptons' ladys." This porch has a small chamber over the entrance, concerning which these remarks appear in Lysons' "Environs:"—"This was originally intended, as I suppose, for a church-house, a building of which figure representing a human head; there are also corbel heads at the angles beneath the basin. The carving is of the Perpendicular period, and is in a fair state of preservation, although somewhat worn with age and disfigured with paint. The figures, as well as the font, were re-chiselled in 1854 by a local tradesman, at a charge of £5. This font is probably as old as the present church; the roses carved upon it correspond with those on the door-

TOTTENHAM CHURCH.

traces are to be found in the records of almost every parish. They were, as our vestries are now, places where the inhabitants assembled to transact the parish business." In this room there formerly resided, for many years, an old almswoman, named Elizabeth Fleming; she died in 1790, a veritable centenarian. Of late years this upper chamber was used as a school-room for the children of the parish. There is a hagioscope, or "squint," made in the wall of the church, so that the occupant of this room over the porch might be enabled to see the altar.

The font is octagonal in shape, having ornamental panels enclosing quatrefoils, within which are roses, a three-leafed plant enclosing berries, a pelican, a mermaid, a dragon or wyvern, and a ways of the porch, from which we may infer that it was made early in the fifteenth century.

The monuments and brasses are somewhat numerous; but in consequence of the alterations recently made in the building, few of them retain their original position. Some of the more ancient brasses have altogether disappeared. They are fully described in Robinson's "History of Tottenham." The oldest brass still remaining is a small plate to the memory of Thomas Hynnyngham; it bears the date 1499. Mr. George Waight, in his "History of Tottenham," to which we are indebted for much of the information here given, describes a few of the existing monuments, some of which are of peculiar interest. At the east end of the south aisle is one to the memory of Richard

VIEWS IN TOTTENHAM.

Candeler, Esq., who died in 1602, and Eliza his wife, 1622: they are represented kneeling before desks, on which are placed books. Adjoining this monument is another to the memory of Sir Ferdinando Heyborne, Gentleman of the Privy Chamber to Queen Elizabeth and James I., dated 1618, and his wife, the daughter of Richard Candeler, who died in 1612. A mural monument, with effigies, commemorates Sir John Melton, Keeper of the Great Seal for the north of England; he died in 1640. A large and curious monument in the north aisle, ornamented after the fashion of the period in which it was set up, is to the memory of Maria, wife of Sir Robert Barkham, of the county of Lincoln, and daughter of Richard Wilcocks, of Tottenham. She died in 1644. Upon this monument are busts of the deceased and her husband, and beneath are the effigies of their twelve children. A sum of money was left by the family of the deceased for the purpose of keeping this monument in good condition. In the chancel was the gravestone of the Rev. William Bedwell, who was many years vicar of this church, and also rector of St. Ethelburga's, in Bishopsgate Street. The epitaph—which commenced with some account of his daughter, who was married to one Mr. or Dr. Clark, and died December 20th, 1662—concluded as follows:—

> "Here lies likewise interred in
> this chancel the body of Mr. William
> Bedwell her father, some time
> Vicar of this Church, and one of
> King James's translators of the
> Bible, and for Easterne tongues
> as learned a man as most lived
> in these modern times, aged 70,
> dyed May 5th, 1632."

He was the author of the "History of Tottenham" mentioned above, and also of a book called the "Traveller's Calendar."

In 1875–7 the church underwent a thorough "restoration" and enlargement, after the fashion of the time. The additions to the fabric on this occasion consist of one new bay at the east end of the nave and aisles (or rather the old chancel and its aisles), with a new chancel, north and south transepts, an organ-chamber, double vestries, with a furnace-room for heating the church beneath one of them, and a north porch. The old chancel, with the addition of the new bay mentioned above, now becomes part of the nave, and is furnished with seats for the congregation. To meet the case of so greatly enlarged a church, all the new roofs are at a considerably higher level than they were originally. A clerestory, with windows on each side of it, has been put upon the new bay of the nave, the windows being absolutely necessary, as is proved by the unsightly skylights which had in former days been inserted in various parts of the roof. The new work has been carried out in red brick and stone in harmony with the fine red brick and stone south porch. The choir part of the chancel is fitted up with oak and walnut-wood seats and desks, and is paved with tiles. The eastern part, or sanctuary, is arcaded in stone on its sides and east end, with a central reredos behind the altar-table. Marble shafts and marble in various forms are used in this part of the chancel, on the south side of which is a graduated sedilia of two seats, and also a credence, very beautifully designed and executed. A large east window of five lights fills the gable end at a high level. The ceiling above is vaulted in wood and plaster, and is delicately painted in colours, in which a grey-blue predominates, with stars and flowers. The east five-light chancel window, the south three-light transept window, and another three-light window in the new bay of the south aisle, are filled with stained glass, presented by various persons as memorials.

"From the occurrence of a priest with half a hide of land at 'Totanam,' in the Doomsday Survey, the existence of a church may be fairly presumed at least as early as the Conquest, although we have no mention of it as a benefice till the twelfth century, when it was given to the canons of the Holy Trinity by Aldgate, soon after the foundation of their house by David, King of Scotland,* to whom it was appropriated, and a vicarage endowed about the beginning of the thirteenth century by Bishop William de Sanctæ de Mariæ Ecclesiæ."†

"The rudeness of construction and plainness of the oldest parts of the building," observes Mr. George Waight, in his work above mentioned, "make it very probable that the original church, of which they formed part, was built by one of the great lords of the manor, for there is always a marked difference observable between churches built by the lords of the soil and those built by monks and ecclesiastics—*i.e.*, between rectorial churches and vicarial churches. The vicarial churches having been built by the monks, who possessed more architectural skill and probably larger means than the lords of the soil, for that reason, almost uniformly present a greater elegance of design and magnitude than the former. It must be borne in mind that the church of Tottenham did not become vicarial until after it was given by David, King of Scotland, to the canons of the Holy

* Dugd. "Mon.," vol. ii., p. 80. † Newc. "Rep.," vol. i., p. 753.

Trinity, London. Up to that time the church and advowson had been appended to the manor, which had remained entire. There are many things," he adds, "which point to this conclusion; the mention of a priest in the Domesday Survey, the existence of the manorial house called Bruce Castle, the former lordship of the place (the road leading to it being still called Lordship Lane), and the close proximity of the church to both, all testify to the antiquity of the church as a religious foundation. The charter by which David, King of Scotland, granted the church, probably soon after it was built, to the canons of the Holy Trinity, was directed to Gilbert, Bishop of London (surnamed Universalis), who was Bishop of London in the reign of Henry I., from 1128 to 1134, and was confirmed by William de Sancta Maria, who was Bishop of London from the tenth year of Richard I. (1198) to the sixth year of Henry III. (1221)."

A chantry was founded in this church by John Drayton, citizen and goldsmith of London, as appears by his will, dated 27th September, 1456, "to find two priests daily, one to say divine service at St. Paul's, London, and the other at the Church of All Saints, Tottenham, at the altar of the blessed virgin and martyr St. Katherine; and the same priest also, on Wednesdays and Fridays, to perform the like service in the Chapel of St. Anne, called the Hermitage, in this parish, near the king's highway; also for the souls of King Richard II., Anne his queen, and others, his own two wives, parents and benefactors, and all the faithful deceased."

The bells in the old tower are six in number, and one of them, called the Saints' Bell, is ornamented with medallions and other figures and ornamentation. This bell was taken at the siege of Quebec—it having served originally as the alarm-bell of that town—and was given to the parish at the commencement of this century. The old vestry, at the eastern end of the church, was built and endowed by Lord Coleraine, in 1696, upon condition that he and his family should possess the ground beneath as a place of interment; the building was circular, and had originally a dome and an obelisk, but these were removed in 1855, they having become decayed, and ultimately the building was entirely demolished.

Tottenham Grammar School dates from the early part of the last century, when it was endowed under the will of Sarah, Dowager Duchess of Somerset. At one time there is reason to believe that it must have been in a fairly flourishing condition, as among its head-masters we find the name of the learned William Baxter, the nephew of the celebrated Richard Baxter. Of late years it had fallen into disrepute, and had, in fact, become a mere parish elementary school; but about the year 1872 a change of trustees having taken place, steps were taken to place the school upon a more efficient footing. A scheme was accordingly drawn up, the school premises were enlarged, and at the commencement of the year 1877 it was re-opened as a second-grade school.

Down to comparatively recent times, Tottenham could boast of other antiquities besides those we have already described; for in the "Ambulator" (1774) we read that St. Loy's Well, in this parish, is said to be "always full, and never to run over; and the people report many strange cures performed at Bishop's Well." The field in which the first-mentioned well is situated is called "South Field at St. Loy's," in a survey of the parish taken in 1619. It is situated on the west side of the high road, near the footpath leading past the Wesleyan chapel, and across the field to Philip Lane. Bedwell speaks of St. Loy's Well, in his history of the parish, as being in his time "nothing else but a deep pit in the highway, on the west side thereof;" he also adds that "it was within memory cleaned out, and at the bottom was found a fair great stone, which had certain letters or characters on it; but being broken or defaced by the negligence of the workmen, and nobody near that regarded such things, it was not known what they were or meant." The condition of the well has not much improved since Bedwell's time, having become nothing more nor less than "a dirty pool of water, full of mud and rubbish." Dr. Robinson, in his "History of Tottenham" (1840), describes the well as being surrounded by willows, about 500 feet from the highway, and adds that it was bricked up on all sides, square, and about four feet deep. The water of this spring was said to excel, in its medicinal qualities, those of any other near it; and in a foot-note, Robinson says that the properties of the water are similar to the water of Cheltenham springs.

The Chapel or "Offertory" of St. Loy is described by Bedwell as "a poore house, situate on the west side of the great road, a little off from the bridge where the middle ward was determined." It has long since disappeared. St. Loy, or St. Eloy, was one of the greatest oaths which men swore by in the Middle Ages. In Chaucer's "Canterbury Tales," for instance, the carter, encouraging his horses to draw his cart out of a slough, says,

"I pray God save thy body and St. Eloy."

Bishop's Well is described by Bedwell as "a spring issuing out of the side of a hill, in a field opposite to the vicarage, and falling into the Mosel afore it hath run many paces." The ground near it was formerly called Well Field, but now forms part of the cemetery. The water was said never to freeze, and, like that of St. Loy's Well, to be efficacious in the cure of certain bodily ailments.

White Hart Lane, mentioned above, the road leading to Wood Green, has long been built upon. Indeed, in the "Beauties of England and Wales," as far back as 1816, we find it spoken of as containing "several capacious villas, and some modern houses, of less magnitude, which are desirable in every respect, except that of standing in a crowded row. On the left hand of this lane," adds the writer, "at the distance of three quarters of a mile from the village of Tottenham, is the handsome residence of Henry P. Sperling, Esq. This is accounted the manor-house of the Pembrokes, but has, in fact, been long alienated from that estate. The building was, till within these very few years, surrounded by a moat, over which was a drawbridge. The moat was filled up by the present proprietor, probably to the advantage of his grounds, which are of a pleasing and rural character." Pembroke House is stated by Dyson, in his "History of Tottenham," to have been built for Mr. Soames, one of the Lords of the Admiralty, about the year 1636, at which time "the moat was dug and walled in."

At Wood Green are the almshouses belonging to the Printers' Pension, Almshouse, and Orphan Asylum Corporation. The objects of this institution, which was founded in the year 1827, are the maintaining and educating of orphans of deceased members of the printing profession, as well as granting of pensions, ranging from £8 to £25, to aged and infirm printers and their widows. The almshouses are a picturesque block of buildings, with a handsome board-room and offices in the centre, containing, with the two wings, residences for twenty-four inmates. The original portion of the building was erected in 1849, and the additional wings in 1871.

Tottenham Wood, in the fifteenth century, was celebrated for its medicinal spring; it bore the name of St. Dunstan's Well. Of the Wood itself, there are three old proverbs extant. To express a thing impossible, the people here used to say, "You may as well try to move Tottenham Wood," which was of great extent. Another, "Tottenham is turned French," meaning that it is as foolish as other places to leave the customs of England for foreign ones. And a third—

"When Tottenham Wood is all on fire,
Then Tottenham Street is nothing but mire."

This means, when a thick fog-like smoke hangs over Tottenham Wood, it is a sign of rain, and therefore of mud and dirt. We need hardly add that the task of removing Tottenham Wood has been accomplished, and that such part of it as is still unbuilt upon, is under arable cultivation. So much for the familiar "sayings" connected with Tottenham. But there is also a metrical satire which requires some brief mention. This is a mock heroic poem, known as the "Tournament of Tottenham," which appears to be a kind of satire on the dangerous and costly tournaments of the fifteenth and sixteenth centuries, and is supposed by Warton to have been written in the reign of Henry VII. The full title of the work is "The Turnament of Tottenham, or the wooeing, winning, and wedding of Tybbe, the Reeve's daughter there;" and the poem is descriptive of a contest between some five or six lusty bachelors, bearing the aristocratic names of "Perkyn, Hawkya, Dawkya, Tomkyn," &c., from "Hysseldon, Hackenaye," and other country districts, for the hand of the fair Tybbe, a rustic maiden, the daughter of a "reeve," or manciple of the place, whose marriage portion was a gray mare, a spotted sow, a dun cow, and "coppel, a brode hen that was brought out of Kent." The scene is the "Croft" at Tottenham; the rushing of the doughty warriors at each other in the lists, the broken heads and limbs, the falls from their horses, more accustomed to the plough than the jousts, and the winning of the fair Tybbe by the stalwart Perkyn; the carrying home of the defeated and drunken combatants; and finally, the wedding procession to Tottenham Church, in which Perkyn, Tybbe, and the reeve are the foremost characters—all these things are described in a style which excellently takes off the ballad style which has so often been used to portray a genuine tournament of knights, that the reader might almost be pardoned for indulging in the supposition that the affair really happened at Tottenham.

It does honour to the good sense of our nation, as Bishop Percy remarks, that whilst all Europe was captivated by the bewitching charms of chivalry and romance, two of our writers in the ruder times could see through the false glare that surrounded them, and could discover and hold up to the eyes of all what was absurd in them both. Chaucer wrote his "Rhyme of Sir Thopas" in ridicule of the latter, and in the "Turnament of Tottenham" we have a most humorous burlesque of the former. It is well known, of course, that the tournament, as an institution of the Middle Ages, did much to encourage the spirit of duelling —under another name—and that it continued to flourish in spite of the vigorous denunciations of the authorities both of Church and State. Such being the case, the author of the "Tournament" has availed himself of the keen weapon of ridicule in order to show up the absurd custom in its true colours. With this view he here introduces with admirable humour a parcel of country clowns and bumpkins, imitating at the Croft in Tottenham all the solemnities of the tourney. Here we have the regular challenge, the appointed day, the lady for the prize, the formal preparations, the display of armour, the oaths taken on entering the lists, the various accidents of the encounter, the victor leading off the prize, and the magnificent feasting, with all the other solemn fopperies that usually attended the pompous "tournament."

The "Turnament of Tottenham," it may be added, though now rendered popular by its being placed by Bishop Percy in his "Reliques," was first printed from an ancient MS. in 1631, by the Rev. William Bedwell, Rector of Tottenham, who, as stated above, was one of the translators of the Bible, and who tells us that its author was Gilbert Pilkington, thought by some to have been also in his day parson of the parish, and the author of another piece called "Passio Domini." Bedwell, however, though a learned man, does not seem to have appreciated the wit of his predecessor, and really imagines that the verses are a description of a veritable tournament written before the time of Edward III., in whose reign tournaments were prohibited. A perusal of the "Turnament" itself will be sufficient to dispel this matter-of-fact view of the poem, which is, perhaps, the best piece of mock-heroic writing that has come down to us since the "Battle of the Bees," so admirably portrayed by Virgil in his fourth Georgic.

We quote the following stanza, which describes the situation of the contending parties subsequent to the combat, and may serve as a specimen of the production:—

"To the rich feast came many for the nonce;
Some came hop-halte, and some tripping on the stones;
Some with a staffe in his hand, and some two at once;
Of some were the heads broken, of some the shoulder-bones;
With sorrow came they hither.
Wo was Hawkin; wo was Harry;
Wo was Tymkin; wo was Tirry;
And so was all the company,
But yet they came togither."

It may be added that the poem, in its entirety, is given in the various histories of Tottenham, by Bedwell, Oldfield, and Dyson, as well as in Percy's "Reliques of Ancient Poetry."

Before quitting Tottenham, we may state that here was born, in 1557, the learned civilian and statesman, Sir Julius Cæsar, who was some time Master of the Rolls, and as we have already had occasion to observe, lived to such a great age, that he was said to be "kept alive, beyond Nature's course, by the prayers of the many poor whom he daily relieved." He was in attendance on his friend Lord Bacon at the time of his last illness, and was present with him when he died.* In 1598 Sir Julius resided at Mitcham, in Surrey, where he was visited by Queen Elizabeth. He lived near the High Cross, and died in 1636.

Here, in 1842, died William Hone, the author of very many popular works, and among others of the "Every-day Book." "I am going out to Tottenham this morning," writes Charles Dickens, "on a cheerless mission I would willingly have avoided. Hone is dying, and he sent Cruickshank yesterday to beg me to go and see him, as, having read no books but mine of late, he wanted to see me, and shake hands with me 'before he went.'" The request so asked, Charles Dickens performed with his usual tender-heartedness. In a month afterwards he paid a second visit to Tottenham. It was to attend Hone's funeral.

In concluding this chapter, we may be pardoned for referring to the sanitary condition of Tottenham. In 1837, when the Registrar-General's Department was first established, the village was a decidedly healthy place, and its healthiness was further improved by the establishment, about twenty years later, of an excellent system of drainage and water-supply, which reduced for some years the death-rate from fever by nearly one-half. About the year 1860 the population of Tottenham began to increase very rapidly, and owing mainly to the supineness of the leading inhabitants, the Local Board of Health neglected to extend the area of the drainage and water-supply, and likewise supplemented its water-supply from wells in the chalk by land-spring water drawn from highly-manured land. The Board also became remiss in dealing with nuisances. The result was that the death-rate rose rapidly, and by 1870 it was 20 per cent. higher than formerly, while the death-rate from the seven principal zymotic diseases had nearly doubled. Typhoid fever became prevalent, and in 1873 was epidemic. The leading inhabitants becoming alarmed, formed themselves into a sanitary association, elected efficient men on to the Local Board of Health, and devoted themselves to the speedy carrying out of numerous sanitary reforms. Sewers were freely ventilated, additional sewers were constructed, the polluted

* See *ante*, p. 405.

land-spring water was excluded from the water-supply, ditches and water-courses were cleansed, nuisances of all kinds were abated. The Local Board issued a handbill to every occupier, urging the need of house-drain ventilation, and, better still, began to insist upon efficient drain ventilation in the case of all new buildings. An immediate improvement in the public health followed upon these measures. The death-rate during 1876 was only 16·7 per 1,000; the rate from the seven principal zymotic diseases only 1·9 per 1,000; and that from fever less than ·2 per 1,000. The water-supply, as shown by the monthly reports furnished to the Registrar-General, stands, in respect of freedom from organic impurity, at the very head of all the waters supplied by the metropolitan water companies. Sanitary reform has not only diminished the number of deaths and the amount of illness, but has also, as a consequence, greatly increased the prosperity of Tottenham.

THE "BELL" AT EDMONTON. (*From an Old View.*)

CHAPTER XLVI.

NORTH TOTTENHAM, EDMONTON, &c.

"Away went Gilpin, neck or nought,
Away went hat and wig."—*Cowper.*

The "Bell" and "Johnny Gilpin's Ride"—Mrs. Gilpin on the Stile—How Cowper came to write "Johnny Gilpin"—A Supplement to the Story—Historic Reminiscences of the "Bell" at Edmonton—Charles Lamb's Visit there—Lamb's Residence at Edmonton—The Grave of Charles Lamb—Edmonton Church—The "Merry Devil of Edmonton"—The Witch of Edmonton—Archbishop Tillotson—Edmonton Fairs—Southgate—Arno's Grove—Bush Hill Park.

WE have stated in the preceding chapter that the main road northwards runs through the centre of the village, and indeed forms the principal street of Tottenham High Cross. It continues straight on for some two miles or more towards Edmonton. This bit of roadway has acquired some celebrity, for Londoners at least, as the scene of Johnny Gilpin's famous ride, as related by Cowper. Indeed, we might ask, what traveller has ever refreshed himself or herself at the "Bell," and not thought of Johnny Gilpin, and his ride from London and back, nor sympathised with his worthy spouse on the disasters of that day's outing? The "Bell" inn, where Gilpin and his wife *should* have dined, is on the left-hand side of the road, as we proceed along from Tottenham. The balcony which the house possessed in Cowper's time has been removed, and the place, in fact, otherwise much altered. It has, however, a capacious "banqueting hall," and large pleasure-gardens "abounding with all kinds of shrubs and flowers;" no wonder, therefore, that it is a favourite resort for London holiday-makers. A painting of Johnny Gilpin's ride is fixed outside the tavern, and the house is commonly known as "Gilpin's Bell;" the landlord, however, designates it "The Bell and Johnny Gilpin's Ride."

EDMONTON CHURCH, 1790.

In his "Library of English Literature," Professor Henry Morley thus tells the story of that ever-popular favourite ballad:—"Lady Austen one evening told Cowper the story of 'John Gilpin,' which, as told by her, tickled his fancy so much that he was kept awake by fits of laughter during great part of the night after hearing it, and must needs turn it into a ballad when he got up. Mrs. Unwin's son sent it to the *Public Advertiser*, where it appeared without an author's name. John Henderson, an actor from Bath, who took the London playgoers by storm in 1777 as Shylock, Hamlet, and Falstaff, was then giving readings at the Freemason's Tavern. He had succeeded almost to Garrick's fame. His feeling was so true, his voice so flexible, that Mrs. Siddons and John Kemble often went to hear him read. Henderson finding 'John Gilpin' in print, but not yet famous, chose it for recitation. Mrs. Siddons heard it with delight, and in the spring of 1785 its success was the event of the season. It was reprinted in many forms, and talked of in all circles; prints of 'John Gilpin,' were familiar in shop-windows; and Cowper, who was finishing the 'Task,' felt that his more serious work would be helped if it were published with this 'John Gilpin,' as an avowed piece by the same author." It is now fairly established as the most popular classic, and almost every English child knows it by heart. Indeed, so famous has the ballad, and consequently the "Bell" at Edmonton, become, that Mr. Mark Boyd tells us in his "Social Gleanings," that some American friends, who had come to England, declared that they had seen the two places most worth a visit in the metropolis, namely, "St. Paul's Cathedral, and the house connected with John Gilpin's famous ride."

Mr. John Timbs, in his "Century of Anecdote," gives a similar version of the story of John Gilpin:—"This little poem was composed by Cowper about the year 1782, upon a story told to the poet by Lady Austen, in order to relieve one of the poet's fits of depressive melancholy. Lady Austen, it so happened, remembered the tale from the days of her childhood in the nursery, and its effects on the fancy of Cowper had the air almost of enchantment, for he told her the next morning that he had been kept awake during the greater part of the night by convulsions of irrepressible laughter, brought on by the recollection of her story, and that he had turned the chief facts of it into a ballad. Somehow or other it found its way into the newspapers, and Henderson, the actor, perceiving how true it was to nature, recited it in some of his public readings. Southey, whose judgment on such subjects is worth having and recording, conjectured that possibly the tale might have been first suggested to Cowper by a poem written by Sir Thomas More in his youthful days, entitled 'The Merry Jest of the Serjeant and Freere;' and it is quite within the range of probability that the tale which Lady Austen remembered and related may have originally come from this source, for there is next to nothing really new under the sun."

It has been much disputed, as probably our readers are aware, whether or not "John Gilpin" was an entirely fictitious romance, a creation of Cowper's brain, or whether its author founded his poem upon an adventure, or rather a mis-adventure, in the life of a real personage. The quotation above given from John Timbs, and the opinion of Southey, would certainly seem to give support to the former supposition; but in one of the volumes of the *Gentleman's Magazine* towards the close of the last century there is an entry which certainly looks quite the other way. According to that, the name of the individual who was really the subject of Cowper's inimitable ballad was Jonathan Gilpin, and he died at Bath, in September, 1790. The following notice appears in the *Gentleman's Magazine* for November of that year:—"The gentleman who was so severely ridiculed for bad horsemanship under the title of John Gilpin died, a few days ago, at Bath, and has left an unmarried daughter, with a fortune of £20,000." If this was really the case, then, in all probability, the memorable ride from London to the "Bell" at Edmonton and back again, the loss of wig, and the other accessories of the story, were not matters of pure invention, but some of the stern realities of life to a certain civic dignitary whose name has passed away.

It may not be generally known, though Mr. William Hone has recorded the fact in his amusing "Table-Book," that Cowper afterwards added an amusing little episode to John Gilpin's ride, which was found in the poet's own handwriting among the papers of his friend, Mrs. Unwin, illustrated with a comical sketch by George Romney. The episode consisted of three stanzas, which ran as follows:—

"Then Mrs. Gilpin sweetly said
Unto her children three,
'I'll clamber o'er the style so high,
And you climb after me.'

"But having climbed unto the top,
She could no farther go;
But sat, to every passer-by
A spectacle and show.

"Who said, 'Your spouse and you to-day
Both show your horsemanship;
And if you stay till he comes back
Your horse will need no whip.'"

It is much to be regretted that no more lines of this interesting ballad were discovered, as they were evidently intended to form an addendum to the "Diverting History of Johnny Gilpin," for it is supposed that in the interval between dinner and tea Mrs. Gilpin, finding the time to hang rather heavily on her hands, during her husband's involuntary absence, rambled out with her children into the fields at the back of the "Bell," where she met with the embarrassment recorded on ascending one of those awkward gates and stiles which abound in the neighbourhood of Edmonton and Tottenham. The droll picture of Mrs. Gilpin seated astride on the stile will be found in the pleasant pages of Mr. Hone.

We may state here that the "Bell" at Edmonton was a house of good repute as far back as the days of James I., as will appear from the following extract from John Savile's tractate, entitled, "King James's Entertainment at Theobalds, with his Welcome to London." Having described the vast concourse of people that flocked forth to greet their new sovereign on his approach to the metropolis, honest John says:—"After our breakfast at Edmonton, at the sign of the 'Bell,' we took occasion to note how many would come down in the next hour; so coming up into a chamber next to the street, where we might both best see, and likewise take notice of all passengers, we called for an hour-glass, and after we had disposed of ourselves who should take the number of the horse, and who the foot, we turned the hour-glass, which before it was half run out, we could not possibly truly number them, they came so exceedingly fast; but there we broke off, and made our account of 309 horses, and 137 footmen, which course continued that day from four o'clock in the morning till three o'clock in the afternoon, and the day before also, as the host of the house told us, without intermission." Besides establishing the existence of the renowned "Bell" at this period, the foregoing passage we have quoted is curious in other respects.

Charles Lamb, the last years of whose life were passed at Edmonton, and whose boyhood is so pleasantly connected with Christ's Hospital,* was in the habit of repairing to the "Bell" with any of his friends who may have visited him, when on their return; and here he used to take a parting glass, generally of porter, with them.

Lamb—"that frail good man," as Wordsworth affectionately called him—was the beloved and honoured friend of the leading intellectual lights of his day. From his early school days to his death he was the bosom friend of the poet Coleridge, and the intimate of Leigh Hunt, Rogers, Southey, and Talfourd. By the last-named gentleman his biography, including his letters, &c., was published in 1848. The writings of Lamb, like those of Goldsmith, and especially the "Essays of Elia," mirror forth the gentleness and simplicity of their author's nature. To his wit, Moore's lines on Sheridan most admirably apply:—

> "Whose wit, in the combat, as gentle and bright,
> Ne'er carried a heart-stain away on its blade."

Macaulay has paid the following tribute to his memory:—"We admire his genius; we love the kind nature which appears in all his writings; and we cherish his memory as much as if we had known him personally." On one occasion Lamb and Coleridge were conversing together on the incidents of the latter's early life, when he was beginning his career in the Church, and Coleridge was describing some of the facts in his usual tone, when he paused, and said, "Pray, Mr. Lamb, did you ever hear me preach?" To this the latter replied, "I never heard you do anything else."

Lucy Aikin, in one of her letters, gives her estimate of the character of Charles Lamb in the following words:—"There is no better English than that of poor Charles Lamb—a true and original genius; the delight of all who knew, and much more of all who read him, and a man whom none who had once seen him could ever forget."

Having already travelled somewhat farther northward than we had at first intended, we must forbear passing on to Enfield, where Lamb appears also at one time to have resided; but we may be pardoned for introducing one or two scraps of correspondence having reference to that fact.

Charles Lamb writes to a friend from Enfield Chase, Oct. 1, 1827: "Dear R——, I am settled, and for life I hope, at Enfield. I have taken the prettiest, compactest house I ever saw." And the same friend writes in similar terms: "I took the stage to Edmonton, and walked thence to Enfield. I found them—*i.e.*, Charles and Mary Lamb—in their new house, a small but comfortable place, and Charles Lamb quite delighted with his retirement. He does not fear the solitude of the situation, though he seems to be almost without an acquaintance (here), and dreads rather than seeks visitors."

In a letter addressed by Lamb, about this time, to his friend Tom Hood, we get a glimpse of the "inner life" of the Lambs at Enfield. "If I have anything in my head," he writes, "I will send it to Mr. Watts. Strictly speaking, he should have had my album-verses, but a very intimate friend importun'd me for the trifles, and I believe I forgot Mr. Watts, or lost sight at the time of his similar *souvenir*. Jamieson conveyed the farce from me to Mrs. C. Kemble; *he* will not be in town before the 27th. Give our kind loves to all at Highgate, and tell them that we have finally torn ourselves outright away from Colebrooke, where I had *no* health, and are about to domiciliate for good at Enfield, where I have experienced *good*.

> 'Lord, what good hours do we keep!
> How quietly we sleep!'

"See the rest in the 'Complete Angler.'

"We have got our books into our new house. I am a dray-horse, if [I] was not ashamed of the undigested, dirty lumber, as I toppled 'em out of the cart, and blest Becky that came with 'em for her having an unstuff'd brain with such rubbish. We shall get in by Michael's Mass. 'Twas with some pain we were evuls'd from Colebrooke. You may find some of our flesh sticking to the door-posts. To change habitations is to die to them; and in my time I have died seven deaths. But I don't know whether every such change does not bring with it a rejuvenescence. 'Tis an enterprise; and shoves back the sense of death's approximating, which, tho' not terrible to me, is at all times particularly distasteful. My house-deaths have generally been periodical, recurring after seven years; but this last is premature by half that time. Cut off in the flower of Colebrook! The Middletonian stream, and all its echoes, mourn. Even minnows dwindle. *A parvis fiunt minima!* I fear to invite Mrs. Hood!"

Lamb, it is stated, was addicted to the practice

* See Vol. II., p. 370.

of smoking, and on being asked one day how he had acquired the habit, he replied, "By striving after it, as other men strive after virtue."

Charles Lamb survived his earliest friend and schoolfellow, Coleridge, only a few months. One morning, it is said, he showed a friend the mourning ring which the author of "Christabel" had left him, and exclaimed sorrowfully, "Poor fellow! I have never ceased to think of him from the day I first heard of his death!" Only five days after he had thus expressed himself—namely, on the 27th of December, 1834—Charles Lamb died, in his sixtieth year.

We leave the house in which he lived and died, Bay Cottage, on the right-hand side of Church Street, as we walk from the main road towards Edmonton Church. It is a small white house, standing back from the roadway, and next door to the large brick-built dwelling, known as the "Lion House," from the heraldic lions supporting shields on the tops of the gate-piers.

Poor Lamb was buried in the old churchyard close by, and the tall upright stone which marks his grave, near the south-west corner of the church, bears upon it the following lines, written by his friend, the Rev. Henry F. Cary, the translator of Dante :—

"Farewell, dear Friend—that smile, that harmless mirth,
No more shall gladden our domestic hearth;
That rising tear, with pain forbid to flow,
Better than words—no more assuage our woe;
That hand outstretch'd from small, but well-earn'd store,
Yield succour to the destitute no more.
Yet art thou not all lost: through many an age,
With sterling sense and humour, shall thy page
Win many an English bosom, pleas'd to see
That old and happier vein reviv'd in thee;
This for our earth; and if with friends we share
Our joys in heaven, we hope to meet thee there."

Mary Lamb continued to live on here after her brother's death. She died at St. John's Wood in 1847, but was buried in the same grave with her brother; so it may truly be said of them, that they "were lovely and pleasant in their lives, and in their death they were not divided."

Church Street has another literary memory, for here, from 1810 till 1816, resided John Keats, whilst serving his apprenticeship to a Mr. Hammond, a surgeon; here he wrote his "Juvenile Poems," which were published in 1817.

The parish church of Edmonton, dedicated to All Saints', is a large edifice, chiefly of Perpendicular architecture. At the west end is a square tower of stone, embattled, and profusely overgrown with ivy. The remainder of the building was encased with brickwork in the year 1772, and, at the same time, most reprehensible liberties were taken with the original character of the fabric. "A bricklayer and a carpenter," says the author of the "Beauties of England and Wales," "at that period possessed influence over the decisions of the vestry. A general casing of brick was evidently advantageous to the former; and the carpenter obtained permission to remove the stone mullions of the venerable windows, and to substitute wooden framework! The interference of higher powers prevented his extending the *job* to the windows of the chancel, which yet retain their ancient character, and would appear to be of the date of the latter part of the fourteenth century." In 1866 the interior of the church was carefully restored, new Perpendicular windows of stained glass being inserted in the chancel, and a south aisle added to it. The nave has a north aisle, separated from it by pointed arches sustained by octangular pillars. There are galleries at the western end, and in the north aisle. The chancel and its side aisles are separated from the nave by a bold arch. Weever mentions several monuments in this church, which do not exist in the present day; and Norden, in his MS. additions to his "Speculum Britanniæ," observes that, "There is a fable of one Peter Fabell that lyeth here, who is sayde to have beguyled the Devyll for monie: he was verye subtile that could deceyve him that is deceyt itselfe." This Peter Fabell is supposed by Weever to have been "some ingenious conceited gentleman, who did use some sleightie tricks for his own disport." There is a scarce pamphlet, entitled "The Life and Death of the Merry Devil of Edmonton, with the Pleasant Pranks of Smug the Smith," &c. In this book we are informed that Peter Fabell was born at Edmonton, and lived and died there in the reign of Henry VII. His story was made the groundwork of a drama, called the "Merry Devil of Edmonton," which is stated to have been "sundry times acted by his Majesties Servants, at the Globe on the Bankeside." Notwithstanding that this drama has the letters "T. B." appended to it as the initials of the author's name, it was long the fashion to attribute it to Shakespeare, just as it was in later times to ascribe it to Michael Drayton. In the prologue to the play we are informed that the "merry devil" was "Peter Fabel, a renowned scholar;" and are further told that—

"If any here make doubt of such a name
In Edmonton, yet fresh unto this day,
Fix'd in the wall of that old ancient church,
His monument remaineth to be seen."

As we have intimated above, however, this monument has long since disappeared.

Edmonton appears to have produced not only a "merry devil," but also a witch of considerable notoriety—

"The town of Edmonton has lent the stage
A Devil and a Witch—both in an age."

If we may believe the compiler of the "Beauties of England and Wales," the wretched and persecuted woman alluded to in the above lines was named Sawyer; and many particulars concerning her may be found in a pamphlet, published in 1621, under the title of "The wonderfull discoverie of Elizabeth Sawyer, a witch, late of Edmonton; her conviction, her condemnation, and death; together with the relation of the Devil's accesse to her, and their conference together. Written by Henry Goodcole, minister of the Word of God, and her continual visitor in the Gaole of Newgate." A play, by Ford and Dekker, was founded on this unhappy female.

At a short distance from the church, on the road leading towards Bush Hill, in a mansion called the Rectory House, Dr. Tillotson resided for several years, whilst Dean of St. Paul's, and occasionally also after he became Archbishop of Canterbury. "The day previous to his consecration as Archbishop," remarks the compiler of Tillotson's works, "he retired hither, and prepared himself, by fasting and prayer, for an entrance on his important and dignified duties with becoming humility of temper."

The ancient fair of Edmonton, with all its mirth and drollery, its swings and roundabouts, its spiced gingerbread, and wild-beast shows, is now a thing of the past. There were, in fact, three fairs annually held within the parish of Edmonton. Two of these, termed Beggar's Bush Fairs, arose from a grant made by James I., when he laid out a part of Enfield Chase into Theobalds Park. The third was called Edmonton Statute Fair, and was formerly held for the hiring of servants; it, however, became perverted to the use of holiday-people, chiefly of the lower ranks, and, in common with similar celebrations of idleness in the vicinity of the metropolis, became a source of great moral degradation.

In 1820, one of the chief attractions of the fair was a travelling menagerie, whose keeper walked into the den of a lioness, and nursed her cubs in his lap. He then paid his respects to the husband and father, a magnificent Barbary lion. After the usual complimentary greetings between them, the man, somewhat roughly, thrust open the monster's jaws, and put his head into his mouth. This he did with impunity. A few days afterwards, having travelled a little farther north with his show, the keeper repeated his performance, and fell a victim to his rashness.

Southgate, the favourite haunt of Leigh Hunt's childhood, is a detached hamlet, or village, belonging to Edmonton, and derives its name from having been the southern gate to Enfield Chase, which stretches away northward. The village of Southgate lies on the road towards Muswell Hill. Christ Church, a handsome edifice of Early-English architecture, dates its erection from 1862, when it was built in place of the old Weld Chapel.

Minchenden House, in the village, was the seat of the Duchess of Chandos early in the present century. It is said that George II., on coming here to visit the duke's father or grandfather, was obliged to pass through Bedstiles Wood, which was a trespass. The man who kept the gate, being ordered to open it for his Majesty, refused, saying, "If he be the D—— himself, he shall pay me before he passes." The king had to pay; but the result was that the duke threw open the road.

Arno's Grove is another mansion of some note in the hamlet of Southgate. It stands on the site of a more ancient structure, termed Arnold's, which some two centuries ago belonged to Sir John Weld. After some intermediate transmissions, it was purchased, early in the last century, by Mr. James Colebrooke, father of Sir George Colebrook, Bart., who eventually inherited the property. Among its subsequent owners was Sir William Mayne, Bart., who was in 1776 raised to the peerage with the title of Lord Newhaven.

Bush Hill Park, in the neighbourhood of Southgate, between Edmonton and Enfield, was formerly the seat of a rich merchant, named Mellish (who was M.P. for Middlesex), and afterwards of Mr. A. Raphael, and of the Moorat family. Its grounds are said to have been laid out by Le Notre. In the hall there was a curious carving in wood, by Grinling Gibbons, representing the stoning of St. Stephen. "It stood for some time," writes Lambert, "in the house of Mr. Gibbons, at Deptford, where it attracted the attention of his scientific neighbour, Mr. Evelyn, the author of 'Silvia,' who was induced by this specimen of his work to recommend him to Charles II. This carving was purchased for the Duke of Chandos, for his seat at Canons, near Edgware, whence it was brought to Bush Hill." The estate is now broken up and built over with villas. In the grounds of an adjoining mansion are the remains of a circular encampment, of considerable dimensions, about which antiquaries are divided in opinion as to whether they formed part of a Roman or a British camp.

OLD BOW BRIDGE.

CHAPTER XLVII.

THE LEA, STRATFORD-LE-BOW, &c.

" Longarum hæc meta viarum."—*Virgil.*

The River Lea—Bow Bridge—Stratford-atte-Bowe, and Chaucer's Allusion thereto—Construction of the Road through Stratford—Alterations and Repairs of the Bridge—Don Antonio Perez, and other Noted Residents at Stratford—The Parish Church of Stratford-le-Bow—The School and Market House—The Parish Workhouse—Bow and Bromley Institute—King John's Palace at Old Ford—St. John's Church—The Town Hall—West Ham Park—West Ham Abbey—Abbey Mill Pumping Station—Stratford New Town—The Great Eastern Railway Works—"Hudson Town"—West Ham Cemetery and Jews' Cemetery—St. Leonard's Convent, Bromley—The Chapel converted into a Parish Church—Bromley Church rebuilt—Allhallows' Church—The Church of St. Michael and all Angels—The Manor House—The Old Palace—Wesley House—The Old Jews' Cemetery—The City of London and Tower Hamlets Cemetery.

In order to make our way to London Bridge, which is our destined starting-point in the next and concluding volume, we may now drop quietly down the river Lea, passing between green and flowery meadows, and re-visiting on our way some of those shady nooks by which, as we have seen in our wanderings northward, Izaak Walton so much loved to lounge when engaged in his favourite pastime of angling. We shall in due course find ourselves at Bow Bridge, which crosses the Lea between Whitechapel Church and Stratford.

The river, after it leaves Clapton and Hackney, passes on by the Temple Mills to Stratford, or as it is frequently called, Stratford-le-Bow, which lies between Hackney and Whitechapel parishes. Here it divides its course into several channels, the principal stream being that which is spanned by Bow Bridge. The name of Stratford evidently points to the existence near this spot of a ford which doubtless connected London with the old Roman road to Camalodunum, whether that were at Maldon or at Colchester. In the course of time, however, the primitive ford was superseded by a bridge, which appears to have been called "Bow" Bridge, from the arches (*arcus*), which supported and really formed the structure; or possibly because it was constructed of a single arch, as suggested by the writers of the "Beauties of England and Wales." Hence the village was called "Stratford-atte-Bowe," under which name it is immortalised by Chaucer, in the Prologue to the "Canterbury Tales," in terms which seem to imply that five centuries ago it was a well-known place of education for young ladies. Most of our readers will remember the comely prioress, how, in the words of the poet—

> "French she spake full fayre and fetisly,
> After the scole of Stratforde-attè-Bowe,
> For French of Paris was to her unknowe."

We may be pardoned for suggesting as a solution of the meaning of this allusion, that in the adjoining parish of Bromley, within a mile of the bridge, stood the Convent of St. Leonard's, usually termed the Priory in Stratford, and that the nuns of that religious house probably taught the French language among other accomplishments to the young ladies of that favourite suburb.

But it is time that we said something about the old bridge, which was really an historic structure. Fortunately we have to guide us, not only the "Survey" of Stow, and the "Collectanea" of Leland, but also a document, the substance of which was given upon oath at an inquisition taken before two justices of the peace in the year 1303, and which is to be found at length in Lysons' "Environs of London."

"The jurors," writes Lysons, "declared that at the time when Matilda, the good Queen of England, lived, the road from London to Essex was by a place called the Old Ford, where there was no bridge, and during great inundations was so extremely dangerous that many passengers lost their lives; which, coming to the good queen's ears, she caused the road to be turned where it now is—namely, between the towns of Stratford and Westham, and of her bounty caused the bridges and road to be made, except the bridge called Chaner's Bridge, which ought to be made by the Abbot of Stratford. They said further, that Hugh Pratt, living near the roads and bridges in the reign of King John, did of his own authority keep them in repair, begging the aid of passengers. After his death his son William did the same for some time, and afterwards, through the interest of Robert Passelowe, the King's Justice, obtained a toll, which enabled him to make an iron railing upon a certain bridge, called Lock Bridge, from which circumstance he altered his name from Pratt to Bridgewryght; and thus were the bridges repaired, till Philip Bagset and the Abbot of Waltham, being hindered from passing that way with their wagons in the late reign, broke down the railing; whereby the said William, being no longer able to repair it, left the bridge in ruins; in which state it remained till Queen Eleanor of her bounty ordered it to be repaired, committing the charge of it to William de Capella, keeper of her chapel. After which, one William Carlton (yet living) repaired all the bridges with the effects of Bartholomew de Castello, deceased. The jurors added that the bridges and roads had always been repaired by 'bounties,' and that there were no lands or tenements charged with their repair except for Chaner's Bridge, which the Abbot of Stratford was bound to keep in repair."

In the early part of the present century Bow Bridge consisted of three arches. It was very narrow, and bore marks of venerable age; but the numerous alterations and repairs of four centuries had obscured its original plan, and, indeed, left it doubtful how much of it was the work of the good Queen Matilda, and, indeed, whether any part of the original structure remained. The bridge was taken down about the year 1835, and superseded by a lighter and wider structure.

Stratford-le-Bow has few historical or personal associations for us to record. It may, however, be remembered that it was the residence of Don Antonio Perez, who endeavoured to obtain the crown of Spain and Portugal, but who, failing in the attempt, fled for refuge to England as an asylum. He is said to have lived here whilst negotiating with Elizabeth for aid in support of his pretensions, and his residence here is rendered all the more probable from the fact that the parish register contains the entry of the burial of a foreigner who is called his treasurer. Another resident in Stratford was Edmund, Lord Sheffield, who distinguished himself so much in the sea-fights off our coast against the Spanish Armada. Lysons states that John Le Neve, the author of "Monumenta Anglicana" and other learned antiquarian works, also had a house within the parish. The exact situation, however, of these two residences is not known.

The church of Stratford-le-Bow was built as a chapel of ease to Stepney early in the fourteenth century, in consequence of a petition from the inhabitants of this place and of Old Ford, stating the distance of their homes from their parish church, and the difficulty of the roads, which in winter were often impassable on account of the floods. In consequence, Baldock, Bishop of London, issued a licence for the erection of a new chapel upon a site taken from "the king's highway" for that purpose. The chapel ultimately blossomed into a separate parish church, and was consecrated as such in 1719. It consists of a chancel, nave, and aisles, separated from the nave by octangular pillars supporting pointed arches.

At the west end is a belfry tower, rather low, with graduated buttresses, and embattled. The edifice, we may add, stands in the middle of the high road, the houses receding slightly from the straight line on either side, so as to allow of a roadway on each side of the church.

A little to the east of the church was formerly a building which had been used at various times as a school and as a market-house. Brewer, in his "History of Middlesex," when speaking of Bow, says: "At a small remove from the church towards the east is a building which appears to have been used as a market-house. A room over the open part of this building had long been occupied as a charity school, on the foundation of Sir John Jolles, established in 1613, and intended for thirty-five boys of Stratford, Bow, and St. Leonard, Bromley." About the year 1830 this building was removed in order to enlarge the churchyard, and a new school-room erected in its stead at Old Ford.

At a short distance, on the north side of the main street, stood the parish workhouse, which evidently was at one time a mansion of handsome proportions, its rooms being ornamented with fine ceilings and carved chimney-pieces. It was pulled down several years ago, its site being converted to business purposes.

On the north side of the high road, at a short distance westward of Bow Church, stands a large and attractive building, the upper part of which, known as the Bow and Bromley Institute, is used occasionally for concerts, lectures, and similar entertainments. The ground floor serves as the Bow Station of the North London Railway, which here runs below the road. In the roadway close by is a statue of Mr. Gladstone, presented by Mr. H. T. Bryant in 1882.

The hamlet of Old Ford is situated a little to the north of Bow. "In this place," write the compilers of the 'Beauties of England and Wales,' "stood an ancient mansion, often termed King John's Palace, but which does not appear to have been at any time vested in the Crown. The site of this mansion was given to Christ's Hospital by a citizen of London named William Williams, in 1665. A brick gallery, which has been recently covered with cement, is now the only relic of the ancient building. The present (1816) lessee of the estate is Henry Manley, Esq., who has here a handsome residence, and has much improved the grounds and neighbourhood." The last vestige of this building was demolished a few years ago.

Stratford—the "ford of the street, or Roman way from London to Colchester"—lies on the east side of the river Lea, and is consequently in the county of Essex. It is also on the Great Eastern Railway, whence the Colchester and the Cambridge, and the Blackwall and Woolwich, and the Woodford and the Tilbury branch lines diverge; and it is a ward of the parish of West Ham. The church, dedicated to St. John, is a large and handsome edifice, in the centre of the town, and is in the Early English style. Its site is on land which, up to the time of its erection, in 1834, had been an unenclosed village green. At first the church was founded as a chapel of ease to the parish church of West Ham; but about 1859 it was constituted a vicarage, and Stratford became a parish of itself.

The Town Hall, in the Broadway, at the corner of West Ham Lane, was opened in 1869. It is a handsome building, in the classic style, and has a frontage of about 100 feet each way. It has a tower about 100 feet in height, and the building is surmounted by various figures and groups of statuary, illustrative of the arts, science, agriculture, manufacture, commerce, &c. The lower part of the building comprises some commodious public offices, and on the first floor is a spacious hall, artistically decorated.

At a short distance eastward is West Ham Park, a large plot of ground open for the purpose of recreation for the inhabitants of this district. It was formed a short time ago, under the auspices of Sir Antonio Brady, and occupies what was formerly Upton Park, the seat and property of the Gurneys. The mansion has been taken down. The park was laid out with the aid of City funds. In December, 1876, a grant was voted—£1,500 for necessary works carried out, and £675 for the annual maintenance of the grounds.

Stratford (or West Ham) Abbey was founded here in 1135, for monks of the Cistercian order, the abbot of which was a lord of Parliament. There are considerable remains of the building.

Abbey Mill Pumping Station, close by, is an extensive range of works, in connection with the main drainage of North London. As the works here are very similar to those already described in connection with the Pumping Station at Chelsea,* there is no occasion for entering upon a further account of them.

Stratford being, as stated above, the point where the two main branches of the Great Eastern Railway leading respectively to Cambridge and Colchester diverge, has of late years given birth to a new town, which has become quite a railway

* See *ante*, pp. 41, 42.

colony. Here the company has its chief depôt for carriages, engines, and rolling stock, and yards for their repairs. The works, which were established here about the year 1847, cover a very large extent of ground, and give employment to upwards of 2,500 hands, independently of about 600 others engaged in the running sheds. The various buildings used as workshops for the different branches of work required to be done, either in the construction or the repair of engines, &c., are large and well lighted, and embrace foundries for casting, forges, fitting rooms, braziers' shops, carpenters' shops, saw-mills, &c. The principal erecting shops are about 120 yards in length, by sixty in breadth. The machinery throughout is of the most perfect description, and adapted for almost all kinds of work; one shop alone contains upwards of 100 machines for the performance of the most delicate work. One of the latest and most useful pieces of machinery in operation in the smiths' shop is the hydraulic riveting-machine. To give some idea of the amount of labour accomplished in these works, we may state that about 500 engines, 3,000 carriages, and 10,000 wagons are here kept in constant repair, and that the sum paid weekly in wages in the locomotive department alone amounts, on an average, to about £6,000.

The new town which has sprung up in the neighbourhood of the works is the residence of several hundreds of skilled *employés*—engineers, drivers, and others. At first it was called Hudson Town, in compliment to the "Railway King;" but when he lost his crown, the name fell into disuse. In 1871 the New Town numbered some 23,000 souls; and now probably the population has nearly doubled itself. The town, it may be added, has its literary institution, a "temperance" public-house, besides numerous places of worship.

At a short distance eastward of the railway works, by the side of Forest Road, which runs parallel with the Colchester line, stands an industrial school, with spacious grounds attached, in the rear of which is the West Ham Cemetery, and the Jews' Cemetery. In the latter, which covers about eleven acres of ground, and was formed in 1858, on the closing of the Jews' Cemetery at Mile End, are the vaults of the Goldsmid and the Lucas families, of Sir David Salomons, and other leading members of the Jewish community, together with a dome-crowned mausoleum for the members of the house of Rothschild.

Adjoining Bow on the south-east, in the parish of Bromley, was, as above-mentioned, a convent dedicated to St. Leonard, stated by some historians to have been founded in the reign of William the Conqueror, by William, Bishop of London, for a prioress and nine nuns; other writers, however, are of opinion that it was founded at a much earlier period. Indeed, when, or by whom, the convent was really founded, seems a very difficult matter now to decide. Stow says it was founded by Henry II., in the first year of his reign (1154); but Dugdale, in the "Monasticon," says, "This is a mistake, it was in being before." Weever fixed the foundation still later, by saying that "this religious structure was sometime a monastery replenished with white monks, dedicated to the honour of our Saviour Jesus Christ, and Saint Leonard; founded by Henry II., in the twenty-third year of his reign." But Strype, in his "Survey of London," says, respecting this statement of Weever:—"How to reconcile the said antiquary with an elder than he, namely, John Leland, and the 'Monasticon Anglicanum,' I cannot tell, for Weever writes that this monastery was replenished with white monks, and founded by King Henry II., in the twenty-third year of his reign; whereas Leland and the 'Monasticon' reports it a religious house for nuns, founded by William, Bishop of London, that lived in the Conqueror's time," which was nearly a century earlier. Lysons, in his "Environs of London," attempts to unravel the apparently opposite statements of Stow, Weever, Leland, Dugdale, and others, by supposing Weever to have been altogether in error, he having confounded the Abbey of Monks at Stratford (the remaining vestiges of which is now called West Ham Abbey), in Essex, with the Convent of Nuns, in Middlesex, which convent, says Lysons, was invariably said in ancient wills to have been at Stratford, Bow, on account of its contiguity to that place. And he further says, respecting these two religious houses: "It is difficult to distinguish them in the calendars in the Tower; nor can it be always done without referring to the original will, where the word 'Prioresse' will determine the grants which belong to this house at Bromley, even if 'Beati Leonardi' should not follow."

Weever states that the convent of which he was speaking was in Middlesex, and dedicated to St. Leonard; whereas, the convent at Stratford he knew to be in Essex, which he says that he visited himself "after going over 'Bow Bridge,' in his journey towards West Ham." Leland, who was engaged in making historical collections relating to religious houses, by order of Henry VIII., is reported to have met with but little encouragement, and to have died insane in the neighbourhood of St. Paul's; "uncertain," says Fuller, "whether his brains were broken with weight of work or want of wages." This report of Leland's—for such it really is—was printed in Latin, and entitled "Antiquarii de rebus;" and in it he says, respecting the Priory at Bromley, "Gul. Episcopus London fundator." Historians generally have followed this dictum, since Leland wrote, and ascribed the first foundation, both of the structure and religious society of St. Leonard, to William, Bishop of London, in the Conqueror's reign. But Speed, in his "History of England and its Monasteries," speaks of the Norman bishop, with respect to the Priory at Bromley, as a "benefactor" only; and this is quoted against Leland in the "Monasticon." Mr. Dunstan, in his "History of Bromley and St. Leonard," says: "That William, Bishop of London, was a benefactor there can be no doubt; nay, more, it is probable that he enlarged the original priory about the period mentioned. He might also have much enlarged the Lady Chapel attached to the priory which was dedicated to St. Mary; and this will account for the mixed style of the old church, it having been partly of Gothic, partly of Saxon, and partly of Norman architecture, which would indicate that the structure was not all the work of one hand, nor even of one age; for whilst the round-headed arches in one part were both Saxon and Norman, the pointed arches, yea, even the main or principal doorway, and heavy buttresses, were purely Gothic, and therefore of more ancient date, in the other. It is very probable," he continues, "that William, Bishop of London, might have removed some portions of the original chapel, and added others of more extensive and lofty dimensions, suited to the style of Norman architecture." This hypothesis is particularly strengthened by the fact that when the old chapel or church was taken down in 1842, a considerable quantity of old building materials, chiefly consisting of very ancient wrought stone, was found embedded in various parts of the walls; evidently the fragments of some very ancient religious structure, which probably had occupied the same, or nearly the same site, anterior to the episcopacy of William, in the Conqueror's reign. Moreover, the arches which were found blocked up and plastered over, and covered with many generations of whitewash within, and rough-coat without, in 1825, were all of the Gothic style, and evidently led into some building (as Lysons conceives) on the south side; whereas, according to Newcourt and others, the nunnery or convent in the days of Henry VIII. was at the west end of the chapel; and the lofty arch at the western end of the church contained the screen which separated the chapel from the convent and cloisters.

"Speed, therefore, views the antiquity of the Convent of St. Leonard as being anterior to that of Henry II., as mentioned by Stow and Weever, and considers Henry II. as a benefactor only; and in the same light he considers all the others whose benefactions and confirmations have been named, including William, Bishop of London, among the rest. And, therefore, in tracing that antiquity to a reasonable, nay, to a probable source, it does appear from the many foregoing considerations that the original foundation of the Convent or Priory of St. Leonard at Bromley may, with the greatest propriety, be attributed to the time of Edgar's reign, about one hundred years before William the Conqueror landed on the British shores—namely, somewhere about the middle of the tenth century, or nearly coeval with the re-establishment of the monastery at Westminster." All trace of the old priory buildings, with the exception of the chapel, has long since passed away. The chapel was dedicated to St. Mary, and at the dissolution of the religious houses it was converted into a parochial church. Lysons says that "the chapel of St. Mary, with the convent of St. Leonard, Bromley, is mentioned in several ancient wills." The fabric consisted of a nave and chancel, and the latter was separated from the former by a chancel-screen and by being raised one step. The principal entrance, at the western end, was in the same situation as that in the present building, but consisted of a Gothic arched doorway. This doorway, it is conjectured, was inserted when the old chapel first became appropriated as a parish church, as upon the removal of the north wall there was found, bricked up and plastered over, a very ancient doorway of small dimensions and of Norman architecture. The chancel of the old church occupied precisely the same position with that of the present church, as portions of the walls of the old building are now standing, both in the north and south-eastern ends of the present church. In the chancel are five stone stalls, or *sedilia*, through one of which was a small doorway opening at once into the churchyard. At the western end of the nave was a capacious gallery, and the body of the church was fitted up with pews of the orthodox fashion. In 1692 the chancel was lengthened by Sir William Benson, the then lord of the manor, "by the addition of a projecting recess in which was placed the communion-table." At the west end of the church was a large round-headed arch, ornamented with lozenge and other Saxon or early Norman mouldings; this was much disfigured by the galleries inside, and also by the vestry-room outside. It has been suggested that the church as it remained down to the present period was only the chancel and lady chapel of a much larger edifice; and that the arch here spoken of was that which separated it from a nave, of which every trace has long since perished. In 1843 the new church was opened, the old fabric having been demolished piecemeal. It is a plain brick-built structure, consisting of a nave, chancel, and side-aisles, with a tower and dwarf spire at the south-west corner. The style of architecture adopted is that of the Norman period, and some of the windows are enriched with coloured glass.

The font is of Norman design, and of the usual size; it is said to have been for many years expelled from the church, and to have lain in the churchyard. In 1825, when the old church was repaired and "beautified," the churchwardens had the antique device on the font re-cut, and it was placed upon a Gothic pedestal. Although it was so far restored to its original position, it appears to have been discarded by the officiating minister; a small portable font having been used for many years. It has, however, now been fully re-installed, and the Gothic character of the pedestal changed into Norman.

The old church was particularly rich in monuments and funeral hatchments. In the nave formerly lay a large stone which contained the brasses of a man and woman, with much ornamental work over their heads. "They seem," says Strype, "to be some nobleman and his wife interred in this religious house. Perhaps the Earl [John De Bohun] and his wife, already mentioned." If so, it would have dated from about 1336. The stone was afterwards removed to the entrance of the old church, and formed a part of the floor; it is now placed in the floor of the tower. Against the south wall of the church was a large mural monument of marble, to the memory of William Ferrars, and dated 1625. On the erection of the new church this monument was placed against the north wall. Busts of the deceased and his wife, who was Jane, daughter of Sir Peter Van-Lore, are represented under arches supported by pillars of the Corinthian order. The man is habited in a doublet and ruff, and the hands of both are united, resting on a skull. In a panel over the effigies is the motto—

"Live well, and dye never,
Dye well, and live ever."

A curious and interesting monument is that of Abraham Jacob, Esq., who died in the year 1629. The figures of himself and his wife are represented kneeling under arches, the monument being adorned with the arms of the family and its alliances. The monument is particularly chaste and emblematical. The principal feature in the ornamentation is the representation of a vine, on the leaves of which are written the names of his twelve children. The names of five that were married, and their respective alliances, are expressed by the quartering of their several coats of arms; whilst the younger offshoots indicate the fruits of the respective unions, on the leaves of which offshoots are inscribed the names of their children. The names of the seven unmarried remain above on the leaves of the old vine. This monument was erected by Sir John Jacob, who, after the death of his father, Abraham Jacob, had purchased the manor and advowson of Bromley, in 1634. He is said to have been a very rich and loyal citizen, and one of the "farmers of the customs." He was a great sufferer during the Civil War, and was at one time confined as a prisoner in Crosby House.

Bromley possesses also three or four other churches, besides chapels and meeting-houses for members of various denominations. Allhallows' Church, an edifice of Early English architecture, was built in 1874, from the proceeds of the sale of the church of Allhallows Staining, Mark Lane, and is in the patronage of the Grocers' Company. The large church of St. Michael and All Angels, which is of similar architecture, and consecrated in 1865, contains sittings for about 1,300 worshippers.

About the middle of the seventeenth century Sir John Jacob built a "large brick edifice" on the site of the old priory. The house was surrounded by a small park and gardens, the east side of which was washed by the river Lea. The building, which was called the Manor House, was demolished early in the present century, and its site covered by rows of small cottages, whilst some portion of the grounds was added to the churchyard.

That Bromley in its time has had a fair share of aristocratic inhabitants may be seen from the fact that, in the parish rate-books of the seventeenth century, besides the name of Sir J. Jacob, appear those of Sir Henry Ferrers, Sir William Turner, Sir John Poole, Sir Nicholas Crisp, Sir J. Fleetwood, Sir John Chambers, Sir Richard Mundy, Lady Stanhope, Lady Munden, and several other titled personages.

At a short distance westward of the church, a large brick-built mansion—one of the former glories of the place—is still standing, but cut up into three or four tenements. It is commonly known as the Old Palace, and is sometimes called Queen Anne's Palace. The building is very lofty, and has a slightly projecting wing at either end.

The interior bears numerous traces of its original splendour in the shape of stuccoed ceilings, carved panellings and chimney-pieces, as well as marble floors. A long row of wooden houses standing at right angles with the mansion, and forming one side of another street, occupies the site of the ancient stables. Another curious old house in this street, with the words "Wesley House" painted over the doorway, is said to have been one of the first meeting-houses in which John Wesley preached.

Before quitting Bromley, we must not omit to mention the bowling-green, the village stocks, the whipping-post, the pond and ducking-stool, and the parish pound, all of which remained in full operation down to the latter part of the last century.

Adjoining Bromley, and at the eastern end of the Mile End Road, not far from Bow and Old Ford, is the disused Jewish Cemetery, formerly belonging to the Great German Synagogue in Duke's Place. Here are buried nearly all the members of the Jewish religion who have been connected with the City and the East End of London. Among them lies Baron Nathan Rothschild, the great millionaire, and head of the well-known banking and financial house which bears his name. He died in 1836, and his funeral was perhaps the most imposing ever witnessed in these districts. This cemetery was closed in 1858, on the opening of the new Jewish Cemetery near Stratford New Town, as mentioned above. The burial-grounds for Jews are mostly laid out and planted in a manner similar to other cemeteries. Formerly their burial-place was "outside the City Wall, at Leyrestowe, without Cripelgate."

In this neighbourhood—at South Grove, Mile End—is the Cemetery of the City of London and Tower Hamlets Company. It occupies about thirty acres of ground, north of Bow Common, and is skirted on the south-east side by a branch of the Great Eastern Railway, on its way from Stepney Station to Bow Road and Stratford. The cemetery, which is altogether a dreary place, now holds the remains of many thousands of persons, mostly of the poorer classes, many of whom occupy nameless graves.

It now only remains to remind our readers that in the course of the present volume we have endeavoured to act as their guides over a far larger extent of ground than that which we traversed in all our previous volumes. We have lounged in their company about the old mansions of Chelsea and Kensington; we have wandered with them through the green fields of Bayswater and Paddington, of Marylebone and the Regent's Park; we have climbed with them the "northern heights" of Hampstead and Highgate Hills; and lastly, we have reconnoitred the northern outskirts of Dalston and Hackney, Stoke Newington and Tottenham; and roamed hand in hand with them the pleasant meadows that fringe the river Lea. Here we must leave our readers for a time, purposing in the following volume to take them through quite another tract of country, not romantic in its outward features, but full of historic interest, on the south bank of the Thames, feeling assured that but scanty justice will have been done to "London, Old and New," unless we include in our perambulations both Southwark and Lambeth, Bermondsey and Deptford, Kennington and Walworth, Wandsworth and Putney, Fulham and Hammersmith; in each, and all of which, once rural villages, though now large and populous towns and busy "hives of industry," we shall studiously endeavour so to blend the present with the past as to avoid, and, if possible, to escape the risk of proving ourselves dull and profitless companions.